W9-DGD-505

To the Student

This text was created to provide you with a high-quality educational resource. As a publisher specializing in college texts for business and economics, our goal is to provide you with learning materials that will serve you well in your college studies and throughout your career.

The educational process involves the retention and application of concepts and principles. You can accelerate your learning efforts by utilizing the supplements accompanying this text.

The STUDY GUIDE, prepared by Ula Motekat, Old Dominion University, is designed to help you better your performance in your Advanced Accounting course. The guide contains outlines of each chapter, true-false questions, and exercises with solutions.

The WORKING PAPERS, prepared by Don Vickrey includes forms needed to solve the end-of-chapter problems. The forms contain captions and information that you would otherwise have to copy from the text.

These learning aids are designed to improve your performance in the course by highlighting key points in the text and providing you with assistance in mastering basic concepts. Check your local bookstore or ask the manager to place an order for you today.

We at Irwin sincerely hope that ADVANCED ACCOUNTING will assist you in reaching your goals both now and in the future.

SEVENTH EDITION

Advanced Accounting

James R. Boatsman, Ph.D.
Arizona State University

Charles H. Griffin, Ph.D.
The University of Texas at Austin

Don W. Vickrey, Ph.D.
Arizona State University West

Thomas H. Williams, Ph.D.
University of Wisconsin, Madison

IRWIN

Burr Ridge, Illinois
Boston, Massachusetts
Sydney, Australia

The previous edition of this text was published under the
authorship of Griffin, Williams, Boatsman, and Vickrey.

The previous edition of this text was published under the
authorship of Griffin, Williams, Boatsman, and Vickrey.

Material from the Uniform CPA Examination Questions and Unofficial
Answers © 1974, 1975, 1976, 1977, 1978, 1979, 1980, 1981, 1982,
1983, and 1984 by the American Institute of Certified Public
Accountants, Inc., is reprinted (or adapted) with permission.

© RICHARD D. IRWIN, INC., 1966, 1971, 1977, 1980, 1985, 1991, and
1994

Senior sponsoring editor: Jeff Shelstad
Developmental editor: Shelley McDonald Taylor
Marketing manager: Cindy L. Ledwith
Project editor: Jean Lou Hess
Production manager: Ann Cassady
Art coordinator: Heather Burbridge
Compositor: Better Graphics, Inc.
Typeface: 10/12 Times Roman
Printer: R. R. Donnelley & Sons Company

Library of Congress Cataloging-in-Publication Data

Boatsman, James R.
   Advanced accounting / James R. Boatsman, Don W. Vickrey, Thomas H.
Williams.—7th ed.
      p.   cm.
   Rev. ed. of: Advanced accounting / Charles H. Griffin . . . [et
al.]. 6th ed. 1991.
   Includes index.
   ISBN 0-256-10819-6
   1. Accounting.   I. Vickrey, Don William, date.   II. Williams,
Thomas Howard.   III. Griffin, Charles H. Advanced accounting.
IV. Title.
HF5635.B6797   1994
657'.046—dc20   93-10648
                                                            CIP

Printed in the United States of America
1 2 3 4 5 6 7 8 9 0   DOC   0 9 8 7 6 5 4 3

The Irwin Series in Undergraduate Accounting

Preface

We are very pleased you are using this new edition of *Advanced Accounting*. We have made every effort to see that our text and instructional materials satisfy the needs of instructors and students. As long-time teachers of advanced accounting, we believe we appreciate both. Our goal continues to be a book that is up-to-date, comprehensive, well organized, logical, and clear.

The Seventh Edition Revision

A major objective of this edition was to improve the clarity of exposition and understandability of the principles of business combinations and consolidated financial statements in Chapters 1 through 5. We believe that we have achieved this goal through a major reorganization of the topics.

Following an overview of business combinations in Chapter 1, a complete introduction to consolidated financial statements is presented in Chapter 2—without the complications associated with purchase accounting. More technical topics, including comprehensive coverage of the allocation of the purchase price based on the fair values of the acquired firm's assets and liabilities, are presented in Chapters 3 and 4. Chapter 5 introduces the ac-counting issues associated with a variety of types of corporate restructurings, including leveraged buyouts and joint ventures. The accounting issues in these restructurings have a common theme—should the assets and liabilities be revalued? The elements of this theme are briefly reviewed in the context of the 1992 FASB discussion memorandum, *New Basis of Accounting*.

A second objective was to provide a means of introducing complex financial reporting issues requiring research and analysis beyond the coverage included in intermediate and advanced accounting texts. This goal has been achieved through the case book that is packaged with the text. In addition to a variety of cases of varying difficulty, the case book also includes a brief summary of the critical elements of financial reporting research. Students' understanding and appreciation of the full dimension of the financial reporting environment will be significantly enhanced, we believe, by working several of these cases.

A third objective was to streamline our coverage of the fundamentals of intercompany profits and bond holdings in consolidated financial statements. To this end, we have adopted the modified equity method. This change highlights the basic principles of, and simplifies the mechanics associated with, intercompany profits and bond holdings in Chapters 6 through 8. Coverage of the (full) equity method entries for intercompany profits and bond holdings is provided in the context of an investor-investee relationship.

Our final objective was to update and expand textual and problem materials. In this regard, we have expanded our treatment of foreign currency transactions and translation so that essential material is covered more completely, and we have updated our discussion of international financial reporting. We also cover all pertinent FASB and GASB pronouncements released in time to be discussed in this edition. In particular, we provide an extended discussion of GASB *Statement No. 11*, "Measurement Focus and Basis of Accounting—Government Fund Operating Statements." Nevertheless, our examples and end-of-chapter materials are designed to be consistent with both current pronouncements and GASB *Statement No. 11*.

Instructional Materials

For the Student:

- *Study Guide*. Prepared by Ula Motekat of Old Dominion University.
  Provides chapter outlines, self-review questions, and computational exercises.

- *Working Papers*. Developed by Don Vickrey. Contains all significant forms needed for solving homework assignments. Working Papers include captions, column headings, account balances, and other information the student would otherwise have to copy from the text.

- *Check Figures*
  Provide key figures from solutions for each exercise and problem. Enables students to check solutions while working through assignments.

- *Case Book*
  Includes a variety of cases of varying levels of

difficulty. Also included is a summary of financial reporting research methods.

For the Instructor:

- *Solutions Manual*
  Includes answers and solutions to all questions exercises, and problems provided in the text.

- *Solutions Transparencies*
  Provide solutions to selected exercises and problems.

- *Test Bank*. Prepared by Ula Motekat.
  Includes true/false and multiple-choice questions. Each question is coded by level of difficulty.

- *Computest 3*
  Irwin's computerized testing software.

Acknowledgments

Professor Janice Bell
California State University-Northridge

Professor JoAnn DeVries
Central State University

Professor Richard B. Griffin
University of Tennessee at Martin

Professor John G. Hamer
University of Lowell

Professor Al Massimini
LaSalle University

Professor Enrico Petri
State University of New York-Albany

Professor Robert Terrell
Central State University

Professor Mark Trombley
University of Arizona

Irwin's Commitment to Quality

We recognize the importance of accuracy in accounting texts. Carefully checked examples, exhibits, exercises, problems, and cases are crucial to a quality classroom experience. The authors and publisher have invested a significant amount of time and effort to ensure the accuracy of this text and its ancillaries.

In addition to the usual accuracy checking procedures, all numerical elements were checked again during the production process by three individuals: Vicky Arnold of Arizona State University West; Edward Schwan of Susquehanna University; and Donn Vickrey of the University of San Diego. We also thank the many users and reviewers of our text, who continually provide excellent feedback.

Request for Comments

There have been many changes in the content and style of *Advanced Accounting* over its seven editions, most of which we hope have improved the quality of the text. We would greatly appreciate any comments you have to help us improve it further. We hope that you enjoy using the Seventh Edition.

James R. Boatsman
Charles H. Griffin
Don W. Vickrey
Thomas H. Williams

Contents

UNIT V

Fiduciary and Institutional Accounting   807

Accounting for Combined Corporate Entities

CHAPTER

1

Economic and Accounting Issues in Business Combinations

Chapter Outline

There are various ways two or more corporations can join under common ownership. We use the term *business combination* to refer to these transactions, regardless of the way the transaction is done. Thousands of business combinations occur annually. In many, at least one of the combining companies is quite large. Because of the number of business combinations that occur and the size of the firms involved, accounting for business combinations is an important topic. This topic is the principal focus of Units I and II of this text. We begin with the economic motivations for buiness combinations.

ECONOMIC MOTIVATIONS FOR BUSINESS COMBINATIONS

The decision to enter into a business combination is a type of capital budgeting decision. Consider first a firm's decision to acquire a single asset, say, a machine. According to the net present value criterion, the machine should be acquired if its value to the firm exceeds its purchase price. The value to the firm is the present value of the cash flow it can generate when added to the configuration of the firm's existing assets. Its purchase price is its value in the market for machines. Thus, net present value arises when the purchasing firm can use the asset in a way that other participants in the market for machines do not envision. Purchasing the machine will create incremental value equal to the net present value.

Now consider the decision to acquire several assets in a basket purchase; that is, purchasing a portfolio of assets in a single transaction. Again, the net present value criterion specifies that the basket should be purchased if doing so will add value to the acquiring firm.

Finally, consider a business combination. A business combination involves obtaining the net assets of an entire firm by obtaining the firm's common shares. Common shares represent ownership claims to the firm's net assets. Accordingly, there is little fundamental difference between a basket purchase of the firm's net assets and purchasing its common shares. And like the purchase of a single asset or a basket purchase of assets, a business combination is motivated by a desire to add value.

There are several reasons why value can be created in a business combination. One reason is *eliminating duplicate fixed costs*. This would be expected when two companies with similar productive processes are combined. A second reason is *coordinating successive phases of a production process*. This would be expected with combinations involving one firm that produces another firm's input. A third reason is *more efficient asset management*. If the assets of one of the combining firms are underutilized due to mismanagement, a business combination provides an opportunity for bringing such assets under a second firm's more talented management. Fourth, value can arise through *capturing otherwise unused tax advantages*. For example, the net operating loss carryforward of an acquired firm might never be realized without an enhancement of its profits.

Of course, mere expectation of added value does not guarantee that any will materialize. If synergies exist and the price paid is reasonable, the combination should be successful. Otherwise, it may join the many business combinations undertaken with the best of intentions that are subsequently dissolved because the anticipated increase in value did not occur.

MECHANISMS FOR BUSINESS COMBINATIONS

Business combinations are often accomplished by exchanging cash for common stock or common stock for common stock. Let's consider the exchange of cash for common stock. Aspects of two combining firms, *each owned by a single individual,* before the combination are:

A Corporation		B Corporation	
The Corporation	*Individual 1*	*The Corporation*	*Individual 2*
Cash	Common stock of A	Net assets	Common stock of B
Other net assets			

Before the combination, items owned by A Corporation are cash for the business combination and other net assets (other assets less liabilities). The owner of A, Individual 1, holds all the outstanding common stock of A. Similarly, B Corporation has net assets, and its owner, Individual 2, holds all the outstanding common stock of B. A Corporation then acquires control of B's net assets by exchanging cash for the stock of B owned by Individual 2. After the exchange, the diagram is:

A Corporation		B Corporation	
The Corporation	*Individual 1*	*The Corporation*	*Individual 2*
Other net assets	Common stock of A	Net assets	Cash
Common stock of B			

B Corporation is now owned by A Corporation. Therefore, the net assets of B are controlled by a *different* individual, Individual 1. Individual 2 now holds only cash and has been removed from the affairs of either corporation. In this case, we clearly see that the ownership of something, the net assets of B, has changed hands. In substance, A Corporation has *purchased* the net assets of B Corporation.

Now consider a business combination involving a common stock for common stock exchange. Aspects of two combining firms, each owned by a single individual, are:

A Corporation		B Corporation	
The Corporation	*Individual 1*	*The Corporation*	*Individual 2*
Net assets	Common stock of A	Net assets	Common stock of B
Common stock of A			

Items owned by A Corporation include net assets and unissued shares of its common stock (or treasury shares). Other features are the same as in the case of the cash for common stock exchange. A Corporation now acquires control of B's net assets by exchanging its unissued shares (or treasury shares) for the shares of B owned by Individual 2. After the exchange, the diagram is:

A Corporation		B Corporation	
The Corporation	*Individual 1*	*The Corporation*	*Individual 2*
Net assets	Common stock of A	Net assets	Common stock of A
Common stock of B			

As in the cash for common stock exchange, B Corporation is now owned by A Corporation. Also, Individual 1 and B Corporation are in the same position they were in after the cash for common stock exchange. However, it is the position of Individual 2 after the combination that is important. Individual 2 has *not* been removed from the affairs of both corporations. Instead, Individual 2 remains involved through ownership of some of the outstanding shares of A Corporation. In this case, it is not obvious that something has been bought and sold. Before the transaction, the net assets of A and the net assets of B were owned by Individuals 1 and 2. After the transaction, the net assets of A and the net assets of B are still owned by these same individuals. There is a *continuity of ownership*. It appears that Individuals 1 and 2 have *pooled* their investments in net assets.

Both the cash for common stock and the common stock for common stock exchanges illustrated above are called *acquisitions*. The distinctive feature of an acquisition is that A Corporation and B Corporation continue as legal entities. B Corporation is called a *subsidiary,* and A Corporation is called a *parent*. Each corporation normally continues to operate its own distinct accounting system which produces financial statements at the end of accounting periods. The accounting issues, then, for acquisitions are:

1. How should the separate statements of the parent show its investment in the subsidiary?
2. How should the separate statements of the subsidiary show the acquisition?
3. How should *consolidated financial statements* be prepared? That is, how should the separate statements of the parent and subsidiary be combined to produce a single set of financial statements showing the financial affairs of the combined economic entity?

A *merger* can be illustrated by changing the circumstances of either the cash for common stock or common stock for common stock examples. Consider A Corporation and B Corporation after A acquires B:

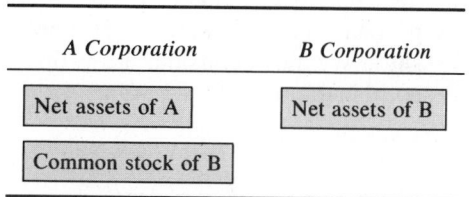

B Corporation now distributes its net assets to its owner (A Corporation) as a liquidating dividend. The outstanding common stock of B is retired, and B Corporation ceases to exist as a legal entity. All of the assets are now owned by A Corporation, as shown below:

	A Corporation	B Corporation
	Net assets of A	
	Net assets of B	

The distinctive feature of a merger is that only one of the constituent firms in the business combination continues as a legal entity. Because of this, only one accounting system remains in operation, and the only financial statements produced are those of the surviving entity. The accounting issue, then, for a merger is "How should the surviving entity account for net assets received from its merger partner?"

Now, suppose that a new legal entity, C Corporation, is formed. A Corporation distributes all of its net assets, including those received from B Corporation, to C Corporation. This new corporation then issues shares of its stock to the owners of A Corporation (Individuals 1 and 2 or just Individual 1, depending on whether the initial transaction was a cash for common stock or common stock for common stock exchange). The A Corporation shares are then retired. A Corporation and B Corporation cease existing, and C Corporation is the surviving legal entity. This illustrates a *consolidation*. Although there are more direct ways of liquidating two (or more) corporations into a newly created corporation, the distinctive feature of a consolidation is that a newly created corporation receives the net assets of its liquidating predecessors. Thus, as with a merger, there is only one surviving entity, one accounting system, and one set of financial statements. The accounting issue, then, for a consolidation is "How should the new corporation account for the net assets transferred to it by its predecessors?"

In all three cases (the acquisition, the merger, and the consolidation), Individual 2 might have received cash or common stock. If cash were received, there is a *purchase* since ownership of net assets changed hands. If common stock were received, a purchase is less obvious since a continuity of ownership on the part of Individual 2 is present. Regardless of the form of the combination, we must therefore determine whether the substance of a business combination is (1) a purchase of net assets or (2) a pooling of investments with no change in ownership. We now consider how this question relates to accounting for business combinations.

Accounting Methods for Business Combinations— An Overview

In the United States, there are two accepted methods of accounting for business combinations. These are called the *purchase method* and the *pooling of interests method*. One may not, however, freely choose between the methods. If 12 criteria are all met, the pooling of interests method must be used. Otherwise, the purchase method is used.

We can see the basic difference between the methods by considering a merger, such that any issues relating to the separate company statements of the parent and subsidiary do not arise.[1] The only financial statements produced are those of the surviving firm. If the combination is accounted for as a *purchase*, the financial statements of the surviving firm are identical to those produced if the firm had made a basket purchase of net assets.

Suppose that Corporation A purchases all the net assets of Corporation B for the cash price of $100. At the purchase date, these net assets had the following values:

---

[1] Also in an acquisition, the possibility of acquiring less than 100 percent of the outstanding shares of the subsidiary complicates a discussion of the difference between the two methods.

	Value from B's Financial Statements (Book Value)	Fair Value
Inventory	$ 50	$ 60
Plant and equipment	100	120
Total assets	$150	$180
Liabilities	$100	$ 90
Net assets	$ 50	$ 90

Corporation A will record the assets and liabilities (including the implied goodwill) at fair value:

```
Inventory  . . . . . . . . . . . . . . . . . . . . . . . . . . . . . . . . .    60
Plant and Equipment . . . . . . . . . . . . . . . . . . . . . . . . . . . .   120
Goodwill . . . . . . . . . . . . . . . . . . . . . . . . . . . . . . . . . .    10
    Liabilities . . . . . . . . . . . . . . . . . . . . . . . . . . . . . . . .         90
    Cash . . . . . . . . . . . . . . . . . . . . . . . . . . . . . . . . . . .        100
```

Now, suppose A Corporation purchases all the outstanding common shares of B for $100. A Corporation will record the share purchase with the following entry:

```
Investment in B Company  . . . . . . . . . . . . . . . . . . . . . . . . . .   100
    Cash . . . . . . . . . . . . . . . . . . . . . . . . . . . . . . . . . . .        100
```

B Corporation then merges with A Corporation (distributing its net assets in a liquidating dividend). A Corporation will record the receipt of B's net assets with the following entry:

```
Inventory  . . . . . . . . . . . . . . . . . . . . . . . . . . . . . . . . .    60
Plant and Equipment . . . . . . . . . . . . . . . . . . . . . . . . . . . .   120
Goodwill . . . . . . . . . . . . . . . . . . . . . . . . . . . . . . . . . .    10
    Liabilities . . . . . . . . . . . . . . . . . . . . . . . . . . . . . . . .         90
    Investment in B Company . . . . . . . . . . . . . . . . . . . . . . . . .        100
```

At this point, B's net assets appear on A's books at fair value, just as if they had been acquired in a basket purchase. Thus, the purchase method recognizes the basic equivalence of purchasing a firm's net assets or purchasing its common shares.

In contrast, the *pooling of interests* method of accounting ignores fair values of assets as of the date of the business combination. The financial statements of the surviving company are identical to those produced if the constituent firms had been operating as a single entity throughout their entire history. Accordingly, the basis of accounting for B's net assets remains at their $50 book value. Suppose that this book value consists of capital stock of $30 and retained earnings of $20, and that A obtains all of B's shares by issuing A shares with a par value of $30. The former shareholders of A and B now jointly own the surviving firm (A

Corporation). Neither shareholder group has sold out to the other. Instead, they have pooled their investment interests. A Corporation will record its investment in B shares with the following entry:

Investment in B Company (book value of B's net assets)	50	
Capital Stock		30
Retained Earnings		20

A Corporation will then record the merger as follows:

Inventory	50	
Plant and Equipment	100	
Liabilities		100
Investment in B Company		50

B's asset, liability, and equity valuations have been recorded on A's books. At this point, A's books will appear as if it had acquired and used B's net assets in exactly the same fashion as B acquired and used them.

Since the purchase and pooling of interests methods involve different initial net asset valuations, income statements subsequent to the business combination will differ. These differences are summarized as follows:

	Purchase	Pooling of Interests
Cost of goods sold	$ 60	$ 50
Depreciation of plant and equipment	120	100
Goodwill amortization	10	—
Amortization of discount on liabilities	10	—
Total expenses	$200	$150

Assuming the same amount of revenue, the purchase method will result in $50 less future net income than the pooling of interests method. Clearly, the difference is due to the excess of fair value of net assets over their historical costs.

Fair values tend to exceed historical cost valuations. Because of this, purchase accounting tends to result in lower postcombination income than does pooling of interests accounting. Since managers of firms are often compensated on the basis of accounting income, we expect that managers often prefer having a business combination accounted for as a pooling of interests. Or management's preference might be based on factors not directly related to compensation. For example, higher earnings improve the debt/equity ratio. And this ratio might be used to determine whether a borrower is in technical default on debt covenants.

Historically, the tendency for managers to favor the pooling of interests method has been a source of conflict between accountants and managers. The conflict exists because many transactions are not as clear-cut as in our previous examples involving cash for common stock and common stock for common stock. When all the outstanding shares of one firm are acquired for cash, an ownership change is obvious and purchase accounting is appropriate. Similarly, when all the stockholders of one firm surrender their common shares for common shares of another firm, continuity of ownership is clear and pooling of interests accounting is indicated.

However, between these two extremes are a large number of possibilities. Many combinations involve acquisitions of less than 100 percent of the outstanding shares of a combining company. Many involve payment in the form of a mixture of cash and common stock. Others involve issuing debt instruments and/or preferred stock plus cash and/or common stock. And the debt and/or preferred stock may or may not be convertible. In such exchanges, it is difficult to determine whether or not a change in ownership has taken place. Because of the ambiguity of such transactions, accountants historically had a hard time arguing against the position of managers that these exchanges be accounted for as a pooling of interests.

In 1970, the Accounting Principles Board (APB) clarified the circumstances in which pooling of interests accounting is appropriate. In its *Opinion No. 16,* ''Accounting for Business Combinations,'' the Board identified 12 conditions, all of which must be met, in order for a pooling of interests to be acceptable. All transactions failing to meet one or more of these conditions must be accounted for as purchases. In short, the Board acted consistently with the principle of conservatism. Unclear cases are to be resolved in favor of the method which records less current income. And the purchase method, with its higher depreciation and amortization, usually records less current income.

Criteria for a Pooling of Interests

The board's 12 conditions are as follows.

I. Attributes of the Combining Companies

1. Each of the combining companies must be autonomous and must not have been a subsidiary or division of another corporation during the two-year period prior to the initiation of the combination plan. However, this does not exclude companies that were newly incorporated within the preceding two years, unless they were successors to part or all of a company that was not autonomous.
2. At the dates the plan of combination is initiated and consummated, none of the combining companies can hold as intercorporate investments more than 10 percent of the outstanding voting common stock of any combining company, unless the shares held

were exchanged for shares that are issued to effect the combination plan. In other words, each of the combining companies must be independent of the other combining companies.[2]

II. Method of Combining Stockholder Interests

3. The combination must be effected by a single transaction or in accordance with a specific plan within one year after the plan is initiated.

4. The surviving (or parent) corporation must issue *only* common stock with rights identical to those of the majority of its outstanding voting common stock, in exchange for "substantially all" of the voting common stock of the other combining companies outstanding at the date the plan of combination is consummated. *APB Opinion No. 16* specifies a detailed set of procedures for determining whether the requirement is satisfied that substantially all of the voting common stock be exchanged. The essence of the requirement is that 90 percent or more of the outstanding common stock of a combining company must be exchanged (between the dates the plan of combination is initiated and consummated) for the voting common stock issued by the surviving or parent corporation.

5. Each of the combining companies must maintain substantially the same voting common stock interest. That is, none of the companies may change those interests by exchanges, retirements, or distributions to stockholders in contemplation of effecting the combination.

6. The combining companies may reacquire shares of voting common stock *only* for purposes other than business combinations, and no company may reacquire more than a normal number of shares after the plan of combination is begun.

7. The ratio of the interest of an individual common stockholder to those of other common stockholders in a combining company must remain the same as a result of the exchange of stock to effect the combination.

8. The voting rights of the common stock interests in the combined corporation must be exercisable by the stockholders. No

---

[2] However, *Statement of Financial Accounting Standards No. 10,* "Extension of 'Grandfather' Provisions for Business Combinations," provides a permanent exception for companies which held a minority interest in other companies on October 31, 1970 (the date *APB Opinion No. 16* became effective), if the stockholder corporations eventually increase their investments to establish control. In these cases, the stockholder companies may have owned up to 50 percent of the investee's outstanding stock on October 31, 1970, and still qualify for a pooling of interests, so long as the other pooling of interest conditions are satisfied.

mechanisms such as a voting trust can be used to deprive or restrict the common stockholders from exercising their voting rights.

9. The combination must be resolved at the date the plan is consummated, with no pending provision of the plan relating to the issue of securities or other consideration. Thus, the combined corporation cannot agree to contingent issuances of additional shares or other consideration to the former stockholders of a combining company.

III. Prohibited Postcombination Transactions

10. The combined corporation must not agree directly or indirectly to retire or reacquire all or part of the common stock issued to effect the combination.

11. The combined corporation must not enter into other financial arrangements for the benefit of the former stockholders of a combining company, such as a guaranty of loans secured by stock issued in the combination.

12. The combined corporation must not intend to dispose of a significant part of the assets of the combining companies within two years after the combination, except to eliminate duplicate facilities or excess capacity and those assets that would have been disposed of in the ordinary course of business of the combining company.

These conditions specify a situation where ownership interests in net assets have not been transferred from one group of owners to another. There is a clear continuity of ownership. Condition 4 is fundamental, and often the critical criterion. It requires that the surviving (or parent) corporation issue *only* common stock, with rights identical to those of the majority of its outstanding voting common stock, in exchange for "substantially all" (defined to mean 90 percent or more) of the voting common stock of the other combining company. This means that the common stockholders of both combining companies continue as voting common stockholders of the combined company. Control of the combined company is shared by the common stockholders of both combining companies. Since neither of the stockholder groups loses its ownership position, the combination does *not* involve the sale of one company to another. It is *not* a purchase/sale transaction. In one way or another, each of the 12 conditions adds to the conclusion that neither company is being sold to the other and that the operations and ownership interests of each combining company are continued through the combined company. For example, conditions 5, 6, and 10 prevent bypassing condition 4 through treasury stock transactions. Conditions 5 and 6 rule out either firm buying shares from stockholders who do not favor a future common stock for common stock exchange. Such a treasury stock transaction results in a change in ownership and therefore is a purchase. Similarly, condition 10 rules out an agreement by which shareholders initially receive common shares and then sell these shares back to the issuing corporation after the combination.

As a practical matter, it is difficult to determine the motive of treasury stock transactions. The Securities and Exchange Commission (SEC) has provided guidance in determining whether treasury stock transactions are violations of conditions 5, 6, and 10. Treasury stock transactions within a two-year period prior to initiation of a business combination, or between initiation and consummation of the combination, are presumed to violate the conditions. This presumption is overturned only in the case of treasury stock transactions which are consistent with an established pattern of treasury stock acquisitions (e.g., purchasing 1,000 shares annually in order to honor executive stock options).[3]

Despite the specificity of *APB Opinion No. 16,* transactions that are difficult to classify as purchases or pooling of interests still occur. Thus, accountants still must make hard decisions regarding the accounting for business combinations. Interestingly, the United States and the United Kingdom are virtually the only industrialized countries in which the pooling of interests method is acceptable. Perhaps this is due to the difficulty of conceiving of business combinations that result in genuine continuity of ownership. This concept is particularly difficult when the shares of the constituent firms are actively traded in an organized market. Ownership of such firms changes regularly. Nonetheless, many business combinations involving publicly traded companies meet the criteria specified by *APB Opinion No. 16* and are accounted for as a pooling of interests. Historically, about 60 percent of business combinations in the United States are classified as a pooling of interests.

Unopposed and Opposed Business Combinations

It is difficult for one corporation to obtain at least 90 percent of the outstanding common shares of another without cooperation on the part of both firms' management. It is common for one management to approach another with a proposal to exchange shares of one corporation for all the outstanding shares of the other. If the managements negotiate mutually satisfactory terms, the proposed exchange can be placed on the agenda for a stockholder meeting. Typically, a two-thirds favorable vote is enough to bind all stockholders to the transaction such that the 90 percent requirement for a pooling of interests is met.

In many cases, however, the management of a target for acquisition opposes the transaction and refuses to place a proposed exchange before a vote of the stockholders. The only option this leaves the potential acquiring firm is to deal directly with the stockholders of the target firm. That is, the acquiring firm must make a *tender offer* (an offer to acquire shares directly from individual share-

---

[3] *SEC Accounting Guide* (Chicago: Commerce Clearing House, Inc., 1984), par. 3552.

holders). This can be difficult since the target management can use corporate resources in resisting a takeover attempt.

It is unusual for a tender offer to result in acquisition of 90 percent of the outstanding shares. Accordingly, business combinations resulting from tender offers are usually classified as purchases. Moreover, the acquiring firm typically must offer a substantial premium over market value as an inducement for shareholders to sell their shares. A large premium virtually guarantees that the purchase price will exceed the book value of net assets acquired and therefore reduces postcombination income when the purchase method is used.

Many takeover attempts fail. The tender offer does not result in the would-be acquirer purchasing the desired number of shares. In many cases, the takeover target then buys the shares the would-be acquirer was successful in obtaining. The price paid for these treasury shares is often higher than even the premium price paid by the acquirer.[4] This practice of obtaining treasury shares at premium prices is termed *greenmail*. Payment of greenmail creates the presumption that the excess of price over the fair value of the treasury shares should not be recorded as a reduction of stockholders' equity. Rather, it should be recorded as current expense.[5]

Associated with takeovers is a colorful vocabulary extending beyond the term *greenmail*. To avoid takeover, the management of a target firm may seek to be acquired by or merge with a third firm more to the liking of the target management. Such a third firm is termed a *white knight*. Or the management may enter into agreements to liquidate prime assets in the event of takeover. Honoring such an agreement is termed *taking a poison pill*. On occasion, the management and/or employees of a target may seek to take over the firm in a transaction termed a *leveraged buyout* (the accounting for which is discussed in Chapter 5). Finally, many corporations have executive compensation contracts providing for generous payments to individuals displaced as a result of takeover. These contracts are termed *golden parachutes*.

TAX FACTORS AFFECTING BUSINESS COMBINATIONS

Taxation can be a very important aspect of business combinations. Depending on how the transaction is structured, the shareholders of the acquired corporation may have a gain or loss. Similarly, the acquired corporation may be treated as

---

[4] In a well-known case, Walt Disney Productions in 1984 paid investor Saul Steinberg over $325 million for his 11.1% interest in exchange for his promise not to issue a tender offer to acquire additional stock. Following the transaction, the market price of Disney stock fell almost 20 percent.

[5] Financial Accounting Standards Board, *FASB Technical Bulletin No. 85–6*, ''Accounting for a Purchase of Treasury Shares at a Price Significantly in Excess of the Current Market Price of the Shares and the Income Statement Classification of Costs Incurred in Defending against a Takeover Attempt'' (Norwalk, CT: FASB, 1985).

having sold its net assets and repurchased them at fair value. Last, the parent and subsidiary corporations may elect to file consolidated tax returns and be taxed as if they were a single entity. Such tax aspects affect the financial reporting of business combinations in various ways.[6]

Taxable and Nontaxable Acquisitions

An investor who sells shares of stock usually has a gain or loss equal to the difference between their sales price and tax basis. However, the sale will not be a taxable transaction to the seller if:

1. The transaction is a merger under state law and a significant part of the total consideration received is common stock of the acquiring corporation; or
2. The transaction involves the acquisition of at least 80 percent of the acquired corporation's common shares solely in exchange for common shares of the acquiring corporation.

Tax Basis of Acquired Corporation's Assets

When a business combination is a nontaxable transaction for the shareholders of the acquired corporation, there are no immediate tax consequences for the corporation itself. The corporation is not treated as having sold its net assets. Accordingly, the tax bases of those net assets remain the same as they were prior to the business combination.

If the business combination is taxable for the shareholders of the acquired corporation, however, the corporation itself can *elect* to be taxed as if it had sold its net assets and repurchased them at fair value.[7] If the fair value of these assets exceeds their current tax bases, the effects of the election are current taxable income on the implied sale of assets and higher tax bases for those assets. Unless the acquired corporation has a net operating loss or other carryforwards that would offset the current gain, there is little incentive to make this selection to step up tax bases of assets. Higher depreciation deductions in future years would be obtained at the cost of current gain on sale of assets. Unless the gain is taxed at a reduced rate, the election involves paying the tax now in exchange for not paying later. Declining to make the election avoids current gain recognition on the part of the acquired corporation and leaves the tax bases in its net assets unchanged.

Most business combinations that are taxable transactions for the shareholders of the acquired corporation are, for financial reporting purposes, accounted for using the purchase method. Recall that the purchase method involves reporting

---

[6] Much of the material in this section is taken from *Tax Strategies and Planning* (New York: Coopers & Lybrand, 1988).

[7] In some circumstances, the acquired corporation is *deemed* to have made the election, even though it did not actually do so.

acquired assets at their fair values. If the acquired corporation does not elect to step up the tax bases of its assets, the fair values of these assets will not, in general, coincide with their tax bases. In Chapter 3, we discuss the implication of using the purchase method when fair values of assets are not equal to their tax bases.

Consolidated Tax Returns

An election to file a separate or consolidated tax return is available to member corporations of the affiliated group. To qualify as an affiliated group, a parent must own at least 80 percent of the common shares of its subsidiary. If a consolidated tax return is filed, intercompany dividends escape taxation. In addition, losses of one affiliate may be used to offset current income of another. Last, profits on sales of assets from one affiliate to another are not taxed until the purchasing affiliate sells the assets to a nonaffiliate. The financial reporting implications of taxation as an affiliated group as opposed to separate entities are discussed in Chapters 4 and 7.

Summary

We began this chapter with the economic motivations for one corporation to obtain the common shares of another. Such transactions, like the acquisition of a single asset and basket purchase of assets, are undertaken with the expectation of generating added value through synergies of combination.

Subsequent to the business combination, the acquired corporation can continue to exist as a legal entity. Such transactions are termed *acquisitions*. Or the acquired corporation can distribute its net assets to the acquiring corporation and cease existing. If so, the transaction is termed a *merger*. Finally, a newly created corporation can receive the net assets of the combining corporations. This type of business combination is termed a *consolidation*.

An important accounting issue in business combinations is whether the transaction involves a continuity of ownership. When there is a continuity of ownership, the *pooling of interests* method is used to account for the business combination. Among the characteristics of this method is continued valuation of acquired firm assets at historical cost. When a business combination involves a change in ownership, the *purchase* method is used to account for the transaction. Assets of the acquired firm are recorded at fair value under the purchase method. *APB Opinion No. 16* provides guidance in determining whether a continuity of ownership exists.

Business combinations can be taxable or nontaxable events for the shareholders of the acquired firm. If the business combination is nontaxable, the acquired corporation does not alter the tax bases of its net assets. If the business combination is taxable, the acquired corporation can elect to be taxed as if it has sold its assets and repurchased them at fair value. Following some business combinations, the constituent corporations can elect to be taxed as a single entity.

Appendix: Negotiating Purchase Price

Recall that the economic motivation for business combinations is to generate additional market value. Whether the transaction is a cash for common stock or common stock for common stock exchange, negotiating the purchase price involves allocating the anticipated synergy between the shareholders of the acquiring and acquired firms.

First consider a cash for common stock exchange. Suppose a target firm has a current market value of $20 million. The target is a supplier of input for the acquiring firm. When acquired, the target will be more efficient since inventory production can be timed to coincide with parent company demands. Accordingly, inventory storage costs can be eliminated. In addition, marketing expenses can be reduced. Because of these factors, the target firm is expected to be worth $25 million when controlled by the acquiring firm.

The purchase price paid to the shareholders of the target firm will be between $20 million and $25 million. At a price of $20 million, the $5 million in synergistic value is allocated to the shareholders of the acquiring firm. At a price of $25 million, the added value is allocated to the shareholders of the acquired firm. The actual price will depend on the relative bargaining power of the two groups of shareholders.

Unfortunately, the factors that give rise to bargaining power are not well understood. It has been suggested that competition among several would-be acquirers gives bargaining power to the shareholders of the target firm. More bargaining power in the hands of the target firm shareholders will drive the actual price toward the $25 million price. Evidence on this subject is mixed.

The same principles apply in common stock for common stock exchanges. The *stock exchange ratio,* defined as the number of shares of the issuing firm to be given in exchange for one share of the acquired firm, is a "price" that allocates anticipated market value between the two shareholder groups. Consider the actual combination of General Electric and Utah International. At the time, this business combination was the largest in U.S. history. The combination was done through an exchange of new General Electric shares for all the outstanding shares of Utah International. Data relating to these two companies before the exchange were:

	General Electric	Utah International
Market value per share	$45.75	$47.50
Shares outstanding	182,855,000	31,540,000
Total market value	$8,365,616,000	$1,498,150,000

Shortly after the exchange, the market value of the combined firm's outstanding shares was $11,976,350,000. This amount is greater than the sum of the precombination values of the two firms by $2,112,584,000, a substantial synergistic effect. If we assume this actual combined firm value is a good estimate for what was anticipated, then the upper bound for the exchange ratio is the maximum that the General Electric stockholders would accept. It is the exchange ratio that gives all the anticipated synergistic market value of $2,112,584,000 to the Utah International stockholders and leaves the General Electric stockholders with only their original $8,365,616,000 in market value.

Let S denote the additional shares of General Electric that are issued in exchange for the outstanding Utah International shares. The percentage ownership interest of the

General Electric stockholders in the combined firm is then

$$\frac{182,855,000}{182,855,000 + S}$$

and the market value associated with this ownership percentage is

$$\frac{182,855,000}{182,855,000 + S}(\$11,976,350,000)$$

The value of S which leaves the General Electric stockholders with only their original $8,365,616,000 in market value is the solution to the equation

$$\frac{182,855,000}{182,855,000 + S}(\$11,976,350,000) = \$8,365,616,000$$

The solution for S is 78,923,000 additional shares. This implies the exchange ratio

$$\frac{78,923,000}{31,540,000} = 2.50:1$$

which is the largest price the General Electric stockholders would be willing to pay for the Utah International shares. With this exchange ratio, all the $2,112,584,000 in additional market value is given to the Utah International stockholders.

The lowest price the Utah International stockholders are willing to accept is similarly reached. The percentage ownership of the Utah International stockholders in the combined firm is

$$\frac{S}{182,855,000 + S}$$

and the market value associated with this ownership percentage is

$$\frac{S}{182,855,000 + S}(\$11,976,350,000)$$

The value of S which leaves the Utah International stockholders with only their original $1,498,150,000 in market value is the solution to the equation

$$\frac{S}{182,855,000 + S}(\$11,976,350,000) = \$1,498,150,000$$

The solution for S is now 26,144,000, which imples the exchange ratio

$$\frac{26,144,000}{31,540,000} = .83:1$$

With this exchange ratio, all the $2,112,584,000 in added market value is given to the General Electric stockholders.

According to the analysis, the actual exchange ratio in the General Electric/Utah International exchange should have been between 2.50 and .83. It was! In fact, 41,002,000 additional General Electric shares were issued in exchange for the 31,540,000 outstanding Utah International shares. The actual exchange ratio was

$$\frac{41,002,000}{31,540,000} = 1.30:1$$

Apparently, the General Electric shareholders had more bargaining power than those of Utah International. The actual exchange ratio was closer to the .83 minimum price than it was to the 2.50 maximum price.

The exchange ratio will affect the postcombination earnings per share of the acquiring company. The size of the effect will depend on the precombination price/earnings ratios of the acquiring and acquired firms. When a high price/earnings ratio firm acquires a low price/earnings ratio firm, the business combination tends to increase the acquirer's postcombination earnings per share. This is because earnings (the numerator) are increased relatively more than are shares outstanding (the denominator). Thus, common stock for common stock business combinations provide a vehicle for manipulating earnings per share.

Questions

1. What is the economic motivation for business combinations? Is this different from the motivation to acquire any asset?

2. Business combinations often result in additional market value. What are some reasons that this increase might materialize?

3. Explain the main differences among business combinations that are classified as acquisitions, mergers, and consolidations.

4. Explain the relationship between the method of payment (cash or stock) and the issue of whether the ownership of the acquired company has changed hands. Also explain the relationship between changes in ownership and the methods of accounting for business combinations.

5. What are the balance sheet differences between a purchase and a pooling of interests? What are the income statement differences?

6. Explain the effect of treasury stock transactions on whether a business combination results in a change in ownership and hence is accounted for as a purchase.

7. Under what conditions is a sale of shares a nontaxable transaction for the owner of the shares? When the transaction is nontaxable, are there tax consequences for the corporation whose shares have been sold?

8. When an investor sells shares in a taxable transaction, the corporation whose shares are sold may elect to step up the bases of its net assets. What are the tax consequences of doing so?

9. Explain the basic differences between consolidated and separate company tax returns.

10. In a business combination facilitated through an exchange of common shares, the share exchange ratio is negotiated. Fair values of each combining company's assets and liabilities play a role in such negotiations. Accordingly, both sets of fair values are in some sense confirmed. The pooling of interests method ignores these fair values, despite their confirmation through an arm's length negotiation. Why are fair values ignored despite their having been confirmed?

Exercises

Exercise 1–1   (Purchase and Pooling of Interests Methods)

Identify whether each of the following acquisitions appears to satisfy the criteria for a pooling of interests.

a. A Company acquired 95 percent of the outstanding common shares of B Company. Fifty-one percent of the B shares were acquired for cash. The remaining 44 percent were acquired in a common stock for common stock exchange.

b. A Company acquired all the outstanding common shares of B Company in a common stock for common stock exchange. A Company obtained the A shares given in the exchange as treasury shares shortly prior to the combination.

c. A Company acquired 95 percent of the outstanding common shares of B Company in exchange for shares of A Company's fully participating preferred stock.

d. A Company acquired 95 percent of the outstanding common shares of B Company in a common stock for common stock exchange.

e. B Company acquired 15 percent of its outstanding common shares shortly before its acquisition by A Company. These shares had been owned by C Company with the expectation that C Company would systematically increase its ownership of B to 51 percent. The acquisition of B Company by A Company was achieved by A Company issuing its common shares in exchange for 95 percent of B Company's then outstanding common shares.

f. P Company acquired a 100 percent interest in S Company on December 31, 19X0, by issuing 500,000 shares of P Company $1 par common stock in exchange for S Company shares. The current market price of the P Company common stock is $40 per share. Additionally, P Company guaranteed that the market price of its shares will be at least $60 at December 31, 19X2. If the market price of P Company stock is less than $60 per share on this date, P Company will issue additional shares with a current market value equal to the difference between the total guaranteed value and the current market value of the shares previously issued.

g. A Company, a subsidiary of B Company, was acquired by C Company after it was spun off by B (by distributing the shares of A to the shareholders of B).

Exercise 1–2   (Pooling of Interests Method)

Company P has made a tender offering for all the common shares of S. The S management is opposed to P's offer and is aware that it is extremely important to P management that any P/S combination be accounted for as a pooling of interests. The S management identified a "white knight" company, X Company, willing to make a competing tender offer for 11 percent of the common shares of S. The S management encouraged the S owners to accept X Company's offer.

Required:

a. Explain why it might be important to the P management to have a P/S combination accounted for as a pooling of interests.

b. Explain why X Company's tender offer will be an effective tactic to fight the takeover of S by P.

Exercise 1-3   (Purchase Method)

Data relating to B Corporation appear below:

	Book Value	Fair Value
Current assets	$200,000	$220,000
Plant and equipment	400,000	500,000
Liabilities	250,000	250,000
Capital stock	200,000	
Retained earnings	150,000	

A Corporation acquired B's assets and assumed its liabilities for a cash payment of $600,000.

Required:
Prepare the entry on A's books to record the basket purchase.

Exercise 1-4   (Purchase Method)

Refer to the data in Exercise 1-3. Assume, however, that A purchased all the outstanding common shares of B for $600,000 cash in a business combination classified as a merger.

Required:
Prepare the entries on A's books to record the share purchase and merger.

Exercise 1-5   (Purchase Method)

Refer to the data in Exercise 1-3. Assume, however, that A purchased all the outstanding common shares of B for $600,000 cash. The transaction was taxable to the B shareholders and there was no election to step up the basis of B's plant and equipment. B's tax basis of the plant and equipment was equal to book value.

Required:
Do you think that B has an unrecorded liability because the fair value of its plant and equipment is $100,000 in excess of book value? If so, do you think A has implicitly assumed this liability?

Exercise 1-6   (Pooling of Interests Method)

Refer to the data in Exercise 1-3. Assume, however, that A obtained all of B's outstanding common shares by issuing A Company shares with a par value of $200,000. The business combination is classified as a merger and accounted for as a pooling of interests.

Required:

Prepare the entries on A's books to record the share exchange and merger.

Exercise 1–7   (Pooling of Interests Method)

Curt Crandall and Adam Boatsman own lawn care businesses. The assets of each business consist of a truck, lawn mowers, and miscellaneous garden tools. Crandall's business assets have a book value of $5,000, and he believes that it would cost approximately $6,000 to replace them. Boatsman's business assets have a book value of $3,000, and he believes their replacement cost to be approximately $4,000.

Crandall and Boatsman agree that their individual economic interests would be well served by combining their operations. The basis for this belief is elimination of duplicate costs of soliciting customers. Boatsman contributes the assets of his firm to Crandall's firm in exchange for a 40 percent ownership interest in Crandall's firm.

Required:

a. Does this transaction satisfy the normal accounting notions for realization such that Boatsman can be said to have realized a profit of $1,000 as a result of the transaction?

b. Does the transaction confirm the appreciation of Boatsman's assets to any greater extent than it confirms the appreciation of Crandall's assets?

c. Would either of the above answers change if Boatsman contributed the stock of his firm to Crandall's firm instead of contributing its assets?

d. Explain how your answers relate to the pooling of interests method of accounting for a business combination.

Exercise 1–8   (Purchase Method)

Curt Crandall and Adam Boatsman own lawn care businesses. The assets of each business consist of a truck, lawn mowers, and miscellaneous garden tools. Crandall's business assets have a book value of $5,000, and he believes that it would cost approximately $6,000 to replace them. Boatsman's business assets have a book value of $3,000, and he believes their replacement cost to be approximately $4,000.

Crandall and Boatsman agree that their individual economic interests would be well served by combining their assets into a single economic entity. The basis for this belief is elimination of duplicate costs of soliciting customers. Boatsman transfers the assets of his firm to Crandall's firm in exchange for $4,000 cash. Crandall's firm borrowed the $4,000 to pay Boatsman.

Required:

a. Does this transaction satisfy the normal accounting notions for realization such that Boatsman can be said to have realized a profit of $1,000 as a result of the transaction?

b. Does the transaction confirm the appreciation of Boatsman's assets to any greater extent than it confirms the appreciation of Crandall's assets?

c. Would either of the above answers change if Boatsman contributed the stock of his firm to Crandall's firm instead of contributing its assets?

d. Explain how your answers relate to the purchase method of accounting for a business combination.

Problems

Problem 1-9   (Purchase Method)

Howerton Company acquired 100 percent of the outstanding shares of Penney, Inc., for $500,000 cash. Immediately prior to the transaction, Howerton's balance sheet was as follows:

Cash	$ 1,000,000
Other current assets	2,000,000
Plant and equipment	8,000,000
Total assets	$11,000,000
Current liabilities	$ 2,000,000
Long-term liabilities	6,000,000
Total liabilities	$ 8,000,000
Capital stock	$ 2,000,000
Retained earnings	1,000,000
Total stockholders' equity	$ 3,000,000
Total liabilities and stockholders' equity	$11,000,000

On the acquisition date, data relating to the net assets of Penney were:

	Fair Value	Book Value
Cash	$ 200,000	$200,000
Other current assets	200,000	150,000
Plant and equipment	600,000	400,000
Total assets	$1,000,000	$750,000
Current liabilities	$ 100,000	$100,000
Long-term liabilities	450,000	500,000
Total liabilities	$ 550,000	$600,000
Total net assets	$ 450,000	$150,000

If the Howerton/Penney combination is accounted for as a purchase, the postcombination balance sheet of the combined entity would appear as:

Cash	$ 700,000
Other current assets	2,200,000
Plant and equipment	8,600,000
Goodwill	50,000
Total assets	$11,550,000
Current liabilities	$ 2,100,000
Long-term liabilities	6,450,000
Total liabilities	$ 8,550,000
Capital stock	$ 2,000,000
Retained earnings	1,000,000
Total stockholders' equity	$ 3,000,000
Total liabilities and stockholders' equity	$11,550,000

Required:

a. Assume that instead of purchasing Penney shares, Howerton purchased all of Penney's assets and assumed Penney's liabilities. Also assume that Howerton paid Penney's owners $500,000 cash in this transaction. Prepare the journal entry to record the transaction on the books of Howerton.

b. Under the assumptions above, prepare Howerton's balance sheet immediately after the purchase of Penney's net assets. Compare this balance sheet with postcombination balance sheet given earlier.

c. Is the purchase of net assets fundamentally different from the purchase of the shares of another company? If so, in what respect?

Problem 1–10   (Pooling of Interests Method)

Penny Company acquired 100 percent of the outstanding shares of Nickel, Inc., by issuing 200,000 shares of its $1 par common stock ($1.10 market value). Right before the transaction, Penny's balance sheet was:

Current assets	$ 3,000,000
Plant and equipment	8,000,000
Total assets	$11,000,000
Current liabilities	$ 2,000,000
Long-term liabilities	6,000,000
Total liabilities	$ 8,000,000
Capital stock	$ 2,000,000
Retained earnings	1,000,000
Total stockholders' equity	$ 3,000,000
Total liabilities and stockholders' equity	$11,000,000

Nickel was organized one year ago by issuing 200,000 shares of its $1 par common stock at $1 per share. The proceeds were invested in a savings account that has earned 10 percent interest. Right before its acquisition by Penny, Nickel's balance sheet was:

Current assets	$220,000
Total assets	$220,000
Capital stock	$200,000
Retained earnings	20,000
Total stockholders' equity	$220,000

If the Penny/Nickel combination is accounted for as a pooling of interests, the postcombination balance sheet of the combined entity would appear as:

Current assets	$ 3,220,000
Plant and equipment	8,000,000
Total assets	$11,220,000
Current liabilities	$ 2,000,000
Long-term liabilities	6,000,000
Total liabilities	$ 8,000,000
Capital stock	$ 2,200,000
Retained earnings	1,020,000
Total stockholders' equity	$ 3,220,000
Total liabilities and stockholders' equity	$11,220,000

Required:

a. Assume that one year ago, Penny issued 200,000 shares of its common stock at $1 per share. Also assume that the proceeds were invested in a savings account that has earned 10 percent interest during the past year. Prepare the journal entry to record the issuance of the 200,000 Penny shares and investment of proceeds in the savings account.

b. Under the assumptions above, prepare the journal entry to record the collection of one year's interest on Penny's investment in the savings account.

c. Under the assumptions above, prepare Penny's balance sheet as of one year after the issuance of 200,000 shares and investment of proceeds in the savings account. Compare this balance sheet with the postcombination balance sheet given above.

Problem 1-11   (Purchase and Pooling of Interests Methods)

Charles Christian owns two assets: a truck and a trailer. Christian believes both assets have fair values in excess of their historical cost values. The truck is sold for cash to Reneau Company. The purchase price is the fair value envisioned by Christian. Christian then transfers ownership in the trailer to Reneau, receiving in exchange a 20 percent ownership interest in Reneau.

Required:

a. Has the fair value of the truck been confirmed by virtue of its sale to Reneau?

b. Has the fair value of the trailer been confirmed by virtue of its exchange for a 20 percent ownership interest in Reneau?

c. In light of your answers to *(a)* and *(b)*, should Reneau use a fair value basis of accounting for both the truck and trailer?

d. Now assume that the truck and trailer are owned by a corporation which is, in turn, owned by Christian. Christian transfers all the stock of this corporation to Reneau, receiving cash equal to the fair value of the truck and a 20 percent ownership interest in Reneau. Does this alteration in circumstances change your answers to *(a)*, *(b)*, or *(c)*?

e. Would the transaction in *(d)* be accounted for by Reneau as a purchase or pooling of interests?

Problems for Appendix

Problem 1-12   (Share Exchange Ratio)

Data relating to the acquisition of B by A appear below:

	A	B	Combined Entity
Net income	$ 2,000,000	$1,000,000	$ 3,000,000
Shares outstanding	8,000,000	2,000,000	?
Market value of common	$10,000,000	$4,000,000	$20,000,000
Price/earnings ratio	5.00	4.00	6.67

Required:

a. Calculate the minimum stock exchange ratio of A shares to B shares acceptable to the owners of B.

b. Calculate the maximum stock exchange ratio of A shares to B shares acceptable to the owners of A.

Problem 1–13   (Share Exchange Ratios)

A Company acquires 100 percent of the outstanding common shares of B Company in a stock for stock business combination properly accounted for as a pooling of interests. Data relating to A Company, B Company, and the combined entity are:

	A Company	B Company	Combined
Fair value	$10,000	$5,000	$20,000
Earnings	$ 1,000	$ 800	$ 2,000
Earnings per share	$ .50	$ .80	
Shares outstanding	2,000	1,000	

Required:

Assume that the negotiated share exchange ratio is the minimum acceptable to the owners of B Company. Compute the postcombination earnings per share of the combined entity (A Company and its subsidiary B Company).

Problem 1–14   (Share Exchange Ratios)

Data for the combination of Drake Company and Week Company (to be facilitated through an exchange of common shares) appear below:

	Drake	Week	Combined Entity
Net income	$ 6,000,000	$ 4,000,000	$10,000,000
Shares outstanding	5,000,000	1,000,000	?
Market value of common	$12,000,000	$20,000,000	$32,000,000
Price/earnings ratio	2.00	5.00	3.20

Required:

Assuming that one objective of the combination is to maximize the growth in EPS of the acquiring firm, would it be better for Drake to acquire Week or vice versa?

Fundamentals of Consolidated Statements

Recall that businesss combinations can be acquisitions, mergers, or consolidations. And depending on how the combination is structured, any of the three forms of combination can be a purchase or pooling of interests. Thus, there are six possibilities:

1. Acquisition accounted for as a purchase.
2. Acquisition accounted for as a pooling of interests.
3. Merger accounted for as a purchase.
4. Merger accounted for as a pooling of interests.
5. Consolidation accounted for as a purchase.
6. Consolidation accounted for as a pooling of interests.

In this chapter we concentrate on *acquisitions accounted for as poolings of interests*. In an acquisition, a parent corporation acquires the common shares of a subsidiary corporation which continues to exist as a legal entity. Both corporations normally continue to operate accounting systems which produce financial statements at the ends of accounting periods. Thus, one issue is how to account for the subsidiary on the books of the parent company. A second accounting issue involves combining the separate company statements of the parent and subsidiary into a single set of statements of the combined economic entity. Such statements are termed *consolidated statements*.[1]

Reasons for the Acquisition Form of Business Combination

There are many reasons that a business combination will take the form of an acquisition. In a corporate takeover, there is little point in owning 100 percent of the voting shares of the target. Control can be achieved with a significantly lower ownership interest. A merger generally requires at least 90 percent ownership.[2] Additionally, legal requirements for shareholder approvals are minimized when business combinations take the form of an acquisition.

Business combinations are undertaken with the expectation of adding market value. However, the expectations may not materialize. In the event a business combination is ultimately rescinded, it may be easier to sell the subsidiary's shares than to sell the subsidiary's assets individually. Only the latter option would be available had the subsidiary been merged into the parent.

A characteristic of corporations is limited liability on the part of shareholders. In the case of an acquisition, the parent is a shareholder of the subsidiary. Thus, the parent enjoys limited liability.

---

[1] Use of the term *consolidated statements* sometimes creates confusion, since the business combination is an *acquisition* (as opposed to a *consolidation*). However, as is discussed later, the economic entity composed of the parent company and the subsidiary company for which the consolidated statements are prepared is analogous to the new legal entity resulting from a consolidation.

[2] §11.04, *Model Business Corporation Act.*

Acquisitions may, however, be unattractive from a tax standpoint. In many states, corporations pay a franchise tax. A franchise tax is a tax on net assets. When the parent uses the equity method to account for its investment in the subsidiary, the parent's share of the subsidiary's net assets appears among the parent's assets (in the form of the investment account) as well as on the books of the subsidiary. Franchise taxes are normally assessed at the individual corporation level. Thus, the parent's share of subsidiary assets is effectively taxed to both the parent and subsidiary. This double franchise taxation would not occur if the subsidiary were merged into the parent.

REQUIREMENTS FOR CONSOLIDATED AND SEPARATE COMPANY STATEMENTS

The authoritative literature recognizes that both consolidated and separate company financial statements have merit. In its *Regulation S-X*, the SEC states a *presumption* that consolidated statements are more meaningful than separate company statements. This view of the paramount importance of consolidated statements is affirmed by the FASB in *Statement of Financial Accounting Standards No. 94*.[3] *Statement No. 94* requires consolidated presentation of investments in majority-owned subsidiaries unless control is likely to be temporary or if control does not reside with the majority shareholders. In short, if a consolidated presentation is required, any separate company presentations are supplements to the consolidated presentation.

It is common for annual reports to shareholders to include only consolidated statements. In reports filed with the SEC, however, a consolidated presentation with supplemental separate company presentations is sometimes required. *Regulation S-X* requires supplemental parent company statements when there are material restrictions on the transfer of assets to the parent from the subsidiary. The regulation also requires supplemental subsidiary financial statements in some circumstances.[4]

Control

The consolidation requirement in *Statement No. 94* is majority ownership of voting shares. SEC requirements, on the other hand, tend to focus on control. In most cases, control is evidenced by majority ownership and the two requirements coincide. However, it is possible for control to exist without majority ownership

---

[3] FASB, *Statement of Financial Accounting Standards No. 94*, "Consolidation of All Majority-Owned Subsidiaries" (Norwalk, CT: FASB, 1987).

[4] Specifics of these requirements are complex and are beyond the scope of this text. See SEC, *Financial Reporting Release No. 1*, "Codification of Financial Reporting Policies" (Washington, D.C.: SEC, 1982), sec. 213.

and for majority ownership to be insufficient for control. In those rare situations where control does not coincide with majority ownership, the apparent conflict between the two consolidation requirements would be resolved in favor of the SEC position that a subsidiary should be consolidated if controlled.

Circumstances beyond voting share ownership must be examined to determine whether control exists. As an example, imagine P Company owns 10 percent of the voting shares of S Company. However, P Company also holds convertible debt of S Company. This debt can be converted whenever P Company wishes. If the debt is converted, P Company's ownership of S Company's voting shares would increase to 90 percent. In addition, the debt has covenants which prevent S Company from issuing any additional debt or common stock such that P Company's ability to convert and own a 90 percent interest cannot be diluted. Last, the debt agreement requires that the executives of S Company serve at the pleasure of P Company. In this case, P Company controls S Company despite owning only 10 percent of S Company's voting shares.[5]

As a second example, imagine that P Company owns 90 percent of the voting shares of S Company. However, S Company is in legal reorganization or bankruptcy. In this case, control does not rest with P Company even though it owns 90 percent of the S Company shares.

In determining whether control exists, it is useful to think about reasons why a parent company might want to structure an acquisition to give the appearance that control doesn't exist when, in substance, it does. One common reason is to avoid reporting debt. In the financial statements of the parent company, any debt of the subsidiary is "buried" in the investment account. If a subsidiary is consolidated, however, the debt is reported separately as a liability. Therefore, avoiding consolidation results in reporting a lower debt/equity ratio. If the parent has debt covenants which restrict the debt/equity ratio, and if compliance with these covenants is to be determined from financial statements issued to shareholders, an otherwise binding covenant can be "undone" by avoiding consolidation in statements issued to shareholders.

RECORDING THE ACQUISITION

Recall from Chapter 1 that the effect of applying *pooling of interests accounting* to a business combination is a set of financial statements that is identical to the statements that would have been produced if the combining firms had been operating as a single entity throughout their entire histories. Book values are

---

[5] The circumstances of this example are similar to those described in a recent SEC enforcement action involving the financial statements of Digilog, Inc., in which control was determined to exist.

carried forward without adjustment for changes in fair values, and the incomes of the two companies are simply combined for all periods. This accounting treatment is appropriate when the combination is not viewed as a purchase of one company by the other, but rather a blending together of existing shareholder interests to continue the formerly separate companies under joint control. There is continuity of ownership and management. Prior to the adoption of *APB Opinion No. 16*, the principal authority for determining the method of accounting for a business combination was provided by *Accounting Research Bulletin No. 48*. This pronouncement provided broad factors which should be considered in determining the appropriate accounting. Unfortunately, standard setters concluded that this judgmentally based approach was being severely abused in practice, and the result was the set of 12 specific, somewhat legalistic, criteria contained in *Opinion No. 16*.

A business combination can be accounted for as a pooling of interests under *Opinion No. 16* if, in addition to satisfying the other 11 conditions, the "acquiring" company (the parent) issues shares of its common stock for at least 90 percent of the common stock of the "acquired" company (the subsidiary). An acquisition in which 100 percent of the acquired company's stock is acquired is recorded by the parent company by debiting the investment account for the book value of the subsidiary's net assets, and crediting Paid-in Capital and Retained Earnings for the amounts reflected on the subsidiary's books.[6]

For example, assume S Company has net assets with a book value of $100, and its shareholders' equity is composed of common stock, $10, additional paid-in capital, $50, and retained earnings, $40. We also assume that P company issues its *no par* common stock in exchange for all of the common stock of S Company and that the combination qualifies as a pooling of interests.[7] The entry to record the exchange of shares is:

Investment in S Company	100	
Capital Stock (no par)		60
Retained Earnings		40

The credit to Capital Stock (no par) is for the total paid-in capital of S Company (capital stock, $10, and additional paid-in capital, $50), and the retained earnings of S Company is carried forward and combined with the retained earnings of P Company.

If P Company does not acquire all of the common stock of S Company (but does acquire more than the 90 percent minimum for a pooling of interests), the

---

[6] The credits to shareholders' equity may be different when the acquiring company issues common stock with a *par or stated value* which exceeds the *combined* paid-in capital of the combining companies. The procedure for dealing with these types of unusual circumstances is discussed in Appendix B.

[7] Our assumption that *no par* stock is issued by the parent allows us to avoid at this time the problems of allocating the paid-in capital between capital stock and additional paid-in capital. This process is illustrated in Appendix B.

amounts recorded to the paid-in capital and retained earnings components are based upon the *acquired ownership percentage*. For example, assume P Company had acquired only 95 percent of S Company's outstanding common stock, but that the transaction still qualified as a pooling of interests. The entry to record the exchange of shares in this case would be:

Investment in S Company (95% × $100)	95	
Capital Stock (no par) (95% × $60)		57
Retained Earnings (95% × $40)		38

CONSOLIDATED BALANCE SHEET

In this section, we confine our attention to a consolidated balance sheet prepared immediately after a subsidiary is acquired by its parent. There is no particular reason that a business combination would occur on the last day of an accounting period. Accordingly, a consolidated balance sheet as of the date of acquisition might never be prepared in actual practice. However, focusing on the consolidated balance sheet at the date of acquisition is a convenient starting point to illustrate the basic principles of consolidated financial statements.

The Nature of a Consolidated Balance Sheet

On the date of acquisition, the consolidated balance sheet is similar to the balance sheet of the parent. Differences are confined to detail. We develop this notion through a series of cases arranged in order of increasing complexity. For simplicity, we use small numerical values. Recall that all combinations are classified as a pooling of interests.

Case 1. Acquisition of a 100 Percent Interest

Assume P Company acquires 100 percent of the common shares of S Company in exchange for its no par common stock. At acquisition, S Company's balance sheet consists of current assets, $10; plant and equipment, $190; and liabilities, $100. The stockholders' equity is composed of capital stock of $25 and retained earnings of $75. P Company's entry to record the acquisition is:

Investment in S Company	100	
Capital Stock		25
Retained Earnings		75

The investment account is set equal to the book value of S Company's net assets, and the paid-in capital and retained earnings of S Company are carried forward.

Now assume that after the combination is recorded, P Company's balance sheet is:

Current assets	$100
Investment in S Company	100
Plant and equipment	200
Total assets	$400
Liabilities	$200
Stockholders' equity	200
Total liabilities and stockholders' equity	$400

Since the balance in the investment account equals the book value of the net assets acquired, S Company's individual assets and liabilities can be substituted in place of the investment account by adding the book values of S Company assets and liabilities to corresponding P Company amounts. The result would be:

Current assets ($100 + $10)	$110
Investment in S Company	–0–
Plant and equipment ($200 + $190)	390
Total assets	$500
Liabilities ($200 + $100)	$300
Stockholders' equity	200
Total liabilities and stockholders' equity	$500

This exercise has produced a *consolidated balance sheet.* The difference between the parent company balance sheet and the consolidated balance sheet is a matter of detail. In the parent company balance sheet, the book values of the subsidiary's individual assets and liabilities are added together in the investment account. On the consolidated balance sheet, these values are reported individually (i.e., the $10 book value of current assets is reported with the parent's current assets, the $190 book value of plant and equipment is added to P Company's plant and equipment, and the $100 book value of liabilities is included with the liabilities).

For our next case, it will be convenient to think about the differences between the separate company balance sheet of the parent and the consolidated balance sheet in T account format. In this format, the differences between the presentations of S Company's net assets on the separate company balance sheet of P Company and the consolidated balance sheet are:

Parent Company Balance Sheet	Consolidated Balance Sheet
	Current Assets
	10
Investment in S Company	**Plant and Equipment**
100	190
	Liabilities
	100

On its separate company balance sheet, P's investment in S Company is presented in a single account (the investment account). On the consolidated balance sheet, this single account presentation is replaced with a multiple account presentation.

Case 2. Acquisition of Less than 100 Percent Interest

Assume P Company acquires 90 percent of the common shares of S Company in exchange for shares of its no par common stock. At acquisition, S Company's assets, liabilities, and owners' equity are as in Case 1.

The book value of S Company's recorded net assets is $100. Therefore, the book value of a claim to 90 percent of these net assets is $90 (90% × $100). In this case, there are two ways in which the $90 appearing in P Company's investment account could be disaggregated in order to prepare a consolidated balance sheet. In T account format, the first of these is as follows:

Parent Company Balance Sheet	Consolidated Balance Sheet
	Current Assets
	90% × 10 = 9
Investment in S Company	**Plant and Equipment**
90	90% × 190 = 171
	Liabilities
	90% × 100 = 90

On the consolidated balance sheet, the individual assets and liabilities of S Company are presented at 90 percent of book value. This alternative is termed *proportionate consolidation*.

Although proportionate consolidation is used in some circumstances (discussed in Chapter 5), the method has distinct limitations. P Company *controls* the utilization of *all* of S Company's net assets, not just 90 percent of them. Imagine assessing the asset management performance of P's management by, say, computing the return on total assets. Clearly, we would want to include all the assets under the control of P's management in the denominator and all the income generated with these assets in the numerator. Consolidated financial statements prepared using proportionate consolidation would not permit this since only 90 percent of S Company's asset and liability values appear on the consolidated balance sheet.

The alternative to proportionate consolidation is to present 100 percent of the book values of S Company's assets and liabilities on the consolidated balance sheet. However, 100 percent of these book values sums to $100, but P Company's investment account balance is only $90. This dilemma can be remedied by adding an additional item to the consolidated balance sheet. The additional item, with a $10 credit balance, is termed *minority interest*. In T account format, the differences between the presentations on the parent balance sheet and the consolidated balance sheet are:

Parent Company Balance Sheet		**Consolidated Balance Sheet**	
		Current Assets	
		10	
		Plant and Equipment	
Investment in S Company		190	
90			
		Liabilities	
			100
		Minority Interest	
			$10\% \times 100 = 10$

All the book values of S Company's assets and liabilities appear on the consolidated balance sheet. Although P Company *controls* all these assets and liabilities, it *owns* only 90 percent of them. The remaining 10 percent is owned by S Company's other shareholders. These shareholders are termed *minority shareholders*.

The minority interest item on the consolidated balance sheet represents the claim of the minority shareholders to S Company's net assets.

This method of presentation is termed *full consolidation*. The consolidated balance sheet contains all the assets under the control of P Company's management, and reflects the claims of three groups against these assets: creditors, P Company shareholders, and the minority shareholders of S Company. Full consolidation is the prevailing method in current practice and is used throughout this text.

Consolidated Balance Sheet Working Paper

A consolidated balance sheet can be prepared by simply changing amounts on the parent company's balance sheet; that is, increasing the parent's current assets, plant and equipment, and liabilities, eliminating the investment account, and establishing minority interest. When the parent and subsidiary balance sheets contain many accounts, however, it is easier to use a working paper to develop a consolidated balance sheet.

Case 3. Illustration of Working Paper

Assume that P Company acquires 90 percent of the common shares of S Company in exchange for shares of P Company's no par common stock. On the date of acquisition, but before the transaction is recorded by P Company, the balance sheets of P Company and S Company are:

	P Company	S Company
Current assets	$100	$ 10
Plant and equipment	300	190
	$400	$200
Liabilities	$200	$100
Capital stock (no par)	100	50
Retained earnings	100	50
	$400	$200

The entry on P Company's books to record the acquisition as a pooling of interests is:

```
Investment in S Company  . . . . . . . . . . . . . . . . . . . . . . . . . . . . . . . . . . . . .  90
    Capital Stock (90% × $50) . . . . . . . . . . . . . . . . . . . . . . . . . . . . . . . . . .     45
    Retained Earnings (90% × $50)  . . . . . . . . . . . . . . . . . . . . . . . . . . . . . .     45
```

A working paper to prepare the consolidated balance sheet appears in Illustration 2–1. The first two columns contain the balance sheets of P Company and

S Company, respectively. The next two columns contain debit and credit eliminations. The final column contains the consolidated balance sheet, and is produced
by adding across (keeping in mind that debit eliminations increase debit balance
accounts, credit eliminations increase credit balance accounts, and so on).

In a journal entry format, the required elimination entry is:

Capital Stock—S Company	50	
Retained Earnings—S Company	50	
Minority Interest (10% × $100)		10
Investment in S Company		90

ILLUSTRATION 2-1

P COMPANY AND SUBSIDIARY S COMPANY
Consolidated Balance Sheet Working Paper
(Acquisition Date)

	P Company	*S* Company	Eliminations *Dr.*	Eliminations *Cr.*	*Consoli-dated*
Current assets	100	10			110
Investment in S Company	90			(1) 90	–0–
Plant and equipment	300	190			490
	490	200			600
Liabilities	200	100			300
Minority interest				(1) 10	10
Capital stock	145	50	(1) 50		145
Retained earnings	145	50	(1) 50		145
	490	200	100	100	600

This working paper elimination entry, called the *investment elimination entry,*
causes several results:

a. The capital stock and retained earnings accounts of S Company are
eliminated.

b. The parent company's investment account is eliminated.

c. The minority interest in the net assets of S Company is established.

The investment elimination entry effectively substitutes the assets and liabilites of
the subsidiary for the investment account of the parent company, with the claim of
minority shareholders reflected in the Minority Interest account. At present,
Minority Interest is normally disclosed between liabilities and shareholders'
equity.

Presenting elimination entries in journal entry format is often helpful in understanding their function on the working paper. This journal entry format will be used frequently throughout this text. However, it is important to be mindful that these are *working paper entries only*. They are not actual journal entries recorded on the books of either the parent or the subsidiary. To help in maintaining this distinction, working paper entries are shaded throughout this text. Actual journal entries made by the parent or subsidiary are not shaded. Additionally, we have numbered all components of the entry in the working paper. The benefits of numbering will become apparent when there are more elimination entries.

Other Intercompany Transactions and Subsidiary Treasury Stock

We have emphasized the intercompany transaction establishing the parent-subsidiary relationship. However, other intercompany transactions may be reflected on the separate company financial statements. Their effects must also be eliminated. The consolidated statements portray the affairs of the parent and subsidiary as if they were a single economic entity. A single economic entity cannot have claims to and from itself. Consequently, all accounts classified as assets on one affiliate's balance sheet for which the originating transaction created a liability on the balance sheet of a second affiliate must be totally eliminated. The amount of the elimination is *not* dependent on the parent's proportionate ownership of the subsidiary. The full amount is always eliminated.

For example, the two companies may have previously engaged in transactions which resulted in an open trade receivable/payable of $5,000 on the date of acquisition. Assume the receivable is on the parent company's books and the payable is on the subsidiary company's books. No adjustment is made to the book value of the net assets of the subsidiary because of this intercompany payable in determining the entry recorded by the parent company. However, in the consolidated balance sheet working paper prepared on the date of acquisition, the following eliminating entry would be made:

Accounts Payable 5,000
    Accounts Receivable   5,000

A purchased subsidiary may hold *treasury stock* at the date of acquisition. The entire amount of the subsidiary's stockholders' equity accounts must be eliminated on the working paper, including any amounts relating to treasury stock.

Properties of Consolidated and Separate Company Balance Sheets

Balance sheets are intended to provide information about an entity's financial position. Illustration 2–1 reveals that the consolidated and parent company balance sheets do not provide identical portrayals of financial position.

First, note that parent company capital stock and retained earnings are identical to consolidated capital stock and retained earnings. On the parent company balance sheet, however, S Company's assets, liabilities, and minority interest are added together in the investment account. Because of this, various important financial statistics will be different on the parent and consolidated balance sheets. Consider the debt/total asset ratio. On the consolidated balance sheet, the debt/total asset ratio is 50 percent (300/600 = .50). On the parent balance sheet, the ratio is 40.8 percent (200/490 = .408). Similarly, current assets are $110 on the consolidated balance sheet and $100 on the parent company balance sheet.

Such differences can be quite dramatic. In 1987, General Motors Corporation did not report its investment in General Motors Acceptance Corporation (GMAC) on a consolidated basis. Accordingly, GMAC's substantial liabilities were netted against its assets in the parent company's investment account. In 1988, General Motors reported its investment in GMAC on a consolidated basis. The effect of the difference in reporting was to increase the debt/equity ratio from 50 to 250 percent.

Which of the two balance sheets provides the correct financial position? Neither is correct to the exclusion of the other. For example, suppose a reader were interested in assessing parent liquidity. The consolidated balance sheet reports larger current assets. If the parent company can easily obtain S Company's current assets (by having its subsidiary declare a dividend or loan monies to the parent), the consolidated amount of $110 is relevant. However, if there were some reason the parent could not access S Company's current assets (perhaps because covenants on S Company's debt preclude dividend payments or loans), the consolidated balance sheet overstates the parent's liquidity.

ACCOUNTING FOR INVESTMENT AFTER ACQUISITION

The preparation of consolidated statements following a period of subsidiary operations is complicated, at least in part, by the introduction of two new variables: the elapsed time since the acquisition of subsidiary shares *and* the parent company's method of accounting for the investment. At date of acquisition, the investment is recorded at cost or book value, depending on whether it is a purchase or pooling of interests. Subsequently, an election must be made by the parent as to whether this measurement should be preserved without change *or* periodically adjusted to reflect the activities and operations of the subsidiary. The former, more traditional, approach is the *cost, or legal basis, method*. The latter approach is referred to as the *equity method*. These two alternative methods of accounting for the parent company's investment are summarized below. However, it may be noted at this point that regardless of which method is employed by the parent to account for its investment *in a subsidiary that is to be included in the consolidation,* the formal consolidated statements remain unaffected. That is, only the separate company statements of the parent differ. The working paper eliminations are designed to compensate for the differences between the two methods.

The Cost Method

The cost method of accounting for stock investments presumes that cost is an accurate reflection of the market value of the investment at date of acquisition,[8] and that this valuation should remain undisturbed in most instances by the influence of subsequent operations of the company whose stock is held. Accordingly, under the cost method, subsidiary profits are not recorded by the parent when they are reported by the subsidiary. Similarly, losses of a subsidiary are not recorded by the parent *unless* there is convincing evidence that indicates the incurrence of a material and apparently permanent impairment of the value of the investment. Income is recognized by the parent company only when the subsidiary declares a cash dividend. At this time, the parent company debits Dividends Receivable and credits Dividend Income for its share of the subsidiary dividends.[9]

The Equity Method

Under the equity method, the parent company's equity in the postacquisition earnings of a subsidiary is recorded by debiting the investment account and crediting a suitably named account, such as Equity in Subsidiary Earnings. All or part of this "equity" may be in "undistributed" earnings, which emphasizes the unique *realization* criterion underlying the recognition of a subsidiary's contribution to the parent's net income. Historically, when the traditional realization concept was applied to stock investments, it was interpreted as a requirement that income not be recognized by the stockholder until declared as dividends by the issuing company. The equity method involves a significant relaxation of this traditional criterion. In essence, the equity method is based on the argument that the economic impact of a corporation's reported profits and losses immediately accrues to its stockholders, regardless of the timing of dividend declarations.

Postacquisition losses sustained by a subsidiary affiliate are recorded in a similar manner by the parent. Equity in Subsidiary Earnings is debited with a corresponding credit to the investment account. Such losses result from a decrease in the underlying subsidiary net assets. The parent's entry formally recognizes the unfavorable economic circumstance.[10]

---

[8] This presumption is clearly unjustified when the parent company records the investment at the book value of the acquired company's net assets under pooling of interests accounting.

[9] If a cash dividend paid by a subsidiary is in excess of the accumulated, undistributed earnings of the subsidiary since the date the parent acquired the subsidiary, such excess is properly classified (from the point of view of the parent) as a *liquidating dividend*. Liquidating dividends received by the parent are credited to the investment account rather than Dividend Income.

[10] However, if the recording of losses would result in reducing the investment account below zero, the equity method is abandoned in favor of the cost method (unless the parent has guaranteed the obligations of its subsidiary).

The parent company's receipt of a cash dividend from the subsidiary is recorded by debiting Cash and crediting the investment account. The entry reflects the financial realization of the parent's equity in subsidiary profits in the amount of the assets transferred. Accordingly, the receipt of dividends is treated as a reduction in the investment account balance. The effect produced on the parent company's books is merely a transformation in asset form—from a claim against subsidiary net assets to cash.

Comparison of Methods

The entries made by the parent company using both the cost and equity methods are shown in Illustration 2–2. A comparison of these entries reveals some of the principal differences between the two methods. Note that the entries shown in Illustration 2–2 are those recorded on the books of the parent company. They should not be confused with eliminating entries required for consolidated statement working papers.

ILLUSTRATION 2–2   Parent Company Entries

Cost Method			*Equity Method*		

A 90% investment in subsidiary stock is acquired in exchange for shares of the parent company's no par stock. The subsidiary's stockholders' equity was capital stock, $30,000, and retained earnings, $20,000.

Investment in			Investment in		
Subsidiary	45,000		Subsidiary	45,000	
Capital Stock		27,000	Capital Stock		27,000
Retained Earnings		18,000	Retained Earnings		18,000

Cash dividends of $4,000 are paid by the subsidiary during the first year of its operations.

Cash	3,600		Cash	3,600	
Dividend Income		3,600	Investment in Subsidiary		3,600

The subsidiary reports net income of $10,000 for the first year's operations.

No entry.			Investment in		
			Subsidiary	9,000	
			Equity in Subsidiary		
			Earnings		9,000

Cash dividends of $3,000 are paid by the subsidiary during the second year.

Cash	2,700		Cash	2,700	
Dividend Income		2,700	Investment in Subsidiary		2,700

The subsidiary reports a net loss of $2,000 for the second year.

No entry.			Equity in Subsidiary		
			Earnings	1,800	
			Investment in Subsidiary		1,800

Although either method of accounting for the investment in the stock of the subsidiary may be used, many companies shifted from the cost method to the equity method following the adoption of *APB Opinion No. 18,* "The Equity Method of Accounting for Investment in Common Stock." Strictly speaking, this *Opinion* imposes a financial reporting requirement, not an accounting requirement, and it has an impact *on consolidated statements* only for investments in unconsolidated affiliates. Although the formal consolidated statements are unaffected by the choice of accounting method (cost or equity) for investments in subsidiaries that are consolidated, *the mechanics of consolidation are affected by the accounting method used.* Since we believe that the equity method is now the prevalent method used by most instructors, we have elected to base the primary explanations and illustrations on the assumption that the parent company has employed the equity method. However, important differences in consolidated working paper techniques for investments carried under the cost method are presented in chapter appendixes or separately identified sections.

STATEMENTS OF CONSOLIDATED INCOME AND RETAINED EARNINGS

Following a period of subsidiary operations, consolidated statements of income and retained earnings are prepared in addition to the consolidated balance sheet. A consolidated income statement combines the revenues and expenses of the parent and subsidiary companies after elimination of those account balances that result from transactions between the affiliates. The process of combination includes a deduction from the combined net incomes of all the affiliated companies, after eliminations, for the amounts of minority interests in the net incomes of the subsidiary affiliates. The residual, so determined, is then assignable to the majority (parent company) shareholders and is designated *consolidated net income.*

An alternative definition of consolidated net income is based on the *entity theory,* which makes no distinction between minority shareholders and the parent company interest. Under this perspective, the amount of income allocated to minority interests is treated as a *distribution* of consolidated net income rather than a *deduction necessary to determine* consolidated net income.

We support the first definition presented above primarily because it emphasizes the equity of parent company stockholders. The significance of consolidated statements clearly stems from the informational needs of parties that have interests in the parent company; that is, parent company creditors and stockholders. Defining consolidated net income as the portion of combined net income accruing to the parent is fully consistent with this dominant statement function. This focus on the shareholders of the parent company is called the *parent company theory* of consolidated statements. Subsequent development is based on this theory unless otherwise noted.

The consolidated statement of retained earnings is simply a sequential ordering of the consolidated retained earnings at the beginning of an accounting period, increased by consolidated net income, and reduced by the parent company's dividends declared. The algebraic sum of these amounts is the balance of consolidated retained earnings at the end of the accounting period.

THE THREE-DIVISION WORKING PAPER—FIRST YEAR SUBSEQUENT TO ACQUISITION

The basic data for preparation of consolidated financial reports are contained in the financial statements of the separate affiliates. When the source information is in financial statement form, the three-division working paper is both an efficient and a logical basis for the development of consolidated statement information. On some occasions, the trial balances of the affiliates are provided. In these instances, the trial balances can be reclassified in financial statement form to accommodate the three-division working paper format. In the remaining discussion of consolidated statements, trial balances of affiliated companies are given as the source information for consolidated working papers in order to minimize the space devoted to underlying detail. Nonetheless, the three-division working paper format will usually be employed because it provides a logical framework for analysis.

Case 4. Data for First Year

Assume that P Company issued shares of its no par common stock for 90 percent of the capital stock of S company on January 1, 19X1 when S Company's stockholders' equity consisted of capital stock, $50,000, and retained earnings, $10,000. The investment was recorded by P Company at $54,000, with credits of $45,000 to capital stock and $9,000 to retained earnings. The trial balances for the two affiliates at December 31, 19X1, are as follows:

	P Company		S Company	
Cash	$ 29,500		$ 8,000	
Accounts Receivable	18,000		3,000	
Inventory (1/1)	16,000		4,000	
Investment in S Company	67,500			
Other Assets	73,000		62,000	
Accounts Payable		$ 22,000		$ 5,000
Other Liabilities		6,000		
Capital Stock (no par)		100,000		50,000
Retained Earnings (1/1)		40,000		10,000
Dividends Declared	10,000		5,000	
Sales		78,000		40,000
Equity in Subsidiary Earnings		18,000		
Purchases	42,000		20,000	
Operating Expenses	8,000		3,000	
	$264,000	$264,000	$105,000	$105,000
Inventory (12/31)	$ 10,000		$ 7,000	

Note that Retained Earnings is a beginning of year balance (otherwise income statement accounts would have already been closed into Retained Earnings). Also, the adjusting entries relating to Cost of Sales have not yet been made (otherwise only Cost of Sales and Ending Inventory would appear on the trial balance). The Dividends Declared account is a special classification refinement that facilitates the analysis in the retained earnings statement division of the consolidated statement working paper. The account has the following properties: it is debited when dividends are declared (rather than Retained Earnings); and at the end of the period, it is closed (along with other nominal accounts) to Retained Earnings. Even if the accounting system of a company does not actually incorporate this refinement, the consolidated working paper can be set up as if the account existed. Should one choose not to identify dividends declared separately in the consolidated statement working paper, then all consolidation entries that otherwise would affect this account would be made directly against Retained Earnings.

The consolidated statement working paper relating to Case 4 appears in Illustration 2–3. Note that the trial balance data have been reclassified into income statement, retained earnings statement, and balance sheet formats.

Elimination Entries for Case 4

The working paper contains three elimination entries. Collectively, these elimination entries:

1. Prevent double counting that would otherwise occur when parent and subsidiary account balances are added together.
2. Reclassify amounts that appear on the consolidated statements as minority interest.

In order to appreciate the role played by elimination entries on the working paper, it is helpful to consider the entries made by the parent company during 19X1. The parent recorded its equity in S Company's 19X1 earnings as follows:

Investment in S Company (90% × 20,000) 18,000
    Equity in Subsidiary Earnings 18,000

The parent company recorded receipt of dividends from S Company as follows:

Cash (90% × 5,000) 4,500
    Investment in S Company 4,500

At acquisition, the investment account was set equal to 90 percent of S Company's net assets. The above two equity method entries preserve this relation. During 19X1, S Company's net assets increased due to $20,000 in earnings and decreased due to $5,000 in dividends. The parent company adjusted the investment account by 90 percent of these amounts. Accordingly, the December 31, 19X1, balance of the investment account continues to equal 90 percent of S Company's net assets (90% × 75,000). This property of the equity method plays an important role in the working paper elimination entries.

ILLUSTRATION 2-3

P COMPANY AND SUBSIDIARY S COMPANY
Consolidated Statement Working Paper
For Year Ended December 31, 19X1

	P Company	S Company	Eliminations Dr.	Eliminations Cr.	Consolidated
Income Statement					
Sales	78,000	40,000			118,000
Equity in subsidiary earnings	18,000		(1) 18,000		
Total credits	96,000	40,000			118,000
Cost of sales	48,000	17,000			65,000
Operating expenses	8,000	3,000			11,000
Total debits	56,000	20,000			76,000
	40,000	20,000			42,000
Minority interest expense			(2) 2,000		2,000
Net income	40,000	20,000	20,000		40,000
Retained Earnings Statement					
Retained earnings (1/1):					
P Company	40,000				40,000
S Company		10,000	(3) 10,000		
Net income	40,000	20,000	20,000		40,000
	80,000	30,000			80,000
Dividends declared:					
P Company	10,000				10,000
S Company		5,000		(1) 4,500	
				(2) 500	
Retained earnings (12/31)	70,000	25,000	30,000	5,000	70,000
Balance Sheet					
Cash	29,500	8,000			37,500
Accounts receivable	18,000	3,000			21,000
Inventory	10,000	7,000			17,000
Investment in S Company	67,500			(1) 13,500	
				(3) 54,000	
Other assets	73,000	62,000			135,000
	198,000	80,000			210,500
Accounts payable	22,000	5,000			27,000
Other liabilities	6,000				6,000
Capital stock:					
P Company	100,000				100,000
S Company		50,000	(3) 50,000		
Retained earnings	70,000	25,000	30,000	5,000	70,000
Minority interest				(2) 1,500	7,500
				(3) 6,000	
	198,000	80,000	80,000	80,000	210,500

Explanation of eliminations:
(1) To eliminate parent's share of subsidiary earnings and dividends.
(2) To account for the minority's share of subsidiary earnings and dividends.
(3) To eliminate January 1, 19X1, stockholders' equity balances.

The first working paper elimination entry reverses these equity method entries. In journal entry format, the entry is:

1. Equity in Subsidiary Earnings 18,000
      Investment in S Company 13,500
      Dividends Declared—S Company 4,500

The debit to Equity in Subsidiary Earnings prevents double counting P Company's share of S Company's 19X1 net income. That is, P Company's net income includes 90 percent of S Company's net income, and simply adding parent and subsidiary revenue and expense accounts would overstate the income of the combined economic entity by this amount. The credit to Dividends Declared eliminates the intercompany dividend paid by S Company to P Company. The credit to Investment in S Company restores the balance of $54,000 at January 1 and allows us to make the investment elimination entry in the same manner as we have done for a consolidated balance sheet.

The second elimination entry adjusts the minority interest for earnings and dividends during the year. For our case, the entry is:

2. Minority Interest Expense (10% × $20,000) 2,000
      Dividends Declared—S Company (10% × $5,000) 500
      Minority Interest 1,500

The debit to Minority Interest Expense reduces the entity's combined income by the amount accruing to the minority shareholders of the subsidiary. This is consistent with the entries recorded by the parent company which accrue only the parent's 90 percent share of the subsidiary's income. The credit to Dividends Declared—S Company completes the elimination of all of S Company's dividends (together with elimination [1]). Consequently, only dividends to parent company shareholders appear in the consolidated statements. The credit to Minority Interest increases the equity of the minority shareholders in the consolidated balance sheet for their share (10%) of the excess of the subsidiary's net income over its dividends declared. When this amount is added to the minority shareholders' interest in the net assets of the subsidiary at the begining of the year (from the investment elimination entry below), the balance reflects the minority shareholders' claim against the net assets of the subsidiary at the end of the period. Accordingly, the Minority Interest account in the consolidated balance sheet will reflect this amount ($7,500 in Illustration 2–3, which is 10 percent of $75,000).

The third elimination entry, which is the familiar investment elimination entry, is:

3. Capital Stock—S Company	. . . .	50,000	
Retained Earnings—S Company	. . . .	10,000	
Investment in S Company (90% × $60,000)	. . . .		54,000
Minority Interest (10% × $60,000)	. . . .		6,000

Each division of the consolidated working paper provides the requisite data for the preparation of one of the series of consolidated statements. While the working paper is subdivided for this purpose, the links that unite the various divisions are also clearly evident. All items on the "net income" line of the income statement division, including elimination debits and credits, are carried forward to the same line description in the retained earnings statement division. Similarly, the totals on the ending retained earnings line are carried forward to the identical line description in the balance sheet division. These divisions, each representing a formal consolidated statement, articulate with each other. It may be observed that equality of amounts of elimination debits and credits is not preserved in the first two divisions of the working paper; yet total elimination debits and credits for the three divisions are necessarily balanced.

Study of the working paper in Illustration 2–3 will reveal a number of important relations. First observe the differences between the Parent Company and Consolidated columns in the balance sheet division. The investment account balance of $67,500 does not appear on the consolidated balance sheet. In its place are S Company's assets, liabilities, and the claim of the minority shareholders to these net assets:

Cash	$ 8,000
Accounts receivable	3,000
Inventory	7,000
Other assets	62,000
Accounts payable	(5,000)
Minority interest	(7,500)
	$67,500

Apart from this distinction, the consolidated balance sheet is identical to the parent company balance sheet. Parent company Capital Stock and Retained Earnings amounts equal amounts of consolidated Capital Stock and Retained Earnings. The equity method is often described as a "one-line consolidation," because subsidiary assets, liabilities, and minority interest on the consolidated balance sheet are added together in a single-line item (the investment account) on the parent company balance sheet.

Also note the composition of the two elimination entries relating to the minority interest. The $6,000 credit is the minority interest in the subsidiary's net assets as of January 1, 19X1. The $1,500 credit is the minority's share of the excess of S Company's 19X1 net income over 19X1 dividends. The final balance of $7,500 is therefore the claim of the minority shareholders to the $75,000 net assets of S Company which appear on the consolidated balance sheet.

Now observe the differences between the Parent and Consolidated columns in the income statement division of the working paper. Equity in Subsidiary Earnings has been eliminated. S Company's revenue and expenses, and the minority interest in these revenue and expenses, are substituted in its place:

Sales	$40,000
Cost of sales	(17,000)
Expenses	(3,000)
Minority interest in earnings	(2,000)
	$18,000

The parent company's income statement also constitutes a "one-line consolidation" in the sense that subsidiary revenue and expenses and minority interest expense appear as a single-line item in the parent company income statement. Therefore, parent company net income necessarily equals consolidated net income.

Finally, observe the Parent Company and Consolidated columns in the retained earnings division of the working paper. Parent company amounts of beginning retained earnings, net income, and dividends all equal their consolidated counterparts.

The formal consolidated statements for Case 4 are shown in Illustration 2–4.

THE THREE-DIVISION WORKING PAPER—SECOND YEAR SUBSEQUENT TO ACQUISITION

The consolidated statement working paper for subsequent years is essentially the same, in respect to details of format, eliminations, and extensions, as in the working paper for the year of acquisition. Nonetheless, it is useful to review the mechanics of the elimination entries for a second (or later) year to emphasize the specific steps that are followed.

Case 5. Data for Second Year

Preparation of a consolidated statement working paper for the second year after acquisition is illustrated by modifying the data for Case 4 to include the following 19X2 activities:

	P Company	S Company
Net income for 19X2	$44,900	$28,000
Dividends declared, 19X2	15,000	10,000

The investment account at December 31, 19X2, has a balance of $83,700, as reflected below:

Investment in S Company

Acquisition, January 1, 19X1	54,000	Dividends received from S in 19X1	4,500
Equity in S's 19X1 earnings	18,000	Balance, December 31, 19X1	67,500
	72,000		72,000
Balance, December 31, 19X1	67,500	Dividends received from S in 19X2	9,000
Equity in S's 19X2 earnings	25,200	Balance, December 31, 19X2	83,700
	92,700		92,700
Balance December 31, 19X2	83,700		

Elimination Entries for Case 5

The consolidated statement working paper relating to Case 5 appears in Illustration 2–5. Values for accounts that are not carried forward from 19X1 are arbitrarily selected. The elimination entries play the same role on the working paper as in Illustration 2–3. However, amounts are different due to the passage of an additional year. The elimination entries are:

1. Equity in Subsidiary Earnings	25,200	
Investment in S Company		16,200
Dividends Declared—S Company (90% × 10,000)		9,000
2. Minority Interest Expense (10% × 28,000)	2,800	
Dividends Declared—S Company (10% × 10,000)		1,000
Minority Interest		1,800
3. Capital Stock—S Company	50,000	
Retained Earnings—S Company	25,000	
Investment in S Company (90% × 75,000)		67,500
Minority Interest (10% × 75,000)		7,500

ILLUSTRATION 2-4

P COMPANY AND SUBSIDIARY S COMPANY
Consolidated Income Statement
For Year Ended December 31, 19X1

Sales	$118,000
Cost of sales	65,000
Gross profit	$ 53,000
Operating expenses	11,000
Combined net income	$ 42,000
Minority interest in subsidiary net income	2,000
Consolidated net income	$ 40,000

P COMPANY AND SUBSIDIARY S COMPANY
Consolidated Statement of Retained Earnings
For Year Ended December 31, 19X1

Retained earnings, January 1, 19X1	$40,000
Consolidated net income	40,000
Total	$80,000
Dividends declared	10,000
Retained earnings, December 31, 19X1	$70,000

P COMPANY AND SUBSIDIARY S COMPANY
Consolidated Balance Sheet
December 31, 19X1

Assets		Equities	
Cash	$ 37,500	Liabilities:	
Accounts receivable	21,000	Accounts payable	$ 27,000
Inventory	17,000	Other liabilities	6,000
Other assets	135,000	Minority interest	7,500
		Shareholders' equity:	
		Capital stock	100,000
		Retained earnings	70,000
Total assets	$210,500	Total equities	$210,500

Study of Illustration 2–5 reveals the same relationships as in Illustration 2–3. Parent company net income and stockholders' equity balances equal their counterparts in the consolidated statements. Consolidated dividends declared includes only dividends to parent comany shareholders. The minority interest on the balance sheet consists of the minority shareholders' claim to January 1, 19X2, S Company net assets, increased by the minority shareholders' claim to 19X2 earnings, and reduced by dividends to minority shareholders. Investment in S Company on the parent company balance sheet is replaced by S Company's assets, liabilities, and minority interest on the consolidated balance sheet. Equity in subsidiary earnings on the parent company income statement is replaced by S Company's revenue and expenses, and minority interest expense, on the consolidated income statement.

ILLUSTRATION 2–5

P COMPANY AND SUBSIDIARY S COMPANY
Consolidated Statement Working Paper
For Year Ended December 31, 19X2

	P Company	S Company	Eliminations Dr.		Eliminations Cr.		Consolidated
Income Statement							
Sales	96,000	63,000					159,000
Equity in subsidiary earnings	25,200		(1)	25,200			
Total credits	121,200	63,000					159,000
Cost of sales	53,800	26,900					80,700
Operating expenses	22,500	8,100					30,600
Total debits	76,300	35,000					111,300
	44,900	28,000					47,700
Minority interest expense			(2)	2,800			2,800
Net income	44,900	28,000		28,000			44,900
Retained Earnings Statement							
Retained earnings (1/1):							
P Company	70,000						70,000
S Company		25,000	(3)	25,000			
Net income	44,900	28,000		28,000			44,900
	114,900	53,000					114,900
Dividends declared:							
P Company	15,000						15,000
S Company		10,000			(1)	9,000	
					(2)	1,000	
Retained earnings (12/31)	99,900	43,000		53,000		10,000	99,900
Balance Sheet							
Cash	31,000	12,000					43,000
Accounts receivable	22,000	19,000					41,000
Inventory	14,200	9,200					23,400
Investment in S Company	83,700				(1)	16,200	
					(3)	67,500	
Other assets	83,000	64,300					147,300
	233,900	104,500					254,700
Accounts payable	30,000	9,000					39,000
Other liabilities	4,000	2,500					6,500
Capital stock:							
P Company	100,000						100,000
S Company		50,000	(3)	50,000			
Retained earnings	99,900	43,000		53,000		10,000	99,900
Minority interest					(2)	1,800	9,300
Minority interest					(3)	7,500	
	233,900	104,500		103,000		103,000	254,700

Explanation of eliminations:

(1) To eliminate parent's share of subsidiary earnings and dividends.

(2) To account for the minority's share of subsidiary earnings and dividends.

(3) To eliminate January 1, 19X1, stockholders' equity balances.

OTHER INTERCOMPANY TRANSACTIONS

Our discussion of intercompany relationships has included the investment account, reciprocal debtor-creditor relationships among affiliates, and the declaration of subsidiary dividends. If there are other intercompany transactions, their effects must also be eliminated. One such transaction which occurs with relative frequency is the sale of merchandise by one affiliate to another. Since the consolidated income statement should exhibit only revenue and expenses which result from transactions with nonaffiliates, it is appropriate to eliminate the *total amount* of intercompany sales by a debit to Sales and a credit to Cost of Sales in the consolidated working paper. Special elimination problems arise if some of the items in the intercompany merchandise shipments are not subsequently resold by the purchasing affiliate during the current period and are accordingly included in its final inventory. The complications created by the profit residue in the final inventory are dealt with in detail in Chapter 6.

Other types of intercompany revenue-expense transactions that must be similarly eliminated in the consolidated working papers include transactions arising from intercorporate financing, or the rendering of services by one affiliate to another. All evidences of these transactions must be removed from the consolidated statements to avoid duplicate measurement. Accounts for which eliminating entries must be made in the consolidated statement working paper include interest income–interest expense, management fee income–management fee expense, commissions earned–commissions expense, and various others.

MULTICOMPANY AFFILIATIONS

Our examples to this point have assumed two-party affiliations, a parent company and a single subsidiary. We now consider the case of a three-party affiliation. It should be noted that an increase in the number of subsidiaries only increases the number of accounts to be dealt with and the eliminations to be made. The principles of consolidated statement preparation developed in the context of two-party affiliations remain unchanged.

Corporate affiliations can be quite complex. Not only can a parent own several subsidiaries, but the subsidiaries can, in turn, own subsidiaries. Or one subsidiary can own shares of another subsidiary (or own shares of the parent). Analysis of complex affiliations is often simplified by preparing an *affiliation diagram* in which percentages and directions of share ownership are portrayed in a graphic format. Affiliation diagrams are especially helpful in analyzing the complex affiliations discussed in Chapter 10.

Case 6. Parent and Two Subsidiaries

On January 1, 19X1, P Company acquires 90 percent of the outstanding common shares of Y Company and 95 percent of the outstanding common shares of Z Company in exchange for common stock of P Company. The combinations are

ILLUSTRATION 2–6

P COMPANY AND SUBSIDIARIES
Trial Balances
For the Year Ended December 31, 19X1

	P Company		Y Company		Z Company	
Cash	$ 34,300		$ 8,000		$ 4,000	
Accounts Receivable	18,000		3,000		6,000	
Inventory (1/1)	16,000		4,000		3,000	
Investment in Y Company	67,500					
Investment in Z Company	51,300					
Other Assets	29,850		62,000		44,000	
Accounts Payable		$ 22,000		$ 5,000		$ 4,000
Other Liabilities		6,000				1,000
Capital Stock		100,000		50,000		40,000
Retained Earnings (1/1)		40,000		10,000		5,000
Dividends Declared	10,000		5,000		6,000	
Sales		78,000		40,000		30,000
Equity in Subsidiary Earnings		32,250				
Purchases	42,000		20,000		12,000	
Operating Expenses	9,300		3,000		5,000	
	$278,250	$278,250	$105,000	$105,000	$80,000	$80,000
Inventory (12/31)	$ 10,000		$ 7,000		$ 5,000	

Additional information:

(1) On January 1, 19X1, P Company acquired 90 percent of the capital stock of Y Company and 95 percent of the capital stock of Z Company. Both acquisitions were classified as poolings of interests.

(2) On December 30, 19X1, P Company transferred $1,000 cash to Z Company in partial settlement of a $3,000 obligation, classified by P Company as "Other Liabilities." As of December 31, this transfer was not yet recorded by Z Company.

(3) The sales of merchandise by Y Company to Z Company during 19X1 were $5,000 (ignore the question of unconfirmed, or unrealized, inventory profit).

classified for accounting purposes as poolings of interests. An affiliation diagram for this multicompany affiliation is as follows:

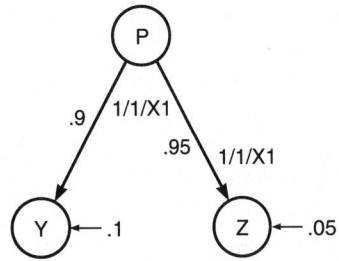

The December 31, 19X1, trial balances for companies P, Y, and Z are given in Illustration 2–6. Note carefully the additional information included at the foot of the trial balances because this information provides the basis for the eliminations

ILLUSTRATION 2–7

P COMPANY AND SUBSIDIARIES
Consolidated Statement Working Paper
For Year Ended December 31, 19X1

	P Company	Y Company	Z Company	Eliminations Dr.	Eliminations Cr.	Consolidated
Income Statement						
Sales	78,000	40,000	30,000	(6) 5,000		143,000
Equity in subsidiary earnings*	32,250			(2) 32,250		
Total credits	110,250	40,000	30,000			143,000
Cost of sales	48,000	17,000	10,000		(6) 5,000	70,000
Operating expenses	9,300	3,000	5,000			17,300
Total debits	57,300	20,000	15,000			87,300
	52,950	20,000	15,000			55,700
Minority interest expense†				(3) 2,750		2,750
Net income	52,950	20,000	15,000	40,000	5,000	52,950
Retained Earnings Statement						
Retained earnings (1/1):						
P Company	40,000					40,000
Y Company		10,000		(4) 10,000		
Z Company			5,000	(4) 5,000		
Net income	52,950	20,000	15,000	40,000	5,000	52,950
	92,950	30,000	20,000			92,950
Dividends declared:						
P Company	10,000					10,000
Y Company		5,000			(2) 4,500	
					(3) 500	
Z Company			6,000		(2) 5,700	
					(3) 300	
Retained earnings (12/31)	82,950	25,000	14,000	55,000	16,000	82,950

in the consolidated statement working paper. This working paper appears in Illustration 2–7.

Observe in Illustration 2–7 that again the parent company's net income and stockholders' equity are equal in amount to consolidated net income and stockholders' equity. Further, the elimination entries for the two subsidiaries are determined for each subsidiary in the same manner previously illustrated for single subsidiary cases. The elimination of intercompany sales is handled in accordance with the discussion in the preceding section and produces amounts for consolidated sales and cost of sales that reflect transactions with outside parties. Finally, an additional entry is necessary to reflect the unrecorded transfer of cash from P Company. This adjustment corrects an error and, unlike eliminations, would also be recorded on the books of Z Company.

ILLUSTRATION 2-7 *(continued)*

	P Company	Y Company	Z Company	Eliminations Dr.		Eliminations Cr.		Consolidated
Balance Sheet								
Cash	34,300	8,000	4,000	(1)	1,000			47,300
Accounts receivable	18,000	3,000	6,000			(1)	1,000	24,000
						(5)	2,000	
Inventory	10,000	7,000	5,000					22,000
Investment in Y	67,500					(2)	13,500	
						(4)	54,000	
Investment in Z	51,300					(2)	8,550	
						(4)	42,750	
Other assets	29,850	62,000	44,000					135,850
	210,950	80,000	59,000					229,150
Accounts payable	22,000	5,000	4,000					31,000
Other liabilities	6,000		1,000	(5)	2,000			5,000
Capital stock:								
P Company	100,000							100,000
Y Company		50,000		(4)	50,000			
Z Company			40,000	(4)	40,000			
Retained earnings	82,950	25,000	14,000		55,000		16,000	82,950
Minority interest—Y Company						(3)	1,500	7,500
						(4)	6,000	
Minority interest—Z Company						(3)	450	2,700
						(4)	2,250	
	210,950	80,000	59,000		148,000		148,000	229,150

*Equity in subsidiary earnings = (90% × $20,000) + (95% × $15,000)

                      = $32,250

†Minority interest expense   = (10% × $20,000) + (5% × $15,000)

                      = $2,750

Explanation of adjustments and eliminations:

(1) Adjustment for unrecorded cash receipt by Z Company.

(2) To eliminate parent's share of subsidiary earnings and dividends.

(3) To account for the minority's share of subsidiary earnings and dividends.

(4) To eliminate January 1, 19X1, stockholders' equity balances (investment elimination entries).

(5) To eliminate intercompany debt.

(6) To eliminate intercompany sales.

Reconsideration of Basic Definitions

In grappling with the various consolidated statement working paper techniques, one must be careful not to lose touch with the objectives of the process and the underlying definitions that guide our efforts. The objective is to combine the assets, liabilities, revenue, and expenses of the affiliates such that the consolidated financial statements reflect the activities and financial position of the group as if it were a single economic entity. In pursuit of this objective, the definitions of consolidated net income and consolidated retained earnings (see page 44) guide our procedural efforts. It is useful at this point to reconsider and elaborate upon these basic definitions in the context of the numerical data in Case 6.

Consolidated Net Income.   Consolidated net income was previously defined as a residual value accruing to the majority shareholders (i.e., the shareholders of the parent company). This residual value is produced in the consolidated working paper by combining the revenue and expenses of the affiliated companies after eliminating intercompany transactions and the parent's recorded equity in subsidiary earnings, and then deducting minority interest. But consolidated net income can also be determined independent of the working paper. An independent determination will often be useful in understanding material in subsequent chapters. There are two methods by which consolidated net income can be determined independent of the working paper.

A Residual Determination of Consolidated Net Income.   Consolidated net income is that portion of the combined entity's income accruing to parent shareholders. One method of determining consolidated net income begins with a computation of the combined entity's net income. This combined entity income accrues to two shareholder groups: the shareholders of the parent and the minority shareholders of the subsidiaries. Therefore, deducting the minority's share of subsidiary income from the combined entity's income necessarily produces consolidated net income. Using the data from Case 6, this residual determination of consolidated net income is:

P Company's net income for 19X1		$52,950
Y Company's net income for 19X1		20,000
Z Company's net income for 19X1		15,000
		$87,950
Less income of Y Company and Z Company included		
in P Company's net income		32,250
Combined entity income		$55,700
Less minority's share of subsidiary income:		
Y Company (10% × $20,000)	$2,000	
Z Company (5% × $15,000)	750	2,750
Consolidated net income		$52,950

Note that the combined entity's net income is not the sum of the reported net incomes of the three affiliates. Since P Company uses the equity method to account for its investments in Y and Z, $18,000 of Y Company's net income and $14,250 of Z Company's net income are included in P Company's recorded net income. The sum of the reported net incomes overstates combined entity income due to this double counting. Accordingly, $32,250 is subtracted from reported income in arriving at the combined entity's net income.

This residual determination of consolidated net income closely parallels the working paper. On the working paper, the income statement items of the affiliates are first summed. Then any double counting in this summation is eliminated, and the minority interest is deducted.

An Incremental Determination of Consolidated Net Income. Consolidated net income can also be determined without first computing the combined entity's net income. The portion of the combined entity's net income accruing to the parent shareholders is the sum of (1) the parent company's income from its own operations (i.e., excluding the equity in subsidiary earnings), and (2) the parent company's equity in the net incomes of its subsidiaries. Using the data from Case 6, this incremental determination of consolidated net income is:

P Company's income from its own operations		
(52,950 − 32,250)		$20,700
Plus:		
Equity in Y Company's net income (90% × $20,000) .	$18,000	
Equity in Z Company's net income (95% × $15,000) . .	14,250	32,250
Consolidated net income		$52,950

Consolidated Retained Earnings. Consolidated retained earnings may be analyzed in a manner similar to that used to analyze consolidated net income. However, when the parent company uses the equity method of accounting, this analysis is generally not a productive venture. Therefore, we merely note again for possible computational convenience that consolidated retained earnings simply may be viewed as consolidated retained earnings at the beginnning of the period, increased by consolidated net income, and reduced by the parent company's dividends declared. Applying this definition to the data of Case 6, and recalling that consolidated retained earnings at the date of acquisition is equal to the parent company's retained earnings, the December 31, 19X1, consolidated retained earnings balance is calculated as follows:

Consolidated retained earnings, January 1, 19X1	$40,000
Consolidated net income for 19X1	52,950
	$92,950
P Company dividends declared in 19X1	10,000
Consolidated retained earnings, December 31, 19X1	$82,950

Summary

The contents of this chapter have focused on the nature and preparation of consolidated statements accounted for using the pooling of interests method. We began with the nature and justification for consolidated statements. Next, the relation between the consolidated balance sheet and the parent company balance sheet was examined.

The consolidated balance sheet is simply the parent company balance sheet with the investment account disaggregated into individual assets, liabilities, and minority interest. A working paper technology to facilitate this process was illustrated.

Next, we reviewed the cost and equity methods of accounting for investments in subsidiaries. Focusing on the equity method, we illustrated a working paper technology to prepare an income statement, retained earnings statement, and balance sheet as of the end of the year of the acquisition year. Then, we extended this illustration to the subsequent year. In both illustrations, the "one-line consolidation" property of the equity method was emphasized. That is to say, the difference between the parent company income statement and the consolidated income statement is a matter of detail. Subsidiary revenue, expenses, and the minority interest expense appearing on the consolidated income statement are all combined into Equity in Subsidiary Earnings on the parent company income statement. Similarly, subsidiary assets, liabilities, and the minority claim to these assets and liabilities appearing on the consolidated balance sheet are combined together in the investment account on the parent balance sheet.

Appendix A: Illustration of Consolidated Statement Working Paper Techniques When the Investment Account Is Carried under the Cost Method

The consolidated statement techniques described in this and succeeding chapters *are usually based on the assumption that the investment account is carried under the equity method*. However, the following paragraphs illustrate briefly the mechanics of consolidation under the cost method. Recall that regardless which method is used by the parent company to account for its investment in the subsidiary, *the consolidated financial statements will be the same in all respects*. To emphasize this point, the data used for our two illustrations will reflect the same economic events as are assumed in Cases 4 and 5 in the main body of the chapter.

Consolidated Statement Working Paper—First Year Subsequent to Acquisition (Case A–1)

It is assumed, as in Case 4, that P Company issued shares of its no par common stock for 90 percent of the capital stock of S Company on January 1, 19X1, when S Company's stockholders' equity consisted of capital stock, $50,000 and retained earnings, $10,000. The trial balances for the two affiliates at December 31, 19X1, are as follows:

	P Company		S Company	
Cash	$ 29,500		$ 8,000	
Accounts Receivable	18,000		3,000	
Inventory (1/1)	16,000		4,000	
Investment in S Company	54,000			
Other Assets	73,000		62,000	
Accounts Payable		$ 22,000		$ 5,000
Other Liabilities		6,000		
Capital Stock (no par)		100,000		50,000
Retained Earnings (1/1)		40,000		10,000
Dividends Declared	10,000		5,000	
Sales		78,000		40,000
Dividend Income		4,500		
Purchases	42,000		20,000	
Operating Expenses	8,000		3,000	
	$250,500	$250,500	$105,000	$105,000
Inventory (12/31)	$ 10,000		$ 7,000	

The account balances in this trial balance correspond exactly with the balances in Case 4 in the chapter, except for differences due to use of the cost method.

The consolidated statement working paper for this case appears in Illustration 2–8. In journal entry format, the first elimination entry is:

1. Dividend Income (90% × $5,000) 4,500
      Dividends Declared—S Company   4,500

This entry prevents double counting in income and eliminates the intercompany dividend paid to the parent by the subsidiary. The second elimination entry is:

2. Minority Interest Expense (10% × $20,000) 2,000
      Minority Interest   1,500
      Dividends Declared—S Company (10% × $5,000)   500

The entry establishes minority interest expense and the minority's share of income, net of dividends paid. Finally, the third elimination entry eliminates the date of acquisition balances of S Company's stockholders' equity and the investment account. In addition, it reclassifies 10 percent of the beginning of year balances as minority interest.

3. Capital Stock—S Company 50,000
      Retained Earnings—S Company 10,000
      Investment in S Company   54,000
      Minority Interest   6,000

ILLUSTRATION 2–8

P COMPANY AND SUBSIDIARY S COMPANY
Consolidated Statement Working Paper
For Year Ended December 31, 19X1

	P Company	S Company	Eliminations Dr.	Eliminations Cr.	Consolidated
Income Statement					
Sales	78,000	40,000			118,000
Dividend income	4,500		(1) 4,500		
Total credits	82,500	40,000			118,000
Cost of sales	48,000	17,000			65,000
Operating expenses	8,000	3,000			11,000
Total debits	56,000	20,000			76,000
	26,500	20,000			42,000
Minority interest expense			(2) 2,000		2,000
Net income	26,500	20,000	6,500		40,000
Retained Earnings Statement					
Retained earnings (1/1):					
P Company	40,000				40,000
S Company		10,000	(3) 10,000		
Net income	26,500	20,000	6,500		40,000
	66,500	30,000			80,000
Dividends declared:					
P Company	10,000				10,000
S Company		5,000		(1) 4,500	
				(2) 500	
Retained earnings (12/31)	56,500	25,000	16,500	5,000	70,000
Balance Sheet					
Cash	29,500	8,000			37,500
Accounts receivable	18,000	3,000			21,000
Inventory	10,000	7,000			17,000
Investment in S Company	54,000			(3) 54,000	
Other assets	73,000	62,000			135,000
	184,500	80,000			210,500
Accounts payable	22,000	5,000			27,000
Other liabilities	6,000				6,000
Capital stock:					
P Company	100,000				100,000
S Company		50,000	(3) 50,000		
Retained earnings	56,500	25,000	16,500	5,000	70,000
Minority interest				(2) 1,500	7,500
				(3) 6,000	
	184,500	80,000	66,500	66,500	210,500

Explanation of eliminations:

(1) To eliminate intercompany dividends received by parent company.

(2) To account for the minority's share of subsidiary earnings and dividends.

(3) To eliminate January 1, 19X1, stockholders' equity balances.

Note that all amounts in the consolidated columns of Illustration 2–8 and Illustration 2–3 are identical. Thus, as was previously asserted, the choice between the cost and the equity methods of accounting for the investment on the books of the parent company does not affect the results reflected in the consolidated statements. The choice does affect the sources and amounts of income as well as the balance of the investment account on the parent company's books and in the separate company statements of the parent. This can be confirmed by comparing the first columns of the two working papers.

Consolidated Statement Working Paper—Second Year Subsequent to Acquisition (Case A–2)

The data for Case A–1 are modified to include the following 19X2 activities:

	P Company	S Company
Net income for 19X2	$28,700	$28,000
Dividends declared, 19X2	15,000	10,000

Note that P Company's net income again differs from that shown in Case 5 in the chapter because the parent company is recognizing income from S Company's operations on the basis of dividends declared by S Company during 19X2, not income reported by S Company for 19X2.

The consolidated statement working paper for this case appears in Illustration 2–9. In journal entry format, the first elimination entry is:

```
1. Dividend Income (90% × $10,000) . . . . . . . . . . . . . . . . . . . . .   9,000
      Dividends Declared—S Company . . . . . . . . . . . . . . . . . . . .           9,000
```

This entry plays the same role as its counterpart in Case A–1. The second elimination entry is:

```
2. Minority Interest Expense (10% × $28,000) . . . . . . . . . . . . . . . .   2,800
      Minority Interest . . . . . . . . . . . . . . . . . . . . . . . . . . . .           1,800
      Dividends Declared—S Company (10% × $10,000) . . . . . . . . . .           1,000
```

It also plays the same role as its counterpart in Case A–1. The third entry, the investment elimination entry, is:

```
3. Capital Stock—S Company . . . . . . . . . . . . . . . . . . . . . . . . .  50,000
   Retained Earnings—S Company . . . . . . . . . . . . . . . . . . . . . . .  25,000
      Investment in S Company . . . . . . . . . . . . . . . . . . . . . . .          54,000
      Minority Interest [10% × ($50,000 + $25,000)] . . . . . . . . . . .           7,500
      Retained Earnings—P Company [90% × ($25,000 − $10,000)] . . .          13,500
```

ILLUSTRATION 2-9

P COMPANY AND SUBSIDIARY S COMPANY
Consolidated Statement Working Paper
For Year Ended December 31, 19X2

	P Company	S Company	Eliminations Dr.	Eliminations Cr.	Consolidated
Income Statement					
Sales	96,000	63,000			159,000
Dividend income	9,000		(1) 9,000		
Total credits	105,000	63,000			159,000
Cost of sales	53,800	26,900			80,700
Operating expenses	22,500	8,100			30,600
Total debits	76,300	35,000			111,300
	28,700	28,000			47,700
Minority interest expense			(2) 2,800		2,800
Net income	28,700	28,000	11,800		44,900
Retained Earnings Statement					
Retained earnings (1/1):					
P Company	56,500			(3) 13,500	70,000
S Company		25,000	(3) 25,000		
Net income	28,700	28,000	11,800		44,900
	85,200	53,000			114,900
Dividends declared:					
P Company	15,000				15,000
S Company		10,000		(1) 9,000	
				(2) 1,000	
Retained earnings (12/31)	70,200	43,000	36,800	23,500	99,900
Balance Sheet					
Cash	31,000	12,000			43,000
Accounts receivable	22,000	19,000			41,000
Inventory	14,200	9,200			23,400
Investment in S Company	54,000			(3) 54,000	
Other assets	83,000	64,300			147,300
	204,200	104,500			254,700
Accounts payable	30,000	9,000			39,000
Other liabilities	4,000	2,500			6,500
Capital stock:					
P Company	100,000				100,000
S Company		50,000	(3) 50,000		
Retained earnings	70,200	43,000	36,800	23,500	99,900
Minority interest				(2) 1,800	9,300
				(3) 7,500	
	204,200	104,500	86,800	86,800	254,700

Explanation of eliminations:

(1) To eliminate intercompany dividends received by parent company.

(2) To account for the minority's share of subsidiary earnings and dividends.

(3) To eliminate January 1, 19X2, stockholders' equity balances.

This entry differs from its counterpart in Case A–1 by the credit to the parent's retained earnings *at the beginning of the year* for the parent's share of the subsidiary's *undistributed earnings since acquisition*. The undistributed earnings since acquisition are measured by the difference between the subsidiary's retained earnings at the beginning of the current year ($25,000) and the subsidiary's retained earnings *on the date of acquisition* ($10,000). Thus, in Case A–1, the undistributed earnings since acquisition were zero. When we prepare the consolidated statement working paper for the year ended December 31, 19X3, this credit will be $29,700 [90% × ($43,000 − $10,000)]. The credit effectively converts the parent's retained earnings at the beginning of the year *from the cost method to the equity method*.

Appendix B: Recording the Investment under Pooling of Interests Accounting When the Stock Issued Has Par or Stated Value

The procedures for recording an investment under pooling of interests accounting must be expanded when the parent issues common stock with a par or stated value. However, the basic principles remain unchanged. The investment account is debited for the book value of the net assets of the acquired company, and shareholders' equity is credited based upon the paid-in capital and retained earnings components of the combining companies. In unusual cases where the par or stated value of the shares of the parent company that are outstanding after the acquisition exceeds the total paid-in capital of the combining companies prior to combination, the full retained earnings of the combining companies will not be carried forward. In less extreme cases, the division of paid-in capital between capital stock and additional paid-in capital will be modified because of the difference in the total par value of the capital stock outstanding.[11]

For all of our examples, we use the following shareholders' equity data for the combining companies immediately prior to the combination:

	P Company	S Company
Common stock:		
P Company ($5 par)	$ 50,000	
S Company ($1 par)		$20,000
Additional paid-in capital	100,000	30,000
Retained earnings	125,000	40,000
Total shareholders' equity	$275,000	$90,000

---

[11] The basic authority covering these situations is paragraph 53 of *APB Opinion No. 16:* "The stockholders' equities of the separate companies are also combined as a part of the pooling of interests method of accounting. The combined corporation records as capital the capital stock and capital in excess of par or stated value of outstanding stock of the separate companies. Similarly, retained earnings or deficits of the separate companies are combined and recognized as retained earnings of the combined corporation. . . . The amount of outstanding shares of stock of the combined corporation at par or stated value may exceed the total amount of capital stock of the separate combining companies; the excess should be deducted first from the *combined* other contributed capital and then from the combined retained earnings." (Emphasis added.)

To illustrate a number of unique accounting situations, we vary the number of shares of P Company stock that are issued to acquire S Company stock. Additionally, we assume for simplicity that all 20,000 shares of S Company are acquired. If less than 100 percent of the shares were acquired, the analysis would be based upon the pro rata portion of the accounts. Since the book value of S Company's net assets is $90,000, in all cases the investment account is debited for $90,000. Only the components of shareholders' equity that are carried forward vary among the cases.

Case B–1. Par Value of Stock Issued by P Company Is Less Than S Company's Capital Stock.   Assume P Company issues 3,000 shares of its common stock for all of the common stock of S Company. In this case, the total paid-in capital of S Company ($50,000) exceeds the par value of the stock issued by P Company ($15,000). Thus, the $50,000 paid-in capital and the $40,000 retained earnings will be carried forward. Since the par value of the stock issued by P Company ($15,000) is less than the capital stock previously recorded by S Company ($20,000), the difference is credited to Additional Paid-in Capital. The entry is:

Investment in S Company	90,000	
Capital Stock ($5 par) ($3,000 × 5)		15,000
Additional Paid-In Capital*		35,000
Retained Earnings		40,000
*$30,000 + ($20,000 − $15,000)		

Case B–2. Par Value of Stock Issued by P Company Is More Than S Company's Capital Stock, but Difference Is Less Than S Company's Additional Paid-In Capital.   Assume P Company issues 9,000 shares of its common stock for all of the common stock of S Company. In this case, the total paid-in capital of S Company ($50,000) again exceeds the par value of the stock issued by P Company ($45,000). Thus, the $50,000 paid-in capital and the $40,000 retained earnings will again be carried forward. However, the $25,000 excess of the par value of the stock issued by P Company ($45,000) over the par value of the capital stock previously recorded by S Company ($20,000) is deducted from the *combined* Additional Paid-in Capital of the two companies. *Recall that these entries are recorded on P Company's books.* Accordingly, the "deduction" can be achieved by picking up only $5,000 of the $30,000 additional paid-in capital on S Company's books. The entry is:

Investment in S Company	90,000	
Capital Stock ($5 par) ($9,000 × $5)		45,000
Additional Paid-In Capital*		5,000
Retained Earnings		40,000
*$30,000 − ($45,000 − $20,000)		

Case B–3. Par Value of Stock Issued by P Company Is More Than S Company's Capital Stock, and Difference Is More Than S Company's Additional Paid-In Capital but Less Than Combined Additional Paid-In Capital.   Assume P Company issues 21,000 shares of its common stock for all of the common stock of S Company. In this case, the total paid-in capital of S Company ($50,000) does *not* exceed the par value of the stock issued by P Company ($105,000). Thus, the excess ($55,000) must be offset against the additional paid-in capital *on P Company's books*. With this deduction, the total paid-in capital of the *combined* companies will be the same ($200,000) after the pooling of interests as it was before, and the *combined* retained earnings ($165,000) will also remain constant. The entry is:

Investment in S Company	90,000	
Additional Paid-In Capital*	55,000	
Capital Stock ($5 par) ($21,000 × $5)		105,000
Retained Earnings		40,000

*$30,000 − ($105,000 − $20,000)

Case B–4. Par Value of Stock Issued by P Company Is More Than S Company's Capital Stock, and Difference Is More Than Combined Additional Paid-In Capital. Assume P Company issues 35,000 shares of its common stock for all of the common stock of S Company. In this case, the total paid-in capital of S Company ($50,000) does *not* exceed the par value of the stock issued by P Company (\$175,000), *and* the difference of \$125,000 exceeds the additional paid-in capital of P Company by \$25,000. This \$25,000 must be offset against the combined retained earnings. Thus, the combined paid-in capital will be \$25,000 more after the combination than before, and the combined retained earnings will be \$25,000 less. Because of the large amount assigned to capital stock, the combined company has effectively capitalized \$25,000 of its precombination retained earnings. The entry for this case is:

Investment in S Company	90,000	
Additional Paid-In Capital	100,000	
Capital Stock ($5 par) ($35,000 × $5)		175,000
Retained Earnings*		15,000

*$40,000 − ($175,000 − $20,000 − $30,000 − $100,000)

Questions

1. Why might a corporation prefer the acquisition form of business combination as opposed to the merger or consolidation forms?
2. What is the principal motivation for presentations of consolidated statements?
3. What is the criterion for a consolidated presentation of an investment?
4. Is majority ownership of voting shares necessary for control? Explain.
5. Interpretation of consolidated statements requires careful consideration of the inherent limitations of these statements. What are some of these inherent limitations?
6. For a business combination accounted for as a pooling of interests, what value is assigned to the investment account when the combination is recorded?
7. What is minority interest?
8. Explain the two variables that complicate the preparation of consolidated financial statements when the statements are prepared subsequent to the date of a subsidiary's acquisition by a parent.
9. For subsidiary shareholdings, what are the basic differences between the entries recorded by a parent company under the two alternative methods of accounting for the investment?
10. How does the realization criterion underlying the equity method differ from that underlying the cost method?
11. What differences exist in the formal consolidated financial statements when the equity method is used instead of the cost method for consolidated subsidiaries?

12. Is the cost or equity method preferred as a method of accounting for investments in subsidiaries?

13. Describe the reasoning underlying the two alternative views (the parent company theory and the entity theory) of consolidated net income.

14. What is the composition of the consolidated retained earnings statement?

15. When using the three-division working paper, do the "debits equal the credits" in *each* of the three sections of the Eliminations columns? If so, why? If not, why not?

16. How is the minority interest in a subsidiary's net income calculated? Is this amount added to or subtracted from the combined net incomes of the affiliates in order to determine "consolidated net income"?

17. For a company using the equity method, describe the relationship between the parent company's net income and the consolidated net income, and between the parent company's retained earnings balance and the consolidated retained earnings balance.

18. For an investment carried under the equity method, what is the relationship between the investment account balance and the net assets of the subsidiary at any point in time?

19. Identify five types of intercompany transactions which create elimination entries in the consolidation process.

Exercises

Exercise 2-1   (Consolidated Net Income)

Select the best answer for each of the following:

1. What is the effect on the financial statements if an unconsolidated subsidiary is accounted for by the equity method but consolidated statements are being prepared with other subsidiaries?
    a. All of the unconsolidated subsidiary's accounts will be included individually in the consolidated statements.
    b. The consolidated retained earnings will *not* reflect the earnings of the unconsolidated subsidiary.
    c. The consolidated retained earnings will be the same as if the subsidiary had been included in the consolidation.
    d. Dividend revenue from the unconsolidated subsidiary will be reflected in consolidated net income.

2. How is the part of the affiliates' combined earnings to be assigned to minority interest in consolidated financial statements determined?
    a. The net income of the parent is subtracted from the subsidiary's net income to determine the minority interest.
    b. The subsidiary's net income is the minority interest.
    c. The amount of the subsidiary's earnings is multiplied by the minority's percentage ownership.
    d. The amount of consolidated earnings determined on the consolidated working papers is multiplied by the minority interest percentage at the balance sheet date.

3. Aaron, Inc., owns 95 percent of the outside stock of Belle, Inc. Compare (I) consolidated net earnings of Aaron and Belle with (II) Aaron's net earnings if it does *not* consolidate with Belle.
   a. I is greater than II.
   b. I equals II.
   c. I is less than II.
   d. Cannot be determined.

Exercise 2–2   (Consolidated Net Income and the Equity Method)

Select the best answer for each of the following.

1. Parent, Inc., owns a 90 percent interest in Sub, Inc., which is recorded on a *cost* basis. During the calendar year 19X1, Parent reported net income of $50,000 and Sub reported net income of $20,000. Intercompany interest on bonds was $800. Sub declared and paid a $3,000 dividend during the year. How much is 19X1 *consolidated* net income?
   a. $64,500.
   b. $65,300.
   c. $66,100.
   d. $68,000.

2. On January 1, 19X1, Bedard Corporation issued its own no par stock in exchange for 60,000 shares of Biggs Company's common stock, which represents a 90 percent investment in Biggs. On this date, Biggs' net assets were $600,000. Bedard received a dividend of $1 per share from Biggs in 19X1. Biggs reported net income of $320,000 for the year ended December 31, 19X1. The balance in the Investment in Biggs Company account at December 31, 19X1, under the equity method is
   a. $768,000.
   b. $774,000.
   c. $800,000.
   d. $828,000.

                                                                          (AICPA adapted)

Exercise 2–3   (Equity Method and Working Paper Entries)

On January 1, 19X1, Howard Company acquired a 90 percent interest in Thomas Company in exchange for Howard no par common stock. On this date, Thomas Company had capital stock of $50,000 and retained earnings of $30,000. The combination is a pooling of interests.

   During 19X1, Thomas Company reported net income of $20,000 and paid cash dividends of $10,000.

Required:

a. Prepare all entries on the books of Howard Company in 19X1 related to its investment in Thomas Company under (1) the cost method and (2) the equity method.

b. Assuming Howard Company uses the equity method of accounting for its investment, prepare the elimination entries for a consolidated statement working paper on December 31, 19X1.

Exercise 2–4   (Equity Method and Working Paper Entries)

Bit Company acquired a 90 percent interest in Crunch Company on January 1, 19X1, in exchange for no par common shares of Bit. On this date, Crunch Company had capital stock of $20,000 and retained earnings of $30,000.

During 19X1 and 19X2, Crunch Company reports net income of $20,000 per year and pays cash dividends of $5,000 each year. The combination is a pooling of interests. Bit Company uses the equity method of accounting for its investment in Crunch Company.

Required:

a. Determine the balance of the investment account on December 31, 19X1, and December 31, 19X2.
b. Prepare the elimination entries for a consolidated statement working paper on December 31, 19X1, and December 31, 19X2.

Exercise 2–5   (Equity Method and Working Paper Entries)

On January 1, 19X1, Harm Company acquired a 90 percent interest in Todd Company in exchange for no par common stock. On this date, Todd Company had capital stock of $30,000 and retained earnings of $70,000. The combination is a pooling of interests.

During 19X1, Todd Company reports net income of $40,000 and pays a cash dividend of $10,000. During 19X2, Todd Company reports a net loss of $10,000 and pays a cash dividend of $5,000. Harm Company uses the equity method of accounting for its investment in Todd Company.

Required:

a. Prepare the entries on Harm Company's books in 19X1 and 19X2 related to its investment in Todd Company.
b. Prepare the elimination entries for a consolidated statement working paper on December 31, 19X1, and December 31, 19X2.

Exercise 2–6   (Equity Method and Working Paper Entries)

On January 1, 19X1, Vale Company acquired a 90 percent interest in CPW Company in exchange for Vale no par common shares. On this date, CPW Company had capital stock of $10,000 and retained earnings of $30,000. The combination is a pooling of interests.

During 19X1 and 19X2, CPW Company reports net income of $15,000 each year and pays cash dividends of $10,000 each year. Vale Company uses the equity method of accounting for its investment in CPW Company.

Required:

a. Determine the balance of the investment account on December 31, 19X1, and December 31, 19X2.
b. Prepare the elimination entries for a consolidated statement working paper on December 31, 19X1, and December 31, 19X2.

Exercise 2–7 (Equity Method and Working Paper Entries)

Snyder Company has a 95 percent interest in Holland Company, acquired in 19X1 in exchange for Snyder no par stock. The combination was accounted for as a pooling of interests. Snyder Company uses the equity method of accounting for its investment in Holland Company.

During 19X5, Snyder Company recorded the following entries:

1. Investment in Holland Company 19,000
    Equity in Subsidiary Earnings 19,000

2. Cash 4,750
    Investment in Holland Company 4,750

At December 31, 19X5, Holland Company reported capital stock of $50,000 and retained earnings of $100,000 (including 19X5 income and dividends).

Required:

a. Determine the balance of the investment account on December 31, 19X5.
b. Calculate the value of the minority interest in net income for 19X5 and the total value of the minority interest in Holland Company at December 31, 19X5.
c. Prepare the elimination entries for a consolidated statement working paper on December 31, 19X5.

Exercise 2–8 (Equity Method and Allocation of Income)

P Company made the following investments on January 1, 19X1, in exchange for P Company no par stock:

> 90% of the capital stock of Y Company
> 95% of the capital stock of Z Company
> 90% of the capital stock of W Company

Additional data concerning these companies are:

	P Company	*Y Company*	*Z Company*	*W Company*
Capital stock (no par)	$200,000	$100,000	$50,000	$40,000
Retained earnings,				
January 1, 19X1	100,000	50,000	20,000	10,000
Net income (loss), 19X1	80,500	40,000	20,000	(5,000)
Cash dividends, 19X1	10,000	5,000	4,000	–0–

P Company carries its investment in subsidiaries on an equity basis; it reported a profit from its own operations in 19X1 of $30,000. All the combinations were pooling of interests.

Required:

a. Prepare journal entries for 19X1 on the books of P Company reflecting its transactions with, or interests in, subsidiary companies.
b. Calculate the amount of consolidated net income for 19X1 and the balance of consolidated retained earnings as of December 31, 19X1.
c. Calculate the amounts of minority interest in the 19X1 net income (loss) and the December 31, 19X1, retained earnings of subsidiary companies.

Exercise 2–9   (Equity Method and Allocation of Income)

The following data relate to companies M, G, and R for the two-year period ending December 31, 19X1:

	M Company	G Company	R Company
Capital stock	$220,000	$103,500	$51,000
Retained earnings (deficit), January 1, 19X0	250,000	40,000	(20,000)
Net income (excluding equity in subsidiary profits):			
19X0	90,000	60,000	30,000
19X1	75,000	40,000	40,000
Dividends paid:			
19X0	20,000	4,000	–0–
19X1	20,000	10,000	5,000

In each of the following independent cases, investments in subsidiary stock are carried by the parent on an equity basis, and all combinations are pooling of interests.

Case 1: M Company acquired 90 percent of the capital stock of G Company on January 1, 19X0, in exchange for M no par common stock.

Case 2: G Company acquired 90 percent of the capital stock of R Company on January 1, 19X0, in exchange for G no par common stock.

Case 3: M Company acquired 95 percent of the capital stock of G Company on January 1, 19X1, in exchange for M no par common stock.

Case 4: M Company acquired 100 percent of the capital stock of R Company on January 1, 19X0, and 90 percent of the capital stock of G Company on January 1, 19X1, in exchange for M no par common stock.

Required:

In each of the above cases:

a. Calculate the balance of the investment account on December 31, 19X1.
b. Calculate the amount of consolidated net income for 19X0 and 19X1, and the balance of consolidated retained earnings on December 31, 19X1.

Exercise 2–10   (Consolidated Net Income)

Ashton Corporation has a 90 percent interest in Hubbard Household Equipment Company. During 19X1, Hubbard reported net income of $20,000, and in 19X2, Hubbard reported a loss of $10,000. Ashton had net income from its own operations of $50,000 each year.

Required:

Calculate consolidated net income for 19X1 and 19X2.

Exercise 2–11   (Consolidated Net Income)

P Company acquired a 90 percent interest in S Company on January 1, 19X1, in exchange for P Company no par common stock. The combination is a pooling of interests. You are given the following information for the companies' earnings and dividends:

	P Company	S Company
Retained earnings, December 31, 19X0	$100,000	$50,000
Net incomes from own operations:		
19X1	20,000	15,000
19X2	30,000	20,000
Dividends declared and paid:		
19X1	10,000	5,000
19X2	15,000	5,000

Required:

a. Using the incremental approach, calculate consolidated net income for 19X1 and 19X2.
b. Using the residual approach, calculate consolidated net income for 19X1 and 19X2.
c. Compute consolidated retained earnings as of December 31, 19X1, and December 31, 19X2.

Exercise 2–12   (Consolidated Net Income)

A Company acquired 95 percent of the capital stock of B Company on January 1, 19X0, and 90 percent of the capital stock of C Company on January 1, 19X1, in exchange for A no par stock. The combinations were pooling of interests. The following two-year operating summary relates to the affiliated companies:

	A Company	B Company	C Company
Retained earnings, January 1, 19X0	$70,000	$40,000	$35,000
19X0 net income from own operations	40,000	20,000	30,000
19X0 cash dividends	–0–	10,000	5,000
19X1 net income from own operations	10,000	15,000	20,000
19X1 cash dividends	4,000	6,000	10,000

Required:

a. Using the incremental approach, calculate consolidated net income for 19X0 and 19X1.
b. Using the residual approach, calculate consolidated net income for 19X0 and 19X1.
c. Calculate consolidated retained earnings as of December 31, 19X0, and December 31, 19X1.

Exercise 2–13   (Consolidated Net Income)

P Company acquired a 90 percent interest in the capital stock of Y Company on January 1, 19X1, and a 95 percent interest in the capital stock of Z Company on the same day. The combinations were pooling of interests. You are given the following information for the companies' earnings and dividends:

	P Company	Y Company	Z Company
Retained earnings, January 1, 19X1	$60,000	$30,000	$15,000
Net incomes (loss) from own operations:			
19X1	13,200	8,000	(5,000)
19X2	8,400	4,000	7,000
Dividends declared and paid:			
19X1	5,000	2,000	–0–
19X2	–0–	1,000	2,000

Required:

a. Calculate consolidated net income for 19X1 and 19X2.
b. Calculate consolidated retained earnings on December 31, 19X1, and December 31, 19X2.

Exercise 2-14   (Equity Method and Allocation of Income)

On January 1, 19X1, Box Corporation made the following investments:

1. Acquired 90 percent of the outstanding common stock of Valley Corporation in exchange for Box no par common stock. The stockholders' equity of Valley on January 1, 19X1, consisted of the following:

Common stock, par value $50	$50,000
Retained earnings	20,000

2. Acquired 90 percent of the outstanding common stock of May Corporation in exchange for Box no par common stock. The stockholders' equity of May on January 1, 19X1, consisted of the following:

Common stock, par value $20	$60,000
Capital in excess of par value	20,000
Retained earnings	40,000

The following information on the companies' earnings and dividends for 19X1 is provided:

	Box	Valley	May
Net income (loss) from own operations	$104,600	$36,000	$(12,000)
Dividends declared and paid	40,000	16,000	9,000

Box Corporation uses the equity method to account for its investments in Valley and May. Both combinations were classified as pooling of interests.

Required:

a. What entries should have been made on the books of Box Corporation during 19X1 to record the following?
   (1) Investments in subsidiaries.
   (2) Parent's share of subsidiary income or loss.
   (3) Subsidiary dividends received.
b. Compute the amount of minority interest in each subsidiary's stockholders' equity at December 31, 19X1.
c. Assuming that Box Corporation's retained earnings on January 1, 19X1, amounted to $240,000, what amount should be reported as consolidated retained earnings of Box Corporation and subsidiaries as of December 31, 19X1?

(AICPA adapted)

Problems

Problem 2–15   (Working Paper)

Hanna Company acquired 90 percent of the capital stock of Taylor Corporation on January 1, 19X1, in exchange for Hanna no par common stock, when Taylor's capital stock and retained earnings were $50,000 and $10,000, respectively. The combination is a pooling of interests. Trial balances prepared on December 31, 19X1, disclose the following:

| | December 31, 19X1 | |
	Hanna Company	Taylor Corporation
Cash	$ 8,000	$ 5,000
Accounts Receivable	21,000	17,000
Inventory (1/1)	15,000	8,000
Investment in Taylor Corporation	63,000	
Other Assets	50,000	48,000
Dividends Declared	10,000	5,000
Purchases	90,000	20,000
Operating Expenses	10,000	7,000
	$267,000	$110,000
Accounts Payable	$ 3,500	$ 6,000
Advances from Hanna		4,000
Other Liabilities	5,000	
Capital Stock (no par)	100,000	50,000
Retained Earnings	40,000	10,000
Sales	105,000	40,000
Equity in Subsidiary Earnings	13,500	
	$267,000	$110,000
Inventory (12/31)	$ 20,000	$ 10,000

Required:

a. Prepare a consolidated statement working paper for the year ended December 31, 19X1.

b. Prepare formal consolidated statements.

Problem 2–16   (Working Paper)

The Parnelli Company acquired 95 percent of the capital stock of Foyt Company on January 1, 19X1, in exchange for Parnelli common stock. One year later, the following trial balances are prepared:

	Parnelli Company	Foyt Company
Cash	$ 14,000	$ 23,000
Inventory (12/31)	45,000	30,000
Investment in Foyt Company	114,000	
Other Assets	106,000	80,000
Cost of Sales	87,000	65,000
Operating Expenses	14,000	16,000
Dividends Declared	20,000	10,000
	$400,000	$224,000
Accounts Payable	7,000	10,000
Other Liabilities	1,500	3,000
Capital Stock (no par)	200,000	100,000
Retained Earnings	64,000	20,000
Sales	118,000	91,000
Equity in Subsidiary Earnings	9,500	
	$400,000	$224,000

Required:

Prepare a consolidated statement working paper for the year ended December 31, 19X1.

Problem 2–17   (Working Paper)

Cruse Company acquired 90 percent of the capital stock of Summers, Inc., on January 1, 19X1, in exchange for Cruse common stock. On this date, Summers' stockholders' equity consisted of capital stock, $50,000, and retained earnings, $12,000. The combination is classified as a pooling of interests. Two years later, the trial balances of the companies were:

	December 31, 19X2	
	Cruse Company	*Summers, Inc.*
Cash	$ 22,000	$ 12,500
Accounts Receivable	5,000	17,000
Inventory (1/1)	28,000	11,000
Investment in Summers, Inc.	90,000	
Other Assets	49,400	80,500
Dividends Declared	8,500	5,000
Purchases	161,000	83,000
Freight-in	1,000	200
Selling Expenses	18,000	11,100
Administrative Expenses	9,300	5,700
	$392,200	$226,000
Accounts Payable	$ 13,700	$ 12,000
Other Liabilities	3,000	16,000
Capital Stock (no par)	100,000	50,000
Retained Earnings	44,500	27,000
Sales	205,000	121,000
Equity in Subsidiary Earnings	25,200	
Interest Income	800	
	$392,200	$226,000
Inventory (12/31)	$ 41,000	$ 18,000

The accounts payable of Summers, Inc., include $3,000 payable to Cruse Company.

Required:

Prepare a three-division consolidated statement working paper for the year ended December 31, 19X2.

Problem 2–18   (Working Paper)

Weeks Company acquired a 95 percent interest in Knight Company in 19X1 in exchange for Weeks common stock. The combination was a pooling of interests. On December 31, 19X5, the companies prepare the following trial balances:

	Weeks Company	Knight Company
Cash	$ 14,000	$ 23,000
Inventory (12/31)	45,000	30,000
Investment in Knight Company	123,500	
Other Assets	108,000	80,000
Cost of Sales	87,000	65,000
Operating Expenses	14,000	16,000
Dividends Declared	20,000	10,000
	$411,500	$224,000
Accounts Payable	$ 10,500	$ 3,000
Capital Stock (no par)	200,000	100,000
Retained Earnings	64,000	20,000
Sales	118,000	101,000
Equity in Subsidiary Earnings	19,000	
	$411,500	$224,000

Required:

Prepare a three-division consolidated statement working paper for the year ended December 31, 19X5.

Problem 2–19   (Working Paper)

Bransford Company acquired a 90 percent interest in Strandberg Company on January 1, 19X1, in exchange for Bransford common stock. On this date, Strandberg's shareholders' equity consisted of capital stock, $300,000, and retained earnings, $20,000. The combination was classified as a pooling of interests. On December 31, 19X3, the companies prepare the following trial balances:

	Bransford Company	Strandberg Company
Cash	$ 42,000	$ 69,000
Inventory (1/1)	126,000	105,000
Investment in Strandberg Company	351,000	
Other Assets	343,500	240,000
Purchases	270,000	180,000
Operating Expenses	42,000	48,000
Dividends Declared	60,000	30,000
	$1,234,500	$672,000
Accounts Payable	$ 30,500	$ 9,000
Capital Stock (no par)	600,000	300,000
Retained Earnings	196,000	60,000
Sales	354,000	303,000
Equity in Subsidiary Earnings	54,000	
	$1,234,500	$672,000
Inventory (12/31)	$ 135,000	$ 90,000

During 19X3, Strandberg sold merchandise to Bransford in the amount of $53,000. At December 31, 19X3, Strandberg's Other Assets included a receivable of $6,500 from Bransford (which is included in Bransford's Accounts Payable).

Required:

Prepare a three-division consolidated statement working paper for the year ended December 31, 19X3.

Problems for Appendixes

Problem 2–20(A)   (Working Paper)

On January 1, 19X1, Central Company acquired 90 percent of the capital stock of Western Company in exchange for Central common stock. The combination is a pooling of interests. On December 31, 19X1, their trial balances are as follows:

	Central Company	Western Company
Cash	$ 8,000	$ 5,000
Accounts Receivable	21,000	17,000
Inventory (1/1)	15,000	8,000
Investment in Western Company	54,000	
Other Assets	50,000	48,000
Dividends Declared	10,000	5,000
Purchases	90,000	20,000
Operating Expenses	10,000	7,000
	$258,000	$110,000
Accounts Payable	$ 3,500	$ 6,000
Other Liabilities	5,000	
Advances from Central		4,000
Capital Stock (no par)	100,000	50,000
Retained Earnings	40,000	10,000
Sales	105,000	40,000
Dividend Income	4,500	
	$258,000	$110,000
Inventory (12/31)	$ 20,000	$ 10,000

Central Company uses the *cost* method of accounting for its investment in Western Company.

Required:

On December 31, 19X1, prepare consolidated statements supported by a three-division working paper.

Problem 2–21(A)   (Working Paper)

Cruse Company acquired 90 percent of the capital stock of Summers, Inc., on January 1, 19X1, in exchange for Cruse common stock. On this date, Summers' stockholders' equity consisted of capital stock, $50,000, and retained earnings, $12,000. Cruse Company uses the *cost* method of accounting for its investment in Summers. The combination is classified as a pooling of interests. Two years later, the trial balances of the companies were:

	December 31, 19X2	
	Cruse Company	*Summers, Inc.*
Cash	$ 22,000	$ 12,500
Accounts Receivable	5,000	17,000
Inventory (1/1)	28,000	11,000
Investment in Summers, Inc.	55,800	
Other Assets	49,400	80,500
Dividends Declared	8,500	5,000
Purchases	161,000	83,000
Freight-in	1,000	200
Selling Expenses	18,000	11,100
Administrative Expenses	9,300	5,700
	$358,000	$226,000
Accounts Payable	$ 13,700	$ 12,000
Other Liabilities	3,000	16,000
Capital Stock (no par)	100,000	50,000
Retained Earnings	31,000	27,000
Sales	205,000	121,000
Dividend Income	4,500	
Interest Income	800	
	$358,000	$226,000
Inventory (12/31)	$ 41,000	$ 18,000

The accounts payable of Summers, Inc., include $3,000 payable to Cruse Company.

Required:

Prepare a three-division consolidated statement working paper for the year ended December 31, 19X2.

Problem 2-22(A)   (Working Paper)

Bransford Company acquired a 90 percent interest in Strandberg Company on January 1, 19X1, in exchange for Bransford common stock. The combination was classified as a pooling of interests. On this date, Strandberg's stockholders' equity consisted of capital stock, $300,000, and retained earnings, $20,000. Bransford Company uses the *cost* method of accounting for its investment in Strandberg. On December 31, 19X3, the companies prepare the trial balances as shown below.

During 19X3, Strandberg sold merchandise to Bransford in the amount of $53,000. At December 31, 19X3, Strandberg's Other Assets included a receivable of $6,500 from Bransford (which is included in Bransford's Accounts Payable).

	Bransford Company	Strandberg Company
Cash	$ 42,000	$ 69,000
Inventory (1/1)	126,000	105,000
Investment in Strandberg Company	288,000	
Other Assets	343,500	240,000
Purchases	270,000	180,000
Operating Expenses	42,000	48,000
Dividends Declared	60,000	30,000
	$1,171,500	$672,000
Accounts Payable	$ 30,500	$ 9,000
Capital Stock (no par)	600,000	300,000
Retained Earnings	160,000	60,000
Sales	354,000	303,000
Dividend Income	27,000	
	$1,171,500	$672,000
Inventory (12/31)	$ 135,000	$ 90,000

Required:

Prepare a three-division consolidated statement working paper for the year ended December 31, 19X3.

Issues in Purchase Combinations

In Chapter 2, we described the fundamentals of consolidated statements for acquisitions classified as a *pooling of interests*. In this chapter, the additional issues that arise because the acquisition is classified as a *purchase* are examined. These issues include the allocation of the purchase cost to the acquired assets and liabilities on the basis of their fair values on the date of acquisition and the subsequent amortization of these allocated costs. In all other respects, the basic elements of the consolidation process described in the previous chapter remain the same.

Determining the Cost of an Acquired Company

With the purchase method, the acquisition of stock of the subsidiary is accounted for in accordance with the traditional principles of the purchase of assets. The acquiring company debits its investment account for the cost of the acquired company. The cost is measured by the fair value of the consideration given or received, whichever is more clearly evident. Note that the consideration given may include cash, noncash assets, debt, and/or stock of the acquiring company.

Acquisition Date

The cost of an acquired company is determined on the date of acquisition. Normally, the acquisition date is the date that assets and securities are exchanged. However, the parties to the combination transaction may choose the effective date of the combination to be the end of an accounting period between the dates the combination is initiated and consummated. When this occurs, the cost of the investment is reduced (and interest expense recognized) by the imputed interest on assets given, liabilities incurred, or preferred stock distributed from the acquisition date to the transfer date.[1]

Direct and Indirect Costs

Only the direct, incremental costs of an acquisition are included in the cost of the investment. Indirect and general expenses related to acquisitions (e.g., the costs of an "acquisitions" department) are expensed as incurred.[2] Similarly, costs of closing duplicate facilities are not part of the cost of an acquired company.[3]

---

[1] *APB Opinion No. 16*, pars. 93–94.

[2] AICPA, *APB Opinion No. 16, Accounting Interpretation No. 33*, "Costs of Maintaining an 'Acquisitions' Department" (New York: AICPA, 1970), par. 76.

[3] FASB, *Technical Bulletin No. 85-5*, "Issues Relating to Accounting for Business Combinations. . ." (Norwalk, CT: FASB, 1985), par. 2.

Declared but Unpaid Subsidiary Dividend

The parent company may purchase shares of an acquired company between the declaration date and record date of a dividend. If so, the total price paid includes the purchase of the right to receive the unpaid dividend. Accordingly, the acquisition entry reflects the purchase of two assets: investment in the subsidiary and dividends receivable. Immediately following the acquisition, the parent's balance sheet includes dividends receivable relating to dividends payable on the subsidiary's balance sheet. If a consolidated balance sheet is prepared on the date of acquisition, a working paper elimination entry debiting Dividends Payable and crediting Dividends Receivable is required.

Registration Costs

Securities issued in an acquisition must often be registered with the SEC. When costs of registering and issuing equity securities used in an acquisition are incurred, the "otherwise determinable" fair value of the securities is reduced by the amount of these costs. The value assigned to the investment account is the sum of these registration costs and the net value of the equity securities.[4] For example, assume that P Company issues 5,000 shares of its no-par common stock for all of the common stock of S Company and pays registration costs of $2,000. The estimated fair market value of the stock issued by P Company (when registered) is $30 per share. In this case, the value of the stock issued by P Company is $150,000 ($30 × 5,000), less registration costs of $2,000, or a net value of $148,000. The entry recording the purchase is:

Investment in S Company	150,000	
Cash		2,000
Capital Stock		148,000

If unregistered equity securities are issued in an acquisition with an agreement for later registration, the estimated amount of these registration costs is accrued as a liability, and the net fair value of the shares issued is determined as above.[5]

Contingent Consideration

The terms of a business combination may provide additional consideration based on future specified events or transactions. In this situation, the general measurement guidelines applied are as follows:

> Contingent consideration usually should be recorded when the contingency is resolved and consideration is issued or becomes issuable. In general, the issue of additional

---

[4] Accounting Principles Board, *APB Opinion No. 16*, "Business Combinations" (New York: AICPA, 1970), par. 76.

[5] AICPA, *APB Opinion No. 16, Accounting Interpretation No. 35*, "Registration Costs in a Purchase" (New York: AICPA, 1972).

securities or distribution of other consideration at resolution of contingencies *based on earnings* should result in an additional element of cost of an acquired company. In contrast, the issue of additional securities or distribution of other consideration at resolution of contingencies *based on security prices* should not change the recorded cost of an acquired company.[6]

These general guidelines are discussed in paragraphs 77–86 of *Opinion No. 16*.

An example of contingent consideration is provided in the acquisition by General Motors Corporation of Hughes Aircraft Company. The price paid for Hughes was $2.7 billion in cash and cash equivalents and 100 million shares of General Motors Class H common stock. In addition, for each share issued and held by the Howard Hughes Medical Institute four years after acquisition, General Motors agreed to pay the Institute the amount by which the market value of the Class H common stock might be below $30 per share, provided that such payment would not exceed $20 per share. This is, of course, a contingency based on security prices. If the agreement had specified a payment contingent on earnings per share of the Class H common stock reaching some target level after four years, the contingency would be one based on earnings.

ALLOCATING PURCHASE COST

In the preparation of consolidated statements under the purchase method, we must deal with the difference between the cost of the investment and the parent's interest in the book value of the subsidiary's net assets. This is accomplished by substituting the book values of the subsidiary's assets and liabilities for a portion of the investment account and allocating the difference to the individual assets and liabilities of the subsidiary on the basis of their fair values.

The allocation process is presented in three cases. The first case assumes a 100 percent acquisition in which the value assigned to each individual asset and liability is equal to its fair value. The second case covers the situation in which less than 100 percent of the shares are acquired and the values assigned are less than the full fair values. In both cases, the purchase price exceeds the parent's interest in the fair value of the net assets acquired and the excess is assigned to goodwill. The third case examines the circumstance in which the price paid is less than the fair value of the net assets acquired (the *residual credit* case).

---

[6] *APB Opinion No. 16*, par. 79. [Emphasis added.]

Case 1. Acquisition of 100 Percent Interest at Cost Unequal to Book Value

Assume P Company acquires 100 percent of S Company's common shares for the cash price of $150, and the book value of S Company's net assets is only $100. Apparently

1. The fair values of S Company's *recorded* assets and liabilities do not equal their book values, and/or
2. S Company has *unrecorded* assets or liabilities.

To follow up on these implications, assume S Company's recorded assets and liabilities are as follows:

	Book Value	Fair Value	Difference
Current assets	$ 10	$ 10	$–0–
Plant and equipment	190	220	30
	$200	$230	$30
Liabilities	100	100	–0–
Net assets	$100	$130	$30

It is clear that $30 of the $50 excess of purchase price over book value is because the recorded book value of the plant and equipment does not equal its fair value. Therefore, the remaining $20 of purchase price represents payment for unrecorded assets (net of any unrecorded liabilities). Absent any additional information, we must conclude that the unrecorded asset is goodwill with a fair value of $20. The $150 purchase price can thus be allocated as follows:

Current assets acquired	$ 10
Plant and equipment acquired	220
Goodwill acquired	20
	$250
Liabilities assumed	100
Purchase price	$150

On the consolidated balance sheet, the individual assets and liabilities of S Company are presented at their respective book values plus any excess of fair value over book value. In T account format, this allocation of the $150 investment cost is reflected in the consolidated balance sheet as follows:

Parent Company Balance Sheet	Consolidated Balance Sheet
	Current Assets
	10
Investment in S Company	**Plant and Equipment**
150	190 + 30 = 220
	Goodwill
	20
	Liabilities
	100

Case 2. Acquisition of Less than 100 Percent Interest at Cost Unequal to Book Value

Assume P Company acquires 90 percent of S Company's common shares for the cash price of $135. At acquisition, book values and fair values of S Company's recorded assets and liabilities are as follows:

	Book Value	Fair Value	Difference
Current assets	$ 10	$ 10	$-0-
Plant and equipment	190	220	30
	$200	$230	$30
Liabilities	100	100	-0-
Net assets	$100	$130	$30

Note that these are the same amounts as in Case 1. If $135 is the fair value of 90 percent of S Company's shares, the fair value of 100 percent of S Company's shares is \$150 (\$135 ÷ 90%). And absent additional information, we again conclude that S Company has \$20 in goodwill.

There are two ways in which the \$135 appearing in P Company's investment account might be disaggregated in order to prepare a consolidated balance sheet. In T account format, the first of these is as follows:

Parent Company Balance Sheet	**Consolidated Balance Sheet**
	Current Assets
	10	
	Plant and Equipment
	220	
Investment in S Company	**Goodwill**
135		20	
	Liabilities
		100
	Minority Interest
		10% × 150 = 15

On the consolidated balance sheet, the individual assets and liabilities of S Company are presented at 100 percent of their respective fair values. Accordingly, the minority interest claim to these assets is also based on fair value.

Full consolidation done in this fashion is an application of the *entity theory,* which asserts that the audience of the consolidated statements includes both the parent shareholders and the minority shareholders of S Company. Application of the entity theory is rare in current practice. Prevailing practice is to apply the *parent company theory.* Under this perspective, only the parent company's proportionate interest in differences between fair values and book values is included on the consolidated balance sheet. In T account format, application of the parent company theory results in the following allocations to individual accounts:

Parent Company Balance Sheet	Consolidated Balance Sheet

Current Assets

	10

Plant and Equipment

190 + (90% × 30) = 217	

Investment in S Company	Goodwill
135	(90% × 20) = 18

Liabilities

	100

Minority Interest

	(10% × 100) = 10

On the consolidated balance sheet, S Company's individual assets and liabilities are presented at book value plus the parent's share of any difference between book value and fair value.

The basis of accounting for minority interest is *book value*. According to the parent company theory, the owners of the accounting equity are the parent company shareholders. Accordingly, the minority interest is classified as either a liability or as a "mezzanine" item between liabilities and stockholders' equity. As we noted in Chapter 2, the parent company theory is assumed throughout this text.

There are a number of ways in which amounts allocated to individual assets and liabilities can be determined. However, the following schedular format will be useful as our attention shifts to a working paper format for preparation of the consolidated balance sheet:

Purchase price		$135
Parent's proportionate interest in book value of subsidiary's recorded net assets (90% × $100)		90
Debit differential		$ 45
Allocation of debit differential:		
Plant and equipment [90% × ($220 − $190)]	$ 27	
Other assets and liabilities	–0–	27
Goodwill		$ 18

The difference between the purchase price and the parent's proportionate interest in the book value of the subsidiary's recorded net assets is termed the *differential*. Usually the differential is a positive number and is referred to as a *debit differential*. The differential is then "explained" to the extent possible. In the preceding example, $27 of the debit differential is due to the acquisition of 90 percent of S Company's undervalued plant and equipment. Since no other assets or liabilities have fair values different from book values, the remaining "unexplained" debit differential of $18 is attributed to goodwill. "Explaining" the differential is synonymous with allocating it: $27 of the differential is allocated to plant and equipment, and $18 is allocated to goodwill. On the consolidated balance sheet, individual assets and liabilities are presented at their book values plus amounts of differential allocated to them:

	Book Value	Differential Allocation	Consolidated Statement Valuation
Current assets	$ 10	$-0-	$ 10
Plant and equipment	190	27	217
Goodwill	-0-	18	18
	$200	$ 45	$245
Liabilities	100	-0-	100
Net assets	$100	$ 45	$145

Case 3. Residual Credit after Differential Allocation

The process of allocating the differential can result in a residual credit balance. This occurs when the purchase price is less than the parent's proportionate share of the fair value of the subsidiary's assets and liabilities. Assume P Company purchases 100 percent of S Company's outstanding common shares for $150. At acquisition, data relating to S Company's net assets are as follows:

	Fair Value	Book Value
Current assets	$ 10	$ 5
Marketable securities (noncurrent)	70	50
Plant and equipment	120	105
Intangibles (not including goodwill)	50	20
Liabilities	(80)	(80)
	$170	$100

The standard differential allocation here results in a residual credit:

Purchase price		$150
Parent's proportionate share of book value of		
subsidiary's recorded net assets		100
Debit differential		$ 50
Allocation of debit differential:		
Current assets ($10 − $5)	$ 5	
Marketable securities ($70 − $50)	20	
Plant and equipment ($120 − $105)	15	
Intangibles ($50 − $20)	30	$ 70
Residual credit		($ 20)

The presence of this residual credit might be explained in the following ways:

1. The former shareholders of S Company have acted irrationally. If they had sold S Company's assets individually and used the proceeds to pay debtors, they would have received a net amount of $170. Selling S Company shares netted them only $150. Apparently, the firm as a whole has "negative goodwill."
2. The fair values used in making the initial differential allocation contain measurement error.

The first alternative, although possible, is unlikely. The second is quite likely. Estimating fair values of noncurrent assets is a subjective process, except for the investments in marketable securities. Apparently, the estimated fair values of plant and equipment and intangibles are overstated, resulting in the residual credit.

APB Opinion No. 16 specifies that, instead of allocating a negative value to goodwill, the amounts assigned to *noncurrent assets* (other than marketable securities) should be reduced proportionately.[7] Of the total fair value of non-current assets (other than marketable securities), plant and equipment composes 71 percent and intangibles 29 percent:

	Fair Value	*Percent*
Plant and equipment	$120	71
Intangibles	50	29
	$170	100

[7] *APB Opinion No. 16*, par 87.

Thus, the amount assigned to plant and equipment should be reduced by $14 (71% × $20), and the amount assigned to intangibles should be reduced by $6 (29% × $20). The ultimate differential allocation is as follows:

Current assets	$ 5
Marketable securities	20
Plant and equipment ($15 − $14)	1
Intangibles ($30 − $6)	24
Differential to be allocated	$50

When the excess of fair value over purchase price is large, it is possible that noncurrent asset values could be reduced to zero without eliminating the residual credit differential. In such cases, any remaining residual credit differential is classified as a deferred credit and amortized to income.[8]

DETERMINING FAIR VALUES

In a business combination accounted for using the purchase method, the differential (difference between purchase price and parent's share of the book values of acquired assets and liabilities) is allocated to individual assets and liabilities. This allocation requires estimates of the fair values of the subsidiary's assets and liabilities. In practice, determining these fair values can be complex.

Basic Authoritative Guidance

APB Opinion No. 16 provides the following guidelines for determining fair values:

1. Marketable securities: at current net realizable values.
2. Receivables: at present values of amounts to be received determined at appropriate current interest rates, less allowances for uncollectibility and collection costs.
3. Inventories:
   a. Finished goods: at estimated selling prices less the sum of disposal costs and a reasonable profit allowance for the selling effort.
   b. Work in process: at estimated selling prices of finished goods less the sum of costs to complete, costs of disposal, and a reasonable profit allowance for the completion and selling efforts.

---

[8] See footnote 7.

4. Plant and equipment:
   a. To be used: at current replacement costs for similar capacity unless the expected future use of the assets indicates a lower value to the acquirer.
   b. To be sold or held for later sale rather than used: at current net realizable value.
   c. To be used temporarily: at current net realizable value recognizing future depreciation for the expected period of use.
5. Intangible assets that can be identified and named, including contracts, patents, franchises, customer and supplier lists, and favorable leases: at appraised values.
6. Other assets, including land, natural resources, and nonmarketable securities: at appraised values.
7. Accounts and notes payable, long-term debt, and other claims payable: at present values of amounts to be paid determined at appropriate current interest rates.
8. Other liabilities and commitments, including unfavorable leases, contracts, commitments, and plant closing expense incident to the acquisition: at present values of amounts to be paid determined at appropriate current interest rates.

Pension Liabilities

Statement of Financial Accounting Standards No. 87 provides guidance on determining the fair value of pension plans. Liabilities are valued at the excess of projected benefit obligations over plan assets. Assets are valued at the excess of plan assets over projected benefit obligations.[9] Note that it is the projected benefit obligation, not the accumulated benefit obligation, that enters into the determination of pension assets and liabilities.

Deferred Taxes

Special problems arise when the consolidated statement values of assets and liabilities are not equal to their tax bases (e.g., when the acquired corporation does not elect to step up tax bases to fair value). When an asset's assigned value exceeds its tax basis, a deferred tax liability is created.

First, consider purchasing an asset for $100. Assume the asset will generate pretax revenues of $110, tax deductions equal to its $100 purchase price, and a 30 percent tax rate. Using the asset will result in payment of $3 in taxes, as illustrated

---

[9] FASB, *Statement of Financial Accounting Standards No. 87,* "Employers' Accounting for Pensions" (Norwalk, CT: FASB, 1985), par. 74.

in the first column below. Now, assume that the tax deductions are only $60. Use of the asset will result in payment of $15 in taxes, as illustrated in the second column below.

	$100 Tax Basis	$60 Tax Basis
Revenues	$110	$110
Tax deductions	100	60
Taxable income	$ 10	$ 50
Tax rate	×.30	×.30
Tax	$ 3	$ 15

Purchasing the asset in the first column for $100 will result in an after-tax profit of $7 ($110 − $3 − $100). To earn this same $7 profit from the asset in the second column, the purchase price would have to be $12 less (because of the incremental $12 in taxes). In a sense, purchasing the asset in the second column for $88 ($100 − $12) involves acquiring an asset with a value of $100 and assuming a tax liability of $12.

Statement of Financial Accounting Standards No. 109 requires this treatment in business combinations accounted for as a purchase. The consolidated statement value of an acquired company's deferred taxes is equal to the tax rate times the difference between the consolidated statement values and the tax bases of its identified assets and liabilities.[10] With a 30 percent tax rate, an asset with an assigned value of $100 and a $60 tax basis requires a $12 consolidated statement valuation of deferred taxes [30% × ($100 − $60)]. If the asset generates $110 in pretax revenues, pretax accounting income will be $10 ($110 − $100), and taxable income will be $50 ($110 − $60). Accordingly, the provision for income taxes will be as follows:

Current (30% × $50)	$15
Deferred [30% × ($60 − $100)]	(12)
Provision for income taxes	$ 3

---

[10] FASB, *Statement of Financial Accounting Standards No. 109,* "Accounting for Income Taxes" (Norwalk, CT: FASB, 1992). Note that deferred taxes arise from assigned value/tax basis differences of *identified* assets and liabilities. Goodwill is not an identified asset. Therefore, the consolidated statement value of deferred taxes does not include any amount due to goodwill.

Net Operating Loss Carryforwards

At the date of acquisition, a subsidiary's net operating loss carryforward can be assigned a consolidated statement value if, under the laws of the applicable taxing jurisdiction, it can reduce the parent's tax liability.[11] Any value so assigned reduces the amount otherwise assigned to deferred taxes, which effectively reduces the assigned value of goodwill.

If a net operating loss carryforward is not assigned a value at acquisition, its subsequent realization is reflected on the consolidated statements first as a reduction of goodwill from the acquisition and then to other noncurrent intangibles related to the acquisition. After these assets have been reduced to zero, realization is reflected on the consolidated statement as a reduction of income tax expense.[12]

Preacquisition Contingencies

It is often the case that the acquired company has unrecorded contingent assets and liabilities at the acquisition date. A common example is pending litigation. If the status of the contingency changes such that it is recorded by S Company during the *allocation period* (generally understood to mean one year following the acquisition date), this *hindsight* information is reflected in the determination of fair values at the date of acquisition.[13]

For example, assume P Company purchases 100 percent of S Company's common shares on January 1, 19X1, for $100. On this date, the book value and fair value of S Company's recorded net assets are $80. However, S Company has an unrecorded contingent liability by virtue of being a defendant in a lawsuit. As of the acquisition date, the $20 differential ($100 − $80) is allocated to goodwill. Prior to December 31, 19X1, the status of the lawsuit changes such that it is now probable that S Company will eventually pay $15. The effect of this change in status is to retroactively reduce S Company's net assets from $80 to $65 and thus increase goodwill from $20 to $35. If the change in status occurs after the end of the allocation period, the effect is a charge to earnings.

Litigation arising from the acquisition itself (e.g., antitrust actions or actions relating to the tax treatment of the acquisition) is not considered a preacquisition contingency. Rather, such actions are contingencies of the purchaser.[14]

---

[11] See footnote 10.

[12] See footnote 10.

[13] FASB, *Statement of Financial Accounting Standards No. 38,* "Accounting for Preacquisition Contingencies of Purchased Enterprises" (Norwalk, CT: FASB, 1980).

[14] See footnote 14.

DIFFERENTIAL ALLOCATION IN THE WORKING PAPER

The following example introduces the working paper processes and integrates many of the issues discussed to this point. The facts involve an acquisition accounted for using the purchase method. The purchase price exceeds the parent's proportionate interest in the subsidiary's recorded assets and liabilities. The consolidated statement values of the subsidiary's assets and liabilities do not coincide with their tax bases.

Case 4. Comprehensive Differential Allocation

P Company purchases 80 percent of the outstanding common shares of S Company for the cash price of $1,800. Immediately after the acquisition, the balance sheets of P Company and S Company are as follows:

	P Company	S Company
Current assets	$ 500	$ 200
Investment in S Company	1,800	
Plant and equipment	3,000	2,000
	$5,300	$2,200
Liabilities	$2,000	$1,000
Deferred taxes	300	60
Capital stock	2,000	500
Other contributed capital		200
Retained earnings	1,000	440
	$5,300	$2,200

The book value of S Company's net assets (i.e., stockholders' equity) is $1,140 ($500 + $200 + $440). Accordingly, the debit differential is as follows:

Purchase price	$1,800
Parent's proportionate interest in book value of subsidiary recorded net assets (80% × $1,140)	(912)
Debit differential	$ 888

To allocate this differential, you determine the following data relating to S Company's assets and liabilities (excluding the deferred taxes):

	Fair Value	Book Value	Tax Basis
Current assets	$ 300	$ 200	$ 200
Plant and equipment	2,500	2,000	1,800
Liabilities	(900)	(1,000)	(1,000)
	$1,900	$1,200	$1,000

The consolidated statement values of these assets and liabilities are their book values plus 80 percent of any differences between fair values and book values:

Current assets [$200 + 80% × ($300 − $200)]	$ 280
Plant and equipment [$2,000 + 80% × ($2,500 − $2,000)]	2,400
Liabilities [$1,000 + 80% × ($900 − $1,000)]	(920)
	$1,760

Assuming a 30 percent tax rate, the consolidated statement value of S Company's deferred taxes is 30 percent of the excess of these assigned values over their tax bases:

Assigned values	$1,760
Tax bases	1,000
Excess of assigned values over tax bases	$ 760
Tax rate	× .30
Deferred taxes	$ 228

Since the book value of S Company's deferred taxes is $60, the portion of the debit differential allocated to deferred taxes is $168 ($228 − $60).

All of the above implies that the consolidated statement value of goodwill is as follows:

Debit differential		$888
Allocation of debit differential:		
Current assets [80% × ($300 − $200)]	$ 80	
Plant and equipment [80% × ($2,500 − $2,000)]	400	
Liabilities [80% × ($1,000 − $900)]	80	
Deferred taxes	(168)	$392
Goodwill		$496

The working paper used to prepare a consolidated balance sheet appears in Illustration 3–1. In journal entry format, the two elimination entries are as follows:

1. To eliminate S Company's stockholders' equity and P Company's investment account and to establish the debit differential and minority interest:

Capital Stock	500	
Other Contributed Capital	200	
Retained Earnings	440	
Differential [1,800 − (80% × $1,140)]	888	
Minority Interest (20% × $1,140)		228
Investment in S Company		1,800

ILLUSTRATION   3–1

P COMPANY AND SUBSIDIARY S COMPANY
Consolidated Balance Sheet Working Paper
(Acquisition Date)

	P Company	S Company	Eliminations Dr.		Eliminations Cr.		Consolidated
Current assets	500	200	(2)	80	(1)	1,800	780
Investment in S Company	1,800				(1)	1,800	
Plant and equipment	3,000	2,000	(2)	400			5,400
Goodwill			(2)	496			496
Differential			(1)	888	(2)	888	
	5,300	2,200					6,676
Liabilities	2,000	1,000	(2)	80			2,920
Deferred taxes	300	60			(2)	168	528
Minority interest					(1)	228	228
Capital stock	2,000	500	(1)	500			2,000
Other contributed capital		200	(1)	200			
Retained earnings	1,000	440	(1)	440			1,000
	5,300	2,200		3,084		3,084	6,676

2. To allocate the debit differential:

Current Assets 80		
Plant and Equipment [80% × ($2,500 − $2,000)] 400		
Goodwill 496		
Liabilities [80% × ($1,000 − $900)] 80		
Deferred Taxes ($228 − $60)	168	
Differential	888	

Although not necessary for the preparation of the consolidated balance sheet working paper, P Company's purchase price can be explained in terms of the fair values of assets purchased and liabilities assumed:

Current assets		$ 300
Plant and equipment		2,500
Goodwill ($496/80%)		620
Liabilities		(900)
Total fair value before consideration		
of implicit deferred tax liability		$2,520
Parent's proportionate interest		× .80
		$2,016
Deferred tax liability	$228	
Assumed by minority shareholders (20% × $60)	12	$ 216
Purchase price		$1,800

TREATMENT OF DIFFERENTIALS SUBSEQUENT TO DATE OF ACQUISITION

Subsequent to acquisition, allocated differential amounts are accounted for consistent with the accounting for the particular asset (or liability) to which they are assigned. Thus, amounts allocated to accounts whose balances are not normally subject to systematic amortization (e.g., land) will continue to be reported at the same, originally allocated values. Amounts allocated to accounts whose balances are expensed or periodically amortized will be accorded similar treatment in consolidated financial statements.

Recall that an unallocated debit differential is classified as goodwill. This value, like the values of all intangible assets, should be amortized on the basis of the estimated life of the specific asset (in this case, goodwill). It should not be written off in the period of acquisition. The Accounting Principles Board set an arbitrary maximum life of 40 years for the amortization of goodwill. Generally, straight-line amortization should be applied. This amortization of goodwill does not create a difference for temporary income tax allocation purposes, and thus tax allocation is inappropriate.[15]

An unallocated credit differential (after the specified reallocation to noncurrent assets) similarly should be amortized systematically to income over the period of time estimated to benefit therefrom, but not to exceed 40 years. No part of this deferred credit should be added directly to stockholders' equity at the date of acquisition.[16]

Application of these principles at the end of an accounting period generally results in a set of expense adjustments, the total of which is referred to as the *amortization of the differential for the period* (or sometimes simply *differential amortization*).

Since a differential is part of the cost incurred by the parent company, the amortization of this cost is allocated wholly to the majority shareholders. The value of the interest of minority shareholders is calculated, as before, on the basis of accumulations recorded in the subsidiary's equity accounts.

In addition to recognizing the differential amortization in the consolidated statement working paper the parent company must also recognize this expense on its books. *APB Opinion No. 18* states: "The difference between consolidation and the equity method lies in the details reported in the financial statements. Thus, an investor's net income for the period and its stockholders' equity at the end of the period are the same whether an investment in a subsidiary is accounted for under the equity method or the subsidiary is consolidated."[17] Accordingly, at the same time that the parent records its equity in subsidiary earnings for the period, an additional entry must be made to record the amortization of the differential for the period.

The specific accounting procedures that are employed to reflect the differential amortization are illustrated in two integrated examples which follow. The first case deals with the year of acquisition, and the second case considers the year subsequent to the acquisition year. Each example illustrates the eliminating entries required for the preparation of a consolidated statement working paper and the formal journal entries recorded on the books of the parent company.

Case 5. Amortization of Differential—Year of Acquisition

On January 1, 19X1, P Company purchased an 80 percent interest in S Company for $300,000. On this date, S Company had capital stock of $50,000 and retained earnings of $120,000.

---

[15] APB, *APB Opinion No. 17*, "Intangible Assets" (New York: AICPA, 1970), pars. 23–30.

[16] APB, *APB Opinion No. 16*, "Business Combinations" (New York: AICPA, 1970), pars. 91–92.

[17] APB, *APB Opinion No. 18*, "The Equity Method of Accounting for Investments in Common Stock" (New York: AICPA, 1971), par. 19.

Assume that an examination of S Company's identifiable assets and liabilities revealed that all were recorded at amounts that approximated their fair values except for inventory, plant and equipment, and land. The analysis of these differences is provided as follows:

	Book Value	Fair Value	Excess of Fair Value over Book Value	P Company's 80% Interest in Excess
Inventory	$ 20,000	$ 25,000	$ 5,000	$ 4,000
Plant and equipment (net)	80,000	155,000	75,000	60,000
Land	40,000	65,000	25,000	20,000
	$140,000	$245,000	$105,000	$84,000

The differential generated by this acquisition follows:

Investment cost	$300,000
P Company's equity in recorded net assets of S Company (80% × $170,000)	136,000
Differential	$164,000

Since the investment cost exceeds the parent's equity in the recorded net assets of the subsidiary, the differential is a debit differential. Based upon the examination of the identifiable assets and liabilities of S Company, $84,000 of the differential is allocated to the three specific assets. The remaining unallocated debit differential of $80,000 is classified as goodwill in the consolidated statements.

Each allocated portion of the differential is amortized in accordance with the accounting for the asset to which it is assigned. For purposes of this illustration, we assume that the following determinations were made:

1. The inventory on hand on January 1, 19X1, was all sold during 19X1.
2. On January 1, 19X1, the plant and equipment had an expected remaining life of 10 years.
3. The land is not subject to amortization.

The goodwill requires, of course, an independent assessment of expected useful life. We assume that P Company decided to amortize the goodwill acquired in the combination over the maximum period of 40 years. Based upon these facts, a schedule of differential amortization is presented in Illustration 3–2.

Assume finally that S Company reported net income of $50,000 for the year ended December 31, 19X1, and paid $12,500 cash dividends during the year.

ILLUSTRATION 3-2   **Schedule of Differential Amortization**

	Allocated Amount	Annual Amortization		
		Year 1	Years 2–10	Years 11–40
Inventory	$ 4,000	$ 4,000	–0–	–0–
Plant and equipment (net)	60,000	6,000	$6,000	–0–
Land	20,000	–0–	–0–	–0–
Goodwill	80,000	2,000	2,000	$2,000
	$164,000	$12,000	$8,000	$2,000

Parent Company Entries—Year 1.   Based upon the information presented in the case and the schedule of differential amortization developed in Illustration 3–2, the parent company makes the following entries during 19X1:

1. To record the receipt of dividends from S Company:

   Cash (80% × $12,500) 10,000
       Investment in S Company   10,000

2. To recognize the equity in S Company's reported earnings:

   Investment in S Company (80% × 50,000) 40,000
       Equity in Subsidiary Earnings   40,000

3. To recognize the differential amortization for the period (see Illustration 3–2):

   Equity in Subsidiary Earnings 12,000
       Investment in S Company   12,000

Amortization of the differential for the period is charged against the parent company's equity in reported subsidiary earnings because the differential represents the portion of the total investment cost that has not (implicitly) been taken into account in the calculation of subsidiary net income. Of course, entries (2) and (3) can be combined into a single entry recognizing P Company's equity method income:

Investment in S Company [(80% × 50,000) − 12,000] 28,000
    Equity in Subsidiary Earnings   28,000

Note the effects of these entries on the balance of the investment account. On January 1, 19X1, the balance of the investment account was equal to 80 percent of S Company's stockholders' equity plus the unamortized differential:

ILLUSTRATION 3-3

P COMPANY AND SUBSIDIARY S COMPANY
Consolidated Statement Working Paper
For Year Ended December 31, 19X1

	P Company	S Company	Eliminations Dr.	Eliminations Cr.	Consolidated
Income Statement					
Sales	520,000	290,000			810,000
Equity in subsidiary earnings	28,000		(1) 28,000		
Total credits	548,000	290,000			810,000
Cost of sales	258,000	140,000	(5) 4,000		402,000
Operating expenses	160,000	100,000	(5) 8,000		268,000
Total debits	418,000	240,000			670,000
	130,000	50,000			140,000
Minority interest expense			(2) 10,000		10,000
Net income	130,000	50,000	50,000		130,000
Retained Earnings Statement					
Retained earnings (1/1):					
P Company	410,000				410,000
S Company		120,000	(3) 120,000		
Net income	130,000	50,000	50,000		130,000
	540,000	170,000			540,000
Dividends declared:					
P Company	40,000				40,000
S Company		12,500		(1) 10,000	
				(2) 2,500	
Retained earnings (12/31)	500,000	157,500	170,000	12,500	500,000

Eighty percent of S Company's stockholders' equity

80% × ($50,000 + $120,000) $136,000

Unamortized differential 164,000

$300,000

During 19X1, S Company's stockholders' equity increased by $37,500 (the net of its earnings and dividends). The first two entries above increase the investment account by 80 percent of $37,500. After these two entries, the balance in the investment account is 80 percent of S Company's December 31, 19X1, stockholders' equity plus the original unamortized differential. The third entry decreases the investment account by the 19X1 differential amortization. Thus, at December 31, 19X1, the balance of the investment account is 80 percent of

ILLUSTRATION 3-3 *(Continued)*

	P Company	S Company	Eliminations Dr.		Eliminations Cr.		Consolidated
Balance Sheet							
Cash	50,000	28,000					78,000
Accounts receivable	100,000	60,000					160,000
Inventory	82,000	30,000	(4)	4,000	(5)	4,000	112,000
Investment in S Company	318,000				(5)	18,000	
					(1)	18,000	
					(3)	300,000	
Land	50,000	40,000	(4)	20,000			110,000
Plant and equipment	150,000	72,000	(4)	60,000	(5)	6,000	276,000
Differential			(3)	164,000	(4)	164,000	
Goodwill			(4)	80,000	(5)	2,000	78,000
	750,000	230,000					814,000
Accounts payable	50,000	22,500					72,500
Capital stock:							
P Company	200,000						200,000
S Company		50,000	(3)	50,000			
Retained earnings	500,000	157,500		170,000		12,500	500,000
Minority interest					(2)	7,500	41,500
					(3)	34,000	
	750,000	230,000		548,000		548,000	814,000

Explanation of eliminations:

(1) To eliminate parent's share of subsidiary earnings and dividends.

(2) To account for the minority's share of subsidiary earnings and dividends.

(3) To eliminate January 1, 19X1, stockholders' equity balances and establish differential.

(4) To allocate differential.

(5) To amortize differential.

S Company's December 31, 19X1, stockholders' equity plus the December 31, 19X1, unamortized differential:

Eighty percent of S Company's stockholders' equity	
80% × ($50,000 + $120,000 + $50,000 − $12,500)	$166,000
Unamortized differential ($164,000 − $12,000)	152,000
	$318,000

This relationship persists when the parent uses the equity method. At all points in time, the balance of the investment account is the parent's percentage ownership times the subsidiary stockholders' equity plus the unamortized differential.

Consolidated Statement Working Paper—Year 1. The consolidated statement working paper for the year ended December 31, 19X1, appears in Illustration 3–3.

The balances in the working paper are arbitrarily chosen, except where it is required that they correspond with data previously presented in Case 5.

Note first the income statement division of the working paper. Consistent with the "one-line consolidation" properties of the equity method, parent company income equals consolidated income. In the Consolidated column, the $28,000 equity in subsidiary earnings balance in the P Company column is disaggregated into the following:

Sales	$290,000
Cost of sales ($140,000 + $4,000)	(144,000)
Operating expenses ($100,000 + $8,000)	(108,000)
Minority interest expense	(10,000)
	$ 28,000

which is:

S Company net income	$50,000
Differential amortization	(12,000)
Minority interest expense	(10,000)
	$28,000

or 80 percent of S Company's net income less differential amortization.

Also note the balance sheet division of the working paper. Consistent with the "one-line consolidation" properties of the equity method, parent company stockholders' equity equals consolidated stockholders' equity. The differences in the assets and liabilities between the P Company column and the Consolidated column result from the disaggregation of the $318,000 balance in the investment account into the following:

Cash	$ 28,000
Accounts receivable	60,000
Inventory	30,000
Land ($40,000 + $20,000)	60,000
Plant and equipment ($72,000 + $60,000 − $6,000)	126,000
Goodwill ($80,000 − $2,000)	78,000
Accounts payable	(22,500)
Minority interest	(41,500)
	$318,000

which is 80 percent of S Company's stockholders' equity plus unamortized differential.

The elimination entries on the working paper follow:

1. Equity in Subsidiary Earnings	28,000	
Investment in S Company		18,000
Dividends Declared—S Company (80% × $12,500)		10,000

This entry eliminates double counting of equity method income in the income statement division of the working paper and the intercompany dividends paid by the subsidiary to the parent.

2. Minority Interest Expense (20% × $50,000)	10,000	
Dividends Declared—S Company (20% × $12,500)		2,500
Minority Interest		7,500

Entry 2 establishes minority interest expense and the minority share of income, net of dividends paid.

3. Capital Stock—S Company	50,000	
Retained Earnings—S Company	120,000	
Differential	164,000	
Investment in S Company		300,000
Minority Interest [20% × ($50,000 + $120,000)]		34,000

This entry eliminates S Company stockholders' equity accounts *as of the beginning of the year,* eliminates the remainder of the investment account, establishes the unamortized differential *as of the beginning of the year,* and establishes the minority interest *as of the beginning of the year.*

4. Inventory	4,000	
Plant and Equipment	60,000	
Land	20,000	
Goodwill	80,000	
Differential		164,000

Entry 4 allocates the *beginning of the year* differential.

5. Cost of Sales	4,000	
Operating Expenses	8,000	
Inventory		4,000
Plant and Equipment		6,000
Goodwill		2,000

This entry records the 19X1 amortization of the differential. Note that the reductions of inventory, plant and equipment, and goodwill correspond to the amounts in Illustration 3–2. By assumption, all of the inventory to which the $4,000 differential applies was sold during 19X1. This assumption is consistent with first-in, first-out (FIFO) inventory valuation. If it had been assumed that none of the inventory to which the differential applies was sold during 19X1 (consistent with last-in, first-out [LIFO] inventory valuation), the debit to Cost of Sales and the credit to Inventory would not be necessary.

Case 6. Amortization of Differential—Year Subsequent to Acquisition Year. Assume that S Company reported net income of $40,000 for the year ended December 31, 19X2, and again paid $12,500 cash dividends during the year. Note that 19X2 is the second year the companies have operated as a combined entity.

Parent Company Entries—Year 2

Based upon the assumed income and dividend figures of Case 6 and again referencing illustration 3–2 for the differential amortization for 19X2, P Company makes the following entries during 19X2:

1. To record receipts of dividends from S Company:

Cash (80% × $12,500)	10,000	
Investment in S Company		10,000

2. To recognize equity in S Company's reported earnings:

Investment in S Company	32,000	
Equity in Subsidiary Earnings (80% × $40,000)		32,000

3. To recognize differential amortization for the period (from Illustration 3–2):

Equity in Subsidiary Earnings	8,000	
Investment in S Company		8,000

Consolidated Statement Working Paper—Year 2. The consolidated statement working paper for Case 6 appears in Illustration 3–4. As before, the balances in the working paper are arbitrarily chosen, except where it is required that they correspond with assumed data. Note again that the "one-line consolidation" properties of the equity method persist. Parent net income equals consolidated net income. Parent stockholders' equity equals consolidated stockholders' equity.

ILLUSTRATION 3-4

P COMPANY AND SUBSIDIARY S COMPANY
Consolidated Statement Working Paper
For Year Ended December 31, 19X2

	P Company	S Company	Eliminations Dr.	Eliminations Cr.	Consolidated
Income Statement					
Sales	586,000	250,000			836,000
Equity in subsidiary earnings	24,000		(1) 24,000		
Total credits	610,000	250,000			836,000
Cost of sales	252,000	100,000			352,000
Operating expenses	198,000	110,000	(5) 8,000		316,000
Total debits	450,000	210,000			668,000
	160,000	40,000			168,000
Minority interest expense			(2) 8,000		8,000
Net income	160,000	40,000	40,000		160,000
Retained Earnings Statement					
Retained earnings (1/1):					
P Company	500,000				500,000
S Company		157,500	(3) 157,500		
Net income	160,000	40,000	40,000		160,000
	660,000	197,500			660,000
Dividends declared:					
P Company	50,000				50,000
S Company		12,500		(1) 10,000	
				(2) 2,500	
Retained earnings (12/31)	610,000	185,000	197,500	12,500	610,000
Balance Sheet					
Cash	130,000	36,000			166,000
Accounts receivable	150,000	80,000			230,000
Inventory	110,000	50,000			160,000
Investment in S Company	332,000			(1) 14,000	
				(3) 318,000	
Land	50,000	40,000	(4) 20,000		110,000
Plant and equipment	128,000	64,000	(4) 54,000	(5) 6,000	240,000
Differential			(3) 152,000	(4) 152,000	
Goodwill			(4) 78,000	(5) 2,000	76,000
	900,000	270,000			982,000
Accounts payable	90,000	35,000			125,000
Capital stock:					
P Company	200,000				200,000
S Company		50,000	(3) 50,000		
Retained earnings	610,000	185,000	197,500	12,500	610,000
Minority interest				(2) 5,500	47,000
				(3) 41,500	
	900,000	270,000	551,500	551,500	982,000

Explanation of eliminations:

(1) To eliminate parent's share of subsidiary earnings and dividends.

(2) To account for the minority's share of subsidiary earnings and dividends.

(3) To eliminate January 1, 19X2, stockholders' equity balances and establish differential.

(4) To allocate differential.

(5) To amortize differential.

ILLUSTRATION 3-5   Schedule of Unamortized Differential (Allocations as of January 1, 19X2)

	Original Amounts Allocated— January 1, 19X1	Amortization for 19X1	Unamortized Amounts— January 1, 19X2
Inventory	$ 4,000	$ 4,000	$ -0-
Plant and equipment (net)	60,000	6,000	54,000
Land	20,000	-0-	20,000
Goodwill	80,000	2,000	78,000
	$164,000	$12,000	$152,000

The five numbered elimination entries are analogous to their prior year counterparts. The first three of these are as follows:

1. Equity in Subsidiary Earnings	24,000	
Investment in S Company		14,000
Dividends Declared—S Company (80% × $12,500)		10,000
2. Minority Interest Expense (20% × $40,000)	8,000	
Dividends Declared—S Company (20% × $12,500)		2,500
Minority Interest		5,500
3. Capital Stock—S Company	50,000	
Retained Earnings—S Company	157,500	
Differential	152,000	
Investment in S Company		318,000
Minority Interest [20% × ($50,000 + $157,500)]		41,500

As a consequence of these three working paper elimination entries, the unamortized differential as of January 1, 19X2, is set up in the working paper. This amount is derived in Illustration 3–5. The fourth working paper entry allocates this differential:

4. Plant and Equipment	54,000	
Land	20,000	
Goodwill	78,000	
Differential		152,000

The final working paper entry records differential amortization for 19X2:

5. Operating Expenses	8,000	
Plant and Equipment		6,000
Goodwill		2,000

Treatment of Separate Accumulated Depreciation Account

In Cases 5 and 6, plant and equipment was presented net of any accumulated depreciation to focus on the substance of differential allocation and amortization. Consolidating a subsidiary's balance sheet which includes both the gross value of plant and equipment and the related accumulated depreciation changes nothing of a fundamental nature. But it does add slightly to the complexity of the elimination entries. Assume that the $80,000 date of acquisition book value of plant and equipment assumed in Cases 5 and 6 consists of the following:

Plant and equipment	$240,000
Accumulated depreciation (20 years at $8,000)	(160,000)
Net value of plant and equipment	$ 80,000

Accordingly, the subsidiary continues to report depreciation expense at the rate of $8,000 per year.

At date of acquisition, the consolidated statement values of the plant and equipment and accumulated depreciation are $140,000 ($80,000 + [80% × ($155,000 − $80,000)]) and zero, respectively. Such values are consistent with principles of valuation of any newly purchased asset. Given the assumed remaining life of 10 years, the consolidated statements therefore reflect depreciation expense of $14,000 ($140,000/10) per year.

The balances of accumulated depreciation reported on S Company's balance sheet and the consolidated balance sheet as of December 31, 19X1, and December 31, 19X2, are as follows:

	S Company	Consolidated
December 31, 19X1	$168,000	$14,000
December 31, 19X2	$176,000	$28,000

Given these data, the fourth and fifth working paper elimination entries from Case 5 must be modified to these:

```
4. Inventory ...................................    4,000
   Accumulated Depreciation ($168,000 − $8,000) ...........  160,000
   Land ......................................   20,000
   Goodwill ..................................   80,000
        Plant and Equipment ($240,000 − $140,000) ...........         100,000
        Differential ............................         164,000


5. Cost of Sales ...............................    4,000
   Operating Expenses ..........................    8,000
        Inventory ..............................           4,000
        Accumulated Depreciation ($14,000 − $8,000) ..........           6,000
        Goodwill ...............................           2,000
```

The debit to Accumulated Depreciation in entry (4) eliminates all accumulated depreciation except for that recorded by S Company during 19X1. The credit to Accumulated Depreciation in entry (5) increases the balance by the excess of the consolidated statement depreciation expense over the amount reported by S Company. Accordingly, the December 31, 19X1, consolidated statement valuation of accumulated depreciation is established at $14,000 ($168,000 − $160,000 + $6,000).

The fourth and fifth working paper entries for Case 6 must be modified as follows:

```
4. Accumulated Depreciation ($160,000 − $6,000) ...........  154,000
   Land ......................................   20,000
   Goodwill ..................................   78,000
        Plant and Equipment ($240,000 − $140,000) ...........         100,000
        Differential ............................         152,000


5. Operating Expenses ..........................    8,000
        Accumulated Depreciation ....................           6,000
        Goodwill ...............................           2,000
```

The debit to Accumulated Depreciation in entry (4) is the amount eliminated in the prior year ($160,000) less the prior year's differential amortization relating to the plant and equipment ($6,000). The above entries establish the December 31, 19X2, consolidated statement valuation of accumulated depreciation at $28,000 ($176,000 − $154,000 + $6,000).

Summary

When a business combination is classified as a *purchase,* the investment is recorded at *cost.* Therefore, the chapter began with a review of the elements determining the cost of an acquired company. Next, the principles applicable to the allocation of the difference between cost and book value were examined, and the working paper procedures to facilitate this process were illustrated. Finally, we examined the treatment of the differential subsequent to acquisition, including modification of equity method entries on the parent's books and eliminating entries in the consolidated statement working paper to reflect the periodic amortization.

Appendix: Illustration of Consolidated Statement Working Paper Eliminating Entries for Differential Allocation and Amortization When the Investment Account Is Carried under the Cost Method

The fundamentals of consolidated statement preparation when the parent company uses the cost method to account for its investment were discussed in Appendix A to Chapter 2. These fundamentals are changed little with the introduction of a differential. We illustrate these changes using the data in Case 6 of this chapter.

The consolidated statement working paper as of December 31, 19X2, appears in Illustration 3–6. The Parent Company column differs from its equity method counterpart in Illustration 3–4 only because of the difference in parent company accounting methods. The first elimination entry is as follows:

1. Dividend Income (80% × $12,500)	10,000	
Dividends Declared—S Company		10,000

This entry eliminates double counting in income and eliminates the intercompany dividends paid to the parent by the subsidiary. This entry is unaffected by the debit differential.

The second working paper elimination entry follows:

2. Minority Interest Expense (20% × 40,000)	8,000	
Minority Interest		5,500
Dividends Declared—S Company (20% × $12,500)		2,500

This entry records the minority interest expense for 19X2 and the minority share of income, net of dividends paid. This entry is also unaffected by the debit differential.

ILLUSTRATION 3-6

P COMPANY AND SUBSIDIARY S COMPANY
Consolidated Statement Working Paper
For Year Ended December 31, 19X2

	P Company	S Company	Eliminations Dr.	Eliminations Cr.	Consolidated
Income Statement					
Sales	586,000	250,000			836,000
Dividend income	10,000		(1) 10,000		
Total credits	596,000	250,000			836,000
Cost of sales	252,000	100,000			352,000
Operating expenses	198,000	110,000	(5) 8,000		316,000
Total debits	450,000	210,000			668,000
	146,000	40,000			168,000
Minority interest expense			(2) 8,000		8,000
Net income	146,000	40,000	26,000		160,000
Retained Earnings Statement					
Retained earnings (1/1):					
P Company	482,000			(3) 18,000	500,000
S Company		157,500	(3) 157,500		
Net income	146,000	40,000	26,000		160,000
	628,000	197,500			660,000
Dividends declared:					
P Company	50,000				50,000
S Company		12,500		(1) 10,000	
				(2) 2,500	
Retained earnings (12/31)	578,000	185,000	183,500	30,500	610,000
Balance Sheet					
Cash	130,000	36,000			166,000
Accounts receivable	150,000	80,000			230,000
Inventory	110,000	50,000			160,000
Investment in S Company	300,000			(3) 300,000	
Land	50,000	40,000	(4) 20,000		110,000
Plant and equipment	128,000	64,000	(4) 54,000	(5) 6,000	240,000
Differential			(3) 152,000	(4) 152,000	
Goodwill			(4) 78,000	(5) 2,000	76,000
	868,000	270,000			982,000
Accounts payable	90,000	35,000			125,000
Capital stock:					
P Company	200,000				200,000
S Company		50,000	(3) 50,000		
Retained earnings	578,000	185,000	183,500	30,500	610,000
Minority interest				(2) 5,500	47,000
				(3) 41,500	
	868,000	270,000	537,500	537,500	982,000

Explanation of eliminations:

(1) To eliminate intercompany dividends received by parent company.

(2) To account for the minority's share of subsidiary earnings and dividends.

(3) To eliminate January 1, 19X2, stockholders' equity balances and establish differential.

(4) To allocate differential.

(5) To amortize differential.

The third working paper elimination entry follows:

```
3. Capital Stock—S Company  . . . . . . . . . . . . . . . . . . . . . .    50,000
   Retained Earnings—S Company  . . . . . . . . . . . . . . . . . .   157,500
   Differential  . . . . . . . . . . . . . . . . . . . . . . . . . . . . . . . . .   152,000
      Investment in S Company . . . . . . . . . . . . . . . . . . . . . . .              300,000
      Minority Interest (20% × $207,500) . . . . . . . . . . . . . .               41,500
      Retained Earnings—P Company
      [(80% × $37,500) − $12,000] . . . . . . . . . . . . . . . . . .               18,000
```

This entry differs from its counterpart in Appendix A to Chapter 2 in recognizing two aspects of the differential. First, the unamortized differential at the beginning of the year ($152,000) is recognized. Second, the credit to P Company's retained earnings for the parent's share of the subsidiary's undistributed earnings since acquisition (80% × $37,500) must be adjusted for the *cumulative differential amortization* from acquisition to the beginning of the current year ($12,000). With this latter adjustment, the credit again effectively converts the parent's retained earnings at the beginning of the year *from the cost method to the equity method.*

The fourth and fifth working paper entries allocate and amortize the differential. Since the amount of differential and its amortization do not depend on whether the parent company uses the cost or equity methods, these entries are identical to their counterparts in Illustration 3–4.

```
4. Plant and Equipment  . . . . . . . . . . . . . . . . . . . . . . . . . .    54,000
   Land . . . . . . . . . . . . . . . . . . . . . . . . . . . . . . . . . . . . . .    20,000
   Goodwill . . . . . . . . . . . . . . . . . . . . . . . . . . . . . . . . . . .    78,000
      Differential  . . . . . . . . . . . . . . . . . . . . . . . . . . . . . .              152,000

5. Operating Expenses . . . . . . . . . . . . . . . . . . . . . . . . . .     8,000
      Plant and Equipment . . . . . . . . . . . . . . . . . . . . . . . .                6,000
      Goodwill . . . . . . . . . . . . . . . . . . . . . . . . . . . . . . . . . .                2,000
```

Note that the Consolidated columns of Illustration 3–4 and 3–6 are identical. The consolidated statements do *not* depend on whether the parent company uses the cost or equity method. Differences in the parent company accounting method are accommodated by differences in the elimination entries.

Questions

1. What is the general rule for determining the date of acquisition of a newly acquired subsidiary? Are there any exceptions to this general rule?
2. Describe how the following items related to a business combination classified as a purchase are treated:

  a. Costs of your "acquisitions" department.
  b. Declared but unpaid dividends on the stock you purchase in the acquisition of a new subsidiary.
  c. Estimated costs to register shares issued as payment for the subsidiary.
  d. Contingent consideration given as part of an acquisition.

3. What is a differential? How is it explained?

4. After the differential has been allocated to identifiable assets and liabilities, any remaining unallocated debit differential is classified as goodwill. How is this classification justified?

5. If a residual credit remains after the initial differential has been allocated to identifiable assets and liabilities, what procedures are followed? How are these procedures justified?

6. In the determination of the fair values of subsidiary assets and liabilities, describe how the following items are valued:
  a. Pension liabilities.
  b. Deferred taxes.
  c. Net operating loss carryforwards.
  d. Preacquisition contingencies.

7. What do you think is the rationale for the "allocation period" during which preacquisition contingencies enter into the purchase price allocation?

8. What is the basic principle of accounting for differentials subsequent to the date of acquisition?

9. How does differential amortization affect the value of the minority interest?

10. For an investment carried under the equity method, what is the relationship between the investment account balance and the net assets of the subsidiary at any point in time?

Exercises

Exercise 3–1   (Differential Allocation)

Select the best answer in each of the following two situations.

1. On April 1, Bone Company paid $400,000 for all the issued and outstanding common stock of Dean Corporation in a transaction accounted for as a purchase. The assets and liabilities of Dean Corporation on April 1 follow:

Cash	$ 40,000
Inventory	120,000
Property and equipment (net of accumulated depreciation of $160,000)	240,000
Liabilities	(90,000)

On April 1, it was determined that the inventory of Dean had a fair value of $95,000 and the property and equipment (net) had a fair value of $280,000.

What is the amount recognized as goodwill in a consolidated balance sheet prepared on April 1?

a. $0.

b. $25,000.

c. $75,000.

d. $90,000.

2. P Company purchased all of the outstanding stock of S Company for $80,000. On the date of purchase, S Company had no long-term investments in marketable securities and $10,000 (book and fair value) of liabilities. The fair values of S Company's assets on the date of purchase were as follows:

Current assets	$ 40,000
Noncurrent assets	60,000
	$100,000

How is the $10,000 difference between the fair value ($90,000) of S Company's net assets and the investment cost ($80,000) handled in the consolidated balance sheet working paper prepared on the acquisition date?

a. The $10,000 difference should be credited to retained earnings.

b. The noncurrent assets should be valued at $50,000.

c. The current assets are valued at $36,000, and the noncurrent assets are valued at $54,000.

d. A deferred credit of $10,000 is established.

(AICPA adapted)

Exercise 3–2   (Differential Allocation)

Madison Company acquired 70 percent of the outstanding stock of Vail Corporation. The separate balance sheet of Madison right after the acquisition and the consolidated balance sheet are shown below.

Of the excess of purchase price over 70 percent of book value, $10,000 was allocated to undervaluation of its fixed assets; the balance of the excess was allocated to goodwill. Current assets of Vail included a $2,000 receivable from Madison, which arose before they became related on an ownership basis.

The following two items relate to Vail's separate balance sheet prepared at the time Madison acquired its 70 percent interest in Vail. Select the best answer.

	Madison	Consolidated
Assets		
Current assets	$106,000	$146,000
Investment in Vail	100,000	—
Goodwill	—	8,100
Fixed assets (net)	270,000	370,000
Total assets	$476,000	$524,100
Equities		
Current liabilities	$ 15,000	$ 28,000
Capital stock	350,000	350,000
Minority interest	—	35,100
Retained earnings	111,000	111,000
Total equities	$476,000	$524,100

1. What was the total of the current assets on Vail's separate balance sheet at the time Madison acquired its 70 percent interest?
   a. $38,000.
   b. $40,000.
   c. $42,000.
   d. $104,000.

2. What was the total stockholders' equity on Vail's separate balance sheet at the time Madison acquired its 70 percent interest?
   a. $64,900.
   b. $70,000.
   c. $100,000.
   d. $117,000.

(AICPA adapted)

Exercise 3–3   (Contingent Consideration)

P Company acquired a majority interest in S Company on 1/1/X1 by issuing 500,000 shares of no-par, common stock (current market price—$10 per share) for S Company shares. Treat each of the two situations below as independent cases, and select the best answer.

1. Assume that P Company guaranteed that if the market price of its shares fell below $10 per share at the end of one year, it would issue additional shares to restore the total market value of the consideration given to $5 million. Further assume that the market price at the end of the year was $5 per share and that P Company issued an additional 500,000 shares to meet its obligation. Issuance
   of the additional 500,000 shares would be recorded by P Company:

   a. Investment in S Company 2,500,000
      Capital Stock   2,500,000
   b. Investment in S Company 5,000,000
      Capital Stock   5,000,000
   c. Goodwill 2,500,000
      Capital Stock   2,500,000

    d. Some other entry would be made.

    e. No entry would be made.

2. Assume P Company guaranteed that it would issue additional shares worth $1 million (at 12/31/X1 market prices) if S Company's earnings for 19X1 exceed a specific amount. Further assume that the condition was satisfied and P Company issued 50,000 additional shares (at a 12/31/X1 market price of $20 per share). Issuance of the additional 50,000 shares at 12/31/X1 would be recorded by P Company.

    a. Investment in S Company 1,000,000
        Capital Stock   1,000,000

    b. Investment in S Company   500,000
        Capital Stock   500,000

    c. Goodwill 1,000,000
        Capital Stock   1,000,000

    d. Some other entry would be made.

    e. No entry would be made.

(It may be helpful to review paragraphs 77–86 of *APB Opinion No. 16.*)

Exercise 3–4   (Working Paper Entries)

Prepare working paper elimination entries for the Pacific Company and its subsidiary, Ocean Company, for each of the conditions listed below:

	Acquired Interest	Amount Paid	Ocean Capital Balances		
			Capital Stock	Other Contributed Capital	Retained Earnings (Deficit)
a.	100%	1,450,000	1,000,000	250,000	300,000
b.	90	1,125,000	1,000,000	325,000	(100,000)
c.	75	1,000,000	1,000,000	200,000	120,000

Exercise 3–5   (Acquisition and Working Paper Entries)

On December 1, 19X1, Valley-View Company declared a dividend of $2.50 per share on its outstanding 100,000 shares for shareholders of record, January 10, 19X2. On December 31, 19X1, Texton Company acquired 90,000 shares of Valley-View Company for a cash outlay of $2 million. Valley-View Company had the following balances in its capital accounts at December 31:

Capital stock ($10 par) $1,020,000
Treasury stock (recorded at par)   20,000
Other contributed capital   500,000
Retained earnings   400,000

Required:

a. Prepare working paper elimination entry for Texton Company as of December 31, 19X1.

b. Give the journal entry Texton Company would make to record the acquisition.

Exercise 3–6   (Residual Credit)

On January 1, 19X1, P Company purchased 90 percent of S Company for a cash outlay of $124,000. At the time of the investment, the book values of all S Company's assets and liabilities were equal to their fair values. S Company's balance sheet on January 1, 19X1, was as follows:

	S Company
Assets	
Cash	$ 10,000
Accounts receivable	5,000
Inventory	50,000
Long-term investments in marketable securities	15,000
Plant and equipment (net)	50,000
Land	60,000
Total assets	$190,000
Equities	
Accounts payable	$ 15,000
Notes payable	25,000
Capital stock	50,000
Retained earnings	100,000
Total equities	$190,000

Required:

a. Prepare a working paper elimination entry for P Company as of January 1, 19X1.

b. Give the elimination entry (entries) necessary to allocate the differential (if not incorporated in [a]).

Exercise 3–7   (Residual Credit)

P Company purchased an 80 percent interest in S Company for $84,800 on July 1, 19X1. S Company's balance sheet on that date was as follows:

	S Company
Assets	
Cash	$15,000
Receivables	20,000
Inventory	30,000
Long-term investments in marketable securities	12,000
Plant and equipment (net)	11,000
Patents	4,000
Total assets	$92,000
Equities	
Payables	$12,000
Capital stock	30,000
Retained earnings	50,000
Total equities	$92,000

A study of S Company's assets and liabilities revealed the following information:

	Fair Value
Inventory	$40,000
Long-term investments in marketable securities	15,000
Plant and equipment (net)	20,000
Patents	12,000

The fair values of the remainder of the assets and liabilities were equal to their book values.

Required:

a. Prepare working paper elimination entries for a consolidated balance sheet at July 1, 19X1.

b. Give the elimination entry (entries) necessary to allocate the differential (if not incorporated in [a]).

Exercise 3–8 (Asset Valuation in Purchase Transactions)

Shriver Enterprises is involved in crude oil trading. At January 1, 19X1, Shriver holds 100 barrels of oil, the historical cost of which is $14 per barrel. Shriver has no other assets and no liabilities.

On January 2, 19X1, Shriver sells 90 percent of its inventory of crude oil for $18. Accordingly, the historical cost basis of Shriver's assets is increased to $1,760 [(90 × $18) + (10 × $14)].

Required:

Assume that the January 2, 19X1, transaction involved Shriver's owners selling 90 percent of its common shares for $1,620 instead of selling 90 barrels at $18. Would you argue that in either case the ownership of 90 percent of Shriver's assets has changed hands? If so, is there any basis for valuing Shriver's assets differently when its owners sell 90 percent of their stock as opposed to the company itself selling 90 percent of its assets? How would Shriver's assets be valued in consolidated statements immediately following acquisition of 90 percent of its common shares?

Exercise 3–9   (Differential Allocation)

P Company acquired an 80 percent interest in S Company by issuing cash and other stock valued at $975,000. The investment elimination entry in P Company's consolidated statement working paper on the date of acquisition follows:

Capital Stock—S Company	100,000	
Retained Earnings—S Company	400,000	
Differential	575,000	
Minority Interest		100,000
Investment in S Company		975,000

An analysis of the identifiable assets and liabilities of S Company produced the following data:

	Book Value	Fair Value
Cash	$ 50,000	$ 50,000
Receivables	150,000	130,000
Inventory	250,000	310,000
Plant and equipment (net)	350,000	500,000
Patents	–0–	100,000
Land	100,000	150,000
Goodwill	50,000	–0–
	$950,000	$1,240,000
Accounts and notes payable	$300,000	$ 280,000
Accruals	50,000	40,000
Deferred income tax liability	100,000	–0–
	$450,000	$ 320,000
Net assets	$500,000	$ 920,000

Required:

a. Prepare the eliminating entry to allocate the differential to specific assets and liabilities. Assume assigned values equal tax bases.

b. The determination of "fair value" requires the application of different valuation bases (models) to different categories of assets and liabilities. Based upon the general guidelines established in paragraphs 88–89 of *APB Opinion No. 16* and *Statement of Financial Accounting Standards No. 109,* indicate the probable valuation basis that was used to estimate the fair value for each asset and liability.

Exercise 3–10   (Differential Allocation)

Lacy Company purchased 90 percent of the common shares of Wyndelts Company for $350,000 when the stockholders' equity of Wyndelts was as follows:

Capital stock	$100,000
Retained earnings	200,000
	$300,000

The sum of the fair values of the acquired net assets was $380,000. The sum of their tax bases was $300,000. Wyndelts Company had no recorded deferred taxes at the acquisition date. Its tax rate is 30 percent.

Required:

a. Compute the amount of the debit differential.

b. Compute the consolidated statement value of Wyndelts Company's assets and liabilities (other than deferred taxes).

c. Compute the consolidated statement value of Wyndelts Company's deferred taxes.

d. Compute the consolidated statement value of goodwill.

Exercise 3–11   (Consolidated Statement Relationships)

Items 1 through 5 are based on the following trial balance data relating to the combination of X Company and Y Company, in which X Company acquired 80 percent of the outstanding stock of Y Company several years ago:

	X Company	Y Company
Investment in Y Company	$ 30,000	
Other Assets	600,000	$50,000
Dividends Declared	8,000	5,000
Expenses	200,000	20,000
	$838,000	$75,000
Equity in Y Income	$ 14,000	
Sales	300,000	$40,000
Liabilities	330,000	20,000
Capital Stock	100,000	10,000
Retained Earnings	94,000	5,000
	$838,000	$75,000

All of the unamortized differential is allocable to goodwill.

1. The total expenses (including minority interest expense) which will appear on the consolidated income statement will be
   a. $200,000.
   b. $226,000.
   c. $220,000.
   d. $222,000.

2. The amount of goodwill appearing on the consolidated balance sheet will be
   a. $6,000.
   b. $2,000.
   c. $4,000.
   d. None of the above.

3. The total assets appearing on the consolidated balance sheet will be
   a. $838,000.
   b. $656,000.
   c. $650,000.
   d. $630,000.

4. The consolidated net income will be
   a. $114,000.
   b. $116,000.
   c. $120,000.
   d. $113,000.

5. The minority interest on the consolidated balance sheet will be
   a. $6,000.
   b. $5,800.
   c. $7,000.
   d. $3,000.

Exercise 3–12   (Equity Method and Working Paper Entries)

On January 1, 19X1, P Company purchased an 80 percent interest in S Company for $120,000. On this date, S Company had capital stock of $25,000 and retained earnings of $50,000.

An examination of S Company's assets and liabilities revealed that book values were equal to fair values for all except plant and equipment (net), which had a book value of $50,000 and a fair value of $75,000. The plant and equipment had an expected remaining life of five years. P Company planned to amortize any goodwill acquired in the combination over 20 years.

During 19X1 and 19X2, P Company reported net income from its own operations of $20,000, and S Company's income was $10,000 per year. S Company did not pay dividends either year.

Required:

a. Prepare the entries that P Company would have made in 19X1 and 19X2 in respect to its investment in S Company.

b. Prepare the eliminating entries for consolidated statement working papers on December 31, 19X1, and December 31, 19X2.

c. Calculate consolidated net income for 19X1 and 19X2.

Exercise 3–13   (Equity Method and Working Paper Entries)

On January 1, 19X1, P Company had capital stock of $60,000 and retained earnings of $40,000.

An examination of S Company's assets and liabilities revealed that book values were equal to fair values. P Company planned to amortize any goodwill acquired in the combination over the maximum period of 40 years.

During 19X1 and 19X2, P Company's net income from its own operations was $30,000 per year, and S Company's net income amounted to $20,000 per year.

Required:

a. Prepare the entries that P Company would have made in 19X1 and 19X2 in respect to its investment in S Company.

b. Prepare the eliminating entries for consolidated statement working papers on December 31, 19X1, and December 31, 19X2.

c. Calculate consolidated net income for 19X1 and 19X2.

Exercise 3–14   (Effects of Differential Amortization)

Assume that General Motors acquired all of the outstanding common stock of IBM in an exchange of shares on December 31, 19X1. The combination was accounted for as a purchase, and on this date the fair market value of the shares exchanged was determined to be approximately $37 billion.

The following information was taken from the financial statements of the (assumed) combination participants:

	General Motors	IBM
Recorded net assets,		
December 31, 19X1	$13,000,000,000	$11,000,000,000
Net income for 19X1	1,250,000,000	2,000,000,000

Assume that all of the differential is allocated to goodwill, and that it will be amortized over the maximum time period.

Required:

a. Assuming that the two companies had earnings from their own operations in 19X2 equal to the 19X1 amounts and that there were no intercompany transactions during the year, calculate consolidated net income for 19X2.

b. Prepare the eliminating entries to allocate the differential and to recognize differential amortization for 19X2.

c. If consolidated statements were prepared on January 1, 19X2, what percentage of consolidated net assets was represented by the "purchased" goodwill?

d. Assuming that General Motors had 290 million common shares outstanding in 19X1 and that it issued 610 million additional common shares to acquire IBM, calculate consolidated earnings per share for 19X2. How does this compare to General Motors' earnings per share in 19X1?

Exercise 3–15   (Equity Method and Working Paper Entries)

On January 1, 19X1, P Company purchased an 80 percent interest in S Company for $140,000. On this date, S Company had capital stock of $25,000 and retained earnings of $50,000.

An examination of S Company's assets and liabilities revealed that book values were equal to fair values for all except plant and equipment (net), which had a book value of $30,000 and a fair value of $75,000. The plant and equipment had an expected remaining life of 10 years. P Company planned to amortize any goodwill acquired in the combination over 40 years.

During 19X1 and 19X2, P Company reported net income from its own operations of $20,000, and S Company's income was $20,000 in 19X1 and $15,000 in 19X2. S Company did not pay dividends either year.

Required:

a. Prepare the entries that P Company would have made in 19X1 and 19X2 in respect to its investment in S Company.
b. Prepare the eliminating entries for consolidated statement working papers on December 31, 19X1, and December 31, 19X2.
c. Calculate consolidated net income for 19X1 and 19X2.

Exercise 3–16   (Equity Method and Working Paper Entries)

On January 1, 19X1, P Company purchased a 60 percent interest in S Company for $220,000. On this date, S Company had capital stock of $60,000 and retained earnings of $40,000.

An examination of S Company's recorded assets and liabilities revealed that book values were equal to fair values. P Company planned to amortize any goodwill acquired in the combination over the maximum period of 40 years.

During 19X1 and 19X2, P Company's net income from its own operations was $30,000 per year, and S Company's net income amounted to $10,000 in 19X1 and $15,000 in 19X2.

Required:

a. Prepare the entries that P Company would have made in 19X1 and 19X2 in respect to its investment in S Company.
b. Prepare the eliminating entries for consolidated statement working papers on December 31, 19X1, and December 31, 19X2.
c. Calculate consolidated net income for 19X1 and 19X2.

Exercise 3–17   (Composition of Investment Account)

Jones Company purchased in the open market 80 percent of the capital stock of Vernon, Inc., on January 1, 19X1, at $50,000 more than 80 percent of its book value. The differential was allocated totally to goodwill, with an estimated life of 20 years. During the following five years, Vernon, Inc., reported cumulative earnings of $200,000 and paid $50,000 in dividends. On January 1, 19X6, minority shareholders in Vernon, Inc., had an equity of $70,000 in net assets of the company.

Required:

If the parent company carries its investment in subsidiary stock on an equity basis,

a. Determine the January 1, 19X1, cost of the investment.

b. Calculate the investment carrying value on December 31, 19X5.

Exercise 3–18   (Composition of Investment Account)

Smith Company purchased in the open market 60 percent of the capital stock of Mori Company on January 1, 19X1, at $100,000 more than 60 percent of its book value. The differential was allocated $40,000 to plant and equipment (net) and $60,000 to goodwill. The plant and equipment had an estimated remaining life of 10 years, and the goodwill was estimated to have a life of 20 years.

On January 1, 19X4, minority shareholders in Mori Company have an equity of $96,000 in the net assets of the company.

Required:

If the parent company carries its investment in subsidiary stock on an equity basis,

a. Determine the net assets of Mori Company on January 1, 19X4.

b. Calculate the investment carrying value on January 1, 19X4.

Problems

Problem 3–19   (Working Paper)

Bunker Company purchased 80 percent of the capital stock of Hampton Corporation on January 1, 19X1, for $71,200, when the latter's capital stock and retained earnings were $50,000 and $10,000, respectively. Book values were equal to fair values for all assets and liabilities of Hampton Corporation except inventory, which had a fair value of $12,000 on January 1, 19X1. The inventory on hand on January 1 was all sold during 19X1. Bunker planned to amortize any goodwill over 10 years.

Trial balances prepared on December 31, 19X1, disclose the following:

	Bunker Company	Hampton Corporation
Cash	$ 8,000	$ 5,000
Accounts Receivable	21,000	17,000
Inventory (1/1)	15,000	8,000
Investment in Hampton	74,000	
Other Assets	33,800	48,000
Dividends Declared	10,000	5,000
Purchases	90,000	20,000
Operating Expenses	10,000	7,000
	$261,800	$110,000

	Bunker Company	Hampton Corporation
Accounts Payable	$ 5,000	$ 10,000
Other Liabilities	5,000	
Capital Stock	100,000	50,000
Retained Earnings	40,000	10,000
Sales	105,000	40,000
Equity in Subsidiary Earnings	6,800	
	$261,800	$110,000
Inventory (12/31)	$ 20,000	$ 10,000

Required:

a. Prepare the eliminating entries for a consolidated statement working paper for the year ended December 31, 19X1.

b. Prepare a consolidated statement working paper for the year ended December 31, 19X1.

Problem 3–20   (Working Paper)

P Company purchased 60 percent of the capital stock of S Company on January 1, 19X1, for $46,000 when the latter's capital stock and retained earnings were $30,000 and $10,000, respectively. Book values were equal to fair values for all assets and liabilities of S Company except plant and equipment (net), which had a fair value $20,000 in excess of book value. The plant and equipment had an estimated remaining life of five years, and any goodwill arising from the combination should be amortized over 10 years.

Trial balances for the companies on December 31, 19X2, follow:

	P Company	S Company
Cash	$ 28,800	$ 30,000
Inventory (1/1)	30,000	15,000
Investment in S Company	51,200	
Plant and Equipment (net)	80,000	40,000
Dividends Declared	20,000	5,000
Purchases	48,000	23,000
Operating Expenses	12,000	7,000
	$270,000	$120,000
Accounts Payable	$ 24,400	$ 20,000
Capital Stock	100,000	30,000
Retained Earnings	50,000	20,000
Sales	90,000	50,000
Equity in Subsidiary Earnings	5,600	
	$270,000	$120,000
Inventory (12/31)	$ 20,000	$ 10,000

Required:

a. Prepare the eliminating entries for a consolidated statement working paper for the year ended December 31, 19X2.

b. Prepare a consolidated statement working paper for the year ended December 31, 19X2.

Problem 3–21   (Separate Accumulated Depreciation Account)

On January 1, 19X1, United Distributors purchased 1,200 shares of Texas Wholesalers, Inc., capital stock for $200,000. On this date, Texas Wholesalers had capital stock of $150,000 and retained earnings of $50,000. Book values were equal to fair values for all assets and liabilities of the subsidiary except land and building. Information provided by an appraisal survey completed shortly after the investment indicated the following:

	Replacement Cost New	Fair Value
Land	$ 50,000	$ 50,000
Building	280,000	140,000

The original estimate of service life in respect to the building remained unchanged by the appraisal, that is, original estimate, 20 years; remaining life, 10 years.

The December 31, 19X2, trial balances are as follows:

	United Distributors	Texas Wholesalers, Inc.
Inventory (1/1)	$ 50,000	$ 20,000
Land	100,000	40,000
Building	400,000	200,000
Other Assets	790,000	135,000
Investment in Texas Wholesalers, Inc.	229,600	
Dividends Declared	10,000	5,000
Purchases	200,000	70,000
Operating Expenses	50,000	10,000
	$1,829,600	$480,000
Liabilities	$ 296,000	$ 20,000
Accumulated Depreciation—Building	100,000	120,000
Sales	300,000	120,000
Equity in Subsidiary Earnings	20,800	
Capital Stock (par, $100)	742,000	150,000
Retained Earnings	370,800	70,000
	$1,829,600	$480,000
Inventory (12/31)	$ 75,000	$ 10,000

Required:

a. Prepare the eliminating entries for a consolidated statement working paper for the year ended December 31, 19X2.

b. Prepare a consolidated statement working paper for the year ended December 31, 19X2.

Problem 3–22   (Residual Credit Differential)

On January 1, 19X1, X Company purchased 80 percent of the voting common shares of Y Company for the cash price of $300,000. On this date, data relating to Y Company's assets and liabilities were as follows:

	Book Value	Fair Value
Current assets	$ 20,000	$ 25,000
Marketable equity securities	30,000	40,000
Plant and equipment	400,000	600,000
Liabilities	(200,000)	(150,000)
Total net assets	$250,000	$515,000

Required:

Compute the values which will appear on a consolidated balance sheet as of the date of acquisition relating to each of Y Company's assets, liabilities, and minority interest. Record your solutions using the following format.

Current assets	_____
Marketable equity securities	_____
Plant and equipment	_____
Liabilities	_____
Minority interest	_____
Total purchase price	_____

Problem 3–23   (Working Paper)

The December 31, 19X1, balance sheet information of X Company, a petroleum refinery, and companies Y and Z, two of its crude oil suppliers, is as follows:

	X Company	Y Company	Z Company
Assets			
Cash	$ 10,400,000	$ 570,000	$ 1,100,000
Marketable Securities	27,300,000		
Accounts Receivable	29,000,000	1,200,000	3,200,000
Notes Receivable			1,500,000
Inventory	55,900,000	2,240,000	10,800,000
Long-Lived Assets (net)	187,000,000	3,900,000	14,600,000
Other Assets	4,320,000	100,000	200,000
Total Assets	$313,920,000	$8,010,000	$31,400,000
Equities			
Accounts Payable	$ 36,900,000	$1,200,000	$ 1,800,000
Notes Payable, Z Company		1,500,000	
Dividends Payable (Note 1)		100,000	
Accrued Expenses	1,820,000	570,000	700,000
Bonds Payable	100,000,000		10,000,000
Capital Stock:			
$100 Par	100,000,000		
$10 Par		2,000,000	
No Par (100,000 shares)			17,400,000
Other Contributed Capital	47,800,000	1,800,000	
Retained Earnings	27,400,000	840,000	1,500,000
Total Equities	$313,920,000	$8,010,000	$31,400,000

NOTE 1: Cash dividends were declared December 28, 19X1, payable on January 25, 19X2, to stockholders of record, January 5, 19X2.

On January 1, 19X2, X Company purchased a controlling interest in the capital stock of companies Y and Z to ensure continuity of supply of crude oil. The acquisition of stock was as follows:

1. Purchased 160,000 shares of Y Company's capital stock in the open market for 25^{5}/_{8}$ per share. Payment was made by check.
2. Acquired 90,000 shares of Z Company's capital stock by issuing 80,000 shares of X Company's stock to the individual stockholders of Z Company. On January 1, 19X2, the capital stock of X Company was quoted at $250 per share. The acquisition is classified as a purchase.

Required:

Prepare a consolidated balance sheet working paper as of January 1, 19X2. Assume any differential is allocated to goodwill.

Problem 3–24   (Deferred Taxes at Acquisition)

On January 1, 19X1, X Company purchased 90 percent of the outstanding common shares of Y Company, after which the following balance sheet information was prepared:

	X Company	Y Company
Assets		
Cash	$ 10,000	$ 8,000
Accounts receivable	40,000	30,000
Other current assets	60,000	15,000
Investment in Y Co.	300,000	
Plant and equipment	200,000	160,000
Other assets	30,000	10,000
	$640,000	$223,000
Equities		
Accounts payable	$ 20,000	$ 10,000
Long-term debt	150,000	50,000
Deferred taxes	10,000	3,000
Capital stock	250,000	60,000
Retained earnings	210,000	100,000
	$640,000	$223,000

In addition, the following data relating to book values, fair values, and tax bases of Y Company's assets and liabilities were compiled (all assets and liabilities not included have equal book values, fair values, and tax bases):

	Fair Value	Book Value	Tax Basis
Other current assets	$ 20,000	$ 15,000	$ 15,000
Plant and equipment	200,000	160,000	150,000
Other assets	12,000	10,000	10,000
Long-term debt	(60,000)	(50,000)	(50,000)

Y Company's income tax rate is 30 percent.

Required:

a. Prepare a schedule to compute and allocate the differential relating to the purchase of Y Company shares.

b. Prepare the eliminating entries for a consolidated balance sheet working paper as of January 1, 19X1.

Problem 3–25   (Working Paper)

Refer to the data in Problem 3–24.

Required:

Prepare a consolidated balance sheet working paper as of January 1, 19X1.

Problems for Appendix

Problem 3–26   (Working Paper)

P Company purchased 60 percent of the capital stock of S Company on January 1, 19X1, for $46,000 when the latter's capital stock and retained earnings were $30,000 and $10,000, respectively. Book values were equal to fair values for all assets and liabilities of S Company except plant and equipment (net), which had a fair value of $20,000 in excess of book value. The plant and equipment had an estimated remaining life of five years, and any goodwill arising from the combination should be amortized over 10 years.

Trial balances for the companies on December 31, 19X2, follow:

	P Company	S Company
Cash	$ 28,800	$ 30,000
Inventory (1/1)	30,000	15,000
Investment in S Company	46,000	
Plant and Equipment (net)	80,000	40,000
Dividends Declared	20,000	5,000
Purchases	48,000	23,000
Operating Expenses	12,000	7,000
	$264,800	$120,000
Accounts Payable	$ 24,400	$ 20,000
Capital Stock	100,000	30,000
Retained Earnings	47,400	20,000
Sales	90,000	50,000
Dividend Income	3,000	
	$264,800	$120,000
Inventory (12/31)	$ 20,000	$ 10,000

P Company uses the *cost* method to account for its investment in S Company.

Required:

a. Prepare the eliminating entries for a consolidated statement working paper for the year ended December 31, 19X2.

b. Prepare a consolidated statement working paper for the year ended December 31, 19X2.

Problem 3–27   (Separate Accumulated Depreciation Account)

On January 1, 19X1, United Distributors purchased 1,200 shares of Texas Wholesalers, Inc., capital stock for $200,000. On this date, Texas Wholesalers had capital stock of $150,000 and retained earnings of $50,000. Book values were equal to fair values for all assets and liabilities of the subsidiary except land and building. Information provided by an appraisal survey completed shortly after the investment indicated the following:

	Replacement Cost New	Fair Value
Land	$ 50,000	$ 50,000
Building	280,000	140,000

The original estimate of service life in respect to the building remained unchanged by the appraisal, that is, original estimate, 20 years; remaining life, 10 years.

The December 31, 19X2, trial balances are shown below.

	United Distributors	Texas Wholesalers, Inc.
Inventory (1/1)	$ 50,000	$ 20,000
Land	100,000	40,000
Building	400,000	200,000
Other Assets	790,000	135,000
Investment in Texas Wholesalers, Inc.	200,000	
Dividends Declared	10,000	5,000
Purchases	200,000	70,000
Operating Expenses	50,000	10,000
	$1,800,000	$480,000
Liabilities	$ 296,000	$ 20,000
Accumulated Depreciation —Building	100,000	120,000
Sales	300,000	120,000
Dividend Income	4,000	
Capital Stock ($100 par)	742,000	150,000
Retained Earnings	358,000	70,000
	$1,800,000	$480,000
Inventory (12/31)	$ 75,000	$ 10,000

United Distributors uses the *cost* method to account for its investment in Texas Wholesalers, Inc.

Required:

a. Prepare the eliminating entries for a consolidated statement working paper for the year ended December 31, 19X2.

b. Prepare a consolidated statement working paper for the year ended December 31, 19X2.

Additional Measurement and Reporting Issues

Chapter Outline

In the preceding two chapters, the fundamental processes associated with recording a business combination, accounting for the investment on the parent's books, and preparing consolidated statements have been described. This chapter focuses on several measurement and reporting topics that have unique elements when encountered in the preparation or use of consolidated statements. These topics include business combinations that occur during the fiscal year, trend analyses for combined entities, and the new principles associated with consolidated cash flow statements and consolidated earnings per share measures.

Interim Purchases

Thus far, we have assumed that the date of acquisition coincides with the first day of an accounting period. For combinations accounted for as *purchases,* acquisition at an interim date requires special treatment in the acquisition year, because *only earnings subsequent to acquisition are included in equity method income and consolidated net income.* Although the accrual of income is restricted to post-acquisition activities, there are two views on how the acquisition year revenues and expenses of the subsidiary should be reported in the consolidated income statement.

One possibility is to include only post-acquisition subsidiary revenues and expenses in the consolidated income statement. The difficulty with this presentation is that partial-year subsidiary revenues and expenses are combined with whole-year parent revenues and expenses. Since only the total of these partial-year and whole-year amounts is reported, a financial statement user cannot easily estimate annualized revenues and expenses. Therefore, the acquisition year consolidated income statement may not be helpful in forecasting the revenues and expenses of subsequent periods (which will consist of whole-year amounts for both the parent and subsidiary). And subsequent year revenues and expenses cannot be meaningfully compared with those reported in the acquisition year.

The alternative view is to include whole-year amounts of subsidiary revenues and expenses in the consolidated income statement, with preacquisition earnings deducted as an additional expense. This expense is created in the working paper eliminations, and is titled *purchased preacquisition earnings.* Both alternatives are sanctioned in the authoritative literature.[1] However, when an interim purchase of shares represents an additional interest in an existing subsidiary, the whole-year amounts of the subsidiary's revenue and expenses are already part of the consolidated income statement. Therefore, the adjustment for preacquisition earnings must be made.[2] For this reason and because of its advantages to financial

---

[1] AICPA, *Accounting Research Bulletin No. 51,* "Consolidated Financial Statements" (New York: AICPA, 1959), par. 11.

[2] The problem of dealing with the acquisition of blocks of shares at several different dates is covered in Chapter 9.

statement users, we elect only to illustrate the inclusion of whole-year amounts of subsidiary revenues and expenses.

Case 1. No Subsidiary Dividends

Assume that P Company acquired 80 percent of the capital stock of S Company on April 1, 19X1, for $124,000. Assume further that on January 1, 19X1, S Company had outstanding capital stock of $100,000 and retained earnings of $50,000, that the fair values of S Company's assets and liabilities are equal to book values, and that the two companies reported the following operating information for the year ended December 31, 19X1:

			S Company	
			4/1–12/31	1/1–3/31
	P Company	*Total*	*(estimated)*	*(estimated)*
Sales	$200,000	$100,000	$75,000	$25,000
Cost of sales	$ 90,000	$ 60,000	$45,000	$15,000
Other expenses	50,000	20,000	15,000	5,000
	$140,000	$ 80,000	$60,000	$20,000
Net income	$ 60,000*	$ 20,000	$15,000	$ 5,000

* Excluding P Company's interest in S Company's earnings.

Amounts in the two estimated columns implicitly assume that allocating S Company's earnings uniformly over the year is appropriate. The consolidated income statement can be prepared directly from these data, including the adjustment for preacquisition earnings, as follows:

Sales ($200,000 + $100,000)		$300,000
Expenses:		
Cost of sales ($90,000 + $60,000)	$150,000	
Other expenses ($50,000 + $20,000)	70,000	220,000
		$ 80,000
Less:		
Minority interest expense (20% × $20,000)	$ 4,000	
Purchased preacquisition earnings (80% × $5,000)	4,000	8,000
Consolidated net income		$ 72,000

Consolidated net income can be verified using the incremental approach as follows:

P Company's income from its own operations	$60,000
P Company's equity in S Company's *post-acquisition* earnings (80% × $15,000)	12,000
Consolidated net income	$72,000

The working paper elimination entries at December 31, 19X1, follow:

1. Equity in Subsidiary Earnings (80% × $15,000)	12,000	
Investment in S Company		12,000
2. Minority Interest Expense (20% × $20,000)	4,000	
Minority Interest		4,000
3. Capital Stock—S Company	100,000	
Retained Earnings—S Company	50,000	
Purchased Preacquisition Earnings (80% × $5,000)	4,000	
Investment in S Company		124,000
Minority Interest (20% × $150,000)		30,000

The parent company's equity method income is 80 percent of S Company's post-acquisition earnings. Accordingly, only this amount is eliminated in the first entry. The second entry recognizes the minority's share of the subsidiary's *whole-year* earnings. In entry 3, the investment elimination entry, note that the January 1, 19X1, balance of Retained Earnings must be eliminated, even though the acquisition took place April 1, 19X1. The consolidated statement working paper for Case 1 appears in Illustration 4–1. As is our practice, the balances in the working paper are arbitrarily chosen except for those accounts for which we have specified a balance.

In the event the subsidiary had declared cash dividends in the current period *prior* to acquisition, the elimination entries would require some modification. Case 2 illustrates this modification.

Case 2. Cash Dividends Paid by Subsidiary

Assume S Company's Retained Earnings balance was $60,000 on January 1, 19X1, and that S Company declared a cash dividend of $10,000 on March 15, 19X1, and $11,000 on September 15, 19X1. The net effect of these assumptions is to leave S Company's book value at April 1 the same as it was in Case 1, but with different balances in the stockholders' equity accounts. The dividends paid by the subsidiary after acquisition are handled in the normal manner. Using the rest of the Case 1 data, we determine that the working paper elimination entries are as follows:

ILLUSTRATION 4–1

P COMPANY AND SUBSIDIARY S COMPANY
Consolidated Statement Working Paper
For the Year Ended December 31, 19X1

	P Company	S Company	Eliminations Dr.	Eliminations Cr.	Consolidated
Income Statement					
Sales	200,000	100,000			300,000
Equity in subsidiary income	12,000		(1) 12,000		–0–
	212,000	100,000			300,000
Cost of sales	90,000	60,000			150,000
Other expenses	50,000	20,000			70,000
Purchased preacquisition earnings			(3) 4,000		4,000
	140,000	80,000			224,000
	72,000	20,000			76,000
Minority interest expense			(2) 4,000		4,000
Net income	72,000	20,000	20,000	–0–	72,000
Retained Earnings Statement					
Retained earnings (1/1):					
P Company	165,000				165,000
S Company		50,000	(3) 50,000		–0–
Net income	72,000	20,000	20,000	–0–	72,000
	237,000	70,000			237,000
Dividends declared:					
P Company	32,000				32,000
S Company		–0–			–0–
Retained earnings (12/31)	205,000	70,000	70,000	–0–	205,000
Balance Sheet					
Other assets	694,000	230,000			924,000
Investment in S Company	136,000			(1) 12,000	–0–
				(3) 124,000	
	830,000	230,000			924,000
Liabilities	225,000	60,000			285,000
Capital stock:					
P Company	400,000				400,000
S Company		100,000	(3) 100,000		–0–
Retained earnings	205,000	70,000	70,000	–0–	205,000
Minority interest				(2) 4,000	34,000
				(3) 30,000	
	830,000	230,000	170,000	170,000	924,000

Explanation of eliminations:

(1) To eliminate parent's share of subsidiary earnings *after acquisition.*

(2) To account for the minority's share of subsidiary earnings *for the year.*

(3) To eliminate *January 1, 19X1* stockholders' equity balances, and recognize *purchased preacquisition earnings* for first three months.

1. Equity in Subsidiary Earnings (80% × $15,000) 12,000
     Investment in S Company 3,200
       Dividends Declared—S Company (80% × $11,000) 8,800

2. Minority Interest Expense (20% × $20,000) 4,000
     Dividends Declared—S Company (20% × $11,000) 2,200
       Minority Interest 1,800

3. Capital Stock—S Company 100,000
     Retained Earnings—S Company 60,000
     Purchased Preacquisition Earnings (80% × $5,000) 4,000
       Investment in S Company 124,000
       Dividends Declared—S Company 10,000
       Minority Interest
         [20% × ($100,000 + $60,000 − $10,000)] 30,000

The consolidated statement working paper for this case appears in Illustration 4–2. Note that the additional $11,000 dividend in September causes an adjustment to both firms' Other Assets accounts and the Investment in S Company account.

REALIGNMENT OF SUBSIDIARY'S SHAREHOLDERS' EQUITY

Among the more common ways of altering a corporation's capital structure are the declaration of stock dividends, changing the par value of outstanding stock, and appropriations of retained earnings. Such actions by a subsidiary do not affect consolidated net income or retained earnings, but in the year of their occurrence, they do require special attention in the consolidated statement working paper.

Stock Dividends

The parent company, like any investor, records the receipt of dividend shares of stock only by a memorandum entry. The entry made by the issuing company depends upon the size of the stock dividend, but in any case, it will decrease

ILLUSTRATION 4–2

P COMPANY AND SUBSIDIARY S COMPANY
Consolidated Statement Working Paper
For the Year Ended December 31, 19X1

	P Company	S Company	Eliminations Dr.	Eliminations Cr.	Consolidated
Income Statement					
Sales	200,000	100,000			300,000
Equity in subsidiary income	12,000		(1) 12,000		–0–
	212,000	100,000			300,000
Cost of sales	90,000	60,000			150,000
Other expenses	50,000	20,000			70,000
Purchased preacquisition earnings			(3) 4,000		4,000
	140,000	80,000			224,000
	72,000	20,000			76,000
Minority interest expense			(2) 4,000		4,000
Net income	72,000	20,000	20,000	–0–	72,000
Retained Earnings Statement					
Retained earnings (1/1):					
P Company	165,000				165,000
S Company		60,000	(3) 60,000		–0–
Net income	72,000	20,000	20,000	–0–	72,000
	237,000	80,000			237,000
Dividends declared:					
P Company	32,000				32,000
S Company		21,000		(1) 8,800	–0–
				(2) 2,200	
				(3) 10,000	
Retained earnings (12/31)	205,000	59,000	80,000	21,000	205,000
Balance Sheet					
Other assets	702,800	219,000			921,800
Investment in S Company	127,200			(1) 3,200	–0–
				(3) 124,000	
	830,000	219,000			921,800
Liabilities	225,000	60,000			285,000
Capital stock:					
P Company	400,000				400,000
S Company		100,000	(3) 100,000		–0–
Retained earnings	205,000	59,000	80,000	21,000	205,000
Minority interest				(2) 1,800	31,800
				(3) 30,000	
	830,000	219,000	180,000	180,000	921,800

Explanation of eliminations:

(1) To eliminate parent's share of subsidiary earnings and dividends *after acquisition.*

(2) To account for the minority's share of subsidiary earnings *for the year* and dividends *after acquisition.*

(3) To eliminate *January 1, 19X1*, stockholders' equity balances and recognize *purchased preacquisition earnings* and subsidiary dividends for first three months.

retained earnings and increase the subsidiary's paid-in capital. Therefore, in the year a stock dividend is distributed by a subsidiary, an additional elimination entry must be made on the working paper. This entry reverses the entry made by the subsidiary to record the stock dividend. Accordingly, it restores the subsidiary's stockholders' equity accounts to their *beginning of year* balances—the balances eliminated in the standard working paper elimination entries.

For example, assume that an 80 percent–owned subsidiary declared a stock dividend during the current year that was recorded by the subsidiary as follows:

Dividends Declared	100,000	
Capital Stock		10,000
Other Contributed Capital		90,000

The additional elimination entry is as follows:

Capital Stock	10,000	
Other Contributed Capital	90,000	
Dividends Declared		100,000

In subsequent years, the additional elimination entry will no longer be necessary.

There is an accounting convention that the sources of stock dividends are the earliest accumulated earnings. It is possible, however, that a subsidiary stock dividend can be large enough that earnings accumulated since acquisition are capitalized. The parent's equity in these earnings is included in its retained earnings and in consolidated retained earnings. However, the included amount is unavailable for distribution to parent shareholders. One position on this circumstance is that the restriction imposed by the capitalization of post-acquisition subsidiary earnings warrants classification of this amount as additional paid-in capital in the consolidated balance sheet. However, this position is rejected in current accounting policy with the following argument:

> Occasionally, subsidiary companies capitalize earned surplus [retained earnings] arising since acquisition, by means of a stock dividend or otherwise. This does not require a transfer to capital surplus [additional paid-in capital] on consolidation, inasmuch as the retained earnings in the consolidated financial statements should reflect the accumulated earnings of the consolidated group not distributed to the shareholders of, or capitalized by, the parent company.[3]

Although the capitalized post-acquisition subsidiary earnings need not therefore be transferred to additional paid-in capital in the consolidated balance sheet, we believe that disclosure (parenthetically or by footnote) of this permanent limitation on dividend availability should be made in the formal consolidated statements.

---

[3] *Accounting Research Bulletin No. 51,* "Consolidated Financial Statements" (New York: AICPA, 1959), par. 18.

Changes in Par Value of Subsidiary Stock

A subsidiary may change the legal status of its capital stock, either in the amount of the par value, from par value to no-par value, or no-par value to par value. Such an action has no effect on the investment account of the parent company or on consolidated net income and retained earnings. In the consolidated statement working paper for the year of the change, the original journal entry is reversed in a fashion analogous to the reversal of a stock dividend.

Appropriation of Retained Earnings

In the event that the subsidiary has an appropriation of retained earnings, this balance should merely be included with the unappropriated retained earnings in the consolidated statement working paper. No special disclosure is necessary in the consolidated statements unless the amount of appropriated retained earnings exceeds the retained earnings existing at the date of acquisition, in which case the temporary limitation on dividend availability may be disclosed.

INCOME TAX CONSIDERATIONS

If a subsidiary is not included in a consolidated tax return (perhaps because it is less than 80 percent owned or it is a foreign subsidiary), the parent company may have to pay income tax on a portion of its recognized interest in the subsidiary's undistributed earnings at some future date. The tax on currently distributed earnings will of course have been paid and recognized by the parent company. The potential tax on the subsidiary's undistributed earnings may be levied upon a future distribution of cash dividends by the subsidiary (usually subject to an 80 percent dividends received deduction), or perhaps on the proceeds of sale upon disposition of all or part of the stock interest.

In view of this potential tax liability of the parent, *APB Opinion No. 23,* as amended by *Statement of Financial Accounting Standards No. 109,* requires the parent to make a deferred income tax provision on the subsidiary's undistributed earnings. The parent company should debit Income Tax Expense and credit Deferred Tax Liability for the deferred income tax on the subsidiary's undistributed earnings of the current period (taking into account the dividends received deduction or other special income tax provisions that might be applicable). When the equity method is applied to a less than 50 percent owned investee, *APB Opinion No. 24* requires tax allocation. The deferred tax is calculated and recorded in the same manner as for a subsidiary.

Assume that P Company owns 70 percent of the outstanding common shares of S Company and that P's equity method income from its investment is $150,000. In addition, assume that this equity method income includes $40,000 in debit differential amortization that is not tax deductible. Last, assume that P Company received $60,000 in dividends from S Company, that these dividends are subject to the 80 percent dividend deduction, and that P's applicable income tax rate is 30 percent. The calculation of P Company's deferred taxes on undistributed earn-

---

ILLUSTRATION 4-3   Calculation of Deferred Taxes on Undistributed Subsidiary Earnings

---

P Company's equity method earnings	$150,000
Add debit differential amortization	40,000
Earnings which eventually will be received in dividends	$190,000
Dividends received deduction (80%)	152,000
Equity method earnings ultimately subject to taxation	$ 38,000
Tax rate	× .30
P Company's income tax expense due to equity method earnings	$ 11,400
Dividends received from S Company	$ 60,000
Dividends received deduction (80%)	48,000
Taxable income	$ 12,000
Tax rate	× .30
Taxes currently payable	$ 3,600
Income tax expense	$ 11,400
Taxes currently payable	3,600
Deferred taxes	$ 7,800

---

ings of S Company appears in Illustration 4–3. Based on this calculation, P Company records income tax expense of $11,400, taxes currently payable of $3,600, and deferred taxes of $7,800.

When a subsidiary files a separate income tax return (federal or state), the tax paid is a determinant of its net income for the period. Thus, the parent's equity is based upon the subsidiary's reported net income after taxes—as it normally should be. However, when the subsidiary pays income tax in the current period on profits that are considered unrealized on a consolidated basis (unconfirmed intercompany profits), these taxes must be deferred. The procedures applicable to these circumstances are explained in Chapter 7.

In subsequent chapters, we assume that the affiliates have filed consolidated tax returns and/or that deferral of income taxes is inappropriate, unless otherwise indicated.

CONSOLIDATED STATEMENT OF CASH FLOWS

Statement of Financial Accounting Standards No. 95 requires a statement of cash flows as part of a full set of financial statements. The statement breaks down cash flows into three categories: cash flows from operating activities, cash flows from investing activities, and cash flows from financing activities.[4]

---

[4] *Statement of Financial Accounting Standards No. 95,* "Statement of Cash Flows" (Norwalk, CT: FASB, 1987).

The statement encourages reporting cash flows from operating activities *directly* by showing major classes of operating cash receipts and payments. Alternatively, cash flows from operating activities can be reported *indirectly* by adjusting net income to reconcile it to net cash flows from operating activities. If the direct method is used, however, a reconciliation of net income with net cash flows from operating activities is to be provided as a separate schedule. Thus, net income must be reconciled with operating cash flows whether the direct or indirect reporting format is used in the statement of cash flows. Inherent in the reconciliation is adding to net income the increases in accounts payable and any expenses not involving expenditure of cash in the current period (e.g., depreciation and amortization). Increases in receivables, inventory, and so on are deducted.

When the statement of cash flows is prepared on a *consolidated basis,* the reconciliation of net income with operating cash flows must add minority interest expense to consolidated net income. This happens because the minority interest expense, like depreciation and amortization, is an expense not requiring a current expenditure of cash. Moreover, if a subsidiary has been acquired during the year, the changes in receivables, inventory, payables, and so forth included in the reconciliation must be *net* of any changes in these items resulting from the acquisition. That is to say, only changes not resulting from the investing activity of acquiring a subsidiary are included as reconciling items.

Because the acquisition of a subsidiary is an investing activity, the purchase price (net of subsidiary cash purchased) is reported as a cash outflow from investing. And if the purchase were financed with debt or newly issued parent company stock, the proceeds would be reported as a cash inflow from financing activities. Dividends paid to minority shareholders are reported as outflows from financing activities.

Additional complexities are introduced with foreign subsidiaries. These issues are discussed in Chapter 14.

A consolidated statement of cash flows and the reconciliation of net income with net cash provided by operating activities can be prepared directly from consolidated balance sheets and the consolidated income statement. The process is much the same as in the case of a single entity. Alternatively, the statement and reconciliation can be prepared from the separate company statements and reconciliations with the aid of a working paper. Such a working paper appears in Illustration 4–4. Amounts in this illustration are consistent with those in Illustration 3–4. The upper portion of the working paper contains the statement of cash flows under the direct method. The lower portion contains the reconciliation of net income with net cash flows provided by operating activities. Note that the upper portion includes the $10,000 in dividends paid by S Company to P Company as a cash inflow from operating activities on P Company's statement of cash flows. This $10,000 is also included in the $12,500 amount of cash outflow from financing activities on S Company's statement. Accordingly, $10,000 in intercompany dividends is eliminated in arriving at consolidated amounts. The consolidated statement shows only the $50,000 in dividends distributed to P Company shareholders and the $2,500 distributed to the minority shareholders of S Company.

ILLUSTRATION 4–4

P COMPANY AND SUBSIDIARY S COMPANY
Consolidated Statement of Cash Flows and Reconciliation Working Papers
For the Year Ended December 31, 19X2

	P Company	S Company	Eliminations	Consolidated
Working Paper—Consolidated Statement of Cash Flows				
Cash flows from operating activities:				
Cash received from customers	536,000	230,000		766,000
Dividends from S Company	10,000		(10,000)	
Cash paid to suppliers and employees	(416,000)	(209,500)		(625,500)
Net cash provided	130,000	20,500	(10,000)	140,500
Cash flows from financing activities:				
Dividends paid	(50,000)	(12,500)	10,000	(52,500)
Change in cash	80,000	8,000	–0–	88,000
Beginning cash balance	50,000	28,000		78,000
Ending cash balance	130,000	36,000	–0–	166,000
Working Paper—Reconciliation of Net Income with Net Cash Provided by Operating Activities				
Net income	160,000	40,000	(40,000)	160,000
Add (subtract):				
Depreciation expense	22,000	8,000	8,000	38,000
Increase in accounts receivable	(50,000)	(20,000)		(70,000)
Increase in inventory	(28,000)	(20,000)		(48,000)
Increase in current payables	40,000	12,500		52,500
Equity in S Company income	(24,000)		24,000	
Dividends from S Company	10,000		(10,000)	
Minority interest expense			8,000	8,000
Net cash provided by operating activities	130,000	20,500	(10,000)	140,500

Eliminations in the reconciliation of net income with net cash provided by operating activities are made for the following reasons:

1. The entire amount of S Company's net income is eliminated.
2. The depreciation expense added to net income by the separate companies is augmented by differential amortization of $8,000.
3. The equity method income subtracted in P Company's reconciliation is unnecessary since all of S Company's net income has already been eliminated.
4. The minority interest expense is added back since it represents an expense not requiring the current expenditure of cash.
5. Adding back the dividends received from S Company is unnecessary since this represents only a movement of cash within the consolidated entity.

TREND ANALYSES FOR COMBINED ENTITIES

The purchase and pooling of interests methods are not alternatives for each other. When the conditions outlined in Chapter 1 are satisfied, the pooling of interests method is required. When they are not, the purchase method is required. Without specific knowledge of fair values of acquired assets and liabilities, it is not possible to transform earnings reported under one method into what they would have been under the other method. Nonetheless, it is generally accepted that the purchase method normally results in lower earnings.

Evidence on this issue is obtainable from the annual report of CGA Computer, Inc. and Subsidiaries. During 1981, CGA acquired Allen Services in a business combination initially accounted for as a pooling of interests. Subsequently, the Securities and Exchange Commission determined that the initial reporting was inappropriate. As part of a settlement with the Commission, CGA agreed to report under *both* the purchase and pooling of interests methods. This unique example of dual reporting affords an opportunity to observe the differences between the methods in the context of an actual business combination.

Allen Services developed and marketed computer software products. Due to the normal accounting for research and development costs, the fair values of rights to market such products greatly exceeded their book values. In addition, Allen had substantial goodwill. Thus, the purchase method involved amortizing fair values of software products and purchased goodwill. The pooling of interests method involved no goodwill amortization and amortization of only the book value of software products. For the year ended April 30, 1984, CGA's dual presentation revealed 1984 amortization under the purchase method of $4,314,000. The counterpart number under the pooling of interests method was $648,000. The effect on pretax income was the difference of $3,666,000. After taxes, the difference was $2,679,000. Since net income under the pooling of interests method was $3,444,000, the effect of including differential amortization in the determination of net income was a 78 percent reduction.

Of course, the CGA experience is anecdotal. There is no way of knowing the extent to which such dramatic differences exist in the general population of business combinations. In addition to this problem, however, the financial statement user must also consider carefully the effect of business combinations on historical summaries and trend analyses.

One method of evaluating the current position and future expectations of a business entity involves the examination of a firm's past financial trends and history. To facilitate this type of analysis, published financial reports usually include comparative financial statements for the past two to five years. Additionally, financial summaries (which focus upon such items as sales, earnings, earnings per share, and selected ratios) are frequently provided for as many as the past 10 to 15 years. The preparation and interpretation of these comparative statements and financial summaries are particularly difficult if the period covered by the analysis includes one or more business combinations.

A business combination is usually a critical event in the history of a business entity. Managerial identity, ownership positions, legal structure, the nature of operations and resources, and many other significant aspects of the entity may undergo dramatic change as the result of a combination. Indeed, it can be argued that many business combinations involve such sweeping changes that meaningful comparisons between the combined entity and its precombination constituents are virtually impossible. Nevertheless, there persists a desire for information that may be relevant to future decisions, which has accented the importance of trend analysis extending over periods that include business combinations.

The most basic problem involved in trend analysis of combined business entities relates to the precombination operating periods. What data of these periods are comparable to the post-combination financial statements? Two alternative approaches to resolving this data selection problem are utilized. One method is to select the reported precombination financial statements of the *acquiring* firm as the relevant data to compare with the post-combination financial statements of the combined entity. This approach is consistent with the *purchase method* of accounting. If a combination is interpreted as a purchase of assets and assumption of liabilities, adjustments of precombination statements are not warranted. Thus, historical financial summaries and comparative financial statements prepared in accordance with the purchase method do *not* involve retroactive combining of precombination financial data. The past financial statements of the *acquiring* firm as originally reported are the comparative base.

An alternative approach to historical trend analysis involves restatement of the precombination financial statements to retroactively reflect the combination. This method is a natural counterpart to *pooling of interests accounting*. Under the pooling perspective, a combined entity involves nothing more substantive than the merging of two businesses into a single enterprise. Both continue to exist as one combined entity. Given this perspective, it is consistent to retroactively combine precombination financial statements. Such recast statements should be comparable to post-combination statements. Therefore, after a pooling of interests combination, any financial reference to precombination periods should be expressed in terms of combined data. For example, when a pooling of interests combination occurs after a balance sheet date but before statements are prepared, the subsequently prepared statements should be prepared on a combined basis.

The decision as to whether or not precombination financial data are restated has a significant impact upon the trends displayed by historical comparisons. Case 3 exhibits the differences between the two approaches.

Case 3. Comparison of Approaches

For several years, G Company and H Company have enjoyed a 10 percent growth rate in their sales, earnings, and earnings per share. For 19X1, these firms reported the following data:

	G Company	H Company
Sales	$1,000,000	$750,000
Earnings	$ 100,000	$ 75,000
Outstanding shares	100,000	75,000
Earnings per share	$1.00	$1.00

G Company acquired 100 percent of H Company's stock on January 1, 19X2, in a common stock for common stock exchange. The exchange ratio was set at 0.6:1. During 19X2, G Company and its subsidiary maintained their historical 10 percent growth rates. Financial data for 19X2 were as follows:

	G Company	H Company	Consolidated
Sales	$1,100,000	$825,000	$1,925,000
Earnings (excluding parent's equity in subsidiary earnings)	$ 110,000	$ 82,500	$ 192,500
Outstanding shares			145,000*
Earnings per share			$1.33

*100,000 + (60% × 75,000) = 145,000.

The historical comparisons under the alternative disclosures are presented in Illustration 4–5. Significantly, the restatement of precombination data results in the 10 percent growth rate being maintained. Thus, if growth rates in sales, earnings, and other operating data are important variables in the decision makers' predictions of future success, restatement would seem appropriate. The large growth rates displayed by comparisons with the unadjusted base are primarily caused by the combination itself. They are not likely to be maintained over several future periods. Maintaining such growth rates requires increasingly large business combinations. Indeed, the size of the firms to be acquired would have to increase at a geometrical rate.

It must be reemphasized that the restatement approach is employed only when combinations are accounted for as poolings of interests. The unadjusted disclosure is used if the purchase method is followed.[5] Case 3 was based on the implicit assumption of unique circumstances in which the differences between the purchase and pooling of interests methods did not affect 19X2 combined net income. Consequently, the difference in the reported trends was attributable entirely to the restatement or nonrestatement of the data of precombination periods.

---

[5] However, under the purchase method, *APB Opinion No. 16* requires an additional, one-time disclosure in the first financial statements issued after the combination. Specifically, the requirement is for footnote disclosure of the current and immediately preceding periods' results of operations based on a pro forma restatement as if the combination had taken place at the beginning of the preceding period. See *APB Opinion No. 16,* "Business Combinations" (New York: AICPA, 1970), par. 96.

ILLUSTRATION 4–5   **Historical Comparisons of Financial Data**

	19X1 Data		19X2 Data	
	Absolute Amounts	*As a Percentage of 19X0 Amounts**	*Absolute Amounts*	*As a Percentage of 19X1 Amounts*
With retroactive adjustments:				
Sales	$1,750,000	110	$1,925,000	110
Earnings	175,000	110	192,500	110
Earnings per share	$1.21	110	$1.33	110
Without retroactive adjustments:				
Sales	$1,000,000	110	$1,925,000	192.5
Earnings	100,000	110	192,500	192.5
Earnings per share	$1.00	110	$1.33	133

* The annual growth rate for sales, earnings, and earnings per share was assumed to be 10 percent for years prior to 19X2.

This case displays the sharp discontinuities that can occur in historical earnings per share trends when combinations involve traditional common stock for common stock exchanges. The critical factor that causes this phenomenon is the relative size of the combining firms' price/earnings ratios. Retroactive adjustments (used primarily with pooling of interests accounting) are attempts to report growth trends that are consistent with internal operations. However, it must be recognized that data once reported are probably never completely overturned in the minds of investors, no matter how forcefully the retroactive adjustments may be emphasized.

CONSOLIDATED EARNINGS PER SHARE

One of the most critical items of information that is drawn from accounting reports is earnings per share (EPS). As a summary indicator of current success and future expectations of success, the amount, periodic variation, and growth rate of earnings per share probably have more informational significance than any other data that can be extracted from financial statements. Nonetheless, accountants frequently warn against the dangers of placing an exaggerated emphasis on earnings per share. This summary indicator should always be interpreted in light of all of the other information obtainable from financial statements and other sources. Prudent accountants acknowledge that proper analysis of all available data is superior to undue reliance on any single item such as earnings per share. Nevertheless, earnings per share continues to be of great importance to the investing community.

The large number of business combinations has been accompanied by an increasing variety of financing methods. Many of these methods have an immediate or potential impact on earnings per share calculations. Even with the employment of more traditional financing methods, the examples above showed that the act of combination can cause a sharp discontinuity in the historical trend of earnings per share. As a result, the meaning and reliability of earnings per share calculations must be viewed circumspectly. Understanding these problems and attempts to resolve them is a requisite part of comprehending the broader subject of accounting for business combinations.

In addition to this relationship between earnings per share issues and business combinations, *the calculations of earnings per share for consolidated financial statements and for investor companies that use the equity method must be made in accordance with special procedures.* Further, unique problems can occur if the securities of one affiliate are convertible into a security of the other affiliate. Thus, earnings per share calculations are an important issue to be understood in the context of learning how to prepare and interpret consolidated financial statements.

Earnings per Share Calculations Involving Affiliates

Any corporation may have outstanding common stock equivalents or senior securities that involve potential dilution of earnings per share. Additionally, when companies have intercorporate stock investments and the investor corporation uses the equity method or prepares consolidated statements, earnings per share calculations for the investor corporation may be affected by the nature of the securities issued by the investee corporation. In other words, if a corporation's net income includes equity method earnings from holding stock of another corporation, the earnings per share calculations for the stockholder corporation must give explicit consideration to potential dilution associated with the investee corporation's earnings. This is also true regarding earnings per share calculations for consolidated financial statements.

To accomplish this objective, primary and fully diluted earnings per share for the investee corporation must first be calculated.[6] Next, in the calculations for the investor corporation, the investor corporation's net income derived from use of the equity method must be recomputed under whatever assumptions have been used in the calculation of the investee corporation's earnings per share. These assumptions can alter the investor corporation's equity method earnings in at least two ways. First, an assumed conversion of dilutive securities increases the investee corporation's earnings available for common dividends. Second, all assumed conversions of convertible securities and exercises of warrants and options change the number of investee corporation common shares outstanding, and thus can alter the investor corporation's ownership interest.[7] Moreover, in

---

[6] A review of basic earnings per share concepts is provided in Appendix A.

[7] Changing the investor corporation's ownership interest can result in some rather subtle second-order effects in the calculation of equity method income. Elimination of intercompany profit as discussed in Chapters 6, 7, and 8 can be affected by a changed ownership interest. Also, increases and decreases in ownership interest can affect amortization of differentials, as discussed in Chapter 9.

determining the alteration of the investor corporation's ownership interest, it is necessary to consider whether any additional common shares assumed to be issued would be issued to the investor corporation. Ownership interest is a fraction, the numerator of which is common shares held by the investor corporation. The denominator is investee corporation common shares outstanding. If the investor corporation holds any of the convertible securities, options, or warrants that are assumed to have been converted or exercised, the numerator and denominator of ownership interest will increase. The investor corporation's recalculated equity in investee income, *before differential amortization,* can be expressed as shown in Illustration 4–6. Note that if the denominator of the left term is moved to the right term, the expression becomes the product of (1) investee shares held (or assumed to be held) and (2) investee earnings per share—that is, the investor's equity in investee earnings per share. The investor corporation's earnings per share is then computed using the recalculated equity in investee income (*after* differential amortization) instead of the recorded equity method income.

Case 4. Consolidated Primary Earnings per Share

The following data are applicable to the consolidated primary earnings per share calculation for P Company and its 90 percent owned subsidiary, S Company:

	P Company	S Company
Net income (excluding equity in subsidiary income for P Company)	$150,000	$ 50,000
Common stock (par value, $1)	$ 75,000	$ 40,000
Preferred stock, 9%	$ 30,000	
Preferred stock, 8%, convertible into common stock at the rate of 4 common shares per $100 of preferred stock (This is **not** classified as a common stock equivalent.)		$ 20,000

Warrants:

  P Company has warrants outstanding for 10,000 shares at an exercise price of $10 per share. The average market price during the period was $20 per share, and the ending market price was $25 per share.

  S Company has warrants outstanding for 5,000 shares at an exercise price of $6 per share. The average market price during the period was $10 per share, and the ending market price was $8 per share.

Other information:

  P Company owns 36,000 shares of S Company's common stock and 1,000 of S Company's outstanding warrants.

  Differential amortization for the period was $6,000.

ILLUSTRATION 4–6   Recalculated Equity in Investee Income (before Differential Amortization)

$$\frac{\text{Investee common shares held by investor} + \text{Additional investee common shares issued to investor through assumed conversion or exercise of dilutive securities}}{\text{Investee common shares outstanding} + \text{Additional investee common shares assumed issued through conversion or exercise of dilutive securities}} \times \left[\text{Net income available for common dividends, as reported by investee} + \text{Increase in net income through assumed conversion of dilutive securities} \right]$$

Recalculated investor corporation's ownership interest consistent with assumptions made in calculation of investee corporation's earnings per share

Recalculated investee corporation net income available for common dividends consistent with assumptions made in calculation of investee corporation's earnings per share

The first step is to calculate S Company's primary earnings per share. This calculation, which is presented in Illustration 4–7, uses only basic earnings per share principles. Our next step, which is unique to earnings per share calculations involving affiliated companies, is to make a pro forma calculation of P Company's equity in investee income reflecting the assumptions incorporated in S Company's primary earnings per share computation. Using the basic relationship depicted in Illustration 4–6, this calculation is shown in Illustration 4–8. Note that we have included in P Company's holdings 400 shares of the 2,000 shares of common stock that it is assumed will be issued (net of repurchases) when the 5,000 warrants are exercised. Since P Company holds 20 percent (1,000/5,000) of the warrants, the same proportion of the 2,000 shares is assigned to the parent. After calculating the parent's share of S Company's pro forma income available for common stock and common stock equivalents, differential amortization for the period is deducted. The result is the parent's pro forma equity in S Company's income. Finally, consolidated primary earnings per share is calculated in Illustration 4–9. Using the recalculated equity in investee income, this calculation is relatively straightforward.

Consolidated net income for the period is *unchanged* by the pro forma earnings per share calculations. In this case, consolidated net income is as follows:

ILLUSTRATION 4-7   **Calculation of S Company Primary Earnings per Share**

	Shares	*Income*
Reported net income		$50,000
Common shares outstanding	40,000	
Dividend requirement on preferred stock (8% × $20,000) . . .		(1,600)
Assumed exercise of warrants:		
Shares issued	5,000	
Assumed repurchase [(5,000 × $6)/$10]	(3,000)	2,000	
	42,000	$48,400
Primary EPS ($48,400/42,000)		$1.15

P Company income, excluding equity in S company income	$ 150,000
Equity in S Company reported income (90% × $50,000)	45,000
Differential amortization	(6,000)
Consolidated net income	$ 189,000

Consolidated net income is used to establish the "base" earnings per share for the materiality threshold test. In this case, the base earnings per share is calculated as follows:

Consolidated net income	$ 189,000
Dividend requirement for preferred stock	(2,700)
Income available for common shareholders	$ 186,300
Base EPS ($186,300/75,000)	$ 2.48

Since the consolidated primary earnings per share of $2.29 is less than 97 percent of this base, the 3 percent materiality test is satisfied, and primary and fully diluted earnings per share must be reported.

Calculation of consolidated fully diluted earnings per share is left as an exercise for the reader. Additionally, a more complex illustration of consolidated earnings per share calculations is presented in Appendix B.

Additional Issues

Subsidiary Securities Convertible into Parent Securities.   Some subsidiaries issue securities (or warrants) that are convertible (or exercisable) into common stock of the parent. Obviously, the conversion or exercise of these securities would not

---

ILLUSTRATION 4-8   Pro Forma Calculation of Equity in Subsidiary Income

---

Equity interest in S Company:	
Number of common shares owned	36,000
Additional S Company shares that would be acquired due to assumed	
exercise of S Company warrants (1,000/5,000 × 2,000)	400
Pro forma common stock and common stock equivalents held by P Company	36,400
Pro forma common stock and common stock equivalents that S Company's	
primary EPS calculation assumes to be outstanding (Illustration 4–7)	42,000
Pro forma percentage interest (36,400/42,000)	86.7%
Pro forma income available for S Company's common stock and common	
stock equivalents (Illustration 4–7)	$48,400
Pro forma equity in S Company income, before differential amortization	
(86.7% × $48,400)	$41,963
Differential amortization	6,000
Pro forma equity in S Company income	$35,963

ILLUSTRATION 4-9   Calculation of Consolidated Primary Earnings per Share

---

	Shares	*Income*
Reported net income		
(excluding equity in subsidiary income)		$150,000
Common shares outstanding	75,000	
Pro forma equity in S Company income		
(Illustration 4–8)		35,963
Dividend requirement on preferred stock		
(9% × $30,000)		(2,700)
Assumed exercise of warrants:		
Shares issued	10,000	
Assumed repurchase [(10,000 × $10)/$20]	(5,000)	5,000	
	80,000	$183,263
Primary EPS ($183,263/80,000)		$2.29

---

dilute the subsidiary's earnings per share. Therefore, subsidiary calculations need reflect only the appropriate deductions for current cash payments (e.g., dividends) to holders of such securities.

In calculations for the parent, however, such securities must be classified as common stock equivalents or as potentially dilutive securities. If their effects are dilutive, the assumed conversion or exercise of these securities must be incorporated in parent calculations. In so doing, consideration must be given to the fact that the subsidiary's earnings per share calculations may have involved deductions for payments to the holders of the securities which are convertible into the parent's stock. Thus, if conversion of those securities is assumed in parent calculations, the subsidiary's deductions for payments to the security holders must be restored to earnings, since no payments to outsiders would have been made if the securities had been converted.[8]

Contingent Stock Issuances.   Many business combinations are financed, in part, with deferred payments of an indeterminate number of common shares. The amount to be issued may depend on future earnings of the acquired firm or on the market value of the stock at some future date. Both primary and fully diluted computations of earnings per share may require special refinements when such contingent stock issuances are outstanding.

In an attempt to resolve the difficulties imposed by contingent stock issuances, the APB recommended specific rules to follow. With respect to primary earnings per share, stock issuances that depend on future earnings levels should be included to the extent that shares will be issued if earnings are maintained at current levels. Further, if the number of shares to be issued depends on the future market price of the stock, the market price at the most recent balance sheet date should be used to estimate the assumed number of shares to be issued.

Fully diluted earnings per share calculations should also reflect contingent stock issuances. But they should not be constrained by the primary calculation requirement that limits the issuance to an amount satisfied by the maintenance of current earnings. Thus, fully diluted calculations should assume the highest reasonable dilution level that can occur. The required increase in earnings (to attain the highest dilution level) should also be added to current earnings in the numerator of the statistic. As in the case of primary calculations, the stock price at the close of the period being reported should be used if the contingent issuances are dependent on future stock prices.[9]

Restatement of Prior Periods' Earnings per Share.   Several conditions may justify restating the earnings per share statistics that relate to prior periods. Such restatements would be disclosed in the presentation of comparative statements and in historical financial summaries. Among the events that would lead to restatement of prior periods' earnings per share are the following: (1) the number of common shares outstanding changes due to stock dividends, stock splits, or reverse stock splits; (2) prior period adjustments of net income are made; (3) a business combination has occurred and was accounted for as a *pooling of interests;* (4) prior periods' statistics include contingent stock issuances and at the termination of the

---

[8] In an interpretation of *APB Opinion No. 15,* 100 percent of the restored subsidiary payments is allocated to the parent. This method is followed even when the parent owns less than 100 percent of the subsidiary. There is no obvious rationale for such a treatment. A more logical method would restore the subsidiary's payments to the subsidiary's income in order to determine the parent's equity in subsidiary earnings. See *Accounting Interpretation No. 93 of APB Opinion No. 15,* "Securities Issued by Subsidiaries" (New York: AICPA, 1970).

[9] *APB Opinion No. 15,* pars. 62–64.

contingency agreement the conditions have not been met; and (5) contingent stock issuances, which were included in the statistics of prior periods and remain contingently effective, are dependent on future earnings and/or stock prices, and the current (end-of-period) price and/or earnings level indicates that the assumptions which were previously used in reporting earnings per share should be modified. However, "previously reported earnings per share data should not be restated to give retroactive effect to shares subsequently issued as a result of attainment of specified increased earnings levels."[10]

Summary

This chapter introduced several new principles underlying consolidated financial statements. The first issue addressed was acquisition of shares of a subsidiary which occurred during the fiscal year and was accounted for under the purchase method. The basic principle is that only post-acquisition income of the newly acquired subsidiary is included in consolidated net income. However, it is appropriate to include the revenue and expenses of the subsidiary for the entire year in the consolidated income statement.

A second major issue presented was the preparation of a consolidated cash flow statement. In the same manner as the other primary financial statements, the consolidated cash flow statement must include only cash flows with outside parties. Any intercompany elements must be eliminated. We also examined briefly the effects of business combinations on various aspects of financial statement analysis, including the impact that alternative methods have on the magnitude of consolidated net income and the trends in critical performance measures.

Finally, we reviewed the new issues that must be confronted in the computation of consolidated earnings per share. The basic principle is that the equity in investee income that is included in the consolidated or equity method earnings per share calculation should be based on the same assumptions that are incorporated in the earnings per share calculations for the affiliate.

Appendix A: Review of Basic Earnings per Share Concepts

Earnings per share is a financial statistic of long standing. Traditionally, it was calculated as a quotient, the numerator of which was net income less preferred dividends declared (including current arrearages) and the denominator of which was the weighted-average number of common shares outstanding. The significance of this calculation as a basic success indicator was implicitly accepted for many years. However, increasing usage of convertible securities, common stock warrants, and stock option plans rendered this traditional calculation misleading and inadequate. As a substitute for this summary statis-

---

[10] Ibid., par. 62.

tic, accountants developed two calculations: primary earnings per share and fully diluted earnings per share. Controversy continues as to the importance of these measures as indicants of future business success. Nevertheless, they represent the only evident means of providing the information that was once supplied by the traditional earnings per share calculation.[11]

Primary Earnings per Share

Primary earnings per share is based on a concept of "common stock equivalents" which are added to common stock presently outstanding[12] to determine the denominator in the calculation. In fact, the primary earnings per share statistic is frequently reported in financial statements as "earnings per common share and common equivalent share." The Accounting Principles Board (APB) defined the concept of "common stock equivalent" as follows:

> A common stock equivalent is a security which is not, in form, a common stock but which usually contains provisions to enable its holder to become a common stockholder and which, because of its terms and the circumstances under which it was issued, is in substance equivalent to a common stock. The holders of these securities can expect to participate in the appreciation of the value of the common stock resulting principally from the earnings and earnings potential of the issuing corporation. This participation is essentially the same as that of a common stockholder except that the security may carry a specified dividend or interest rate yielding a return different from that received by a common stockholder.[13]

The most prominent types of securities that are, or may be, common stock equivalents are (1) those which are convertible into common stock and (2) common stock options and warrants that allow the holder to purchase common shares at specified prices.

It should be apparent that the definition of common stock equivalents requires some more specific operational criteria that may be used to decide whether a specific security should be classified as a common stock equivalent or as a senior security. Without such a definitive standard, the earnings per share calculations of business firms would probably not be based on comparable classifications. With respect to all convertible securities, the APB stated the following classification criterion:

> . . . a convertible security should be considered as a common stock equivalent at the time of issuance if, based on its market price, it has a cash yield of less than 66⅔ percent of the then current bank prime interest rate. For any convertible security which has a change in its cash interest rate or cash dividend rate scheduled within the first five years after issuance, the lowest scheduled rate during such five years should be used in determining the cash yield of the security at issuance.[14]

---

[11] The principal computational and reporting requirements for earnings per share are contained primarily in *APB Opinion No. 15*, which was published in 1968. However, in 1978, the FASB issued *Statement No. 21*, which exempted nonpublic companies from the reporting requirements of *APB Opinion No. 15*. But if a nonpublic company *chooses* to report earnings per share data, it must follow the *APB Opinion No. 15* requirements.

[12] The amount to be added is the number of common shares that could be issued through conversion or exercise of the common stock equivalents less the number the company could repurchase using the cash proceeds from the exercise of options and warrants.

[13] *APB Opinion No. 15*, "Earnings per Share," par. 25.

[14] Ibid., par. 33. If no market price is available at the time of issuance, this test is based on the fair value of the security.

More recently, the Financial Accounting Standards Board (FASB) altered the criterion by substituting the average Aa corporate bond yield in place of the bank prime interest rate. The bank prime rate is a short-term rate. Substitution of the average Aa corporate bond yield thus makes the classification criterion more internally consistent in that convertible securities are classified by comparing their yield with $66^2/_3$ percent of the average yield of securities of similar maturity. In addition, the effective yield has been substituted for the cash yield. For securities with a fixed maturity date, the effective yield is the discount rate which equates the present value of the interest payments and maturity value with the price at issuance. For securities without a fixed maturity date (for example, preferred stock), the effective yield is the ratio of the security's stated annual interest or dividend payments to its market price at issuance.[15] The classification criterion is applied only at the time of issue, and the classification status remains unchanged as long as the security remains outstanding.

With respect to common stock options, warrants, and similar obligations, the established criterion is that they be included in the common stock equivalent class at all times. This inclusion is consistent with the fact that such securities generally have no cash yield and therefore derive their value "from the right to obtain common stock at specified prices for an extended period."[16]

In respect to the calculation of primary earnings per share, it should be recognized that the assumed conversion or exercise of a common stock equivalent may be either *dilutive* or *antidilutive*. That is, the effect of the assumed conversion may be either to decrease or to increase the earnings per share figure. However, the underlying purpose of the development of the primary earnings per share statistic was to recognize that some securities (other than common stock) are likely to participate in the value increments of common stock that result from growth in earnings. If earnings are not maintained at a level that would eventually make it profitable for security holders to convert or exercise their securities, it can be assumed that such conversions may not take place. As a consequence, the calculation of primary earnings per share is based on the assumed conversion and exercise of common stock equivalents, *only if the effects of the assumed conversions or exercises are dilutive*. Given several different common stock equivalents, there are obviously several different possible earnings per share amounts, depending upon how each common stock equivalent is treated—conversion assumed, or not. The correct treatment of the common stock equivalents is that which results in the lowest earnings per share amount.

Special consideration must be given to the treatment of common stock warrants (and stock options) in the calculation of primary earnings per share. So long as the number of common shares that are issuable upon the exercise of warrants is 20 percent or less of the total number of common shares outstanding at the end of the period, the treatment of warrants in this calculation is described as the *treasury stock* method. The cash proceeds from the anticipated exercise of warrants are assumed to be used to repurchase shares of common stock at the average market price during the period. If the exercise price of the warrants is less than the average market price of common stock, more common shares will have been issued than will have been repurchased; thus, the net number of common shares outstanding is increased and the warrants are *dilutive* in effect. However, if the exercise

---

[15] *Statement of Financial Accounting Standards No. 55,* "Determining Whether a Convertible Security Is a Common Stock Equivalent" (Norwalk, CT: FASB, 1982), and *Statement of Financial Accounting Standards No. 85,* "Yield Test for Determining Whether a Convertible Security Is a Common Stock Equivalent" (Norwalk, CT: FASB, 1985).

[16] *APB Opinion No. 15,* par 35.

price of the warrants is greater than the average price of common stock, the cash proceeds from the assumed exercise of the warrants would provide for repurchasing more common shares than were issued when the warrants were exercised; thus, the net number of common shares outstanding is decreased and the warrants are *antidilutive*. In the latter situation, the warrants should be disregarded in calculating primary earnings per share, notwithstanding the fact that they are classified as common stock equivalents.

In the event that the number of common shares issuable upon the exercise of warrants and options exceeds 20 percent of the number of common shares outstanding at the end of the period, the previously described treasury stock method is modified in the belief that it may not provide an adequate reflection of the potential dilution associated with warrants. The APB described the alternative method to be utilized, as follows:

> . . . all the options and warrants should be assumed to have been exercised and the aggregate proceeds therefrom to have been applied in two steps:
> a. As if the funds were first applied to the repurchase of outstanding common shares at the average market price during the period (treasury stock method) but not to exceed 20 percent of the outstanding shares; and then
> b. As if the balance of the funds were applied first to reduce any short-term or long-term borrowings and any remaining funds were invested in U.S. government securities or commercial paper, with appropriate recognition of any income tax effect.
>
> The results of steps (a) and (b) of the computation (whether dilutive or antidilutive) should be aggregated and, if the net effect is dilutive, should enter into the earnings per share computation.[17]

To summarize, the denominator in primary earnings per share calculations includes the weighted average of the number of common shares outstanding plus the number of common shares that would have been issued if each dilutive common stock equivalent were converted or exercised. In general, the numerator includes (1) net income, less dividend declarations (including current arrearages) to preferred shares that are classified as senior securities and (2) the interest charges, less tax effect, on convertible bonds that are classified as dilutive common stock equivalents, and on debt that would have been retired with the proceeds from the exercise of dilutive warrants.

Fully Diluted Earnings per Share

Primary earnings per share calculations provide no indication of the potential impact upon common stockholders of possible future conversions or exercises of potentially dilutive securities not classified as common stock equivalents. To communicate the estimated effect of such contingencies, attention is directed to fully diluted earnings per share. The fully diluted calculation "reflects the dilution of earnings per share that would have occured if *all* contingent issuances of common stock that would individually reduce earnings per share had taken place at the beginning of the period (or time of issuance of the convertible security, etc, if later)."[18] Fully diluted earnings per share should be reported concurrently with primary earnings per share whenever present contingencies may result in future common stock issuances that would materially dilute primary earnings per share. It

---

[17] Ibid., par. 38.

[18] Ibid., par. 15. A reduction of less than 3 percent in primary earnings per share is not considered by the board to be significant enough to warrant the presentation of fully diluted earnings per share.

should also be reported if conversions taking place during the current period would have materially diluted primary earnings per share had they taken place at the beginning of the period (or date of issuance, if later).

The fully diluted calculation closely parallels the calculation for primary earnings per share. The principal difference between the two statistics is that fully diluted calculations include the assumed conversion and exercise of *all* dilutive securities; alternatively, the primary calculations assume the conversion and exercise only of dilutive common stock equivalents. Since the essential purpose of the fully diluted statistic is to show the maximum potential dilution, "the computations of fully diluted earnings per share for each period should exclude those securities whose conversion, exercise or other contingent issuance would have the effect of increasing the earnings per share amount or decreasing the loss per share amount for such period."[19] Regarding the fully diluted calculations, one important modification in the previously described primary earnings per share calculations relates to the assumed exercise of warrants and options. In the primary calculations, it is assumed (under the treasury stock method) that the cash proceeds are used to repurchase common stock at the *average* market price during the period. In fully diluted calculations, "the market price at the close of the period reported upon should be used to determine the number of shares which would be assumed to be repurchased . . . if such market price is higher than the average price used in computing primary earnings per share.[20]

Changing Conversion Rates or Exercise Prices

Several types of corporate securities and transactions may cause particular difficulty in earnings per share calculations. For example, a convertible security may stipulate a changing rate of conversion with the passage of time. Similarly, the price to exercise stock warrants may change. The obvious difficulty in such cases is to determine which conversion rate or exercise price shoud be used in computations of primary and fully diluted earnings per share. With respect to *fully diluted* earnings per share, it is reasonable to utilize the rate or price that will be most favorable to the security holders. Such a rate is consistent with the basic implication of the fully diluted statistic—the implication of portraying the maximum dilution that can occur, given current contingencies. However, conversion rates or exercise prices that are effective only in the distant future probably have little relevance to current security holders. Thus, the APB concluded that the most attractive rate or price during *only* the 10 years following the latest fiscal period should be used.[21]

Selecting an appropriate conversion rate or exercise price for primary earnings per share calculations is somewhat more arbitrary. As a general rule, it seems appropriate to use the rate or price that is in effect during the period covered by the calculation. The board provided for the following specific exceptions to this general rule:

If options, warrants or other common stock equivalents are not immediately exercisable or convertible, the earliest effective exercise price or conversion rate if any during the succeeding five years should be used. If a convertible security having an increasing conversion rate is issued in exchange for another class of security of the issuing company and is convertible back into the

---

[19] Ibid., par. 40.
[20] Ibid., par. 42.
[21] Ibid., par. 58.

same or a similar security, and if a conversion rate equal to or greater than the original rate becomes effective during the period of convertibility, the conversion rate used in the computation should not result in a reduction in the number of common shares (or common share equivalents) existing before the original exchange took place until a greater rate becomes effective.[22]

Appendix B: A Complex Consolidated Earnings per Share Example

Case B–1. Primary Earnings per Share

Western Calculations, Inc., reported net income of $8 million for 19X1. The firm's common stock is traded actively on the New York Stock Exchange and had an average market price of $50 during the year; the December 31, 19X1, price was $80. The following securities of Western Calculations were outstanding throughout 19X1:

Long-term debt:	
10% bonds, due 19X9	$ 5,000,000
10.5% 30-year bonds, due 20 years hence, and convertible into common stock at the rate of three shares per $100; at issuance, the average Aa corporate bond yield was 16.5%; the bonds were issued at par	$10,000,000
Stockholders' equity:	
Preferred stock, cumulative as to dividends of $6, callable at $100, and convertible into common stock at the rate of two shares for each share of preferred; at issuance, the average Aa corporate bond yield was 13%; issue price, $100	150,000 shares
Preferred stock, cumulative as to dividends of $2.50, callable at $35, and convertible into common stock at the rate of one share for each share of preferred; at issuance, the average Aa corporate bond yield was 14%; issue price, $20	400,000 shares
Common stock	1,500,000 shares
Warrants to purchase common stock:	
100,000 shares at $20.	
200,000 shares at $52.	

Primary earnings per share calculations require a determination of which securities should be classified as common stock equivalents. Applying the aforementioned rules, the classification process is summarized in Illustration 4–10, and the computation of primary earnings per share is presented in Illustration 4–11.

---

[22] Ibid., par. 57.

ILLUSTRATION 4-10   Classification of Securities—Western Calculations, Inc.

Security	Effective Yield	Average Aa Corporate Bond Yield at Issuance	Classification	Criterion
10% bonds			Senior	No common stock characteristics
10.5% bonds	10.5%	16.5%	C/S equivalent	Yield was less than ²/₃ of Aa rate
$6.00 preferred stock	6.0	13%	C/S equivalent	Yield was less than ²/₃ of Aa rate
$2.50 preferred stock	12.5	14.0	Potentially dilutive security	Yield was greater than ²/₃ of Aa rate
Warrants at $20			C/S equivalent	Always C/S equivalent
Warrants at $52			C/S equivalent	Always C/S equivalent

ILLUSTRATION 4-11   Primary Earnings per Share—Western Calculations, Inc.

	Shares	Earnings
Reported net income		$8,000,000
Common shares outstanding	1,500,000	
Dividend requirements on $2.50 preferred stock ($2.50 × 400,000)		(1,000,000)
		$7,000,000
Effect of assumed conversion or exercise of dilutive common stock equivalents:*		
10.5% convertible bonds:		
[3($10,000,000/$100)]	300,000	
[54% × (10.5% × $10,000,000)]		567,000
$6.00 convertible preferred stock (2 × 150,000)	300,000	
Warrants for 100,000 at $20: 100,000		
(100,000 × $20)/$50 . . . . (40,000)	60,000	
Warrants for 200,000 at $52: 200,000		
(200,000 × $52)/$50 . . . . (208,000)		
	2,160,000	$7,567,000
Primary earnings per share		$3.50

* It should be noted that each of the common stock equivalent securities for which conversion or exercise was assumed had the effect of diluting earnings per share. The warrants for 200,000 common shares at $52 were not included in the calculation since the effect of including them would have been to increase earnings per share. The earnings effect of the 10.5 percent bond conversion is after taxes (assuming a 46 percent rate).

Case B–2. Fully Diluted Earnings per Share

This case assumes the same data as these presented in Case B–1. The calculation of fully diluted earnings per share requires the assumed conversion of all dilutive securities including the one designated as a potentially dilutive security in Illustration 4–10. The computation of fully diluted earnings per share is presented in Illustration 4–12.

ILLUSTRATION 4-12   **Fully Diluted Earnings per Share—Western Calculations, Inc.**

	Shares	*Earnings*
Reported net income		$8,000,000
Common shares outstanding	1,500,000	
Effect of assumed conversion of dilutive common stock equivalents and potentially dilutive securities:		
10.5% convertible bonds:		
3($10,000,000/$100)	300,000	
[54% × (10.5% × $10,000,000)]		567,000
$6.00 convertible preferred stock (2 × 150,000)	300,000	
$2.50 convertible preferred stock (1 × 400,000)	400,000	
Warrants for 100,000 at $20:		
Shares issued 100,000		
(100,000 × $20)/$80 .... (25,000)	75,000	
Warrants for 200,000 at $52:*		
Shares issued 200,000		
(200,000 × $52)/$80 .... (130,000)	70,000	
	2,645,000	$8,567,000
Fully diluted earnings per share		$3.24

---

* Note that the warrants for 200,000 common shares at $52, although common stock equivalents, become dilutive only in the fully diluted earnings per share calculations. This was caused by the increase in the common stock market price from the $50 average price during the year to $80 at the end of the year.

Case B-3. Consolidated Earnings per Share

Western Calculations, Inc., which was analyzed in Cases B–1 and B–2, is now assumed to be a subsidiary of Northern Computers Corporation. Northern has a simple capital structure with no securities outstanding other than 2 million shares of common stock. The following data are drawn from the records of Northern:

Investments in Western Calculations, Inc.:		
Common stock, acquired at book value		1,200,000 shares
Warrants to purchase common stock at $20		80,000 warrants
Warrants to purchase common stock at $52		40,000 warrants
Net income for 19X1, excluding subsidiary earnings		$10,000,000
Equity in subsidiary earnings:		
Subsidiary net income	$8,000,000	
Preferred dividends:		
$2.50 preferred	(1,000,000)	
$6.00 preferred	(900,000)	
Earnings allocated to common stock	$6,100,000	
Northern equity therein:		
(1,200,000/1,500,000) × $6,100,000		4,880,000
Reported net income (equals consolidated net income)		$14,880,000

Northern does not have any potential dilution in its capital structure. Nevertheless, it should be emphasized that earnings per share for Northern is *not* determined by dividing Northern's reported net income ($14,880,000) by the number of common shares outstanding (2,000,000). Instead, primary earnings per share is calculated as indicated in Illustration 4–13. Since the $52 warrants were antidilutive in the calculation of primary earnings per share for Western (see Illustration 4–11), they are ignored in the comparable calculation for Western's parent (Illustration 4–13). However, Northern's ownership of $20 warrants must be incorporated in the calculation since they had a dilutive effect on the subsidiary's earnings per share. In Illustration 4–11, the assumed exercise of these $20 warrants had a net result of 60,000 additional common shares outstanding and the assumed conversions of the 10.5 percent convertible bonds and $6 convertible preferred stock resulted in another 600,000 common shares. Since Northern owns 80 percent of the $20 warrants, it would have received 48,000 additional shares (net). Receipt of only 48,000 of 660,000 additional shares issued would drop Northern's ownership interest from 80 percent (1,200,000/1,500,000) to 57.8 percent. In addition, the assumed conversion of the 10.5 percent convertible bonds and $6 convertible preferred stock increased Western's net income available to common stock from $6,100,000 to $7,567,000. Thus, for purposes of computing Northern's primary earnings per share, Northern's equity in the income of Western is recalculated according to these assumed effects.

Fully diluted earnings per share for Northern Computers Corporation amounts to $7.06, which is not materially less than primary earnings per share. The calculations to confirm this $7.06 amount are left for the reader's exercise.

ILLUSTRATION 4–13   Primary Earnings per Share Calculation, Parent Company or Consolidated Statements—Northern Computers Corporation

Number of Western common shares held by Northern	1,200,000
Additional Western common shares assumed to be issued to Northern through exercise of $20 warrants (see Illustration 4–11), 60,000(80,000/100,000)	48,000
Numerator of Northern's ownership interest	1,248,000
Number of Western common shares outstanding	1,500,000
Additional Western common shares assumed to be issued through conversion of 10.5% convertible bonds, $6 convertible preferred stock, and exercise of $20 warrants (see Illustration 4–11)	660,000
Denominator of Northern's ownership interest	2,160,000
Recalculated Northern ownership interest (1,248,000/2,160,000)	57.8%
Recalculated Western income available for common dividends (see Illustration 4–11)	$ 7,567,000
Recalculated Northern ownership interest	× 57.8%
Recalculated Northern equity in Western income	$ 4,373,726
Primary Northern income, excluding equity method income	10,000,000
Recalculated Northern primary income	$14,373,726
Number of Northern common shares outstanding	2,000,000
Northern primary earnings per share ($14,373,726/2,000,000)	$7.19

Questions

1. When a subsidiary is purchased during the year, how is its net income for the year reported on the consolidated income statement?

2. When a subsidiary is purchased during the year, there are two acceptable methods for including the subsidiary's revenue in the consolidated income statement. Describe and evaluate the alternatives.

3. If a stock dividend is declared by a subsidiary, what special steps must be taken in the consolidated statement working paper in the year the dividend is declared? In subsequent years?

4. Should deferred taxes be provided on the parent's share of undistributed earnings of subsidiaries not included in consolidated tax returns? On the investor's share of undistributed earnings of an investee?

5. What entry is made to recognize deferred taxes on undistributed earnings of affiliates?

6. Describe how the following items are reflected in the consolidated cash flow statement: (a) minority interest expense; (b) minority interest; (c) subsidiary dividend payments; and (d) differential amortization.

7. In post-combination periods, the method of presenting financial data that relate to precombination periods is dependent upon how the combination is classified. Explain the difference between the purchase and pooling of interests methods with respect to the presentation of precombination financial information.

8. In respect to the earnings per share calculations of a parent company, what is the potential significance of common stock equivalents and other potentially dilutive securities that have been issued by a subsidiary?

9. Describe the effect on consolidated earnings per share of subsidiary dilutive securities which are held by the parent.

10. List five situations in which previously reported earnings per share data should be restated in financial presentations referring to prior periods.

Exercises

Exercise 4–1   (Stock Dividends and Working Paper Entries)

P Company purchased an 80 percent interest in S Company on January 1, 19X1, for $40,000, when S Company had capital stock of $20,000 and retained earnings of $30,000.

During 19X1, S Company reported net income of $10,000 and paid cash dividends of $5,000. Additionally, S Company paid a 10 percent stock dividend on October 15, 19X1, on which it made the following entry:

Dividends Declared	7,000	
Additional Paid-In Capital		5,000
Capital Stock		2,000

Required:

a. Prepare the entries that P Company would make in 19X1 in respect to its investment in S Company.

b. Prepare the elimination entries for a consolidated statement working paper for the year ended December 31, 19X1.

Exercise 4–2   (Interim Purchase)

P Company purchased an 80 percent interest in S Company on March 1, 19X1, for $38,400. On January 1, 19X1, S Company had capital stock of $20,000 and retained earnings of $25,000.

The companies' operating data for 19X1 are as follows:

	P Company*	S Company
Sales	$300,000	$60,000
Cost of sales	$180,000	$30,000
Other expenses	40,000	12,000
	$220,000	$42,000
Net income	$ 80,000	$18,000

* Excluding P Company's interest in S Company earnings.

It is assumed that S Company's revenue is earned and expenses are incurred uniformly throughout the year. Neither company paid any dividends in 19X1.

Required:

a. Prepare a consolidated income statement for 19X1.

b. Prepare elimination entries for a consolidated statement working paper for the year ended December 31, 19X1.

Exercise 4–3   (Interim Purchase)

P Company purchased a 70 percent interest in S Company on September 1, 19X1, for $70,000. On January 1, 19X1, S Company had capital stock of $50,000 and retained earnings of $30,000.

The companies' operating data for 19X1 are as follows:

	P Company*	S Company
Sales	$140,000	$90,000
Cost of sales	$ 60,000	$45,000
Other expenses	30,000	15,000
	$ 90,000	$60,000
Net income	$ 50,000	$30,000

* Excluding P Company's interest in S Company earnings.

It is assumed that S Company's revenue is earned and expenses are incurred uniformly throughout the year. Neither company paid any dividends in 19X1.

Required:

a. Prepare a consolidated income statement for 19X1.

b. Prepare elimination entries for a consolidated statement working paper for the year ended December 31, 19X1.

Exercise 4–4   (Interim Purchase)

P Company purchased 90 shares of S Company capital stock on May 1, 19X1, in the open market for $16,200. A partial trial balance as of December 31, 19X1, discloses the following balances:

	P Company	*S Company*
Capital Stock ($100 par)	$100,000	$10,000
Retained Earnings (1/1)	40,000	5,000
Dividends Declared	5,000	2,000
Sales	200,000	40,000
Cost of Sales	130,000	20,000
Operating Expenses	40,000	8,000
Equity in Subsidiary Earnings	?	

S Company declared a $10 dividend per share on February 1 and July 1. It is assumed that subsidiary net income is earned uniformly throughout the year.

Required:

a. Prepare the entries made by P Company in 19X1 for its investment in S Company.

b. Prepare the elimination entries for a consolidated statement working paper for the year ended December 31, 19X1.

c. Prepare the consolidated income statement for the year ended December 31, 19X1.

Exercise 4–5   (Income Taxes)

Amos Company's 19X1 operations included equity method earnings from its investment in 70 percent of the outstanding common shares of Charlotte Chemical Company, computed as follows:

70 percent of Charlotte's reported 19X1 net income	$80,000
Differential amortization	15,000
Equity method earnings	$65,000

During 19X1, Charlotte declared and distributed a dividend in the amount of $50,000. The dividend received by Amos was subject to the 80 percent dividends received deduction. Amos pays income tax at a 30 percent rate.

Required:

Calculate the income tax expense, deferred taxes, and current tax liability due to Amos Company's investment in Charlotte Chemical Company.

Exercise 4–6   (Purchase and Pooling Characteristics)

Statements 1–8 below are made in reference to accounting for business combinations. Select from the phrases (*a*)–(*d*) the one which is consistent with each statement: (*a*) pooling of interests, (*b*) purchase, (*c*) neither pooling of interests nor purchase, and (*d*) either pooling of interests or purchase.

1. If an acquisition results in a debit differential, the assets of the acquired firm will be valued at less than their book value on the books of the acquired firm.
2. Given credit balances in the retained earnings of the combining companies, consolidated retained earnings are generally higher under this method.
3. The existence of a credit differential due to an overvalued building on the books of the acquired firm would result in consolidated earnings per share for the next year being lower under this method.
4. The combination was finalized nine months after the plan for combination was initiated.
5. The difference between book value and investment cost is recognized under this method.
6. Consolidated retained earnings is always equal to the sum of the retained earnings of the constituents under this method.
7. If investment cost is higher than the book value of the net assets of the acquired firm, it is possible that goodwill resulting from the combination will appear in the consolidated statements.
8. Several years after the combination, consolidated financial summaries pertaining to precombination periods will depict the historical data of only the acquired firm.

Exercise 4–7   (Consolidated Fully Diluted Earnings per Share)

Using the information in Case 4 in the chapter, calculate consolidated fully diluted earnings per share.

Exercise 4–8   (Earnings per Share)

South Sail Company had the following securities outstanding throughout 19X1:

Common stock, $10 par, average market price during 19X1 was $60, ending market price was $60	20,000 shares
Warrants to purchase 7,000 common shares at $50 per share.	
Bonds payable, 7%, issued at par, market price throughout 19X1 was approximately par	$200,000

South Sail Company earned $50,000 net income during 19X1. The effective income tax rate is 46 percent.

Required:

Calculate primary and fully diluted earnings per share for 19X1.

Exercise 4–9   (Earnings per Share)

P Company purchased 6,000 of S Company's 10,000 outstanding common shares at book value. S Company has convertible bonds and common stock warrants outstanding, but P Company does not own any of these securities. S Company has net income of $24,000 and primary earnings per share of $2. P Company has net income of $40,000, excluding its equity in S Company's earnings, and has 26,000 common shares outstanding. Also, P Company has outstanding warrants to purchase 5,000 common shares at $10. The average market price of P Company common stock during the year was $50.

Required:

a. Calculate the primary earnings per share of P Company.
b. Now assume that P Company also owns 1,500 of S Company's 1,800 outstanding common stock warrants. Also assume that S Company's calculation of primary earnings per share involved the assumed exercise of the 1,800 warrants for 1,800 common shares and that the cash proceeds from the exercise of warrants was used to repurchase 600 common shares. Calculate P Company's primary earnings per share.
c. Calculate consolidated net income for P Company and its subsidiary.

Exercise 4–10   (Earnings per Share)

Company A owns 20,000 of 25,000 outstanding shares of B Company. Data relating to A and B are as follows:

	A	B
Earnings excluding equity method earnings	$50,000	$20,000
Equity in B earnings	16,000	—
Common shares outstanding	80,000	25,000
Net common shares that would be issued upon the assumed exercise of warrants and proceeds used to acquire treasury shares at average common price during year	—	6,000
Number of B warrants held by A	40%	—

Required:

Compute A Company's primary earnings per share.

Problems

Problem 4–11   (Purchase and Pooling Characteristics)

On January 1, 19X3, Fox, Inc., issued 100,000 common shares in exchange for all of the outstanding common stock of Weber Company. Fox, Inc., employs the equity method of accounting for its investment in Weber Company; Weber Company has never declared dividends. The combination between Fox, Inc., and Weber Company complied with all of the criteria for a pooling of interests. During 19X3 and 19X4, Weber company sold merchandise to Fox, Inc., at prices equal to Weber Company's cost. These sales amounted to $50,000 each year. Selected financial data for each of the two companies are as follows:

	19X1	19X2	19X3	19X4
Sales:				
Fox	$400,000	$440,000	$450,000	$500,000
Weber	350,000	400,000	360,000	400,000
Net income:				
Fox (includes subsidiary earnings)	100,000	150,000	200,000	280,000
Weber	80,000	100,000	80,000	120,000
Earnings per share:				
Fox	$1.00	$1.50	$1.00	$1.40
Weber	0.40	0.50	0.40	0.60

Required:

a. Prepare a four-year financial summary of sales, net income, and earnings per share for Fox, Inc., and its subsidiary, to be included in the 19X4 annual report of Fox, Inc.

b. Assume that the combination did not comply with all of the criteria for a pooling of interests because some of the shares issued by Fox, Inc., to effect the combination were placed in a voting trust which restricted the voting rights of the stockholders. Fox, Inc.'s common stock is actively traded, and its market price has been stable at $40. The book value of Weber Company's common stock was $2,250,000 at the date of the combination. As a result of an analysis of Weber Company's assets and liabilities, the difference between the fair market value of Fox, Inc.'s investment and its equity in Weber Company's recorded net assets was allocated as follows: one half of the difference to fixed assets that have 10 years estimated remaining useful life and one half of the difference to goodwill, which management decided to amortize over 40 years. Prepare a four-year financial summary similar to that required in (a).

Problem 4–12   (Statement of Cash Flows)

Separate company balance sheet data of P Company as of December 31, 19X1, and consolidated balance sheet data of P Company and Subsidiary S Company as of December 31, 19X2, appear below:

	P Company 12/31/X1	Consolidated 12/31/X2
Cash	$100,000	$149,000
Receivables	10,000	55,000
Inventory	20,000	50,000
Total assets	$130,000	$254,000
Accounts payable	$ 30,000	$125,000
Minority interest		11,000
Capital stock	80,000	80,000
Retained earnings	20,000	38,000
Total equities	$130,000	$254,000

Consolidated income statement data for the year ended December 31, 19X2, are as follows:

Sales		$80,000
Operating expenses	$60,000	
Minority interest expense	2,000	62,000
Net income		$18,000

On January 1, 19X2, P Company purchased 80 percent of the outstanding shares of S Company for $40,000. Balance sheet data relating to S Company on this date are as follows:

Cash	$50,000
Receivables	5,000
Inventory	10,000
Total assets	$65,000
Accounts payable	$15,000
Capital stock	30,000
Retained earnings	20,000
Total equities	$65,000

At the date of acquisition, all of S Company's assets and liabilities had book values equal to fair values. In addition, S Company paid a $5,000 cash dividend on July 1, 19X2. P Company paid no dividends during 19X2.

Required:

Prepare a consolidated statement of cash flows for the year ended December 31, 19X2. Use the indirect method of reporting cash flows from operating activites.

Problem 4–13

P Company owns 80 percent of S Company. Statements of cash flows and reconciliations of net income with net cash provided by operating activities for the year ended December 31, 19X1, are as follows:

	P Company	S Company
Cash flows from operating activities:		
Cash received from customers	$268,000	$115,000
Dividends from S Company	5,000	
Cash paid to suppliers and employees	(208,000)	(104,750)
Net cash provided by operating activities	$ 65,000	$ 10,250
Cash flows from investing activities:		
Loan to S Company	$ (50,000)	
Net cash applied to investing activities	$ (50,000)	
Cash flows from financing activities:		
Dividends	$ (25,000)	$ (6,250)
Proceeds of loan from P Company		50,000
Net cash provided by financing activities	$ (25,000)	$ 43,750
Change in cash	$ (10,000)	$ 54,000
Beginning cash balance	25,000	14,000
Ending cash balance	$ 15,000	$ 68,000

Reconciliation of Net Income with Net Cash Provided by Operating Activities

	P Company	S Company
Net income	$ 80,000	$ 20,000
Add (subtract):		
Depreciation	11,000	4,000
Increase in accounts receivable	(25,000)	(10,000)
Increase in inventory	(14,000)	(10,000)
Increase in current payables	20,000	6,250
Equity in S Company income	(12,000)	
Dividends from S Company	5,000	
Net cash provided by operating activities	$ 65,000	$ 10,250

Required:

Prepare working papers for a consolidated statement of cash flows and reconciliation of net income with net cash provided by operating activities.

Problem 4–14   (Earnings per Share)

P Company has income from its own operations of $50,000 and equity in subsidiary earnings of $30,000. The equity method income arises from holding 6,000 of 8,000 outstanding S Company shares. P Company has 20,000 outstanding shares. In addition to the 8,000 shares, S Company has outstanding warrants exercisable into 800 S Company shares at an exercise price of $30. The average price of S common during the year is $40. One fourth of the S Company warrants are held by P Company. S Company also has outstanding $100,000 face, 10 percent, convertible bonds. The bonds were sold at face value several years ago when the average Aa bond yield was 12 percent. They are convertible into 10,000 S Company shares. The marginal tax rate of both companies is 40 percent.

Required:

Calculate P Company's primary earnings per share, ignoring any considerations of materiality.

Problem 4–15   (Earnings per Share)

Several years ago, Walker Transportation Company purchased 80 percent of Bonanza, Inc.'s outstanding common stock. The differential was fully amortized in prior years. For 19X1, selected financial information for the two companies is presented below. The effective income tax rate is 40 percent. Walker does not own any of the Bonanza warrants.

	Walker	*Bonanza*
Net income (excluding earnings from subsidiary)	$ 51,000	$ 30,000
Common stock market prices during 19X1:		
Average	90	80
Ending	135	80
Outstanding securities:		
Bonds payable, 6%, due 20 years hence, convertible into common		
stock at the rate of two shares per $100; bonds issued at par;		
at the date of issuance, average Aa corporate bond yield was 8%		100,000
Preferred stock, $100 par, 5%, cumulative as to dividends	100,000	
Common stock, $50 par	500,000	300,000
Warrants to purchase common:		
1,000 Bonanza shares at $40		
1,500 Walker shares at $90		

Required:

In respect to the 19X1 consolidated income statement of Walker Transportation Company and its subsidiary, calculate

a. Primary earnings per share.

b. Fully diluted earnings per share.

Problem 4–16   (Earnings per Share)

Toy, Inc., owns 900 shares of Ball Company's outstanding common stock and 360 warrants to purchase Ball Company common stock at $50 per share. The following information pertains to these companies' financial operations and status during 19X1:

	Toy, Inc.	Ball Company
Net income, excluding subsidiary earnings	$20,000	$ 5,000
Common shares outstanding	5,600	1,000
Preferred stock, 7%, cumulative, issued at par ($100), convertible into common at $20 (i.e., 5 shares of common for 1 share of preferred). Average Aa corporate bond yield at issuance was 12 percent. Shares outstanding	800	
Average price of common stock during 19X1	$ 100	$ 300
6%, 30-year bonds, issued at par, convertible into common stock at $200 (a $1,000 bond can be exchanged for 5 common shares). Average Aa corporate bond yield at issuance was 10 percent. The corporate income tax rate is 40 percent. Bonds outstanding		$200,000

In addition to the above, Ball Company has issued and outstanding 600 warrants to purchase Ball Company common stock at $50 per share. Ball Company also issued warrants to purchase 500 common shares of Toy, Inc., at $20 per share. All of the warrants are outstanding.

Required:

a. Calculate primary earnings per share for Ball Company.

b. Calculate primary earnings per share for Toy, Inc., and its consolidated subsidiary.

c. Calculate consolidated net income.

Problem 4–17   (Consolidated Fully Diluted Earnings per Share)

Using the information in Case B–3 in Appendix B to the chapter, calculate consolidated fully diluted earnings per share.

Accounting for Corporate Restructurings and Alternative Organizational Forms

Chapter Outline

In the preceding chapters, we examined the principles for preparing consolidated financial statements for a parent and its subsidiaries under both purchase and pooling of interests accounting. In this chapter, we extend our scope to incorporate alternative organizational forms for business combinations and some important types of corporate restructurings.

ACCOUNTING FOR ACQUISITIONS, MERGERS, AND CONSOLIDATIONS

The distinguishing characteristic of an *acquisition* is the legal continuity of the affiliated companies through a parent-subsidiary relationship. The distinguishing characteristic of a *merger* is that only one of the affiliates remains in existence. The distinguishing characteristic of a *consolidation* is that a new legal entity is formed and none of the predecessor affiliates remain in existence.

Recall that each of these three legal forms of combination can, for accounting purposes, be classified as a purchase transaction or as a pooling of interests. In purchase transactions, acquired net assets are valued at their purchase prices. Also, accumulated earnings from these net assets in the hands of a previous owner are not recorded by their purchaser. The pooling of interests method portrays combined companies *as if* they had always operated as a single economic entity. Accordingly, predecessor company valuations are carried over on the financial statements of the combined entity. Moreover, the balance sheet of the combined entity will include the precombination retained earnings of the affiliates.

The following five cases provide a comparative review of these features of the purchase and pooling of interests methods in the context of acquisitions, mergers, and consolidations. All cases are based on the following data.

On January 1, 19X1, P Company acquires 100 percent of the outstanding no-par common shares of S Company by issuing 1,000 shares of $5 par common shares. The market price of the P Company shares is $10. Thus, the fair value of the shares issued is $10,000. At the date of acquisition, data relating to S Company are as follows:

	Book Value	*Fair Value*
Current assets	$1,000	$ 1,000
Plant and equipment	8,000	9,000
	$9,000	$10,000
Liabilities	800	700
Net assets	$8,200	$ 9,300
Composed of:		
Capital stock	$6,000	
Retained earnings	2,200	
	$8,200	

During 19X1, S Company earned $1,000 in net income. All elements of the $1,800 ($10,000 − $8,200) differential associated with the purchase method have a remaining life of 10 years.

Case 1. Acquisition/Purchase

Assuming the business combination is an acquisition accounted for using the purchase method, P Company's entry to record the transaction at date of acquisition follows:

Investment in S Company (1,000 × $10)	10,000	
Capital Stock (1,000 × $5)		5,000
Additional Paid-In Capital		5,000

Consistent with the purchase method, P Company's basis in S Company's acquired net assets is the $10,000 fair value of the consideration surrendered to obtain them. Also, P Company does not record S Company's $2,200 retained earnings. The entire equity claim to the $10,000 increase in P Company's assets is contributed capital.

P Company's equity method income for 19X1 consists of 100 percent of S Company's 19X1 income, less differential amortization in the amount of $180 ($1,800/10). P Company's entry to record its equity in S Company's 19X1 earnings is as follows:

Investment in S Company ($1,000 − $180)	820	
Equity in Subsidiary Earnings		820

As of December 31, 19X1, the consolidated statement working paper entries are as follows:

Equity in Subsidiary Earnings	820	
Investment in S Company		820
Capital Stock—S Company	6,000	
Retained Earnings—S Company	2,200	
Differential	1,800	
Investment in S Company		10,000
Plant and Equipment ($9,000 − $8,000)	1,000	
Goodwill ($10,000 − $9,300)	700	
Liabilities ($800 − $700)	100	
Differential		1,800
Expenses	180	
Plant and Equipment ($1,000/10)		100
Goodwill ($700/10)		70
Liabilities ($100/10)		10

The above parent company entries and consolidated statement working paper entries are entirely consistent with the procedures discussed in Chapter 3. On the consolidated balance sheet, S Company's assets and liabilities appear at book values plus P Company's proportionate share (100 percent) of the differences between fair values and book values (less 19X1 depreciation and amortization). S Company's stockholders' equity is eliminated, and the equity in S Company's net assets consists of P Company's $10,000 contribution to acquire S Company's net assets plus P Company's earnings from these assets subsequent to their acquisition. That is to say, the assets acquired from S Company are valued as follows:

Initial purchase price	$10,000
Increase in value due to earnings (net of $180 amortization)	820
Total value of subsidiary net assets on December 31, 19X1, consolidated balance sheet	$10,820

and the equity claim to these net assets consists of

Capital stock	$ 5,000
Additional paid-in capital	5,000
Retained earnings	820
Total equity claim to subsidiary net assets on December 31, 19X1, consolidated balance sheet	$10,820

Case 2. Merger/Purchase

The above relationships are more apparent if the business combination is a merger in which P Company receives the net assets of S Company, after which S Company ceases to exist. P Company's entry to record the merger involves recording individual assets and liabilities as if they had been purchased outright:

Current Assets	1,000	
Plant and Equipment	9,000	
Goodwill	700	
Liabilities		700
Capital Stock		5,000
Additional Paid-In Capital		5,000

S Company's net assets are now recorded on the books of P Company. As these assets earn $820 in income, P Company increases their values in amounts totaling $820. The corresponding credit ultimately appears as P Company retained earnings. Thus, the equity claim to the $10,820 in net assets value appears on P Company's December 31, 19X1, balance sheet as

Capital stock	$ 5,000
Additional paid-in capital	5,000
Retained earnings	820
	$10,820

Case 3. Acquisition/Pooling of Interests

Assuming the business combination is an acquisition accounted for as a pooling of interests, P Company's entry to record the transaction at the date of acquisition is the following:

Investment in S Company	8,200	
Capital Stock (1,000 × $5)		5,000
Additional Paid-In Capital		1,000
Retained Earnings		2,200

S Company's $8,200 book value is carried over as the basis of P Company's investment. Similarly, P Company records total contributed capital (the amounts in Capital Stock plus Additional Paid-In Capital) at the $6,000 amount of S Company's total contributed capital. However, the mix of capital stock/other paid-in capital differs from the counterpart mix on S Company's books. This is because P Company must record the par value of its 1,000 newly issued shares in its Capital Stock account. The credit to Additional Paid-In Capital is simply whatever amount is necessary to increase P Company's total contributed capital to $6,000. Last, P Company records S Company's $2,200 retained earnings.[1]

The effects of P Company's entry are to record the book values of S Company's net assets in the investment account and to record the equity claims to these net assets in the same paid-in capital/earned capital mix as appears on S Company's books. Apart from the fact that the book values of S Company's net assets are added together in the investment account, P Company has added S Company's balance sheet to its own. In this sense, P Company's balance sheet is *as if* P Company has absorbed the entire accounting history of S Company.

---

[1] Recall from Chapter 2 that the objective is to bring S Company's contributed and earned capital onto P Company's books. However, if the par value of P Company's shares is quite large, it may be that P Company must debit Additional Paid-in Capital in order to retain the combined companies' contributed capital/earned capital mix. If P Company's Additional Paid-in Capital is not large enough to absorb such a debit, there is no alternative but to reduce P Company's Additional Paid-in Capital to zero and absorb the remainder against the combined retained earnings. These situations are illustrated in Appendix B to Chapter 2.

P Company's equity method income for 19X1 consists of 100 percent of S Company's 19X1 income. *There is no differential amortization,* since the pooling of interests method involves recording acquired net assets at book value. Therefore, P Company's equity method earnings exceed their purchase method counterpart by $180 in differential amortization. P Company's entry to record its equity in S Company's 19X1 earnings follows:

Investment in S Company	1,000	
Equity in Subsidiary Earnings		1,000

As of December 31, 19X1, the consolidated statement working paper entries are as follows:

Equity in Subsidiary Earnings	1,000	
Investment in S Company		1,000
Capital Stock—S Company	6,000	
Retained Earnings—S Company	2,200	
Investment in S Company		8,200

Since S Company's date of acquisition stockholders' equity has been added to P Company's balance sheet, the above elimination entries simply facilitate adding S Company's 19X1 income statement amounts to those of P Company (after eliminating P Company's equity method earnings) and adding the book values of S Company's assets and liabilities to those of P Company (after eliminating P Company's investment account). Thus, the consolidated balance sheet appears *as if* P Company and S Company have always operated as a single entity.

Case 4. Merger/Pooling of Interests

As in Case 2, if the business combination is a merger in which P Company receives the net assets of S Company, after which S Company ceases to exist, the financial statement effects of a pooling of interests are explicitly reflected in P Company's entry to record the merger. S Company's individual assets, liabilities, and contributed capital/earned capital mix are recorded using S Company's book values:

Current Assets	1,000	
Plant and Equipment	8,000	
Liabilities		800
Capital Stock		5,000
Additional Paid-In Capital		1,000
Retained Earnings		2,200

S Company's net assets are now recorded on the books of P Company. As these assets earn $1,000 in income, P Company increases their values in amounts totaling $1,000. The corresponding credit ultimately appears as P Company's retained earnings, exactly *as if* P Company and S Company had always operated as a single entity.

Case 5. Consolidations

In the consolidation form of business combination, a newly created accounting entity is formed to receive the net assets of two or more predecessors. If the consolidation is accounted for as a purchase transaction, the new entity records the individual assets and liabilities of the *purchased* company (or companies) at their fair values. The new entity records the assets and liabilities received from the *acquiring* company at their book values (analogous to the values carried forward for the surviving company when the combination is structured as a merger).

In contrast, a consolidation accounted for as a pooling of interests involves the new entity recording the individual assets and liabilities of all the predecessor companies at their book values. In addition, the contributed capital/earned capital mixes of the predecessors are recorded as stockholders' equity of the new entity. Thus, the entire accounting histories of the predecessors are recorded by the new entity. Immediately following the combination, the balance sheet of the new entity appears *as if* it were a seasoned entity which had undertaken all the transactions of the predecessors.

REPORTING ON SUBSIDIARIES—PUSH-DOWN ACCOUNTING

When a parent company controls a subsidiary, and the control is not likely to be temporary, consolidated financial statements are the primary financial statements of the reporting entity. Reports to the SEC may also include supplemental parent company statements and supplemental separate company statements of the subsidiary. Separate company statements of the subsidiary are also issued to (1) the minority shareholders of the subsidiary, (2) preferred shareholders of the subsidiary, and (3) holders of any subsidiary public debt. We now focus on the implications of a business combination for the separate company statements of the subsidiary.

Staff Accounting Bulletin No. 54 and *Staff Accounting Bulletin No. 73* relate to the use of *push-down* accounting in separate company statements. The term *push-down accounting* refers to "pushing down" consolidated statement accounting to the separate company statements of the subsidiary. When push-down accounting is used, the fair value basis of accounting used in the consolidated statement is also used in the separate company statements of the subsidiary.

For example, in the series of cases in Chapter 3 introducing purchase accounting, one scenario (Case 2) involved the cash purchase for $135 of 90 percent of S Company's common stock when the book and fair values for S Company were as follows:

	Book Value	Fair Value
Current assets	$ 10	$ 10
Plant and equipment	190	220
	$200	$230
Liabilities	100	100
Net assets	$100	$130

The differential is $45 [$135 − (90% × $100)], which is allocated as follows:

	Book Value	Differential Allocation	Consolidated Statement Valuation
Current assets	$ 10	$-0-	$ 10
Plant and equipment	190	27	217
Goodwill	-0-	18	18
	$200	$ 45	$245
Liabilities	100	-0-	100
Net assets	$100	$ 45	$145
Minority interest (10% × $100)			$ 10

With these values, the separate company balance sheet of the subsidiary issued on a *push-down* basis is shown in Illustration 5–1.

Note that the subsidiary assets and liabilities are valued precisely as in the consolidated statements; that is, book values plus any allocated shares of the debit differential. Note as well that no retained earnings appears as of the date of acquisition. Stockholders' equity consists only of capital stock and is valued at the $135 price paid by the parent company plus the $10 minority interest. Thus, the appearance is essentially one of a newly created accounting entity.[2]

Staff Accounting Bulletin No. 54 requires push-down accounting whenever there is a substantial change in ownership of the subsidiary in a single transaction *unless*

1. The subsidiary has public debt outstanding.
2. The subsidiary has preferred stock outstanding.

---

[2] If the subsidiary were indeed a newly created accounting entity, the basis of accounting for new assets and liabilities would be 100 percent of fair value. *EITF Consensus Position No. 86–16* specifies valuation at book value plus the parent's share of any excess of fair value over book value. This position is consistent with the parent company theory and inconsistent with the entity theory.

ILLUSTRATION 5–1

S COMPANY
Balance Sheet
(Push-Down Basis)

Current assets	$ 10
Plant and equipment	217
Goodwill	18
Total assets	$245
Liabilities	$100
Capital stock	145
Total liabilities and stockholders' equity	$245

A substantial change in ownership is generally understood to mean acquisition of at least 90 percent of a company's common shares. The idea is that a substantial change in ownership in a single transaction is tantamount to the creation of a new accounting entity. The exceptions for public debt and preferred stock exist in order to prevent violation of contractual agreements with debtors and/or preferred stockholders merely because of the ownership change.[3] Push-down accounting is *permitted* when the ownership change is less than substantial as long as a majority of the subsidiary's shares are acquired in a single transaction.

ACCOUNTING FOR JOINT VENTURES

Thus far, we have focused on affiliations in which one corporation controls another corporation. We also need to consider alternatives in which the investee is not necessarily organized in corporate form. We refer to these noncorporate investees as *joint ventures*. A joint venture is an entity that is owned and operated by a small group of investors termed *venturers*. Each venturer usually plays an active role in the management of the joint venture, such that no one venturer can be said to be in control. That is, control is usually joint in the sense that consent of all venturers is required to decide major operating and financing issues. Joint ventures are utilized as a convenient means of entering foreign markets (e.g., a domestic corporation enters into a joint venture with a foreign corporation, or even with a foreign government). They are also utilized to enter into particularly risky undertakings requiring large capital investment, such as construction and operation of nuclear power plants, real estate development, and oil and gas exploration.

---

[3] Push-down accounting can alter the subsidiary's debt/equity ratio. The subsidiary may have debt covenants making the debt immediately due when the debt/equity ratio exceeds a stipulated number. It would be unfair for such an event to occur only because the subsidiary was acquired.

A joint venture may assume any of the following legal forms:

1. A corporate joint venture—in which the venture is organized as a corporation. Rights and rewards of ownership are determined on the basis of shares held.
2. A general partnership—in which the venture is organized as a partnership with each partner assuming unlimited liability. Rights and rewards of ownership are determined by the partnership agreement.
3. A limited partnership—in which the venture is organized as a partnership, but one or more general partners have unlimited liability, and one or more limited partners have limited liability. Rights and rewards of ownership are determined by the partnership agreement. General partners usually manage the jointly owned net assets, subject to restrictions placed upon them by limited partners.
4. An undivided interest (often termed an *unincorporated joint venture*)—in which ownership of net assets takes neither the form of a corporation nor a partnership. Rights and rewards of ownership are determined by contract among the venturers.

In recent years, the joint venture has been used with increasing frequency. Because of this, the accounting for an investment in a joint venture on the part of a venturer is an important matter. Unfortunately, there is little authoritative guidance on accounting for investments in joint ventures. Extant guidance reflects a disturbing degree of legal form dominating substance. Custom is also reflected.

Corporate Joint Ventures

APB Opinion No. 18, "The Equity Method of Accounting for Investments in Common Stock," paragraph 16, mandates the equity method of accounting for investments in corporate joint ventures (in financial statements issued to shareholders). However, no mention is made of the venturer's ability to exercise significant influence over the operating and financial policies of the venture. Thus, the equity method is apparently sanctioned even if the venturer holds a quite small percentage of the shares of the venture. Presumably, this endorsement of the equity method is a consequence of the usual case in which the venture is subject to the *joint* control of all venturers (such that *each* venturer thus exercises a significant influence). However, paragraph 3 defines a subsidiary as a corporation that is controlled by another corporation. If one venturer indeed exercises control over the corporate joint venture, the venture is deemed a subsidiary, *not* a corporate joint venture. Thus, the controlling venturer would account for its investment by applying the principles applicable to investments in subsidiaries (i.e., issue consolidated statements if control is not expected to be temporary). Similarly, the other venturers would account for their investment using either the cost method or the equity method, depending upon whether they exercise significant influence over the operating and financial policies of the venture.

Partnerships and Undivided Interests

An interpretation of *APB Opinion No. 18* deals with use of the equity method in the case of joint ventures organized as partnerships or undivided interests. However, the interpretation states only that "many of the provisions of *APB Opinion No. 18* would be appropriate in accounting for these unincorporated entities."[4] The interpretation provides examples of these provisions in which a venturer includes in its income the venturer's share of profits or losses of the joint venture and eliminates intercompany profits and losses.[5] Moreover, since income tax effects of partnerships and undivided interests accrue directly to the venturers but are not recorded by the venture, a venturer should accrue income tax effects attributable to the venturer's share of profits or losses.

Particular care must be exercised in determining a venturer's share of profits and losses, and in accruing income tax effects attributable to these profits and losses. For example, a venture agreement may purport to allocate all depreciation expense to one venturer and to allocate all other revenue and expense items equally. However, the agreement may also stipulate that all cash distributions (including those made in liquidation) are to be divided equally. In such an agreement, the purported allocation of depreciation expense has no substance. Therefore, all venturers would record equal shares of the venture profit or loss.

Proportionate Consolidation

In some industries, especially the oil and gas industry, investments in *undivided interests* are reported on a *proportionate consolidation* basis. Recall that proportionate consolidation involves reporting on the consolidated statements only the investor's proportionate interest in assets, liabilities, revenues, and expenses. Accordingly, no minority interest is reported. *Interpretation No. 2* sanctions this method of reporting in cases in which it is an established industry tradition.

Balance sheet and income statement data relating to a venturer and a joint venture (in which a 60 percent interest is held) are displayed in the first two columns of Illustration 5–2. It is assumed that the venturer uses the equity method for bookkeeping purposes. The last two columns of Illustration 5–2 display conventional and proportionate consolidations. Comparison of the income statement data as portrayed in the conventional and proportionate consolidations reveals equal amounts of net income. In the case of conventional consolidation, all of the venture's revenue and expense items are included, with the attendant recognition of minority interest in the amount of 40 percent of venture net income. In the case of proportionate consolidation, the income statement simply excludes 40 percent of the venture's sales, cost of sales, and other expenses. With respect to the

---

[4] *Accounting Interpretation No. 2 of APB Opinion No. 18,* "Investments in Partnerships and Ventures" (New York, AICPA, 1971).

[5] Intercompany profits and losses are discussed in Chapters 6, 7, and 8.

ILLUSTRATION 5-2

VENTURER AND JOINT VENTURE
Conventional Consolidation and Proportionate Consolidation

	Venturer	*Joint Venture*	*Conventional Consolidation*	*Proportionate Consolidation*
Income statement:				
Sales	$1,000,000	$ 300,000	$1,300,000	$1,180,000
Equity in venture earnings	60,000			
	$1,060,000	$ 300,000	$1,300,000	$1,180,000
Cost of sales	$ 500,000	$ 150,000	$ 650,000	$ 590,000
Other expenses	240,000	50,000	290,000	270,000
Minority interest in venture earnings			40,000	
	$ 740,000	$ 200,000	$ 980,000	$ 860,000
Net income	$ 320,000	$ 100,000	$ 320,000	$ 320,000
Balance sheet:				
Cash	$ 420,000	$ 40,000	$ 460,000	$ 444,000
Inventory	600,000		600,000	600,000
Investment in venture	480,000			
Other assets	1,500,000	1,060,000	2,560,000	2,136,000
	$3,000,000	$1,100,000	$3,620,000	$3,180,000
Accounts payable	$2,000,000	$ 300,000	$2,300,000	$2,180,000
Minority interest			320,000	
Capital stock	600,000		600,000	600,000
Retained earnings	400,000		400,000	400,000
Venturers' equity		800,000		
	$3,000,000	$1,100,000	$3,620,000	$3,180,000

balance sheet data, the conventional consolidation includes all of the venture's assets and liabilities, with attendant recognition of minority interest in the amount of 40 percent of the venture's net assets. In contrast, the proportionate consolidation simply excludes 40 percent of the venture's cash, inventory, other assets, and accounts payable.

Real Estate Joint Ventures

Interestingly, a committee of the AICPA has recommended that accounting for investments in real estate joint ventures be determined by control, not legal form.[6] That is, if any single venturer controls the venture, that venturer should consolidate the investment. Thus, corporate joint ventures, general partnerships, limited

---

[6] *Statement of Position 78-9,* "Accounting for Investments in Real Estate Ventures" (New York: AICPA, 1978).

partnerships, and undivided interests would all be consolidated by a controlling venturer. Other venturers would use the cost or equity method, depending on their ability to exercise significant influence over the operating and financial policies of the venture. If the venture is subject to joint control, all venturers would use the equity method. However, the scope of the recommendation is limited to real estate ventures, and its relevance beyond that industry is unclear.

Valuing Nonmonetary Assets Contributed by Venturers

In the formation of joint ventures, the investors often contribute nonmonetary assets with a difference between carrying value and fair value. The difference may be substantial, and thus it is important how these assets are accounted for on the books of the joint venture. If a stepped-up basis is adopted, the venturer who contributed the assets will probably recognize an immediate gain, and in subsequent periods, the joint venture income will reflect the effects of the higher cost. On the other hand, if the assets are carried over at their book values to the contributing venturer, no gain or loss will be immediately recognized, but joint venture income will be higher in the future.

In 1979, a task force of the Accounting Standards Executive Committee (AcSEC) composed a document, *Joint Venture Accounting,* which identified a number of issues that needed resolution. On this matter of establishing a value for nonmonetary assets contributed by the venturers, the task force concluded (albeit by a close vote) the following (par. 53):

1. The formation of a joint venture establishes a new reporting entity, and existing book values for assets and liabilities contributed to the joint venture should not be carried forward.
2. It is assumed that amounts agreed upon by the venturers for contributed assets and liabilities will reflect fair values. In the absence of evidence to the contrary, the agreed-upon amounts should be used to value the assets and liabilities on the books of the joint venture.

While this issue is among many on the current agenda of the Financial Accounting Standards Board (FASB) (discussed below), the SEC staff has taken the position that a step-up in the basis of nonmonetary assets contributed to a joint venture is acceptable *only* when the alleged fair value is matched by cash contributions to the joint venture by the other venturer(s). When some or all the cash contributed by one venturer is paid to the venturer contributing nonmonetary assets, a partial step-up is usually allowed (again to the extent of the cash contributed).

Case 6. Determining Asset Values upon the Formation of a Joint Venture

Assume that a new 50/50 joint venture is formed by investors A and B, and that investor A contributes nonmonetary assets with a book value of $50,000 and an estimated fair value of $200,000. We will determine the value assigned to the nonmonetary assets contributed by A to the joint venture under three alternatives for investor B's contribution:

Alternative	Investor B's Contribution to the Joint Venture
I	Cash of $200,000
II	The joint venture sells 50% of the joint venture to investor B for $100,000 and then distributes the $100,000 cash to investor A.
III	A nonmonetary asset with a book value of $130,000 and an estimated fair value of $200,000

Under the SEC staff position, these scenarios would result in the assignment of the following values to the nonmonetary assets contributed by investor A to the joint venture:

Alternative	Value Assigned to Nonmonetary Assets Contributed by Investor A	Explanation of Calculated Value
I	$200,000	Investor B contributed cash that matched the estimated fair value of the nonmonetary asset contributed by investor A.
II	$125,000	The 50% interest sold to investor B is valued at $100,000, which is investor B's cost. The 50% interest contributed by investor A is valued at $25,000, which is A's book value for this one-half interest (50% × $50,000).
III	$ 50,000	Since no cash was contributed by investor B, the book value of the nonmonetary asset contributed by A is carried over as the value for the asset on the books of the joint venture. The nonmonetary asset contributed by investor B will also be valued at its book value, or $130,000.

ACCOUNTING FOR LEVERAGED BUYOUTS (LBOS)

Closely related to the issue of push-down accounting is accounting for a class of transactions termed *leveraged buyouts,* or simply LBOs. In a typical LBO, a newly created holding company acquires all the outstanding common shares of an existing operating entity. For simplicity, we refer to the newly created company as *Newco* and the existing operating entity as *Oldco.* After acquisition of Oldco by Newco, Oldco is merged into Newco; that is, Oldco distributes its net assets to Newco and ceases to exist. Essentially all of Newco's capital is debt, hence the term *leveraged* buyout. Newco's small amount of equity capital is usually contributed by a subset of Oldco shareholders, often managers of Oldco. A third-party investor may also contribute equity capital to Newco. The fundamental accounting issue in an LBO is the basis of accounting for the Oldco net assets received by Newco. *Consensus Position No. 88–16* of the Emerging Issues Task Force specifies rules for determining this accounting basis.[7]

The basis of accounting for net assets distributed from Oldco to Newco depends upon the *residual interest* of any Oldco shareholders who become Newco shareholders and are part of whatever group of shareholders control Newco. Determining (1) residual interest of such continuing shareholders and (2) which of these continuing shareholders are part of the Newco control group can be quite complicated. We confine our discussion to a simplified setting in which residual interest of continuing shareholders and control group membership are relatively obvious.

Case 7. An LBO Example

The following data relate to Oldco immediately prior to its acquisition by Newco:

	Book Value	Fair Value
Fixed assets	$2,000	$12,000
Other net assets	400	400
Goodwill	–0–	7,600
Owners' equity	$2,400	$20,000

Oldco has 1,000 outstanding common shares, 50 of which are held by Oldco management (5 percent management ownership). Newco is formed with an outside investor contributing $1,000 in cash. In addition, the managers of Oldco contribute their 50 Oldco shares, which have a market value of $1,000 (5% × $20,000). The outside investor and the Oldco managers each own 50 percent of Newco since each contributed $1,000 in market value.

Newco then borrows $18,000 from a bank, using the proceeds and the $1,000 contributed by the outside investor to purchase the remaining 950 outstanding Oldco shares (95 percent). Oldco is then merged into Newco.

It is clear that control of Oldco has changed hands. Oldco shareholders who held 950 shares (95 percent) have sold these shares for cash and no longer have any economic interest in Oldco's net assets. But Oldco management, which held the remaining 50 shares (5 percent), continues its economic interest in Oldco's net assets by virtue of owning 50 percent of Newco. In this example, the Oldco managers are the continuing shareholders of Newco. Their residual interest is 5 percent and they, along with the outside investor, control Newco. At issue is Newco's accounting basis in the 5 percent of Oldco's assets contributed by the

---

[7] See J. Gorman, "LBO Accounting: Consensus at Last!" *Journal of Accountancy,* August 1989, pp. 68–78, for a more extensive discussion of the *Consensus Position.*

continuing shareholders. Should it be $1,000; that is, 5 percent of the $20,000 fair value? Or should it be only $120; that is, 5 percent of the $2,400 book value?

According to the *Consensus Position,* only 95 percent of Oldco's net assets have been purchased. Thus, only 95 percent of the $17,600 excess of the fair values over book values has been confirmed through a purchase transaction ($17,600 = $20,000 − $2,400). This 95 percent is recorded. The remaining 5 percent has not been confirmed since there has been no change in ownership of 5 percent of Oldco's net assets. This remaining 5 percent is not recorded. Thus, Newco's accounting basis in Oldco's net assets is as follows:

	95 Percent Purchased	Remaining 5 Percent	Total
Book value	$ 2,280	$120	$ 2,400
$17,600 excess of fair values over book values	16,720	–0–	16,720
	$19,000	$120	$19,120

Journal entries *on the books of Newco* to record the LBO are as follows:

1. To record the $1,000 cash contribution of equity capital by the third-party investor:

    Cash 1,000
      Capital Stock   1,000

2. To record the contribution of 50 shares of Oldco stock by the continuing shareholders. Basis of accounting is 5 percent of Oldco book value:

    Investment in Oldco (5% × $2,400)   120
      Capital Stock   120

3. To record the bank financing:

    Cash 18,000
      Payable to Bank   18,000

4. To record purchase of 950 Oldco shares with available cash of $19,000:

    Investment in Oldco 19,000
      Cash   19,000

5. To record the merger of Oldco into Newco. Assets are valued at Oldco book values plus 95 percent of any excess of fair values over book values:

    Fixed Assets [$2,000 + (95% × ($12,000 − $2,000))] 11,500
    Other Net Assets   400
    Goodwill (95% × $7,600) 7,220
      Investment in Oldco   19,120

In this example, Newco borrowed $18,000 of the cash used to acquire Oldco. It is obvious that this debt is properly included on Newco's balance sheet. However, what if the third-party investor and the Oldco managers borrowed the $18,000, pledging Newco's assets as collateral for the loan? In form, the Newco owners, not Newco itself, have incurred debt. In substance, however, the debt is Newco debt since Newco assets will be the source of cash to service the debt. *Staff Accounting Bulletin No. 73* requires reporting on Newco's balance sheet any debt which is, in substance, Newco debt. It does not matter whether Newco's owners signed notes as individuals or agents of Newco.

The above example illustrates how LBO accounting parallels the parent company theory as it relates to the purchase method of accounting for business combinations. Both involve recording assets and liabilities at book values plus only a portion of any excess of fair values over book values. We again emphasize that determining residual interest and control group membership can, in some transactions, be complicated. The *Consensus Position* should be carefully considered on a case-by-case basis.

COMBINED FINANCIAL STATEMENTS

Combined financial statements report the affairs of two or more entities with a common owner or management as if they were a single entity. One entity does not control the other(s) as in the case of consolidated financial statements. For example, an individual investor may own several businesses and wish to report their affairs as if they were a single entity. If so, combined financial statements would be prepared.

Preparation of combined financial statements is analogous to preparation of consolidated financial statements. Separate company account balances are added together after eliminating any effects of intercompany transactions (e.g., intercompany receivables and payables). However, since there is no parent/subsidiary relationship, a simple combining of accounts results in no double counting of net assets, earnings, or dividends. Therefore, the standard elimination entries for the consolidated statement working paper have no counterparts in the preparation of combined financial statements.

CURRENT FASB AGENDA ISSUES

In 1982, the FASB added to its agenda a major project dealing with consolidations and related matters (initially called the *reporting entity* project). As it has evolved over the past 10 years, the board has organized the project into the following phases:[8]

---

[8] *Discussion Memorandum: Consolidation Policy and Procedures,* (Norwalk, CT: FASB, September 10, 1991), par. 5.

1. Reconsideration of the *Accounting Research Bulletin No. 51* "nonhomogeneity" exception to the presumption that a majority-owned subsidiary would be consolidated. (This phase was completed with the issuance in 1987 of *SFAS No. 94, "Consolidation of All Majority-Owned Subsidiaries."*)

2. Review of consolidation policies and procedures presently incorporated into the authoritative literature and/or applied in practice. (These issues are addressed in the FASB's September 1991 discussion memorandum, *Consolidation Policy and Procedures*.)

3. Determination of appropriate accounting for investments in entities that are not consolidated, including reconsideration of the equity method guidelines incorporated in *APB Opinion No. 18*. An important issue in this phase is accounting for joint ventures.

4. Determination of the conditions and events that warrant a "new basis of accounting" for the assets and liabilities of an entity. (These issues are addressed in the FASB's December 1991 discussion memorandum, *New Basis Accounting*.)

5. Disclosure of disaggregated information. (Current policy is provided in *SFAS No. 14, "Financial Reporting for Segments of a Business Enterprise."*)

6. Application of principles developed for these issues to not-for-profit entities.

Because this project will have an important impact on the accounting for affiliated companies, we briefly review below some of the major issues that have been formulated in the two recent discussion memoranda.

New Basis of Accounting

The crux of the problem in this phase of the consolidations project was addressed earlier in the chapter in the context of various forms of combinations and/or restructurings. When, and by what amount, do we change the accounting basis for assets and liabilities from their previously recorded carrying values? We know that under business combinations accounted for as a purchase, the assets and liabilities of the acquired company are adjusted closer to their fair values (depending upon the percentage interest acquired), but that in a pooling of interests, no new basis is established for the assets and liabilities. And we have seen that in an LBO, the basis for assets and liabilities contributed by continuing shareholders is different from those acquired from outside parties. Or at the formation of a joint venture, the basis of nonmonetary assets contributed by a venturer depends upon the amount of cash contributed by other venturers. Are the principles of existing GAAP consistent across these different types of transactions?

The FASB discussion memorandum, *New Basis Accounting,* identifies the fundamental issue as "What transactions or other events, if any, should result in recognizing a new basis of accounting?"[9] The bulk of the discussion memorandum focuses on conditions and criteria that potentially can provide an answer to this fundamental question. The discussion memorandum also examines several questions that must be addressed when it is decided that a change in basis is appropriate (e.g., should we recognize the full difference between fair and book value, or only a portion?).

At this stage of the deliberations, the FASB has developed four categories of transactions or events that may provide a rationale for adopting a new basis of accounting for assets and liabilities. The classes of transactions are presented in Illustration 5–3.

A very large number of economic transactions are described in this discussion memorandum. Nonetheless, the Board hopes to identify criteria that can be consistently applied across the different categories. A preliminary set of factors that may have a bearing on whether a new basis of accounting should be recognized are included in the discussion. These factors are as follows:[10]

1. Is there a change in voting control?
2. Does the entity participate in the transaction or event?
3. Does a new legal entity result?
4. Have the users of the entity's external financial statements, or the needs of these users, changed?
5. Did the settlement include monetary consideration?

These factors are, of course, not entirely new. For example, we noted above that the existence of monetary consideration is necessary to justify a step-up in basis for nonmonetary assets contributed to a joint venture, and a change in voting control is one of the factors that define a business combination accounted for under purchase accounting. We may expect to see some combination of these factors in the new accounting principles that result from this phase of the project.

Consolidation Policy and Procedures

This discussion memorandum examines different concepts of consolidated financial statements (primarily the entity theory and the parent company theory) and the implications of these concepts for the various consolidation policies and procedures. As we noted in previous chapters, these concepts affect such things as the amount of goodwill to be recognized, the classification of minority interest, and the definition of consolidated net income.

Another important issue in this phase of the project is the relevance of *control* and *ownership* to the decision to consolidate affiliated companies, and the degree

---

[9] *Discussion Memorandum: New Basis Accounting* (Norwalk, CT: FASB, December 18, 1991), par. 19.

[10] Ibid., par. 23.

ILLUSTRATION 5-3   **Four Possible Rationales for Recognizing a New Basis of Accounting**[11]

Categories of Transactions	Examples
1. When an external party or group values the entity in conjunction with the purchase of a majority residual interest in it	• Tender offer by one firm for all or most of another firm's stock • Initial public offering (IPO) of a majority of a firm's stock • Change of ownership of majority of stock without change in voting control
2. When a third-party lender values the entity in conjunction with a borrowing transaction in which the lender puts a substantial amount of debt capital at risk to the entity's performance	• Leveraged recapitalization as a takeover defense • Parent pledges majority of subsidiary stock as collateral
3. When related parties value the entity in conjunction with a capital restructuring or reorganization in which the entity's stockholders exchange one configuration of the entity's assets or rights for another	• Reorganization in bankruptcy • Quasi-reorganization • Unleveraged recapitalization • Spinoff of subsidiary
4. When participants in a corporate joint venture value the entity in conjunction with its formation or the subsequent sale of interests therein	• Formation of 50/50 joint venture without any cash investment • Cash sale of a 50% interest by an investor in a joint venture

and form these variables must assume to justify consolidation. For example, present GAAP generally assumes that a controlling company must hold, or have the ability to acquire, a majority of the common stock of an affiliate in order to consolidate it. But is this necessary? What if a firm holds 40 percent of the common stock and the remainder of the ownership is widely dispersed? When these fundamental issues are resolved, there probably will be a number of changes in specific measurement procedures and presentation practices to implement consistently the underlying concepts.

Summary

In this chapter, we extended the focus of our study beyond business combinations structured as acquisitions to incorporate alternative organizational forms and to review the accounting issues associated with some important types of corporate restructurings.

---

[11] This table was prepared from the specifications of these groups and the associated examples in FASB, *Discussion Memorandum: New Basis Accounting,* par. 18.

In the business combination area, we contrasted purchase and pooling of interests accounting for acquisitions and mergers and observed that for the same accounting method, the financial statements of the surviving company in a merger are equivalent to the consolidated statements for the combination consummated as an acquisition. We also briefly summarized the accounting for a business combination effected as a consolidation and noted the obvious similarities to accounting for a merger.

On the corporate restructurings topic, we reviewed the accounting issues associated with joint ventures and leveraged buyouts, as well as the concept of push-down accounting for subsidiaries reporting separately. This overview identified some basic valuation issues that are analogous to those encountered with business combinations. A primary question that emerges from the variety of circumstances is under what conditions should a new basis of accounting be established for the assets and liabilities of a reporting entity? Since this question is the subject of a current FASB project, we reviewed briefly the approach that the Board is following. We also commented on the basic issues that are the subject of the Board's study of consolidation policy and procedures.

Questions

1. Contrast the purchase and pooling of interests methods of accounting with respect to (*a*) the valuation of net assets, (*b*) the valuation of individual assets and liabilities, and (*c*) the amount of retained earnings reported by the combined company.

2. In the event a business combination results in a parent-subsidiary relationship between the combining companies, what is the amount recorded in the parent's investment account
   a. If the purchase method of accounting is employed?
   b. If the pooling of interests method is employed?

3. Describe the parent's entry to record a pooling of interests when the par value of parent shares issued is not equal to the par value of the subsidiary's outstanding capital stock.

4. How are the assets and liabilities of the combining companies recorded when the combination is structured as a consolidation?

5. Explain the concept of "push-down" accounting.

6. Under what conditions does the SEC require that push-down accounting be implemented in the separate financial statements of a subsidiary?

7. What is a joint venture? Describe the legal forms a joint venture can assume.

8. How are the assets contributed to the joint venture by the venturers valued on the books of the joint venture?

9. How do the venturers account for their interests in the joint venture?

10. What are leveraged buyouts (LBOs)? After the LBO, how are the assets of the surviving company valued?

11. In an LBO, the third-party investors and the former managers often borrow the funds to make the acquisition and pledge the LBO company's assets as collateral. How is this debt reported in the financial statements of the LBO company?

12. What are combined financial statements? How are they like consolidated financial statements?

13. What are the phases of the FASB project dealing with consolidations and related matters?

14. What is the fundamental question in the FASB's study of "new basis accounting"? How is the FASB examining this question?

15. What are the objectives of the FASB's study of "consolidation policy and procedures"?

Exercises

Exercise 5–1   (Pooling of Interests)

On January 1, 19X1, P Company issued 50,000 of its common shares in exchange for all the outstanding common shares of S Company. The P Company shares had a market value of $10 per share and a par value of $2 per share. The transaction met all the requirements for a pooling of interests. Data relating to S Company on the date of its acquisition by P Company follow:

	Book Value	Fair Value
Current assets	$100,000	$120,000
Plant and equipment	500,000	630,000
Other assets	200,000	200,000
Current liabilities	(50,000)	(50,000)
Long-term debt	(400,000)	(450,000)
Capital stock	(200,000)	
Retained earnings	(150,000)	

Required:

Prepare the parent company entry to record the acquisition of the subsidiary on January 1, 19X1. *Also* prepare in journal entry form the elimination entry that would appear on a consolidated statement working paper as of the date of acquisition.

Exercise 5–2   (Pooling of Interests)

Holtz Company and Frantz, Inc., have agreed to combine their businesses in a stock for stock transaction, after which Holtz Company will act as the parent and Frantz, Inc., as the subsidiary. According to the agreement, Holtz issued common stock in exchange for 100 percent of Frantz, Inc.'s outstanding shares. Before the stock exchange, which qualified as a pooling of interests, the stockholders' equity accounts of the two companies were as follows:

	Holtz Company	Frantz, Inc.
Common stock ($100 par)	$ 80,000	$80,000
Other contributed capital		20,000
Retained earnings	100,000	40,000

Required:

Prepare the entry on the books of Holtz Company to record the issuance of stock for each of the following independent situations. Also show the investment elimination entry at date of combination and calculate consolidated retained earnings in each case.

a. Holtz Company issued 1,200 shares.

b. Holtz Company issued 900 shares.

c. Holtz Company issued 500 shares.

Exercise 5–3   (Purchase and Pooling Characteristics)

Effective December 31, Alpha proposes to issue additional shares of its common stock in exchange for all of the assets and liabilities of Bravo and Echo, after which the latter two corporations will distribute the Alpha shares to their shareholders in complete liquidation and dissolution. The plan complies with all of the criteria for a pooling of interests. Balance sheets for each of the three companies immediately prior to the merger are given below. The common stock exchange ratios were each negotiated to be 1:1.

	Alpha	Bravo	Echo
Assets			
Current assets	$ 2,000,000	$ 500,000	$ 25,000
Fixed assets (net)	10,000,000	4,000,000	200,000
Total assets	$12,000,000	$4,500,000	$225,000
Equities			
Current liabilities	$ 1,000,000	$ 300,000	$ 20,000
Long-term debt	3,000,000	1,000,000	105,000
Common stock ($10 par)	3,000,000	1,000,000	50,000
Retained earnings	5,000,000	2,200,000	50,000
Total equities	$12,000,000	$4,500,000	$225,000

Required:

a. Prepare Alpha's journal entries to record the combination of Alpha, Bravo, and Echo.

b. Assume that the combination fails to meet the criteria for a pooling of interests because Bravo and Echo have not been autonomous entities for two years prior to the combination. The identifiable assets and liabilities of Bravo and Echo are all reflected in the balance sheet (above), and their recorded amounts are equal to their current fair market values. Alpha's common stock is traded actively. An appropriate market price per share is $45. Prepare Alpha's journal entries to record the combination.

(AICPA adapted)

Exercise 5–4   (Purchase and Pooling Characteristics)

Items 1 through 6 are based on the following data relating to the acquisition on January 1, 19X1, of 100 percent of the outstanding common shares of Y Company.

Y Company was acquired by issuing 80 parent company shares with a par value of $1 per share and a market value of $10 per share. During 19X1, Y Company earned net income in the amount of $70. Book values and fair values of Y Company's net assets on January 1, 19X1, were as follows:

	Book Value	Fair Value
Cash	$100	$100
Receivables	150	150
Inventory	200	200
Plant and equipment (5-year remaining life)	500	600
Liabilities	(250)	(250)
Capital stock ($10 par)	(100)	
Retained earnings	(600)	

1. Assuming that the acquisition is classified as a purchase, 19X1 equity method income is
   a. $50.
   b. $70.
   c. $40.
   d. None of the above.

2. Assuming that the acquisition is classified as a pooling of interests, 19X1 equity method income is
   a. $50.
   b. $70.
   c. $40.
   d. None of the above.

3. Assuming that the acquisition is classified as a purchase, the parent entry to record the acquisition would increase total contributed capital (Capital Stock and Other Contributed Capital) by
   a. $80.
   b. $800.
   c. $100.
   d. $600.

4. Assuming that the acquisition is classified as a pooling of interests, the parent entry to record the acquisition would increase total contributed capital (Capital Stock and Other Contributed Capital) by
   a. $80.
   b. $800.
   c. $100.
   d. $600.

5. Assuming that the acquisition is classified as a pooling of interests, the parent entry to record the acquisition would increase retained earnings by
   a. $600.
   b. $100.
   c. $72.
   d. There would be no increase in parent retained earnings.

6. Assuming that the acquisition is classified as a purchase, the parent entry to record the acquisition would increase retained earnings by
   a. $600.
   b. $100.
   c. $72.
   d. There would be no increase in retained earnings.

Exercise 5–5   (Purchase and Pooling Characteristics)

For each of the following, select the one best answer that either completes the statement or answers the question.

1. Consider a business combination in which the purchase method would result in a credit differential that would be allocated to depreciable assets. What would be the future income statement effect of structuring the combination to meet the pooling of interests requirements instead of accounting for it as a purchase?
   a. Smaller net incomes.
   b. Larger reported revenues.
   c. Smaller reported expenses.
   d. Larger net incomes.

2. On November 1, 19X1, Wilkins, Inc., issued shares of its voting common stock in exchange for all of the voting common stock of Dow Company in a business combination appropriately accounted for by the pooling of interests method. Both companies have a December 31 year-end. Net income for each company is as follows:

	Wilkins, Inc.	Dow Company
12 months ended December 31, 19X1	$1,300,000	$800,000
2 months ended December 31, 19X1	240,000	170,000

Assuming that the net income of Wilkins, Inc., given above does not include its equity in the earnings of Dow Company, the consolidated net income for the year ended December 31, 19X1, should be
   a. $410,000.
   b. $2,100,000.
   c. $1,470,000.
   d. $1,300,000.

3. On December 31, 19X1, Franklin, Inc., has 2 million shares of authorized $10 par value, voting common stock of which 1,600,000 were issued and outstanding. On December 1, 19X2, Franklin issued 250,000 additional shares of its $10 par value voting common stock in exchange for all 100,000 shares of Burkey Company's outstanding $20 par value voting common stock in a business combination appropriately accounted for by the pooling of interests method. The market value of Franklin, Inc.'s common stock was $30 per share on the date of the business combination. What is the *consolidated common stock* issued and outstanding for Franklin and its subsidiary, Burkey, on December 31, 19X2?
   a. $17,000,000.
   b. $22,500,000.

    c. $18,500,000.

    d. $55,500,000.

4. Buffer Corporation issued voting common stock with a stated value of $90,000 and a market value of $180,000 in exchange for *all* of the outstanding common stock of Plate Company. The combination was properly accounted for as a pooling of interests. The stockholders' equity section of Plate Company on the date of the combination was as follows:

Common stock	$ 70,000
Other contributed capital	7,000
Retained earnings	50,000
	$127,000

What should be the increase in stockholders' equity of Buffer Corporation on the date of acquisition as a result of this business combination?

    a. $37,000.

    b. $90,000.

    c. $180,000.

    d. $127,000.

Exercise 5–6.   (Push-Down Accounting)

P Company purchased 100 percent of the outstanding common shares of S Company for $30,000. Data relating to S Company's net assets as of date of acquisition are as follows:

	Fair Value	*Book Value*
Current assets	$ 2,000	$ 1,000
Marketable equity securities	14,000	10,000
Plant and equipment	24,000	22,000
Intangibles (not including goodwill)	10,000	4,000
Liabilities	(16,000)	(16,000)
	$34,000	$21,000

Required:

a. Compute the consolidated statement valuations of the above assets and liabilities as of date of acquisition.

b. Prepare S Company's separate company balance sheet on a push-down basis.

Exercise 5–7   (Joint Venture)

Beaver, Inc. is general partner in a joint venture organized as a limited partnership. The limited partners are two individuals. The partnership was formed in 19X0. The partnership agreement specifies that revenues and expenses except depreciation expense are to be divided equally among the three partners. Depreciation expense is to be allocated entirely to Beaver. However, all cash distributions, including those made in liquidation, are to be divided equally among the three partners.

The partnership income statement for 19X1 was as follows:

Revenues	$300,000
Depreciation expense	$ 30,000
Other expenses	90,000
Total expenses	$120,000
Net income	$180,000

Beaver's tax rate is 40 percent.

Required:

Prepare all entries on the part of Beaver relating to its partnership investment during 19X1.

Exercise 5–8   (Leveraged Buyout)

The managers of X Company own 1,000 of its 10,000 outstanding common shares. Y Company is formed with an outside investor contributing $2,000 cash and X Company management contributing its 1,000 X Company shares. Y Company then borrows $16,000 from a bank and purchases 9,000 X Company shares for $18,000. X Company is then merged into Y Company. Data relating to X Company immediately prior to the leveraged buyout are as follows:

	Book Value	Fair Value
Current assets	$ 1,000	$ 1,000
Plant and equipment	19,000	29,000
Goodwill		5,000
Liabilities	(12,000)	(15,000)
Stockholders' equity	$ 8,000	$20,000

Required:

Complete the following table of values relating to Y Company's balance sheet immediately following the leveraged buyout:

Current assets	_____
Plant and equipment	_____
Goodwill	_____
Liabilities	_____
Stockholders' equity	_____

Exercise 5–9   (Joint Venture)

JV Corporation is incorporated on July 1, 19X1, by investors A Corporation and B Corporation to produce and market a new measuring device that improves the efficiency of products sold by both A and B. The two investor corporations each receive an equal number of shares of JV's no-par capital stock, and both will participate equally in the management of the joint venture.

Required:

For each of the following independent cases, prepare the entry on the books of JV Corporation to record the contribution of assets and the issuance of shares of stock. Assume the transactions took place on July 1 and that the companies are subject to SEC jurisdiction.

Case 1: Investor A contributes equipment with a fair value of $250,000 and a book value of $110,000, and investor B contributes $250,000 cash.

Case 2: Investor A contributes equipment with a fair value of $250,000 and a book value of $110,000, and investor B contributes patents with a fair value of $250,000 and a book value of $32,000.

Case 3: Investor B sells a 50 percent interest in a patent for $125,000 cash to investor A. The patent has a fair value of $250,000 and a book value of $32,000. Both investors then contribute their interests in the patent to JV Corporation.

Case 4: Investor A contributes equipment with a fair value of $250,000 and a book value of $110,000, and investor B contributes $200,000 cash and land with a fair value of $50,000 and a book value of $14,000.

Problems

Problem 5–10   (Purchase and Pooling Characteristics)

X Company combines with Y Company. X issues 10,000 of its $5 par common stock in exchange for 100 percent of Y Company's outstanding common shares. An appropriate market price of X Company stock is $20 per share. Data relating to Y Company as of the date of combination are as follows:

	Fair Value	Book Value
Assets	$190,000	$120,000
Liabilities	80,000	40,000
Capital stock	120,000	60,000
Retained earnings (credit balance)		20,000

Required:

a. Prepare X's entry to record the investment, assuming the transaction is a purchase/merger with X as the surviving entity.

b. Prepare X's entry to record the investment, assuming the transaction is a pooling/merger with X as the surviving entity.

c. Prepare X's entry to record the investment, assuming the transaction is a pooling/acquisition.

d. Prepare X's entry to record the investment, assuming the transaction is a purchase/acquisition.

Problem 5–11   (Purchase and Pooling Characteristics)

Falcon Company issued additional common shares in exchange for 100 percent of Jones, Inc., outstanding stock. The following information pertains to the two firms on the day immediately before the combination occurred:

	Falcon Company	Jones, Inc.
Common stock outstanding, $100 par	$300,000	
Common stock outstanding, $50 par		$100,000
Other contributed capital		40,000
Retained earnings	100,000	60,000

Falcon Company issued 1,200 additional shares (market value of $250 per share) for Jones, Inc., and the combination was accounted for as a pooling of interests.

Required:

a. What differential would be recognized in preparing consolidated statements?

b. What would be consolidated retained earnings on the date of combination?

c. In general journal form, present the entry on the books of Falcon Company to record the stock issuance.

d. In general journal form, present the working paper elimination entry for a consolidated balance sheet on the date of combination.

e. Assume now that the combination should be classified as a purchase. Under this assumption, present the entry on the books of Falcon Company to record the stock issuance.

f. Assuming the combination is a purchase, present in general journal form the working paper elimination entry for a consolidated balance sheet on the date of combination.

Problem 5–12   (Purchase and Pooling Characteristics)

Companies P and S agree to combine. On the date of combination, the books reflect the following data:

	P	S
Assets	$142,000	$75,000
Liabilities	67,000	12,000
Stockholders' equity:		
Capital stock ($1 par)	25,000	10,000
Other contributed capital	7,000	4,000
Retained earnings	43,000	49,000

S's assets have a fair market value of $95,000, and the fair market value of S's liabilities is equal to the book value.

Required:

1. Assuming that P issues 30,000 shares of its stock (fair market value of $5 per share) for all of the outstanding stock of S, that S continues to exist as a separate corporation, and that the combination is classified as a *pooling of interests:*
   a. Prepare the entry on P's books to record the acquisition of S's stock.
   b. Prepare the working paper eliminating entry or entries that would be made in order to prepare a consolidated balance sheet immediately following the acquisition.

2. Assume now that S is merged into P, rather than continuing to exist as a separate corporation, and that the same combination is classified as a *purchase;* all other conditions are the same. Under these new assumptions, prepare the entry on P's books to record the acquisition of the assets and liabilities of S.

Problem 5–13   (Pooling of Interests)

On January 1, 19X1, P Company acquired all the outstanding common shares of S Company by issuing 5,000 P Company shares. The par value of these shares was $10. The acquisition met all the criteria for pooling of interests accounting. Trial balance data relating to P Company and S Company as of December 31, 19X1, are as follows:

	P Company	S Company
Cash	$ 34,500	$ 8,000
Accounts Receivable	18,000	3,000
Inventory (1/1)	16,000	4,000
Investment in S	75,000	
Other Assets	140,500	62,000
Dividends Declared	10,000	5,000
Purchases	42,000	20,000
Expenses	8,000	3,000
	$344,000	$105,000

Accounts Payable	$ 22,000	$ 5,000
Other Liabilities	6,000	
Capital Stock	150,000	50,000
Retained Earnings (1/1)	50,000	10,000
Sales	96,000	40,000
Equity in S Earnings	20,000	
	$344,000	$105,000
Inventory (12/31)	$ 10,000	$ 7,000

Required:

a. Prepare all of P Company's entries relating to its investment in S Company during 19X1.

b. Prepare a consolidated statement working paper for the year ended December 31, 19X1.

Problem 5–14   (Push-Down Accounting)

On January 1, 19X1, P Company purchased 90 percent of the outstanding common shares of S Company, after which the following balance sheet information was prepared:

	P Company	S Company
Assets		
Cash	$ 10,000	$ 8,000
Accounts receivable	40,000	30,000
Other current assets	60,000	15,000
Investment in S Co.	300,000	
Plant and equipment	200,000	160,000
Other assets	30,000	10,000
	$640,000	$223,000
Equities		
Accounts payable	$ 20,000	$ 10,000
Long-term debt	150,000	50,000
Deferred taxes	10,000	3,000
Capital stock		
P Company	250,000	
S Company		60,000
Retained earnings:		
P Company	210,000	
S Company		100,000
	$640,000	$223,000

In addition, the following data relating to book values, fair values, and tax bases of S Company's assets and liabilities were compiled (all assets and liabilities not included have equal book values, fair values, and tax bases):

	Fair Value	Book Value	Tax Basis
Other current assets	$ 20,000	$ 15,000	$ 15,000
Plant and equipment	200,000	160,000	150,000
Other assets	12,000	10,000	10,000
Long-term debt	(60,000)	(50,000)	(50,000)

S Company's income tax rate is 30 percent.

Required:

Prepare a separate company balance sheet for S Company as of January 1, 19X1, on a push-down basis.

Problem 5–15   (Proportionate Consolidation of Joint Venture)

Boynton Company holds a 55 percent interest in a joint venture organized as an undivided interest. Financial statement data relating to Boynton and the joint venture follow:

	Boynton	Joint Venture
Income statement:		
Sales	$200,000	$ 85,000
Equity in venture earnings	13,750	
	$213,750	$ 85,000
Cost of sales	$100,000	$ 45,000
Operating expenses	50,000	15,000
	$150,000	$ 60,000
Net income	$ 63,750	$ 25,000
Balance sheet:		
Cash	$ 50,000	$ 20,000
Receivables	100,000	40,000
Inventory	75,000	50,000
Investment in venture	38,500	
Other assets	35,000	10,000
	$298,500	$120,000
Accounts payable	$ 50,000	$ 20,000
Other liabilities	80,000	30,000
Capital stock	50,000	
Retained earnings	118,500	
Venturers' equity		70,000
	$298,500	$120,000

Required:

Prepare a consolidated balance sheet and income statement for Boynton and its undivided interest using proportionate consolidation.

Problem 5-16   (Leveraged Buyout)

In the text example of an LBO, 5 percent of Oldco's net assets were valued as if they had not been recently purchased (i.e., their book values were retained). In contrast, 95 percent of Oldco's net assets were valued as newly purchased. Assume that instead of the LBO described in the text, a corporate investor purchased 950 Oldco shares for $19,000 (i.e., 95 percent of Oldco's fair value of $20,000). Continue to assume the $2,400 book value of Oldco's net assets.

Required:

a. At what values will Oldco's net assets appear on the consolidated balance sheet of the corporate investor and its subsidiary Oldco?
b. What will be the value of the minority interest on this consolidated balance sheet?
c. On the basis of your answers to (a) and (b), explain how accounting for an LBO is analogous to accounting for a business combination?

Problem 5-17   (Combined Statements)

Hondo Nelson is the sole stockholder of two corporations: Luckenbach Taverns, Inc., and Luckenbach Long Neck Distributors. Financial statements for these companies follow:

	Statements of Financial Position December 31, 19X1	
	Luckenbach Taverns, Inc.	*Luckenbach Long Neck Distributors*
Assets		
Cash	$ 10,000	$ 25,000
Receivables	35,000	5,000
Inventory	125,000	100,000
Due from Luckenbach Taverns, Inc.		50,000
Long-lived assets	20,000	150,000
Total assets	$190,000	$330,000
Equities		
Current liabilities	$ 20,000	$ 50,000
Long-term debt	100,000	80,000
Stockholders' equity:		
Capital stock	10,000	10,000
Retained earnings	60,000	190,000
Total equities	$190,000	$330,000

| | Income Statements For Year Ended December 31, 19X1 | |
	Luckenbach Taverns, Inc.	*Luckenbach Long Neck Distributors*
Sales	$300,000	$500,000
Cost of sales	$160,000	$200,000
Other expenses	100,000	150,000
Total expenses	$260,000	$350,000
Net income	$ 40,000	$150,000

Mr. Nelson wishes to make an application for a large bank loan in January 19X2, and his accountant suggests that he prepare combined financial statements for his two separate business interests. Mr. Nelson agrees, and the accountant develops the following additional data in the review of the records:

1. During 19X1, Luckenbach Long Neck Distributors made sales of $100,000 to Luckenbach Taverns, Inc. None of these goods remained in the December 31, 19X1, inventory of Luckenbach Taverns, Inc.
2. On December 31, 19X1, Luckenbach Taverns, Inc., owed $50,000 to Luckenbach Long Neck Distributors. This debt was included with a note payable to the bank in "long-term debt." No interest was payable on the debt on December 31, 19X1.

Required:

Prepare a combined statement of financial position on December 31, 19X1, and a combined income statement for 19X1 for Mr. Nelson's two businesses. It is not necessary to prepare a working paper.

Consolidated Statements: An Expanded Analysis

Consolidated Statements— Unconfirmed Profits on Inventory Transfers

---

Chapter Outline

Unit I provides an introduction to business combinations and explains the basic principles of consolidated financial statements. In this unit, we examine a number of issues that complicate the preparation of consolidated statements. The first issue examined is the effect of unrealized profits on intercompany transfers of assets. This chapter covers unrealized profits resulting from the sale of merchandise between affiliated companies. Chapter 7 deals with unrealized profits arising from intercompany sales of assets other than inventory.

OVERVIEW OF THE MERCHANDISE TRANSFER PROBLEM

Consolidated financial statements are summaries of the assets, liabilities, revenues, and expenses of affiliates, *calculated on the basis of transactions with nonaffiliates.* From the *economic (or consolidated) entity's perspective,* intercompany sales of merchandise are not transactions with nonaffiliates. They are *intraentity* transactions that should be excluded from the consolidated statements. Nevertheless, the separate financial statements of the affiliates, which are the source data for preparing consolidated statements, contain the effects of intercompany sales. Thus, these effects must be eliminated in preparing consolidated statements.

Two types of eliminations are employed. The first elimination, which was introduced in Chapter 2, removes the total intercompany sales and the total intercompany purchases from the income statement section of the consolidated statement working paper. Only transactions with nonaffiliates are reflected in the Sales and Cost of Sales accounts in the consolidated income statement. This elimination is made any time there are intercompany sales. It does not matter whether the inventory has been resold to nonaffiliates or is still in the possession of the purchasing affiliate.

The second set of eliminations removes intercompany profits produced by intercompany sales *when the inventory has not been resold to nonaffiliates.* More specifically, the *unconfirmed* portions of these profits are *deferred* to a future period.[1] These portions are eliminated (and deferred) because they are *unrealized from a consolidated viewpoint,* even though they are realized from the perspective of the selling affiliate. Intercompany profits are unconfirmed until the related goods are resold (in original or modified form) to nonaffiliates. Unconfirmed profits are realized, and become confirmed, in the period the goods are resold to nonaffiliates. The essentials of this issue are clarified in the following example. Assume that S Company, a 90 percent owned subsidiary, sells goods with a $1,000 gross profit to P Company, its parent company. Since the revenue realization test is satisfied for S Company, as a separate legal entity, the $1,000 profit is recognized in its financial statements. However, this test is not satisfied from the consolidated viewpoint until the goods are resold to nonaffiliates. Thus, until the

---

[1] Note that the term *deferred profit* is probably too general to use in referring specifically to unconfirmed profits, since many types of profits other than unconfirmed profits also are characterized correctly as deferred profits.

goods are resold to nonaffiliates, the $1,000 intercompany (gross) profit is an unconfirmed profit. When the goods are resold to nonaffiliates, the $1,000 profit is realized, and confirmed, from the consolidated perspective. At this point, the profit is recognized in the consolidated income statement.

Eliminating unconfirmed profits requires the removal of several overstatements. In the period in which unconfirmed profits arise, *the ending inventory of the purchasing affiliate is overstated by an amount equal to the unconfirmed profits*. This overstatement is eliminated from the purchasing affiliate's ending inventory in the balance sheet division of the consolidated statement working paper. At the same time, its cost of sales is increased by the same amount in the income statement division of the working paper. Increasing cost of sales removes (and defers) the unconfirmed profit from consolidated net income. In the following period, *the beginning inventory of the purchasing affiliate is overstated by an amount equal to the unconfirmed profits*. This overstatement is removed from the purchasing affiliate's beginning inventory by reducing cost of sales in the income statement section of the consolidated statement working paper. This reduction recognizes the profit which was confirmed this period in consolidated net income. The series of eliminations just described embodies a fundamental property of consolidated income statements. *In the long run, the total profit reported by the economic entity (before assignment of the minority share) is the sum of the affiliates' net incomes from their own operations, irrespective of the existence of unconfirmed profits*.

Two additional conceptual issues must be resolved. These issues are (1) identifying the amount of unconfirmed profits to be eliminated and (2) determining how the eliminated profits are allocated between the majority shareholder (the parent company) and the minority shareholders.

DETERMINATION OF AMOUNT OF UNCONFIRMED PROFIT TO ELIMINATE

The *basic accounting policy* on the amount of unconfirmed profit to eliminate is established in *Accounting Research Bulletin No. 51,* "Consolidated Financial Statements."

> The amount of intercompany profit or loss to be eliminated . . . is not affected by the existence of a minority interest. The *complete elimination* of the intercompany profit or loss is consistent with the underlying assumption that consolidated statements represent the financial position and operating results of a single business enterprise.[2]

---

[2] Committee on Accounting Procedure, *Accounting Research Bulletin No. 51,* "Consolidated Financial Statements" (New York: AICPA, 1959), par. 14 (emphasis added). A possible exception to this basic policy is discussed in the appendix to this chapter. Another exception is introduced in *Accounting Interpretation No. 1 of APB Opinion No. 18,* which is discussed later in the chapter in "Accounting for Unconfirmed Profits for Investor–Investee Affiliations." See also Thomas E. King and Valdean C. Lembke, "Reporting Investor Income under the Equity Method," *Journal of Accountancy,* September 1976, for additional discussion.

Thus, all of the unconfirmed profit is eliminated in preparing consolidated financial statements under *basic policy*.

But what is the *measure* of profit? We believe that the elimination of the selling affiliate's *gross profit* is the appropriate measure. Thus, the first step in dealing with unconfirmed profit on an intercompany sale under uncomplicated conditions is identifying the amount of the gross profit recognized by the selling affiliate. This amount is determined by applying the selling affiliate's *gross profit rate* to the sales price. This rate is superior to the *net profit rate* since the latter implicitly includes operating expenses in inventory. For example, assume that S Company, a 100 percent owned subsidiary, sells merchandise to its parent, P Company, for $500. Also assume a $200 cost for these goods and operating expenses of $150. At the end of the period, P Company's inventory includes its $500 cost. If the profit elimination is based on the gross profit rate of 60 percent (($500 − $200)/$500), $300 (60% × $500) is removed from inventory, and the acquired inventory is stated correctly at $200. Alternatively, if the elimination is based on the net profit rate of 30 percent [($500 − $200 − $150)/$500], only $150 (30% × $500) is removed from inventory. The resulting balance for the acquired inventory is $350. The $150 difference between the two values for this inventory is the $150 in operating expenses that is inventoried under the net profit rate method. Thus, as indicated, we recommend the use of the gross profit rate in eliminating unconfirmed profits. Other issues such as transportation costs on intercompany sales, inventory market adjustments, and interperiod income tax allocation effects can further complicate this measurement. In the presence of these factors, the gross profit rate becomes the starting point in identifying the amount of unconfirmed profit to eliminate. These measurement issues are discussed later in this chapter.[3]

The gross profit rate may be based on either sales or cost. For example, with a cost of $100 and a selling price of $125, the $25 gross profit may be expressed either as a markup of 25 percent on cost ($25/$100) or 20 percent on selling price ($25/$125). Thus, in deriving the unconfirmed gross profit based on the transfer price of the merchandise acquired from an affiliate and the gross profit rate, the form of the calculation differs depending on whether the rate is based on cost or selling price. For example, if a company has $6,000 of inventory purchased in an intercompany transaction and the gross profit rate of the selling affiliate is

---

[3] A complication that arises in eliminating unconfirmed profits that is important to mention now is the use of LIFO. *Practice Bulletin No. 2,* "Elimination of Profits Resulting from Intercompany Transfers of LIFO Inventories" (New York: AICPA, 1987), deals with intercompany transfers of inventories between or from LIFO pools resulting in LIFO inventory liquidations. Such transfers affect the amount of intercompany profit to be eliminated. The bulletin (par. 04) recommends the adoption of an approach to eliminating such profits "that, if consistently applied, defers reporting intercompany profits from transfers within a reporting entity until such profits are realized by the reporting entity through dispositions outside the consolidated group." The procedure suggested in this bulletin is entirely consistent with the procedures we discuss in this and subsequent chapters. Thus, except for this discussion, we do not refer to the specific methods used by affiliates in accounting for their inventories.

50 percent *based on selling price,* the intercompany profit in the inventory is $3,000 (50% × $6,000). On the other hand, if the 50 percent rate is *based on cost,* we calculate the gross profit as follows:

$$150\% \times \text{Cost} = \$6,000$$
$$\text{Cost} = \$6,000/1.5$$
$$= \$4,000$$

$$\text{Gross profit} = \text{Selling price} - \text{Cost}$$
$$= \$6,000 - \$4,000$$
$$= \$2,000$$

Clearly, it is easier to calculate the unconfirmed profit when the gross profit rate is based on selling price.

ALLOCATION OF UNCONFIRMED PROFIT

Having established the amount of unconfirmed profit to eliminate under GAAP, we consider the allocation of this profit between the majority shareholder (the parent company) and the minority shareholders. When consolidation policy was set by *Accounting Research Bulletin 51,* the usual practice was to eliminate unconfirmed profits wholly against the majority shareholder's interest either because of the nonexistence, or the immateriality, of the minority interest (see below). However, this bulletin also states that unconfirmed profit "*may* be allocated proportionately between the majority and minority interests." Thus, two alternatives permitted by GAAP for allocating unconfirmed profit are the following:

1. Pro rata allocation—the eliminated profit is proportionally allocated between majority and minority shareholders.
2. 100 percent allocation—the eliminated profit is wholly allocated to the majority shareholder (the parent company).

Effect of Alternatives on Consolidated Net Income

In considering the allocation of unconfirmed profit and its effect on consolidated net income, we begin by identifying the circumstances in which the alternatives produce the same effects on the majority and minority shareholders. If the parent company is the selling affiliate, the sale is a *downstream sale,* and the unconfirmed profit naturally is wholly allocated to the majority shareholder, or parent, since the minority shareholders have no interest in this profit. On the other hand, if the subsidiary is the selling affiliate, the sale is an *upstream sale,* and the minority shareholders have an interest in the unconfirmed profit. In this case, the eliminated unconfirmed profit may be allocated to the majority and minority shareholders using 100 percent or pro rata allocation. Under 100 percent allocation, the unconfirmed profit from an upstream sale is wholly allocated to the majority shareholder, irrespective of the minority interest percent. Similarly, if the sale is upstream and the subsidiary is 100 percent owned, the unconfirmed profit naturally is wholly allocated to the majority shareholder under pro rata allocation since there is no minority interest. In each of these cases, the effects of eliminating the unconfirmed profit on the majority and minority shareholders are the same. Thus, the only case in which 100 percent and pro rata allocation produce differing shareholder effects is that of an upstream sale by a less than 100 percent owned subsidiary. The effects of pro rata and 100 percent allocation on majority and minority shareholders are shown below for a $3,000 unconfirmed profit.

		Selling Affiliate	
	Parent	*100 Percent Owned Subsidiary*	*80 Percent Owned Subsidiary*
Pro rata allocation			
Allocation to:			
Majority shareholder	$3,000	$3,000	$2,400
Minority shareholders	–0–	–0–*	600
100 percent allocation			
Allocation to:			
Majority shareholder	$3,000	$3,000	$3,000
Minority shareholders	–0–	–0–*	–0–

* There are no minority shareholders in these situations.

When the two alternatives give the same shareholder effects, there is no differential effect on consolidated net income. However, when a less than 100 percent owned subsidiary makes an upstream sale, there will be a difference. For example, assume that S Company, an 80 percent owned subsidiary of P Company, sells merchandise to its parent in 19X1 for $10,000 and records a gross profit of $3,000. Also, assume that the goods are unsold at year-end and that the companies' 19X1 net incomes from their own operations are P Company, $30,000, and S Company, $20,000. Remember, our phrase "net income from own operations" excludes the parent's equity in subsidiary earnings. However, it does *not* exclude the profit recorded by an affiliate on an intercompany sale. Therefore, the $3,000 unconfirmed profit at the end of 19X1 is included in S Company's $20,000 net income. Consolidated net income under the two alternatives is calculated in Illustration 6–1. Note that the $3,000 unconfirmed profit is subtracted under each alternative. These deductions are correct since, as we illustrate in this chapter and in Chapter 7, the full amount of unconfirmed profit always is eliminated (under current GAAP) in the income statement division of the consolidated statement working paper. Remember, eliminating intercompany sales against intercompany purchases ($10,000 in this illustration) does not affect consolidated net income.

ILLUSTRATION 6-1   Calculations of Consolidated Net Income under Alternative Methods of Allocating the Eliminated Unconfirmed Profit between Majority and Minority Shareholders

	Alternative 1 (Eliminated Profit Allocated Pro Rata to Majority and Minority Shareholders)	Alternative 2 (All of Eliminated Profit Allocated to Majority Shareholder)
P Company's net income from own operations	$30,000	$30,000
S Company's net income	20,000	20,000
Sum of affiliates' net incomes from own operations	$50,000	$50,000
Less: Unconfirmed profit in P Company's ending inventory	3,000	3,000
Combined entity income	$47,000	$47,000
Less: Minority interest in S Company's net income:		
Alternative 1		
[20% × ($20,000 − $3,000)]	3,400	
Alternative 2		
(20% × $20,000)		4,000
Consolidated net income	$43,600	$43,000

The $600 difference between the two alternatives is the minority interest in the $3,000 unconfirmed profit (20% × $3,000). Consolidated net income is $600 higher under pro rata allocation because the elimination of the unconfirmed profit reduces the minority interest in S Company's net income by $600. This type of difference reverses automatically in the year in which unconfirmed profits become confirmed. Thus, if the $3,000 profit is confirmed in the next year (which usually is the case), the minority's share of the confirmed profit ($600) is deducted (as part of the minority interest in S Company's 19X2 net income) in arriving at consolidated net income under pro rata allocation. In this case, 19X2 consolidated net income is $600 higher under 100 percent allocation than under pro rata allocation. Although total consolidated net income is the same over the two-year period (as clarified later), the existence of differences in consolidated net income for the individual years leads us to identify the preferable method of allocating eliminated unconfirmed profits.

Evaluation of the Alternatives

When *Accounting Research Bulletin No. 51* was adopted (1959), most consolidated entities had few, if any, minority shareholders. At that time, consolidated statements with large minority interests were even discouraged. The practice was to eliminate unconfirmed profits wholly against the majority interest either because of the nonexistence, or the immateriality, of the minority interest. Providing for unusual situations (i.e., large minority interests) might have been the principal motivation of the Committee on Accounting Procedure in accepting pro rata allocation. Since 1959, however, the character of parent-subsidiary relationships has changed substantially. It is now common to have large minority interests. This change implies that the effects of minority interests cannot be ignored because of immateriality. This implication, along with the representational intent of consolidated financial statements, argues strongly that pro rata allocation is the preferred alternative.

Recall that the intent of consolidated financial statements is to show the economic effects of transactions with nonaffiliates. Thus, from the consolidated viewpoint, the income statement for the year in which an unconfirmed profit arises preferably reflects results of operations *as if the related intercompany sale never occurred*. Following this reasoning, assume that the intercompany sale creating the unconfirmed profit in the previous illustration did not occur. With this assumption, S Company's net income from its own operations is $17,000 ($20,000 − $3,000), and consolidated net income is calculated as follows:

P Company's net income from own operations	$30,000
S Company's net income	17,000
Combined entity income	$47,000
Less: Minority interest in S Company's net income (20% × $17,000)	3,400
Consolidated net income	$43,600

Compare this figure for consolidated net income with the amounts calculated in Illustration 6–1. This comparison shows that the hypothetical no-sale situation gives consolidated net income equal to that produced under pro rata allocation. In contrast, 100 percent allocation results in consolidated net income $600 lower than if the intercompany sale had not occurred. Thus, pro rata allocation is consistent with the intent of consolidated financial statements. It reports results of operations as if intercompany sales are not present. Consequently, we strongly recommend the use of pro rata allocation in allocating eliminated unconfirmed profits among majority and minority shareholders. We also note that this method is frequently used in practice and is strongly supported by the AICPA Accounting Standards Executive Committee in a 1981 Issues Paper entitled "Certain Issues that Affect Accounting for Minority Interest in Consolidated Financial Statements." In future discussions and illustrations, *pro rata allocation is used unless otherwise noted* because of our preference for this method.[4]

---

[4] Another alternative for eliminating unconfirmed profits is fractional elimination. See the appendix for discussion.

Reported and Confirmed Incomes of Affiliates

The residual calculations in the above illustrations suggest that unconfirmed profits must be incorporated into our incremental approach to calculating consolidated net income. Under the incremental approach, and assuming *pro rata allocation of eliminated profits*, consolidated net income for a given period is redefined as follows:

Parent company's confirmed net income from its own operations, plus (minus) its equity in its subsidiary's confirmed net income (loss), and minus (plus) debit (credit) differential amortization.

In this definition, the phrase "confirmed net income" refers to net income that has been *realized through transactions with nonaffiliates*. Thus, this definition emphasizes the importance of the realization of profit before it is included in consolidated net income (and consolidated retained earnings).

The crucial element in the incremental calculation of consolidated net income is determining the affiliates' confirmed incomes. Returning to the case of the $3,000 unconfirmed profit resulting from an upstream sale, S Company's confirmed net income for 19X1 is calculated as follows:

S Company's 19X1 net income	$20,000
Less: Unconfirmed profit included in S Company's 19X1 net income	3,000
S Company's 19X1 confirmed net income	$17,000

Note that *all* of the unconfirmed profit is deducted in the period it arises (or is added in the period it is confirmed) in arriving at S Company's confirmed net income. P Company's confirmed net income from its own operations equals its net income from own operations ($30,000) since it did not engage in downstream sales that resulted in unconfirmed profits at the end of 19X1. Given the above values for the affiliates' confirmed incomes for 19X1, consolidated net income is calculated incrementally as follows:

P Company's 19X1 (confirmed) net income from its own operations	$30,000
Plus: P Company's equity in S Company's 19X1 *confirmed* net income	
(80% × $17,000)	13,600
Consolidated net income for 19X1	$43,600

This result equals the amount previously determined using residual calculation under pro rata allocation, but differs from the related 100 percent allocation value (see Illustration 6–1). Thus, the new definition of consolidated net income generally is appropriate only under pro rata allocation.[5] Also, note that the pro rata allocation of unconfirmed profit between majority and minority shareholders is automatically achieved in the incremental calculation of consolidated net income by using the subsidiary's confirmed net income as the basis for calculating the parent's equity in subsidiary earnings.

As mentioned, the total profit reported by the economic entity (*before assignment of the minority share*) is the sum of the affiliates' net incomes from their own operations in the long run, irrespective of the existence of unconfirmed profits. This point is illustrated by showing the equality of the total *confirmed net income* from own operations and total *net income* from own operations of a parent and its subsidiary over a period including both the creation and the realization of an unconfirmed profit. Continuing the preceding example, assume that S Company's 19X2 net income is $15,000 and P Company's 19X2 net income from its own operations is $40,000. Also, assume that the merchandise purchased by P Company from S Company in 19X1 is sold to nonaffiliates in 19X2. Given no additional unconfirmed profits arising in 19X2, total confirmed net income from own operations and total net income from own operations for the period 19X1 to 19X2 are calculated as follows:

	19X1	19X2	Total for 19X1 and 19X2
P Company's net income from own operations	$30,000	$40,000	$ 70,000
Add: S Company's net income	20,000	15,000	35,000
Total net income from own operations	$50,000	$55,000	$105,000
Add (subtract):			
Reported, but unconfirmed, intercompany profit	(3,000)		(3,000)
Confirmed, but unreported, intercompany profit		3,000	3,000
Total *confirmed* net income from own operations	$47,000	$58,000	$105,000

Total confirmed net income from own operations differs from total net income from own operations in each of the two years because the $3,000 unconfirmed profit is recognized by the consolidated entity a year later than by S Company. However, the totals for the two-year period are equal. *Therefore, the net incomes from own operations of the affiliates are the ultimate determinants of long-run consolidated net income.*

---

[5] Consolidated net income differs in the case of an upstream sale by a less than 100 percent owned subsidiary.

Logically, the net incomes from own operations of the affiliates are the ultimate determinants of long-run consolidated net income since the sum of the reported profits of the purchasing and selling affiliates relating to an intercompany sale of merchandise equals the profit realized by the consolidated entity from these goods. For example, in our illustration, S Company sells merchandise to P Company in 19X1 for $10,000 and reports a profit of $3,000. Thus, the related cost of goods sold is $7,000. Assume further that P Company sells the merchandise to nonaffiliates for $15,000 in 19X2. Given its purchase cost of $10,000, P Company reports a profit of $5,000. From the consolidated entity's perspective, the total profit on the goods is as follows:

Selling price to nonaffiliates	$15,000
Cost of merchandise	7,000
Profit to consolidated entity	$ 8,000

The $8,000 profit to the entity is the sum of the reported profits of S Company ($3,000) and P Company ($5,000). Thus, the sum of the reported profits of the affiliates equals the profit realized by the consolidated entity. Since these profits are included in the net incomes from own operations of the affiliates, these income figures are the logical determinants of long-run consolidated net income.

Similarly, the subsidiary's reported net incomes are the ultimate determinants of long-run minority interest expense and the minority shareholders' claims against the net assets of the subsidiary. The sales prices for intercompany sales govern the actual transfers of assets between the affiliates and partially determine the subsidiary's net income figures even though they do not result from arm's length bargaining. For example, note in the above cases that the intercompany sales price of $10,000 determines the transfer of resources from P Company to S Company and partially determines S Company's net income. In turn, S Company's net income and the unconfirmed profit of $3,000 determine its confirmed net income of $17,000 ($20,000 − $3,000). The confirmed net income value is the basis for calculating the $3,400 (20% × $17,000) minority interest expense. Thus, the subsidiary's net incomes are the proper determinants of long-run minority interest in subsidiary net income even if these values are influenced by nonarm's length intercompany sales prices.[6] Similarly, these values are the ultimate determinants of the minority shareholders' claims against the net assets of the subsid-

---

[6] It is possible to argue that intercompany sales prices are reasonable exchange prices. Under this argument, the view that the subsidiary's net incomes are the proper determinants of long-run minority interest in subsidiary net income is strengthened. See Chapter 7, "Transfer Profits before Affiliation," for related discussion.

iary even if they result partially from sales prices influenced significantly by the parent.

As mentioned, the new definition of consolidated net income generally is appropriate only under pro rata allocation. We emphasize this definition because we strongly prefer pro rata allocation. Nevertheless, a similar definition applies to the 100 percent allocation alternative. Under the incremental approach, and assuming *100 percent allocation of eliminated profits,* consolidated net income for a given period is defined as follows:

Parent company's confirmed net income from its own operations, plus (minus) its equity in its subsidiary's net income (loss), minus (plus) debit (credit) differential amortization, and minus (plus) its subsidiary's unconfirmed profit arising (becoming confirmed) during the period.

Applying this definition to our illustrative data for 19X1, we obtain

P Company's 19X1 (confirmed) net income from its own operations	$30,000
Plus: P Company's equity in S Company's 19X1 net income (80% × $20,000)	16,000
Minus: S Company's unconfirmed profit arising during the period	3,000
Consolidated net income for 19X1	$43,000

You can verify that this result equals the amount previously determined using residual calculation under 100 percent allocation (see Illustration 6–1).

EQUITY METHOD ENTRIES FOR UNCONFIRMED PROFITS

We previously observed that the equity method is like a "one-line consolidation." Thus, if profits recognized on intercompany transactions are unconfirmed from a consolidated point of view, they should also be excluded from recognition under the equity method. *APB Opinion 18* confirms this view: "Intercompany profits and losses should be eliminated until realized by the investor or investee as if a subsidiary, corporate joint venture or investee company were consolidated."[7]

When entries are made on the investor's books to record the effects of intercompany profits, the equity method is referred to as the *full* (or *complete*) equity method. When these entries are not recorded, the equity method being implemented is classified as a *modified* (or *partial*) equity method. As in prior

---

[7] *APB Opinion 18,* "The Equity Method of Accounting for Investments in Common Stock" (New York: AICPA, 1971), par. 19.

chapters in dealing with the cost method, the same consolidated statements are prepared regardless of the method of accounting followed by a parent company. This is equally true in the case of the full and modified equity methods. But differences in the parent's accounting method do require minor variations in the eliminating entries. Therefore, to eliminate unnecessary distractions as new topics are introduced, the method we use consistently in our illustrations is the *modified* equity method, which recognizes all events that are "permanent," such as the investor's share of an affiliate's reported income and differential amortization, but ignores events such as intercompany profits which reverse over time. The reasons for this choice are twofold. First, it is not necessary to record unconfirmed profits on the parent's books to reflect the deferral in the consolidated statements. Only corporate joint ventures and 20 to 50 percent owned investee companies are reported separately in the consolidated statements with values determined under the equity method. With *SFAS No. 94,* there are very few unconsolidated subsidiaries, and the limitations in *ARB 51* precluding consolidation of a majority-owned subsidiary are also now applied as limitations on the use of the equity method.[8] Therefore, we illustrate the entries for investee companies later in this chapter. The second reason is clarity of focus. Since the parent company's method of accounting does not affect the consolidated statements, we have attempted to deal with the effects of unconfirmed profits on the consolidation process first and then illustrate the equity method entries in the more relevant context of 20 to 50 percent owned investee companies.

UNCONFIRMED INVENTORY PROFITS IN THE CONSOLIDATED STATEMENT WORKING PAPER

The techniques used in dealing with unconfirmed profits in the consolidated statement working paper are explained using two, 2-year cases. The first case illustrates the techniques for a downstream sale, and the second example explains the procedures for an upstream sale (with a 90 percent majority interest in both). Again, we stress the assumption of *pro rata allocation* unless noted otherwise. Also, we emphasize two critical variables to keep in mind in studying the examples.

1. Whether the sale generating the unconfirmed profit is upstream or downstream.
2. Whether the unconfirmed profit is in the beginning or ending inventory of the purchasing affiliate.

---

[8] *Statement of Financial Accounting Standards No. 94,* "Consolidation of All Majority-owned Subsidiaries" (Norwalk, CT: FASB, par. 15d., 1987).

The first variable is pertinent in determining if there is a minority interest in the unconfirmed profit. If the sale is upstream and there is a minority interest in the unconfirmed profit, pro rata portions of the profit are allocated to the majority and the minority shareholders. The second variable is relevant in determining whether we have a reported profit that must be deferred or a previously deferred profit that must be recognized. In the year of sale, the unconfirmed profit is in the ending inventory of the purchasing affiliate and, consequently, is unconfirmed at year-end. This profit is in the purchasing affiliate's beginning inventory the second year and, therefore, is assumed confirmed in that year.

As indicated, in our first case, the parent is the selling affiliate; in the second case, a 90 percent owned subsidiary is the selling company. The companies' net income from their separate operations are the same in each case. Therefore, consolidated net income *for the two-year period* is the same in both cases. Consolidated net income is, however, different in each of the two years because the unconfirmed profits are allocated wholly to the majority shareholder in the downstream sale case and are allocated pro rata in the upstream sale example. Finally, our cases avoid complexities such as differentials to focus exclusively on the effects of unconfirmed profits.

Case 1. Downstream Sale

Assume that P Company acquires its 90 percent interest in S Company on January 1, 19X1, at a cost of $90,000, when S Company has capital stock of $50,000 and retained earnings of $50,000. There is only one intercompany transaction between the affiliates in 19X1. Near the end of 19X1, P Company sells merchandise to S Company for $8,000, generating a $3,000 intercompany (gross) profit. All of this merchandise is in S Company's 19X1 ending inventory; thus, the unconfirmed profit at the end of 19X1 is $3,000. During 19X2, S Company sells these goods to nonaffiliates and, consequently, the profit on this intercompany transaction is confirmed in 19X2. There are no intercompany transactions in 19X2. The companies' net incomes from their separate operations are as follows.

	19X1	*19X2*
P Company	$30,000	$30,000
S Company	10,000	10,000

Remember, P Company's 19X1 net income from its own operations includes the $3,000 unconfirmed profit but does not include its equity in subsidiary earnings. This $3,000 unconfirmed profit is included in S Company's ending inventory in 19X1 and in its beginning inventory in 19X2.

Working Paper Entries for 19X1.   The working paper elimination entries for 19X1 are as follows:[9]

1. To reverse the parent's equity method entries for the year:

Equity in Subsidiary Earnings (90% × $10,000)	9,000	
Investment in S Company		9,000

2. To account for the minority's share of subsidiary earnings during the year:

Minority Interest Expense (10% × $10,000)	1,000	
Minority Interest		1,000

3. To eliminate investment account against beginning-of-year shareholders' equity accounts of subsidiary:

Capital Stock—S Company	50,000	
Retained Earnings—S Company	50,000	
Investment in S Company		90,000
Minority Interest (10% × $100,000)		10,000

4. To eliminate intercompany sales:

Sales	8,000	
Cost of Sales		8,000

---

[9] The working paper procedures for unconfirmed inventory profits apply with equal force to periodic and perpetual inventory systems. In this context, our procedures assume that the affiliates' Cost of Sales account balances are known (which always would be the case if financial statements of any type are to be prepared). Note also that our procedures can be modified easily to accommodate the display of beginning and ending inventories and purchases, rather than cost of sales, in the three-division consolidated statement working paper.

5. To eliminate unconfirmed profit in ending inventory:

Cost of Sales	3,000	
Inventory		3,000

The consolidated statement working paper for 19X1 is shown in Illustration 6–2. Except for the account balances specifically given, the balances in this and subsequent working papers are arbitrarily chosen.

The circumstances of this illustration are such that the first three eliminations are unchanged from prior chapters. Since the parent is using the *modified equity method,* its share of the subsidiary's reported income (90% × $10,000) is recorded in Equity in Subsidiary Earnings, but no entry is made for the unconfirmed profit of $3,000 at the end of the period. Thus, the elimination of Equity in Subsidiary Earnings continues to be for the amount of the parent's share of the subsidiary's reported income (net of differential amortization when it exists). Of course, in a more general sense, we always eliminate whatever amount the parent has recorded in Equity in Subsidiary Earnings (whether or not it was recorded correctly).

In entry (2), the minority interest expense (10% × $10,000) is based on the subsidiary's *reported income.* The unconfirmed profit has no effect because it arose from a *downstream* sale. When we consider *upstream* sales in the next case, we will see that, *under pro rata elimination of unconfirmed profits,* the calculation of minority interest expense reflects the minority's share of the unconfirmed profit.

Entry (3), the investment elimination entry, remains unchanged. We have chosen a format for our eliminations so that the investment elimination remains unaffected by the existence of unconfirmed profits due to intercompany transactions.

Eliminations (4) and (5) deal with the intercompany transactions, including the unconfirmed profit. Entry (4), which we have seen before, eliminates the full amount of intercompany sales during the period. If all of the merchandise has been resold to nonaffiliates so that there are no unconfirmed profits at the end of the period, this entry completely accounts for the intercompany activity. Note that in Illustration 6–2 we have disaggregated Sales and Inventory to identify the intercompany portion and highlight the effects of the eliminations.[10] Cost of Sales is not disaggregated. The reason for this is that the cost of sales elimination is

---

[10] Once the pattern of these entries is clear, it is unnecessary and inconvenient to include this classificational detail.

ILLUSTRATION 6–2   Downstream Sale—19X1

P COMPANY AND SUBSIDIARY S COMPANY
Consolidated Statement Working Paper
For the Year Ended December 31, 19X1

	P Company	S Company	Eliminations Dr.		Eliminations Cr.		Consolidated
Income Statement							
Sales							
To nonaffiliates	92,000	50,000					142,000
Intercompany	8,000	–0–	(4)	8,000			–0–
Equity in subsidiary income	9,000		(1)	9,000			–0–
	109,000	50,000					142,000
Cost of sales	60,000	35,000	(5)	3,000	(4)	8,000	90,000
Operating expenses	10,000	5,000					15,000
Minority interest expense			(2)	1,000			1,000
	70,000	40,000					106,000
Net income	39,000	10,000		21,000		8,000	36,000
Retained Earnings Statement							
Retained earnings (1/1):							
P Company	–0–						–0–
S Company		50,000	(3)	50,000			–0–
Net income	39,000	10,000		21,000		8,000	36,000
Retained earnings (12/31)	39,000	60,000		71,000		8,000	36,000
Balance Sheet							
Other assets	10,000	100,000					110,000
Inventory							
Acquired from nonaffiliates	30,000	2,000					32,000
Acquired from affiliates	–0–	8,000			(5)	3,000	5,000
Investment in S Company	99,000				(1)	9,000	–0–
					(3)	90,000	
	139,000	110,000					147,000
Capital stock:							
P Company	100,000						100,000
S Company		50,000	(3)	50,000			–0–
Retained earnings	39,000	60,000		71,000		8,000	36,000
Minority interest					(2)	1,000	11,000
					(3)	10,000	
	139,000	110,000		121,000		121,000	147,000

Explanation of eliminations:

(1) To eliminate parent's share of subsidiary earnings.

(2) To account for the minority share of subsidiary earnings.

(3) To eliminate the January 1, 19X1, stockholders' equity balances.

(4) To eliminate intercompany sales.

(5) To eliminate unconfirmed profit in ending inventory.

against the purchasing affiliate's cost of sales when the goods have been resold but against the selling affiliate's cost of sales when the goods are still on hand at the end of the period. Fortunately, entries (4) and (5) can be made against the aggregated cost of sales without worrying about which affiliate's cost of sales is being eliminated.

We diverge briefly from the data of our case to illustrate the effect of eliminating intercompany sales. Assume that P Company sold merchandise costing $120 to its 90 percent owned subsidiary S Company for $160, and in the same period S Company sold the merchandise to nonaffiliates for $190. Ignoring any other transactions, the effect of eliminating intercompany sales is shown below in the income statement section of a consolidated statement working paper:

	P Company	S Company	Eliminations Dr.	Eliminations Cr.	Consolidated
Sales					
To nonaffiliates	–0–	190			190
Intercompany	160	–0–	(1) 160		–0–
Cost of sales	120	160		(1) 160	120
Gross profit	40	30			70
Minority interest expense					
(10% × 30)			(2) 3		3
Net income	40	30	163	160	67

The intercompany sales of $160 are eliminated, leaving sales of $190 to nonaffiliates and the original cost of $120 to P Company. Note that because the original cost of the intercompany transaction is on the books of the selling company, the elimination of cost of sales is against the inflated value on the books of the company making the final sale to nonaffiliates. As we observed earlier in the chapter, the gross profit on a consolidated basis ($70) is the sum of the gross profits recorded by the two affiliates. And it is the recorded profits that provide the basis for the allocation of the total profit between the parent company shareholders and the minority shareholders.

Entry (5) in Illustration 6–2 eliminates the total unconfirmed profit ($3,000) by crediting Inventory, to reduce it to cost, and debiting Cost of Sales. The effect of the $3,000 debit to Cost of Sales is to defer the profit recognized on P Company's books because it has not been confirmed on a consolidated basis.

Returning to our simplified example, we can observe the effect of these entries by now assuming that S Company did not resell the goods to nonaffiliates before the end of the period. The partial working paper for this scenario follows:

	P Company	S Company	Eliminations Dr.	Eliminations Cr.	Consolidated
Sales					
To nonaffiliates	–0–	–0–			–0–
Intercompany	160	–0–	(1) 160		–0–
Cost of sales	120	–0–	(2) 40	(1) 160	–0–
Gross profit	40	–0–			–0–
Minority interest expense					
Net income	40	–0–	200	160	–0–
Inventory					
From nonaffiliates	–0–	–0–			
Intercompany	–0–	160		(2) 40	120

The effects described above for entry (5) are easily observed in this working paper. Note here that the cost of sales elimination is against the parent's accounts because the subsidiary has not yet resold the inventory. Also, consider the *combined effect* of the two eliminations for intercompany transactions:

Sales	160	
Cost of Sales		120
Inventory		40

This single entry can always be substituted for the two entries to eliminate intercompany transactions by debiting Sales for the total amount of intercompany sales for the period, crediting Inventory for the unconfirmed profit at the end of the period, and crediting Cost of Sales for the difference.

Calculations of 19X1 Consolidated Net Income.   Consolidated net income for 19X1 is shown in the consolidated statement working paper as $36,000. Using the incremental approach, it is calculated as follows:

P Company's 19X1 *confirmed* net income from its own operations ($39,000 − $9,000 − $3,000)	$27,000
Plus: P Company's equity in S Company's 19X1 net income (90% × $10,000)	9,000
Consolidated net income for 19X1	$36,000

P Company's confirmed net income from its own operations is determined by subtracting two amounts from its net income under the modified equity method: (1) its equity in subsidiary net income of $9,000 and (2) its unconfirmed profit of $3,000. The first subtraction gives P Company's net income from its own operations, and the second yields its confirmed net income from its own operations. S Company's net income is not adjusted since it contains no unconfirmed profits. We emphasize again that consolidated net income ($39,000) is *not* equal to P Company's net income because we are using the modified equity method.

Consolidated net income also can be calculated using the residual approach. We modify slightly the residual approach illustrated earlier by adding a section that adds or subtracts the effects of the working paper entries on the sum of the *affiliates' net incomes.* By using this procedure, the residual calculation of consolidated net income continues to closely parallel the one found in the consolidated statement working paper.

P Company's 19X1 net income	$39,000	
S Company's 19X1 net income	10,000	
Sum of affiliates' net incomes		$49,000
Plus (minus): Effects of working paper entries on sum of affiliates' net incomes:		
Elimination of equity in subsidiary earnings	($9,000)	
Elimination of unconfirmed profit	(3,000)	
Minority interest expense	(1,000)	(13,000)
Consolidated net income for 19X1		$36,000

Tracing these numbers back to the income statement division of the consolidated statement working paper clarifies the procedure used in the working paper in calculating consolidated net income.

Working Paper Entries for 19X2.   The working paper entries for 19X2 follow:

1. To reverse the parent's equity method entries for the year:

> Equity in Subsidiary Earnings (90% × $10,000)   9,000
>   Investment in S Company   9,000

2. To account for the minority's share of subsidiary earnings during the year:

```
Minority Interest Expense (10% × $10,000)  . . . . . . . . . . . .   1,000
    Minority Interest  . . . . . . . . . . . . . . . . . . . . . . . . . . . . .              1,000
```

3. To eliminate investment account against beginning-of-year shareholders' equity accounts of subsidiary:

```
Capital Stock—S Company  . . . . . . . . . . . . . . . . . . . . . .   50,000
Retained Earnings—S Company  . . . . . . . . . . . . . . . . . .   60,000
    Investment in S Company  . . . . . . . . . . . . . . . . . . . .             99,000
    Minority Interest  . . . . . . . . . . . . . . . . . . . . . . . . . . . .              11,000
```

4. To recognize confirmation of profit in beginning inventory:

```
Retained Earnings, 1/1/X2—P Co. (100% × $3,000)  . . . . . . . .   3,000
    Cost of Sales  . . . . . . . . . . . . . . . . . . . . . . . . . . . . . . .             3,000
```

There were no intercompany sales in 19X2; therefore, no eliminations are required for intercompany sales and purchases and unconfirmed profit at year-end. The consolidated statement working paper for 19X2 is shown in Illustration 6–3.

The first two entries are unchanged from the 19X1 eliminations because the affiliates' incomes are the same.[11] Entry (3) is changed only to reflect the January 1, 19X2, balances of S Company's Retained Earnings and investment accounts. Entry (4) recognizes the confirmation during 19X2 of the unconfirmed profit in the beginning inventory of S Company. The credit of $3,000 to Cost of Sales adds back the profit that was deferred in 19X1. This profit is wholly allocated to the parent company shareholders (by not adjusting the minority interest expense computation) because the intercompany sale was downstream. To understand the reason for the debit to P Company's beginning retained earnings, recall that P Company recognized the profit in 19X1. Therefore, after closing, P Company's retained earnings were $3,000 higher than consolidated retained earnings (see Illustration 6–2), and this overstatement is reflected in P Company's January 1, 19X2, balance in the retained earnings statement section of the 19X2 working paper (see Illustration 6–3). The debit in entry (4) adjusts the account to its proper consolidated basis.

---

[11] If the parent company were using the *full* equity method, which requires recognition of unconfirmed profits, these entries would be different even though the incomes from their separate operations were unchanged.

ILLUSTRATION 6-3   Downstream Sale—19X2

P COMPANY AND SUBSIDIARY S COMPANY
Consolidated Statement Working Paper
For the Year Ended December 31, 19X2

	P Company	S Company	Eliminations Dr.	Eliminations Cr.	Consolidated
Income Statement					
Sales					
To nonaffiliates	100,000	50,000			150,000
Intercompany	–0–	–0–			–0–
Equity in subsidiary income	9,000		(1) 9,000		–0–
	109,000	50,000			150,000
Cost of sales	60,000	35,000		(4) 3,000	92,000
Operating expenses	10,000	5,000			15,000
Minority interest expense			(2) 1,000		1,000
	70,000	40,000			108,000
Net income	39,000	10,000	10,000	3,000	42,000
Retained Earnings Statement					
Retained earnings (1/1):					
P Company	39,000		(4) 3,000		36,000
S Company		60,000	(3) 60,000		–0–
Net income	39,000	10,000	10,000	3,000	42,000
Retained earnings (12/31)	78,000	70,000	73,000	3,000	78,000
Balance Sheet					
Other assets	50,000	105,000			155,000
Inventory					
Acquired from nonaffiliates	20,000	15,000			35,000
Acquired from affiliates	–0–	–0–			–0–
Investment in S Company	108,000			(1) 9,000	–0–
				(3) 99,000	
	178,000	120,000			190,000
Capital stock:					
P Company	100,000				100,000
S Company		50,000	(3) 50,000		–0–
Retained earnings	78,000	70,000	73,000	3,000	78,000
Minority interest				(2) 1,000	12,000
				(3) 11,000	
	178,000	120,000	123,000	123,000	190,000

Explanation of eliminations:

(1) To eliminate parent's share of subsidiary earnings.

(2) To account for the minority share of subsidiary earnings.

(3) To eliminate the January 1, 19X1, stockholders' equity balances.

(4) To recognize confirmation of profit in beginning inventory.

Calculations of 19X2 Consolidated Net Income.   Consolidated net income for 19X2 is determined to be $42,000 in the consolidated statement working paper in Illustration 6–3. This amount can be verified using an incremental calculation as follows:

P Company's 19X2 *confirmed* net income from its own operations	
($39,000 − $9,000 + $3,000)	$33,000
Plus: P Company's equity in S Company's 19X2 (confirmed) net income	
(90% × $10,000)	9,000
Consolidated net income for 19X2	$42,000

P Company's confirmed net income from its own operations is determined via two adjustments to its net income: (1) the balance of equity in subsidiary earnings of $9,000 is subtracted and (2) the $3,000 profit confirmed during the period is added. The subtraction of equity in subsidiary earnings yields P Company's net income from its own operations. The addition of the confirmed profit gives the company's confirmed net income from its own operations. S Company's net income is not adjusted since it neither contains unconfirmed profits nor excludes confirmed profits.

Using the residual approach, consolidated net income is determined as follows:

P Company's 19X2 net income	$39,000	
S Company's 19X2 net income	10,000	
Sum of affiliates' net incomes		$49,000
Plus (minus): Effects of working paper entries on sum of affiliates' net incomes:		
Elimination of equity in subsidiary earnings	($9,000)	
Confirmation of profit	3,000	
Minority interest expense	(1,000)	($7,000)
Consolidated net income for 19X2		$42,000

Again, tracing these values to the income statement section of the consolidated statement working paper aids in understanding the working paper calculation of consolidated net income.

Case 2. Upstream Sale

The Case 1 data are used in this example, *except* that we now assume that S Company, the 90 percent owned subsidiary, is the selling affiliate. The unconfirmed profit at the end of 19X1 is still $3,000, but now this profit is contained in P Company's December 31, 19X1, inventory. An important feature of this example is that the 19X1 and 19X2 consolidated net income figures differ from those of the prior case because the unconfirmed profit is allocated pro rata in this case, but this profit is wholly allocated to the majority shareholder in the first example. Note, however, that the two-year consolidated net income figures are the same in the two cases.

The working paper procedures for this case are similar to those of Case 1. However, some important new issues are introduced.

Working Paper Entries for 19X1.   The working paper entries for 19X1 follow:

1. To reverse the parent's equity method entries for the year:

> Equity in Subsidiary Earnings (90% × $10,000)   9,000
>   Investment in S Company   9,000

2. To account for the minority's share of subsidiary *confirmed* income during the year:

> Minority Interest Expense   700
>   Minority Interest [10% × ($10,000 − $3,000)]   700

3. To eliminate investment account against beginning-of-year shareholders' equity accounts of subsidiary:

> Capital Stock—S Company 50,000
> Retained Earnings—S Company 50,000
>   Investment in S Company   90,000
>   Minority Interest (10% × $100,000)   10,000

4. To eliminate intercompany sales:

> Sales   8,000
>   Cost of Sales   8,000

5. To eliminate unconfirmed profit in ending inventory:

> Cost of Sales   3,000
>   Inventory   3,000

The consolidated statement working paper for 19X1 is shown in Illustration 6-4.

ILLUSTRATION 6-4   **Upstream Sale—19X1**

P COMPANY AND SUBSIDIARY S COMPANY
Consolidated Statement Working Paper
For the Year Ended December 31, 19X1

	P Company	S Company	Eliminations Dr.		Eliminations Cr.		Consoli-dated
Income Statement							
Sales							
To nonaffiliates	100,000	42,000					142,000
Intercompany	–0–	8,000	(4)	8,000			–0–
Equity in subsidiary income	9,000		(1)	9,000			–0–
	109,000	50,000					142,000
Cost of sales	60,000	35,000	(5)	3,000	(4)	8,000	90,000
Operating expenses	10,000	5,000					15,000
Minority interest expense			(2)	700			700
	70,000	40,000					105,700
Net income	39,000	10,000		20,700		8,000	36,300
Retained Earnings Statement							
Retained earnings (1/1):							
P Company	–0–						–0–
S Company		50,000	(3)	50,000			–0–
Net income	39,000	10,000		20,700		8,000	36,300
Retained earnings (12/31)	39,000	60,000		70,700		8,000	36,300
Balance Sheet							
Other assets	10,000	100,000					110,000
Inventory							
Acquired from nonaffiliates	22,000	10,000					32,000
Acquired from affiliates	8,000	–0–			(5)	3,000	5,000
Investment in S Company	99,000				(1)	9,000	–0–
					(3)	90,000	
	139,000	110,000					147,000
Capital stock:							
P Company	100,000						100,000
S Company		50,000	(3)	50,000			–0–
Retained earnings	39,000	60,000		70,700		8,000	36,300
Minority interest					(2)	700	10,700
					(3)	10,000	
	139,000	110,000		120,700		120,700	147,000

Explanation of eliminations:

(1) To eliminate parent's share of subsidiary earnings.

(2) To account for the minority share of *confirmed* subsidiary earnings.

(3) To eliminate the January 1, 19X1, stockholders' equity balances.

(4) To eliminate intercompany sales.

(5) To eliminate unconfirmed profit in ending inventory.

All of the eliminating entries are the same as those for Case 1 except for the recognition of minority interest expense. Since S Company was the selling affiliate on the intercompany transaction and we elected to use pro rata allocation of unconfirmed profits, the $3,000 unconfirmed profit must be allocated between the parent company shareholders and the minority shareholders. This allocation is accomplished in elimination (2) by calculating minority interest expense on S Company's *confirmed* 19X1 income. The minority's share is $300 lower than in the case of the downstream sale. The remaining $2,700 is allocated to the majority shareholders.

Calculations of 19X1 Consolidated Net Income

The working paper in Illustration 6–4 shows consolidated net income of $36,300. This is verified by incremental calculation as follows:

P Company's 19X1 net income from its own operations ($39,000 − $9,000)	$30,000
Plus: P Company's equity in S Company's 19X1 *confirmed* net income	
[90% × ($10,000 − $3,000)]	6,300
Consolidated net income for 19X1	$36,300

With the upstream sale, the unconfirmed profit is included in S Company's reported net income. Therefore, $3,000 is subtracted from S Company's income to calculate its confirmed net income. P Company's confirmed net income is equal to its income from its own operations.

The residual calculation of consolidated net income is as follows:

P Company's 19X1 net income	$39,000	
S Company's 19X1 net income	10,000	
Sum of affiliates' net incomes		$49,000
Plus (minus): Effects of working paper entries on sum of affiliates' net incomes:		
Elimination of equity in subsidiary earnings	($9,000)	
Deferral of unconfirmed profit	(3,000)	
Minority interest expense	(700)	(12,700)
Consolidated net income for 19X1		$36,300

Again, tracing these numbers back to the income statement section of the consolidated statement working paper in Illustration 6–4 enhances understanding of the underlying consolidation principles.

Relationship between Minority Interest and Net Assets of Subsidiary.   In Case 1, minority interest in the consolidated balance sheet is the product of the minority interest percent and the subsidiary's stockholders' equity at year-end. When the subsidiary is the selling affiliate on transactions producing an unconfirmed profit and we have chosen to use pro rata allocation, this relationship is modified. Since the subsidiary's *confirmed* net income is less than its net income in the year in which an unconfirmed profit arises from an upstream sale, its year-end *confirmed* retained earnings (and *confirmed* stockholders' equity) is less than its year-end retained earnings (and stockholders' equity). Thus, when a subsidiary's upstream sale produces a profit that is unconfirmed at year-end, minority interest in the consolidated balance sheet is the product of the minority interest percent and the subsidiary's *confirmed* stockholders' equity. In Case 2, minority interest for the consolidated balance sheet in 19X1 is calculated as follows:

S Company's capital stock (12/31)		$ 50,000
S Company's *confirmed* retained earnings (12/31):		
S Company's retained earnings (12/31)	$60,000	
S Company's unconfirmed profit (12/31)	(3,000)	57,000
S Company *confirmed* stockholders' equity (12/31)		$107,000
Minority interest for consolidated balance sheet (12/31)		
(10% × $107,000)		$ 10,700

Working Paper Entries for 19X2.   The working paper entries for 19X2 follow:

1. To reverse the parent's equity method entries for the year:

Equity in Subsidiary Earnings (90% × $10,000)	9,000	
Investment in S Company		9,000

2. To account for the minority's share of subsidiary *confirmed* earnings during the year:

Minority Interest Expense	1,300	
Minority Interest [10% × ($10,000 + $3,000)]		1,300

3. To eliminate investment account against beginning-of-year shareholders' equity accounts of subsidiary:

Capital Stock—S Company	50,000	
Retained Earnings—S Company	60,000	
Investment in S Company		99,000
Minority Interest (10% × $110,000)		11,000

4. To recognize confirmation of profit in beginning inventory:

Retained Earnings, 1/1/X2—P Company (90% × $3,000)	2,700	
Minority Interest (10% × $3,000)	300	
Cost of Sales		3,000

Since there are no intercompany transactions in 19X2, there are no eliminations for intercompany sales and unconfirmed profits at year-end. The consolidated statement working paper for 19X2 is shown in Illustration 6–5.

The eliminating entries for 19X2 are very similar to those for Case 1 except for the allocation of the unconfirmed profit in entries (2) and (4). With pro rata allocation and an upstream sale, $3,000 confirmed profit is allocated between the minority shareholders and the parent company shareholders by calculating minority interest expense in elimination (2) on S Company's *confirmed* 19X1 income of $13,000. The minority's share is $300 higher, and the majority's share $300 less, than in the case of the downstream sale. In entry (4), the $3,000 credit to Cost of Sales recognizes the deferred profit just as it did in Case 1. However, with an upstream sale in this case, the debit is allocated between the parent company and minority shareholders. On a consolidated basis, P Company's beginning retained earnings is overstated by $2,700 because no entry was made on the parent's books for its share of the 19X1 unconfirmed profit. Similarly, the minority interest at the beginning of the year is established in the investment elimination entry based on the S Company book values. Since these recorded values include the unconfirmed profit in 19X1, the minority's share of the unconfirmed profit at the beginning of the year is debited to Minority Interest. Recall that the minority is credited for its share of the confirmed profit in 19X2 in the calculation of minority interest expense, so that the year-end minority interest is equal to 10 percent of S Company's net assets.

Calculations of 19X2 Consolidated Net Income.   The working paper in Illustration 6–5 shows consolidated net income of $41,700. This is verified by incremental calculation as follows:

P Company's 19X2 net income from its own operations ($39,000 − $9,000)	$30,000
Plus: P Company's equity in S Company's 19X2 *confirmed* net income	
[90% × ($10,000 + $3,000)]	11,700
Consolidated net income for 19X2	$41,700

The $3,000 unconfirmed profit in S Company's 19X1 reported net income was deferred because it had not been realized on a consolidated basis. Therefore, $3,000 is added to S Company's 19X2 reported net income to calculate its 19X2 confirmed net income. Again, in this upstream case, P Company's confirmed net income is equal to its income from its own operations.

ILLUSTRATION 6-5   Upstream Sale—19X2

P COMPANY AND SUBSIDIARY S COMPANY
Consolidated Statement Working Paper
For the Year Ended December 31, 19X2

	P Company	S Company	Eliminations Dr.		Eliminations Cr.		Consolidated
Income Statement							
Sales							
To nonaffiliates	100,000	50,000					150,000
Intercompany	–0–	–0–					–0–
Equity in subsidiary income	9,000		(1)	9,000			–0–
	109,000	50,000					150,000
Cost of sales	60,000	35,000			(4)	3,000	92,000
Operating expenses	10,000	5,000					15,000
Minority interest expense			(2)	1,300			1,300
	70,000	40,000					108,300
Net income	39,000	10,000		10,300		3,000	41,700
Retained Earnings Statement							
Retained earnings (1/1):							
P Company	39,000		(4)	2,700			36,300
S Company		60,000	(3)	60,000			–0–
Net income	39,000	10,000		10,300		3,000	41,700
Retained earnings (12/31)	78,000	70,000		73,000		3,000	78,000
Balance Sheet							
Other assets	50,000	105,000					155,000
Inventory							
Acquired from nonaffiliates	20,000	15,000					35,000
Acquired from affiliates	–0–	–0–					–0–
Investment in S Company	108,000				(1)	9,000	–0–
					(3)	99,000	
	178,000	120,000					190,000
Capital stock:							
P Company	100,000						100,000
S Company		50,000	(3)	50,000			–0–
Retained earnings	78,000	70,000		73,000		3,000	78,000
Minority interest			(4)	300	(2)	1,300	12,000
					(3)	11,000	
	178,000	120,000		123,300		123,300	190,000

Explanation of eliminations:

(1) To eliminate parent's share of subsidiary earnings.

(2) To account for the minority share of *confirmed* subsidiary earnings.

(3) To eliminate the January 1, 19X1, stockholders' equity balances.

(4) To recognize confirmation of profit in beginning inventory.

The residual calculation of consolidated net income is as follows:

P Company's 19X2 net income	$39,000	
S Company's 19X2 net income	10,000	
Sum of affiliates' net incomes		$49,000
Plus (minus): Effects of working paper entries on sum of affiliates' net incomes:		
Elimination of equity in subsidiary earnings	($9,000)	
Recognition of confirmed profit	3,000	
Minority interest expense	(1,300)	(7,300)
Consolidated net income for 19X2		$41,700

Summary of Consolidated Net Income for Both Cases

The working papers for the two cases show the following values for consolidated net income:

	19X1	*19X2*	*Total*
Downstream sale (Case 1)	$36,000	$42,000	$78,000
Upstream sale (Case 2)	36,300	41,700	78,000

The differences in the individual years arise because 100 percent of the unconfirmed profit is allocated to the parent company in Case 1, but only 90 percent of this profit is allocated in Case 2. Since unconfirmed profits are merely moved from one year to another without changing total reported income for the two-year period, the difference in 19X1 reverses automatically in 19X2, the year in which unconfirmed profit becomes confirmed. Thus, the two-year totals for consolidated net income are equal. They are the same as the consolidated net income figure that is produced if the accounting period is extended to cover two years. In this longer period, there are no unconfirmed profits because the goods from the intercompany sale are resold to nonaffiliates during the period. Assuming a two-year accounting period, consolidated net income is calculated incrementally as follows:

P Company's 19X1 to 19X2 net income from its own operations ($30,000 + $30,000)	$60,000
Plus: P Company's equity in S Company's 19X1 to 19X2 net income [90% × ($10,000 + $10,000)]	18,000
Consolidated net income for 19X1 to 19X2	$78,000

Effect of 100 Percent Allocation

If 100 percent allocation were used in Case 2 (the *upstream* sale example), all of the unconfirmed profit is allocated to the majority shareholder. Under these conditions, the working paper entries and the calculations (with minor changes in terminology for the incremental calculation) are the same as those illustrated in Case 1, the *downstream* sale example. Calculations of consolidated net income for 19X1 for Case 2 are shown below, assuming 100 percent allocation. The incremental calculation follows:

P Company's 19X1 net income from its own operations, less 100 percent of S Company's unconfirmed profit ($39,000 − $9,000 − $3,000)	$27,000
Plus: P Company's equity in S Company's 19X1 net income (90% × $10,000)	9,000
Consolidated net income for 19X1	$36,000

P Company's confirmed net income from its own operations is determined by subtracting only its equity in subsidiary net income of $9,000 since its sales produced no unconfirmed profits in 19X1. S Company's unconfirmed profit of $3,000 is subtracted from P Company's confirmed net income from its own operations since 100 percent allocation is assumed. S Company's net income is not adjusted under 100 percent allocation even though the sale producing the unconfirmed profit is upstream.

Consolidated net income is calculated residually as follows:

P Company's 19X1 net income	$39,000	
S Company's 19X1 net income	10,000	
Sum of affiliates' net incomes		$49,000
Plus (minus): Effects of working paper entries on sum of affiliates' net incomes:		
Elimination of equity in subsidiary earnings	($9,000)	
Elimination of unconfirmed profit	(3,000)	
Minority interest expense	(1,000)	(13,000)
Consolidated net income for 19X1		$36,000

Unconfirmed Profit in Both Beginning and Ending Inventories

Our cases isolate the treatment of unconfirmed profits in either beginning or ending inventory. The working paper entry for unconfirmed profit in beginning inventory recognizes its confirmation during the year, and the entry for unconfirmed profit in ending inventory defers unconfirmed profit arising during the year to a subsequent year. It is possible for unconfirmed profits to appear in both beginning and ending inventories in a given year. Assuming that unconfirmed profits of $3,000 appear in both the beginning and ending inventories in 19X1, the 19X1 working paper entries for the unconfirmed profits in Cases 1 and 2 are as follows:

	Case 1— Downstream Sale		Case 2— Upstream Sale	
1. To confirm profit in the *beginning* inventory:				
Retained Earnings, 1/1/X1—P Company	3,000		2,700	
Minority Interest			300	
Cost of Sales		3,000		3,000
2. To eliminate profit in the *ending* inventory:				
Cost of Sales	3,000		3,000	
Inventory		3,000		3,000

When unconfirmed profits appear in both beginning and ending inventories, the calculations of consolidated net income and minority interest illustrated above are easy to modify. The main point to keep in mind is that the *confirmed* income for the selling affiliate (either parent or subsidiary, or both) is calculated by adding the unconfirmed profits becoming confirmed during the year and subtracting the unconfirmed profits arising during the year.

Effect of Parent Carrying Investment Account on Cost or Full Equity Method

The parent company may account for its investment in its subsidiaries with a method other than the *modified equity method* that we used in our illustrations. If so, some modifications in the eliminations for unconfirmed profits *may* be required.

If the parent uses the *cost method,* no changes in the eliminations for unconfirmed profits are required. Of course, the investment elimination entry would have to be modified in the normal way for the cost method.

If the parent chooses the *full equity method,* the effects of unconfirmed profits are booked. For upstream sales, the initial deferral is recorded by debiting Equity in Subsidiary Earnings and crediting Investment in Subsidiary for the parent's share of the unconfirmed profit. For downstream sales, several alternative methods of recording the deferral are available, including the same entry as for upstream sales. Assuming that this latter choice is made for all unconfirmed profits, the working paper entry to recognize the confirmation of the deferred profit in the second year is modified to debit the parent's investment account rather than the parent's beginning retained earnings account. The reason for this change is that because the parent has booked the deferral of the unconfirmed profit, the parent's beginning retained earnings is equal to consolidated retained earnings. But recording the unconfirmed profit by crediting the investment account changes the normal relationship between the investment account balance and the subsidiary's stockholders' equity at the beginning of the year. The debit to the investment account in the working paper entry restores the usual proportional relationship. Other than this one change in the working paper entry to recognize the confirmation of intercompany profits, no other changes in the working paper entries for unconfirmed profits are required.

COMPLICATING FACTORS IN THE ELIMINATION OF UNCONFIRMED PROFITS

The selling affiliate's gross profit rate is recommended in eliminating unconfirmed profits. When complicating factors are present, this rate is the starting point in identifying the amount of unconfirmed profit to eliminate. Three factors that complicate the elimination of unconfirmed profits are discussed below.

Transportation Costs on Intercompany Sales

The transportation costs on intercompany sales of merchandise are valid inventory costs to the consolidated entity. If these costs are paid by the purchasing affiliate and are included in its inventory value, no special adjustment is needed. However, if the selling affiliate pays the transportation costs, or if the purchasing affiliate has not capitalized them, the amount of the seller's unconfirmed profit is reduced by these costs in determining the adjusted amount of unconfirmed profit to eliminate.

For example, assume that P Company sells merchandise to its subsidiary, S Company, for $1,000. Also, assume that P Company pays transportation costs of $100 to ship the goods to S Company and records these costs as selling expense. P Company's gross profit rate (on selling price) on this merchandise is 40 percent. By assuming P's profit is unconfirmed at year-end, the adjusted unconfirmed profit is calculated as follows:

Unconfirmed profit recorded by P Company (40% × $1,000)	$ 400
Cost of the merchandise to P Company ($1,000 − $400)	600
Cost of the merchandise recorded by S Company (invoice price)	1,000
Inventoriable cost to the economic entity ($600 + $100)	700
Amount of adjusted unconfirmed profit ($400 − $100)	300

Eliminating the adjusted unconfirmed profit of $300 against the $1,000 inventory cost recorded by S Company gives a $700 value for the inventory in the consolidated statements. This procedure capitalizes the transportation costs recorded by P Company as selling expense.

Inventory Market Adjustments

The purchasing affiliate may have applied the lower-of-cost-or-market rule to intercompany merchandise in its ending inventory. If this affiliate's market adjustment is less than the selling affiliate's unconfirmed profit, it is used in determining the adjusted amount of unconfirmed profit to eliminate. Alternatively, if the adjustment is greater than, or equal to, this profit, no elimination of unconfirmed profit is required.

For example, assume that P Company sells merchandise that cost $200 to its subsidiary, S Company, for $300. S Company pays transportation costs of $10 and records the merchandise at $310. At the end of the period, S Company applies the lower-of-cost-or-market rule to reduce the value of this inventory to $280—a $30 reduction. Under these conditions, the adjusted unconfirmed profit is $70 ($100 − $30). Eliminating $70 from the inventory figure of $280 gives a $210 value for the merchandise in the consolidated statements. This amount is correct since the cost of the inventory to the consolidated entity is P Company's cost of $200, plus S Company's transportation costs of $10.

Income Tax Effects

If a consolidated income tax return is filed by the affiliates and unconfirmed profits exist, the consolidated statements do not require interperiod income tax allocation because the unconfirmed profits are not taxed. However, if the affiliates file separate income tax returns and unconfirmed profits exist, temporary timing differences are produced. Under these conditions, interperiod income tax allocation is applied.

For example, assume that P Company sells merchandise to its subsidiary, S Company and that a $1,000 unconfirmed profit results. The federal income tax rate is 40 percent. If the companies file separate tax returns, the $1,000 profit is taxed to P Company in the current period. However, this profit is deferred until the goods are resold to nonaffiliates for consolidated statement purposes, and a temporary timing difference is created. Thus, under the principles of interperiod income tax allocation, the related income taxes of $400 (40% × $1,000) also are deferred to this later period. These procedures, in effect, eliminate the unconfirmed profit net of tax in the current period. In the later period, the $1,000 profit is confirmed from the consolidated statement perspective. Since the timing difference has reversed, this profit and the related taxes of $400 are matched in the consolidated income statement under interperiod income tax allocation. An explanation of the procedures for interperiod income tax allocation in the presence of unconfirmed profits is included in Chapter 7.

ACCOUNTING FOR UNCONFIRMED PROFITS FOR INVESTOR-INVESTEE AFFILIATIONS

We observed earlier that there are various ways to deal wtih unconfirmed profits when accounting for a subsidiary under the equity method. Since the parent's accounting method does not affect the consolidated statements, we elected to use the *modified equity method* to provide the sharpest focus on the treatment of unconfirmed profits in the working papers. For investments in affiliates that provide *only significant influence but not control* (usually 20–50 percent ownership interests), the unrealized profits arising from intercompany transactions must be recorded under the *full equity method* since these values will be reflected directly in the financial statements.

Amount of Unconfirmed Profit to Eliminate

The general rule for the amount of the intercompany profit to be eliminated under the full equity method is the investor's share of the full unconfirmed profit (pro rata method). This share is the ownership interest in the investee for upstream sales and 100 percent for downstream sales. However, *Accounting Interpretation No. 1 of APB Opinion No. 18* authorizes, for certain cases, the use of the ownership interest in the investee for *both* upstream and downstream sales. The cases for which this exception for downstream sales is appropriate are not explicitly specified. But GAAP does stipulate that its use is *not* justified under the following circumstances:

> When an investor controls an investee through majority voting interest and enters into a transaction with an investee which is not on an "arm's length" basis, none of the intercompany profit or loss from the transaction should be recognized in income by the investor until it has been realized through transactions with third parties. The same treatment also applies for an investee established with the cooperation of an investor (including an investee established for the financing and operation or leasing of property sold to the investee by the investor) when control is exercised through guarantees of indebtedness, extension of credit and other special arrangements by the investor for the benefit of the investee, or because of ownership by the investor of warrants, convertible securities, etc. issued by the investee.[12]

By putting these exclusions together with certain general principles for revenue realization, the use of the ownership interest to eliminate intercompany profit for both upstream and downstream sales seems to be appropriate if the following apply:

1. The investor does not control, directly or indirectly, the investee company.

---

[12] *Accounting Interpretation No. 1 of APB Opinion 18.*

2. The exchange price in the transaction generating the intercompany profit is verifiable.
3. The realization of the exchange price is reasonably assured.
4. There is an effective sharing of the risk of ownership among investors in the investee company (e.g., capital contributions by the various owners are sufficient to absorb their shares of possible losses).

An Upstream Example

Assume that Vanguard Company acquires a 30 percent ownership interest in Leno Controls on January 1, 19X1, for $340,000 when the book and fair values of Leno's net assets are $1,000,000. The differential of $40,000 is assigned to goodwill and is amortized over 40 years. During 19X1, Leno reports net income of $200,000. Also during 19X1, Leno records a profit of $15,000 on a sale of merchandise to Vanguard that remains in Vanguard's December 31, 19X1, inventory. Vanguard's entries under the *full* equity method are as follows:

---

1. To record Vanguard's equity in Leno's reported 19X1 net income:

Investment in Leno	60,000	
Equity in Investee Earnings (30% × $200,000)		60,000

2. To recognize amortization of differential:

Equity in Investee Earnings ($40,000/40)	1,000	
Investment in Leno		1,000

3. To defer Vanguard's share of the $15,000 unconfirmed profit on the upstream sale:

Equity in Investee Earnings (30% × $15,000)	4,500	
Investment in Leno		4,500

19X1 Equity in Investee Earnings = $54,500

The balance in the Equity in Investee Earnings account of $54,500 reflects Vanguard's equity in Leno's 19X1 *confirmed* income [30% × ($200,000 − $15,000)] less the $1,000 differential amortization. When this account is added to Vanguard's income from its own operations, 19X1 net income is completely analogous to a calculation of consolidated net income for a parent/subsidiary relationship.

In 19X2, we assume that the unconfirmed profit is confirmed when Vanguard sells the merchandise to nonaffiliates and that Leno reports net income of $120,000. The entries to record Vanguard's investment in Leno for 19X2 follow:

1. To record Vanguard's equity in Leno's reported 19X2 net income:

Investment in Leno 36,000
    Equity in Investee Earnings (30% × $120,000)   36,000

2. To recognize amortization of differential:

Equity in Investee Earnings ($40,000/40) 1,000
    Investment in Leno   1,000

3. To recognize Vanguard's share of the $15,000 unconfirmed profit that was confirmed during 19X2:

Investment in Leno 4,500
    Equity in Investee Earnings (30% × $15,000)   4,500

19X2 Equity in Investee Earnings = $39,500

The 19X2 entries recognize the confirmation of the intercompany profit by crediting Vanguard's share (30% × $15,000) to its Equity in Investee Earnings. This offsets the deferral in 19X1, and for the two-year period, of the equity in investee earnings of $94,000 is equal to 30 percent of Leno's reported income ($320,000), less two years' differential amortization of $2,000. Again, this exactly mirrors the treatment of unconfirmed profits we have examined in the context of consolidated financial statements.

Accounting Interpretation No. 1 of APB Opinion 18 permits some flexibility in the way the unconfirmed profit is recorded. In particular, since Vanguard's ending inventory includes the $15,000 intercompany profit, an alternative entry for the unconfirmed profit is to reduce inventory by Vanguard's $4,500 share of the profit. If this entry is made in 19X1, Cost of Sales must be debited in 19X2 to reflect the parent's actual profit on its sale of the merchandise to third parties and, as before, Equity in Investee Earnings is credited. This alternative form of the entries for the unconfirmed profit is shown below:

19X1

3A. To defer Vanguard's share of the $15,000 unconfirmed profit on the upstream sale:

Equity in Investee Earnings (30% × $15,000) 4,500
    Inventory   4,500

19X2

3B. To recognize Vanguard's share of the $15,000 unconfirmed profit that was confirmed during 19X2:

Cost of Sales 4,500
     Equity in Investee Earnings (30% × $15,000) 4,500

A Downstream Example

For this example, assume the same facts as the upstream case except that Vanguard is the seller on the intercompany transaction and the $15,000 unconfirmed profit at the end of 19X1 is reflected in Leno's ending inventory. We also assume that the risk of realization of the $15,000 profit is now shared with the other owners of Leno and that *the transaction satisfies all of the conditions for elimination of only the parent's ownership percentage.* Accordingly, $4,500 is again the amount eliminated, resulting in Vanguard realizing a profit in 19X1 of $10,500 on the downstream sale to an affiliate.

The entries for Vanguard's equity "pickup" and the amortization of the differential are the same as for the upstream case. Since the $15,000 intercompany profit is reflected in Vanguard's regular operations, not in its equity in investee earnings, the deferral of the unconfirmed profit in 19X1 is recorded as follows:

3. To defer Vanguard's share of the $15,000 unconfirmed profit on the downstream sale:

Deferred Intercompany Profit 4,500
     Deferred Credit for Intercompany Profit 4,500

The balance of Deferred Intercompany Profit is deducted from gross profit in Vanguard's income statement, and the balance of Deferred Credit for Intercompany Profit is shown as a current liability in its balance sheet. The entry in 19X2 to recognize the confirmation of the intercompany profit follows:

3. To recognize Vanguard's share of the $15,000 unconfirmed profit that was confirmed during 19X2:

Deferred Credit for Intercompany Profit 4,500
     Realized Intercompany Profit 4,500

If Vanguard did not satisfy the conditions for this exception to the general rule for the amount of the unconfirmed profit to be eliminated, entry (3) would be for $15,000 instead of $4,500. Obviously, in some circumstances, the decision to eliminate only the investor company's ownership interest in an unconfirmed intercompany profit on a downstream sale can have a substantial impact on the income reported by the investor company in the year of sale.

Summary

This chapter covered the basic procedures for dealing with unconfirmed profits resulting from intercompany sales of merchandise. Intercompany sales of goods are not transactions with nonaffiliates. Thus, their unrealized effects are not included in the consolidated statements.

Intercompany sales produce two effects that are eliminated in preparing consolidated statements. First, the total intercompany sales and the total intercompany purchases are eliminated since they result from intraentity transactions. Second, the unconfirmed portions of the intercompany profits from the intercompany sales are eliminated because they are unrealized from a consolidated viewpoint. In all cases, 100 percent of the unconfirmed profits are eliminated under current GAAP, and the superior rate for measuring the amount of unconfirmed profit is the selling affiliate's gross profit rate. There are two accepted alternatives for allocating the eliminated profit on upstream sales:

1. Pro rata allocation—the eliminated profit is proportionally allocated between majority and minority shareholders.
2. 100 percent allocation—the eliminated profit is wholly allocated to the majority shareholder (the parent company).

The choice of allocation method affects periodic consolidated net income, although long-run consolidated net income is the same irrespective of the choice. Nevertheless, this choice is important since the amount shown for periodic consolidated net income is a significant issue. For conceptual reasons, we strongly prefer pro rata allocation. Recall, however, that the choice between pro rata allocation and 100 percent allocation is important only in the case of an upstream sale by a less than 100 percent owned subsidiary. Similar results are produced in all other cases either because the sale is downstream or because it is an upstream sale by a 100 percent owned subsidiary.

Intercompany profits are unconfirmed until the related merchandise is resold (in original or modified form) to nonaffiliates. Unconfirmed profits are realized, and become confirmed, in the periods the goods are resold to nonaffiliates. Once realized, they are recognized as confirmed in the consolidated statements. Confirmed profits are recognized using the preferred pro rata allocation procedure or 100 percent allocation, depending on which method is used to eliminate unconfirmed profits. As in the case of the initial deferral, the procedure used is important only if the intercompany sale is an upstream sale by a less than 100 percent owned subsidiary.

Appendix: Fractional Elimination of Unconfirmed Profits

Recall that under current GAAP, *all* of the unconfirmed profit is eliminated using pro rata or 100 percent allocation. As shown, pro rata and 100 percent allocation differ only in the case of upstream sales by less than 100 percent owned subsidiaries. An additional method of measuring the *amount* of the unconfirmed profit to be eliminated is *fractional elimination*.

Under fractional elimination, which is not explicitly authorized under GAAP, only the parent's share of an unconfirmed profit on an *upstream* sale is considered to be unrealized. Accordingly, only the parent's share of unconfirmed profit from an upstream sale is eliminated from inventory under fractional elimination. The argument supporting fractional elimination is that the minority shareholders' portion of a profit arising from an upstream sale is realized in the sense that it represents a legitimate claim against the net assets of the subsidiary by these shareholders and, consequently, should not be eliminated. Additionally, this claim by the minority shareholders is appropriately added to the inventory cost when the consolidated statements are prepared from the point of view of the parent company shareholders (the parent company theory). Fractional elimination is similar to pro rata allocation in the sense that both methods produce the same consolidated net income and consolidated retained earnings values.

To illustrate this approach, assume that P Company's 90 percent owned subsidiary, S Company, sells merchandise costing $5,000 to P Company for $8,000 in 19X1. The unconfirmed gross profit in P Company's ending inventory is $3,000 ($8,000 − $5,000). P Company and S Company report net incomes from their own operations of $30,000 and $10,000, respectively.

As indicated, fractional elimination and pro rata allocation are similar. The most important similarity is that they produce the same consolidated net income and consolidated retained earnings values. Also, as mentioned, the minority interest figures are the same under fractional elimination and 100 percent allocation. The following tabulation contrasts the three methods on consolidated financial statement variables when differences occur. Once the unconfirmed profit becomes confirmed, the financial statement differences disappear.

	Fractional Elimination	Total (100 Percent) Elimination	
		Pro Rata Allocation	100 Percent Allocation
P Company's carrying value for inventory	$ 8,000	$ 8,000	$ 8,000
Less: Amount eliminated	2,700	3,000	3,000
Value of inventory in consolidated balance sheet	$ 5,300	$ 5,000	$ 5,000
Minority interest in S Company's net income	$ 1,000	$ 700	$ 1,000
Consolidated net income (by residual calculation): Sum of affiliates' net incomes from own operations	$40,000	$40,000	$40,000
Less: Unconfirmed profit eliminated from P Company's inventory	2,700	3,000	3,000
Combined entity income	$37,300	$37,000	$37,000
Less: Minority interest in net income	1,000	700	1,000
Consolidated net income	$36,300	$36,300	$36,000

Questions

1. Describe the general treatment of profits recognized on the sale of merchandise between affiliates.
2. Identify the preferred profit rate for use in determining the amount of unconfirmed inventory profit to be eliminated, and explain the reason for this choice.
3. How are transportation costs incurred in transferring goods between affiliates accounted for in determining the amount of unconfirmed profit to eliminate?
4. Assume that two affiliates with intercompany sales of merchandise utilize the "lower-of-cost-or-market" method in pricing their inventories. What is the effect on the unconfirmed profit elimination if year-end market price is lower than selling price?
5. What are the alternatives under *Accounting Research Bulletin No. 51,* "Consolidated Financial Statements," regarding the elimination of unconfirmed profit?
6. Contrast the effects of pro rata allocation and 100 percent allocation on the consolidated financial statements, including the effects on consolidated net income, inventory, and minority interest expense.
7. Why is it important to distinguish between upstream and downstream sales in the analysis of intercompany profits?
8. Explain how unconfirmed inventory profit becomes "confirmed," or "realized" from the point of view of the consolidated, or economic, entity?
9. What is the relationship between a subsidiary's confirmed and reported net incomes in the year of an intercompany sale generating an unconfirmed profit? In a year in which the previously unconfirmed profit is confirmed? Over the total period of time encompassing sale and subsequent confirmation of the intercompany profit?
10. How is consolidated net income redefined under the incremental approach to give effect to the new variable—unconfirmed profit?
11. What is the effect of an unconfirmed profit at the end of an accounting period on the relationship between the total minority interest and the recorded net assets of the subsidiary?
12. Describe the alternatives under GAAP for the amount of unconfirmed profits to be eliminated for investor-investee relationships.

Exercises

Exercise 6–1   (Lower-of-Cost-or-Market Rule)

Item A: X Corporation manufactures at a finished cost of $20 per unit and sells to Y Corporation at $25 per unit. Y Corporation leaves its inventory in the warehouse of X Corporation, withdrawing it only as needed, and pays to

X Corporation storage at the rate of 50 cents per unit per month. The units in the inventory of Y Corporation at December 31 had been purchased six months previously. Y Corporation resells at $40 FOB shipping point, which is the same price at which X Corporation sells to others.

Item B: X Corporation owns and operates a mine from which item B is extracted. The average cost of mining item B is $5 per ton. The cost of the mine and development thereof is subject to depletion at the rate of $2.50 per ton. The cost of loading on freight cars averages $1 per ton. Y Corporation purchases from X Corporation at cost, FOB the mine, and transports the product to its plant, paying freight of $1.50 per ton. X Corporation sells approximately 75 percent of its mined product to others at a price of $15 per ton, FOB the mine, and Y Corporation sells at a substantial profit after refinement.

Item C: X Corporation buys manufacturing supplies at a price of $50 per unit, less trade discounts of 10/10/20. A portion of the supplies purchased by X Corporation is resold to Y Corporation at a price of $41 FOB Y Corporation's plant. The freight, paid by X Corporation, amounts to 50 cents per unit. Y Corporation does not have access to the market from which X Corporation buys.

Item D: X Corporation manufactures this item at an average cost of $29 per unit and sells its total output to Y Corporation at $35 per unit, FOB X Corporation's plant under terms of a firm contract. The freight amounts to $2 per unit. The amount obtainable from X Corporation is only about 50 percent of the quantity required by Y Corporation. The balance of Y Corporation's requirements are obtained from other sources at a price of $32.50 per unit, FOB Y's plant. Y resells this item at a price that yields $34 per unit after allowing for sales and handling expense.

Item E: X Corporation manufactures at a cost of $6 per unit and sells to Y Corporation and others at $5 per unit, FOB X Corporation's plant. The freight to Y's plant amounts to 75 cents per unit. Y Corporation processes this item and sells it at a profit.

Required:

Assume that there are 10 units of each of the five items in the inventory of each corporation at the end of the concurrent fiscal years. For each item, determine the appropriate lower-of-cost-or-market inventory valuation:

a. In the separate financial statements of X Corporation and Y Corporation.

b. In the consolidated financial statements, assuming Y Corporation is a 90 percent owned subsidiary of X Corporation.

Provide a brief explanation for your answers.

Exercise 6–2   (Alternative Investor Entries for Deferring Unconfirmed Profits)

Wilson Company has a 35 percent interest in Forsythe Company and uses the full equity method to account for its investment. During 19X1, Forsythe Company reports net income of $20,000. Annual differential amortization is $1,200. Additionally, at the end of the year, there is a $15,000 unconfirmed profit on purchases from the affiliate.

Required:

a. Assuming that the intercompany transaction was an upstream sale, prepare Wilson Company's entries at the end of 19X1 to record its equity in Forsythe Company's net income and to defer the unconfirmed profit.

b. Assuming that the intercompany transaction was a downstream sale and Wilson satisfied the conditions for pro rata elimination, prepare Wilson Company's entries at the end of 19X1 to record its equity in Forsythe Company's net income and to defer the unconfirmed profit.

c. Assuming that Wilson Company had income from its own operations of $60,000 (including the transaction with Forsythe in the downstream case but excluding equity in investee earnings), calculate Wilson's 19X1 net income for both (*a*) and (*b*).

Exercise 6–3   (Eliminations and Minority Interest Expense—Pro Rata Allocation)

P Company has an 80 percent interest in S Company. During 19X1, S Company reports net income of $40,000, and there is an unconfirmed inventory profit of $5,000 at the end of the year. P Company accounts for its investment in S Company using the modified equity method and eliminates unconfirmed profits using pro rata allocation.

Required:

a. Assuming that S Company is the seller on the transaction producing the unconfirmed profit:
(1) Prepare the eliminating entry for the consolidated statement working paper at December 31, 19X1, for the unconfirmed profit.
(2) Calculate 19X1 minority interest expense.

b. Assuming that P Company is the seller on the transaction producing the unconfirmed profit:
(1) Prepare the eliminating entry for the consolidated statement working paper at December 31, 19X1, for the unconfirmed profit.
(2) Calculate 19X1 minority interest expense.

Exercise 6–4   (Incremental and Residual Calculations—Pro Rata Allocation)

Kersbergen owns 80 percent of Algoe Ltd.'s common stock. Algoe sells merchandise to Kersbergen with a markup of 50 percent on cost. During 19X0 and 19X1, such sales (at transfer or sales prices) amount to $90,000 and $60,000, respectively. At the end of each year, Kersbergen has in inventory one half of the amount purchased from Algoe that year. Assume that each firm reports $50,000 net income from its own operations during 19X1 and that Kersbergen allocates unconfirmed profit pro rata to majority and minority shareholders. Kersbergen uses the modified equity method to account for its investment in Algoe Ltd.

Required:

Prepare calculations of consolidated net income for 19X1 using the

a. Incremental approach.

b. Residual approach.

Exercise 6–5   (Working Paper Entries, Incremental and Residual Calculations, and Minority Interest Expense—Pro Rata Allocation)

Hart Company owns 90 percent of the capital stock of Lake Company. During 19X1, Hart Company sells merchandise to Lake Company for $10,000 and purchases $5,000 of merchandise from Lake Company. Twenty percent of all intercompany purchases remains in the ending inventory of the purchasing affiliate. The beginning inventory of Hart Company includes $500 of merchandise purchased in the previous period from Lake Company. Each company marks merchandise to sell at 25 percent above cost.

   The 19X1 net incomes from own operations of Hart Company and Lake Company are $20,000 and $10,000, respectively. Hart Company uses the modified equity method to account for its investment in Lake Company.

Required:

a. Prepare all 19X1 working paper entries related to the intercompany sales. Assume unconfirmed profits are allocated pro rata to majority and minority shareholders.

b. Calculate 19X1 minority interest expense.

c. Calculate 19X1 consolidated net income incrementally and residually.

Exercise 6–6   (100 Percent Allocation Version of Exercise 6–5)

Use the information of Exercise 6–5, except now assume that 100 percent allocation is used. With this change, complete the requirements of Exercise 6–5.

Exercise 6–7   (Working Paper Entries, Incremental and Minority Interest Expense Calculations—Pro Rata Allocation)

P Company owns 80 percent of the capital stock of S Company. For the year ended December 31, 19X1, P Company and S Company report net incomes from their own operations of $30,000 and $8,000, respectively. The January 1, 19X1, inventory of P Company includes a $2,000 profit recorded by S Company on 19X0 sales. During 19X1, P Company and S Company make intercompany sales of $10,000 and $15,000, respectively. Both companies have a gross profit rate (on selling prices) of 30 percent. The ending inventory of P Company includes $2,000 of these goods, and S Company's ending inventory includes $3,000 of goods purchased from P Company.

   P Company carries its investment in S Company under the modified equity method. Unconfirmed profits are allocated pro rata to majority and minority shareholders.

Required:

a. Prepare all working paper entries related to the intercompany sales and unconfirmed profits for a consolidated statement working paper for the year ended December 31, 19X1.

b. Calculate 19X1 minority interest expense.

c. Calculate consolidated net income for 19X1 incrementally.

Exercise 6–8   (100 Percent Allocation Version of Exercise 6–7)

Use the information of Exercise 6–7, except now assume that 100 percent allocation is used. With this change, complete the requirements of Exercise 6–7.

Exercise 6-9   (Basic Relationships)

P Company purchases (in the open market) 90 percent of the capital stock of
S Company on January 1, 19X1, for $2,200 less than its purchased equity in the book
value of S Company's stock. The parent uses the modified equity method. The credit
differential is assigned to land. On December 31, 19X2, the consolidated balance sheet
discloses the value of the minority interest to be $8,608. Other information for the years
19X1 and 19X2 is as follows:

	19X1	*19X2*
Consolidated net income	$109,200	$116,900
P Company's net income from its own operations	80,000	60,000

Additionally, an analysis of intercompany sales reveals the existence of the following
unconfirmed profits:

	December 31, 19X1	*December 31, 19X2*
In the inventory of		
P Company	$2,000	$1,000
S Company	5,000	3,000

Unconfirmed profits are allocated pro rata to majority and minority shareholders. S Company pays cash dividends of $20,000 in both 19X1 and 19X2.

Required:

a. Calculate the net assets of S Company at December 31, 19X2.

b. Calculate S Company's reported net income for 19X1 and 19X2.

c. Calculate the investment cost on January 1, 19X1.

d. Calculate the balance in the investment account on December 31, 19X2.

Exercise 6-10   (100 Percent Allocation Version of Exercise 6-9)

Use the information of Exercise 6-9, except now assume that 100 percent allocation is
used. With this change, complete the requirements of Exercise 6-9.

**Exercise 6-11   (Working Paper Entries, Incremental and Residual Calculations, and
Minority Interest Expense—Pro Rata Allocation)**

Volks Company owns 80 percent of the voting common stock of Oddi Company. Volks
Company sells goods to Oddi Company for $8,000 in 19X1. In this year, Volks
Company also purchases $6,000 of merchandise from Oddi Company. Forty percent of
the intercompany purchases remains in the affiliates' ending inventories in 19X1. The
beginning inventory of Volks Company includes $1,000 of goods purchased from Oddi
Company in 19X0. Each company marks its goods up 33$\frac{1}{3}$ percent based on cost.

The 19X1 net incomes from the separate operations of Volks Company and Oddi Company are $30,000 and $20,000, respectively. Volks Company accounts for its interest in Oddi Company using the modified equity method.

Required:

a. Prepare all 19X1 working paper entries related to the intercompany sales. Assume unconfirmed profits are allocated pro rata to majority and minority shareholders.
b. Calculate 19X1 minority interest expense.
c. Calculate consolidated net income incrementally and residually.

Exercise 6–12   (Working Paper Entries and Incremental and Minority Interest Expense Calculations—Pro Rata Allocation)

P Company owns 90 percent of the voting common stock of S Company. During 19X1, P Company and S Company have net incomes from their own operations of $40,000 and $20,000, respectively. The January 1, 19X1, inventory of P Company includes a $5,000 unconfirmed profit recorded by S Company in 19X0. During 19X1, P Company and S Company make intercompany sales of $15,000 and $20,000, respectively. Both companies have gross profit rates on selling price of 40 percent. The ending inventory of P Company includes $5,000 of the goods acquired from S Company, and S Company's ending inventory includes $4,000 of goods purchased from P Company.

P Company accounts for its investment in S Company using the modified equity method. Unconfirmed profits are allocated pro rata to majority and minority shareholders.

Required:

a. Prepare all 19X1 working paper entries related to the intercompany sales and unconfirmed profits for a consolidated statement working paper.
b. Calculate 19X1 minority interest expense.
c. Calculate 19X1 consolidated net income incrementally.

Exercise 6–13   (Alternative Investor Entries for Deferring Unconfirmed Profits)

Jonas Company has a 25 percent interest in Hampton Company and uses the full equity method to account for its investment. During 19X1, Hampton Company reports net income of $100,000. Annual differential amortization is $3,700. Additionally, at the end of the year, there is a $24,000 unconfirmed profit on purchases from the affiliate.

Required:

a. Assuming that the intercompany transaction was an upstream sale, prepare Jonas Company's entries at the end of 19X1 to record its equity in Hampton Company's net income and to defer the unconfirmed profit.
b. Assuming that the intercompany transaction was a downstream sale and Jonas satisfied the conditions for pro rata elimination, prepare Jonas Company's entries at the end of 19X1 to record its equity in Hampton Company's net income and to defer the unconfirmed profit.

c. Assuming that Jonas Company had income from its own operations of $75,000 (including the transaction with Hampton in the downstream case but excluding equity in investee earnings), calculate Jonas's 19X1 net income for both (*a*) and (*b*).

Problems

Problem 6-14   (Equity Method Entries, Working Paper, and Related Calculations—Pro Rata Allocation)

More Company purchases 80 percent of the voting capital stock of Less Company on January 1, 19X1, for $100,000. On this date, Less Company has capital stock of $80,000 and retained earnings of $45,000.

At the beginning of 19X2, More Company's inventory contains merchandise purchased from Less Company in 19X1 for $5,000. During 19X2, Less Company sells goods to More Company for $30,000. Twenty percent of these goods remains in More Company's 19X2 ending inventory. Less Company's gross profit rate based on selling price is 40 percent.

Less Company earns net income of $26,000 and pays dividends of $8,000 in 19X1. On January 1, 19X1, More Company's retained earnings is $40,000. During 19X1, More Company earns net income from its own operations of $35,000 and pays cash dividends of $12,000.

More Company accounts for its investment in Less Company using the modified equity method. Unconfirmed profits are allocated pro rata between majority and minority shareholders.

The following information is available from the companies' December 31, 19X2, trial balances.

| | December 31, 19X2 | |
	More Company	Less Company
Sales	$150,000	$100,000
Cost of Sales	50,000	40,000
Operating Expenses	44,000	42,000
Inventory	25,000	10,000
Dividends Declared	8,000	6,000
Other Assets	197,200	145,000
Capital Stock	200,000	80,000

Required:

a. Prepare all entries made by More Company in 19X1 and 19X2 related to its investment in Less Company.
b. Calculate the balances of the following accounts:
   (1) Equity in Subsidiary Earnings for 19X1 and 19X2.
   (2) Retained Earnings at January 1, 19X2, for both companies.
   (3) Investment in Less Company at December 31, 19X2.
c. Prepare a consolidated statement working paper for 19X2.
d. Calculate 19X2 consolidated net income incrementally.

Problem 6–15   (100 Percent Allocation Version of Problem 6–14)

Use the information of Problem 6–14, except now assume that 100 percent allocation is used in allocating unconfirmed profits. With this change, complete the requirements of Problem 6–14.

Problem 6–16   (Full Equity Method Version of Problem 6–14)

Use the information of Problem 6–14, except now assume that More Company uses the full equity method to account for its investment in Less Company. With this change, complete the requirements of Problem 6–14.

Problem 6–17   (Cost Method Version of Problem 6–14)

Use the information of Problem 6–14, except now assume that More Company uses the *cost* method to account for its investment in Less Company. With this change, complete the requirements of Problem 6–14, except under requirement (*b*), calculate the balances in the Dividend Income account for 19X1 and 19X2 rather than the balances in Equity in Subsidiary Earnings account for these years.

Problem 6–18   (Equity Method Entries, Working Paper, and Related Calculations—Pro Rata Allocation)

On January 1, 19X1, Moyer Company purchases 90 percent of the capital stock of Bedford Company at a cost of $72,000. On this date, Bedford Company has capital stock of $50,000 and retained earnings of $30,000.

During 19X2, Bedford Company sells merchandise to Moyer Company for $20,000. Of this 19X2 shipment, 30 percent remains in the inventory of Moyer Company on December 31, 19X2. At the beginning of the year (January 1, 19X2), Moyer Company's inventory contains goods purchased from Bedford Company in 19X1 for $3,600. Bedford Company's gross profit rate (on selling price) on intercompany sales is 50 percent.

In 19X1, Bedford Company reports net income of $25,000 and pays cash dividends of $10,000. On January 1, 19X1, the balance of Moyer's Retained Earnings account is $50,000. During 19X1, Moyer's net income from its own operations is $30,000, and it pays cash dividends of $10,000.

Moyer Company uses the modified equity method to account for its investment in Bedford Company. Unconfirmed profits are allocated pro rata between majority and minority shareholders.

The following information is available from the companies' trial balances at December 31, 19X2:

	December 31, 19X2	
	Moyer Company	*Bedford Company*
Sales	$144,000	$93,000
Cost of Sales	44,000	22,000
Operating Expenses	54,000	52,000
Inventory	24,000	12,000
Dividends Declared	10,000	5,000
Other Assets	123,500	97,000
Capital Stock	100,000	50,000

Required:

a. Prepare all entries made by Moyer Company in 19X1 and 19X2 associated with its investment in Bedford Company.

b. Calculate the balances of the following accounts:
   (1) Equity in Subsidiary Earnings for 19X1 and 19X2.
   (2) Retained Earnings at January 1, 19X2, for Moyer Company and Bedford Company.
   (3) Investment in Bedford Company at December 31, 19X2.

c. Using the information presented in the problem and the amounts calculated in (b) above, prepare a consolidated statement working paper for the year ended December 31, 19X2.

d. Calculate consolidated net income for 19X2 using the incremental approach.

Problem 6-19   (100 Percent Allocation Version of Problem 6-18)

Use the information of Problem 6-18, except now assume that 100 percent allocation is used in allocating unconfirmed profits. With this change, complete the requirements of Problem 6-18.

Problem 6-20   (Full Equity Method Version of Problem 6-18)

Use the information of Problem 6-18, except now assume that Moyer Company uses the full equity method. Assume that unconfirmed profits are allocated pro rata between majority and minority shareholders. With this change, complete the requirements of Problem 6-18.

Problem 6-21   (Cost Method Version of Problem 6-18)

Use the information of Problem 6-18, except now assume that Moyer Company uses the cost method to account for its investment in Bedford Company. Continue to assume that unconfirmed profits are allocated pro rata between majority and minority shareholders. With this change, complete the requirements of Problem 6-18. (Under requirement (b), calculate Dividend Income for 19X1 and 19X2 rather than Equity in Subsidiary Earnings for these years.)

Problem 6–22 **(Balance Sheet Working Paper and Differential—Unspecified Allocation Method)**

On June 30, 19X6, Ayr Corporation acquires all of the outstanding voting common stock of Duke Corporation for cash of $19 per share. Both companies continue to operate as separate entities, and both companies have calendar fiscal years.

On June 30, 19X6, after closing the nominal accounts, Duke's condensed balance sheet is as follows:

Assets	
Cash	$ 700,000
Accounts receivable, net	600,000
Inventories	1,400,000
Property, plant, and equipment, net	3,300,000
Other assets	500,000
Total assets	$6,500,000
Liabilities and Stockholders' Equity	
Accounts payable and other current liabilities	$ 700,000
Long-term debt	2,600,000
Other liabilities	200,000
Common stock, par value $1 per share	1,000,000
Additional paid-in capital	400,000
Retained earnings	1,600,000
Total liabilities and stockholders' equity	$6,500,000

On June 30, 19X6, Duke's assets and liabilities with fair values different from their book values are as follows:

	Fair Value
Property, plant, and equipment, net	$16,400,000
Other assets	200,000
Long-term debt	2,200,000

The differences between fair values and book values result in a charge or credit to depreciation or amortization in the consolidated statements for the year ending December 31, 19X6, as follows:

Property, plant, and equipment, net	$500,000	charge
Other assets	10,000	credit
Long-term debt	5,000	charge
	$495,000	charge

The amount paid by Ayr Corporation in excess of the fair value of the net assets of Duke is attributable to expected future earnings of Duke and will be amortized over the maximum allowable period. On June 30, 19X6, there are no intercompany receivables or payables.

During the six-month period ending December 31, 19X6, Duke acquires merchandise from Ayr at an invoice price of $500,000. The cost of the merchandise to Ayr is $300,000. At December 31, 19X6, one half of the merchandise had not been sold, and Duke had not paid for any of the merchandise.

The 19X6 net income (loss) figures for the companies are as follows:

	Ayr	Duke
January 1 to June 30	$ 250,000	($750,000)
July 1 to December 31	1,600,000	1,250,000

The $1,600,000 net income of Ayr includes its equity in the net income of Duke.

On December 31, 19X6, after closing the nominal accounts, the consolidated balance sheets for both companies are as follows:

	Ayr	Duke
Assets		
Cash	$ 3,500,000	$ 600,000
Accounts receivable, net	1,400,000	1,500,000
Inventories	1,000,000	2,500,000
Property, plant, and equipment, net	2,000,000	3,100,000
Investment in subsidiary, at equity	20,250,000	—
Other assets	100,000	500,000
Total assets	$28,250,000	$8,200,000
Liabilities and Stockholders' Equity		
Accounts payable and other current liabilities	$ 1,500,000	$1,100,000
Long-term debt	4,000,000	2,600,000
Other liabilities	750,000	250,000
Common stock, par value $1 per share	10,000,000	1,000,000
Additional paid-in capital	5,000,000	400,000
Retained earnings	7,000,000	2,850,000
Total liabilities and stockholders' equity	$28,250,000	$8,200,000

Required:

a. Prepare a consolidated balance sheet working paper for December 31, 19X6.

b. Calculate consolidated net income for 19X6.

(AICPA adapted)

Problem 6-23   (Working Paper and Differential—Pro Rata Allocation)

P Company acquires 80 percent of the stock of S Company on January 1, 19X1, in the open market for a cash payment of $254,400. On that date, the balances of S Company's shareholders' equity accounts are Capital Stock, $100,000, and Retained Earnings, $50,000.

An examination of S Company's assets and liabilities on January 1, 19X1, reveals that book values are equal to fair values for all assets and liabilities except the following:

	Book Value	Fair Value
Inventory	$ 32,000	$ 40,000
Property, plant, and equipment, net	260,000	320,000

The inventory on hand on January 1, 19X1, is consumed during 19X1, and the property, plant, and equipment on hand on January 1, 19X1, have an estimated remaining life of 10 years. Any goodwill arising from the combination is to be amortized over the maximum allowable time period.

Both companies regularly sell to each other with a markup of 30 percent on selling price. During 19X5 and 19X6, the intercompany sales and the amounts remaining in the inventories of the purchasing affiliates follow:

Selling Affiliate	Intercompany Sales		Remaining in Ending Inventory of Purchasing Affiliate, 12/31	
	19X5	*19X6*	*19X5*	*19X6*
P Company	$50,000	$60,000	$10,000	$15,000
S Company	30,000	20,000	4,000	2,000

P Company accounts for its investment in S Company using the modified equity method. Assume that both companies have properly recorded all transactions and eliminations.

The trial balances of the two companies at December 31, 19X6, are provided below:

	P Company	*S Company*
Property, Plant, and Equipment, net	$ 249,980	$200,000
Inventory (1/1/X6):		
Acquired from nonaffiliates	71,000	20,000
Acquired from affiliate	4,000	10,000
Investment in S Company	255,200	

Purchases		
From nonaffiliates	400,000	100,000
From affiliate	20,000	60,000
Operating Expenses	55,000	10,000
Dividends Declared	40,000	15,000
	$1,095,180	$415,000
Liabilities	$ 110,000	$ 40,000
Capital Stock	250,000	100,000
Retained Earnings (1/1/X6)	166,980	100,000
Sales:		
To nonaffiliates	495,000	155,000
Intercompany	60,000	20,000
Equity in Subsidiary Earnings	13,200	
	$1,095,180	$415,000
Inventory (12/31/X6):		
Acquired from nonaffiliates	$ 68,000	$ 35,000
Acquired from affiliate	2,000	15,000

Required:

a. Prepare a consolidated statement working paper for the year ended December 31, 19X6. Unconfirmed profits are allocated pro rata to majority and minority shareholders on upstream sales.

b. Calculate consolidated net income for 19X6 using the incremental approach.

Problem 6–24   (Working Paper, Differential, and Incremental Calculation—Pro Rata Allocation)

On January 1, 19X1, P Company acquires an 80 percent interest in S Company. The cost of the acquisition, which is for cash in the open market, is $700,000. On the date of acquisition, S Company has capital stock of $250,000 and retained earnings of $150,000. In their evaluation of the fair value of the assets and liabilities of S Company, the management of P Company determines that only one asset, land, has a fair value different from book value. The fair value of the land, which is included in property, plant, and equipment, is $50,000 higher than its book value. P Company decides that the amount allocated to goodwill is to be amortized over 20 years.

The affiliates regularly engage in transactions with each other. During 19X5, P Company has sales of $180,000 to S Company, and S Company has sales of $80,000 to P Company. The following information pertains to unconfirmed profits in the beginning and ending inventories of the affiliates:

	Unconfirmed Profit in Inventory	
	January 1, 19X5	*December 31, 19X5*
Profits recognized by P Company as selling affiliate	$9,000	$13,500
Profits recognized by S Company as selling affiliate	3,600	1,800

P Company accounts for its investment in S Company using the modified equity method. All transactions and adjustments have been properly recorded. The trial balances of the affiliates at December 31, 19X5, are as follows:

	P Company	S Company
Cash	$ 90,000	$ 10,000
Accounts Receivable	110,000	40,000
Property, Plant, and Equipment	549,940	550,000
Investment in S Company	799,000	
Inventory	210,000	150,000
Cost of Goods Sold	1,275,000	420,000
Operating Expenses	175,000	35,000
Dividends Declared	120,000	45,000
	$3,328,940	$1,250,000
Accounts Payable	$ 150,000	$ 20,000
Other Liabilities	180,000	100,000
Common Stock	750,000	250,000
Retained Earnings	530,940	350,000
Sales	1,675,000	530,000
Equity in Subsidiary Earnings	43,000	
	$3,328,940	$1,250,000

Required:

a. Prepare a consolidated statement working paper for the year ended December 31, 19X5. Unconfirmed profits are allocated pro rata to majority and minority shareholders on upstream sales.

b. Calculate consolidated net income for 19X5 using the incremental approach.

Problem 6–25   (Working Paper, Differential, and Incremental Calculation—Pro Rata Allocation)

P Company purchases 60 percent of the capital stock of S Company on January 1, 19X1, for $100,000—when the latter's capital stock and retained earnings are $50,000 and $30,000, respectively. Book values are equal to fair values for all assets and liabilities of S Company, except plant and equipment (net), which have a fair value of $50,000 in excess of book value. The plant and equipment have an estimated remaining life of 6 years, and the goodwill arising from the combination is being amortized over 20 years.

S Company regularly sells merchandise to the parent company. During 19X2, the subsidiary has sales of $30,000 to the parent. The unconfirmed profit in P Company's beginning inventory is $5,000, and in P Company's December 31, 19X2, inventory it is $1,500.

P Company uses the modified equity method to account for its investment in S Company.

Trial balances for the companies on December 31, 19X2, are as follows:

	P Company	S Company
Cash	$ 53,600	$ 56,000
Property, Plant, and Equipment, net	160,000	80,000
Investment in S Company	111,800	
Inventory	40,000	20,000
Cost of Sales	116,000	56,000
Operating Expenses	28,000	18,000
Dividends Declared	40,000	10,000
	$549,400	$240,000
Accounts Payable	$ 44,800	$ 36,000
Capital Stock	200,000	50,000
Retained Earnings	108,700	50,000
Sales	184,000	104,000
Equity in Subsidiary Earnings	11,900	
	$549,400	$240,000

Required:

a. Prepare a consolidated statement working paper for the year ended December 31, 19X2. Unconfirmed profits are allocated pro rata to majority and minority shareholders on upstream sales.

b. Calculate consolidated net income for 19X2 using the incremental approach.

Problem 6–26   (Full Equity Method Version of Problem 6–25)

Use the information of Problem 6–25, except now assume that P Company uses the full equity method.

Required:

a. Adjust P Company's trial balance in Problem 6–25 to reflect the use of the full equity method.

b. Complete the requirements of Problem 6–25.

Consolidated Statements— Unconfirmed Profits on Intercompany Transfers of Other Assets

Chapter Outline

This chapter completes our coverage of unconfirmed profits on asset transfers. We first examine the treatment of intercompany sales of depreciable assets. We then briefly look at intercompany sales of nondepreciable assets and services. Finally, the chapter describes the application of income tax accounting to the scenario involving unconfirmed profits on asset transfers. There also is a short appendix describing the treatment of profits on asset transfers between affiliates prior to the date of combination.

INTERCOMPANY SALES OF DEPRECIABLE ASSETS

On occasion, affiliates engage in upstream and downstream sales of plant and equipment. These intercompany sales, like intercompany merchandise sales, produce unconfirmed profits. The unconfirmed profits existing at year-end are deferred in the current consolidated statements and recognized in subsequent periods as they are confirmed.

Many of the procedures used in dealing with unconfirmed profits on intercompany inventory transfers remain applicable. However, an intercompany sale of a *depreciable* fixed asset produces a new conceptual issue—determining when the unconfirmed profit becomes confirmed. There is no problem in the case of unconfirmed inventory profit because the point of resale of merchandise to nonaffiliates is a natural point in time for recognizing confirmed profit—*a point in time which corresponds to the consumption of the inventory from the consolidated viewpoint*. But fixed assets transferred between affiliates are not intended for resale to nonaffiliates. They are retained for use in the operating activities of the consolidated entity. Thus, it is more difficult to decide when unconfirmed profits from intercompany sales of depreciable fixed assets are realized. *In dealing with this problem, we assume that the amount of unconfirmed profit realized during the period equals the extra depreciation expense recorded from the consolidated viewpoint by the purchasing affiliate as a consequence of the intercompany sale.* For example, assume that on January 1, 19X2, P Company sells a fixed asset for $12,000 to its 90 percent owned subsidiary, S Company. The asset's cost and accumulated depreciation are $20,000 and $17,000, respectively. The unconfirmed profit equals the $9,000 gain on the sale [$12,000 − ($20,000 − $17,000)]. Assuming a remaining useful life of three years for the asset, straight-line depreciation, and no salvage value, the 19X2 depreciation expense recorded on the asset by S Company is $4,000 ($12,000/3). However, 19X2 depreciation expense from the consolidated entity's perspective is based on the unamortized cost of the asset to P Company and is $1,000 [($20,000 − $17,000)/3]. Thus, from the consolidated viewpoint, depreciation expense is overstated by $3,000 ($4,000 − $1,000). To compensate for this overstatement, we assume that the unconfirmed profit realized in 19X2 equals the extra depreciation expense—$3,000. The basis for this assumption is our view that the process of using an intercompany fixed asset is *comparable* to the resale of intercompany merchandise to nonaffiliates since both result in the *consumption* of the asset from the consolidated viewpoint. When intercompany merchandise is resold, the related unconfirmed profit is realized, in a sense, because the goods are *consumed* from the consolidated view. In this case, the unconfirmed profit equals the *extra* cost of the goods recorded by the purchasing affiliate. Thus, under our view, when an intercompany fixed asset is used, the related unconfirmed profit becomes realized since the asset is being *consumed* from the consolidated perspective. Similar to the inventory case, the amount of profit realized in a given period equals the *extra* cost to the purchasing affiliate— the extra depreciation expense. Note that the total extra depreciation expense recorded by the purchasing affiliate always equals the unconfirmed profit from the sale.[1]

To this point, our discussion implicitly assumes that the extra depreciation expense is not capitalized as a cost of goods in process or finished goods. If it is inventoried, the related unconfirmed profit is not realized until the manufactured goods are sold to nonaffiliates. We ignore the capitalization of extra depreciation expense to avoid unnecessary complexity in our explanations. However, if material, this capitalization cannot be ignored in practice. Allowing for the capitalization of the extra depreciation expense is easy once you understand the basic techniques for dealing with unconfirmed profits from intercompany sales of plant and equipment as illustrated below.

We explain the procedures for unconfirmed profits arising from intercompany sales of depreciable fixed assets with a two-year case. The case illustrates the techniques for an upstream sale of equipment by a 60 percent owned subsidiary. We assume pro rata allocation. The procedures for downstream sales and for upstream sales with no minority interest follow the same principles, but there is no allocation to minority interest. A two-year example is sufficient to explain all of the principles for dealing with unconfirmed profits from intercompany transfers of depreciable plant and equipment, even though the confirmation of the unconfirmed profits from such sales often requires more than two years.

Case 1. Upstream Sale of Plant and Equipment

Assume that P Company acquires a 60 percent interest in S Company on January 1, 19X1, for $60,000 when S Company's stockholders' equity accounts are Capital Stock, $75,000, and Retained Earnings, $25,000. There are no intercompany sales of merchandise during 19X1 or 19X2. On January 1, 19X1, S Company sells equipment with a book value of $10,000 (cost $20,000 and accumulated depreciation $10,000) to P Company for $15,000. The gain of $5,000 is recorded by S Company in its Gain on Sale of Plant and Equipment account. The equipment has a remaining useful life of five years, and straight-line depreciation with a zero

---

[1] Issues similar to those of intercompany sales of depreciable fixed assets also arise in connection with capitalizable leases between affiliates. The consolidated statement procedures applicable to such leases are similar to those used in relation to intercompany sales of depreciable fixed assets.

salvage value is used by both affiliates. S Company's net income figures for 19X1 and 19X2 are $32,000 and $20,000, respectively. P Company accounts for its investment in S Company using the modified equity method.

Analysis of Unconfirmed Profit Confirmation.   The unconfirmed profit on the date of sale is S Company's recorded gain of $5,000. This profit is eliminated in the year of sale. It is confirmed as P Company, the purchasing affiliate, uses the equipment. The following schedule shows the pattern of profit confirmation over the equipment's remaining useful life.

| | **Depreciation Expense** | | |
	Recorded by P Company	*From Viewpoint of Consolidated Entity*	*Extra Recorded Each Year = Unconfirmed Profit Assumed Confirmed Each Year*
19X1	$ 3,000	$ 2,000	$1,000
19X2	3,000	2,000	1,000
19X3	3,000	2,000	1,000
19X4	3,000	2,000	1,000
19X5	3,000	2,000	1,000
	$15,000	$10,000	$5,000

P Company records depreciation expense of $3,000 each year since its cost for the asset is $15,000. However, the unamortized cost of the asset to the consolidated entity is $10,000—the book value of the asset before the upstream sale. Thus, annual depreciation expense from a consolidated perspective is $2,000. The difference between the two depreciation figures ($1,000) is the extra depreciation expense recorded each year by the purchasing affiliate because of the intercompany sale. The amount of usage reflected in the extra depreciation measures the confirmed profit each year.

Working Paper Entries for 19X1.   Besides recognizing the deferral and subsequent confirmation of profit, the 19X1 working paper entries correct several misstatements that *exist from the consolidated viewpoint alone* as of the sale date. First, the intercompany equipment is recorded on P Company's books at its $15,000 cost. This cost is not correct. From the view of the consolidated entity, the asset's cost is $20,000—its original cost to S Company—since the cost of an asset cannot be increased by the profit from an intercompany transfer. Furthermore, P Company's accumulated depreciation on this asset on the sale date is zero. From the consolidated entity's perspective, accumulated depreciation is $10,000—the accumulated depreciation shown by S Company on this date. The misstatement of accumulated depreciation from the consolidated perspective becomes smaller over time since P Company records an extra $1,000 in depreciation expense each year. At any time, the net misstatement equals the remaining

ILLUSTRATION 7-1   **Recorded and Consolidated Basis Values (for Asset Sold to P Company by S Company in Case 1)**

	January 1, 19X1	January 1, 19X2	January 1, 19X3
Plant and equipment:			
Correct balance—			
consolidated entity	$20,000	$20,000	$20,000
Balance on purchasing			
affiliate's books	(15,000)	(15,000)	(15,000)
Understatement of cost to			
consolidated entity	$ 5,000	$ 5,000	$ 5,000
Accumulated depreciation:			
Correct balance—			
consolidated entity	($10,000)	($12,000)	($14,000)
Balance on purchasing			
affiliate's books	–0–	(3,000)	(6,000)
Understatement of			
accumulated depreciation			
to consolidated entity	($10,000)	($ 9,000)	($ 8,000)
Unconfirmed profit	($ 5,000)	($ 4,000)	($ 3,000)

unconfirmed profit on the intercompany sale. These observations are summarized in Illustration 7–1 for January 1, 19X1 to 19X3.

The working paper elimination entries for 19X1 are as follows:

1. To reverse the parent's equity method entry for the year:

Equity in Subsidiary Earnings (60% × $32,000)	19,200	
Investment in S Company		19,200

2. To account for the minority's share of subsidiary *confirmed* income during the year:

Minority Interest Expense	11,200	
Minority Interest [40% × ($32,000 − $5,000 + $1,000)] ..		11,200

3. To eliminate investment account against beginning-of-year shareholders' equity accounts of subsidiary:

Capital Stock—S Company	75,000	
Retained Earnings—S Company	25,000	
Investment in S Company		60,000
Minority Interest (40% × $100,000)		40,000

4. To defer gain on intercompany sale of plant and equipment as of date of exchange:

Gain on Sale of Plant and Equipment	5,000	
Plant and Equipment	5,000	
Accumulated Depreciation		10,000

5. To recognize confirmation of profit through use of equipment:

Accumulated Depreciation	1,000	
Depreciation Expense		1,000

The consolidated statement working paper for 19X1 is presented in Illustration 7–2.

Working paper entry (2) is the same as in the case of an upstream inventory sale, although the calculation of the subsidiary's confirmed net income differs. We emphasize that confirmed subsidiary net income *in the year of an intercompany sale of a depreciable fixed asset* equals its net income, less the unconfirmed profit recorded on the transfer, plus the profit confirmed during the year ($32,000 − $5,000 + $1,000 in this case). Entries (4) and (5) are new. Entry (4) eliminates the unconfirmed profit recorded on the sale date and corrects the misstatements of asset cost and accumulated depreciation existing on this date. Entry (5) eliminates the extra depreciation recorded by P Company and, consequently, reflects the profit confirmed during 19X1 (by reducing expense). In combination, entries (4) and (5) produce the correct year-end balance for accumulated depreciation ($12,000 = $10,000 + $2,000) on the consolidated statement working paper—the balance that would be shown if the intercompany sale did not occur. Consistent with the principles established in Chapter 6, all of the unconfirmed profit is eliminated, and pro rata allocation is applied via entry (2)—which records minority interest expense on the basis of confirmed subsidiary net income.

Working Paper Entries for 19X2. The working paper eliminations for 19X2 follow:

1. To reverse the parent's equity method entry for the year:

Equity in Subsidiary Earnings (60% × $20,000)	12,000	
Investment in S Company		12,000

ILLUSTRATION 7-2   Upstream Sale–19X1

P COMPANY AND SUBSIDIARY S COMPANY
Consolidated Statement Working Paper
For The Year Ended December 31, 19X1

	P Company	S Company	Eliminations Dr.		Eliminations Cr.		Consolidated
Income Statement							
Sales	120,000	80,000					200,000
Equity in subsidiary earnings	19,200		(1)	19,200			–0–
Gain on sale of plant and equipment	–0–	5,000	(4)	5,000			–0–
Total credits	139,200	85,000					200,000
Cost of sales	84,000	48,000					132,000
Operating expenses (except depreciation)	12,000	5,000					17,000
Depreciation expense	3,000				(5)	1,000	2,000
Minority interest expense			(2)	11,200			11,200
Total debits	99,000	53,000					162,200
Net income	40,200	32,000		35,400		1,000	37,800
Retained Earnings Statement							
Retained earnings, 1/1/X1:							
P Company	40,000						40,000
S Company		25,000	(3)	25,000			–0–
Net income	40,200	32,000		35,400		1,000	37,800
Retained earnings, 12/31/X1	80,200	57,000		60,400		1,000	77,800
Balance Sheet							
Other assets	125,800	141,000					266,800
Inventory	30,000	12,000					42,000
Investment in S Company	79,200				(1)	19,200	–0–
					(3)	60,000	
Plant and equipment	15,000	–0–	(4)	5,000			20,000
	250,000	153,000					328,800
Accumulated depreciation	3,000	–0–	(5)	1,000	(4)	10,000	12,000
Liabilities	66,800	21,000					87,800
Capital stock:							
P Company	100,000						100,000
S Company		75,000	(3)	75,000			–0–
Retained earnings	80,200	57,000		60,400		1,000	77,800
Minority interest					(2)	11,200	51,200
					(3)	40,000	
	250,000	153,000		141,400		141,400	328,800

Explanation of eliminations:

(1) To eliminate parent's share of subsidiary earnings.

(2) To account for the minority's share of *confirmed* subsidiary earnings.

(3) To eliminate January 1, 19X1, stockholders' equity balances.

(4) To defer unconfirmed gain on date of sale.

(5) To recognize confirmation of profit.

277

2. To account for the minority's share of subsidiary *confirmed* income during the year:

Minority Interest Expense	8,400	
Minority Interest [40% × ($20,000 + $1,000)]		8,400

3. To eliminate investment account against beginning-of-year shareholders' equity accounts of subsidiary:

Capital Stock—S Company	75,000	
Retained Earnings—S Company	57,000	
Investment in S Company		79,200
Minority Interest (40% × $132,000)		52,800

4. To adjust for unconfirmed gain at beginning of year:

Retained Earnings, 1/1/X2—P Company		
[60% × ($5,000 − $1,000)]	2,400	
Minority Interest [40% × ($5,000 − $1,000]	1,600	
Plant and Equipment	5,000	
Accumulated Depreciation		9,000

5. To recognize confirmation of profit through use of equipment:

Accumulated Depreciation	1,000	
Depreciation Expense		1,000

The consolidated statement working paper for 19X2 is presented in Illustration 7–3.

Working paper entry (2) is the same, in concept, as it was in 19X1. It accounts for the minority's share of confirmed subsidiary income in 19X2. Since no new unconfirmed profit must be deferred, we need only to adjust the subsidiary's reported net income for the amount of the intercompany profit that was confirmed ($1,000) during 19X2. Entry (4) is completely analogous to the entry in the second year of an upstream inventory sale. It eliminates the remaining unconfirmed gain on the equipment sale as of January 1, 19X2, from Plant and Equipment and Accumulated Depreciation and allocates it against the parent company's January 1 Retained Earnings and Minority Interest. All of these accounts are overstated on

ILLUSTRATION 7-3 Upstream Sale—19X2

P COMPANY AND SUBSIDIARY S COMPANY
Consolidated Statement Working Paper
For The Year Ended December 31, 19X2

	P Company	S Company	Eliminations Dr.	Eliminations Cr.	Consolidated
Income Statement					
Sales	140,000	85,000			225,000
Equity in subsidiary earnings	12,000		(1) 12,000		–0–
Total credits	152,000	85,000			225,000
Cost of goods sold	98,000	51,000			149,000
Operating expenses (except depreciation)	16,500	14,000			30,500
Depreciation expense	3,000			(5) 1,000	2,000
Minority interest expense			(2) 8,400		8,400
Total debits	117,500	65,000			189,900
Net income	34,500	20,000	20,400	1,000	35,100
Retained Earnings Statement					
Retained earnings (1/1/X2):					
P Company	80,200		(4) 2,400		77,800
S Company		57,000	(3) 57,000		–0–
Net income	34,500	20,000	20,400	1,000	35,100
Retained earnings (12/31/X1)	114,700	77,000	79,800	1,000	112,900
Balance Sheet					
Other assets	170,600	163,000			333,600
Inventory	25,000	15,000			40,000
Investment in S Company	91,200			(1) 12,000	–0–
				(3) 79,200	
Plant and equipment	15,000	–0–	(4) 5,000		20,000
	301,800	178,000			393,600
Accumulated depreciation	6,000	–0–	(5) 1,000	(4) 9,000	14,000
Liabilities	81,100	26,000			107,100
Capital stock:					
P Company	100,000				100,000
S Company		75,000	(3) 75,000		–0–
Retained earnings	114,700	77,000	79,800	1,000	112,900
Minority interest			(4) 1,600	(2) 8,400	59,600
				(3) 52,800	
	301,800	178,000	162,400	162,400	393,600

Explanation of eliminations:

(1) To eliminate parent's share of subsidiary earnings.

(2) To account for the minority's share of *confirmed* subsidiary earnings.

(3) To eliminate January 1, 19X2, stockholders' equity balances.

(4) To adjust for unconfirmed gain at beginning of year.

(5) To recognize confirmation of profit.

a consolidated basis.[2] Entry (5) recognizes the confirmed profit in 19X2 in the same way as in the 19X1 consolidated statement working paper. In contrast to the inventory case, note that only a portion of the unconfirmed gain is confirmed each year. Thus, we continue to make eliminations (4) and (5) in subsequent years, but the amount of the remaining unconfirmed gain is decreasing by $1,000 each year.

Calculations of Consolidated Net Income.   The amounts shown in the consolidated statement working papers for consolidated net income in 19X1 and 19X2 can be calculated incrementally and residually. Using the incremental approach, we obtain the following:

	19X1	*19X2*
P Company's (confirmed)net income from its own operations:		
19X1: ($40,200 − $19,200)	$21,000	
19X2: ($34,500 − $12,000)		$22,500
Plus: P Company's equity in S Company's *confirmed* net income:		
19X1: [60% × ($32,000 − $5,000 + $1,000)]	16,800	
19X2: [60% × ($20,000 + $1,000)]		12,600
Consolidated net income	$37,800	$35,100

In each year, P Company's confirmed net income from its own operations equals its net income, less the balance of equity in subsidiary earnings, since the intercompany sale is upstream. With a downstream sale, P Company's 19X1 confirmed net income from its own operations would be determined by subtracting both its balance for equity in subsidiary earnings and the profit remaining unconfirmed at the end of 19X1 from its 19X1 net income. P Company's 19X2 confirmed net income from its own operations would be calculated by reducing its 19X2 net income by its balance for equity in subsidiary earnings and increasing this figure by the profit assumed confirmed during 19X2.

Using the residual approach, we obtain the following calculations of consolidated net income:

---

[2] If the parent company chooses an alternative to the modified equity method to account for its investment in the subsidiary, the necessary changes in the eliminations for unconfirmed profits are the same as they were in the inventory case in Chapter 6. If the parent uses the cost method, no changes are necessary. If the full equity method is used, the debit to the parent's beginning retained earnings is changed to a debit to the parent's investment account. (See Chapter 6 for an explanation of this change.)

	19X1	*19X2*
P Company's net income	$40,200	$34,500
S Company's net income	32,000	20,000
Sum of affiliate's net incomes	$72,200	$54,500
Plus (minus): Effects of working paper entries on sum of affiliates' net incomes:		
Elimination of equity in subsidiary earnings	($19,200)	($12,000)
Elimination of unconfirmed profit	(5,000)	—
Confirmation of profit	1,000	1,000
Minority interest expense	(11,200)	(8,400)
	($34,400)	($19,400)
Consolidated net income	$37,800	$35,100

Tracing the values used in these calculations to the consolidated statement working papers aids in understanding the procedures used in the working papers in dealing with intercompany sales of depreciable plant and equipment.

Relationship between Minority Interest and Net Assets of Subsidiary.   Minority interest in the consolidated balance sheet for both 19X1 and 19X2 is the product of the minority interest percent and the subsidiary's year-end *confirmed* stockholders' equity. In a given year, this latter value is the sum of the subsidiary's year-end capital stock and year-end confirmed retained earnings. Assuming no complications other than an upstream sale, the subsidiary's year-end confirmed retained earnings equals its year-end retained earnings less any profit remaining unconfirmed at year-end. The 19X1 and 19X2 consolidated balance sheet minority interest values for our example are calculated in the following schedule.

	December 31	
	19X1	*19X2*
S Company's capital stock	$ 75,000	$ 75,000
Calculation of S Company's *confirmed* retained earnings:		
S Company's retained earnings	$ 57,000	$ 77,000
S Company's profit remaining unconfirmed at year-end	(4,000)	(3,000)
S Company's *confirmed* retained earnings	$ 53,000	$ 74,000
S Company's *confirmed* stockholders' equity	$128,000	$149,000
Minority interest for consolidated balance sheet:		
19X1: (40% × $128,000)	$ 51,200	
19X2: (40% × $149,000)		$ 59,600

If the intercompany sale were downstream, the 19X1 minority interest would be the product of the minority interest percent and the subsidiary's recorded stockholders' equity at year-end, or $52,800 [40% × ($75,000 + $57,000)]. For 19X2, this value would be $60,800 [40% × ($75,000 + $77,000)].

INTERCOMPANY SALES OF LAND AND SERVICES

Transfers of Land

To this point, we have considered the treatment of unconfirmed profits related to inventories (nondepreciable assets) and depreciable fixed assets. However, intercompany sales of nondepreciable assets other than inventory also occur, and these sales produce unconfirmed profits. These profits are eliminated using the general principles illustrated previously: (1) the unconfirmed profit is deferred until the asset is consumed (either through sale to nonaffiliates or use) and (2) the acquired asset's carrying value is adjusted to its cost to the selling affiliate. The unconfirmed profit eliminated each year until the transferred asset is disposed of is *constant* if the asset is nondepreciable. For example, assume an unconfirmed profit of $2,000 arising from the *downstream* sale of land is to be eliminated. The working paper entry to eliminate this profit in the year of sale is as follows:

Gain on Sale of Land	2,000	
Land		2,000

Assuming that land is not disposed of, the entry for *each subsequent year* follows:

Retained Earnings, 1/1—P Company	2,000	
Land		2,000

This entry is made each year until the land is disposed of because the profit remains unconfirmed until this time. In the year the land is disposed of, the gain or loss on disposition is based on the cost of the land to the purchasing affiliate. Therefore, the following working paper entry is made:

Retained Earnings, 1/1—P Company	2,000	
Gain on Sale of Land		2,000

If the sale is upstream and pro rata allocation is used, the entry for years subsequent to the intercompany sale by an 80 percent owned subsidiary is the following:

Retained Earnings, 1/1—P Company (80% × $2,000)	1,600	
Minority Interest (20% × $2,000)	400	
Land		2,000

Of course, like the other intercompany sales of assets, the entry in the year of sale is the same whether it is upstream or downstream. The confirmed income of the subsidiary is, however, adjusted in the year of sale for an upstream sale.

Providing Intercompany Services

Besides having intercompany sales of assets, affiliates also engage in intercompany sales of services. In some cases, the cost of the services is capitalized by the purchasing affiliate. For example, a parent company might perform management consulting services for its subsidiary, with the cost of these services being capitalized by the subsidiary as an intangible asset. Since intangibles are amortized, the working paper techniques for this case are virtually identical to those for the sale of a depreciable fixed asset. On the other hand, many transfers of services are treated by the purchasing affiliate as period expenses. In these cases, confirmation of the selling affiliate's profit occurs during the same year as the transfer of the services since the services are consumed in this year. Thus, no working paper entries are required to eliminate the seller's profit in these cases. Nevertheless, the related intercompany sale is offset against the recorded expense by an entry in the consolidated statement working paper.

INCOME TAX ACCOUNTING FOR UNCONFIRMED PROFITS

As discussed in Chapter 6, if a parent and its subsidiaries file separate income tax returns and unconfirmed profits exist, temporary differences are produced. Specifically, if an unconfirmed profit results from an intercompany sale, the profit is taxed to the selling affiliate in the year of the sale but is deferred to a later period when eliminated for consolidated statement purposes. In the period in which the profit is confirmed, the timing difference reverses. In this later period, the profit is recorded for the consolidated financial statements, even though it is taxed in an earlier period. Under these conditions, interperiod income tax allocation is applied. In the first period, the income taxes on the unconfirmed profit are deferred to the period in which the profit becomes confirmed and is recorded. In this period, the profit and the related taxes are matched in the consolidated income statement. As discussed in Chapter 6, these procedures, *in effect,* eliminate the unconfirmed profit net of tax in the year in which it arises. They recognize the profit net of tax, *in effect,* in the year it is confirmed.

According to current accounting standards, the net of tax treatment is appropriate under the equity method for investor-investee relationships.[3] That is, under the equity method, the investor's entries to defer and to recognize the confirmation of unconfirmed profits are made *net of tax.* This procedure maintains the "one-line" consolidation property of the *full* equity method.

Under *Statement of Financial Accounting Standards No. 109,* the *asset and liability* method is used in applying interperiod income tax allocation in the consolidated statements.[4] Case 2 illustrates the application of interperiod income tax allocation in the presence of an unconfirmed inventory profit. Case 3 illustrates these principles in the context of an unconfirmed profit from an intercompany sale of a depreciable fixed asset.

Case 2. Unconfirmed Inventory Profits and Interperiod Income Tax Allocation

Assume that P Company's 80 percent owned subsidiary, S Company, reports net income of $50,000 in both 19X1 and 19X2. Further, assume that an unconfirmed profit of $10,000, produced by an upstream sale, is in P Company's 19X1 ending inventory. This profit is confirmed in 19X2. The companies file separate income tax returns, and the income tax rate is 40 percent.

Working Paper Entries for 19X1 and 19X2.   Under the asset and liability method, the unconfirmed profit is deferred in the normal manner, and the Deferred Income Taxes account is created. The balance of this account equals the income tax expense to be deferred to later years. In this example, the income tax expense deferred from 19X1 is recognized as income tax expense in 19X2 (the year the profit is confirmed).

---

[3] See, for example, *Accounting Interpretation No. 1 of APB Opinion No. 18.*

[4] *Statement of Financial Accounting Standards No. 109,* "Accounting for Income Taxes" (Norwalk, CT: FASB, 1992). Throughout this chapter and its problems, we assume that the existing conditions justify recording deferred tax assets—which will appear on balance sheets (as opposed to reductions in noncurrent deferred tax liabilities). This assumption is made for simplicity and almost always could hold in the case of intercompany inventory sales. It could not always hold in the case of intercompany sales of fixed assets. We also assume that tax rates are constant and do not distinguish between current and noncurrent deferred income tax assets for simplicity.

The working paper entries related to the unconfirmed profit in 19X1 are as follows:

1. To eliminate unconfirmed profit in P Company's ending inventory:

```
Cost of Sales  . . . . . . . . . . . . . . . . . . . . . . . . . . . . . . . . . . .  10,000
    Inventory  . . . . . . . . . . . . . . . . . . . . . . . . . . . . . . . . .          10,000
```

2. To defer income tax expense related to unconfirmed profit:

```
Deferred Income Taxes (40% × $10,000)  . . . . . . . . . . . . . . .  4,000
    Income Tax Expense  . . . . . . . . . . . . . . . . . . . . . . . . .          4,000
```

The first entry is like all prior entries to eliminate unconfirmed profit from ending inventory. Working paper entry (2) records deferred income tax expense and reduces the selling affiliate's income tax expense. The credit to Income Tax Expense produces an income tax expense figure for the consolidated statements that is the same as if the intercompany sale did not occur. Besides recording deferred taxes and reducing Income Tax Expense, the interperiod income tax allocation procedure introduces a new element into the calculation of the subsidiary's 19X1 confirmed net income and confirmed retained earnings at the end of 19X1. The *net of tax amount of unconfirmed profit* (rather than unconfirmed profit) is subtracted from the subsidiary's 19X1 net income and end of 19X1 retained earnings in arriving at these values. S Company's 19X1 confirmed net income is $44,000 [$50,000 − ($10,000 − $4,000)].

The working paper entry for the confirmed profit in 19X2 follows:

1. To recognize confirmation of profit, *net of tax*, in beginning inventory:

```
Retained Earnings, 1/1/X2—P Company
    [80% × ($10,000 − $4,000)]  . . . . . . . . . . . . . . . . . . . . .  4,800
Minority Interest [20% × ($10,000 − $4,000)]  . . . . . . . . . . .  1,200
Income Tax Expense (40% × $10,000)  . . . . . . . . . . . . . . .  4,000
    Cost of Sales  . . . . . . . . . . . . . . . . . . . . . . . . . . . . . . .          10,000
```

This entry recognizes the confirmation of the unconfirmed profit in the beginning inventory ($10,000) by crediting Cost of Sales. Under interperiod income tax allocation, the income tax expense related to this profit is matched with the profit in the consolidated income statement. Thus, Income Tax Expense is debited for $4,000 (40% × $10,000)—producing a $4,000 reduction in income. The $6,000 net of tax amount of unconfirmed profit is allocated pro rata between Minority Interest and the beginning-of-year balance in P Company's Retained Earnings. Confirmed subsidiary net income for 19X2 is \$56,000 [\$50,000 + (\$10,000 − \$4,000)]. In this case, the net of tax amount of the profit becoming confirmed during the period is added in calculating S Company's confirmed net income.

Case 3. Unconfirmed Profits on Fixed Asset Transfers and Interperiod Income Tax Allocation

This example uses the data of Case 1. In addition to its data, assume that the companies file separate income tax returns and the income tax rate is 40 percent. The numbers for the entries are referenced to those in Illustration 7–2.

Working Paper Entries for 19X1 and 19X2. The 19X1 working paper entries related to the unconfirmed profit are as follows:

4a. To defer gain on intercompany sale of plant and equipment as of the date of exchange:

Gain on Sale of Plant and Equipment	5,000	
Plant and Equipment	5,000	
Accumulated Depreciation		10,000

4b. To defer income tax expense related to unconfirmed profit:

Deferred Income Taxes (40% × \$5,000)	2,000	
Income Tax Expense		2,000

5a. To recognize confirmation of profit through use of equipment:

Accumulated Depreciation	1,000	
Depreciation Expense		1,000

5b. To record income tax expense on confirmed profit:

Income Tax Expense (40% × \$1,000)	400	
Deferred Income Taxes		400

These entries are the same as in Case 1, except for entries (4b) and (5b). Entry (4b) records the balance for Deferred Income Taxes as of the date of asset transfer. Entry (5*b*) matches the income tax on the profit confirmed during the year with the confirmed profit in the consolidated income statement.

The working paper entries related to the unconfirmed profit for 19X2 are the following:

4. To adjust for unconfirmed gain and related tax effects at beginning of year:

Retained Earnings, 1/1/X2—P Company (60% × $2,400)	1,440	
Minority Interest (40% × $2,400)	960	
Deferred Income Taxes (40% × $4,000)	1,600	
Plant and Equipment	5,000	
Accumulated Depreciation		9,000

5*a*. To recognize confirmation of profit through use of eqiupment:

Accumulated Depreciation	1,000	
Depreciation Expense		1,000

5*b*. To record income tax expense on confirmed profit:

Income Tax Expense (40% × $1,000)	400	
Deferred Income Taxes		400

Entries (5*a*) and (5*b*) are the same as the corresponding entries in 19X1. An entry corresponding to 19X1 entry (4*b*) is not needed in 19X2 since all of the income taxes on the unconfirmed profit are paid in 19X1. Entry (4) eliminates the remaining net of tax amount of unconfirmed profit at the beginning of the year (60% × $4,000) by correcting the misstatements of Plant and Equipment and Accumulated Depreciation at the beginning of the year and recording the deferred income tax expense on the full amount of this profit (40% × $4,000). The net of tax amount of the unconfirmed profit is allocated pro rata between Minority Interest and the beginning-of-year balance in P Company's Retained Earnings.

Summary

A major topic covered in this chapter is unconfirmed profits from the intercompany sales of assets other than inventory and intercompany sales of services. The chapter explains how these profits are eliminated using the general principles illustrated in Chapter 6: (1) the whole unconfirmed profit is deferred until the asset is consumed (either through sale to nonaffiliates or use) and (2) assuming that an asset is transferred, the asset's carrying value is adjusted to its cost to the selling affiliate. The general principles for the confirmation of profit illustrated in Chapter 6 also apply in these cases, although it is more difficult to determine when profit is confirmed on intercompany sales of depreciable fixed assets. In dealing with this problem, we assume that the amount of unconfirmed profit realized during the period equals the extra depreciation expense recorded from the consolidated viewpoint by the purchasing affiliate as a consequence of the intercompany sale.

The chapter also covers the relationship between unconfirmed profits and interperiod income tax allocation. It shows that if the affiliates file separate income tax returns and unconfirmed profits exist, this produces temporary differences that require the use of interperiod income tax allocation.

Appendix: Transfer Profits before Affiliation

Accountants do not agree on the elimination of profits on assets transferred between companies before their affiliation. The basic issue is whether the transferred assets are stated correctly from the consolidated perspective. The position we endorse is that the profit on an asset transferred prior to affiliation is not eliminated from the related asset balance, even if the transfer occurs during negotiations between the eventual combining companies. Under the assumption that the transfer occurs prior to negotiations, our position is based on the usual *presumption* of historical cost accounting theory that transactions between separate legal entities are arm's length. Under this view, all accounts of the eventual combining companies are stated correctly from the perspectives of the separate legal entities. Thus, there is no reason to distinguish between this case and the situation in which no assets are transferred between the combining companies prior to affiliation. Consequently, there is no reason to eliminate the seller's profit in preparing consolidated statements. Alternatively, assume that the transfer occurs during negotiations. Under these conditions, the transfer may not appear to result from arm's length bargaining. Nevertheless, the managements of the selling and purchasing companies have a fiduciary responsibility to their shareholders, and their actions during negotiations tend to be carefully scrutinized. Consequently, we believe that the sales prices of assets sold during negotiations usually constitute reasonable values for recording the transfers. Thus, under this view, all accounts of the eventual combining companies usually are reasonably stated from the perspectives of the separate legal entities. When this view holds, there is no distinction between this case and the situation in which no assets are transferred prior to affiliation, and there is no reason to eliminate the seller's profit. Further, if misstatement occurs under the assumed conditions, the proper medium for recording needed adjustment is existing accounting conventions—not the arbitrary elimination of the seller's profit. For example, if asset overstatement results from sales prior to affiliation, the assets are written down to "market" under *historical cost accounting theory*. Under this basic theory, no adjustment is made for asset understatement arising, for example, from bargain purchases. Nevertheless, under *consolidated theory*, understated assets of the subsidiary acquired in a *purchase* combination are restated at amounts approaching their fair market values at date of acquisition in preparing consolidated financial statements. Consistent with historical cost theory, understated parent company assets are not written up to compensate for their understatement.

A second position favors eliminating the profits on assets transferred between companies before their affiliation. This treatment was popular in practice at least until the middle of the 1950s. This position is based primarily on a desire for conservative asset valuation and on the view that the date of acquisition is not necessarily the appropriate date for determining whether an unconfirmed profit exists (especially when the asset transfer occurs during negotiations). Our feeling is that a conservative asset value is recorded only if there is a choice between two or more reasonable alternatives and that this choice usually is not present in the case of assets transferred between eventual combining companies (as argued above). Further, if misstatement occurs in this case, the proper medium for recording needed adjustment is existing accounting conventions. We also believe that the issue of whether date of acquisition is the appropriate point in time for determining whether an unconfirmed profit exists is irrelevant to the main issue of whether transferred assets are stated correctly from the consolidated viewpoint. Also, the definition of unconfirmed profit (a profit arising from a transaction between affiliates) implies that date of acquisition is the proper point in time for determining whether an unconfirmed profit exists. Under this definition, if a profit occurs before date of acquisition, it cannot be an unconfirmed profit.

Questions

1. Describe the general treatment of unconfirmed profits from intercompany sales of plant and equipment and services.
2. What options exist under *Accounting Research Bulletin No. 51* regarding the elimination and allocation of unconfirmed profit?
3. Contrast the consolidated financial statement effects of pro rata and 100 percent allocation in the context of an upstream sale of a depreciable fixed asset.
4. Why is it important to distinguish between upstream and downstream asset transfers in the analysis of confirmed or unconfirmed intercompany profits?
5. When is the unconfirmed profit arising from the intercompany sale of plant and equipment confirmed, or realized, from the viewpoint of the consolidated entity?
6. When is the unconfirmed profit arising from the intercompany sale of land confirmed, or realized, from the viewpoint of the consolidated entity?
7. When is the unconfirmed profit arising from the intercompany sale of services that are capitalized on the books of the purchasing affiliate confirmed, or realized, from the viewpoint of the consolidated entity?
8. What is the relationship between a subsidiary's confirmed and reported incomes from operations in the year it is the seller of depreciable plant and equipment generating an unconfirmed profit? In a year in which a portion of the profit becomes confirmed? Over the period of time encompassing the sale and the confirmation of all of the profit?
9. How are the incremental calculations of consolidated net income presented in the prior chapter modified for the existence of unconfirmed profits from sales of depreciable fixed assets?

10. What is the effect of an unconfirmed profit from the intercompany sale of depreciable plant and equipment on the relationship between minority interest and the subsidiary's net assets?

11. How are income taxes related to unconfirmed profits treated under the equity method for an investor-investee relationship?

12. Assuming that the affiliates file separate income tax returns, how are income taxes related to unconfirmed profits treated in the consolidated statements?

Exercises

Exercise 7–1   (Minority Interest Expense and Fixed Asset Balance Sheet Amounts—Pro Rata Allocation)

Select the best answer for each of the following questions:

1. Eltro Company acquires a 70 percent interest in Samson Company in 19X2. For the years ended December 31, 19X3 and 19X4, Samson reports net income of $80,000 and $90,000, respectively. During 19X3, Samson sells land to Eltro for $10,000 at a gain of $2,000. The land is later resold to nonaffiliates for $15,000 during 19X4. Unconfirmed profits are allocated pro rata. For consolidation purposes, what is the minority interest's share of Samson's confirmed net income for 19X3 and 19X4, respectively?

   a. $23,400 and $27,600.
   b. $24,000 and $27,000.
   c. $24,600 and $26,400.
   d. $26,000 and $25,000.

2. On January 1, 19X5, Jonas Company sold equipment to its 100 percent owned subsidiary, Neptune Company, for $1,800,000. The equipment cost Jonas $2 million, and accumulated depreciation on the sale date was $500,000. Jonas was depreciating the equipment over 20 years using the straight-line method and assuming no salvage value, a procedure that Neptune continued. On the consolidated balance sheet at December 31, 19X5, the cost and accumulated depreciation of the equipment, respectively, are

   a. $1,500,000 and $600,000.
   b. $1,800,000 and $100,000.
   c. $1,800,000 and $500,000.
   d. $2,000,000 and $600,000.

(AICPA adapted)

Exercise 7–2   (Unconfirmed Profit—Materials Used in Constructing Fixed Asset)

During the fiscal year ended October 31, 19X1, S Company, a 100 percent owned subsidiary of P Company, sold to the latter, at a profit, materials that P Company used in constructing a new building for its own use. State (*a*) how the profit on the sale of the materials should be treated in preparing the 19X1 consolidated financial statement working papers assuming the new building is not completed and (*b*) how it should be treated in preparing working papers in subsequent years assuming the building is completed.

(AICPA adapted)

Exercise 7–3   (Fixed Asset Sale, Working Paper Entries, Incremental Calculation, and Minority Interest Expense—Pro Rata Allocation)

P Company has a 90 percent interest in the capital stock of S Company. On January 1, 19X1, S Company sells equipment, which cost $80,000 five years ago, to P Company for $60,000. The original estimate of useful life was 10 years, and P Company decided that a remaining life of 5 years is reasonable.

During 19X1 and 19X2, the companies report net incomes from their own operations of $60,000 (P Company) and $50,000 (S Company). P Company uses the modified equity method, and unconfirmed profits are allocated pro rata.

Required:

a. Prepare working paper entries related to the asset transfer for a consolidated statement working paper on December 31, 19X1.
b. Prepare working paper entries related to the asset transfer for a consolidated statement working paper on December 31, 19X2.
c. Calculate consolidated net income for both 19X1 and 19X2 incrementally.
d. Calculate minority interest in confirmed subsidiary net income for both 19X1 and 19X2.

Exercise 7–4   (Fixed Asset Sale, Working Paper Entries, Incremental Calculation, and Minority Interest Expense—Pro Rata Allocation)

P Company acquires 60 percent of the capital stock of S Company on January 1, 19X1. On January 1, 19X4, equipment originally costing S Company $40,000 five years ago is sold to P Company for $60,000. Accumulated depreciation to the date of sale (based upon a 10-year useful life) is $20,000. The net incomes of the companies from their own operations are as follows:

	19X4	19X5
P Company	$80,000	$70,000
S Company	60,000	40,000

P Company uses the modified equity method, and unconfirmed profits are allocated pro rata.

Required:

a. Prepare working paper entries related to the equipment transfer for consolidated statement working papers for the years ended December 31, 19X4 and 19X5.
b. Calculate minority interest expense for both 19X4 and 19X5.
c. Calculate consolidated net income for both 19X4 and 19X5 incrementally.

Exercise 7–5   (Fixed Asset Sale, Working Paper Entries, Incremental Calculation, and Minority Interest Expense—Pro Rata Allocation)

On January 1, 19X1, White Company purchased 90 percent of Black Company's outstanding stock. On this date, Black Company sold a truck to White Company for $15,000. The truck was carried on Black Company's books at a cost of $18,000, with accumulated depreciation of $12,000. The truck was expected to have a remaining life of five years, which was consistent with the 15-year life that Black Company originally estimated.

Each firm reported net income from its own operations of $30,000 during 19X1 and 19X2. White Company uses the modified equity method to account for its investment in Black Company, and unconfirmed profits are allocated pro rata.

Required:

a. Prepare the working paper entries related to the truck transfer for 19X1 and 19X2 consolidated statement working papers.
b. Calculate consolidated net income for both 19X1 and 19X2 incrementally.
c. Calculate minority interest expense for both 19X1 and 19X2.

Exercise 7–6   (100 Percent Allocation Version of Exercise 7–5)

Use the information of Exercise 7–5, except now assume that 100 percent allocation is used. With this change, complete the requirements of Exercise 7–5.

Exercise 7–7   (Inventory Profits, Working Paper Entries, Incremental and Residual Calculations, Minority Interest Expense, and Tax Allocation—Pro Rata Allocation)

P Company owns 90 percent of the capital stock of S Company. For the year ended December 31, 19X1, P Company and S Company report net income from their own operations of $30,000 and $10,000, respectively. The January 1, 19X1, inventory of P Company includes $2,000 of profit recorded by S Company on 19X0 sales. During 19X1, P Company and S Company make intercompany sales of $8,000 and $12,000, respectively. Both companies have a gross profit rate on selling price on intercompany sales of 20 percent. The ending inventory of P Company includes $2,000 of goods purchased from S Company, and S Company's ending inventory includes $3,000 of goods purchased from P Company.

P Company uses the modified equity method to account for its investment in S Company, and unconfirmed profits are allocated pro rata. The affiliates file separate income tax returns. The income tax rate is 40 percent.

Required:

a. Prepare the working paper entries related to the intercompany sales for a 19X1 consolidated statement working paper.
b. Calculate 19X1 minority interest expense.
c. Calculate consolidated net income for 19X1 both incrementally and residually.

Exercise 7–8   (Fixed Asset Sale, Working Paper Entries, Incremental Calculation, Minority Interest Expense, and Tax Allocation—Pro Rata Allocation)

P Company holds 90 percent of the outstanding stock of S Company. On January 1, 19X1, S Company sells equipment to P Company for $25,000. The equipment's cost and accumulated depreciation are $40,000 and $20,000, respectively. The equipment has a remaining life of two years.

P Company uses the modified equity method to account for its investment in S Company, and intercompany profits are allocated pro rata. During 19X1 and 19X2, each company reports net income from its own operations of $10,000.

The affiliates file separate income tax returns. The income tax rate is 40 percent.

Required:

a. Prepare the working paper entries related to the intercompany sale for 19X1 and 19X2 consolidated statement working papers.

b. Calculate minority interest expense for both 19X1 and 19X2.

c. Calculate consolidated net income for both 19X1 and 19X2 incrementally.

Exercise 7–9   (100 Percent Allocation Version of Exercise 7–8)

Use the information of Exercise 7–8, except now assume that 100 percent allocation is used. With this change, complete the requirements of Exercise 7–8.

Exercise 7–10   (Fixed Asset Sale, Working Paper Entries, Incremental Calculation, and Minority Interest Expense—Pro Rata Allocation)

Great Company purchased 80 percent of Small Company's voting common stock on January 1, 19X1. On this date, Small Company sold Great Company a lathe for $15,000. The lathe was recorded on Small Company's books at a cost of $10,000; the related accumulated depreciation was $4,000. At date of sale, the lathe had an estimated remaining useful life of six years with an expected salvage value of zero. These estimates are consistent with the original estimates made by Small Company's management. The lathe has been, and will continue to be, depreciated using the straight-line method.

Each company earned net income from its own operations of $40,000 during 19X1 and 19X2. Great Company accounts for its investment in Small Company using the modified equity method, and unconfirmed profits are allocated pro rata.

Required:

a. Prepare the 19X1 and 19X2 working paper entries related to the sale of the lathe.

b. Calculate 19X2 consolidated net income incrementally.

c. Calculate both 19X1 and 19X2 minority interest expense.

Exercise 7–11   (Fixed Asset Sale, Working Paper Entries, Incremental Calculation, Minority Interest Expense, and Income Tax Allocation—Pro Rata Allocation)

P Company holds 80 percent of the voting stock of S Company. On January 1, 19X1, S Company sells P Company a milling machine for $20,000. The machine's cost and accumulated depreciation on this date are $30,000 and $20,000, respectively. The remaining useful life of the milling machine is expected to be five years.

P Company accounts for its investment in S Company using the modified equity method, and unconfirmed profits are allocated pro rata. During 19X1 and 19X2, each company earned net income from its own operations of $15,000.

P Company and S Company file separate income tax returns. The income tax rate is 40 percent.

Required:

a. Prepare the 19X1 and 19X2 working paper entries related to the sale of the milling machine.

b. Calculate both 19X1 and 19X2 minority interest expense.

c. Calculate both 19X1 and 19X2 consolidated net income incrementally.

Exercise 7-12   (Equity Method Income for Investor Company)

On January 1, 19X1, Donn Company enters into a joint venture with two other companies to manufacture and sell frisbees. The three companies plan to share profits from the joint venture equally.

During 19X1, Donn Company manufactures equipment for the joint venture. The equipment is delivered on December 31, 19X1, at a price of $225,000. Donn Company's manufacturing cost is $150,000. The equipment has an expected useful life of five years.

The joint venture begins operations in 19X2, following the receipt of the equipment. It has no income or loss in 19X1. Its 19X2 net income is $60,000.

Donn Company reports net income from its own operations in 19X1 of $125,000. In 19X2, Donn Company's income from its own operations is $100,000.

Required:

a. Prepare Donn Company's equity method entries for both 19X1 and 19X2.

b. Calculate Donn Company's net income for both 19X1 and 19X2.

Problems

Problem 7-13   (Fixed Asset Sale and Working Paper—Pro Rata Allocation)

Master Company owns 90 percent of Wilson Company's voting common stock. Wilson Company sells a fixed asset to Master Company on January 1, 19X1, for $50,000. This asset was purchased 20 years earlier by Wilson Company for $60,000. Its estimated remaining useful life is 10 years, and the estimated residual value is zero. Accumulated depreciation to the date of sale under the straight-line method amounts to $40,000. The companies file consolidated income tax returns.

The December 31, 19X2, trial balances of the affiliates are given below.

	Master Company	Wilson Company
Current Assets	$ 80,000	$ 65,000
Inventory	57,500	60,000
Fixed Assets	200,000	140,000
Investment in Wilson Company . . .	199,800	
Dividends Declared	10,000	5,000
Cost of Goods Sold	200,000	90,000
Operating Expenses	70,000	60,000
	$817,300	$420,000
Accumulated Depreciation	$ 30,000	$ 20,000
Liabilities	80,000	23,000
Capital Stock	100,000	70,000
Retained Earnings	174,300	87,000
Sales	370,000	220,000
Equity in Subsidiary Earnings	63,000	
	$817,300	$420,000

Master Company accounts for its investment in Wilson Company using the modified equity method. Unconfirmed profits are allocated pro rata.

Required:

Prepare a consolidated statement working paper for the year ended December 31, 19X2.

Problem 7–14   (Fixed Asset Sale and Working Paper—Pro Rata Allocation)

Banner Company owns 80 percent of the capital stock of Ribbon Company. On January 1, 19X1, Ribbon Company sells fixed assets to Banner Company for $45,000. These assets were purchased 10 years earlier by Ribbon Company for $50,000. Accumulated depreciation for the 10 years to the date of sale (estimated total useful life of 25 years) amounts to $20,000. The companies file consolidated income tax returns.

On December 31, 19X2, the trial balances of the affiliates were as follows:

	Banner Company	Ribbon Company
Inventory	$ 13,500	$ 5,900
Fixed Assets	180,000	64,000
Other Assets	115,620	149,700
Investment in Ribbon Company . . .	150,080	
Dividends Declared	10,000	8,000
Cost of Goods Sold	78,500	64,100
Operating Expenses	42,000	37,400
	$589,700	$329,100

	Banner Company	Ribbon Company
Liabilities	$ 23,000	$ 8,000
Accumulated Depreciation	31,200	24,000
Sales	152,000	119,000
Equity in Subsidiary Earnings	14,000	
Capital Stock	250,000	100,000
Retained Earnings	119,500	78,100
	$589,700	$329,100

Banner Company uses the modified equity method to account for its investment in Ribbon Company. Unconfirmed profits are allocated pro rata.

Required:

Prepare a consolidated statement working paper for the year ended December 31, 19X2.

Problem 7–15   (Fixed Asset and Merchandise Sales, Working Paper, and Incremental Calculation—Pro Rata Allocation)

P Company acquired 90 percent of the stock of S Company on January 1, 19X1, for $78,500. On this date, the balances of S Company's stockholders' equity accounts were Capital Stock, $50,000, and Retained Earnings, $10,000.

An examination of S Company's assets and liabilities on January 1, 19X1, revealed that book values were equal to fair values for all items except merchandise, which had a book value of $12,000 and a fair value of $17,000. These goods were sold in 19X1. Goodwill arising from the combination is being amortized over 20 years.

On January 1, 19X4, S Company sold a building to P Company for $50,000. On this date, the building was carried on S Company's books (net of accumulated depreciation) at $40,000. The building was estimated to have a remaining life of 10 years on the sale date.

P Company regularly sells merchandise to S Company with a markup of 40 percent on selling price. During 19X5, intercompany sales amount to $20,000, of which $6,000 remains in the ending inventory of S Company. Additionally, S Company's January 1, 19X5, inventory includes $3,000 of merchandise purchased in the preceding year from P Company.

P Company accounts for its investment in S Company using the modified equity method. Unconfirmed profits are allocated pro rata.

The trial balances of the two companies at December 31, 19X5, are provided below:

	P Company	S Company
Other Assets	$ 37,800	$110,000
Inventory	50,000	15,000
Building, net	40,000	
Investment in S Company	109,500	
Cost of Goods Sold	100,000	45,000
Operating Expenses	70,000	20,000
Dividends Declared	30,000	5,000
	$437,300	$195,000
Liabilities	$ 40,000	$ 20,000
Capital Stock	100,000	50,000
Retained Earnings (1/1/X5)	89,300	50,000
Sales	200,000	75,000
Equity in Subsidiary Earnings	8,000	
	$437,300	$195,000

Required:

a. Prepare a consolidated statement working paper for the year ended December 31, 19X5.

b. Calculate consolidated net income for 19X5 incrementally.

Problem 7–16   (Fixed Asset and Merchandise Sales, Working Paper, and Incremental Calculation—Pro Rata Allocation)

P Company owns 90 percent of the common stock of S Company. On December 31, 19X4, the trial balances of the affiliates are as follows:

	P Company	S Company
Cash	$ 26,700	$ 45,000
Accounts Receivable	30,000	120,000
Property, Plant, and Equipment	75,000	
Investment in S Company	164,250	
Inventory	75,000	22,500
Cost of Goods Sold	150,000	67,500
Operating Expenses	105,000	30,000
Dividends Declared	45,000	7,500
	$670,950	$292,500

	P Company	S Company
Accounts Payable	$ 60,000	$ 30,000
Accumulated Depreciation	15,000	
Common Stock	150,000	75,000
Retained Earnings	133,950	75,000
Sales	300,000	112,500
Equity in Subsidiary Earnings	12,000	
	$670,950	$292,500

At December 31, 19X3, the unamortized differential was $24,000. The differential is allocated to goodwill with a remaining useful life of 16 years as of December 31, 19X3.

S Company regularly sells merchandise to P Company. During 19X4, intercompany sales amounted to $30,000. At the beginning of 19X4, P Company's inventory included unconfirmed profit of $2,000. At December 31, 19X4, the unconfirmed profit in P Company's inventory was $4,000.

On January 1, 19X3, S Company sold a warehouse to P Company for $75,000. At that time, the warehouse was carried on S Company's books at a cost of $240,000 with accumulated depreciation (under the straight-line method) of $180,000. The remaining useful life of the warehouse was estimated to be 10 years on this date. P Company is depreciating the warehouse using the straight-line method.

P Company accounts for its investment in S Company using the modified equity method. Pro rata allocation is used.

Required:

a. Prepare a consolidated statement working paper for the year ended December 31, 19X4.

b. Calculate consolidated net income for 19X4 incrementally.

Problem 7–17   (Fixed Asset Sale, Working Paper, and Incremental Calculation—Pro Rata Allocation)

P Company has a 60 percent interest in S Company. The ownership interest was acquired several years ago, and there is no unamortized differential. Normally, the affiliates do not engage in intercompany transactions. However, on January 1, 19X1, S Company sold P Company some equipment it no longer needed for $50,000. On this date, the equipment had a cost of $80,000 and accumulated depreciation of $40,000. The equipment is estimated to have a remaining useful life of five years, and straight-line depreciation is to continue.

The trial balances of the affiliates at December 31, 19X1, were as follows:

	P Company	S Company
Other Assets	$ 394,580	$426,600
Plant and Equipment	$ 50,000	
Investment in S Company	242,220	
Inventory	93,000	37,200
Cost of Goods Sold	260,400	148,800
Operating Expenses	48,500	20,500
Dividends Declared	8,000	5,000
	$1,096,700	$638,100
Accumulated Depreciation	$9,300	
Liabilities	212,180	60,100
Common Stock	310,000	232,500
Retained Earnings	134,000	82,500
Sales	375,000	253,000
Equity in Subsidiary Earnings	56,220	
Gain on Sale of Equipment		$ 10,000
	$1,096,700	$638,100

P Company accounts for its investment in S Company using the modified equity method. Pro rata allocation is used.

Required:

a. Prepare a consolidated statement working paper for the year ended December 31, 19X1.

b. Calculate consolidated net income for 19X1 incrementally.

Problem 7–18   (Merchandise Sales, Tax Allocation, Incremental and Residual Calculations, Minority Interest Expense, and Working Paper Entries—Pro Rata Allocation)

Buckley Company purchased 90 percent of the capital stock of Carson Company and 60 percent of the capital stock of Diamond Company on January 1, 19X0. Intercompany sales of merchandise during 19X1 were as follows:

From	*To*	*Sales*	*Remaining in Purchaser's 12/31 Inventory*
Buckley	Carson	$30,000	$3,000
Carson	Buckley	20,000	2,000
Diamond	Carson	25,000	4,000

Intercompany sales of merchandise during 19X0 were the following:

From	To	Sales	Remaining in Purchaser's 12/31 Inventory
Carson	Buckley	$15,000	$3,000
Diamond	Carson	10,000	2,000

Gross profit rates (based on selling price) for 19X0 and 19X1 were as follows:

Buckley	20%
Carson	25
Diamond	30

During 19X1, the companies reported net incomes from their own operations as follows:

Buckley	$50,000
Carson	40,000
Diamond	30,000

Buckley Company uses the equity method to account for its investments in Carson and Diamond Companies. Unconfirmed profits are allocated pro rata.

The affiliates file separate income tax returns. The income tax rate is 40 percent.

Required:

a. Calculate the unconfirmed profits in the 19X1 beginning and ending inventories both gross and net of tax.

b. Calculate 19X1 consolidated net income incrementally.

c. Calculate 19X1 minority interest expenses.

d. Prepare the working paper entries related to the intercompany merchandise transactions for a 19X1 consolidated statement working paper.

e. Calculate 19X1 consolidated net income residually.

Consolidated Statements— Preference Interests

Chapter Outline

This chapter covers the effects of preference interests on consolidated financial statements and on the equity method. The first topic covered is intercompany bond holdings. An intercompany bond holding is created when one affiliate's bonds are acquired by another through purchase from a nonaffiliate. The other topic dealt with is the effect of subsidiary preferred stock on the consolidated statements and on the equity method. The existence of preferred stock introduces new features into our analysis whether or not the parent owns some of the preferred shares.

INTERCOMPANY BONDS—GENERAL COMMENTS

There are various motivations for the purchase of an affiliate's bonds. Perhaps the most obvious motivation involves convertible bonds of a subsidiary. Consider the case of a parent owning 51 percent of a subsidiary's common shares. If the subsidiary's capital structure contains a large number of convertible bonds held by nonaffiliates, conversion of the bonds can reduce the parent's ownership interest below 50 percent. The parent can ensure against such a dilution by purchasing 51 percent of the subsidiary's bonds from nonaffiliates. Acquisition of nonconvertible senior securities may be for any of the diverse reasons motivating any company to reacquire its own outstanding debt.

When a company reacquires its own bonds before maturity, a gain or loss on their retirement is recorded. The gain or loss is the difference between the amount paid for the bonds and their book value on the retirement date. A similar situation occurs when one affiliate purchases the bonds of another affiliate from *a nonaffiliate*. In this case, an intercompany bond holding is created, and the bonds are *no longer outstanding from the consolidated viewpoint*, although they remain outstanding legally. Since the intercompany bonds are no longer outstanding from the consolidated view, a gain or loss on their retirement is recognized in the consolidated financial statements.[1] Also, the intercompany bond investment and bond liability do not appear on the consolidated statements. In preparing the statements, these intercompany items are eliminated like other intercompany receivables and payables.

For reasons expressed in Chapter 6, we continue to assume that the parent company uses the *modified equity method* to account for its investment in subsidiaries. Therefore, no entry is made on the parent's books for its share of the gain or loss on the retirement of the bonds.

To illustrate the basic concepts, assume that P Company pays $11,000 to acquire 10 of the outstanding bonds of its 90 percent owned subsidiary, S Company. On the date they are acquired, the bonds have a par value of $10,000 and unamortized discount of $2,000 on S Company's books. In this case, a loss on

---

[1] Such a gain or loss is considered to be a gain or loss on early extinguishment of debt. See *Statement of Financial Accounting Standards No. 4,* "Reporting Gains and Losses from Extinguishment of Debt" (Norwalk, CT: FASB, 1975).

retirement of $3,000 [$11,000 − ($10,000 − $2,000)] is recognized for consolidated statement purposes. A loss occurs because a liability with a book value of $8,000 ($10,000 − $2,000) is liquidated by an $11,000 payment by the consolidated entity. Note that the loss also equals the sum of P Company's premium ($1,000) and S Company's unamortized discount ($2,000). The general principle is that *a gain or loss from an intercompany bond acquisition equals the algebraic sum of any unamortized discounts or premiums recorded on the affiliates' books on the date the bonds are acquired* (where the sign of a debit (credit) balance account is a plus (minus)). *The premium or discount of the purchasing affiliate is referred to as its contribution to the gain or loss. Similarly, the unamortized premium or discount on the issuing affiliate's books is referred to as its contribution to the gain or loss.* Note that P Company's share of the loss in our example does not equal the entire loss. In general, if the parent is involved in an intercompany bond acquisition, *its share of the gain or loss from the acquisition equals the algebraic sum of its unamortized discount or premium on the date the bonds are acquired and the product of the ownership percent and the subsidiary's unamortized discount or premium on this date.* Thus, P Company's share of the loss is $2,800 [$1,000 + (90% × $2,000)]. The parent's share of the gain or loss on an intercompany bond acquisition equals the effect of the gain or loss on consolidated net income. Thus, consolidated net income is decreased by $2,800 because of the $3,000 loss. Finally, P Company's $11,000 bond investment and S Company's net bond liability of $8,000 do not appear on the consolidated statements since they are intercompany items.

We emphasize that intercompany bonds remain outstanding legally. Thus, the affiliate that issued the bonds continues to pay interest on them and to amortize related bond premium or discount. Similarly, the affiliate purchasing the bonds receives interest on them and amortizes its bond premium or discount.

INTERCOMPANY BONDS—INTRODUCTORY CASES

In brief, when intercompany bonds are acquired, they are no longer outstanding from the consolidated view, and a gain or loss on their retirement is recognized in the consolidated financial statements. Also, the intercompany bond investment and the intercompany bond liability are eliminated like other intercompany receivables and payables. The following simplified examples illustrate these points and introduce the consolidated statement working paper techniques for intercompany bond holdings.

Case 1. 100 Percent Ownership and Noninterest-Bearing Bonds Issued at Par

Assume that P Company acquires a 100 percent interest in S Company on December 31, 19X0, at book value. S Company has *noninterest-bearing* bonds outstanding that were issued at par of $10,000.[2] Neither affiliate has any transactions during 19X1, 19X2, and 19X3, except that P Company purchases S Company's bonds from a nonaffiliate on December 31, 19X1, for $9,700 (i.e., at a discount of $300). The bonds mature in two years—on December 31, 19X3. The gain on the intercompany bond acquisition is $300—an amount equal to P Company's discount (a credit balance account).

Subsidiary's Entries in 19X1, 19X2, and 19X3.   Normally, a company issuing bonds pays cash interest on the bonds and amortizes bond premium or discount. However, S Company's bonds are noninterest bearing and were issued at par. Thus, S Company's only entry for its bonds over the period 19X1 to 19X3 records their *actual* retirement on December 31, 19X3:

Bonds Payable	10,000	
Cash		10,000

Parent's Entries in 19X1.   The first entry made by P Company in 19X1 is to record the purchase of the bonds. Normally, this entry would involve a debit to Investment in S Company Bonds for $9,700 and a credit to Cash for $9,700. However, illustrating the effects of discounts and premiums is clarified if we assume that the Investment in S Company Bonds account is carried at par value and the $300 discount is recorded in a contra account (Discount on Bond Investment). With this assumption, P Company's entry to record the bond purchase is as follows:[3]

Investment in S Company Bonds	10,000	
Discount on Bond Investment		300
Cash		9,700

Note that P Company amortizes no discount in 19X1 since the bonds are acquired on December 31, 19X1.

Parent's Entries in 19X2 and 19X3.   Since the bonds are noninterest bearing, P Company's only 19X2 entry related to the bonds is for discount amortization. Assuming straight-line amortization of discount, this entry is as follows:[4]

Discount on Bond Investment ($300/2)	150	
Bond Interest Income		150

---

[2] This unrealistic assumption is meant to simplify our initial scenario.

[3] Any reader uncomfortable with the use of a separate discount or premium account may substitute Investment in S Company Bonds in place of all references to Discount on Bond Investment or Premium on Bond Investment.

[4] Straight-line amortization of bond premium and discount minimizes complicating detail in explaining the procedures related to intercompany bonds. Recall that *APB Opinion No. 21* requires the use of the effective interest method in amortizing bond premium and discount if the amounts involved are material. Case 5 illustrates effective interest amortization.

P Company's 19X3 entries are exactly as in 19X2 with one exception. P Company records S Company's redemption of the bonds at maturity as follows:

Cash 10,000
    Investment in S Company Bonds   10,000

Working Paper Entries for 19X1. The consolidated statement working paper techniques for intercompany bonds can be relatively complex. As a starting point in explaining these procedures, we focus on 19X1 and 19X2 in this simplified example. In 19X1, the working paper entries for the bonds are as follows:

1. To record the gain on retirement of bonds from consolidated perspective:

Discount on Bond Investment   300
    Gain on Purchase of Affiliate's Bonds   300

2. To eliminate intercompany bond holding:

Bonds Payable 10,000
    Investment in S Company Bonds   10,000

These entries are relatively simple for several reasons: the bonds are noninterest bearing, there is no discount amortization (since the bonds are acquired at year-end), and S Company recorded no discount or premium when the bonds were issued (at par). Entry (1) recognizes the gain on the constructive retirement of the bonds by eliminating the discount recorded by P Company when the bonds are acquired. It illustrates the principle that a gain or loss from the acquisition of intercompany bonds equals the algebraic sum of any unamortized discounts or premiums recorded on the affiliates' books on the date the bonds are acquired. This point is elaborated on as our examples become more complex. Entry (2) offsets the intercompany receivable, Investment in S Company Bonds, against the related intercompany payable, Bonds Payable.

Working Paper Entries for 19X2

The 19X2 working paper elimination entries for the bonds are as follows:

1. To eliminate income statement effect of bonds recorded on P Company's books, eliminate P Company's year-end unamortized discount, and *adjust* the beginning-of-year balance in P Company's Retained Earnings for the confirmed but unrecognized gain on the retirement of bonds:

Discount on Bond Investment	150	
Bond Interest Income	150	
Retained Earnings, 1/1/X2—P Company		300

2. To eliminate intercompany bond holding:

Bonds Payable	10,000	
Investment in S Company Bonds		10,000

Entry (2) is the same as in 19X1. Entry (1) has three functions. First, it eliminates the bonds' 19X2 income statement effect—the bond interest income recorded via discount amortization in 19X2. This elimination is consistent with the principle that the income statement effects of discount and premium amortization related to intercompany bonds do not affect consolidated net income. Second, entry (1) eliminates the unamortized discount on P Company's books at the end of 19X2. This balance is eliminated since the bonds no longer exist from the consolidated viewpoint and, consequently, the discount no longer exists from this perspective. Last, it adjusts the beginning-of-year balance in P Company's Retained Earnings for the $300 gain on the retirement of S Company's bonds. The gain was recognized in the 19X1 consolidated income statement and thus belongs in beginning-of-year consolidated retained earnings. Entry (1) accomplishes this.

Case 2. 100 Percent Ownership and Noninterest-Bearing Bonds Issued at Discount

In this case, add to the information of Case 1 that S Company has $100 of unamortized discount on the bonds when they are acquired. Under these conditions, the gain on the constructive retirement of the bonds is $200, the difference between the $9,900 book value of the bonds and the $9,700 acquisition price.

The 19X1 working paper entries for the bonds are similar to those for Case 1.

1. To record gain on retirement of bonds from consolidated perspective:

Discount on Bond Investment	300	
Gain on Purchase of Affiliate's Bonds		300
Gain on Purchase of Affiliate's Bonds	100	
Discount on Bonds Payable		100

2. To eliminate intercompany bond holding:

Bonds Payable	10,000	
Investment in S Company Bonds		10,000

The entries in (1) record the $200 gain on the bonds ($300 − $100) by eliminating both the discount recorded by P Company when the bonds are acquired and the unamortized discount on S Company's books on this date. These entries recognize the gain consistently with the principle that a gain or loss on an intercompany bond acquisition equals the algebraic sum of any unamortized discounts or premiums recorded on the affiliates' books on the date the bonds are acquired. Entry (2) is the same as in Case 1.

The 19X2 working paper entries for the bonds are as follows:

1. To eliminate the income statement effect of bonds recorded on P Company's books, eliminate P Company's year-end unamortized discount, and *adjust* the beginning-of-year balance in P Company's Retained Earnings:

Discount on Bond Investment	150	
Bond Interest Income	150	
Retained Earnings, 1/1/X2—P Company		300

2. To eliminate the income statement effect of bonds recorded on S Company's books, eliminate S Company's year-end unamortized discount, and *adjust* the beginning-of-year balance in P Company's Retained Earnings:

Retained Earnings, 1/1//X2—P Company	100	
Bond Interest Expense		50
Discount on Bonds Payable		50

3. To eliminate intercompany bond holding:

Bonds Payable	10,000	
Investment in S Company Bonds		10,000

The explanations of entries (1) and (3) are the same as in Case 1. Entry (2) eliminates the bonds' income statement effect recorded on S Company's books. The credit to Bond Interest Expense is needed because S Company increases Bond Interest Expense when it amortizes its discount. This elimination also is consistent with the principle that the income statement effects of discount and premium amortization related to intercompany bonds do not affect consolidated net income. Entry (2) also eliminates the unamortized discount on S Company's books at the end of 19X2. As in the case of P Company's discount, S Company's discount no longer exists from the consolidated perspective. Finally, entry (2) adjusts the beginning-of-year balance of P Company's Retained Earnings for its share (100% in this case) of the confirmed but unrecorded loss arising from the discount on Bonds Payable on S Company's books.

ALLOCATING GAINS AND LOSSES FROM INTERCOMPANY BOND ACQUISITIONS

When minority interests exist, the gain or loss from intercompany bond acquisitions must be allocated between the parent company and the minority shareholders. Three general principles apply to this allocation process. The first, as seen before, is that the total gain or loss to be allocated equals the algebraic sum of any unamortized discounts or premiums recorded on the affiliates' books on the bonds' acquisition date. Note that the affiliates involved in an intercompany bond holding may be the parent and a subsidiary or two subsidiaries. The second principle is that if the parent is involved in an intercompany bond acquisition, its share (and the consolidated net income effect) of the related gain or loss equals the algebraic sum of its unamortized discount or premium on the date the bonds are acquired and the product of the ownership percent and the subsidiary's unamortized discount or premium on this date. The third principle covers the case in which two subsidiaries are party to the intercompany bond holding. The parent's share of the resulting gain or loss is the product of the ownership percent for the first subsidiary and its unamortized discount or premium on the acquisition date, plus the product of the ownership percent for the second subsidiary and its unamortized discount or premium on the acquisition date (with appropriate signs being attached to discount and premium). For example, assume that P Company has 80 percent and 70 percent interests in S Company and T Company, respectively. Also, assume that S Company purchases bonds of T Company from a nonaffiliate at a premium of $1,000 at a time when the unamortized premium on these bonds on T Company's books is $500. In this case, P Company's share of the loss of $500 [$1,000 + (−$500)] is $450 [(80% × $1,000) + (70% × (−$500))]. The effect of the loss on consolidated net income also is $450.

The second and third principles mentioned above are consistent with the concept of *pro rata allocation*. Recall that the intent of consolidated financial statements is to show the economic effects of transactions with nonaffiliates. Also, recall in the case of an intercompany sale that pro rata allocation is consistent with this intent. It reports results of operations as if the intercompany sale is not present. In the asset sale case, we are dealing with a recorded, but unconfirmed, profit. The intent of consolidated financial statements is the same in the case of an intercompany bond acquisition. However, we have here a gain or loss from a transaction with a nonaffiliate that is *confirmed, but unrecorded*, from the consolidated perspective. Nevertheless, if pro rata allocation is used, the consolidated statement account balances are as if the intercompany bonds do not exist (i.e., actually have been retired)—which is the consolidated perspective with respect to such bonds. Cases 3 and 4 illustrate that pro rata allocation produces results that are as if the intercompany bonds are retired. As before, the use of pro rata allocation implies that consolidated net income and the minority interest values are calculated on the basis of the affiliates' confirmed net incomes from their own separate operations and the subsidiary's confirmed stockholders' equity. These points also are illustrated in Cases 3 and 4.

Although we prefer pro rata allocation, 100 percent allocation also can be used on gains and losses from intercompany bond acquisitions.[5] Assuming 100 percent allocation, the entire loss of $500 calculated in the above example is allocated to the parent company. Consolidated net income is thus reduced by $500 under 100 percent allocation, and the minority interest values are based on the subsidiary's recorded net income and stockholders' equity. Although we do not illustrate the techniques of 100 percent allocation, the exercises and problems of this chapter cover this procedure. The procedures of 100 percent allocation are relatively easy once the techniques of pro rata allocation are understood.

INTERCOMPANY BONDS—ADVANCED CASES

The previous cases are simplified in several ways. First, the ownership percent is 100. Second, the intercompany bonds are acquired at year-end. Third, the bonds are noninterest bearing. Fourth, the earlier cases ignore the working paper entries except those related to the bonds. And last, consolidated net income and minority interest calculations are not made. The following cases deal with these issues. Cases 3 and 4 are the same, except that the bonds are acquired at year-end in Case 3, but at the beginning of the year in Case 4. The year-end acquisition assumption is retained in Case 3 for clarity in explaining intercompany bond procedures.

Case 3. Subsidiary's Bonds Acquired by Parent at Year-End

On January 1, 19X0, S Company issued $5,000 (par) of 9 percent, 10-year bonds, due 10 years later on January 1, 19X10. Interest is payable semiannually on July 1 and January 1. The cash proceeds from the issue were $6,250, and the $1,250 premium is being amortized over the 10-year bond life at the rate of $125 per year.

---

[5] Note that GAAP is silent on the issue of whether pro rata or 100 percent allocation is to be used in the case of intercompany bond holdings. Since either technique is allowed in the case of unconfirmed profits, we infer that either procedure is acceptable in the case of intercompany bond holdings.

On January 1, 19X7, P Company purchased 80 percent of S Company's common stock for $80,000. On this date, S Company had common stock of $100,000 and zero retained earnings. Book and fair values of assets and liabilities were equal. On December 31, 19X7, P Company purchased the S Company bonds for $5,140, plus $225 accrued interest for six months. P Company's premium of $140 is being amortized over the remaining two years of bond life at a rate of $70 per year. The gain on the intercompany bond acquisition is $110 [$140 + (−$250)] and is allocated pro rata. P Company's contribution is a reduction of $140, and S Company's contribution is $250. P Company's share of the gain is $60 [$140 + (80% × (−$250))].

Subsidiary's Entries. S Company's entries for its bonds include the entry to record their issuance, annual entries to record interest expense and premium amortization, and the entry to record the bonds' redemption at maturity. These entries are as follows:

1. To record issuance of the bonds on January 1, 19X0:

Cash	6,250	
Bonds Payable		5,000
Premium on Bonds Payable		1,250

2. To record payment of cash interest on July 1 of each year through 19X9:

Bond Interest Expense	225	
Cash		225

3. To accrue interest expense on December 31 of each year through 19X9:

Bond Interest Expense	225	
Accrued Interest Payable		225

4. To amortize premium on December 31 of each year through 19X9:

Premium on Bonds Payable	125	
Bond Interest Expense		125

5. To record payment of cash interest on January 1 of each year through 19X10 (except 19X0):

Accrued Interest Payable	225	
Cash		225

6. To record retirement of bonds on January 1, 19X10:

Bonds Payable	5,000	
Cash		5,000

Parent's Entries in 19X7. In 19X7, P Company records its investments in S Company's common stock and bonds and its equity method entries. S Company's net income figures for 19X7 and 19X8, along with the details of its interest expense and premium amortization for these years, are summarized below.

	19X7	*19X8*
S Company's net income, excluding the effect of interest	$20,000	$10,000
Less: Annual interest expense at nominal rate (9% × $5,000)	(450)	(450)
Plus: Premium amortization	125	125
S Company's net income	$19,675	$ 9,675

Given these data, P Company's 19X7 entries are as follows:

1. To record purchase of S Company stock on January 1, 19X7:

| Investment in S Company Stock | 80,000 | |
| Cash | | 80,000 |

2. To record purchase of S Company bonds on December 31, 19X7:

Investment in S Company Bonds	5,000	
Premium on Bond Investment	140	
Accrued Interest Receivable	225	
Cash		5,365

3. To record equity in S Company's net income:

| Investment in S Company Stock (80% × $19,675) | 15,740 | |
| Equity in Subsidiary Earnings | | 15,740 |

The following table summarizes pertinent account balances of the two companies at the end of 19X7.

	December 31, 19X7	
DR (CR)	*P Company*	*S Company*
Bonds Payable		($5,000)
Premium on Bonds Payable		(250)
Accrued Interest Payable		(225)
Interest Expense		325
Income before Interest Expense and Equity in Subsidiary Earnings	($30,000)	(20,000)
Investment in S Company Bonds	5,000	
Premium on Bond Investment	140	
Accrued Interest Receivable	225	
Investment in S Company Stock	95,740	
Equity in Subsidiary Earnings	(15,740)	

Working Paper Entries for 19X7.   The following are the working paper entries for 19X7:

1. To reverse the parent's equity method entry for the year and to account for the minority share of *confirmed* subsidiary net income:[6]

Minority Interest Expense		
[20% × ($19,675 + $250)]	3,985	
Equity in Subsidiary Earnings	15,740	
Investment in S Company Stock		15,740
Minority Interest		3,985

2. To eliminate the investment account against the beginning-of-year stockholders' equity accounts of the subsidiary:

Capital Stock—S Company	100,000	
Retained Earnings—S Company	0	
Investment in S Company Stock		80,000
Minority Interest		20,000

3. To record gain on the constructive retirement of the bonds from a consolidated perspective:

3a. Gain on Purchase of Affiliate's Bonds	140	
Premium on Bond Investment		140
3b. Premium on Bonds Payable	250	
Gain on Purchase of Affiliate's Bonds		250

4. To eliminate intercompany bond holding:

Bonds Payable	5,000	
Investment in S Company Bonds		5,000

---

[6] In the absence of subsidiary dividends, it is convenient to combine the first two working paper entries presented in prior chapters. We follow this convention throughout this chapter.

5. To eliminate intercompany interest payable and interest receivable:

Accrued Interest Payable	225	
Accrued Interest Receivable		225

A partial consolidated statement working paper for 19X7 is presented in Illustration 8–1. The working paper is partial since it excludes accounts that are not pertinent to the case of intercompany bonds. We also assume for simplicity that the parent's beginning retained earnings is zero.

Note in working paper entry (1) that *confirmed* subsidiary net income ($19,925) equals S Company's net income, plus its contribution to the gain on the bonds ($19,675 + $250). S Company's contribution to the gain is added because it represents confirmed, but unrecorded, income from the perspective of the consolidated entity and the minority shareholders.[7] The working paper entries in (3) recognize the $110 gain on the constructive retirement of the bonds in the consolidated statements. They recognize the gain by eliminating both the premium recorded by P Company on the bond acquisition date and the unamortized premium on S Company's books on this date. This reflects the principle that a gain or loss on an intercompany bond acquisition equals the algebraic sum of any unamortized discounts or premiums recorded on the affiliates' books on the acquisition date. Working paper entries (4) and (5) offset intercompany receivables and payables.

Parent's Entries in 19X8.   In 19X8, P Company records the interest received or due from S Company, the amortization of its premium, and its equity method entries. Its 19X8 entries are as follows:

1. To record receipt of cash interest on July 1.

Cash	225	
Bond Interest Income		225

---

[7] If the bonds are retired earlier in the year, the portion of S Company's contribution to the gain *recorded* on its books by year-end—an amount equal to its premium amortization for the year—is subtracted from this result in calculating confirmed subsidiary net income (see Case 4). Thus, the calculation of confirmed subsidiary net income in the year that intercompany bonds are acquired is the *opposite* of the corresponding calculation in the year of an intercompany sale of a depreciable fixed asset. As shown in Chapter 7, confirmed subsidiary net income in the year of an intercompany sale of a depreciable fixed asset equals the subsidiary's net income, less the unconfirmed profit recorded on the sale date, plus the profit confirmed by year-end. These opposite results are produced because a confirmed, but unrecorded, profit is being *recognized* in the bond case, while a recorded, but unconfirmed, profit is being *deferred* in the fixed asset case.

ILLUSTRATION 8-1   Subsidiary's Bonds Acquired by Parent at Year-End

P COMPANY AND SUBSIDIARY S COMPANY
Partial Consolidated Statement Working Paper
For the Year Ended December 31, 19X7

	P Company	S Company	Eliminations Dr.		Eliminations Cr.		Consolidated
Income Statement							
Net income before items shown below	30,000	20,000					50,000
Equity in subsidiary earnings	15,740		(1)	15,740			-0-
Bond interest expense		(325)					(325)
Gain on purchase of affiliate's bonds			(3a)	140	(3b)	250	110
Minority interest expense			(1)	3,985			(3,985)
Net income	45,740	19,675		19,865		250	45,800
Retained Earnings Statement							
Retained earnings 1/1/X7:							
P Company	-0-						-0-
S Company		-0-	(2)	-0-			-0-
Net income	45,740	19,675		19,865		250	45,800
Retained earnings, 12/31/X7	45,740	19,675		19,865		250	45,800
Balance Sheet							
Investment in S Company stock	95,740				(1)	15,740	-0-
					(2)	80,000	
Investment in S Company bonds	5,000				(4)	5,000	-0-
Premium on bond investment	140				(3a)	140	-0-
Accrued interest receivable	225				(5)	225	-0-
Bonds payable		5,000	(4)	5,000			-0-
Premium on bonds payable		250	(3b)	250			-0-
Accrued interest payable		225	(5)	225			-0-
Capital stock—S Company		100,000	(2)	100,000			-0-
Minority interest					(1)	3,985	23,985
					(2)	20,000	
(deduction)							

Explanation of eliminations:

(1) To reverse the parent's equity method entries and recognize minority interest in *confirmed* subsidiary net income.

(2) To eliminate beginning-of-year investment account balance against beginning-of-year S Company stockholders' equity accounts.

(3) To record gain on retirement of bonds from consolidated perspective.

(4) To eliminate intercompany bond holding.

(5) To eliminate intercompany interest payable and interest receivable.

2. To accrue interest income on December 31:

Accrued Interest Receivable	225	
Bond Interest Income		225

3. To amortize premium on December 31:

Bond Interest Income	70	
Premium on Bond Investment		70

4. To record equity in S Company's net income:

Investment in S Company Stock (80% × $9,675)	7,740	
Equity in Subsidiary Earnings		7,740

Working Paper Entries for 19X8.   The following are the working paper elimination entries for 19X8:

1. To reverse the parent's equity method entries for the year and account for the minority's share of *confirmed* subsidiary net income:

Minority Interest Expense		
[20% × ($9,675 − $125)]	1,910	
Equity in Subsidiary Earnings	7,740	
Investment in S Company Stock		7,740
Minority Interest		1,910

2. To partially eliminate the income statement effect of bonds recorded on P Company's books, eliminate P Company's year-end unamortized premium, and *adjust* beginning-of-year balance in P Company's retained earnings:

Retained Earnings, 1/1—P Company	140	
Bond Interest Income		70
Premium on Bond Investment		70

3. To partially eliminate income statement effect of bonds recorded on S Company's books, eliminate S Company's year-end unamortized premium, and *adjust* beginning-of-year balances in P Company's Retained Earnings and Minority Interest:

Premium on Bonds Payable	125	
Bond Interest Expense	125	
Retained Earnings, 1/1—P Company (80% × $250)		200
Minority Interest (20% × $250)		50

4. To eliminate investment account against beginning-of-year stockholders' equity accounts:

Capital Stock—S Company	100,000	
Retained Earnings—S Company	19,675	
Investment in S Company stock		95,740
Minority Interest (20% × $119,675)		23,935

5. To eliminate intercompany bond holding:

Bonds Payable	5,000	
Investment in S Company Bonds		5,000

6. To eliminate intercompany interest payable and interest receivable:

Accrued Interest Payable	225	
Accrued Interest Receivable		225

7. To eliminate intercompany interest income and expense recorded at nominal rate:

Bond Interest Income	450	
Bond Interest Expense		450

The partial consolidated statement working paper for 19X8 is presented in Illustration 8–2.

Again, working paper entry (1) is standard under *pro rata allocation*. In 19X8, confirmed subsidiary net income ($9,550) equals S Company's net income, less its 19X8 premium amortization ($9,675 − $125). The amortization of premium is subtracted because it is an income statement effect of the bonds that already has been reflected in consolidated net income (in 19X7).

Working paper entries (2) and (3) are new to this case. Like the corresponding entry in Case 1, entry (2) has three functions. First, it eliminates a portion of the bonds' income statement effect recorded on P Company's books in 19X8—the reduction in bond interest income recorded by premium amortization. Again, this elimination is consistent with the principle that the income statement effects of premium and discount amortization related to intercompany bonds should not affect consolidated net income because the premium or discount was recognized in the gain or loss on constructive retirement of the bonds. Second, entry (2)

ILLUSTRATION 8-2   Subsidiary's Bonds Acquired by Parent at Year-End

P COMPANY AND SUBSIDIARY S COMPANY
Partial Consolidated Statement Working Paper
For the Year Ended December 31, 19X8

	P Company	S Company	Eliminations Dr.		Eliminations Cr.		Consoli- dated
Income Statement							
Net income before items shown below	25,000	10,000					35,000
Equity in subsidiary earnings	7,740		(1)	7,740			-0-
Bond interest income	380		(7)	450	(2)	70	-0-
Bond interest expense		(325)	(3)	125	(3)	450	-0-
Minority interest expense			(1)	1,910			(1,910)
Net Income	33,120	9,675		10,225		520	33,090
Retained Earnings Statement							
Retained earnings, 1/1/X8:							
P Company	45,740		(2)	140	(3)	200	45,800
S Company		19,675	(4)	19,675			-0-
Net income	33,120	9,675		10,225		520	33,090
Retained earnings, 12/31/X8	78,860	29,350		30,040		720	78,890
Balance Sheet							
Investment in S Company stock	103,480				(1)	7,740	-0-
					(4)	95,740	
Investment in S Company bonds	5,000				(5)	5,000	-0-
Premium on bond investment	70				(2)	70	-0-
Accrued interest receivable	225				(6)	225	-0-
Bonds payable		5,000	(5)	5,000			-0-
Premium on bonds payable		125	(3)	125			-0-
Accrued interest payable		225	(6)	225			-0-
Capital stock—S Company		100,000	(4)	100,000			-0-
Minority interest					(1)	1,910	25,895
					(3)	50	
					(4)	23,935	
(deduction)							

Explanation of eliminations:

(1) To reverse the parent's equity method entries and recognize minority interest in *confirmed* subsidiary net income.

(2) To partially eliminate income statement effect of bonds recorded on P Company's books, eliminate P Company's year-end unamortized premium, and *adjust* beginning-of-year balance in parent's Retained Earnings.

(3) To partially eliminate income statement effect of bonds recorded on S Company's books, eliminate S Company's year-end unamortized premium, and *adjust* beginning-of-year balances in parent's Retained Earnings and Minority Interest.

(4) To eliminate investment account against beginning-of-year stockholders' equity accounts.

(5) To eliminate intercompany bond holding.

(6) To eliminate intercompany interest payable and interest receivable.

(7) To eliminate intercompany interest income and expense recorded at nominal rate.

eliminates the unamortized premium on P Company's books at the end of 19X8. This balance is eliminated since the bonds no longer exist from the consolidated viewpoint. Last, it adjusts the beginning-of-year balance in P Company's Retained Earnings for the parent's unrecognized (through amortization) contribution to the gain on retirement of the bonds.

Entry (3) is similar to entry (2), but it pertains to S Company's premium. Thus, entry (3) eliminates the unamortized premium on S Company's books at the end of 19X8 (since it also no longer exists from the consolidated perspective). Entry (3) also eliminates a portion of the bonds' income statement effect recorded on S Company's books in 19X8—the reduction in bond interest expense recorded through premium amortization. Finally, the beginning-of-year unrecognized S Company contribution of $250 to the gain on retirement of bonds (recognized in 19X7 consolidated net income) is allocated to beginning consolidated retained earnings and minority interest.

Working paper entries (4), (5), and (6) are the same as in 19X7. Entry (7) is new. It eliminates the intercompany bond interest income and bond interest expense recorded at the nominal rate of 9 percent during the period. This entry is similar to the entry made in the case of an intercompany sale of services in which the cost of the services is treated as a period expense by the purchasing affiliate (see discussion in Chapter 7). Recall that the confirmation of the selling affiliate's profit on such a sale occurs during the same year as the transfer of the services since the services are assumed to be consumed in this year. Thus, no entry is required to eliminate the seller's profit in this case, although an entry is needed to offset the related intercompany sale and expense. In this context, the interest revenue recorded by P Company is confirmed since the *lending* services related to the interest expense on S Company's books are consumed in the year the expense is recorded. Thus, no adjustment for the interest revenue and interest expense recorded at the nominal rate by the affiliates is required in calculating their confirmed net incomes from their own operations.

P Company's 19X9 working paper entries are not illustrated and discussed because they follow the same pattern as those for 19X8. However, a bond elimination schedule for this case is given in Illustration 8–3. This schedule identifies the bond-related account balances and the modifications of these balances that are needed for consolidated statement purposes. The schedule also summarizes the bond-related working paper entries for the period 19X7 to 19X9. To enhance your understanding, you may want to prepare the 19X9 working paper entries without first referring to Illustration 8–3.

Calculations of Consolidated Net Income. The amounts shown in the partial consolidated statement working papers for consolidated net income in 19X7 and 19X8 are calculated incrementally as follows:

	19X7	*19X8*
P Company's *confirmed* net income from its own operations:		
19X7: ($45,740 − $15,740 − $140)	$29,860	
19X8: ($33,120 − $7,740 + $70)		$25,450
Plus: P Company's equity in S Company's *confirmed* net income:		
19X7: (80% × $19,675 + $250)	15,940	
19X8: (80% × $9,675 − $125)		7,640
Consolidated net income	$45,800	$33,090

In each year, P Company's confirmed net income from its own operations equals its net income, less Equity in Subsidiary Earnings, plus or minus the effect of the premium on the bond investment. In 19X7, the date of acquisition premium (its contribution to the gain) is subtracted because it reduces the gain on the bonds. In 19X8, the premium amortization is added back since the total deduction was recognized in the consolidated statements in 19X7. S Company's confirmed net income figures are calculated similarly. In 19X7, S Company's net income is increased by its acquisition date unamortized premium (its contribution to the gain) since the premium on bonds payable (credit balance) increases the gain on the bonds. In 19X8, the amortization reflected in the subsidiary's reported income (an increase) is adjusted—again to avoid counting the premium twice.

Using the residual approach, we obtain the following calculations of consolidated net income:

	19X7	*19X8*
P Company's net income	$45,740	$33,120
S Company's net income	19,675	9,675
Sum of affiliates' net incomes	$65,415	$42,795
Plus (minus): Effects of working paper entries on sum of affiliates' net incomes:		
Elimination of equity in subsidiary earnings	($15,740)	($ 7,740)
Recording of gain on bonds ($250 − $140)	110	
Elimination of premium amortization ($125 − $70)		(55)
	($15,630)	($ 7,795)
Combined entity income	$49,785	$35,000
Less: Minority interest in S Company's *confirmed* net income:		
19X7: 20% × ($19,675 + $250)	3,985	
19X8: 20% × ($9,675 − $125)		1,910
Consolidated net income	$45,800	$33,090

ILLUSTRATION 8–3 Bond Elimination Schedule

	December 31, 19X7			December 31, 19X8			December 31, 19X9		
	Recorded Amounts	Amount Eliminated or Recorded in Working Paper	Consolidated Amount	Recorded Amount	Amount Eliminated or Recorded in Working Paper	Consolidated Amount	Recorded Amount	Amount Eliminated or Recorded in Working Paper	Consolidated Amount
Accounts on the books of P Company: Investment in									
S Company Bonds	$5,000	($5,000)	–0–	$5,000	($5,000)	–0–	$5,000	($5,000)	–0–
Premium on Bond Investment	140	(140)	–0–	70	(70)	–0–	–0–	–0–	–0–
Bond Interest Income	–0–	–0–	–0–	(380)	380	–0–	(380)	380	–0–
Accrued Interest Receivable	225	(225)	–0–	225	(225)	–0–	225	(225)	–0–
Accounts on the books of S Company:									
Bonds Payable	(5,000)	5,000	–0–	(5,000)	5,000	–0–	(5,000)	5,000	–0–
Premium on Bonds Payable	(250)	250	–0–	(125)	125	–0–	–0–	–0–	–0–
Bond Interest Expense	325	–0–	$325	325	(325)	–0–	325	(325)	–0–
Accrued Interest Payable	(225)	225	–0–	(225)	225	–0–	(225)	225	–0–
Account created by working paper entries:									
Gain on Purchase of Affiliate's Bonds	–0–	(110)	(110)	–0–	–0–	–0–	–0–	–0–	–0–

DR (CR)

Below are working paper entries to accomplish the above:

	December 31, 19X7		December 31, 19X8		December 31, 19X9	
	Debit	Credit	Debit	Credit	Debit	Credit
Bonds Payable	5,000		5,000		5,000	
Investment in S Company Bonds		5,000		5,000		5,000
Accrued Interest Payable	225		225		225	
Accrued Interest Receivable		225		225		225
Bond Interest Income	—		450		450	
Bond Interest Expense		—		450		450
Gain on Purchase of Affiliate's Bonds	140		—		—	
Premium on Bond Investment		140		—		—
Premium on Bonds Payable	250		—		—	
Gain on Purchase of Affiliate's Bonds		250		—		—
Retained Earnings, 1/1 —P Company	—		140		70	
Bond Interest Income		—		70		70
Premium on Bond Investment		—		70		—
Premium on Bonds Payable	—		125		—	
Bond Interest Expense	—		125		125	
Retained Earnings, 1/1— P Company		—		200		100
Minority Interest		—		50		25

Tracing the values used in these calculations to the partial consolidated statement working papers aids in understanding the procedures used in the working papers in dealing with intercompany bonds.

Relationship between Minority Interest and Net Assets of Subsidiary.   Minority interest in the consolidated balance sheet for both 19X7 and 19X8 is the product of the minority interest percent and the subsidiary's year-end confirmed stockholders' equity. In a given year, this latter value is the sum of the subsidiary's year-end capital stock and year-end confirmed retained earnings. Assuming no complications other than an intercompany bond holding, the subsidiary's year-end confirmed retained earnings equals its year-end retained earnings, less any portion of its contribution to the gain or loss from the intercompany bond acquisition not recorded on its books through amortization. The unrecorded gain is equal to the balance of the premium on bonds payable at year-end. The 19X7 and 19X8 consolidated balance sheet minority interest values for this case are calculated in the following schedule.

	December 31	
	19X7	*19X8*
S Company's capital stock	$100,000	$100,000
Calculation of S Company's *confirmed* retained earnings:		
S Company's retained earnings	$ 19,675	$ 29,350
Portion of S Company's contribution to gain		
unrecorded at year-end	250	125
S Company's *confirmed* retained earnings	$ 19,925	$ 29,475
S Company's *confirmed* stockholders' equity	$119,925	$129,475
Minority interest for consolidated balance sheet:		
19X7: (20% × $119,925)	$ 23,985	
19X8: (20% × $129,475)		$ 25,895

Generality of This Case.   This case is very general since it illustrates all the basic techniques that are pertinent in dealing with intercompany bond holdings. Nevertheless, a few additional comments are appropriate. First, although in this example P Company acquires all of S Company's bonds, intercompany bond holdings are likely to be partial. If one affiliate acquires only a portion of the bonds of another, no fundamental modification of the working paper entries is needed. As in this case, these entries are made in relation to the *portion of the bonds acquired by the affiliate.* For example, only the portion of the issuing company's bond liability held by its affiliate is eliminated for consolidated statement purposes. Similarly, only the portions of the issuing company's accrued interest payable, interest expense at the nominal rate, unamortized premium or discount, and discount or premium amortization pertaining to its affiliate are eliminated.

Second, the cases in this chapter assume that intercompany bonds are acquired either the first or last day of the year (and on an interest date unless the bonds are noninterest bearing). In practice, intercompany bonds often are acquired on interim dates and between interest dates. However, no conceptual difficulties are introduced in these cases. The only practical consideration is that the amount of discount or premium amortization to be eliminated is related to the period of time subsequent to the acquisition date of the bonds.

Third, the intercompany bond holding may be between two subsidiaries. In this case, the procedures illustrated for S Company in Cases 3 and 4 are applied to both subsidiaries. The only change in the entries is the recognition of a minority interest effect in both entries allocating the beginning-of-year discount or premium between the parent's (consolidated) retained earnings and minority interest.

Case 4. Subsidiary's Bonds Acquired by Parent at Beginning of Year

This example is like Case 3, except the bond acquisition date is January 1, 19X7, and the purchase price of the bonds is $5,210. P Company's premium of $210 is being amortized over the remaining three years of bond life at a rate of $70 per year, and there is no accrued interest. The gain on the intercompany bond acquisition now is $165 [$210 + (− $375)]. P Company's share of the gain is $90 [$210 + (80% × (− $375))]. The main difference between the two cases is in the working paper entries. Although many of the working paper entries remain the same, all the 19X7 and 19X8 working paper entries are presented for clarity. Partial consolidated statement working papers are not displayed since their consolidated balances are almost identical to those of Case 3. Also, we do not present the entries recorded on the books of the two companies since they are basically the same (in structure) as previously illustrated.

Working Paper Entries for 19X7. The working paper entries for 19X7 are as follows:

1. To reverse the parent's equity method entries for the year and account for the minority's share of *confirmed* subsidiary net income:

Minority Interest Expense		
[20% × ($19,675 + $375 − $125)]	3,985	
Equity in Subsidiary Earnings		
(80% × $19,675)	15,740	
Investment in S Company Stock		15,740
Minority Interest		3,985

2. To eliminate investment account balance against beginning-of-year stockholders' equity accounts of subsidiary:

Capital Stock—S Company	100,000	
Retained Earnings—S Company	0	
Investment in S Company Stock		80,000
Minority Interest		20,000

3. To record gain on retirement of bonds from consolidated perspective, partially eliminate income statement effect of bonds recorded on P and S companies' books, and eliminate P and S companies' year-end unamortized premiums:

Gain on Purchase of Affiliate's Bonds	210	
Premium on Bond Investment		140
Bond Interest Income		70
Premium on Bonds Payable	250	
Bond Interest Expense	125	
Gain on Purchase of Affiliate's Bonds		375

4. To eliminate intercompany bond holding:

Bonds Payable	5,000	
Investment in S Company Bonds		5,000

5. To eliminate intercompany interest payable and interest receivable:

Accrued Interest Payable	225	
Accrued Interest Receivable		225

6. To eliminate intercompany interest income and expense recorded at nominal rate:

Bond Interest Income	450	
Bond Interest Expense		450

Working paper entries (2), (4), and (5) are the same as in Case 3. Entry (6) is needed in this case because the acquisition date of the bonds is the first day of the year. Entry (1) also is the same as in Case 3; however, the calculations of the amounts in this entry differ slightly. Confirmed subsidiary net income, which is the basis for the debit to Minority Interest Expense, is calculated by increasing S Company's reported net income by the *difference* in its contribution to the gain and the portion of the gain it records by year-end through premium amortization. Entry (3) reflects this same modification for amortization of the premiums recorded by the companies in 19X7.

Working Paper Entries for 19X8.   The following are the working paper entries for 19X8, which are identical to those of Case 3:

1. To reverse the parent's equity method entries for the year and account for the minority's share of *confirmed* subsidiary net income:

Minority Interest Expense [20% × ($9,675 − $125)]	1,910	
Equity in Subsidiary Earnings (80% × $9,675)	7,740	
Investment in S Company Stock		7,740
Minority Interest		1,910

2. To partially eliminate income statement effect of bonds recorded on P Company's books, eliminate P Company's year-end unamortized premium, and *adjust* beginning-of-year balance in P Company's retained earnings:

Retained Earnings, 1/1—P Company	140	
Bond Interest Income		70
Premium on Bond Investment		70

3. To partially eliminate income statement effect of bonds recorded on S Company's books, eliminate S Company's year-end unamortized premium, and *adjust* beginning-of-year balances in P Company's Retained Earnings and Minority Interest:

Premium on Bonds Payable	125	
Bond Interest Expense	125	
Retained Earnings, 1/1—P Company (80% × $250)		200
Minority Interest (20% × $250)		50

4. To eliminate investment account balance against beginning-of-year stockholders' equity accounts:

Capital Stock—S Company	100,000	
Retained Earnings—S Company	19,675	
Investment in S Company Stock		95,740
Minority Interest (20% × $119,675)		23,935

5. To eliminate intercompany bond holding:

Bonds Payable	5,000	
Investment in S Company Bonds		5,000

6. To eliminate intercompany interest payable and interest receivable:

Accrued Interest Payable	225	
Accrued Interest Receivable		225

7. To eliminate intercompany interest income and expense recorded at nominal rate:

Bond Interest Income	450	
Bond Interest Expense		450

Residual Calculations of Consolidated Net Income.   Using the residual approach, we can calculate consolidated net income as follows:

	19X7	19X8
P Company's net income	$45,740	$33,120
S Company's net income	19,675	9,675
Sum of affiliates' net incomes	$65,415	$42,795
Plus (minus): Effects of working paper entries on sum of affiliates' net incomes:		
Elimination of equity in subsidiary earnings	($15,740)	($ 7,740)
Recording of gain on bonds ($375 − $210)	165	
Elimination of premium amortization ($125 − $70)	(55)	(55)
	($15,630)	($ 7,795)
Combined entity income	$49,785	$35,000
Less: Minority interest in S Company's *confirmed* net income:		
19X7: [20% × ($19,675 + $375 − $125)]	3,985	
19X8: [20% × ($9,675 − $125)]		1,910
Consolidated net income	$45,800	$33,090

Except for the amount of the gain and the premium elimination shown in 19X7, these calculations are identical to those of Case 3.

Case 5. *Effective Interest Amortization*

For simplicity, previous cases have assumed straight-line amortization. We now relax this assumption in favor of effective interest amortization. However, we emphasize that the introduction of effective interest amortization merely adds computational complexity. Nothing of a fundamental nature is changed. Accordingly, some readers may wish to skip this case.

Assume that on January 1, 19X1, S Company was a wholly owned subsidiary of P Company. On this date, P Company purchased $10,000 of S Company's 10 percent bonds. The bonds pay interest annually on December 31 and mature December 31, 19X2. When originally issued, the bonds were priced to yield 12 percent. Accordingly, the book value of the bonds on January 1, 19X1, was $9,662 (Bonds Payable of $10,000 less Discount on Bonds Payable of $338). Consistent with the effective interest method of amortization, this $9,662 book value is the present value (at a 12 percent discount rate) of the two remaining interest payments of $1,000 plus the present value (also at a 12 percent discount rate) of the December 31, 19X2, principal repayment.

Assume that P Company paid $9,829 for the bonds. At this price, P Company earns an 11 percent rate of return on its bond investment. The constructive retirement of bonds carried at $9,662, at a price of $9,829, results in a loss (from a consolidated perspective) of $167.

Subsidiary's Entry in 19X1.   S Company will make only one entry relating to the bonds during 19X1. This entry records interest expense in the amount of $1,159 (12% × $9,662). Of this amount, $1,000 is the cash payment, and the remainder is discount amortization. S Company's only entry is as follows:

To record interest expense, payment of interest, and discount amortization.

Interest Expense	1,159	
Discount on Bonds Payable		159
Cash		1,000

For simplicity, assume that S Company made no other entries during 19X1.

Parent's Entries in 19X1.   Assume that P Company's only activity during 19X1 was the purchase of the S Company bonds. Accordingly, its 19X1 entries are as follows:

1. To record purchase of S Company bonds on January 1, 19X1.

Investment in S Company Bonds	10,000	
Discount on Bond Investment		171
Cash		9,829

2. To record interest income, receipt of interest, and discount amortization.

Cash	1,000	
Discount on Bond Investment	81	
Interest Income (11% × $9,829)		1,081

3. To record equity in S Company's net income (loss).

Equity in Subsidiary Earnings (100% × $1,159) 1,159
    Investment in S Company Stock   1,159

The following table summarizes selected account balances of the companies at the end of 19X1.

		December 31, 19X1	
DR (CR)		*P Company*	*S Company*
Bonds Payable			($10,000)
Discount on Bonds Payable ($338 − $159)			179
Interest Expense			1,159
Investment in S Company Bonds		$10,000	
Discount on Bond Investment ($171 − $81)		(90)	
Interest Income		(1,081)	
Equity in Subsidiary Earnings		1,159	

From a consolidated viewpoint, S Company's bonds were retired on January 1, 19X1, at a loss of $167 (the difference between the $9,829 purchase price and the $9,662 book value of the bonds). Moreover, as assumed, no other items of revenue or expense will be reported on the consolidated income statement. Accordingly, the working paper entries for 19X1 eliminate *all* of the above account balances. In their place is substituted the $167 loss on bond retirement.

Working Paper Entries for 19X1.   The following are the working paper entries for 19X1 (in a condensed format):

1. To reverse the parent's equity method entries for the year:

Investment in S Company Stock 1,159
    Equity in Subsidiary Earnings   1,159

2. To eliminate all accounts relating to intercompany bonds and establish the loss on constructive retirement of the bonds:

Loss on Purchase of Affiliate's Bonds 167
Interest Income 1,081
Discount on Bond Investment 90
Bonds Payable 10,000
    Interest Expense   1,159
    Discount on Bonds Payable   179
    Investment in S Company Bonds   10,000

PREFERRED STOCK—GENERAL COMMENTS

Many corporations issue preferred stock as well as common stock. Several complications arise in preparing consolidated financial statements if a subsidiary has outstanding preferred stock. Even if the parent holds none of the preferred stock, the preferences of the preferred stock often require the allocation of part of the subsidiary's retained earnings or net income to the preferred shareholders. If the parent holds some of the preferred stock, its investment in the preferred stock, *which is accounted for using the cost method*, is eliminated in preparing the consolidated financial statements. Prior to making this entry, the subsidiary's retained earnings balance frequently is allocated between the preferred and common shareholders, depending on the preferences of the preferred. Similarly, if the parent holds some of the preferred, the subsidiary's net income often is allocated between the preferred and the common shareholders because of the features of the preferred stock.

ALLOCATING SUBSIDIARY EARNINGS

The allocation of a subsidiary's net income and retained earnings between its preferred and common shareholders depends on the characteristics of the preferred stock. Preferred stock always is preferred with respect to dividends. Additionally, it may be cumulative, partially participating, or fully participating. Once the net income and retained earnings of a subsidiary are allocated between its preferred and common shareholders, these amounts are further allocated between the majority and minority shareholders. This allocation depends on whether the parent holds any of the preferred stock and the ownership percents for the preferred and the common. Some general rules for allocating a subsidiary's retained earnings and net income between its preferred and common shareholders under only the *more common conditions* are given below:

1. **Noncumulative, nonparticipating preferred stock.** If the subsidiary's preferred stock is noncumulative and nonparticipating, its retained earnings is allocated totally to its common shareholders. The allocation of the subsidiary's net income depends on whether the subsidiary declares dividends. If dividends are declared, subsidiary net income, up to the amount of the preferred dividend requirement, is allocated to the preferred shareholders (if possible), with any excess being allocated to the common shareholders. If no dividends are declared, the subsidiary's net income is allocated wholly to the common shareholders.

2. **Cumulative, nonparticipating preferred stock.** If the subsidiary's preferred stock is cumulative and nonparticipating, subsidiary retained earnings up to any dividend arrearage is allocated to the preferred shareholders, with any excess being allocated to the common shareholders. Whether or not dividends are declared, subsidiary net

income, up to the amount of the preferred dividend requirement, is allocated to the preferred shareholders. If subsidiary net income is at least as great as the preferred dividend requirement, there is no further complication. However, if subsidiary net income is less than this requirement, the deficiency is allocated to the common shareholders.

3. **Noncumulative, fully participating preferred stock.** If the subsidiary's preferred stock is noncumulative and fully participating, subsidiary retained earnings is allocated pro rata between the preferred and the common shareholders.[8] If dividends are declared, subsidiary net income, up to the amount of the preferred dividend requirement, is allocated to the preferred shareholders, with any excess being allocated to the common shareholders. If subsidiary net income is greater than or equal to the preferred dividend requirement, the common shareholders receive a dividend up to a percentage (on total par) equal to that of the preferred shareholders before further participation by the preferred shareholders occurs.[9] Once the common shareholders receive this equal percentage, any remaining net income is allocated pro rata between the preferred and the common shareholders.

4. **Cumulative, fully participating preferred stock.** If the subsidiary's preferred stock is cumulative and fully participating, subsidiary retained earnings up to any arrearage is allocated to the preferred shareholders, with any remainder being allocated pro rata between the preferred and the common shareholders. If there is no arrearage, the subsidiary's retained earnings is allocated pro rata between the preferred and common shareholders. Whether or not dividends are declared, subsidiary net income, up to the amount of the preferred dividend requirement, is allocated to the preferred shareholders. If subsidiary net income is greater than or equal to the preferred dividend requirement, the common shareholders receive a dividend up to a percentage (on total par) equal to that of the preferred shareholders before further participation by the preferred shareholders occurs.[10] Once the common shareholders receive this equal percentage, any remaining net income is allocated pro rata between the preferred and the common shareholders. If subsidiary net income is less than the preferred dividend requirement, the deficiency is allocated to the common shareholders.

We illustrate the consolidated financial statement procedures for nonparticipating preferred stock in Cases 6 and 7. Although not an exhaustive treatment of the topic of preferred stock, these cases clarify many of the issues that are involved when a parent company holds some of its subsidiary's preferred stock.

---

[8] The pro rata allocation referred to here and below is based on the relative total par values of the preferred and common shares outstanding.

[9] The common shareholders can receive this percentage only if the dividend declared is at least as large as the product of the related percent and the sum of the total par values of the outstanding preferred and common stock.

[10] See footnote 9.

Case 6. Consolidated Financial Statements and Noncumulative, Nonparticipating Preferred Stock

On December 31, 19X1, P Company purchases 90 percent of the common stock of S Company for $126,000 and 30 percent of its noncumulative, nonparticipating, 8 percent preferred stock at book value for $1,500. As indicated, P Company accounts for the preferred stock under the cost method. Relevant date of acquisition account balances for the two companies are as follows:

	December 31, 19X1	
	P Company	*S Company*
Investment in S Company Common Stock	$126,000	
Investment in S Company Preferred Stock	1,500	
Other Assets	192,620	$145,600
Common Stock ($100 par)	200,000	100,000
Preferred Stock ($100 par)		5,000
Retained Earnings	100,000	40,000

Assume also that P and S companies' net incomes from own operations for 19X2 are $20,000 and $1,000, respectively. S Company's dividend declared (and paid) in 19X2 is $400, an amount equal to its preferred dividend requirement (8% × $5,000).

Parent's Entries in 19X2.   S Company's 19X2 dividend declared of $400 is less than its net income of $1,000. Thus, a portion of S Company's net income equal to the preferred dividend is allocated to its preferred shareholders. The remainder of S Company's net income of $600 ($1,000 − $400) is allocated to its common shareholders, and this amount is the basis for recording P Company's equity in subsidiary earnings in 19X2. In other words, in this common situation, *the parent's entry to record its equity in subsidiary net income is based on the subsidiary's net income available to common shareholders*. Given the above allocations, P Company's 19X2 entries are as follows:

1. To record receipt of cash dividend on preferred stock under cost method:

   Cash (30% × $400) 120
       Dividend Income—Preferred Stock 120

2. To record equity in S Company's net income:

   Investment in S Company Common Stock
   [90% × ($1,000 − $400)] 540
       Equity in Subsidiary Earnings 540

Working Paper Entries for 19X2.   The following are the 19X2 working paper entries:

1. To eliminate the intercompany portion of S Company's preferred dividend and record minority interest expense related to preferred stock:

> Minority Interest Expense (70% × $400) 280
> Dividend Income—Preferred Stock 120
>   Dividends Declared   400

2. To eliminate double counting of equity method income and record minority interest related to common stock:

> Minority Interest Expense (10% × $600) 60
> Equity in Subsidiary Earnings 540
>   Investment in S Company Common Stock   540
>   Minority Interest   60

3. To eliminate beginning-of-year Preferred Stock investment account balance against beginning-of-year S Company preferred stock account and establish beginning-of-year minority interest related to preferred stock:

> Preferred Stock 5,000
>   Investment in S Company Preferred
>   Stock (30% × $5,000)   1,500
>   Minority Interest   3,500

4. To eliminate beginning-of-year investment account balance against beginning-of-year S Company common stockholders' equity accounts and establish beginning of year minority interest related to common stock:

> Common Stock—S Company 100,000
> Retained Earnings—S Company 40,000
>   Investment in S Company Common Stock   126,000
>   Minority Interest   14,000

The consolidated statement working paper for this case is presented in Illustration 8–4.

Working paper entry (1) offsets P Company's dividend income against S Company's Dividends Declared account so that consolidated dividends declared equals P Company's dividends declared (zero in this case). This entry also records the minority interest expense in S Company's net income related to the preferred

---

ILLUSTRATION 8-4   Noncumulative, Nonparticipating Preferred Stock

---

P COMPANY AND SUBSIDIARY S COMPANY
Consolidated Statement Working Paper
For The Year Ended December 31, 19X2

	P Company	S Company	Eliminations Dr.		Eliminations Cr.		Consoli-dated
Income Statement							
Net income before items shown below	20,000	1,000					21,000
Dividend income—Preferred stock	120		(1)	120			-0-
Equity in subsidiary earnings	540		(2)	540			-0-
Minority interest expense			(1)	280			340
			(2)	60			
Net income	20,660	1,000		1,000			20,660
Retained Earnings Statement							
Retained earnings 1/1/X2:							
P Company	100,000						100,000
S Company		40,000	(4)	40,000			-0-
Net income	20,660	1,000		1,000			20,660
	120,660	41,000					120,660
Dividends declared:		400			(1)	400	-0-
Retained earnings, 12/31/X2	120,660	40,600		41,000		400	120,660
Balance Sheet							
Investment in S Company:							
Common stock	126,540				(2)	540	-0-
					(4)	126,000	
Preferred stock	1,500				(3)	1,500	-0-
Other assets	192,620	145,600					338,220
	320,660	145,600					338,220
Preferred stock		5,000	(3)	5,000			-0-
Common stock:							
P Company	200,000						200,000
S Company		100,000	(4)	100,000			-0-
Retained earnings	120,660	40,600		41,000		400	120,660
Minority interest					(2)	60	17,560
					(3)	3,500	
					(4)	14,000	
	320,660	145,600		146,000		146,000	338,220

Explanation of eliminations:

(1) To eliminate the intercompany portion of S Company's preferred dividend and record minority interest expense related to preferred stock.

(2) To reverse the parent's equity method entry and recognize minority interest expense related to common stock.

(3) To eliminate beginning-of-year preferred stock investment account balance against beginning-of-year S Company preferred stock account and establish beginning-of-year minority interest related to preferred stock.

(4) To eliminate beginning-of-year investment account balance against beginning-of-year S Company common stockholders' equity accounts and establish beginning-of-year minority interest related to common stock.

shareholders. Entry (2) is standard, except that it records the minority interest expense in S Company's net income (pertaining to common shareholders) on the basis of net income available to common shareholders. Working paper entry (3) is a cost method investment elimination entry related to the preferred stock (see subsequent discussion under the subsection entitled "Differentials on Cumulative, Nonparticipating Preferred Stock"). Entry (4) is a standard (common stock-related) investment elimination entry.

Incremental Calculation of Consolidated Net Income.   Consolidated net income is calculated incrementally as follows:

	19X2
P Company's net income from its own operations	
($20,660 − $120 − $540)	$20,000
Plus: P Company's equity in S Company's 19X2 net income:	
Amount related to common shares (90% × $600) $540	
Amount related to preferred shares (30% × $400) 120	660
Consolidated net income	$20,660

This calculation agrees with the consolidated net income figure shown in Illustration 8–4. It also agrees with P Company's equity method net income figure; thus, P Company's equity method entry maintains the one-line consolidation property of the equity method.

Case 7. Consolidated Financial Statements and Cumulative, Nonparticipating Preferred Stock

On December 31, 19X1, P Company purchases 90 percent of the common stock of S Company for $126,000 and 30 percent of its cumulative, nonparticipating, 8 percent preferred stock for $14,000. Dividends are not in arrears on this date. Pertinent date of acquisition account balances for the two companies are as follows:

	December 31, 19X1	
	P Company	*S Company*
Investment in S Company Common Stock	$126,000	
Investment in S Company Preferred Stock	14,000	
Other Assets	160,000	$190,000
Common Stock ($100 par)	200,000	100,000
Preferred Stock ($100 par)		50,000
Retained Earnings	100,000	40,000

Again, assume that P and S companies' net incomes from own operations for 19X2 are $20,000 and $1,000, respectively. S Company's dividend declared (and paid) in 19X2 is $4,000.

Differentials on Cumulative, Nonparticipating Preferred Stock.   The $14,000 cost of the preferred stock is $1,000 less than its book value [30% × ($50,000 − $14,000)]. Thus, a credit differential exists on the preferred stock on its acquisition date. Nevertheless, the existence of a differential on nonparticipating preferred stock on this date fails to imply that the book values of the assets or liabilities of the subsidiary differ from their fair values on this date.[11] A differential on such stock normally is the result of changes in interest rates subsequent to the issuance of the stock. Additionally, from the consolidated perspective, the purchase of preferred stock by a parent company is comparable to the retirement of the stock (as in the case of the acquisition of intercompany bonds). For these reasons, differentials on nonparticipating preferred stock are treated similar to differences between the costs and par values of retired shares. Thus, a credit differential, such as the one in this example, is allocated (added) to Other Contributed Capital. A debit differential is allocated to (subtracted from) Other Contributed Capital up to the balance in this account, with any excess being allocated to the parent company's Retained Earnings. The cost method working paper elimination entry that allocates the credit differential in this case to Other Contributed Capital is as follows:

Preferred Stock	50,000	
Investment in S Company Preferred Stock		14,000
Other Contributed Capital		1,000
Minority Interest		35,000

This entry is incorporated into the date of acquisition consolidated statement working paper for this case shown in Illustration 8–5 (see entry (2)). It is appropriate since there is no dividend arrearage at date of acquisition. Given an arrearage on this date, S Company retained earnings equal to the arrearage is allocated to the preferred shareholders (if the balance in Retained Earnings is sufficient), and retained earnings equal the product of the preferred ownership percent and the allocated amount is eliminated in the investment elimination entry for the preferred. Assuming an arrearage equal to one year's preferred dividend requirement of $4,000 (8% × $50,000), the cost method date of acquisition investment elimination entry in this case is the following:

---

[11] A differential on preferred stock is more likely to imply that book values differ from fair values if the stock is participating.

ILLUSTRATION 8-5   Cumulative, Nonparticipating Preferred Stock—19X1

P COMPANY AND SUBSIDIARY S COMPANY
Consolidated Balance Sheet Working Paper
December 31, 19X1

	P Company	S Company	Eliminations Dr.	Eliminations Cr.	Consolidated
Investment in S Company stock:					
Preferred stock	14,000			(1) 14,000	-0-
Common stock	126,000			(2) 126,000	-0-
Other assets	160,000	190,000			350,000
	300,000	190,000			350,000
Preferred stock		50,000	(1) 50,000		-0-
Common stock:					
P Company	200,000				200,000
S Company		100,000	(2) 100,000		-0-
Retained earnings:					
P Company	100,000				100,000
S Company		40,000	(2) 40,000		-0-
Other contributed capital				(1) 1,000	1,000
Minority interest				(2) 14,000	49,000
				(1) 35,000	
	300,000	190,000	190,000	190,000	350,000

Explanation of eliminations:

(1) To eliminate beginning-of-year preferred stock investment account balance against beginning-of-year S Company preferred stock account and establish beginning-of-year minority interest related to preferred stock.

(2) To eliminate beginning-of-year investment account balance against beginning-of-year S Company common stockholders' equity accounts and establish beginning-of-year minority interest related to common stock.

Preferred Stock	50,000	
Retained Earnings—S Company	1,200	
Investment in S Company Preferred Stock		14,000
Other Contributed Capital		2,200
Minority Interest		35,000

S Company's retained earnings is reduced in this example since it has no other contributed capital.

Parent's Entries in 19X2.   Notice that S Company's 19X2 net income of $1,000 is less than its preferred dividend requirement of $4,000. Nevertheless, the preferred shareholders are allocated their share of this requirement (with the deficiency being allocated to the common shareholders) since the preferred stock is cumulative. Furthermore, this allocation is appropriate whether or not a dividend equal to the preferred dividend requirement is declared. *APB Opinion No. 18* states:

> When an investee has outstanding cumulative preferred stock, an investor should compute its share of earnings (losses) after deducting the investee's preferred dividends, whether or not such dividends are declared.[12]

An allocation schedule for our example follows:

	Allocated to		
	S Company Common Share- holders	S Company Preferred Share- holders	Total
First amount of S Company's net income allocated equals preferred dividend requirement		$4,000	$4,000
Remainder of S Company's net income ($1,000 − $4,000 —a deficiency) allocated next	($3,000)		(3,000)
Totals	($3,000)	$4,000	$1,000
Allocation of above on consolidated statement working paper and under equity method:			
Common shareholders:			
Majority Interest [(90% × (−$3,000)) + (30% × $4,000)]			($1,500)
Minority Interest [10% × (−$3,000)]			(300)
Preferred shareholders other than P Company (70% × $4,000)			2,800
Total			$1,000

The above allocation is recorded on P Company's books in 19X2 as follows:

1. To record receipt of cash dividend on preferred stock under cost method:

Cash (30% × $4,000)	1,200	
Dividend Income—Preferred Stock		1,200

2. To record equity in S Company's net income:

Equity in Subsidiary Earnings (90% × $3,000)	2,700	
Investment in S Company Common Stock		2,700

---

[12] APB, *Opinion No. 18*, "The Equity Method of Accounting for Investments in Common Stock" (New York: AICPA, 1971), par. 19(k).

Working Paper Entries for 19X2.   The 19X2 working paper entries are as follows:

1. To eliminate the intercompany portion of S Company's preferred dividend and record minority interest expense related to preferred stock:

Minority Interest Expense	2,800	
Dividend Income—Preferred Stock	1,200	
Dividends Declared		4,000

2. To eliminate double counting of equity method income and record minority interest expense (a credit) related to common stock:

Minority Interest	300	
Investment in S Company Common Stock	2,700	
Equity in Subsidiary Earnings		2,700
Minority Interest Expense		300

3. To eliminate beginning-of-year preferred stock investment account balance against beginning-of-year S Company preferred stock account and establish beginning-of-year minority interest related to preferred stock:

Preferred Stock	50,000	
Investment in S Company Preferred Stock		14,000
Other Contributed Capital		1,000
Minority Interest		35,000

4. To eliminate beginning-of-year investment account balance against beginning-of-year S Company common stockholders' equity accounts and establish beginning-of-year minority interest related to common stock:

Common Stock—S Company	100,000	
Retained Earnings—S Company	40,000	
Investment in S Company Common Stock		126,000
Minority Interest		14,000

The consolidated statement working paper for this case is presented in Illustration 8–6.

Working paper entry (1) offsets P Company's dividend income against S Company's dividends declared account to ensure that consolidated dividends

ILLUSTRATION 8-6   Cumulative, Nonparticipating Preferred Stock—19X2

P COMPANY AND SUBSIDIARY S COMPANY
Consolidated Statement Working Paper
For The Year Ended December 31, 19X2

	P Company	S Company	Eliminations Dr.		Eliminations Cr.		Consoli-dated
Income Statement							
Net income before items shown below	20,000	1,000					21,000
Dividend income—Preferred stock	1,200		(1)	1,200			-0-
Equity in subsidiary earnings	(2,700)				(2)	2,700	-0-
Minority interest expense			(1)	2,800	(2)	300	(2,500)
Net income	18,500	1,000		4,000		3,000	18,500
Retained Earnings Statement							
Retained earnings 1/1/X2:							
P Company	100,000						100,000
S Company		40,000	(4)	40,000			-0-
Net income	18,500	1,000		4,000		3,000	18,500
	118,500	41,000					118,500
Dividends declared:		4,000			(1)	4,000	-0-
Retained earnings, 12/31/X2	118,500	37,000		44,000		7,000	118,500
Balance Sheet							
Investment in S Company:							
Common stock	123,300		(2)	2,700	(4)	126,000	-0-
Preferred stock	14,000				(3)	14,000	-0-
Other assets	181,200	187,000					368,200
	318,500	187,000					368,200
Preferred stock		50,000	(3)	50,000			-0-
Common stock:							
P Company	200,000						200,000
S Company		100,000	(4)	100,000			-0-
Retained earnings	118,500	37,000		44,000		7,000	118,500
Other contributed capital					(3)	1,000	1,000
Minority interest			(2)	300	(3)	35,000	48,700
					(3)	14,000	
	318,500	187,000		197,000		197,000	368,200

(deduction)

Explanation of eliminations:

(1) To eliminate the intercompany portion of S Company's preferred dividend and record minority interest expense related to preferred stock.

(2) To reverse the parent's equity method entries and recognize minority interest expense (a credit) related to common stock.

(3) To eliminate beginning-of-year preferred stock investment account balance against beginning-of-year S Company preferred stock account and establish beginning-of-year minority interest related to preferred stock.

(4) To eliminate beginning-of-year investment account balance against beginning-of-year S Company common stockholders' equity accounts and establish beginning-of-year minority interest related to common stock.

declared equals P Company's dividends declared (zero in this case). This entry also records minority interest expense related to the preferred shareholders as calculated in the above allocation schedule. Entry (2) is standard, except that it records minority interest expense (a credit) pertaining to the common shareholders calculated in the allocation schedule. Working paper entry (3) is discussed in the preceding section of the chapter. Entry (4) is the standard investment elimination entry. Recall that the preferred shareholders have no interest in S Company's retained earnings since dividends are not in arrears.

Cumulative, Nonparticipating Preferred Stock, Consolidated Net Income, and the One-Line Consolidation Property of the Equity Method   Consolidated net income is calculated incrementally as follows:

			19X2
P Company's net income from its own operations			
($18,500 − $1,200 + $2,700)			$20,000
Plus: P Company's equity in S Company's 19X2 net income:			
Amount related to common shares [90% × (−$3,000)]	($2,700)		
Amount related to preferred shares (30% × $4,000)	1,200	($1,500)	
Consolidated net income			$18,500

This calculation of consolidated net income agrees with the consolidated net income figure shown in Illustration 8–6. It also agrees with P Company's equity method net income value.

The equality of consolidated net income and equity method net income occurs because the preferred dividend is declared. An interesting issue arises if this dividend is not declared. Since P Company accounts for its investment in S Company's preferred stock using the cost method, it does not record its share of the preferred dividend ($1,200) if it is not declared under traditional accounting thought. Thus, P Company's equity method net income is $17,300 ($18,500 − $1,200) under this assumption. However, consolidated net income still is $18,500. This value is unchanged since the sum of the affiliates' net incomes from their own operations ($21,000) and the minority interest expense figures shown in the allocation schedule (−$300 and $2,800) are the same whether or not the dividend is declared. Thus, if the dividend is not declared, the one-line consolidation property of the equity method is not maintained. Nevertheless, this property is preserved if the parent company accrues its share of the preferred dividend by debiting Dividends Receivable and crediting Dividend Income. The argument supporting this alternative is persuasive. If the parent owns enough shares of the subsidiary to warrant the preparation of consolidated financial statements, it also owns enough shares to significantly influence the subsidiary's preferred dividend policy. Thus, the parent can ensure (subject to cash availability) that an accrued dividend eventually is paid and, consequently, appears justified in accruing the dividend. Additionally, recall that *APB Opinion No. 18* requires that the preferred shareholders are allocated their share of the preferred dividend even if it is in arrears (with the arrearage being allocated to the common shareholders). Since any arrearage is allocated to the common shareholders, consistency dictates increasing the income from the preferred stock held by the common shareholders by an amount equal to the arrearage. Thus, *APB Opinion No. 18* also provides indirect support for the parent's accrual of the dividend. As indicated, this approach preserves the one-line consolidation property of the equity method.

Summary

This chapter covers the effects of preference interests on the preparation of consolidated financial statements and on the equity method. One topic dealt with is intercompany bond holdings. An intercompany bond holding occurs when one affiliate purchases the bonds of another affiliate from a nonaffiliate. Since the intercompany bonds are no longer outstanding from the consolidated view, a gain or loss on their retirement is recognized in the consolidated financial statements. Also, several other bond related effects, including the intercompany bond investment and bond liability, are eliminated in preparing the consolidated statements.

One principle illustrated in the chapter is that the gain or loss from an intercompany bond acquisition equals the algebraic sum of any unamortized discounts or premiums recorded on the affiliate's books on the date the bonds are acquired (where the sign of a debit (credit) balance account is a plus (minus)). In this context, the premium or discount of the purchasing affiliate is its contribution to the gain or loss. Similarly, the unamortized premium or discount on the issuing affiliate's books is its contribution to the gain or loss. If the parent is involved in the intercompany bond acquisition, its share of the gain or loss from the acquisition equals the algebraic sum of its unamortized discount or premium on the date the bonds are acquired and the product of the ownership percent and the subsidiary's unamortized discount or premium on this date. Alternatively, if two subsidiaries are involved in an intercompany bond acquisition, the parent's share of the resulting gain or loss is the product of the ownership percent for the first subsidiary and its unamortized discount or premium on the acquisition date, plus the product of the ownership percent for the second subsidiary and its unamortized discount or premium on the acquisition date (with appropriate signs being attached to discount and premium). Another general principle is that the income statement effects of discount and premium amortization related to intercompany bonds do not affect consolidated net income because they have been previously recognized in the year the bonds were constructively retired.

The overall treatment of intercompany bond acquisitions described above is consistent with the concept of pro rata allocation. We prefer the use of pro rata allocation in the case of intercompany bond holdings. Recall that the intent of consolidated financial statements is to show the economic effects of transactions with nonaffiliates. If gains and losses from intercompany bond acquisitions are allocated pro rata, this intent is satisfied. More specifically, if pro rata allocation is used, the consolidated financial statements' account balances are as if the intercompany bonds do not exist (i.e., actually have been retired). The use of pro rata allocation on intercompany bond holdings implies that consolidated net income and the minority interest values are calculated on the basis of the affiliates' confirmed net incomes from own operations and the subsidiary's confirmed stockholders' equity.

The other topic dealt with in this chapter is the effect of subsidiary preferred stock on the consolidated statements and on the equity method. Several complications arise in preparing consolidated financial statements if a subsidiary has outstanding preferred stock. Whether or not the parent holds some of the subsidiary's preferred stock, the rights provided by this stock often require the allocation of part of the subsidiary's retained earnings or net income to the preferred shareholders.

In the simpler case covered in this chapter (noncumulative, nonparticipating preferred), subsidiary net income equal to the preferred dividend declared is allocated to the preferred shareholders (provided that the subsidiary's net income is at least this large). In this case, both the parent's equity in subsidiary net income and consolidated net income are based on the subsidiary's net income available to common shareholders. Since the parent holds some of the preferred stock in this case, its investment in the preferred stock is eliminated (under the cost method) in preparing the consolidated financial statements. If a differential exists, it is allocated to other contributed capital or to the parent company's retained earnings.

The second case dealt with in this chapter is that of cumulative, nonparticipating preferred stock. This case results in increased complexity if dividends are in arrears at date of acquisition or because of a subsequent declaration deficiency. The chapter focuses primarily on the equity method and working paper techniques under the latter possibility. It shows that the allocation of a subsidiary's net income is complicated even in this relatively simple situation. Once the subsidiary's net income is allocated between its common and preferred shareholders, the allocated amounts provide the basis for recording the parent's equity in subsidiary net income and for determining consolidated net income. The preferred stock investment elimination entry in the case of cumulative, nonparticipating preferred stock has a complicating feature if dividends are in arrears at date of acquisition. In this instance, subsidiary retained earnings equal to the arrearage (if possible) are allocated to the preferred shareholders, and the parent's share of this amount is eliminated in the investment elimination entry. As in the case of noncumulative, nonparticipating preferred, if a differential exists, it is allocated to other contributed capital or the parent company's retained earnings.

Questions

1. To what extent does the purchase by one affiliate of the bonds of another affiliate parallel the acquisition and retirement by one company of all (or part) of its own outstanding bond issue?

2. Explain the nature of the gain or loss on the acquisition of intercompany bonds. Identify the general principle which governs determination of this amount. What are the affiliates' contributions to the gain or loss? To what extent should it be allocated between the participating affiliates?

3. What is the argument for pro rata allocation of the gain or loss on the purchase of intercompany bonds?

4. With respect to intercompany bonds, discount and premium amortization of the relevant affiliates is eliminated in consolidated statement working papers to avoid recording their contributions to the gain or loss twice. Explain why these eliminations are necessary. Identify the general principle related to these eliminations.

5. In regard to unconfirmed profit on an intercompany sale of a depreciable asset, the effect of the working paper entries is to defer the profit recorded by the selling affiliate initially and to recognize it over the remaining life of the asset subsequently. Compare these results with those produced by the working paper entries related to intercompany bond holdings.

6. What complexity is introduced in the working papers if an affiliate's bonds are purchased between interest dates?

7. Describe, in general terms, the earnings allocation problem associated with the preparation of consolidated financial statements as a result of the subsidiary having both common and preferred stock outstanding.

8. Assume that a subsidiary has both common and noncumulative, nonparticipating preferred stock outstanding. How is the retained earnings of the subsidiary allocated between preferred and common shareholders for the purpose of preparing the investment elimination entry? How does your answer differ if the preferred stock is cumulative, in arrears, and fully participating?

9. Suppose a subsidiary has $100,000 of 9 percent, nonparticipating, cumulative, preferred stock outstanding that is owned entirely by nonaffiliates. Since 1975, the parent has owned 100 percent of the subsidiary's common stock. On December 31, 1985, the preferred stock is three years in arrears. On the consolidated income statement for 1985, minority interest expense is either $9,000 or $27,000. Which is correct? Explain why.

10. Refer to Question 9. Suppose the retained earnings balance of the subsidiary on December 31, 1985, is $20,000. What amount is included in the consolidated balance sheet as minority interest in retained earnings?

11. Refer to Question 9. Suppose the subsidiary earns net income of $30,000 and pays dividends of $40,000 during 1986. What is minority interest expense on the consolidated income statement in 1986?

Exercises

Exercise 8–1   (Gains and Losses on Bonds—Pro Rata Allocation)

Each of the following independent situations pertains to a parent company (P), which owns 80 percent of a subsidiary company (S). In each case, determine the gain or loss on the acquisition of the affiliate's bonds, the portion of the gain or loss contributed by the issuer of the bonds, and the amount of the gain or loss contributed by the purchaser of the bonds. Assume pro rata allocation.

Case A: P Company issues at par $50,000 of 20-year, 8 percent bonds. Four years later, S Company purchases 50 percent of these bonds at par.

Case B: P Company issues $50,000 of 20-year, 8 percent bonds at 106 percent of par. S Company purchases 40 percent of the bonds directly from P Company.

Case C: P Company issues $50,000 of 20-year, 8 percent bonds at 84 percent of par. Five years later, S Company purchases 100 percent of these bonds for $48,000.

Case D: S Company issues $80,000 of 10-year, 9 percent bonds at 95 percent of par. After four years, P Company purchases 75 percent of these bonds for $61,000.

Case E: S Company issues $80,000 of 12-year, 9 percent bonds at 105 percent of par. After seven years, P Company purchases 60 percent of these bonds for $49,000.

Exercise 8–2   (Working Paper Entries—Pro Rata Allocation)

On December 31, 1995, Racket Corporation acquires 90 percent of Net Corporation's outstanding stock for $90,000. On the same date, Net Corporation purchases 100 percent of Racket Corporation's outstanding bonds for $9,000, plus accrued interest of $450. Interest on the bonds is paid January 1 and July 1, and both companies amortize premiums or discounts using the straight-line method. Gains and losses on intercompany bond holdings are allocated pro rata. Racket Corporation uses the modified equity method. The following data relate to the companies immediately after the purchases occur:

	December 31, 1995	
	Racket Corporation	*Net Corporation*
9% bonds payable (due December 31, 1999)	$10,000	
Discount on bonds payable	500	
Accrued interest payable	450	
Investment in net corporation stock	90,000	
Investment in racket corporation bonds		$10,000
Accrued interest receivable		450
Discount on bond investment		1,000
Common stock		70,000
Retained earnings		30,000
1995 and 1996 net income (excluding the effects of interest and equity in subsidiary earnings)	–0–	15,000

Required:

a. Present all of the working paper entries for consolidated statement working papers on
   (1) December 31, 1995.
   (2) December 31, 1996.

b. Calculate consolidated net income for 1995 and 1996.

Exercise 8–3   (Working Paper Entries—Pro Rata Allocation)

Use the information of Exercise 8–2, except now assume that the bonds were purchased on January 1, 1996.

Required:

a. Present all of the working paper entries for a consolidated statement working paper on December 31, 1996.

b. Calculate consolidated net income for 1996.

Exercise 8–4   (100 Percent Allocation Version of Exercise 8–2)

Use the information in Exercise 8–2, except now assume that 100 percent allocation is used. With this change, complete the requirements of Exercise 8–2.

Exercise 8–5   (Working Paper Entries—Pro Rata Allocation)

On January 1, 19X0, Raines Company issued $200,000 of 8 percent, 10-year bonds at 105 percent of par. Interest is payable July 1 and January 1. On January 1, 19X8, Rapco Company, which is a 90 percent owned subsidiary of Raines Company, acquired $100,000 of these bonds, paying 102 percent of par. Assume that both companies use straight-line amortization of premiums and discounts and the use of pro rata allocation. Assume additionally that on January 1, 19X8, Rapco had common stock of $60,000 and retained earnings of $40,000, and that there is no differential.

During 19X8, the net incomes of the two companies, excluding the effects of interest and equity in subsidiary earnings, are as follows: Raines, $40,000, and Rapco, $20,000. Neither company pays dividends during 19X8. Raines Corporation uses the modified equity method.

Required:

a. Prepare all the working paper entries for a December 31, 19X8, consolidated statement working paper.
b. Calculate consolidated net income for 19X8.

Exercise 8–6   (Working Paper Entries—Pro Rata Allocation)

On July 1, 1994, Kinkel Company purchased $200,000 of Brennon Company's 8 percent bonds in the open market at 111½, plus accrued interest. These bonds are part of an original issue of $1,000,000 of bonds sold on January 1, 1986, at 105. Interest is paid annually on January 1. The bonds mature on January 1, 2006. Straight-line amortization is recorded by each company, and gains and losses on intercompany bond holdings are allocated pro rata.

Required:

Assuming that Kinkel Company owns a 90 percent interest in Brennon Company and uses the modified equity method, make the working paper entries relating to the intercompany bonds for the year ended December 31, 1995.

Exercise 8–7   (100 Percent Allocation Version of Exercise 8–6)

Use the information of Exercise 8–6, except now assume that 100 percent allocation is used. With this change, complete the requirements of Exercise 8–6.

Exercise 8–8   (Working Paper Entries—Pro Rata Allocation)

Parent Company owns 80 percent of Subsidiary Company's outstanding common stock. On January 1, 19X1, Parent Company paid $22,000 for all of Subsidiary Company's outstanding 11 percent bonds, which have a par value of $18,000 and which pay interest semiannually on July 1 and January 1. On January 1, 19X1, subsidiary company's records showed an unamortized premium on bonds payable of $1,000. The bonds mature on January 1, 19X5, and both companies amortize premiums and discounts on a straight-line basis. Subsidiary Company's net income for 19X2 is $50,000, excluding the effects of interest expense. Gains and losses on intercompany bonds are allocated pro rata. Parent Company uses the modified entry method.

Required:

a. Calculate the gain or loss on the purchase of the affiliate's bonds and identify the amounts contributed by each affiliate.
b. Calculate 19X2 minority interest expense.
c. Prepare the working paper entries related to the bonds for a 19X2 consolidated statement working paper.

Exercise 8–9   (Bonds, Effective Interest Amortization and Working Paper Entries— Pro Rata Allocation)

On January 1, 19X1, P Company purchased $10,000 of S Company's 10 percent bonds. The bonds mature on December 31, 19X3, and pay interest annually on December 31. On January 1, 19X1, the book value of the bonds was $9,520. This amount is the present value of remaining principal and interest payments discounted at 12 percent. Thus, S Company uses the effective interest method of discount amortization. P Company purchased the bonds for $10,000.

S Company earned net income of $12,000 during 19X1 and 19X2. P Company accounts for its 90 percent interest in S Company's common stock using the modified equity method and pro rata allocation.

Required:

Prepare working paper entries relating to the intercompany bonds for consolidated statement working papers on
a. December 31, 19X1.
b. December 31, 19X2.

Exercise 8–10   (Preferred Stock and Working Paper Entries)

On December 31, 19X5, A Company acquires 80 percent of B Company's common stock for $200,000 and 60 percent of B Company's 8 percent, preferred stock for $50,000. Account balances for the companies are as follows:

	A Company	*B Company*
Preferred Stock, $100 par		$ 80,000
Common Stock, $50 par	$400,000	100,000
Other Contributed Capital		15,000
Retained Earnings	200,000	20,000

Required:

Prepare working paper entries for consolidated statement working papers on December 31, 19X5, under each of the following conditions:

a. The preferred stock is cumulative, nonparticipating, and is *not* in arrears.

b. The preferred stock is noncumulative and fully participating.

c. The preferred stock is cumulative, fully participating, and one year in arrears.

d. The preferred stock is cumulative, nonparticipating, and two years in arrears.

Exercise 8–11   (Preferred Stock and Balance Sheet Working Paper Entries)

Bolts, Inc., acquires 90 percent of Washer, Inc.'s common stock and 60 percent of its 9 percent, preferred stock on December 31, 19X1, at which date the companies had the following stockholders' equity account balances:

	Bolts, Inc.	Washer, Inc.
Preferred Stock, $100 par		$100,000
Common Stock, $50 par	$300,000	150,000
Other Contributed Capital	10,000	30,000
Retained Earnings	90,000	40,000

Required:

Prepare working paper entries for a December 31, 19X1, consolidated balance sheet working paper under each of the following circumstances:

a. The preferred stock is cumulative and nonparticipating, and dividends are not in arrears. Bolts, Inc., pays $100,000 for the preferred stock and $250,000 for the common stock.

b. The preferred stock is cumulative, nonparticipating, and two years in arrears. Bolts, Inc., pays $70,000 for the preferred stock and $250,000 for the common stock.

c. The preferred stock is cumulative, fully participating, and dividends are not in arrears. Bolts, Inc., pays $75,000 for the preferred stock and $200,000 for the common stock.

Exercise 8–12   (Preferred Stock, Consolidated Net Income, and Minority Interest Expense)

Franks Company, a subsidiary of Moore Company, has $100,000 of 9 percent, preferred stock outstanding and $200,000 of common stock outstanding. Calculate (*a*) the amount of Franks Company's net income that is included in consolidated net income and (*b*) minority interest expense under each of the following independent situations.

Case A: Moore Company owns 60 percent of the preferred stock and 90 percent of the common stock. The preferred stock is cumulative, nonparticipating, and not in arrears. Net income of Franks Company is $50,000.

Case B: Moore Company owns 50 percent of the preferred stock and 70 percent of the common stock. The preferred is cumulative, nonparticipating, and not in arrears. Net income of Franks Company is $3,000.

Case C: Moore Company owns none of the preferred stock and 80 percent of the common stock. The preferred stock is cumulative, nonparticipating, and two years in arrears. Net income of Franks Company is $5,000.

Case D: Moore Company owns 40 percent of the preferred stock and 60 percent of the common stock. The preferred stock is cumulative, fully participating, and not in arrears. Net income of Franks Company is $30,000, of which $27,000 was declared and paid as dividends.

Exercise 8-13   (Bonds and Working Paper Entries—Pro Rata Allocation)

Katz Company owns 80 percent of the voting common stock of Ratz Company. On July 1, 1996, Katz Company purchased $100,000 of Ratz Company's 10 percent bonds in the open market at 105³/₄, plus accrued interest. These bonds were issued on January 1, 1988, at 98. Interest on the bonds is paid annually on January 1. The bonds mature on January 1, 2008. Straight-line amortization is recorded by each company, and gains and losses on intercompany bond holdings are allocated pro rata. Katz Company uses the modified equity method.

Required:

Prepare the working paper entries related to the intercompany bonds for the year ended December 31, 1997.

Problems

Problem 8-14   (Bonds, Working Paper Entries, and Incremental and Residual Calculations—Pro Rata Allocation)

On January 1, 1993, Alpha Company owns 90 percent of the voting common stock of Beta Company and 80 percent of the voting common stock of Gamma Company. On January 1, 1987, Beta Company issued $200,000 of 10 percent, 10-year bonds to nonaffiliates at 98. The bonds pay interest on January 1 and July 1. On January 1, 1993, Gamma Company acquires $40,000 of these bonds at 106. The following data pertain to the period January 1, 1993, through December 31, 1994.

	Alpha Company	*Beta Company*	*Gamma Company*
Retained earnings (1/1/93)	$550,000	$500,000	$450,000
Net income (exclusive of interest and equity in subsidiary earnings):			
1993	200,000	150,000	100,000
1994	260,000	220,000	180,000

The companies amortize premium and discount using the straight-line method. Gains and losses on intercompany bond holdings are allocated pro rata. Alpha Company uses the modified equity method.

Required:

a. Prepare the working paper entries related to the intercompany bonds for consolidated statement working papers for the years ended December 31, 1993, 1994, 1995, and 1996.

b. Calculate consolidated net income for both 1993 and 1994 incrementally.

c. Calculate consolidated net income for both 1993 and 1994 residually.

Problem 8–15   (Bonds, Working Paper Entries, and Income Statement Working Paper— Pro Rata Allocation)

Superior Company acquired 80 percent of the voting common stock of Inferior Company in 19X0. On January 1, 19X4, Inferior Company had a $400,000, 12 percent bond issue outstanding. The bonds pay interest on January 1 and July 1. The unamortized discount on the bonds as of January 1, 19X4, was $12,000. The bonds are due January 1, 19X7. On April 1, 19X4, Superior Company acquires $100,000 of Inferior Company's bonds at 1.022, plus accrued interest. The 19X4 net incomes of the affiliates, excluding interest and Superior Company's equity in subsidiary earnings, are given below.

Superior Company	$200,000
Inferior Company	$100,000

The companies amortize premium and discount using the straight-line method. Gains and losses on intercompany bond holdings are allocated pro rata. Superior Company uses the modified equity method.

Required:

a. Prepare the working paper entries related to the intercompany bonds for consolidated statement working papers for the years ended December 31, 19X4, 19X5, and 19X6.

b. Prepare a consolidated income statement working paper for the year ended December 31, 19X4.

Problem 8–16   (100 Percent Allocation Version of Problem 8–15)

Use the information of Problem 8–15, except now assume that 100 percent allocation is used. With this change, complete the requirements of Problem 8–15.

Problem 8–17   (Bonds, Working Paper Entries, and Incremental and Residual Calculations—Pro Rata Allocation)

On January 1, 1995, White Company owns 80 percent of the capital stock of Kaplan Company and 60 percent of the capital stock of Jensen Company. On January 1, 1989,

Kaplan Company issued $300,000 of 8 percent, 10-year bonds to nonaffiliates at 94. On January 1, 1995, Jensen Company acquires $60,000 of these bonds at 104. The bonds pay interest on January 1 and July 1.

The following data relate to the period January 1, 1995, through December 31, 1996:

	White Company	*Kaplan Company*	*Jensen Company*
Retained earnings (1/1/95)	$415,000	$283,000	$196,000
Net income (exclusive of interest and equity in subsidiary earnings):			
1995	110,000	60,000	80,000
1996	90,000	50,000	40,000

The companies amortize premium and discount using the straight-line method. Gains and losses on intercompany bonds are allocated pro rata. White Company uses the modified equity method.

Required:

a. Prepare the working paper entries related to the intercompany bonds for consolidated statement working papers for the years ended December 31, 1995, 1996, 1997, and 1998.

b. Calculate consolidated net income for both 1995 and 1996 incrementally.

c. Calculate consolidated net income for both 1995 and 1996 residually.

Problem 8–18   (Interim Purchase of Bonds, Working Paper Entries, and Income Statement Working Paper)

South Company has a controlling interest in North Corporation, having acquired 80 percent of its capital stock in 19X0. On January 1, 19X6, North Corporation had outstanding a $300,000 issue of 8 percent bonds (interest payable on January 1 and July 1). The unamortized discount on these bonds as of January 1 19X6, was $9,000. The bonds are due January 1, 19X9. On May 1, 19X6, South Company acquires $75,000 of these bonds at 101.6 plus accrued interest. The 19X6 net incomes of the affiliates, excluding interest and South Company's equity in North Corporation's earnings, are as follows:

South Company	$80,000
North Corporation	$60,000

The companies amortize premium and discount using the straight-line method. Gains and losses on intercompany bonds are allocated pro rata. South Company uses the modified equity method.

Required:

a. Prepare the working paper entries related to the intercompany bonds for 19X6 through 19X8.

b. Prepare a consolidated income statement working paper for the year ended December 31, 19X6.

Problem 8–19 (Comprehensive Alternative Requirements for Problem 8–18)

Use the information of Problem 8–18 in completing the requirements listed below.

a. Calculate the 19X6 to 19X8 interest expense at the nominal rate on the intercompany bonds and the related year-end accrued interest figures.

b. Calculate the unamortized discount on the intercompany bonds on their acquisition date and discount amortization on these bonds for a full year, the period January 1, 19X6, to April 30, 19X6, and the period May 1, 19X6, to December 31, 19X6.

c. Repeat (*b*) for the bond premium.

d. Identify the affiliates' contributions to the gain or loss on the bonds.

e. Calculate the gain or loss on the bonds.

f. Calculate the effect of the gain or loss on consolidated net income.

g. Prepare the working paper entries related to the intercompany bonds for 19X6, 19X7, and 19X8.

h. Calculate consolidated net income for both 19X6 and 19X7 incrementally, assuming the 19X6 income figures given also apply to 19X7.

i. Calculate minority interest expense for both 19X6 and 19X7, assuming the 19X6 income figures given also apply to 19X7.

j. Prepare the income statement section of the 19X6 consolidated statement working paper.

Problem 8–20 (Bonds, Incremental Calculation, Minority Interest Expense, and Working Paper Entries—Pro Rata Allocation)

On December 31, 19X0, Allen Company purchased, in the open market, $1 million par value of Dahl Company's bonds. The bonds mature December 31, 19X5, pay interest at the rate of 12 percent annually on December 31, and were sold originally to yield 10 percent. The purchase price on December 31, 19X0, allows Allen to earn an annual rate of 14 percent. Allen accounts for its investment in the bonds using the effective interest method of amortization. Similarly, Dahl accounts for its bonds payable using the effective interest method.

Allen owns 80 percent of the outstanding common shares of Dahl. Allen's income from its own operations was $200,000 annually during the period 19X0 through 19X5. Dahl's income during the same period was $150,000 annually. Allen accounts for its investment in Dahl Company stock using the modified equity method and allocates gains or losses on intercompany bonds pro rata.

Required:

a. Compute the carrying value of the bonds payable as it would appear on Dahl's balance sheet as of December 31, 19X0.

b. Compute the price Allen paid for the bonds on December 31, 19X0.

c. Compute the gain or loss on the intercompany bonds that is reported in the 19X0 consolidated financial statements.

d. Compute consolidated net income incrementally and minority interest expense for the years 19X0 through 19X5.

e. Prepare the working paper entries relating to the intercompany bonds for 19X0 and 19X1.

Problem 8–21   (Preferred Stock, Parent's Entries, Minority Interest Expense, Working Paper Entries, and Consolidated Net Income)

On January 1, 19X1, X Company acquires 900 shares of Y Company's common stock for $20,000 and 160 shares of its 9 percent cumulative, nonparticipating preferred stock for $15,000. On this date, dividends are not in arrears, and the stockholders' equity accounts of Y Company are as follows:

Common Stock ($10 par value)	$10,000
Preferred Stock ($100 par value)	20,000
Retained Earnings	12,000

Assume that any differential on common stock is allocated to land. During 19X1, Y Company reports earnings of $10,000 and pays $7,000 in dividends. In 19X1, X Company earns $20,000 excluding its equity in subsidiary earnings and dividend income.

Required:

a. Prepare X Company's entries to record its equity in subsidiary earnings and dividend income for 19X1. Also record X Company's receipt of dividends.

b. Calculate 19X1 consolidated net income incrementally.

c. Calculate 19X1 minority interest expense.

d. Prepare the working paper entries for a December 31, 19X1, consolidated statement working paper.

e. Suppose Y Company pays no dividends in 19X2. Describe X Company's alternative accounting treatments related to the dividends arrearage. Contrast the effects of the alternatives on X Company's (unconsolidated) financial statements and the consolidated financial statements.

f. Return your attention to 19X1. Assuming that the preferred stock is cumulative and fully participating, calculate 19X1 consolidated net income and minority interest expense.

Problem 8–22   (Bonds, Merchandise Sale, and Income Statement Working Paper)

	Balances, December 31, 1995			
	P Company		S Company	
	Debit	*Credit*	*Debit*	*Credit*
Cash	$ 23,000		$ 30,000	
Accounts Receivable	94,000		60,000	
Inventory	80,000		45,000	
Investment in Stock of S	166,000			
Investment in Bonds of S	51,800			
Other Assets	445,000		210,000	
Current Liabilities		$ 163,000		$ 17,100
Bonds Payable—5%				200,000
Bond Premium				5,400
Sales		630,000		340,000
Cost of Goods Sold	510,000		306,000	
Operating Expenses	92,000		70,000	
Other Expenses	22,000		15,500	
Interest		3,800		
Dividends Declared	20,000		10,000	
Retained Earnings (1/1/95)		107,000		84,000
Common Stock		600,000		100,000
	$1,503,800	$1,503,800	$746,500	$746,500

Additional information:

a. The investment in stock of S Company represents a 90 percent interest which was acquired January 1, 1995, for $175,000. At the same time, $50,000 par value of bonds of S was acquired for $52,000. These bonds had been issued on January 1, 1985, at 106 and are due January 1, 2005. S Company has recorded the amortization of the bond premium applicable to 1995 as an adjustment of interest expense. The stock and the bonds were purchased in the open market. Any difference between the stock purchase cost and book value is related to land owned by S Company.

b. Included in S Company's purchases is a total of $180,000 of goods bought from P Company at 120 percent of cost to P Company. The closing inventory of S Company is estimated to include the same proportion of these purchases as other purchases. S Company's total purchases were $485,000.

c. Although P Company uses the equity method, it has not yet recorded its equity in subsidiary earnings.

Required:

Prepare the income statement section of a consolidated statement working paper for the year ended December 31, 1995.

(AICPA adapted)

Problem 8–23   (Preferred Stock and Balance Sheet Working Paper)

Four years ago, American Company acquired 50 percent of the preferred stock of Banner Corporation for $55,000 and 90 percent of that corporation's common stock for $195,000. At the acquisition date, Banner Corporation had retained earnings of $60,000, and dividends on its 5 percent, cumulative preferred stock were not in arrears. The investments were incorrectly recorded by American Company at the book value shown by Banner Corporation at date of acquisition. However, the excess of book value over the cost of the common stock was known to relate to overvalued land on the books of Banner Corporation. Management has now decided that the investment in the Banner Corporation preferred stock should have been maintained using the cost method.

Consolidated statements are now being prepared as of December 31, 1995, for American Company and its subsidiary. The financial position of the individual companies was as follows on that date:

AMERICAN COMPANY

Assets		Equities	
Miscellaneous assets	$116,000	Liabilities	$ 50,000
Investments:		Preferred stock (4%)	100,000
Banner preferred	50,000	Common stock	100,000
Banner common	234,000	Retained earnings	150,000
Total assets	$400,000	Total equities	$400,000

BANNER CORPORATION

Assets		Equities	
Miscellaneous assets	$400,000	Liabilities	$ 60,000
		Preferred stock (5%)*	100,000
		Common stock	200,000
		Retained earnings	40,000
Total assets	$400,000	Total equities	$400,000

* Preferred stock dividends are three years in arrears. No dividends have been paid on common since acquisition by American Company. Profit in 1992 was $8,000, but losses during the past three years have totaled $23,000.

Required:

a. Prepare the working paper entries for December 31, 1995.

b. Prepare a consolidated balance sheet working paper as of December 31, 1995.

(AICPA adapted)

Problem 8–24   (Comprehensive Review Problem—Chapters 6, 7, and 8)

Mass Company purchased a controlling interest in Able Company on January 1, 19X1, by paying $690,000 cash in exchange for 90 percent of Able's outstanding common stock. On date of acquisition, Able had the following stockholders' equity account balances:

Preferred Stock (9%, cumulative, nonparticipating, $20 par,
    10,000 shares outstanding, no dividend arrearage) $200,000
Common Stock ($10 par, 50,000 shares outstanding)   500,000
Retained Earnings   80,000

An analysis of Able Company's asset and liability accounts on January 1, 19X1, revealed the following differences between book values and market values: land costing $150,000 had a market value of $170,000, and buildings with a book value of $208,000 had a market value of $260,000. The buildings had 13 years of remaining useful life and an estimated salvage value of zero. Mass Company decided that any goodwill arising from the acquisition should be amortized over 40 years.

On January 1, 19X1, Able Company sold Mass Company equipment having a cost of $40,000 and a book value of $20,000. Mass Company paid Able $30,000. The estimated remaining useful life of the equipment on the date of transfer was eight years, and the straight-line method (with zero salvage value) is being used by Mass Company to depreciate the equipment.

On July 1, 19X1, Mass Company purchased $40,000 of Able Company's 8 percent bonds on the open market at 111½ plus accrued interest. These bonds are part of an original $200,000 issue of 20-year bonds that were sold 8½ years before Mass Company's purchase of the bonds. The original sales price was 110. Interest is paid annually on January 1. The companies amortize premium and discount using the straight-line method.

On January 1, 19X2, Mass Company acquired 2,000 shares of Able Company's preferred stock on the open market at a cost of $37,500. Dividends were not in arrears at the time of purchase.

Able Company sold merchandise to Mass Company for $17,000 in 19X1 and for $40,000 in 19X2. Able Company marked this merchandise to sell at 20 percent above its cost. Thirty percent of the 19X2 sales remain in the inventory of Mass Company on December 31, 19X2. On January 1, 19X2, Mass Company's inventory contained goods purchased from Able Company in 19X1 for $7,200 (also billed to Mass Company at a markup of 20 percent on Able Company's cost).

On December 31, 19X2, Mass Company owed Able Company $4,000 on open account. This debt is related to the merchandise purchased in 19X2.

Able Company's net income and dividend declarations for 19X1 and 19X2 were as follows:

| | | Dividends | |
Year	Net Income	To Preferred	To Common
19X1	$68,000	$18,000	$10,000
19X2	60,000	18,000	10,000

Required:

a. Prepare working paper entries for a consolidated *balance sheet* working paper on January 1, 19X1. Show calculations to support the allocation of the differential and the amounts to be amortized in future years.

b. Prepare journal entries to record Mass Company's purchase of the Able Company bonds, the accrual and receipt of related interest, and the amortization of premium or discount on the bond investment during 19X1 and 19X2.

c. Prepare journal entries to record Mass Company's receipt of dividends and equity in subsidiary earnings for 19X1 and 19X2. Mass Company uses the modified equity method.

d. Prepare working paper entries for consolidated statement working papers for December 31, 19X1, and for December 31, 19X2.

e. Calculate minority interest expense for both 19X1 and 19X2.

Consolidated Statements— Changes in Parent Companies' Ownership Percents

Chapter Outline

As shown in Chapters 6 through 8, unconfirmed profits and intercompany bond holdings complicate the preparation of consolidated financial statements. Another complication in preparing these statements results from the changes in parent companies' ownership percents. These percents change in response to a variety of transactions involving subsidiary shares. This chapter covers the consolidated statement and equity method techniques related to these changes.

INCREASES IN PARENTS' OWNERSHIP PERCENTS

An investor company's ownership percent increases when (1) it acquires additional shares of an affiliate in the open market, (2) it acquires a disproportionately large number of newly issued (or reissued) shares of an affiliate, or (3) an affiliate acquires a disproportionately small number of treasury shares from the investor.[1] We refer to the first two cases—the cases in which the ownership percent increases as a consequence of the investor's acquisition of shares subsequent to its initial acquisition—as *block purchases*.[2] *These three situations affect working paper techniques, consolidated statement values, and equity method entries similarly.* Thus, they are grouped in this section for explanatory purposes.

Block Purchase—General Comments

One company may acquire a controlling interest in another through a single purchase of shares or through block purchases. In the latter case, the ownership percent increases over time until control is obtained. Control may be obtained in three ways through block purchases. First, the parent may make open-market block purchases. Second, the parent may acquire newly issued (or reissued) shares directly from the subsidiary. And third, a combination of open-market and direct acquisitions of subsidiary shares may be made by the parent. In either case, consolidated statements are not prepared until the ownership percent is more than 50 percent. Examples pertaining to these cases are presented below.

When control is acquired through block purchases, the relationships between the costs of blocks of shares and pertinent parent company interests in subsidiary stockholders' equities are analyzed in identifying differentials and determining

---

[1] The phrase *disproportionately large number*, as used in (2), implies that the precntage of the newly issued shares acquired by the parent is larger than its previously held percentage of the subsidiary's shares. Similarly, the phrase *disproportionately small number*, as used in (3), implies that the percentage of the treasury shares acquired from the parent is smaller than its previously held percentage of the subsidiary's shares. These phrases are used similarly throughout this chapter.

[2] Note that the phrase *block purchase* could be defined to include any subsidiary stock transaction which yields an increase in the ownership percent. As indicated, we use this phrase to describe situations in which shares are acquired by the investor and the ownership percent increases.

consolidated retained earnings at date of control. Currently, accounting policy allows two methods of analysis: (1) step-by-step analysis and (2) date-of-control analysis.[3] The latter procedure fails to allow for the existence of differentials until control is established and excludes the investor's share of undistributed investee earnings accumulated prior to date of control from consolidated retained earnings. This procedure is justified under current policy in terms of convenience.[4] We strongly recommend step-by-step analysis because of its conceptual superiority. Thus, the following cases employ this technique.

Case 1. Block Purchase—Open Market

Assume that S Company has capital stock of $50,000 ($100 par) and retained earnings of $20,000 on January 1, 19X1. S Company's net income in each of the years 19X1 through 19X3 is $10,000. P Company's net income from its own operations in 19X3 is $25,000. P Company acquires shares of S Company (and related ownership percents) through open-market block purchases as indicated below.[5]

Date	Number (%) of Shares	Cost
January 1, 19X1	200 (40%)	$30,000
January 1, 19X2	100 (20%)	17,500
January 1, 19X3	100 (20%)	20,000

The following differences in fair values and book values for *different* elements of plant and equipment exist on the various block purchase dates.

	Plant and Equipment (net)	
	Fair Value	Book Value
January 1, 19X1	$29,500	$28,250
January 1, 19X2	34,500	32,000
January 1, 19X3	47,500	40,000

[3] Committee on Accounting Procedure, *Accounting Research Bulletin No. 51,* "Consolidated Financial Statements" (New York: AICPA, 1959), par. 10; and APB, *APB Opinion No. 18,* "The Equity Method of Accounting for Investments in Common Stock" (New York: AICPA, 1971), par. 19m.

[4] We believe that date-of-control analysis can be justified only on the basis of materiality. Differential calculation, allocation, and amortization procedures for this technique are covered in the appendix to this chapter.

[5] Acquisitions and sales of shares are assumed to occur at the start of business on the days indicated throughout this chapter. This assumption implies in this case, for example, that an ownership percent of 80 applies throughout all of 19X3.

Each element of plant and equipment has a remaining life of 5 years on the related block purchase date, and goodwill arising from a given block purchase has a life of 10 years. Straight-line amortization is assumed throughout this chapter.

Differentials—Calculation, Allocation, and Amortization.   Under step-by-step analysis, *there usually is a debit or credit differential related to each block of stock*. The sum of the separate differentials is the *total differential (ignoring amortization)*. The calculations of the separate differentials for this case are shown below.

	First Block (40%)	Second Block (20%)	Third Block (20%)
Cost of block	$30,000	$17,500	$20,000
Less: Purchased interest in			
S Company's stockholders' equity:			
First block (40% × $70,000)	28,000		
Second block (20% × $80,000)		16,000	
Third block (20% × $90,000)			18,000
Separate differential	$ 2,000	$ 1,500	$ 2,000

The total differential is $5,500 ($2,000 + $1,500 + $2,000). *Notice that the separate differentials also can be calculated by focusing on the differences in P Company's interests in S Company's stockholders' equity before and after the acquisitions of the various blocks of stock.* For example, P Company's interest in S Company's stockholders' equity right before the acquisition of the third block is $54,000 (60% × $90,000). Immediately after this acquisition, its interest is $72,000 (80% × $90,000). The difference in these values is $18,000. Since (80% × $90,000) − (60% × $90,000) equals (20% × $90,000), the $18,000 difference is identical to the interest in S Company's stockholders' equity related to the third block calculated above. Thus, the separate differential for the third block also equals this block's cost less the related difference in P Company's after and before acquisition interests in S Company's stockholders' equity. *This method of calcualting a separate differential is important when an ownership percent increases because of a subsidiary stock transaction (see below).*

The differential allocation and amortization procedures under the step-by-step approach are identical to those illustrated in Chapter 4, except that more than one block of stock is involved. Differential allocation values related to the different elements of plant and equipment (net) in this case are calculated in the following schedule.

	Plant and Equipment (net)			
	Fair Value	*Book Value*	*Fair Value − Book Value (Excess)*	*Block Ownership Percent × Excess*
First block (40%)	$ 29,500	$ 28,250	$ 1,250	$ 500
Second block (20%)	34,500	32,000	2,500	500
Third block (20%)	47,500	40,000	7,500	1,500
Totals	$111,500	$100,250	$11,250	$2,500

This schedule implies goodwill related to the three blocks of $1,500 ($2,000 − $500), $1,000 ($1,500 − $500), and $500 ($2,000 − $1,500), respectively. Thus, total goodwill is $3,000. Annual differential amortization for the first block is $250 [($500/5) + ($1,500/10)] for each of the five years beginning January 1, 19X1. Of this amount, $100 ($500/5) pertains to plant and equipment (net), and $150 ($1,500/10) is related to goodwill. The corresponding value for the second block beginning January 1, 19X2, is $200 [($500/5) + ($1,000/10)]—with $100 ($500/5) related to plant and equipment (net) and $100 ($1,000/10) pertaining to goodwill. The annual differential amortization figure for the third block is $350 [($1,500/5) + ($500/10)] for each of the five years beginning January 1, 19X3—with $300 ($1,500/5) pertaining to plant and equipment (net) and $50 ($500/10) related to goodwill. These amounts are summarized for the years 19X1 through 19X3 in Illustration 9–1.

Parent's Entries 19X1–19X3. P Company's equity method entries for the years 19X1 through 19X3 allow for its varying ownership percents and the related differential amortization figures. The pertinent ownership percents are 40, 60, and 80 for 19X1, 19X2, and 19X3, respectively (see footnote 5). Ignoring P Company's entries to record the block purchases, its equity method entries for the three years (including its equity method pick up and differential amortization entries) are as follows:

```
19X1   Investment in S Company (40% × $10,000) ...............  4,000
           Equity in Subsidiary Earnings  ....................          4,000

       Equity in Subsidiary Earnings  ........................   250
           Investment in S Company ...........................           250

19X2   Investment in S Company (60% × $10,000) ..............  6,000
           Equity in Subsidiary Earnings  ....................          6,000

       Equity in Subsidiary Earnings  ........................   450
           Investment in S Company ...........................           450
```

ILLUSTRATION 9-1   Differential Amortization by Blocks (Case 1)

	Differential Amortization		
	19X1	*19X2*	*19X3**
First block:			
Plant and equipment (net)	$100	$100	$100
Goodwill	150	150	150
Total	$250	$250	$250
Second block:			
Plant and equipment (net)		$100	$100
Goodwill		100	100
Total		$200	$200
Third block:			
Plant and equipment (net)			$300
Goodwill			50
Total			$350
Combined:			
Plant and equipment (net)	$100	$200	$500
Goodwill	150	250	300
Total	$250	$450	$800

*The values in this column also pertain to 19X4 and 19X5, assuming no further ownership percent changes, and so on. The 19X4 figures are relevant to Case 6.

```
19X3   Investment in S Company (80% × $10,000) . . . . . . . . . . . . . . .  8,000
           Equity in Subsidiary Earnings  . . . . . . . . . . . . . . . . . . . . .        8,000

       Equity in Subsidiary Earnings  . . . . . . . . . . . . . . . . . . . . . . .   800
           Investment in S Company  . . . . . . . . . . . . . . . . . . . . . . . .          800
```

Working Paper Entries and Incremental Calculation of Consolidated Net Income for 19X3. Absent subsidiary dividends, it is convenient to combine the first two working paper entries made in prior chapters. We follow this convention throughout this chapter. The working paper entries for 19X3 are the following:

1. To eliminate double counting of equity method income and record minority interest in subsidiary net income:

```
   Minority Interest Expense (20% × $10,000)  . . . . . . . . . . . . .  2,000
   Equity in Subsidiary Earnings ($8,000 − $800) . . . . . . . . . . .  7,200
       Investment in S Company  . . . . . . . . . . . . . . . . . . . . .          7,200
       Minority Interest  . . . . . . . . . . . . . . . . . . . . . . . . . . .          2,000
```

2. To eliminate investment account balance against beginning-of-year
   S Company stockholders' equity accounts and establish beginning-of-
   year minority interest:

Capital Stock—S Company   50,000
Retained Earnings—S Company
  ($20,000 + $20,000)   40,000
Differential [$5,500 − ($250 + $450)]   4,800
    Investment in S Company
      [$30,000 + $17,500 + $20,000 +
      (40% × $10,000 − $250) +
      (60% × $10,000 − $450)]   76,800
    Minority Interest [(20% × ($50,000 + $40,000)]   18,000

3. To allocate the differential:

Plant and Equipment (net)
  [$2,500 − ($100 + $200)] . . . . , ...   2,200
Goodwill [$3,000 − ($150 + $250)]   2,600
    Differential   4,800

4. To record differential amortization:

Depreciation Expense   500
Amortization of Goodwill   300
    Plant and Equipment (net)   500
    Goodwill   300

The working paper entries for this case are consistent with those of earlier
chapters, *except that the investment account balance eliminated does not equal
the beginning-of-year balance, and the working paper entries are not based on the
beginning-of-year ownership percent.* In this case, the beginning-of-year balance
is $56,800 [$30,000 + $17,500 + (40% × $10,000) − $250 + (60% × $10,000) −
$450]. This balance changes immediately to $76,800 on January 1, 19X3, when the
new shares are acquired for $20,000 (see footnote 5). Similarly, the beginning-of-
year ownership percent is 60, and this percent changes immediately to 80 upon the
acquisition of the new shares. *Notice in the remaining examples in this chapter
that the investment account balance eliminated usually does not equal the beginning-of-year balance and that the working paper entries are not based on the
beginning-of-year ownership percent.*

Circumstances of the type found in this case also alter the calculation of consolidated net income slightly. This calculation now incorporates the varying ownership percents applying during the year rather than only the beginning-of-year ownership percent. For example, consolidated net income is calculated incrementally as follows in this case.

P Company's 19X3 net income from its own operations	$25,000
Plus: P Company's equity in S Company's 19X3 net income	
[(60% × $0) + (80% × $10,000)]	8,000
Less: Differential amortization for 19X3	(800)
Consolidated net income for 19X3	$32,200

Case 2. Interim Block Purchase—Open Market

This case is exactly like Case 1, except that we assume the third block of shares is acquired on March 31, 19X3, and S Company earns its annual net income *uniformly* (i.e., without seasonality). This case combines the procedures discussed above and the interim purchase techniques of Chapter 4. We present P Company's equity method entries for 19X1 through 19X3, the working paper entries for 19X3, and an incremental calculation of consolidated net income for 19X3 below with little discussion because the procedures used have, in effect, been illustrated previously.

In this case, the differential for the third block is $1,500 [($20,000 − 20% × ($90,000 + 25% × $10,000)]. This calculation allows for the $2,500 increase in S Company's retained earnings occurring between January 1, 19X3, and March 31, 19X3, under the uniformity assumption. This differential is allocated wholly to plant and equipment (net) since [20% × ($47,500 − $40,000)] equals $1,500. Since each element of plant and equipment has a remaining life of five years when the related block is acquired, one full year's differential amortization for the third block is $300 ($1,500/5). Thus, after the acquisition of the third block, a full year's differential amortization for several more years is $750 [with $500 ($300 + $200) pertaining to plant and equipment and $250 related to goodwill]. Also, the total differential now is $5,000 ($2,000 + $1,500 + $1,500).

P Company's equity method entries for the years 19X1 through 19X3 are presented below (ignoring the entries to record its share purchases). The entries for 19X1 and 19X2 are the same as in Case 1. The entries for 19X3 allow for the interim purchase. Thus, they record P Company's equity in S Company's net income for the first quarter of 19X3 using the prepurchase ownership percent of 60 and its equity in S Company's net income for the last three quarters of 19X3 using the postpurchase ownership percent of 80. The related differential amortization entries reflect the change in the total differential occurring because of the acquisition of the third block.

19X1 Investment in S Company (40% × $10,000) 4,000
　　　　　Equity in Subsidiary Earnings . . . . 　　　4,000

　　　　Equity in Subsidiary Earnings . . . . 　250
　　　　　Investment in S Company . . . . 　　　250

19X2 Investment in S Company (60% × $10,000) 6,000
　　　　　Equity in Subsidiary Earnings . . . . 　　　6,000

　　　　Equity in Subsidiary Earnings . . . . 　450
　　　　　Investment in S Company . . . . 　　　450

19X3 Investment in S Company [60% × (25% × $10,000)] 1,500
　　　　　Equity in Subsidiary Earnings . . . . 　　　1,500

　　　　Equity in Subsidiary Earnings (25% × $450) . . . . 　113
　　　　　Investment in S Company . . . . 　　　113

　　　　Investment in S Company [80% × (75% × $10,000)] 6,000
　　　　　Equity in Subsidiary Earnings . . . . 　　　6,000

　　　　Equity in Subsidiary Earnings (75% × $750) . . . . 　562
　　　　　Investment in S Company . . . . 　　　562

These are the working paper entries for 19X3:

1. To eliminate double counting of equity method income and record minority interest in subsidiary net income.

> Minority Interest Expense (20% × $10,000) 2,000
> Equity in Subsidiary Earnings
> 　($1,500 − $113 + $6,000 − $562) 6,825
> 　　Investment in S Company . . . . 　　　6,825
> 　　Minority Interest . . . . 　　　2,000

2. To eliminate investment account balance against beginning-of-year S Company's stockholders' equity accounts, record purchased preacquisition earnings, and establish beginning-of-year minority interest:

> Capital Stock—S Company 50,000
> Retained Earnings—S Company
> 　($20,000 + $20,000) 40,000
> Differential [$5,000 − ($250 + $450)] 4,300
> Purchased Preacquisition Earnings
> 　[(80% − 60%) × $2,500] 500
> 　　Investment in S Company (see prior case) . . . . 　　　76,800
> 　　Minority Interest [20% × ($50,000 + $40,000)] . . . . 　　　18,000

3. To allocate the differential:

Plant and Equipment (net)
[$2,500 − ($100 + $200)] 2,200
Goodwill [$2,500 − ($150 + $250)] 2,100
   Differential 4,300

4. To record differential amortization:

Depreciation Expense [(25% × $200) + (75% × $500)] 425
Amortization of Goodwill 250
   Plant and Equipment (net) 425
   Goodwill 250

The working paper entries for this case are entirely consistent with those of the "Interim Purchase" section of Chapter 4. For example, the purchased preacquisition earnings value is calculated using the increase in the ownership percent.[6] The one new complexity is the presence of an amortizable differential. As shown, the procedures for dealing with such a differential in the case of an interim open-market block purchase parallel the differential related procedures explained previously.

Calculations of consolidated net income are slightly more complicated when interim open-market block purchases occur; they allow for the changes in the ownership percents resulting from the purchases and the related interim changes in differential amortization. Consolidated net income for 19X3 is calculated incrementally as follows in this case.

P Company's 19X3 net income from its own operations		$25,000
Plus: P Company's equity in S Company's 19X3 net income:		
First quarter—[60% × (25% × $10,000)]	$1,500	
Last three quarters—[80% × (75% × $10,000)]	6,000	7,500
Less: Differential amortization for 19X3:		
First quarter—(25% × $450)	$113	
Last three quarters—(75% × $750)	562	(675)
Consolidated net income for 19X3		$31,825

---

[6] In Chapter 4, the ownership percent increases from zero to a controlling interest (e.g., 80).

Ownership Percent Increasing Subsidiary Stock Transactions— General Comments.

In the previous increase in ownership percent cases, the subsidiary is not involved in the transactions leading to the ownership percent increases. *However, the subsidiary necessarily is involved in the transaction leading to an ownership percent increase when (1) its parent acquires a disproportionately large number of its newly issued shares or (2) it acquires a disproportionately small number of treasury shares from its parent.* Such transactions are referred to as *ownership percent increasing subsidiary stock transactions*. These transactions lead to a new consideration in preparing consolidated statements—*they produce changes in subsidiaries' stockholders' equities*. Since these transactions affect subsidiaries' stockholders' equities, they also change parents' interests in these equities (which may increase or decrease). These changes are incorporated into the related differential calculation procedures. The justification for this treatment is given below.

As mentioned, when a subsidiary engages in an ownership percent increasing stock transaction, the parent's interest in the subsidiary's stockholders' equity changes. *Exactly* the same changes can be produced through a properly structured open-market block purchase.[7] Given this observation, we recommend that the account balances resulting from a subsidiary's ownership percent increasing stock transaction be the same as those which would have resulted from a properly structured open-market block purchase. For these balances to be the same, changes in parents' interests in subsidiaries' stockholders' equities must be allowed to affect differential calculations when subsidiaries' ownership percent increasing stock transactions occur. From an overall perspective, our recommendation is based on the principle of substance over form. That is, the substance of an ownership percent increasing subsidiary stock transaction is that of a properly structured open-market block purchase. Thus, we believe that such cases are best accounted for as though they are open-market block purchases.

Case 3. Block Purchase—Disproportionately Large Number of Newly Issued Shares Acquired by Parent

Assume that S Company has capital stock of $100,000 ($100 par) and retained earnings of $150,000 initially on January 1, 19X1. At this time, P Company holds 800 S Company shares (which implies an ownership percent of 80), and its

---

[7] Although we do not show the validity of this observation formally, the validity of a similar, but more interesting, observation is demonstrated in the appendix to this chapter. See the section of this chapter entitled "Ownership Percent Decreasing Subsidiary Stock Transactions—General Comments" for further discussion.

Investment in S Company account has a balance of $260,000. Since P Company's interest in S Company's initial stockholders' equity is $200,000 (80% × $250,000), its Investment in S Company account includes an unamortized differential of $60,000 at the start of 19X1. Based on the above values, the book value of each of S Company's outstanding shares is $250 ($250,000/1,000). On January 1, 19X1, P Company acquires an additional 200 shares of S Company at $340 per share directly from the latter. The purchase price of the new shares is $68,000 (200 × $340). P Company's net income from its own operations in 19X1 is $25,000, and S Company's 19X1 net income is $12,000. All unamortized differentials are allocated to elements of plant and equipment with 20-year remaining lives at January 1, 19X1.

The sale of the new shares increases S Company's Capital Stock balance to $120,000 [$100,000 + (200 × $100)] and increases its Other Contributed Capital balance to $48,000 [($340 − $100) × 200]. It also increases P Company's ownership percent from 80 to 83.33 (or 1,000/1,200) and, thus, is a block purchase. Since the ownership percent increases, the acquisition of the new shares by P Company is treated as an *appropriately structured open-market block purchase*. Another effect of the acquisition is a $65,000 increase in P Company's interest in S Company's stockholders' equity. As shown below, this value is pertinent in calculating the differential related to the newly acquired shares. The following table shows the calculation of this amount and reveals the details of the changes brought about by the ownership percent increasing subsidiary stock transaction.

	S Company's Stockholders' Equity		P Company's Interest in S Company's Stockholders' Equity		
	Before Transaction	*After Transaction*	*Before Transaction (80%)*	*After Transaction (83.33%)*	*Increase in P Company's Interest*
Capital stock	$100,000	$120,000	$ 80,000	$100,000	$20,000
Retained earnings	150,000	150,000	120,000	125,000	5,000
Other contributed capital	–0–	48,000	–0–	40,000	40,000
	$250,000	$318,000	$200,000	$265,000	$65,000

Differentials—Calculation, Allocation, and Amortization.   In this case, step-by-step analysis also implies a separate differential for each block of stock. In this instance, only two differentials are present, and the total differential is the sum of the two. The calculations of the separate differentials are shown below.

	First Block	Second Block
Amount in investment account		
on January 1, 19X1	$260,000	$68,000
Less: Initial interest in S Company's		
stockholders' equity (80% × $250,000)	200,000	
Less: Increase in interest in S Company's		
stockholders' equity		65,000
Separate differential	$ 60,000	$ 3,000

The total differential is $63,000 ($60,000 + $3,000). *We emphasize that the separate differential for the second block is related to the increase in P Company's interest in S Company's stockholders' equity just as the separate differentials arising from open-market block purchases are related to such increases.* Given the allocation of unamortized differentials to elements of plant and equipment with remaining lives of 20 years, differential amortization for 19X1 is $3,150 ($63,000/20).

Notice also that the separate differential for the second block is related to the excess of the $340 sales price of each newly issued share over its $250 presale book value. That is, given an ownership percent increase, a debit differential of this type occurs when the sales price exceeds the presale book value. If the sales price equals the presale book value and an ownership percent increase occurs, the issuance of new shares to a parent produces no differential. Also, if the sales price is less than the presale book value and this percent increases, a credit differential is produced. These observations are illustrated using data from the following table—which are based on sales prices of $250 and $190, respectively.

	S Company's Stockholders' Equity		P Company's Interest in S Company's Stockholders' Equity		Increase in P Company's Interest
	Before Transaction	After Transaction	Before Transaction (80%)	After Transaction (83.33%)	
Sales price of $250	$250,000	$300,000	$200,000	$250,000	$50,000
Sales price of $190	250,000	288,000	200,000	240,000	40,000

The cost of the second block is $50,000 (200 × $250) given a sales price of $250. Thus, no differential is produced on this block when the sales price is $250 since its $50,000 cost equals the related increase in P Company's interest. In contrast, when the purchase price is $190, the second block's cost is $38,000 (200 × $190), and a credit differential of $2,000 ($38,000 − $40,000) is produced. Accounting policy currently is silent on the treatment of credit differentials arising subsequent to the acquisition of the first block of stock.

Parent's 19X1 Entries, Related Working Paper Entries, and Incremental Calculation of Consolidated Net Income. After the acquisition of the second block of stock at $340 per share, P Company's ownership percent rises to 83.33. Ignoring P Company's entry to record its share purchase, its equity method entries for 19X1 (including its equity method income and differential amortization entries) are as follows:

Investment in S Company (83.33% × $12,000)	10,000	
Equity in Subsidiary Earnings		10,000
Equity in Subsidiary Earnings	3,150	
Investment in S Company		3,150

The working paper entries for 19X1 are as follows:

1. To eliminate double counting of equity method income and record minority interest in subsidiary net income:

Minority Interest Expense (16.67% × $12,000)	2,000	
Equity in Subsidiary Earnings		
($10,000 − $3,150)	6,850	
Investment in S Company		6,850
Minority Interest		2,000

2. To eliminate investment account balance against S Company stockholders' equity accounts and establish related minority interest:

Capital Stock—S Company	120,000	
Retained Earnings—S Company	150,000	
Other Contributed Capital	48,000	
Differential	63,000	
Investment in S Company		
($260,000 + $68,000)		328,000
Minority Interest		
[16.67% × ($120,000 + $150,000 + $48,000)]		53,000

3. To allocate the differential:

Plant and Equipment (net)	63,000	
Differential		63,000

4. To record differential amortization:

Depreciation Expense	3,150	
Plant and Equipment (net)		3,150

The working paper entries for this case are consistent with those made above and in earlier chapters with one exception. *In entry (2), the end-of-period subsidiary paid-in capital balances are eliminated. This new technique is employed because these balances change during the year. This procedure is used in all situations in which such changes occur.*[8]

The calculation of consolidated net income in this case also is consistent with procedures illustrated previously. Consolidated net income is calculated incrementally below.

P Company's 19X1 net income from its own operations	$25,000
Plus: P Company's equity in S Company's 19X1	
net income (83.33% × $12,000)	10,000
Less: Differential amortization for 19X1	(3,150)
Consolidated net income for 19X1	$31,850

Case 4. Interim Block Purchase—Disproportionately Large Number of Newly Issued Shares Acquired by Parent

This case is exactly like Case 3, except that we assume P Company acquires the newly issued shares of S Company on March 31, 19X1, and S Company's net income is earned uniformly. This case combines the procedures illustrated above and the interim purchase techniques of Chapter 4.

The issuance of the new shares again increases S Company's Capital Stock balance to $120,000 [$100,000 + (200 × $100)] and its Other Contributed Capital balance to $48,000 [200 × ($340 − $100)]. P Company's ownership percent again is increased from 80 percent to 83.33 percent (1,000/1,200). Since the ownership percent increases, the acquisition of the new shares by P Company again is treated as a properly structured open-market block purchase. Another effect of the

---

[8] Technically, end-of-period paid-in capital balances always are eliminated in the investment elimination entry. In earlier chapters, it is correct to emphasize the elimination of beginning-of-period balances because paid-in capital usually does not change during the period. One situation in which paid-in capital changes in earlier chapters is the case of the declaration of a subsidiary stock dividend (Chapter 4). Although we emphasize the elimination of beginning-of-period balances in that case, the effect of our procedures is to eliminate end-of-period balances.

acquisition is a $65,100 increase in P Company's interest in S Company's stockholders' equity. The following table shows the calculation of this amount and other changes brought about by the ownership percent increasing subsidiary stock transaction.

	S Company's Stockholders' Equity		P Company's Interest in S Company's Stockholders' Equity		Increase in P Company's Interest
	Before Transaction	*After Transaction*	*Before Transaction (80%)*	*After Transaction (83.33%)*	
Capital stock	$100,000	$120,000	$ 80,000	$100,000	$20,000
Retained earnings	153,000*	153,000*	122,400	127,500	5,100
Other contributed capital	-0-	48,000	-0-	40,000	40,000
	$253,000	$321,000	$202,400	$267,500	$65,100

* $150,000 + (25% × $12,000)

Differentials—Calculation, Allocation, and Amortization.   The separate differentials for this case implied by step-by-step analysis are calculated below.

	First Block	*Second Block*
Amount in investment account on January 1, 19X1	$260,000	
Amount in investment account on March 31, 19X1		$68,000
Less: Initial interest in S Company's stockholders' equity (80% × $250,000)	200,000	
Less: Increase in interest in S Company's stockholders' equity		65,100
Separate differential	$ 60,000	$ 2,900

The total differential now is $62,900 ($60,000 + $2,900). Again, the separate differential for the second block is related to the increase in P Company's interest in S Company's stockholders' equity just as the separate differentials arising from open-market block purchases are related to such increases. Since the unamortized differentials are allocated to elements of plant and equipment with remaining 20-year lives, differential amortization for 19X1 is $3,109 [($60,000/20) + (75% × $2,900/20)].

Parent's 19X1 Entries, Related Working Paper Entries, and Incremental Calculation of Consolidated Net Income.   After the acquisition of the second block of stock, P Company's ownership percent increases to 83.33. Thus, its equity method entries for 19X1 (ignoring the entry to record its share purchase) are as follows:

```
Investment in S Company [80% × (25% × $12,000)]  . . . . . . . . . . . . . 2,400
    Equity in Subsidiary Earnings  . . . . . . . . . . . . . . . . . . . . . . . . .       2,400

Equity in Subsidiary Earnings [25% × ($60,000/20)]  . . . . . . . . . . . . .  750
    Investment in S Company  . . . . . . . . . . . . . . . . . . . . . . . . . . . .        750

Investment in S Company [83.33% × (75% × $12,000)] . . . . . . . . . . . . 7,500
    Equity in Subsidiary Earnings  . . . . . . . . . . . . . . . . . . . . . . . . .       7,500

Equity in Subsidiary Earnings
    [75% × ($60,000/20 + $2,900/20)]  . . . . . . . . . . . . . . . . . . . . . . 2,359
    Investment in S Company  . . . . . . . . . . . . . . . . . . . . . . . . . . . .      2,359
```

The working paper entries for 19X1 are as follows.

1. To eliminate double counting of equity method income and record minority interest in subsidiary net income:

```
Minority Interest Expense
    (16.67% × $12,000)  . . . . . . . . . . . . . . . . . . . . . . . . .  2,000
Equity in Subsidiary Earnings
    ($2,400 − $750 + $7,500 − $2,359) . . . . . . . . . . . . . . .  6,791
        Investment in S Company  . . . . . . . . . . . . . . . . . . .         6,791
        Minority Interest  . . . . . . . . . . . . . . . . . . . . . . . . .         2,000
```

2. To eliminate the investment account balance against S Company stockholders' equity accounts, record purchased preacquisition earnings, and establish related minority interest:

```
Capital Stock—S Company . . . . . . . . . . . . . . . . . . . . .  120,000
Retained Earnings—S Company  . . . . . . . . . . . . . . . . . .  150,000
Other Contributed Capital . . . . . . . . . . . . . . . . . . . . . .   48,000
Differential . . . . . . . . . . . . . . . . . . . . . . . . . . . . . . . .   62,900
Purchased Preacquisition Earnings
    [(83.33% − 80%) × ($3,000)] . . . . . . . . . . . . . . . . . . .      100
        Investment in S Company
            ($260,000 + $68,000)  . . . . . . . . . . . . . . . . . . . .         328,000
        Minority Interest
            [16.67% × ($120,000 + $150,000 + $48,000)]  . . . . . . .          53,000
```

3. To allocate the differential:

Plant and Equipment (net)	62,900	
Differential		62,900

4. To record differential amortization:

Depreciation Expense	3,109	
Plant and Equipment (net)		3,109

As shown, the entries for this case are very much like those of the previous one. The new feature of significance is the recording of purchased preacquisition earnings in working paper entry (2). As in the interim open-market block purchase case (Case 2), this value is based on the increase in the ownership percent.

The incremental calculation of consolidated net income in this case parallels the calculation made in the interim open-market block purchase case. Thus, the calculation allows for the change in the ownership percent resulting from the purchase of the newly issued shares and the related interim change in differential amortization. Consolidated net income for 19X1 is calculated incrementally as follows:

P Company's 19X1 net income from its own operations		$25,000
Plus: P Company's equity in S Company's 19X1 net income:		
First quarter—[80% × (25% × $12,000)]	$2,400	
Last three quarters—[83.33% × (75% × $12,000)]	7,500	9,900
Less: Differential amortization for 19X1:		
First quarter—[25% × ($60,000/20)]	$750	
Last three quarters—[75% × ($62,900/20)]	2,359	(3,109)
Consolidated net income for 19X1		$31,791

Extension to Acquisitions of Other Proportions of Shares by Parent

In the previous two cases, the parent acquired all the newly issued shares. *Nevertheless, exactly the same procedures apply in any case in which the parent acquires a disproportionately large number of newly issued shares.* If a parent and the related minority shareholders acquire newly issued shares ratably (e.g., when the common shareholders' preemptive rights are exercised), neither the ownership percent nor the minority interest percent changes. Under these conditions, the cost of the parent's shares exactly equals the change in its interest in the subsidiary's stockholders' equity, and there is no change in the total differential or in any other consolidated statement related value. The case in which a parent acquires a disproportionately small number of newly issued subsidiary shares is covered later in this chapter.

Case 5. Disproportionately Small Number of Treasury Shares Acquired from Minority Shareholders on Interim Date

Assume the data of Case 4 except that S Company acquires 100 of its own shares on March 31, 19X1, from minority shareholders (rather than P Company acquiring 200 newly issued shares) and accounts for these treasury shares using the cost method.[9] The cost of each share is $300—implying a total cost of $30,000 (100 × $300).

The purchase of the treasury shares decreases S Company's stockholders' equity by $30,000. It also increases P Company's ownership percent from 80 to 88.89 (or 800/900). Since the ownership percent increases, the purchase of the treasury shares is accounted for by P Company as though it acquired shares itself in the open market at no cost. Another effect of the acquisition is a $4,178 decrease in P Company's interest in S Company's stockholders' equity. As shown below, this value is pertinent in calculating the increase in the total differential related to the acquisition of the treasury shares. The following table shows the calculation of this amount and reveals the details of the changes brought about by the ownership percent increasing subsidiary stock transaction.

	S Company's Stockholders' Equity		P Company's Interest in S Company's Stockholders' Equity		Increase (Decrease) in P Company's Interest
	Before Transaction	*After Transaction*	*Before Transaction (80%)*	*After Transaction (88.89%)*	
Capital stock	$100,000	$100,000	$ 80,000	$ 88,889	$ 8,889
Retained earnings	153,000*	153,000*	122,400	136,000	13,600
Treasury stock (assuming cost method)	–0–	(30,000)	–0–	(26,667)	(26,667)
	$253,000	$223,000	$202,400	$198,222	($ 4,178)

* $150,000 + (25% × $12,000)

---

[9] We ignore the case in which treasury shares are acquired on the first day of the year for brevity.

Differentials—Calculation, Allocation, and Amortization.   In this case, an increase in the total differential also is implied. The calculations supporting this conclusion are shown below:

	First Block	Treasury Stock Transaction
Amount in investment account on January 1, 19X1	$260,000	
Amount in investment account on March 31, 19X1		$-0-
Less: Original interest in S Company's stockholders' equity (80% × $250,000)	200,000	
Less: Decrease in interest in S Company's stockholders' equity		(4,178)
Separate differential	$ 60,000	$4,178

The total differential now is $64,178 ($60,000 + $4,178). In this case, the increase in the total differential equals the decrease in P Company's interest in S Company's stockholders' equity. Thus, the decrease in P Company's interest is treated as though it is an additional cost of its S Company shares.[10] This additional cost is interpreted as a separate differential even though no new shares actually have been acquired. Since the unamortized differentials are allocated to elements of plant and equipment with remaining 20-year lives, differential amortization for 19X1 is $3,157 [($60,000/20) + 75% × ($4,178/20)].

Parent's 19X1 Entries, Related Working Paper Entries, and Incremental Calculation of Consolidated Net Income.   After the purchase of the treasury shares, P Company's ownership percent rises to 88.89. Thus, its equity method entries for 19X1 are as follows:

Investment in S Company [80% × (25% × $12,000)]	2,400	
Equity in Subsidiary Earnings		2,400
Equity in Subsidiary Earnings [25% × ($60,000/20)]	750	
Investment in S Company		750
Investment in S Company [88.89% × (75% × $12,000)]	8,000	
Equity in Subsidiary Earnings		8,000

---

[10] This decrease is accounted for as a purchase even if the combination was accounted for originally as a pooling of interests. See *APB Opinion No. 16*, pars. 5 and 43, and *Accounting Interpretation No. 26* of *APB Opinion No. 16.*

Equity in Subsidiary Earnings
[75% × ($60,000/20 + $4,178/20)] 2,407
     Investment in S Company   2,407

The working paper entries for 19X1 are presented below.

1. To offset balance in Treasury Stock against pertinent S Company stockholders' equity accounts (see Chapter 2):

Capital Stock (100 × $100) 10,000
Retained Earnings 20,000
    Treasury Stock (100 × $300)   30,000

2. To eliminate double counting of equity method income and record minority interest in subsidiary net income:

Minority Interest Expense (11.11% × $12,000) 1,333
Equity in Subsidiary Earnings
   ($2,400 − $750 + $8,000 − $2,407) 7,243
    Investment in S Company   7,243
    Minority Interest   1,333

3. To eliminate investment account balance against S Company stockholders' equity accounts, record purchased preacquisition earnings, and establish related minority interest:

Capital Stock—S Company
   ($100,000 − $10,000) 90,000
Retained Earnings—S Company
   ($150,000 − $20,000) 130,000
Differential 64,178
Purchased Preacquisition Earnings
   [(88.89% − 80%) × $3,000]   266
    Investment in S Company   260,000
    Minority Interest
      [11.11% × ($90,000 + $130,000)]   24,444

4. To allocate the differential:

Plant and Equipment (net) 64,178
    Differential   64,178

5. To record differential amortization:

Depreciation Expense	3,157	
Plant and Equipment (net)		3,157

The working paper entries for this case parallel those of the previous case. The calculation of consolidated net income also parallels the calculation made in the previous case. Consolidated net income is calculated incrementally as follows for 19X1.

P Company's 19X1 net income from its own operations		$25,000
Plus: P Company's equity in S Company's 19X1 net income:		
First quarter—80% × (25% × $12,000)	$2,400	
Last three quarters—88.89% × (75% × $12,000)	8,000	10,400
Less: Differential amortization for 19X1:		
First quarter—25% × ($60,000/20)	$ 750	
Last three quarters—75% × ($64,178/20)	2,407	(3,157)
Consolidated net income for 19X1		$32,243

Extension to Acquisitions of Other Proportions of Treasury Shares

In Case 5, all of the treasury shares are acquired from minority shareholders. *Nevertheless, exactly the same procedures apply in any case in which a subsidiary acquires a disproportionately small number of treasury shares from its parent.* If treasury shares are acquired ratably, neither the ownership percent nor the minority interest percent changes. Under these conditions, there is no change in the total differential or in any other consolidated statement related value. The case in which a subsidiary acquires a disproportionately large number of treasury shares from its parent is covered later in this chapter.

DECREASES IN PARENTS' OWNERSHIP PERCENTS

An investor company's ownership percent decreases when (1) it sells shares of an affiliate to nonaffiliates, (2) it acquires a disproportionately small number of newly issued shares of an affiliate, or (3) an affiliate acquires a disproportionately large number of treasury shares from the investor. *These three situations affect working paper techniques, consolidated statement values, and equity method entries similarly.* Consequently, we group them in this section for explanatory purposes.

Sales of Subsidiary Shares to Nonaffiliates—General Comments

A sale of subsidiary shares to a nonaffiliate by a parent is accounted for similarly to other disposals of parent company assets. That is, the investment account first is adjusted through the point of sale using equity method procedures. Subsequently, the carrying value of the shares sold is matched against the sales price to determine the gain or loss on the sale.[11] The carrying value of the shares sold may be calculated using several procedures, including the specific identification, first-in, first-out, and weighted-average methods. We recommend the use of the weighted-average method since the shares held are interchangeable and have the same economic significance.[12]

Case 6. Sales of Subsidiary Shares to Nonaffiliates

This case is a continuation of Case 1. It assumes that (1) P Company sells 100 shares (or 20 percent) of S Company on March 31, 19X4, to nonaffiliates for $26,000, (2) P Company's 19X4 net income from its own operations is $25,000 (excluding any gain or loss from the sale of the shares), (3) S Company's uniformly earned net income in 19X4 is $10,000, and (4) the weighted-average method is used in accounting for sales of subsidiary shares in financial statements. Recall that S Company has capital stock of $50,000 ($100 par) and retained earnings of $20,000 on January 1, 19X1, and that its net income in each of the years 19X1 through 19X3 is $10,000. Recall also that P Company acquires shares of S Company (and related ownership percents) through open-market block purchases as indicated below.

Date	Number (%) of Shares	Cost
January 1, 19X1	200 (40%)	$30,000
January 1, 19X2	100 (20%)	17,500
January 1, 19X3	100 (20%)	20,000

---

[11] See *APB Opinion No. 18*, par. 19f.

[12] Under current tax law, either specific identification or first-in, first-out must be used in accounting for sales of subsidiary shares. Thus, if the weighted-average method is used for these sales for financial accounting purposes, temporary differences are produced, and interperiod tax allocation procedures are applied. We ignore the tax allocation procedures related to sales of subsidiary shares in this chapter for simplicity. These procedures are covered in intermediate accounting texts.

Finally, recall the following differences in fair values and book values for different elements of plant and equipment at the various block purchase dates.

	Plant and Equipment (net)	
	Fair Value	*Book Value*
January 1, 19X1	$29,500	$28,250
January 1, 19X2	34,500	32,000
January 1, 19X3	47,500	40,000

Each element of plant and equipment still is assumed to have a remaining life of 5 years on the related block purchase date, and goodwill arising from individual block purchases still is to be amortized over 10 years. The differential amortization figures pertinent to this case are found in Illustration 9–1. This illustration reveals the following amortization values for 19X4.

Plant and equipment (net)	$500
Goodwill	300
Total	$800

Parent's Entries in 19X4.   Our discussion of P Company's 19X4 equity method entries begins by analyzing the changes in its Investment in S Company account through the sale of its S Company shares on March 31, 19X4. These changes are tabulated below.

Cost of first block (200 shares)—January 1, 19X1	$30,000
Add: P Company's equity in S Company's	
19X1 net income (40% × $10,000)	4,000
Less: 19X1 differential amortization	(250)
Balance December 31, 19X1	$33,750
Cost of second block (100 shares)—January 1, 19X2	17,500
Add: P Company's equity in S Company's	
19X2 net income (60% × $10,000)	6,000
Less: 19X2 differential amortization	(450)
Balance December 31, 19X2	$56,800
Cost of third block (100 shares)—January 1, 19X3	20,000
Add: P Company's equity in S Company's	
19X3 net income (80% × $10,000)	8,000
Less: 19X3 differential amortization	(800)
Balance December 31, 19X3	$84,000

Add: P Company's equity in S Company's net income
for the period January 1, 19X4–March 31, 19X4
[80% × (25% × $10,000)]   2,000
Less: Differential amortization for the period
January 1, 19X4–March 31, 19X4 (25% × $800) . . . .   (200)
Balance March 31, 19X4 . . . . $85,800

This analysis implies that the weighted-average cost of each of the S Company shares on March 31, 19X4, is $214.50 ($85,800/400). Thus, the weighted-average cost of the shares sold is $21,450 (100 × $214.50), and the gain on the sale is $4,550 ($26,000 − $21,450).

After the sale of the shares, P Company's ownership percent drops from 80 to 60 percent, and the balance in the Investment in S Company account is reduced to $64,350 ($85,800 − $21,450). Notice that the preceding tabulation implies that P Company's equity method entries are based on the presale ownership percent (80%) through the sale date. Subsequently, its equity method entries are based on the post-sale ownership percent (60%). The latter percent is 75 percent of the former (60%/80%). This relationship provides a simple means of calculating differential amortization for periods of time subsequent to the sale. Thus, after the sale, a full year's differential amortization equals 75 percent of any previously calculated amount. For example, if the sale had not occurred, 19X5 differential amortization would have been $800. Given the sale, this value is $600 (75% × $800). Similarly, if the sale had not occurred, differential amortization for the last three quarters of 19X4 would have been $600 (75% × $800). Given the sale, differential amortization for this period is $450 (75% × $600). These calculational procedures are correct since the investment account contains only 75 percent of its presale amounts once the sale is recorded. More specifically, the Investment in S Company account contains only 75 percent of P Company's presale interest in S Company's stockholders' equity and 75 percent of its presale unamortized differential once the sale is recorded. These observations are demonstrated below.

	Investment in S Balance	
	Presale	*Post-sale*
P Company's interest in S Company's stockholders' equity:		
[80% × ($50,000 + $20,000 + $30,000 + 25% × $10,000)]	$82,000	
75% × $82,000 or 60% × $102,500		$61,500
Unamortized differential:		
($5,500 − $250 − $450 − $800 − $200)	3,800	
75% × $3,800		2,850
	$85,800	$64,350

Given the preceding values, P Company's equity method entries for 19X4 are as follows:

1. To record P Company's equity in S Company's net income through the point of sale of the 10 subsidiary shares (i.e., through March 31, 19X4):

Investment in S Company [80% × (25% × $10,000)]   2,000
    Equity in Subsidiary Earnings   2,000

2. To record differential amortization through the point of sale of the subsidiary shares:

Equity in Subsidiary Earnings (25% × $800)   200
    Investment in S Company   200

3. To record the sale of the subsidiary shares using the weighted-average method:

Cash 26,000
    Investment in S Company (25% × $85,800)   21,450
    Gain on Sale of Stock   4,550

4. To record P Company's equity in S Company's net income for the portion of the year subsequent to the sale of the shares:

Investment in S Company [60% × (75% × $10,000)]   4,500
    Equity in Subsidiary Earnings   4,500

5. To record differential amortization for the portion of the year subsequent to the sale of the shares:

Equity in Subsidiary Earnings [75% × (75% × $800)]   450
    Investment in S Company   450

As indicated, the first two equity method entries are based on the presale ownership percent of 80, and the last two entries are based on the post-sale ownership percent of 60. The third equity method entry records the gain on the sale of the subsidiary shares. The last entry reflects the procedures explained above for making post-sale differential amortization calculations.

Calculations of Parent's 19X4 Net Income and Incremental Calculation of 19X4 Consolidated Net Income.   A partial consolidated statement working paper is provided for this case in Illustration 9–2. This illustration shows that P Company's 19X4 net income is $35,400 under the equity method. This balance includes the gain on the sale of stock of $4,550 and equity in subsidiary earnings of $5,850 ($2,000 − $200 + $4,500 − $450). Illustration 9–2 also reveals that consolidated net income is $35,400. Thus, the one-line consolidation property of the equity method (see Chapter 2) is maintained in the context of parent company sales of subsidiary shares to nonaffiliates. As implied, consolidated net income is defined to include gains or losses on such sales. Thus, consolidated net income is calculated incrementally in this case as follows.

ILLUSTRATION 9-2   **Sale of Subsidiary Shares to Nonaffiliates (Case 6)**

P COMPANY AND SUBSIDIARY S COMPANY
Partial Consolidated Statement Working Paper
For the Year Ended December 31, 19X4

| | *P* Company | *S* Company | Eliminations | | Consoli- dated |
			Dr.	*Cr.*	
Income Statement					
Net income (excluding gain on sale of stock and equity in subsidiary earnings)	25,000	10,000	(4) 600		34,400
Gain on sale of stock	4,550				4,550
Equity in subsidiary earnings	5,850		(1) 5,400		450
	35,400	10,000			39,400
Minority interest expense			(1) 4,000		4,000
Net income	35,400	10,000	10,000	–0–	35,400
Retained Earnings Statement					
Retained earnings (1/1/X4):					
P Company	80,000				80,000
S Company		50,000	(2) 50,000		–0–
Net income	35,400	10,000	10,000		35,400
Retained earnings, (12/31/X4)	115,400	60,000	60,000	–0–	115,400

P Company's 19X4 net income from its own operations (excluding gain)		$25,000
Plus: Gain on sale of stock		4,550
		$29,550
Plus: P Company's equity in S Company's 19X4 net income:		
First quarter—[80% × (25% × $10,000)]	$2,000	
Last three quarters—[60% × (75% × $10,000)]	4,500	6,500
Less: Differential amortization for 19X4:		
First quarter—(25% × $800)	$200	
Last three quarters—[75% × (75% × $800)]	450	(650)
Consolidated net income for 19X4		$35,400

Values from this calculation are used below in explaining the working paper
techniques pertaining to sales of subsidiary shares to nonaffiliates.

Working Paper Entries for 19X4.   The working paper entries for 19X4 are presented below. These entries reflect several new features which are explained
subsequently. *For now, note that the entries are made as though the post-sale*

ownership and minority interest percents prevailed throughout the entire year. In this context, notice that several of the values in the entries are calculated using the ratio of the post-sale and presale ownership percents of 75 percent emphasized above.

1. To eliminate double counting of equity method income and record minority interest in subsidiary net income as though the post-sale ownership and minority interest percents prevailed throughout the year.

Minority Interest Expense (40% × $10,000)	4,000	
Equity in Subsidiary Earnings		
[(60% × $10,000) − $600]	5,400	
Investment in S Company		5,400
Minority Interest		4,000

2. To eliminate investment account balance against beginning-of-year S Company stockholders' equity accounts and establish beginning-of-year minority interest as though the post-sale ownership and minority interest percents prevailed throughout the year:

Capital Stock—S Company	50,000	
Retained Earnings—S Company		
($20,000 + $30,000)	50,000	
Differential [75% × (5,500 − ($250 + $450 + $800))]	3,000	
Investment in S Company (75% × $84,000)		63,000
Minority Interest [40% × ($50,000 + $50,000)]		40,000

3. To allocate the differential at the beginning of the year as though the post-sale ownership percent prevailed throughout the year:

Plant and Equipment (net)		
[75% × ($2,500 − ($100 + $200 + $500))]	1,275	
Goodwill [75% × ($3,000 − ($150 + $250 + $300))]	1,725	
Differential		3,000

4. To record differential amortization as though the post-sale ownership percent prevailed throughout the year:

Depreciation Expense (75% × $500)	375	
Amortization of Goodwill (75% × $300)	225	
Plant and Equipment (net)		375
Goodwill		225

As indicated earlier, a partial consolidated statement working paper for this case is presented in Illustration 9–2.

The mechanics of the above entries are self-explanatory once you understand that they are made as if the post-sale ownership and minority interest percents applied during the entire year. Nevertheless, such understanding fails to provide insights into the effects of this procedure. First, notice that working paper entry (1) contains a debit to Equity in Subsidiary Earnings amounting to $5,400 [(60% × $10,000) − (75% × $800)]. The actual balance in this account is $5,850 ($2,000 − $200 + $4,500 − $450). *Thus, entry (1) leaves a balance in Equity in Subsidiary Earnings equaling $450 ($5,850 − $5,400).*[13] This balance equals the difference in two quantities: (1) the excess of P Company's recorded equity in S Company's net income for the first quarter of 19X4 ($2,000) over the corresponding value for this equity assuming the ownership percent had been 60 percent for the entire year ($1,500 = 60% × $2,500) and (2) the excess of the recorded differential amortization for this period ($200) over the differential amortization that would have been recorded during this period if the ownership percent had been 60 percent for the entire year ($150 = 75% × $200). This calculation is summarized as $450 = [($2,000 − $1,500) − ($200 − $150)].[14] This $450 must be left in the Equity in Subsidiary Earnings account (or other accounts—see footnote 14) in order for the consolidated statement working paper to produce the correct consolidated net income figure of $35,400 (as calculated above incrementally). The working paper would show consolidated net income of only $34,950 if this $450 is eliminated.

The second insight into our procedures pertains to the use of the post-sale ownership and minority interest percents in the working paper entries. *These percents are used because consolidated balance sheets are based on post-sale ownership and minority interest percents, irrespective of how these percents change during the year.* If other percents were used, numerous accounts would be misstated. For example, in this case, year-end minority interest equals $44,000 [40% × ($50,000 + $20,000 + $40,000)], and this value would not appear in the consolidated statement working paper if the beginning-of-year minority interest percent of 20 percent is used in the working paper entries. Similarly, the unamortized differential at year-end is $2,400 [75% × ($5,500 − $2,300)], given that P Company owns only 60 percent of S Company at year-end. This amount is allocated to goodwill and S Company's depreciable fixed assets through working paper entries (3) and (4). If these entries were not based on the post-sale ownership percent, goodwill and S Company's depreciable fixed assets would be misstated in the consolidated balance sheet.

----

[13] Note that this is the first time that our working paper procedures have left a balance in Equity in Subsidiary Earnings.

[14] For convenience, we leave this $450 in the Equity in Subsidiary Earnings account. The $500 component of this value related to P Company's equity method pickup can be offset against Minority Interest Expense in the consolidated statement working paper (or consolidated income statement). Similarly, the $50 component related to differential amortization can be broken down into its parts and included with the depreciation and amortization figures in the working paper (or the income statement). Comments such as these apply to all cases below in which a balance is left in Equity in Subsidiary Earnings.

Reconciliation of Subsidiary Net Income and the Sum of Parent's Equity and Minority Interest in Subsidiary Net Income. S Company's 19X4 net income is $10,000. However, examination of the preceding incremental calculation of consolidated net income and working paper entries reveals that P Company's equity in S Company's 19X4 net income is $6,500 [(80% × (25% × $10,000)) + (60% × (75% × $10,000))] and that minority interest expense is $4,000 (40% × $10,000). The sum of these two amounts is $10,500—an amount which is $500 higher than S Company's net income. Thus, it appears that an extra $500 of subsidiary net income has materialized and has been allocated between the majority and minority shareholders. This apparent discrepancy disappears once you realize that there are two $500 inflows of net assets related to the 100 shares of S Company sold. The first of these inflows occurs when S Company earns its first quarter's income of $2,500 and equals .20 percent of this amount. Until the S Company shares are sold, this $500 accrues to P Company. The second inflow occurs when P Company sells the 100 shares of S Company to nonaffiliates. At this point, the nonaffiliates, in effect, compensate P Company for its claim to the first $500 inflow by implicitly including $500 in the $26,000 purchase price of the shares. Once the shares are sold, the minority shareholders (including the nonaffiliates to whom the shares were sold) have a 40 percent claim on S Company's income, and this claim includes the original $500 inflow. Thus, both the majority and minority stockholders' interests are increased by $500 as a consequence of S Company's net income for the first quarter of 19X4 and the sale of shares.

Extension to Subsequent Years. Sales of subsidiary shares to nonaffiliates produce no complications in subsequent years. For example, parent companies' equity method entries are based on post-sale ownership percents. Similarly, all working paper entries are based on these percents. In this context, Equity in Subsidiary Earnings account balances are completely eliminated via the working paper entries. Finally, differential related values continue to be recorded consistently with the differential reductions resulting from sales of subsidiary shares to nonaffiliates.

Ownership Percent Decreasing Subsidiary Stock Transactions— General Comments

The previous decrease in ownership percent case covers a situation in which the subsidiary is not involved in the transaction leading to the ownership percent decrease—a sale of subsidiary shares to nonaffiliates. *However, the subsidiary necessarily is involved in the transaction leading to an ownership percent decrease when (1) its parent acquires a disproportionately small number of its newly issued shares, or (2) it acquires a disproportionately large number of treasury shares from its parent.* Transactions such as these are referred to as *ownership percent decreasing subsidiary stock transactions*. These transactions, like ownership percent increasing subsidiary stock transactions, *produce changes in subsidiaries' stockholders' equities*. Since they affect subsidiaries' stockholders' equities, they also change parents' interests in these equities (which may increase or decrease). These changes are incorporated into the calculation of gains and losses from the transactions. The justification for this treatment is provided below.

As mentioned, when a subsidiary engages in an ownership percent decreasing stock transaction, the parent's interest in the subsidiary's stockholders' equity changes. As shown in the appendix to this chapter, *exactly* the same changes can be produced through a properly structured parent company sale of subsidiary shares to nonaffiliates. Given this observation, we recommend that the account balances resulting from a subsidiary's ownership percent decreasing stock transaction be the same as those which would have resulted from a properly structured parent company sale of subsidiary shares to nonaffiliates. For these balances to be the same, changes in parent's interests in subsidiaries' stockholders' equities must be allowed to affect the gains and losses from subsidiaries' ownership percent decreasing stock transactions.[15] Our recommendation again is based on the principle of substance over form. That is, the substance of an ownership percent decreasing subsidiary stock transaction is that of a properly structured parent company sale of subsidiary shares to nonaffiliates. Thus, we believe that such cases are best accounted for as though they are properly structured parent company sales of subsidiary shares to nonaffiliates.

Case 7. Disproportionately Small Number of Newly Issued Shares Acquired by Parent

Assume that S Company has capital stock of $100,000 ($100 par) and retained earnings of $150,000 initially on January 1, 19X1. At this time, P Company holds 800 of S Company's shares (implying an 80 percent ownership percent), and its Investment in S Company account has a balance of $260,000. The book value of each S Company share is $250 ($250,000/1,000). S Company's net income for 19X1 is $12,000. P Company's 19X1 net income from its own operations is $25,000, excluding any gains or losses on subsidiary stock transactions. On January 1, 19X1, S Company sells an additional 200 shares of its stock to nonaffiliates at $340 per share. The total sales price of the newly issued shares is $68,000 (200 × $340). Since P Company's interest in S Company's stockholders' equity is $200,000 (80% × $250,000) prior to the sale of the shares, the investment account includes a presale unamortized differential of $60,000. The following presale differential allocation and amortization values pertain to 19X1.

---

[15] Some accountants prefer to credit the portions of these gains related to changes in parents' interests to consolidated paid-in capital. Our position is that these amounts are part of consolidated net income. The reasonableness of this view is demonstrated in the appendix to this chapter. This position is supported in the June 1980 AICPA Accounting Standards Executive Committee issues paper entitled "Accounting in Consolidation for Issuances of a Subsidiary's Stock" and by *Staff Accounting Bulletin 51* of the SEC (May 1983).

	Unamortized Differential before Issuance of New Shares	19X1 Amortization
Plant and equipment (net)	$15,000	$1,500
Goodwill	45,000	3,000
Total	$60,000	$4,500

The sale of the new shares increases S Company's Capital Stock balance to $120,000 [$100,000 + (200 × $100)] and increases its Other Contributed Capital balance to $48,000 [200 × ($340 − $100)]. It also decreases P Company's ownership percent from 80% to 66.67 percent (800/1,200). Since the ownership percent decreases, the sale of the new shares by S Company is treated as a sale of shares to nonaffiliates by P Company. Another effect of the sale is a $12,000 increase in P Company's interest in S Company's stockholders' equity. As shown below, this value is relevant in determining the gain or loss from the ownership percent decreasing subsidiary stock transaction. The following table shows the calculation of this amount and the details of the changes brought about by this transaction.

	S Company's Stockholders' Equity		P Company's Interest in S Company's Stockholders' Equity		Increase (Decrease) in P Company's Interest
	Before Transaction	After Transaction	Before Transaction (80%)	After Transaction (66.67%)	
Capital stock	$100,000	$120,000	$ 80,000	$ 80,000	$-0-
Retained earnings	150,000	150,000	120,000	100,000	(20,000)
Other contributed capital	-0-	48,000	-0-	32,000	32,000
	$250,000	$318,000	$200,000	$212,000	$12,000

Parent's Entries in 19X1.   We begin our analysis of P Company's 19X1 equity method entries by calculating the gain or loss resulting from the issuance of the subsidiary shares. First, note that the ratio of the post-sale and presale ownership percent is 83.33 (66.67%/80%). Since the sale of the new shares by S Company is treated as a sale of shares to nonaffiliates by P Company, the unamortized differential is reduced precisely as in the case of such a sale. Thus, the value of the differential after the sale of the subsidiary shares is $50,000 (83.33% × $60,000). The $10,000 difference ($60,000 − $50,000) in the differential before and after the sale is a component of the gain or loss on the ownership percent decreasing subsidiary stock transaction. The other component of this gain or loss is the $12,000 increase in P Company's interest in S Company's stockholders' equity calculated above. Specifically, the gain is $2,000; it equals the increase just mentioned less the decrease in the differential ($12,000 − $10,000). *More gener-*

ally, the gain or loss from an ownership percent decreasing subsidiary stock transaction equals the difference between two quantities: (1) the cash disbursed to acquire new shares (or cash received when the subsidiary repurchases treasury shares) and (2) the increase (decrease) in the parent's interest in the subsidiary's stockholders' equity less the decrease in the differential.

Given the above values, including the post-sale ownership percent of 66.67, P Company's 19X1 equity method entries are as follows:

1. To record P Company's equity in S Company's net income:

Investment in S Company (66.67% × $12,000)	8,000	
Equity in Subsidiary Earnings		8,000

2. To record the gain on the ownership percent decreasing subsidiary stock transaction:

Investment in S Company	2,000	
Gain on Subsidiary Stock Transaction		2,000

3. To record differential amortization:

Equity in Subsidiary Earnings (83.33% × $4,500)	3,750	
Investment in S Company		3,750

Working Paper Entries for 19X1 and Incremental Calculation of Consolidated Net Income. The 19X1 working paper entries, which are self-explanatory, are as follows.

1. To eliminate double counting of equity method income and record minority interest in subsidiary net income as though the post-sale ownership and minority interest percents prevailed throughout the year:

Minority Interest Expense (33.33% × $12,000)	4,000	
Equity in Subsidiary Earnings ($8,000 − $3,750)	4,250	
Investment in S Company		4,250
Minority Interest		4,000

2. To eliminate investment account balance against S Company stockholders' equity accounts and establish related minority interest as though the post-sale ownership and minority interest percents prevailed throughout the year:

Capital Stock—S Company	120,000	
Retained Earnings—S Company	150,000	
Other Contributed Capital	48,000	
Differential (83.33% × $60,000)	50,000	
Investment in S Company ($260,000 + $2,000)		262,000
Minority Interest [33.33% × ($120,000 + $150,000 + $48,000)]		106,000

3. To allocate the differential as though the post-sale ownership percent prevailed throughout the year:

Plant and Equipment (net) (83.33% × $15,000)   12,500
Goodwill (83.33% × $45,000)   37,500
   Differential   50,000

4. To record differential amortization as though the post-sale ownership percent prevailed throughout the year:

Depreciation Expense (83.33% × $1,500)   1,250
Amortization of Goodwill (83.33% × $3,000)   2,500
   Plant and Equipment (net)   1,250
   Goodwill   2,500

Consolidated net income for 19X1 is calculated incrementally below.

P Company's 19X1 net income from its own operations (excluding gain)	$25,000
Plus: Gain on subsidiary stock transaction	2,000
Plus: P Company's equity in S Company's 19X1 net income (66.67% × $12,000)	8,000
Less: Differential amortization for 19X1 (83.33% × $4,500)	(3,750)
Consolidated net income for 19X1	$31,250

Relationships among Book Value of Subsidiary Shares, Issuance Price, and Parent's Interest in Subsidiary Stockholders' Equity. The sales price of S Company's shares is $340 per share, and their presale book value is $250. These conditions result in a $12,000 increase in P Company's interest in S Company's stockholders' equity. In general, if sales price exceeds presale book value in a case such as this one (i.e., one with an ownership percent decrease), the value of the parent's interest in subsidiary stockholders' equity increases. If the sales price equals the presale book value, a situation of this type produces no change in the parent's interest. Also, if the sales price is less than the presale book value in such a case, a decrease in the parent's interest occurs. These observations are illustrated via the following table—which is based on sales prices of $250 and $190, respectively.

	S Company's Stockholders' Equity		P Company's Interest in S Company's Stockholders' Equity		Increase (Decrease) in P Company's Interest
	Before Transaction	*After Transaction*	*Before Transaction (80%)*	*After Transaction (66.67%)*	
Sales price of $250	$250,000	$300,000	$200,000	$200,000	$–0–
Sales price of $190	250,000	288,000	200,000	192,000	(8,000)

Case 8. Disproportionately Small Number of Newly Issued Shares Acquired by Parent on Interim Date

This case is a modification of Case 7. It is exactly like Case 7, except that S Company sells the additional 200 shares on March 31, 19X1 (rather than January 1, 19X1), and S Company's 19X1 net income of $12,000 is assumed to be earned uniformly.

The sale of the new shares again increases S Company's Capital Stock balance to $120,000 [$100,000 + (200 × $100)] and increases its Other Contributed Capital balance to $48,000 [200 × ($340 − $100)]. It also decreases P Company's ownership percent from 80 to 66.67 (800/1,200). Since the ownership percent decreases, the sale of the new shares by S Company again is treated as a sale of shares to nonaffiliates by P Company. In this case, the sale of the new shares produces an $11,600 increase in P Company's interest in S Company's stockholders' equity. The following tabulation shows the calculation of this amount and the details of the changes brought about by the ownership percent decreasing subsidiary stock transaction.

	S Company's Stockholders' Equity		P Company's Interest in S Company's Stockholders' Equity		Increase (Decrease) in P Company's Interest
	Before Transaction	*After Transaction*	*Before Transaction (80%)*	*After Transaction (66.67%)*	
Capital stock	$100,000	$120,000	$ 80,000	$ 80,000	$–0–
Retained earnings	153,000*	153,000*	122,400	102,000	(20,400)
Other contributed capital	–0–	48,000	–0–	32,000	32,000
	$253,000	$321,000	$202,400	$214,000	$11,600

* $150,000 + (25% × $12,000)

Parent's Entries in 19X1. The ratio of the post-sale and presale ownership percents again is 83.33 (66.67/80). Since the sale of the new shares by S Company is treated as a sale of shares to nonaffiliates by P Company, the unamortized differential is reduced accordingly. The value of the differential after the issuance of the subsidiary shares is $49,063 [83.33% × ($60,000 − (25% × $4,500))]. The $9,812 difference [($60,000 − $1,125) − $49,063] in the differential before and after the sale of shares is a component of the gain or loss on the ownership percent decreasing subsidiary stock transaction. The other component of this gain or loss is the $11,600 increase in P Company's interest in S Company's stockholders' equity calculated previously. Specifically, the gain is $1,788; it equals the increase just mentioned less the decrease in the differential ($11,600 − $9,812).

Given the above values, including the post-sale ownership percent of 66.67%, P Company's 19X1 equity method entries are as follows:

1. To record P Company's equity in S Company's net income for the first quarter of 19X1:

   Investment in S Company [80% × (25% × $12,000)] 2,400
       Equity in Subsidiary Earnings   2,400

2. To record differential amortization for the first quarter of 19X1:

   Equity in Subsidiary Earnings (25% × $4,500) 1,125
       Investment in S Company   1,125

3. To record the gain on the ownership percent decreasing subsidiary stock transaction:

   Investment in S Company   1,788
       Gain on Subsidiary Stock Transaction   1,788

4. To record P Company's equity in S Company's net income for the last three quarters of 19X1:

   Investment in S Company [66.67% × (75% × $12,000)] 6,000
       Equity in Subsidiary Earnings   6,000

5. To record differential amortization for the last three quarters of 19X1:

   Equity in Subsidiary Earnings [83.33% × (75% × $4,500)] 2,813
       Investment in S Company   2,813

Working Paper Entries for 19X1 and Incremental Calculation of Consolidated Net Income. The 19X1 working paper entries are as follows. Note that these entries also are made as if the post-sale ownership and minority interest percents prevailed during the entire year. Since these percents are the same as in Case 7, the working paper entries are also the same as in Case 7.

1. To eliminate double counting of equity method income and record minority interest in subsidiary net income as though the post-sale ownership and minority interest percents prevailed throughout the year:

Minority Interest Expense (33.33% × $12,000) 4,000
Equity in Subsidiary Earnings [(66.67% × $12,000) −
   (83.33% × $4,500)] 4,250
    Investment in S Company 4,250
    Minority Interest 4,000

2. To eliminate investment account balance against S Company stockholders' equity accounts and establish related minority interest as though the post-sale ownership and minority interest percents prevailed throughout the year:

Capital Stock—S Company 120,000
Retained Earnings—S Company 150,000
Other Contributed Capital 48,000
Differential (83.33% × $60,000) 50,000
    Investment in S Company
      [$260,000 + $1,788 + ($4,462 − $4,250)] 262,000
    Minority Interest
      [33.33% × ($120,000 + $150,000 + $48,000)] 106,000

3. To allocate the differential as though the post-sale ownership percent prevailed throughout the year:

Plant and Equipment (net) (83.33% × $15,000) 12,500
Goodwill (83.33% × $45,000) 37,500
    Differential 50,000

4. To record differential amortization as though the post-sale ownership percent prevailed throughout the year:

Depreciation Expense (83.33% × $1,500) 1,250
Amortization of Goodwill (83.33% × $3,000) 2,500
    Plant and Equipment (net) 1,250
    Goodwill 2,500

Note that entry (1) contains a debit to Equity in Subsidiary Earnings amounting to $4,250 [(66.67% × $12,000) − (83.33% × $4,500)]. The actual balance in this account is $4,462 ($2,400 − $1,125 + $6,000 − $2,813). Thus, as in Case 6, entry (1) leaves a balance in Equity in Subsidiary Earnings. This balance is $212 ($4,462 − $4,250). It equals the difference in (1) the excess of P Company's recorded equity in S Company's net income for the first quarter of 19X1 ($2,400) over the corresponding value of this equity assuming the ownership percent has been 66.67 for the entire year [($2,000 = (66.67% × $3,000)] and (2) the excess of the recorded differential amortization for this period ($1,125) over the differential amortization that would have been recorded during this period if the ownership percent had been 66.67 for the entire year ($937 = 83.33% × $1,125). This calculation is summarized as $212 = [($2,400 − $2,000) − ($1,125 − $937)]. Similar to Case 6, this $212 must be left in the Equity in Subsidiary Earnings account in order for the consolidated statement working paper to produce the correct consolidated net income figure. Also, as in Case 6, the post-sale owner-ship and minority interest percents are used in the working paper entries so that the correct values are produced for the consolidated balance sheet.

As mentioned earlier, the working paper entries for this example are the same as in Case 7. Thus, there are only two substantive differences in this case and Case 7. First, in this example, $212 is left in the Equity in Subsidiary Earnings account, but the balance in this account is completely eliminated in Case 7. Second, the gain on the subsidiary stock transacation is $1,788 in this exam-ple, but it is $2,000 in Case 7. Although these two differences exist, there is no difference in consolidated net income in the two cases (i.e., since $1,788 + $212 = $2,000). Consolidated net income for this case is calculated incrementally for 19X1 as follows.

P Company's 19X1 net income from its own operations (excluding gain)		$25,000
Plus: Gain on subsidiary stock transaction		1,788
		$26,788
Plus: P Company's equity in S Company's 19X1 net income:		
First quarter—[80% × (25% × $12,000)]	$2,400	
Last three quarters—[66.67% × (75% × $12,000)]	6,000	
		8,400
Less: Differential amortization for 19X1:		
First quarter—(25% × $4,500)	$1,125	
Last three quarters—[83.33% × (75% × $4,500)]	2,813	
Consolidated net income for 19X1		(3,938)
		$31,250

Case 9. Disproportionately Large Number of Treasury Shares Acquired from Parent

This case is a modification of Case 8. Rather than assuming that S Company sells an additional 200 shares to nonaffiliates on March 31, 19X1, it assumes that S Company purchases 100 of its own shares from P Company on this date.[16]

---

[16] As mentioned in footnote 9, we ignore cases in which treasury shares are acquired on the first day of the year for brevity.

The cost of each share is $100—implying a total cost of $10,000 (100 × $100). S Company accounts for treasury shares using the cost method.

The purchase of the treasury shares decreases S Company's stockholders' equity by $10,000. This purchase also decreases P Company's ownership percent from 80 to 77.78 (or 700/900). Since the ownership percent decreases, the purchase of the treasury shares is accounted for by P Company as though it sold shares to nonaffiliates. Another effect of the treasury stock transaction is a $13,400 decrease in P Company's interest in S Company's stockholders' equity. The following table shows the calculation of this amount and the details of the changes brought about by the ownership percent decreasing subsidiary stock transacation.

	S Company's Stockholders' Equity		P Company's Interest in S Company's Stockholders' Equity		Increase (Decrease) in P Company's Interest
	Before Transaction	*After Transaction*	*Before Transaction (80%)*	*After Transaction (77.78%)*	
Capital stock	$100,000	$100,000	$ 80,000	$ 77,778	$ (2,222)
Retained earnings	153,000*	153,000*	122,400	119,000	(3,400)
Treasury stock (assuming cost method)	–0–	(10,000)	–0–	(7,778)	(7,778)
	$253,000	$243,000	$202,400	$189,000	$(13,400)

* $150,000 + (25% × $12,000)

Parent's Entries in 19X1. In this case, the ratio of the post-sale and presale ownership percents is 97.22 (77.78/80). Since the purchase of the treasury shares is treated as a sale of shares to nonaffiliates by P Company, the unamortized differential is reduced accordingly. The value of the unamortized differential is $57,240 [97.22% × ($60,000 − 25% × $4,500)] after the purchase of the treasury shares. The $1,635 difference [($60,000 − $1,125) − $57,240] in the unamortized differential before and after the purchase of these shares is a component of the gain or loss on the ownership percent decreasing subsidiary stock transaction. Another component of this gain or loss is the $13,400 decrease in P Company's interest in S Company's stockholders' equity calculated above. Specifically, the loss is $5,035; it equals the excess of the decrease just mentioned and the decrease in the differential (− $13,400 − $1,635) over the $10,000 received for the shares.

Given the above values, including the post-sale ownership percent of 77.78%, P Company's 19X1 equity method entries are as follows:

1. To record P Company's equity in S Company's net income for the first quarter of 19X1:

Investment in S Company [80% × (25% × $12,000)]	2,400	
Equity in Subsidiary Earnings		2,400

2. To record differential amortization for the first quarter of 19X1:

Equity in Subsidiary Earnings (25% × $4,500) 1,125
    Investment in S Company   1,125

3. To record the loss on the ownership percent decreasing subsidiary stock transaction:

Cash 10,000
Loss on Subsidiary Stock Transaction 5,035
    Investment in S Company
      ($13,400 + $1,635)   15,035

4. To record P Company's net income for the last three quarters of 19X1:

Investment in S Company [77.78% × (75% × $12,000)] 7,000
    Equity in Subsidiary Earnings   7,000

5. To record differential amortization for the last three quarters of 19X1:

Equity in Subsidiary Earnings [97.22% × (75% × $4,500)] 3,281
    Investment in S Company   3,281

Working Paper Entries for 19X1 and Incremental Calculation of Consolidated Net Income. The 19X1 working paper entries are given below. These entries also are made as if the post-sale ownership and minority interest percents prevailed during the entire year.

1. To offset the balance in Treasury Stock against pertinent S Company stockholders' equity accounts (see Chapter 2):

Capital Stock (100 × $100) 10,000
    Treasury Stock   10,000

2. To eliminate double counting of equity method income and record minority interest in subsidiary net income as though the post-sale ownership and minority interest percents prevailed throughout the year:

Minority Interest Expense (22.22% × $12,000) 2,667
Equity in Subsidiary Earnings
    [(77.78% × $12,000) − (97.22% × $4,500)] 4,959
    Investment in S Company   4,959
    Minority Interest   2,667

3. To eliminate investment account balance against S Company stockholders' equity accounts and establish related minority interest as

though the post-sale ownership and minority interest percents prevailed throughout the year:

```
Capital Stock—S Company
  ($100,000 − $10,000) . . . . . . . . . . . . . . . . . . . . . . . . . .   90,000
Retained Earnings—S Company  . . . . . . . . . . . . . . . . . .  150,000
Differential (97.22% × $60,000)  . . . . . . . . . . . . . . . . . .   58,333
    Investment in S Company
      [$260,000 − $15,035 + ($4,994 − $4,959)]  . . . . . . . . .              245,000
    Minority Interest
      [22.22% × ($90,000 + $150,000)]   . . . . . . . . . . . . .               53,333
```

4. To allocate the differential as though the post-sale ownership percent prevailed throughout the year:

```
Plant and Equipment (net) (97.22% × $15,000)   . . . . . . . . .   14,583
Goodwill (97.22% × $45,000) . . . . . . . . . . . . . . . . . . . .   43,750
    Differential  . . . . . . . . . . . . . . . . . . . . . . . . . . . . . .               58,333
```

5. To record differential amortization as though the post-sale ownership percent prevailed throughout the year:

```
Depreciation Expense (97.22% × $1,500)   . . . . . . . . . . . . .    1,458
Amortization of Goodwill (97.22% × $3,000)   . . . . . . . . . . .    2,917
    Plant and Equipment (net) . . . . . . . . . . . . . . . . . . . .                1,458
    Goodwill  . . . . . . . . . . . . . . . . . . . . . . . . . . . . . . .                2,917
```

Note that entry (2) contains a debit to Equity in Subsidiary Earnings amounting to $4,959 [(77.78% × $12,000) − (97.22% × $4,500)]. The actual balance in this account is $4,994 ($2,400 − $1,125 + $7,000 − $3,281). Thus, entry (2) leaves a balance in Equity in Subsidiary Earnings equaling $35 ($4,994 − $4,959). This balance is the difference in (1) the excess of P Company's recorded equity in S Company's net income for the first quarter of 19X4 ($2,400) over the corresponding value for this equity given that the ownership percent of 77.78 had applied for the entire year ($2,333 = 77.78% × $3,000) and (2) the excess of the recorded differential amortization for this period ($1,125) over the differential amortization that would have been recorded during this period if the ownership percent had been 77.78 for the entire year ($1,093 = 97.22% × $1,125). This calculation is summarized as $35 = [($2,400 − $2,333) − ($1,125 − $1,093)]. As before, this $35 is left in the Equity in Subsidiary Earnings account so that the consolidated statement working paper produces the correct consolidated net income figure. Also, the post-sale ownership and minority interest percents again are used in the working paper entries so that the correct consolidated balance sheet values are produced.

Consolidated net income for this case is calculated incrementally for 19X1 as follows.

P Company's 19X1 net income from its own operations (excluding loss)		$25,000
Less: Loss on subsidiary stock transaction		5,035
		$19,965
Plus: P Company's equity in S Company's 19X1 net income:		
First quarter—[80% × (25% × $12,000)]	$2,400	
Last three quarters—[77.78% × (75% × $12,000)]	7,000	9,400
Less: Differential amortization for 19X1:		
First quarter—(25% × $4,500)	$1,125	
Last three quarters—[97.22% × (75% × $4,500)]	3,281	(4,406)
Consolidated net income for 19X1		$24,959

CONFIRMED PROFITS ON UPSTREAM SALES AND SUBSIDIARIES' CONTRIBUTIONS TO GAINS AND LOSSES FROM INTERCOMPANY BOND HOLDINGS

When unconfirmed profits arising from an upstream sale become confirmed during a period in which an ownership percent change occurs, the profits becoming confirmed can be divided into two groups: (1) a group containing profits becoming confirmed prior to the change and (2) a group containing profits becoming confirmed after the change. Given these groups, two procedures can be used in calculating the parent's pre-change and post-change interests in its subsidiary's stockholders' equity and in making related working paper entries. Under the first approach, this calculation and the entries are based on the subsidiary's *confirmed* net income and retained earnings on the date of the ownership percent change. Under the second approach, the calculation and entries are based on the subsidiary's actual net income and retained earnings on the date of the change. We prefer the first approach because it is consistent with the concept of pro rata allocation—the method of allocating unconfirmed profits which we recommend (see Chapter 6). Comments paralleling all of those made above also apply to the calculation of the parent's interest in subsidiary stockholders' equity and amounts for related working paper entries when an intercompany bond holding is present.

Summary

This chapter covers the consolidated statement and equity method techniques related to changes in parents' ownership percents. These percents increase as consequences of various transactions. One way parents' ownership percents increase is through open-market block purchases of subsidiary shares. They also increase as a result of two types of subsidiary stock transactions: (1) acquisitions of disproportionately large numbers of newly issued subsidiary shares by parents and (2) acquisitions of disproportionately small numbers of treasury shares from parents. These two classes of transaction are accounted for as though they are open-market block purchases of subsidiary shares. Since all ownership percent increasing transactions are accounted for similarly, they usually produce separate debit or credit differentials, usually yield purchased preacquisition earnings figures in interim purchase situations, and require the use of year-end ownership and minority interest percents in making working paper entries. Also, related calculations of consolidated net income and equity method entries are structured so that they reflect increases in ownership percents occurring during the year.

Parents' ownership percents also decrease as a result of a variety of transactions. One way parents' ownership percents decrease is through sales of subsidiary shares to nonaffiliates. They also decrease as a consequence of two types of subsidiary stock transactions: (1) acquisitions of disproportionately small numbers of newly issued subsidiary shares by parents and (2) acquisitions of disproportionately large numbers of treasury shares from parents. These transactions are accounted for as though they are sales of subsidiary shares to nonaffiliates. Since all ownership percent decreasing transactions are accounted for similarly, they tend to produce gains and losses related to subsidiary shares, result in reductions in unamortized differentials, require the use of year-end ownership and minority interest percents in making working paper entries, and usually leave balances in Equity in Subsidiary Earnings accounts in interim cases. The related calculations of consolidated net income and equity method entries also are structured so that they reflect decreases in ownership percents occurring during the year.

The appendix to this chapter covers two additional topics related to changes in parents' ownership percents. First, it illustrates differential calculation, allocation, and amortization procedures using date-of-control analysis. This technique is inferior to step-by-step analysis because it fails to allow for the existence of differentials until control is established and it excludes the investor's share of undistributed investee earnings accumulated prior to date of control from consolidated retained earnings. Second, the appendix shows informally that properly structured parent company sales of subsidiary shares to nonaffiliates produce exactly the same results as ownership percent decreasing subsidiary stock transactions. Given the principle of substance over form, this conclusion implies the reasonableness of accounting for ownership percent decreasing subsidiary stock transactions as though they are properly structured parent company sales of subsidiary shares to nonaffiliates. The appendix implies analogously that it is reasonable to account for ownership percent increasing subsidiary stock transactions as though they are properly structured open-market block purchases.

Appendix: Date-of-Control Analysis and Equivalence of Sales of Subsidiary Shares to Nonaffiliates and Other Ownership Percent Decreasing Transactions

This appendix covers two topics. First, it covers procedures pertinent to differentials under date-of-control analysis. This technique is mentioned briefly in the section of the chapter entitled "Block Purchase—General Comments." The second topic covered is the equivalence of properly structured parent company sales of subsidiary shares to nonaffiliates and ownership percent decreasing subsidiary stock transactions. This topic is discussed initially in the section of the chapter entitled "Ownership Percent Decreasing Subsidiary Stock Transactions—General Comments."

Date-of-Control Analysis—Calculation, Allocation, and Amortization of Differentials

The data for the example contained in this section are similar to those of Case 1. They are used in illustrating differential calculation, allocation, and amortization procedures under date-of-control analysis (as opposed to step-by-step analysis).

Assume that S Company has capital stock of $50,000 ($100 par) and retained earnings of $20,000 on January 1, 19X1. S Company's net income in each of the years 19X1 through 19X3 is $10,000. P Company's net income from its own operations is $25,000 in 19X3. P Company acquires shares of S Company (and related ownership percents) through open-market block purchases as indicated in the following schedule:

Date	Number (%) of Shares	Cost
January 1, 19X1	200 (40%)	$30,000
January 1, 19X2	100 (20%)	21,000
January 1, 19X3	100 (20%)	20,000

The following differences in fair values and book values for different elements of plant and equipment exist on the last two block purchase dates:

	Plant and Equipment (net)	
Date	Fair Value	Book Value
January 1, 19X2	64,000	60,250
January 1, 19X3	47,500	40,000

Each element of plant and equipment has a remaining life of 5 years on the related block purchase date, and goodwill arising from individual block purchases is to be amortized over 10 years.

Under date-of-control analysis, the first block is treated as though it is not acquired until control is obtained. The *initial* separate differential is related to all of the block acquired through date of control. There also may be separate differentials related to each block of stock acquired subsequently. The sum of the separate differentials again is the total differential. The calculations of the separate differentials using date-of-control analysis are shown below.

	First Two Blocks (60%)	Third Block (20%)
Cost of block(s)	$51,000	$20,000
Less purchased interest in S Company's stockholders' equity:		
First two blocks (60% × $80,000)	48,000	
Second block (20% × $90,000)		18,000
Separate differential	$ 3,000	$ 2,000

The total differential is $5,000 ($3,000 + $2,000) under date-of-control analysis.

The differential allocation and amortization procedures under the date-of-control approach are identical to those of Chapter 4 once control is obtained. Differential allocation values related to the different elements of plant and equipment (net) in this case are calculated in the following schedule.

	Plant and Equipment (net)			
	Fair Value	Book Value	Fair Value − Book Value (Excess)	Block Ownership Percent × Excess
First two blocks (60%)	$ 64,000	$ 60,250	$ 3,750	$2,250
Third block (20%)	47,500	40,000	7,500	1,500
Totals	$111,500	$100,250	$11,250	$3,750

This schedule implies goodwill pertinent to the first two and third blocks of $750 ($3,000 − $2,250) and $500 ($2,000 − $1,500), respectively. Thus, total goodwill is $1,250. Annual differential amortization for the first two blocks is $525 [($2,250/5) + ($750/10)] for each of the five years beginning January 1, 19X2. Of this amount, $450 ($2,250/5) is related to plant and equipment (net), and $75 ($750/10) pertains to goodwill. Annual differential amortization for the third block is $350 [($1,500/5) + ($500/10)] beginning January 1, 19X3—with $300 ($1,500/5) related to plant and equipment (net) and $50 ($500/10) pertaining to goodwill. These amounts are summarized below for 19X2 and 19X3.

	Differential Amortization	
	19X2	*19X3*
First block:		
Plant and equipment (net)	$450	$450
Goodwill	75	75
Total	$525	$525
Second block:		
Plant and equipment (net)		$300
Goodwill		50
Total		$350
Combined:		
Plant and equipment (net)	$450	$750
Goodwill	75	125
Total	$525	$875

Equivalence of Properly Structured Sales of Subsidiary Shares to Nonaffiliates and Other Ownership Percent Decreasing Transactions

We use the basic data of Case 7 to illustrate informally that properly structured parent company sales of subsidiary shares to nonaffiliates produce exactly the same results as ownership percent decreasing subsidiary stock transactions. In this example, we assume that on January 1, 19X1, S Company sells 200 of its unissued shares ratably to majority and minority shareholders for $340 per share and that P Company immediately sells the 160 (80% × 200) shares it acquires to nonaffiliates for the same price (rather than assuming S Company issues 200 shares to nonaffiliates at this price).[17] Pertinent data from Case 7 are repeated below for convenience.

Assume that S Company has capital stock of $100,000 ($100 par) and retained earnings of $150,000 initially on January 1, 19X1. At this time, P Company holds 800 of S Company's shares, and its Investment in S Company account has a balance of $260,000. S Company's net income for 19X1 is $12,000. P Company's 19X1 net income from its own operations is $25,000. Since P Company's interest in S Company's stockholders' equity is $200,000 (80% × $250,000) prior to the sale of the shares, the investment account includes a presale unamortized differential of $60,000. Assume the following presale differential allocation and amortization values pertinent to 19X1.

---

[17] Results similar to those of this example occur if we assume that P Company sells 133¹/₃ of its S Company shares to nonaffiliates for $340 per share. This assumption produces a smaller cash inflow for the consolidated entity and yields a different minority interest value for the consolidated balance sheet.

	Unamortized Differential before Issuance of New Shares	19X1 Amortization
Plant and equipment (net)	$15,000	$1,500
Goodwill	45,000	3,000
Total	$60,000	$4,500

Parent's Entries in 19X1

Given the above assumptions, the post-sale ownership percent is 66.67 (800/1,200). P Company's 19X1 equity method entries, which are based on this percent, are presented below (ignoring the entry to record the purchase of the shares). Notice that these entries produce exactly the same effects as the equity method entries of Case 7, since the Investment in S Company is debited for $54,400 (160 × $340) when P Company purchases its pro rata portion of the newly issued S Company shares.

1. To record P Company's equity in S Company's net income:

Investment in S Company (66.67% × $12,000)	8,000	
Equity in Subsidiary Earnings		8,000

2. To record the sale of the subsidiary shares using the weighted-average method:

Cash	54,400	
Investment in S Company [160 × ($260,000 + 54,400)/960]		52,400
Gain on Sale of Stock		2,000

3. To record differential amortization:

Equity in Subsidiary Earnings (83.33% × $4,500)	3,750	
Investment in S Company		3,750

Working Paper Entries for 19X1 and Incremental Calculation of Consolidated Net Income

The 19X1 working paper entries are given below. These entries also produce exactly the same effects as those of Case 7.

1. To eliminate double counting of equity method income and record minority interest in subsidiary net income:

Minority Interest Expense (33.3% × $12,000)	4,000	
Equity in Subsidiary Earnings ($8,000 − $3,750)	4,250	
Investment in S Company		4,250
Minority Interest		4,000

2. To eliminate investment account balance against S Company's stockholders' equity accounts and establish related minority interest:

Capital Stock—S Company	120,000	
Retained Earnings—S Company	150,000	
Other Contributed Capital	48,000	
Differential (83.33% × $60,000)	50,000	
Investment in S Company ($260,000 +		
$54,400 − $52,400)		262,000
Minority Interest [33.33% × ($120,000 +		
$150,000 + $48,000)]		106,000

3. To allocate the differential:

Plant and Equipment (net) (83.33% × $15,000)	12,500	
Goodwill (83.33% × $45,000)	37,500	
Differential		50,000

4. To record differential amortization:

Depreciation Expense (83.33% × $1,500)	1,250	
Amortization of Goodwill (83.33% × $3,000)	2,500	
Plant and Equipment (net)		1,250
Goodwill		2,500

Consolidated net income for 19X1 is calculated incrementally below. Notice that this calculation is identical to the incremental calculation related to Case 7 (except for the account title associated with the gain).[18]

P Company's 19X1 net income from its own operations	
(excluding gain)	$25,000
Plus: Gain on sale of stock	2,000
Plus: P Company's equity in S Company's 19X1 net income	
(66.7% × $12,000)	8,000
Less: Differential amortization for 19X1 (83.33% × $4,500)	(3,750)
Consolidated net income for 19X1	$31,250

---

[18] This identity supports the reasonableness of our view that portions of gains related to changes in parents' interests in subsidiaries' stockholders' equities arising from ownership percent decreasing subsidiary stock transactions should be included in consolidated net income rather than in consolidated paid-in capital (see discussion in the section of this chapter entitled "Ownership Percent Decreasing Subsidiary Stock Transactions—General Comments").

From an overall perspective, the above example shows informally that properly structured parent company sales of subsidiary shares to nonaffiliates generate exactly the same results as ownership percent decreasing subsidiary stock transactions. Given the principle of substance over form, this conclusion implies that it is reasonable to account for ownership percent decreasing subsidiary stock transactions as though they are properly structured parent company sales of subsidiary shares to nonaffiliates.

Questions

1. Identify the types of transactions that cause investor companies' ownership percents to increase.
2. Discuss the two ways of handling block purchases of subsidiary shares. Identify the differences produced by the two methods. Also, indicate how each of the methods is justified, and identify the conceptually superior alternative.
3. Identify the cases in which the subsidiary is involved in ownership percent increasing transactions. Discuss the primary differences that arise when such transactions occur as opposed to when a parent acquires shares from nonaffiliates. Explain how these differences affect the differential.
4. Discuss the rationale for accounting for ownership percent increasing subsidiary stock transactions as though they are properly structured open-market block purchases.
5. Identify the types of transactions that cause investor companies' ownership percents to decrease.
6. Discuss the general procedures used in accounting for sales of subsidiary shares to nonaffiliates and the alternatives available for determining the book values of the shares sold. Identify the preferable method and indicate why this method is preferable.
7. Identify the cases in which the subsidiary is involved in ownership percent decreasing transactions. Discuss the primary differences that arise when such transactions occur as opposed to when a parent sells subsidiary shares to nonaffiliates. Explain how these differences affect the gains or losses of parent companies.
8. Discuss the rationale for accounting for ownership percent decreasing subsidiary stock transactions as though they are parent company sales of subsidiary shares to nonaffiliates.
9. Identify the alternative treatments of portions of gains related to changes in parents' interests in subsidiaries' stockholders' equities arising from ownership percent decreasing subsidiary stock transactions. Indicate how these treatments are supported conceptually and officially.
10. Discuss the alternative methods of dealing with unconfirmed profits from upstream sales becoming confirmed during a period in which the parent's ownership percent changes. Identify the preferable alternative. Indicate how the alternative methods apply to intercompany bond holdings.

Exercises

Exercise 9–1   (Open-Market Block Purchases)

On January 1, 19X1, S Company has outstanding capital stock (par $10) of $10,000 and retained earnings of $90,000. P Company makes open-market block purchases of S Company shares as indicated below.

February 1, 19X1	600 shares (cost $70,000)
October 1, 19X1	200 shares (cost $27,000)

Block purchases are accounted for using the step-by-step method. S Company's 19X1 uniformly earned net income is $30,000, and P Company's net income from its own operations in 19X1 is $40,000. All differentials pertain to nonamortizable assets.

Required:

a. Record P Company's equity in S Company's 19X1 net income.

b. Prepare the entries for a 19X1 consolidated statement working paper.

c. Calculate 19X1 consolidated net income incrementally.

Exercise 9–2   (Open-Market Block Purchases)

On January 1, 19X1, S Company has outstanding capital stock (par $10) of $20,000 and retained earnings of $80,000. P Company holds 1,200 S Company shares, and the Investment in S Company account has a balance of $90,000. On this date, P Company purchases an additional 600 shares of S Company stock in the open market for $50,000. Block purchases are accounted for using the step-by-step method. S Company's 19X1 net income is $30,000.

The prepurchase unamortized differential is allocated $11,000 to plant and equipment (net) and the remainder to goodwill. The fair market value of S Company's plant and equipment (net) on January 1, 19X1, is $200,000, and the related book value is $170,000. The fair values and book values of all other assets and liabilities are equal on this date. The estimated remaining lives of plant and equipment and goodwill on January 1, 19X1, are 5 and 20 years, respectively.

Required:

a. Allocate the differentials on January 1, 19X1.

b. Prepare P Company's 19X1 equity method entries, ignoring its entry to record its block purchase.

c. Prepare the entries for a 19X1 consolidated statement working paper.

Exercise 9–3   (Parent's Sale of Subsidiary Shares to Nonaffiliates)

On January 1, 19X1, S Company has outstanding capital stock (par $10) of $10,000 and retained earnings of $30,000. P Company holds 800 S Company shares, and the Investment in S Company account has a balance of $48,000. On January 1, 19X1,

P Company sells 100 of its 800 S Company shares to nonaffiliates for $50 per share. P Company uses the weighted-average method in determining gains and losses on sales of shares. Assume that the unamortized differential is allocated to plant and equipment (net) (with a remaining life of five years) immediately before the sale.

S Company's 19X1 net income is $15,000. P Company's net income from own operations in 19X1, exclusive of any gain or loss from the sale of the subsidiary shares, is $25,000.

Required:

a. Prepare P Company's 19X1 equity method entries.

b. Reconcile the balance in Investment in S Company at December 31, 19X1, with the sum of P Company's interest in S Company's stockholders' equity and the unamortized differential.

c. Prepare the working paper entries for a December 31, 19X1, consolidated statement working paper.

d. Calculate 19X1 consolidated net income incrementally.

Exercise 9–4   (Subsidiary's Sale of Shares to Nonaffiliates)

On January 1, 19X1, S Company has outstanding capital stock (par $10) of $20,000 and retained earnings of $80,000. P Company holds 1,800 S Company shares, and the Investment in S Company account has a balance of $105,000. On this date, S Company issues an additional 1,000 shares of stock to nonaffiliates at $80 per share. Assume that the unamortized differential is allocated to goodwill (with a remaining life of 20 years) immediately before the sale.

Required:

a. Calculate P Company's gain or loss from the sale of the shares.

b. Prepare P Company's equity method entry related to the sale of the shares.

c. Prepare the investment elimination entry for a January 1, 19X1, post-sale consolidated balance sheet working paper.

d. Prepare P Company's equity method entry to record 19X1 differential amortization.

Exercise 9–5   (Subsidiary's Sale of Shares to Nonaffiliates)

On January 1, 19X1, S Company has outstanding capital stock (par $10) of $20,000 and retained earnings of $80,000. P Company holds 1,800 S Company shares, and the Investment in S Company account has a balance of $105,000. On this date, S Company issues an additional 1,000 shares of stock to nonaffiliates at $40 per share. Assume that the unamortized differential is allocated to goodwill (with a remaining life of 20 years) immediately before the sale.

Required:

a. Calculate P Company's gain or loss from the sale of the shares.

b. Prepare P Company's equity method entry related to the sale of the shares.

c. Prepare the investment elimination entry for a January 1, 19X1, post-sale consolidated balance sheet working paper.

d. Prepare P Company's equity method entry to record 19X1 differential amortization.

Exercise 9–6   (Block Purchase of Newly Issued Subsidiary Shares)

On January 1, 19X1, S Company has outstanding capital stock (par $10) of $20,000 and retained earnings of $80,000. P Company holds 1,800 S Company shares, and the Investment in S Company account has a balance of $130,000. On this date, S Company issues an additional 2,000 shares of stock to P Company at $80 per share.

Assume that $15,000 of the unamortized differential is allocated to plant and equipment (net) with a remaining life of five years immediately before the purchase. The remainder of the differential is allocated to goodwill with a remaining life of 20 years at this time. Assume also that the fair value of the plant and equipment (net) is $400,000 and the related book value is $360,000 on January 1, 19X1. The fair values and book values of all other assets and liabilities are the same on this date.

Required:

a. Calculate the change in P Company's interest in S Company's stockholders' equity and the separate differential resulting from the purchase.

b. Record P Company's purchase of the shares.

c. Prepare the investment elimination entry for a January 1, 19X1, post-purchase consolidated balance sheet working paper.

d. Allocate the differentials to plant and equipment (net) and goodwill.

e. Prepare P Company's equity method entry to record 19X1 differential amortization.

Exercise 9–7   (Block Purchase of Newly Issued Subsidiary Shares)

On January 1, 19X1, S Company has outstanding capital stock (par $10) of $20,000 and retained earnings of $80,000. P Company holds 1,800 S Company shares, and the Investment in S Company account has a balance of $130,000. On this date, S Company issues an additional 2,000 shares of stock to P Company at $40 per share.

Assume that $15,000 of the unamortized differential is allocated to plant and equipment (net) with a remaining life of five years immediately before the purchase. The remainder of the differential is allocated to goodwill with a remaining life of 20 years at this time. Assume also that the fair value of the plant and equipment (net) is $400,000 and the related book value is $360,000 on January 1, 19X1. The fair values and book values of all other assets and liabilities are the same on this date.

Required:

a. Calculate the change in P Company's interest in S Company's stockholders' equity and the separate differential resulting from the purchase.

b. Record P Company's purchase of the shares.

c. Prepare the investment elimination entry for a January 1, 19X1, post-purchase consolidated balance sheet working paper.

d. Allocate the differentials to plant and equipment (net) and goodwill.

e. Prepare P Company's equity method entry to record 19X1 differential amortization.

Exercise 9–8   (Ownership Percent Increasing Purchase of Treasury Shares)

On January 1, 19X1, S Company has outstanding capital stock (par $10) of $20,000 and retained earnings of $80,000. P Company holds 1,800 S Company shares, and the

Investment in S Company account has a balance of $110,000. On this date, S Company purchases 200 shares of its own stock from nonaffiliates at $100 per share. S Company accounts for treasury shares using the cost method.

Assume that $14,000 of the unamortized differential is allocated to plant and equipment (net) with a remaining life of four years immediately before the purchase. The remainder of the differential is allocated to goodwill with a remaining life of 10 years at this time. Assume also that the fair value of the plant and equipment (net) is $100,000 and the related book value is $60,000 on January 1, 19X1. The fair values and book values of all other assets and liabilities are the same on this date.

Required:

a. Calculate the change in P Company's interest in S Company's stockholders' equity and the change in the unamortized differential.

b. Prepare any journal entries that would be made by P Company.

c. Prepare the treasury stock and investment elimination entries for a January 1, 19X1, post-purchase consolidated balance sheet working paper.

d. Allocate the differentials to plant and equipment (net) and goodwill.

e. Prepare P Company's equity method entry to record 19X1 differential amortization.

Exercise 9–9 (Ownership Percent Decreasing Purchase of Treasury Shares)

On January 1, 19X1, S Company has outstanding capital stock (par $10) of $20,000 and retained earnings of $80,000. P Company holds 1,800 S Company shares, and the Investment in S Company account has a balance of $110,000. On this date, S Company purchases 400 of its own shares from P Company at $40 per share. S Company accounts for treasury shares using the cost method.

Assume that $14,000 of the unamortized differential is allocated to plant and equipment (net) with a remaining life of five years immediately before the purchase. The remainder of the differential is allocated to goodwill with a remaining life of 10 years at this time.

Required:

a. Calculate P Company's gain or loss from the purchase of shares.

b. Record P Company's gain or loss from the purchase of the shares.

c. Prepare the treasury stock and investment elimination entries for a January 1, 19X1, post-purchase consolidated balance sheet working paper.

d. Allocate the differential to plant and equipment (net) and goodwill.

e. Prepare P Company's equity method entry to record 19X1 differential amortization.

Exercise 9–10 (Ownership Percent Decreasing Purchase of Treasury Shares)

On January 1, 19X1, S Company has outstanding capital stock (par $10) of $10,000 and retained earnings of $40,000. P Company holds 700 S Company shares, and the Investment in S Company account has a balance of $38,500. On this date, S Company purchases 400 of its own shares at $60 per share (with 300 shares acquired from P Company and the remainder acquired from nonaffiliates). S Company accounts for treasury shares using the cost method.

Required:

a. Calculate P Company's gain or loss from the purchase of the shares.

b. Record P Company's gain or loss from the purchase of the shares.

c. Prepare the treasury stock and investment elimination entries for a January 1, 19X1, post-purchase consolidated balance sheet working paper.

Exercise 9–11   (Ownership Percent Increasing Purchase of Treasury Shares)

On January 1, 19X1, S Company has outstanding capital stock (par $10) of $10,000 and retained earnings of $40,000. P Company holds 700 S Company shares, and the Investment in S Company account has a balance of $38,500. On this date, S Company purchases 400 of its own shares at $60 per share (with 200 shares acquired from P Company and the remainder acquired from nonaffiliates). S Company accounts for treasury shares using the cost method.

Required:

a. Calculate the change in P Company's interest in S Company's stockholders' equity and the change in the unamortized differential.

b. Record P Company's sale of S Company shares.

c. Prepare the treasury stock and investment elimination entries for a January 1, 19X1, post-purchase consolidated balance sheet working paper.

Exercise 9–12   (Ownership Percent Decreasing Sale of Shares to Parent and Nonaffiliates)

On January 1, 19X1, S Company has outstanding capital stock (par $100) of $100,000 and retained earnings of $150,000. P Company holds 800 S Company shares, and the Investment in S Company account has a balance of $260,000. On this date, S Company issues an additional 200 shares at $340 per share (with 100 shares purchased by P Company and the remainder acquired by nonaffiliates).

Assume that $12,000 of the unamortized differential is allocated to plant and equipment (net) immediately before the sale. The remainder of the differential is allocated to goodwill.

Required:

a. Calculate P Company's gain or loss from the sale of the shares.

b. Prepare any journal entries that would be made by P Company.

c. Prepare the investment elimination entry for a January 1, 19X1, post-sale consolidated balance sheet working paper.

d. Allocate the differential to plant and equipment (net) and goodwill.

Exercise 9–13   (Ownership Percent Increasing Sale of Shares to Parent and Nonaffiliates)

On January 1, 19X1, S Company has outstanding capital stock (par $100) of $100,000 and retained earnings of $100,000. P Company holds 600 S Company shares, and the Investment in S Company account has a balance of $140,000. On this date,

S Company issues an additional 1,000 shares at $250 per share (with 800 shares purchased by P Company and the remainder acquired by nonaffiliates).

Required:

a. Calculate the change in P Company's interest in S Company's stockholders' equity and the related separate differential.
b. Record P Company's purchase of the shares.
c. Prepare the investment elimination entry for a January 1, 19X1, post-sale consolidated balance sheet working paper.

Exercise 9–14   (Sale of Shares Ratably to Parent and Nonaffiliates)

On January 1, 19X1, S Company has outstanding capital stock (par $100) of $100,000 and retained earnings of $150,000. P Company holds 800 S Company shares, and the Investment in S Company account has a balance of $260,000. On this date, S Company issues an additional 200 shares ratably to majority and minority shareholders.

Required:

a. Show that the increase in P Company's interest in S Company's stockholders' equity equals the cost of its new shares regardless of the relationship between the sales price of the new shares and the book value of its old shares for each of the following sales prices.
   (1) $250 per share.
   (2) $340 per share.
   (3) $190 per share.
b. Prepare the investment elimination entry for a January 1, 19X1, post-sale consolidated balance sheet working paper for each of the alternative sales prices.

Exercise 9–15   (Ownership Percent Decreasing Sale of Shares to Parent and Nonaffiliates)

On January 1, 19X1, S Company has outstanding capital stock (par $100) of $100,000 and retained earnings of $150,000. P Company holds 800 S Company shares, and the Investment in S Company account has a balance of $260,000. On this date, S Company issues an additional 200 shares at $190 per share (with 100 shares purchased by P Company and the remainder acquired by nonaffiliates).

Assume that $12,000 of the unamortized differential is allocated to plant and equipment (net) immediately before the sale. The remainder of the differential is allocated to goodwill.

Required:

a. Calculate P Company's gain or loss from the sale of the shares.
b. Prepare any journal entries that would be made by P Company.
c. Prepare the investment elimination entry for a January 1, 19X1, post-sale consolidated balance sheet working paper.
d. Allocate the differential to plant and equipment (net) and goodwill.

Exercise 9–16   (Ownership Percent Increasing Sale of Shares to Parent and Nonaffiliates)

On January 1, 19X1, S Company has outstanding capital stock (par $100) of $100,000 and retained earnings of $100,000. P Company holds 600 S Company shares, and the Investment in S Company account has a balance of $140,000. On this date, S Company issues an additional 1,000 shares at $150 per share (with 800 shares purchased by P Company and the remainder acquired by nonaffiliates).

Required:

a. Calculate the change in P Company's interest in S Company's stockholders' equity and the related separate differential.

b. Record P Company's purchase of the shares.

c. Prepare the investment elimination entry for a January 1, 19X1, post-sale consolidated balance sheet working paper.

Exercise 9–17   (Purchase of Treasury Shares Ratably from Parent and Nonaffiliates)

On January 1, 19X1, S Company has outstanding capital stock (par $10) of $20,000 and retained earnings of $80,000. P Company holds 1,800 S Company shares, and the Investment in S Company account has a balance of $110,000. On this date, S Company purchases 500 of its own shares ratably from majority and minority shareholders. S Company accounts for treasury shares using the cost method.

Required:

a. Show that the decrease in P Company's interest in S Company's stockholders' equity equals the proceeds from the acquisition of its shares regardless of the relationship between their purchase price and book value for each of the following purchase prices.
   (1) $50 per share.
   (2) $60 per share.
   (3) $40 per share.

b. Prepare the treasury stock and investment elimination entries for a January 1, 19X1, post-purchase consolidated balance sheet working paper for each of the alternative purchase prices.

Problems

Problem 9–18   (Open-Market Block Purchases)

Minor Company has capital stock of $60,000 ($120 par) and retained earnings of $40,000 on January 1, 19X1. Minor Company's uniformly earned net income in each of the years 19X1 through 19X3 is $15,000. Major Company's net income from own operations in 19X3 is $45,000. Major Company acquires shares of Minor Company (and related ownership percents) through open-market block purchases as indicated in the following schedule.

Date	Number (%) of Shares	Cost
January 1, 19X1	100 (20%)	$25,000
January 1, 19X2	200 (40%)	49,000
April 1, 19X3	100 (20%)	30,750

The following differences in fair values and book values for different elements of plant and equipment exist at the various block purchase dates.

Date	Plant and Equipment (net)	
	Fair Value	Book Value
January 1, 19X1	$31,250	$26,250
January 1, 19X2	35,000	31,000
April 1, 19X3	45,000	38,000

The various elements of plant and equipment are assumed to have remaining lives of 5 years on each block purchase date, and goodwill arising from individual block purchases is to be amortized over 10 years.

Required:

a. Calculate the differentials, including the total differential, arising from the block purchases.
b. Allocate the differentials.
c. Prepare a differential amortization schedule for the years 19X1 through 19X3.
d. Prepare Major Company's equity method entries for the years 19X1 through 19X3, ignoring its entries to record its block purchases.
e. Prepare the working paper entries for a 19X3 consolidated statement working paper.
f. Calculate 19X3 consolidated net income incrementally.

Problem 9–19   (Block Purchase of Newly Issued Subsidiary Shares)

Mini Company has capital stock of $150,000 ($150 par) and retained earnings of $200,000 on January 1, 19X1. On this date, Maxi Company holds 800 Mini Company shares, and its Investment in Mini Company account has a balance of $320,000. Maxi Company acquires an additional 600 shares of stock at $380 per share from Mini Company on March 31, 19X1. All unamortized differentials are to be allocated to elements of plant and equipment with 25-year remaining lives at January 1, 19X1.

Maxi Company's net income from own operations in 19X1 is $50,000. Mini Company's uniformly earned 19X1 net income is $16,000.

Required:

a. Determine the change in Maxi Company's interest in Mini Company's stockholders' equity arising from the acquisition of the second block.

b. Calculate the unamortized differentials, including the total unamortized differential, after the second block purchase.

c. Prepare Maxi Company's equity method entries for 19X1, ignoring its entry to record its block purchase.

d. Prepare the working paper entries for a 19X1 consolidated statement working paper.

e. Calculate 19X1 consolidated net income incrementally.

Problem 9–20   (Subsidiary's Acquisition of Treasury Shares from Nonaffiliates)

Dominatee Company has capital stock of $150,000 ($150 par) and retained earnings of $200,000 on January 1, 19X1. On this date, Dominator Company holds 600 Dominatee Company shares, and its Investment in Dominatee Company account has a balance of $250,000. Dominatee Company acquires 100 of its own shares on March 31, 19X1, from minority shareholders at $600 per share and accounts for these treasury shares using the cost method. All unamortized differentials are to be allocated to elements of plant and equipment with 10-year remaining lives at January 1, 19X1.

Dominator Company's net income from own operations in 19X1 is $60,000. Dominatee Company's uniformly earned 19X1 net income is $24,000.

Required:

a. Determine the change in Dominator company's interest in Dominatee Company's stockholders' equity arising from the treasury stock transaction.

b. Calculate the unamortized differentials, including the total unamortized differential, after the treasury stock transaction.

c. Prepare Dominator Company's equity method entries for 19X1.

d. Prepare the working paper entries for a 19X1 consolidated statement working paper.

e. Calculate 19X1 consolidated net income incrementally.

Problem 9–21   (Parent's Sale of Subsidiary Shares to Nonaffiliates)

This problem assumes that Problem 9–18 has been worked. Besides engaging in the transactions mentioned in Problem 9–18, Major Company sells 100 shares of Minor Company on March 31, 19X4, to nonaffiliates for $48,000 and uses the weighted-average method in accounting for sales of subsidiary shares. Ignoring any gain or loss on the sale of the Minor Company shares, Major Company's net income from its own operations in 19X4 is $45,000. Major Company's retained earnings is $150,000 on January 1, 19X4. Minor Company's uniformly earned net income in 19X4 is $20,000.

Required:

a. Calculate the balance in the Investment in Minor Company account immediately prior to the sale of the shares.

b. Calculate the gain or loss on the sale of the Minor Company shares.

c. Calculate the differential remaining in the Investment in Minor Company account immediately after the sale of the Minor Company shares.

d. Prepare Major Company's 19X4 equity method entries.

e. Calculate 19X4 consolidated net income incrementally.

f. Prepare the working paper entries for a 19X4 consolidated statement working paper, and prepare a partial 19X4 working paper.

g. Analyze the balance remaining in Equity in Subsidiary Earnings.

Problem 9–22   (Subsidiary's Sale of Shares to Nonaffiliates)

Under Company has capital stock of $150,000 ($150 par) and retained earnings of $200,000 on January 1, 19X1. On this date, Over Company holds 900 Under Company shares, and its Investment in Under Company account has a balance of $340,000. Under Company's uniformly earned net income for 19X1 is $24,000. Over Company's 19X1 net income from its own operations is $50,000, excluding any gains or losses from subsidiary stock transactions. Under Company sells an additional 600 shares of its stock to nonaffiliates at $400 per share on March 31, 19X1. The following presale differential allocation and amortization values are pertinent to 19X1.

	Unamortized Differential before Issuance of New Shares	19X1 Amortization
Plant and equipment (net)	$10,000	$1,000
Goodwill	15,000	3,000
Total	$25,000	$4,000

Required:

a. Determine the change in Over Company's interest in Under Company's stockholders' equity arising from the sale of the Under Company shares.

b. Calculate the gain or loss related to the sale of the Under Company shares.

c. Prepare Over Company's 19X1 equity method entries.

d. Prepare the working paper entries for a 19X1 consolidated statement working paper.

e. Calculate 19X1 consolidated net income incrementally.

f. Analyze the balance remaining in Equity in Subsidiary Earnings.

Problem 9–23   (Subsidiary's Acquisition of Treasury Shares from Parent)

Poco Company has capital stock of $150,000 ($150 par) and retained earnings of $200,000 on January 1, 19X1. On this date, Grande Company holds 800 Poco Company shares, and its Investment in Poco Company account has a balance of $305,000. Poco Company's uniformly earned net income for 19X1 is $24,000. Grande Company's 19X1 net income from its own operations is $60,000, exluding any gains or losses from subsidiary stock transactions. Poco Company purchases 200 shares of its own stock from Grande Company on March 31, 19X1, for $160 per share and accounts for these treasury shares using the cost method. The following presale differential allocation and amortization values are pertinent to 19X1.

	Unamortized Differential before Issuance of New Shares	19X1 Amortization
Plant and equipment (net)	$10,000	$1,000
Goodwill	15,000	3,000
Total	$25,000	$4,000

Required:

a. Determine the change in Grande Company's interest in Poco Company's stockholders' equity arising from the treasury stock transaction.

b. Calculate the gain or loss related to the treasury stock transaction.

c. Prepare Grande Company's 19X1 equity method entries.

d. Prepare the working paper entries for a 19X1 consolidated statement working paper.

e. Calculate 19X1 consolidated net income incrementally.

f. Analyze the balance remaining in Equity in Subsidiary Earnings.

Problem 9–24   (Open-Market Block Purchases)

Moon Company has capital stock of $100,000 ($200 par) and retained earnings of $80,000 on January 1, 19X1. Moon Company's uniformly earned net income in each of the years 19X1 through 19X3 is $20,000. Sun Company's net income from own operations in 19X3 is $65,000. Sun Company acquires shares of Moon Company (and related ownership percents) through open-market block purchases as indicated in the following schedule.

Date	Number (%) of Shares	Cost
January 1, 19X1	125 (25%)	$51,000
January 1, 19X2	200 (40%)	84,000
June 30, 19X3	125 (25%)	62,500

The following differences in fair values and book values for different elements of plant and equipment exist at the various block purchase dates.

Date	Plant and Equipment (net)	
	Fair Value	Book Value
January 1, 19X1	$36,000	$28,000
January 1, 19X2	33,500	31,000
June 30, 19X3	50,000	38,000

The various elements of plant and equipment are assumed to have remaining lives of 5 years on each block purchase date, and goodwill arising from individual block purchases is to be amortized over 10 years.

Required:

a. Calculate the differentials, including the total differential, arising from the block purchases.

b. Allocate the differentials.

c. Prepare a differential amortization schedule for the years 19X1 through 19X3.

d. Prepare Sun Company's equity method entries for the years 19X1 through 19X3, ignoring its entries to record its block purchases.

e. Prepare the working paper entries for a 19X3 consolidated statement working paper.

f. Calculate 19X3 consolidated net income incrementally.

Problem 9–25   (Block Purchase of Newly Issued Subsidiary Shares)

Micro Company has capital stock of $200,000 ($200 par) and retained earnings of $300,000 on January 1, 19X1. On this date, Macro Company holds 700 Micro Company shares, and its Investment in Micro Company account has a balance of $400,000. Macro Company acquires an additional 500 shares of stock at $550 per share from Micro Company on June 30, 19X1. All unamortized differentials are to be allocated to elements of plant and equipment with 25-year remaining lives at January 1, 19X1.

Macro Company's net income from own operations in 19X1 is $70,000. Micro Company's uniformly earned 19X1 net income is $40,000.

Required:

a. Determine the change in Macro Company's interest in Micro Company's stockholders' equity arising from the acquisition of the second block.

b. Calculate the unamortized differentials, including the unamortized total differential, after the second block purchase.

c. Prepare Macro Company's equity method entries for 19X1, ignoring its entry to record its block purchase.

d. Prepare the working paper entries for a 19X1 consolidated statement working paper.

e. Calculate 19X1 consolidated net income incrementally.

Problem 9–26   (Subsidiary's Acquisition of Treasury Shares from Nonaffiliates)

Private Company has capital stock of $200,000 ($200 par) and retained earnings of $300,000 on January 1, 19X1. On this date, General Company holds 700 Private Company shares, and its Investment in Private Company account has a balance of $370,000. Private Company acquires 200 of its own shares on June 30, 19X1, from minority sharesholders at $625 per share and accounts for these treasury shares using the cost method. All unamortized differentials are to be allocated to elements of plant and equipment with 10-year remaining lives at January 1, 19X1.

General Company's net income from own operations in 19X1 is $80,000. Private Company's uniformly earned 19X1 net income is $50,000.

Required:

a. Determine the change in General Company's interest in Private Company's stockholders' equity arising from the treasury stock transaction.

b. Calculate the unamortized differentials, including the total unamortized differential, after the treasury stock transaction.

c. Prepare General Company's equity method entries for 19X1.

d. Prepare the working paper entries for a 19X1 consolidated statement working paper.

e. Calculate 19X1 consolidated net income incrementally.

Problem 9-27   (Parent's Sale of Subsidiary Shares to Nonaffiliates)

This problem assumes that Problem 9-24 has been worked. Besides engaging in the transactions mentioned in Problem 9-24, Sun Company sells 150 shares of Moon Company on June 30, 19X4, to nonaffiliates for $84,000 and uses the weighted-average method in accounting for sales of subsidiary shares. Ignoring any gain or loss on the sale of the Moon Company shares, Sun Company's net income from its own operations in 19X4 is $80,000. Sun Company's retained earnings is $200,000 on January 1, 19X4. Moon Company's uniformly earned net income in 19X4 is $30,000.

Required:

a. Calculate the balance in the Investment in Moon Company account immediately prior to the sale of the shares.

b. Calculate the gain or loss on the sale of the Moon Company shares.

c. Calculate the differential remaining in the Investment in Moon Company account immediately after the sale of the Moon Company shares.

d. Prepare Sun Company's 19X4 equity method entries.

e. Calculate 19X4 consolidated net income incrementally.

f. Prepare the working paper entries for a 19X4 consolidated statement working paper, and prepare a partial 19X4 working paper.

g. Analyze the balance remaining in Equity in Subsidiary Earnings.

Problem 9-28   (Subsidiary's Sale of Shares to Nonaffiliates)

Solar Company has capital stock of $200,000 ($200 par) and retained earnings of $300,000 on January 1, 19X1. On this date, Galaxy Company holds 700 Solar Company shares, and its Investment in Solar Company account has a balance of $400,000. Solar Company's uniformly earned net income for 19X1 is $40,000. Galaxy Company's 19X1 net income from its own operations is $80,000, excluding any gains or losses from subsidiary stock transactions. Solar Company sells an additional 250 shares of its stock to nonaffiliates at $300 per share on June 30, 19X1. The following presale differential allocation and amortization values are pertinent to 19X1.

	Unamortized Differential before Issuance of New Shares	19X1 Amortization
Plant and equipment (net)	$20,000	$2,000
Goodwill	30,000	1,000
Total	$50,000	$3,000

Required:

a. Determine the change in Galaxy Company's interest in Solar Company's stockholders' equity arising from the sale of the Solar Company shares.

b. Calculate the gain or loss related to the sale of the Solar Company shares.

c. Prepare Galaxy Company's 19X1 equity method entries.

d. Prepare the working paper entries for a 19X1 consolidated statement working paper.

e. Calculate 19X1 consolidated net income incrementally.

f. Analyze the balance remaining in Equity in Subsidiary Earnings.

Problem 9–29   (Subsidiary's Acquisition of Treasury Shares from Parent)

Ess Company has capital stock of $200,000 ($200 par) and retained earnings of $300,000 on January 1, 19X1. On this date, Pea Company holds 900 Ess Company shares, and its Investment in Ess Company account has a balance of $525,000. Ess Company's uniformly earned net income for 19X1 is $60,000. Pea Company's 19X1 net income from its own operations is $90,000, excluding any gains or losses from subsidiary stock transactions. Ess Company purchases 200 shares of its own stock from Pea Company on June 30, 19X1, for $220 per share and accounts for these treasury shares using the cost method. The following presale differential allocation and amortization values are pertinent to 19X1.

	Unamortized Differential before Issuance of New Shares	19X1 Amortization
Plant and equipment (net)	$30,000	$ 3,000
Goodwill	45,000	9,000
Total	$75,000	$12,000

Required:

a. Determine the change in Pea Company's interest in Ess Company's stockholders' equity arising from the treasury stock transaction.

b. Calculate the gain or loss related to the treasury stock transaction.

c. Prepare Pea Company's 19X1 equity method entries.

d. Prepare the working paper entries for a 19X1 consolidated statement working paper.

e. Calculate 19X1 consolidated net income incrementally.

f. Analyze the balance remaining in Equity in Subsidiary Earnings.

Problem 9–30   (Step-by-Step and Date-of-Control Methods)

On January 1, 19X1, S Company has outstanding capital stock (par $10) of $10,000 and retained earnings of $30,000. P Company makes the following open-market block purchases in 19X1.

January 1, 19X1	50 shares (cost $ 2,500)
July 1, 19X1	100 shares (cost $ 5,500)
October 1, 19X1	750 shares (cost $45,000)

Block purchases are accounted for using the step-by-step method.

S Company's uniformly earned 19X1 net income is $20,000. P Company's net income from its own operations for 19X1 is $50,000. All differentials are allocated to nonamortizable assets.

Required:

a. Record P Company's equity in S Company's 19X1 net income.

b. Prepare the working paper entries for a 19X1 consolidated statement working paper through the investment elimination entry.

c. Calculate 19X1 consolidated net income incrementally.

d. Repeat the above requirements assuming that the date-of-control method is used.

Problem 9–31   (Parent's Sale of Subsidiary Shares to Nonaffiliates)

On January 1, 19X1, S Company has outstanding capital stock (par $5) of $10,000 and retained earnings of $50,000. P Company holds 1,800 S Company shares, and the Investment in S Company account has a balance of $84,000. The differential is allocated to land.

On September 30, 19X1, P Company sells 600 of its S Company shares to nonaffiliates for $25 per share. P Company uses the weighted-average method in determining gains and losses on such sales.

S Company's uniformly earned 19X1 net income is $20,000. P Company's 19X1 net income from own operations, excluding any gain or loss on the sale of subsidiary shares, is $50,000.

Required:

a. Record P Company's 19X1 equity method entries.

b. Reconcile the balance of the Investment in S Company account with the sum of P Company's interest in S Company's stockholders' equity and the differential at December 31, 19X1.

c. Prepare the working paper entries for a 19X1 consolidated statement working paper through the investment elimination entry.

d. Calculate 19X1 consolidated net income incrementally.

Problem 9–32   (Parent's Sale of Subsidiary Shares to Nonaffiliates)

On January 1, 19X1, S Company has outstanding capital stock (par $10) of $20,000 and retained earnings of $80,000. P Company holds 1,800 S Company shares, and the Investment in S Company account has a balance of $117,000. The differential is allocated to goodwill with a remaining life of 10 years.

On July 1, 19X1, P Company sells 200 of its S Company shares to nonaffiliates for $80 per share. P Company uses the weighted-average method in determining gains and losses on such sales.

S Company's uniformly earned 19X1 net income is $10,000. P Company's 19X1 net income from own operations, excluding any gain or loss on the sale of subsidiary shares, is $20,000.

Required:

a. Record P Company's 19X1 equity method entries.

b. Reconcile the balance of the Investment in S Company account with the sum of P Company's interest in S Company's stockholders' equity and the unamortized differential at December 31, 19X1.

c. Prepare the working paper entries for a December 31, 19X1, consolidated statement working paper.

d. Calculate 19X1 consolidated net income incrementally.

Problem 9–33   (Subsidiary's Sale of Shares to Nonaffiliates)

On January 1, 19X1, S Company has outstanding capital stock (par $5) of $10,000 and retained earnings of $50,000. P Company holds 1,800 S Company shares, and the Investment in S Company account has a balance of $84,000. The differential is allocated to goodwill with a remaining life of 10 years. On July 1, 19X1, S Company sells 1,000 of its shares to nonaffiliates for $70 per share.

S Company's uniformly earned 19X1 net income is $20,000. P Company's 19X1 net income from own operations, excluding any gain or loss on the sale of subsidiary shares, is $50,000. P Company's January 1, 19X1, Retained Earnings balance is $100,000.

Required:

a. Calculate P Company's gain or loss from the sale of the shares.

b. Prepare P Company's 19X1 equity method entries.

c. Reconcile the balance of the Investment in S Company account with the sum of P Company's interest in S Company's stockholders' equity and the unamortized differential at December 31, 19X1.

d. Prepare the working paper entries for a December 31, 19X1, consolidated statement working paper.

e. Prepare a partial consolidated statement working paper (i.e., the income statement and retained earnings sections) for 19X1.

f. Calculate 19X1 consolidated net income incrementally.

Problem 9–34   (Block Purchase of Newly Issued Subsidiary Shares)

On January 1, 19X1, S Company has outstanding capital stock (par $10) of $20,000 and retained earnings of $80,000. P Company holds 1,800 S Company shares, and the Investment in S Company account has a balance of $130,000. As of January 1, 19X1, the differential is allocated to goodwill with a remaining life of 10 years. On July 1, 19X1, S Company sells 2,000 newly issued shares to P Company for $100 per share. On this date, the fair values and book values of all of S Company's assets and liabilities are the same. Goodwill arising from the sale of shares is to be amortized over the remaining life of the existing goodwill.

S Company's uniformly earned 19X1 net income is $20,000. P Company's 19X1 net income from own operations, excluding any gain or loss on the sale of subsidiary shares, is $50,000. P Company's January 1, 19X1, Retained Earnings balance is $100,000.

Required:

a. Calculate the change in P Company's interest in S Company's stockholders' equity and the related separate differential.

b. Prepare P Company's 19X1 equity method entries, ignoring its entry to record its block purchase.

c. Reconcile the balance of the Investment in S Company account with the sum of P Company's interest in S Company's stockholders' equity and the unamortized differential at December 31, 19X1.

d. Prepare the working paper entries for a December 31, 19X1, consolidated statement working paper.

e. Prepare a partial consolidated statement working paper (i.e., the income statement and retained earnings sections) for 19X1.

f. Calculate 19X1 consolidated net income incrementally.

Problem 9–35   (Unconfirmed Profits)

P Company purchases 800 shares of S Company on January 1, 19X1, for $120,000. On this date, S Company has outstanding capital stock ($100 par) of $100,000 and retained earnings of $50,000. P Company purchases an additional 100 shares of S Company on July 1, 19X2, for $17,700. On July 1, 19X3, S Company sells 200 newly issued shares to nonaffiliates for $40,000. Differentials, if any, are allocated to nonamortizable assets.

Unconfirmed profits from upstream sales exist as follows:

1. Unconfirmed inventory profit of $2,000 reported in 19X1 (confirmed during the last half of 19X2).

2. Unconfirmed inventory profit of $1,000 reported during the first half of 19X2 (confirmed during the first half of 19X3).

3. Unconfirmed profit of $10,000 on sale of plant and equipment on July 2, 19X2 (this asset has a remaining life of 10 years).

Calculations of changes in equity are based on confirmed profits. Also, pro rata allocation is used.

During each year mentioned above, P Company has net income from its own operations of $100,000 (ignoring the gain or loss related to the subsidiary stock transaction). S Company's uniformly earned net income over each of these years is $20,000.

Required:

a. Calculate 19X2 consolidated net income incrementally.

b. Calculate 19X3 consolidated net income incrementally.

Problem 9–36 (Parent's Sale of Subsidiary Shares to Nonaffiliates and Unconfirmed Profits)

Presented below are the trial balances of P Company and its subsidiary, S Company, at December 31, 19X3.

	P Company	S Company
Cash	$ 486,000	$ 249,600
Accounts Receivable	235,000	185,000
Inventories (12/31)	475,000	355,000
Machinery and Equipment (net)	2,231,000	530,000
Investment in S Company Bonds	58,000	
Investment in S Company Stock	954,000	
Unamortized Discount on Bonds Payable		2,400
Cost of Sales	2,982,000	1,015,000
Operating Expenses	400,000	377,200
Interest Expense		7,800
Dividends Declared	170,000	100,000
	$7,991,000	$2,822,000
Accounts Payable	$ 384,000	$ 62,000
Bonds Payable		120,000
Common Stock	1,200,000	250,000
Other Contributed Capital		50,000
Retained Earnings (1/1)	2,100,000	640,000
Sales	4,000,000	1,700,000
Equity in Subsidiary Earnings	232,000	
Dividend Income	75,000	
	$7,991,000	$2,822,000

Additional Information:

1. On January 3, 19X1, P Company acquired from John Simmons (the sole stockholder of S Company), a patent valued at $40,000 and 80 percent of the outstanding stock of S Company for $440,000 cash. The net book value of S Company's stock on the date of acquisition was $500,000, and the book values of its individual assets and liabilities were equal to their fair values.

P Company charged the entire $440,000 to the Investment in S Company Stock account. The patent, for which no amortization has been recorded, had a remaining legal life of four years as of January 3, 19X1.

2. On July 1, 19X3, P Company reduced its investment in S Company to 75 percent by selling S Company shares to a nonaffiliate for $70,000 at a profit of $16,000. P Company recorded the proceeds as a credit to its investment account.

3. For the six months ended June 30, 19X3, S Company had net income of $140,000. P Company recorded 80 percent of this amount prior to the sale.

4. During 19X2, S Company sold merchandise to P Company for $130,000. The markup on this sale was 30 percent over S Company's cost. On January 1, 19X3, $52,000 of this merchandise remained in P Company's inventory. This merchandise was sold by P Company in February 19X3 at a profit of $8,000.

5. In November 19X3, P Company sold merchandise to S Company for the first time. P Company's cost for this merchandise was $80,000, and the sale was made at 120 percent of cost. S Company's inventory at December 31, 19X3, contained $24,000 of merchandise purchased from P Company.

6. On December 31, 19X3, a $45,000 payment was in transit from S Company to P Company. Accounts receivable and accounts payable include intercompany receivables and payables.

7. In December 19X3, S Company declared and paid cash dividends of $100,000 to its stockholders.

8. On December 31, 19X3, P Company purchased 50 percent of the outstanding bonds of S Company for $58,000. The bonds mature on December 31, 19X7, and were originally issued at a discount. On December 31, 19X3, the balance in S Company's Unamortized Discount on Bonds Payable account was $2,400. P Company's management intends to hold these bonds until their maturity.

Required:

a. Prepare a consolidated statement working paper for the year ended December 31, 19X3. Intercompany profits are to be 100 percent eliminated and allocated pro rata to majority and minority shareholders.

b. Calculate 19X3 consolidated net income incrementally.

(AICPA adapted)

Problem 9–37   (Open-Market Block Purchases and Parent's Purchase of Treasury Shares)

P Company acquired control of S Company on June 30, 19X1, by purchasing 2,800 of its shares in the open market for $394,800. On this date, S Company had 4,000 issued shares of $100 par value common stock—of which 500 shares were held as treasury stock (carried at par).

On January 1, 19X3, P Company acquired 200 additional shares at a cost of $35,000 from a minority stockholder. On December 31, 19X3, P Company acquired the 500 treasury shares for $90,000 (with agreement by the minority stockholder).

An analysis of S Company's Other Contributed Capital and Retained Earnings is as follows:

	Other Contributed Capital	Retained Earnings
Credits		
June 30, 19X1	$ 74,300	$ 43,745
Earnings, 6/30 to 12/31/X1		35,306
Earnings, 19X2		65,754
Earnings, 19X3		51,025
Premium on sale of treasury stock	40,000	
	$114,300	$195,830
Debits		
Dividends paid, 12/1/X1		$ 35,000
Dividends paid, 12/5/X2		35,000
Dividends paid, 12/15/X3		40,000
	–0–	$110,000
Balance, 12/31/X3	$114,300	$ 85,830

On the dates of each acquisition of S Company shares, the book and fair values of S Company's assets and liabilities were equal. Goodwill arising from an acquisition is to be amortized over a 10-year period beginning on the acquisition date.

The following information has been excerpted from the companies' December 31, 19X3, trial balances.

	P Company	S Company
Other Assets	$300,000	$680,130
Investment in S Company	?	
Accounts Payable	100,000	80,000
Capital Stock	200,000	400,000
Other Contributed Capital	300,000	114,300
Retained Earnings—P Company:		
From own operations, excluding any effects of		
investment in S Company	129,514	
From investment in S Company	?	
Retained Earnings—S Company		85,830

Required:

a. Assuming that P Company uses the equity method to account for its investment in S Company, calculate the correct balances at December 31, 19X3, for

  (1) Investment in S Company.

  (2) Retained Earnings—P Company.

b. Using the balances calculated in (*a*) above, prepare a consolidated balance sheet working paper at December 31, 19X3.

(AICPA adapted)

Problem 9–38   (Open-Market Block Purchases and Unconfirmed Profits)

The December 31, 19X3, trial balances of Pulsar Corporation and its subsidiary, Shaker Corporation, are presented below:

	Pulsar	Shaker
Cash	$ 167,250	$101,000
Accounts Receivable	178,450	72,000
Notes Receivable	87,500	28,000
Dividends Receivable	36,000	
Inventories	122,000	68,000
Property, Plant, and Equipment (net)	370,000	188,000
Investment in Shaker	240,800	
	$1,202,000	$457,000
Accounts Payable	$ 222,000	$ 76,000
Notes Payable	79,000	89,000
Dividends Payable		40,000
Common Stock	400,000	100,000
Retained Earnings	501,000	152,000
	$1,202,000	$457,000

Pulsar initially acquired 60 percent of the outstanding common stock of Shaker in 19X1. There was no differential related to this purchase. As of December 31, 19X3, the percentage of Shaker's comon stock owned by Pulsar is 90 percent. An analysis of the Investment in Shaker account is provided below.

Date	Description	Amount
12/31/X1	Acquired 6,000 shares	$ 70,800
12/31/X2	60% of 19X2 net income of $78,000	46,800
9/1/X3	Acquired 3,000 shares	92,000
12/31/X3	Subsidiary income for 19X3	67,200*
12/31/X3	90% of dividends declared	(36,000)
		$240,800

* Subsidiary income for 19X3:

(60% × $96,000)		$57,600
[30% × (4/12) × $96,000]		9,600
		$67,200

Assume that Shaker's net income is earned ratably during the year. Any differential is to be allocated to goodwill and amortized over 60 months.

On December 15, 19X3, Shaker declared a $4 cash dividend on its common stock. This dividend is payable to shareholders on January 7, 19X4.

During 19X3, Pulsar sold merchandise to Shaker. Pulsar's cost for this merchandise was $68,000, and the sale was made at 125 percent of cost. Shaker's inventory at December 31, 19X3, included merchandise purchased from Pulsar at a cost to Shaker of $35,000.

In December 19X2, Shaker sold merchandise to Pulsar for $67,000. The sale was made at a markup of 35 percent over Shaker's cost. On January 1, 19X3, $54,000 of this merchandise remained in Pulsar's inventory. This merchandise was sold by Pulsar at a profit of $11,000 during the first six months of 19X3.

On October 1, 19X3, Shaker sold excess equipment to Pulsar for $42,000. Data relating to this equipment are as follows:

Book value on Shaker's books	$36,000
Method of depreciation	Straight-line
Estimated remaining life on 10/1/X3	10 years

Near the end of 19X3, Shaker reduced the balance of its intercompany account payable to Pulsar to zero by transferring $8,000 to Pulsar. This payment was in transit on December 31, 19X3.

Required:

Prepare a consolidated balance sheet working paper at December 31, 19X3, for Pulsar Corporation and its subsidiary, Shaker Corporation. Show your supporting computations in good form. Intercompany profits are eliminated 100 percent using pro rata allocation.

(AICPA adapted)

Consolidated Statements— Special Ownership Configurations

Chapter Outline

Previous chapters dealt with corporate affiliations in which a parent company controls one or more subsidiaries. In such affiliations, control is *directly* exercised by the parent company over all members of the affiliation. This chapter deals with multilevel affiliations in which the parent controls a subsidiary which, in turn, controls a subsidiary. The second-level subsidiary might also control a third-level subsidiary, and so on. In multilevel affiliations, the parent's control over second- and lower-level subsidiaries is *indirect*. This chapter also deals with bilateral stockholdings in which one affiliate owns shares of a second affiliate, which owns shares of the first affiliate.

Affiliation diagrams were introduced as an analytical tool in Chapter 2. Analyses of multilevel affiliations and bilateral stockholdings are often simplified by depicting the affiliation in an affiliation diagram.

MULTILEVEL AFFILIATIONS

In a multilevel affiliation, at least one company other than the parent company is an investor company, and each investor company carries its investment in affiliates using the equity method. Accordingly, the calculation of amounts for the working paper entries, minority interests, equities in affiliates' earnings, and so forth, are based on the results of applying the equity method. Otherwise, parent company entries are made and consolidated statement working paper techniques applied as described in previous chapters.

The following two cases illustrate multilevel affiliations. The account balances related to each of these examples are as follows:

| | January 1, 19X1 | | |
	P Company	*Y Company*	*Z Company*
Capital stock	$200,000	$100,000	$50,000
Retained earnings	80,000	20,000	10,000

Assume that each company reported income, exclusive of any equity in affiliates' earnings, of $10,000 each year. Additionally, for reasons of simplicity, assume that no dividends were declared and that all differentials relate to nonamortizable assets.

Case 1. A Simple Multilevel Affiliation

Y Company purchased 80 percent of the capital stock of Z company on January 1, 19X1, for $50,000. One year later, P Company purchased 90 percent of the capital stock of Y Company for $125,000. As a consequence of these transactions, the affiliation diagram for this multilevel affiliation is as follows:

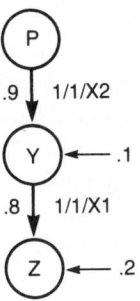

Since both P Company and Y Company hold stock investments in affiliates, each records an equity in an affiliate's earnings and each is subject to an elimination entry in the consolidated statement working paper. The purchased equity in the affiliates and the related differential for each of these two investments are analyzed below:

	P Company in Y Company (1/1/X2)	Y Company in Z Company (1/1/X1)
Investment cost	$125,000	$50,000
Purchased equity in affiliate's net assets:		
Capital stock	$ 90,000	$40,000
Retained earnings	34,200*	8,000
	$124,200	$48,000
Differential	$ 800	$ 2,000

* (90% × $38,000).

Y Company's purchased equity in Z Company is based on the amounts for capital stock and retained earnings at January 1, 19X1. P Company purchased the shares of Y Company one year later, when Y Company's retained earnings balance is $38,000. During 19X1, Y Company's income, *under the equity method,* is $18,000 [$10,000 + (80% × $10,000)], and thus its retained earnings balance on January 1, 19X2 is $38,000.

At the end of 19X2, each company records its equity in affiliates' 19X2 earnings (if any). In order to properly pick up the full equity at each level, the calculations of these equity interests *begin at the lowest level of the affiliation structure and work upward.* Thus, in our example, we begin with Z Company. Z Company holds no ownership interest in affiliates, and as a result its equity method net income is equal to its income from operations ($10,000). Moving up one level to Company Y, its equity in Z Company's 19X2 equity method net income amounts to $8,000 (80% × $10,000). Adding this equity in affiliates' earnings to income from operations of $10,000 yields 19X2 equity method net income for Company Y of $18,000. Finally, moving to the top level of the affiliation structure, P Company's equity in Y Company's 19X2 equity method net income is $16,200 (90% × $18,000), which when combined with P Company's income from operations of $10,000 produces equity method net income for 19X2 for P Company of $26,200.

A partial consolidated statement working paper for this affiliation for the year ended December 31, 19X2, is presented in Illustration 10–1. Note that minority interests are based simply on the subsidiaries' recorded incomes and net assets, which in the case of Y Company reflects Y Company's equity interest in Z Company.

Consolidated net income for 19X2 is calculated incrementally as follows:

P Company's income from its own operations	$10,000
Plus: Equity in Y Company's reported	
(equity method) income (90% × $18,000)	16,200
Consolidated net income for 19X2	$26,200

Case 2. A More Complex Multilevel Affiliation

On January 1, 19X1, P Company purchased 80 percent of the capital stock of Y Company for $100,000 and 70 percent of the capital stock of Z Company for $43,000. One year later, Y Company purchased 20 percent of the capital stock of Z Company for $15,000.

The affiliation diagram and the analysis of the purchased equities in affiliates are as follows:

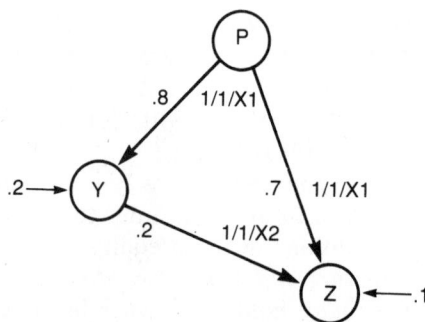

ILLUSTRATION 10-1

P COMPANY AND SUBSIDIARIES
Partial Consolidated Statement Working Paper
For the Year Ended December 31, 19X2

	P Company	Y Company	Z Company	Eliminations Dr.		Eliminations Cr.		Consolidated
Income Statement								
Net income from own operations	10,000	10,000	10,000					30,000
Equity in earnings of affiliates	16,200	8,000		(1)	24,200			
Minority interest expense—Company Y				(1)	1,800			(1,800)
Minority interest expense—Company Z				(1)	2,000			(2,000)
Net income	26,200	18,000	10,000		28,000			26,200
Retained Earnings Statement								
Retained earnings (1/1):								
P Company	90,000							90,000
Y Company		38,000		(2)	38,000			
Z Company			20,000	(2)	20,000			
Net income	26,200	18,000	10,000		28,000			26,200
Retained earnings (12/31)	116,200	56,000	30,000		86,000			116,200
Balance Sheet								
Investment in Y Company	141,200					(1)	16,200	
						(2)	125,000	
Investment in Z Company		66,000				(1)	8,000	
						(2)	58,000	
Differential—P Company in Y Company				(2)	800			800
Differential—Y Company in Z Company				(2)	2,000			2,000
Capital stock:								
P Company	200,000							200,000
Y Company		100,000		(2)	100,000			
Z Company			50,000	(2)	50,000			
Retained earnings	116,200	56,000	30,000		86,000			116,200
Minority interest—Y Company						(1)	1,800	15,600
						(2)	13,800	
Minority interest—Z Company						(1)	2,000	16,000
						(2)	14,000	
(deduction)								

Explanation of eliminations:

(1) To eliminate interests in earnings of affiliates.

(2) To eliminate January 1, 19X2, stockholders' equity balances and establish differential.

	P Company in Y Company (1/1/X1)	P Company in Z Company (1/1/X1)	Y Company in Z Company (1/1/X2)
Investment cost	$100,000	$43,000	$15,000
Purchased equity in affiliates:			
Capital stock	$ 80,000	$35,000	$10,000
Retained earnings	16,000	7,000	4,000*
	$ 96,000	$42,000	$14,000
Differential	$ 4,000	$ 1,000	$ 1,000

* (20% × $20,000).

In Case 1, Y Company was, technically, both a "parent" and a subsidiary, and P Company's control over Z Company was indirect through Y Company. In this example, however, P Company exercises direct control over both subsidiaries and only obtains additional indirect control over Z Company through Y Company's 20 percent equity in Z Company.

Y Company should again carry its investment in Z Company using the equity method because *significant influence* is clearly exerted over the financial and operating policies of Z Company. Even if a second-level *investor company* holds less than a 20 percent interest in another affiliate in a multilevel affiliation, the equity method is justified under *APB Opinion No. 18* when significant influence and/or control is exerted through a combination of direct and indirect shareholdings. Note that if the acquisitions had been reversed, that is, if Y Company had first acquired its interest in Z Company and then P Company had acquired controlling interests in the two companies, the acquisition of Z Company would be in essence a step-by-step acquisition that would require a retroactive adjustment of Y Company's investment account if it were not previously carried under the equity method. In the event a second-level investor company does not carry its investment under the equity method, a working paper adjustment would be required to convert it to the equity method prior to the preparation of other working paper entries.

A partial consolidated statement working paper for this affiliation for the year ended December 31, 19X2, is presented in Illustration 10–2. As in the previous example, the investment accounts are carried under the equity method, and minority interest calculations are based on the subsidiaries' recorded incomes and stockholders' equity values.

ILLUSTRATION 10–2

P COMPANY AND SUBSIDIARIES
Partial Consolidated Statement Working Paper
For the Year Ended December 31, 19X2

	P Company	Y Company	Z Company	Eliminations Dr.	Eliminations Cr.	Consolidated
Income Statement						
Net income from own operations	10,000	10,000	10,000			30,000
Equity in earnings of affiliates	16,600	2,000		(1) 18,600		
Minority interest expense—Company Y				(1) 2,400		(2,400)
Minority interest expense—Company Z				(1) 1,000		(1,000)
Net income	26,600	12,000	10,000	22,000		26,600
Retained Earnings Statement						
Retained earnings (1/1):						
P Company	105,000*					105,000
Y Company		30,000		(2) 30,000		
Z Company			20,000	(2) 20,000		
Net income	26,600	12,000	10,000	22,000		26,600
Retained earnings (12/31)	131,600	42,000	30,000	72,000		131,600
Balance Sheet						
Investment in Y Company	117,600†				(1) 9,600	
					(2) 108,000	
Investment in Z Company	57,000‡				(1) 7,000	
					(2) 50,000	
Investment in Z Company		17,000§			(1) 2,000	
					(2) 15,000	
Differential—P Company in Y Company				(2) 4,000		4,000
Differential—P Company in Z Company				(2) 1,000		1,000
Differential—Y Company in Z Company				(2) 1,000		1,000
Capital stock:						
P Company	200,000					200,000
Y Company		100,000		(2) 100,000		
Z Company			50,000	(2) 50,000		
Retained earnings	131,600	42,000	30,000	72,000		131,600
Minority interest—Y Company					(1) 2,400	28,400
					(2) 26,000	
Minority interest—Z Company					(1) 1,000	8,000
					(2) 7,000	
(deduction)						

* $80,000 + $10,000 + (80% × $10,000) + (70% × $10,000)

† $100,000 + (80% × $10,000) + (80% × $12,000)

‡ $43,000 + (70% × $10,000) + (70% × $10,000)

§ $15,000 + (20% × $10,000)

Explanation of eliminations:

(1) To eliminate interests in earnings of affiliates.

(2) To eliminate January 1, 19X2, stockholders' equity balances and establish differential.

Consolidated net income for 19X2 is calculated incrementally as follows:

P Company's income from its own operations		$10,000
Plus: Equity in affiliates' reported (equity method) incomes		
Y Company (80% × $12,000)	$9,600	
Z Company (70% × $10,000)	7,000	16,600
Consolidated net income for 19X2		$26,600

Effects of Differential Amortization

In the previous two illustrations, we assumed that all differentials were allocated to nonamortizable assets. If these differentials were allocated to amortizable assets, as they normally would be, differential amortization would have to be taken into account in calculating consolidated net income and the minority interests in subsidiaries with investments in other affiliates. As long as all affiliates use the equity method to account for investments in other affiliates, differential amortization poses no special problem in the calculation of consolidated net income and minority interest.

Since differential amortization is recorded by the subsidiary in calculating its equity method net income, the parent company automatically recognizes its proper share of this expense when it records its equity in the subsidiary on the basis of the subsidiary's equity method net income. Thus, the customary equality between parent company and consolidated net income is preserved. In addition, the minority interest expense is the minority ownership percentage times the subsidiary's equity method net income. Of course, on the consolidated statement working paper, the differentials are allocated to specific assets and liabilities, and appropriate amortizations recognized.

Chain Control (Indirect) Less than 50 Percent

On occasion, intercorporate stock ownership arrangements may indicate a chain of interests, the product of which does not represent control of the lower-level subsidiary, where control is defined in terms of majority ownership. The following diagram is an example of such an affiliation:

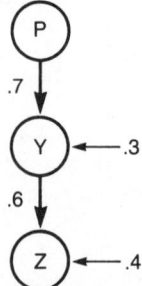

In this instance, the preparation of consolidated statements is still warranted, notwithstanding the 42 percent indirect interest of P Company in Z Company. The question of control relates to *direct* share ownership. In the illustration depicted above, control is confirmed by the percentages of stock owned independently by P Company and Y Company. Although the product of ownership percents in the chain is a factor in the determination of consolidated net income and consolidated retained earnings, it is not a determinant in establishing a minimal condition for preparation of consolidated financial statements.

Intercompany Profit in Multilevel Affiliations

Previous discussion of the elimination of the intercompany profit on asset transfers focused on affiliations in which the subsidiary is one level removed from the parent company. The calculation of consolidated net income is not fundamentally altered by the intercompany profit element existing at any level of a multilevel affiliation. Assuming pro rata allocation, the equity in an affiliate's net income is calculated using the affiliate's *confirmed* equity method net income for the period. Similarly, in the consolidated statement working paper, minority interest expense is based upon the subsidiary's confirmed equity method net income. This procedure allocates the intercompany profit on the basis of the direct and/or indirect ownership interest in the selling affiliate.[1]

Consider the following data and affiliation diagram in respect to companies P, Y, and Z:

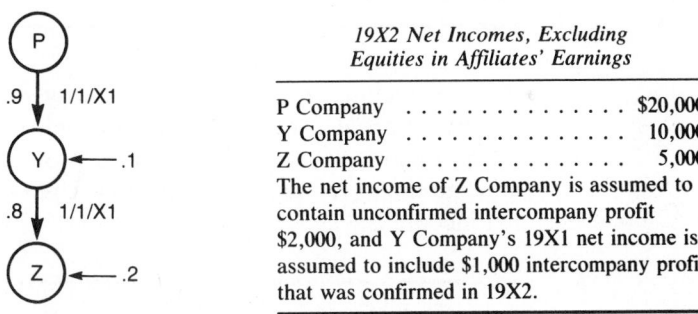

	19X2 Net Incomes, Excluding Equities in Affiliates' Earnings	
P Company	. . . .	$20,000
Y Company	. . . .	10,000
Z Company	. . . .	5,000

The net income of Z Company is assumed to contain unconfirmed intercompany profit $2,000, and Y Company's 19X1 net income is assumed to include $1,000 intercompany profit that was confirmed in 19X2.

Assuming pro rata allocation, consolidated net income for 19X2 may be determined using the incremental approach working from the lowest level upward as follows:

---

[1] When the 100 percent elimination is allocated wholly to the majority shareholders regardless of the selling affiliate, the calculations of consolidated net income and minority interests in net income are based upon the subsidiaries' equity basis net incomes, *unadjusted* for intercompany profits, with the entire amount of the intercompany profit allocated to the parent. This procedure results in a different measure of consolidated net income.

Z Company's confirmed net income = ($5,000 − $2,000) = $3,000

Y Company's confirmed net income (including its equity in Z Company's confirmed net income) = $10,000 + (80% × $3,000) + $1,000 = $13,400

Consolidated net income = $20,000 + (90% × $13,400) = $32,060

The effect of allocating unconfirmed profits may be seen from a different perspective by calculating P Company's interest in the equity method net income of Y Company, unadjusted for intercompany profits, and then deducting directly therefrom the parent's interest in the confirmed and unconfirmed profits. This approach is displayed below:

Y Company's equity method income, unadjusted for unconfirmed profits [$10,000 + (80% × $5,000)]	$14,000
P Company's equity method income, unadjusted for unconfirmed profits [$20,000 + (90% × $14,000)]	$32,600
Add (deduct) P company's interest, direct and/or indirect, in confirmed (unconfirmed) intercompany profits:	
Direct interest in Y Company's $1,000 confirmed profit (90% × $1,000)	900
Indirect interest in Z Company's $2,000 unconfirmed profit (90% × 80% × $2,000)	(1,440)
Consolidated net income	$32,060

This calculation reveals that the majority shareholders are allocated $900 of the confirmed profit and $1,440 of the unconfirmed profit; the remainder is allocated to the minority shareholders. It also provides the basis for comparing pro rata allocation and 100 percent allocation. Under 100 percent allocation consolidated net income is:

P Company's equity method income, unadjusted for unconfirmed profits	$32,600
Add (deduct): The full amount of confirmed (unconfirmed) profits:	
Confirmed profit	1,000
Unconfirmed profit	(2,000)
Consolidated net income	$31,600

The difference in the two amounts of consolidated net income is reflected in the amounts assigned to the minority interests in Companies Y and Z.

BILATERAL STOCKHOLDINGS—TRADITIONAL ALLOCATION METHOD

In all of our previous examples, we focused attention on unilateral ownership by one or more companies of corporate shares of other affiliated companies. On occasion, one may encounter a bilateral stockholding, wherein two or more of the affiliated companies are related through the reciprocal ownership of corporate stock. In the discussion to follow, we consider the problems associated with bilateral stockholdings. First, the traditional method of allocating the affiliates' income between majority and minority shareholders is explained. For purposes of this explanation, we introduce a new term: *equity basis* net income. This term refers to an income number resulting from solution of a system of linear equations. Unlike a parent's equity method net income, which equals consolidated net income, equity basis net income is an intermediate number used in calculating consolidated net income. Equity basis net incomes of subsidiaries are similarly used in calculating minority interest expense. After explaining the traditional method of allocating the affiliates' net incomes, we briefly outline an alternative method—the treasury stock method.

Case 3. Bilateral Stockholdings Not Involving Parent Company

Consider the following affiliation diagram:

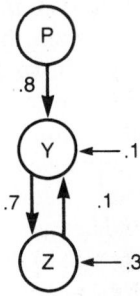

If the net incomes of companies P, Y, and Z *from their own operations* are $50,000, $20,000, and $10,000, respectively, their equity basis net incomes can be determined by solving a system of linear equations. These equity basis net incomes are ultimately allocated to majority and minority shareholders. We term this approach the *traditional allocation method.*

Assume the following notation:

$$Y = \text{Net income of Y Company on an equity basis}$$

$$Z = \text{Net income of Z Company on an equity basis.}$$

With this notation, the equity basis net incomes of Y and Z are the following:

$$Y = \$20,000 + 70\%Z$$

$$Z = \$10,000 + 10\%Y.$$

There is no need for an equation for P Company's net income since neither Y Company nor Z Company owns P Company shares. That is to say, the equity basis net income of P Company does not enter into the determination of the equity basis net incomes of Y Company and Z Company.

Substituting the second equation into the first and simplifying provides the equity basis net income of Y Company:

$$Y = \$20,000 + 70\% \times (\$10,000 + 10\%Y)$$

$$Y = \$20,000 + \$7,000 + 70\%Y$$

$$93\%Y = \$27,000$$

$$Y = \$29,032.26.$$

Substituting this value into the equation $Z = \$10,000 + 10\%Y$ and simplifying provides the equity basis net income of Z Company:

$$Z = \$10,000 + (10\% \times \$29,032.26)$$

$$Z = \$10,000 + \$2,903.23$$

$$Z = \$12,903.23.$$

Solving a system of linear equations using substitution can become quite cumbersome when the number of affiliates (and therefore the number of equations) is large. In such circumstances, matrix algebra may be the only practical way to solve the system of equations. Use of matrix algebra is illustrated in a subsequent section of this chapter.

The equity basis incomes which solve the system of equations have a natural economic interpretation. Assume that both Y Company and Z Company initially pay dividends equal to their income from their own operations. Thus, Y receives $7,000 (70% × $10,000) from Z, and Z receives $2,000 (20% × $20,000) from Y. Then, each company pays another dividend equal to the dividend just received. In this second round of distributions, Y receives $1,400 (70% × $2,000) and Z receives $700 (10% × $7,000). This process continues until the dividends become arbitrarily small. Each company's equity basis net income is the total amount of dividends paid.[2] Moreover, each company's equity in the earnings of its affiliate is the total amount of dividends received. Accordingly, the *net cash outflow* for each company equals its net income from operations. This is precisely the outcome if each company merely pays a dividend equal to its equity basis net income. Thus,

---

[2] This interpretation was suggested by Roman Weil, "Reciprocal or Mutual Holdings: Allocating Earnings and Selecting the Accounting Method," *The Accounting Review*, October 1987, p. 753.

the equity basis net incomes uniquely determine the amount that can be distributed in the form of dividends and still maintain the net assets of the firms at their beginning-of-year levels. This property provides strong theoretical support for the traditional allocation method.[3] However, as is discussed later in connection with the entries to be made by the affiliates, this conclusion reveals certain possible inconsistencies in *APB Opinion No. 18*.

Once the equity basis net incomes are determined, the traditional allocation method proceeds to allocate these incomes to majority and minority shareholders. This allocation is illustrated below:

P Company's net income from its own operations	$50,000.00	
80% of Y Company's equity basis net income		
(80% × $29,032.26)	23,225.81	
Consolidated net income		$73,225.81
Minority interest expense—Y Company		
10% of Y Company's equity basis net income		
(10% × $29,032.26)		2,903.22
Minority interest expense—Z Company:		
30% of Z Company's equity basis net income		
(30% × $12,903.23)		3,870.97
Total net incomes of affiliate companies		
from their own operations		$80,000.00

Note that, although the total equity basis net incomes of Y Company and Z Company exceeds their total income from operations, the allocation process results in consolidated net income and minority interest which sum to the total operating incomes of the three affiliates. This is a sensible result. The total operating incomes must accrue to the shareholders of P Company and the minority shareholders of Y Company and Z Company.

Case 4. Parent Company Involvement

Case 3 dealt with mutually related subsidiary affiliates. The calculation of equity basis net incomes is not essentially different when the parent is also bilaterally related to one or more affiliates. However, since the outside shareholder interest in the parent company is less than 100 percent (because one or more of the affiliates own stock in the parent), the parent's equity basis net income must be allocated to the outside shareholders in the same way that the subsidiaries' equity basis net incomes were allocated to the minority shareholders in the previous case.

---

[3] Ibid., p. 754.

Consider the following affiliation diagram:

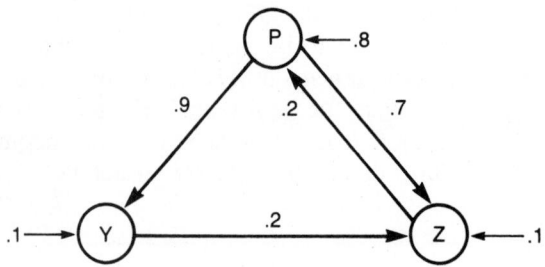

Companies P, Y, and Z are again assumed to have net incomes from their own operations of $50,000, $20,000, and $10,000.

The equity basis net incomes of the affiliates are calculated algebraically as follows:

P = Net income of P Company on an equity basis
Y = Net income of Y Company on an equity basis
Z = Net income of Z Company on an equity basis

$$P = \$50,000 + 90\%Y + 70\%Z$$
$$Y = \$20,000 + 20\%Z$$
$$Z = \$10,000 + 20\%P$$

$$P = \$50,000 + [90\% \times (\$20,000 + 20\%Z) + 70\%Z]$$
$$P = \$50,000 + \$18,000 + 18\%Z + 70\%Z$$
$$P = \$68,000 + 88\%Z$$
$$P = \$68,000 + [88\% \times (\$10,000 + 20\%P)]$$
$$P = \$68,000 + \$8,800 + 17.6\%P$$
$$82.4\%P = \$76,800$$
$$P = \$93,203.88$$

$$Z = \$10,000 + (20\% \times \$93,203.88)$$
$$Z = \$10,000 + \$18,640.78$$
$$Z = \$28,640.78$$

$$Y = \$20,000 + (20\% \times \$28,640.78)$$
$$Y = \$20,000 + \$5,728.16$$
$$Y = \$25,728.16$$

The equity basis net incomes of the three affiliates are allocated to majority and minority shareholder interests as follows:

Consolidated net income:
   80% of P Company's equity basis net income (80% × \$93,203.88) \$74,563.10
Minority interest expense—Y Company:
   10% of Y Company's equity basis net income (10% × \$25,728.16) 2,572.82
Minority interest expense—Z Company:
   10% of Z Company's equity basis net income (10% × \$28,640.78) 2,864.08
      Total net incomes of affiliates from their own operations \$80,000.00

In consolidated net income determination, only the nonaffiliate shareholders of the parent company constitute the majority interest. In this case, 20 percent of P Company's stock is held by Z Company; accordingly, the outside interest in P Company of 80 percent is the equity multiplier in calculating consolidated net income.

Case 5. Intercompany Profit on Asset Transfers—Parent Not Involved in Bilateral Stockholding

The basic principles governing elimination of intercompany profit on the transfer of assets between affiliates extend to cases involving bilateral stockholdings. Assume the following affiliation diagram:

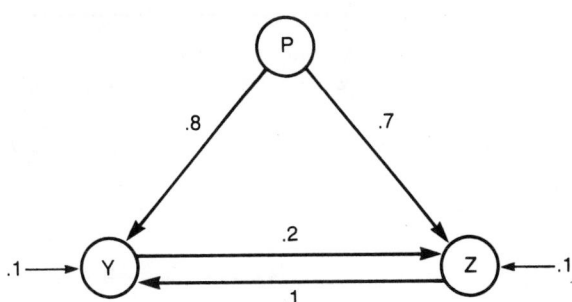

Also assume that unconfirmed profit from the sale of inventory from Z Company to an affiliate is \$9,800.
   Assume the following notation:

P_E = Interest of P Company in the unconfirmed profit on an equity
     basis
Y_E = Interest of Y Company in the unconfirmed profit on an equity
     basis
Z_E = Interest of Z Company in the unconfirmed profit on an equity
     basis

The various interests in the unconfirmed profit in ending inventory are reflected as follows:

$$P_E = 80\%Y_E + 70\%Z_E$$
$$Y_E = 20\%Z_E$$
$$Z_E = \$9,800 + 10\%Y_E$$

By substitution and simplification, solution values are determined to be as follows:

$$P_E = \$8,600$$
$$Y_E = \$2,000$$
$$Z_E = \$10,000$$

In the consolidated working paper, the entry relating to unconfirmed profit is as follows:

Cost of Goods Sold 9,800	
Inventory	9,800

Assuming pro rata allocation, minority shareholders must absorb a ratable amount of the eliminated unconfirmed profit, calculated as follows:

Minority interest expense—Y Company (10% × $2,000)	$ 200
Minority interest expense—Z Company (10% × $10,000)	1,000
	$1,200

Thus, the total elimination of $9,800 is allocated

To the majority shareholders	$8,600
To the minority shareholders	1,200
	$9,800

Each affiliate's confirmed equity basis net income may be determined by subtracting these interests in the unconfirmed inventory profit from its equity basis net income calculated as before.

If we are interested only in the amounts assigned to majority and minority interests with pro rata allocation, confirmed equity basis net incomes may be calculated directly in one algebraic solution by incorporating the unconfirmed profit(s) with the affiliates' net incomes from their own operations. For example, given net incomes from their own operations of $50,000, $20,000, and $10,000 for companies P, Y, and Z, respectively, and the $9,800 unconfirmed inventory profit reported by Z, the equation system for the mutually related subsidiaries would take the following form:

$$Y = \$20,000 + 20\%Z$$
$$Z = \$200 + 10\%Y$$

Z Company's net income in the second equation is reduced to $200 by deducting the $9,800 of unconfirmed inventory profit from the recorded net income of $10,000. By substituting and simplification, solution values are as follows:

$$Y = \$20,448.98$$
$$Z = \$2,244.90$$

Allocation of the net incomes of the affiliate companies is then made as follows:

P Company's net income from its own operations	$50,000.00	
80% of Y Company's equity basis net income		
(80% × $20,448.98)	16,359.18	
70% of Z Company's equity basis net income		
(70% × $2,244.90)	1,571.43	
Consolidated net income		$67,930.61
Minority interest expense—Y Company:		
10% of Y Company's equity basis net income		
(10% × $20,448.98)		2,044.90
Minority interest expense—Z Company:		
10% of Z Company's equity basis net income		
(10% × $2,244.90)		224.49
Total confirmed net incomes of affiliates		$70,200.00

This method implicitly deducts the majority and minority interests in the unconfirmed inventory profit, as calculated above, from the allocated shares of total net income.

Case 6. Intercompany Profit on Asset Transfers—Parent Involved in Bilateral Stockholding

The following is an illustration of an affiliation involving unconfirmed profit in which the parent is bilaterally related to one subsidiary:

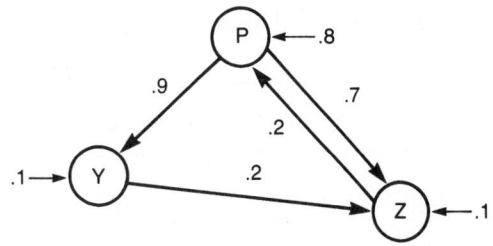

Unconfirmed profit in ending inventory currently recognized by Z Company is assumed to be $8,240.

Let

P_E = Interest of P Company in the unconfirmed profit on an equity basis

Y_E = Interest of Y Company in the unconfirmed profit on an equity basis

Z_E = Interest of Z Company in the unconfirmed profit on an equity basis

The interests in the unconfirmed inventory profit are the following:

$$P_E = 90\%Y_E + 70\%Z_E$$
$$Y_E = 20\%Z_E$$
$$Z_E = \$8,240 + 20\%P_E$$

By substitution and simplification, solution values are

$$P_E = \$8,800$$
$$Y_E = \$2,000$$
$$Z_E = \$10,000$$

Since consolidated net income is but 80 percent of the parent company's equity basis net income (recall that only the parent company's shares held by nonaffiliate interests are determinants of consolidated net income), the effect of the above unconfirmed profit elimination is a reduction of consolidated net income by $7,040 (80% × $8,800).

The consolidated working paper eliminating entry is as follows:

Cost of Goods Sold	8,240	
Inventory		8,240

The amounts of minority interests in the unconfirmed profit on a consolidated basis are calculated as follows:

Minority interest expense—Y Company (10% × $2,000)	$ 200
Minority interest expense—Z Company (10% × $10,000)	1,000
	$1,200

Thus, the total elimination of $8,240 is allocated as follows:

To the majority shareholders (80% × $8,800)	$7,040
To the minority shareholders	1,200
	$8,240

Effects of Differential Amortization

Our illustrations of allocating income between majority and minority shareholders in a bilateral stockholding have ignored the existence of differential amortization. Normally, affiliates with an investment in another affiliate have a differential that must be allocated and amortized, and thus differential amortization must be incorporated into our calculations.

In the case of multilevel affiliations, it was pointed out that the use of a subsidiary's equity basis net income results in a proper allocation of the differential amortization between majority and minority shareholders. In bilateral affiliations, the same effect can be achieved by deducting each affiliate's differential amortization for the period from its income from operations and then calculating the affiliates' equity basis net incomes. Alternatively, the proper allocations of the affiliates' differential amortizations may be separately calculated in the same manner as was illustrated for unconfirmed intercompany profits. Note that if the parent company is bilaterally related to one or more of the subsidiaries, a portion of the parent company's differential amortization is allocated to the minority shareholders. In all previous circumstances, the parent company's differential amortization was borne wholly by the majority shareholders.

Recording Equity in Affiliates' Earnings

There is a problem in determining the proper carrying value for the investment when the parent company is bilaterally related to one or more of its subsidiaries.[4] In particular, should the parent company record (1) its *equity basis* net income as calculated in the examples above or (2) the majority interest in its equity basis net income? Although we have previously observed that the equity basis net income value seems to reflect the basic equity method concept, recall that *APB Opinion No. 18* states the following application principle: "The difference between consolidation and the equity method lies in the details reported in the financial statements. Thus, an investor's *net income for the period and its stockholders' equity at the end of the period* are the same whether an investment in a subsidiary is accounted for under the equity method or the subsidiary is consolidated. . . ."[5] In view of this stated principle, the appropriate value to be recorded for a parent

---

[4] It is possible to construct hypothetical mutual stockholdings for which determination of the "parent" company is a moot point—for example, A Company owns 60 percent of B Company and B Company owns 60 percent of A Company. Although such stockholdings would seldom be encountered in practice, the situation tantalized us briefly in 1982 when Bendix Corporation and Martin Marietta were engaged in their classic takeover battle.

[5] APB, *APB Opinion No. 18,* "The Equity Method of Accounting for Investments in Common Stock" (New York: AICPA, 1971), par. 19. (Emphasis added.)

company under existing accounting authority appears to be the majority interest in the parent's equity basis net income.[6]

Recording the majority interest in the parent's equity basis net income achieves equality between the parent company's net income and consolidated net income, as prescribed in *APB Opinion No. 18*. However, achieving the prescribed equality between the parent company's stockholders' equity and consolidated stockholders' equity is a problem that appears insoluble when the parent company and a subsidiary are bilaterally related. In consolidation, the subsidiary's investment in the parent company is eliminated against the parent's stockholders' equity accounts. But there is no apparent way of achieving this elimination on the parent company's books that has any economic justification. Thus, in general, the parent company's stockholders' equity is greater than consolidated stockholders' equity.[7]

In our consideration of multilevel affiliations earlier in this chapter, it was asserted that subsidiaries with an investment in another affiliate should carry the investment under the equity method. Use of this method provides relevant information to the subsidiary's minority shareholders, facilitates the consolidation process, and seems generally consistent with the *significant influence* criterion of *APB Opinion No. 18*. It is debatable, however, whether these same arguments can be used to justify the equity method for subsidiaries involved in a bilateral stockholding. Particularly, is this true when the reciprocal stockholdings exist between a subsidiary and the parent company? Accordingly, no general rule is appropriate for the method of accounting for a subsidiary's investment in an affiliate when mutual stockholdings are involved. Rather, each case must be evaluated on its individual merits.

Matrix Algebra for Complex Affiliations

When the number of affiliates is large, matrix algebra provides the only practical means of computing each affiliate's equity method income. Operations on large matrices, however, require computer assistance. Fortunately, popular spreadsheet software for personal computers includes a capacity for matrix operations. The reader should note that the material in this section merely illustrates the use of matrix algebra as a means of computing equity basis net incomes in a case involving a quite complex bilateral stockholding. Nothing of a conceptual nature is introduced. Accordingly, many readers may wish to skip this section.

---

[6] Whether this conclusion is equally valid for mutually related companies not in a parent-subsidiary relationship is less clear. An interesting situation of this type involved two of Hong Kong's largest companies—Hongkong Land and Jardine Matheson. Each company held approximately a 40 percent equity in the other company, and their adoption in 1981 of the equity method of accounting generated a great deal of comment in the financial press. See Financial Times, *World Accounting Report* (New York: FT Publications, Inc., October 1981 and November 1981).

[7] Apparently, when *APB Opinion No. 18* was prepared, the Accounting Principles Board did not consider the special case of mutual stockholdings.

Assume the following affiliation diagram:

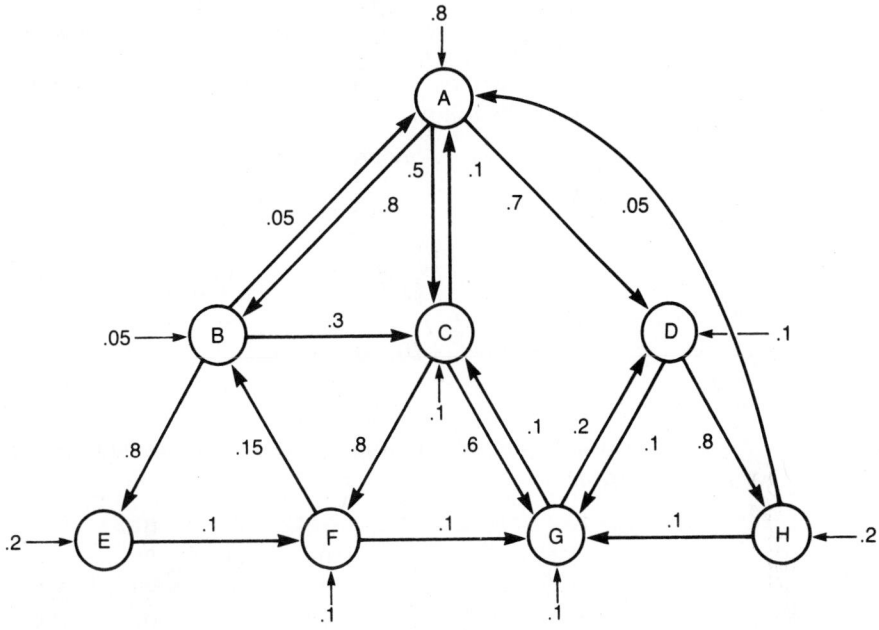

Also assume that the affiliates' net incomes from their own operations for the year 19X1 are as follows:

A Company	$ 40,000
B Company	30,000
C Company	30,000
D Company	40,000
E Company	10,000
F Company	20,000
G Company	10,000
H Company	20,000
	$200,000

As illustrated previously, the equity basis net incomes of the individual companies may be defined in algebraic form. Letting $A, B, \ldots, H$ denote net incomes of the respective companies on an equity basis

$$A = \$40{,}000 + 80\%B + 50\%C + 70\%D$$
$$B = \$30{,}000 + 80\%E + 30\%C + 5\%A$$
$$C = \$30{,}000 + 80\%F + 60\%G + 10\%A$$
$$D = \$40{,}000 + 80\%H + 10\%G$$

$$E = \$10{,}000 + 10\%F$$
$$F = \$20{,}000 + 15\%B + 10\%G$$
$$G = \$10{,}000 + 10\%C + 20\%D$$
$$H = \$20{,}000 + 5\%A + 10\%G$$

These equations may be arranged in a form exhibiting the underlying matrix structure as follows:

$$
\begin{array}{llllllll}
+ \quad A - 80\%B - 50\%C - 70\%D & & & = \$40{,}000 \\
- 5\%A + \quad B - 30\%C \qquad\qquad - 80\%E & & & = \$30{,}000 \\
- 10\%A \qquad\quad + \quad C \qquad\qquad\qquad - 80\%F - 60\%G & & & = \$30{,}000 \\
\qquad\qquad\qquad\quad + \quad D \qquad\qquad\qquad\qquad - 10\%G - 80\%H & & & = \$40{,}000 \\
\qquad\qquad\qquad\qquad\quad + \quad E - 10\%F & & & = \$10{,}000 \\
\quad - 15\%B \qquad\qquad\qquad\qquad\quad + \quad F - 10\%G & & & = \$20{,}000 \\
\qquad\quad - 10\%C - 20\%D \qquad\qquad\qquad + \quad G & & & = \$10{,}000 \\
- 5\%A \qquad\qquad\qquad\qquad\qquad\qquad - 10\%G + \quad H & & & = \$20{,}000
\end{array}
$$

Based upon this equation system, the problem may be easily expressed in matrix form:

$$
\begin{bmatrix}
1 & -80\% & -50\% & -70\% & 0 & 0 & 0 & 0 \\
-5\% & 1 & -30\% & 0 & -80\% & 0 & 0 & 0 \\
-10\% & 0 & 1 & 0 & 0 & -80\% & -60\% & 0 \\
0 & 0 & 0 & 1 & 0 & 0 & -10\% & -80\% \\
0 & 0 & 0 & 0 & 1 & -10\% & 0 & 0 \\
0 & -15\% & 0 & 0 & 0 & 1 & -10\% & 0 \\
0 & 0 & -10\% & -20\% & 0 & 0 & 1 & 0 \\
-5\% & 0 & 0 & 0 & 0 & 0 & -10\% & 1
\end{bmatrix}
\begin{bmatrix}
A \\ B \\ C \\ D \\ E \\ F \\ G \\ H
\end{bmatrix}
=
\begin{bmatrix}
\$40{,}000 \\ \$30{,}000 \\ \$30{,}000 \\ \$40{,}000 \\ \$10{,}000 \\ \$20{,}000 \\ \$10{,}000 \\ \$20{,}000
\end{bmatrix}
$$

In matrix notation, the above is as follows:

$$\mathbf{XY} = \mathbf{Z}$$

where **X** denotes the 8 × 8 coefficient matrix, **Y** denotes the 8 × 1 matrix of equity basis net incomes, and **Z** denotes the 8 × 1 matrix of the affiliates' net incomes from their own operations. Thus, the solution for **Y** is as follows:

$$\mathbf{Y} = \mathbf{X^{-1}Z}$$

where $\mathbf{X^{-1}}$ denotes the inverse of the coefficient matrix. With our numbers, the above equation is as follows:

$$
\begin{bmatrix}
A \\ B \\ C \\ D \\ E \\ F \\ G \\ H
\end{bmatrix}
=
\begin{bmatrix}
1.19654 & 1.09201 & 1.01394 & 1.01372 & 0.87361 & 0.89852 & 0.88069 & 0.81097 \\
0.10622 & 1.15050 & 0.43101 & 0.13985 & 0.92040 & 0.43685 & 0.32746 & 0.11188 \\
0.14971 & 0.27266 & 1.24678 & 0.28506 & 0.21813 & 1.01924 & 0.90131 & 0.22805 \\
0.05244 & 0.05040 & 0.06535 & 1.08473 & 0.04032 & 0.05631 & 0.24009 & 0.86778 \\
0.00185 & 0.01763 & 0.00784 & 0.00455 & 1.01410 & 0.10768 & 0.10629 & 0.00364 \\
0.10848 & 0.17631 & 0.07843 & 0.04552 & 0.14105 & 1.07685 & 0.16293 & 0.03642 \\
0.02546 & 0.03735 & 0.13775 & 0.24545 & 0.02988 & 0.11319 & 1.13815 & 0.19636 \\
0.06237 & 0.05834 & 0.06447 & 0.07523 & 0.04667 & 0.05624 & 0.15785 & 1.06018
\end{bmatrix}
\begin{bmatrix}
\$40{,}000 \\ \$30{,}000 \\ \$30{,}000 \\ \$40{,}000 \\ \$10{,}000 \\ \$20{,}000 \\ \$10{,}000 \\ \$20{,}000
\end{bmatrix}
$$

Thus, the following are the equity basis net incomes:

$$
\begin{bmatrix} A \\ B \\ C \\ D \\ E \\ F \\ G \\ H \end{bmatrix} = \begin{bmatrix} \$203,322 \\ \$\ 80,741 \\ \$\ 99,114 \\ \$\ 70,245 \\ \$\ 13,550 \\ \$\ 35,507 \\ \$\ 33,961 \\ \$\ 33,562 \end{bmatrix}
$$

Consolidated net income for 19X1 and minority interest expense are calculated as before:

Allocation of net incomes:		
Consolidated net income (80% × $203,322)		$162,658
Minority interest expense:		
B Company (5% × $80,741)	$4,037	
C Company (10% × $99,114)	9,911	
D Company (10% × $70,245)	7,025	
E Company (20% × $13,550)	2,710	
F Company (10% × $35,507)	3,551	
G Company (10% × $33,961)	3,396	
H Company (20% × $33,562)	6,712	37,342
Total net income of affiliates		$200,000

The increased number of affiliates and the additional involvements of the intercorporate stockholdings obviously introduce a number of complications in the arithmetic calculations of the equity basis net incomes. However, once these values are determined, the allocation of net incomes is only slightly more tedious than less complex affiliation structures.

A desirable property of the matrix method derives from the *permanence* of the inverse of the coefficient matrix. If there are no changes in the intercorporate shareholdings, the equity basis net incomes are easily determined each period (month, quarter, and so forth) with one matrix multiplication. This characteristic of the matrix representation greatly alleviates the arithmetic complexities, as a single calculation of the inverse of the coefficient matrix provides a continuing basis for the relatively simple calculation of the affiliates' equity basis net incomes in subsequent periods. Multiplication of these values by the appropriate majority or minority shareholder interests then gives the desired solutions.[8]

---

[8] Weil, "Reciprocal or Mutual Holdings," has shown that the second step of multiplying by the external shareholder interests may also be incorporated into the matrix solution, thus reducing the calculation to a single matrix multiplication.

BILATERAL STOCKHOLDINGS—TREASURY STOCK METHOD

Some accountants take the position that the purchase of a parent company's stock by a subsidiary is essentially like the parent's acquisition of *treasury shares*. When such stockholdings are accorded the status of treasury shares, it is appropriate to deduct the cost of these shares from the amounts of contributed capital and retained earnings of the parent company in the preparation of consolidated financial statements. It should be noted that the traditional allocation method, explained above, also removes the parent company's shares held by affiliates from the consolidated balance sheet through the elimination of the affiliate's investment account against the stockholders' equity accounts of the parent. Thus, both methods are in conformity with current accounting policy, which states: "Shares of the parent held by a subsidiary should not be treated as outstanding stock in the consolidated balance sheet."[9]

The methods do differ, however, in their conception of the nature of the transaction and their allocation of equities in net income and net assets between majority and minority interests. The treasury stock method presumes that the subsidiary is acting on behalf of the parent, and thus the investment in the parent company's shares should be accounted for in the same manner as if the parent had reacquired the shares. In order to achieve total equivalence, minority interest calculations (in net income and retained earnings) must exclude dividends received by the subsidiary from its investment in the parent. Although this practice is advocated by some accountants, we believe that it is unwarranted. Each time the parent declares a cash dividend, the majority shareholders incur an explicit cost for this use of subsidiary assets. The amount of the cost equals the minority's share of the dividend received by the subsidiary. Accordingly, it seems appropriate to calculate minority interest expense on the basis of the subsidiary's recorded net income (including the dividend income from the parent). As a consequence of these procedures, the minority interest in the consolidated balance sheet remains equal to the minority shareholders' percentage ownership interest multiplied by the net assets of the subsidiary. The traditional allocation method, on the other hand, recognizes this cost on an "accrual basis" by allocating a portion of the parent's current income to the shares held by the subsidiary. This method yields measures of majority and minority interests which reflect current equities in the net assets (excluding the bilateral stockholdings) of the two companies, rather than basing them, in part at least, on the dividend policies of the parent company.

If consolidated statements are prepared on the date reciprocal ownership of shares is established, the traditional allocation and treasury stock methods produce similar results (varying only in the amount of the differential in this transaction). Also, if the *total* amount of the subsidiaries' outstanding shares are held

---

[9] Committee on Accounting Procedure, *Accounting Research Bulletin No. 51,* "Consolidated Financial Statements" (New York: AICPA, 1959), par. 13. Also reproduced in FASB, *Accounting Standards—Current Text* (Norwalk, CT: FASB, sec. C51.114).

either by the parent or other subsidiaries, the effects produced on consolidated statements are again essentially the same. However, when neither condition prevails, the allocated amounts from applying the two methods often continue to diverge, in some instances materially, depending upon the dividend policy of the parent company.

In the following example, consolidated balance sheets are prepared both on the date of bilateral affiliation and on a subsequent date.

Case 7. Treasury Stock Method

On January 1, 19X1, P Company purchased 80 percent of the capital stock (par $100) of Y Company concurrent with the latter's purchase of 20 percent of the capital stock (par $100) of P Company. The balance sheets of each company after the investment transactions are illustrated in the following table:

	P Company	Y Company
Assets		
Investments in corporate stock:		
P Company		$ 50,000
Y Company	$120,000	
Other assets	170,000	95,000
Total assets	$290,000	$145,000
Equities		
Liabilities	$ 10,000	$ 5,000
Capital stock	200,000	100,000
Retained earnings	80,000	40,000
Total equities	$290,000	$145,000

A consolidated balance sheet on this date using the treasury stock method follows:

P COMPANY AND SUBSIDIARY
Consolidated Balance Sheet
(Treasury Stock Method)
January 1, 19X1

Assets

Other assets		$265,000
Other assets (differential)		8,000
Total assets		$273,000

Equities

Liabilities		$ 15,000
Minority interest:		
Capital stock, Y Company	$ 20,000	
Retained earnings, Y Company	8,000	28,000

P COMPANY AND SUBSIDIARY (continued)

Owner's equity:
Capital stock, P Company:

Issued	$200,000	
Held by Y Company	(40,000)	
Held by nonaffiliates		160,000
Retained earnings:		
P Company retained earnings	$ 80,000	
Less: Premium on treasury stock purchased	(10,000)	70,000
Total equities		$273,000

Note that the traditional allocation solution, incorporating the elimination of Y Company in P Company, would add to the consolidated balance sheet a $6,000 credit differential (contra to the $8,000 debit differential) and reduce consolidated retained earnings to $64,000 (P's retained earnings of $80,000, less the $16,000 investment elimination of Y Company in P Company).

Case 8. Continuation of Case 7

In this example, the data of Case 7 are repeated, adjusted for 19X1 earnings. It is assumed that the net income of each affiliate from its own operations for 19X1 is $30,000, with a corresponding increase in the amount of other assets, and no dividends are paid by either company. Differential amortization is ignored.

A consolidated balance sheet on December 31, 19X1, follows (treasury stock method):

P COMPANY AND SUBSIDIARY
Consolidated Balance Sheet
(Treasury Stock Method)
December 31, 19X1

Assets

Other assets	$325,000
Other assets (differential)	8,000
Total assets	$333,000

Equities

Liabilities		$ 15,000
Minority interest:		
Capital stock, Y Company	$ 20,000	
Retained earnings, Y Company	14,000	34,000
Owner's equity:		
Capital stock, P Company:		
Issued	$200,000	
Held by Y Company	(40,000)	
Held by nonaffiliates		160,000

P COMPANY AND SUBSIDIARY (continued)

Retained earnings:
P Company retained earnings . . . . $134,000 *
   Less: Premium on treasury stock purchased . . . . (10,000)   124,000

Total equities $333,000

* [$80,000 + $30,000 + 80% × $30,000)]

Use of the traditional allocation method yields different allocations of retained earnings between majority and minority shareholders. At acquisition, the following working paper eliminations are made:

	Debit (Credit)	
	P Company in Y Company	*Y Company in P Company*
Capital stock	$ 100,000	$ 40,000
Retained earnings	40,000	16,000
Differential	8,000	(6,000)
Minority interest	(28,000)	
Investment	$(120,000)	$(50,000)

The conventional solution provides for the elimination of the "investment" of Y Company in P Company, in addition to the principal investment elimination of P Company in Y Company. All of Y Company's stockholders' equity is eliminated, with 20 percent reclassified as minority interest. Only 20 percent of P Company's stockholders' equity is eliminated since the remaining 80 percent is properly classified as the equity of the majority shareholders.

The interdependency structure with respect to the allocation of the affiliates' net incomes may be represented as follows:

$$P = \text{Net income of P Company on an equity basis}$$
$$Y = \text{Net income of Y Company on an equity basis}$$

$$P = \$30,000 + 80\%Y$$
$$Y = \$30,000 + 20\%P$$

By substitution and simplification, solution values are as follows:

$$P = \$64,285.71; \quad 80\% \text{ whereof} = \$51,428.57$$
$$Y = \$42,857.14; \quad 20\% \text{ whereof} = \$8,571.43$$

It follows that at December 31, 19X1, the allocation of retained earnings of companies P and Y is as follows:

Consolidated retained earnings ($64,000 + $51,428.57)	$115,428.57
Minority interest expense ($8,000 + $8,571.43)	16,571.43
Total	$132,000.00

In the previously illustrated treasury stock treatment, the following allocation was made:

Consolidated retained earnings (net of premium on treasury stock purchased)	$124,000
Minority interest expense [20% × ($40,000 + $30,000)]	14,000
Total	$138,000

The difference of $6,000 ($138,000 − $132,000) is attributable to the aforementioned alternative of either eliminating 20 percent of the retained earnings of the parent company ($16,000) or charging the premium on the treasury stock ($10,000) against consolidated retained earnings. However, the important difference exhibited in the post-acquisition consolidated balance sheets is the disparity in the relative shares of the remaining retained earnings; this difference is a function of the different allocation ratios inherent in each method.

The allocation differences are magnified as the nonaffiliate shareholder interests in the mutually related affiliates increase; additionally, these differences continue to increase in succeeding consolidated financial statements.[10]

Summary

In this chapter, we considered special consolidation problems, the first of which involves multilevel affiliations. In a multilevel affiliation, a parent company controls a subsidiary which, in turn, controls its own subsidiary, and so on. In preparing consolidated statements, the number of working paper eliminations is expanded. It is convenient to think of these eliminations in stages. Imagine that P Company controls Y Company which, in turn, controls Z Company. In the first stage, the eliminations are *as if* Y Company were merely consolidating its subsidiary Z Company. In the second stage, the eliminations are *as if* P Company were consolidating its subsidiary Y Company.

Additional complexities are introduced by bilateral stockholdings; that is, when a parent controls a subsidiary which owns shares of its parent. The principal problem with

---

[10] A technique incorporating the treasury stock method for calculating consolidated net income and the traditional allocation method for calculating, as supplementary information, minority interest is proposed in Enrico Petri and Ronald Minch, "The Treasury Stock Method and Conventional Method in Reciprocal Stockholdings—An Amalgamation," *The Accounting Review,* April 1974. Its validity, like the validity of the two methods individually, depends upon one's conception of the nature of a transaction wherein the subsidiary acquires the parent's stock.

bilateral stockholdings involves allocating the combined income (and retained earnings) between the majority and minority shareholders. The traditional allocation method of dealing with this problem involves computing the equity method income of all affiliates by solving simultaneous equations (perhaps with the aid of matrix algebra). Consolidated net income is the product of the parent's equity method income and the fraction of parent shares not held by affiliates. An alternative method of allocating combined income assumes that a subsidiary's investment in its parent is, in substance, a treasury stock transaction on the part of the parent.

Questions

1. Define *multilevel affiliation* and illustrate by example (diagram) such an affiliation.
2. In a multilevel affiliation, what method of accounting is used for a subsidiary's 30 percent investment in another affiliate? A 10 percent investment?
3. How is differential amortization recorded by a subsidiary with an investment in another affiliate allocated between majority and minority shareholders?
4. When intercompany profit exists at the second level of a multilevel affiliation, how is minority interest expense calculated if the elimination is allocated pro rata between majority and minority shareholders? If the elimination is allocated wholly against the majority shareholders?
5. A Company is the owner of 55 percent of the outstanding stock of B Company, and B Company holds 60 percent of the shares of C Company. Are consolidated statements justified? What is the criterion to apply in making such a decision?
6. Define *bilateral stockholding* and illustrate by example (diagram) such an affiliation.
7. What is meant by equity basis net incomes of reciprocally related members of an affiliation?
8. Given a situation in which the affiliates of a consolidated entity have reciprocal stockholdings, explain why the sum of the equity basis net incomes exceeds the sum of the affiliates' net incomes from their own operations, notwithstanding the fact that the ultimate determination of majority and minority interests are equal in total to the summed net incomes from the affiliates' own operations.
9. Explain any additional complications in the calculation of consolidated net income that result from a situation in which the bilateral stockholdings involve the parent.
10. How is the elimination of intercompany profits on the transfer of assets complicated by the existence of reciprocal stockholdings?
11. How is differential amortization allocated between majority and minority shareholders in a bilateral stockholding?
12. When the parent company is bilaterally related to one or more of its subsidiaries, what amount is recorded by the parent company to recognize its equity in affiliates?
13. What do you see as the principal advantage of the matrix method over the substitution method in determining the equity basis net incomes of reciprocally related affiliates?
14. How does the determination of minority interests differ between the treasury stock method and the traditional allocation method?

Exercises

Exercise 10–1   (Multilevel Affiliation)

On January 1, 19X1, P Company acquired a 90 percent interest in R Company, R Company acquired an 80 percent interest in S Company, and S Company acquired a 70 percent interest in T Company. Each of the companies earned $5,000 from its own operations during 19X1, except P Company, which as a holding company had no income from operations.

No dividends were paid by any of the affiliates during 19X1. Ignore differentials.

Required:

Calculate consolidated net income for 19X1 using the incremental approach.

Exercise 10–2   (Multilevel Affiliation)

Bravo Company purchased 70 percent of Charlie Company's outstanding stock on January 1, 19X1. Alpha Company purchased 80 percent of Bravo Company's outstanding stock on January 1, 19X2. Each of the three companies earned $10,000 from its own operations during 19X1 and 19X2. Each of the three companies declared annual dividends of $6,000 during 19X1 and 19X2. Each of the three firms had retained earnings of $50,000 on January 1, 19X1.

Assume that differentials are allocated to nonamortizable assets.

Required:

a. What is Alpha Company's purchased equity in Bravo Company's retained earnings on January 1, 19X2?

b. Prepare the entries made on the books of Alpha Company and Bravo Company during 19X2 to account for their interests in affiliates.

c. Calculate consolidated net income for 19X2 using the incremental approach.

d. Calculate consolidated retained earnings at December 31, 19X2.

Exercise 10–3   (Multilevel Affiliation)

On January 1, 19X1, P Company acquired a 90 percent interest in Y Company and Y Company acquired a 70 percent interest in Z Company. In these investment transactions, P Company had a debit differential of $25,000 and Y Company had a debit differential of $15,000. Both differentials were allocated wholly to goodwill, which is to be amortized over a 10-year period.

During 19X1, the companies reported the following incomes from their own operations:

P Company	$30,000
Y Company	20,000
Z Company	10,000

Required:

a. Prepare the entries made on the books of P Company and Y Company at the end of 19X1 to record their equities in affiliates' earnings and differential amortization.

b. Calculate consolidated net income for 19X1 using the incremental approach.

Exercise 10–4   (Intercompany Profit in Multilevel Affiliation)

On January 1, 19X1, P Company purchased 80 percent of the outstanding stock of Y Company and 70 percent of the outstanding stock of Z Company. On the same date, Y Company acquired 20 percent of Z Company's stock.

During 19X1, the companies reported the following incomes from their own operations:

P Company	$40,000
Y Company	30,000
Z Company	20,000

The net income of Z Company for 19X1 contains an element of unconfirmed profit in the amount of $5,000. Uncomfirmed profits are allocated pro rata.

Required:

a. Calculate consolidated net income for 19X1 using the incremental approach.

b. Calculate consolidated net income for 19X1 using the residual approach.

Exercise 10–5   (Intercompany Profit in Multilevel Affiliation)

On January 1, 19X1, Seydel, Inc., purchased 90 percent of White Corporation's outstanding stock and concurrently White Corporation purchased 80 percent of Hanson Company's outstanding stock. On January 2, 19X1, Hanson sold a truck to Seydel for $15,000. The truck had a book value to Hanson of $10,000 and was expected to be useful for another five years.

Each of the three firms reported net income from its own operations of $10,000 during 19X1. Intercompany profit eliminations are allocated pro rata to majority and minority shareholders.

Required:

a. Prepare the working paper entries relating to the truck sale that would be necessary for a consolidated statement working paper for the year ended December 31, 19X1.

b. Calculate consolidated net income for 19X1.

c. Calculate minority interest expense for 19X1.

Exercise 10–6   (Bilateral Stockholdings)

A Company owns 80 percent of the capital stock of B Company, 70 percent of the capital stock of C Company, 60 percent of the capital stock of D Company, and 70 percent of the capital stock of E Company. Additionally, B Company owns 20 percent of the capital stock of C Company, D Company owns 30 percent of the capital stock of

E Company, C Company owns 10 percent of the capital stock of B Company, and E Company owns 20 percent of the capital stock of D Company.

Net incomes from operations in 19X1 were as follows:

Company A	$ 54,000
Company B	30,000
Company C	26,400
Company D	40,000
Company E	39,000
	$189,400

Required:

Using the traditional allocation method, compute consolidated net income for 19X1 and minority interest expense. (*Solution hint:* Draw the affiliation diagram.)

Exercise 10–7   (Bilateral Stockholdings)

The financial facts shown below pertain to corporations R and S that had mutual holdings of capital stock during and at the end of the fiscal year ended December 31, 19X1.

	Corporation	
	R	**S**
Of the issued capital stock:		
R owns	10%	50%
S owns	20%	10%
Net assets (exclusive of investment accounts),		
December 31, 19X1	$540,000	$590,000

There has been no change in the mutual holdings during the year.

Required:

Compute the dollar equity of outside shareholders in the total net assets of R and S, respectively.

(AICPA adapted)

Exercise 10–8   (Bilateral Stockholdings)

P Company owns 80 percent of the capital stock of S Company, and S Company owns 10 percent of the capital stock of P Company. During 19X1, the companies' net incomes from their own operations were as follows:

P Company	$20,000
S Company	15,000

Differentials have been completely amortized in prior years. No dividends were paid by P Company in 19X1.

Required:

a. Using the traditional allocation method, compute consolidated net income for 19X1 and minority interest expense.
b. Using the treasury stock method, compute consolidated net income for 19X1 and minority interest expense.

Exercise 10–9   (Bilateral Stockholdings)

A Company owns 90 percent of the capital stock of B Company, 80 percent of the capital stock of C Company, and 80 percent of the capital stock of D Company. Additionally, C Company owns 80 percent of the capital stock of E Company, and E Company holds 5 percent of the outstanding stock of C Company.

During 19X1, the companies reported the following incomes from their own operations:

A Company	$50,000
B Company	30,000
C Company	32,000
D Company	30,000
E Company	20,000

Required:

Using the traditional allocation method, compute consolidated net income for 19X1 and minority interest expense. (*Hint:* Draw the affiliation diagram.)

Problems

Problem 10–10   (Multilevel Affiliation)

On January 1, 19X1, B Company purchased an 80 percent interest in C Company. A Company purchased a 90 percent interest in B Company on January 1, 19X3. Both A and B utilize the equity method in accounting for their interests in subsidiaries.

Relevant data for 19X3 are as follows:

	A Company	B Company	C Company
Common stock, January 1, 19X3	$200,000	$100,000	$50,000
Retained earnings, January 1, 19X3	100,000	26,000	18,000
Investment in C Company, January 1, 19X3		56,400	
Investment in B Company, January 1, 19X3	120,000		
Net income for 19X3, excluding equity in affiliates' income	20,000	10,000	10,000
Dividends paid in 19X3	10,000	5,000	6,000

Assume both differentials are allocated to Land.

Required:

a. Prepare the working paper entries for consolidated financial statements on January 1, 19X3.

b. Prepare a partial consolidated statement working paper for 19X3.

c. Calculate consolidated net income for 19X3 using the incremental approach.

Problem 10–11   (Multilevel Affiliation)

On January 1, 19X1, P Company acquired an 80 percent interest in Y Company at a cost of $78,000, and Y Company acquired a 90 percent interest in Z Company at a cost of $56,000. The stockholders' equity accounts of the affiliates on this date were the following:

	P Company	Y Company	Z Company
Capital stock	$50,000	$40,000	$20,000
Retained earnings	30,000	20,000	20,000

The differentials are to be allocated wholly to goodwill and are to be amortized over a 10-year period.

Each of the three companies earned $10,000 from its own operations during 19X1 and 19X2. No dividends were paid by any of the affiliates.

Required:

a. Prepare the entries made on the books of P Company and Y Company at the end of 19X2 to record their equities in affiliates' earnings for 19X2 and differential amortization for 19X2.

b. Prepare a partial consolidated statement working paper for the year ended December 31, 19X2. (*Hint:* Make the income statement division eliminations for differential amortization against "net income, excluding equity in affiliates' earnings.")

c. Prepare a calculation of consolidated net income for 19X2 using the incremental approach.

Problem 10–12   (Intercompany Profit in Multilevel Affiliation)

Y Company purchased 80 percent of Z Company's outstanding stock on January 1, 19X1, for $32,000, and on January 1, 19X2, P Company purchased 80 percent of Y Company's stock for $57,600. Each of the three companies earned $20,000 from its own operations during 19X1 and 19X2, and each had capital stock and retained earnings of $10,000 and $30,000, respectively, on January 1, 19X1.

The net income of Z Company for 19X1 contains unconfirmed profits of $5,000, and Z Company's net income for 19X2 contains unconfirmed profits at the end of that year of $2,000. All unconfirmed profits are due to intercompany sales of inventory. Assume that unconfirmed profits are allocated pro rata.

No dividends were paid by the affiliates during 19X1 or 19X2. Differentials, if any, are assumed to be allocated to nonamortizable assets.

Required:

a. Calculate consolidated net income for 19X2
   (1) Using the incremental approach
   (2) Using the residual approach.
b. Calculate the balances at December 31, 19X2, of the two investment accounts.
c. Prepare a partial consolidated statement working paper for the year ended December 31, 19X2. (*Hint:* Make the income statement division eliminations for intercompany profits in beginning and ending inventory against "net income, excluding equity in affiliates' earnings.")

Problem 10–13   (Bilateral Stockholdings)

For the year 19X1, companies X, Y, and Z have net incomes from their own operations of $30,000, $20,000 and $9,500, respectively.

Required:

Using the traditional allocation method, compute the consolidated net income and the minority interest expense for the year 19X1 in each of the following independent cases:

Case 1: X Company has an 80 percent interest in Y Company, and Y Company has a 10 percent interest in X Company.
Case 2: X Company owns 80 percent of the stock of Y Company, Y Company owns 80 percent of the stock of Z Company, and Z Company has a 10 percent interest in Y Company.
Case 3: X Company has a 90 percent interest in Y Company, Y Company has a 60 percent interest in Z Company, and Z Company has a 10 percent interest in X Company.

Problem 10–14   (Intercompany Profit with Bilateral Stockholdings)

On January 1, 19X0, Gregory Company purchased 80 percent of the capital stock of Morris Company and 60 percent of the capital stock of Adams Company. On January 1,

19X1, Morris Company purchased 30 percent of the capital stock of Adams Company. Also on January 1, 19X1, Adams Company purchased 20 percent of the capital stock of Gregory Company.

During 19X1, the net incomes from operations were as follows:

Gregory Company	$42,800
Morris Company	40,000
Adams Company	10,000

Required:

a. Calculate consolidated net income for 19X1.

b. Calculate the interests of the majority and minority shareholders in intercompany profit, assuming that the unconfirmed profit is included in the selling affiliates' 19X1 incomes as follows:

Morris Company	$3,000
Adams Company	2,000

c. Still assuming the existence of the unconfirmed profits, calculate consolidated net income for 19X1 and minority interest expense when the eliminated intercompany profit is allocated

(1) Pro rata to majority and minority shareholders.

(2) Wholly to majority shareholders.

Problem 10–15   (Intercompany Profit with Bilateral Stockholdings)

A diagram depicting the intercompany stock ownership of companies X, Y, and Z on January 1, 19X1, follows:

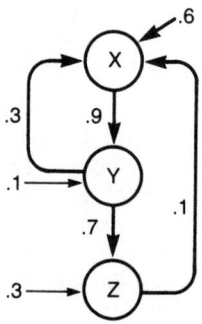

Net incomes from operations for 19X1 were the following:

X Company	$71,000
Y Company	37,600
Z Company	35,400

Y Company's net income includes $3,000 of unconfirmed profit in the ending inventory of X Company; the originating sale was made during 19X1.

Required:

Prepare the working paper entry for unconfirmed profit and calculate consolidated net income and minority interest expense for 19X1 assuming

a. Pro rata allocation of the unconfirmed profit.

b. Allocation of the unconfirmed profit wholly to the majority shareholders.

Problem 10–16   (Traditional and Treasury Stock Methods)

On January 1, 19X1, P Company acquires 90 percent of the capital stock of S Company for $37,000, and S Company acquires 20 percent of the capital stock of P Company for $20,000. The stockholders' equity accounts of the companies on this date were as follows:

	P Company	*S Company*
Capital stock	$20,000	$10,000
Retained earnings	50,000	20,000

The differentials are to be allocated wholly to goodwill and are to be amortized over a 10-year period.

Each company earned $10,000 from its own operations during 19X1, and neither paid any dividends.

Required:

a. Using the traditional allocation method, calculate consolidated net income for 19X1 and minority interest expense.

b. Using the treasury stock method, calculate consolidated net income for 19X1 and minority interest expense.

c. Calculate the values that would be shown for minority interest and stockholders' equity in the December 31, 19X1, consolidated balance sheet under each of the two methods.

Problem 10–17   (Bilateral Stockholdings)

P Company owns 80 percent of S company, and S Company owns 30 percent of P Company. Each company uses the equity method to account for its investments. Trial balances of the two companies are as follows:

	P Company	S Company
Noninvestment Assets	$154,000	$ 73,000
Investment in P		78,316
Investment in S	117,053	
Expenses	20,000	10,000
	$291,053	$161,316
Accounts Payable	$ 10,000	$ 5,000
Capital Stock	100,000	50,000
Retained Earnings (1/1)	90,000	45,000
Sales	50,000	40,000
Equity in P Earnings		21,316
Equity in S Earnings	41,053	
	$291,053	$161,316

Required:

a. Verify that the amounts reported in the two equity method income accounts are correct.

b. Prepare in journal entry format the working paper entries for a three-division working paper.

c. Prepare the three-division consolidated statement working paper.

Problem 10–18   (Treasury Stock Method)

P Company owns 80 percent of S Company, and S Company owns 30 percent of P Company. S Company uses the cost method to account for its investment in P Company. Trial balances of the two companies are as follows:

	P Company	S Company
Noninvestment Assets	$154,000	$ 73,000
Investment in P		57,000
Investment in S	100,000	
Expenses	20,000	10,000
	$274,000	$140,000
Accounts Payable	$ 10,000	$ 5,000
Capital Stock	100,000	50,000
Retained Earnings (1/1)	90,000	45,000
Sales	50,000	40,000
Equity in S Earnings	24,000	
	$274,000	$140,000

Required:

a. Prepare in journal entry format the working paper entries for a three-division consolidated statement working paper assuming the treasury stock method.

b. Prepare the three-division consolidated statement working paper.

Problem 10–19   (Bilateral Stockholdings)

P Company owns 80 percent of R Company. R Company owns 60 percent of S Company. S Company owns 30 percent of P Company. All investments were made on the same date, and all companies use the equity method to account for their investments. Trial balances of the three companies are as follows:

	P Company	R Company	S Company
Noninvestment Assets	$182,000	$ 73,000	$ 85,000
Investment in P			68,972
Investment in R	97,907		
Investment in S		89,383	
Expenses	30,000	30,000	30,000
	$309,907	$192,383	$183,972
Accounts Payable	50,000	40,000	5,000
Capital Stock	100,000	40,000	50,000
Retained Earnings (1/1)	50,000	20,000	45,000
Sales	60,000	60,000	60,000
Equity in P Earnings			23,972
Equity in R Earnings	49,907		
Equity in S Earnings		32,383	
	$309,907	$192,383	$183,972

Required:

a. Verify that the amounts reported in the three equity method income accounts are correct.

b. Prepare in journal entry format the working paper entries for a three-division consolidated statement working paper.

c. Prepare the three-division consolidated statement working paper.

Branch Accounting; Segmental and Interim Reporting

Chapter Outline

Previous chapters in Units I and II of this text dealt exclusively with issues relating to consolidated financial reporting. In this chapter, we address two topics which bear a close relation to consolidated financial reporting. In the first of these, a home office/branch relationship between units of a single legal entity replaces the parent/subsidiary relationship of previous chapters. The second topic is, in many respects, the antithesis of consolidated financial reporting. Consolidated financial reporting involves aggregating financial statements of separate companies. Segmental reporting, on the other hand, involves breaking apart amounts reported on the consolidated statements. This breaking apart process proceeds according to the reporting entity's industrial and geographical activities, and bears no necessary relationship to a simple disaggregation of consolidated amounts into those of a parent and its subsidiaries. In addition to branch accounting and segmental reporting, the chapter addresses issues involved in reporting for periods of time shorter than one year.

BRANCH ACCOUNTING

Major business expansion projects generally entail significant organizational changes. Such expansions often occur through mergers or acquisitions. On other occasions, expansion may be accomplished by the creation of new sales—and perhaps production—outlets to exploit heretofore undeveloped geographic areas or to more intensively cultivate existing markets. In the latter instance, agencies or branch offices are often the optimal organizational forms.

Agencies and Branches

Although both the agency and the branch office are vehicles for enlarging sales volume, they exhibit a number of significant operational differences. An agency usually carries sample or display merchandise and accepts orders for delivery by the home office only. The credit status of prospective buyers is appraised by the home office; and the customers' remittances are normally made to the home office. On the other hand, a branch normally carries a full complement of merchandise, makes the usual warranties respecting quality, makes collections of accounts receivable, and functions in many respects as an autonomous and formally structured business unit.

Although these characteristics are descriptive in general terms of the typical agency and branch, it is not unusual to find compromise forms of business subdivisions. On occasions, the agency may carry a full line of merchandise, make collections of accounts receivable, or otherwise accept responsibilities normally reserved to the branch. Similarly, a branch may sometimes be denied some of the autonomy of operation previously noted.

The extent of branch self-management is a function of corporate policy in regard to decentralized operating and administrative control. Although different branches within the same company may be accorded different degrees of administrative authority, the status of each branch as an operating subdivision is usually established by general standards which extend company wide.

The data accumulation process for the operations of agencies does not introduce any new accounting problems because an agency is essentially little more than an extension of existing sales territories. Consequently, the discussion that follows is confined to accounting for branches. As will become apparent, most of the special aspects of branch accounting are analogous to concepts and procedures previously discussed in our coverage of consolidated financial statements.

Branch Accounts

Branch accounting is essentially an application of the controlling account principle in which the subsidiary records are those of a reasonably independent operating unit. With respect to transactions with the branch, it is conventional for the home office to adopt an account terminology that clearly identifies and describes branch operations. The accounts are selected on the basis of expected frequency of use, their relevance to branch operations, and their contribution to overall accounting control. The general ledger controlling account is variously referred to as Branch Current, Branch Account, or Investment in Branch.

Equivalence of debit and credit balances is preserved in the branch ledger by the use of a Home Office Current account, which is reciprocal to the Branch Current account. The Home Office Current account has a number of properties that traditionally characterize a proprietorship account, particularly with respect to the branch closing process; branch profits and losses are periodically closed to this account. However, viewed more precisely, the account has no special identity, and its balance is perhaps best described as merely the algebraic sum of all other account balances in the branch ledger.

The Branch Current account is normally charged with the cost of assets or services contributed to the branch by the home office and is credited with remittances from the branch. Periodically, the account is adjusted to give effect to branch net income or loss. When there are numerous branches, the use of separate current accounts for each branch is often desirable. Although there is no evident consensus as to the specific accounts most appropriate for inclusion in the branch records, it is usual to find only accounts most closely allied with branch operations, such as those which relate to sales, accounts receivable, inventories, expenses incurred by the branch, and so forth. It is not uncommon to find the accounts for the branch fixed assets in the home office records; yet, depreciation expense may be recorded by the branch making use of the property. In some instances, other expenses incurred by the home office that are in support of branch operations may also be allocated to the benefiting branch. Notice of such expense assignment should be given the relevant branch for purposes of entry in the branch records. Such an identification of expenses with specific branches makes it possible to measure more accurately the operating efficiency of each branch as an independent entity. Those expenses incurred by the home office for the benefit of several branches that do not accommodate to convenient allocation, however, are best reflected in aggregates in combined financial statements of the branches and the home office. If expenses applicable to one or more branches are not formally assigned to (and recorded by) the branches, these expenses are usually charged against the branch net income or loss recorded by the home office in its closing process.

Illustrative Entries

The following transactions relate to the establishment of a branch and its first month's operations:

1. Cash is transferred to the branch, $1,000.
2. Merchandise costing $5,000 is shipped to the branch. Billing of home office shipments to the branch is at cost.
3. Expenses are incurred and paid by the branch, $200.
4. Additional merchandise, costing $2,500, is acquired by the branch from outside wholesalers.
5. Branch credit sales are $8,000.
6. Branch collections on account amount to $4,700.
7. Cash remitted by the branch to the home office is $1,000.
8. Closing entries are prepared by the branch; a monthly operating summary is submitted to the home office. The month-end branch inventory is $1,800.

Journal entries for these transactions are recorded on the books of the home office and the branch in Illustration 11–1. Additional entries by the home office are necessary to close the revenue and expense accounts from its own operations. It should be noted that the Shipments to Branch account (on the home office books) is a contra account to Purchases or Cost of Goods Manufactured on the books of the home office; consequently, it necessarily *always* reflects the *cost* of goods shipped and is closed at the end of the accounting period. Similarly, the Shipments from Home Office account (on the branch books) is equivalent to a Purchases account and accordingly reflects the intracompany billing price; it also is closed at the end of the accounting period. These reciprocal accounts are used for the purpose of maintaining accounting control of intracompany merchandise shipments.

At completion of a period of branch operations, it is customary for the branch to render operating and position statements to the home office, supported in most instances by transaction details in respect to branch inventories and the Home Office Current account. The latter information may be especially useful for foreign branches or where there are numerous cash remittances to and from the home office. Once these data are compiled, it is frequently desirable to prepare combined financial statements of the home office and branch.

ILLUSTRATION 11-1   Journal Entries for Branch's First Month of Operations

Home Office Books			*Branch Books*		
(1) Branch Current 1,000			(1) Cash 1,000		
Cash		1,000	Home Office Current		1,000
(2) Branch Current 5,000			(2) Shipments from Home Office 5,000		
Shipments to Branch		5,000	Home Office Current		5,000
			(3) Expenses 200		
			Cash		200
			(4) Purchases 2,500		
			Accounts Payable		2,500
			(5) Accounts Receivable 8,000		
			Sales		8,000
			(6) Cash 4,700		
			Accounts Receivable		4,700
(7) Cash 1,000			(7) Home Office Current 1,000		
Branch Current		1,000	Cash		1,000
(8) Branch Current 2,100			(8) Sales 8,000		
Branch Net Income		2,100	Merchandise Inventory 1,800		
			Purchases		2,500
			Shipments from Home		
			Office		5,000
			Expenses		200
			Income Summary		2,100
			Income Summary 2,100		
			Home Office Current		2,100

Combined Financial Statements

Although the separate statements of the branch and home office disclose useful information relating to the operations of each division, they do not adequately convey important analytical data about the composite business unit. Merely to include in the home office operating statement a single figure for branch net income or loss is not fully informative. Summary disclosures concerning total sales, cost of sales, and operating expenses of the business unit as a whole are often more meaningful than data revealed in the separate statements of the affiliate divisions.

Combined statements of the home office and branch are needed to reflect the effects of transactions of the total business entity with outside interests. Accordingly, the effects of transactions between the home office and branches (or between branches) must be eliminated to avoid overstatement or duplicate measurement in the accounts. Combined statements make use of the *principle of substitution*—the branch's asset, liability, and operating accounts are substituted for the Branch Current account. This is accomplished in a combined statement working paper by *eliminating* the Branch Current account against the Home Office Current account. To the extent that there are evidences in other accounts of intracompany transactions, their effects must also be eliminated. For example, balances found in the reciprocal Shipments to Branch–Shipments from Home Office accounts, and Remittances to Home Office–Remittances from Branch accounts (the latter accounts reflecting periodic cash transfers) must also be eliminated because they represent only the internal movements of company resources. *The eliminating entries are working paper entries only;* accordingly, they are not entered on the books of either the home office or the branch.

One familiar form of combined statement working paper is given in Illustration 11–2. As a basis for this illustration, the trial balance information for the home office and branch of X Company on December 31, 19X1, follows:

	Home Office	Branch
Cash	$ 40,000	$15,000
Accounts Receivable	22,000	20,000
Merchandise (1/1)	15,000	
Branch Current	17,000	
Other Assets	14,000	
Purchases	65,000	9,000
Shipments from Home Office		12,000
Expenses	7,000	4,000
	$180,000	$60,000
Liabilities	$ 8,000	$12,000
Capital Stock	50,000	
Retained Earnings	10,000	
Home Office Current		17,000
Sales	100,000	31,000
Shipments to Branch	12,000	
	$180,000	$60,000
Merchandise (12/31)	$ 10,000	$ 4,000

The working paper is divided into three divisions to accommodate the preparation of the income statement, the retained earnings statement, and the balance sheet. The balances in the reciprocal accounts are eliminated as noted. Observe that the accounts composing cost of goods sold are shown separately on the working paper. Also note that the working paper refers to retained earnings balances of both the home office and the branch. As noted earlier, the branch does not ordinarily accumulate branch profits and losses in a retained earnings account; rather, it records such profits and losses as adjustments in the Home Office Current account, and the beginning balance of "retained earnings" of the branch

ILLUSTRATION 11-2

X COMPANY
Combined Statement Working Paper
For the Year Ended December 31, 19X1

	Home Office	Branch	Eliminations Dr.	Eliminations Cr.	Combined
Income Statement					
Sales	100,000	31,000			131,000
Merchandise (12/31)	10,000	4,000			14,000
Shipments to branch	12,000		(2) 12,000		–0–
Total credits	122,000	35,000			145,000
Merchandise (1/1)	15,000				15,000
Purchases	65,000	9,000			74,000
Shipments from home office		12,000		(2) 12,000	–0–
Expenses	7,000	4,000			11,000
Total debits	87,000	25,000			100,000
Net income	35,000	10,000	12,000	12,000	45,000
Retained Earnings Statement					
Retained earnings 1/1/X1	10,000	–0–			10,000
Net income	35,000	10,000	12,000	12,000	45,000
Retained earnings 12/31/X1	45,000	10,000	12,000	12,000	55,000
Balance Sheet					
Cash	40,000	15,000			55,000
Accounts receivable	22,000	20,000			42,000
Merchandise (12/31)	10,000	4,000			14,000
Branch current	17,000			(1) 17,000	–0–
Other assets	14,000				14,000
	103,000	39,000			125,000
Liabilities	8,000	12,000			20,000
Capital stock	50,000				50,000
Retained earnings	45,000	10,000*	12,000	12,000	55,000
Home office current		17,000	(1) 17,000		–0–
	103,000	39,000	29,000	29,000	125,000

* Increment to Home Office Current due to periodic branch net income.

is always necessarily zero. Accordingly, variation in the balances of the Home Office Current account as found in the combined statement working paper and as reported in the branch's period-end balance sheet may be explained in terms of the branch's periodic profit or loss. However, the working paper format does indicate the total retained earnings for the composite entity at the end of the period, that is, the accumulated earnings of the home office increased or decreased by the branch net profit or loss for the period.

The formal combined statements are easily prepared using the data found in the Combined column of the working paper. The combined statements for X Company are presented in Illustration 11–3.

Branch Billing in Excess of Cost

When the home office ships merchandise to the branch, it may elect to bill the branch at a value in excess of cost—either at retail price or at a selected percentage markup on cost. Under either of these conditions, the branch manager frequently is not given complete information concerning the cost of branch shipments. Therefore, net profit as computed by the branch necessarily requires

---

ILLUSTRATION 11–3

X COMPANY
Income Statement
For the Year Ended December 31, 19X1

Sales			$131,000
Cost of sales:			
Merchandise, January 1, 19X1		$15,000	
Purchases		74,000	
		$89,000	
Merchandise, December 31, 19X1		14,000	75,000
Gross margin			$ 56,000
Expenses			11,000
Net income			$ 45,000

X COMPANY
Retained Earnings Statement
For the Year Ended December 31, 19X1

Retained earnings, January 1, 19X1	$10,000
Net income, 19X1	45,000
Retained earnings, December 31, 19X1	$55,000

X COMPANY
Balance Sheet
December 31, 19X1

Assets		Equities	
Cash	$ 55,000	Liabilities	$ 20,000
Accounts receivable	42,000	Capital stock	50,000
Merchandise	14,000	Retained earnings	55,000
Other assets	14,000		
Total assets	$125,000	Total equities	$125,000

adjustment by the home office to the extent of realized intracompany profit; only the intracompany profit in the unsold branch merchandise is deferred. Consider the following transactions that illustrate the accounting consequences of this type of billing:

1. Merchandise costing the home office $4,000 is billed to the branch at $5,000. The branch is not informed of the merchandise cost.
2. One half of the above shipment is sold by the branch for $3,000.
3. The branch closes its books and reports its net income to the home office.

The journal entries for these transactions, as recorded on the books of the home office and branch, appear in Illustration 11–4.

The net income calculation of the branch is based upon the transfer price of the merchandise. The home office, possessed of complete information about intracompany billing, is able to make appropriate adjustment for the intracompany inventory profit. That amount of the profit on the original shipment subsequently *confirmed* by branch sales is appropriately transferred in the home office closing process to branch net income. The amount of profit identified with unsold branch merchandise is reserved as a credit in the Intracompany Inventory Profit account until the relevant units are sold. The balance in the Intracompany Inventory Profit account should be reported as a deduction from the balance in the Branch Current account in the balance sheet of the home office. In combined statements prepared before closing, the Intracompany Inventory Profit account is eliminated as a part of the Shipments to Branch–Shipments from Home Office elimination and accordingly does not appear as an extended value in the combined statement working paper. Additionally, the unconfirmed profit in the ending inventory of the branch is eliminated.

Illustrative Problem

The following illustrative problem introduces a combined statement working paper involving residual intracompany inventory profit. The trial balances of the home office and branch on December 31, 19X1, are as follows:

	Home Office	Branch
Cash	$ 40,000	$ 15,000
Accounts Receivable	22,000	20,000
Merchandise (1/1)	15,000	12,000
Branch Current	53,000	
Other Assets	14,000	50,000
Purchases	65,000	9,000
Shipments from Home Office		36,000
Expenses	7,000	4,000
	$216,000	$146,000

ILLUSTRATION 11-4 Journal Entries for Intracompany Inventory Shipments with Transfer Prices in Excess of Cost

Home Office Books

(1)	Branch Current	5,000	
	Shipment to Branch (at cost)		4,000
	Intracompany Inventory Profit		1,000
(3)	Branch Current	500	
	Branch Net Income		500
	Intracompany Inventory Profit	500	
	Branch Net Income		500

Branch Books

(1)	Shipments from Home Office		
	(at billing Price)	5,000	
	Home Office Current		5,000
(2)	Accounts Receivable	3,000	
	Sales		3,000
(3)	Merchandise Inventory	2,500	
	Sales	3,000	
	Shipments from Home Office		5,000
	Income Summary		500

	Home Office	Branch
Liabilities	$ 18,000	$ 12,000
Capital Stock	50,000	
Retained Earnings	10,000	
Home Office Current		53,000
Sales	100,000	81,000
Shipments to Branch	30,000	
Intracompany Inventory Profit	8,000	
	$216,000	$146,000
Merchandise (12/31)	$ 10,000	$ 4,800

The home office bills all shipments to the branch at 20 percent above cost. The branch's beginning and ending inventories consist exclusively of merchandise purchased from the home office.

The combined statement working paper for this problem is shown in Illustration 11–5. Observe that the beginning inventory of the branch, $12,000, is profit inflated to the extent of $2,000. This amount must be eliminated from both the Merchandise (1/1) and Intracompany Inventory Profit accounts. Similarly, Shipments from Home Office, $36,000, contains a profit factor of $6,000, which reconciles the contra shipment accounts. It is important that the reciprocal shipment accounts be eliminated, together with the residual $6,000 of intracompany inventory profit. Finally, there remains an elimination of the profit element in the final inventory of the branch. The branch inventory, $4,800, contains $800 of intracompany profit. It is sufficient to make this elimination by merely reducing the inventory value as it appears in the income statement division and also as it appears in the balance sheet division of the combined statement working paper.

In journal entry format, these working paper entries are as follows:

1.	Home Office Current	53,000	
	Branch Current		53,000
2.	Intracompany Inventory Profit	2,000	
	Merchandise (1/1)		2,000
3.	Intracompany Inventory Profit	6,000	
	Shipments to Branch	30,000	
	Shipments from Home Office		36,000
4.	Merchandise (12/31—income statement)	800	
	Merchandise (12/31—balance sheet)		800

ILLUSTRATION 11–5

X COMPANY
Combined Statement Working Paper
For the Year Ended December 31, 19X1

	Home Office	Branch	Eliminations Dr.		Eliminations Cr.		Combined
Income Statement							
Sales	100,000	81,000					181,000
Merchandise (12/31)	10,000	4,800	(4)	800			14,000
Shipments to branch	30,000		(3)	30,000			–0–
Total credits	140,000	85,800					195,000
Merchandise (1/1)	15,000	12,000			(2)	2,000	25,000
Purchases	65,000	9,000					74,000
Shipments from home office		36,000			(3)	36,000	–0–
Expenses	7,000	4,000					11,000
Total debits	87,000	61,000					110,000
Net income	53,000	24,800		30,800		38,000	85,000
Retained Earnings Statement							
Retained earnings 1/1/X1	10,000	–0–					10,000
Net income	53,000	24,800		30,800		38,000	85,000
Retained earnings 12/31/X1	63,000	24,800		30,800		38,000	95,000
Balance Sheet							
Cash	40,000	15,000					55,000
Accounts receivable	22,000	20,000					42,000
Merchandise (12/31)	10,000	4,800			(4)	800	14,000
Branch current	53,000				(1)	53,000	–0–
Other assets	14,000	50,000					64,000
	139,000	89,800					175,000
Liabilities	18,000	12,000					30,000
Capital stock	50,000						50,000
Retained earnings	63,000	24,800*		30,800		38,000	95,000
Home office current		53,000	(1)	53,000			–0–
Intracompany inventory profit	8,000		(2)	2,000			–0–
			(3)	6,000			
	139,000	89,800		91,800		91,800	175,000

* Increment to Home Office Current due to periodic branch net income.

Reconciling Adjustments

All intracompany reciprocal account balances must be eliminated in the preparation of a combined financial statement for the branch and home office. Sometimes these accounts will *not* carry equivalent balances on specified statement dates. It is accordingly necessary to determine the reason(s) for the discrepancies and to make adjustments to establish reciprocity prior to making the eliminating entries. The following are three common sources of difference between the Branch Current account and the Home Office Current account:

1. End-of-period billings by the home office for the branch's share of expenses recorded on the books of the home office that have not been recorded by the branch.
2. Cash remittances in transit between the branch and the home office (or vice versa) that have not been recorded in the same accounting period by the recipient entity.
3. Merchandise shipments in transit between the home office and the branch (or vice versa) that have not been recorded in the same accounting period by the recipient entity.

Identification of these and other sources of discrepancy between the Branch Current and Home Office Current accounts is accomplished by reviewing records of end-of-period transactions as recorded on both sets of books and on occasion by reconciling recorded figures. For example, if all of the branch's acquisitions of merchandise are shipments from the home office, the total merchandise accounted for by the branch (as reflected by the sum of its cost of sales and ending inventory) should equal the value of merchandise made available to it during the period (as reflected by the sum of its beginning inventory and the value of shipments from the home office). These reconciling adjustments may be entered on the combined statement working paper in the same manner as the other working paper entries; they are, however, usually identified by a different system of indexing.

Interbranch Shipments of Merchandise

Economic conditions may sometimes make it necessary for one branch to ship merchandise previously received from the home office to another branch. In such a circumstance, it is important that each branch record the transaction so as to give appropriate recognition to the effect produced *on the home office books*. For example, the receiving branch should debit the accounts of the assets received and credit the Home Office Current account; similarly, the shipping branch should reduce by appropriate entries both its Home Office Current account and the accounts for the assets transferred. It is unusual for branches to carry current accounts with other branches; rather, interbranch transactions are ordinarily analyzed in terms of accountability to the home office.

Freight on assets transferred by the home office to a branch is properly included as an element of asset cost to the receiving branch. However, when assets are shipped from one branch to another, it is appropriate to include in the cost of the asset only that amount of freight that would have been paid had the shipment been directed originally from the home office to the ultimate branch recipient. Payments in excess of this amount are normally charged to expense by the home office, the assumption being that the home office is at least nominally responsible for the excess charge resulting from indirect routing.

Freight on branch shipments is illustrated below. It is assumed that merchandise costing the home office $1,000 is shipped to Branch A. Freight on this shipment, $80, is paid by the home office. Subsequently, these goods are shipped to Branch B, with the payment of additional freight of $40 by Branch A. It is determined that direct routing from the home office to Branch B would have resulted in an aggregate freight cost of $100. Entries for these transactions are as follows:

Home Office

Branch A Current	1,080	
Shipments to Branch A		1,000
Cash		80
Shipments to Branch A	1,000	
Shipments to Branch B		1,000
Branch B Current	1,100	
Excess Freight on Branch Transshipment	20	
Branch A Current		1,120

Branch A

Shipments from Home Office	1,000	
Freight-In	80	
Home Office Current		1,080
Home Office Current	1,120	
Shipments from Home Office		1,000
Freight-In		80
Cash		40

Branch B

Shipments from Home Office	1,000	
Freight-In	100	
Home Office Current		1,100

Other Accounting Systems

On occasion, the home office may elect to centralize the accounting for all branch operations within the structure of home office records. This may result in the creation of a separate set of accounts to identify the details of branch operations, or these operations may be subsumed in the same system of accounts as are used in nonbranch transactions. In either circumstance, the documentary evidences of all branch transactions must be regularly submitted to the home office for entry. Such a system is not essentially unlike that used for agencies.

On other occasions, the accounting system may take the form of a complete record-keeping by *both* branch and home office with respect to all branch transactions. Necessarily, this duplication has disadvantages. Yet the more complete dissemination of accounting information may, in fact, promote greater operating efficiencies in the administrative decentralization than the added cost of maintaining duplicate records appears to indicate.

SEGMENTAL REPORTING

A number of advantages and risks are associated with diversified business operations. The natural growth of prospering firms has often led to internally generated diversification as well as surges of diversification by the *external* process of business combination.

It should be recognized that the unique accounting problems of reporting the operations of highly diversified businesses are not confined to combined corporate entities. Nevertheless, the processes of combining business enterprises frequently give rise to special accounting problems associated with reporting the results of diversified business activity. An obvious objective of many combinations is diversification. As a consequence, a rounded examination of accounting for combined business entities must include reference to the special problems of accounting for diversified business entities.

The Need for Segmental Reports

The basic advantages and limitations associated with consolidated statements were outlined in Chapter 2. Compared with the alternative of presenting only the parent's financial statements, consolidated statements have uniquely important informational significance. These reports clearly are a primary source of information for anyone concerned with the operations and financial position of the parent's sphere of control. It should be understood that the interest in, and need for, more detailed reporting on diversified companies does not negate the need for consolidated reports. The movement toward more detailed reporting is rather an *expansion* of the basic consolidated information. Reports that cover significant segments of a diversified firm should be perceived, therefore, as complementary to the consolidated statements. In fact, the method of reporting on segments may involve simply expanding the consolidated statements to include more detail within these statements.

Taken alone, consolidated financial statements do not provide sufficient information regarding the various types of business activity undertaken by the consolidated entity. Revenues, expenses, and assets may be associated with vastly disparate operations; yet they are aggregated and reported in total. It should be apparent that decisions concerning widely diversified firms can often be facilitated by information as to the relative significance to the firm of distinct subunit operations. A prominent study defines a diversified company in a manner that emphasizes these informational needs.

> A diversified company is . . . a company which either is so managerially decentralized, so lacks operational integration, or has such diversified markets that it may experience rates of profitability, degrees of risk, and opportunities for growth which vary within the company to such an extent that an investor requires information about these variations in order to make informed decisions.[1]

It is not possible to specify the precise role played by segmental reports in the decision process of investors. Nevertheless, the need for such information on diversified firms has become widely recognized.

Beginning in 1969, segmental information was required in certain reports filed with the SEC. Currently, the primary requirements for reporting segmental information are contained in FASB *Statement No. 14.* In general, enterprises are required to disclose segmental information whenever they issue a complete set of financial statements that present financial position at the fiscal year-end and results of operations for that year in conformity with generally accepted accounting principles.[2] In *Statement No. 21,* the FASB exempted nonpublic enterprises from the segmental reporting requirements. Also, when an enterprise's financial statements are presented in another enterprise's financial report (i.e., the primary reporting enterprise) and certain limiting conditions are satisfied, FASB *Statement No. 24* eliminates the requirements for the financial statements so included (but not for the primary reporting enterprise). Finally, *Statement No. 18* exempted interim financial statements from segmental reporting requirements.[3]

Identifying Significant Segments of a Firm

Several alternative ways of segmenting a diversified firm may result in reports that have informational significance to investors. Three important alternatives are (1) geographical divisions, (2) product line or industrial divisions, and (3) divisions

---

[1] R. K. Mautz, *Financial Reporting by Diversified Companies* (New York: Financial Executives Research Foundation, 1968), pp. 7–8.

[2] FASB, *Statement of Financial Accounting Standards No. 14,* "Financial Reporting for Segments of a Business Enterprise" (Norwalk, CT: FASB, 1976), par. 3.

[3] FASB, *Statement of Financial Accounting Standards No. 21,* "Suspension of the Reporting of Earnings per Share and Segment Information by Nonpublic Enterprises" (Norwalk, CT: FASB, 1978), par. 12; FASB, *Statement of Financial Accounting Standards No. 24,* "Reporting Segmental Information in Financial Statements That Are Presented in Another Enterprise's Financial Report" (Norwalk, CT: FASB, 1978), par. 5; and FASB, *Statement of Financial Accounting Standards No. 18,* "Financial Reporting for Segments of a Business Enterprise—Interim Financial Statements" (Norwalk, CT: FASB, 1977), par. 7.

that conform to the internal structure of managerial control. Of course, other possible bases for segmenting a firm's operations may have significance, particularly in specific industries. For example, a division between government and private operations might provide especially relevant information for firms such as those engaged in defense contracting.

Arguments can be marshaled in support of each of the three primary alternatives mentioned above. As a general rule, the necessary data can probably be accumulated most accurately and at the smallest additional cost when the basis for division conforms to the internal structure of managerial control. On the other hand, segmentation that meaningfully reflects differences in profitability, degrees of risk, and growth opportunities frequently follows the product lines or industrial categories in which a firm is active. Of course, for many enterprises, the industrial classification would conform fairly closely to the above-mentioned managerial units of control. A geographical basis of segmentation may be highly informative for some companies, particularly in its ability to accent important distinctions between domestic and foreign operations.

FASB *Statement No. 14* calls for the information to be presented on each of three items:

a. The enterprise's operations in different industries.

b. Its foreign operations and export sales.

c. Its major customers.[4]

With respect to item (*b*), if the export sales of the domestic operations are significant in amount, they should be reported in the aggregate and by appropriate geographical areas. Such sales are considered significant if they amount to 10 percent or more of the company's consolidated sales.[5]

Foreign operations are identified as operations that are located in foreign countries *and* that generate revenue from sales to unaffiliated customers or from intraenterprise sales or simply from transfers between geographical areas. Without specifying the criteria by which foreign operations in different countries should be grouped, *Statement No. 14* indicates that foreign geographical areas may consist of one or more countries and requires that certain information be presented separately for each significant geographical area and in the aggregate for those geographical areas which are not individually significant. A geographical area is deemed to be significant if its revenues from unaffiliated customers or its identifiable assets are 10 percent or more of the related consolidated amounts.[6]

Given these definitions, *Statement No. 14* requires that for domestic operations and for each foreign geographical area, the following information be reported: (1) sales to unaffiliated customers, (2) intraenterprise sales and transfers between geographical areas, (3) operating profit (loss) or net income or some other

---

[4] FASB, *Statement No. 14*. par. 3.

[5] Ibid., par. 36.

[6] Ibid., pars. 331–34.

measure of profitability between operating profit (loss) and net income, and (4) identifiable assets.[7]

Regarding major customers, the fact and the amount of revenue to each major customer must be reported. The customers need not be individually identified by name, but the industry segment or segments making the sales must be identified. A major customer is one to whom sales equal 10 percent or more of the company's total sales. If several entities are under common control, they are "regarded as a single customer, and the federal government, a state government, a local government . . . or a foreign government [are each] considered as a single customer."[8]

In addition to the above types of information, FASB *Statement No. 14* calls for a system of segmental reporting based upon an industrial segmentation of the entity. Reporting based on industrial segments closely parallels reporting based on geographical areas. Sales to unaffiliated customers and sales or transfers to other industrial segments are reported, as are operating profits or losses and identifiable assets. In addition, depreciation, amortization, and additions to property, plant, and equipment are disclosed for each reportable industry segment. If the operations of an investee accounted for under the equity method are vertically integrated with those of a reportable segment, that fact is also disclosed.[9]

Identifying the industrial segments of a firm requires that its products and services be grouped by industrial lines. The definition of an "industry segment" requires that its sales be primarily to unaffiliated customers. In identifying the segments, attention should be given to the nature of the products produced, the nature of the production process involved, and the markets and marketing methods employed to sell the products. Differences in these factors help to identify different segments.[10]

A problem relating to the selection of a basis for segmentation is to determine how finely segmented the reports should be. Addressing this question, the FASB stated that an entity should present reports on each industry segment for which one or more of the following tests are satisfied during the year for which financial statements are to be presented:

(A) Its revenue (including both sales to unaffiliated customers and intersegment sales or transfers) is 10 percent or more of the combined revenue (sales to unaffiliated customers and intersegment sales or transfers) of all of the enterprise's industry segments.

(B) The absolute amount of its operating profit or operating loss is 10 percent or more of the greater, in absolute amount, of:

    (i) The combined operating profit of all industry segments that did not incur an operating loss, or

---

[7] Ibid., par. 35.

[8] FASB, *Statement of Financial Accounting Standards No. 30,* "Disclosures of Information about Major Customers" (Norwalk, CT: FASB, 1979), par. 6.

[9] FASB *Statement No. 14,* pars. 23–27.

[10] Ibid., pars. 10–14, 100.

(ii) The combined operating loss of all industry segments that did incur an operating loss.

(C) Its identifiable assets are 10 percent or more of the combined identifiable assets of all industry segments.[11]

For example, consider the following data relating to a firm with five segments:

Segment	Revenue (Including Intersegment Sales)	Operating Profit	Operating Loss	Identifiable Assets
A	$1,000	$ 200		$ 2,000
B	2,000	250		4,000
C	1,500	600		6,000
D	150	75		600
E	50		$25	400
Totals	$4,700	$1,125	$25	$13,000

The revenues (including intersegment sales) of segments A, B, and C are all 10 percent or more of the combined revenues of $4,700. Accordingly, segments A, B, and C are reportable segments. The revenues of segments D and E are not at least 10 percent of $4,700. Moreover, the absolute values of the operating profits of neither D nor E are at least 10 percent of $1,125 (the greater of segmental operating profits and segmental operating losses). Finally, the identifiable assets of neither D nor E are at least 10 percent of $13,000. Thus, segments A, B, and C are the only reportable segments. Revenues, operating profits, and identifiable assets of segments D and E can be combined and reported in an "other" category.

The FASB recognized that abnormal results for a single period may result in a segment meeting one of the 10 percent tests when past periods and future expectations do not support separate reporting of the segment. In such a case, the segment need not be reported. Alternatively, a normally significant segment may happen to fail the tests in a single year, in which case it should be treated as a reportable segment. Also, if a single segment accounts for more than 90 percent of the firm's revenue, operating profit or loss, and identifiable assets, but no other industry segment meets any of the 10 percent tests previously mentioned, reports for that segment need not be presented separate from the consolidated statements for the firm as a whole.[12]

On the other hand, some firms consist of many small segments, most of which may not meet the 10 percent tests listed above. To ensure that a substantial portion of a firm's operations be presented in segmental reports, *Statement No. 14*

---

[11] Ibid., par. 15.
[12] Ibid., pars. 16, 20

requires that the reports on specific segments should disclose at least 75 percent of the combined revenue from sales to unaffiliated customers. Otherwise, additional industry segments should be identified as reportable segments until the 75 percent test is met.[13]

The SEC apparently concluded that in following the FASB's rules, many firms were not dividing their operations into enough segments. As a consequence, *Accounting Series Release No. 244* was issued. That *Release* discusses the segmentation problem at some length but does not proclaim additional rules for segmentation. Instead, it warns managements to make sure that their segmental disclosures include enough segments to most usefully assist investors in analyzing the registrants' businesses.[14] In essence, the matter of defining segments remains quite subjective, but the SEC stands ready to question and even reject a company's financial statements if they fail to reflect reasonable, informative disclosures according to the FASB's rules.

Intersegmental Transfer Pricing

An important problem that must be resolved for the purposes of segmental reporting is the pricing of intrafirm transfers of goods and services between reporting segments. Some segments may exist entirely for the purpose of providing goods or services to outside customers. Others may be concerned with outside sales *and* intrafirm transfers. To the extent that transfers are made between segments, the reported profits of both the *selling* and *purchasing* segments are directly affected by the prices at which the transfers are recorded.

An ideal basis for setting transfer prices would be the independent market prices for the same goods and services, given a perfectly competitive market. However, good approximations of these conditions rarely exist. One is more likely to discover highly imperfect markets for goods or services that are transferred between segments within an enterprise. Independent market prices for similar goods (given a sensitivity to the quantities being sold) would, however, be a reasonable basis for recording transfer prices whenever such information is available.

As a practical matter, it is perhaps impossible to select a single basis for transfer pricing that would be best in all situations. The FASB *Statement* apparently recognizes this difficulty and simply concludes that the transfer prices used should be those which are used by the company to price the intersegment sales or transfers.[15]

---

[13] Ibid., pars. 17–18.

[14] Securities and Exchange Commission, *Securities Act Release No. 5910, Securities Exchange Act Release 14523*, "Interpretations, Guidelines and Administrative Determinations of the Commissions's Staff Regarding Classification by Registrants of Their Business into Industry Segments" (Washington, DC: SEC March 3, 1978).

[15] FASB, *Statement No. 14*, par. 10.

Allocating Common Costs and Measuring Segmental Profitability

Regardless of the means by which a firm is divided into subunits for reporting purposes, some expenses are common to two or more of the reporting segments. Typical examples of such expenses include interest, income taxes, top-management compensation, and general corporate administrative expenses. Depending on the nature of the company's operations, many of the noninventoried expenses may be at times common to more than one subunit.

The allocation of common costs to reporting segments is constrained by two conflicting objectives. On the one hand, the bases of allocation should not be arbitrary. Given this single objective, the accountant would be led to leave many common costs unallocated. Allocations that are patently arbitrary may result in the data being more misleading than informative. On the other hand, one of the primary objectives of segmental reporting is to provide information concerning each segment's contribution to the profitability of the firm. When common costs remain unallocated, this objective is only partially fulfilled.

The ability to allocate most common costs depends largely upon the organization and operating procedures of each firm. Consequently, *general rules* of allocation are very difficult to prescribe. And there exist some common expenses (and revenues) for which reasonable allocations between segments are virtually impossible.

In regard to calculating the *operating profit or loss* of each segment, FASB *Statement No. 14* concludes that nine specific items should not be allocated to segments. They are (1) revenue earned at the corporate level but not from the operations of an industry segment; (2) general corporate expenses; (3) interest expense, unless it refers to a segment whose operations are essentially financial in nature; (4) income taxes; (5) equity in income or loss from unconsolidated subsidiaries and other unconsolidated investees; (6) gain or loss on discontinued operations; (7) extraordinary items; (8) minority interest expense; and (9) the cumulative effect of a change in an accounting principle.[16] On the other hand, the *Statement* does not preclude the possibility of presenting additional measures of segmental profitability (other than operating profit) that would involve allocating some or all of the nine items listed above.

Identifying Segmental Assets

Adequate evaluation of segmental performance requires that the operating profit of each segment be related to the investment of resources in segmental operations. However, a complete balance sheet for each segment obviously cannot be prepared. Corporate equities (including liabilities) generally represent undivided interests in the entire net assets of the business, notwithstanding the fact that some may enjoy special rights in the event of insolvency. The measurement of

---

[16] Ibid., par. 10.

segmental investment is therefore limited to an allocation of assets between the reporting segments.

Some assets are easily identified with a specific segment because they are used exclusively by that segment. Other assets are shared by more than one segment, and a reasonable basis of determining each segment's usage must be identified and used to allocate the assets between the segments.

A few assets such as cash, marketable securities, and other assets that are used at the company's central office should not be allocated to industry segments. Also, the assets identified with a segment should not include investments accounted for by the equity method. This is consistent with the requirement that earnings from equity method investments not be included in the revenues or operating profits of a segment. However, if an unconsolidated subsidiary or other equity method investee is vertically integrated into the operations of a segment, separate disclosure must be made of the enterprise's equity in the net income from the investment and in the net assets of the investee.[17]

An Example of Segmental Reporting

Illustration 11–6 presents an example of segmental reports and related footnotes for a broadly diversified firm. Operations of the firm include activities other than those disclosed as electronics, chemicals, and machine manufacturing. However, none of these other activities satisfied the 10 percent tests of a reportable segment listed by the FASB.

The procedures necessary to prepare such reports depend in large part on the nature of the internal accounting system employed by the firm. Segmental reports may be virtually complete as a consequence of maintaining administrative and budgetary control within the firm. A major factor necessarily is the degree of similarity between reporting segments and the internal structure of control.

INTERIM REPORTING

The term *interim reporting* refers to reporting for periods shorter than an annual accounting period (e.g., monthly or quarterly periods). Although interim reports can include all three basic financial statements, our focus is on issues relating to reporting results of operations on an interim basis. Public companies report abbreviated quarterly results of operations. Such reports normally include revenues, provision for income taxes, net income, and earnings per share data. Any special income statement items, such as extraordinary items, discontinued operations, and the cumulative effect of a change in accounting principle, are included as well. Normally, these items are reported for the current quarter of the current

---

[17] Ibid., pars. 7, 10, 27.

ILLUSTRATION 11-6

INFORMATION ABOUT THE COMPANY'S OPERATIONS IN DIFFERENT INDUSTRIES

For the Year Ended December 31, 19X1
($000)

	Electronics	Chemicals	Machine Manufacturing	Other Industries	Eliminations	Consolidated
Sales to unaffiliated customers	$1,000	$2,000	$1,500	$ 200		$ 4,700
Intersegment sales	200		500		$(700)	
Total revenue	$1,200	$2,000	$2,000	$ 200	$(700)	$ 4,700
Operating profit	$ 200	$ 290	$ 600	$ 50	$ (40)	$ 1,100
Equity in net income of Electro Company						100
General corporate expenses						(100)
Interest expense						(200)
Income from continuing operations before income taxes						$ 900
Identifiable assets on December 31, 19X1	$2,000	$4,050	$6,000	$1,000	$ (50)	$13,000
Investment in net assets of Electro Company						400
Corporate assets						1,600
Total assets at December 31, 19X1						$15,000

NOTES: The Company operates principally in three industries, electronics, chemicals, and machine manufacturing. The electronics operations involve the development and manufacture of microcircuitry. Chemical operations involve the manufacture of a variety of petroleum based chemicals for industrial usage. Machine manufacturing operations involve the development and manufacture of precision measuring and cutting instruments for industrial usage. Intersegment sales are accounted for at market values.

Operating profit is total revenue less operating expenses. In computing operating profit, none of the following items has been added or deducted: general corporate expenses, interest expense, income taxes, equity in income from unconsolidated investee, loss from discounted operations of the Raychem Division (which was part of the Company's operations in the chemical industry), and an extraordinary gain that occurred in the Machine Manufacturing segment of the Company's operations. Operations in the electronics industry had depreciation of $80 and capital expenditures of $100. In the chemical industry they were $100 and $200, respectively, and in machine manufacturing they were $150 and $400, respectively.

The Company has a 40% interest in Electo Company, whose operations are in the United States and are vertically integrated with the Company's operations in electronics.

Identifiable assets by industry are those assets of the Company that are used exclusively in or are reasonably allocable to operations in each industry. Assets employed at the Company's central administrative office are principally cash and marketable securities.

To reconcile industry information with consolidated amounts, the following eliminations have been made; $700 of intersegment sales; $40 relating to the net change in intersegment operating profit in beginning and ending inventories; and $50 intersegment operating profit in ending inventory.

SOURCE: Adapted from FASB *Statement No. 14*, Appendix F.

year and for the current quarter of the prior year. In addition, year-to-date amounts are reported for the current and prior years. Fourth-quarter results are not normally reported since, as is discussed below, they are generally apparent from the differences between (1) amounts reported for the year and (2) year-to-date amounts reported for the third quarter.

Two Viewpoints from Which to Resolve Interim Reporting Issues

An interim period can be viewed as a *stand-alone* accounting period or as an integral part of an annual accounting period. Income taxation provides a ready example of the difference between these two perspectives. Imagine a firm which earns pretax income uniformly during an annual accounting period. For simplicity, assume that the income tax rate is 10 percent on the first $25,000 of pretax income and 50 percent on any excess over $25,000. During the first quarter, the firm generates $20,000 of pretax earnings. If the first quarter is viewed as a stand-alone accounting period, income tax expense would be computed by applying the rate structure to the $20,000 in first-quarter earnings. Accordingly, net income would be computed as follows:

Income before income taxes	$20,000
Income tax expense (10% × $20,000)	2,000
Net income	$18,000

Income taxation is a distinctively annual phenomenon, and viewing the first quarter as a stand-alone accounting period has diminished the usefulness of first-quarter net income as a predictor of annual net income. Knowing only that the firm's operations are not seasonal and that first-quarter net income is $18,000, a seemingly reasonable prediction of annual net income is $72,000 [$18,000 × 4]. Because of the way income tax expense has been computed, however, $72,000 is not a very good prediction of annual net income. If pretax earnings continue at $20,000 for the remaining three quarters, annual net income will be as follows:

Income before income taxes	$80,000
Income tax expense	
[(10% × $25,000) + (50% × ($80,000 − $25,000))]	30,000
Net income	$50,000

If each of the four quarters is viewed in this stand-alone fashion, $18,000 would be reported for each of the four quarters. Accordingly, the quarterly net income numbers will not sum to annual net income. Or if they are forced to sum to annual net income, the fourth quarter will necessarily contain *catch-up* income tax expense of $24,000 [$30,000 − 3 × $2,000], resulting in a net loss of $4,000

($20,000 − $24,000). This fourth-quarter loss creates the false impression that profitability has suddenly changed for the worse.

In contrast, viewing interim periods as integral portions of the annual accounting period tends to avoid these problems. Under this view, income tax expense for the first quarter would be computed by (1) *forecasting* the average tax rate which will apply to annual pretax earnings and (2) applying this rate to the $20,000 in first-quarter earnings. If annual pretax earnings are expected to be $80,000, then $30,000 in annual income tax expense is expected. Therefore, the forecast of the average tax rate for the year is as follows:

$$\begin{array}{l}\text{Expected} \\ \text{annual} \\ \text{average} \\ \text{rate}\end{array} = \begin{array}{l}\text{Expected annual} \\ \text{income tax expense} \\ \hline \text{Expected annual} \\ \text{pretax income}\end{array} = \frac{\$30{,}000}{\$80{,}000} = 37.5\%$$

When this rate is applied to pretax first-quarter earnings, net income is as follows:

Income before income taxes	$20,000
Income tax expense (37.5% × $20,000)	7,500
Net income	$12,500

On the basis of this $12,500 in first-quarter net income, and knowledge that the firm's operations are not seasonal, a reasonable prediction of annual net income would be $50,000 [$12,500 × 4]. If the $80,000 in annual pretax earnings implicit in the 37.5 percent tax rate calculation indeed materialize, this prediction will be absolutely correct. Moreover, the fourth-quarter net income will not have to be compromised in order for the quarterly net incomes to sum to annual net income. Note, however, that these effects are not achieved without cost. Obtaining them places a forecasting burden on the reporting firm. That is to say, accounting for interim periods requires a forecast of events beyond the end of the interim periods in question.

In its *Opinion No. 28*, the APB decided in favor of viewing an interim period as an integral portion of an annual accounting period.[18] The view was continued by the FASB in its *Statement No. 3*.[19] Remaining sections of this chapter involve implications of viewing interim periods as integral portions of an annual accounting period.

---

[18] APB, *Opinion No. 28*, "Interim Financial Reporting" (New York: AICPA, 1973).

[19] FASB, *Statement of Financial Accounting Standards No. 3*, "Reporting Accounting Changes in Interim Financial Statements" (Norwalk, CT: FASB, 1974).

Income Tax Issues

The preceding example of accounting for income taxes was simplified by the implicit assumption that all accounting income is subject to taxation. More realistically, accounting and taxable income do not coincide. Nonetheless, the basic principle is unaltered. The numerator of the expected annual average rate is whatever income tax expense number is expected to appear on the annual income statement. Differences between accounting and taxable income will cause this number to differ from the expected value of income taxes currently payable. The denominator is expected annual pretax accounting income. Thus, their quotient is a *rate of financial accounting income tax expense per dollar of pretax financial accounting income.*

Additional complexity is introduced by operating losses. One possibility is an operating loss in an interim period with the expectation of annual income. If the firm has an established seasonal pattern of loss in early interim periods offset by income in later interim periods, realization of the tax benefit of the early operating loss is reasonably certain. Accordingly, the tax benefit is reported in the loss period. This tax benefit is calculated by applying the expected annual average rate to the operating loss. For example, assume that a firm expects annual income and an average annual rate of 20 percent. The tax benefit of, say, a $10,000 loss in the first quarter is $2,000 (20% $\times$ $10,000). On the other hand, realization of tax benefit of an early operating loss may not be reasonably certain (e.g., the firm does not normally have a seasonal pattern of early loss followed by income). In such cases, no tax benefit is reported in the loss period. No income tax expense is reported in subsequent periods until year-to-date operations become profitable.

Other possible patterns involve year-to-date income with expectation of an operating loss for the year and year-to-date loss with expectation of an operating loss for the year. In both cases, the numerator of the expected annual average rate is the tax benefit which is expected to appear on the annual income statement, giving due consideration to the firm's carryback/carryforward position. The denominator is the expected operating loss for the year. The rate so computed is then used to allocate tax expense or tax benefit to interim periods.

Costs Associated with Revenue

A firm using LIFO inventory valuation may, at an interim date, liquidate a LIFO layer that is expected to be replaced by year-end. If so, strict adherence to LIFO is abandoned in the interim period. Cost of goods sold for the interim period is based on the expected replacement cost of the liquidated layer.[20] For example, consider the following data relating to the first quarter:

---

[20] *APB Opinion No. 28,* par. 14.

	Units	Unit Cost	Amount
Beginning inventory	300	$1.00	$300
Purchase—February	50	2.50	100

Sales during the first quarter were 75 units. Thus, when the first quarter is viewed as a stand-alone accounting period, 25 units of the beginning LIFO inventory were liquidated. Suppose, however, that the $2.50 current purchase price is expected to prevail throughout the year and that units purchased are expected to exceed units sold *for the year*. Accordingly, cost of goods sold computed on an annual basis includes none of the cost of beginning inventory. Under such conditions, the cost of goods sold for the first quarter is $187.50 ($2.50 × 75), *not* $150 [$2.50 × 50 + $1.00 × 25].

In applying the lower-of-cost-or-market rule, an interim period loss that is expected to be permanent should be reported in the interim period in which the loss occurs. If that loss is recovered as a result of increases in market valuation during the same annual period, a gain is recorded in the interim period in which the recovery occurs. The amount of the gain cannot, however, exceed the loss previously recorded. Interim period losses which are expected to be recovered by the end of the annual period are ignored.[21]

Interim period purchase price, volume, or capacity cost variances that are expected to be absorbed by the end of the annual period are ignored. However, if variances are not expected to be absorbed by the end of the annual period, such variances are reported in the interim period in which they occur.[22]

Other Costs, Special Items, and Earnings per Share

Annual period costs must be allocated to interim periods. The method of allocation should not be arbitrary.[23] If, for example, revenues are used as a basis for allocating annual fixed cost to interim periods, the annual fixed cost becomes variable in interim periods.

For example, assume annual fixed costs of $100,000 and revenues of $200,000 for the first quarter. Also assume that annual revenues are estimated to be $1,600,000. With these assumptions, the amount of annual fixed cost allocated to the first quarter is $12,500 [($200,000/$1,600,000) × $100,000]. If annual revenues unfold according to estimate, fixed cost allocated to the remaining three quarters is $87,500 [($1,400,000/$1,600,000) × $100,000].

---

[21] Ibid., par. 14.

[22] Ibid., par. 14.

[23] Ibid., par. 15.

Extraordinary items and discontinued operations which are of sufficient materiality to be reported separately in the annual income statement are reported separately in interim periods. Contingencies that affect the fairness of presentation of interim data are disclosed in the same fashion required for annual reporting.[24]

Recall from Chapter 5 that the denominator of earnings per share is affected by share prices when the firm's capital structure includes warrants and/or options. Share price fluctuations can therefore result in interim period denominators which differ from one another and also differ from the denominator used for the annual computation. Accordingly, interim earnings per share numbers do not necessarily sum to annual earnings per share.[25]

Variation in the denominators of interim earnings per share can also result from issuing or repurchasing shares during the year. For example, a firm with 1,000 shares outstanding on January 1 which issues an additional 600 shares on March 1 uses 1,200 shares $[1,000(3/3) + 600(1/3)]$ in computing first-quarter earnings per share. Second-, third-, and fourth-quarter computations involve 1,600 shares. In computing annual earnings per share, however, 1,500 shares are used $[1,000(12/12) + 600(10/12)]$. Variation in the denominators of earnings per share due to changes in shares outstanding may also preclude interim results from summing to their annual counterparts.

Accounting Changes

Reporting the cumulative effect of an accounting change presents no special problems if the change occurs during the first quarter. Recall that the cumulative effect reported on the annual income statement is as of the beginning of the change *year*. When the change occurs during the first quarter, the cumulative effect as of the beginning of the change *quarter* equals the amount reported on the annual income statement. All quarterly incomes, as well as annual income, will be reported on the basis of the new accounting method.

Problems arise when the change does not occur during the first quarter. Consider an accounting change during the second quarter. A first-quarter report has already been issued on the basis of the old accounting method. The second-, third-, and any fourth-quarter reports will be on the basis of the new accounting method. Since the annual report will be based on the new accounting method as well, interim earnings will not add to annual earnings. Year-to-date data relating to the first quarter which are reported in the second, third, and fourth quarters can, however, be restated *as if* the change occurred in the first quarter. Interim data

---

[24] Ibid., par. 22.

[25] AICPA, *Interpretation No. 64 of APB Opinion No. 15,* "Total of Quarters May Not Equal EPS" (New York: AICPA, 1970).

restated in this fashion add to their annual counterparts. Such restatements are required by FASB *Statement No. 3.* Assume an accounting change during the second quarter of 19X2. Net income data under the old and new accounting methods are as follows:

	Net Income		
	Old Method	*New Method*	*Difference*
Prior to 19X2	$100,000	$120,000	$20,000
First quarter 19X2	10,000	11,000	1,000
Second quarter 19X2	11,000	13,000	2,000

Since the change is not made until after the first-quarter report is issued, the first-quarter report will include old method net income of $10,000. Moreover, no cumulative effect of the change will be reported. Year-to-date amounts included in the second-quarter report will be restated *as if* the change were made in the first quarter. Net income before cumulative effect of change in accounting principle will be based on the new accounting method, and the cumulative effect of change in accounting principle will be as of the beginning of the first quarter. The second quarter report will appear as follows:

	3 Months Ended June 30, 19X2	*6 Months Ended June 30, 19X2*
Net income before cumulative effect of change in accounting principle	$13,000	$24,000
Cumulative effect of change in accounting principle	–0–	20,000
Net income	$13,000	$44,000

Pro forma disclosures of the 19X1 second-quarter and year-to-date amounts, computed on the basis of the new method, would also be included in the second-quarter 19X2 report.

The effect of a change in accounting estimate is accounted for in the quarter in which the change in estimate is made. No restatement of previously reported interim information is made for changes in estimate. A common change in accounting estimate is an interim revision of beliefs about annual pretax accounting income in conjunction with determination of the expected annual average rate. Accordingly, income tax expense for the quarter in which a revision occurs contains a positive or negative *catch-up* adjustment. The amount of this adjustment is the cumulative difference between tax expense previously reported and tax expense based on the new rate forecast.

Summary

Branch accounting closely parallels accounting for business combinations. The Branch Current account is similar to the investment account and the Home Office Current account is similar to the subsidiary stockholders' equity accounts. Combined financial statements are similar to consolidated financial statements in the sense that amounts are combined after eliminating reciprocal accounts.

Segmental reporting is the antithesis of consolidated financial reporting. Consolidated amounts are broken apart and reported according to geographical areas of operating and industrial segments. The existence of major customers is also disclosed.

Judgment is required in determining what constitutes the firm's geographical areas and industry segments. Once this judgment has been exercised, various materiality tests are performed in order to determine which of the identified areas or industry segments are material and therefore reported separately. Sales to unaffiliated customers, as well as intersegment or interarea transfers, are reported for each segment or geographical area, as are operating profits or losses and identifiable assets. In determining operating profits to be reported, common costs are allocated. However, nine specific elements of revenue and expense are never allocated. Similarly, in allocating identifiable assets to segments and geographical areas, assets which are used at the central office level are not allocated. Neither are investments accounted for using the equity method.

Interim reporting issues are resolved by viewing an interim period as an integral portion of an annual accounting period. This view has little to do with reporting interim revenues. Revenues are reported in the interim period in which they are realized. On the other hand, interim reporting of many costs and expenses requires forecasting amounts on the forthcoming annual income statement and using these forecasts in allocating the costs and expenses to interim periods. With the exception of reporting earnings per share data, two objectives drive this allocation of costs and expenses. First, interim amounts should be useful in forecasting their annual counterparts. Second, interim amounts should sum to their annual counterparts. When an accounting change occurs in other than the first interim period, subsequent interim reports are restated *as if* the change occurred in the first interim period.

Questions

1. What is the relationship between and the function of the Branch Current and Home Office Current accounts?
2. What is meant by the "principle of substitution" as applied to branch accounting?
3. If the home office elects to bill the branch for merchandise at a price in excess of cost, why is it preferable to use a price above cost but less than retail?
4. What are "reconciling adjustments" in branch accounting?
5. List three alternative bases for segmenting a diversified firm. Which of the three is preferred?

6. With respect to segmental reports, the allocation of common costs between segments is constrained by two conflicting objectives. What are they?

7. List four major problems the accountant faces in preparing segmental financial statements for a diversified company.

8. What tests are required by the FASB to determine whether or not an industry segment is significant enough to warrant separate financial disclosure?

9. In deciding upon an appropriate basis for pricing goods and services that are transferred between industry segments, what conclusions were reached by the FASB?

10. Should the income from an investment accounted for by the equity method be included in the operating profit of an industry segment? Under what conditions do equity method investments require separate disclosure in the industrially segmented reports?

11. Identify the problems associated with viewing an interim period as a *stand-alone* accounting period. What problem is substituted in their place by viewing an interim period as an integral portion of an annual accounting period?

12. Under what circumstances is the tax benefit of a first-quarter operating loss reported in the first quarter?

13. Explain the accounting for liquidation of a LIFO layer which is expected to be replenished prior to year-end.

14. For what reasons may interim earnings per share not sum to annual earnings per share?

15. If an investor views the four quarterly reports as they were originally issued, will the four income numbers sum to annual income if the reporting firm has changed accounting methods during the third quarter?

Exercises

Exercise 11–1   (Branch Accounting)

Edwards Company opened a Dallas branch in January 19X7. During 19X7, Edwards recorded merchandise transfers to the branch and merchandise returns from the branch with the following entries:

Branch Current	156,000	
Sales		156,000
Sales Returns	3,900	
Branch Current		3,900

Transfers to and from the branch were recorded by Edwards at 130 percent of Edwards' cost.

The Dallas branch reported to the home office a net loss of $12,000 for 19X7. In addition, the branch reported a closing inventory of $65,000, all of which was acquired from the home office.

Required:

Assume that the home office books have not been closed for 19X7. Prepare the journal entries on the books of the home office that are necessary at the end of 19X7 to (1) correct the accounts of the home office and (2) recognize the results of branch activities during 19X7.

Exercise 11–2   (Branch Accounting)

On July 1, the Demaris Company, central distributor for Arlo Metal Castings, Inc., organized a southwest sales outlet in El Paso. Following are the home office–branch transactions for the month of July:

July 1   The Demaris Company transferred $2,500 to its El Paso branch.
  2   Merchandise costing the home office $3 per unit was shipped to the branch at an invoice price of $5 per unit. One thousand units were shipped on July 2; a second order was to be filled by local suppliers.
  2   Shipping costs on the above were paid as follows:

By the home office	$150
By the branch	50

  5   Additional merchandise was acquired by the El Paso branch from regional distributors, 500 units at $3.10.
  7   Display equipment was purchased by the home office, cost $3,600, and was delivered to the El Paso branch. Fixed asset accounts are kept by the home office.
  10   Branch sales for the period July 3–10: on account, 800 units at $5.
  18   Branch collections on account, $3,200.
  25   Branch sales for the period July 11–24: on account, 500 units at $5.
  29   Cash remittance by branch to home office, $1,000.
  30   Monthly summary of branch cash expenses:

Advertising	$ 40
Sales commissions	650
Miscellaneous	10

  31   Depreciation recorded by the Demaris Company for July included $150 that related to the display equipment used by the El Paso branch. Insurance on this equipment was amortized by the home office in the amount of $25.
  31   Inventories of merchandise at El Paso on July 31 included the following:

From the home office	150 units @ $5.00
From local suppliers	50 units @ $3.10

Required:

Journalize the above transactions on the books of the Demaris Company and the El Paso branch office and prepare closing entries for July month-end statements.

Exercise 11–3 (Determination of Reportable Segments)

Jason Company's operations involve four industry segments: A, B, C, and D. During the most recent year, the operating profits or losses of the segments were as follows:

Industry Segment	Operating Profit (Loss)
A	$(200)
B	400
C	50
D	(400)

Required:

Apply the "operating profit or loss" test required by the FASB to determine which of the four industry segments should be treated as reportable segments.

Exercise 11–4 (Segmental Reporting—General)

Western Company's consolidated income statement appears as follows:

WESTERN COMPANY
Statement of Consolidated Income
For the Year Ended July 31, 19X1

Net sales	$38,041,200
Other revenue	407,400
Total revenue	$38,448,600
Cost of products sold	$27,173,300
Selling and administrative expenses	8,687,500
Interest expense	296,900
Total cost and expenses	$36,157,700
Income before income taxes	$ 2,290,900
Provision for income taxes	1,005,200
Net income	$ 1,285,700

Ray Bach, a security analyst, visited the corporate office of Western Company to obtain more information about the company's operations. In the annual report, Western's president stated that Western was engaged in the pharmaceutical, food processing, toy manufacturing, and metal-working industries. Mr. Bach complained that the income statement was of limited utility in his analysis of the firm's operations. He said analysis of Western's operations required more detailed information showing the profit earned in each of its component industries.

Required:

a. Explain what is meant by the term *conglomerate* company.

b. Discuss the accounting problems involved in measuring net profit by industry segments within a company.

c. With reference to Western Company's statement of consolidated income, identify the specific items for which it may be difficult to measure the profit earned by each of its industry segments and explain the nature of the difficulty.

(AICPA adapted)

Exercise 11–5   (Allocation of Costs to Segments)

Reneau Company operates in three different industries, each of which is appropriately regarded as a reportable segment. Reneau's manufacturing segment contributed 60 percent of total sales. Sales for the manufacturing segment were $900,000, and traceable costs were $400,000. Total common costs for Reneau were $600,000. This amount does not include $100,000 of general corporate expenses and $300,000 of interest expense. Reneau allocates common costs based on relative sales, an appropriate (not arbitrary) method of allocation.

Required:

Compute the manufacturing segment's operating profit.

Exercise 11–6   (Determination of Reportable Segments)

Adam Enterprises includes seven industry segments. Operating profits (losses) relating to these segments are as follows:

Segment	Operating Profit (Loss)
A	$100
B	500
C	400
D	(295)
E	(600)
F	(100)
G	(105)

Required:

Based only on the above operating profit (loss) information, which of Adam's segments would be reported separately?

Exercise 11-7   (Income Taxes in Interim Periods)

Click Company's quarterly pretax income numbers, all of which coincide with taxable income, are as follows:

First quarter	$ 20,000
Second quarter	20,000
Third quarter	10,000
Fourth quarter	50,000
Annual	$100,000

As of the end of the first, second, and third quarters, annual net income of $100,000 was expected. Click's tax rate is 25 percent on the first $25,000 of taxable income and 50 percent on any excess over $25,000.

Required:

Compute Click's net income for each of the four quarters. Describe how your results would change if the forecast of annual net income were revised during the year.

Exercise 11-8   (Inventory Liquidations in Interim Periods)

LIFO inventory data relating to Beth Duncan Enterprises are as follows:

	Units	Unit Cost	Amount
Beginning inventory	100	$1	$100
Purchase—January 15	20	2	40
Purchase—April 1	90	3	270

On March 30, Beth Duncan Enterprises sold 50 units. An additional 55 units were sold on December 1.

Required:

Compute cost of goods sold for the first quarter and annual period.

Exercise 11-9   (Interim EPS)

Regier Company had 1,000 outstanding common shares as of January 1, 19X1. In an effort to combat a hostile takeover, Regier acquired 600 of these shares on March 1, 19X1. Quarterly earnings were the following:

First quarter	$10,000
Second quarter	6,000
Third quarter	6,000
Fourth quarter	6,000
Annual	$28,000

Regier's capital structure includes no dilutive securities.

Required:

Compute primary earnings per share data for each quarter and the annual period.

Problems

Problem 11–10   (Branch Accounting)

The Cincinnati home office of The Geis Company regularly acquires merchandise at a cost of $4 a unit, which is subsequently marked to sell at $6 a unit by both the home office and its Athens branch. During 19X7, the home office purchased 4,000 units, sold 3,000 units, and shipped 500 units to the branch. During 19X8, the home office purchased an additional 4,500 units, sold 3,200 units, and made a second shipment of 1,000 units to the Athens branch.

Branch sales of units acquired from the home office were 400 units in 19X7 and 900 units in 19X8.

Required:

a. Journalize all transactions on the books of The Geis Company and its Athens branch (including closing entries) for the years 19X7 and 19X8 *if* the home office bills merchandise shipped to the branch at $4 a unit.

b. Same conditions as in (a) except that the home office bills merchandise shipped to the branch at $5 a unit.

Problem 11–11   (Branch Accounting)

Using the data of Problem 11-10, prepare working papers for a *combined* income statement for The Geis Company and its Athens branch for the years 19X7 and 19X8 *if*

a. The home office bills merchandise shipped to the branch at $4 a unit.

b. The home office bills merchandise shipped to the branch at $5 a unit.

Problem 11–12   (Branch Accounting)

Longley Company of Indianapolis regularly distributes its products through branch retail outlets. Shipments to its Muncie branch, which was established at the beginning of the year, are billed as follows: Case A, at cost; Case B, 25 percent above cost; and Case C, retail price at date of shipment.

During the year, the Muncie branch received merchandise from the home office, cost, $60,000. Additionally, the branch recorded credit sales of $81,000; made collections on account, $64,000; paid expenses, $14,000; and remitted cash to the Indianapolis home office, $61,200. The December 31 final inventory of the branch was Case A, $6,000; Case B, $7,500; and Case C, $9,000.

The trial balance of the Indianapolis home office on December 31 was as follows:

	Case A	Case B	Case C
Cash	$ 39,000	$ 39,000	$ 39,000
Accounts Receivable	45,000	45,000	45,000
Branch Current	(1,200)	13,800	28,800
Purchases	150,000	150,000	150,000
Expenses	17,200	17,200	17,200
	$250,000	$265,000	$280,000
Accounts Payable	$ 20,000	$ 20,000	$ 20,000
Shipments to Branch	60,000	60,000	60,000
Intracompany Inventory Profit	–0–	15,000	30,000
Capital Stock	40,000	40,000	40,000
Sales	130,000	130,000	130,000
	$250,000	$265,000	$280,000
Merchandise (12/31)	$ 8,000	$ 8,000	$ 8,000

Required:

a. Journalize the transactions of the branch for the year, as recorded by the Indianapolis home office and the Muncie branch.

b. Prepare closing entries for the branch and home office.

c. Prepare a combined statement working paper (Case C only).

Problem 11–13   (Branch Accounting)

Sales distribution of Electronic Transistor Company is principally conducted by its home office and one centrally located branch. Units of merchandise shipped to the branch are uniformly priced at 120 percent of cost. The trial balances of the home office and branch at December 31, 19X1, are as follows:

	December 31, 19X1	
	Home Office	*Branch*
Cash	$ 125,200	$ 17,600
Marketable Securities	229,000	
Accounts Receivable (net)	172,700	84,300
Inventory (1/1)	341,000	133,200
Branch Current	122,300	
Fixed Assets (net)	1,172,600	
Purchases	2,450,000	
Expenses	381,000	78,100
Shipments from Home Office		811,200
	$4,993,800	$1,124,400
Accounts Payable	$ 397,000	$ 12,400
Accrued Expenses	14,100	1,700
Capital Stock	1,000,000	
Retained Earnings	172,300	
Home Office Current		72,300
Sales	2,547,000	1,038,000
Shipments to Branch	701,000	
Intracompany Inventory Profit	162,400	
	$4,993,800	$1,124,400
Inventory (12/31)	$ 284,000	$ 120,000

An examination of duplicate deposit tickets on January 3, 19X2, discloses that the branch made a $20,000 deposit to the credit of the home office on December 31, 19X1. In addition, merchandise was in transit to the branch on December 31, 19X1.

Required:

a. Prepare a working paper for a combined statement for the home office and branch for the year ended December 31, 19X1.

b. Journalize adjusting and closing entries for the branch and home office.

Problem 11–14   (Branch Accounting)

The trial balance of Johnson Export Company at December 31, 19X3, is as follows:

	Home Office	*Branch*
Cash	$ 15,000	$ 2,000
Accounts Receivable	20,000	17,000
Inventory (12/31/X3)	30,000	8,000
Fixed Assets (net)	150,000	
Branch Office Current	44,000	
Cost of Sales	220,000	93,000
Expenses	70,000	41,000
	$549,000	$161,000

	Home Office	Branch
Accounts Payable	$ 23,000	
Mortgage Payable	50,000	
Capital Stock	100,000	
Retained Earnings (1/1/X3)	26,000	
Sales	350,000	$150,000
Accrued Expenses		2,000
Home Office Current		9,000
	$549,000	$161,000

The following additional information is available:

1. The branch receives all of its merchandise from the home office. The home office bills goods to the branch at 125 percent of cost. During 19X3, the branch was billed for $105,000 on shipments from the home office.

2. The home office credits Sales for the invoice price of goods shipped to the branch.

3. On January 1, 19X3, the inventory of the home office was $25,000. The branch books showed a $6,000 inventory. In addition, merchandise was in transit to the branch on December 31, 19X3.

4. The home office billed the branch for $12,000 on December 31, 19X3, representing the branch's share of expenses paid at the home office. The branch has not recorded this billing.

5. All cash collections made by the branch are deposited in a local bank to the account of the home office. Deposits of this nature included the following:

Amount	Date Deposited by Branch	Date Recorded by Home Office
$5,000	December 28, 19X3	December 31, 19X3
3,000	December 30, 19X3	January 2, 19X4
7,000	December 31, 19X3	January 3, 19X4
2,000	January 2, 19X4	January 5, 19X4

6. Expenses incurred locally by the branch are paid from an imprest bank account that is reimbursed periodically by the home office. Just prior to the end of the year, the home office forwarded a reimbursement check in the amount of $3,000 that was not received by the branch office until January 19X4.

7. It is not necessary to make provisions for federal income tax.

Required:

a. Prepare a working paper for a combined statement for the home office and branch for the year ended December 31, 19X3.

b. Prepare a reconciliation of the Branch Office Current and Home Office Current accounts showing the correct book balance.

(AICPA adapted)

Problem 11–15   (Branch Accounting)

Koufax Sporting Goods Company of Los Angeles decided on July 1 to establish sales branches in Chicago and New York as a means of expanding and improving its services to customers in these areas. Transactions with these branches for the month of July are as follows:

July 1 The home office transferred $75,000 cash to the Chicago branch and $100,000 to the New York branch to be used as working funds.

  2 Merchandise costing $310,000 was shipped to the New York branch and was billed at 140 percent of cost. Freight charges, paid by the home office, amounted to $1,400.

  3 Merchandise costing $225,000 was shipped to the Chicago branch and was billed at a 25 percent markup on the invoice price. Freight charges of $888 were paid by the Chicago branch.

  10 Fixed assets costing $400,000 were purchased for the use of the Chicago branch, and $500,000 were purchased for the New York branch. General ledger control over fixed assets is maintained by the home office.

  15 Timely reporting is facilitated by the use of electronic data processing equipment; as a consequence, the first semimonthly summary of operating data was received on July 15 and disclosed the following:

	Branches	
	Chicago	*New York*
Credit sales	$42,000	$57,000
Collections on account	34,000	41,000
Expenses	8,000	12,000
Payments on account	6,400	9,700

  17 Merchandise previously shipped to Chicago was transshipped to New York. These goods, on which freight charges amounted to $147, had been billed to Chicago at $20,000. Additional freight paid by the New York branch for the transshipment amounted to $68. Had the shipment been initially directed to New York, transportation costs would have totaled $175.

  20 The home office shipped additional merchandise to branches as follows: Chicago, $150,000 cost; and New York, $200,000 cost. The terms of branch billing remained unchanged. Freight charges, paid by the home office, were $700 on the Chicago shipment and $1,150 on the New York shipment.

  31 The semimonthly operating summary is as follows:

	Branches	
	Chicago	*New York*
Credit sales	$122,100	$150,800
Collections on account	97,700	128,100
Expenses	19,000	27,000
Payments on account	19,600	26,300

July 31   Cash remittances to the home office were as follows:

New York branch	$125,000
Chicago branch	100,000

Required:

a. Prepare journal entries for July for each branch and the home office. (In the home office books, use separate accounts with respect to the transactions of each branch.)

b. Prepare closing entries, given the following additional information:
  (1) Inventories, July 31:

New York branch	$560,000
Chicago branch	360,000

Inventories are determined by physical count; freight charges on merchandise shipments are not allocated to inventory.

  (2) Depreciation on fixed assets is regularly recorded by the home office. Depreciation expense for the month of July follows:

Property at New York branch	$500
Property at Chicago branch	400

Problem 11-16   (Reporting Industrial Segments)

A partial consolidated income statement for X Company appears below:

Sales		$4,700
Cost of sales	$3,000	
Selling, general, and administrative expense	700	
Interest expense	200	3,900
		$ 800
Equity in net income of Z Company		100
Income from continuing operations before taxes		$ 900

Selected industrial segment information follows:

	Industry A	Industry B	Industry C
Sales to unaffiliated customers	$1,000	$2,000	$1,500
Intersegment sales	200		500
Operating profit	200	290	600

The intersegment sales are from Industries A and C to Industry B. Industry B's beginning inventory includes $20 in unconfirmed profit, and its ending inventory includes $60 in unconfirmed profit. The selling, general, and administrative expense shown in the consolidated income statement includes $100 of general corporate administrative expense.

Required:

Prepare the industrial segment report relating to revenues and operating profits, including reconciliations with consolidated amounts.

Problem 11–17   (Reporting Geographical Segments)

Refer to the partial consolidated income statement in Problem 11–16. Selected information relating to domestic and foreign operations follows:

	United States	Area A	Area B
Sale to unaffiliated customers	$3,000	$1,000	$700
Transfer between geographical areas	1,000		
Operating profit	800	400	100

The transfers between geographical areas are from the United States to Geographical Area A, resulting in $200 unconfirmed profit from U.S. operations.

Required:

Prepare the geographical segment report relating to revenues and operating profits, including reconciliations with consolidated amounts.

Problem 11–18   (Determination of Reportable Segments)

The operations of Cedar Falls Corporation involve eight different industries. Information on these eight industrial segments for the most recent year is as follows:

Industry Segment	Revenue from Unaffiliated Customers	Intersegment Sales	Operating Profit (Loss)	Identifiable Assets
1	$ 300	$ 100	$ (50)	$ 800
2	800	200	200	1,200
3	5,000	1,000	200	5,000
4	8,000	—	1,100	6,500
5	9,500	—	500	8,500
6	1,200	400	400	1,500
7	1,000	500	(600)	2,000
8	2,000	—	(100)	3,000

An investigation of the operations of recent years suggests that the most recent data are not unusual.

Required:

In anticipation of the need to prepare financial reports on the important segments in which Cedar Falls Corporation operates, and using the criteria required by the FASB, determine which of the eight industry segments should be treated as reportable segments. In other words, for which of the eight should separate financial information be presented?

Problem 11–19   (Segmental Reporting—General)

Jamestown Company is a broadly diversified company whose operations involve five major industries: A, B, C, D, and E. Management of Jamestown Company plans to include in the annual report for 19X1 a segmented financial report prepared in accordance with FASB *Statement No. 14*. Financial data relating to segmental operations during 19X1 follow:

	A	B	C	D	E
Sales	$7,000	$19,000	$150,000	$ 6,000	$12,000
Cost of goods sold	$3,000	$12,000	$ 80,000	$ 1,400	$ 7,000
Administrative expenses	1,000	4,000	24,000	1,000	1,000
Selling expenses	1,000	7,000	29,000	1,600	3,000
Total operating expenses	$5,000	$23,000	$133,000	$ 4,000	$11,000
Operating profit	$2,000	$(4,000)	$ 17,000	$ 2,000	$ 1,000
Identifiable assets	$8,000	$15,000	$ 95,000	$16,000	$35,000

Additional Information:

a. Included in the sales of segment E are $4,000 which were sales to segment C. None of the items sold to C remains in the December 31, 19X1, assets of C.

b. In addition to the assets identified with industrial segments, the corporate offices have assets of $18,000 on December 31, 19X1.

c. Income taxes amount to 30 percent of net operating profits.

Required:

a. Determine which of the industry segments should be reported separately in segmental reports and state the basis for your decision in each case.

b. Prepare a summarized financial report by segments which is reconciled with summarized consolidated data.

Problem 11-20   (Income Taxes in Interim Periods)

Star Service Company expects annual pretax accounting income in the amount of $100,000. Taxable income for the year is expected to be $60,000. The entire $40,000 disparity is due to differences in the timing of revenue recognition. Applicable tax rates are 25 percent on the first $25,000 of taxable income and 50 percent on any excess over $25,000.

During the first quarter, Star experienced a pretax operating loss of $30,000. First-quarter operating losses are part of a normal seasonal pattern leading to income for the year.

Required:

Compute Star's first-quarter net income.

Problem 11-21   (Fixed Costs in Interim Periods)

Sunshine Products, Inc., budgets its 19X1 operations as follows:

Sales (100,000 units @ $10)		$1,000,000
Variable costs (100,000 @ $6)	$600,000	
Fixed costs	300,000	900,000
Net income before taxes		$ 100,000

Sunshine's revenues are seasonal with the following pattern:

	Percent
First quarter	10
Second quarter	20
Third quarter	20
Fourth quarter	50

During the first quarter of 19X1, Sunshine produced and sold 10,500 units at the expected price of $10 per unit. Variable costs were the $6 expected amount per unit. Sunshine reported a first quarter pretax loss of $33,000.

Required:

a. How has Sunshine apparently computed first-quarter results? Is this consistent with *APB Opinion No. 28?*

b. How might Sunshine improve the predictive properties of its interim earnings numbers?

Problem 11-22   (Accounting Changes in Interim Periods)

Yogi Pet Supplies changes from one depreciation method to another during the second quarter of 19X2. Data relating to interim earnings under the old and new depreciation methods are as follows:

Quarter	Year	Old Method	New Method	Difference
1	19X1	$10,000	$11,000	$1,000
2	19X1	15,000	17,000	2,000
3	19X1	15,000	16,000	1,000
4	19X1	20,000	21,000	1,000
1	19X2	22,000	21,000	(1,000)
2	19X2	24,000	25,000	1,000
3	19X2	30,000	33,000	3,000
4	19X2	45,000	47,000	2,000

Yogi had no depreciable assets prior to 19X1.

Required:

Prepare a partial second-quarter 19X2 report for Yogi. The format should include income before cumulative effect of accounting change, cumulative effect of accounting change, and net income for

a. Second quarter of 19X2

b. Second quarter of 19X1

c. Year to date for 19X2

d. Year to date for 19X1

In addition, pro forma net income is reported for items (*a*) through (*d*) above.

Problem 11–23   (Interim Reporting—General)

Selected forecast data relating to Hammer Company appear below:

	1st Quarter	2nd Quarter	3rd Quarter	4th Quarter	Annual
Sales	$12,000	$15,000	$20,000	$30,000	$77,000
Purchases	(5,000)	(12,000)	(15,000)	(7,000)	(39,000)
Depreciation					(20,000)
Goodwill amortization					(10,000)

Hammer uses the LIFO inventory method. It expects inventory quantities to behave in the following fashion:

	1st Quarter	2nd Quarter	3rd Quarter	4th Quarter	Annual
Beginning quantity	2,000	1,500	3,750	6,250	2,000
Purchased quantity	2,500	6,000	7,500	3,500	19,500
Sold quantity	(3,000)	(3,750)	(5,000)	(7,500)	(19,250)
Ending quantity	1,500	3,750	6,250	2,250	2,250

The quantity on hand at the beginning of the first quarter is valued at a LIFO cost of $1 per unit. All purchases are expected to cost $2 per unit and all sales prices are expected to be $4 per unit.

Hammer's statutory tax rate is 30 percent of taxable income. The goodwill amortization is not deductible in computing taxable income.

Required:

Assuming (1) that all Hammer's expectations are met and (2) that annual fixed costs are allocated to interim periods on the basis of revenue, prepare income statements for the four interim periods as well as the annual period.

UNIT III Accounting for International Operations

Chapter Outline

Chapters 12, 13, and 14 cover accounting for the international operations of domestic companies. This chapter deals with certain transactions of domestic companies that involve foreign currencies. Chapter 13 covers the conversion of foreign entities' financial statements into U.S. dollars—the domestic currency of the United States. Chapter 14 examines additional topics in international accounting, including the preparation of consolidated financial statements for domestic companies and their foreign subsidiaries, international accounting standards, and financial reporting by foreign companies.

Foreign Currency Transactions—Introductory Comments

A foreign currency transaction is a transaction that is denominated in a currency other than the entity's functional currency. Stated briefly, *Statement of Financial Accounting Standards No. 52* indicates that a company's functional currency is "the currency of the primary economic environment in which the entity operates."[1] In Chapters 12, 13, and 14, all domestic companies are assumed to be *U.S. companies whose functional currencies are the U.S. dollar.* We also assume in these chapters that the *reporting currency* of these companies is the U.S. dollar. The reporting currency is the currency in which financial statements are prepared. This chapter explains the accounting techniques applying to the major classes of foreign currency transactions between *domestic* companies and *nonaffiliates.* The foreign currency transactions covered produce receivables or payables on the domestic companies' books that are *denominated in (nonfunctional) foreign currencies.* A receivable or payable is denominated in a foreign currency if it is to be settled using that currency.

One example of the type of foreign currency transaction covered in this chapter is a trading transaction (i.e., an export or import transaction) resulting in a receivable or payable on the domestic company's books that is denominated in a foreign currency. Another transaction of this type is a speculative transaction which results in a receivable or a payable on the domestic company's books that is denominated in a foreign currency. As indicated, a receivable or payable is denominated in a foreign currency if it is to be settled using that currency. The initial problem in accounting for a receivable or payable denominated in a foreign currency is determining the amount at which it is to be recorded *in the domestic currency* (i.e., the U.S. dollar in Chapters 12, 13, and 14). The second difficulty in dealing with receivables and payables denominated in foreign currencies is accounting for their *exchange gains or losses.* These gains and losses are referred to more specifically as *transaction exchange gains and losses.*[2] They occur because of changes in the *current* values of the receivables and payables resulting from

---

[1] *Statement of Financial Accounting Standards No. 52,* "Foreign Currency Translation" (Norwalk, CT: FASB, 1981) is the current pronouncement dealing with foreign currency transactions. The phrase *functional currency* is defined and discussed in this pronouncement. We elaborate on this concept in Chapter 13.

[2] A second type of exchange gain or loss is a *conversion exchange gain or loss.* Conversion exchange gains and losses are dealt with initially in Chapter 13.

fluctuations in exchange rates among the domestic and foreign currencies. The third problem related to receivables and payables denominated in foreign currencies is accounting for the *hedging transactions* that are entered because of their existence. These transaction are designed to largely eliminate the effects of exchange gains or losses from the receivables and payables. The three problems just described are the primary focus of this chapter.

CURRENCY EXCHANGE RATES

From the perspective of a domestic company, foreign currencies are like commodities (especially securities) that have *prices* expressed in the domestic currency. These prices are called *exchange rates*. Exchange rates *express the relative values* of two currencies and govern their exchanges in the international money markets—markets that provide for both immediate and future deliveries of the currencies. Historically, these rates were based on the gold content of the different currencies. Gold content no longer is a factor in determining exchange rates. Currently, two main types of exchange rates are important: (1) *free* rates—which are functions of the changing economic values of currencies (viewed as economic goods) resulting from supply and demand factors and (2) *official* rates—which are established by governments. A country can have several official rates, each of which is related to a type of economic activity and is a consequence of its government's attitude toward the activity. For example, the government of a developing country might apply a favorable rate to exporters supplying the country with capital goods. In contrast, it might apply a less favorable rate to dividend payments made to residents of another country.

Since an exchange rate for two currencies is a ratio of the relative values of the currencies, it can be stated in terms of either country's currency. If the exchange rate is *directly quoted,* it expresses the price of one unit of the foreign currency in terms of the domestic currency. For example, if the directly quoted free exchange rate for the U.S. dollar and the British pound is 1.25, one pound can be acquired for $1.25 (1 × $1.25). If the exchange rate is *indirectly quoted,* it expresses the price of one unit of the domestic currency in terms of the foreign currency. Thus, if the indirectly quoted free exchange rate for the British pound and the U.S. dollar is .8, one dollar can be acquired for .8 pounds (1 × .8 pounds). Directly and indirectly quoted exchange rates are reciprocals of each other. *Note that we do not put currency designations* (e.g., $) *on exchange rates unless they are used in calculations* (as illustrated above). Thus, we tend to express exchange rates the way they are expressed in the financial press.

Exchange rates also are classified as *spot* rates and *forward* (or future) rates. If currencies are exchanged in the market for immediate delivery, the pertinent exchange rate is the spot rate. If they are exchanged in the futures market (the market specifying future delivery, for example, in 30, 90, or 180 days), the relevant rate is the forward rate. A forward rate is a currently existing rate governing agreed-upon future exchanges of currency. The futures market allows companies to engage in the hedging transactions intended to largely eliminate the effects of transaction exchange gains or losses from receivables and payables denominated in foreign currencies. In the United States, exchange rates currently are quoted both directly and indirectly. For example, on September 24, 1991, *The Wall Street Journal* reported the following Bankers Trust Co. (free) spot rate quotations for 3:00 P.M. (Eastern time) on September 23, 1991.

Country (Currency)	U.S. Dollar Price of One Foreign Currency Unit (Direct Quotation)	Foreign Currency Price of One U.S. Dollar (Indirect Quotation)
Britain (pound)	1.744000	.5734
Japan (yen)	.007536	132.7000
Switzerland (franc)	.686100	1.4575

Forward (free) rates also are reported in the financial press.

Export and Import Transactions—Fundamental Issues

As indicated, *Statement of Financial Accounting Standards No. 52,* "Foreign Currency Translation," is the current pronouncement dealing with foreign currency transactions. The cases in this chapter cover the accounting treatments for various types of foreign currency transactions under this standard. The cases of this section introduce the principles applying to export and import transactions and related hedges through forward exchange contracts. The first four cases are introductory since all settlements related to the export and import transactions and their hedges are made in the same reporting periods as the transactions. Also, these cases are introductory since pertinent spot and forward rates are assumed to be the same.

Case 1. Export Transaction with Receivable Denominated in Foreign Currency

In an export transaction, a domestic company sells goods to a foreign company.[3] If the sale is on credit, a receivable is recorded on the domestic company's books. Depending on the agreement with the foreign company, the receivable is denominated in the domestic currency (the U.S. dollar in Chapters 12, 13, and 14) or in the foreign currency. If denominated in the domestic currency, no exchange risk is borne by the domestic seller (i.e., it is borne by the foreign purchaser since the purchaser has a payable denominated in dollars). Also, no new accounting prob-

---

[3] Note that export transactions may require disclosures under *Statement of Financial Accounting Standards No. 14,* "Financial Reporting for Segments of a Business Enterprise" (Norwalk, CT: FASB, 1976). See the section entitled "Segmental Disclosures Related to Operations of Consolidated Foreign Subsidiaries and Export Sales" in Chapter 14 for further discussion.

lems arise. However, if the receivable is denominated in the foreign currency, the exchange risk of the transaction is borne by the domestic company (and no exchange risk is borne by the foreign purchaser since its payable is denominated in its currency). The domestic company experiences exchange risk since the *current* value of its receivable changes as the spot rate for the companies' currencies fluctuates. As indicated, these changes produce transaction exchange gains and losses. Additionally, if the receivable is denominated in the foreign currency, a variety of new accounting issues emerge.[4] As mentioned, the three primary problems for a receivable are: (1) recording it in the domestic currency, (2) accounting for any related transaction exchange gains or losses, and (3) accounting for hedging transactions intended to largely eliminate the effects of these gains or losses. The following two export examples illustrate the basic accounting techniques related to these problems. To focus clearly on these procedures, the examples illustrate the domestic company's entries under two assumptions: *(a)* its receivable is denominated in the domestic currency and *(b)* its receivable is denominated in the foreign currency. All exchange rates used in our examples and in the problems at the end of the chapters are assumed to be *directly quoted, free rates* unless indicated otherwise.

Assume that Leader Corporation, an American company, sells merchandise to East Indies Company, a British company, on January 1, 19X0—when the spot rate for the dollar and the pound is 1.50. Depending on the companies' contract, the billing on the sale is expressed in dollars or pounds. If expressed in dollars, the assumed billing is $15,000, and Leader Corporation's receivable is denominated in dollars. Alternatively, if the billing is expressed in pounds, its amount is 10,000 pounds (15,000/1.5 pounds), and the receivable is denominated in pounds. In *either case,* the sale is recorded by Leader Corporation *in the domestic currency* at $15,000. We emphasize that if the billing is expressed in pounds, East Indies Corporation delivers 10,000 pounds to Leader Corporation on the settlement date for the receivable (January 31, 19X0). The spot rate on this date is 1.52. We assume that Leader Corporation exchanges any pounds received for dollars immediately using the services of an exchange broker. The examples of this chapter ignore the commissions and other service charges of exchange brokers for simplicity and since these factors are dealt with easily. Note also that dollar amounts assigned to receivables and payables *denominated in foreign currencies (fc)* are shaded in this chapter and in Chapter 14. *In solving homework problems,*

---

[4] As indicated, a receivable or payable is denominated in a foreign currency if it is to be settled using that currency. More generally, any asset or liability is *denominated* in a particular currency if its amount is fixed in that currency. Thus, the criterion of whether an asset or liability is denominated in a given currency also distinguishes between monetary and nonmonetary assets and liabilities, since monetary items' amounts are fixed in terms of currencies (while nonmonetary items' amounts are not fixed in this way). Also, note that *any* asset or liability amount can be expressed in any currency, irrespective of the currency in which it is denominated. For example, a firm's cash balance in a U.S. bank is denominated in U.S. dollars, but this balance can be expressed in any currency. Similarly, the balance for a nonmonetary asset (e.g., land), which is not denominated in any currency since the asset is nonmonetary, can be expressed in any currency.

you may want to place "fc" in parentheses next to the titles of accounts that are denominated in foreign currencies as an aid in keeping track of accounts which may need adjustment because of exchange rate fluctuations [e.g., Accounts Receivable (fc)]. The entries for this example are shown in Illustration 12–1.

The entries in column *(b)* of Illustration 12–1 require explanation. Entry (1) records Leader Corporation's sale—which leads to a receivable denominated in a foreign currency. Thus, the $15,000 values for the sale and the receivable are determined by multiplying the billing of 10,000 pounds by the sale date spot rate of 1.5. *The debit to the receivable illustrates the general principle that receivables and payables denominated in foreign currencies arising from nonspeculative transactions are accounted for at all significant points in time at their current values.* Thus, their values are recorded or adjusted using *current spot rates* on transaction and financial statement dates. On January 31, 19X0, East Indies Company delivers 10,000 pounds to Leader Corporation in settlement of its debt. Leader Corporation records the receipt of the 10,000 pounds in entry (2) by debiting Foreign Currency—Pounds. This debit equals the product of the number of pounds received and the spot rate on the date they are received (10,000 × $1.52). It is analogous to the debit recorded if 10,000 shares of a security are purchased for $1.52 per share. The transaction exchange gain recorded in entry (2) equals the product of the 10,000 pounds and the change in the spot rate between the sale date and the settlement date [10,000 × ($1.52 − $1.5)]. This gain occurs because the *dollar weakens* in relation to the pound between the sale date and the settlement date. The domestic currency weakens in relation to a foreign currency when the spot rate increases since such an increase implies that it takes more dollars to acquire one unit of the foreign currency. Even though the dollar weakens, a gain occurs because the 10,000 pounds yield more dollars under the

ILLUSTRATION 12-1   Export Transaction

			(a) Billing in Domestic Currency (Dollars)		(b) Billing in Foreign Currency (Pounds)	
1.	1/1/X0	Accounts Receivable	15,000		15,000	
		Sales		15,000		15,000
2.	1/31/X0	Cash	15,000			
		Foreign Currency—Pounds			15,200	
		Exchange Gain				200
		Accounts Receivable		15,000		15,000
3.	1/31/X0	Cash			15,200	
		Foreign Currency—Pounds				15,200

NOTE: Dollar values assigned to receivables, payables, and other accounts denominated in foreign currency units are shaded here and throughout this chapter.

1.52 exchange rate than under the 1.5 rate. This observation is illustrated by entry (3). This entry records Leader Corporation's immediate exchange (through the exchange broker) of the pounds received for $15,200 (10,000 × $1.52). If the dollar did not weaken, only $15,000 (10,000 × $1.5) would have been received. Illustration 12–2 summarizes the exchange gain and loss effects produced by fluctuations in exchange rates.

Case 2. Hedging Exchange Risk on an Export Transaction

Assume the information of Case 1, except now assume specifically that the billing is in pounds. Assume also that Leader Corporation decides to minimize its exchange risk by entering into a forward exchange contract. In other words, assume that Leader Corporation decides to hedge its exchange risk using a forward exchange contract entered through the futures market. In general, a hedge *related to a receivable* denominated in a foreign currency is achieved by *selling* units of the foreign currency *through an exchange broker* on the date of the export transaction at a particular forward rate. Such hedges are referred to as *hedges of exposed asset positions* since they hedge the exchange risks related to assets denominated in foreign currencies. The hedging transaction is arranged so the delivery date of the foreign currency sold (10,000 pounds in our example) coincides with the settlement date of the receivable. Thus, the forward rate at which the foreign currency is sold is the rate for the period of time from the date of the export transaction to the settlement date of its receivable. The 30-day forward rate is pertinent here since the date of the export transaction is January 1, 19X0, and the settlement date of the receivable is January 31, 19X0. We assume the 30-day forward rate equals the spot rate on the date of the export transaction (1.5) to illustrate an ideal hedge—one that eliminates all exchange risk. We emphasize that these rates usually are not equal and, therefore, that hedges usually do not eliminate all exchange risk. Cases in which these rates differ are covered later. The entries for this example are presented in Illustration 12–3. The first column in

---

ILLUSTRATION 12-2   Fluctuations in Exchange Rates and Exchange Gains and Losses

	Receivable Denominated in Foreign Currency	*Payable Denominated in Foreign Currency*
Domestic currency weakens— exchange rate increases	Exchange gain occurs	Exchange loss occurs
Domestic currency strengthens— exchange rate decreases	Exchange loss occurs	Exchange gain occurs

ILLUSTRATION 12-3   **Hedging Exchange Risk on Export Transaction**

			Export Transaction—Billing in Foreign Currency (Pounds)		Hedging Transaction	
1.	1/1/X0	Accounts Receivable	15,000			
		Sales		15,000		
2.	1/1/X0	Dollars Due from Exchange Broker			15,000	
		Pounds Due to Exchange Broker				15,000
3.	1/31/X0	Foreign Currency—Pounds	15,000			
		Exchange Gain or Loss		200		
		Accounts Receivable		15,000		
4.	1/31/X0	Pounds Due to Exchange Broker			15,000	
		Exchange Gain or Loss			200	
		Foreign Currency—Pounds				15,200
5.	1/31/X0	Cash			15,000	
		Dollars Due from Exchange Broker				15,000

this illustration pertains to the export transaction, and the second column is related to the hedging transaction.[5]

Entries (1) and (3) in Illustration 12-3 are the same as entries (1) and (2) in column (b) of Case 1. Entry (2) in this case records Leader Corporation's forward exchange contract (its hedge). In this entry, the debit to Dollars Due from Exchange Broker (a receivable) is the product of the *forward rate* (1.5) and the number of pounds sold (10,000). This receivable is denominated in dollars; thus, its existence does not expose Leader Corporation to exchange risk. Also, its value is not changed over the life of the hedging contract. *This treatment of the balance for Dollars Due from Exchange Broker illustrates the general principle that receivables and payables denominated in the domestic currency are not adjusted over time since their current values do not change in response to fluctuations in exchange rates.* In this context, note that Leader Corporation definitely receives

---

[5] Since a forward exchange contract is an executory contract (i.e., the exchange of a promise for a promise), current accounting standards do not require an entry to be made on the date of such a contract. However, these principles require recognition of exchange gains or losses on the contract at the settlement date and at intervening financial statement dates. In this context, *Statement of Financial Accounting Standards No. 52* discusses forward exchange contracts only in terms of determining their exchange gains or losses—the multiplication of a particular foreign currency exposure (e.g., a receivable denominated in a foreign currency) by the change in a specified exchange rate. For pedagogical reasons, we believe that it is important to record the implicit values of receivables and payables related to forward exchange contracts. Thus, we follow this practice in this chapter. The gains and losses recognized by this procedure are the same as those produced under *Statement of Financial Accounting Standards No. 52*. By offsetting the receivables and payables recorded in our entries, you get the balance sheet elements recognized under *Statement of Financial Accounting Standards No. 52*.

$15,000 from the exchange broker when it delivers the sold pounds on January 31, 19X0, since the receivable, Dollars Due from Exchange Broker, is denominated in dollars. In contrast, the account credited in entry (2), Pounds Due to Exchange Broker, is a payable that is denominated in a foreign currency (pounds). Consequently, its existence exposes Leader Corporation to exchange risk. Exchange risk occurs in this case since the current value of the payable changes as the spot rate for the two companies' currencies fluctuates. As in the case of a receivable denominated in a foreign currency, these changes produce transaction exchange gains and losses. Also, similar to the receivable case, the existence of a payable denominated in a foreign currency produces three accounting problems: (1) recording it in the domestic currency, (2) accounting for related transaction exchange gains or losses, and (3) accounting for hedging transactions intended to largely eliminate the effects of these gains or losses (which is not an issue in this example). These problems are dealt with in entries (2) and (4) in our example. Entry (2) credits Pounds Due to Exchange Broker for an amount equaling the product of the *spot rate* on the export transaction date (also 1.5) and the number of pounds sold (10,000). Entry (4) records the exchange gain or loss related to this account. More specifically, Leader Corporation records the delivery of the 10,000 pounds to the exchange broker in entry (4) by crediting Foreign Currency— Pounds. This credit equals the carrying value of the pounds recorded in entry (3). Since the pounds have been delivered, Leader Corporation debits Pounds Due to Exchange Broker for its carrying value to eliminate the debt to the exchange broker. The exchange loss recorded in entry (4) equals the product of the 10,000 pounds and the change in the spot rate between the export sale date and the settlement date [10,000 × ($1.52 − $1.5)]. This loss occurs because the dollar weakens in relation to the pound between these dates. In other words, the loss occurs because Leader Corporation has to deliver pounds to the exchange broker that are worth $15,200 (10,000 × $1.52), while it would have had to deliver pounds worth only $15,000 (10,000 × $1.5) if the spot rate did not change. Note that the loss recorded in (4) exactly offsets the gain recorded in (3). Thus, Leader Corporation's hedge is perfect; it eliminates all exchange risk. Entry (5) records the receipt of the (fixed) $15,000 sales price of the pounds from the exchange broker.

Case 3. *Import Transaction with Payable Denominated in Foreign Currency*

In an import transaction, a domestic company purchases merchandise from a foreign company. If the purchase is on credit, a payable is recorded on the domestic company's books. Depending on the companies' contract, the payable is denominated in the domestic currency or in the foreign currency. If denominated in the domestic currency, no exchange risk is borne by the domestic purchaser (it is borne by the foreign seller), and no new accounting issues arise. However, if the payable is denominated in the foreign currency, the exchange risk of the transaction is borne by the domestic company (not the foreign seller). The domestic company experiences exchange risk since the current value of its payable changes as the spot rate for the two companies' currencies fluctuates. Again, these changes produce transaction exchange gains and losses. Also, as indicated above, the existence of a payable denominated in a foreign currency produces several accounting problems: (1) recording the payable in the domestic currency, (2) accounting for any related exchange gains or losses, and (3) accounting for hedging transactions intended to largely eliminate the effects of these gains or losses. The basic accounting techniques pertinent to these issues are examined via the following two import examples. The first example also illustrates the domestic company's entries under two assumptions: *(a)* its payable is denominated in the domestic currency and *(b)* its payable is denominated in the foreign currency.

Assume that Leader Corporation purchases goods from Alps Company, a Swiss Company, on January 1, 19X0—when the spot rate for the dollar and the (Swiss) franc is .50. Depending on the agreement between Leader Corporation and Alps Company, the billing is expressed in dollars or francs. If expressed in dollars, the assumed billing is $25,000, and Leader Corporation's payable is denominated in dollars. Alternatively, if the billing is expressed in francs, its amount is 50,000 francs (25,000/.5 francs), and the receivable is denominated in francs. In *either case,* the purchase is recorded by Leader Corporation *in the domestic currency* at $25,000. If the billing is expressed in francs, Leader Corporation delivers 50,000 francs to Alps Company on the settlement date for the payable (January 31, 19X0). The spot rate on this date is .51. If the payable is settled in francs, Leader Corporation must acquire the needed francs through an exchange broker. Assume the francs are acquired on the settlement date. The entries for this example are shown in Illustration 12–4.

Again, the entries in column *(b)* need explanation. Entry (1) records Leader Corporation's purchase. Note that its payable is denominated in francs. Thus, the $25,000 values for the purchase and the payable are obtained by multiplying the billing of 50,000 francs by the purchase date spot rate of .5. On January 31, 19X0, Leader Corporation acquires the 50,000 francs it must deliver to Alps Company in

---

ILLUSTRATION 12-4　Import Transaction

			(a) Billing in Domestic Currency (Dollars)		(b) Billing in Foreign Currency (Francs)	
1.	1/1/X0	Purchases	25,000		25,000	
		Accounts Payable		25,000		25,000
2.	1/31/X0	Foreign Currency—Francs			25,500	
		Cash				25,500
3.	1/31/X0	Accounts Payable	25,000		25,000	
		Exchange Loss			500	
		Foreign Currency—Francs				25,500
		Cash		25,000		

settlement of its debt. Leader Corporation records the purchase of the 50,000 francs in entry (2) by debiting Foreign Currency—Francs. This debit equals the product of the number of francs purchased and the spot rate on the date they are acquired (50,000 × $.51). This debit is analogous to the debit made if 50,000 shares of a security are purchased for $.51 per share. Entry (3) records the exchange loss on the payable. The loss recorded equals the product of the 50,000 francs and the change in the spot rate between the purchase date and the settlement date [50,000 × ($.51 − $.5)]. This loss occurs because the dollar weakens in relation to the franc between these dates (see Illustration 12–2). In other words, the loss occurs because Leader Corporation has to pay more dollars to obtain the francs needed to liquidate its debt (50,000 × $.51) than it would have had to pay if the spot rate had not changed (50,000 × $.5).

Case 4. Hedging Exchange Risk on an Import Transaction

Assume the information of Case 3, except now assume specifically that the billing is in francs. Assume again that Leader Corporation decides to hedge its exchange risk using a forward exchange contract entered through the futures market. In general, a hedge *related to a payable* denominated in a foreign currency is accomplished by *purchasing* units of the foreign currency through an exchange broker on the date of the import transaction at a particular forward rate. Such hedges are referred to as *hedges of exposed liability positions* since they hedge the exchange risks related to obligations denominated in foreign currencies. The hedging transaction is arranged so that the receipt date of the foreign currency purchased (50,000 francs in this example) corresponds with the settlement date of

---

ILLUSTRATION 12–5   Hedging Exchange Risk on Import Transaction

			Import Transaction—Billing in Foreign Currency (Francs)		Hedging Transaction	
1.	1/1/X0	Purchases	25,000			
		Accounts Payable		25,000		
2.	1/1/X0	Francs Due from Exchange Broker			25,000	
		Dollars Due to Exchange Broker				25,000
3.	1/31/X0	Foreign Currency—Francs			25,500	
		Exchange Gain or Loss				500
		Francs Due from Exchange Broker				25,000
4.	1/31/X0	Dollars Due to Exchange Broker			25,000	
		Cash				25,000
5.	1/31/X0	Accounts Payable	25,000			
		Exchange Gain or Loss	500			
		Foreign Currency—Francs		25,500		

the payable. Thus, the forward rate at which the foreign currency is purchased is the rate for the period of time from the date of the import transaction to the settlement date of its payable. Again, the 30-day forward rate is pertinent in our example since the date of the import transaction is January 1, 19X0, and the settlement date of the payable is January 31, 19X0. We assume that the 30-day forward rate equals the spot rate on the date of the import transaction (.5) to illustrate a perfect hedge. We emphasize once more that these rates usually are not equal and, therefore, that hedges usually do not eliminate all exchange risk. The entries for this example are presented in Illustration 12–5. The first column in this illustration pertains to the import transaction, and the second column is related to the hedging transaction.

Entries (1) and (5) in Illustration 12–5 are identical to entries (1) and (3) of column *(b)* in Case 3. Entry (2) records Leader Corporation's forward exchange contract (hedge). The credit to Dollars Due to Exchange Broker (a payable) is the product of the *forward rate* (.5) and the number of francs purchased (50,000). This payable is denominated in dollars; thus, its existence does not expose Leader Corporation to exchange risk, and its balance is not adjusted over time. Note that Leader Corporation definitely pays the exchange broker $25,000 when it receives the purchased francs on January 31, 19X0, since the payable, Dollars Due to Exchange Broker, is denominated (fixed) in dollars. In contrast, the account debited in entry (2), Francs Due from Exchange Broker, is a receivable denominated in francs. Thus, its existence exposes Leader Corporation to exchange risk. As usual, exchange risk occurs since the current value of the receivable changes as the spot rate for the two companies' currencies fluctuates. Entry (2) debits Francs Due from Exchange Broker for an amount equal to the product of the *spot rate* on the import transaction date (also .5) and the number of francs purchased (50,000). Entry (3) records the receipt of the francs delivered by the exchange broker by debiting Foreign Currency—Francs for the value of the francs recieved—an amount equaling the product of the number of francs received and the spot rate on the settlement date (50,000 × $.51). Since the exchange broker has delivered the francs, entry (3) eliminates the balance in Francs Due from Exchange Broker. Entry (3) also records the exchange gain from the hedging transaction—$500. This gain equals the product of the number of francs purchased and the change in the spot rate between the import date and the settlement date [50,000 × ($.51 − $.5)]. It occurs because Leader Corporation only pays $25,000 for francs obtained from the exchange broker that are worth $25,500 (50,000 × $.51) on the settlement date (i.e., because the dollar weakens in relation to the franc between the import date and the settlement date). Note that the gain recorded in (3) exactly offsets the loss recorded in (5). Thus, Leader Corporation's hedge again is perfect; it eliminates all exchange risk. Entry (4) records the $25,000 payment to the exchange broker for the purchased francs.

To this point, our discussions assume that all transactions are settled within the same reporting period and that all pertinent forward rates and spot rates are the same. The next two cases relax these assumptions.

Additional Discussion of Forward Rates and Values on Financial Reporting Dates

As indicated, we assume in Cases 5 and 6 that relevant spot rates and forward rates are not the same and that settlements related to various transactions and their hedges are not made in the same reporting periods. Thus, additional discussion of forward rates, the existence of differences in these rates and pertinent spot rates, and the values for receivables and payables denominated in foreign currencies on financial reporting dates is appropriate.

Note first that spot rates and forward rates usually differ at least slightly. For example, consider the following September 23, 1991, quotations for the Japanese yen and the Canadian dollar reported on September 24, 1991, in *The Wall Street Journal*:

	(Direct Quotation) U.S. Dollar Price of	
	One Japanese Yen	One Canadian Dollar
Spot rate	$0.007536	$0.8818
Forward rates:		
30-day forward	0.007527	0.8797
90-day forward	0.007517	0.8755
180-day forward	0.007516	0.8706

When the forward rate is lower (as on both of the above currencies), the difference between the two rates is called a *discount*. When the forward rate is higher, the difference between the two rates is referred to as a *premium*. Although many factors affect discounts and premiums at any time, they generally are attributable to interest rate differentials between currencies in the Euromarket for currencies.[6]

The existence of discounts and premiums alters the accounting techniques illustrated previously only minimally in the context of hedges of exchange risk on export and import transactions. That is, they are accounted for separately from the exchange gains and losses from these transactions and are included in the determination of net income over the duration of the forward exchange contracts. This procedure is illustrated in Cases 5 and 6.

---

[6] The Euromarket for currencies is an international market for currencies that is free of regulations. The market consists of deposits and loans of freely convertible currencies, with interest rates reflecting the supply and demand for the currencies. The related market for dollars is called the *Eurodollar market*. Whenever the discount or premium in the futures market fails to reflect the interest rate differentials in the Euromarket, there is a chance for arbitrage transactions, which restore the equality.

The issue of the values of receivables and payables denominated in foreign currencies on financial reporting dates in the context of export and import transactions and related hedges is more substantive in terms of the accounting procedures required. That is, these values must be adjusted on each financial reporting date using current spot rates (i.e., the spot rates in existence on the statement dates). The need to adjust such account balances again reflects the general principle that receivables and payables denominated in foreign currencies arising from nonspeculative transactions are reported on all financial reporting dates at their current values (i.e., using current spot rates). The required adjustment techniques also are illustrated in Cases 5 and 6.

Case 5. Export Transaction and Hedge—Advanced Example

Assume the information of Case 2, except now assume that the related receivable will be settled on March 2, 19X0, and that January 31, 19X0, is an interim reporting date. Assume also that the spot rate on March 2, 19X0, is 1.56 and that the 60-day forward rate is 1.55. Recall that the January 1, 19X0, and January 31, 19X0, spot rates are 1.50 and 1.52, respectively. Again, Leader Corporation decides to minimize its exchange risk by entering into a forward exchange contract. In this case, the hedging transaction is arranged so that the delivery date of the foreign currency sold (10,000 pounds) is March 2, 19X0. Thus, the 60-day forward rate is pertinent in recording the Dollars Due from Exchange Broker balance arising from the hedging transaction. In contrast, current spot rates are used in accounting for the Accounts Receivable and the Pounds Due to Exchange Broker balances at all significant points in time, including the sale date, the interim financial reporting date, and, in effect, the settlement date. The entries for this example are presented in Illustration 12–6. The first column in this illustration pertains to the export transaction, and the second column is related to the hedging transaction. With the exceptions of the amounts in entries (3) and (4), the entries are not explained for the sake of brevity; the remainder of the amounts are easily derived using the exchange rates given above. The amounts in entries (3) and (4) equal the product of the change in the spot rate between 1/1/X0 and 1/31/X0 (1.52 − 1.50) and the 10,000 pound values involved in the contracts.

Case 6. Import Transaction and Hedge—Advanced Example

Assume the information of Case 4, only now assume that the related payable will be settled on March 2, 19X0, and that January 31, 19X0, is an interim reporting date. Assume also that the spot rate on March 2, 19X0, is .53 and that the 60-day forward rate is .55. As before, the January 1, 19X0, and January 31, 19X0, spot rates are .50 and .51, respectively. Once again, Leader Corporation decides to minimize its exchange risk by entering into a forward exchange contract. In this

ILLUSTRATION 12-6   **Hedging Exchange Risk on Export Transaction—Advanced Example**

			Export Transaction— Billing in Foreign Currency (Pounds)		Hedging Transaction	
1.	1/1/X0	Accounts Receivable	15,000			
		Sales		15,000		
2.	1/1/X0	Dollars Due from Exchange Broker			15,500	
		Pounds Due to Exchange Broker				15,000
		Deferred Premium on Forward Contract				500
3.	1/31/X0	Accounts Receivable	200			
		Exchange Gain or Loss		200		
4.	1/31/X0	Exchange Gain or Loss			200	
		Pounds Due to Exchange Broker				200
5.	1/31/X0	Deferred Premium on Forward Contract				
		(.5 × $500)			250	
		Other Income				250
6.	3/2/X0	Foreign Currency—Pounds	15,600			
		Exchange Gain or Loss		400		
		Accounts Receivable		15,200		
7.	3/2/X0	Pounds Due to Exchange Broker			15,200	
		Exchange Gain or Loss			400	
		Foreign Currency—Pounds				15,600
8.	3/2/X0	Cash			15,500	
		Dollars Due from Exchange Broker				15,500
9.	3/2/X0	Deferred Premium on Forward Contract				
		(.5 × $500)			250	
		Other income				250

case, the hedging transaction is arranged so that the acquisition date of the foreign currency purchased (50,000 francs) is March 2, 19X0. Thus, the 60-day forward rate is relevant in recording the Dollars Due to Exchange Broker balance arising from the hedging transaction. In contrast, current spot rates are used in accounting for the Accounts Payable and the Francs Due from Exchange Broker balances at all significant points in time, including the sale date, the interim financial reporting date, and, in effect, the settlement date. The entries for this example are given in Illustration 12-7. The first column in this illustration pertains to the import transaction, and its second column is related to the hedging transaction. Again, the entries are not explained for the sake of brevity with the exception of the amounts in entries (3) and (4). These amounts equal the product of the change in the spot rate between 1/1/X0 and 1/31/X0 (.51 − .50) and the 50,000 franc values related to the contracts.

ILLUSTRATION 12-7   Hedging Exchange Risk on Import Transaction—Advanced Example

			Import Transaction—Billing in Foreign Currency (Francs)		Hedging Transaction	
1.	1/1/X0	Purchases	25,000			
		Accounts Payable		25,000		
2.	1/1/X0	Francs Due from Exchange Broker			25,000	
		Deferred Premium on Forward Contract			2,500	
		Dollars Due to Exchange Broker				27,500
3.	1/31/X0	Exchange Gain or Loss	500			
		Accounts Payable		500		
4.	1/31/X0	Francs Due from Exchange Broker			500	
		Exchange Gain or Loss				500
5.	1/31/X0	Other Expense (.5 × $2,500)			1,250	
		Deferred Premium on Forward Contract				1,250
6.	3/2/X0	Foreign Currency—Francs			26,500	
		Exchange Gain or Loss				1,000
		Francs Due from Exchange Broker				25,500
7.	3/2/X0	Dollars Due to Exchange Broker			27,500	
		Cash				27,500
8.	3/2/X0	Accounts Payable	25,500			
		Exchange Gain or Loss	1,000			
		Foreign Currency—Francs		26,500		
9.	3/2/X0	Other Expense			1,250	
		Deferred Premium on Forward Contract				1,250

Discussion of Exchange Gains and Losses from Export and Import Transactions

The procedures described above for recording transaction exchange gains and losses are consistent with the two-transaction perspective on these gains and losses. Under this view, the decision to export or import goods is separate from the decision to assume the exchange risk related to an export or import transaction. Furthermore, the billing on an export or import transaction denominated in a foreign currency is viewed as resulting from arm's length bargaining based partially on the exchange rate prevailing on the purchase or sale date and ignoring possible fluctuations in this rate. Thus, under the two-transaction perspective, transaction gains and losses do not affect the recorded amounts of sales or purchases. These amounts are as though the billing is denominated in the domestic currency. Additionally, under this viewpoint, transaction exchange gains or losses resulting from exporting and importing companies' decisions not to hedge are disclosed in their income statements separately as items which are related to financial, rather than operating, decisions.[7] The two-transaction perspective obtained authoritative support initially through *Statement of Financial Accounting Standards No. 8.*[8] *Statement of Financial Accounting Standards No. 52* retains this support since it requires separate disclosure of transaction exchange gains and losses.

The alternative to the two-transaction view is the one-transaction perspective. Under this view, transaction exchange gains or losses affect the recorded amounts of sales or purchases from export and import transactions. More specifically, they either increase or decrease these amounts, depending on whether they are debits or credits. For example, if a sale of $10,000 is recorded and a related transaction exchange loss (a debit) of $500 occurs, the sales value ultimately recorded is $9,500. This treatment is a result of viewing a purchase or sale and the future payment or collection as components of a single transaction. This perspective is not appropriate under existing pronouncements.

FORWARD EXCHANGE CONTRACTS—ADDITIONAL ISSUES

The cases presented above combine forward exchange contracts with export and import transactions to introduce the accounting procedures related to the hedging opportunities of exporters and importers. Note, however, that forward exchange contracts are used by firms to manage additional types of exchange rate risk and to speculate in exchange rate fluctuations. Speculative contracts are foreign currency transactions by definition since they produce receivables and payables denominated in foreign currencies.

The accounting principles pertaining to a forward exchange contract depend on the contract's type. For accounting purposes, there are two pertinent classes of forward exchange contracts: (1) hedging contracts and (2) speculative contracts. In addition, different accounting treatments are applied to the various types of forward exchange hedging contracts. From the perspective of accounting treat-

---

[7] Transaction exchange gains and losses usually are recognized in the income statement. Nevertheless, there are two cases noted in *Statement of Financial Accounting Standards No. 52* (par. 20) where all, or some portion, of such a gain or loss is not shown in the income statement: (1) the transaction producing the gain or loss is designated, and effective, as an economic hedge of a net investment (ownership interest) in a foreign entity or (2) the gain or loss results from a long-term intercompany investment transaction between companies reporting through consolidated financial statements or under the equity method. In these cases, all, or some portion, of related exchange gains or losses are accumulated in shareholders' equity accounts in the same manner as translation adjustments (i.e., in Cumulative Foreign Exchange Translation Adjustments accounts). See Chapters 13 and 14 for further discussion.

[8] FASB, *Statement of Financial Accounting Standards No. 8,* "Accounting for the Translation of Foreign Currency Transactions and Foreign Currency Financial Statements" (Norwalk, CT: FASB, 1975).

ment, the relevant classes of forward exchange hedging contracts are: (1) hedges of identifiable foreign currency commitments, (2) hedges of exposed asset and liability positions (such as receivables and payables from export and import transactions as illustrated in Cases 2, 4, 5, and 6), and (3) hedges of net investments (ownership interests) in foreign entities (see discussion in Chapter 14). In illustrating the accounting procedures for these classes below, we assume that settlements related to various transactions and their hedges are made in different reporting periods and that pertinent spot rates and forward rates are not the same.

Case 7. Hedging an Identifiable Foreign Currency Commitment

A hedge of an identifiable foreign currency commitment is undertaken because exchange rate risk can be experienced before an accounting transaction is recorded. For example, a domestic company might enter a contract to manufacture merchandise for a foreign company at a fixed price denominated in the foreign company's currency. Since the contract is executory, the sales entry is not made until the goods are delivered. However, the domestic company is exposed to exchange risk once the contract is signed. *The exchange risk is the same as if a receivable and the related sale are recorded on the contract date.* Thus, the domestic company has the opportunity to enter a forward exchange contract on the contract date to minimize this risk. Such a contract is classified, for accounting purposes, as a hedge of an identifiable foreign currency commitment.[9] Although we illustrate the hedge of an identifiable foreign currency commitment only in relation to an export transaction, note that such hedges also are pertinent in the case of import transactions.

Except for a few details, the procedures related to hedges of foreign currency commitments are like those of the earlier cases given. Thus, in this case, the (export) sale is recorded using the spot rate on the sale date. Additionally, when recording the hedge, the debit to Dollars Due from Exchange Broker is based on the forward rate on the date the forward exchange contract is entered, and the credit to Marks Due to Exchange Broker (a payable denominated in marks) is based on the spot rate on this date. The more important features of this case are: (1) the need to adjust the Marks Due to Exchange Broker balance prior to settlement, (2) the use of a Deferred Exchange Gain or Loss account, and (3) the existence of a deferred premium on the hedging transaction. The need to adjust the Marks Due to Exchange Broker account (again) reflects the general principle that receivables and payables denominated in foreign currencies arising from nonspeculative transactions are accounted for at all significant points in time at their current values (using current spot rates). That is, as illustrated earlier,

---

[9] *Statement of Financial Accounting Standards No. 52* (par. 21) establishes the following conditions for this type of hedge: (1) "the foreign currency transaction is designated as, and is effective as, a hedge of a foreign currency commitment" and (2) "the foreign currency commitment is firm."

receivables and payables denominated in foreign currencies and related exchange gains and losses (deferred or otherwise) are adjusted using the spot rates on financial reporting dates. Additionally, these accounts are adjusted on the sale date so that sales revenue is determined properly (see below). The need to use a Deferred Exchange Gain or Loss account occurs because the forward exchange contract is entered prior to the sale date. Thus, this account is used to accumulate transaction exchange gains or losses occurring through the point of sale. On the sale date, the balance of this account is closed to Sales under the theory that related hedging activities are intended to protect the selling company's gross profit.[10] The existence of a deferred premium on the hedging transaction arises because the spot rate and the pertinent forward rate are different on the date of the forward exchange contract. There are two alternatives for dealing with deferred premiums and discounts from forward exchange contracts hedging sales related to identifiable foreign currency commitments: (1) amortize them over the duration of the forward exchange contract with amortization up to the point of sale being closed to Sales and (2) amortize them against income, in general, over this period (at a rate corresponding to their interest rate differential characteristics). We illustrate the former procedure in the following example because it is the procedure usually used in practice.

Assume that a domestic company contracts on July 15, 19X1, to manufacture merchandise for a customer in Germany on December 15, 19X1, for 300,000 marks. On July 15, the spot rate for marks is .50, and the domestic company's expected cost of sales is $100,000. Thus, the contract provides a gross margin of $50,000 based on the current spot rate [300,000 × $.50) − $100,000]. However, the domestic company does not have a binding claim against its customer until the merchandise is delivered. Thus, the sale is not recorded until delivery of the goods. Assume further that the terms of the contract allow 30 days for payment. Thus, payment is not received until January 14, 19X2. During the six-month period between the contract date and the settlement date, the domestic company is exposed to exchange rate risk because of possible fluctuations in the mark's spot rate. The company decides to hedge its risk by entering a forward exchange contract to sell 300,000 marks in six months at the July 15, 19X1, 180-day forward rate of .51. Recall that the forward rate fixes the number of dollars [$153,000 = 300,000 × $.51] that the company receives from the exchange broker in return for the 300,000 marks on the settlement date. The obligation to deliver the 300,000 marks to the exchange broker represents a hedge of the foreign currency commitment for the first five months of the contract. The function of the forward exchange contract generating the hedge is to protect the domestic company's $50,000 gross profit as far as possible. The difference of .01 in the spot rate and the 180-day forward rate on July 15, 19X1, is the premium on the mark. The product of the premium and the 300,000 marks to be delivered [$3,000 = (300,000 × $.01)]

---

[10] Note that *Statement of Financial Accounting Standards No. 52* (par. 21) indicates that losses are not deferred beyond the current period "if it is estimated that deferral would lead to recognizing losses in later periods."

is the premium on the forward exchange contract. The following future spot rates are assumed: September 30, 19X1—.55 and December 15, 19X1—.58. These rates are needed to adjust the balance of marks due to exchange broker on the interim financial statement date of September 30, 19X1, and on the sale date of December 15, 19X1. The entries for this example are presented in Illustration 12–8. The entries cover the period from the contract date to the date the sale is recorded.

Entry (1) in Illustration 12–8 is consistent with the Case 2 entry to record the hedge on the export transaction. That is, the debit of $153,000 to Dollars Due from Exchange Broker equals the product of the 300,000 marks sold and the .51 July 15, 19X1, 180-day forward rate. Also, the credit of $150,000 to Marks Due to Exchange Broker equals the product of the 300,000 marks sold and the July 15, 19X1, spot rate. The credit to Deferred Premium on Forward Contract is the difference between the debit and the credit just mentioned; this amount is calculated above. Entry (2) adjusts the Marks Due to Exchange Broker balance and records the related Deferred Exchange Gain or Loss for the September 30, 19X1, financial statements. The amount of this entry equals the current value of the Marks Due to Exchange Broker account less the balance in this account recorded on July 15, 19X1. The current value of this account is the product of the 300,000 marks sold

---

ILLUSTRATION 12-8   Hedging an Identifiable Foreign Currency Commitment

	Sales Transaction	Forward Exchange Contract
1. On July 15, 19X1 (contract date):		
Dollars Due from Exchange Broker		
(300,000 × $.51)		153,000
Deferred Premium on Forward Contract		
(300,000 × $.01)		3,000
Marks Due to Exchange Broker		
(300,000 × $.50)		150,000
2. On September 30, 19X1 (for quarterly financial statements):		
Deferred Exchange Gain or Loss		15,000
Marks Due to Exchange Broker		
[(300,000 × $.55) − $150,000]		15,000
3. On December 15, 19X1 (sale date):		
Deferred Exchange Gain or Loss		9,000
Marks Due to Exchange Broker		
[(300,000 × $.58) − $165,000]		9,000
Accounts Receivable	174,000	
Sales (300,000 × $.58)		174,000
Sales		24,000
Deferred Exchange Gain or Loss		
($15,000 + $9,000)		24,000
Deferred Premium on Forward Contract		2,500
Sales (5/6 × $3,000)		2,500

and the September 30, 19X1, spot rate of .55. The first entry in (3) adjusts the Marks Due to Exchange Broker balance and the Deferred Exchange Gain or Loss balance as of the sale date. The amount of this entry is the current value of the Marks Due to Exchange Broker account less the balance in this account recorded through September 30, 19X1 ($150,000 + $15,000). The current value of this account is the product of the 300,000 marks sold and the December 15, 19X1, spot rate of .58. The second entry in (3) records the sale, and the third entry in (3) closes the Deferred Exchange Gain or Loss account to the Sales account. The final entry in (3) amortizes the portion of the Deferred Premium on Forward Contract balance applicable to the period July 15, 19X1, to December 15, 19X1, to the Sales account.

The balance for Sales resulting from the entries in Illustration 12–8 is $152,500 ($174,000 − $24,000 + $2,500). Ignoring the credit to Sales for deferred premium amortization, the balance in Sales is $150,000. Thus, except for the amount of the deferred premium amortization, the forward exchange contract generating the hedge protects the domestic company's gross profit completely. As indicated above, the purpose of the contract is to protect this profit as much as possible. Generally, a forward exchange contract cannot protect a company's gross profit perfectly because there usually is a difference in the pertinent spot and forward rates. Illustration 12–8 also reveals that the following receivables and payables exist on December 15, 19X1:

	Balance December 15, 19X1
Claims denominated in marks:	
Accounts Receivable	$174,000
Marks Due to Exchange Broker	174,000
Claims denominated in dollars:	
Dollars Due from Exchange Broker	153,000

The two claims denominated in marks have the same balance because each represents a claim to 300,000 marks. The obligation to the exchange broker will be satisifed with the marks received from the German customer on the settlement date. These balances are pertinent in the following case.

Case 8. *Hedging an Exposed Asset Position*

By continuing the example begun in Case 7 over the period December 16, 19X1, to January 14, 19X2, a hedging contract falling into the hedges of exposed asset and liability positions category is illustrated. During this period, the forward exchange contract hedges the receivable from the sale to the German customer—which is denominated in marks. The procedures of this case are essentially the same as those of Cases 2 and 5 since each involves a hedge of an exposed asset position. Specifically, we continue to value all accounts denominated in a foreign currency (marks in this case) using the spot rate on the valuation date. Also, the transaction exchange gains or losses arising in this case are recorded consistently with the earlier cases. The more important features of this case are: (1) adjusting Marks Due to Exchange Broker and Accounts Receivable prior to settlement and (2) amortizing the deferred premium from the forward exchange contract. The need to adjust Marks Due to Exchange Broker and Accounts Receivable arises because a financial reporting date occurs between December 15, 19X1, and January 14, 19X2. The need to amortize the deferred premium balance occurs because premiums or discounts from forward exchange contracts are amortized over the lives of the contracts (whether or not they affect sales revenue). In continuing our example, we assume the following spot rates: December 31, 19X1—.56 and January 14, 19X2—.62. The entries for Case 8 are found in Illustration 12–9. Although we only illustrate the hedge of an exposed asset position in the context of a sales-related foreign currency commitment in this section of the chapter, recognize that similar principles also apply to hedges of exposed liability positions in the context of purchase-related foreign currency commitments.

The entries in (1) in Illustration 12–9 are adjusting entries needed at December 31, 19X1, the annual financial statement date. The first entry adjusts Marks Due to Exchange Broker and records the related exchange gain. The amount of

---

ILLUSTRATION 12-9   Hedging an Exposed Asset Position

	Exposed Asset Position		Forward Exchange Contract	
1. On December 31, 19X1 (for annual financial statements):				
Marks Due to Exchange Broker			6,000	
Exchange Gain or Loss [(300,000 × $.56) − $174,000]				6,000
Exchange Gain or Loss	6,000			
Accounts Receivable [(300,000 × $.56) − $174,000]		6,000		
Deferred Premium on Forward Contract			250	
Other income [1/2 × ($3,000 − $2,500)]				250
2. On January 14, 19X2 (maturity of forward contract and collection of acount receivable):				
Foreign Currency—Marks (300,000 × $.62)	186,000			
Exchange Gain or Loss		18,000		
Accounts Receivable		168,000		
Marks Due to Exchange Broker			168,000	
Exchange Gain or Loss			18,000	
Foreign Currency—Marks				186,000
Cash			153,000	
Dollars Due from Exchange Broker				153,000
Deferred Premium on Forward Contract			250	
Other Income				250

this entry is the current value of the Marks Due to Exchange Broker account less the balance in this account recorded through December 15, 19X1 ($150,000 + $15,000 + $9,000). The current value of this account is the product of the 300,000 marks sold and the December 31, 19X1, spot rate of .56. In this case, the adjustment reduces the balance in Marks Due to Exchange Broker. The second entry in (1) adjusts Accounts Receivable and records the associated exchange loss. This entry's amount equals the current value of the Accounts Receivable account less the balance in this account recorded on the sale date of December 15, 19X1 ($174,000). The current value of the Accounts Receivable balance is the product of the 300,000 marks to be delivered by the German customer and the December 31, 19X1, spot rate of .56. The final entry in (1) records amortization of the deferred premium for the period December 15, 19X1, through December 31, 19X1. The last entry of (2) records amortization of the deferred premium for the period January 1, 19X2, through January 14, 19X2. Except for this entry, the entries of (2) are much like those of earlier cases (and, thus, are not discussed).

From an overall perspective, the hedge of the exposed asset position largely eliminates all of the domestic company's exchange risk. That is, the exchange gain on the receivable denominated in marks for the period December 16, 19X1, through January 14, 19X2 ($18,000 − $6,000) is completely offset by the exchange loss ($18,000 − $6,000) from the payable denominated in marks (Marks Due to Exchange Broker) over this period. The only income statement effect of the portion of the forward exchange contract hedging the exposed asset position is the (total) $500 credit to Other Income from the final entries in (1) and (2). Effects of this type are virtually unavoidable since pertinent spot rates and forward rates almost always are different.

Case 9. Speculation in Foreign Currency Exchange Price Fluctuations

The purpose of a forward exchange contract entered for speculation is to realize a gain from a favorable fluctuation in the pertinent exchange rate. The accounting procedures for such contracts are similar in form to those for exposed asset and liability positions. For example, transaction exchange gains and losses are recorded on these contracts on the settlement date and on intervening financial statement dates. Nevertheless, the rate used in determining the gain or loss for a period on a speculative contract differs from the one used in the case of a hedge of an exposed asset or liability position. The rate used on a speculative contract is the forward rate pertaining to the remaining life of the contract. Another difference between the accounting procedures for a speculative forward exchange contract and those for a hedge of an exposed asset or liability position is that *both* the receivable and the payable related to the speculative contract are recorded initially using the forward rate relevant to the period covered by the contract (e.g., the 90-day forward rate, if the contract covers a 90-day period). Since both the receivable and the payable are recorded using the same rate, no premium or discount is recorded on such a contract. The following example illustrates the principles just mentioned.

Assume that the management of a domestic company believes the exchange rate between U.S. and Canadian dollars will increase over the next three months and, consequently, decides to purchase Canadian dollars to be received in the future. Specifically, assume that the company purchases 100,000 Canadian dollars on December 1, 19X1, for delivery in 90 days. On this date, the spot rate for the Canadian dollar is .75, and the 90-day forward rate is .74. Assume also that the 60-day forward rate is .76 on December 31, 19X1, and that the spot rate on March 1, 19X2, is .72. The company's entries for its speculative forward exchange contract are shown in Illustration 12–10.

The first entry in Illustration 12–10 records the speculative forward exchange contract. The amounts in this entry are based on the 90-day forward rate of .74. Entry (2) adjusts the receivable denominated in the foreign currency, Canadian Dollars Due from Exchange Broker, and records the related exchange gain for the annual financial statements. The amount of this adjustment is based on the 60-day forward rate of .76, since there are 60 days remaining on the contract at December 31, 19X1. Specifically, the adjustment equals the product of this rate and the 100,000 Canadian Dollars purchased, less the balance of Canadian Dollars Due from Exchange Broker recorded on the contract date. The entries in (3) record the settlement of the speculative contract at maturity. The first of these entries

---

ILLUSTRATION 12–10   Speculation in Foreign Currency Exchange Price Fluctuations

		Speculative Forward Exchange Contract
1.	On December 1, 19X1 (contract date):		
	Canadian Dollars Due from Exchange Broker		
	(100,000 × $.74)	74,000	
	U.S. Dollars Due to Exchange Broker		74,000
2.	On December 31, 19X1 (for annual financial statements):		
	Canadian Dollars Due from Exchange Broker		
	[(100,000 × $.76) − $74,000]	2,000	
	Exchange Gain or Loss		2,000
3.	On March 1, 19X2 (maturity of forward contract):		
	U.S. Dollars Due to Exchange Broker	74,000	
	Cash		74,000
	Foreign Currency—Canadian Dollars		
	(100,000 × $.72)	72,000	
	Exchange Gain or Loss	4,000	
	Canadian Dollars Due from Exchange Broker		
	($74,000 + $2,000)		76,000

records the payment of the (fixed) number of U.S. dollars ($74,000) to the exchange broker. The second entry in (3) records the receipt of the Canadian dollars from the broker. The debit to Foreign Currency—Canadian Dollars equals the current value of the currency received determined using the spot rate on the settlement date. The loss recorded is the difference in the current value of the Canadian dollars received and the balance in Canadian Dollars Due from Exchange Broker recorded through entries (1) and (2) ($74,000 + $2,000). From an overall perspective, the domestic company incurs a $2,000 loss on the speculative contract—the difference between the $74,000 cash paid to the exchange broker and the $72,000 value of the Canadian dollars received. This loss occurs because the value of the U.S. dollar strengthened relative to the Canadian dollar (from the perspective of the December 1, 19X1, 90-day forward rate of .74 and the March 1, 19X2, spot rate of .72).[11] Although we illustrate only the purchase of units of a foreign currency, sales of such units are handled similarly.

MULTIPLE EXCHANGE RATES

If commitments or accounts are denominated in a foreign currency that has multiple exchange rates, the following rates are used:

1. At the transaction date, the transaction is recorded using the rate at which that particular type of transaction can be settled immediately.
2. At future financial statement dates, receivables and payables are valued using the rates at which they can be settled immediately.

Normally, the same rate is used over the period including the transaction and settlement dates.

---

[11] In this example, the speculative forward contract is specifically identified. In principle, the same accounting treatment seems pertinent to the amount of any hedging contract in excess of the related foreign currency exposure. While *Statement of Financial Accounting Standards No. 52* adheres to the substance of this observation, two points are relevant. First, and more important, the measure of excess amount includes recognition of the related tax effect. For example, under this standard (par. 21), if a forward exchange contract that exceeds the related foreign currency commitment is entered to provide a hedge on an after-tax basis, the excess part of the hedge covering the tax effect also is deferred and recognized as an offset in the period the tax effect is recognized (*Statement of Financial Accounting Standards No. 52*—par. 129—also discusses the recognition of the after-tax effects of hedges of net investments in foreign entities). Second, *Statement of Financial Accounting Standards No. 52* is unclear on the valuation of the exchange gain or loss on the after-tax excess. Specifically, it is ambiguous on whether forward rates are used in this context only on contracts that are *classified as speculative* or on *all* contracts that are *determined* to be speculative. Because exchange gains and losses are produced by *changes* in rates over pertinent time periods, using either spot rates or forward rates probably tends to yield the same results.

Summary

This chapter covers the accounting procedures applying to various foreign currency transactions (including forward exchange contracts entered for speculative purposes). Foreign currency transactions result in receivables or payables on domestic companies' books that are *denominated in foreign currencies*. A receivable or payable is denominated in a foreign currency if it is to be settled using that currency. The main problems arising in connection with such receivables and payables are: (1) determining the amounts at which they are recorded in the domestic currency, (2) accounting for their related transaction exchange gains or losses (which occur because of changes in the values of the receivables and payables resulting from fluctuations in the exchange rates between the domestic and foreign currencies), and (3) accounting for forward exchange contracts that are entered to hedge the transaction exchange gains and losses. The hedging transactions are designed to largely eliminate the effects of the exchange gains or losses from the receivables and payables.

The accounting principles pertaining to a forward exchange contract depend on the contract's type. For accounting purposes, there are two relevant classes of forward exchange contracts: (1) hedging contracts and (2) speculative contracts. Furthermore, different accounting treatments are pertinent to different types of forward exchange hedging contracts. The major classes of forward exchange hedging contracts are: (1) hedges of identifiable foreign currency commitments, (2) hedges of exposed asset and liability positions, and (3) hedges of net investments (ownership interests) in foreign entities. The accounting procedures applying to forward exchange contracts are summarized in Illustration 12–11.

Both hedges of identifiable foreign currency commitments and hedges of exposed asset and liability positions are related to export and import transactions. The procedures we illustrate for dealing with transaction exchange gains and losses from these transactions are consistent with the two-transaction perspective—which views the decision to export or import goods as separate from the decision to assume the exchange risk related to the export or import transaction. Under the two-transaction perspective, transaction exchange gains and losses do not affect the recorded amounts of sales or purchases. These amounts are recorded as though the billing is denominated in the domestic currency. Additionally, under this viewpoint, transaction exchange gains or losses resulting from exporting or importing companies' decisions not to hedge are disclosed in their income statements separately as items resulting from financial, rather than operating, decisions.

Questions

1. What is a currency exchange rate?
2. Distinguish between free and official rates of exchange.
3. Distinguish between quoting an exchange rate for a given currency directly and indirectly.
4. Distinguish between spot and forward rates of exchange.
5. What relationship exists between directly and indirectly quoted exchange rates?

ILLUSTRATION 12-11   Accounting Procedures for Forward Exchange Contracts

Type	Exchange Rate Used to Value Receivables and Payables Denominated in Foreign Currency	Treatment of Transaction Exchange Gains and Losses	Treatment of Amortization of Discounts and Premiums
1. Hedges of identifiable foreign currency commitments	Spot rate	Defer to date of transaction and then close to Sales or Purchases	Treat the same as exchange gain or loss or show separately in income statement
2. Hedges of exposed asset and liability positions	Spot rate	Include in income statement	Include in income statement
3. Hedge of net investments in foreign entities (see Chapter 14)	Spot rate	Include as separate component of shareholders' equity	Treat the same as exchange gain or loss or show separately in income statement
4. Speculative contracts	Forward rate (for time period equal to remaining life of contract)	Include in income statement	Not recorded

---

6. Briefly explain the concept of functional currency.

7. What is a foreign currency transaction?

8. When do exchange gains and losses occur on export/import transactions?

9. How are exchange gains and losses arising from export/import transactions reported?

10. Briefly explain how hedging is achieved through forward exchange contracts.

11. Summarize current accounting policy related to export/import transactions which result in receivables and payables denominated in foreign currencies.

12. Identify and explain the major accounting categories of forward exchange contracts and summarize current accounting policy related to these contracts.

13. When multiple exchange rates exist, what rate is used in accounting for foreign currency transactions?

Exercises

Exercise 12-1   (Exchange Rate Calculations)

Bill Branch is planning a trip through several foreign countries. He plans to purchase and evaluate a variety of products sold in each country for sale in his import shop. In anticipation of his trip, Branch purchases $500 of currency for each country he plans to visit. He receives the following amounts:

Country	Currency	Amount Received
Belgium	Franc	29,500
Denmark	Krone	5,750
France	Franc	4,900
Italy	Lira	935,000

Required:

Calculate the exchange rate between U.S. dollars and each foreign currency purchased by Branch both directly and indirectly.

Exercise 12–2   (Export and Import Transactions)

Journalize the following transactions of Black and White Company (a New York company) arising from its export/import operations:

June 1   Purchased merchandise from an Edinburgh, Scotland, manufacturer at an invoice cost of 1,000 pounds. On this date, the exchange rate for pounds is 1.20.

5   Purchased merchandise from a Glasgow, Scotland, manufacturer. The billing is $2,000. The exchange rate for pounds is 1.21.

7   Sold merchandise to a Toronto wholesaler. The billing price is 4,000 Canadian dollars, and the exchange rate for Canadian dollars is .80.

15   Paid 500 pounds on account to the Edinburgh manufacturer. The exchange rate is 1.15.

20   Paid the amount due to the Glasgow manufacturer. The exchange rate is 1.18.

25   Returned merchandise to the Edinburgh manufacturer and received credit for 100 pounds. The exchange rate is 1.15.

28   Received full payment on account from the Toronto wholesaler. The exchange rate is .76.

30   Remitted final payment to the Edinburgh manufacturer. The exchange rate is 1.16.

Exercise 12–3   (Export and Import Transactions and Hedges)

Prepare the journal entries to record the following transactions on the books of Schwab Company.

a. Schwab Company purchases merchandise from Zee Company of Portugal for 300,000 escudos when the exchange rate for escudos is .007. At the same time, Schwab Company purchases 100,000 escudos for future delivery at .007.

b. Schwab Company pays Zee Company for the purchase in (a) when the exchange rate for the escudo is .005. The escudos purchased in (a) are received from the exchange broker.

c. Schwab Company sells merchandise to Dee Company of Finland for 20,000 markkas when the exchange rate for the markka is .18. Also, Schwab Company sells 5,000 markkas for future delivery at .18.

d. Schwab Company receives payment from Dee Company related to *(c)* when the exchange rate for the markka is .16. The markkas sold in *(c)* are delivered to the exchange broker.

Exercise 12–4   (Export and Import Transactions and Hedges)

X Company, a U.S. company whose functional currency is the dollar, engages in the following international transactions during December 19X1 (all billings are denominated in a foreign currency):

1. X Company sells merchandise to Y Company of Italy for 2 million lira when the exchange rate for the lira is .00052. X Company also sells 1 million lira for future delivery at .00052.

2. X Company receives payment from Y Company related to (1) when the exchange rate for the lira is .0006. The lira sold in (1) are delivered to the exchange broker.

3. X Company purchases merchandise from A Company of Great Britain for 5,000 pounds when the exchange rate for the pound is 1.20. Concurrently, X Company purchases 5,000 pounds for future delivery at 1.20.

4. X Company receives the pounds related to (3) from the exchange broker. X Company then pays A Company for the merchandise purchased in (3) using these pounds. On this date, the exchange rate for the pound is 1.25.

5. X Company sells merchandise to B Company of Mexico for 100,000 pesos when the exchange rate for the peso is .0045.

6. X Company purchases merchandise from C Company of Mexico for 200,000 pesos when the exchange rate for the peso is .0045.

Required:

a. Prepare the journal entries to record the above transactions on X Company's books.

b. Assuming that the receivable and payable created by the last two transactions remain unsettled on December 31, 19X1, discuss their valuation if the exchange rate is .005. Would your answer be different if X Company had purchased and sold pesos for future delivery instead of merchandise?

Exercise 12–5   (Speculation in Foreign Currency)

McCaskill, Inc., decides to speculate in the forward market. On May 1, 19X1, McCaskill purchases 1 million Japanese yen for delivery in 90 days. On this date, the spot rate for the yen is .004, and the 90-day forward rate is .0042.

McCaskill's fiscal year ends on June 30. On this date, the spot rate for the yen is .0044, and selected forward rates are 30-day—.00445 and 90-day—.0046.

Required:

Prepare the May 1 and June 30 journal entries related to McCaskill's forward exchange contract.

Exercise 12–6   (Calculations of Exchange Gains or Losses)

Choose the best answer for each of the following questions.

1. Corvus Company, a U.S. company, orders a machine from Walker Company of New Zealand on July 15, 19X4, for 100,000 New Zealand dollars when the spot rate is .4955. Walker Company ships the machine on September 1, 19X4, and bills Corvus Company for 100,000 New Zealand dollars. The spot rate is .4875 on this date. On October 25, 19X4, when the spot rate is .4855, Corvus Company buys 100,000 New Zealand dollars and pays its invoice. On Corvus Company's December 31, 19X4, income statement, the amount of the transaction exchange gain is
   a. $0.
   b. $200.
   c. $800.
   d. $1,000.

2. On October 1, 19X1, Rock Company loans $120,000 to a foreign supplier, evidenced by an interest-bearing note due on October 1, 19X2. The note is denominated in the currency of the borrower and is equivalent to 840,000 local currency units (LCU) on the loan date. The note's principal is correctly included at $140,000 in the receivables section of Rock Company's December 31, 19X1, balance sheet. The principal is repaid to Rock Company on its October 1, 19X2, due date—when the exchange rate is 8 LCU to $1. On Rock Company's December 31, 19X2, income statement, the amount of the transaction exchange gain or loss is
   a. $0.
   b. $15,000 loss.
   c. $15,000 gain.
   d. $35,000 loss.

3. Jones Company, a domestic company, buys machine parts from Klaus Company of Germany on March 1, 19X1, for 30,000 marks—when the spot rate for marks is .4895. Jones Company's year-end is March 31, 19X1. On this date, the spot rate for the mark is .4845. Jones buys 30,000 marks and pays its invoice on April 20, 19X1— when the spot rate is .4945. What amount does Jones Company show for exchange gains or losses in its 19X1 and 19X2 income statements?
   a. $0 $0
   b. $0 $150 loss
   c. $150 loss $0
   d. $150 gain $300 loss

4. On November 30, 19X0, Pabst Publishing Company, located in Wisconsin, executes a contract with Joan Coors, an author from Canada. The contract provides for payment of 10 percent royalties on Canadian sales of Coors' book. Payment is to be made in Canadian dollars each January 10 for the previous year's sales. Canadian sales of the book for the year ended December 31, 19X1, total 50,000 Canadian dollars. Pabst pays Coors her 19X1 royalties on January 10, 19X2. Pabst Company's 19X1 financial statements are issued on February 1, 19X2. Selected spot rates for Canadian dollars are

   November 30, 19X0—.87.
   January 1, 19X1—.88.
   December 31, 19X1—.89.
   January 10, 19X2—.90.

The amount of Pabst Company's royalty accrual on December 31, 19X1 is

a. $4,350.

b. $4,425.

c. $4,450.

d. $4,500.

(AICPA adapted)

Exercise 12–7   (Expressing and Denominating Items in Foreign Currencies)

The Financial Accounting Standards Board discusses accounting for foreign currency transactions in *Statement of Financial Accounting Standards No. 52*. Included in its discussion is consideration of the distinction between financial statement items being expressed in a currency and being denominated in that currency.

Required:

Explain the distinction between a financial statement item being expressed in a currency and being denominated in that currency based on the discussions and examples of this chapter. Also provide a brief example that illustrates this distinction.

(AICPA adapted)

Exercise 12–8   (Exchange Gains and Losses on Intercompany Accounts)

A domestic parent company has two types of intercompany accounts in 19X5 with its French subsidiary:

1. An advance to the subsidiary of 1 million francs to provide working capital. This advance is evidenced by a demand note, denominated in francs. The note has been outstanding without change for the three years since the French affiliate was acquired, and the chief financial officer indicates that the parent does not plan to require payment in the foreseeable future.

2. Trade receivables (denominated in francs) arising from sales to the affiliate. Although individual invoices are paid in the normal 30-day credit period, there has been an average balance of 500,000 francs outstanding during the past several years, and the balance on the aggregate invoices outstanding at any time has not fallen below 400,000 francs since the two companies affiliated. At December 31, 19X5, the total receivable is 600,000 francs. The chief financial officer expects the aggregate receivable to exceed 500,000 francs for the foreseeable future. During 19X5, the parent company recorded a net exchange gain on the intercompany trade receivables of $18,000.

At January 1, 19X5, the spot rate for francs was .10, and at December 31, 19X5, it was .12.

Required:

Explain how the parent company calculates and accounts for the exchange gains or losses realized during 19X5 on the intercompany accounts. (Hint: You may wish to consult *Statement of Financial Accounting Standards No. 52* and other relevant authoritative sources for additional guidance.)

Exercise 12–9 (Classification of Exchange Gains and Losses)

During 19X6, Bell International Banks, a domestic company, realized exchange losses of $300,000 on a series of forward exchange contracts in which it purchased pounds sterling. These contracts were intended to hedge the rental contract on its London office. Bell International signed this contract at the beginning of the year; it commits the firm to a fixed rental price denominated in pounds sterling. In view of this designated purpose, the controller of Bell International takes the position that its losses should be included with rent expense in its 19X6 consolidated financial statements.

Required:

Discuss the propriety of the controller's position. Include in your answer discussion of any additional facts that need to be determined. (Hint: You may wish to consult *Statement of Financial Accounting Standards No. 52* and other relevant authoritative sources for additional guidance.)

Exercise 12–10 (Export Transaction)

Betty Company, a domestic company, sells merchandise to Laurie Company, a British company, on January 1, 19X0—when the spot rate for the dollar and the pound is 1.25. The billing on the contract is expressed in pounds. In dollars, the billing would have been $12,500. The settlement date of the receivable is January 31, 19X0. The spot rate on this date is 1.26. Betty Company exchanges any pounds received for dollars immediately through an exchange broker.

Required:

Prepare Betty Company's journal entries related to the export transaction.

Exercise 12–11 (Import Transaction)

Shiva Company, a domestic company, purchases goods from Nancy Company, a Swiss company, on January 1, 19X0—when the spot rate for the dollar and the (Swiss) franc is .4. The billing on the contract is expressed in francs. In dollars, the billing would have been $32,000. The settlement date of the payable is January 31, 19X0. The spot rate on this date is .5. Shiva Company acquires any needed francs on the settlement date through an exchange broker.

Required:

Prepare Shiva Company's journal entries related to the import transaction.

Exercise 12–12 (Speculation in Foreign Currency)

Sharyl Company believes the exchange rate between U.S. and Canadian dollars will increase over the next three months and, thus, decides to purchase Canadian dollars to be received in the future. Sharyl Company purchases 50,000 Canadian dollars on December 1, 19X1 for delivery in 90 days. On this date, the spot rate for the Canadian dollar is .39, and the 90-day forward rate is .37. The 60-day forward rate is .38 on

December 31, 19X1. The spot rate on March 1, 19X2, is .36. Sharyl Company's fiscal year ends on December 31, 19X1.

Required:

Prepare Sharyl Company's journal entries related to the forward exchange contract.

Problems

Problem 12–13   (Identifiable Foreign Currency Commitment and Hedge)

On October 1, 19X1, Advanced Electronics Company, a domestic company, secured an order from a company located in France for a new computer to be delivered on April 1, 19X2. The sales price, which is payable in francs, is 200,000 francs. The 180-day delivery schedule allows for custom manufacture, delivery, and installation. Payment is due on delivery.

The spot rate for francs on October 1, 19X1, is .13. To protect itself from foreign currency fluctuations, Advanced Electronics Company sells 200,000 francs for delivery in 180 days at a price of .12 in the futures market. Selected additional exchange rates are

1. December 31, 19X1:
   a. Spot rate—.11
   b. Forward rate for 90-day delivery—.10.
2. April 1, 19X2: Spot rate—.09.

Advanced Electronics elects to offset any discount or premium amortization related to its forward exchange contract against sales.

Required:

a. Prepare Advanced Electronics Company's entries on
   (1) October 1, 19X1.
   (2) December 31, 19X1 (when the firm's annual report is prepared).
   (3) April 1, 19X2.
b. Identify the December 31, 19X1, financial statement balances (and their classification) resulting from the above entries.

Problem 12–14   (Identifiable Foreign Currency Commitment and Hedge)

On December 1, 19X3, Micro Systems Company, a domestic company, placed an order with a company located in the Netherlands for laboratory equipment to be delivered in 60 days. The purchase price, which is payable in guilders, is 400,000 guilders. Payment is due on delivery.

The spot rate for guilders on December 1, 19X3, is .21. On this date, Micro Systems decides to hedge its foreign currency commitment by purchasing 300,000 guilders for delivery in 60 days at a price of .23 in the futures market. Selected additional exchange rates are

1. December 31, 19X3:
    a. Spot rate—.24.
    b. Forward rate for 30-day delivery—.23.
2. January 30, 19X4: spot rate—.17.

Micro Systems elects to amortize any discount or premium related to its forward exchange contract against income, in general, using the straight-line method.

Required:

a. Prepare Micro Systems entries on
    (1) December 1, 19X3.
    (2) December 31, 19X3 (when the firm's annual report is prepared).
    (3) January 30, 19X4.
b. Identify the December 31, 19X3, financial statement balances (and their classifications) resulting from the above entries.

Problem 12–15   (Hedge of Exposed Asset Position and Related Speculation)

Daley International, a Chicago firm, enters a 90-day forward exchange contract on December 1, 19X1, to deliver 500,000 units of a foreign currency. On this date, the 90-day forward rate is 1.75. Management engages in this transaction for two reasons: (1) to hedge an exposed asset position of 300,000 units of the foreign currency arising from its export/import operations and (2) to speculate in exchange rate fluctuations on the excess of the foreign currency units sold and the exposed asset position. The spot rate on December 1, 19X1, is 1.77. Selected additional exchange rates are

1. December 31, 19X1:
    a. Spot rate—1.82.
    b. Forward rate for
        (i) 60-day delivery—1.80.
        (ii) 90-day delivery—1.79.
2. March 1, 19X2:
    a. Spot rate—1.85.
    b. Forward rate for:
        (i) 60-day delivery—1.835.
        (ii) 90-day delivery—1.83.

Required:

a. Prepare Daley International's entries on the forward exchange contract on
    (1) December 1, 19X1.
    (2) December 31, 19X1 (when the firm's annual report is prepared).
    (3) March 1, 19X2.
b. Identify the December 31, 19X1, financial statement balances (and their classifications) resulting from the above entries.
c. Prepare a reconciliation of the total gain or loss ultimately realized on the forward exchange contract with the expense or income recognized in the 19X1 and 19X2 income statements.

Problem 12–16 (Export Transaction and Hedge)

Cody Company, a Texas company, sells merchandise to Armadillo Company, an English firm, on January 1, 19X0—when the spot rate for the dollar and the pound is 1.60. The billing on the sale is expressed in pounds. In dollars, the billing would have been $80,000. The settlement date of the receivable is January 31, 19X0. The spot rate on this date is 1.62.

Cody Company decides to minimize its exchange risk by entering a forward exchange contract on January 1, 19X0, to sell 50,000 pounds through an exchange broker. The 30-day forward rate for dollars and pounds is the same as the spot rate on January 31, 19X0.

Required:

a. Prepare Cody Company's journal entries related to the export transaction and the forward exchange contract.

b. Indicate the extent to which Cody Company's hedge minimizes its exchange risk.

Problem 12–17 (Import Transaction and Hedge)

Nod Company, a domestic company, purchases goods from Yerkciv Company, a Swiss company, on January 1, 19X0—when the spot rate for the dollar and the (Swiss) franc is .6. The billing on the contract is expressed in francs. In dollars, the billing would have been $36,000. The settlement date of the payable is January 31, 19X0. The spot rate on this date is .62.

Nod Company decides to hedge its exchange risk by entering a forward exchange contract to purchase 60,000 francs on January 1, 19X0. The 30-day forward rate for dollars and francs equals the spot rate on the date of the import transaction.

Required:

a. Prepare Nod Company's journal entries related to the import transaction and the forward exchange contract.

b. Indicate the extent to which Nod Company's hedge minimizes its exchange risk.

Problem 12–18 (Identifiable Foreign Currency Commitment and Hedge)

Domestic Company contracts on July 15, 19X1, to manufacture and deliver merchandise to Foreign Company, a German company, on December 15, 19X1, for 600,000 marks. On July 15, the spot rate for marks is .50. Domestic Company's expected cost of sales is $200,000. The contract requires Foreign Company to pay for the goods on January 14, 19X2.

Domestic Company decides to hedge its risk on its foreign currency commitment and the related exposed asset position by entering a forward exchange contract to sell 600,000 marks in six months at the July 15, 19X1, 180-day forward rate of .51. Domestic Company amortizes any deferred premium or discount from a forward exchange contract that hedges a sales contract over the duration of the forward contract with amortization up to the point of sale being closed to Sales.

The following future spot rates are assumed: September 30, 19X1—.55; December 15, 19X1—.58; December 31, 19X1—.56; and January 14, 19X2—.62. Domestic Company's fiscal year ends on December 31, and it prepares quarterly financial statements.

Required:

a. Prepare all of Domestic Company's journal entries related to the export transaction and forward exchange contract.

b. Identify the December 31, 19X1, financial statement balances (and their classifications) resulting from the above entries.

c. Indicate the extent to which Domestic Company's hedge protects its gross profit.

Problem 12–19   (Identifiable Foreign Currency Commitment and Hedge)

On August 15, 19X1, Jones Company, a domestic company, signed a contract with a Swiss customer to construct and deliver machinery on or before February 15, 19X2. The price specified in the contract is 150,000 Swiss francs, and the spot rate for the Swiss franc on the contract date was .42.

The price of the Swiss franc fell over the next two weeks. To partially hedge its foreign currency commitment, Jones entered a forward exchange contract on September 1, 19X1, to deliver 100,000 Swiss francs in 180 days. On this date, the spot rate for Swiss francs was .40, and the 180-day forward rate was .41.

On December 11, 19X1, after the Swiss franc had strengthened to .50, Jones reached an agreement with the exchange broker to close the contract for $9,000—the difference between the current value of the Swiss francs ($50,000) and the broker's U.S. dollar obligation to Jones ($41,000). Jones paid the $9,000, and the contract was canceled.

Required:

a. Prepare Jones Company's 19X1 entries related to its foreign currency transactions.

b. Describe how the exchange loss and the premium on the forward contract are reported in Jones Company's 19X1 financial statements. (*Hint:* You may wish to consult *Statement of Financial Accounting Standards No. 52* and other relevant authoritative sources for additional guidance.)

Problem 12–20   (Export Transaction and Hedge with Adjustments)

Allyson Company, an American company, sells merchandise to Sanmarcus Company, an English firm, on January 1, 19X0—when the spot rate for the dollar and the pound is 1.60. The billing on the sale is expressed in pounds. In dollars, the billing would have been $32,000. The settlement date of the receivable is March 2, 19X0, and January 31, 19X0, is a financial reporting date. The spot rates on these dates are 1.67 and 1.63, respectively.

Allyson Company decides to minimize its exchange risk by entering a forward exchange contract on January 1, 19X0, to sell 20,000 pounds through an exchange broker. The 60-day forward rate for dollars and pounds is 1.64. Allyson Company accounts for premiums and discounts on forward contracts over the duration of the contracts.

Required:

Prepare Allyson Company's journal entries related to the export transaction and the forward exchange contract.

Problem 12–21   (Import Transaction and Hedge with Adjustments)

Wordman Company, a domestic company, purchases goods from Allycat Company, a Swiss company, on January 1, 19X0—when the spot rate for the dollar and the (Swiss) franc is .60. The billing on the contract is expressed in francs. In dollars, the billing would have been $36,000. The settlement date of the payable is March 2, 19X0, and January 31, 19X0, is a financial reporting date. The spot rates on these dates are .66 and .62, respectively.

Wordman Company decides to hedge its exchange risk by entering a forward exchange contract to purchase 60,000 francs on January 1, 19X0. The 60-day forward rate for dollars and francs is .65. Wordman Company accounts for premiums and discounts on forward contracts over the duration of the contracts.

Required:

Prepare Wordman Company's journal entries related to the import transaction and the forward exchange contract.

Chapter Outline

This chapter covers the second major topic in accounting for international operations—the conversion of foreign entities' financial statements into the domestic currency. This conversion process is the first step in preparing consolidated financial statements for a domestic parent company and its foreign subsidiary and in accounting for a domestic company's investment in a foreign affiliate under the equity method. The consolidated statement and equity method aspects of international operations are covered in Chapter 14.

THE FUNCTIONAL CURRENCY CONCEPT

We introduce the FASB's concept of functional currency in Chapter 13. Generally, it is the "currency of the primary economic environment in which the entity operates: normally, that is the currency of the environment in which an entity primarily generates and expends cash."[1] The FASB's approach to the conversion of foreign entities' financial statements into the domestic currency is a functional currency approach. *Statement of Financial Accounting Standards No. 52* (par. 69) indicates that this approach encompasses the following:

  a. Identifying the functional currency of the (foreign) entity's economic environment.
  b. Measuring all elements of the financial statements in the functional currency.
  c. Using the current exchange rate for translation from the functional currency to the reporting currency, if they are different.
  d. Distinguishing the economic impact of changes in exchange rates on a net investment from the impact of such changes on individual assets and liabilities that are receivable or payable in currencies other than the functional currency.

We continue to assume, as in Chapter 12, that all *domestic* companies are U.S. companies whose functional and reporting currencies are the U.S. dollar. Recall that an entity's reporting currency is the currency in which its financial statements are prepared. Although the functional currency of a domestic company normally is apparent, determining the functional currency of a foreign entity can be difficult. *Statement No. 52* discusses the factors relevant to this determination. The FASB observes that a foreign subsidiary of a domestic parent might be one of two extreme types. The first class includes foreign subsidiaries that are primarily integral components, or extensions, of parent companies' operations. Membership in this class implies that a subsidiary's day-to-day operations are dependent on the economic environment of the parent's currency and that its cash flows

---

[1] FASB, *Statement of Financial Accounting Standards No. 52,* "Foreign Currency Translation" (Norwalk, CT: FASB, 1981), par. 5.

impact directly on the cash flows of the parent. In this case, the functional currency of the subsidiary is the U.S. dollar—the domestic parent's currency. *This conclusion applies even if the subsidiary primarily generates and expends cash and keeps its records in its local currency.* A subsidiary's local currency is the currency of the country in which it is domiciled (e.g., the franc for a French subsidiary). At the other extreme, a foreign subsidiary might be highly independent, with its operations applying primarily to a particular foreign economic environment. In this case, the day-to-day operations of the subsidiary are not nearly as dependent on the economic environment of the parent's currency and its cash flows impact less directly on the cash flows of the parent. Under these conditions, the subsidiary's functional currency is its local currency.

Many cases lie between these two relatively well-defined extremes. Thus, the FASB elaborates (in Appendix A) on the indicators that are pertinent in identifying the functional currencies of foreign subsidiaries. The essence of this discussion is summarized as follows:

1. **Cash flow indicators**—Do the cash flows of the subsidiary impact on the parent company's cash flows on a regular basis?

2. **Sales price indicators**—Are the subsidiary's prices responsive to short-term shifts in exchange rates?

3. **Sales market indicators**—Are the subsidiary's products sold in its local market at prices denominated in its local currency or in the parent's environment?

4. **Expense indicators**—Are costs mainly incurred in local markets or from the parent's environment?

5. **Financing indicators**—Are debts denominated in, and serviced through, foreign currency or via the parent's currency?

6. **Intercompany transactions and arrangements indicators**—Are the operations and management of the subsidiary relatively independent, and are there relatively few intercompany transactions and control arrangements?

In deciding on a foreign subsidiary's functional currency, these factors are used in determining which currency better satisfies the *translation* objectives of *Statement No. 52.* The objectives in translating a foreign subsidiary's financial statements from its functional currency into the reporting currency of its parent under this standard (par. 4) are to:[2]

---

[2] Note that we refer to *translation objectives* in this discussion. As explained below, the FASB's approach to converting a foreign entity's financial statements into the domestic currency is best described as the process of *translating its financial statements from its functional currency into the reporting currency.* The translation process also may include the conversion procedure referred to as *remeasurement.* Hereafter, we refer to the *conversion* of a foreign subsidiary's financial statements into the reporting currency when we do not wish to distinguish between translation, remeasurement, or any other particular restatement approach.

a. Provide information that is generally compatible with the expected economic effects of a rate change on an enterprise's cash flows and equity.

b. Reflect in consolidated statements the financial results and relationships of the individual consolidated entities as measured in their *functional currencies* in conformity with U.S. generally accepted accounting principles (GAAP).[3]

These objectives are contrasted to some extent with other conversion objectives in the next section. Although conversion objectives have changed over time, one unchanging element of these objectives is the preparation of financial statements in accordance with GAAP. Thus, if a foreign subsidiary's statements are not stated using GAAP, all material deficiencies are remedied prior to conversion.

Note two additional points related to the functional currency concept. First, once a foreign subsidiary's functional currency is determined, it is not changed unless the underlying economic circumstances change significantly. Second, if a foreign subsidiary has distinct operations in different economic environments, each operation can have a different functional currency. For example, if a French subsidiary has separate operations in France and England, it may have two functional currencies—the franc and the pound.

EVOLUTION OF CONVERSION PRINCIPLES

A variety of methods of converting foreign subsidiaries' financial statements into the (domestic) reporting currency has been used. We emphasize that the primary reasons for converting these statements into the reporting currency are the preparation of consolidated financial statements for domestic parent companies and their foreign subsidiaries and the application of the equity method by domestic investors in foreign companies. Since the consolidated statements of domestic parent companies (and similar equity method results) are supposed to be consistent with GAAP, a major criterion for evaluating conversion methods is whether or not they produce results that are consistent with previously applied GAAP.

The first conversion method that was widely accepted is the *current-noncurrent* method.[4] Under this technique, current assets and current liabilities are converted using the spot rate on the balance sheet date (the current rate). All other

---

[3] Most of the discussion in *Statement No. 52* refers directly to the consolidated financial statement aspects of translation. However, this statement also applies to translation in the context of the application of the equity method, whether or not the preparation of consolidated statements is appropriate. The statement does not cover translation of foreign entity financial statements for any purpose other than the preparation of consolidated financial statements or the application of the equity method (par. 2).

[4] This method is described in the Committee on Accounting Procedure's *Accounting Research Bulletin No. 4,* "Foreign Operations and Foreign Exchange" (New York: AICPA, 1939).

assets and equities are converted at the spot rate in effect when they were acquired (their historical rates).[5] Under this approach, conversion gains are deferred, but conversion losses are included in income. In general, conversion gains and losses occur because conversion processes seldom maintain the equality of balance sheet debits and credits. Under any conversion method, such gains and losses are produced *only on assets and liabilities converted at the current rate*. Thus, under the current-noncurrent method, conversion gains and losses are related to current assets and current liabilities. This method is arbitrary since its conversion rate distinction is based on the current-noncurrent dichotomy. This arbitrariness results in dissimilar treatments for tangible assets, such as inventories and fixed assets, and for liabilities with differing maturities.

Because of its conceptual weakness, the current-noncurrent method was gradually replaced in practice (without formal authoritative support) by the *monetary-nonmonetary* method. Under this approach, monetary assets and liabilities are converted at the current rate, and nonmonetary assets and equities are converted at their historical rates. The disclosure of conversion gains and losses varied under this technique—as is expected when accounting practice is evolving.

In 1972, an AICPA research study proposed the use of the *temporal* method.[6] This technique emphasizes the conversion of assets and equities so that the previously applied *accounting principles applied to them are retained*. For example, if land is on a foreign affiliate's balance sheet at its original historical cost, its balance is converted using its historical rate. Similarly, since an account receivable is on such a balance sheet at the current rate, its balance is converted using the current rate. This method is important conceptually since it maintains previously applied GAAP. Note also that as long as the techniques of historical cost accounting are used, the temporal and monetary-nonmonetary methods produce essentially the same results. In 1975, *Statement of Financial Accounting Standards No. 8* provided the temporal method with additional authoritative support.[7] According to the FASB (in 1975), the temporal method is conceptually sound since it maintains previously applied GAAP. In discussing conversion, the FASB emphasizes the importance of maintaining previously applied GAAP as follows:

> For the purpose of preparing an enterprise's financial statements, the objective of translation is to measure and express *(a)* in dollars and *(b)* in conformity with U.S. generally accepted accounting principles the assets, liabilities, revenue[s], or expenses

---

[5] We emphasize that the balance sheet date, spot rate is referred to as the *current rate* in Chapters 13 and 14. We refer to the *spot rate in existence when an asset or a liability is acquired* (including the investment in a foreign subsidiary by a domestic parent) as its historical rate in these chapters. As in Chapter 12, exchange rates are assumed to be directly quoted, free rates in Chapters 13 and 14 unless indicated otherwise.

[6] Leonard Lorenson, *Accounting Research Study No. 12,* "Reporting Foreign Operations of U.S. Companies in U.S. Dollars" (New York: AICPA, 1972).

[7] FASB, *Statement of Financial Accounting Standards No. 8,* "Accounting for the Translation of Foreign Currency Transactions and Foreign Currency Financial Statements" (Norwalk, CT: FASB, 1975).

that are measured or denominated in foreign currency. Remeasuring in dollars the assets, liabilities, revenue[s], or expenses measured or denominated in foreign currency should not affect either the measurement bases for assets and liabilities or the timing of revenue and expense recognition otherwise required by generally accepted accounting principles. That is, translation should change the *unit of measure* without changing accounting principles.

As explained in detail later, the conversion gains and losses produced by the temporal method are similar to the transaction exchange gains and losses of Chapter 12. For now, note that the conversion gains and losses from this method are related to the foreign entity's *foreign currency exposure*—which is either an *exposed net monetary asset or exposed net monetary liability position*. For example, assume that the excess of a 100 percent owned foreign subsidiary's monetary liabilities over its monetary assets, both of which are denominated in pounds, is a constant 10,000 pounds during the accounting period. In this case, the company's foreign currency exposure is an exposed net monetary liability position of 10,000 pounds for the period. Thus, if the dollar weakens (strengthens), a conversion loss (gain) is produced. Under the temporal method, both conversion gains and losses are recognized in the income statement currently.

Subsequent to the adoption of *Statement No. 8,* the dollar began to weaken in relation to most major currencies. Also, companies tended to have large exposed net monetary liability positions related to their investments in foreign affiliates. Thus, many companies were reporting large conversion losses on these investments. To many managers, the reported results seemed inconsistent with economic reality. Their view was based on a different perspective on the foreign investments and the related foreign currency risks—one that combines a foreign entity's nonmonetary items with their exposed net monetary liability position and converts all assets and liabilities at the current rate. When the *net investment* in a foreign entity with an exposed net monetary liability position is viewed this way, its foreign currency exposure usually changes to a net asset. Under this view, if the dollar weakens in relation to a foreign currency, a gain, not a loss, occurs. For example, assume that the foreign subsidiary in the case mentioned above has 25,000 pounds of nonmonetary assets and no nonmonetary liabilities. Under the managers' views, its foreign currency exposure is a net asset of 15,000 pounds. Now, if the dollar weakens, a gain is produced.

A method that reflects the view of foreign currency exposure just described is the *current rate* method. Under this procedure, all assets and liabilities are converted using the current rate. The major objection to this method is that it fails to maintain previously applied GAAP. For example, if land purchased 10 years ago is converted to dollars using the current rate, its historical cost is not maintained. Furthermore, the resulting value is not likely to equal the current market value of the land. Thus, in general, the interpretation of converted values for nonmonetary items is unclear under the current rate method. Nevertheless, the current rate method is consistent with (but not equivalent to) movement toward current value financial reporting—a movement which we support in general. Despite this consistency, the failure of the current rate method to maintain previously applied GAAP is serious enough to suggest that it is inappropriate for financial reporting given the goal of maintaining previously applied GAAP. Nevertheless, the FASB agreed to reconsider the issue of the conversion of foreign entity financial statements because of the widespread managerial dissatisfaction with the temporal method. The result of the FASB's comprehensive (and controversial) study of this matter is *Statement of Financial Accounting Standards No. 52.*

Under this statement, the *current rate method is used in translating foreign entities' financial statements from their functional currencies into the reporting currency.*[8] The FASB discusses its functional currency approach extensively; the following comments (pars. 94, 95, and 98) illustrate its reasoning.

> Fundamental to the functional currency approach to translation is the view that, generally, a U.S. enterprise is exposed to exchange risk to the extent of its net investment in a foreign operation. This view derives from a broad concept of economic hedging. An asset, such as plant and equipment, that produces revenues in the functional currency of an entity can be an effective hedge of debt that requires payments in that currency. Therefore, functional currency assets and liabilities hedge one another, and only the net assets are exposed to exchange risk.
>
> If all of a foreign entity's assets and liabilities are measured in its functional currency and are translated at the current exchange rate, the net accounting effect of a change in the exchange rate is the effect on the net assets of the entity. That accounting result is compatible with the broad concept of economic hedging on which the net investment view is based. No gains or losses arise from hedged assets and liabilities and the dollar equivalent of the unhedged net investment increases or decreases when the functional currency strengthens or weakens.
>
>   *   *   *   *   *
>
> A foreign entity's assets, liabilities, and operations exist in the economic environment of its functional currency. Its costs are incurred in its functional currency and its revenues are produced in its functional currency. Use of a current exchange rate retains those historical costs and other measurements but restates them in terms of the reporting currency, thereby preserving the relationships established in the entity's economic environment. . . . If a foreign entity is producing net income in its functional currency, the dollar equivalent of that net income will be reflected in the consolidated statements. . . . At the extreme, if different [exchange] rates are used for monetary and nonmonetary items, the results of operations for a foreign entity that, in fact, is operating profitably . . . may be converted to a loss merely as a result of the mechanical translation process. The Board believes that by preserving the actual [functional currency] indicators of performance and financial condition of each component entity, the consolidated financial statements will portray the best information about the enterprise as a whole.

---

[8] The use of this method reflects a change from a single unit of measure concept to a multiple units of measure concept when a foreign affiliate's functional currency differs from the parent's reporting currency. This change is due to the FASB's determination (with three members dissenting) that it is possible to meaningfully aggregate companies' financial statements only if the functional currency relationships are maintained.

Although the FASB's reasoning is similar to that of the managers mentioned above, note that certain conversion (specifically translation) gains and losses are not recognized in the income statement under the functional currency approach. They are accumulated in a separate account in stockholders' equity (i.e., the Cumulative Foreign Exchange Translation Adjustments account).[9] This treatment is based on the FASB's view that translation gains or losses are not directly related to the foreign entity's operating cash flows. We elaborate on the functional currency approach below.

As mentioned in footnote 2, the conversion process under *Statement No. 52* is best described as the process of *translating the foreign entity's financial statements from its functional currency into the reporting currency.* We refer to this process simply as *translation.* In short, the overall objective of translation is to convert the foreign entity's financial statements into dollars in a way that preserves the economic results and relationships existing in its functional currency statements.

In discussing translation, the examples in this chapter focus initially on the commonly encountered cases in which only two currencies are involved in the translation process. In this context, *if the foreign entity's functional and local currencies are the same, translation reduces to the current rate method.* Note that the entity's transactions are recorded in its local currency in this case (or there would be no need for translation). Alternatively, *if the foreign entity's functional and reporting currencies are the same and its transactions are recorded in its local currency, translation reduces to the temporal method* (which preserves previously applied GAAP). Recall that a foreign subsidiary's functional and reporting currencies can be the same, even if its transactions are recorded in its local currency, if the subsidiary is primarily an integral component, or extension, of the parent company's operations. The FASB refers to the temporal method as *remeasurement* in *Statement No. 52.* According to the FASB, the objective of remeasurement, which is consistent with the overall objective of translation, is to produce the same financial statement values that would have been produced if the foreign entity's transactions had been recorded in its functional currency in the first place. *In contrast to translation gains and losses, remeasurement gains and losses are recognized in the income statement.* This treatment is based on the view that the foreign entity is exposed to exchange risk on transactions that are denominated in a currency other than its functional currency and that the resulting gains and losses affect operating cash flows.

Later in the chapter, we cover the relatively rare case in which the foreign entity's functional and reporting currencies are different and its transactions are recorded in a third currency. In this case, its statements first are remeasured into

---

[9] If the investment in the foreign entity is sold or partially liquidated, the cumulative translation gain or loss applicable to the sold interest is removed from shareholders' equity and included in the gain or loss on the sale.

its functional currency. Subsequently, they are translated from the functional currency into the reporting currency. This situation is easy to deal with once the commonly encountered cases are understood.

As indicated above, *Statement No. 52* is a complicated document. Illustration 13–1 summarizes many of its features.[10] Its more important features are illustrated in the examples that follow. Several of the examples begun in this chapter are continued in Chapter 14—which covers their consolidated statement and equity method aspects. *The cases begin with the temporal method since this approach is simpler than the current rate method from an overall perspective (especially in the context of consolidated statements and the equity method).* Nevertheless, this chapter is structured so that the latter method can be studied first—by reading the given data of Case 1 and then moving to the current rate method section. The cases of this chapter assume that the ownership percent is 100 and that purchase accounting is appropriate. No generality is lost by making these assumptions.

TRANSLATION WITH REMEASUREMENT ALONE—SUBSIDIARY'S FUNCTIONAL AND REPORTING CURRENCIES THE SAME

Our first two cases deal with situations in which the foreign subsidiary's functional and reporting currencies are the same, and its transactions are recorded in its local currency. As indicated, translation reduces to the temporal method (remeasurement) under these conditions. Recall that the objective of this process is to create the same financial statement values that would have resulted if the subsidiary's transactions had been recorded in its functional currency initially. We use the phrase *temporal method* and the word *remeasurement* interchangeably below.

---

[10] A foreign affiliate may reside in a country whose economy is highly inflationary. In these cases, the financial statement values assigned to long-lived assets are likely to lack economic substance when converted at either their historical rates or the current rate. The FASB considered several solutions to this problem and decided that the financial statements of a foreign affiliate operating in a highly inflationary economy should be *remeasured as if the affiliate's functional currency is the parent's reporting currency.* In other words, the FASB decided that the currency of a highly inflationary economy cannot be an entity's functional currency. *Statement of Financial Accounting Standards No. 52* provides guidelines for determining whether an economy is highly inflationary. In its most definitive statement, the FASB indicates that if the cumulative inflation for the past three years is approximately 100 percent or more, an economy is highly inflationary. Nevertheless, the FASB indicates that this criterion is to be applied with judgment (par. 109). One judgmental factor mentioned by the FASB is the trend of inflation for the current three-year period (as contrasted with the cumulative rate for this period)

ILLUSTRATION 13–1   Translating Foreign Currency Financial Statements

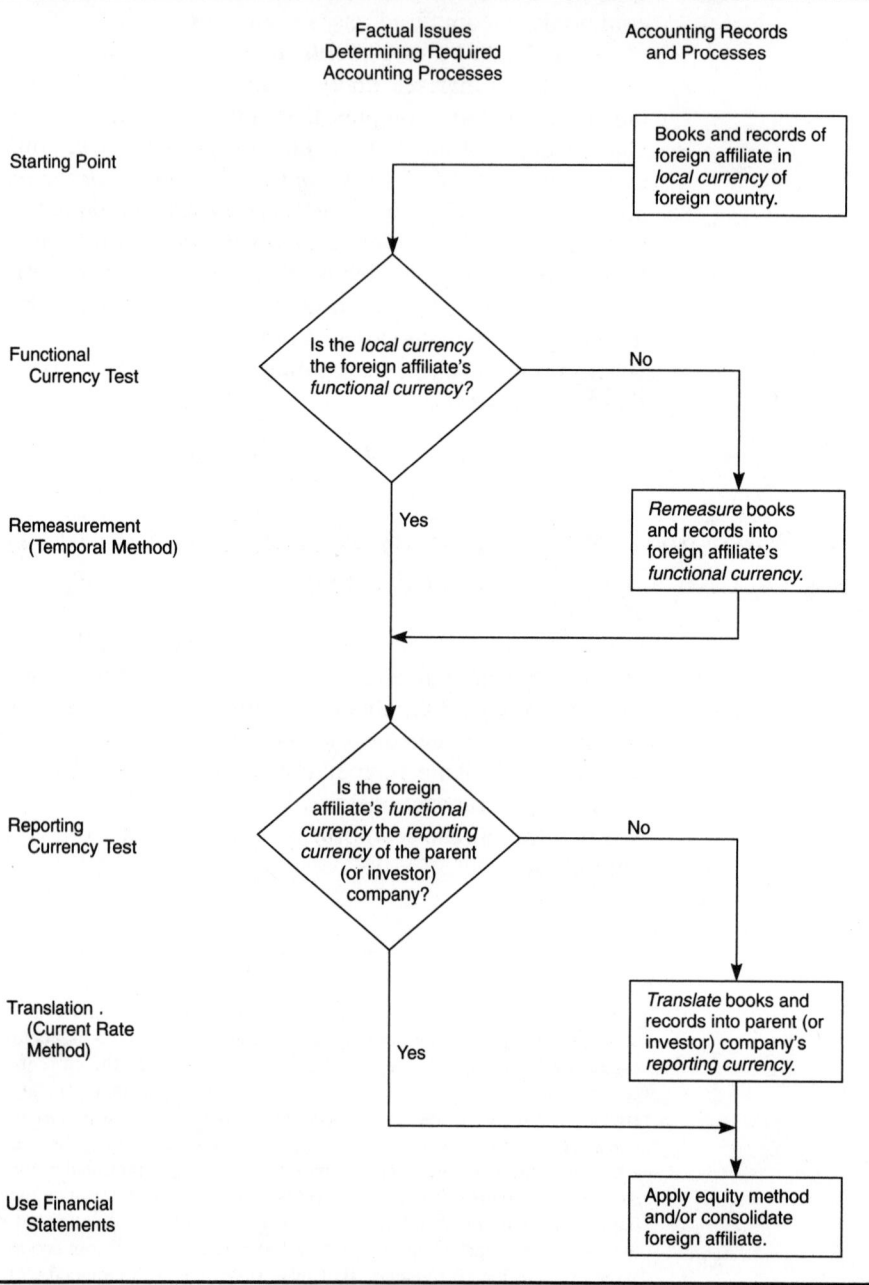

Case 1. Remeasurement with No Long-Term Intercompany Payable

Assume that Monroe Co. (a Texas company) purchases 100 percent of the outstanding capital stock of Bordeaux Company (a French company) on January 1, 19X1, for $150,000. On this date, the directly quoted, spot rate is .125, and Bordeaux Company's balance sheet is expressed in francs as follows:

Accounts	Francs
Assets	
Cash and receivables	200,000
Plant and equipment (net)	1,000,000
Total assets	1,200,000
Liabilities and Owners' Equity	
Current payables	100,000
Long-term debt	700,000
Capital stock	100,000
Retained earnings	300,000
Total liabilities and owners' equity	1,200,000

On date of acquisition, the temporal method is applied by multiplying each of Bordeaux Company's account balances by the balance sheet date, spot rate (the current rate) of .125. *Subsequently, this rate is interpreted as the historical rate for assets and equities on Bordeaux Company's books at date of acquisition.* The historical rates for assets and equities acquired after this date are the spot rates on their acquisition dates. The results of applying remeasurement to Bordeaux Company's accounts on date of acquisition are as follows:

	Francs	Exchange Rate	Dollars
Cash and receivables	200,000	.125	25,000
Plant and equipment (net)	1,000,000	.125	125,000
	1,200,000		150,000
Current payables	100,000	.125	12,500
Long-term debt	700,000	.125	87,500
Capital stock	100,000	.125	12,500
Retained earnings	300,000	.125	37,500
	1,200,000		150,000

Assume further that Bordeaux Company's trial balance at December 31, 19X1, is as follows:

Accounts	Francs
Debits	
Cash and Receivables	1,150,000
Plant and Equipment (net)	750,000
Depreciation Expense	250,000
Other Expenses	350,000
Totals	2,500,000
Credits	
Current Payables	200,000
Long-Term Debt	700,000
Sales	1,200,000
Capital Stock	100,000
Retained Earnings (1/1)	300,000
Totals	2,500,000

The current rate on December 31, 19X1, is .10, and the weighted-average exchange rate for 19X1 is .11. All of Bordeaux Company's monetary assets and liabilities are denominated in francs. The only change in its Plant and Equipment (net) during 19X1 is from recording depreciation expense of 250,000 francs.

Subsequent to date of acquisition, monetary assets and monetary liabilities are converted using the current rate under remeasurement. All other balance sheet items and direct charges and credits to Retained Earnings (e.g., dividends) are converted at their historical rates. In concept, income statement items also are converted at their historical rates under the temporal method. However, *Statement No. 52* (par. 12) provides an exception to this principle based on practicality. Specifically, the FASB believes that converting income statement items (including purchases) at their historical rates often is impractical because of their large number; thus, these items can be converted using "an appropriately weighted average exchange rate for the period." This type of simplification, which also arises in several other conversion-related situations, seems reasonable when the values under consideration are accumulated approximately uniformly over the accounting period. Note that converting depreciation expense figures at their historical rates usually is feasible because these rates are the same as the historical rates applying to the conversion of the related asset balances. A similar observation sometimes applies to the purchases component of cost of goods sold.

An account balance not obtained by conversion under the temporal method, except at date of acquisition, is the dollar amount of beginning-of-period retained earnings. This balance simply is set equal to the dollar value of retained earnings at the end of the prior period (or at date of acquisition)—which always is known. The *remeasurement* (conversion) gain or loss resulting from the temporal method is almost always recognized in the subsidiary's income statement (in dollars). Thus, the balance of this account usually is included in the end-of-period retained earnings figure. Remeasurement gains and losses are discussed further below. For

ILLUSTRATION 13–2   Temporal Method

BORDEAUX COMPANY
Foreign Currency Translation Working Paper
For the Year Ended December 31, 19X1

	Trial Balance (in francs)	Exchange Rate Code	Exchange Rate Rate	Trial Balance (in dollars)	Income Statement (in dollars)	Balance Sheet (in dollars)
Cash and receivables	1,150,000	C	.100	115,000		115,000
Plant and equipment (net)	750,000	H	.125	93,750		93,750
Depreciation expense	250,000	H	.125	31,250	31,250	
Other expenses	350,000	W	.110	38,500	38,500	
Net income (including remeasurement gain)					68,750	
	2,500,000			278,500	138,500	208,750
Current payables	200,000	C	.100	20,000		20,000
Long-term debt	700,000	C	.100	70,000		70,000
Sales	1,200,000	W	.110	132,000	132,000	
Capital stock	100,000	H	.125	12,500		12,500
Retained earnings (1/1)	300,000	P		37,500		37,500
Remeasurement gain (19X1)				6,500	6,500	
Net income (including remeasurement gain)						68,750
	2,500,000			278,500	138,500	208,750

Code:
C = Current exchange rate at December 31, 19X1.
W = Weighted-average exchange rate for 19X1.
H = Historical exchange rate.
P = Dollar balance end of preceding period.

now, note that they are calculated indirectly in temporal method working papers. Calculated indirectly, they are the "plug" figures that balance the debits and credits in these working papers. The temporal method working paper for Bordeaux Company for 19X1 is shown in Illustration 13–2.

The converted values in Illustration 13–2 are consistent with the general rules for applying the temporal method given above. The Cash and Receivables, Current Payables, and Long-Term Debt balances all are remeasured at the current rate, and the remaining assets and equities, except beginning retained earnings, are remeasured at their historical rates. The beginning-of-period retained earnings figure is set equal to the dollar value calculated for the Retained Earnings account at date of acquisition. All of the income statement items, except depreciation expense, are remeasured using the weighted-average rate for the period. Depreciation expense is converted using the historical rate for Plant and Equipment. The remeasurement gain is calculated indirectly as the "plug" figure that balances the debits and the credits in the Trial Balance (in dollars) column. Bordeaux Company's net income for 19X1 is $62,250, ignoring the remeasurement gain. Including this gain, its net income is $68,750. Bordeaux Company's ending Retained Earnings balance is $106,250 ($37,500 + $68,750). This value is the beginning-of-period retained earnings figure for next year's temporal method working paper. An income statement and a balance sheet for this case are presented in Illustration 13–7.

Remeasurement Gains and Losses

Under the temporal method, only monetary assets and monetary liabilities are remeasured using current rates—since only these items are denominated in a foreign currency. Recall that conversion gains and losses are related only to balance sheet items converted using current rates. Thus, under the temporal method, remeasurement gains and losses are related to the foreign entity's *exposed net monetary asset or exposed net monetary liability position* (i.e., the excess of its monetary assets over its monetary liabilities, or vice versa). The entity's exposed net monetary asset or liability position is its foreign currency exposure under this method. As indicated, remeasurement gains and losses are similar to the transaction exchange gains and losses of Chapter 12. That is, they occur because the monetary assets and monetary liabilities of companies for which remeasurement is appropriate are denominated in foreign currencies.

In our example, Bordeaux Company's exposed net monetary asset [(liability)] position is determined as follows for the end and the beginning of 19X1:

	In Francs	
	12/31/X1	*1/1/X1*
Assets translated at current rate—		
Cash and Receivables	1,150,000	200,000
Less: Liabilities translated at current rate—		
Current payables	200,000	100,000
Long-term debt	700,000	700,000
	900,000	800,000
Exposed net monetary asset [(liability)] position	250,000	(600,000)

During 19X1, Bordeaux Company has both an exposed net monetary liability position and an exposed net monetary asset position. The exposed net monetary liability position of 600,000 francs at the beginning of the year is converted to an exposed net monetary asset position of 250,000 francs by year-end. The net change in foreign currency exposure of 850,000 francs occurs because of an inflow of net monetary assets from sales (1,200,000 francs) and an outflow of net monetary assets related to other expenses (350,000 francs). From an overall perspective, a remeasurement gain occurs in our example because the dollar strengthens in relation to the franc (i.e., the spot rate moves from .125 to .1) over a period (19X1) in which Bordeaux Company's exposed net monetary liability position *dominates* its exposed net monetary asset position.

One way of calculating the 19X1 remeasurement gain is as follows:

Gain on beginning exposed net monetary liability position	
[−600,000 × ($.125 − $.10)]	($15,000)
Loss on net monetary asset inflow over the year	
[850,000 × ($.11 − $.10)]	8,500
Remeasurement gain	($ 6,500)

The gain on the beginning net monetary liability position more than offsets the loss on the net monetary asset inflow, even though this inflow is larger than the beginning position. This result occurs because: (1) the calculation assumes implicitly that the inflow occurs abruptly when the spot rate equals the weighted-average rate of .11 and (2) the difference between the beginning-of-year spot rate and the weighted-average rate exceeds the difference between the weighted-average rate and the end-of-year spot rate. These points are clarified through the following alternative calculation of the remeasurement gain. This calculation assumes explicitly that Bordeaux Company's net monetary position changes when the exchange rate equals the weighted average of .11.

Gain for first part of year on net monetary liability position	
[−600,000 × ($.125 − $.11)]	($9,000)
Loss for subsequent portion of year on net monetary asset	
position [(850,000 − 600,000) × ($.11 − $.10)] =	
[(250,000) × ($.11 − $.10)]	2,500
Remeasurement gain	($6,500)

This calculation reveals the similarity between remeasurement gains and losses and transaction exchange gains and losses. This similarity is revealed because the calculation emphasizes the periods over which Bordeaux Company's foreign currency exposure is assumed to be (1) an exposed net monetary liability position and (2) an exposed net monetary asset position, as well as the assumed changes in spot rates over these periods.

Case 2. Remeasurement with Long-Term Intercompany Payable

This case is essentially the same as Case 1. The main difference is that the *long-term debt is assumed to be the result of an intercompany foreign currency transaction that is of a long-term investment nature (i.e., settlement is not anticipated in the foreseeable future).* Thus, assume this debt results from an $87,500 advance to Bordeaux Company by Monroe Company occurring immediately after acquisition on January 1, 19X1. Also assume that Monroe Company does not expect this debt to be settled in the foreseeable future. We still assume that this debt is denominated in francs. Finally, assume that the proceeds of Monroe Company's loan are used to purchase plant and equipment on date of acquisition by Bordeaux Company for 700,000 francs (i.e., after the $87,500 is converted to 700,000 francs (87,500/.125 francs) by Bordeaux Company). Under this assumption, the balance for Plant and Equipment (net) at acquisition is 50,000 francs. Except for the 700,000 franc purchase, the only change in Plant and Equipment (net) in 19X1 is from recording depreciation expense of 250,000 francs.

Statement No. 52 calls for special treatment of transaction gains and losses from the type of debt described above when consolidated statements are to be prepared eventually (as in this case) (pars. 15, 20, 120, 122, and 131).[11] These gains and losses are not disclosed in the income statement. Instead, they are accumulated in the Cumulative Foreign Exchange Translation Adjustments account in shareholders' equity.[12] The temporal method working paper for this case is presented in Illustration 13-3.

The remeasurement gain or loss (a loss in this case) still is the "plug" that balances the debits and credits in the Trial Balance (in dollars) column of the working paper. However, one more value must be known to determine this "plug"—the amount of the translation adjustment (i.e., a gain or loss). The translation adjustment of $17,500 (a gain) is the product of the balance in Long-Term Debt—Monroe (700,000) and the change in the spot rate for 19X1 (.125 − .1). This adjustment is a gain since the dollar strengthens in relation to the franc. On Bordeaux Company's December 31, 19X1, balance sheet, this amount is combined with the zero beginning balance in Cumulative Foreign Exchange Translation Adjustments to obtain the ending balance for this account (see Illustration 13-7 for the financial statements for this case). In general, the beginning-of-period balance in Cumulative Foreign Exchange Translation Adjustments is obtained exactly as in the case of beginning-of-period Retained Earnings—by setting this figure equal to the dollar value of the Cumulative Foreign Exchange

---

[11] If debt of the type in this case is denominated in the functional currency (dollars), no special accounting treatment is required since the related transaction is not a foreign currency transaction. Recall from Chapter 12 that a foreign currency transaction is a transaction that results in a balance sheet account that is denominated in a currency other than the entity's functional currency.

[12] The FASB's apparent reason for this treatment is that intercompany foreign currency transactions of a long-term investment nature augment parent companies' net investments in foreign investee companies and, consequently, do not affect functional currency cash flows.

ILLUSTRATION 13-3   Temporal Method—Long-Term Intercompany Payable

BORDEAUX COMPANY
Foreign Currency Translation Working Paper
For the Year Ended December 31, 19X1

	Trial Balance (in francs)	Exchange Rate		Trial Balance (in dollars)	Income Statement (in dollars)	Balance Sheet (in dollars)
		Code	Rate			
Cash and receivables	1,150,000	C	.100	115,000		115,000
Plant and equipment (net)	750,000	H	.125	93,750		93,750
Depreciation expense	250,000	H	.125	31,250	31,250	
Other expenses	350,000	W	.110	38,500	38,500	
Remeasurement loss (19X1)				11,000	11,000	
Net income (including remeasurement loss)					51,250	
	2,500,000			289,500	132,000	208,750
Current payables	200,000	C	.100	20,000		20,000
Long-term debt—Monroe	700,000	C	.100	70,000		70,000
Sales	1,200,000	W	.110	132,000	132,000	
Capital stock	100,000	H	.125	12,500		12,500
Retained earnings (1/1)	300,000	P		37,500		37,500
Net income (including remeasurement loss)						51,250
Cumulative foreign exchange translation adjustments (1/1)		P		–0–		–0–
Translation gain (19X1)				17,500		17,500
	2,500,000			289,500	132,000	208,750

Code:
 C = Current exchange rate at December 31, 19X1.
 W = Weighted-average exchange rate for 19X1.
 H = Historical exchange rate.
 P = Dollar balance end of preceding period.

Translation Adjustments account at the end of the prior period (or at date of acquisition). The remeasurement loss is calculated directly as follows:

Loss for first part of year on net monetary asset position [100,000 × ($.125 − $.11)]	$ 1,500
Loss for subsequent portion of year on net monetary asset position [950,000 × ($.11 − $.10)]	9,500
Remeasurement loss	$11,000

Note that Bordeaux Company's foreign currency exposure is calculated ignoring the Monroe Company debt since the related gain or loss is not allowed to affect the remeasurement gain or loss. Finally, note that the requirements of *Statement No. 52* convert a net income figure of $68,750 to $51,250 by converting a remeasurement gain of $6,500 to remeasurement loss of $11,000, although the underlying circumstances of Cases 1 and 2 are essentially the same.

TRANSLATION WITHOUT REMEASUREMENT—SUBSIDIARY'S FUNCTIONAL AND REPORTING CURRENCIES DIFFERENT

The next case deals with the situation in which the foreign subsidiary's functional and reporting currencies are different, and its transactions are recorded in its functional currency. As indicated, translation reduces to the current rate method under these conditions. This method is meant to convert the foreign entity's financial statements into dollars in a way that preserves the economic results and relationships existing in its functional currency statements. *We refer to the conversion process described in this section as the current rate method for clarity, although it also is accurate to refer to it as translation.* We do not refer to this process as translation since the word *translation* also encompasses the procedures of remeasurement under *Statement No. 52.*

Case 3. Current Rate Method

The assumptions of this case are the same as in Case 1, except that Bordeaux Company's functional and reporting currencies are different, and its transactions are recorded in its functional currency. Its functional currency is the franc, and its reporting currency is the functional currency of Monroe Company—the U.S. dollar. We repeat Bordeaux Company's date of acquisition (January 1, 19X1) balance sheet below for convenience.

Accounts	Francs
Assets	
Cash and receivables	200,000
Plant and equipment (net)	1,000,000
Total assets	1,200,000
Liabilities and Owners' Equity	
Current payables	100,000
Long-term debt	700,000
Capital stock	100,000
Retained earnings	300,000
Total liabilities and owners' equity	1,200,000

On date of acquisition, the current rate method and the temporal method are identical. Thus, the former is applied in this case by multiplying each of Bordeaux Company's account balances by the current rate of .125. *This rate is used in the future only in converting elements of contributed capital under the current rate method.* The results of applying the current rate method to Bordeaux Company's accounts on date of acquisition are as follows:

	Francs	Exchange Rate	Dollars
Cash and receivables	200,000	.125	25,000
Plant and equipment (net)	1,000,000	.125	125,000
	1,200,000		150,000
Current payables	100,000	.125	12,500
Long-term debt	700,000	.125	87,500
Capital stock	100,000	.125	12,500
Retained earnings	300,000	.125	37,500
	1,200,000		150,000

Bordeaux Company's trial balance at December 31, 19X1, again is as follows:

Accounts	Francs
Debits	
Cash and Receivables	1,150,000
Plant and Equipment (net)	750,000
Depreciation Expense	250,000
Other Expenses	350,000
Totals	2,500,000
Credits	
Current Payables	200,000
Long-Term Debt	700,000
Sales	1,200,000
Capital Stock	100,000
Retained Earnings (1/1)	300,000
Totals	2,500,000

Recall from Case 1 that the current exchange rate on December 31, 19X1, is .10 and that the weighted-average rate for 19X1 is .11. Also, as in Case 1, all monetary assets and liabilities are denominated in francs (Bordeaux Company's functional currency in this case), and the only change in Plant and Equipment (net) during 19X1 is from recording depreciation expense of 250,000 francs.

Subsequent to date of acquisition, all assets and liabilities are converted using the current rate under the current rate method. Contributed capital, direct charges and credits to Retained Earnings (e.g., dividends), and income statement balances are converted at their historical rates under this method. However, *Statement No. 52* (par. 12) also makes an exception to this rule on income statement items because of their large number. Thus, as under remeasurement, these items (including depreciation expense and cost of goods sold) can be converted using an appropriately determined weighted-average exchange rate for the period. The beginning-of-period retained earnings balance is obtained exactly as under the temporal method—by setting this figure equal to the dollar value of retained earnings at the end of the prior period (or at date of acquisition). *As indicated, the period's translation (conversion) gain or loss resulting from the current rate method is included on Bordeaux Company's December 31, 19X1 balance sheet in shareholders' equity in the Cumulative Foreign Exchange Translation Adjustments account.* The beginning-of-period balance in this account is obtained exactly as in the case of beginning-of-period retained earnings. Translation gains and losses are discussed further below. For now, note that the period's translation gain or loss is calculated indirectly in a current rate method working paper. Thus, it is the "plug" figure that balances the debits and credits in such a working paper. The current rate method working paper for Bordeaux Company for 19X1 is provided in Illustration 13–4.

The converted values in Illustration 13–4 result from applying the general rules of the current rate method mentioned above. The Cash and Receivables, Plant and Equipment (net), Current Payables, and Long-Term Debt balances all are converted at the current rate, and Capital Stock is converted using its historical rate. The beginning-of-period retained earnings figure is set equal to the dollar value calculated for retained earnings at date of acquisition. All of the income statement items are converted using the weighted-average rate for the period. The translation loss is the "plug" figure that balances the debits and credits in the Trial Balance (in dollars) column. Bordeaux Company's net income for 19X1 is $66,000. Its ending retained earnings balance is $103,500 ($37,500 + $66,000). This value is the beginning-of-period retained earnings figure for next year's current rate method working paper. The income statement and balance sheet for this case are shown in Illustration 13–7.

Translation Gains and Losses

Under the current rate method, all assets and liabilities are translated using current rates. As mentioned, conversion gains and losses are related only to balance sheet items converted using current rates. Thus, under the current rate method, translation gains and losses are related to the foreign entity's net asset position.

ILLUSTRATION 13-4   **Current Rate Method**

BORDEAUX COMPANY
Foreign Currency Translation Working Paper
For the Year Ended December 31, 19X1

	Trial Balance (in francs)	Exchange Rate Code	Exchange Rate Rate	Trial Balance (in dollars)	Income Statement (in dollars)	Balance Sheet (in dollars)
Cash and receivables	1,150,000	C	.100	115,000		115,000
Plant and equipment (net)	750,000	C	.100	75,000		75,000
Depreciation expense	250,000	W	.110	27,500	27,500	
Other expenses	350,000	W	.110	38,500	38,500	
Translation loss (19X1)				16,000		
Net income					66,000	
	2,500,000			272,000	132,000	190,000
Current payables	200,000	C	.100	20,000		20,000
Long-term debt	700,000	C	.100	70,000		70,000
Sales	1,200,000	W	.110	132,000	132,000	
Capital stock	100,000	H	.125	12,500		12,500
Retained earnings (1/1)	300,000	P		37,500		37,500
Net income						66,000
Cumulative foreign exchange translation adjustments (1/1)		P		–0–		–0–
Translation loss (19X1)						(16,000)
	2,500,000			272,000	132,000	190,000

Code:
C = Current exchange rate at December 31, 19X1.
W = Weighted-average exchange rate for 19X1.
H = Historical exchange rate.
P = Dollar balance end of preceding period.
(debit)

In this example, Bordeaux Company's net asset position is calculated as follows for the end and the beginning of 19X1:

	In Francs	
	12/31/X1	1/1/X1
Assets translated at current rate— All	1,900,000	1,200,000
Less: Liabilities translated at current rate— All	900,000	800,000
Net asset position	1,000,000	400,000

Under the current rate method, Bordeaux Company's foreign currency exposure is a net asset during all of 19X1. During 19X1, this position changes from 400,000 francs to 1,000,000 francs as a consequence of net asset inflows. A translation loss occurs in our example because the dollar strengthens in relation to the franc (i.e., the spot rate moves from .125 to .1) over a period (19X1) in which Bordeaux Company's foreign currency exposure is a net asset. One way of calculating the 19X1 translation loss is as follows:

Loss on beginning net asset position	
[400,000 × ($.125 − $.10)]	$10,000
Loss on net asset inflow over the year	
[600,000 × ($.11 − $.10)]	6,000
Translation loss	$16,000

This calculation assumes implicitly that the net asset increase occurs when the spot rate equals the 19X1 weighted-average rate of .11. This assumption is made apparent by the following calculation which assumes explicitly that Bordeaux Company's net asset position changes when the exchange rate for the year equals the weighted average of .11.

Loss for first part of year on net asset position	
[400,000 × ($.125 − $.11)]	$ 6,000
Loss for subsequent portion of year on net asset position	
[1,000,000 × ($.11 − $.10)]	10,000
Translation loss	$16,000

This calculation is easier to interpret than the preceding one since it emphasizes the periods over which Bordeaux Company's foreign currency exposure is assumed to be at different levels, as well as the assumed changes in spot rates over these periods.

Long-Term Intercompany Payables under Current Rate Method

We assume in (temporal method) Case 2 that Bordeaux Company's long-term debt, which is denominated in francs, results from an intercompany foreign currency transaction that is of a long-term investment nature. Under the temporal method, transaction gains and losses on this type of debt are given special treatment under *Statement No. 52;* they are accumulated in the Cumulative Foreign Exchange Translation Adjustments account. Gains and losses of this type do not require special consideration (or separate calculation) under the current rate method since this method's conversion procedure automatically includes them in the period's translation gain or loss (which becomes part of the balance of Cumulative Foreign Exchange Translation Adjustments). They are included in the period's translation gain or loss under the current rate method because they are part of the foreign entity's foreign currency exposure—its net asset or net liability position.

TRANSLATION WITH BOTH REMEASUREMENT AND CURRENT RATE METHOD

As indicated earlier, there is a relatively rare case in which the foreign entity's functional and reporting currencies are different and its transactions are recorded in a third currency. In this case, its statements first are remeasured in its functional currency. Subsequently, they are translated from the functional currency into the reporting currency. This situation is covered in Case 4.

Case 4. Remeasurement and Current Rate Methods Combined

Assume the data of Case 1, except that Bordeaux Company is a Canadian Company whose functional currency is the Canadian dollar and that the exchange rates given in Case 1 pertain to the Canadian dollar and the franc. Since Bordeaux Company conducts its business exclusively with French customers and all related settlements are made in francs, its transactions are recorded in francs. Also, since Bordeaux Company is a subsidiary of Monroe Company, a U.S. Company whose reporting currency is the U.S. dollar, two steps are required in converting Bordeaux Company's financial statements into the reporting currency of its parent company. First, they are remeasured from francs into Canadian dollars since Bordeaux Company's functional currency is the Canadian dollar. Illustration 13–5 provides the temporal method working paper reflecting this step. Second, the resulting statement values are translated from Canadian dollars into U.S. dollars using the current rate method. Directly quoted exchange rates between the U.S. and Canadian dollars pertinent to this application of the current rate method are assumed to be: (1) date of Monroe Company's acquisition of Bordeaux Company—.9, (2) December 31, 19X1—1.1, and (3) weighted-average rate for 19X1—.96. The related current rate method working paper is given in Illustration 13–6.

ILLUSTRATION 13–5   **Temporal Method**

BORDEAUX COMPANY
Foreign Currency Translation Working Paper
For the Year Ended December 31, 19X1

	Trial Balance (in francs)	Exchange Rate — Code	Exchange Rate — Rate	Trial Balance (in Canadian dollars)	Income Statement (in Canadian dollars)	Balance Sheet (in Canadian dollars)
Cash and receivables	1,150,000	C	.100	115,000		115,000
Plant and equipment (net)	750,000	H	.125	93,750		93,750
Depreciation expense	250,000	H	.125	31,250	31,250	
Other expenses	350,000	W	.110	38,500	38,500	
Net income (including remeasurement gain)					68,750	
	2,500,000			278,500	138,500	208,750
Current payables	200,000	C	.100	20,000		20,000
Long-term debt	700,000	C	.100	70,000		70,000
Sales	1,200,000	W	.110	132,000	132,000	
Capital stock	100,000	H	.125	12,500		12,500
Retained earnings (1/1)	300,000	P		37,500		37,500
Remeasurement gain (19X1)				6,500	6,500	
Net income (including remeasurement gain)						68,750
	2,500,000			278,500	138,500	208,750

Code:
C = Current exchange rate at December 31, 19X1.
W = Weighted-average exchange rate for 19X1.
H = Historical exchange rate.
P = Dollar balance end of preceding period.

INCOME STATEMENTS AND BALANCE SHEETS— TEMPORAL AND CURRENT RATE METHODS

Comparative 19X1 income statements and December 31, 19X1, balance sheets for the examples of this chapter are given in Ilustration 13–7. They emphasize the treatment of certain amounts under *Statement No. 52*—remeasurement gains and losses, translation gains and losses, and cumulative foreign exchange translation adjustments.

ILLUSTRATION 13-6 Current Rate Method

BORDEAUX COMPANY
Foreign Currency Translation Working Paper
For the Year Ended December 31, 19X1

	Trial Balance (in Canadian dollars)	Exchange Rate Code	Exchange Rate Rate	Trial Balance (in U.S. dollars)	Income Statement (in U.S. dollars)	Balance Sheet (in U.S. dollars)
Cash and receivables	115,000	C	1.10	126,500		126,500
Plant and equipment (net)	93,750	C	1.10	103,125		103,125
Depreciation expense	31,250	W	0.96	30,000	30,000	
Other expenses	38,500	W	0.96	36,960	36,960	
Net income (including remeasurement gain)					66,000	
	278,500			296,585	132,960	229,625
Current payables	20,000	C	1.10	22,000		22,000
Long-term debt	70,000	C	1.10	77,000		77,000
Sales	132,000	W	0.96	126,720	126,720	
Capital stock	12,500	H	0.90	11,250		11,250
Retained earnings (1/1)	37,500	P		33,750*		33,750
Remeasurement gain (19X1)	6,500	W	0.96	6,240	6,240	
Translation gain (19X1)				19,625		19,625
Net income (including remeasurement gain)					132,960	66,000
	278,500			296,585	132,960	229,625

Code:
C = Current exchange rate at December 31, 19X1.
W = Weighted-average exchange rate for 19X1.
H = Historical exchange rate.
P = Dollar balance end of preceding period.
* = .9 × (.125 × 300,000)

ILLUSTRATION 13-7   **Account Balance Effects of Temporal and Current Rate Methods**

BORDEAUX COMPANY
Comparative 19X1 Income Statements and Balance Sheets
(in dollars)

	Temporal Method		Current Rate Method	Both Methods
	Case 1	Case 2	Case 3	Case 4
19X1 Income statements:				
Sales	132,000	132,000	132,000	126,720
Expenses, gains, and losses:				
Depreciation expense	31,250	31,250	27,500	30,000
Other expenses	38,500	38,500	38,500	36,960
Remeasurement (gain) or loss	(6,500)	11,000	–0–	(6,240)
Net income	68,750	51,250	66,000	66,000
December 31, 19X1, balance sheets:				
Cash and receivables	115,000	115,000	115,000	126,500
Plant and equipment (net)	93,750	93,750	75,000	103,125
Total assets	208,750	208,750	190,000	229,625
Current payables	20,000	20,000	20,000	22,000
Long-term debt	70,000	70,000	70,000	77,000
Capital stock	12,500	12,500	12,500	11,250
Retained earnings	106,250	88,750	103,500	99,750
Cumulative foreign exchange translation adjustments [(debit)]	–0–	17,500	(16,000)	19,625
Total equities	208,750	208,750	190,000	229,625

INVENTORIES AND THE LOWER-OF-COST-OR-MARKET RULE

If a foreign entity's records are not kept in its functional currency, the application of the lower-of-cost-or-market rule under *Statement No. 52* (par. 49) requires remeasurement of the relevant cost and market values into the functional currency. Once remeasured, the lower-of-cost-or-market rule is applied in the *functional currency* as appropriate for the entity (i.e., on the individual item, inventory category, or inventory whole basis). This procedure is particularly pertinent to the frequently encountered case in which the entity's functional and reporting currencies are the same, and its transactions are recorded in its local currency. In this case, translation reduces to the temporal method. The following example illustrates these points.

Case 5. Lower-of-Cost-or-Market Rule—Remeasurement

Assume that a British subsidiary whose functional and reporting currencies are the U.S. dollar has an item of inventory at December 31, 19X1, costing 1,000 pounds. Its local currency is the pound. The inventory item was acquired when the directly quoted, spot rate for the pound was 5. Assume also that the individual item approach is followed in applying the lower-of-cost-or-market rule. We consider two independent situations. The data for the two situations are presented below.

	Situation 1	*Situation 2*
Market (replacement price, ceiling, or floor)—pounds	1,100	900
Spot rate for pound—12/31/X1	4	6

The costs and market values for the item of inventory are remeasured in dollars as follows:

	Situation 1	*Situation 2*
Cost (1,000 × $5)	$5,000	$5,000
Market:		
(1,100 × $4)	4,400	
(900 × $6)		5,400
Lower of cost or market:		
Market	4,400	
Cost		5,000

In situation 1, cost (1,000) is lower than market (1,100) in pounds. However, once these values are remeasured into dollars, market ($4,400) is lower than cost ($5,000). Comparing cost and market in the functional currency yields a remeasured inventory value of $4,400 for the company's reporting currency financial statements. Thus, the item is written down $600 ($5,000 − $4,400) for these statements. In situation 2, market (900) is lower than cost (1,000) in pounds. After remeasurement into dollars, cost ($5,000) is lower than market ($5,400). In this situation, the item is shown in the reporting currency financial statements at its remeasurement cost of $5,000. The opposite results occur in the two situations because the spot rate moves in different directions subsequent to acquisition of the inventory item.

FOREIGN BRANCHES

Branch operations usually are closely connected to the operations of the dominant organizational unit of a company. Thus, in most cases the functional currency of a foreign branch is the reporting currency of the home office. In these cases, the temporal method is used to convert most of the branch foreign currency account balances into the reporting currency. Note, however, that branch reciprocal accounts are converted by setting them equal to the balances of their counterparts on the home office books. This procedure produces the same results as those yielded if each transaction recorded in the reciprocal accounts is converted using its historical rate.

MULTIPLE EXCHANGE RATES

When multiple exchange rates exist, the rate used in converting a foreign entity's financial statements usually is the rate that pertains to its dividend payments. This rate is specified in *Statement No. 52* (par. 138) because it governs the conversion of cash flows from a foreign affiliate's operations into the reporting currency.

Using the dividend payment rate for converting foreign entity financial statements occasionally creates a difference between intercompany receivables and payables. For example, assume that a domestic parent's intercompany receivable is to be settled at a rate differing from the dividend payment rate. In this case, the conversion of the foreign subsidiary's payable at the dividend payment rate produces an amount that differs from the carrying value of the receivable. Differences of this sort are treated as receivables or payables in consolidated financial statements until the related accounts are settled.

INCOME TAX ALLOCATION—FOREIGN CURRENCY TRANSLATION

For simplicity, the analyses of Chapters 12, 13, and 14 ignore income tax allocation issues. However, under *Statement No. 52* (pars. 22, 23, 24, 134, and 135), *Statement No. 96* (par. 43) and *Statement No. 109* (par. 118), income tax allocation is appropriate in several cases:[13]

1. Situations in which taxable transaction exchange gains and losses are included in income in a different period for financial statement purposes than for income tax purposes (interperiod income tax allocation).

---

[13] FASB, *Statement of Financial Accounting Standards No. 109,* "Accounting for Income Taxes" (Norwalk, CT: FASB, 1992) is the current authoritative pronouncement covering income tax accounting.

2. Situations in which potential future tax effects partially offset the increases or decreases in entities' net assets from translation adjustments (interperiod income tax allocation).

3. Situations in which some of the current period's income taxes are applicable to transaction exchange gains and losses and translation adjustments in shareholders' equity (intraperiod income tax allocation).

4. Certain situations reflecting temporary differences of foreign assets and liabilities occurring after a change in exchange rates (interperiod income tax allocation).[14]

FINANCIAL STATEMENT DISCLOSURES—FOREIGN CURRENCY TRANSLATION

Statement No. 52 (pars. 30 and 31) requires the following specific disclosures related to foreign currency translation in the financial statements or related footnotes:

1. The remeasurement gain or loss included in net income and
2. An analysis of the period's change in the Cumulative Foreign Exchange Translation Adjustments account which reveals as a minimum:
   a. The beginning and ending balance of this account;
   b. The aggregate change in this balance from translation adjustments and gains and losses from transactions that are (i) designated as, and are effective as, hedges of a net investment in a foreign entity and (ii) intercompany foreign currency transactions of a long term investment nature;
   c. The income taxes for the period allocated to translation adjustments; and
   d. The amounts transferred from Cumulative Foreign Exchange Translation Adjustments and included in determining net income for the period as a result of the sale, complete liquidation, or substantially complete liquidation of an investment in a foreign entity.

Note that the account title, Cumulative Foreign Exchange Translation Adjustments, is ours and is not specified in *Statement No. 52*.

---

[14] *APB Opinion No. 23,* "Accounting for Income Taxes—Special Areas," (par. 12) requires that deferred taxes not be provided for unremitted earnings of a subsidiary if "sufficient evidence shows that the subsidiary has invested or will invest the undistributed earnings indefinitely or that the earnings will be remitted in a tax-free liquidation." In these cases, *Statement No. 52* (par. 23) specifies that deferred taxes are not provided on translation adjustments. Note also that *Statement No. 96* (par. 44) discusses translation of foreign entities' deferred foreign tax assets and liabilities after a change in exchange rates. If the functional and reporting currencies are the same, this statement allows the related transaction exchange gain or loss to be reported in the amount of deferred tax benefit or expense when this presentation is deemed more useful. *Statement 109* (par. 230) reaffirms this view and indicates that such gains and losses still are included in the aggregate transaction gain or loss for the period as required under *Statement No. 52*.

Summary

This chapter deals with the conversion of foreign entities' financial statements into the reporting currency—which usually is the domestic currency of investor companies. This conversion process is the first step in preparing consolidated financial statements for a domestic parent company and its foreign subsidiary and in accounting for a domestic company's investment in a foreign affiliate under the equity method. Under *Statement No. 52,* this conversion process is a functional currency approach.

An entity's functional currency frequently is the currency of the primary economic environment in which it operates—the currency of the environment in which the entity primarily generates and expends cash. Nevertheless, a foreign entity's functional currency can be the reporting currency of a domestic affiliate, even if it records its transactions in its local currency. The objectives of translating a foreign entity's financial statements from its functional currency into the reporting currency of its parent (or investing affiliate) under *Statement No. 52* are to:

a. Provide information that is generally compatible with the expected economic effects of a rate change on an enterprise's cash flows and equity and

b. Reflect in consolidated statements [and under the equity method] the financial results and relationships of the individual . . . entities as measured in their *functional currencies* in conformity with U.S. generally accepted accounting principles.

Under *Statement No. 52,* the conversion process is best described as the process of translating the foreign entity's financial statements from its functional currency into the reporting currency. This process is referred to as *translation.* There are two commonly encountered situations requiring translation. First, the foreign entity's functional and local currencies can be the same, with its transactions recorded in the local currency. In this case, translation reduces to the current rate method. This technique is meant to convert the foreign entity's financial statements into dollars in a way that preserves the economic results and relationships existing in its functional currency statements. Under this method, all assets and liabilities are converted at the balance sheet date spot rate. Second, the foreign entity's functional and reporting currencies can be the same, with its transactions recorded in its local currency. This situation occurs if a foreign subsidiary is primarily an integral component, or extension, of its parent company's operations. In this case, translation reduces to the temporal method (remeasurement). The objective of remeasurement is to produce the same financial statement values that would have been produced if the foreign entity's transactions had been recorded in its functional currency in the first place. Thus, this method preserves GAAP. Under the temporal method, only monetary assets and monetary liabilities are converted using the balance sheet date, spot rate. All other assets and equities are remeasured using their historical rates.

Both the current rate and temporal methods produce conversion gains and losses. These gains and losses are related only to assets and liabilities converted at the balance sheet date spot rate. We refer to the conversion gains and losses arising under the current rate method as translation exchange gains and losses. These gains and losses are not included in calculating net income; they are accumulated in shareholders' equity in the Cumulative Foreign Exchange Translation Adjustments account. This treatment is based on the FASB's view that translation gains or losses are not directly related to the foreign entity's operating cash flows. We refer to the conversion gains and losses occurring under the temporal method as remeasurement gains and losses. These gains and losses are recognized in the income statement. This treatment is based on the view that the foreign entity is exposed to exchange risk on transactions that are denominated in a currency other than its functional currency and that the resulting gains and losses affect operating cash flows.

Questions

1. How is the *Statement of Financial Accounting Standards No. 52* approach to the conversion of foreign currency financial statements best described?
2. What are the objectives of the FASB's functional currency approach to the conversion of foreign currency financial statements?
3. What is the objective of the current rate method?
4. What is the objective of the temporal method?
5. How are assets and liabilities in foreign currency financial statements translated under the current rate method?
6. How are revenue and expense items in foreign currency financial statements translated under the current rate method?
7. How are the translation gains and losses arising from the translation of foreign currency financial statements under the current rate method reported under current accounting policy?
8. How are assets and liabilities in foreign currency financial statements remeasured under the temporal method?
9. How are revenue and expense items in foreign currency financial statements remeasured under the temporal method?
10. How are the remeasurement gains and losses arising from the remeasurement of foreign currency financial statements under the temporal method reported under current accounting policy?
11. Explain the process used to identify the appropriate method for converting an affiliate's foreign currency financial statements into the reporting currency.
12. Explain the concept of functional currency.
13. What is a highly inflationary economy? What is the significance of this concept for foreign currency translation?
14. How are the assets and liabilities of a newly acquired foreign subsidiary translated on date of acquisition? What is the significance of the rates used in later periods?
15. How are the shareholders' equity accounts of a foreign subsidiary translated into the parent's reporting currency?
16. How is the Cumulative Foreign Exchange Translation Adjustment account shown in financial statements under the current rate method and the temporal method?

17. Explain the application of the lower-of-cost-or-market rule to inventory when the temporal method is used.
18. When multiple exchange rates exist, what rate is used in translating foreign currency financial statements?
19. When does the translation of foreign currency financial statements require income tax allocation?
20. What is the significance of intercompany foreign currency transactions of a long-term investment nature in the context of foreign currency translation?

Exercises

Exercise 13–1   (Rates Used under Temporal Method)

Identify the rates used in remeasuring the following accounts on the books of a foreign subsidiary into its parent's reporting currency.

1. Patents.
2. Accrued Wages Payable.
3. Marketable Equity Securities (at cost).
4. Deferred Income.
5. Inventory (at cost).
6. Allowance for Doubtful Accounts.
7. Inventory (at net realizable value).
8. Property, Plant, and Equipment.
9. Accumulated Depreciation.
10. Advances to Unconsolidated Subsidiaries.

Exercise 13–2   (Rates Used under Temporal Method)

Dhia Products Company was incorporated in Virginia in 19X0 to manufacture medical supplies and equipment. Dhia has doubled in size about every three years and now is considered one of the leading medical supply companies in the country.

During January 19X4, Dhia established a subsidiary, Ban Company, in the emerging nation of Shatha. Dhia Company owns 90 percent of the outstanding capital stock of Ban Company. The remaining 10 percent of Ban Company's outstanding capital stock is held by Shatha citizens, as required by Shatha's constitutional law. The investment in Ban Company, accounted for by Dhia Company using the equity method, represents about 18 percent of the total assets of Dhia Company at December 31, 19X7 (the end of the current fiscal year for both companies). The management of Dhia Company has determined that Ban Company's functional currency is the dollar.

Required:

a. What criteria are applied in deciding whether consolidated financial statements should be prepared for Dhia Products Company and its subsidiary for the year ended December 31, 19X7? Explain your answer. (Hint: You may wish to consult *Statement of Financial Accounting Standards No. 94* for guidance.)

b. Assume that Dhia and Ban Companies prepared consolidated financial statements consistently with GAAP for the years 19X4 to 19X7. For each of Ban Company's accounts listed below, identify the exchange rate (e.g., weighted-average exchange rate for 19X7, current exchange rate at December 31, 19X7, etc.) to be used in converting the account balance into dollars. Explain why each selected rate is appropriate. Number your answers to correspond with each account listed below.

1. Cash in Shatha National Bank.
2. Trade Accounts Receivable (all from 19X7 revenues).
3. Supplies Inventory (all purchased during the last quarter of 19X7).
4. Land (purchased in 19X4).
5. Short-Term Note Payable to Shatha National Bank.
6. Capital Stock (no par or stated value, and all issued in January 19X4).
7. Retained Earnings (January 1, 19X7).
8. Sales Revenue.
9. Depreciation Expense (on buildings).
10. Salaries Expense.

(AICPA adapted)

Exercise 13–3   (Balances and Rates under Temporal and Current Rate Methods)

Select the best answers for the following questions under each of two alternative assumptions: *(a)* the current rate method is used in converting foreign entity financial statements into dollars and *(b)* the temporal method is used in this conversion.

1. Certain balance sheet accounts of a foreign subsidiary of the Brown Company have been translated into dollars as follows at December 31, 19X7:

	Converted at	
	Current Rate	Historical Rate
Marketable equity securities (at cost)	$100,000	$110,000
Marketable equity securities (at current market price)	120,000	125,000
Inventories (at cost)	130,000	132,000
Inventories (at net realizable value)	80,000	84,000
	$430,000	$451,000

What amount is shown in Brown's balance sheet at December 31, 19X7?
a. $430,000.
b. $436,000.
c. $442,000.
d. $451,000.

2. When converting the fixed assets of a foreign subsidiary, the appropriate exchange rate is the
a. Current exchange rate.
b. Weighted-average exchange rate for the current year.

    c. Historical exchange rate.

    d. Weighted-average exchange rate over the life of each fixed asset.

3. The year-end balance of accounts receivable on the books of a foreign subsidiary is converted by the parent company for consolidation purposes at the

    a. Historical rate.

    b. Current rate.

    c. Negotiated rate.

    d. Spot rate.

4. If a parent company bills all sales to a foreign subsidiary in dollars and is to be repaid in the same number of dollars, the Purchases account of the subsidiary is converted to dollars using

    a. The weighted-average exchange rate for the period.

    b. The exchange rate at the beginning of the period.

    c. The exchange rate at the end of the period.

    d. The amount of the parent's sales to the subsidiary.

5. United Company purchases with dollars all the outstanding common stock of Wilson Company, a Canadian corporation. At purchase, a portion of the investment account was appropriately allocated to goodwill. One year later, after an exchange rate decrease, the goodwill should be shown in the consolidated balance sheet at what amount? (*Hint:* You may wish to consult Chapter 14 for guidance.)

    a. An increased amount, less amortization.

    b. The same amount, less amortization.

    c. A lesser amount, less amortization.

    d. An increased or lesser amount depending on management policy, less amortization.

(AICPA adapted)

Exercise 13–4   (Balances under Current Rate and Temporal Methods)

Select the best answers for the following questions under each of two alternative assumptions: *(a)* the current rate method is used in converting foreign entity financial statements into dollars and *(b)* the temporal method is used in this conversion.

1. Ben Company had a receivable from a foreign customer which was payable in the local currency of the foreign customer. On December 31, 19X6, this receivable was included in the accounts receivable section of Ben Company's balance sheet at $450,000. When the receivable was collected on January 4, 19X7, Ben Company converted the local currency of the foreign customer into $440,000. Ben Company also owns a foreign subsidiary—on which a conversion gain of $45,000 was produced in 1987 as a consequence of foreign currency translation. What amount, if any, should be included as an exchange gain or loss in Ben's 19X7 consolidated income statement?

    a. $0.

    b. $10,000 exchange loss.

    c. $35,000 exchange gain.

    d. $45,000 exchange gain.

2. On January 1, 19X8, James Company formed a foreign subsidiary. On February 15, 19X8, James Company's subsidiary purchased 100,000 local current units (LCU) of

inventory. Twenty-five thousand LCU of this inventory made up the subsidiary's entire inventory on December 31, 19X8. The exchange rates were 2.2 LCU to $1 from January 1, 19X8, to June 30, 19X8, and 2 LCU to $1 from July 1, 19X8, to December 31, 19X8. The December 31, 19X8, inventory balance for James Company's subsidiary is translated into dollars of

a. $10,500.
b. $11,364.
c. $11,905.
d. $12,500.

3. Seed Company owns a foreign subsidiary with 2,400,000 local currency units (LCU) of property, plant, and equipment before accumulated depreciation at December 31, 19X8. Of this amount, 1,500,000 LCU were acquired in 19X6 when the rate of exchange was 1.5 LCU to $1, and 900,000 LCU were acquired in 19X7 when the rate of exchange was 1.6 LCU to $1. The weighted-average exchange rate for 19X8 was 1.8 LCU to $1. Assuming that the property, plant, and equipment are depreciated using the straight-line method over a 10-year period with no salvage value, how much depreciation expense relating to the foreign subsidiary's property, plant, and equipment is included in Seed Company's consolidated income statement for 19X8?

a. $126,316.
b. $133,333.
c. $150,000.
d. $156,250.

(AICPA adapted)

Exercise 13–5   (Balances and Rates under Temporal and Current Rate Methods)

Select the best answers for the following questions.

1. The balance in Davong Corporation's foreign exchange loss account from 19X1 transactions with foreign suppliers is $6,500 at December 31, 19X1, before any necessary year-end adjustment(s) relating to the following:
   a. Davong had a $10,000 translation loss resulting from the translation of the accounts of its wholly owned foreign subsidiary from its functional currency into dollars for the year ended December 31, 19X1.
   b. Davong had an account payable to an unrelated foreign supplier payable in the local currency of the foreign supplier on January 12, 19X2. The dollar equivalent of the payable was $50,000 on the November 13, 19X1, invoice date, and it was $53,000 on December 31, 19X1.

   In Davong's 19X1 consolidated income statement, what amount is included as a foreign exchange loss?
   a. $19,500.
   b. $16,500.
   c. $9,500.
   d. $6,500.

2. A subsidiary's functional currency is the local currency, which has not experienced significant inflation. The appropriate exchange rate for translating the depreciation on plant assets in the income statement of the foreign subsidiary is the
   a. Exit exchange rate.
   b. Historical exchange rate.

    c. Weighted-average exchange rate over the economic life of each plant asset.

    d. Weighted-average exchange rate for the current year.

3. Losses resulting from the process of translating a foreign entity's financial statements from the functional currency (which is experiencing a 3 percent inflation rate) to dollars is included as a (an)

    a. Deferred charge.

    b. Separate component of stockholder's equity.

    c. Component of income from continuing operations.

    d. Extraordinary item.

4. Tate Corporation had a $20,000 translation loss adjustment resulting from the translation of the accounts of its wholly owned foreign subsidiary from its functional currency into dollars for the year ended December 31, 19X5. Tate also had a receivable at the beginning of the year from a foreign customer, which was payable in the local currency of the foreign customer. On December 31, 19X4, this receivable for 100,000 local currency units (LCU) was included in Tate's balance sheet at $55,000. When the receivable was collected on February 10, 19X5, the exchange rate was 2 LCU to $1. In Tate's 19X5 consolidated income statement, what amount is included as a foreign exchange loss?

    a. $0.

    b. $5,000.

    c. $20,000.

    d. $25,000.

5. On January 1, 19X2, Norton Company established a wholly owned foreign subsidiary. The subsidiary purchased merchandise at a cost of 720,000 local currency units (LCU) on February 15, 19X2. The purchase price was equivalent to $180,000 on this date. The subsidiary's inventory at December 31, 19X2, consisted solely of merchandise purchased on February 15, 19X2, and amounted to 240,000 LCU. The exchange rate was 6 LCU to $1 on December 31, 19X2, and the average rate of exchange was 5 LCU to $1 for 19X2. Assume that the LCU is the functional currency of the subsidiary. In Norton Company's December 31, 19X2 consolidated balance sheet, the subsidiary's inventory balance of 240,000 LCU is translated into dollars at

    a. $40,000.

    b. $48,000.

    c. $60,000.

    d. $84,000.

(AICPA adapted)

Exercise 13–6   (Changes in Functional Currency)

Statement of Financial Accounting Standards No. 52 indicates that determining a functional currency is a judgmental matter involving a number of guidelines. However, once management has selected a functional currency, this decision is consistently applied unless significant changes in economic circumstances indicate clearly that the functional currency has changed.

    Explain the accounting implications of the functional currency changing *(a)* from a foreign currency to the reporting currency and *(b)* from the reporting currency to a foreign currency. (*Hint:* You may wish to consult extant authoritative pronouncements for guidance.)

Exercise 13-7 (Lower-of-Cost-or-Market Rule under Temporal Method)

Inventory on hand at December 31, 19X1, has a cost of 10,000 local currency units (LCU). The inventory was acquired when the exchange rate was LCU 1 = $.70. The lower-of-cost-or-market rule is used to value the inventory. For each of the following cases, calculate the dollar value that is assigned to the inventory under the temporal method.

	Case 1	Case 2	Case 3	Case 4
Replacement cost	LCU 11,000	LCU 11,000	LCU 9,000	LCU 9,000
Net realizable value	14,000	16,000	10,000	10,000
Net realizable value, less an approximately normal profit margin	10,000	12,000	7,000	7,000
Exchange rate—12/31/X1	$.60	$.50	$.80	$.75

Problems

Problem 13-8 (Current Rate Method Working Paper and Statements)

Mission Company is a foreign subsidiary of a U.S. parent. Mission Company's trial balance at the beginning and end of 19X1 are shown below in local currency units (LCU):

	12/31/X1	1/1/X1
Cash	300,000	300,000
Plant and Equipment (net)	2,400,000	2,000,000
Depreciation Expense	200,000	
Other Expenses	500,000	
	3,400,000	2,300,000
Current Payables	50,000	150,000
Long-Term Debt	1,000,000	1,000,000
Capital Stock	500,000	500,000
Retained Earnings (1/1/X1)	650,000	650,000
Sales	1,200,000	
	3,400,000	2,300,000

The following additional information is available:

1. Mission's functional currency is its local currency.
2. The exchange rates between the dollar and the LCU for 19X1 are the following: January 1, 19X1—.30.

Weighted average for 19X1—.36.
December 31, 19X1—.40.
Date of acquisition—.25.

3. There has been no change in Mission Company's capital structure. On December 31, 19X0, Mission Company's Retained Earnings had a credit balance of $175,000, and the Cumulative Foreign Exchange Translation Adjustments account had a credit balance of $45,000.

4. There were no retirements of plant and equipment during 19X1.

Required:

a. Prepare a foreign currency translation working paper for Mission Company for the year ended December 31, 19X1. (Note that this problem is integrated with Exercise 14–5.)

b. Prepare Mission Company's 19X1 income statement and its December 31, 19X1, balance sheet.

Problem 13–9   (Temporal Method Working Paper and Statements)

Assume the information of Problem 13–8, except now assume that Mission Company's functional currency is the dollar. Assume also that Mission Company's plant and equipment and long-term debt were on its books at date of acquisition and that its January 1, 19X1, retained earnings is $54,000. With these changes, complete the requirements of Problem 13–8. (Note that this problem is integrated with Exercise 14–6.)

Problem 13–10   (Translation and Remeasurement Gains or Losses)

Use the data of Problems 13–8 and 13–9, respectively, to calculate Mission Company's 19X1 translation gain or loss and 19X1 remeasurement gain or loss directly.

Problem 13–11   (Temporal Method Working Paper)

This problem extends the data presented in this chapter for Monroe Company and its French subsidiary, Bordeaux Company, to the year 19X2. It deals with the case in which there is no long-term intercompany payable. In solving this problem, you may need to refer to the text for 19X1 data.

Bordeaux Company's trial balance at December 31, 19X2, is as follows:

	Francs
Cash	1,200,000
Receivables	400,000
Plant and Equipment (net)	1,300,000
Depreciation Expense	300,000*
Other Expenses	500,000
	3,700,000

	Francs
Current Payables	300,000
Long-Term Debt	900,000
Sales	1,500,000
Capital Stock	100,000
Retained Earnings (1/1)	900,000
	3,700,000

* Depreciation expense is higher in 19X2 than in 19X1 because
some assets are being depreciated using the units-of-service
approach.

The directly quoted, spot rate for the franc at December 31, 19X2, is .12. The weighted-average exchange rate for 19X2 is .105. For simplicity, assume that the newly acquired plant and equipment is purchased in 19X2 when the spot rate equals the weighted-average rate for the year and that Bordeaux Company does not depreciate new equipment in the year of acquisition. Assume Bordeaux Company's functional currency is the dollar in this problem.

Required:

Prepare a foreign currency translation working paper for Bordeaux Company for the year ended December 31, 19X2. (Note that this problem is integrated with Problems 14-9, 14-10, and 14-11.)

Problem 13-12   (Remeasurement Gain or Loss and Statements)

Use the information of Problem 13-11 (1) to calculate Bordeaux Company's remeasurement gain or loss directly and (2) to prepare its 19X2 income statement and December 31, 19X2, balance sheet.

Problem 13-13   (Current Rate Method Working Paper)

Use the information of Problem 13-11, except now assume that Bordeaux Company's functional currency is the franc. With these changes, complete the requirements of Problem 13-11. (Note that this problem is integrated with Problems 14-12, 14-13, 14-14, and 14-15.)

Problem 13-14   (Translation Gain or Loss and Statements)

Use the information of Problem 13-13 (1) to calculate Bordeaux Company's translation gain or loss directly and (2) to prepare its 19X2 income statement and December 31, 19X2 balance sheet.

Problem 13-15   (Temporal Method Working Paper)

This problem extends the data presented in this chapter for Monroe Company and its French subsidiary, Bordeaux Company, to the year 19X2. It deals with the case in which there is a long-term intercompany payable. In solving this problem, you may need to refer to the text for 19X1 data.

Bordeaux Company's trial balance at December 31, 19X2, is as follows:

	Francs
Cash	1,200,000
Receivables	400,000
Plant and Equipment (net)	1,300,000
Depreciation Expense	300,000*
Other Expenses	500,000
	3,700,000
Current Payables	300,000
Long-Term Debt—Monroe	700,000
Other Long-Term Debt	200,000
Sales	1,500,000
Capital Stock	100,000
Retained Earnings (1/1)	900,000
	3,700,000

*Depreciation expense is higher in 19X2 than in 19X1 because some assets are being depreciated using the units-of-service approach.

The directly quoted, spot rate for the franc at December 31, 19X2, is .12. The weighted-average exchange rate for 19X2 is .105. Assume that Bordeaux Company's functional currency is the reporting currency (the dollar) in this problem. For simplicity, assume that the newly acquired plant and equipment is purchased in 19X2 when the spot rate equals the weighted-average rate for the year and that Bordeaux Company does not depreciate new equipment in the year of acquisition.

Required:

Prepare a foreign currency translation working paper for Bordeaux Company for the year ended December 31, 19X2. (Note that this problem is integrated with Problems 14–16, 14–17, and 14–18.)

Problem 13–16   (Translation Gain or Loss, Remeasurement Gain or Loss, and Statements)

Use the information of Problem 13–15 (1) to calculate Bordeaux Company's translation gain or loss directly, (2) to calculate its remeasurement gain or loss directly, and (3) to prepare its 19X2 income statement and December 31, 19X2, balance sheet.

Problem 13–17   (Temporal Method Working Paper and Statements)

May Company, a Seattle firm, holds an 80 percent ownership interest in Seneque Company, a South African corporation. This interest was acquired when Seneque Company was chartered. The dollar is Seneque Company's functional currency.

Seneque Company's trial balance at December 31, 19X7, is presented below.

	Rands
Cash	60,000
Accounts Receivable	100,000
Airplanes (net)	500,000
Depreciation Expense	80,000
Other Expenses	160,000
	900,000
Allowance for Doubtful Accounts	10,000
Notes Payable	200,000
Capital Stock	100,000
Retained Earnings (1/1)	290,000
Revenue	300,000
	900,000

The capital stock was issued seven years ago when the company was formed to provide charter air service. On this date, the exchange rate was .80. The current fleet of airplanes was acquired three years ago when the exchange rate was .90. The notes were given to a local bank at the same time. The spot rates for rands in 19X7 were as follows:

January 1	.57
Weighted average	.53
December 31	.50

Seneque Company's retained earnings was $333,700 in its converted December 31, 19X6, balance sheet.

Required:

a. Prepare a foreign currency translation working paper for Seneque Company for the year ended December 31, 19X7. (Note that this problem is integrated with Problem 14–19.)

b. Prepare Seneque Company's 19X7 income statement and its December 31, 19X7, balance sheet.

Problem 13–18   (Current Rate Method Working Paper and Statements)

Use the information of Problem 13–17, except now assume that (1) Seneque Company's functional currency is the rand, (2) its December 31, 19X6, Retained Earnings balance was $200,000, and (3) its December 31, 19X6, Cumulative Foreign Exchange Translation Adjustments balance was a debit balance of $57,700. With these changes, complete the requirements of Problem 13–17. (Note that this problem is integrated with Problem 14–20.)

Problem 13–19   (Remeasurement and Translation Gains or Losses)

Use the data of Problems 13–17 and 13–18, respectively, to calculate Seneque Company's 19X7 remeasurement gain or loss and 19X7 translation gain or loss directly. Assume that Seneque Company's net monetary liability position on January 1, 19X7, is 190,000 rands and that its net asset position on this date is 390,000 rands.

Problem 13–20   (Temporal Method Working Paper and Statements)

Faison Importers Company, an Arizona company, holds a 70 percent interest in Mommessin Company, a French company. This ownership interest was acquired when Mommessin Company was initially incorporated. The dollar is Mommessin Company's functional currency.

Ꮐ   The trial balance of Mommessin Company at December 31, 19X1, is as follows.

	Francs
Cash	40,000
Accounts Receivable	20,000
Inventory	60,000
Plant and Equipment (net)	100,000
Cost of Goods Sold	110,000
Depreciation Expense	20,000
Other Expenses	50,000
	400,000
Notes Payable	60,000
Capital Stock	100,000
Retained Earnings (1/1)	60,000
Sales	180,000
	400,000
Beginning Inventory	70,000

The capital stock was issued and plant and equipment acquired four years ago when the exchange rate was .30. The beginning (ending) inventory was acquired when the spot rate was .23 (.21). The weighted-average exchange rate for 19X1 was .22. Retained earnings was $15,200 in the converted December 31, 19X0, balance sheet of Mommessin Company. The spot rate for the franc on January 1, 19X1, was .23, and at December 31, 19X1, it was .20.

Required:

a. Prepare a foreign currency translation working paper for Mommessin Company for the year ended December 31, 19X1. (Note that this problem is integrated with Problem 14–21.)

b. Prepare Mommessin Company's 19X1 income statement and its December 31, 19X1, balance sheet.

Problem 13–21   (Current Rate Method Working Paper and Statements)

Use the information of Problem 13–20, except now assume that (1) Mommessin Company's functional currency is the franc, (2) its December 31, 19X0, Retained Earnings balance was $25,000, and (3) its December 31, 19X0, Cumulative Foreign Exchange Translation Adjustments balance was a debit of $18,200. With these changes, complete the requirements of Problem 13–20. (Note that this problem is integrated with Problem 14–22.)

Problem 13–22   (Remeasurement and Translation Gains or Losses)

Use the data of Problems 13–20 and 13–21, respectively, to calculate Mommessin Company's 19X1 remeasurement gain or loss and 19X1 translation gain or loss directly. Assume Mommessin Company's net monetary liability position on January 1, 19X1, is 30,000 francs and that its net asset position on this date is 160,000 francs.

Problem 13–23   (Working Paper to Convert Branch Accounts and Closing Entries)

The adjusted trial balances of the Dallas Company and its Dutch branch were as follows on December 31, 19X7:

	Home Office (Dollars)		Branch (Guilders)	
Cash	27,800		18,300	
Accounts Receivable	32,000		30,000	
Allowance for Doubtful Accounts		400		300
Merchandise Inventory (1/1)	24,000		9,000	
Plant and Equipment	140,000		68,000	
Accumulated Depreciation		25,000		12,000
Accounts Payable		20,000		7,000
Shipments from Home Office			30,000	
Shipments to Branch		7,000		
Branch Current	17,360			
Home Office Current				76,000
Sales		100,000		78,000
Purchases	76,360		10,000	
Expenses	12,000		8,000	
Capital Stock		150,000		
Retained Earnings		27,120		
	329,520	329,520	173,300	173,300
Merchandise Inventory (12/31)	18,000		10,000	

The plant and equipment carried on the books of the branch was acquired in Dutch markets in 19X1 when the exchange rate was .26.

The branch inventory on January 1 included 7,000 guilders of merchandise received from the home office. These goods were billed at the home office cost of $1,470. The remainder of the branch inventory was acquired from local suppliers in the Netherlands when the exchange rate was .23. All shipments to the branch during 19X7 were billed at cost.

The December 31 branch inventory consisted of 5,500 guilders of merchandise acquired by current shipment from the home office. The home office cost of this merchandise was $1,250. All other merchandise was purchased locally throughout the year. Annual adjustments for depreciation (5 percent annual rate) and doubtful accounts (1 percent of receivable balance) have been made.

Pertinent exchange rates are as follows:

January 1, 19X7	.23
December 31, 19X7	.20
Weighted average for 19X7	.24

Branch operations are fully integrated with home office operations. Thus, the functional currency of the branch is the dollar.

Required:

a. Prepare a foreign currency translation working paper to convert the branch's trial balance to dollars.

b. Journalize closing entries for the home office.

Problem 13–24   (Temporal and Current Rate Method Working Papers)

This problem extends the data presented in this chapter for Monroe Company and its subsidiary, Bordeaux Company, to the year 19X2. It deals with the case in which Bordeaux Company is a Canadian Company. In solving this problem, you may need to refer to the text for 19X1 data.

Bordeaux Company's trial balance at December 31, 19X2, is as follows:

	Francs
Cash and Receivables	1,200,000
Receivables	400,000
Plant and Equipment (net)	1,300,000
Depreciation Expense	300,000*
Other Expenses	500,000
	3,700,000

Current Payables	300,000
Long-Term Debt	900,000
Sales	1,500,000
Capital Stock	100,000
Retained Earnings (1/1)	900,000
	3,700,000

* Depreciation expense is higher in 19X2 than in 19X1 because some assets are being depreciated using the units-of-service approach.

The directly quoted, spot rate between the Canadian dollar and the franc at December 31, 19X2, is .12. The related weighted-average exchange rate for 19X2 is .105. For simplicity, assume that the newly acquired plant and equipment is purchased in 19X2 when the spot rate equals the weighted-average rate for the year and that Bordeaux Company does not depreciate new equipment in the year of acquisition. Assume that Bordeaux Company's functional and reporting currencies are Canadian and U.S. dollars, respectively, in this problem. Pertinent directly quoted exchange rates between the U.S. and Canadian dollars are weighted average for 19X2—1.06 and December 31, 19X2—1.2.

Required:

Prepare temporal and current rate method foreign currency translation working papers for Bordeaux Company for the year ended December 31, 19X2.

Additional Topics in International Financial Reporting

Chapter Outline

This chapter provides an explanation of the preparation of consolidated financial statements for domestic companies and their foreign subsidiaries. Related major topics covered in this chapter are the application of the equity method by domestic investors in foreign investees and hedges of net investments (ownership interests) in foreign entities. The chapter also deals with two general topics pertinent to consolidated statements: (1) the extent to which consolidated financial statements are prepared and encouraged from a worldwide perspective and (2) international financial accounting. The coverage of international financial accounting includes general discussions of the setting of international financial accounting standards, the harmonization of financial accounting standards, the factors impacting on national financial accounting systems, financial reporting by foreign companies, and approaches to transnational financial reporting. These discussions show, among other things, that diversity is the rule in international financial accounting. An understanding of this diversity is important because the financial statements of domestic and foreign subsidiaries must reflect common standards on material matters or the usefulness of related consolidated statements is impaired. From a more general perspective, it also is important to understand the international financial accounting standard-setting and reporting processes and the forces that shape these processes and impact on international financial reporting diversity.

CONSOLIDATED FINANCIAL STATEMENTS AND THE EQUITY METHOD FOR DOMESTIC PARENTS AND FOREIGN SUBSIDIARIES—GENERAL COMMENTS

Chapter 13 deals with the conversion of foreign entities' financial statements into the domestic currency. As indicated, this process is the first step in preparing consolidated financial statements for a domestic parent company and its foreign subsidiary (as well as in applying the equity method by a domestic investor with significant influence over the operations of a foreign affiliate). The consolidation of foreign subsidiaries is required in the United States in most cases by *Statement of Financial Accounting Standards No. 94,* "Consolidation of All Majority Owned Subsidiaries."[1] This statement (par. 13) indicates that a majority-owned foreign subsidiary is to be consolidated unless it "operates under foreign exchange restrictions, controls, or other governmentally imposed uncertainties so

---

[1] FASB, *Statement of Financial Accounting Standards No. 94,* "Consolidation of All Majority Owned Subsidiaries" (Norwalk, CT: FASB, 1987).

severe that they cast significant doubt on the parent's ability to control the subsidiary.''[2]

Although we focus on the preparation of consolidated statements and the application of the equity method for domestic parent companies below, our explanation also applies to the general use of the equity method under *APB Opinion No. 18,* ''The Equity Method of Accounting for Investments in Common Stocks.'' The examples used in this chapter are continued from Chapter 13.[3] Thus, we still assume the use of purchase accounting and that the ownership percent is 100. The preparation of consolidated financial statements and the related application of the equity method for domestic parent companies and their foreign subsidiaries is considered next.

CONSOLIDATION AND EQUITY METHOD—TEMPORAL METHOD

As indicated in Chapter 13, the temporal method (remeasurement) is the simpler of the two conversion techniques covered by *Statement of Financial Accounting Standards No. 52.* Thus, we begin by explaining the preparation of consolidated financial statements and the application of the equity method under this procedure.

Case 1. Consolidation and Equity Method with No Long-Term Intercompany Payable

This case uses the information of Case 1 from Chapter 13 along with additional data. We integrate the original and new data and repeat related calculations and working papers below for convenience.

Assume that Monroe Co. (a Texas company) purchases 100 percent of the outstanding capital stock of Bordeaux Company (a French company) on January 1, 19X1, for $150,000 and accounts for this investment using the *equity method.* On this date, the directly quoted spot rate is .125. The current exchange rate on

---

[2] *Statement No. 94* (par. 15d) also requires the application of the equity method to a less than majority-owned foreign affiliate unless foreign exchange restrictions, controls, or other governmentally imposed uncertainties cast doubt on the investor's ability to significantly influence the affiliate's operations.

[3] This chapter, like Chapters 12 and 13, ignores income tax allocation issues for simplicity. See the section entitled ''Income Tax Allocation—Foreign Currency Translation'' in Chapter 13 for discussion of situations requiring income tax allocation.

December 31, 19X1, is .10, and the weighted-average exchange rate for 19X1 is
.11. Also, assume that (1) all of Bordeaux Company's monetary assets and
liabilities are denominated in francs, (2) the only change in its plant and equipment
(net) balance during 19X1 results from recording depreciation expense of 250,000
francs, (3) the remaining useful life of its plant and equipment is 4 years at date of
acquisition, (4) the components of its plant and equipment are being depreciated
using the straight-line and the units-of-service methods (with zero salvage values),
and (5) goodwill is amortized over 10 years using the straight-line method. Monroe
and Bordeaux Companies' date of acquisition balance sheets expressed in dollars
and francs, respectively, are as follows:

	Monroe Company (Dollars)	Bordeaux Company (Francs)
Assets		
Cash and receivables		200,000
Investment in Bordeaux Company	150,000	
Plant and equipment (net)		1,000,000
Total assets	150,000	1,200,000
Liabilities and Owners' Equity		
Current payables		100,000
Long-term debt		700,000
Capital stock	150,000	100,000
Retained earnings		300,000
Total liabilities and owners' equity	150,000	1,200,000

Note that Monroe Company is only a holding company and, consequently, it has
no revenues or expenses, except those related to its ownership interest in Bordeaux Company. These assumptions are made for simplicity and impact minimally on the generality of the procedures demonstrated.

As shown in Chapter 13, the application of the temporal method on date of
acquisition produces the following balances for Bordeaux Company.

	Francs	Exchange Rate	Dollars
Cash and receivables	200,000	.125	25,000
Plant and equipment (net)	1,000,000	.125	125,000
	1,200,000		150,000
Current payables	100,000	.125	12,500
Long-term debt	700,000	.125	87,500
Capital stock	100,000	.125	12,500
Retained earnings	300,000	.125	37,500
	1,200,000		150,000

Monroe and Bordeaux Companies' December 31, 19X1, trial balances are as follows:

	Monroe Company (Dollars)	Bordeaux Company (Francs)
Debits		
Cash and Receivables		1,150,000
Investment in Bordeaux Company	197,500*	
Plant and Equipment (net)		750,000
Depreciation Expense		250,000
Other Expenses		350,000
Totals	197,500	2,500,000
Credits		
Current Payables		200,000
Long-Term Debt		700,000
Sales		1,200,000
Equity in Subsidiary Earnings	47,500*	
Capital Stock	150,000	100,000
Retained Earnings (1/1)		300,000
Totals	197,500	2,500,000

* The origin of this balance is explained below.

The temporal method working paper for Bordeaux Company in 19X1 is provided in Illustration 14–1. Note that its net income (including its remeasurement gain) is $68,750.

Differentials under the Temporal Method. In preparing consolidated financial statements and applying the equity method under the temporal method, the techniques used in accounting for differentials are almost identical to those of earlier chapters. That is, differentials are calculated, allocated, and amortized. The only difference is that subsidiary amounts related to differentials are remeasured into dollars in calculating and allocating the differentials.[4] To illustrate, assume that the fair value of Bordeaux Company's plant and equipment (net) at date of acquisition is 1,600,000 in francs. Recall that the related book value figure is 1 million francs. Also, assume there are no other differences in fair values and

---

[4] *Statement of Financial Accounting Standards No. 52,* "Foreign Currency Translation" (par. 101) requires differentials to be calculated and allocated using the temporal method if the foreign entity's functional and reporting currencies are the same. Similarly, this statement (par. 101) requires differentials to be calculated and allocated using the current rate method if the foreign entity's functional and local currencies are the same. Thus, differentials are treated differently, depending on the foreign entity's functional currency.

ILLUSTRATION 14-1   Temporal Method

BORDEAUX COMPANY
Foreign Currency Translation Working Paper
For the Year Ended December 31, 19X1

	Trial Balance (in francs)	Exchange Rate Code	Exchange Rate Rate	Trial Balance (in dollars)	Income Statement (in dollars)	Balance Sheet (in dollars)
Cash and receivables	1,150,000	C	.100	115,000		115,000
Plant and equipment (net)	750,000	H	.125	93,750		93,750
Depreciation expense	250,000	H	.125	31,250	31,250	
Other expenses	350,000	W	.110	38,500	38,500	
Net income (including remeasurement gain)					68,750	
	2,500,000			278,500	138,500	208,750
Current payables	200,000	C	.100	20,000		20,000
Long-term debt	700,000	C	.100	70,000		70,000
Sales	1,200,000	W	.110	132,000	132,000	
Capital stock	100,000	H	.125	12,500		12,500
Retained earnings (1/1)	300,000	P		37,500		37,500
Remeasurement gain (19X1)				6,500	6,500	
Net income (including remeasurement gain)						68,750
	2,500,000			278,500	138,500	208,750

Code:
C = Current exchange rate at December 31, 19X1.
W = Weighted-average exchange rate for 19X1.
H = Historical exchange rate.
P = Dollar balance end of preceding period.

book values at date of acquisition. In this case, the differential is calculated as follows at date of acquisition.

Investment cost		$150,000
Less: Monroe Company's equity in recorded net assets of Bordeaux Company—		
Capital stock [100% × ($.125 × 100,000)]	$12,500	
Retained earnings [100% × ($.125 × 300,000)]	37,500	50,000
Differential		$100,000

In this calculation, Bordeaux Company's date of acquisition Capital Stock and Retained Earnings balances of 100,000 and 300,000, respectively, first are remeasured into dollars using the date of acquisition spot rate (.125). Subsequently, the product of the ownership percent and the sum of the remeasured values ($50,000) is subtracted from the cost of the investment to obtain the differential of $100,000. We emphasize that the differential is calculated in dollars in this case.

Consistent with the procedures of Chapter 4, $75,000 of the differential is allocated to plant and equipment (net). This amount is calculated by multiplying the ownership percent by the difference in the remeasured fair value and book value figures for Bordeaux Company's plant and equipment net [100% × [($.125 × 1,600,000) − ($.125 × 1,000,000)]]. This procedure is exactly as in Chapter 4, except that the fair and book value figures are remeasured from a foreign currency into dollars prior to multiplication by the ownership percent. Since $75,000 of the differential is allocated to plant and equipment (net), the remaining $25,000 ($100,000 − $75,000) is allocated to goodwill.[5] We assume for simplicity that the portion of the differential allocated to plant and equipment (net) pertains to assets which are being depreciated using the straight-line method (and no salvage value). Our assumptions yield the differential amortization schedule shown in Illustration 14–2.

Parent Company Entries for 19X1.   Unless there is a long-term intercompany payable resulting from an intercompany foreign currency transaction of a long-term investment nature (see below), equity method entries under the temporal method are exactly like those made in the case of a domestic subsidiary. Thus, in this case, Monroe Company makes the following equity method entries.

Investment in Bordeaux Company (100% × $68,750)   68,750
    Equity in Subsidiary Earnings   68,750

Equity in Subsidiary Earnings   21,250
    Investment in Bordeaux Company   21,250

The first entry records Monroe Company's equity in Bordeaux Company's net income (including the remeasurement gain) as shown in the latter's 19X1 temporal method working paper (see Illustration 14–1). The second equity method entry records Monroe Company's 19X1 differential amortization (see Illustration 14–2). The sum of these entries accounts for both the change in Monroe Company's Investment in Bordeaux Company account during 19X1 and the related balance in

---

[5] Note that the same results are produced if the differential first is calculated and allocated in the foreign currency and subsequently is remeasured into dollars. In our example, the differential calculated in francs is 800,000 ($100,000/$.125). If the differential is allocated in francs, 600,000 [100% × (1,600,000 − 1,000,000)] is allocated to plant and equipment (net) and 200,000 (800,000 − 600,000) is allocated to goodwill. Remeasurement of these values yields the same allocated dollar amounts as calculated previously—$75,000 ($.125 × 600,000) and $25,000 ($.125 × 200,000).

**ILLUSTRATION 14-2   Schedule of Differential Amortization—
Temporal Method (dollars)**

	Allocated Amount	Annual Amortization	
		Years 1–4	Years 5–10
Plant and equipment (net)	$ 75,000	$18,750*	$ –0–
Goodwill	25,000	2,500†	2,500
Totals	$100,000	$21,250	$2,500

* $75,000/4
† $25,000/10

its Equity in Subsidiary Earnings account. Their effects on the Investment account are summarized below.

Initial investment (1/1/X1)	$150,000
Equity in Bordeaux Company's 19X1 net income (including remeasurement gain)	68,750
Differential amortization for 19X1	(21,250)
Investment in Bordeaux Company (12/31/X1)	$197,500*

* As shown in 12/31/X1 Monroe Company trial balance in Case 1.

Working Paper Entries for 19X1. With one exception, the consolidated statement working paper entries for this case have no new features. The exception is that the investment elimination entry (entry 2) eliminates the *remeasured* amounts of the beginning-of-year balances in the subsidiary's stockholders' equity accounts. The entries are as follows:

1. To eliminate double counting of equity method income and record minority interest (zero) in subsidiary net income:

> Equity in Subsidiary Earnings
> ($68,750 – $21,250) 47,500
>   Investment in Bordeaux Company 47,500

2. To eliminate beginning-of-year investment account balance against beginning-of-year Bordeaux Company stockholders' equity accounts,

establish beginning-of-year minority interest (zero), and establish beginning-of-year differential:

Capital Stock—Bordeaux Company		
($.125 × 100,000)	12,500	
Retained Earnings—Bordeaux Company		
($.125 × 300,000)	37,500	
Differential	100,000	
Investment in Bordeaux Company		150,000

3. To allocate the beginning-of-year differential:

Plant and Equipment (net)	75,000	
Goodwill	25,000	
Differential		100,000

4. To record differential amortization:

Depreciation Expense	18,750	
Other Expenses	2,500	
Plant and Equipment (net)		18,750
Goodwill		2,500

A consolidated statement working paper is not presented for this case because of its simplicity. We emphasize, however, that the Bordeaux Company account balances used in such a working paper are the remeasured amounts shown in its 19X1 temporal method working paper. Note also that Bordeaux Company's remeasurement gain is included in the calculation of consolidated net income. Consolidated net income for this case, which equals Monroe Company's (equity method) net income, is calculated incrementally as follows:

Monroe Company's 19X1 (confirmed) net income from its own operations	$ –0–
Plus: Monroe Company's equity in Bordeaux Company's (confirmed) 19X1 net income (100% × $68,750)	68,750
Minus: Differential amortization for 19X1	21,250
Consolidated net income for 19X1	$47,500

Case 2. Consolidation and Equity Method with Long-Term Intercompany Payable

Recall that *Statement No. 52* calls for special treatment of translation gains and losses from long-term debts resulting from intercompany foreign currency transactions of a long-term investment nature when consolidated statements are to be prepared. That is, they are accumulated in the Cumulative Foreign Exchange Translation Adjustments account. Several factors related to such debts cause modification of the equity method and working paper entries explained above. To illustrate, we continue Case 2 from Chapter 13. Thus, assume that Bordeaux Company's long-term debt results from an $87,500 advance from Monroe Company occurring immediately after acquisition on January 1, 19X1, that Monroe Company does not expect this debt to be settled in the foreseeable future, and that this debt is denominated in francs. Also, as in Chapter 13, assume that the proceeds of Monroe Company's loan are used by Bordeaux Company to purchase plant and equipment on date of acquisition for 700,000 francs immediately after these proceeds have been converted into francs ($87,500/$.125). Finally, assume that (1) the long-term debt is noninterest bearing for simplicity, (2) Monroe Company acquires the $87,500 loaned to Bordeaux Company by issuing additional capital stock immediately after acquisition of its subsidiary on January 1, 19X1, and (3) the differential pertains entirely to goodwill. Given the last assumption, differential amortization for each of the 10 years beginning with date of acquisition is $10,000 ($100,000/10) (see differential calculation in Case 1). Monroe and Bordeaux Companies' December 31, 19X1, trial balances are as follows:

	Monroe Company (Dollars)	Bordeaux Company (Francs)
Debits		
Cash and Receivables		1,150,000
Investment in Bordeaux Company	208,750*	
Long-Term Receivable—Bordeaux	70,000	
Plant and Equipment (net)		750,000
Depreciation Expense		250,000
Other Expenses		350,000
Totals	278,750	2,500,000
Credits		
Current Payables		200,000
Long-Term Debt—Monroe		700,000
Sales		1,200,000
Equity in Subsidiary Earnings	41,250*	
Capital Stock	237,500	100,000
Retained Earnings (1/1)		300,000
Cumulative Foreign Exchange Translation Adjustments	–0–*	
Totals	278,750	2,500,000

* The origin of this balance is explained below.

Monroe Company's trial balance differs from the previous case because it now has a long-term receivable from Bordeaux Company and additional capital stock. This trial balance also shows new balances for Investment in Bordeaux Company and Equity in Subsidiary Earnings since Bordeaux Company's net income is different and differential amortization is only $10,000. Although not apparent, Monroe Company's trial balance reflects offsetting entries of $17,500 to the Cumulative Foreign Exchange Translation Adjustment account (which has a zero balance). One of these entries also affects the investment account balance. The origins of these balances are explained below.

The temporal method working paper for this case is repeated in Illustration 14–3 for convenience. This working paper reveals three long-term debt-related factors that cause the equity method and working paper entries for this case to differ from those of the prior case: (1) the translation gain of $17,500

ILLUSTRATION 14-3   **Temporal Method—Long-Term Intercompany Payable**

BORDEAUX COMPANY
Foreign Currency Translation Working Paper
For the Year Ended December 31, 19X1

	Trial Balance (in francs)	Exchange Rate Code	Exchange Rate	Trial Balance (in dollars)	Income Statement (in dollars)	Balance Sheet (in dollars)
Cash and receivables	1,150,000	C	.100	115,000		115,000
Plant and equipment (net)	750,000	H	.125	93,750		93,750
Depreciation expense	250,000	H	.125	31,250	31,250	
Other expenses	350,000	W	.110	38,500	38,500	
Remeasurement loss (19X1)				11,000	11,000	
Net income (including remeasurement loss)					51,250	
	2,500,000			289,500	132,000	208,750
Current payables	200,000	C	.100	20,000		20,000
Long-term debt—Monroe	700,000	C	.100	70,000		70,000
Sales	1,200,000	W	.110	132,000	132,000	
Capital stock	100,000	H	.125	12,500		12,500
Retained earnings (1/1)	300,000	P		37,500		37,500
Net income (including remeasurement loss)						51,250
Cumulative foreign exchange translation adjustments (1/1)		P		–0–		–0–
Translation gain (19X1)				17,500		17,500
	2,500,000			289,500	132,000	208,750

Code:
C = Current exchange rate at December 31, 19X1.
W = Weighted-average exchange rate for 19X1.
H = Historical exchange rate.
P = Dollar balance end of preceding period.

(which equals the balance of Cumulative Foreign Exchange Translation Adjustments at year-end), (2) the conversion of the remeasurement gain of $6,500 to a remeasurement loss of $11,000 (see discussion in Chapter 13), and (3) the intercompany nature of the long-term debt.

Parent Company Entries for 19X1.   Monroe Company makes two types of entries in 19X1 related to its investment in Bordeaux Company: (1) an entry to record its foreign exchange gain or loss on its intercompany receivable from Bordeaux Company and (2) its equity method entries. The entry related to the receivable follows:

```
Cumulative Foreign Exchange
  Translation Adjustments  .............................. 17,500
     Long-Term Receivable—Bordeaux  .....................         17,500
```

This entry records the exchange loss on Monroe Company's intercompany receivable occurring between January 1, 19X1, and December 31, 19X1 [700,000 × ($.125 − $.10)]. An exchange loss occurs because the dollar strengthens in relation to the franc. This loss is recorded consistently with the requirements of *Statement No. 52*; it is debited to the Cumulative Foreign Exchange Translation Adjustments account.

Monroe Company's equity method entries for this case are as follows:

```
Investment in Bordeaux Company (100% × $51,250)  ............. 51,250
   Equity in Subsidiary Earnings  ........................         51,250

Equity in Subsidiary Earnings  ............................ 10,000
   Investment in Bordeaux Company ........................         10,000

Investment in Bordeaux Company (100% × $17,500)  ............. 17,500
   Cumulative Foreign Exchange
     Translation Adjustments ............................         17,500
```

Except for their amounts, the first two entries are the same as in the previous case. The first entry's amount is different because Bordeaux Company's net income (including its remeasurement loss) is $51,250 in this case as compared to $68,750 in the previous example. The amount of the second entry is different because differential amortization is $10,000 in this case rather than $21,250. The third entry requires special consideration. Recall that Bordeaux Company's stockholders' equity is increased because of the 19X1 translation gain related to its intercompany payable. Consequently, Monroe Company's interest in Bordeaux Company's stockholders' equity also is increased. This latter increase is recorded in the third equity method entry. Notice that the credit in this entry is to *Monroe Company's* Cumulative Foreign Exchange Translation Adjustments account (not to Bordeaux Company's working paper account with the same title). Since the equity method is applied to this account, it works exactly like a parent company's Retained Earnings account under the equity method. That is, the balance in a parent's Cumulative Foreign Exchange Translation Adjustments account equals *consolidated* cumulative foreign exchange translation adjustments just as the balance in its Retained Earnings account equals consolidated retained earnings. We emphasize that the $17,500 entries given above are offsetting with respect to Monroe Company's Cumulative Foreign Exchange Translation Adjustments account. This effect occurs because Monroe Company has a loss related to its long-term receivable from Bordeaux Company, but it has a gain of an equal amount related to its equity in Bordeaux Company's gain on its long-term payable to Monroe Company.

In this example, the equity method entries given above account for the change in Monroe Company's Investment in Bordeaux Company account during 19X1, the change in Equity in Subsidiary Earnings, and part of the change in Cumulative Foreign Exchange Translation Adjustments. The effects of these entries on the investment account and Equity in Subsidiary Earnings are summarized below.

Initial investment in Bordeaux Company (1/1/X1)		$150,000
Equity in Bordeaux Company's 19X1 net income		
(including remeasurement gain)	$51,250	
Differential amortization for 19X1	(10,000)	
Equity in subsidiary earnings		41,250
Equity in Bordeaux Company's 19X1 translation		
gain = Part of change in cumulative foreign		
exchange translation adjustments		17,500
Investment in Bordeaux Company (12/31/X1)		$208,750

Working Paper Entries for 19X1. The working paper entries for this case are as follows:

1. To eliminate double counting of equity method income and translation gain recorded by the third equity method entry and to record minority interest (zero) in subsidiary net income and translation gain:

Equity in Subsidiary Earnings		
($51,250 − $10,000)	41,250	
Cumulative Foreign Exchange Translation		
Adjustments—Monroe Company	17,500	
Investment in Bordeaux Company		58,750

2. To eliminate beginning-of-year investment account balance against beginning-of-year Bordeaux Company stockholders' equity accounts, establish beginning-of-year minority interest (zero), and establish beginning-of-year differential:

Capital Stock—Bordeaux Company		
($.125 × 100,000)	12,500	
Retained Earnings—Bordeaux Company		
($.125 × 300,000)	37,500	
Differential	100,000	
Investment in Bordeaux Company		150,000

3. To allocate the beginning-of-year differential:

Goodwill	100,000	
Differential		100,000

4. To record differential amortization:

Other Expenses	10,000	
Goodwill		10,000

5. To eliminate long-term intercompany receivable and payable:

Long-Term Debt—Monroe		
($.1 × 700,000)	70,000	
Long-Term Receivable—		
Bordeaux ($87,500 − $17,500)		70,000

Ignoring the minor differences attributable to the differential, these entries are identical to those of the previous case with two exceptions. First, entry (1) prevents double counting of Bordeaux Company's translation gain (recorded by the third equity method entry) in addition to its usual functions. Second, entry (5) eliminates the intercompany receivable and payable created on date of acquisition. Notice that the balance of each of these accounts now equals its date of acquisition balance of $87,500, less the $17,500 effect of the change in exchange rates between January 1, 19X1, and December 31, 19X1. The consolidated statement working paper for this case is given in Illustration 14–4. Note that Bordeaux Company's translation gain does not affect the calculation of consolidated net income, although its remeasurement loss enters into the calculation of this value.

MONROE COMPANY AND SUBSIDIARY BORDEAUX COMPANY
Consolidated Statement Working Paper
For the Year Ended December 31, 19X1

	Monroe Company	Bordeaux Company	Eliminations Dr.	Eliminations Cr.	Consolidated
Income Statement					
Sales		132,000			132,000
Equity in subsidiary earnings	41,250		(1) 41,250		–0–
Total credits	41,250	132,000			132,000
Depreciation expense		31,250			31,250
Other expenses		38,500	(4) 10,000		48,500
Remeasurement loss		11,000			11,000
Total debits		80,750			90,750
Net income	41,250	51,250	51,250		41,250
Retained Earnings Statement					
Retained earnings 1/1:					
Monroe Company	–0–				–0–
Bordeaux Company		37,500	(2) 37,500		–0–
Net income	41,250	51,250	51,250		41,250
Retained earnings 12/31	41,250	88,750	88,750		41,250
Balance Sheet					
Cash and receivables		115,000			115,000
Long-term receivable—Bordeaux	70,000			(5) 70,000	–0–
Plant and equipment (net)		93,750			93,750
Investment in Bordeaux Company	208,750			(1) 58,750	–0–
				(2) 150,000	
Differential			(2) 100,000	(3) 100,000	–0–
Goodwill			(3) 100,000	(4) 10,000	90,000
	278,750	208,750			298,750
Current payables		20,000			20,000
Long-term debt—Monroe		70,000	(5) 70,000		–0–
Common stock:					
Monroe Company	237,500				237,500
Bordeaux Company		12,500	(2) 12,500		–0–
Retained earnings	41,250	88,750	88,750		41,250
Cumulative foreign exchange translation adjustments	–0–	17,500	(1) 17,500		–0–
	278,750	208,750	388,750	388,750	298,750

Explanation of eliminations:

(1) To eliminate double counting of equity method income and translation gain and to record minority interest (zero) in subsidiary net income and translation gain.

(2) To eliminate beginning-of-year investment account balance against beginning-of-year Bordeaux Company stockholders' equity accounts, establish beginning-of-year minority interest (zero), and establish beginning-of-year differential.

(3) To allocate the beginning-of-year differential.

(4) To record differential amortization.

(5) To eliminate long-term intercompany receivable and payable.

Consolidated net income for this case, which equals Monroe Company's (equity method) net income, is calculated incrementally as follows:

Monroe Company's 19X1 (confirmed) net income from
  its own operations .... $ –0–
Plus: Monroe Company's equity in Bordeaux Company's
  (confirmed) 19X1 net income (100% × $51,250) 51,250
Minus: Differential amortization for 19X1 10,000
Consolidated net income for 19X1 .... $41,250

Investment Elimination for Subsequent Years

The working paper entries shown above fail to illustrate one new point related to long-term debts resulting from intercompany foreign currency transactions of a long-term investment nature. In years subsequent to the year of acquisition, a beginning-of-year balance is likely to exist in a foreign subsidiary's Cumulative Foreign Exchange Translation Adjustments account (i.e., on its temporal method working paper). Since this account is part of the subsidiary's stockholders' equity, its balance is offset in the investment elimination entry just as is the balance in any other subsidiary stockholders' equity account which pertains to its common shareholders. In our example, the 19X2 investment elimination entry is as follows:

Capital Stock—Bordeaux Company
  ($.125 × 100,000) 12,500
Retained Earnings—Bordeaux Company
  ($37,500 + $51,250) 88,750
Cumulative Foreign Exchange Translation
  Adjustments—Bordeaux Company 17,500
Differential ($100,000 − $10,000) 90,000
    Investment in Bordeaux Company 208,750

CONSOLIDATION AND EQUITY METHOD— CURRENT RATE METHOD

This portion of the chapter covers the preparation of consolidated financial statements and the application of the equity method under the current rate method. These procedures are more complicated than under the temporal method primarily because of the effects of the current rate method on the differential and its allocation and amortization.

Case 3. Consolidation and Equity Method

The assumptions of this case are the same as in Case 1, except that Bordeaux Company's functional and reporting currencies are different, and its transactions are recorded in its functional currency. Its functional currency is the franc, and its reporting currency is the functional currency of Monroe Company—the U.S. dollar. Monroe and Bordeaux Companies' date of acquisition balance sheets expressed in dollars and francs, respectively, are repeated below for convenience.

	Monroe Company (Dollars)	Bordeaux Company (Francs)
Assets		
Cash and receivables		200,000
Investment in Bordeaux Company	150,000	
Plant and equipment (net)		1,000,000
Total assets	150,000	1,200,000
Liabilities and Owners' Equity		
Current payables		100,000
Long-term debt		700,000
Capital stock	150,000	100,000
Retained earnings		300,000
Total liabilities and owners' equities	150,000	1,200,000

As shown in Chapter 13, the application of the current rate method on date of acquisition produces the following balances for Bordeaux Company.

	Francs	Exchange Rate	Dollars
Cash and receivables	200,000	.125	25,000
Plant and equipment (net)	1,000,000	.125	125,000
	1,200,000		150,000
Current payables	100,000	.125	12,500
Long-term debt	700,000	.125	87,500
Capital stock	100,000	.125	12,500
Retained earnings	300,000	.125	37,500
	1,200,000		150,000

Monroe and Bordeaux Companies' December 31, 19X1, trial balances are as follows:

	Monroe Company (Dollars)	Bordeaux Company (Francs)
Debits		
Cash and Receivables		1,150,000
Investment in Bordeaux Company	163,000*	
Plant and Equipment (net)		750,000
Depreciation Expense		250,000
Other Expenses		350,000
Totals	163,000	2,500,000
Credits		
Current Payables		200,000
Long-Term Debt		700,000
Sales		1,200,000
Equity in Subsidiary Earnings	47,300*	
Capital Stock	150,000	100,000
Retained Earnings (1/1)		300,000
Cumulative Foreign Exchange Translation Adjustments	(34,300)*	
Totals	163,000	2,500,000

(debit)

* The origin of this balance is explained below.

Similar to Case 2, Monroe Company's trial balance contains a balance for Equity in Subsidiary Earnings that differs from that of Case 1 and a balance for Cumulative Foreign Exchange Translation Adjustments. These balances are explained later.

The current rate method working paper for Bordeaux Company in 19X1 is given in Illustration 14–5. Note that its net income, which excludes its translation loss, is $66,000.

Differentials under the Current Rate Method. The procedures for dealing with differentials under the current rate method are more complicated than those under the temporal method. The complications arise because *Statement No. 52* requires the calculation and allocation of differentials using current rates if the foreign entity's functional and local currencies are the same (see footnote 4). The general procedures for dealing with a differential under the current rate method are: (1) calculate the differential in the foreign currency, (2) allocate the differential in this currency, (3) determine differential amortization in the foreign cur-

ILLUSTRATION 14–5   Current Rate Method

BORDEAUX COMPANY
Foreign Currency Translation Working Paper
For the Year Ended December 31, 19X1

	Trial Balance (in francs)	Exchange Rate Code	Exchange Rate Rate	Trial Balance (in dollars)	Income Statement (in dollars)	Balance Sheet (in dollars)
Cash and receivables	1,150,000	C	.100	115,000		115,000
Plant and equipment (net)	750,000	C	.100	75,000		75,000
Depreciation expense	250,000	W	.110	27,500	27,500	
Other expenses	350,000	W	.110	38,500	38,500	
Translation loss (19X1)				16,000		
Net income					66,000	
	2,500,000			272,000	132,000	190,000
Current payables	200,000	C	.100	20,000		20,000
Long-term debt	700,000	C	.100	70,000		70,000
Sales	1,200,000	W	.110	132,000	132,000	
Capital stock	100,000	H	.125	12,500		12,500
Retained earnings (1/1)	300,000	P		37,500		37,500
Net income						66,000
Cumulative foreign exchange translation adjustments (1/1)		P		–0–		–0–
Translation loss (19X1)						(16,000)
	2,500,000			272,000	132,000	190,000

Code:
C = Current exchange rate at December 31, 19X1.
W = Weighted-average exchange rate for 19X1.
H = Historical exchange rate.
P = Dollar balance end of preceding period.
(debit)

rency, (4) convert the amortization figures into the reporting currency using the weighted-average exchange rate for the period, (5) calculate the translation gain or loss related to the differential in the reporting currency, and (6) make the appropriate equity method and working paper entries related to the differential (based on additional calculations when needed). These procedures are explained below using the information of Case 1. Note that the current rate method procedures for the differential are separate and distinct from the current rate procedures used in translating Bordeaux Company's financial statements into dollars.

Recall that the fair value of Bordeaux Company's plant and equipment (net) at date of acquisition is 1,600,000 in francs and that the related book value figure is 1 million francs. In this case, the differential is calculated as follows *in francs* at date of acquisition.

Investment cost ($150,000/$.125)		1,200,000
Less: Monroe Company's equity in recorded		
net assets of Bordeaux Company—		
Capital stock (100% × 100,000)	100,000	
Retained earnings (100% × 300,000)	300,000	400,000
Differential		800,000

Note that the dollar cost of Monroe Company's investment in Bordeaux Company is converted to francs by dividing by the date of acquisition spot rate. We emphasize that the differential is calculated in francs under the current rate method.[6]

The allocation of the differential under the current rate method at date of acquisition also is consistent with the procedures of Chapter 4, except that the differential is allocated in francs. Thus, 600,000 francs of the differential is allocated to plant and equipment (net). This amount is calculated by multiplying the ownership percent by the difference in the franc-based fair value and book value figures for Bordeaux Company's plant and equipment (net) [100% × (1,600,000 − 1,000,000)]. Since 600,000 francs of the differential is allocated to plant and equipment (net), the remaining 200,000 francs (800,000 − 600,000) is allocated to goodwill. Our assumptions produce the franc-based differential amortization schedule shown in Illustration 14–6.

The next step in dealing with the differential is calculating the differential amortization amounts in the reporting currency—the dollar. These values are calculated by multiplying the franc-based amortization figures by the weighted-average exchange rate for the period. The dollar-based amortization figures for 19X1 are calculated below.

	19X1 Amortization (francs)	19X1 Weighted-Average Rate	19X1 Amortization (dollars)
Plant and equipment (net)	150,000	.11	16,500
Goodwill	20,000	.11	2,200
Totals	170,000		18,700

As implied, the dollar-based amortization figures usually differ from year to year under the current rate method even in years in which the franc-based values are the same. These differences are produced because foreign currency-based amor-

---

[6] The differential also can be calculated in francs by dividing its dollar amount (as determined in Case 1) by the acquisition date spot rate ($100,000/$.125). The amounts of the differential allocated in francs below can be calculated similarly.

ILLUSTRATION 14-6   **Schedule of Differential Amortization—Current Rate Method**

	Allocated Amount (francs)	Annual Amortization (francs)	
		Years 1–4	Years 5–10
Plant and equipment (net)	600,000	150,000*	–0–
Goodwill	200,000	20,000†	20,000
Totals	800,000	170,000	20,000

* 600,000/4.

† 200,000/10.

tization figures always are translated to dollars using the current year's weighted-average rate under the current rate method. In contrast, differences of this type are not produced under the temporal method since it uses historical rates.

The final differential related matter covered in this section is calculating the translation gain or loss related to the differential in the reporting currency. Translation gains and losses on differentials occur under the current rate method because differentials are translated using current rates under this approach. The presumption underlying these gains and losses is that domestic parent companies have foreign currency exposures related to their differentials when their subsidiaries' functional currencies differ from the reporting currency. Translation gains and losses on differentials are calculated similarly to the translation and remeasurement gains and losses of Chapter 13. One way of calculating the 19X1 translation loss on the differential is as follows:

Loss on beginning-of-year unamortized differential [800,000 × ($.125 − $.10)]	$20,000
Gain related to decrease in differential during the year [−170,000 × ($.11 − $.10)]	(1,700)
Translation loss on differential	$18,300

The decrease in the differential shown in this calculation equals the franc-based differential amortization for the year. This calculation assumes implicitly that the decrease in the foreign currency exposure related to the differential occurs when the spot rate equals the 19X1 weighted-average rate of .11. This assumption is clarified in the following calculation, which assumes explicitly that the differential reduction occurs when the exchange rate for the year equals the weighted average of .11.

Loss for first part of year on unamortized differential
[800,000 × ($.125 − $.11)] $12,000
Loss for subsequent portion of year on unamortized differential
[(800,000 − 170,000) × ($.11 − $.10) = 630,000 × $.01]   6,300
Translation loss on differential $18,300

This calculation is easier to interpret than the preceding one since it emphasizes the periods over which the foreign currency exposure related to the differential is assumed to be at different levels, as well as the assumed changes in spot rates over these periods. The accounting treatment of the translation loss on the differential is covered below.

Parent Company Entries for 19X1.   Monroe Company's equity method entries for this case are as follows:

Investment in Bordeaux Company (100% × $66,000) 66,000
    Equity in Subsidiary Earnings   66,000

Equity in Subsidiary Earnings 18,700
    Investment in Bordeaux Company   18,700

Cumulative Foreign Exchange
  Translation Adjustments (100% × $16,000) 16,000
    Investment in Bordeaux Company   16,000

Cumulative Foreign Exchange
  Translation Adjustments 18,300
    Investment in Bordeaux Company   18,300

The first three entries are analogous to the entries of Case 2. They record Monroe Company's equity in Bordeaux Company's 19X1 earnings, its differential amortization (as calculated above), and its equity in Bordeaux Company's translation loss, respectively. The explanation of the third entry is similar to the explanation of the third entry in Case 2. In this case, Bordeaux Company's stockholders' equity is decreased because of its 19X1 translation loss of $16,000. Thus, Monroe Company's interest in Bordeaux Company's stockholders' equity also is decreased. This latter decrease is recorded in the third equity method entry by debiting Monroe Company's Cumulative Foreign Exchange Translation Adjustments account. As in Case 2, the balance in this account equals *consolidated* cumulative foreign exchange translation adjustments. The fourth equity method entry records Monroe Company's translation loss on the differential. This loss is debited to Monroe Company's Cumulative Foreign Exchange Translation Adjustments account since it is a consequence of the conversion process peculiar to the current rate method. The equity method entries in this case account for the change in Monroe Company's Investment in Bordeaux Company account during 19X1 and the related changes in Equity in Subsidiary Earnings and Cumulative Foreign Exchange Translation Adjustments. The effects of these entries are summarized below.

Initial investment in Bordeaux Company (1/1/X1)		$150,000
Equity in Bordeaux Company's 19X1 net income	$ 66,000	
Differential amortization for 19X1	(18,700)	
Equity in subsidiary earnings		47,300
Equity in Bordeaux Company's 19X1		
translation loss	$(16,000)	
Translation loss on differential	(18,300)	
Change in cumulative foreign exchange		
translation adjustments		(34,300)
Investment in Bordeaux Company (12/31/X1)		$163,000

Working Paper Entries for 19X1.   Before examining the working paper entries for this case, a few additional calculations related to working paper entry (3) are needed. This entry has two functions: (1) to allocate the beginning-of-year differential in *dollars* and (2) to record the translation loss on the differential for consolidated statement purposes.

The first set of calculations reveals the allocation of the beginning-of-year differential in dollars. These calculations are as follows:

	Portion of Unamortized Differential Related to	
	Plant and Equipment (net)	*Goodwill*
Balances on date of acquisition (francs)*	600,000	200,000
Less prior years' amortization (francs)	–0–	–0–
Balances January 1, 19X1 (francs)*	600,000	200,000
Times beginning-of-year (or date of		
acquisition) spot rate	× $.125	× $.125
Balances January 1, 19X1 (dollars)	75,000	25,000

* Note that this schedule provides a model for use in all years, including the year of acquisition. Thus, its first and third lines both pertain to January 1, 19X1, since 19X1 is the year of acquisition.

The second set of calculations is related to the loss on the differential. This set separates the loss into components that are related to plant and equipment (net) and goodwill. The following are the pertinent calculations:

Loss for first part of year on unamortized
  differential related to plant and equipment (net)
  [600,000 × ($.125 − $.11)] . . . . $ 9,000
Loss for subsequent portion of year on unamortized
  differential related to plant and equipment (net)
  [(600,000 − 150,000) × ($.11 − $.10) = 450,000 × $.01]   4,500
Translation loss on differential related to
  plant and equipment (net) $13,500

and

Loss for first part of year on unamortized differential
  related to goodwill [200,000 × ($.125 − $.11)] $3,000
Loss for subsequent portion of year on unamortized
  differential related to goodwill
  [(200,000 − 20,000) × ($.11 − $.10) = 180,000 × $.01]   1,800
Translation loss on differential related to goodwill $4,800

Note that the sum of the two losses calculated above equals the translation loss on the differential of $18,300 ($13,500 + $4,800).

    Given both sets of calculations, the working paper entries for this case are as follows:

1. To eliminate double counting of equity method income and subsidiary translation loss recorded by the second equity method entry, eliminate translation loss on differential recorded by the third equity method entry, and record minority interest (zero) in subsidiary net income and subsidiary translation loss:

Equity in Subsidiary Earnings
  ($66,000 − $18,700) 47,300
    Cumulative Foreign Exchange Translation
      Adjustments—Monroe Company
        ($16,000 + $18,300) 34,300
    Investment in Bordeaux Company 13,000

2. To eliminate beginning-of-year investment account balance against beginning-of-year Bordeaux Company stockholders' equity accounts, establish beginning-of-year minority interest (zero), and establish beginning-of-year differential:

Capital Stock—Bordeaux Company
($.125 × 100,000)   12,500
Retained Earnings—Bordeaux Company
($.125 × 300,000)   37,500
Differential   100,000
    Investment in Bordeaux Company   150,000

3. To allocate the beginning-of-year differential and record translation loss on differential:

Cumulative Foreign Exchange
    Translation Adjustments   18,300
Plant and Equipment (net)
($75,000 − $13,500)   61,500
Goodwill ($25,000 − $4,800)   20,200
    Differential   100,000

4. To record differential amortization:

Depreciation Expense   16,500
Other Expenses   2,200
    Plant and Equipment (net)   16,500
    Goodwill   2,200

Working paper entry (1) is similar to the first entry in Case 2; it prevents double counting of Bordeaux Company's translation loss and eliminates the loss on the differential recorded under the equity method in addition to its usual functions. Entry (2) is a standard investment elimination entry and is identical to the investment elimination entries in Cases 1 and 2. Entry (4) records 19X1 differential amortization as calculated above. Entry (3) requires explanation. As indicated, this entry allocates the beginning-of-year differential in dollars and records the translation loss on the differential for consolidated statement purposes. The translation loss is recorded by the debit to Cumulative Foreign Exchange Translation Adjustments. The loss represents a decrease in the differential—a decrease that has not yet been recorded for the consolidated statements. Thus, when the loss is recorded and the differential is allocated in entry (3), the portions of the loss related to the Plant and Equipment (net) and Goodwill accounts ($13,500 and $4,800, respectively) are subtracted from the portions of the beginning-of-year differential allocable to these accounts ($75,000 and $25,000, respectively). To see these effects more clearly, note that the following two entries produce the same results as, and constitute an alternative to, entry (3).

Cumulative Foreign Exchange
   Translation Adjustments 18,300
      Differential 18,300

Plant and Equipment (net) ($75,000 − $13,500) 61,500
Goodwill ($25,000 − $4,800) 20,200
    Differential ($100,000 − $18,300) 81,700

A consolidated statement working paper for this case is presented in Illustration 14–7. Consolidated net income for this case, which equals Monroe Company's (equity method) net income, is calculated incrementally as follows:

Monroe Company's 19X1 (confirmed) net income
  from its own operations .... $ –0–
Plus: Monroe Company's equity in Bordeaux Company's
  (confirmed) 19X1 net income (100% × $66,000) 66,000
Minus: Differential amortization for 19X1 18,700
Consolidated net income for 19X1 .... $47,300

     Notice also in Illustration 14–7 that the consolidated balance for Cumulative Foreign Exchange Translation Adjustments equals Monroe Company's balance for this account. As in Case 2, this phenomenon occurs because the equity method is applied to Monroe Company's Cumulative Foreign Exchange Adjustments account. Recall that such application ensures that the balance in this account works just like a parent company's retained earnings account under the equity method.

Investment Elimination for Subsequent Years

The working paper entries shown above fail to illustrate the form of the investment elimination entry for years subsequent to year of acquisition. As in Case 2, a beginning-of-year balance is likely to exist in a foreign subsidiary's Cumulative Foreign Exchange Translation Adjustments account in years subsequent to acquisition under the current rate method (i.e., in its current rate method working paper). Since this account is part of the subsidiary's stockholders' equity, it is offset in the investment elimination entry just as is the balance in any other subsidiary stockholders' equity account which pertains to its common share-

ILLUSTRATION 14-7   Consolidation under Current Rate Method

MONROE COMPANY AND SUBSIDIARY BORDEAUX COMPANY
Consolidated Statement Working Paper
For the Year Ended December 31, 19X1

	Monroe Company	Bordeaux Company	Eliminations Dr.	Eliminations Cr.	Consolidated
Income Statement					
Sales		132,000			132,000
Equity in subsidiary earnings	47,300		(1) 47,300		-0-
Total credits	47,300	132,000			132,000
Depreciation expense		27,500	(4) 16,500		44,000
Other expenses		38,500	(4) 2,200		40,700
Total debits		66,000			84,700
Net income	47,300	66,000	66,000		47,300
Retained Earnings Statement					
Retained earnings 1/1:					
Monroe Company	-0-				-0-
Bordeaux Company		37,500	(2) 37,500		-0-
Net income	47,300	66,000	66,000		47,300
Retained earnings 12/31	47,300	103,500	103,500		47,300
Balance Sheet					
Cash and receivables		115,000			115,000
Plant and equipment (net)		75,000	(3) 61,500	(4) 16,500	120,000
Investment in Bordeaux Company	163,000			(1) 13,000	-0-
				(2) 150,000	
Differential			(2) 100,000	(3) 100,000	-0-
Goodwill			(3) 20,200	(4) 2,200	18,000
	163,000	190,000			253,000
Current payables		20,000			20,000
Long-term debt		70,000			70,000
Common stock:					
Monroe Company	150,000				150,000
Bordeaux Company		12,500	(2) 12,500		-0-
Retained earnings	47,300	103,500	103,500		47,300
Cumulative foreign exchange translation adjustments	(34,300)	(16,000)	(3) 18,300	(1) 34,300	(34,300)
	163,000	190,000	316,000	316,000	253,000

(deduction)

Explanation of eliminations:

(1) To eliminate double counting of equity method income and subsidiary translation loss, eliminate translation loss on differential, and record minority interest (zero) in subsidiary net income and subsidiary translation loss.

(2) To eliminate beginning-of-year investment account balance against beginning-of-year Bordeaux Company stockholders' equity accounts, establish beginning-of-year minority interst (zero), and establish beginning-of-year differential.

(3) To allocate the beginning-of-year differential and record translation loss on differential.

(4) To record differential amortization.

holders. Thus, the 19X2 investment elimination entry for this example is as follows:

Capital Stock—Bordeaux Company	
($.125 × 100,000)	12,500
Retained Earnings—Bordeaux Company	
($37,500 + $66,000)	103,500
Differential ($100,000 − $18,300 − $18,700)	63,000
Investment in Bordeaux Company	163,000
Cumulative Foreign Exchange Translation	
Adjustments—Bordeaux Company	16,000

Long-Term Intercompany Payables

We assume in Case 2 that Bordeaux Company's long-term debt, which is denomi-nated in francs, results from an intercompany foreign currency transaction that is of a long-term investment nature. As indicated in Chapter 13, the transaction gains and losses related to this type of debt do not require special treatment (or separate calculation) under the current rate method. They also introduce no complications in the preparation of consolidated financial statements or in applying the equity method under this technique. Note, however, that if a debt of this type is denominated in dollars, a minor problem exists. The payable on the subsidiary's books is adjusted using the current rate under the current rate method, and the receivable on the parent's books is stated consistently with conversion at its historical rate (i.e., since it is denominated in its functional currency). Under these conditions, we recommend that any difference between the intercompany receivable and payable be treated as a receivable or payable until the debt is settled. This treatment is consistent with the discussion found in Chapter 13 under "Multiple Exchange Rates."

CONSOLIDATED STATEMENT OF CASH FLOWS

Statement of Financial Accounting Standards No. 95 allows both a direct and an indirect approach to preparing the statement of cash flows.[7] Both of these ap-proaches report cash flows from operating, investing, and financing activities. The direct approach requires a separate schedule that reconciles net income with net cash provided by operating activities. In the next two cases, we illustrate consoli-dated statement of cash flows working papers for the direct approach for Monroe Company and its subsidiary, Bordeaux Company. The following schedule pro-

---

[7] FASB, *Statement of Financial Accounting Standards No. 95,* "Statement of Cash Flows" (Norwalk, CT: FASB, 1987).

vides supplementary data related to Bordeaux Company's Cash and Receivables account and summarizes previously given data related to its Current Payables account.

	December 31, 19X1		January 1, 19X1	
	Dollars	*Francs*	*Dollars*	*Francs*
Cash	100,000	1,000,000	15,000	120,000
Receivables	15,000	150,000	10,000	80,000
Total	115,000	1,150,000	25,000	200,000
Current Payables	20,000	200,000	12,500	100,000

Case 4. Consolidated Statement of Cash Flows—Temporal Method

This case is a continuation of Case 2. It deals with the preparation of a consolidated statement of cash flows and the required reconciliation using the direct approach under the temporal method. Illustration 14–8 contains the working papers for this case. Formal statements are not presented for Cases 4 and 5 since they are, in effect, shown in the consolidated columns of the working papers.

Six figures from Illustration 14–8 require explanation—"Equity in undistributed subsidiary income," "Cash received from customers," "Cash paid to suppliers and employees," the investing and financing activities figures related to the purchase of plant and equipment, and "Effect of rate changes on cash." The equity in undistributed subsidiary income figure is found in the "Reconciliation of Net Income with Net Cash Provided by Operating Activities" working paper. This value is subtracted in the Monroe Company column of the reconciliation since it is a part of Monroe Company's net income that provides no cash. In this case, the amount subtracted equals Monroe Company's equity in Bordeaux Company's 19X1 net income since the latter paid no dividends in 19X1. The remaining values to be explained are contained in the "Consolidated Statement of Cash Flows" working paper. The cash received from customers figure of $124,300 equals Bordeaux Company's remeasured sales, less its 19X1 remeasured increase in accounts receivable [.11 × (1,200,000 − (150,000 − 80,000))]. Similarly, the cash paid to suppliers and employees value of $27,500 equals Bordeaux Company's remeasured other expenses, less its 19X1 remeasured increase in current payables [.11 × (350,000 − (200,000 − 100,000))]. The investing and financing values of $87,500 both equal the product of the 700,000 francs borrowed and invested and the exchange rate in effect on the date these transactions occurred (.125).[8] The direct calculation of the effect of rate changes on cash is more

---

[8] *Statement No. 95* (par. 144) indicates that investing and financing activity amounts are converted using the rates in effect at the times of the cash flows in preparing consolidated statements of cash flows under both the temporal and the current rate methods.

ILLUSTRATION 14-8   Temporal Method with Long-Term Intercompany Payable

MONROE COMPANY AND SUBSIDIARY BORDEAUX COMPANY
Working Papers—Consolidated Statement of Cash Flows and Reconciliation
For the Year Ended December 31, 19X1

Working Paper—Consolidated Statement of Cash Flows:

	Monroe Company	Bordeaux Company	Elimi- nations	Consoli- dated
Cash flows from operating activities:				
Cash received from customers		124,300		124,300
Cash paid to suppliers and employees		27,500		27,500
Net cash provided by operating activities		96,800		96,800
Cash flows from investing activities:				
Long-term loan—Bordeaux	87,500		(87,500)	
Purchase of plant and equipment		87,500		87,500
Net cash used in investing activities	87,500	87,500	(87,500)	87,500
Cash flows from financing activities:				
Proceeds from long-term loan—Monroe		87,500	(87,500)	
Proceeds from issuing capital stock	87,500			87,500
Net cash provided by financing activities	87,500	87,500	(87,500)	87,500
Effect of rate changes on cash		(11,800)		(11,800)
Net change in cash and cash equivalents	–0–	85,000		85,000
Cash and cash equivalents (1/1/X1)	–0–	15,000		15,000
Cash and cash equivalents (12/31/X1)	–0–	100,000	–0–	100,000

Working Paper—Reconciliation of Net Income with Net Cash Provided by Operating Activities:

	Monroe Company	Bordeaux Company	Elimi- nations	Consoli- dated
Net income	41,250	51,250	(51,250)	41,250
Add [(subtract)]:				
Depreciation and amortization	10,000	31,250		41,250
Increase in accounts receivable		(7,700)		(7,700)
Increase in current payables		11,000		11,000
Equity in undistributed subsidiary income	(51,250)		51,250	–0–
Remeasurement loss		11,000		11,000
Net cash provided by operating activities	–0–	96,800	–0–	96,800

complicated. Although this value can be calculated indirectly as the "plug" figure that completes the Bordeaux Company column of the working paper, *Statement No. 95* (par. 146) provides guidance on the direct calculation of this value. Before focusing on this calculation, note that Bordeaux Company's 19X1 cash provided by operations in francs is as follows:

Bordeaux Company's 19X1 net income in francs	600,000
Less: Its 19X1 increase in accounts receivable in francs	
(150,000 − 80,000)	70,000
Plus: Its 19X1 increase in current payables in francs	
(200,000 − 100,000)	100,000
Plus: Its 19X1 depreciation expense in francs	250,000
Bordeaux Company's 19X1 cash provided by operations in francs	880,000

Illustration 14–9 shows the direct calculation of the effect of rate changes on cash.

Case 5. Consolidated Statement of Cash Flows—Current Rate Method

This case continues Case 3. It covers the preparation of a consolidated statement of cash flows and the required reconciliation using the direct approach under the current rate method. The working papers for this case are presented in Illustration 14–10. The values and related calculations for this illustration are similar to those of Illustration 14–8. The main difference is the calculation of the effect of rate changes on cash. In this case, the $11,800 effect of rate changes on cash simply equals the sum of the effect on the 19X1 beginning cash balance (− $3,000) and the effect from operating activities for 19X1 (− $8,800) shown in Illustration 14–9. In general, the calculation of the effect of rate changes on cash is the same under both remeasurement and the current rate method since the same exchange rates, and so on, are used in both cases.[9]

HEDGES OF NET INVESTMENT IN A FOREIGN ENTITY

Recall from Chapter 12 that one class of forward exchange hedging contract is hedges of net investments (ownership interests) in foreign entities. For transactions to fall in this class, *Statement No. 52* (par. 20) indicates that they must be "designated as, and effective as, economic hedges of a net investment in a foreign

---

[9] For elaboration, see John G. Hamer and Linda H. Kistler, "The Statement of Cash Flows—An Analysis of Translation and Remeasurement Techniques for Foreign Subsidiaries," *The International Journal of Accounting,* Fall 1987, pp. 29–42.

ILLUSTRATION 14-9   **Temporal Method with Long-Term Intercompany Payable**

BORDEAUX COMPANY
Calculation of the Effect of Rate Changes on Cash Values
For the Year Ended December 31, 19X1

Effect on 19X1 beginning cash balance:			
Beginning cash balance in francs	120,000		
Times change in spot rate			
during 19X1 ($.1 − $.125)	× ($.025)		
			(3,000)
Effect from 19X1 operating activities:			
Cash provided by operations in			
19X1 in francs	880,000		
Times year-end spot rate	× $.1		
Cash provided by operations based			
on year-end rate		88,000	
Less operating cash flows			
shown in working paper		96,800	
Effect from 19X1 operating activities			(8,800)
Effect from 19X1 investing activities:			
Net cash used in investing			
activities in francs	(700,000)		
Times year-end spot rate	× $.1		
Investing cash flows based on			
year-end rate		(70,000)	
Less net cash used in investing activities			
shown in working paper		(87,500)	
Effect from 19X1 investing activities			17,500
Effect from 19X1 financing activities:			
Net cash provided by financing			
activities in francs	700,000		
Times year-end spot rate	× $.1		
Financing cash flows based on			
year-end rate		$70,000	
Less net cash used in financing activities			
shown in working paper		87,500	
Effect from 19X1 financing activities			(17,500)
Effect of rate changes on cash			(11,800)

---

entity. . . ." An example of this type of hedge is a domestic parent company selling units of its subsidiary's foreign functional currency and designating this sale as a hedge of its foreign currency exposure (i.e., the subsidiary's net asset position). To illustrate, assume in Case 3 that Monroe Company decides to hedge its net investment in Bordeaux Company by entering into a forward exchange contract. Specifically, assume that it sells 1,600,000 francs on July 1, 19X1, for delivery on December 31, 19X1 (180 days later). Assume that the spot rate and the 180-day forward rate both are .11 on the sale date. Recall also that Bordeaux

ILLUSTRATION 14-10   Current Rate Method

MONROE COMPANY AND SUBSIDIARY BORDEAUX COMPANY
Working Papers—Consolidated Statement of Cash Flows and Reconciliation
For the Year Ended December 31, 19X1

Working Paper—Consolidated Statement of Cash Flows:

	Monroe Company	Bordeaux Company	Consoli- dated
Cash flows from operating activities:			
Cash received from customers	-0-	124,300	124,300
Cash paid to suppliers and employees	-0-	27,500	27,500
Net cash provided by operating activities	-0-	96,800	96,800
Effect of rate changes on cash	-0-	(11,800)	(11,800)
Net change in cash and cash equivalents	-0-	85,000	85,000
Cash and cash equivalents (1/1/X1)	-0-	15,000	15,000
Cash and cash equivalents (12/31/X1)	-0-	100,000	100,000

Working Paper—Reconciliation of Net Income with Net Cash Provided by Operating Activities:

	Monroe Company	Bordeaux Company	Elimi- nations	Consoli- dated
Net income	47,300	66,000	(66,000)	47,300
Add [(subtract)]:				
Depreciation and amortization	18,700	27,500		46,200
Increase in accounts receivable		(7,700)		(7,700)
Increase in current payables		11,000		11,000
Equity in undistributed subsidiary income	(66,000)		66,000	-0-
Net cash provided by operating activities	-0-	96,800	-0-	96,800

Company experiences a $16,000 translation loss during 19X1. Monroe Company's entries related to the forward exchange contract are as follows:

1.	7/1/X1	Dollars Due from Exchange Broker ($.11 × 1,600,000)	176,000	
		Francs Due to Exchange Broker		176,000
2.	12/31/X1	Cash	16,000	
		Foreign Currency—Francs ($.1 × 1,600,000)	160,000	
		Dollars Due from Exchange Broker		176,000
3.	12/31/X1	Francs Due to Exchange Broker	176,000	
		Foreign Currency—Francs		160,000
		Cumulative Foreign Exchange Translation Adjustments		16,000

Thus, Monroe Company experiences a $16,000 transaction exchange gain. Under *Statement No. 52*, transaction exchange gains and losses resulting from hedges of net investments in foreign entities are accumulated in the Cumulative Foreign Exchange Translations Adjustments account provided they are less than, or equal to, the foreign entity's translation adjustment.[10] Thus, in our example the whole transaction exchange gain is credited to this account.

Note that Monroe Company's hedge is perfect; it exactly offsets Bordeaux Company's translation loss of $16,000. The hedge is perfect because Monroe Company correctly anticipates the year-end spot rate and, consequently, sells exactly the number of francs needed to produce a $16,000 transaction gain. Note also that our assumption that the spot rate and the 180-day forward rate are the same on July 1, 19X1, implies that there is no premium or discount on the hedging transaction. We emphasize that companies' forecasts of future spot rates usually are not exact and that the pertinent spot and forward rates usually are not equal. Premiums and discounts related to this type of hedge are amortized over the life of the forward exchange contract and are recognized in the income statement or in the Cumulative Foreign Exchange Translation Adjustments account (provided the net amount of the domestic company's gain or loss and the amortization does not exceed the foreign entity's translation gain or loss (see footnote 10)).

The consolidated financial statement and consolidated statement of cash flows working papers for this case are presented in Illustrations 14–11 and 14–12, respectively. These working papers are presented without explanation since they are so similar to earlier working papers. Note, however, that Monroe's hedge provides an additional $16,000 in cash.

ELIMINATION OF UNCONFIRMED PROFITS

Domestic parents and foreign subsidiaries also engage in transactions resulting in unconfirmed profits. Thus, the issue of which exchange rate to use in calculating unconfirmed profits arises. *Statement No. 52* (par. 137) concludes that "any intercompany profit occurs on the date of sale or transfer and that exchange rates in effect on that date or reasonable approximations thereof should be used to compute the amount of any intercompany profit to be eliminated." Under this view, subsequent changes in exchange rates on the transferred asset (or related expense) are seen as being the results of changes in exchange rates rather than being functions of intercompany profits. Thus, such changes do not affect the elimination of unconfirmed profits.

---

[10] Under this pronouncement, the excess of the domestic company's gain or loss over the foreign entity's gain or loss is recognized in the income statement as a transaction exchange gain or loss.

MONROE COMPANY AND SUBSIDIARY BORDEAUX COMPANY
Consolidated Statement Working Paper
For the Year Ended December 31, 19X1

	Monroe Company	Bordeaux Company	Eliminations Dr.	Eliminations Cr.	Consolidated
Income Statement					
Sales		132,000			132,000
Equity in subsidiary earnings	47,300		(1) 47,300		–0–
Total credits	47,300	132,000			132,000
Depreciation expense		27,500	(4) 16,500		44,000
Other expenses		38,500	(4) 2,200		40,700
Total debits		66,000			84,700
Net income	47,300	66,000	66,000		47,300
Retained Earnings Statement					
Retained earnings 1/1:					
Monroe Company	–0–				–0–
Bordeaux Company		37,500	(2) 37,500		–0–
Net income	47,300	66,000	66,000		47,300
Retained earnings 12/31	47,300	103,500	103,500		47,300
Balance Sheet					
Cash and receivables	16,000	115,000			131,000
Plant and equipment (net)		75,000	(3) 61,500	(4) 16,500	120,000
Investment in Bordeaux Company	163,000			(1) 13,000	–0–
				(2) 150,000	
Differential			(2) 100,000	(3) 100,000	–0–
Goodwill			(3) 20,200	(4) 2,200	18,000
	179,000	190,000			269,000
Current payables		20,000			20,000
Long-term debt		70,000			70,000
Common stock:					
Monroe Company	150,000				150,000
Bordeaux Company		12,500	(2) 12,500		–0–
Retained earnings	47,300	103,500	103,500		47,300
Cumulative foreign exchange translation adjustments	(18,300)	(16,000)	(3) 18,300	(1) 34,300	(18,300)
	179,000	190,000	316,000	316,000	269,000

(deduction)

Explanation of eliminations:

(1) To eliminate double counting of equity method income and subsidiary translation loss, eliminate translation loss on differential, and record minority interest (zero) in subsidiary net income and subsidiary translation loss.

(2) To eliminate beginning-of-year investment account balance against beginning-of-year Bordeaux Company stockholders' equity accounts, establish beginning-of-year minority interest (zero), and establish beginning-of-year differential.

(3) To allocate the beginning-of-year differential and record translation loss on differential.

(4) To record differential amortization.

ILLUSTRATION 14-12 **Current Rate Method with Hedge of Net Investment in Foreign Entity**

MONROE COMPANY AND SUBSIDIARY BORDEAUX COMPANY
Working Papers—Consolidated Statement of Cash Flows and Reconciliation
For the Year Ended December 31, 19X1

Working Paper—Consolidated Statement of Cash Flows:

	Monroe Company	Bordeaux Company	Consoli- dated
Cash flows from operating activities:			
Cash received from customers		124,300	124,300
Cash paid to suppliers and employees		27,500	27,500
Net cash provided by operating activities		96,800	96,800
Cash flows from financing activities:			
Net proceeds from hedge of net investment			
in Bordeaux Company	16,000		16,000
Net cash provided by financing activities	16,000		16,000
Effect of rate changes on cash		(11,800)	(11,800)
Net change in cash and cash equivalents		85,000	101,000
Cash and cash equivalents (1/1/X1)		15,000	15,000
Cash and cash equivalents (12/31/X1)	16,000	100,000	116,000

Working Paper—Reconciliation of Net Income with Net Cash Provided by Operating Activities:

	Monroe Company	Bordeaux Company	Elimi- nations	Consoli- dated
Net income	47,300	66,000	(66,000)	47,300
Add [(subtract)]:				
Depreciation and amortization	18,700	27,500		46,200
Increase in accounts receivable		(7,700)		(7,700)
Increase in current payables		11,000		11,000
Equity in undistributed				
subsidiary income	(66,000)		66,000	–0–
Net cash provided by operating				
activities	–0–	96,800	–0–	96,800

SEGMENTAL DISCLOSURES RELATED TO OPERATIONS OF CONSOLIDATED FOREIGN SUBSIDIARIES AND EXPORT SALES

Statement of Financial Accounting Standards No. 14, "Financial Reporting for Segments of a Business Enterprise," requires standard segmental reporting for entities' foreign operations. According to *Statement No. 14* (par. 31), an entity's foreign operations include its revenue-producing operations *(except unconsolidated subsidiaries and other unconsolidated investees)* that "*(a)* are located outside of the enterprise's home country . . . and *(b)* are generating revenue either from sales to unaffiliated customers or from intraenterprise sales or transfers between geographic areas.'' The basic segmental disclosures of *Statement No. 14* (par. 32) are required for

(1) an entity's foreign operations, either in aggregate or, if appropriate under paragraph 33 by geographical area, and (2) its domestic operations, if either of the following conditions are met:

a. Revenue generated by the enterprise's foreign operations from sales to unaffiliated customers is 10 percent or more of consolidated revenue as reported in the enterprise's income statement.

b. Identifiable assets of the enterprise's foreign operations are 10 percent or more of consolidated total assets as reported in the enterprise's balance sheet.

DISCLOSURES RELATED TO PREVIOUSLY AND CURRENTLY UNCONSOLIDATED FOREIGN SUBSIDIARIES

Accounting Research Bulletin No. 51 allowed several exceptions to the general rule that subsidiaries are to be consolidated, including an exception (by reference to *Accounting Research Bulletin No. 43*) for foreign subsidiaries. In this context, *Accounting Research Bulletin No. 43* (Chapter 12, par. 8) indicates that

In view of the uncertain values and availability of the assets and net income of foreign subsidiaries subject to controls and exchange restrictions and the consequent unrealistic statements of income that may result from the translation of many foreign currencies into dollars, careful consideration should be given to the fundamental question of whether it is proper to consolidate the statements of foreign subsidiaries with the statements of the United States Companies.

As indicated earlier, *Statement No. 94* requires the consolidation of a majority-owned foreign subsidiary unless it operates under foreign exchange restrictions, controls, or other governmentally imposed uncertainties that cast doubt on the parent's ability to control the subsidiary. One intention of *Statement No. 94* (par. 9) is ''to narrow the [*Accounting Research Bulletin No. 43*] exception for a majority-owned foreign subsidiary from one that permits exclusion from consolidation of any or all foreign subsidiaries to one that effectively eliminates distinctions between foreign and domestic subsidiaries.'' As a consequence of *Statement No. 94,* previously unconsolidated foreign subsidiaries presumably now are being consolidated. In these cases, *Statement No. 94* requires certain disclosures. Specifically, it states (par. 19):

Information that was disclosed under *APB Opinion No. 18,* paragraph 20(c), about majority owned subsidiaries that were unconsolidated in financial statements for fiscal years 1986 and 1987 shall continue to be disclosed for them after they are consolidated pursuant to the provisions of this pronouncement as amended by *Statement No. 94.*

That is, summarized information about the assets, liabilities, and results of operations (or separate statements) shall be provided for those subsidiaries, either individually or in groups, as appropriate, in the consolidated financial statements or notes.

Although one intention of *Statement No. 94* is to reduce the number of unconsolidated foreign subsidiaries, there undoubtedly will be foreign subsidiaries that are not consolidated. The disclosure requirements for such subsidiaries previously were covered in *Accounting Research Bulletin No. 43* (Chapter 12, par. 9) and *Accounting Research Bulletin No. 51* (pars. 19–21). Additionally, *APB Opinion No. 18* (par. 20(c)) called for the disclosure of summarized data about the assets, liabilities, and operating results (or separate statements) for unconsolidated subsidiaries, either individually or in groups (as appropriate), in consolidated financial statements or the related footnotes when the investment in such subsidiaries is material. All of these paragraphs are superseded by *Statement No. 94*. Nevertheless, *Statement No. 94* is vague on disclosures related to *currently* unconsolidated subsidiaries. That is, all of its discussions of disclosures for unconsolidated subsidiaries (pars. 19, 58, and 59) can be interpreted as pertaining only to *previously* unconsolidated subsidiaries. Our feeling is that the FASB's intention is to continue the requirements of *APB Opinion No. 18* (par. 20(c)) mentioned above for unconsolidated subsidiaries.

CONSOLIDATED FINANCIAL STATEMENTS—A WORLDWIDE VIEW

In international financial accounting, the phrase *national* (or *local*) *financial reporting* refers to financial reporting within a country; the phrase *transnational financial reporting* refers to financial reporting across national boundaries. An important issue that arises in both national and transnational reporting is whether consolidated financial statements are to be prepared for companies and their local subsidiaries. A related issue is whether foreign subsidiaries are to be consolidated. As indicated above, a majority-owned foreign subsidiary of a U.S. parent is consolidated unless it operates under foreign exchange restrictions, controls, or other governmentally imposed uncertainties so severe that they cast significant doubt on the parent's ability to control the subsidiary. Nevertheless, the issues just mentioned, like most important financial reporting issues, are dealt with inconsistently internationally (see additional discussion below).[11] Some companies consolidate only local subsidiaries; others consolidate both local and foreign subsidiaries. In these cases, the consolidated statements may be the primary statements, or they may be presented as supplementary information. Addi-

---

[11] Another issue involves the criteria that are applied in deciding whether a company should be consolidated. These criteria also are not consistent internationally. For example, in a few cases, it is permissible to consolidate less than 50 percent owned companies. We do not explore country-to-country differences in consolidation criteria.

tionally, consolidated financial statements are not prepared at all in some countries. Companies in these countries prepare *parent company only* financial statements.

Statistics on the number of countries and firms following particular consolidated statement practices are difficult to obtain. Nevertheless, the international accounting literature provides insights concerning the countries (and their types) in which local or foreign subsidiaries are consolidated. One inference which seems warranted is that both types of subsidiaries tend to be consolidated in the more highly developed countries. For example, Choi and Bavishi indicate that firms in 20 of 24 relatively highly developed countries tended to consolidate local subsidiaries, and companies in 19 of these countries tended to consolidate both local and foreign subsidiaries.[12] As implied, even local subsidiaries related to the group of 20 countries were not consolidated in *all* cases. For example, in West Germany, consolidation was required, historically, only for local subsidiaries whose parent companies were subject to the country's Publicity Law. Firms in West Germany also did not consolidate foreign subsidiaries. Besides West Germany, the countries whose firms were found not to consolidate either local or foreign subsidiaries consistently were Finland, Italy, India, and South Korea. In general, Third World countries are relatively slow to adopt accounting technology such as the preparation of consolidated financial statements. Additionally, in some countries (e.g., Colombia), the preparation of consolidated statements is prohibited by law. From an overall perspective, the preparation of consolidated financial statements is the exception, rather than the rule, internationally.

When consolidated financial statements are prepared, they usually are prepared because they are required by private-sector, policy-setting body mandate, are required legally, or are advocated by the International Accounting Standards Committee (IASC). The United States and Canada are prime examples of countries in which consolidated financial statements are prepared primarily as a result of private-sector, policy-setting body requirements. Japan and West Germany are (or were) good examples of countries in which consolidated statements are (were) required legally, at least for some firms. Note also that European Community (EC or Common Market) countries are expected to be legally required to prepare consolidated financial statements beginning in the 1990s.[13] Multinational compa-

---

[12] Frederick D. S. Choi and Vinod B. Bavishi, "International Accounting Standards: Issues Needing Attention," *Journal of Accountancy,* March 1983, pp. 66–67.

[13] The EC begins the process of setting legally binding standards by issuing EC directives. Once approved by the EC's Council of Ministers, these directives become binding on EC member nations. That is, these nations must modify their laws so that they are consistent with EC directives over a period of years. The EC's Seventh Directive, which was adopted by its Council of Ministers about seven years after it was first proposed, requires countries to modify their laws so that the preparation of consolidated financial statements is required. The deadline for countries to comply with this directive was January 1, 1988, and companies were to have begun preparing consolidated statements after January 1, 1990, under this directive. Note that there are some significant differences between the EC's consolidation policy and that of the FASB.

nies are examples of companies that often prepare consolidated financial statements voluntarily in accordance with the consolidation procedures recommended by the IASC.

The IASC's efforts in setting consolidation standards are attributable to its interest in the *harmonization* of financial accounting standards.[14] The IASC has issued two *International Accounting Standards (IAS)* dealing with the preparation of consolidated financial statements. In 1976, it issued *IAS No. 3,* "Consolidated Financial Statements." Except for the portions dealing with "accounting for investments in affiliates that are not subsidiaries," *IAS No. 3* was superseded in early 1989 by *IAS No. 27,* "Consolidated Financial Statements and Accounting for Investments in Subsidiaries." Under *IAS No. 27* (par. 6), a subsidiary is any company that is *controlled* by another company (called its *parent*), and consolidated financial statements are prepared for a *group*. A group is a parent and *all* of its subsidiaries. Under *IAS No. 27* (par. 10), an enterprise is considered to be controlled if another company directly, or indirectly, owns more than 50 percent of its voting power. One company also controls another with less than, or equal to, 50 percent ownership under *IAS No. 27* (par. 10) provided

1. It has an agreement with other investors giving it power over more than one half of the voting rights of the second company;
2. A statute or agreement gives it the power to govern the financing and operating policies of the second company;
3. It has the power to appoint or remove the majority of the members of the second company's board of directors (or equivalent governing body); or
4. It has the power to cast the majority of votes at meetings of the second company's board of directors (or equivalent governing body).

Although inconsistent with the definitions of control and group just mentioned, a controlled company is not consolidated under *IAS No. 27* (par. 11) if (1) control is intended to be temporary because the company was acquired for disposal in the near future or (2) the company operates under long-term restrictions severe enough to significantly impair its ability to transfer funds to its parent.

AN INTRODUCTION TO INTERNATIONAL FINANCIAL ACCOUNTING

As indicated earlier, this chapter also discusses the topic of international financial accounting. The topics covered below include the setting of international financial accounting standards, the harmonization of financial accounting standards, the factors impacting on national financial accounting systems, financial reporting by

---

[14] As discussed further below, the process of reducing, or eliminating, conceptually unjustified diversity in financial accounting standards is referred to as *harmonization in international accounting.*

foreign companies, and approaches to transnational financial reporting. From the perspective of consolidated financial statements, an analysis of these topics is important because it reveals the diversity that exists internationally in financial accounting. This diversity, when material, must be dealt with prior to the preparation of consolidated financial statements so that their usefulness is not compromised. From a more general perspective, this analysis provides insights into the international financial accounting standard-setting and reporting processes and the forces that shape these processes and affect the diversity in international financial accounting (including consolidation policies).

Financial Accounting Standard Setting—Contrast between U.S. and International Processes

The U.S. and international financial accounting standard-setting processes can be contrasted on various dimensions, including their philosophies, mechanics, outcomes, enforceability of outcomes, and objectives. To provide a basis for such contrasts, the FASB's policy-setting process is described briefly below. Subsequently, an important element of the international financial accounting standard-setting process, the operations of the IASC, is described in more detail and pertinent contrasts are provided.

The FASB's standard-setting process is best characterized as a due-process procedure. It is meant to ensure that financial reporting issues are studied thoroughly prior to the issuance of financial accounting standards and that all interested parties are allowed to participate in the standard-setting process. Since all interested parties participate in the FASB's due-process procedure, it is heavily politicized. This process is heavily politicized in the sense that influential individuals and groups (e.g., managers) expend resources to see that policies which serve their best interests are adopted. Ultimately, the due-process procedure is intended to guarantee that the interests of those affected by the financial reporting process are protected. The essential steps in the FASB's due-process procedure are summarized as follows:

1. An item is placed on the FASB's agenda as a consequence of the efforts of its Agenda Advisory Committee or its Emerging Issues Task Force.
2. A task force is appointed to provide the FASB with advice on the issue, to assess the need for project-related research, and to assist in preparing the related discussion memorandum.
3. A discussion memorandum, along with a request for comments on the memorandum or any other aspect of the issue being considered, is widely distributed to interested parties. The discussion memorandum identifies the reporting problem under consideration, discusses relevant literature and related research, identifies various approaches to resolving the issue, and considers the arguments for, and the implications of, each of the possible solutions.

4. A public hearing is held to allow interested parties to express their opinions on the reporting problem orally, to provide written position papers on the issue, and, generally, to allow the FASB to obtain additional information about the issue.

5. The FASB analyzes the oral and written comments and meets publicly as many times as necessary to discuss the comments and the reporting problem further.

6. The FASB, given that a majority of its members concur, issues an exposure draft which includes, among other things, a discussion of the reporting issue, a presentation of its proposed solution, a discussion of the reasons for its tentative solution, and a request for additional comments from interested parties.

7. The FASB analyzes the written comments on the exposure draft to see if its tentative solution should be modified and to see if additional public meetings should be scheduled.

8. After analyzing the written comments and any additional input from public hearings, three possibilities exist: *(a)* the standard-setting project may be terminated with no resolution to the reporting issue, *(b)* another exposure draft, which reflects modifications of the FASB's tentative solution, may be issued (with attendant repetition of above steps), and *(c)* the tentative solution may be judged to be acceptable.

9. Assuming that the tentative solution is judged to be acceptable (via a majority vote of the FASB's members), the final step in the due-process procedure is the issuance of a *Statement of Financial Accounting Standards (SFAS)*.

10. If an issue has been especially controversial, the FASB may follow up by monitoring the acceptance of the resulting standard through informal communications with interested parties.

SFAS are highly ranked in terms of providing authoritative support (i.e., in general they are dominated only by SEC pronouncements). Nevertheless, they need not be followed legally unless specified by the SEC for firms providing financial information under its jurisdiction. Although not required legally in general, note that rule 203 of the AICPA's *Code of Professional Conduct* prohibits its members from expressing opinions that financial statements conform with GAAP if the statements depart materially from those which would be produced under existing *SFAS* (unless it can be shown that the statements would be misleading otherwise).

In implementing its due-process procedure, the FASB's goal is to ensure the presentation of information that is useful in making economic decisions. Thus, the FASB indicates in *Statement of Financial Accounting Concepts (SFAC) No. 1* that the first broad objective of "general purpose external financial reporting by business enterprises" is to "provide information that is useful to present and potential investors and creditors and other users in making rational investment, credit, and similar decisions.''[15] Given this objective, *SFAC No. 1* (par. 30) emphasizes that the users of interest are those that do not have the power to require managements to disclose the information which they desire. Although the FASB states that financial reporting is directed toward numerous classes of users, it focuses on the decision processes of investors and creditors because they, and their advisers, are the most prominent group of users of financial reporting information, because their decision processes have been studied and described extensively, and because data which are useful to them are apt to be useful to other classes of users. Furthermore, *SFAC No. 1* (par. 34) assumes that users are sophisticated in the sense that they ''have a reasonable understanding of business and economic activities and are willing to study . . . [financial accounting] information with reasonable diligence.'' From the FASB's perspective, information which is useful in forming expectations about cash flows both to and from accounting entities is of primary importance in the context of the economic decisions of individuals. Thus, *SFAC No. 1* (par. 37) says

> Financial reporting should provide information to help present and potential investors and creditors and other users in assessing the amounts, timing, and uncertainty of prospective cash receipts [from accounting entities]. . . . Since investors' and creditors' cash flows are related to enterprise cash flows, financial reporting should provide information to help investors, creditors, and others assess the amounts, timing, and uncertainty of prospective net cash inflows to the related enterprise.

Although the FASB's focus is providing information which is useful to investors and creditors in forming expectations about cash flows, it believes that the same information is pertinent to the decision processes of other individuals and groups.

An important factor, which impacts on the due-process procedure, is the FASB's conceptual framework project. The results of this project—the FASB's *SFAC*—are meant to be useful in setting financial accounting standards. Thus, according to *SFAC No. 1* (par. i) the objective of the conceptual framework project is to ''set forth fundamentals on which financial accounting and reporting standards will be based. . . '' and ''more specifically . . . to establish the objectives and concepts that . . . [will be used] in developing [such] standards. . . .'' To date, four operative *SFAC* dealing with financial reporting have been issued: *SFAC No. 1,* ''Objectives of Financial Reporting by Business Enterprises''; *SFAC No. 2,* ''Qualitative Characteristics of Accounting Information''; *SFAC No. 5,* ''Recognition and Measurement in Financial Statements of Business Enterprises''; and *SFAC No. 6,* ''Elements of Financial Statements.''

The international counterpart to the FASB is the IASC. The IASC was formed in 1973 by leading professional accounting organizations (e.g., the AICPA) in Australia, Canada, France, Germany, Japan, Mexico, the Netherlands, the United Kingdom, Ireland, and the United States. The IASC now represents

---

[15] FASB, *Statement of Financial Accounting Concepts No. 1,* ''Objectives of Financial Reporting by Business Enterprises'' (Norwalk, CT: FASB, 1978), par. 34.

approximately 100 accounting organizations from about 75 countries. This committee's functions are (1) to develop public interest–based, international financial accounting standards which are required for unqualified attestations on financial statements, (2) to promote the worldwide acceptance of these standards, and (3) to work toward the harmonization of financial accounting standards.[16] The IASC's member organizations are committed to promoting worldwide acceptance of its standards by having them adopted by their national standard-setting bodies.

IASC standards are approved by its board—which consists of up to 17 representatives (including 13 representatives from its member professional accounting organizations and up to 4 representatives from nonaccounting international organizations with an interest in financial reporting). In early 1989, the IASC board consisted of representatives from Australia, Canada, Denmark, France, Germany, Italy, Japan, Jordan, Korea, the Netherlands, South Africa, the United Kingdom, and the United States. Thus, both the FASB and the IASC board are designed to provide representation to a variety of interests. As indicated above, IASC standards are referred to as *International Accounting Standards (IAS)*. To date, approximately 30 *IAS* have been issued. These standards deal with various important topics such as the preparation of consolidated financial statements and accounting for investments in subsidiaries *(IAS No. 3* and *IAS No. 27)*, accounting for income taxes *(IAS No. 12)*, segmental reporting *(IAS No. 14)*, inflation accounting *(IAS No. 15)*, the conversion of foreign currency financial statements *(IAS No. 21)*, and accounting for business combinations *(IAS No. 22)*. As implied, the topics dealt with by both the IASC and the FASB are very similar. Additionally, the requirements of IASC standards tend to be heavily influenced by previously existing FASB standards and the U.S. historical cost accounting model in general.

Similar to the FASB, the IASC standard-setting process is a due-process procedure designed to ensure that the interests of those affected by the financial reporting process are protected. However, the IASC process is not quite as involved as that of the FASB. The essential steps in the IASC procedure are the following:

1. An international financial reporting issue is placed on the IASC's agenda.
2. A steering committee of four representatives, which is appointed by the IASC board, studies the issue and drafts a document reflecting the

---

[16] Another influential international accounting body is the International Federation of Accountants (IFAC). This organization, which is the international counterpart of the AICPA, was founded in 1977. The IFAC's functions include developing international auditing procedures, organizing and conducting international accounting congresses, and promoting the exchange of technical information among its members. All professional accounting organizations that are members of the IFAC automatically are members of the IASC. By joint agreement, the IFAC does not infringe on the IASC's role in establishing international accounting standards.

points that it believes should be considered in resolving the reporting issue and submits this document to the board for comments.[17]

3. Given the board's comments, the steering committee prepares a preliminary draft of an *IAS* which includes its proposed solution to the reporting problem and submits the draft to the board.

4. If approved by the board, the preliminary draft is circulated among the IASC membership to obtain comments.

5. After receiving the members' comments, a revised version of the draft is prepared by the steering committee and submitted to the board.

6. Assuming that the revised version is judged to be acceptable (via a two-thirds vote of the IASC board), it is circulated as an exposure draft among professionals and nonprofessionals, including all IASC member organizations, for approximately a six-month period to obtain additional comments from all interested parties.

7. After studying the final set of comments, the steering committee revises its exposure draft and submits the resulting proposed standard to the IASC's board for approval.

8. Assuming that the exposure draft is judged to be acceptable (by a three-fourths vote of the IASC board), the final step in the IASC due-process procedure is the issuance of an *IAS*.

In gaining acceptance for its standards, the IASC strategy is for its members

1. To promote consistency between IASC standards and national standards when the standards are being worked on concurrently or when the national standards are developed subsequently.

2. To encourage the adoption of IASC standards in countries which do not have their own standards.

3. To encourage the elimination of inconsistencies between existing national standards and IASC standards.

4. To encourage changes in the laws of countries that contain reporting requirements differing from those of IASC standards.

The IASC was formed primarily in response to the use of widely differing accounting principles by essentially similar firms, especially multinational firms which have, in effect, outgrown the accounting principles of their countries. This situation is described aptly as follows.

Accounting evolves rather slowly, and larger multinationals have literally transcended the environments of their native countries to reflect a global business environment. (Toyota, for example, probably has more in common with General Motors than it does

---

[17] The steering committee includes at least one board member and at least one representative from a developing country.

with small Japanese companies). Yet most multinational corporations still retain the accounting practices of their native countries.[18]

Thus, as indicated, one of the functions of the IASC is harmonizing financial accounting standards.

As mentioned, the process of reducing, or eliminating, conceptually unjustified diversity in financial accounting standards is referred to as harmonization in international accounting. Although harmonization seems especially reasonable in the case of multinational companies, some concept of harmonization may be appropriate for all companies. Three concepts of harmonization have been identified: (1) absolute harmonization, (2) circumstantial harmonization, and (3) purposive harmonization.[19] Under absolute harmonization, one set of accounting standards applies, irrespective of the conditions leading to the production of the accounting information. Under circumstantial harmonization, the same set of accounting standards applies when the underlying conditions, other than the purpose of the accounting information, are similar. Purposive harmonization adds the purpose of the accounting information to the underlying set of conditions considered. Under this concept, the same set of accounting standards applies when all underlying conditions, including the purpose of the accounting information, are similar. Both the IASC and the FASB appear to be operating more consistently with circumstantial harmonization, since both organizations' activities or statements reflect the attitude that the same information can serve many purposes. Most arguments favoring harmonization tend to be applied to both circumstantial and purposive harmonization. The following are the more important of these arguments:

1. Harmonization aids international investors and information intermediaries by facilitating financial statement analysis.
2. By aiding international investors and information intermediaries, harmonization enhances the abilities of international firms to raise capital and facilitates the international allocation of resources.
3. Harmonization facilitates the internationalization of markets which, in turn, reduces difficulties in international trading and pricing.
4. By eliminating unjustified financial statement differences, harmonization leads to more efficient international financial markets.
5. Harmonization simplifies aspects of, and reduces the costs of, international accounting (e.g., the preparation of consolidated financial statements for domestic parent companies and foreign subsidiaries, managerial control activities, and dealing with the standards of different countries).

---

[18] Gerhard G. Mueller, Helen Gernon, and Gary Meek, *Accounting: An International Perspective* (Homewood, IL: Richard D. Irwin, 1991), pp. 43–44.

[19] These concepts also have been referred to as *the absolute uniformity model, the circumstantial uniformity model,* and the *purposive uniformity model,* respectively.

6. Harmonization makes the valuation of firms easier and, thus, facilitates business combination activities.

7. Harmonization facilitates auditing from the international perspective.

8. Harmonization aids in keeping the standard-setting process out of the hands of governments and the United Nations.

9. Harmonization reduces the costs to developing countries of obtaining accounting standards and allows them to fit into the accounting mainstream immediately.

10. Harmonization reduces the burden of taxing authorities in dealing with foreign income.

Each of these arguments indicates directly, or at least implies, that harmonization will provide one group, or another, with an economic benefit. Those who argue against harmonization are opposed primarily to absolute harmonization. Their argument is that the existence of differences in the characteristics of countries implies that the objectives and nature of financial accounting necessarily differ from country to country and, therefore, that absolute harmonization is undesirable. The types of differences mentioned in this context include educational, sociocultural, political and legal (including taxation), and economic (including the economic consequences of standards) differences. It is difficult to argue that neither circumstantial nor purposive harmonization is desirable from the perspective of an international economy, just as it is difficult to argue that neither of these forms is desirable from the viewpoint of the U.S. economy.[20]

Despite the likely benefits from harmonization, the IASC has experienced only limited success in achieving acceptance of its standards. These are several reasons advanced for this ineffectiveness:

1. The existence of conflicts between IASC standards and those of other national and international bodies.[21]

2. The incorporation of accounting procedures into law in many countries.

3. The view that IASC standards should not be required nationally until it is clear that they are acceptable internationally.

4. The limitations of accounting organizations in some countries to require compliance with either national or international standards.

5. The absence of a conceptual framework, such as the FASB's, upon which to base IASC standards.

---

[20] The argument that the free-market approach to the setting of both national and international accounting standards is the superior approach always can be advanced; however, this argument cannot be proved or disproved.

[21] Examples of bodies which may establish harmonizing accounting policy and which require compliance (or have the influence to elicit significant voluntary compliance) are the FASB, the European Community (EC or Common Market), and the Organization for Economic Cooperation and Development (OECD). Additionally, the United Nations (UN) is interested in harmonizing accounting standards for multinational companies and may become involved in standard setting. To date, the UN has made only certain disclosure recommendations.

6. The lack of recognition of the IASC by national governments and international agreements.

7. The inability of the IASC to require compliance with its standards.

8. The political nature of the IASC's due-process, standard-setting process (which parallels the politicization of the FASB's process).

The IASC also has had little success in interesting nonaccounting groups, such as financial analysts, representatives of stock exchanges, and labor unions, in participating in the international standard-setting process. For example, in 1981, the IASC set up a consultative group to increase the involvement of such groups to enhance the acceptability of its standards. Almost all of these groups refused an invitation to join the IASC for a variety of reasons (not necessarily implying lack of support for the concept of international accounting standards). Nevertheless, the IASC has had some successes. For example, some accounting bodies afford IASC and national financial accounting standards equal status, and other accounting bodies declare support for the concept of international accounting standards and state that acceptance of international accounting standards by their members is desirable.

International Financial Reporting

The argument against absolute harmonization is based on the idea that differences in the characteristics of countries, including educational, sociocultural, political and legal, and economic differences, lead to variations in the objectives and natures of their financial accounting processes. This argument is consistent with the view that financial accounting develops in response to the evolution of its immediate environment. Since countries' environments are different, no two countries' financial accounting systems are identical. To provide an overview of international financial reporting, the following paragraphs identify the environmental factors resulting in national accounting system differences (and similarities), discuss variations in national financial reporting in general, and examine approaches to transnational financial reporting.

As mentioned, in international accounting, the phrase *national* (or *local*) *financial reporting* refers to financial reporting within a country, and the phrase *transnational financial reporting* refers to financial reporting across national boundaries. The environmental factors impacting on national financial reporting processes typically are classified consistently with the differences mentioned above. Thus, they are placed in educational, sociocultural, legal and political, and economic classes. Without being specific about class membership, some of the environmental factors tending to impact on the financial reporting process in a particular country include the following:

1. The general literacy of the population.
2. The availability of accounting education.
3. The society's attitudes toward business and accounting.
4. The government's stability.

5. The extent to which laws dictate accounting standards.

6. The legal congruity between financial and tax accounting.

7. The government's attitude about firms' effects on the environment and economic development in general.

8. The degree of private ownership of productive resources and the extent of governmental involvement in the production and the distribution of goods.

9. The sources of funds for capital investment.

10. The extent of reliance on international trade.

11. The degree of inflation.

12. The stage and type of economic development.

13. The political, legal, and religious systems in general.

14. The nature of financial accounting information users.

15. The government's attitude toward the development of particular industries.

16. The existence and extent of development of financial markets.

17. The tendency to import financial technology.[22]

Although differences in factors such as these account for variations in countries' financial accounting systems, the argument that financial accounting develops in response to the evolution of its immediate environment also implies that countries with similar environments have similar financial accounting systems. Consistently, groups of countries with similar environments and similar accounting systems have been identified. For example, Mueller, Gernon, and Meek identify clusters of nations with similar financial accounting processes.[23] These clusters include countries whose financial accounting processes are *similar enough* on significant dimensions to be considered to be using one of several basic accounting models—the more important of which are the British/American model, the Continental model, and the South American model. Illustration 14–13, which is adapted from *Accounting: An International Perspective,* identifies the countries forming the clusters related to these models.

The British/American model, which is an accrual accounting model, is used by more nations than any other. As implied by the above discussion of the FASB's approach to standard setting, this model emphasizes a conceptual, private-sector approach to standard setting and the provision of information that is useful in making economic decisions. In contrast, the Continental model is a legalistic model. That is, this model results primarily from legal requirements that are intended to satisfy various governmental information needs (e.g., for taxation purposes and for demonstrating compliance with, or contribution to, macro-

---

[22] These sorts of factors often are discussed in the international accounting literature. See, for example, Jeffrey S. Arpan and Lee H. Radebaugh, *International Accounting and Multinational Enterprises* (New York: John Wiley & Sons, 1985).

[23] Mueller et al., *Accounting: An International Perspective,* pp. 15–19.

ILLUSTRATION 14–13   Financial Accounting Model Clusters

British/American Model

Australia	India	Papua New Guinea
Bahamas	Indonesia	Philippines
Barbados	Ireland	Puerto Rico
Benin	Israel	Singapore
Bermuda	Jamaica	South Africa
Botswana	Kenya	Tanzania
Canada	Liberia	Trinidad and Tobago
Cayman Islands	Malawi	Uganda
Central America	Malaysia	United Kingdom
Colombia	Mexico	United States
Cyprus	Netherlands	Venezuela
Dominican Republic	New Zealand	Zambia
Fiji	Nigeria	Zimbabwe
Ghana	Pakistan	
Hong Kong	Panama	

Continental Model

Algeria	Germany	Norway
Angola	Greece	Portugal
Austria	Guinea	Senegal
Belgium	Italy	Sierra Leone
Burkina	Ivory Coast	Spain
Cameroon	Japan	Sweden
Denmark	Luxembourg	Switzerland
Egypt	Mali	Togo
France	Morocco	Zaire

South American Model

Argentina	Chile	Paraguay
Bolivia	Ecuador	Peru
Brazil	Guyana	Uruguay

SOURCE: Adapted from Gerhard G. Mueller, Helen Gernon, and Gary Meek, *Accounting: An International Perspective* (Homewood, IL: Richard D. Irwin, 1991), p. 16.

economic or environmental plans). For example, the Japanese Commercial Code, Justice Ministry orders, taxation laws, and Justice Ministry disclosure requirements work together to require Japanese companies to prepare fiscal year financial reports based on prescribed accounting procedures. In form, the South American model is distinguished from the British/American model primarily by its incorporation of general price-level adjustment procedures which are designed to compensate for the effects of high inflation rates. This model is aimed both at the needs of governmental units and the economic decisions of individuals. For example, in Brazil, financial reporting requirements were based primarily on corporation and income tax law prior to 1976. However, under Brazil's Corporation Law of 1976, Brazilian accounting techniques were updated to emphasize both governmental reporting needs and the presentation of information for economic decisions. As indicated, the resulting set of procedures is very similar to those of the British/American model—with the major difference being the incorporation of general price-level adjustment procedures.

Although similar financial reporting practices are followed in clusters of countries, the variation in national financial reporting procedures is significant. Detailed consideration of the variation in worldwide financial reporting practices is outside the scope of this book. Nevertheless, the following discussion provides insights into the magnitudes of existing differences in national financial reporting. In this context, Choi and Bavishi identify the methods used historically by firms in 24 relatively highly developed nations in dealing with 32 financial reporting issues.[24] Some of the issues considered are accounting for general price-level change, accounting for subsidiaries and other investees, the conversion of foreign entity financial statements, and interperiod income tax allocation. The group of 24 countries studied includes the United States, Canada, Brazil, Mexico, the United Kingdom, West Germany, France, Belgium, the Netherlands, Switzerland, Ireland, Austria, Sweden, Denmark, Finland, Norway, Italy, Spain, Japan, Australia, Malaysia, India, South Korea, and South Africa. The variation in practices employed related to the 32 issues was significant. For example, the following table summarizes Choi and Bavishi's findings on the issues of accounting for 21 to 50 percent owned affiliates and the conversion of foreign entity financial statements:

Reporting Issue	*Number of Countries*
Accounting for 21–50 percent owned affiliates:	
Equity method is predominant practice	9
Equity method with minor modification is predominant practice	1
Cost method is predominant practice	11
Both equity and cost methods used	2
Method used could not be determined	$\underline{1}$
	$\underline{\underline{24}}$
Conversion of foreign entity financial statements:	
Temporal method is predominant practice	2
Current rate method is predominant practice	6
Alternative practices followed with no majority	3
Method used could not be determined or not applicable	4
Temporal method not used and alternative used not specified in study	$\underline{9}$
	$\underline{\underline{24}}$

---

[24] Choi and Bavishi, "International Accounting Standards."

As explained, educational, sociocultural, legal and political, and economic factors impact significantly on national financial reporting. Although these factors also affect transnational financial reporting, other considerations tend to dominate in shaping this form of financial reporting. The primary companies concerned with transnational financial reporting are multinational companies. The main factors impacting on transnational reporting appear to be the *global financing strategies* of multinationals and the *transnational investing activities* of those who invest in foreign companies.[25] Multinationals involved in global financing strategies engage in activities such as listing their securities on the stock exchanges of countries other than their own, issuing bonds in these countries, and obtaining bank loans in these nations. Parties engaging in transnational investing purchase the securities of multinationals for their portfolios. Thus, the global financing strategies of multinationals and transnational investing activities create information demands by financial statement users, such as security exchange personnel, underwriters, security analysts, bankers, and investors, which are satisfied through transnational financial reporting.

Multinational companies engage in at least six practices intended to satisfy varying transnational financial reporting demands:

1. Utilizing their existing financial statements.
2. Preparing convenience translations.
3. Preparing convenience financial statements.
4. Restating financial statements on a limited basis.
5. Preparing secondary financial statements.
6. Preparing financial statements consistent with universally applicable accounting standards.[26]

In many cases, it is possible for multinationals to satisfy transnational reporting needs via their *existing financial statements*. For example, this approach often is sufficient for U.S. companies since English is a widely understood language, the dollar is an internationally known currency, and U.S. financial accounting standards are highly respected. Under the *convenience translation* approach, the multinational translates its existing financial statements into the user's language without changing the currency unit or the accounting standards employed. Multinationals preparing *convenience financial statements* translate their existing financial statements into the user's language and currency unit but also do not alter the underlying accounting standards used. Multinationals *restating financial statements on a limited basis* provide significantly improved information over those using the last two methods mentioned. Under limited restatement, the user's language normally is used in the financial statements, although currency unit translation is not necessarily provided. One approach to limited restatement

---

[25] Mueller et al., *Accounting: An International Perspective*, p. 23.

[26] For a more complete discussion of these alternatives, see Mueller et al., *Accounting: An International Perspective*, pp. 26–36.

is for the company to provide a reconciliation of its existing net income with its net income calculated under the user's accounting standards. Under this method, enough information often is provided to allow restatement of the multinational's balance sheet. The second approach to limited restatement is for the multinational simply to restate selected financial statement items (e.g., net income) under the user's accounting standards. *Preparing secondary financial statements* is a complete approach to transnational reporting. Under this approach, the company's financial statements are recast employing the user's language, currency unit, and accounting standards. The final approach to transnational reporting, *preparing financial statements consistent with universally applicable accounting standards,* also is a complete approach, although it may not satisfy all users. Under this approach, the multinational prepares one set of financial statements that is meant to satisfy all users' needs. The statements are prepared consistently with the company's view of the superior set of accounting standards.

Summary

This chapter explains the preparation of consolidated financial statements (including the consolidated statement of cash flows) for domestic companies and their foreign subsidiaries. In this context, *Statement No. 94* indicates that a majority-owned foreign subsidiary is to be consolidated unless it "operates under foreign exchange restrictions, controls, or other governmentally imposed uncertainties so severe that they cast significant doubt on the parent's ability to control the subsidiary." Additionally, the chapter covers the application of the equity method by domestic investors in foreign investees and hedges of net investments (ownership interests) in foreign entities.

This chapter also deals with two general topics relevant to consolidated statements. The first of these topics is the extent to which consolidated financial statements are prepared and encouraged from a worldwide perspective. The chapter shows that the preparation of consolidated financial statements is the exception, rather than the rule, internationally. Nevertheless, a variety of organizations are working to promote the preparation of such statements. For example, the IASC has issued pronouncements calling for the consolidation of both local and foreign subsidiaries.

The second general topic covered is international financial reporting. One subject dealt with in this context is international financial accounting standard setting. The chapter indicates that the international counterpart of the FASB is the IASC. The IASC's standard-setting process is a due-process procedure, similar to that of the FASB, which is designed to protect the interests of those affected by financial reporting. The IASC was formed primarily in response to the use of widely differing accounting principles by essentially similar firms, especially multinational firms which have, in effect, transcended their national accounting principles. Thus, one of the IASC's goals is the harmonization of financial accounting standards.

The process of reducing, or eliminating, conceptually unjustified variations in financial accounting standards is referred to as *harmonization* in international accounting. Three concepts of harmonization have been identified: (1) absolute harmonization, (2) circumstantial harmonization, and (3) purposive harmonization. Those who argue against harmonization are opposed primarily to absolute harmonization. Their argument is that the existence of differences in the characteristics of countries implies that the objectives and nature of financial accounting necessarily differ from country to country and, therefore, that absolute harmonization is undesirable.

This argument is consistent with the view that financial accounting develops nationally in response to the evolution of its immediate environment (i.e., in response to the development of the educational, sociocultural, legal and political, and economic aspects of its environment). It also is consistent with the existence of identified clusters of countries with similar environments and similar accounting systems. Each cluster includes countries whose financial accounting processes are similar enough on major dimensions to be considered to be using one of three basic accounting models—the British/American model, the Continental model, or the South American model. Despite the existence of these clusters and models, diversity in accounting standards is the rule in international financial accounting.

In contrast to national financial reporting, transnational financial reporting appears to be more heavily influenced by the global financing strategies of multinationals and the transnational investing activities of those who invest in foreign companies. The companies tending to be most concerned with transnational financial reporting are multinational companies. Multinational companies engage in various practices intended to satisfy transnational financial reporting demands, including these:

1. Utilizing their existing financial statements.
2. Preparing convenience translations.
3. Preparing convenience financial statements.
4. Restating financial statements on a limited basis.
5. Preparing secondary financial statements.
6. Preparing financial statements consistent with universally applicable accounting standards.

Questions

1. Identify the requirements of *Statement of Financial Accounting Standards No. 94* with respect to the consolidation of foreign subsidiaries.
2. How is the differential accounted for under the current rate method? How is it accounted for under the temporal method?
3. What entries are recorded by a parent company under the equity method for a foreign subsidiary whose financial statements are translated into the parent's reporting currency using the current rate method?
4. What entries are recorded by a parent company under the equity method for a foreign subsidiary whose financial statements are remeasured into the parent's reporting currency?
5. Contrast the basic consolidated statement working paper entries under the temporal and the current rate methods.

6. Discuss the accounting procedures required by *Statement of Financial Accounting Standards No. 52* for intercompany foreign currency transactions of a long-term investment nature under the temporal and the current rate methods.

7. Discuss the basic requirements for preparing a consolidated statement of cash flows under *Statement of Financial Accounting Standards No. 95.*

8. Discuss the procedures involved in hedging a net investment in a foreign entity. Also, discuss the factors involved in achieving a successful hedge of this type.

9. Identify the exchange rate that should be used in eliminating intercompany profits.

10. Discuss the segmental disclosures related to the operations of consolidated foreign subsidiaries and export sales required by *Statement of Financial Accounting Standards No. 14.*

11. Discuss the disclosures related to previously and currently unconsolidated foreign subsidiaries required by *Statement of Financial Accounting Standards No. 94.*

12. Discuss the preparation of consolidated financial statements from the international perspective.

13. Describe the operations and the standard-setting process of the International Accounting Standards Committee.

14. Contrast the standard-setting processes of the International Accounting Standards Board and the Financial Accounting Standards Board.

15. Discuss the harmonization of financial accounting standards.

16. Identify the 10 factors which you think are most important in shaping national financial accounting systems.

17. Distinguish between national financial reporting and transnational financial reporting.

18. Identify the approaches used by multinational companies in transnational financial reporting.

19. Discuss the British/American, Continental, and South American financial reporting models.

20. Discuss the issue of whether consistency is the exception, rather than the rule, in international financial reporting.

Exercises

Exercise 14–1   (Current Rate Method, Differential, and Related Equity Method Entries)

P Company purchases all of the outstanding stock of its new foreign subsidiary, S Company, on January 1, 19X1, for $40,000. The exchange rate on this date between the dollar and S Company's local currency units (LCU) is LCU 1 = $.40. S Company has net assets of 70,000 LCU on January 1, 19X1. The fair value of S Company's property, plant, and equipment (life of 5 years) is 10,000 LCUs greater than book value on date of acquisition; after prior allocation, any remaining differential is allocated to goodwill (life of 20 years). S Company's functional currency is its local currency.

On December 31, 19X1, the exchange rate is LCU 1 = $.45. The weighted-average exchange rate for 19X1 is LCU 1 = $.42.

Required:

a. Prepare schedules for 19X1 which show differential allocation and amortization related to P Company's application of the equity method.
b. Prepare P Company's 19X1 equity method entries related to the differential.

Exercise 14–2   (Temporal Method, Differential, and Related Equity Method Entries)

Use the information of Exercise 14–1, except now assume that S Company's functional currency is the reporting currency—the dollar. With this change, complete the requirements of Exercise 14–1.

Exercise 14–3   (Temporal Method, Differential, and Related Equity Method Entries)

Carter Company, an Atlanta Company, purchases 100 percent of the outstanding capital stock of Fritz Company, a German Company, on January 1, 19X2, for $380,000. The book and fair values of Fritz Company's assets and liabilities on this date are as follows:

	Marks	
	Book Value	Fair Value
Cash	100,000	100,000
Accounts receivable	150,000	150,000
Inventory	250,000	300,000
Plant and equipment (net)	400,000	600,000
Totals	900,000	1,150,000
Bank notes and bonds payable	300,000	300,000
Net assets	600,000	850,000
Composed of:		
Capital stock	100,000	
Retained earnings	500,000	
Total	600,000	

The inventory was completely sold in 19X2. The plant and equipment has a remaining life of 10 years, and any goodwill arising from the acquisition is amortized over 20 years.

The exchange rate was .40 on January 1, 19X2. It was .35 on December 31, 19X2. The weighted-average exchange rate for 19X2 was .38.

Required:

a. Assuming that Fritz Company's functional currency is the dollar, prepare a differential allocation and amortization schedule covering the life of the differential.
b. Prepare Carter Company's 19X2 equity method entries related to the differential.

Exercise 14–4   (Current Rate Method, Differential, and Related Equity Method Entries)

Use the information of Exercise 14–3, except now assume that Fritz Company's functional currency is the mark. With this change, complete the requirements listed below.

Required:

a. Prepare schedules for 19X2 which show differential allocation and amortization related to Carter Company's application of the equity method.

b. Prepare Carter Company's 19X2 equity method entries related to the differential.

Exercise 14–5   (Current Rate Method and Statement of Cash Flows Working Papers)

Mission Company is a foreign subsidiary of a U.S. parent. Mission Company's trial balances at the beginning and end of 19X1, in local currency units (LCU), are shown below.

	12/31/X1	1/1/X1
Cash	300,000	300,000
Plant and Equipment (net)	2,400,000	2,000,000
Depreciation Expense	200,000	
Other Expenses	500,000	
Totals	3,400,000	2,300,000
Current Payables	50,000	150,000
Long-Term Debt	1,000,000	1,000,000
Capital Stock	500,000	500,000
Retained Earnings (1/1/X1)	650,000	650,000
Sales	1,200,000	
Totals	3,400,000	2,300,000

The following additional information is available:

1. Mission's functional currency is its local currency.
2. The exchange rates between the dollar and the LCU for 19X1 are as follows:
   January 1, 19X1—.30.
   Weighted average for 19X1—.36.
   December 31, 19X1—.40.
   Date of acquisition—.25.
3. There has been no change in Mission Company's capital structure. On December 31, 19X0, Mission Company's Retained Earnings had a credit balance of $175,000, and the Cumulative Foreign Exchange Translation Adjustments account had a credit balance of $45,000.
4. There were no retirements of plant and equipment during 19X1. Mission Company's new plant and equipment was acquired when the spot rate equaled the weighted-average rate for the year.

Required:

a. Prepare a foreign currency translation working paper for Mission Company for the year ended December 31, 19X1 (or review your solution to Problem 13–8).

b. Prepare working papers for a statement of cash flows for Mission Company for the year ended December 31, 19X2, which can be used by its parent company in preparing a consolidated statement of cash flows. Also, calculate the effect of the rate changes on cash.

Exercise 14–6   (Temporal Method and Statement of Cash Flows Working Papers)

Use the information of Exercise 14–5, except now assume that Mission Company's functional currency is the reporting currency—the dollar. With these changes, complete the requirements of Exercise 14–5. Utilize the additional assumptions given in Problem 13–9.

Exercise 14–7   (Hedge of Net Investment in Foreign Entity)

Taylor Company, a New Mexico Company, owns 100 percent of Fosteaux Company, a French Company. Taylor Company decides to hedge its net investment in Fosteaux Company by selling francs on October 1, 19X1, for delivery on December 31, 19X1. On this date, both the spot rate and the 90-day forward rate are .10. All months are assumed to have 30 days. The spot rate at the beginning of the year was .12, and the spot rate at year-end was .08. The weighted-average exchange rate for the year was .095. Taylor Company expects Fosteaux Company to have a $50,000 translation loss for 19X1. Fosteaux Company's functional currency is the franc.

Required:

a. Calculate the number of francs which Taylor Company must sell to produce a perfect hedge assuming Fosteaux Company's actual translation loss for 19X1 is $50,000.

b. Prepare Taylor Company's equity method entry related to Fosteaux Company's translation loss.

c. Prepare Taylor Company's entries related to its hedging transaction.

Exercise 14–8   (Hedge of Net Investment in Foreign Entity)

A U.S. Company purchased a 100 percent interest in a British subsidiary on January 1, 19X1, for 1 million pounds. The exchange rate on this date was 1.20. The functional currency of the subsidiary is the pound. There is no differential.

The parent company borrows 1,500,000 pounds on January 1, 19X1, from a London bank to hedge against a continuing decline in the value of the pound relative to the dollar. This loan, which is denominated in pounds, is designated a hedge, on an after-tax basis, of the net investment in the British subsidiary.

On December 31, 19X1, the exchange rate is 1.10, and the weighted-average exchange rate for 19X1 is 1.14. The subsidiary reports 19X1 net income of 200,000 pounds. The parent does not record deferred taxes on the subsidiary's net income (consistent with *APB Opinion No. 23*) since the evidence implies that the British subsidiary will invest its undistributed earnings indefinitely. (See footnote 14 of Chapter 13 for discussion of conditions under which deferred taxes are not recorded on unremitted subsidiary earnings.)

The loan is outstanding during all of 19X1. Therefore, the exchange gain or loss on the loan creates a timing difference for income tax allocation purposes. The U.S. parent's marginal income tax rate is 40 percent.

Required:

Prepare the entries that the U.S. parent makes on December 31, 19X1, to record its equity in the subsidiary's 19X1 operations (including the translation gain or loss) and to adjust the balance of the loan for exchange rate fluctuation. Assume no prior entries have affected the loan payable and ignore interest. Explain the reasons for your treatment of the exchange gain or loss. (*Hint:* It may be useful to review paragraphs 20–21 and the related paragraphs in the "Basis for Conclusions" section in *Statement of Financial Accounting Standards No. 52.*)

Problems

Problem 14–9   (Temporal Method Working Paper, Differential, and Equity Method Entries)

This problem, and the following two problems, extend the data of Case 1 presented in this chapter for Monroe Company and its French subsidiary, Bordeaux Company, to the year 19X2. In solving these problems, you may need to refer to the text for 19X1 data.

Bordeaux Company's trial balance at December 31, 19X2, is as follows:

	Francs
Cash	1,200,000
Receivables	400,000
Plant and Equipment (net)	1,300,000
Depreciation Expense	300,000*
Other Expenses	500,000
Total	3,700,000
Current Payables	300,000
Long-Term Debt	900,000
Sales	1,500,000
Capital Stock	100,000
Retained Earnings (1/1)	900,000
Total	3,700,000

* Depreciation expense is higher in 19X2 than in 19X1 because some assets are being depreciated using the units-of-service approach.

The directly quoted, spot rate for the franc at December 31, 19X2, is .12. The weighted-average exchange rate for 19X2 is .105. Assume that Bordeaux Company's functional currency is the reporting currency (the dollar) in this problem. For simplicity, assume that the newly acquired plant and equipment is purchased in 19X2 when the spot rate equals the weighted-average rate for the year and that Bordeaux Company does not depreciate new equipment in the year of acquisition. Assume also that the new long-term debt is issued at the same time.

Required:

a. Prepare a foreign currency translation working paper for Bordeaux Company for the year ended December 31, 19X2 (or review your solution to Problem 13–11).

b. Prepare schedules for 19X2 which show differential allocation and amortization related to Monroe Company's application of the equity method.

c. Prepare Monroe Company's 19X2 equity method entries.

Problem 14–10   (Consolidated Statement Working Paper under Temporal Method and Calculation of Consolidated Net Income)

Monroe Company's trial balance at December 31, 19X2, is as follows:

Assets	
Investment in Bordeaux Company	$251,000
Liabilities and Owners' Equity	
Capital Stock	$150,000
Retained Earnings (1/1)	47,500
Equity in Subsidiary Earnings	53,500
	$251,000

This trial balance assumes that Bordeaux Company's functional currency is the dollar and that all 19X2 equity method entries have been made.

Required:

a. Prepare the solution to Problem 14–9 and use the resulting information to prepare a consolidated statement working paper for Monroe Company and its subsidiary, Bordeaux Company, for the year ended December 31, 19X2.

b. Calculate 19X2 consolidated net income incrementally.

Problem 14–11   (Consolidated Statement of Cash Flows under Temporal Method)

Prepare the solutions to Problems 14–9 and 14–10 and use the resulting information to prepare working papers for a consolidated statement of cash flows for Monroe Company and its subsidiary, Bordeaux Company, for the year ended December 31, 19X2. Also, calculate the effect of the rate changes on cash.

Problem 14–12   (Current Rate Method Working Paper, Differential, and Equity Method Entries)

This problem, and the following three problems, extend the data of Case 3 presented in this chapter for Monroe Company and its French subsidiary, Bordeaux Company, to the year 19X2. In solving these problems, you may need to refer to the text for 19X1 data.

Bordeaux Company's trial balance at December 31, 19X2, is as follows:

	Francs
Cash	1,200,000
Receivables	400,000
Plant and Equipment (net)	1,300,000
Depreciation Expense	300,000*
Other Expenses	500,000
Total	3,700,000
Current Payables	300,000
Long-Term Debt	900,000
Sales	1,500,000
Capital Stock	100,000
Retained Earnings (1/1)	900,000
Total	3,700,000

* Depreciation expense is higher in 19X2 than in 19X1 because some assets are being depreciated using the units-of-service approach.

The directly quoted, spot rate for the franc at December 31, 19X2 is .12. The weighted-average exchange rate for 19X2 is .105. Assume that Bordeaux Company's functional currency is the franc in this problem. For simplicity, assume that the newly acquired plant and equipment is purchased in 19X2 when the spot rate equals the weighted-average rate for the year and that Bordeaux Company does not depreciate new equipment in the year of acquisition. Assume also that the new long-term debt is issued at the same time.

Required:

a. Prepare a foreign currency translation working paper for Bordeaux Company for the year ended December 31, 19X2 (or review your solution to Problem 13–13).

b. Prepare schedules for 19X2 which show differential allocation and amortization related to Monroe Company's application of the equity method.

c. Prepare Monroe Company's 19X2 equity method entries.

Problem 14–13   (Consolidated Statement Working Paper under Current Rate Method and Calculation of Consolidated Net Income)

Monroe Company's trial balance at December 31, 19X2, is as follows:

Assets	
Investment in Bordeaux Company	$259,200

Liabilities and Owners' Equity	
Capital Stock	$150,000
Retained Earnings (1/1)	47,300
Cumulative Foreign Exchange	
Translation Adjustments	6,250
Equity in Subsidiary Earnings	55,650
	$259,200

This trial balance assumes that Bordeaux Company's functional currency is the franc and that all 19X2 equity method entries have been made.

Required:

a. Prepare the solution to Problem 14–12 and use the resulting information to prepare a consolidated statement working paper for Monroe Company and its subsidiary, Bordeaux Company, for the year ended December 31, 19X2.

b. Calculate 19X2 consolidated net income incrementally.

Problem 14–14   (Consolidated Statement of Cash Flows under Current Rate Method)

Prepare the solutions to Problems 14–12 and 14–13 and use the resulting information to prepare working papers for a consolidated statement of cash flows for Monroe Company and its subsidiary, Bordeaux Company, for the year ended December 31, 19X2. Also, calculate the effect of the rate changes on cash.

Problem 14–15   (Variation of Problems 14–12, 14–13, and 14–14 Incorporating Hedge of Net Investment)

Assume the information of Problem 14–12, except now assume that the December 31, 19X2, spot rate is .08 and the weighted-average exchange rate for 19X2 is .09. Assume also that Monroe Company decides to hedge its net investment in Bordeaux Company by selling 2,700,000 francs on July 1, 19X2, for delivery on December 31, 19X2. On this date, both the spot rate and the 180-day forward rate are .09. All months are assumed to have 30 days. With these changes, complete the following requirements.

Required:

a. Complete the requirements of Problem 14–12.

b. Prepare Monroe Company's entries related to its hedging transaction.

c. Complete the requirements of Problem 14–13 given the following December 31, 19X2, trial balance for Monroe Company.

Assets	
Cash	$ 27,000
Investment in Bordeaux Company	172,800
Total	$199,800
Liabilities and Owners' Equity	
Capital Stock	$150,000
Retained Earnings (1/1)	47,300
Cumulative Foreign Exchange	
Translation Adjustments	(45,200)
Equity in Subsidiary Earnings	47,700
Total	$199,800

This trial balance assumes that Bordeaux Company's functional currency is the franc and that all 19X2 equity method entries have been made.

d. Complete the requirements of Problem 14–14.

Problem 14–16   (Temporal Method Working Paper, Differential, Equity Method Entries, and Long-Term Intercompany Payable)

This problem, and the following two problems, extend the data of Case 2 presented in this chapter for Monroe Company and its French subsidiary, Bordeaux Company, to the year 19X2. In solving these problems, you may need to refer to the text for 19X1 data.

Bordeaux Company's trial balance at December 31, 19X2, is as follows:

	Francs
Cash	1,200,000
Receivables	400,000
Plant and Equipment (net)	1,300,000
Depreciation Expense	300,000*
Other Expenses	500,000
Total	3,700,000
Current Payables	300,000
Long-Term Debt—Monroe	700,000
Other Long-Term Debt	200,000
Sales	1,500,000
Capital Stock	100,000
Retained Earnings (1/1)	900,000
Total	3,700,000

* Depreciation expense is higher in 19X2 than in 19X1 because some assets are being depreciated using the units-of-service approach.

The directly quoted, spot rate for the franc at December 31, 19X2, is .12. The weighted-average exchange rate for 19X2 is .105. Assume that Bordeaux Company's functional currency is the reporting currency (the dollar) in this problem. For simplicity, assume that the newly acquired plant and equipment is purchased in 19X2 when the spot rate equals the weighted-average rate for the year and that Bordeaux Company does not depreciate new equipment in the year of acquisition. Assume also that the new long-term debt is issued at the same time.

Required:

a. Prepare a foreign currency translation working paper for Bordeaux Company for the year ended December 31, 19X2 (or review your solution to Problem 13–15).

b. Prepare schedules for 19X2 which show differential allocation and amortization related to Monroe Company's application of the equity method.

c. Prepare Monroe Company's 19X2 equity method entries.

d. Prepare Monroe Company's 19X2 entry to record its foreign exchange gain or loss on its intercompany receivable.

Problem 14–17   (Consolidated Statement Working Paper under Temporal Method, Calculation of Consolidated Net Income, and Long-Term Intercompany Payable)

Monroe Company's trial balance at December 31, 19X2, is as follows:

Assets	
Investment in Bordeaux Company	$273,500
Long-Term Receivable—Bordeaux	84,000
Total	$357,500
Liabilities and Owners' Equity	
Capital Stock	$237,500
Retained Earnings (1/1)	41,250
Equity in Subsidiary Earnings	78,750
Total	$357,500

This trial balance assumes that Bordeaux Company's functional currency is the dollar and that all 19X2 equity method entries have been made.

Required:

a. Prepare the solution to Problem 14–16 and use the resulting information to prepare a consolidated statement working paper for Monroe Company and its subsidiary, Bordeaux Company, for the year ended December 31, 19X2.

b. Calculate 19X2 consolidated net income incrementally.

Problem 14–18   (Consolidated Statement of Cash Flows under Temporal Method with Long-Term Intercompany Payable)

Prepare the solutions to Problems 14–16 and 14–17 and use the resulting information to prepare working papers for a consolidated statement of cash flows for Monroe Company and its subsidiary, Bordeaux Company, for the year ended December 31, 19X2. Also, calculate the effect of the rate changes on cash.

Problem 14–19   (Working Papers and Entries under Temporal Method)

May Company, a Seattle firm, holds an 80 percent ownership interest in Seneque Company, a South African corporation. This interest was acquired when Seneque Company was chartered. The dollar is Seneque Company's functional currency. Seneque Company's trial balances at the beginning and end of 19X7 are shown below.

	Rands	
	12/31/X7	*1/1/X7*
Cash	60,000	40,000
Accounts Receivable	100,000	120,000
Airplanes (net)	500,000	580,000
Depreciation Expense	80,000	
Other Expenses	160,000	
Total	900,000	740,000
Allowance for Doubtful Accounts	10,000	20,000
Accounts Payable		130,000
Notes Payable	200,000	200,000
Capital Stock	100,000	100,000
Retained Earnings (1/1)	290,000	290,000
Revenue	300,000	
Totals	900,000	740,000

The capital stock was issued seven years ago when the company was formed to provide charter air service. On this date, the exchange rate was .80. The current fleet of airplanes was acquired three years ago when the exchange rate was .90. The notes were given to a local bank at the same time. The spot rates for rands in 19X7 were as follows:

January 1	.57
Weighted average	.53
December 31	.50

Seneque Company's retained earnings was $333,700 in its converted December 31, 19X6, balance sheet.

Required:

a. Prepare a foreign currency translation working paper for Seneque Company for the year ended December 31, 19X7 (or review your solution to Problem 13–17).

b. Prepare May Company's 19X7 equity method entries related to the conversion of Seneque Company's financial statements into dollars.

c. Prepare May Company's consolidated statement working paper entries for 19X7.

d. Prepare working papers for a statement of cash flows for Seneque Company for the year ended December 31, 19X7, which can be used by May Company in preparing a consolidated statement of cash flows. Also, calculate the effect of the rate changes on cash.

Problem 14–20   (Working Papers and Entries under Current Rate Method)

Use the information of Problem 14–19, except now assume that (1) Seneque Company's functional currency is the rand, (2) its December 31, 19X6, retained earnings was $200,000, and (3) its December 31, 19X6, Cumulative Foreign Exchange Translation Adjustments balance was a debit balance of $57,700. With these changes, complete the requirements listed below.

Required:

a. Prepare a foreign currency translation working paper for Seneque Company for the year ended December 31, 19X7 (or review your solution to Problem 13–18).

b. Prepare May Company's 19X7 equity method entries related to the conversion of Seneque Company's financial statements into dollars.

c. Prepare May Company's consolidated statement working paper entries for 19X7.

d. Prepare working papers for a statement of cash flows for Seneque Company for the year ended December 31, 19X7, which can be used by May Company in preparing a consolidated statement of cash flows. Also, calculate the effect of the rate changes on cash.

Problem 14–21   (Working Papers and Entries under Temporal Method)

Faison Importers Company, an Arizona company, holds a 70 percent interest in Mommessin Company, a French company. This ownership interest was acquired when Mommessin Company was initially incorporated. The dollar is Mommessin Company's functional currency. Mommessin Company's trial balances at the beginning and end of 19X1 are shown below:

	Francs	
	12/31/X1	*1/1/X1*
Cash	40,000	60,000
Accounts Receivable	20,000	10,000
Inventory	60,000	70,000
Plant and Equipment (net)	100,000	120,000
Cost of Goods Sold	110,000	
Depreciation Expense	20,000	
Other Expenses	50,000	
Totals	400,000	260,000
Notes Payable (short term)	60,000	100,000
Capital Stock	100,000	100,000
Retained Earnings (1/1)	60,000	60,000
Sales	180,000	
Totals	400,000	260,000

The capital stock was issued and plant and equipment acquired four years ago when the exchange rate was .30. The beginning (ending) inventory was acquired when the spot rate was .23 (.21). The weighted-average exchange rate for 19X1 was .22. Retained earnings was $15,200 in the converted December 31, 19X0, balance sheet of Mommessin Company. The spot rate for the franc on January 1, 19X1, was .23, and at December 31, 19X1, it was .20. Mommessin Company's notes payable are related to purchases of inventory.

Required:

a. Prepare a foreign currency translation working paper for Mommessin Company for the year ended December 31, 19X1 (or review your solution to Problem 13–20).

b. Prepare Faison Company's 19X1 equity method entries related to the conversion of Mommessin Company's financial statements into dollars.

c. Prepare Faison Company's consolidated statement working paper entries for 19X1.

d. Prepare working papers for a statement of cash flows for Mommessin Company for the year ended December 31, 19X1, which can be used by Faison Company in preparing a consolidated statement of cash flows. Also, calculate the effect of the rate changes on cash.

Problem 14–22   (Working Papers and Entries under Current Rate Method)

Use the information of Problem 14–21, except now assume that (1) Mommessin Company's functional currency is the franc, (2) its December 31, 19X0, retained earnings was $25,000, and (3) its December 31, 19X0, Cumulative Foreign Exchange Translation Adjustments balance was a debit of $18,200. With these changes, complete the requirements listed below.

Required:

a. Prepare a foreign currency translation working paper for Mommessin Company for the year ended December 31, 19X1 (or review your solution to Problem 13–21).

b. Prepare Faison Company's 19X1 equity method entries related to the conversion of Mommessin Company's financial statements into dollars.

c. Prepare Faison Company's consolidated statement working paper entries for 19X1.

d. Prepare working papers for a statement of cash flows for Mommessin Company for the year ended December 31, 19X1, which can be used by Faison Company in preparing a consolidated statement of cash flows. Also, calculate the effect of the rate changes on cash.

UNIT IV

Fiduciary and Institutional Accounting

Chapter Outline

The partnership is a form of business organization wherein two or more individuals associate themselves in a joint profit-making endeavor. A number of problems peculiar to this type of organizational structure call for unique accounting procedures for reporting on partnership operations and for disclosing the economic and legal equities of the various parties having an interest in partnership assets. These accounting techniques will be the focus of attention in this and the following two chapters.

NATURE OF A PARTNERSHIP

Although the common law originally provided the legal framework within which partnership operations were generally conducted, most states have now adopted the Uniform Partnership Act, or some variant thereof, as the controlling statutory authority. Emphasis is hereafter directed toward relevant provisions of this act, which is reproduced in the appendix to this chapter.

Aggregate versus Entity Concept

Section 6 of the Uniform Partnership Act defines a partnership as "an association of two or more persons to carry on as co-owners a business for profit."[1] This definition suggests an aggregate, or proprietary, concept of the partnership as the underlying legal philosophy. A partnership is perceived as being nothing more than an aggregation of the rights and responsibilities of the individual partners. Such a notion was fundamental to the structure of the common law and has been extended in the Uniform Partnership Act in the provision that the individual partners are jointly liable for all debts and obligations of the partnership (Section 15). Yet the dominant theme of the act nonetheless appears to rest on a concept of the partnership as a legal entity, separate and distinct from the individual partners who compose the ownership group. This point of view is implicit in numerous provisions, among which are the following:

1. In the event of liquidation, partnership creditors have priority in respect to the assets of the partnership, and creditors of the individual partners are given priority in respect to the partners' personal assets (Section 40).
2. Title to partnership assets may be vested in the name of the partnership (Section 8).
3. A clear distinction is drawn between the partners' rights to partnership assets and their interests in the partnership entity (Sections 25 and 26).

---

[1] Section 2 defines the words *person* and *business* as they are used in the definition of a partnership; Section 6 provides criteria for the legal determination of the *existence* of a partnership.

4. A continuity of the partnership organization may exist under circumstances which formerly, under the common law, would have caused a dissolution of the partnership (see, for example, Section 23, continuation of the partnership beyond a fixed term, and Section 27, assignment of a partner's interest in the partnership).

Notwithstanding these evidences of the entity concept of the partnership organization, many current accounting practices continue to emphasize the aggregate aspects of the partnership. This is no doubt due in large measure to an inheritance of the proprietary emphasis from both accounting and law, and it derives additional support from current provisions of the Internal Revenue Code. The following two examples illustrate the basic proprietary emphasis of the Code:

1. When individual partners contribute assets to the partnership, the existing tax bases transfer to the partnership, regardless of market values existing at the time of the contribution.
2. The income tax is levied on the individual partners' shares of periodic net income of the partnership and is reported in their separate returns; it is not assessed on the net income of the partnership.

The existence of such tax legislation partially explains the continuing infusion of the aggregate notion in partnership accounting. It does not, however, provide strong theoretical justification for the practice. Specific examples of the aggregate and entity concepts of the partnership will be referred to subsequently in this chapter.

Partnership Agreement

Before a particular organizational form is selected for a business activity, the interested parties should carefully analyze the advantages and disadvantages of alternative types of organizations—the corporation, general partnership, limited partnership, and so forth. If a general partnership is regarded as the best choice, the partners should agree on basic provisions within which they will operate—from initial formation, through operating routines and realignment of ownership interests, to eventual dissolution of the partnership. Appropriate attention to the details of these provisions at the time the partnership is initially formed minimizes or eliminates the subsequent emergence of possible inequities and legal uncertainties regarding the relationship between partners and their relations with outside parties.

The partnership agreement may be either a written or an oral contract. However, a formal, written agreement between the partners, often called the *articles of partnership,* or *copartnership,* is believed to be preferable in delineating the individual partners' rights and responsibilities. The importance of this agreement cannot be overemphasized. Although the Uniform Partnership Act imposes certain obligations on the partnership that may not be avoided or overcome, such as joint liability for all partnership debts, most of the provisions of this act control *only* in the absence of an express agreement to the contrary among the partners. Indeed, judicial remedy is often based on the court's interpretation of the partners' *intent,* when in fact the partners may not have anticipated a particular problem currently in dispute. Consequently, partners would be wise to seek the counsel of both an accountant and an attorney in formulating a comprehensive, *written* agreement indicating their intentions in various areas of partners' responsibilities and interests, which, if omitted or ambiguously drafted, may subsequently cause dispute and possible litigation.

Important provisions in the articles of partnership, including the purpose of the partnership, management rights and authority, and causes of dissolution, should reflect clearly the partners' intentions in terms of prevailing legal doctrine. There are also a number of legally unregulated areas of mutual interest to the several partners that have significant accounting (and equity) implications. The accountant may offer valuable counsel in these areas. Among the more important accounting-related issues that should be addressed in the agreement are the following:

1. The assets that the partners intially are to contribute to the partnership, and the monetary value to be ascribed thereto, should be itemized.

2. A clear distinction should be drawn between the individual partners' initial interests in partnership capital and their interests in subsequent profits or losses. If the initial interest in capital is not consistent with a summation of the agreed-upon values for the contributed assets, the agreement should be specific in regard to the treatment of this difference. For example, if the partners insist on an equal dollar interest in capital even though the valuations of their contributed assets are not equal, two different accounting solutions are possible: either *(a)* a bonus, or capital transfer, may be effected between the partners in order to equalize their capital credits or *(b)* intangible assets, which may derive from unusual managerial ability or widespread customer appeal and which apparently are implicit in such an agreement, may be recognized in the accounts. Although the judgment of the partners should not be the singular criterion for recognizing intangible assets in the partnership books, an explicit indication in the partnership agreement of the purported existence of such intangibles does provide an initial argument for account recognition.

3. The basis for dividing partnership profits should be expressly stated. In the absence of a contrary agreement, Section 18 of the Uniform Partnership Act provides that the partners shall share equally in profits. If it is desired that individual partners be rewarded for their separate capital contributions and/or services to the partnership before any residual profits are allocated according to a profit-sharing ratio, the basis or monetary value for each factor should be specified.

4. If contributed capital is to be a basis for allocating partnership profits, the agreement normally should be responsive to the following questions:
   a. Is the allocation to be based on initial capital contributions, or capital as adjusted by subsequent contributions, profits, and/or withdrawals?

       b. If the allocation is computed upon adjusted capital, is it to be based on beginning, average, or ending capital balances for the year?

       c. In the event that average or ending capital balances are used, what treatment should be accorded current withdrawals? In particular, if it is desired to distinguish between capital withdrawals and withdrawals in anticipation of the current period's profits, the basis for the distinction should be expressly stated. Moreover, when the distinction is made, the accounting treatment of amounts available for withdrawal but permitted to remain in the business must be established.

5. Section 18 of the act further provides that losses are to be shared in the profit-sharing ratio. Thus, if it is desired to protect a partner whose principal contribution is service from incurring a disproportionate share of possible losses, special loss-sharing ratios should be indicated.

6. The bases for calculating the monetary equity of a withdrawing partner, either through retirement or death, should be outlined. A withdrawal may involve consideration of such factors as the possible revaluation of tangible assets and the recognition of implicit intangible asset values.

7. If net income and the partners' drawing accounts are to be closed to the capital accounts at the end of the accounting period, thereby increasing or decreasing the total contributed capital, this closing sequence should be indicated. Such a provision may be important in the event the partnership is dissolved and assets are distributed to the retiring partners.

Although this list of significant provisions is necessarily incomplete, it does indicate the *type* of accounting considerations that are important in a careful formulation of the partnership agreement.

PARTNERSHIP FORMATION

The initial formation of a partnership presents relatively few difficult accounting problems. In the event that there exists a predecessor business, an election must be made as to whether its records are to be preserved; if not, new books must be opened. In the former case, only those entries necessary to record the contributions of partners not previously affiliated with the predecessor are required; in the latter case, all contributions must be entered in the new records. Based on the provisions of the partnership agreement, the opening journal entries for the new partnership call for recording the assets contributed and the liabilities assumed. The partners' respective monetary (dollar) interests in the initial capital of the organization are entered as credits to their individual capital accounts. The following two cases illustrate typical accounting entries to open the books of a new partnership.

Case 1. Initial Capital Balances Equal to Fair Values of Tangible Net Assets Contributed

The partnership agreement of X and Y lists the following assets that are to constitute the resources of the new XY Partnership:

	Contributed by	
	X	*Y*
Cash	$10,000	$20,000
Merchandise		10,000
Building		30,000
Furniture and equipment	5,000	

The building is subject to a mortgage loan of $25,000, which is to be assumed by the partnership. The values represent the partners' best estimates of fair market values.

The journal entry to open the books of the partnership is as follows:

Cash	30,000	
Inventory	10,000	
Building	30,000	
Furniture and Equipment	5,000	
Mortgage Payable		25,000
X, Capital		15,000
Y, Capital		35,000

In this case, the partners' capital credits are based on the fair market value of the net assets contributed by each partner.

Case 2. Equal Initial Capital Balances

Assume that in the previous illustration, the partnership agreement provided that the partners initially should have an equal interest in partnership capital (or partnership net assets).

Two accounting solutions are possible. If the partners wish to record only the tangible assets identified in the partnership agreement, the capital accounts are equalized by transferring capital equity from Y to X so that each partner receives a capital credit of $25,000 (one half of $50,000 net assets).

Cash	30,000	
Inventory	10,000	
Building	30,000	
Furniture and Equipment	5,000	
Mortgage Payable		25,000
X, Capital		25,000
Y, Capital		25,000

Accountants characterize this type of entry as one in which Y pays a *bonus* of $10,000 to X, in the form of the increased monetary equity in the recorded net assets of the firm. One may ask, why would Y agree to pay this bonus? Presumably Y believes that X brings some intangible economic value to the partnership in addition to the assets enumerated in the partnership agreement. Whether this additional value will be realized eventually is uncertain at this time. Accordingly, the bonus method of equalizing the capital credits reflects a traditional accounting "wait and see" attitude toward the worth of the alleged intangible assets.

Alternatively, the different values of contributed net assets may be cited as sufficiently strong evidence to justify recognition of an intangible asset contributed by X to the partnership. In the absence of any other information, this asset is presumed to be goodwill. Assigning a value of $20,000 to the goodwill acknowledges equal contributions of net assets by both X and Y. The entry under this alternative follows:

Cash	30,000	
Inventory	10,000	
Building	30,000	
Furniture and Equipment	5,000	
Goodwill (or some other intangible asset)	20,000	
Mortgage Payable		25,000
X, Capital		35,000
Y, Capital		35,000

The net assets of the partnership following the opening entry, often referred to as the *goodwill method,* are $70,000, including $50,000 of net tangible assets and $20,000 of goodwill. More will be said about the bonus and goodwill methods in Chapter 16.

If the partners' future interests in partnership profits and losses are also to be equal, the choice of either method (bonus or goodwill) will produce no inequity in the relative monetary interest of the two partners because they will share equally in the subsequent gain or loss, of whatever amount, on the realization of the intangible asset. However, recording the goodwill in the partnership books may have a significant effect on the balance sheet of the partnership. If the amount of such goodwill is material, adequate disclosure of the nature of this asset should be included in a partnership balance sheet prepared for the use of third parties.

The preceding examples refer to the source of new partnership assets in terms of the contributing partners. On occasion, one or more of the new partners may contribute the assets and liabilities of an existing business to the new partnership. In such a circumstance, it is important that the assets be appraised at the time the new partnership is formed. Existing book values of the contributed assets may be grossly inadequate as a measure of the relative capital investments of the partners in the new venture.

Income Tax Considerations

Although the problems in income tax accounting are not a principal concern of this text, certain *fundamental* income tax concepts are briefly considered within the context of partnership formation. Basically, the Internal Revenue Code adopts the aggregate theory and treats the partnership as a conduit through which net income of the firm is allocated to the partners *as if* they had individually earned it. With this partnership concept, two value bases are particularly relevant to initial formation of the firm:

1. The tax "basis" of the *assets* contributed to the partnership.
2. The tax "basis" of the partners' dollar *interest* in the partnership.

No taxable gain or loss is assumed to result from the contribution of property to a partnership by an individual partner. Rather, the partnership adopts the same *asset* basis, or unamortized cost, for income tax purposes as applied to the individual partner in respect to the calculation of his or her personal tax liability. It is unlikely that this value will be equivalent to the fair market value of the asset at the date of contribution. Although the market valuation of contributed assets is an important determinant in computing the dollar interest of the partners in the capital of the new firm, the tax-basis valuation necessarily modifies the relative interests of the partners for income tax purposes.

The tax *basis* of a partner's *interest* in the firm at the time of its formation is defined as *the sum of the bases of the individual assets contributed to the firm, increased by that partner's share of any partnership liabilities, and decreased by any personal liabilities assumed by the partnership.* Thus, the sum of the bases of the contributed assets is equal to the sum of the bases of the partners' separate interests in the partnership. It should be noted that partnership liabilities are excluded from this basic equation because they are implicitly included in the bases of the partners' separate interests. The following example illustrates these provisions.

Using the data of Case 1 and assuming that the basis of the building to Y is $20,000, that other assets have a tax basis equal to their present market values, and that X agrees to accept joint liability for the mortgage on the building, the income tax implications of the initial formation may be reflected in the following schedule:

	Tax Bases of the Assets to the Partnership	Tax Bases of the Partners' Interests in the Partnership
Cash	$30,000	
Merchandise	10,000	
Building	20,000	
Furniture and equipment	5,000	
Partner X's interest		$27,500
Partner Y's interest		37,500
Totals	$65,000	$65,000

Note that the sum of the asset bases, $65,000, equals the sum of the bases of the partners' monetary interests. The computation of the interests of X and Y is made as follows:

	X	Y
Bases of assets contributed:		
Cash	$10,000	$20,000
Inventory		10,000
Building		20,000
Furniture and equipment	5,000	
	$15,000	$50,000
Add: Liabilities assumed by X		
(50% of $25,000 mortgage)	12,500	
Deduct: Personal liability transferred to X		(12,500)
	$27,500	$37,500

The implications of the tax bases associated with the partnership formation are to reduce, *for tax purposes,* the depreciable cost of partnership assets by $10,000 and to alter the relative monetary interests of the individual partners. The ultimate effect of these changes is reflected in the periodic determination of taxable net income for the partnership to be allocated to the individual partners, and in the computation of taxable gain or loss in the event that one or both partners elect to dispose of their interests in the firm.

PARTNERSHIP OPERATIONS

Accounting for the operations of a partnership is similar to accounting for other profit-oriented businesses. The primary operational objective of the accounting process continues to be the determination of periodic net income. To this end, a partnership is perceived as a separate and distinct accounting entity. Net income is calculated in the traditional manner; that is, by relating periodic revenues and expenses, with only the salary payments to the partners and interest on capital investments accounted for differently.

The special problems of accounting for partnership operations are classified for discussion purposes as follows:

1. Establishing the nature and determining the amount of the relative interests of the partners in the firm.
2. Determining the proper allocation of partnership net income between the partners.
3. Preparing financial statements for the partnership: the balance sheet, income statement, and statement of partners' capital.

Nature and Amount of Relative Interests

The partners' interests in, and obligations to, the partnership may be dichotomized initially into (1) debtor-creditor relationships and (2) capital equities and/

or deficiencies. In many cases, these divisions are essentially arbitrary in nature, but in light of generally accepted accounting practices, they may materially influence the financial statements of the partnership.

Debtor-Creditor Relationships.   If in addition to contributions to the capital of the firm, a partner loans money to the partnership with the provision that it be repaid within a specified period of time, appropriate recognition of the separateness of the accounting entity and the nature of the transaction requires that such an advance be recorded as a partnership liability. Similarly, loans to individual partners by the partnership, which are to be repaid subsequently to the partnership, are properly classified as partnership receivables. Interest expense and/or income generated by these explicitly conceived contractual obligations are normally included (subtracted or added) in the periodic computation of partnership net income. This treatment is consistent with the classification of the originating transaction as a business loan and with the acceptance of the separate entity status of the partnership.

Capital Equities and/or Deficiencies.   The total capital equity of the partnership is equal to the difference between partnership assets and liabilities. It is necessary, however, that the amount of each partner's capital credit in the firm be independently calculated and recorded. Normally, two accounts are maintained for each partner: (1) a drawing, or personal, account and (2) a capital account. The drawing account is debited with the partner's withdrawals of cash or other assets during the period, presumably in anticipation of his or her share of profits, and is credited with his or her equity in partnership net income. The capital account initially reflects the dollar investment of each partner at the date of formation of the partnership. Subsequently, additional investments or withdrawals that are believed to be relatively permanent in character are entered in the account. If the partners should so elect, the balance of the drawing account may be periodically transferred to the capital account. As will be discussed later, it is possible that a more informative statement of financial position may result from segregating capital transactions from those that summarize profits. When the transactions are thus separated, the closing of the drawing accounts to capital accounts may prove undesirable.

Conventionally, interest credits on capital equities are not accounted for as partnership expenses. Interest credits on partners' loans, however, are deducted as a determinant of partnership net income. Thus, the objectivity of net income determination is at least partially compromised if the partners, at their discretion, can control whether additional equity shall be provided by partners' loans or accumulated profits. However, in this connection, a subtlety often overlooked relates to the implicit interest on *excessive* capital contributions. In the absence of a contrary agreement, Section 18(c) of the Uniform Partnership Act provides that a partner, who in aid of the partnership makes any payment or advance beyond the amount of capital that he or she agreed to contribute, shall be paid interest from the date of the payment or advance. An extension of this argument implies that from a legal point of view, profit accumulations of the partnership *may* be the basis of interest payments to individual partners. In point of fact, little substantive difference exists between accumulated profits and loans to the partnership. It would appear that the accounting problem is eliminated only where there is a complete acceptance of the proprietary theory, wherein no expense or income may be generated in transactions with the owners *or* by a complete acceptance of the entity theory wherein the expense of total capital (creditors' and owners') is recognized.

Allocating Net Income to Partners

Some of the fundamental problems underlying the allocation of partnership net income were discussed earlier in terms of eliminating unnecessary ambiguity from the partnership agreement. Note that the allocation of net income to the partners involves recording the respective shares in the equity accounts of the partners. It does not involve distributions of cash or other assets from the partnership to the individual partners. The problem of determining periodic withdrawals of assets by the partners is a separate matter, and partners may agree that some portion of each partner's allocated net income will be reinvested in the business and not withdrawn.

The three most commonly used bases for allocating partnership net income are the following:

1. Specified ratios.
2. Relative capital investments of the partners.
3. Service contributions of the partners.

Frequently, some weighted combination of these several bases is used to reward the partners.

Case 3. Specified Ratios

Assume that X and Y agree to divide profits from their partnership operations in a ratio of 3:1; that is, 75 percent to X and 25 percent to Y. If net income for the year is $60,000, the following journal entry indicates the allocation of profits:

Income Summary	60,000	
X, Drawing (75% × $60,000)		45,000
Y, Drawing (25% × $60,000)		15,000

In the absence of this specific profit-sharing agreement, each partner would have received $30,000. In both cases, the allocation of profits is uniform. Each partner receives a predetermined percentage of profits, without regard to the magnitude of such profits.

Relative Capital Investments

Because capital is an income-producing factor, it may be important to consider the partners' respective capital investments in allocating partnership net income. If partners are to be rewarded, in part at least, in proportion to the relative magnitudes of their investments of capital, it is imperative that there be an unequivocal statement in the partnership agreement concerning the computation of these capital balances. As indicated earlier, if average or ending capital balances are to be used, the treatment of withdrawals, or amounts available for withdrawal, may pose a problem.

The following data will be used in Cases 4 and 5 to illustrate alternative approaches to the allocation of net income when it is based upon the partners' relative capital investments.

X, Capital

2/1	10,000	1/1 Balance	50,000
		4/1	10,000
		8/1	20,000
		11/1	20,000

X, Drawing

1/1–12/1 ($1,000 per month, per agreement)	12,000		

Y, Capital

4/1	5,000	1/1 Balance	25,000
7/1	10,000	9/1	15,000

Y, Drawing

1/1–12/1 ($1,000 per month, per agreement)	12,000		

Income Summary

		12/31	50,000

It is assumed that withdrawals *in excess of* the $1,000 monthly allowance are permanent reductions in capital (i.e., are not loans from the partnership). Similarly, it is assumed that contributions during the year are permanent infusions of capital (i.e., are not loans to the partnership). Accordingly, both withdrawals in excess of the monthly allowance and capital contributions are recorded in the partners' capital accounts.

Case 4. Interest on Beginning Capital Balances

In this example, it is assumed that each partner is to receive a 6 percent return (interest) on capital investment, calculated in terms of the capital balances at the beginning of the year, with the remaining profit (or loss) to be distributed in a ratio of 4 : 6 to X and Y, respectively. Computation of the allocated partnership net income is as follows:

	X	*Y*	*Total*
Interest :			
6% × $50,000	$ 3,000		$ 3,000
6% × $25,000		$ 1,500	1,500
Remainder (in residual profit-sharing ratio):			
40% × $45,500	18,200		18,200
60% × $45,500		27,300	27,300
	$21,200	$28,800	$50,000

Case 5. Interest on Average Capital Balances

In this example, each partner is assumed to receive a 6 percent return (interest) on his or her *average* capital investment, utilizing the basis previously described for determining capital withdrawals. Since each partner withdrew the total amount allowable each month, no problem arises concerning amounts available for withdrawal but not actually withdrawn. After interest allowances, the residual profit element is again to be allocated in the ratio 4 : 6.

The first step in determining profit allocations is to calculate the average capital balance for each partner by weighting each new capital balance by the number of months (or other appropriate time interval) that the balance remains unchanged; by adding each of these products and dividing by the sum of weights, an average balance is determined. Calculations for the data in this example are as follows:

	Capital Balance	*Weighting Factor— Number of Months*	*Weighted Product*
X's capital balance:			
January 1–February 1	$50,000	1	$ 50,000
February 1–April 1	40,000	2	80,000
April 1–August 1	50,000	4	200,000
August 1–November 1	70,000	3	210,000
November 1–December 31	90,000	2	180,000
		12	$720,000

	Capital Balance	Weighting Factor— Number of Months	Weighted Product
Average capital balance ($720,000/12)			$ 60,000
Y's capital balance:			
January 1–April 1	$25,000	3	$ 75,000
April 1–July 1	20,000	3	60,000
July 1–September 1	10,000	2	20,000
September 1–December 31	25,000	4	100,000
		12	$255,000
Average capital balance ($255,000/12)			$ 21,250

Following the calculation of average capital balances, the several profit elements are allocated as follows:

	X	Y	Total
Interest :			
6% × $60,000	$ 3,600		$ 3,600
6% × $21,250		$ 1,275	1,275
Remainder (in residual profit-sharing ratio):			
40% × $45,125	18,050		18,050
60% × $45,125		27,075	27,075
	$21,650	$28,350	$50,000

The ending capital balances of the partners may also be used as a basis for interest allowances in net profit distribution. Alternatively, the total net profit for the accounting period may be allocated on the basis of relative capital investments. However, it is perhaps more usual for partnership agreements to specify that only a *reasonable* return should accrue from the investment of capital and that additional excess earnings of the partnership should be divided in some specified ratio to compensate the partners for the disproportionate contributions they make to the operation of the business. Furthermore, in determining the base to be used in computing the return on investments, the beginning or average capital balances are frequently preferred—the beginning balance because of the simplicity of calculation, or the average capital balance because it provides a more refined measurement of the actual capital employed by the firm *during* the accounting period.

Services Rendered

In order to reward the individual partners for their different service contributions to the operation of the partnership, salary allowances are often provided as an additional basis for allocating partnership net income. This basis, as in the case of interest allowances on capital investments, is frequently used in combination with negotiated ratios or other allocation bases. When the partners contribute a disproportionate amount of time and talent to partnership activities, inclusion of a provision for salaries in the allocation basis may contribute to a more equitable distribution of the net income of the business.

Case 6. Salary Provision

Using the data of Case 5, with the additional provision that salaries of $6,000 and $12,000 are to be awarded to X and Y, respectively, the net profit is allocated as follows:

	X	Y	Total
Salary allowances	$ 6,000	$12,000	$18,000
Interest credits	3,600	1,275	4,875
Remainder:			
40% × $27,125	10,850		10,850
60% × $27,125		16,275	16,275
	$20,450	$29,550	$50,000

Normally, salary allowances to partners are accounted for as an *allocation* of net income rather than as a *determinant* of net income. This practice has no effect on the ultimate capital accumulations of the various partners. However, it results in an amount of partnership net income that is in excess of that calculated for a corporation wherein salaries to officer-shareholders may have a status comparable to that of partners in a partnership.

If the salary of an officer-stockholder of a closely held corporation is treated as an expense when it meets the test of reasonableness, why is not the salary of a partner similarly a factor in net income determination if it satisfies the same criterion? Oddly enough, the entity theory is adopted in accounting for one type of transaction between the partners and the firm (debtor-creditor relationships); the proprietary theory is reflected in another type of transaction (salaries to partners) between the same parties. Although little theoretical support can be marshaled for the traditional accounting distinction between corporate officers' salaries (expenses) and salaries of partners (allocations of income), it persists in current accounting practice. Because of this inconsistency, net income comparisons between partnerships and corporations often are not meaningful unless adjustments are made for these differences in accounting for salaries.

Order of Distribution

If the net income is insufficient to cover the prescribed allocations for salaries and/ or interest on capital balances, two alternatives are available. First, the partners may elect that the allocation for salaries and interest on investment be made and that the earnings deficiency produced by these allocations be allocated in the residual profit- and loss-sharing ratio. Second, a sequence of allocations may be specified, with the provision that at each stage available net income is to be allocated to the fullest extent possible. This necessarily requires that the relative ratio of the partners' earned salaries or interest on investment be used to allocate that amount of net income remaining after prior allocations, if any, that is insufficient to make a total allocation for a profit-sharing factor. Consider the following data:

	X	Y	Total
Earned salaries	$10,000	$5,000	$15,000
Earned interest	4,000	6,000	10,000

If X and Y agreed that available earnings are to be allocated first for salaries, then for interest on capital investment, and finally in the residual profit-sharing ratio, this second method yields the following types of allocations of earnings when there are insufficient profits to make total allocations for both salaries and interest:

	X	Y	Total
Case I (net income, $9,000):			
Salaries:			
X (67% × $9,000)	$ 6,000		$ 6,000
Y (33% × $9,000)		$3,000	3,000
	$ 6,000	$3,000	$ 9,000
Case II (net income, $20,000):			
Salaries	$10,000	$5,000	$15,000
Interest:			
X (40% × $5,000)	2,000		2,000
Y (60% × $5,000)		3,000	3,000
	$12,000	$8,000	$20,000

The net income would be allocated differently if the first method were employed; that is, salaries and interest would be first allocated, after which the resulting deficiency would be allocated.

This situation reflects yet another instance requiring adequate planning in the formulation of the partnership agreement. In the absence of such an agreement, or where the agreement is silent as to the order of earnings allocation, the first method discussed is usually followed. It may be observed that this method implicitly treats the salaries and interest on capital investments as a partnership expense, and thus makes but one actual allocation of net (residual) income, viz, partnership net income after partners' salaries and interest on their investments.

Correction of Prior Years' Net Income

Accounting policy for prior period adjustments has undergone revision on numerous occasions. Presently, the FASB's definition of prior period adjustments is so narrow that they are practically precluded in all but a very few situations.[2] However, one must keep in mind that the pronouncements of the FASB are guided by objectives that might not apply in many partnership situations. In 1978, the FASB published its objectives for financial reporting. The first stated objective is that "financial reporting should provide information that is useful to present and potential investors and creditors and other users in making rational investment, credit, and similar decisions."[3] To the extent that a general objective such as this implicitly guided previous pronouncements, it may be inappropriate for certain partnership accounting applications. More specifically, the objectives that underlie decisions on prior period adjustments are likely to be quite different than the one quoted above.

In partnership accounting, corrections of prior years' net income may have direct economic implications in terms of how the economic consequences of partnership operations are allocated between the partners. Regardless of the potential impact, if any, on future investment and credit decisions, partners are likely to be most interested in using accounting procedures that provide an equitable allocation of net incomes between the partners.

In some cases, the decision whether to treat an item as a prior period adjustment or as a part of current net income would have no impact on the allocation of net income between partners. This would be so if the identity of the partners is currently the same as in the year to which the adjustments or corrections relate and the profit- and loss-sharing ratios remain unchanged, with no special constraints on allocations of salaries and/or interest.

---

[2] FASB, *Statement No. 16,* pars. 10–14.

[3] FASB, *Statement of Financial Accounting Concepts No. 1,* "Objectives of Financial Reporting by Business Enterprises" (Norwalk, CT, 1978), par. 34.

If these rather restrictive conditions are not fully satisfied, however, one must examine more carefully a proposed correction or adjustment of prior years' net income. In determining whether specific items should be treated as prior period adjustments, the principles to be generally followed have been specified by the APB in *Opinion No. 9* and *Opinion No. 20* and by the FASB in *Statement No. 16*. But, when the income allocation between partners is directly affected by prior period adjustment decisions, the agreed-upon will of the partners should dominate over the pronouncements of the APB, FASB, or other rule-making bodies. For example, partners may feel that a material bad debt that was not adequately allowed for during the period of sale should be treated as a prior period adjustment, notwithstanding the APB and FASB conclusions to the contrary.

Although the APB and FASB pronouncements may be relied on as an expression of norms, consideration should be given to three basic alternatives:

1. The amount of the adjustment is minor. In this circumstance, the adjustment may be absorbed in the current period's net income without material effect on the partners' capital balances.
2. The adjustment is material in amount but is not easily identified with a specific period or periods. An example of such an adjustment may be a correction of the allowance for uncollectible accounts. In this case, the gain or loss resulting from over- or underallowances in prior periods may be absorbed in the current period, or an arbitrary allocation to prior periods may be made, depending on the decision of the partners.
3. The adjustment is material in amount and is identifiable with specific accounting periods. This condition may exist where errors or omissions are discovered. In this type of circumstance, equity would seem to call for a recomputation of the allocations of adjusted net incomes for the affected periods.

Of course, corrections of prior periods' net incomes may not be the only, nor the most significant, adjustments that affect an equitable allocation of partnership net income. The existence of material, extraordinary, or nonrecurring gains or losses raises the question as to the specific period or periods to which they properly relate. Where this problem exists, the traditional realization criterion should be applied until further refinements in accounting methodology permit a more accurate determination of periodic net income.

Financial Statement Presentation

As previously indicated, accounting practice conventionally regards interest on partners' loans as a partnership expense, but it excludes partners' salaries and interest on capital as factors in profit determination. The exclusions (profit elements) are enumerated separately in an appendage to the income statement. The following income statement illustrates the traditional format:

XY PARTNERSHIP
Income Statement
For the Year Ended December 31, 19X1

Sales		$100,000
Cost of goods sold		60,000
Gross profit		$ 40,000
Operating expenses:		
Interest on partners' loans	$ 1,000	
Other expenses	19,000	20,000
Net income		$ 20,000

Allocated as follows:

	X	Y	Total
Partners' salaries	$ 8,000	$4,000	$12,000
Interest on capital	–0–	2,000	2,000
Remainder equally	3,000	3,000	6,000
	$11,000	$9,000	$20,000

If the position is taken that partners' salaries are "reasonable compensation for services rendered," consistent reporting would require disclosure of the $12,000 as an operating expense, with a corresponding reduction of net income to $8,000.

Just as changes in corporate retained earnings are reported separately in a statement of retained earnings, so are the changes in partners' equity reported separately in a statement of partners' capital. This statement typically follows this format:

XY PARTNERSHIP
Statement of Partners' Capital
For the Year Ended December 31, 19X1

	X	Y	Total
Capital, January 1	$10,000	$20,000	$30,000
Net income for the year	11,000	9,000	20,000
	$21,000	$29,000	$50,000
Withdrawals	12,000	10,000	22,000
Capital, December 31	$ 9,000	$19,000	$28,000

The usual partnership balance sheet reflects the proprietary concept in its equity section in that the capital accounts of the partners are separately disclosed. Following is an abbreviated example of this format:

XY PARTNERSHIP
Balance Sheet
December 31, 19X1

Assets		Equities		
Cash	$ 6,000	Current liabilities		$30,000
Accounts receivable	12,000	Loans payable		25,000
Inventory	20,000	Capital:		
Fixed assets (net)	40,000	X	$ 9,000	
Other assets	5,000	Y	19,000	28,000
Total assets	$83,000	Total equities		$83,000

Possibly, a more meaningful disclosure would result if the equity section were divided into capital and accumulated profits divisions. Section 40 of the Uniform Partnership Act makes a vague distinction between partnership capital and accumulated partnership profits. Potentially useful information for the financial management of the business is provided if this distinction is maintained in the balance sheet. Also, for credit purposes, the balances of the partners' accounts are relatively unimportant, because the partners remain jointly liable for partnership obligations. Additionally, the information relating to the partners' equities in the business is reported in detail in the statement of partners' capital.

Summary

This chapter examines a variety of topics regarding the formation and operation of partnerships. Partnerships can be viewed from two different perspectives. Under the aggregate, or proprietary, concept of a partnership, the partnership is considered to be an aggregation of the rights and responsibilities of the individual partners. In contrast, under the entity concept of a partnership, the partnership is seen as a legal entity, separate and distinct from the individual partners. The Uniform Partnership Act reflects the aggregate concept of a partnership; the Internal Revenue Code also tends to emphasize the aggregate concept of a partnership.

The partnership agreement is a written or oral contract which sets forth the individual rights and responsibilities of the partners. Although the Uniform Partnership Act establishes certain legal requirements for the partnership, most of the provisions of the act apply only to issues not addressed in the partnership agreement. The partnership agreement should state clearly the partners' intentions, including the purpose of the partnership, management rights and authority, and causes of dissolution. The partnership agreement should also address significant accounting issues such as the valuation of assets contributed to the partnership, the establishment of interests in capital and profits (losses), the basis for dividing partnership profits (losses), the basis for calculating the monetary equity of a withdrawing partner, and whether or not drawing accounts are to be closed to capital accounts at the end of the accounting period.

The accounting entries required to record the partners' initial interests may take many forms. For example, the individual partners' capital credits may be set equal to the fair market value of the net assets contributed by each partner. On the other hand, the partnership agreement may provide that the partners' initial capital credits should be the same regardless of the fair market value of the assets contributed by each individual partner. A related consideration involves the two income tax value bases: (1) the tax basis of the assets contributed to the partnership and (2) the tax basis of the partners' dollar interest in the partnership.

Accounting for the operations of the partnership involves establishing the nature and amount of the partners' relative interests, determining the proper allocation of partnership net income, and preparing financial statements for the partnership. Establishing the partners' interests in the partnership reflects two distinct issues: (1) debtor-creditor relationships between the partnership and individual partners, and (2) capital equities and/or deficiencies. The allocation of net income involves recording each partner's share in the respective equity accounts. Allocation is generally performed on the basis of specified ratios, relative capital investments, or service contributions. The financial statements prepared by partnerships are the balance sheet, the income statement, and the statement of partners' capital.

Appendix: The Uniform Partnership Act

Part I: Preliminary Provisions

§1.   Name of Act

This act may be cited as Uniform Partnership Act.

§2.   Definition of Terms

In this act, "Court" includes every court and judge having jurisdiction in the case.

"Business" includes every trade, occupation, or profession.

"Person" includes individuals, partnerships, corporations, and other associations.

"Bankrupt" includes bankrupt under the Federal Bankruptcy Act or insolvent under any state insolvent act.

"Conveyance" includes every assignment, lease, mortgage, or encumbrance.

"Real property" includes land and any interest or estate in land.

§3.   Interpretation of Knowledge and Notice

(1)   A person has "knowledge" of a fact within the meaning of this act not only when he has actual knowledge thereof, but also when he has knowledge of such other facts as in the circumstances shows bad faith.

(2)   A person has "notice" of a fact within the meaning of this act when the person who claims the benefit of the notice:

(a)   States the fact to such person, or

(b)   Delivers through the mail, or by other means of communication, a written statement of the fact to such person or to a proper person at his place of business or residence.

§4.   Rules of Construction

(1)   The rule that statutes in derogation of the common law are to be strictly construed shall have no application to this act.

(2)   The law of estoppel shall apply under this act.

(3)   The law of agency shall apply under this act.

(4)   This act shall be so interpreted and construed as to effect its general purpose to make uniform the law of those states which enact it.

(5)   This act shall not be construed so as to impair the obligations of any contract existing when the act goes into effect, nor to affect any action or proceedings begun or right accrued before this act takes effect.

§5.   Rules for Cases Not Provided for in This Act

In any case not provided for in this act the rules of law and equity, including the law merchant, shall govern.

Part II: Nature of Partnership

§6.   Partnership Defined

(1)   A partnership is an association of two or more persons to carry on as co-owners a business for profit.

(2)   But any association formed under any other statute of this state, or any statute adopted by authority, other than the authority of this state, is not a partnership under this act, unless such association would have been a partnership in this state prior to the adoption of this act; but this act shall apply to limited partnerships except in so far as the statutes relating to such partnerships are inconsistent herewith.

§7.   Rules for Determining the Existence of a Partnership

In determining whether a partnership exists, these rules shall apply:

(1)   Except as provided by section 16 persons who are not partners as to each other are not partners as to third persons.

(2)   Joint tenancy, tenancy in common, tenancy by the entireties, joint property, common property, or part ownership does not of itself establish a partnership, whether such co-owners do or do not share any profits made by the use of the property.

(3)   The sharing of gross returns does not of itself establish a partnership, whether

or not the persons sharing them have a joint or common right or interest in any property from which the returns are derived.

(4)   The receipt by a person of a share of the profits of a business is prima facie evidence that he is a partner in the business, but no such inference shall be drawn if such profits were received in payment:

(a)   As a debt by installments or otherwise,

(b)   As wages of an employee or rent to a landlord,

(c)   As an annuity to a widow or representative of a deceased partner,

(d)   As interest on a loan, though the amount of payment varies with the profits of the business,

(e)   As the consideration for the sale of a good-will of a business or other property by installments or otherwise.

§8.   Partnership Property

(1)   All property originally brought into the partnership stock or subsequently acquired by purchase or otherwise, on account of the partnership, is partnership property.

(2)   Unless the contrary intention appears, property acquired with partnership funds is partnership property.

(3)   Any estate in real property may be acquired in the partnership name. Title so acquired can be conveyed only in the partnership name.

(4)   A conveyance to a partnership in the partnership name, though without words of inheritance, passes the entire estate of the grantor unless a contrary intent appears.

Part III: Relations of Partners to Persons Dealing with the Partnership

§9.   Partner Agent of Partnership as to Partnership Business

(1)   Every partner is an agent of the partnership for the purpose of its business, and the act of every partner, including the execution in the partnership name of any instrument, for apparently carrying on in the usual way the business of the partnership of which he is a member binds the partnership, unless the partner so acting has in fact no authority to act for the partnership in the particular matter, and the person with whom he is dealing has knowledge of the fact that he has no such authority.

(2)   An act of a partner which is not apparently for the carrying on of the business of the partnership in the usual way does not bind the partnership unless authorized by the other partners.

(3)   Unless authorized by the other partners or unless they have abandoned the business, one or more but less than all the partners have no authority to:

(a)   Assign the partnership property in trust for creditors or on the assignee's promise to pay the debts of the partnership,

(b)   Dispose of the good-will of the business,

(c)   Do any other act which would make it impossible to carry on the ordinary business of a partnership,

(d)   Confess a judgment,

(e)   Submit a partnership claim or liability to arbitration or reference.

(4)   No act of a partner in contravention of a restriction on authority shall bind the partnership to persons having knowledge of the restriction.

§10.   Conveyance of Real Property of the Partnership

(1)   Where title to real property is in the partnership name, any partner may convey title to such property by a conveyance executed in the partnership name; but the partnership may recover such property unless the partner's act binds the partnership under the provisions of paragraph (1) of section 9, or unless such property has been conveyed by the grantee or a person claiming through such a grantee to a holder for value without knowledge that the partner, in making the conveyance, has exceeded his authority.

(2)   Where title to real property is in the name of the partnership, a conveyance executed by a partner, in his own name, passes the equitable interest of the partnership, provided the act is one within the authority of the partner under the provisions of paragraph (1) of section 9.

(3)   Where title to real property is in the name of one or more but not all the partners, and the record does not disclose the right of the partnership, the partners in whose name the title stands may convey title to such property, but the partnership may recover such property if the partners' act does not bind the partnership under the provisions of paragraph (1) or section 9, unless the purchaser or his assignee, is a holder for value, without knowledge.

(4)   Where the title to real property is in the name of one or more or all the partners, or in a third person in trust for the partnership, a conveyance executed by a partner in the partnership name, or in his own name, passes the equitable interest of the partnership, provided the act is one within the authority of the partner under the provisions of paragraph (1) of section 9.

(5)   Where the title to real property is in the names of all the partners a conveyance executed by all the partners passes all their rights in such property.

§11.   Partnership Bound by Admission of Partner

An admission or representation made by any partners concerning partnership affairs within the scope of his authority as conferred by this act is evidence against the partnership.

§12.   Partnership Charged with Knowledge of or Notice to Partner

Notice to any partner of any matter relating to partnership affairs, and the knowledge of the partner acting in the particular matter, acquired while a partner or then present to his mind, and the knowledge of any other partner who reasonably could and should have communicated it to the acting partner, operate as notice to or knowledge of the partnership, except in the case of a fraud on the partnership committed by or with the consent of that partner.

§13. Partnership Bound by Partner's Wrongful Act

Where, by any wrongful act or omission of any partner acting in the ordinary course of the business of the partnership or with the authority of his co-partners, loss or injury is caused to any person, not being a partner in the partnership, or any penalty is incurred, the partnership is liable therefor to the same extent as the partner so acting or omitting to act.

§14. Partnership Bound by Partner's Breach of Trust

The partnership is bound to make good the loss:

(a)   Where one partner acting within the scope of his apparent authority receives money or property of a third person and misapplies it; and

(b)   Where the partnership in the course of its business receives money or property of a third person and the money or property so received is misapplied by any partner while it is in the custody of the partnership.

§15. Nature of Partner's Liability

All partners are liable

(a)   Jointly and severally for everything chargeable to the partnership under sections 13 and 14.

(b)   Jointly for all other debts and obligations of the partnership; but any partner may enter into a separate obligation to perform a partnership contract.

§16. Partner by Estoppel

(1)   When a person, by words spoken or written or by conduct, represents himself, or consents to another representing him to any one, as a partner in an existing partnership or with one or more persons not actual partners, he is liable to any such person to whom such representation has been made, who has, on the faith of such representation, given credit to the actual or apparent partnership, and if he has made such representation or consented to its being made in a public manner he is liable to such person, whether the representation has or has not been made or communicated to such person so giving credit by or with the knowledge of the apparent partner making the representation or consenting to its being made.

(a)   When a partnership liability results, he is liable as though he were an actual member of the partnership.

(b)   When no partnership liability results, he is liable jointly with the other persons, if any, so consenting to the contract or representation as to incur liability, otherwise separately.

(2)   When a person has been thus represented to be a partner in an existing partnership, or with one or more persons not actual partners, he is an agent of the

persons consenting to such representation to bind them to the same extent and in the same manner as though he were a partner in fact, with respect to persons who rely upon the representation. Where all the members of the existing partnership consent to the representation, a partnership act or obligation results; but in all other cases it is the joint act or obligation of the person acting and the persons consenting to the representation.

§17. Liability of Incoming Partner

A person admitted as a partner into an existing partnership is liable for all the obligations of the partnership arising before his admission as though he had been a partner when such obligations were incurred, except that this liability shall be satisfied only out of partnership property.

Part IV: Relations of Partners to One Another

§18. Rules Determining Rights and Duties of Partners

The rights and duties of the partners in relation to the partnership shall be determined, subject to any agreement between them, by the following rules:

(a)   Each partner shall be repaid his contributions, whether by way of capital or advances to the partnership property and share equally in the profits and surplus remaining after all liabilities, including those to partners, are satisfied; and must contribute towards the losses, whether of capital or otherwise, sustained by the partnership according to his share in the profits.

(b)   The partnership must indemnify every partner in respect of payments made and personal liabilities reasonably incurred by him in the ordinary and proper conduct of its business, or for the preservation of its business or property.

(c)   A partner, who in aid of the partnership makes any payment or advance beyond the amount of capital which he agreed to contribute, shall be paid interest from the date of the payment or advance.

(d)   A partner shall receive interest on the capital contributed by him only from the date when repayment should be made.

(e)   All partners have equal rights in the management and conduct of the partnership business.

(f)   No partner is entitled to remuneration for acting in the partnership business, except that a surviving partner is entitled to reasonable compensation for his services in winding up the partnership affairs.

(g)   No person can become a member of a partnership without the consent of all the partners.

(h)   Any difference arising as to ordinary matters connected with the partnership business may be decided by a majority of the partners; but no act in contravention of any agreement between the partners may be done rightfully without the consent of all the partners.

§19. Partnership Books

The partnership books shall be kept, subject to any agreement between the partners, at the principal place of business of the partnership, and every partner shall at all times have access to and may inspect and copy any of them.

§20. Duty of Partners to Render Information

Partners shall render on demand true and full information of all things affecting the partnership to any partner or the legal representative of any deceased partner or partner under legal disability.

§21. Partner Accountable as a Fiduciary

(1) Every partner must account to the partnership for any benefit, and hold as trustee for it any profits derived by him without the consent of the other partners from any transaction connected with the formation, conduct, or liquidation of the partnership or from any use by him of its property.

(2) This section applies also to the representatives of a deceased partner engaged in the liquidation of the affairs of the partnership as the personal representatives of the last surviving partner.

§22. Right to an Account

Any partner shall have the right to a formal account as to partnership affairs:

(a) If he is wrongfully excluded from the partnership business or possession of its property by his co-partners,

(b) If the right exists under the terms of any agreement,

(c) As provided by section 21,

(d) Whenever other circumstances render it just and reasonable.

§23. Continuation of Partnership beyond Fixed Term

(1) When a partnership for a fixed term or particular undertaking is continued after the termination of such term or particular undertaking without any express agreement, the rights and duties of the partners remain the same as they were at such termination, so far as is consistent with a partnership at will.

(2) A continuation of the business by the partners or such of them as habitually acted therein during the term, without any settlement or liquidation of the partnership affairs, is prima facie evidence of a continuation of the partnership.

Part V: Property Rights of a Partner

§24. Extent of Property Rights of a Partner

The property rights of a partner are (1) his rights in specific partnership property, (2) his interest in the partnership, and (3) his right to participate in the management.

§25.   Nature of a Partner's Right in Specific Partnership Property

(1)   A partner is co-owner with his partners of specific partnership property holding as a tenant in partnership.

(2)   The incidents of this tenancy are such that:

(a)   A partner, subject to the provisions of this act and to any agreement between the partners, has an equal right with his partners to possess specific partnership property for partnership purposes; but he has no right to possess such property for any other purpose without the consent of his partners.

(b)   A partner's right in specific partnership property is not assignable except in connection with the assignment of rights of all the partners in the same property.

(c)   A partner's right in specific partnership property is not subject to attachment or execution, except on a claim against the partnership. When partnership property is attached for a partnership debt the partners, or any of them, or the representatives of a deceased partner, cannot claim any right under the homestead or exemption laws.

(d)   On the death of a partner his right in specific partnership property vests in the surviving partner or partners, except where the deceased was the last surviving partner, when his right in such property vests in his legal representative. Such surviving partner or partners, or the legal representative of the last surviving partner, has no right to possess the partnership property for any but a partnership purpose.

(e)   A partner's right in specific partnership property is not subject to dower, courtesy, or allowances to widows, heirs, or next of kin.

§26.   Nature of Partner's Interest in the Partnership

A partner's interest in the partnership is his share of the profits and surplus, and the same is personal property.

§27.   Assignment of Partner's Interest

(1)   A conveyance by a partner of his interest in the partnership does not of itself dissolve the partnership, nor, as against the other partners in the absence of agreement, entitle the assignee, during the continuance of the partnership, to interfere in the management or administration of the partnership business or affairs, or to require any information or account of partnership transactions, or to inspect the partnership books; but it merely entitles the assignee to receive in accordance with his contract the profits to which the assigning partner would otherwise be entitled.

(2)   In case of a dissolution of the partnership, the assignee is entitled to receive his assignor's interest and may require an account from the date only of the last account agreed to by all the partners.

§28.   Partner's Interest Subject to Charging Order

(1)   On due application to a competent court by any judgment creditor of a partner, the court which entered the judgment, order, or decree, or any other court, may

charge the interest of the debtor partner with payment of the unsatisfied amount of such judgment debt with interest thereon; and may then or later appoint a receiver of his share of the profits, and of any other money due or to fall due to him in respect of the partnership, and make all other orders, directions, accounts and inquiries which the debtor partner might have made, or which the circumstances of the case may require.

(2)   The interest charged may be redeemed at any time before foreclosure, or in case of a sale being directed by the court may be purchased without thereby causing a dissolution:

(a)   With separate property, by any one or more of the partners, or

(b)   With partnership property, by any one or more of the partners with the consent of all the partners whose interests are not so charged or sold.

(3)   Nothing in this act shall be held to deprive a partner of his right, if any, under the exemption laws, as regards his interest in the partnership.

Part VI: Dissolution and Winding Up

§29.   Dissolution Defined

The dissolution of a partnership is the change in the relation of the partners caused by any partner ceasing to be associated in the carrying on as distinguished from the winding up of the business.

§30.   Partnership Not Terminated by Dissolution

On dissolution the partnership is not terminated, but continues until the winding up of partnership affairs is completed.

§31.   Causes of Dissolution

Dissolution is caused:

(1)   Without violation of the agreement between the partners,

(a)   By the termination of the definite term or particular undertaking specified in the agreement,

(b)   By the express will of any partner when no definite term or particular undertaking is specified,

(c)   By the express will of all the partners who have not assigned their interests or suffered them to be charged for their separate debts, either before or after the termination of any specified term or particular undertaking,

(d)   By the expulsion of any partner from the business bona fide in accordance with such a power conferred by the agreement between the partners;

(2)   In contravention of the agreement between the partners, where the circumstances do not permit a dissolution under any other provision of this section, by the express will of any partner at any time;

(3)   By any event which makes it unlawful for the business of the partnership to be carried on or for the members to carry it on in partnership;

(4) By the death of any partner;

(5) By the bankruptcy of any partner or the partnership;

(6) By decree of court under section 32.

§32. Dissolution by Decree of Court

(1) On application by or for a partner the court shall decree a dissolution whenever:

(a) A partner has been declared a lunatic in any judicial proceeding or is shown to be of unsound mind,

(b) A partner becomes in any other way incapable of performing his part of the partnership contract,

(c) A partner has been guilty of such conduct as tends to affect prejudicially the carrying on of the business.

(d) A partner wilfully or persistently commits a breach of the partnership agreement, or otherwise so conducts himself in matters relating to the partnership business that is not reasonably practicable to carry on the business in partnership with him.

(e) The business of the partnership can only be carried on at a loss,

(f) Other circumstances render a dissolution equitable.

(2) On the application of the purchaser of a partner's interest under sections 28 or 29:

(a) After the termination of the specified term or particular undertaking.

(b) At any time if the partnership was a partnership at will when the interest was assigned or when the charging order was issued.

§33. General Effect of Dissolution on Authority of Partner

Except so far as may be necessary to wind up partnership affairs or to complete transactions begun but not then finished, dissolution terminates all authority of any partner to act for the partnership,

(1) With respect to the partners,

(a) When the dissolution is not by the act, bankruptcy or death of a partner; or

(b) When the dissolution is by such act, bankruptcy or death of a partner, in cases where section 34 so requires.

(2) With respect to persons not partners, as declared in section 35.

§34. Right of Partner to Contribution from Co-partners after Dissolution

Where the dissolution is caused by the act, death or bankruptcy of a partner, each partner is liable to his co-partners for his share of any liability created by any partner acting for the partnership as if the partnership had not been dissolved unless

(a) The dissolution being by act of any partner, the partner acting for the partnership had knowledge of the dissolution, or

(b) The dissolution being by the death or bankruptcy of a partner, the partner acting for the partnership had knowledge or notice of the death or bankruptcy.

§35.   Power of Partner to Bind Partnership to Third Persons after Dissolution

(1)   After dissolution a partner can bind the partnership except as provided in paragraph (3)

(a)   By any act appropriate for winding up partnership affairs or completing transactions unfinished at dissolution;

(b)   By any transaction which would bind the partnership if dissolution had not taken place, provided the other party to the transaction

(I)   Had extended credit to the partnership prior to dissolution and had no knowledge or notice of the dissolution; or

(II)   Though he had not so extended credit, had nevertheless known of the partnership prior to dissolution, and having no knowledge or notice of dissolution, the fact of dissolution had not been advertised in a newspaper of general circulation in the place (or in each place if more than one) at which the partnership business was regularly carried on.

(2)   The liability of a partner under paragraph (1b) shall be satisfied out of partnership assets alone when such partner had been prior to dissolution

(a)   Unknown as a partner to the person with whom the contract is made; and

(b)   So far unknown and inactive in partnership affairs that the business reputation of the partnership could not be said to have been in any degree due to his connection with it.

(3)   The partnership is in no case bound by any act of a partner after dissolution

(a)   Where the partnership is dissolved because it is unlawful to carry on the business, unless the act is appropriate for winding up partnership affairs; or

(b)   Where the partner has become bankrupt; or

(c)   Where the partner has no authority to wind up partnership affairs; except by a transaction with one who

(I)   Had extended credit to the partnership prior to dissolution and had no knowledge or notice of his want of authority; or

(II)   Had not extended credit to the partnership prior to dissolution, and, having no knowledge or notice of his want of authority, the fact of his want of authority has not been advised in the manner provided for advertising the fact of dissolution in paragraph (1bII).

(4)   Nothing in this section shall affect the liability under section 16 of any person who after dissolution represents himself or consents to another representing him as a partner in a partnership engaged in carrying on business.

§36.   Effect of Dissolution on Partner's Existing Liability

(1)   The dissolution of the partnership does not of itself discharge the existing liability of any partner.

(2)   A partner is discharged from any existing liability upon dissolution of the partnership by an agreement to that effect between himself, the partnership creditor and the person or partnership continuing the business; and such agreement may be

inferred from the course of dealing between the creditor having knowledge of the dissolution and the person or partnership continuing the business.

(3)   Where a person agrees to assume the existing obligations of a dissolved partnership, the partners whose obligations have been assumed shall be discharged from any liability to any creditor of the partnership who, knowing of the agreement, consents to a material alteration in the nature or time of payment of such obligations.

(4)   The individual property of a deceased partner shall be liable for all obligations of the partnership incurred while he was a partner but subject to the prior payment of his separate debts.

§37.   Right to Wind Up

Unless otherwise agreed the partners who have not wrongfully dissolved the partnership or the legal representative of the last surviving partner, not bankrupt, has the right to wind up the partnership affairs; provided, however, that any partner, his legal representative or his assignee, upon cause shown, may obtain winding up by the court.

§38.   Rights of Partners to Application of Partnership Property

(1)   When dissolution is caused in any way, except in contravention of the partnership agreement, each partner, as against his co-partners and all persons claiming through them in respect of their interests in the partnership, unless otherwise agreed, may have the partnership property applied to discharge its liabilities, and the surplus applied to pay in cash the net amount owing to the respective partners. But if dissolution is caused by expulsion of a partner, bona fide under the partnership agreement and if the expelled partner is discharged from all partnership liabilities, either by payment or agreement under section 36(2), he shall receive in cash only the net amount due him from the partnership.

(2)   When dissolution is caused in contravention of the partnership agreement the rights of the partners shall be as follows:

(a)   Each partner who has not caused dissolution wrongfully shall have,

I.   All the rights specified in paragraph (1) of this section, and

II.   The right, as against each partner who has caused the dissolution wrongfully, to damages for breach of the agreement.

(b)   The partners who have not caused the dissolution wrongfully, if they all desire to continue the business in the same name, either by themselves or jointly with others, may do so, during the agreed term for the partnership and for that purpose may possess the partnership property, provided they secure the payment by bond approved by the court, or pay to any partner who has caused the dissolution wrongfully, the value of his interest in the partnership at the dissolution, less any damages recoverable under clause (2aII) of this section, and in like manner indemnify him against all present or future partnership liabilities.

(c)   A partner who has caused the dissolution wrongfully shall have:

I.   If the business is not continued under the provisions of paragraph (2b) all the rights of a partner under paragraph (1), subject to clause (2aII), of this section,

II.   If the business is continued under paragraph (2b) of this section the right as against his co-partners and all claiming through them in respect of their interests in the partnership, to have the value of his interest in the partnership, less any damages caused to his co-partners by the dissolution, ascertained and paid to him in cash, or the payment secured by bond approved by the court, and to be released from all existing liabilities of the partnership; but in ascertaining the value of the partner's interest the value of the good-will of the business shall not be considered.

§39.   Rights Where Partnership Is Dissolved for Fraud or Misrepresentation

Where a partnership contract is rescinded on the ground of the fraud or misrepresentation of one of the parties thereto, the party entitled to rescind is, without prejudice to any other right, entitled,

(a)   To a lien on, or a right of retention of, the surplus of the partnership property after satisfying the partnership liabilities to third persons for any sum of money paid by him for the purchase of an interest in the partnership and for any capital or advances contributed by him; and

(b)   To stand, after all liabilities to third persons have been satisfied, in the place of the creditors of the partnership for any payments made by him in respect of the partnership liabilities; and

(c)   To be indemnified by the person guilty of the fraud or making the representation against all debts and liabilities of the partnership.

§40.   Rules of Distribution

In settling accounts between the partners after dissolution, the following rules shall be observed, subject to any agreement to the contrary:

(a)   The assets of the partnership are:

I.   The partnership property,

II.   The contributions of the partners necessary for the payment of all the liabilities specified in clause (b) of this paragraph.

(b)   The liabilities of the partnership shall rank in order of payment, as follows:

I.   Those owing to creditors other than partners,

II.   Those owing to partners other than for capital and profits,

III.   Those owing to partners in respect of capital,

IV.   Those owing to partners in respect of profits.

(c)   The assets shall be applied in order of their declaration in clause (a) of this paragraph to the satisfaction of the liabilities.

(d)   The partners shall contribute, as provided by section 18(a) the amount necessary to satisfy the liabilities; but if any, but not all, of the partners are insolvent, or, not being subject to process, refuse to contribute, the other partners shall contribute their share of the liabilities, and, in relative proportions in which they share the profits, the additional amount necessary to pay the liabilities.

(e)   An assignee for the benefit of creditors or any person appointed by the court shall have the right to enforce the contributions specified in clause (d) of this paragraph.

(f)   Any partner or his legal representative shall have the right to enforce the contributions specified in clause (d) of this paragraph, to the extent of the amount which he has paid in excess of his share of the liability.

(g)   The individual property of a deceased partner shall be liable for the contributions specified in clause (d) of this paragraph.

(h)   When partnership property and the individual properties of the partners are in possession of a court for distribution, partnership creditors shall have priority on partnership property and separate creditors on individual property, saving the rights of lien or secured creditors as heretofore.

(i)   Where a partner has become bankrupt or his estate is insolvent the claims against his separate property shall rank in the following order:

I.   Those owing to separate creditors,

II.   Those owing to partnership creditors,

III. Those owing to partners by way of contribution.

§41.   Liability of Persons Continuing the Business in Certain Cases

(1)   When any new partner is admitted into an existing partnership, or when any partner retires and assigns (or the representative of the deceased partner assigns) his rights in partnership property to two or more of the partners, or to one or more of the partners and one or more third persons, if the business is continued without liquidation of the partnership affairs, creditors of the first or dissolved partnership are also creditors of the partnership so continuing the business.

(2)   When all but one partner retire and assign (or the representative of a deceased partner assigns) their rights in partnership property to the remaining partner, who continues the business without liquidation of partnership affairs, either alone or with others, creditors of the dissolved partnership are also creditors of the person or partnership so continuing the business.

(3)   When any partner retires or dies and the business of the dissolved partnership is continued as set forth in paragraphs (1) and (2) of this section, with the consent of the retired partners or the representative of the deceased partner, but without any assignment of his right in partnership property, rights of creditors of the dissolved partnership and of the creditors of the person or partnership continuing the business shall be as if such assignment had been made.

(4)   When all the partners or their representatives assign their rights in partnership property to one or more third persons who promise to pay the debts and who continue the business of the dissolved partnership, creditors of the dissolved partnership are also creditors of the person or partnership continuing the business.

(5)   When any partner wrongfully causes a dissolution and the remaining partners continue the business under the provisions of section 38(2b), either alone or with others, and without liquidation of the partnership affairs, creditors of the dissolved partnership are also creditors of the person or partnership continuing the business.

(6)   When a partner is expelled and the remaining partners continue the business either alone or with others, without liquidation of the partnership affairs, creditors of the dissolved partnership are also creditors of the person or partnership continuing the business.

(7)   The liability of a third person becoming a partner in the partnership continuing the business, under this section, to the creditors of the dissolved partnership shall be satisfied out of partnership property only.

(8)   When the business of a partnership after dissolution is continued under any conditions set forth in this section the creditors of the dissolved partnership, as against the separate creditors of the retiring or deceased partner or the representative of the deceased partner, have a prior right to any claim of the retired partner or the representative of the deceased partner against the person or partnership continuing the business, on account of the retired or deceased partner's interest in the dissolved partnership or on account of any consideration promised for such interest or for his right in partnership property.

(9)   Nothing in this section shall be held to modify any right of creditors to set aside any assignment on the ground of fraud.

(10)   The use by the person or partnership continuing the business of the partnership name, or the name of a deceased partner as part thereof, shall not of itself make the individual property of the deceased partner liable for any debts contracted by such person or partnership.

§42.   Rights of Retiring or Estate of Deceased Partner When the Business Is Continued

When any partner retires or dies, and the business is continued under any of the conditions set forth in section 41(1, 2, 3, 5, 6), or section 38(2b) without any settlement of accounts as between him or his estate and the person or partnership continuing the business, unless otherwise agreed, he or his legal representative as against such persons or partnership may have the value of his interest at the date of dissolution ascertained, and shall receive as an ordinary creditor an amount equal to the value of his interest in the dissolved partnership with interest, or, at his option or at the option of his legal representative, in lieu of interest, the profits attributable to the use of his right in the property of the dissolved partnership; provided that the creditors of the dissolved partnership as against the separate creditors, or the representative of the retired or deceased partner, shall have priority on any claim arising under this section, as provided by section 41(8) of this act.

§43.   Accrual of Actions

The right to an account of his interest shall accrue to any partner, or his legal representative, as against the winding up partners or the surviving partners or the person or partnership continuing the business, at the date of dissolution, in the absence of any agreement to the contrary.

Part VII: Miscellaneous Provisions

§44. When Act Takes Effect

This act shall take effect on the . . . .
day of . . . . one thousand nine hundred and . . . .

§45. Legislation Repealed

All acts or parts of acts inconsistent with this act are hereby repealed.

Questions

1. What is the essential nature of a partnership? What distinguishes it from other forms of business organization?
2. Enumerate five important provisions that should be explicitly considered in the partnership agreement.
3. The partnership agreement of the ABC partnership provides that "profits and losses shall be shared in the ratio of the partners' capital balances. Can you foresee any problems with the language of this profit-sharing arrangement? Should such an agreement be in writing to have full legal effect on the parties?
4. How is the tax "basis" of a partner's interest in the partnership defined? Is this concept different from the tax bases of the assets a partner contributes?
5. What are three commonly used bases for allocating partnership net income to the partners?
6. What is the justification for salary allowances in a partnership agreement? Why is interest on capital balances frequently included in a partnership agreement as a basis for profit distribution?
7. "The pronouncements of the APB and FASB may not always serve as appropriate guidelines for partnership accounting." Explain the basis for this statement.
8. If by agreement the partners wish to begin with equal interests in the partnership net assets yet do not contribute assets of equal value, what methods might be used to record the formation of the partnership?
9. What alternatives exist for correction of prior years' net income when (a) the amount of the adjustment is minor, (b) the adjustment is material in amount but is not easily identifiable with a specific period or periods, or (c) the adjustment is material in amount and is identifiable with specific accounting periods?
10. What advantages may derive from reporting partners' capital accounts on the balance sheet *divided between contributed capital and accumulated profits*? Does present practice more closely approximate the proprietary or entity concept of the partnership?
11. Explain why salaries to partners are typically accounted for as allocations of income rather than as expenses.

12. What advantage would result from reporting the salaries and interest paid on partners' capital balances as *expenses* on the income statement rather than accounting for them as earnings distributions?

Exercises

Exercise 15-1   (Profit- and Loss-Sharing Agreements)

Partnership contracts usually specify a profit and loss ratio. They may also provide for such additional profit- and loss-sharing features as salaries, bonuses, and interest allowances on invested capital.

Required:

a. What is the objective of profit- and loss-sharing arrangements? Why may there be a need for features in addition to a simple profit and loss ratio? Discuss.

b. Discuss the arguments for recording salary and bonus allowances to partners as charges to operations.

c. What are the arguments against treating partnership salary and bonus allowances as expenses? Discuss.

d. In addition to its other profit- and loss-sharing features, a partnership agreement may state that "interest is to be allowed on invested capital." List the additional provisions that should be included in the partnership agreement so that "interest to be allowed on invested capital" can be computed.

(AICPA adapted)

Exercise 15-2   (Miscellaneous Partnership Topics)

For each of the following, select the one best answer that either completes the sentence or answers the question.

1. Which of the following statements concerning partnerships is true?
   a. A dominant theme in the Uniform Partnership Act is that a partnership is a legal entity, separate and distinct from the individual partners.
   b. Individual partners are jointly liable for the debts and obligations of a partnership.
   c. Income tax is levied on the individual partners' shares of the net income of a partnership and is reported in their personal tax returns.
   d. In the event of liquidation, partnership creditors generally have priority in respect to the assets of the partnership and separate creditors in respect to the personal assets of the partners.
   e. All of the above are true.

2. For income tax purposes, the tax basis of a partner's interest in a partnership is generally equal to
   a. The fair market values of the assets at date of contribution.
   b. The unamortized cost of the assets to the partner.

   c. The sum of the fair market values of the assets the partner contributes to the firm, increased by any liabilities of other partners assumed and decreased by any personal liabilities that are assumed by other partners.

   d. The sum of the bases of the individual assets the partner contributes to the firm, decreased by the partner's share of partnership liabilities.

   e. The sum of the bases of the assets the partner contributes, increased by any liabilities of other partners assumed and decreased by any personal liabilities that are assumed by other partners.

3. Which of the following statements about partnership accounts is true?

   a. Two accounts are generally maintained for each partner, a drawing account and a capital account.

   b. The drawing account is credited with the partner's withdrawals of cash or other assets during the period.

   c. The drawing account is credited with the partner's equity in the final allocation of net income.

   d. Answers *(a)* and *(c)* are correct but *(b)* is false.

   e. Answers *(a)*, *(b)*, and *(c)* are all correct.

4. Partners A and B agree that B is to receive a $10,000 salary from their partnership and remaining profits are to be divided in a 3 : 2 ratio. If net income for the year is $75,000, how will the allocation of profits be made?

   a. $32,500 to A and $42,500 to B.

   b. $39,000 to A and $36,000 to B.

   c. $26,000 to A and $49,000 to B.

   d. $45,000 to A and $30,000 to B.

   e. $37,500 to A and $37,500 to B.

5. In the absence of a partnership agreement, income is usually allocated to partners according to the following:

   a. Salaries, and the remainder by capital ratio.

   b. Interest on capital, salaries, and the remainder by capital ratio.

   c. By capital ratio.

   d. Salaries, interest on capital, and the remainder by capital ratio.

   e. Equal amounts of income to each partner.

Exercise 15–3   (Capital Account Balances and Implicit Goodwill)

The partnership of Charles and Michael was formed on February 28, 19X1. At that date, the following assets were contributed:

	Charles	Michael
Cash	$35,000	$ 15,000
Merchandise		45,000
Building		100,000
Furniture and equipment	25,000	

The building is subject to a mortgage loan of $30,000 that is to be assumed by the partnership. The partnership agreement provides that Charles and Michael share profits or losses equally.

Required:

a. What are the capital balances of the partners on February 28, 19X1?

b. If the partnership agreement states that the initial capital balances of the partners should be equal and no recognition should be given to any intangible assets contributed, what are the partners' capital balances on February 28, 19X1?

c. Given the facts stated in requirement *(b)* except that any contributed goodwill should be recognized in the accounts, what are the partners' capital balances on February 28, 19X1? How much goodwill should be recognized?

(AICPA adapted)

Exercise 15–4   (Capital Account Balances and Implicit Goodwill)

The SJ Partnership was formed by Dave Smith and Paula Jones, who contributed tangible assets with the following fair values:

	Contributed by	
	Smith	*Jones*
Cash	$50,000	$10,000
Furniture	10,000	
Building		80,000

The amount of $3,000 is owed on the furniture, and the amount of $50,000 is owed on the building. The partnership assumes both liabilities.

Required:

a. Prepare the partnership formation entry assuming that the partners' capital balances are to be equal and goodwill is to be recorded.

b. Prepare the partnership formation entry assuming that the partners' capital balances are to be equal and contributed goodwill is to be recorded.

Exercise 15–5   (Distribution of Partnership Profits)

Best and Branch are partners in B and B Travel Agency. Their capital account balances on January 1, 19X1, are $40,000 and $20,000, respectively. They agree that partnership profits are to be distributed as follows:

	Best	*Branch*
Salary	$3,000	$9,000
Interest on beginning capital balances	5%	5%
Bonus	25% of net income *after* salaries and bonus *but before* interest has been deducted	None
Residual profits or losses	70%	30%

Required:

Calculate the distribution of 19X1 partnership profits (identifying the profit elements separately) if the partnership net income before salaries, interest, and bonus is $60,000.

Exercise 15–6   (Recording Partnership Formation and Calculating Tax Bases)

Lori and Val joined in the Lorival partnership on January 1, 19X1. The partners share equally in profits, losses, and capital. Val contributed land valued at $10,000 that had a tax basis of $8,000. She also contributed a building valued at $130,000 that had a tax basis of $70,000. The partnership assumed a mortgage loan against the building and land in the amount of $40,000. Lori contributed $50,000 cash, and equipment valued at $50,000 that had a tax basis of $20,000. There was no goodwill contributed.

Required:

a. Prepare a general journal entry to record the formation of the partnership and the contributions of the partners.

b. Prepare a schedule showing the tax bases of the partnership's assets and the bases of the partners' interests in the partnership.

Exercise 15–7   (Distribution of Partnership Profits)

Walker, Wayne, and Monroe are partners sharing profits and losses as follows:

Salaries:	
Walker	$18,000
Wayne	12,000
Monroe	8,000
Interest (6%) on the following average capital balances:	
Walker, capital	100,000
Wayne, capital	50,000
Monroe, capital	80,000

Residual profits or losses are divided equally.

Required:

If the partnership net income for 19X1 is reported to be $26,000, indicate the distribution to each partner. Identify the profit and loss elements separately.

Exercise 15–8   (Error Correction and Distribution of Partnership Profits)

Rogers and Horn share profits 3 : 4 after annual salary allowances of $34,000 and $36,000, respectively; however, if partnership net income is insufficient to make these distributions in full amount, net income shall be divided equally between the partners In 19X1, the following errors were discovered:

1. Depreciation for 19X0 was understated by $8,400.

2. Inventory on December 31, 19X0, was overvalued by $45,600.

The partnership net income for 19X0 was reported to be $98,000.

Required:

Indicate the correcting entry or entries necessary upon discovery of these errors.

Exercise 15-9   (Allocation of Partnership Profits)

A, B, and C are partners and share profits and losses as follows: Salaries of $20,000 to A; $15,000 to B; and none to C. If net income exceeds salaries, then a bonus is allocated to A. The bonus is 5 percent of net income after deducting salaries and the bonus. Residual profits or residual losses are allocated 10 percent to A, 20 percent to B, and 70 percent to C.

Required:

a. If net income before salaries and bonus is $70,000, how should it be allocated among the partners?

b. Suppose that after the allocation of requirement *(a)* was recorded and the books were closed, the partners discovered an error and that correction of the error would reduce net income from $70,000 to $30,000. The error involved understated depreciation expense. Present the journal entry to correct the accounts, and show any supporting calculations.

Exercise 15-10   (Recording Partners' Contributions)

Joe Conn developed an interesting idea for marketing sailboats in Death Valley. He interested Rob White in joining him in a partnership. Following is the information you have collected relative to their original contributions.

Rob contributed $30,000 cash, a tract of land, and delivery equipment. Joe contributed $60,000 cash. After giving special consideration to the tax bases of the assets contributed, the relative usefulness of the assets to the partnership versus the problems of finding buyers for the assets and contributing cash, and other such factors, the partners agreed that Joe's contribution was equal to 40 percent of the partnership's tangible assets, measured in terms of the fair value of the assets *to the partnership*. However, since the marketing idea originated with Joe, it was agreed that he should receive credit for 50 percent of the recorded capital. Recent sales of land similar to that contributed by Rob suggest a market value of $40,000. Likewise, recent sales of delivery equipment similar to that contributed by Rob suggest $40,000 as the market value of the equipment. These sales, of course, were not entirely representative of the particular assets contributed by Rob and therefore may be a better indicator of their *relative* values than their absolute values. In reflecting on their venture, the partners agree that it is a rather risky affair in respect to anticipated profits. Hopefully, however, they will be able to build good customer relations over the long run and establish a permanent business with an attractive long-term rate of return.

Required:

a. Journalize the partners' contributions under the most appropriate method, given the circumstances.

b. Journalize their contributions under another method, probably less appropriate.

c. State why you think method *(a)* is better than *(b)* in this situation.

Problems

Problem 15-11   (Allocating Partnerhip Profits)

Matthew and Lindsey organized the ML partnership on January 1, 19X1. The following entries were made in their capital accounts during 19X1:

	Debit	Credit	Balance
Matthew, capital:			
January 1		$20,000	$20,000
April 1		5,000	25,000
October 1		5,000	30,000
Lindsey, capital:			
January 1		40,000	40,000
March 1	$10,000		30,000
September 1	10,000		20,000
November 1		10,000	30,000

Required:

If the partnership net income, computed without regard to salaries or interest, is $20,000 for 19X1, indicate its division between the partners under the following independent profit-sharing conditions:

a. Interest at 8 percent is allowed on average capital investments, and the remainder is divided equally.

b. A salary of $9,000 is to be credited to Lindsey; 8 percent interest is allowed each partner on his or her ending capital balance; residual profits or losses are divided 60 percent to Matthew and 40 percent to Lindsey.

c. Salaries are allowed Matthew and Lindsey in amounts of $8,300 and $9,500, respectively, and residual profits or residual losses are divided in the ratio of average capital balances.

d. A bonus of 20 percent of partnership net income is credited to Matthew, a salary of $5,000 is allowed to Lindsey, and residual profits or residual losses are shared equally. (The bonus and salary are regarded as "expenses" for purposes of calculating the amount of the bonus.)

Problem 15-12   (Statement of Partners' Capitals and Closing Entries)

David and Paul organize the D & P partnership on January 1, 19X1, with capital contributions of $40,000 and $60,000, respectively. It is agreed that each will be allowed a salary credit of $4,000 annually plus an additional 5 percent credit for interest on the beginning-of-year capital balances. Residual profits are to be divided equally.

Year	Profits before Interest and Salaries	Cash Withdrawals David	Paul
19X1	$20,000	$3,000	$10,500
19X2	17,325	4,500	6,250

Required:

a. Prepare a statement of partners' capital accounts for the two years ended December 31, 19X2.

b. Prepare closing entries as of December 31, 19X2.

Problem 15–13   (Schedule of Partners' Capital Accounts)

Pam, Sarah, and Katie have been partners throughout the year 19X1. The average capital balances for the year and their balances at the end of the year before closing the nominal accounts are as follows:

	Average Balances	Balances December 31, 19X1
Pam	Cr. $80,000	Cr. $60,000
Sarah	Cr. 5,000	Dr. 4,000
Katie	Cr. 15,000	Cr. 19,000

The profit for 19X1 is $64,000 before charging partners' drawing allowance (salaries) and before interest on average balances at the agreed rate of 4 percent per annum. Pam is entitled to a drawing account credit of $10,000, Sarah of $8,000, and Katie of $7,000 per annum. The balance of the profit is to be distributed at the rate of 60 percent to Pam, 30 percent to Sarah, and 10 percent to Katie.

It is intended to distribute amounts of cash to the partners so that after credits and distributions as indicated in the preceding paragraph, the balances in the partners' accounts will be proportionate to their profit-sharing ratio. None of the partners is to pay in any money, but it is desired to distribute the lowest possible amount of cash.

Required:

Prepare a schedule of the partners' capital accounts, showing balances at the end of 19X1 before closing, the allocations of the net profit for 19X1, the cash distributed, and the closing balances.

(AICPA adapted)

Problem 15–14 (Accrual Accounting and the Distribution of Profits)

The Ben-Russ-Mick partnership was formed in 19X0. Ben contributed a major portion of the capital, and Russ and Mick provided important management skills and experience. The partnership agreement specifies that the accounting records shall be maintained on the accrual basis and that the net income shall be distributed to the partners as follows:

1. Each partner shall receive 5 percent interest on the balance in his capital account at the beginning of the year.
2. Russ and Mick shall each receive a commission of 10 percent of net income determined under *cash basis* accounting after deducting the normal allowance for depreciation and the interest on capital. For this purpose, all merchandise purchased is to be regarded as an expense.
3. The net income remaining after deducting the interest on capital and commissions due to Russ and Mick shall be distributed equally, except that the total portion of net income to Ben must not be less than 50 percent of the net income determined under the firm's accrual accounting system.

There were no changes in the partners' capital accounts during 19X1. The partnership comparative balance sheet follows.

BEN-RUSS-MICK PARTNERSHIP
Comparative Balance Sheet

	December 31, 19X0		*December 31, 19X1*	
Assets				
Cash		$ 7,000		$ 11,120
Accounts receivable—customers	$ 5,000		$ 6,000	
Allowance for doubtful accounts	200	4,800	120	5,880
Inventory		26,000		29,000
U.S. government bonds (at cost)				8,000
Fixed assets (at cost)	$120,000		$220,000	
Accumulated depreciation	40,300	79,700	46,300	173,700
Prepaid expenses		600		800
Total assets		$118,100		$228,500
Liabilities and Capital				
Accounts payable—trade		$ 6,200		$ 8,000
Accrued wages		5,500		5,000
Accrued taxes		500		500
Deferred income		5,900		
Bonds payable				90,000
Net income, 19X1				25,000
Partners' capitals:				
Ben	$ 80,000		$ 80,000	
Russ	15,000		15,000	
Mick	5,000	100,000	5,000	100,000
Total liabilities and capital		$118,100		$228,500

Required:

Given the balance sheets above, prepare—

a. A schedule, supported by computational detail, showing the adjustments necessary to convert the net income for 19X1 from an accrual basis to a cash basis.

b. A statement, supported by computational detail, indicating the distribution of 19X1 net income to the partners.

(AICPA adapted)

Problem 15–15   (Partnership Billings and Working Papers)

Deskins and Demaris, architectural designers and interior decorators, combined May 1, 19X1, agreeing to share profits: Deskins, 80 percent; and Demaris, 20 percent. Deskins contributed furniture and fixtures, $3,000, and cash, $2,000; Demaris contributed cash, $500.

They plan to submit monthly bills and make the following arrangements with their clients:

1. The salaries of draftsmen and others who are paid on an hourly basis shall be billed to clients at an hourly rate for time spent on each job, plus 125 percent for overhead and profit and plus 4.50 percent for payroll taxes.
2. Partners' time on jobs shall be billed at $10 an hour.
3. A 10 percent service fee shall be charged on purchases of furniture, drapes, and so forth, installed on the jobs. (Deskins and Demaris will pay the vendors and charge their clients for these purchases but would like to have their operating statements reflect only revenue from services.)
4. There will be no service fee on taxis, telephone, and other expenses identifiable to jobs and charged to clients.

Voucher register totals for May are given below:

Credits	
Vouchers payable	$3,469
Taxes withheld—federal income	93
Taxes withheld—FICA	27
Income from charges to jobs for partners' time	790
Total	$4,379
Debits	
Purchases and expenses chargeable to clients	$1,615
Partners' drawings (Deskins, $100; Demaris, $125)	225
General expenses	784
Jobs in process:	
Draftsmen's salaries	940
Partner's time	790
Petty cash fund	25
Total	$4,379

The first debit column in the voucher register is analyzed as follows:

Purchases subject to 10% fee:		
Client M, Job 51	$1,210	
Client H, Job 52	320	$1,530
Expenses chargeable to clients:		
Client M 51	$ 23	
Client M 54	7	
Client H 52	19	
Client L 53	36	85
		$1,615

The client has not yet authorized them to do Job M 54. The partners are confident, however, that the job will be authorized and the above expenses, as well as charges for time spent by Deskins and a draftsman on preliminary designs, will be billed and collected.

The payroll analysis is summarized below. Partners' time on jobs, charged to the jobs at $5 an hour, is summarized in the payroll analysis for convenience in posting costs to job sheets, although the partners are not paid for direct time on jobs.

	Secretary	Drafters	Deskins	Demaris
Job:				
M 51		$ 312	$120	$150
H 52		276	60	115
L 53		304	65	160
M 54		48	120	
		$ 940	$365	$425
General expenses:				
General office	$160	40		
Idle time		60		
Total payroll	$160	$1,040		

Journal entries recorded depreciation on furniture and fixtures of $25 and the employer's share of federal and state taxes of $54.

There were no cash receipts other than the original investment. The cash disbursements book shows the following totals:

Debit:	Vouchers payable	$2,373
Credit:	Cash	2,358
Credit:	Discount on purchases	15

Required:

a. Compute billings to clients for May.

b. Prepare a working paper showing the balance sheet, profit and loss general ledger accounts, and the profit allocation at May 31, 19X1. Show how you arrive at these balances by entering all May transactions on the working paper. Use the accounts indicated in the voucher register.

(AICPA adapted)

Problem 15-16   (Error Correction and Partnership Financial Statements)

You are engaged to assist B & M Footcover Company, a partnership, that was organized on January 2, 19X1, and has operated one year unsuccessfully. Barnes, who owns Boot Distributors Company, contributed $12,000 in inventory for a 50 percent interest in B & M Footcover Company. On the same date, January 2, 19X1, Monroe, who owns Dress Shoe Distributors Company, contributed $2,000 cash and $10,000 in inventory for a 50 percent interest. All profits and losses are shared equally.

While examining the records of B & M Footcover Company, you determine the following facts:

1. A part-time bookkeeper had discarded all cash register tapes and invoices for expenses and purchases. He also served as bookkeeper for the Dress Shoe Distributors Company.

2. The partners state that the only existing payables are to themselves and are as follows:

Boot Distributors Company	$7,500
Dress Shoe Distributors Company	4,500
	$12,000

3. You prepare the following summary of cash transactions from bank statements and canceled checks:

Cash balance, January 2, 19X1		$2,000
Receipts:		
Sales	$48,000	
Inventory liquidation	6,000	54,000
		$56,000
Disbursements:		
Purchases	$26,000	
Operating expenses	15,000	
Leasehold improvements (five-year lease)	6,000	
Liquidating expenses	4,000	51,000
Cash balance, December 31, 19X1		$ 5,000

4. On December 31, 19X1, each partner was paid $2,500 in partial settlement of the $12,000 liability.

5. The partners indicate that the dollar amounts of regular sales of boots and dress shoes were approximately equal, and that the dollar amounts of liquidation sale of boots and dress shoes were also approximately equal. There was a uniform markup of 20 percent on cost of boots and 50 percent on cost of dress shoes. All sales were for cash. The ending inventory of merchandise was liquidated on December 31, 19X1, for 50 percent of the retail sales price.

6. The partners believe that some dress shoes may have been returned to Dress Shoe Distributors Company; there is no record of such returns, however, on the books of either company.

Required:

a. Estimate the unrecorded amount of dress shoes returned to Dress Shoe Distributors Company, if any.

b. Prepare an income statement for the partnership for 19X1.

c. Prepare a statement of changes in partners' capital accounts in 19X1.

(AICPA adapted)

Problem 15–17   (Partnership Working Paper)

Zef/Fro Company is a partnership that has not maintained adequate accounting records because it has been unable to employ a competent bookkeeper. The company sells hardware items to the retail trade and also wholesales to builders and contractors. As the company's CPA, you have been asked to prepare the company's financial statements as of June 30, 19X1.

Your working papers provide the following post-closing trial balance at December 31, 19X0:

ZEF/FRO COMPANY
Postclosing Trial Balance
December 31, 19X0

Cash	$10,000	
Accounts receivable	9,050	
Allowance for bad debts		$ 600
Merchandise inventory	35,000	
Prepaid insurance	150	
Automobiles	8,200	
Allowance for depreciation—automobiles		4,250
Furniture and fixtures	1,600	
Allowance for depreciation—furniture and fixtures		650
Accounts payable		14,650
Bank loan payable		8,000
Accrued expenses		200
Zef, capital		17,500
Fro, capital		18,150
	$64,000	$64,000

You are able to collect the following information at June 30, 19X1.

1. Your analysis of cash transactions, derived from the company's bank statements and checkbook stubs, is as follows:

Deposits:	
Cash receipts from customers ($30,000 of this amount represents collections on receivables including redeposited protested checks totaling $600)	$48,700
Bank loan, 1/2/X1 (4/2/X1, 10% discounted)	7,800
Bank loan, 4/1/X1 (7/30/X1, 10% discounted)	8,700
Sale of old automobile	45
Total deposits	$65,245
Disbursements:	
Payments to merchandise creditors	$31,000
Payments to Internal Revenue Service on Fro's 19X1 declaration of estimated income tax	3,000
General expenses	7,000
Bank loan, 1/2/X1	8,000
Bank loan, 4/2/X1	8,000
Payment for new automobile	2,400
Protested checks	700
Zef, withdrawals	5,000
Fro, withdrawals	2,500
Total disbursements	$67,600

2. The protested checks include customers' checks totaling $600 that were redeposited and a $100 check from an employee that is still on hand.

3. Accounts receivable from customers for merchandise sales amount to $15,050 and include accounts totaling $800 that have been placed with an attorney for collection. Correspondence with the client's attorney reveals that one of the accounts for $175 is uncollectible. Experience indicates that 1 percent of credit sales will prove uncollectible.

4. On April 1, a used automobile was purchased. The list price of the automobile was $2,900, and $500 was allowed for the trade-in of an old automobile, even though the dealer stated that its condition was so poor that he did not want it. The client sold the old automobile, which cost $1,600 and was fully depreciated at December 31, 19X0, to an auto wrecker for $45. The old automobile was in use up to the date of its sale.

5. Depreciation is recorded by the straight-line method and is computed on acquisitions to the nearest full month. The estimated life for furniture and fixtures is 10 years and for automobiles is three years. (Salvage value is to be ignored in computing depreciation. No asset other than the car in item [4] was fully depreciated prior to June 30, 19X1.)

6. Other data as of June 30, 19X1, include the following:

Merchandise inventory	$32,000
Prepaid insurance	80
Accrued expenses	176

7. Accounts payable to merchandise vendors total $9,750. There is on hand an $800 credit memorandum from a merchandise vendor for returned merchandise; the company will apply the credit to July merchandise purchases. Neither the credit memorandum nor the return of the merchandise had been recorded on the books.

8. Profits and losses are divided equally between the partners.

Required:

Prepare a working paper that provides on the accrual basis information regarding transactions for the six months ended June 30, 19X1, the results of the partnership operations for the period, and the financial position of the partnership at June 30, 19X1.

(AICPA adapted)

Problem 15–18   (Partnership Working Paper)

The Charles, Steve, & Robert Partnership engaged you to adjust its accounting records and convert them uniformly to the accrual basis in anticipation of admitting Dow as a new partner. Some accounts are on the accrual basis, and others are on the cash basis. The partnership's books were closed at December 31 19X1, by the bookkeeper who prepared the general ledger trial balance that appears below:

CHARLES, STEVE, & ROBERT PARTNERSHIP
General Ledger Trial Balance
December 31, 19X1

Cash	$ 18,000	
Accounts Receivable	50,000	
Inventory	26,000	
Land	9,000	
Buildings	50,000	
Allowance for Depreciation—Buildings		$ 19,000
Equipment	56,000	
Allowance for Depreciation—Equipment		6,000
Goodwill	5,000	
Accounts Payable		55,000
Allowance for Future Inventory Losses		4,000
Charles, Capital		40,000
Steve, Capital		60,000
Robert, Capital		30,000
	$214,000	$214,000

Your inquiries disclosed the following:

1. The partnership was organized on January 1, 19X0, with no provision in the partnership agreement for the distribution of partnership profits and losses. During

19X0, profits were distributed equally among the partners. The partnership agreement was amended effective January 1, 19X1, to provide for the following profit and loss ratio: Charles, 50 percent; Steve, 25 percent; and Robert, 25 percent. The amended partnership agreement also stated that the accounting records were to be maintained on the accrual basis and that any adjustments necessary for 19X0 should be allocated according to the 19X0 distribution of profits.

2. The following amounts were not recorded as prepayments or accruals:

	December 31	
	19X1	*19X0*
Prepaid insurance	$ 700	$ 800
Advances from customers	1,550	1,100
Accrued interest expense		450

The advances from customers were recorded as sales in the year the cash was received.

3. In 19X1, the partnership recorded a provision of $4,000 for anticipated declines in inventory prices. You convinced the partners that the provision was unnecessary and should be removed from the books.

4. The partnership charged equipment purchased for $8,000 on January 3, 19X1, to expense. This equipment has an estimated life of 10 years and an estimated salvage value of $1,000. The partnership depreciates its capitalized equipment under the declining balance method at twice the straight-line depreciation rate.

5. The partners agreed to establish an allowance for doubtful accounts at 2 percent of current accounts receivable and 5 percent of past-due accounts. At December 31, 19X0, the partnership had $39,000 of accounts receivable, of which only $4,000 was past due. At December 31, 19X1, 12 percent of accounts receivable was past due, of which $4,000 represented sales made in 19X0 and was generally considered collectible. The partnership had written off uncollectible accounts in the year the accounts became worthless as follows:

	Accounts Written Off in	
	19X1	*19X0*
19X1 accounts	$800	
19X0 accounts	700	$250

Required:

Prepare a working paper showing the adjustments and the adjusted trial balance for the partnership on the accrual basis at December 31, 19X1. All adjustments affecting income should be made directly to partners' capital accounts. Number your adjusting entries. Supporting computations should be in good form.

(AICPA adapted)

In the previous chapter, the formation and operation of partnerships were examined. In this chapter, the analysis is extended to consider realignment of ownership structure due to the admission of a new partner, the death of a partner, or the retirement of a partner.

BASIC LEGAL PROVISIONS

Under common law, any change in the ownership structure of a partnership results in its dissolution, although concurrently a new partnership is often formed. In many instances, the legal dissolution is not perceived to be a reflection of an overt intention to interrupt the continuity of partnership operations. However, the existence of this common-law provision, together with numerous ancillary concepts concerning the nature of partnership dissolution, often has created problems that disrupt and sometimes terminate the operations of the business. Some of the problems created by this legal dissolution are the determination of equitable settlements to the partners and the computation of their taxable net income. Provisions of the Uniform Partnership Act partially ameliorate the dangers of an unexpected dissolution by stating more precisely the nature of a dissolution and also by reducing the number of conditions under which the partnership may be dissolved.

Section 29 of the act defines *dissolution* of a partnership as "the change in the relation of the partners caused by any partner ceasing to be associated in the carrying on as distinguished from the winding up of the business." The following partial enumeration from Sections 31 and 32 indicates the various types of conditions that constitute a legal dissolution of a partnership:

1. By completion of a definite term of existence (or a particular undertaking) specified in the partnership agreement.
2. By the express will of any partner when no definite term of existence is specified in the agreement.
3. By the death of a partner.
4. By decree of a court for various reasons.
5. By the bankruptcy of any partner or the partnership.

It should be noted, however, that sale of an interest in the partnership does not of itself constitute a dissolution (Section 27), and although the admission or retirement of a partner by implication dissolves the partnership, according to Section 41(1), this provision has little *functional* significance if the partnership is immediately reestablished without actually terminating its operations. Furthermore, various states have adapted for their own purposes certain provisions of the Uniform Partnership Act such that the partners are permitted to include in the articles of copartnership further restrictions on dissolution. For example, the Texas Uniform Partnership Act allows a provision to be included in the partnership agreement prescribing that the death of a partner is not a cause of dissolution.

In view of this trend toward greater permanency in the partnership ownership configuration, the *legal* problems associated with ownership realignment need not be emphasized in the following discussion.

In order to facilitate a systematic review of the accounting problems involved in changes in the ownership structure, three general classes of realignment will be considered:

1. Admission of a new partner.
2. Retirement of a partner.
3. Death of a partner.

These classes are obviously not mutually exclusive. For example, a new partner may be admitted to an existing partnership by purchasing the interest of a retiring partner. Nonetheless, the above classes do provide a framework for analyzing most of the basic accounting problems associated with the realignment of ownership interests.

ADMISSION OF A NEW PARTNER

There are two principal bases on which a new partner may be admitted to an existing partnership. Either the new partner may invest cash or other assets in the business so that the net assets of the partnership are increased by his or her contribution, or he or she may purchase an interest directly from one or more of the existing partners. In the latter case, the consideration merely passes between the partners, acting as individuals, and partnership net assets are usually not altered. The firm's potential need for additional resources is often an important determining factor as to the method elected for admitting a new partner. For example, a deficiency in current working capital may be the compelling initial motivation for the admission of a new partner. Once the old partners have selected a basis for admitting a new partner, his or her capital credit must be duly recorded, as well as any necessary adjustments to the capital accounts of the existing partners and/or the assets of the partnership.

Prior to the admission of a new partner, it is important to carefully analyze the partnership's existing asset (and liability) values as well as of the asset values to be contributed by the new partner. In this analysis, three types of assets should be considered:

1. Existing assets, tangible and intangible, presently recorded in the books of the partnership should be appraised and their current market values established. Although the partners may elect not to record appraisal increments, these values should nonetheless be considered in analyzing the basis of the admission "price" to be paid by the new partner.
2. Unrecorded partnership assets, particularly intangible assets, may be implied by comparing the price paid by the new partner for an interest in the partnership and the preexistent capital after adjustment for

appraisal increments. Unrecorded assets may include identifiable tangibles and also goodwill attributable to the existing partners.

3. The assets to be contributed by the new partner must be evaluated. In addition, a comparison of the admission price with the new partner's equity in identifiable assets may suggest that goodwill is being contributed by the new partner.

Once this analysis has been completed, the appropriate capital account balance for each partner can be derived from the related asset and liability values to be recorded.

Admission with Payment to the Partnership

The entries to record the admission of a new partner vary, depending on the results of the analysis described in the previous paragraph. A sequence of three cases will be used to illustrate alternative entries to record the admission of a new partner under varying fact conditions. In each case, the new partner contributes assets to the partnership in payment for being admitted as a partner.

Case 1. No Unrecorded Assets

Assume that X and Y are partners with capital balances of $7,000 and $3,000, respectively. The profit- and loss-sharing ratio is 60 : 40. Z invests tangible assets valued at $15,000 for a 50 percent interest in the capital of the partnership. Concurrently, an appraisal of existing partnership net assets reveals a current market valuation of $15,000.

An analysis of these data indicates that Z is investing $15,000 for a one-half interest in partnership net assets, which after the investment by Z have a total fair market value of $30,000. The data thus imply that unrecorded assets do not exist. However, a choice must be made about whether to record the appraisal increment for existing partnership assets. The alternative entries to record the admission of Z are as follows:

1. Appraisal increment recorded:

Assets	5,000	
X, Capital		3,000
Y, Capital		2,000
Assets	15,000	
Z, Capital		15,000

2. Appraisal increment not recorded:

Assets	15,000	
X, Capital (60% × $2,500)		1,500
Y, Capital (40% × $2,500)		1,000
Z, Capital		12,500

In the first entry, the existing assets are restated to reflect the results of the appraisal. The increment in the value of existing assets is precisely the amount necessary to explain the $30,000 total value of the partnership that is inferred from Z's purchase of a 50 percent interest for $15,000.

Recorded assets prior to Z's admission	$10,000
Value increment per appraisal	5,000
Assets contributed by Z	15,000
Total asset value after Z's admission	$30,000

Since the $30,000 value of identifiable assets fully explains the inferred total value of the partnership, there is no goodwill. Corresponding to the revaluation of assets, the capital accounts of the old partners are credited by an amount equal to the increment in asset values. The increment is allocated between the partners on the basis of their profit-sharing percentages. Note that under this alternative, Z's capital account is credited for the full $15,000 invested.

In the second alternative, Z is merely given a 50 percent interest in the *recorded values* of the net assets (without appraisal increment adjustments) of the new partnership. Note, however, that the $12,500 credit to Z's capital account is $2,500 less than the $15,000 increase in partnership assets. This $2,500 is allocated to X and Y in the profit- and loss-sharing ratio. Suppose that the $5,000 appraisal increment is subsequently recorded (either through sale of the undervalued assets or through the enhanced income which results from recording $5,000 less in depreciation expense). Suppose as well that the profit- and loss-sharing ratio changes to 30 : 20 : 50. When the $5,000 appraisal increment is subsequently recorded, X's capital account will increase by $1,500 (30% × $5,000), Y's capital account will increase by $1,000 (20% × $5,000), and Z's capital account will increase by $2,500 (50% × $5,000). At such time, the difference between the two alternatives will have disappeared. Necessary conditions for the ultimate equivalence of the two methods are discussed in more detail following Cases 2 and 3.

Hereafter, it will be assumed that the *recorded* assets of the firm are properly valued, or that an adjustment for current market values has previously been recorded in the old partners' capital accounts. Further analysis of each situation, however, may disclose the existence of *unrecorded* goodwill.

Consider the following alternatives as to the amount of a new partner's contribution of assets. If the existing (old) partners are assumed to have total capital equities of $20,000, and the incoming (new) partner is called upon to contribute $10,000 for a one-third interest in new partnership capital, it is evident that the new partner is investing on the basis of the *average fractional interest* in capital of the old partners; that is, the retained two-thirds interest in capital of the old partners amounts to $20,000 for which the average one-third interest is

$10,000. In this instance, there is no evidence of intangibles which relate either to the new or old partners. However, should the new partner be required to invest more than $10,000 for a one-third interest in capital, one may argue that the leverage of the old partners in imposing this larger contribution—more than the *average fractional interest*—derives from their assumed possession of unrecorded intangibles (goodwill). On the other hand, should the amount of the required contribution of the new partner be less than $10,000, one may inversely conclude that this concession of a lower contributed amount—less than the *average fractional interest*—indicates the presence of goodwill identifiable with the new partner which is presumed to have value to the partnership in addition to that provided by his or her contribution of tangible assets. The acknowledgment of the existence of goodwill in alternatives two and three does not in itself resolve the question of whether it should be recorded. Whether or not such goodwill should be recorded raises the same questions as did the discussion in Chapter 15 of recording the partners' original contributions to the partnership. Accordingly, the bonus and goodwill methods are also alternative accounting solutions to the admission of a new partner to the partnership.

Case 2. Goodwill Contributed by Existing Partners

X and Y are partners with capital balances of $40,000 and $10,000, respectively. Profits and losses are shared in the ratio of 80 : 20. Z invests tangible assets valued at $30,000 for a 25 percent interest in the capital of the new partnership.

Observe that Z has acquired a $20,000 (25% × $80,000) interest in the tangible net assets of the firm, inclusive of Z's contribution, at a cost of $30,000. Since it is assumed that all tangible assets are properly valued, Z is apparently paying $10,000 for a one-fourth interest in *unrecorded* intangible assets of the partnership. Conventionally, this type of intangible asset is described as partnership *goodwill*. The amount of the goodwill can be determined by applying the following standard procedure:

1. Let C equal the total new capital of the firm, including the as yet undetermined goodwill, and solve the following two equations:
   a. (Fractional interest in capital retained by the old partners) × C = Total recorded capital balances of old partners.
   b. (Fractional interest in capital obtained by the new partner) × C = Investment of the new partner.
2. Determine the amount of implied goodwill by subtracting the total recorded net assets of the *new* firm (including the tangible assets contributed by the new partner) from the larger amount computed for C in (1) above. If *(a)* is larger, we infer that the new partner is contributing goodwill in addition to the assets identified in his or her investment; if *(b)* is larger, we conclude that the partnership possessed goodwill.

This procedure may be applied to the data of Case 2 in the following manner:

1. Computation of alternative capital balances:

$$a. \ .75(C) = \$50,000$$
$$C = \$66,667$$

$$b. \ .25(C) = \$30,000$$
$$C = \$120,000$$

2. Computation of goodwill:

$$\text{Goodwill} = \$120,000 - \$80,000$$
$$= \$40,000$$

To understand why the procedure works, consider the following. If the new partner's cost is larger than his or her interest in recorded assets (as in Case 2), he or she is paying for something (unrecorded goodwill) in addition to the recorded assets. Since the new partner is paying for it, by inference, the old partners already have generated the unrecorded goodwill. Hence, if goodwill is to be recorded, the old partners' capital accounts should be credited with their equity in the goodwill. Prior to making such adjustments, the old partners' capital accounts cannot be relied on to calculate the total capital of the firm, including goodwill. Thus, equation *(a)* does not provide a reliable measure of the firm's total capital. But, since the new partner's cost reflects the value of his or her interest in the firm's total capital, including goodwill, generated by the old partners, equation *(b)* can be used to infer total capital.

The $40,000 valuation for goodwill may also be explained in different terms by reconsidering the details of the investment transaction. It was noted that Z paid $10,000 more than his or her acquired capital interest in the net tangible assets of the new firm. It is now evident that this $10,000 was a payment for a one-fourth interest in the unrecorded goodwill of $40,000.

The two alternative methods for recording the entry of the new partner into the partnership are the following:

1. Bonus method:

Assets 30,000		
X, Capital (80% × $10,000)		8,000
Y, Capital (20% × $10,000)		2,000
Z, Capital (25% × $80,000)		20,000

2. Goodwill method:

Goodwill 40,000		
X, Capital (80% × $40,000)		32,000
Y, Capital (20% × $40,000)		8,000
Assets 30,000		
Z, Capital		30,000

Regardless of which method is used, note that the resultant capital balances are in the agreed-upon percentage relationship; that is, Z has a 25 percent interest while partners X and Y share a 75 percent interest.

	X	Y	Z	Total
Balances prior to Z's entry	$40,000	$10,000	—	$ 50,000
1. Bonus method adjustments	8,000	2,000	$20,000	30,000
Resulting totals	$48,000	$12,000	$20,000	$ 80,000
Percentage of total	60%	15%	25%	100%
Balances prior to Z's entry	$40,000	$10,000	—	$ 50,000
2. Goodwill method adjustments	32,000	8,000	$30,000	70,000
Resulting totals	$72,000	$18,000	$30,000	$120,000
Percentage of total	60%	15%	25%	100%

The equivalence of the two methods with respect to the relative equities of the partners is subject to certain constraints to be investigated at a later point.

These two methods are, in substance, identical with the alternative methods used in Case 1. In Case 2, however, the recorded tangible assets are assumed to be correctly valued. Thus, the choice between the methods turns on beliefs about the propriety of recording implicit goodwill rather than of recording appraisal increments (or decrements). Generally, the evidence supporting the existence and amount of *goodwill* is less persuasive than that provided by an appraisal that indicates the fair values of tangible assets. Nevertheless, the desirability of giving the new partner credit for the full amount of the cost may outweigh the undesirability of recording a subjective valuation for goodwill.

Case 3. Goodwill Contributed by New Partner

X and Y are partners with capital balances of $50,000 and $30,000, respectively. Except for possible goodwill, all assets are assumed to be recorded at their fair values. Profits and losses are shared in the ratio of 70 : 30. Z invests tangible assets valued at $15,000 for a 20 percent interest in the capital of the new partnership.

In this instance, Z acquires an interest of $19,000 (20% × $95,000) in the net tangible assets of the firm at a cost of $15,000. By implication, Z has contributed an additional asset to the partnership for which he or she receives additional capital credit. The standard procedure may again be applied to estimate the amount of the implicit goodwill:

1. Computation of alternative capital balances:

$$a. \quad .80(C) = \$80,000$$
$$C = \$100,000$$

$$b. \quad .20(C) = \$15,000$$
$$C = \$75,000$$

2. Computation of goodwill:

$$\text{Goodwill} = \$100,000 - \$95,000$$
$$= \$5,000$$

Note that equation *(a)* is used to infer the total capital of the firm. Since the new partner is contributing goodwill in addition to tangible assets valued at $15,000, the $15,000 alone does not represent 20 percent of the firm's total capital; thus, equation *(b)* cannot be used. But, the summed capital accounts of the old partners should equal 80 percent of the firm's total capital, and equation *(a)* is appropriate.

In other words, the existing partners have acquired an 80 percent interest in the implicit goodwill contributed by Z when it accrues to the benefit of the partnership. For this interest, they have given to Z a $4,000 interest in partnership assets in excess of the tangible assets he or she contributed to the firm ($19,000 − $15,000). Therefore, the amount of the goodwill, as measured by the price imposed upon Z for his or her interest in net tangible assets, is $5,000 ($4,000/80%).

Either the goodwill or the bonus method may again be used to record this transaction:

1. Bonus method:

Assets	15,000	
X, Capital (70% × $4,000)	2,800	
Y, Capital (30% × $4,000)	1,200	
Z, Capital (20% × $95,000)		19,000

2. Goodwill method:

Assets	15,000	
Goodwill	5,000	
Z, Capital		20,000

Recall that the agreed-upon terms for Z's entry were that Z was to receive a 20 percent interest in capital. Both methods are consistent with that agreement. Under the bonus method, the total recorded capital of the firm is $95,000 ($50,000 + $30,000 + $15,000), and Z's capital account is 20 percent of $95,000, or $19,000. Under the goodwill method, the firm's total recorded capital is $100,000 ($50,000 + $30,000 + $15,000 + $5,000), and Z's capital account is 20 percent of $100,000, or $20,000.

In the previous three cases, it may be observed that *the profit and loss ratios were used when allocating goodwill among the partners or when a bonus was allocated between the partners.* For example, if a bonus were awarded to the new partner, each of the old partners was charged for a portion of the bonus in accordance with his or her profit- and loss-sharing percentage. Similarly, when a bonus was given to the old partners, it was allocated between them on the basis of their profit and loss ratio.

Goodwill can be perceived as being the present value of future net income in excess of normal. If goodwill is not recognized, the future net income will be allocated in accordance with the profit-sharing ratio as the net income is realized. The decision to presently record the present value of that income does not alter the fact that it is income to the partners. Thus, it should be shared in accordance with the profit and loss ratio. In a similar manner, a bonus to the old partners increases their capital accounts in apparent reflection of their operating effectiveness. And, from the perspective of the old partners, the bonus has exactly the same impact as would additional partnership net income; thus, it is also shared in accordance with the profit and loss ratio. If the old partners are charged for a bonus that is given to the new partner, the bonus may be viewed as a cost that is incurred and charged to the old partners. From this perspective, it should be treated like an expense that is chargeable to the old partners.

Also observe that the recipient(s) of the bonus under the bonus method is(are) the contributor(s) of the goodwill to the new partnership. In Case 2, X and Y contributed the goodwill (through the old partnership) and received the bonuses; in Case 3, Z contributed the goodwill and received the bonus.

A Comparison of the Bonus and Goodwill Methods

Accounting problems of recording asset revaluations and/or implicit goodwill have been considered relative to the *bonus* method of recording a new partner's admission with payment to the partnership. However, an understanding of the implications of selecting one method or the other requires further analysis of the conditions under which the two methods are ultimately equivalent in terms of their effects on the relative equities of the individual partners.

Assume that goodwill is recorded and subsequently proves to have been overstated or valueless. A condition of equivalence would require that after the write-down adjustment to eliminate the amount of the recorded goodwill (loss realization), the individual partners' capital accounts should be equivalent to those balances that would have been obtained had the bonus method been used originally. Alternatively, if the bonus method is initially employed and subsequently a determinable amount of goodwill is confirmed by an objective transaction of the partnership, a similar requirement of equality is imposed to establish equivalence.

The conditions necessary to achieve equivalence of these alternative methods will be introduced and tested by means of an example. Using the data of Case 3, the effect of recording the admission of Z with goodwill recognized, and subsequently writing off the total amount of this intangible, is contrasted with the capital balances obtained by initially applying the bonus method (see Illustration 16–1). Interim transactions are ignored in order to isolate the equity effects of the two methods. Three different profit and loss ratios are assumed:

	Profit and Loss Ratios		
	X	Y	Z
Situation 1	56%	24%	20%
Situation 2	49	21	30
Situation 3	60	20	20

Illustration 16–1 isolates in Situation 1 the two conditions necessary for the equivalence of the bonus and goodwill methods:

1. The percentage interest in profits and losses of the new partner must be the same as his or her initial fractional interest in the partnership capital.
2. The new (or adjusted) percentage interests in profits and losses of the old partners must be in the same relative proportion as their old percentage interests.

In Situation 1, Z has a 20 percent interest in profits and losses, which is equal to his or her initial fractional interest in partnership capital, and the new percentage interests in profits and losses of X and Y are in the same relative proportion as their prior percentage interests—80 percent of 70 percent for X, and 80 percent of 30 percent for Y, or 70 : 30 = 56 : 24. In Situation 2, the new percentage interests in profits and losses of the old partners are in the same relative proportion, but the interest of Z in profits and losses exceeds his or her initial fractional interest in capital; consequently, an advantage accrues to X and Y equivalent in amount to the disadvantage to Z. In Situation 3, the new percentage interests of X and Y are in a different proportion than existed prior to the admission of Z, that is, 70 : 30 ≠ 60 : 20; this condition results in an advantage to Y with a corresponding disadvantage to X.

Admission with Payment to the Existing Partner(s)

A second basic method of acquiring an interest in a partnership is to purchase a capital equity directly from one or more of the old partners, without an increase in partnership assets. In this section, two cases will be distinguished:

1. Purchase of a portion of one partner's interest.
2. Purchase of a partial interest uniformly from all of the existing partners.

In both instances, the ownership structure is numerically enlarged by the transfer of an interest in the existing partnership to a new member. The purchase of one partner's total interest in a partnership, thereby replacing the old partner with a new partner, will be discussed in a subsequent section that deals with the retirement of partners.

ILLUSTRATION 16–1

	X	Y	Z	Total
Bonus method:				
Capital balances	$47,200	$28,800	$19,000	$ 95,000
Goodwill method:				
Situation 1:				
Initial capital balances	$50,000	$30,000	$20,000	$100,000
Write-off of goodwill	(2,800)	(1,200)	(1,000)	(5,000)
Ending capital balances	$47,200	$28,800	$19,000	$ 95,000
Difference between methods				
after write-off	–0–	–0–	–0–	–0–
Situation 2:				
Initial capital balances	$50,000	$30,000	$20,000	$100,000
Write-off of goodwill	(2,450)	(1,050)	(1,500)	(5,000)
Ending capital balances	$47,550	$28,950	$18,500	$ 95,000
Difference between methods				
after write-off	$ 350	$ 150	$ (500)	–0–
Situation 3:				
Initial capital balances	$50,000	$30,000	$20,000	$100,000
Write-off of goodwill	(3,000)	(1,000)	(1,000)	(5,000)
Ending capital balances	$47,000	$29,000	$19,000	$ 95,000
Difference between methods				
after write-off	$ (200)	$ 200	–0–	–0–

If an existing partner sells a portion of his or her interest in capital and profits to another individual, the only entry *required* on the books of the partnership is one that establishes the new partner's capital credit by a transfer of the amount of the purchased interest from the capital account of the selling partner. For example, if X and Y are partners, with capital balances of $60,000 and $40,000, respectively, and Y sells one fourth of his or her interest to Z for $12,000, the only entry required on the partnership books is:

Y, Capital (25% × $40,000) 10,000
    Z, Capital   10,000

The cash consideration that moves laterally between the old and new partners is established independently by Y and Z and need not be reflected in the above entry on the partnership books. From the point of view of the partnership entity, Y has merely transferred a personal asset to a new partner, viz, one-fourth of his or her *recorded* interest in partnership capital; only this fact need be recognized in the partnership accounts.

If in the preceding illustration Z had purchased a one-fourth interest in the partnership by means of a direct purchase from *both* X and Y for $30,000 (a ratable transfer of one-fourth of the monetary interest of each in the partnership), the accounting entry to record the capital transfer is essentially the same. Each partner conveys to Z one-fourth of his or her interest in the *recorded* capital of the firm.

X, Capital (25% × $60,000)	15,000	
Y, Capital (25% × $40,000)	10,000	
Z, Capital		25,000

Again, the cash price for the purchased interests is not a compelling factor affecting the partnership accounts because the sale represents an *independent* transaction between the existing partners and the incoming partner. The transaction may be compared to the sale of shares of corporate stock in the open market subsequent to their original issuance; the total stockholders' equity of the corporate entity remains unaffected by the sale. Only the identity and the relative interests of the various owners are changed.

Two problems intrude upon this relatively simple accounting framework for recording the purchase of a partnership interest directly from one or more partners. First, an argument can be made that the cash price established in the sale of an interest should be used as an independent index of the current value of the partnership net assets. If this premise is accepted and if the recorded net assets of the partnership are assumed to reflect current market values, the purchase price may be used to estimate the amount of goodwill possessed by the preexistent partnership. Returning to the previous example in which Z purchased a one-fourth ratable interest from X and Y for $30,000, it is possible to conclude that the total value of the partnership net assets may be $120,000 ($30,000 is one-fourth of the total value). Since the recorded partners' equity presently is only $100,000, implicit goodwill of $20,000 may be inferred from this purchase. If the goodwill were recorded, and assuming X and Y share profits and losses equally, the entries to record the admission of Z are as follows:

Goodwill	20,000	
X, Capital		10,000
Y, Capital		10,000
X, Capital (25% × $70,000)	17,500	
Y, Capital (25% × $50,000)	12,500	
Z, Capital		30,000

In an analogous manner, goodwill identified with the new partner may be computed. The advantages of recording the implicit goodwill in either case, and the requisite conditions for the equivalence of this and the preceding method, are the same as those discussed earlier in this chapter.

A second problem arising from the purchase of an interest from more than one existing partner concerns the distribution settlement of cash to the selling partners. This is ultimately a matter of negotiation between the new partner and each of the old partners or between the old partners. One allocation scheme, consistent with the above data, is the following:

	X	Y	Total
Capital balances, as recorded	$60,000	$40,000	$100,000
Implicit goodwill—allocated in			
profit and loss ratio	10,000	10,000	$20,000
Adjusted capital balances	$70,000	$50,000	$120,000
Retained capital—three fourths			
of adjusted balances	52,500	37,500	90,000
Capital transferred to Z—basis			
for allocation of cash	$17,500	$12,500	$ 30,000

An analysis of this scheme of cash distribution raises several questions. Since the sale was assumed to be independent of the partnership entity, one may take the position that it is inappropriate to utilize present partners' capital balances and provisions of the partnership agreement (i.e., the profit and loss ratios of X and Y) as a basis for determining the cash allocations. In this case, the capital balances are not in the profit- and loss-sharing ratios; consequently, X and Y are surrendering an interest in recorded partnership capital according to one ratio, 60 : 40, and they are forsaking an interest in future profits in another ratio, 50 : 50. The above scheme indicates the accepted method of recording, on the partnership books, the existence of implicit goodwill, and the resulting transfers of capital from X and Y to Z. The scheme, however, may not represent the most appropriate allocation of the $30,000 between the amount paid for an interest in present partnership capital and the amount paid for an interest in future profits and losses. The ultimate decision in respect to cash distributions remains with the old partners.

One may also appropriately question the basic premise underlying the conventional computation of implicit goodwill. It is tacitly assumed that the capital balances of the old partners and the purchase price of the new partner may serve as a basis for inferring the existence of unrecorded goodwill. However, as noted above, the new partner is, in fact, buying an interest in both present capital *and* future profits; accordingly, it is questionable whether only one of these components should be used in computing the amount of goodwill. For example, the price paid for a partnership interest that is in excess of identifiable net assets acquired may be a payment for the excess earning capacity of the business (goodwill); or it may represent the purchase of a greater interest in profits than in capital. If the latter interpretation prevails, the existence and amount of goodwill is an indeterminate element and should be recorded only when supporting evidence is compelling.

Legal Status of a New Partner

Section 27 of the Uniform Partnership Act confers upon any partner the right to convey by assignment to a third party his or her interest in the partnership—which is, as previously noted, personal property. This assignment does not, however, give the assignee authority to participate in the management of the business. Rather, it entitles the assignee merely to receive the profits and in the case of dissolution, to receive an interest in net assets that would normally accrue to the assignor.

However, if the existing partners agree to admit by assignment a new partner to the ownership structure, as is implicitly done when a prospective partner invests assets in the business, the new partner assumes the same rights and obligations as the old partners. This assumption is modified somewhat in Section 17 of the act, in which it is provided that the new partner is personally liable for only those liabilities created subsequent to his or her admission to the firm. Thus, if dissolution should occur shortly after the admission of a new partner, it is necessary to distinguish between "old" and "new" liabilities of the partnership. The reader will note that the accounting treatment previously discussed for the "purchase of an interest" implicitly assumes that the assignee is admitted to the partnership with the status of a new partner, that is, no special equity status is identified.

Tax Basis of a New Partner

The tax basis of a new partner admitted by investing assets in the business is determined in the same manner as was outlined in the preceding chapter, viz, the new partner's basis is the sum of the bases of the contributed assets plus the amount of any partnership liabilities he or she assumed, and less the amount of any personal liabilities of the new partner that is assumed by the existing partners.

For example, assume the following data for the XY Partnership:

	Tax Basis	Book Value
Assets	$50,000	$60,000
Liabilities	18,000	18,000
Capital (interest) of partners:		
X	30,000	25,000
Y	20,000	17,000

Z is admitted to a one-fourth interest in the capital, profits, and losses of XY Partnership by investing $14,000 cash, that is, one-fourth of the net assets of the new firm, $42,000 ($60,000 − $18,000), and he or she assumes a one-fourth responsibility for present partnership obligations.

Assuming that X and Y have equal interests in profits and losses, the tax bases of the contributed assets and relevant capital adjustments are given as follows:

	Tax Bases			
	Assets	*X*	*Y*	*Z*
Prior to Z's entry	$ 50,000	$ 30,000	$ 20,000	—
Adjustments to reflect Z's entry	+ 14,000	− 2,250	− 2,250	$ + 18,500
Adjusted balances	$ 64,000	$ 27,750	$ 17,750	$ 18,500

The basis of Z's interest can be proved:

Basis of assets contributed	$14,000
Partnership liabilities assumed (25% × $18,000)	4,500
	$18,500

Although acquiring a one-fourth interest in future profits and losses of the partnership, Z also assumed responsibility for one-fourth of the existing partnership liabilities. This is recognized in the reduction of X's and Y's tax bases by $2,250 each, the amount of partnership liabilities transferred to Z. Importantly, the sum of the asset tax bases, $64,000 ($50,000 + $14,000), is equal to the sum of the bases of the partners' capital interests in the firm, $64,000 ($27,750 + $17,750 + $18,500).

When a new partner purchases an interest *directly* from one or more of the existing partners, Section 742 of the Internal Revenue Code states that the basis of the new partner's interest in the firm is determined in a similar fashion. In essence, his or her basis is the price paid to acquire the interest, adjusted for liabilities assumed, and/or liabilities that the other partners assume. Thus, the tax basis of the new partner's interest can be different from the tax basis of the old partners' interests. This difference is subject to alternative tax treatments, and partners should obtain expert tax counsel when making decisions on this matter.

RETIREMENT OR DEATH OF A PARTNER

Retirement of a Partner

If one of the partners desires to withdraw from the partnership and is not in violation of the agreement between the partners (Section 31),[1] two sections of the Uniform Partnership Act are relevant. As noted previously, Section 27 permits a partner to convey an interest in the partnership either to the existing partners or to a third party. If sold to a third party, the assignee is admitted to the partnership and is accorded the status of partner *only* with the consent of the continuing partners. If they should disapprove, the assignee is entitled to receive the profits that would have accrued to the assignor. But he or she is not otherwise entitled to management privileges.

If there is no express agreement as to the settlement of accounts with a retiring partner, Section 42 provides that the retiring partner is entitled to have the value of his or her equity at the date of retirement ascertained, and to receive, as an ordinary creditor, an amount equal to this value plus an interest credit on this amount. However, he or she may choose to retain a passive interest in the firm and receive, in lieu of interest, the "profits attributable to the use of his or her right in the property of the dissolved partnership." Determining the value of a retiring partner's equity is often a basic issue in the settlement arrangement. The accounting problems of reclassifying the retiring partner's capital equity as a liability and the treatment of any assigned value increment in excess of recorded capital will be considered in the following discussion.

Sale of an Interest to a New Partner

The sale of a retiring partner's interest to a new partner introduces no special problems other than those relating to a conveyance of an interest. The admission of the new partner is recorded merely by transferring the recorded capital interest of the retiring partner to the new partner; however, the conditions of admission may indicate the presence of partnership goodwill. If goodwill is to be formally recognized in the accounts, the recorded amount is normally the *total* amount of goodwill attaching to the partnership entity, not merely the amount that relates to the retiring partner. However, in the event that goodwill previously existed in the partnership books and is reduced as a consequence of the retirement of a partner, that is, the goodwill attaches primarily to the retiring partner as a separate individual, the purchase transaction may indicate the amount of "lost" goodwill.

---

[1] If the withdrawal and the resulting partnership dissolution are in contravention of the articles of copartnership, the retiring partner is liable for damages suffered by the innocent partners (Section 38).

Sale of an Interest to Continuing Partners

If the continuing partners acquire the interest of a retiring partner, whether negotiating jointly or separately *outside* the partnership or jointly *within* and *through* the partnership entity, the essence of the accounting problem remains substantially unchanged. If the purchase is completed independently of the partnership, the transaction is analogous to the sale of an interest to a third party. And if the retiring partner sells his or her interest to the partnership entity, the substance of the transaction is unchanged but the partnership assumes the obligation to make payment to the retiring partner—essentially a liquidating distribution. As before, partnership goodwill may be inferred if the purchase price (or the computed amount of a liquidating settlement) exceeds the recorded capital of the retiring partner. In this case, however, the evaluation of goodwill is subject to question because the parties to the transaction are not mutually independent. The following case illustrates the sale to the partnership of a retiring partner's interest.

Case 4. Distribution of Partnership Assets to Retiring Partner

Z elects to retire from XYZ Partnership, and the remaining partners agree to purchase Z's interest *through the partnership*. The partners share profits and losses equally. On this date, the balance sheet of the partnership is as follows:

XYZ PARTNERSHIP
Balance Sheet
Date of Proposed Retirement

Assets		Equities	
Assets	$110,000	Liabilities	$ 10,000
		X, capital	30,000
		Y, capital	30,000
		Z, capital	40,000
Total assets	$110,000	Total equities	$110,000

An examination of the values of existing assets and an estimate of prospective earnings for future years indicate that Z's interest is worth considerably more than $40,000. It is determined that the current market value of the partnership assets is $140,000. After negotiation with Z and in consideration of the demonstrated excess earnings potential of the partnership, it is agreed that Z will receive $60,000, payment to be made in four annual installments, with interest of 9 percent accruing annually on the unpaid balance.

As a consequence of Z's retirement, the partnership is legally dissolved. The first accounting objective, therefore, is to determine and record the status of the retiring partner and to establish a proper basis of accounting for the partnership as a continuing entity. From this point of view, it is appropriate to adjust the assets to their current market values. Accordingly, the entry to record the value adjustments is as follows (assuming that profits and losses are shared equally):

Assets 30,000		
X, Capital		10,000
Y, Capital		10,000
Z, Capital		10,000

The entry to adjust the equity of the retiring partner in the continuing partnership may be made in either of two ways. Using a method similar to the bonus method previously discussed, the entry takes the following form:

Method 1:

Z, Capital 50,000		
X, Capital 5,000		
Y, Capital 5,000		
Notes Payable to Z		60,000

Since Z received $10,000 more than the recorded capital interest after adjustments were made for asset revaluations, there is evidence that the partnership has unrecorded goodwill. Should the partners elect to recognize a value for goodwill, the conventional approach is to record it in the following manner:

Method 2:

Z, Capital 50,000		
Goodwill 10,000		
Notes Payable to Z		60,000

If the $10,000 excess payment to Z does, in fact, represent a valid measure of a one-third interest in the unrecorded goodwill, then the total amount of goodwill ($30,000) might be recorded. If the total amount of goodwill is to be recorded, the following entries would be made:

Method 2 (as modified):

Goodwill 30,000		
X, Capital		10,000
Y, Capital		10,000
Z, Capital		10,000
Z, Capital 60,000		
Notes Payable to Z		60,000

These two methods may be analyzed as before for equivalence with respect to their effects on the partners' equities.

Death of a Partner

The death of a partner dissolves a partnership under provisions of the Uniform Partnership Act (Section 31). However, modifications of the act adopted by a number of states permit the partners to prevent dissolution by including a contrary provision in the partnership agreement.

It is important that the partnership agreement specify the procedures to be followed on the death of a partner whether or not legal dissolution is a consequence of the death. Whether the surviving partners acting separately or the partnership as an entity purchases the interest of the deceased partner, a determination of the value of this equity at the date of death is an important first consideration. When the partnership continues as an operating entity under the control of the surviving partners, the agreement may provide that payments for this interest be based on recorded partnership values, or that a revaluation of assets be made and the adjusted capital interests be based thereon. Where the agreement is silent with respect to payments made for a deceased partner's interest, the amount of settlement is the result of negotiations between the estate of the deceased partner and the surviving partners. The estate is accorded the same status under Section 42 as a retiring partner, viz, the option to receive either interest on an unliquidated capital balance, or profits attributable to the use of this equity.

Once the capital interest of the deceased partner is determined, the remaining partners must agree on an acceptable means of settlement. Life insurance covering individual partners is one commonly employed method of meeting this contingency. Two types of life insurance are often used: (1) cross-insurance and (2) entity insurance. If cross-insurance is utilized, the lives of individual partners are insured by the other partners independently of the partnership. When this type of coverage exists, the partnership does not incur an expense. If entity insurance is used, the partnership insures the life of each of the partners, and although nondeductible for income tax purposes, the premium payments represent proper expense charges in determining partnership net income.

If insurance is not available, the partners must decide whether to make a liquidating payment in cash or to make distributions of assets in kind. If the partnership is to be terminated, it is probable that distribution will be made in specific assets. However, if it is anticipated that partnership operations will continue, a method of installment cash payments, with interest, is a common method of discharging the obligation to the estate of the deceased partner.

Legal Status of a Retiring or Deceased Partner

The fact of partnership dissolution does not of itself result in the discharge of individual partners from unpaid partnership debts. However, Section 36 provides that "a partner is discharged from any existing liability upon dissolution of the partnership by an agreement to that effect between himself, the partnership creditors and the person or partnership continuing the business." Assuming that proper notice is given past and prospective creditors, the retiring or deceased partner is, at most, liable for only those obligations existing at the date of dissolution.

Summary

This chapter deals with the realignment of ownership structure due to the admission of a new partner, retirement of a partner, or death of a partner. Under common law, any change in the ownership structure of a partnership results in its dissolution. However, this provision poses no significant problems because the partnership may be immediately reestablished without actually terminating its operations. Furthermore, many states have altered the Uniform Partnership Act to allow partnerships to place restrictions on dissolution.

A new partner may be admitted to an existing partnership in two principal ways. The new partner may either invest cash or other assets in the partnership or purchase an interest directly from one or more existing partners. When a new partner contributes assets to the partnership in order to gain admission, a choice must be made regarding whether to record any appraisal increments for existing partnership assets. Next, it must be determined whether any unrecorded (implied) goodwill exists. If implied goodwill exists, the amount of the goodwill may be recorded using either the goodwill method or the bonus method. Under the goodwill method, the amount of the goodwill is recorded on the books of the partnership. In contrast, the bonus method does not record implied goodwill; instead, the partner's capital accounts are adjusted to reflect the amount of the implied goodwill.

Upon retirement, a partner may convey his or her interest in the partnership to a new partner or to the existing partners. From an accounting standpoint, the transfer of an interest to a new partner often requires only a transfer of the retiring partner's recorded capital interest to the new partner. However, the admission of the new partner may have implications with respect to goodwill. If a retiring partner's interest is sold to existing partners, the transaction may take place outside of the partnership or through the partnership. In either case, the transaction is analogous to the sale of an interest to a third party. However, in the latter case, the obligation to make settlement to the retiring partner is assumed by the partnership entity.

Upon the death of a partner, the partnership may be dissolved, or it may continue to operate, depending on the legal circumstances and the intentions of the remaining partners. If the partnership continues to operate, the deceased partner's interest may be purchased by the individual partners or by the partnership itself. Once the value of the deceased partner's interest has been determined, the surviving partners must agree on an acceptable means of settlement. Payments may be made from the proceeds of life insurance, by the distribution of assets in kind, by a liquidating payment in cash, or by installment payments with interest.

Questions

1. What circumstances or conditions cause a legal dissolution of a partnership?
2. Discuss two alternative explanations and related accounting treatments of the following situation. A new partner is admitted to a partnership on the basis of contributing additional assets. Further, the new partner's agreed-upon interest in the

previously recorded equity of the partnership plus the tangible assets he or she contributed are smaller than the value of the assets he or she contributed.

3. What is the usual accounting procedure for calculating the value of unrecorded goodwill implied in the transaction to admit a new partner who contributes additional assets to the partnership?

4. What two conditions are necessary for the bonus method and goodwill method to have equivalent effects on the relative balances in the capital accounts?

5. Partners A and B have equal capital balances and share profits and losses in a 70 : 30 ratio. Upon admission of C to the partnership, goodwill is recognized and allocated to the capital accounts of A and B. Should the goodwill be allocated on a 50 : 50 basis or a 70 : 30 basis? Why?

6. Partners A and B have equal capital balances and share profits and losses in a 70 : 30 ratio. Upon admission of C to the partnership, C's capital account is credited with a bonus. In charging the bonus to the capital accounts of A and B, on what basis should it be allocated? Why?

7. If a partner sells part of his or her interest in the partnership to another individual, is the consideration reflected on the books of the partnership? Why, or why not?

8. What special problems may arise when a new partner acquires a partnership interest directly from one or more partners?

9. Suppose an existing partnership plans to admit a new partner whose profit- and loss-sharing percentage will be different from his or her percentage interest in partnership capital. In this instance, explain why the conventional approach to calculating goodwill to be recorded with the new partner's admission might not be appropriate.

10. If goodwill is to be recognized at the time of a partner's retirement, should the partnership recognize the entire amount of goodwill or merely that portion of the intangible associated with the retiring partner? Explain.

11. In the event of a partner's death, is there a concurrent dissolution of the partnership or may the enterprise continue in existence?

12. What is the general method for determining the tax basis of a new partner's interest in a partnership?

13. Enumerate several important factors that the accountant should consider in evaluating the appropriateness of recognizing implied goodwill upon the retirement and/or withdrawal of a partner from a partnership.

Exercises

Exercise 16–1   (Admission of a New Partner)

Martin and Adrian are partners sharing profits and losses 70 : 30, respectively. Their capital account balances are Martin, $42,000; and Adrian, $28,000. Journalize the admission of Harrell to the partnership under the following independent conditions:

1. Harrell invests $30,000 for a one-fourth interest in partnership capital. Goodwill implicit in the investment is to be recorded.

2. Harrell invests $10,000 for a one-fifth interest in partnership capital. Total capital after the admission of Harrell is to be $80,000.

3. Harrell purchases one third of the interests of the existing partners, paying $18,000 to each partner. Goodwill implied by the purchase price is to be recorded.

Exercise 16-2   (Admission of a New Partner)

Felix and May share profits equally and have equal investments in their partnership. The partnership's net assets are carried on the books at $28,000. Smith is admitted to the partnership with a one-third interest in profits and net assets. Smith pays $10,000 cash into the partnership for his interest.

   Prepare journal entries to show three possible methods of recording on the partnership books the admission of Smith. State the conditions under which each method would be appropriate.

(AICPA adapted)

Exercise 16-3   (Miscellaneous Partnership Topics)

Select the answer in each of the following that best completes the sentence or answers the question.

1. Which of the following conditions constitutes a legal dissolution of a partnership?
    a. Completion of a definite term of existence specified in the partnership agreement.
    b. Death of a partner.
    c. Bankruptcy of any partner.
    d. Admission or retirement of a partner.
    e. All of the above.

2. When admitting a new partner into an existing partnership, any allocation of goodwill to the old partners is based on
    a. The profit and loss ratio.
    b. An equal distribution among the partners.
    c. The carrying values of the assets each partner has contributed to the partnership.
    d. The fair market values of the assets each partner has contributed to the partnership.
    e. The relative capital balances of the partners.

3. A and B are partners with capital balances of $40,000 and $15,000, respectively. Profits and losses are shared in the ratio of 80 : 20. C invests in the partnership assets valued at $60,000 for a 50 percent interest in capital and profits and losses. Under the bonus method, how will the various capital accounts be affected?
    a. C's, credited $60,000; A's, debited $4,000; B's, debited $1,000.
    b. C's, credited $57,500; A's, credited $2,000; B's, credited $500.
    c. C's, credited $57,500; A's, debited $500; B's, debited $2,000.
    d. C's, credited $60,000; A's, debited $2,500; B's, debited $2,500.
    e. None of the above.

4. John and Sam are partners with capital balances of $20,000 and $10,000, respectively. Profits and losses are shared in the ratio of 60 : 40. Pat invests in the partnership tangible assets valued at $5,000 for a 20 percent interest in capital, profits, and

losses. Assuming that the recorded assets of the firm are properly valued, the amount of goodwill is

a. $7,500.

b. $5,000.

c. $2,500.

d. $2,000.

e. $1,500.

5. Necessary conditions for the bonus and goodwill methods to be equivalent are

   a. The percentage interest in profits and losses and the fractional interest in the partnership capital of the new partner must be the same.

   b. The new (or adjusted) percentage interests in profits and losses of the old partners must be in the same relative proportion as their old percentage interests.

   c. The percentage interests in profits and losses of the old partners must be in proportion to their capital balances.

   d. (1) and (2) are both necessary.

   e. (1) and (3) are both necessary.

Exercise 16–4   (Admission of New Partners: Various Methods)

Journalize the admission of Barr to the partnership of Lawton and Taylor in each of the following independent cases. The capital balances of Lawton and Taylor are $10,000 and $10,000; they share profits and losses equally.

1. Barr is admitted to a one-third interest in capital, profits, and losses with a contribution of $10,000.

2. Barr is admitted to a one-fourth interest in capital, profits, and losses with a contribution of $12,000. Total capital of the new partnership is to be $32,000.

3. Barr is admitted to a one-fifth interest in capital, profits, and losses upon contributing $3,000. Total capital of the new partnership is to be $25,000.

4. Barr is admitted to a one-fifth interest in capital, profits, and losses by the purchase of one-fifth of the interests of Lawton and Taylor for $5,500, paying the money directly to the old partners. Total capital of the new partnership is to be $20,000.

5. Same conditions as in (4), except that the new partnership capital is to be $27,500.

6. Barr is admitted to a one-third interest in capital, profits, and losses upon contributing $7,000, after which each partner is to have an equal capital equity in the new partnership.

7. Barr is admitted to a one-fifth interest in capital, profits, and losses upon contributing $7,000. Total capital of the new partnership is to be $35,000.

Exercise 16–5   (Admitting a New Partner: Various Methods)

A and B, who share profits and losses in the ratio of 60 : 40, agree to admit C to the partnership. C is to pay each of the old partners cash for one third of each partner's interest and thus will own a one-third interest in profits, losses, and capital. The identifiable net assets of the partnership are recorded at their fair values, and A and B each have capital balances of $30,000. The partners wish to decide how C's total cash payment of $25,000 should be distributed between A and B.

Required:

a. Show the traditionally suggested allocation of cash between A and B.

b. Explain why the traditional allocation of cash, calculated in response to requirement (*a*), may not be fair to A.

c. Show the journal entry to record C's entry to the partnership assuming that goodwill is not to be recognized.

Exercise 16–6   (Admitting a New Partner: Various Methods)

Two long-time partners, Pop and Pam, finally decided that their partnership did not have enough push to compete in the modern world. As a consequence, they are considering the admission of Pow to the partnership. Prior to Pow's entry, the capital interests of Pop and Pam are $24,000 and $36,000, respectively. They share profits and losses in a 30 : 70 ratio. Several alternative plans for admitting Pow are being considered, each of which is described below:

1. Pow contributes $18,000 cash to the partnership in exchange for a 25 percent interest in capital, profits, and losses.

2. Pow pays $10,000 to the partners in exchange for a 25 percent interest in capital, profits, and losses. Thus, 25 percent of each partner's interest is transferred to Pow. Pop and Pam agree to distribute the $10,000 between them such that Pop receives $4,000 and Pam receives $6,000.

3. Pow contributes $18,000 to the partnership in exchange for a 20 percent interest in profits, losses, and capital.

Required:

For each of the three alternatives: *(a)* present the journal entries to reflect the goodwill method of recording the events and *(b)* present the journal entries to reflect the bonus method of recording the events.

Exercise 16–7   (Retirement of a Partner)

Bill retired from the Slowball Partnership on January 1, 19X1. In accordance with the provisions of the partnership agreement, Bill was paid $80,000 from the partnership assets in satisfaction of this one-third interest. This amount was based on a formula that was specified in the original partnership agreement. It was determined by such factors as number of years of service to the partnership, capital contributed, and recent years' sales and earnings performance of the partnership. Bill's capital balance on January 1, 19X1, was $60,000. Lucy and Darlene, the other partners, each have one-third interests and $60,000 capital balances. Assume that the tangible assets of the partnership are correctly valued.

Required:

a. Journalize Bill's retirement under each of three alternative methods.

b. Discuss the relative merits of each method, noting the conditions under which each may draw the greatest support. As a part of your answer, state which method appears least appropriate under the circumstances.

Problems

Problem 16–8   (Admitting a New Partner: Bonus and Goodwill Methods)

Adam and Bates are partners in the Lang Company and have capital balances of $67,000 and $48,000, respectively, on December 1, 19X1. Profits and losses are shared 60 : 40. Colin is admitted to the partnership on January 2, 19X2, by investing $45,000 for a one-fourth interest in capital and profits.

Required:

a. Prepare journal entries to record the admission of Colin under both the bonus and goodwill methods.

b. Assuming that the goodwill method is used to record the admission of Colin *and* that subsequently the goodwill is written off, compare the effect of this treatment on the partners' capitals with that of the bonus method under the following three independent conditions (ignore the effects of other changes in capital):

	Percentage Interest in Profits		
	Adam	*Bates*	*Colin*
Case 1	45%	30%	25%
Case 2	40	37	23
Case 3	48	30	22

Problem 16–9   (Admitting a New Partner: Various Methods)

Jinx, Samuels, and Wells are partners. Their profit-sharing ratio and capital balances on December 31, 19X1, are as follows:

Partners	*Profit-Sharing Ratio*	*Capital Balance*
Jinx	60%	$97,000
Samuels	30	65,000
Wells	10	38,000

Brock is admitted to the partnership on January 1, 19X2, by investing $40,000 for a 20 percent interest in capital and profits.

Required:

a. Prepare journal entries for each of three alternative methods of recording the admission of the new partner.

b. Assume that Brock purchased a 20 percent interest in the partnership ratably from the existing partners by paying $42,000 cash directly to the partners. Prepare journal entries for each of two alternative methods of recording the admission of Brock.

Problem 16–10   (Partners' Capital and Drawing Accounts)

A, B, and C decide to practice accounting together as of January 1, 19X1. They enter into an agreement under which they share profits and losses in the proportion of 50 percent, 25 percent, and 25 percent, respectively, and agree to contribute $50,000 in cash in these same proportions to provide working capital. They decide to keep their books on a cash basis.

On January 1, 19X2, B died and the remaining partners agreed to admit D, giving him a 20 percent share in the profits with a minimum guarantee of $10,000 per year whether operations are profitable or not. A and C have percentages of 40 and 40, respectively. This partnership is of one year's duration, and at the end of this period C decides to retire but permits the use of his name in future partnerships subject to the payment to him of $5,000 per annum to be treated as an expense of the partnership.

As of January 1, 19X3, a partnership is formed in which C's name is utilized in accordance with his proposal and to which E is admitted. The partners' interests in this partnership are as follows: A, 40 percent; D, 30 percent; and E, 30 percent.

Since there were no substantial accruals at the end of the year, disbursements for expenses made during any one period were treated as expenses of the then current partnership. These disbursements were $70,000 in 19X1, $90,000 in 19X2, and $90,000 in 19X3.

Receipts of fees were as follows:

		Earned by Partnership	
	No. 1	*No. 2*	*No. 3*
19X1	$ 80,000		
19X2	160,000	$40,000	
19X3		50,000	$60,000

Each new partnership agreement provided for the newly created partnership to purchase from the old partnership the $50,000 capital originally paid in by A, B, and C. The agreements also provided that the partners should bear the cost of acquisition of this amount in the proportion which they shared profits (and losses). However, it was agreed that an incoming partner, or one acquiring an increased percentage, need not make his contribution in cash immediately but could have the same charged to his drawing account. All such partners availed themselves of this privilege. Partners selling all or a part of their interests in capital are credited through their drawing accounts and immediately withdraw the amount of such credit. In addition to drawings made under this agreement, the partners or their heirs made cash drawings as follows:

		A	B	C	D	E
19X1	. . . . . .	$10,500	$27,750	$13,750		
19X2	. . . . . .	40,000	6,000	5,000	$7,000	
19X3	. . . . . .	10,000	8,750	11,250	1,000	$5,000

Required:

Prepare schedules or statements showing the details of transactions in the partners' drawing accounts and capital accounts for each of the years involved. These accounts should be in such form that the balance at the end of each year that was available for withdrawal by each partner is shown in that partner's drawing account. The capital accounts are to reflect only the $50,000 original investment.

(AICPA adapted)

Problem 16–11   (Error Correction and Admission of a New Partner)

Crenshaw and Kite have been operating a business for several years as partners, during which time they have divided profits equally. They need additional capital to expand their business and have agreed to admit Norman to the partnership as of January 1, 19X7, with a one-third interest in profits and in the capital. Norman is to pay cash into the business as additional capital in an amount equal to one half of the combined capital of the present two partners, redetermined as follows:

The average partnership profits, after partners' salaries, for the past two years are to be capitalized at the rate of 10 percent per annum, which will redetermine the aggregate capital of the two present partners. Before such capitalization of profits, the accounts are to be adjusted for errors and omissions.

The business has not followed a strict accrual basis of accounting. As a result, the following items have been omitted from the books:

Item	Balance 12/31/X4	Balance 12/31/X5	Balance 12/31/X6
Accrued expenses	$3,201	$2,472	$3,829
Prepaid expenses	1,010	812	872
Accrued income	—	250	130

In addition, no provision has been made for loss on uncollectible accounts. It is agreed that a provision of $4,500 is needed as of December 31, 19X6, of which $600 is for 19X5 accounts. Charge-offs have been made to expense in 19X4 of 19X3 and prior accounts—$1,200; in 19X5 of 19X4 accounts—$3,100, and of 19X5 accounts—$400; in 19X6 of 19X5 accounts—$2,100, and of 19X6 accounts—$525.

The inventory at December 31, 19X6, contains some obsolete goods carried at cost of $4,400. A 20 percent write-down is to be made to reduce these items to their present value.

In 19X5 and 19X6, salaries of $3,000 for each partner were taken out of the business and charged to expense before determining profits. It has been agreed that the salaries should have been $2,000 each.

The following financial data are available:

Balance Sheet
December 31, 19X6

Assets		Equities	
Cash	$ 23,100	Accounts payable	$ 43,200
Accounts receivable	42,500	Notes payable	25,000
Notes receivable	6,000	Accumulated depreciation—	
		fixtures	5,300
Merchandise	64,000	Crenshaw, capital	38,100
Store fixtures	12,400	Kite, capital	36,400
Total assets	$148,000	Total equities	$148,000

	19X4	19X5	19X6
Profit per books	$ 8,364	$ 8,419	$10,497
Crenshaw, capital	20,000	24,000	38,100
Kite, capital	25,000	33,000	36,400

Required:

Show the computation of the amount that Norman will pay into the partnership, and prepare a balance sheet as it would appear after adjustment for errors and omissions and after redetermination of capital accounts and receipt of Norman's capital contribution as of January 1, 19X7.

(AICPA adapted)

Problem 16–12   (Partnership Working Paper and Admission of a New Partner)

You have been engaged to prepare financial statements for the partnership of Alexander, Randolph, and Ware as of June 30, 19X1. The partnership was formed originally by Alexander and Barnes on July 1, 19X0. At that date, Barnes contributed $400,000 cash. Alexander contributed land, building, and equipment with market values of $110,000, $520,000, and $185,000, respectively. The land and building were subject to securing a mortgage with an 8 percent note (interest rate of similar notes at July 1, 19X0). The note is due in quarterly payments of $5,000 plus interest on January 1, April 1, July 1, and October 1 of each year. Alexander made the July 1, 19X0, principal and interest payment personally. The partnership then assumed the obligation for the remaining $300,000 balance.

The partnership agreement provided that Alexander had contributed a certain intangible benefit to the partnership due to his many years of business activity in the area to be serviced by the new partnership. The assigned value of this intangible asset plus the net tangible assets he contributed gave Alexander a 60 percent initial capital interest in the partnership. Alexander was designated to receive an annual salary of $24,000 plus an annual bonus of 4 percent of net income after deducting his salary but before deducting interest on partners' capital investments (see below). Both the salary and the bonus are operating expenses of the partnership. Each partner is to receive a 6 percent return on his average capital investment, such interest to be an expense of the partnership. All residual profits or losses are to be shared equally.

On October 1, 19X0, Barnes sold his partnership interest and rights as of July 1, 19X0, to Ware for $370,000. Alexander agreed to accept Ware as a partner if he would contribute sufficient cash to meet the October 1, 19X0, payment on the mortgage. Ware made the payment from personal funds.

On January 1, 19X1, Alexander and Ware admitted a new partner, Randolph, who invested $150,000 cash for a 10 percent capital interest based on the initial investments at July 1, 19X0, of Alexander and Barnes. At January 1, 19X1, the book value of the partnership's assets and liabilities approximated their market values. Randolph contributed no intangible benefit to the partnership. Similar to the other partners, Randolph is to receive a 6 percent return on his average capital investment. His investment also entitled him to 20 percent of the partnership's profits or losses as defined above. However, for the year ended June 30, 19X1, Randolph would receive one half of his pro rata share of the profits or losses.

The accounting records show that on February 1, 19X1, Other Miscellaneous Expenses had been charged $3,600 in payment of hospital expenses incurred by Alexander's eight-year-old daughter.

All salary payments to Alexander have been charged to his drawing account. On June 1, 19X1, Ware made a $33,000 withdrawal. These are the only transactions recorded in the partners' drawing accounts. Since Ware's withdrawal is not an expense of the partnership, it is understood to be a reduction in his capital investment. The trial balance as of June 30, 19X1, is as follows:

	Dr. [Cr.]
Current Assets	$ 307,100
Fixed Assets, Net	1,285,800
Current Liabilities	(157,000)
8% Mortgage Note Payable	(290,000)
Alexander, Capital	(515,000)
Randolph, Capital	(150,000)
Ware, Capital	(400,000)
Alexander, Drawing	24,000
Randolph, Drawing	—
Ware, Drawing	33,000
Sales	(872,600)
Cost of Sales	695,000
Administrative Expenses	16,900
Other Miscellaneous Expenses	11,100
Interest Expense	11,700

Required:

Prepare a working paper to adjust the net income (loss) and partners' capital accounts for the year ended June 30, 19X1, and to close the net income (loss) to the partners' capital accounts at June 30, 19X1. Amortization of goodwill, if any, is to be over a 10-year period. Use the following column headings and begin with balances per books as shown.

		Partners' Capital			Other Accounts	
Description	*Net Income (Loss) Cr. (Dr.)*	*Alexander Cr. (Dr.)*	*Randolph Cr. (Dr.)*	*Ware Cr. (Dr.)*	*Amount Dr. (Cr.)*	*Name*
Book balances at June 30, 19X1	$137,900	$515,000	$150,000	$400,000		

(AICPA adapted)

Problem 16–13   (Death of a Partner)

The partnership agreement of Koy, Elway, White, Matthew, and Floyd contained a buy and sell agreement, among numerous other provisions, which would become operative in case of the death of any partner. Some provisions contained in the buy and sell agreement were as follows:

ARTICLE V. *Buy and Sell Agreement*

1. Purposes of the Buy and Sell Agreement.

(a) The partners mutually desire that the business shall be continued by the survivors without interruption or liquidation upon the death of one of the partners.

(b) The partners also mutually desire that the deceased partner's estate shall receive the full value of the deceased partner's interest in the partnership and that the estate shall share in the earnings of the partnership until the deceased partner's interest shall be fully purchased by the surviving partners.

2. Purchase and Sale of Deceased Partner's Interest.

(a) Upon the death of the partner first to die, the partnership shall continue to operate without dissolution.

(b) Upon the decedent's death, the survivors shall purchase and the executor or administrator of the deceased partner's estate shall sell to the surviving partners the deceased partner's interest in the partnership for the price and upon the terms and conditions hereinafter set forth.

(c) The deceased partner's estate shall retain the deceased partner's interest until the amount specified in the next paragraph shall be paid in full by the surviving partners.

(d) The parties agree that the purchase price for the partnership interest shall be an amount equal to the deceased partner's capital account at the date of death. Said amount shall be paid to the legal representative of decedent as follows:

(i) The first installment of 25 percent of said capital account shall be paid within 60 days from the date of death of the partner or within 30 days from the date on which the personal representative of decedent becomes qualified by law, whichever date is later, and

(ii) The balance shall be due in four equal installments which shall be due and payable annually on the anniversary date of said death.

3. Deceased Partner's Estate's Share of the Earnings.

(a) The partners mutually desire that the deceased partner's estate shall be guaranteed a share in the earnings of the partnership over the period said estate retains an interest in the partnership. Said estate shall not be deemed to have an interest in the partnership after the final installment for the deceased partner's capital account is paid even though a portion of the guaranteed payments specified below may be unpaid and may be due and owing.

(b) The deceased partner's estate's guaranteed share of the earnings of the partnership shall be determined from two items and shall be paid at different times as follows:

(i) First, interest shall be paid on the unpaid balance of the deceased partner's capital account at the same date the installment on the purchase price is paid. The amount to be paid shall be an amount equal to accrued interest at the rate of 6 percent per annum on the unpaid balance of the purchase price for the deceased partner's capital account.

(ii) Second, the parties agree that the balance of the guaranteed payment from the partnership earnings shall be an amount equal to 30 percent of the deceased partner's share of the aggregate gross receipts of the partnership for the full 36 months preceding the month of the partner's death. Said amount shall be payable in 48 equal monthly installments without interest, and the first payment shall be made within 60 days following the death of the partner or within 30 days from the date on which the personal representative of the deceased becomes qualified, whichever date is later; provided, however, that the payments so made under this provision during any 12-month period shall not exceed the highest annual salary on a calendar-year basis received by the partner for the three calendar years immediately preceding the date of his death. In the event that said payment would exceed said salary, then an amount per month shall be paid which does not so exceed said highest monthly salary, and the term over which payments shall be paid to the beneficiary shall be lengthened out beyond the said 48 months in order to complete said payments.

Koy and Floyd were both killed simultaneously in an automobile accident on January 10, 19X3. The surviving partners notified the executors of both estates that the first payment due under the buy and sell agreement would be paid on March 10, 19X3, and that subsequent payments would be paid on the 10th day of each month as due.

The following information was determined from the partnership's records:

Partner	*Profit- and Loss- Sharing Ratio*	*Capital Account on January 10, 19X3*	**Annual Salaries to Partners by Years**		
			19X0	*19X1*	*19X2*
Koy	25%	$26,000	$16,500	$16,500	$16,800
Elway	25	21,970	15,000	15,750	16,500
White	20	4,780	12,000	13,000	14,000
Matthew	15	5,860	9,600	10,800	12,000
Floyd	15	6,700	8,400	9,600	11,800

The partnership's gross receipts for the three prior years follows:

19X0	$296,470
19X1	325,310
19X2	398,220

Required:

Prepare a schedule of the amounts to be paid to the Koy Estate and to the Floyd Estate in March 19X3, December 19X3, and January 19X4. The schedule should identify the amounts attributable to earnings and to interest in the guaranteed payments and to capital. Supporting computations should be in good form.

(AICPA adapted)

Problem 16–14 (Admission of a Partner with Goodwill)

The trial balance of AB, a partnership, on January 1, 19X1, is shown below. Profits and losses were to be shared equally by A and B.

	Debit	*Credit*
Cash	$ 68,000	
Accounts Receivable	50,000	
Notes Receivable	40,000	
Merchandise Inventories	35,000	
Land	85,000	
Buildings and Equipment—less		
allowance for depreciation	28,000	
Investments—at cost	35,000	
Prepaid Insurance	6,000	
Office Supplies	3,000	
Bank Loans		$ 45,000
Accounts Payable		48,000
Accrued Taxes		2,500
First-mortgage, 7% long-term notes		55,500
Capital Accounts:		
A		104,000
B		95,000
	$350,000	$350,000

As of December 31, 19X1, C purchased for $100,000 in cash from partners A and B a one-third interest in the partnership; each partner agreed to transfer one third of his individual capital account to C. Prior to C's admission, it was decided that a valuation reserve of $7,000 should be provided with respect to the investments, that an allowance for bad debts should be established in the amount of $8,000, and that the valuation of buildings and equipment should be reduced to $23,000. Profit sharing by C commenced on January 1, 19X2.

As of December 31, 19X2, D was admitted to a one-fourth interest in partnership profits and contributed the following assets from a business he previously operated as a sole proprietor:

Cash	$60,000
Inventory	70,000
Investments	10,000

The following liabilities incurred by D in his previous business were assumed by the new partnership:

Accounts payable	$20,000
Bank loans	24,000

As an inducement to merge his enterprise with the ABC partnership, D was allowed goodwill of $14,000. Profits were to be shared equally by A, B, C, and D in the new firm, commencing January 1, 19X3.

Additional data to be used in the solution of this problem are as follows:

	Year Ended December 31	
	19X1	*19X2*
Profit of the firm	$18,000	$27,000
Drawings:		
A	13,000	10,000
B	7,000	6,000
C	—	14,000

For the purposes of simplicity, it is assumed that profits for each year were realized in cash and that the balance sheet of the firm on January 1, 19X1, did not change during the two-year period, except as indicated in the terms of this problem.

Required:

a. Prepare an interim working paper for the two-year period from January 1, 19X1, through December 31, 19X2. Goodwill is not to be recorded upon C's entry, and only the $14,000 granted to D is to be recorded upon his entry to the partnership.

b. Prepare journal entries to record the admission of C and D, assuming goodwill is implicitly determined and recorded in each instance. In the case of D's entry, record all of the implicit goodwill and disregard the $14,000 limit mentioned previously in the problem.

(AICPA adapted)

Problem 16–15   (Death of a Partner)

Micro World is a family partnership engaged in the wholesale trade. It closes its books at December 31. During the year, all transactions are recorded on a cash receipts and disbursements basis. However, at the end of the fiscal year, adjustment is made to what was termed the *inventory account* for all items necessary to reflect operations and financial position on an accrual basis.

Partner E died on October 31, 19X1. Her will left equal shares in her estate to partners A and C and an outsider, F. For purposes of this problem, assume no probate period and that E's estate was distributed immediately. All remaining partners, together with F, agreed that the business of Micro World would continue as a partnership of A, B, C, D, and F, with beginning interest on November 1, 19X1, as computed on a proper accrual basis to October 31, and after distribution of E's interest on that date.

Depreciation of fixed assets may be ignored.

Balances as shown by the books of the firm were as follows:

	January 1, 19X1	October 31, 19X1
Cash	$ 42,000	$ 55,000
Inventory account	195,000	195,000
Fixed assets	60,000	59,000
Accruals	29,000	16,000
Notes payable	100,000	60,000
Partners' equities	168,000	168,000
Sales	—	2,000,000
Purchases	—	1,725,000
Operating expenses	—	210,000

In addition to the above, the following information concerning the inventory account was available:

At January 1, 19X1: accounts receivable, $80,000; merchandise, $200,000; freight claims (on incoming merchandise), $2,000; prepaid operating expenses, $10,000; accounts payable, $90,000; and allowances due customers, $7,000. At October 31, 19X1: accounts receivable, $83,300; merchandise, $221,000; freight claims (on incoming merchandise), $1,500; prepaid operating expenses, $6,000; accounts payable, $85,000; and allowances due customers, $8,000.

Partners' equities and profit- and loss-sharing ratio are as follows:

	Equities	Profit and Loss Ratio
A	$ 10,500	6.25%
B	52,500	31.25
C	77,000	37.50
D	7,000	12.50
E	21,000	12.50
	$168,000	100.00%

Required:

a. Prepare an income statement for the period January 1 to October 31, 19X1.

b. Prepare a statement of financial position on November 1, 19X1.

(AICPA adapted)

Problem 16–16   (Retirement of a Partner)

Immediately prior to the retirement of Z from the XYZ Partnership, the partnership trial balance was as follows:

	Debit	Credit
Assets	$200,000	
Liabilities		$50,000
X, capital		60,000
Y, capital		60,000
Z, capital		30,000
Totals	$200,000	$200,000

All capital account balances in the above trial balance are aligned in the profit- and loss-sharing ratio.

Z retires from the partnership and receives a partnership note in the face amount of $50,000. Interest is to be paid annually at the rate of 10 percent. As of the date of Z's retirement, an appraisal of partnership assets reveals that their fair value exceeds book value by $30,000.

Required:

a. Prepare the entry to adjust partnership asset values to their fair values.

b. Prepare the entry to record Z's retirement, assuming that no amount of goodwill is to be recorded.

c. Prepare the entry to record Z's retirement, assuming that goodwill in the amount of Z's excess payment is to be recorded.

d. Prepare the entry to record Z's retirement, assuming that the entire amount of goodwill implied by the retirement terms is to be recorded.

Problem 16–17   (Retirement of a Partner)

Immediately prior to the retirement of X from the XYZ Partnership, the partnership balance sheet was as follows:

Assets	$300,000
X, loan	$10,000
X, capital	62,000
Y, capital	58,000
Z, capital	170,000
Total equities	$300,000

X, Y, and Z share profits and losses in the ratio 2 : 2 : 6. X retires from the partnership and receives $100,000 cash. This amount includes $10,000 in full settlement of the partnership liability to X. As of the date of X's retirement, an appraisal of partnership assets reveals that their fair value is $350,000.

Required:

a. Prepare the entry to adjust partnership asset values to their fair value.

b. Prepare the entry to record X's retirement, assuming that no amount of goodwill is to be recorded.

c. Prepare the entry to record X's retirement, assuming that goodwill in the amount of Z's excess payment is to be recorded.

d. Prepare the entry to record X's retirement, assuming that the entire amount of goodwill implied by the retirement terms is to be recorded.

The Liquidation Process

We discussed the nature of partnership dissolution, viz, "the change in the relation of the partners caused by any partner ceasing to be associated in the carrying on as distinguished from the winding up of the business" (Section 29) in Chapter 16. In that chapter, we focused on the continuity of partnership operations. In this chapter, we focus on the accounting problems and procedures involved in the winding up (liquidation) of partnership affairs—the time between legal *dissolution* and effective *termination* of partnership operations.

Accounting Problems in Partnership Liquidation

The basic objectives of the partnership during the liquidation process are (1) to convert the firm's assets to cash with minimum loss in value (*realization* of assets), (2) to discharge valid partnership liabilities, and (3) to distribute cash and any unrealized assets to the individual partners in an equitable manner. The main objective for the accounting function during the liquidation process is to provide information adequate for a fair disbursement of the partnership assets to creditors and partners, in compliance with the law. Thus, the accounting focus is shifted from the measurement of periodic income to the determination of realization gains and losses, the allocation of these gains and losses among the partners, the payment of partnership creditors, and the planning and recording of asset distributions to partners. Careful attention must be given to relevant provisions of the state partnership act, the partnership agreement, and, in some instances, state and federal insolvency (bankruptcy) statutes. It is especially important that the accounting process be guided mainly by legal rights and obligations.

Basic Dichotomy—Partnership Solvency and Insolvency

Since the liquidation of solvent and insolvent partnerships introduces essentially different problems, we discuss each condition separately. In the following discussion, a partnership is regarded as insolvent when its recorded assets are not sufficient to discharge existing partnership liabilities. This is an entity approach to the condition of insolvency. From a purely legal point of view, however, partnership insolvency is defined in terms of the underlying aggregate concept: "The now settled view is that a partnership is insolvent only when the surplus of *individual* assets [of the partners] over *nonpartnership debts* is insufficient, together with partnership assets to pay partnership obligations."[1] This more restrictive definition of partnership insolvency is illustrated as a special condition of entity insolvency.

---

[1] Reed Rowley, *Rowley on Partnership*, vol. II, (New York: Bobbs-Merrill, 1960), p. 85. (Emphasis added.)

In liquidating a partnership that is solvent by the entity definition, there are two alternative approaches. First, under the "simple liquidation" process, all of the partnership assets are realized or converted *before* any distributions are made to the partners. In this case, the accounting treatment is relatively simple. Since the amount of the total liquidation gain or loss is known before asset distributions to partners, the accounting problem is to schedule a distribution of assets that complies with the order or priority established by existing statutes.

Second, under the "installment payments" approach to liquidation, the partners elect to receive liquidating payments in a series of installments *before* partnership assets are completely realized or converted. In this case, the accounting problem is to develop a plan of settlement that produces the same ultimate distribution as if payments had been deferred until all of the noncash assets were converted.

After we examine simple liquidations, the accounting problems for installment payments are analyzed. We consider situations in which there is one insolvent partner separately, so long as all are not insolvent. In the final section of this chapter, we analyze the accounting problems of insolvent partnerships. The rights of both partnership creditors and individual creditors are examined with reference to provisions of the Uniform Partnership Act, the Federal Bankruptcy Act, and certain common-law decisions.

SIMPLE LIQUIDATION

Basic Distributive Rights

In a simple liquidation, all of the partnership assets are converted into cash before any distribution is made to creditors or to individual partners. The distribution of assets is made in the order of priority established in the Uniform Partnership Act where that act is operative. Section 40 (B) of the act states:

> The liabilities of the partnership shall rank in order of payment, as follows:
>
> (I) Those owing to creditors other than partners,
> (II) Those owing to partners other than for capital and profits,
> (III) Those owing to partners in respect of capital,
> (IV) Those owing to partners in respect of profits.

Since the conversion of all noncash assets precedes the distribution of cash to the partners, the total amount of gain or loss on realization is known. Unless a specific *liquidation* gain and loss ratio is indicated in the partnership agreement, the gain or loss should be allocated to the partners in the current profit and loss residual ratio. Salary and interest factors are disregarded. This basis for distribution appears fair, as realization gains or losses often include adjustments of prior years' reported profits, which were distributed on this basis. Also, gains or losses that can be attributed to the *fact* of liquidation are basically elements of the overall profitability of the business. Thus, they should relate to individual partners in the same ratio as normal periodic earnings and losses of the partnership.

When current profits are closed to the partners' capital accounts, priorities (III) and (IV) of Section 40 (B) coalesce. Further, the distinction between capital and profits is of no practical consequence unless a "deficit" in the profits account is not absorbed by, or offset against, capital balances before distributing cash to individual partners. Since an "equitable" settlement is the controlling consideration in most partnership law, a nonabsorbed deficit condition seems unlikely, unless expressly anticipated and provided for in the partnership agreement. Consequently, elements (III) and (IV) are hereafter considered as a single priority status.

The basic rights of creditors and partners in a simple liquidation are illustrated in the paragraphs that follow.

Case 1. No Capital Deficits during Liquidation

The balance sheet of the WaTex Company at the dissolution date is as follows:

Assets		Equities	
Cash	$10,000	Liabilities	$12,000
Noncash assets	80,000	Capital:	
		Able	31,000
		Holmes	20,000
		Thomas	27,000
Total assets	$90,000	Total equities	$90,000

During liquidation, $50,000 is realized from the conversion of the noncash assets. The partners share profits and losses in the ratio 5 : 3 : 2.

Given these data, a *partnership liquidation schedule* is prepared in Illustration 17–1. *The schedule of partnership liquidation is the primary historical statement reflecting partnership transactions during the liquidation period.* The schedule indicates the condition of the partnership at the dissolution date (preliquidation balances), gains and losses from the conversion of noncash assets, the allocation of gains and losses to the partners in their profit and loss ratio, and the distribution of cash in the order of payment specified in Section 40 (B). The same format may be expanded to include other important events during the liquidation process.

Partners' Debit Balances

In the previous illustration, each of the partners had a large enough credit balance in his or her capital account to absorb his or her proportionate share of the realization loss. However, this is not always the case. Often, an individual partner's share of the realization loss is more than his or her capital credit, producing a *debit balance* in his or her capital account. This capital deficiency

ILLUSTRATION 17-1 **Simple Liquidation (Case 1)**

WATEX COMPANY
Schedule of Partnership Liquidation
Dr. (Cr.)

	Assets			Claimants		
				Residual Equities		
	Cash	Noncash	Priority Claims	Able	Holmes	Thomas
Profit and loss ratio				50%	30%	20%
Preliquidation balances	$10,000	$80,000	$(12,000)	$(31,000)	$(20,000)	$(27,000)
Realization of assets and allocation of loss	50,000	(80,000)		15,000	9,000	6,000
Predistribution balances	$60,000	–0–	$(12,000)	$(16,000)	$(11,000)	$(21,000)
Cash distribution:						
Priority claims	(12,000)		12,000			
Partners' residual equities	(48,000)			16,000	11,000	21,000
Termination of partnership	–0–	–0–	–0–	–0–	–0–	–0–

creates a valid claim of the partnership against the partner. Section 18 (A) specifies that "each partner . . . must contribute toward the losses, whether of capital or otherwise, sustained by the partnership according to his share in the profits." Section 40 (D) states that "the partners shall contribute, as provided by Section 18 (A), the amount necessary to satisfy the liabilities; but if any, but not all, of the partners are insolvent, or, not being subject to process, refuse to contribute, the other partners shall contribute their share of the liabilities, and, in the relative proportions in which they share the profits, the additional amount necessary to pay the liabilities."

It is important that the term *liability* in this particular usage be fully understood. Section 40 of the act states that liabilities may be created by accumulated losses from operations, realization losses, or the *loss* incurred when a partner with a debit balance in his or her capital account fails to contribute enough personal assets to remove this deficit. In fact, Section 40 (A) defines the assets of a partnership to include contributions due from the partners for this cause.[2] Thus, a partner's failure to contribute to the extent of his or her capital deficiency is equivalent to a realization loss for the remaining partners. If a debit balance is not collected from the delinquent partner, it is allocated to the remaining partners as if it were a realization loss. The allocation is made in the ratio of the remaining partners' original shares of profits and losses. For example, assume that X, Y, and

---

[2] Note that this provision is consistent with the legal definition of partnership insolvency, whereby insolvency is impossible unless the claims against the individual partners are uncollectible due to a condition of personal insolvency.

Z share profits and losses in the ratio 5 : 3 : 2. If Y should fail to contribute to the partnership the amount of a debit balance in his capital account, X and Z will share this loss (a capital deficiency) in the ratio 5 : 2, that is, 5/7 to X and 2/7 to Z. If X should fail to contribute for a preexistent capital deficiency, Y and Z would share this loss in the ratio 3 : 2, that is 3/5 to Y and 2/5 to Z.

The effects of partners' debit balances on the liquidation process and their treatment in the partnership liquidation schedule are illustrated in the following case.

Case 2. *Capital Deficiencies during Liquidation*

The balance sheet of Super Serv Company immediately before the liquidation of the partnership is as follows:

Assets		Equities	
Cash	$ 5,000	Liabilities	$15,000
Noncash assets	45,000	Capital:	
		Johnson	9,000
		Granof	6,000
		Deakin	20,000
Total assets	$50,000	Total equities	$50,000

The partners share profits and losses in the ratio 4 : 4 : 2. We assume that Johnson and Deakin have enough personal resources to "make good" capital debit balances that might be created during the liquidation process. Granof has no available personal assets. The noncash assets of the partnership are sold for $15,000.

A partnership liquidation schedule based upon these data is shown in Illustration 17–2.

In this case, Granof's uncollectible debit balance creates an additional "realization loss" that must be absorbed by Johnson and Deakin in their relative profit and loss ratio. Johnson contributes personal assets to restore the debit balance in her capital account to zero. Note that even if Johnson had failed to contribute personal assets, the partnership would have remained solvent, since enough cash was available to discharge liabilities to partnership creditors.

Partners' Loans with Simple Liquidation

In the distribution of partnership assets, the Uniform Partnership Act ranks payments for partners' loans ahead of payments on their capital accounts. However, this priority has functional significance *only* when payments on loans are to be made to partners with capital deficiencies. If in liquidation a partner's capital account has a debit balance, the partner is required by Section 18 of the act to contribute an amount equal to his or her debit balance. But the partnership might

ILLUSTRATION 17-2   Partners' Debit Balances (Case 2)

SUPER SERV COMPANY
Schedule of Partnership Liquidation
Dr. (Cr.)

| | Assets | | | Claimants | | |
| | | | | Residual Equities | | |
	Cash	Noncash	Priority Claims	Johnson	Granof	Deakin
Profit and loss ratio				40%	40%	20%
Preliquidation balances	$ 5,000	$45,000	$(15,000)	$(9,000)	$(6,000)	$(20,000)
Realization of assets and						
allocation of loss	15,000	(45,000)		12,000	12,000	6,000
Balances	$20,000	–0–	$(15,000)	$ 3,000	$ 6,000	$(14,000)
Absorption of Granof's						
balance (4 : 2)				4,000	(6,000)	2,000
Balances	$20,000	–0–	$(15,000)	$ 7,000	–0–	$(12,000)
Contribution by Johnson	7,000			(7,000)		
Predistribution balances	$27,000	–0–	$(15,000)	–0–	–0–	$(12,000)
Cash distribution:						
Priority claims	(15,000)		15,000			
Partners' residual equities	(12,000)					12,000
Termination of partnership	–0–	–0–	–0–	–0–	–0–	–0–

be unable to collect this amount from the delinquent partner. Under these circumstances, if partnership assets were first distributed to the partner in repayment of his or her loan, the assets might be permanently lost. To prevent this sequence of events, the rule of *setoff* has been generally accepted by the courts as a way of achieving an equitable settlement. Thus, debit balances are offset against partners' loans to the fullest extent possible, *before* any cash distribution is made.[3]

The rule of setoff is illustrated in the following case.

Case 3. Offset of Loans and Capital Deficiencies

The preliquidation balances of the assets and equities of the Geneva Appliance Partnership are as follows:

---

[3] This general provision may be challenged by the individual creditors of an insolvent partner. If there is such a challenge, the accountant should advise the withholding of cash in an amount equal to the loan balance pending a final determination of priorities.

Assets		Equities		
Cash	$ 20,000	Liabilities		$ 40,000
Noncash assets	80,000	Partners' loans:		
		Bruns	4,000	
		Jensen	5,000	
		Miles	7,000	16,000
		Partners' capital:		
		Bruns	$10,000	
		Jensen	12,000	
		Miles	16,000	
		Schiff	6,000	44,000
Total assets	$100,000	Total equities		$100,000

The partners share profits and losses in the ratio 3 : 3 : 2 : 2. Bruns, Jensen, and Miles are committed to making contributions for any debit balances that might be created by loss absorption and are assumed to have sufficient personal assets for this purpose. Schiff has only $2,000 of available personal assets. The noncash assets are sold during liquidation for $30,000. A partnership liquidation schedule for this case is given in Illustration 17–3.

This case illustrates the offset principle for the loans of two partners (Bruns and Jensen), a contribution by Schiff to reduce part of his capital deficiency, the absorption of the capital debit residue of Schiff by the remaining partners (Bruns, Jensen, and Miles), and a full contribution by Bruns for her debit balance. The occurrence of two separate offsets of Jensen's loan against a debit balance in his capital account was a result of the schedule order. If the complete liquidation relationship between Schiff and the partnership (partial contribution and absorption of residue debit balance) had been established first, only one setoff—$3,750 in amount—would have been required for Jensen. The total effect would remain unchanged.

Liquidation Expenses

In each of the previous cases, the reference to "realization of assets and allocation of loss" indicated the *net* proceeds realized on the disposition of noncash assets. Such a description is correct when an item of expense is directly related to an asset sale, for example, commissions on sales. If, however, expenses incurred during the liquidation process are not directly associated with specific assets but are identifiable only with the liquidation process or period, it may be better to separately disclose such expenses in the liquidation schedule. For example, if one of the partners assumes sole responsibility for managing or directing the liquidation activities and is given a specific fee for the service, the expense can be shown as a separate liquidation expense with a corresponding increase in the partner's capital account. Such an assignment discloses more completely the effect of the

ILLUSTRATION 17–3 Partners' Loans, Debit Balances, and Additional Contributions (Case 3)

GENEVA APPLIANCE PARTNERSHIP
Schedule of Partnership Liquidation
Dr. (Cr.)

	Assets Cash	Assets Noncash	Priority Claims	Bruns Loan	Bruns Capital	Jensen Loan	Jensen Capital	Miles Loan	Miles Capital	Schiff Capital
Profit and loss ratio					30%		30%		20%	20%
Preliquidation balances	$20,000	$80,000	$(40,000)	$(4,000)	$(10,000)	$(5,000)	$(12,000)	$(7,000)	$(16,000)	$(6,000)
Realization of assets and allocation of loss	30,000	(80,000)			15,000		15,000		10,000	10,000
Balances	$50,000	-0-	$(40,000)	$(4,000)	$ 5,000	$(5,000)	$ 3,000	$(7,000)	$ (6,000)	$ 4,000
Offset of loans against debit balances:										
Bruns				4,000	(4,000)					
Jensen						3,000	(3,000)			
Balances	$50,000	-0-	$(40,000)	-0-	$ 1,000	$(2,000)	-0-	$(7,000)	$ (6,000)	$ 4,000
Contribution by Schiff	2,000									(2,000)
Balances	$52,000	-0-	$(40,000)	-0-	$ 1,000	$(2,000)	-0-	$(7,000)	$ (6,000)	$ 2,000
Absorption of Schiff's debit balance (3 : 3 : 2)					750		750		500	(2,000)
Balances	$52,000	-0-	$(40,000)	-0-	$ 1,750	$(2,000)	$ 750	$(7,000)	$ (5,500)	-0-
Additional offset against Jensen's loan balance						750	(750)			
Balances	$52,000	-0-	$(40,000)	-0-	$ 1,750	$(1,250)	-0-	$(7,000)	$ (5,500)	-0-
Contribution by Bruns for debit balance	1,750				(1,750)					
Predistribution balances	$53,750	-0-	$(40,000)	-0-	-0-	$(1,250)	-0-	$(7,000)	$ (5,500)	-0-
Cash distribution:										
Priority claims	(40,000)		40,000							
Partners' loans	(8,250)					1,250		7,000		
Partner's residual equity	(5,500)								5,500	
Termination of partnership	-0-	-0-	-0-	-0-	-0-	-0-	-0-	-0-	-0-	-0-

Claimants / Residual Equities

769

expense on the liquidation process and may prevent a premature distribution of cash to this managing partner, which might be subject to legal challenge should a debit balance ultimately exist in his or her capital account.

INSTALLMENT (PERIODIC) PAYMENTS

Basic Accounting Problem

In a simple liquidation, the total gain or loss on the realization of assets, including the effects of liquidation expenses, is known before cash is distributed to individual partners. However, if the liquidation period is prolonged, it may be desirable to make partial distributions of cash to the partners *before* all of the assets have been realized. In this case, an accountant may assume a fiduciary status for the claims of both partnership creditors and the individual partners against the available cash of the partnership. Therefore, care must be exercised in determining the amount of each installment payment in order to avoid an overdistribution to one or more of the partners. The fiduciary might be held liable for losses that occur due to excessive distributions. Thus, a distribution procedure should preclude any prospect for an overdistribution which might result in personal liability to the fiduciary.

In the traditional approach to this problem, the *largest potential loss* that can be incurred in future realizations of noncash assets is estimated prior to each cash distribution. Since the equities of the partners are based on the book values of the partnership assets, the total recorded value of the noncash assets approximates the maximum potential loss to the partnership.[4] If one *assumes* the actual incurrence of the maximum potential loss, its effect on the individual partners' capital balances can be computed. Any debit balance in a partner's capital account that results from the loss allocation process represents still another *potential* loss to the other partners (because it may not be satisfied by contributions of the deficient partner). Thus, the debit balance should be allocated to the remaining partners—in effect, it is a reallocation of part of the maximum potential loss to the partnership. This sequence of hypothetical loss absorptions ends with one or more partners' capital accounts having credit balances which, in total, are equal to the cash available for distribution to partners. Initially, this amount is the total cash less claims of outside creditors. After obligations to creditors are discharged, the residual amount of cash on hand may be distributed in amounts equal to these adjusted credit balances. Then, if the noncash assets prove worthless and if all debit balances in partners' capital balances must be absorbed, each of the partners' capital accounts will end with a zero balance. Since cash distributions are not made to any partner who conceivably could end up with a debit balance under the worst possible asset realization scenario, the cash payments calculated in this

---

[4] See pages 775 and 777 for a more precise statement of the maximum potential loss.

manner are referred to as *safe payments*. This procedure, expressed as a *partnership liquidation schedule* and supported by a *calculation of safe installment payments,* is illustrated in Case 4.

Case 4. Installment Liquidation—No Loans from Partners

On January 1, 19X1, Dahl, Hersey, and Katz agree to dissolve their partnership. Their preliquidation capital balances and percentage interests in profits and losses are as follows:

Partner	Capital	Ratio
Dahl	$25,000	50%
Hersey	45,000	30
Katz	15,000	20

The partnership has cash of $5,000, noncash assets of $85,000, and liabilities to outside creditors of $5,000. The partners decide to make periodic distributions of all accumulated cash at the end of each month during the liquidation process. The following data relate to the realization of assets:

	Book Values	Net Proceeds
January	$25,000	$20,000
February	40,000	20,000
March	10,000	5,000
April	10,000	2,000

Note that immediately prior to the January distribution, the largest potential loss that can be incurred in future realizations of noncash assets is $60,000 (the book values of noncash assets to be sold during February, March, and April). Immediately prior to the February distribution, the largest potential loss that can be incurred in future realizations is $20,000 (the book values of noncash assets to be sold during March and April). And immediately prior to the March distribution, the largest potential loss that can be incurred in future realizations is $10,000 (the book values of noncash assets to be sold during April).

The partnership liquidation schedule and the supporting calculation of safe installment payments are shown in Illustrations 17–4 and 17–5. Several important conclusions can be drawn from an analysis of the illustrations in this case:

1. The total cash payments to each partner are equal to the amount of a single payment computed under a simple liquidation procedure. This is illustrated as follows:

Simple Liquidation Method

	Dahl	Hersey	Katz
Preliquidation balances	$25,000	$45,000	$15,000
Realization loss ($85,000 − $47,000)	19,000	11,400	7,600
Partners' claims	$ 6,000	$33,600	$ 7,400

Installment Payments Method
(from Illustration 17–4)

	Dahl	Hersey	Katz
January	–0–	$20,000	–0–
February	$2,500	11,500	$6,000
March	2,500	1,500	1,000
April	1,000	600	400
Total payments	$6,000	$33,600	$7,400

2. The ratio of the partners' capital balances at the end of February exhibits a significant relationship: *the ratio of capital balances is equal to the profit and loss ratio.* When this condition exists, all future installment distributions are based on the profit and loss ratio (see March and April installment payments in Illustration 17–4). Any future losses will be allocated on this basis, and thus the availability of cash for distribution to partners indicates that the total equity of the partners exceeds the total potential loss. The computation of safe payments is, in fact, an iterative process that systematically causes the ratio of partners' equities to converge to the profit and loss ratio as rapidly as can be accomplished by controlling cash distributions to partners. Therefore, after one payment is allocated among two or more partners, distributions to these partners are in the same ratio as their relative profit and loss ratio. Also, after a payment has been made to all partners, the ratio of the partners' equities is equal to the profit and loss ratio. This fact is confirmed by Case 4 data with the February installment payment. In this case, a supporting calculation to determine safe payments to partners is unnecessary *after* the February distribution.

3. The order of payments in the schedule of partnership liquidation is consistent with the order of priority established in the Uniform Partnership Act. Distributions are first made to creditors; subsequent payments, as cash becomes available, are made to partners.

ILLUSTRATION 17-4   Installment Payments (Case 4)

DAHL, HERSEY, AND KATZ PARTNERSHIP
Schedule of Partnership Liquidation
Dr. (Cr.)

	Cash	Noncash	Priority Claims	Dahl	Hersey	Katz
	Assets			**Residual Equities**		
				(Claimants)		
Profit and loss				50%	30%	20%
Preliquidation balances	$ 5,000	$85,000	$(5,000)	$(25,000)	$(45,000)	$(15,000)
Realization of assets and						
allocation of loss	20,000	(25,000)		2,500	1,500	1,000
Balances	$25,000	$60,000	$(5,000)	$(22,500)	$(43,500)	$(14,000)
Payment of liabilities	(5,000)		5,000			
Balances	$20,000	$60,000	–0–	$(22,500)	$(43,500)	$(14,000)
January installment payment						
(see supporting schedule—						
Illustration 17–5)	(20,000)				20,000	
Balances	–0–	$60,000	–0–	$(22,500)	$(23,500)	$(14,000)
Realization of assets and						
allocation of loss	20,000	(40,000)		10,000	6,000	4,000
Balances	$20,000	$20,000	–0–	$(12,500)	$(17,500)	$(10,000)
February installment payment						
(see supporting schedule—						
Illustration 17–5)	(20,000)			2,500	11,500	6,000
Balances	–0–	$20,000	–0–	$(10,000)	$ (6,000)	$ (4,000)
Realization of assets and						
allocation of loss	$ 5,000	(10,000)		2,500	1,500	1,000
Balances	$ 5,000	$10,000	–0–	$ (7,500)	$ (4,500)	$ (3,000)
March installment payment						
(see supporting schedule—						
Illustration 17–5)	(5,000)			2,500	1,500	1,000
Balances	–0–	$10,000	–0–	$ (5,000)	$ (3,000)	$ (2,000)
Realization of assets and						
allocation of loss	$ 2,000	(10,000)		4,000	2,400	1,600
Balances	$ 2,000	–0–	–0–	$ (1,000)	$ (600)	$ (400)
Final (April) payment to partners	(2,000)			1,000	600	400
Termination of partnership	–0–	–0–	–0–	–0–	–0–	–0–

Partners' Loans with Installment Payments

We have noted that in partnership liquidation a partner's loan balance should be offset against a debit balance in his or her capital account. Thus, liquidating payments are based on each partner's *total* equity (or net equity in the event of a capital deficit) in the partnership. This principle is equally valid when installment

ILLUSTRATION 17-5 **Safe Payments Calculations for Case 4**

DAHL, HERSEY, AND KATZ PARTNERSHIP
Calculation of Safe Installment Payments
Dr. (Cr.)

	Residual Equities		
	Dahl	*Hersey*	*Katz*
Profit and loss ratio	50%	30%	20%
Computation of January installment:			
Predistribution balances	$(22,500)	$(43,500)	$(14,000)
Potential loss—noncash assets—$60,000	30,000	18,000	12,000
Balances	$ 7,500	$(25,500)	$ (2,000)
Potential loss—Dahl's debit balance	(7,500)	4,500	3,000
Balances	-0-	$(21,000)	$ 1,000
Potential loss—Katz's debit balance		1,000	(1,000)
Safe payments to partners	-0-	$(20,000)	-0-
Computation of February installment:			
Predistribution balances	$(12,500)	$(17,500)	$(10,000)
Potential loss—noncash assets—$20,000	10,000	6,000	4,000
Safe payments to partners	$ (2,500)	$(11,500)	$ (6,000)
Computation of March installment:			
Predistribution balances	$ (7,500)	$ (4,500)	$ (3,000)
Potential loss—noncash assets—$10,000	5,000	3,000	2,000
Safe payments to partners	$ (2,500)	$ (1,500)	$ (1,000)

payments are made to partners during liquidation. The total equity of each partner (the sum of both loan and capital balances) should be entered in the calculation of safe installment payments. Entering the total equity implicitly recognizes the relevance of setoff if a partner's capital balance is completely absorbed when potential losses are allocated. In the schedule of partnership liquidation, however, payments to each partner are traditionally reported first in abatement of loans and second in reduction of capital balances.

Adding partners' loans to a liquidation process involving installment distributions is illustrated in the following case.

Case 5. Installment Liquidation—Loans from Partners

The partners of Jackson Company agree to dissolve their partnership on March 31, 19X1. Their preliquidation capital and loan account balances and the profit and loss ratio are as follows:

Partner	Capital	Loan	Ratio
W	$16,000	$4,000	50%
X	29,000	2,000	20
Y	23,000		20
Z	9,000	1,000	10

The partnership has a cash balance of $10,000, noncash assets of $80,000, and obligations to outside creditors of $6,000. Available cash is to be distributed at the end of each month during the liquidation. Assets are realized as follows:

	Book Values	Net Proceeds
April	$54,000	$30,000
May	24,000	18,000
June	2,000	–0–

The partnership liquidation schedule is given in Illustration 17–6, and the supporting calculation of safe installment payments is shown in Illustration 17–7.

Case 5 accents several concepts previously discussed:

1. Although the total equity (capital and loan balance) of each partner is used in calculating safe installment payments, any cash distribution to a partner is assumed to apply first against the partner's loan account. Remaining payments are matched against his or her capital balance.

2. Since installment payments were made to X, Y, and Z in April, the ratio of their *total equities* at the end of April should be equal to their relative profit and loss ratio. This equality is confirmed by the schedule of partnership liquidation (7200 : 7200 : 3600 = 20 : 20 : 10). The schedule also shows that future distributions to these partners are made in their relative profit and loss ratio (e.g., in May, 5600 : 5600 : 2800 = 20 : 20 : 10). Since an installment payment is made to W in May, all of the partners' equities at May 31 are in their respective profit and loss ratio. Future distributions, if any, would be made on the basis of this ratio.

Liquidation Expenses and Unrecorded Liabilities

We have assumed the total potential loss of a partnership to be equal to the book value of noncash assets. This assumption is true *only* if the assets are determined to be completely worthless, *and* if *additional* expenses are not incurred in the

ILLUSTRATION 17–6 Installment Payments with Partners' Loans (Case 5)

JACKSON COMPANY
Schedule of Partnership Liquidation
Dr. (Cr.)

	Cash	Noncash	Priority Claims	W Loan	W Capital	X Loan	X Capital	Y Capital	Z Loan	Z Capital
	Assets			*(50%)*	*50%*		*20%*	*20%*		*10%*
Profit and loss ratio					50%		20%	20%		10%
Preliquidation balances	$10,000	$80,000	$(6,000)	$(4,000)	$(16,000)	$(2,000)	$(29,000)	$(23,000)	$(1,000)	$(9,000)
Realization of assets and allocation of loss	30,000	(54,000)			12,000		4,800	4,800		2,400
Balances	$40,000	$26,000	$(6,000)	$(4,000)	$(4,000)	$(2,000)	$(24,200)	$(18,200)	$(1,000)	$(6,600)
Payment to creditors	(6,000)		6,000							
Balances	$34,000	$26,000	–0–	$(4,000)	$(4,000)	$(2,000)	$(24,200)	$(18,200)	$(1,000)	$(6,600)
April installment payment (see supporting schedule—Illustration 17–7)	(34,000)					2,000	17,000	11,000	1,000	3,000
Balances	–0–	$26,000	–0–	$(4,000)	$(4,000)	–0–	$(7,200)	$(7,200)	–0–	$(3,600)
Realization of assets and allocation of loss	$18,000	(24,000)			3,000		1,200	1,200		600
Balances	$18,000	$2,000	–0–	$(4,000)	$(1,000)	–0–	$(6,000)	$(6,000)	–0–	$(3,000)
May installment payment (see supporting schedule—Illustration 17–7)	(18,000)			4,000			5,600	5,600		2,800
Balances	–0–	$2,000	–0–	–0–	$(1,000)	–0–	$(400)	$(400)	–0–	$(200)
Realization of assets and allocation of loss	–0–	(2,000)			1,000		400	400		200
Termination of partnership	–0–	–0–	–0–	–0–	–0–	–0–	–0–	–0–	–0–	–0–

ILLUSTRATION 17-7   Safe Payments Calculations for Case 5

JACKSON COMPANY
Calculation of Safe Installment Payments
Dr. (Cr.)

	Residual Equities (Capital and Loan Balances)			
	W	X	Y	Z
Profit and loss ratio	50%	20%	20%	10%
Computation of April installment:				
Predistribution balances	$(8,000)	$(26,200)	$(18,200)	$(7,600)
Potential loss—noncash				
assets—$26,000	13,000	5,200	5,200	2,600
Balances	$ 5,000	$(21,000)	$(13,000)	$(5,000)
Potential loss—W's debit balance	(5,000)	2,000	2,000	1,000
Safe payments to partners	–0–	$(19,000)	$(11,000)	$(4,000)
Computation of May installment:				
Predistribution balances	$(5,000)	$ (6,000)	$ (6,000)	$(3,000)
Potential loss—noncash				
assets—$2,000	1,000	400	400	200
Safe payments to partners	$(4,000)	$ (5,600)	$ (5,600)	$(2,800)

---

process of liquidation, *and* if all partnership liabilities have been properly recorded. However, if liquidation expenses, including disposal costs for noncash assets, are more than the proceeds from asset realization, the actual loss suffered is greater than the assumed loss. Also, unrecorded liabilities to outside creditors might be discovered during the period of liquidation. These claims rank ahead of the residual claims of partners. Therefore, in order to avoid personal liability, the fiduciary should explicitly recognize these items in the liquidation schedule when they can be predicted. In calculating safe installment payments, estimated future liquidation expenses and unrecorded liabilities are incorporated by treating them as additions to the potential loss of total book value. This adjustment reserves cash equal to the total of anticipated liquidation expenses and unrecorded liabilities.

Cash Predistribution Plan

In the previous discussion, we have shown how the fiduciary can move through the period of partnership liquidation, paying creditors and making periodic payments to partners that are reasonably *safe*. In other words, those partners who receive cash payments are not apt to find their capital accounts reduced to debit balances from future partnership losses. These safe payments are made possible by the information provided in the calculations of safe installment payments.

However, at the beginning of the liquidation process, it might be desirable to develop an overall plan for making future cash payments. For example, creditors or partners might ask the fiduciary to estimate when cash is likely to be distributed to them. To answer this inquiry, the fiduciary must first project the timing and amounts of cash receipts from the realization of assets. This will vary greatly, depending on the type of assets involved, the condition and location of the assets, the quantities of assets, and the markets available for selling the assets. Because the problems of making such cash projections vary so much with the particular situation, and because they are not unique to partnership accounting, we do not discuss them further.

But projecting cash receipts from the liquidation of assets is only the first step in responding to inquiries about future cash payments. The second step is to prepare a plan for the future distribution of cash, whenever it becomes available. This plan is called the *cash predistribution plan*. It is designed to show the order and amounts of payments that will be made to creditors and partners if, and when, cash becomes available during the liquidation period.

The following sequence of operations is used in establishing the predetermined order and amount of distribution payments:

1. Using each partner's residual equity (combined capital and loan balances) and percentage interest in profits and losses, compute the partners' *loss-absorption potentials*. The amount of this potential for each partner is the amount of possible loss the partnership might incur before the partner is obliged to contribute new assets to the partnership; that is, his or her residual equity divided by his or her percentage interest in profits and losses.

For example, if Baker and Moore have equities (including loans) of $48,000 and $40,000, respectively, and share profits and losses in the ratio 6 : 4, the table of loss-absorption potential is as follows:

BAKER-MOORE PARTNERSHIP
Loss-Absorption Potentials

Partner	Equities	Profit and Loss Ratio	Loss-Absorption Potentials	Order of Equity Absorption
Baker	$48,000	60%	$ 80,000 = ($48,000/60%)	1
Moore	40,000	40	100,000 = ($40,000/40%)	2

A loss of $80,000 would totally absorb Baker's equity in the partnership (including any possible offset of a loan balance), whereas a loss of $100,000 would be required before Moore's total equity would be absorbed.

2. After calculating the loss-absorption potential of each partner, prepare a schedule of potential losses sequenced such that the amount of each assumed loss is sufficient to absorb the equity of exactly one partner, beginning with the partner

having the smallest loss-absorption potential. The order of this equity absorption follows the order of ascending amounts of loss-absorption potentials.

If the Baker-Moore Partnership has cash of $7,000, noncash assets of $93,000, and liabilities of $12,000, the schedule is as follows:

BAKER-MOORE PARTNERSHIP
Schedule of Loss Absorption
Dr. (Cr.)

	Assumed Losses	Baker	Moore
Profit and loss ratio		60%	40%
Preliquidation balances		$(48,000)	$(40,000)
Potential loss to absorb Baker's equity	$(80,000)	48,000	32,000
Balances		$ –0–	$ (8,000)
Potential loss to absorb Moore's remaining equity	(8,000)		8,000
Balance			$ –0–

In this simple case, the total potential loss is attributed to the degree of realization of noncash assets. Therefore, as noted before, the book value of noncash assets is generally assumed to establish a maximum possible loss. The case does illustrate the important principle that after one partner's equity has been totally eliminated, additional losses are absorbed by the remaining partners in their relative profit and loss ratio. Given the assumption that debit balances will *not* be restored to zero by contributions, no benefit is to be derived by allocating future assumed losses to all partners. Doing so would require a reallocation of the debit balances created in the first allocation. In this example, Moore is the only remaining partner with an equity. Thus, she must absorb 100 percent of all additional losses. A loss of $8,000 completely absorbs her $8,000 equity. In the schedule, the sequence continues until all partners' equities have been reduced to zero, unless the cash on hand exceeds the claims of outside creditors. In this event, the schedule should be continued until partners' capital balances equal the "excess" cash.

3. Using the above schedule, which indicates the effect of loss absorption on the partners' equities, construct a predistribution plan indicating in order the distribution of cash as it is made available to the partnership. This is done by reverse movement through the loss-absorption schedule because the continued availability of cash systematically negates the assumption of potential losses. Recall that the Baker-Moore Partnership has cash of $7,000, noncash assets of $93,000, and liabilities of $12,000. The preliquidation cash of $7,000 obviously should be used to satisfy liabilities, leaving unpaid liabilities of $5,000. Realizing $5,000 from the sale of noncash assets implies a potential loss of $88,000 ($93,000 − $5,000), the amount which eliminates the equities of both partners.

Realizing cash of $5,000 therefore rules out a potential loss greater than the equities of both partners, and the first $5,000 received from the sale of noncash assets should be used to satisfy the remaining liabilities.

Realizing $13,000 from the sale of noncash assets implies a potential loss of $80,000 ($93,000 − $13,000), the amount which eliminates Baker's equity and leaves $8,000 in Moore's capital account. Realizing cash of $13,000 therefore rules out a potential loss greater than the amount which eliminates Moore's equity. Until realized cash exceeds $13,000, any excess over $5,000 can be distributed to Moore without any prospect for a deficit in her capital account.

Realizing more than $13,000 from the sale of noncash assets rules out a potential loss greater than the amount which eliminates Baker's equity. Accordingly, any realized cash in excess of $13,000 can be distributed to Baker and Moore in the profit- and loss-sharing ratio without any prospect for a deficit in either capital account.

The cash predistribution plan for the Baker-Moore Partnership is given below:

BAKER-MOORE PARTNERSHIP
Cash Predistribution Plan

		Distributions		
		Priority Claims	Baker	Moore
Preliquidation cash balance	$ 7,000	100%		
Subsequent collections (on realization of noncash assets):				
First	$ 5,000	100%		
Next	8,000			100%
Next	80,000		60%	40%
Noncash assets	$93,000			
Any additional cash collected			60%	40%

Of course, the percentage amounts might alternatively be stated as dollar amounts. However, this alternative does not indicate explicitly the proper distribution if only a portion of the indicated cash were available.

The cash predistribution plan serves as a guide for cash payments throughout the liquidation period, *if it is interpreted carefully and if certain events do not occur*. First, the process of liquidating a business invariably involves incurring some expenses. These liquidation expenses *are not* estimated and included among the priority claims shown in the cash predistribution plan. Hence, the plan should be interpreted as specifying cash payments to be made from cash balances and receipts, *net* of liquidation expense payments to nonpartners. The total amount to be paid for priority claims before partners receive any cash will therefore often be more than the value listed in the cash predistribution plan.

Second, unrecorded liabilities to outside creditors might be discovered during the liquidation period. If so, the amount of priority claims disclosed in the cash predistribution plan must be increased by the amount of these newly discovered liabilities. Finally, if for some reason one of the partners should contribute additional assets to the partnership, the loss-absorption potential of that partner is enlarged by the contribution. Hence, the original cash predistribution plan is invalidated and a new plan must be prepared.

INSOLVENT PARTNERSHIP

Basic Rights

Recall that we define partnership insolvency to exist when recorded partnership assets are less than partnership liabilities. This definition emphasizes the financial condition of the partnership, viewed as a separate and distinct entity. It ignores the existence and potential value of the partnership claim against the individual partners for debit balances in their capital accounts. At least one such debit balance must exist if partnership liabilities exceed partnership assets. In the following discussion, we assume that partnership creditors first exhaust partnership assets and then make claims against the partners jointly for any remaining unpaid balances of partnership debts. Two conditions are possible:

1. One or more of the individual partners possess enough separate net assets to meet the claims of the partnership creditors (i.e., legally, the partnership is not insolvent).
2. The partners individually do not have sufficient assets to discharge all existing partnership debts (i.e., the partnership is legally insolvent, and considering the claims of partnership creditors, all of the partners are individually insolvent). In this case, the order of distributing the partners' individually owned assets depends on the relative rights of partnership and individual creditors.

To determine the basic rights of creditors, it is important first to segregate or marshal the assets of the partnership and the several partners. This legal doctrine, *marshaling of assets,* prescribes that partnership assets and individual assets constitute separate pools of resources against which partnership creditors and individual creditors, respectively, have initial and separate recourse. If the partnership is insolvent, partnership assets are completely exhausted in the *partial* settlement of partnership debts. If the partnership is solvent, creditors of individual partners have a claim against the remaining partnership assets to the extent of the partner's residual interest therein. Once individual creditors have satisfied their claims against individual assets, the partnership creditors may recover from the partners' separately owned assets to the extent of their unsatisfied claims, *regardless of the equity status of the partner in the firm* (debit or credit balance). A special point of interest in this allocation process is the definition of individual and partnership assets and liabilities. A difficult and legally unresolved problem relates to a debit balance existing in an insolvent partner's capital account (whether or not the *other* partners are insolvent). Section 40 (i) of the Uniform Partnership Act is explicit on this point:

> Where a partner has become bankrupt or his estate is insolvent the claims against his separate property shall rank in the following order:
>   (I)   Those owing to separate creditors,
>   (II) Those owing to partnership creditors,
>   (III) Those owing to partners by way of contribution.

Under this act, the obligation to the partnership, and the remaining partners, for a debit balance does not constitute a *separate* or *individual* liability of the insolvent partner. The language of the Federal Bankruptcy Act, which emphasizes the marshaling principle, also appears to support this position. There is, however, a possible legal *interpretation* of the "contribution obligation" which creates an individual liability of the partner. In this regard, the following observations made at the time the Uniform Partnership Act was initially developed are relevant:

> It is to be hoped that eventually in all our courts of insolvency the liability of the partner to contribute to the payment of partnership liabilities, correctly described by the Act as a partnership asset, will be treated as on a parity with his other liabilities for purpose of distribution of his insolvent estate.[5]

> This [Section 40 (i)] however introduces several changes into the law as it is established by the weight of authority. A partner who has paid the partnership debts can at present [prior to passage of the Act] prove for contribution against the insolvent partner's estate and share *pari passu* with his other separate creditors.[6]

A contrary opinion is expressed in the following terms:

> It is submitted that the partner, by paying the partnership debts, should be held to have stepped into the right of the partnership creditors against the assets of the insolvent partner. He should not obtain, however, in respect to that estate a better position than the person whose claim he has paid. Indeed, if he were allowed to do so, the rule giving priority to separate creditors on the separate estate would be to that extent nullified.[7]

---

[5] Judson A. Crane, "The Uniform Partnership Act—A Criticism," *Harvard Law Review,* June 1915, pp. 784–85.

[6] Ibid., p. 786.

[7] William Draper Lewis, "The Uniform Partnership Act," *Harvard Law Review,* January 1916, pp. 307–8.

The first opinion (by Crane) appears to support the position that a partner's debit balance in his or her capital account, particularly if it is an obligation to a solvent partner who has personally discharged the total claims of partnership creditors, is a separate liability of the insolvent partner. The counterargument, however, focuses on the apparent *equity* of the Uniform Partnership Act provision. We conclude, therefore, that in those states which have not adopted the Uniform Partnership Act, or in federal bankruptcy cases, it is possible that the individual partner's estate may be prorated among his or her separate creditors and his or her obligation to the partnership.[8]

The basic rights of creditors, following the marshaling of assets principle, may then be summarized:

1. Partnership creditors should seek the discharge of partnership debts by first exhausting partnership assets (excluding contributions of partners) to the extent of their claims.

2. A partner's individual creditors should first seek recourse against his or her separate assets to the extent of their claims. Under the Uniform Partnership Act, amounts due to the partnership by way of contribution are not individual liabilities. Under common law, or in federal bankruptcy cases, the contribution requirements *may* be construed as an individual liability sharing *pari passu* with other individual liabilities.

3. To the extent of their unsatisfied claims, partnership creditors may prove against the residual assets of an individual partner after his or her separate creditors have been satisfied, regardless of the amount of the partner's residual interest in the partnership.

4. To the extent of their unsatisfied claims, a partner's individual creditors may prove against the *recorded* interest of the individual partner in the residual assets of a solvent partnership.

5. If a partner pays more than his or her share of partnership liabilities, that partner has a claim, as measured by the resulting credit balance in his or her account, against those partners with debit balances (representing their unrequited share of partnership losses).

Determining amounts to be allocated to the various creditor and equity interests is illustrated under each of the two conditions of insolvency: (1) an insolvent partnership with at least one solvent partner and (2) an insolvent partnership with all partners insolvent.

---

[8] Even other interpretations have been made. In *Robinson* v. *Security Co.,* Ann. Cas. 1915C, 1170, it was held that a judgment should be rendered "dividing the distributable assets belonging to the estate of each partner ratably among the separate creditors of such partners together with the partnership creditors." Marshaling of assets was not applied even *in form* in this case.

Case 6. At Least One Solvent Partner

The trial balance of the ABC Partnership, after realization of assets but before distribution of cash to either creditors or partners, is as follows:

	Debit	Credit
Cash	$20,000	
Liabilities		$30,000
A, capital		10,000
B, capital	5,000	
C, capital	15,000	
	$40,000	$40,000

A, B, and C share profits and losses in the ratio 2 : 4 : 4. The separate financial status of each individual partner, excluding his or her interest in, or obligation to, the partnership, is the following:

	Assets (Realizable Value)	Liabilities
A	$ 5,000	$20,000
B	6,000	4,000
C	30,000	10,000

Given these data, it is apparent that both A and B are insolvent. A's individual liabilities exceed his individual assets and his interest in the firm (even assuming that his partnership interest is recoverable at book value). B's obligations to individual creditors ($4,000) and to the partnership ($5,000) exceed his individual assets. We also assume that partnership creditors obtain a judgment against C and that she makes full payment of the partnership obligations to its outside creditors, using her separate assets as necessary. Schedules of partnership liquidation and distribution of separate assets of the individual partners under the provisions of the Uniform Partnership Act are given in Illustrations 17–8 and 17–9.

If the Uniform Partnership Act is not controlling in this case *and* if the partners' obligations to the firm are judged individual liabilities sharing *pari passu* with other individual obligations, the liquidation schedule is changed only by the amount of B's contribution to the firm (since A, the second insolvent partner,

ILLUSTRATION 17-8   One Solvent Partner (Case 6)

ABC PARTNERSHIP
Schedule of Partnership Liquidation
Dr. (Cr.)

	Cash	Priority Claims	Residual Equities		
			A	B	C
Profit and loss ratio			20%	40%	40%
Balances	$20,000	$(30,000)	$(10,000)	$5,000	$15,000
Payment of liabilities	(20,000)	20,000			
Balances	–0–	$(10,000)	$(10,000)	$5,000	$15,000
Establish status of each partner's personal solvency. Record payment of partnership liabilities by C from her separate assets		10,000			(10,000)
Balances	–0–	–0–	$(10,000)	$5,000	$ 5,000
Contribution by B	$ 2,000			(2,000)	
Balances	$ 2,000	–0–	$(10,000)	$3,000	$ 5,000
Allocation of B's debit balance			1,000	(3,000)	2,000
Balances	$ 2,000	–0–	$ (9,000)	–0–	$ 7,000
Contribution by C	7,000				(7,000)
Balances	$ 9,000	–0–	$ (9,000)	–0–	–0–
Distribution of cash	(9,000)		9,000		
Termination of partnership	–0–	–0–	–0–	–0–	–0–

ILLUSTRATION 17-9   One Solvent Partner (Case 6)

ABC PARTNERSHIP
Schedule of Distribution of Separate Assets

	A	B	C
Separate assets	$ 5,000	$ 6,000	$ 30,000
Separate liabilities (Rank I)	(20,000)	(4,000)	(10,000)
Separate capital (deficit)	$(15,000)	$ 2,000	$ 20,000
Payment of partnership debts (Rank II)			(10,000)
Separate capital (deficit)	$(15,000)	$ 2,000	$ 10,000
Payment of debt to partnership (Rank III)		(2,000)	(7,000)
Separate capital (deficit)	$(15,000)	–0–	$ 3,000
Distribution of cash by partnership	9,000		
Separate capital (deficit)	$ (6,000)	–0–	$ 3,000
Obligations of B to A and C through the partnership	1,000	$(3,000)	2,000
Separate capital (deficit)	$ (5,000)	$(3,000)	$ 5,000

does not have an obligation to contribute to the partnership). The amount of B's contribution is calculated as follows:

	B		
	Liabilities	*Ratio of Assets to Liabilities*	*Asset Settlement*
To partnership	$5,000	$^2/_3$	$3,334
Separate creditors	4,000	$^2/_3$	2,666
	$9,000		$6,000

Under these conditions, A, the only partner with a credit balance, will receive $445 more than under the provisions of the Uniform Partnership Act, C will contribute $889 less to the partnership, and B's personal creditors will receive $1,334 less.

Case 7. All Partners Insolvent

Assume the same facts as in Case 6, except that C has separate assets of $10,000 rather than $30,000. In this case, the partnership is legally insolvent because there are not enough partnership assets and net assets of individual partners to make a full settlement with partnership creditors.

Under the provisions of the Uniform Partnership Act, the partnership creditors will receive the $20,000 of partnership cash and the $2,000 excess assets of B (those not required to discharge separate debts), leaving a deficiency in payments to partnership creditors of $8,000. The $22,000 distribution to these creditors will necessarily be made according to priorities established by law.

If the partners' obligations to the partnership are considered separate (individual) liabilities and are accorded the same status as other separate liabilities, the distribution of separate property is calculated as follows:

	B		
	Liabilities	*Ratio of Assets to Liabilities*	*Asset Settlement*
To partnership	$5,000	$^2/_3$	$3,334
Separate creditors	4,000	$^2/_3$	2,666
	$9,000		$6,000

		C	
	Liabilities	*Ratio of Assets to Liabilities*	*Asset Settlement*
To partnership	$15,000	$^2/_5$	$ 6,000
Separate creditors	10,000	$^2/_5$	4,000
	$25,000		$10,000

The allocation of B's separate assets is unchanged in this case because there was no adjustment of B's financial status. Thus, when the partners' obligations to contribute to the firm for debit balances are confirmed legally and are given an equal status with their separate liabilities, the partnership creditors will receive an additional $7,334 ($1,334 + $6,000) from the partnership, $1,334 being contributed by B and $6,000 being contributed by C. Note, however, that this calculation technique ignores the subtlety introduced by the inherent variability of the obligation to the partnership when two or more partners are involved, that is, the undischarged balance must be absorbed by the remaining partners, which accordingly alters the relative ratio of liabilities to separate creditors and to the partnership.

COMPREHENSIVE ILLUSTRATION

We now illustrate the preparation of a cash predistribution plan, a partnership liquidation schedule, and the related supporting calculations and schedules, given a more complex situation in which four partners decide to liquidate their partnership and one of the four partners is insolvent.

The partners of Slippery Walk Company agree to dissolve their partnership on July 1, 19X1, since the operations of the company have met with financial difficulties. The preliquidation capital and loan account balances and profit and loss ratio are as follows:

	Dr. (Cr.)		
Partner	*Capital*	*Loan*	*Ratio*
James	$(36,000)	$(14,000)	20%
McDonald	(28,000)	4,000*	20
Pearson	(12,000)	(4,000)	50
Quigley	(30,000)		10

* Loan to McDonald from Slippery Walk Company.

Completing the liquidation is anticipated to take about three months. The partners request that available cash be distributed at the end of each month and are interested in knowing when they should expect to participate in cash distributions. Accordingly, a cash predistribution plan is developed. The calculations in support of this plan are shown in Illustration 17–10.

Based on this information and the cash predistribution plan, a forecast of cash distributions to partners and creditors can be developed. The forecast presumes retaining $10,000 cash at the end of July and $4,000 at the end of August as a reserve for future unrecorded liabilities. All liquidation expenses and unrecorded liabilities are presumed to be known by the end of September, at which time a final cash distribution will be made. The forecasted schedule of cash payments is as follows:

Forecasted Schedule of Payments

Payee	July 31 Payments	August 31 Payments	September 30 Payments
Creditors	$130,000		
James	3,333	$17,333	$11,733
McDonald			6,400
Pearson			
Quigley	6,667	8,667	5,867
Total expected payments	$140,000	$26,000	$24,000
Cash to be held in reserve	$ 10,000	$ 4,000	–0–

Of course, the forecast is based on subjective estimates of when and how cash will be generated from liquidating assets. Actual events may differ substantially from expectations.

In contrast to the cash predistribution plan and the forecast of payments (which are statements of what is expected to happen in the future), the schedule of partnership liquidation is a historical document that reports the actual transactions which occur during the liquidation period. The schedule of partnership liquidation for Slippery Walk Company is based on the following events that took place during the three-month liquidation of the company.

	Liquidation of Noncash Assets		
	Discovery of Unrecorded Liabilities	Cash Proceeds Net of Liquidation Expenses	Book Values of Liquidated Assets
During July	–0–	$136,000	$180,000
During August	$8,000	22,000	18,000
During September	–0–	20,000	46,000

ILLUSTRATION 17-10   Comprehensive Illustration

SLIPPERY WALK COMPANY
Supporting Schedules for Cash Predistribution Plan

A. Schedule of Loss-Absorption Potentials

Partner	Equities	Profit and Loss Ratio	Loss-Absorption Potentials	Order of Equity Absorption
James	$50,000	20%	$250,000 = ($50,000/20%)	3
McDonald	24,000	20	120,000 = ($24,000/20%)	2
Pearson	16,000	50	32,000 = ($16,000/50%)	1
Quigley	30,000	10	300,000 = ($30,000/10%)	4

B. Schedule of Loss Absorption, Dr. (Cr.)

	Assumed Losses	James	McDonald	Pearson	Quigley
Profit and loss ratio		20%	20%	50%	10%
Preliquidation equities		$(50,000)	$(24,000)	$(16,000)	$(30,000)
Potential loss to absorb Pearson's equity ($16,000/50%)	$(32,000)	6,400	6,400	16,000	3,200
Balances		$(43,600)	$(17,600)	–0–	$(26,800)
Potential loss to absorb McDonald's equity ($17,600/40%)	(44,000)	17,600	17,600		8,800
Balances		$(26,000)	–0–		$(18,000)
Potential loss to absorb James' equity ($26,000/66²/₃%)	(39,000)	26,000			13,000
Balances		–0–			$ (5,000)
Potential loss to absorb Quigley's remaining equity	(5,000)				5,000
Balance					–0–

ILLUSTRATION 17-11 Comprehensive Illustration

SLIPPERY WALK COMPANY
Schedule of Partnership Liquidation
Dr. (Cr.)

	Assets			Claimants / Residual Equities						
			Priority	James		McDonald		Pearson		Quigley
	Cash	Noncash	Claims	Loan	Capital	Loan	Capital	Loan	Capital	Capital
Profit and loss ratio					20%		20%		50%	10%
Preliquidation balances	$ 6,000	$244,000	$(130,000)	$(14,000)	$(36,000)	$4,000	$(28,000)	$(4,000)	$(12,000)	$(30,000)
Realization of assets and allocation of loss—July	136,000	(180,000)			8,800		8,800		22,000	4,400
Balances	$142,000	$ 64,000	$(130,000)	$(14,000)	$(27,200)	$4,000	$(19,200)	$(4,000)	$ 10,000	$(25,600)
Payment of creditors	(130,000)		130,000							
July 31 installment payment	(2,000)									2,000
Balances on July 31	$ 10,000	$ 64,000	–0–	$(14,000)	$(27,200)	$4,000	$(19,200)	$(4,000)	$ 10,000	$(23,600)
Realization of assets and allocation of gain—August	22,000	(18,000)			(800)		(800)		(2,000)	(400)
Recognition of unrecorded liabilities			$ (8,000)		1,600		1,600		4,000	800
Contribution by Pearson	5,000								(5,000)	
Balances	$ 37,000	$ 46,000	$ (8,000)	$(14,000)	$(26,400)	$4,000	$(18,400)	$(4,000)	$ 7,000	$(23,200)
Payment of creditors	(8,000)		8,000							
August 31 installment	(25,000)			14,000	667					10,333
Balances on August 31	$ 4,000	$ 46,000	–0–	–0–	$(25,733)	$4,000	$(18,400)	$(4,000)	$ 7,000	$(12,867)

Realization of assets and allocation of loss —September	20,000	(46,000)		5,200	5,200		13,000	2,600
Offset of loans against capital accounts					4,000	(4,000)		
Balances	$ 24,000	-0-	-0-	$(20,533)	(9,200)	-0-	$ 16,000	$(10,267)
Allocation of Pearson's capital deficiency				6,400	6,400		(16,000)	3,200
Balances	$ 24,000	-0-	-0-	$(14,133)	$ (2,800)	-0-	-0-	$ (7,067)
September 30 installment	(24,000)			14,133	2,800			7,067
Termination of partnership	-0-	-0-	-0-	-0-	-0-	-0-	-0-	-0-

The assets and liabilities of Slippery Walk Company on July 1, 19X1, are cash, $6,000; noncash assets, $244,000; and liabilities, $130,000. Using the calculations shown in Illustration 17–10 and the information about liabilities, the cash predistribution plan is as follows:

SLIPPERY WALK COMPANY
Cash Predistribution Plan

		Distributions			
	Priority Claims	James	McDonald	Pearson	Quigley
Cash distributions:					
First $130,000	100%				
Next 5,000					100%
Next 39,000		66²/₃%			33¹/₃
Next 44,000		40	40%		20
All additional payments		20	20	50%	10

It is anticipated that the realization of noncash assets will follow this pattern:

July 19X1	$144,000 net cash proceeds
August 19X1	20,000 net cash proceeds
September 19X1	20,000 net cash proceeds

Cash disbursements at the end of each month equaled available cash balances except for a $10,000 cash reserve at the end of July and a $4,000 cash reserve at the end of August. During the month of August, Pearson contributed $5,000 to the partnership to partially compensate for his capital deficiency. He was unable to make any further contributions.

The schedule of partnership liquidation is presented in Illustration 17–11. The actual order of cash distributions is consistent with the cash predistribution plan except for the $8,000 payment for liabilities which were discovered in August, after the cash predistribution plan was prepared. Nevertheless, Pearson's $5,000 cash contribution to the partnership (in August) could have altered the sequence of payments from that indicated by the cash predistribution plan. That plan was constructed on the assumption that none of the partners would be able to make additional investments to cover capital deficiencies. Pearson's $5,000 contribution obviously strengthened his capital position relative to the other partners. Thus, his stronger position would warrant his participation in cash distributions somewhat sooner than was indicated by the cash predistribution plan. However, since the total amount of available cash was not large enough to provide any cash return to Pearson, the actual distribution of cash did in fact conform to the predistribution plan.

ILLUSTRATION 17-12   Comprehensive Illustration

SLIPPERY WALK COMPANY
Schedule of Safe Installment Payments
Dr.(Cr.)

	Partners' Equities			
	James	*McDonald*	*Pearson*	*Quigley*
Profit and loss ratio	20%	20%	50%	10%
Computation of July 31 payment:				
Predistribution balances	$(41,200)	$(15,200)	$ 6,000	$(25,600)
Potential loss, $80,000*	32,000	32,000	(6,000)	16,000
Balances	$ (9,200)	$ 16,800	–0–	$ (9,600)
Potential loss, $16,800	11,200	(16,800)		5,600
Balances	$ 2,000	–0–		$ (4,000)
Potential loss, $2,000	(2,000)			2,000
Safe payment to partner	–0–			$ (2,000)
Computation of August 31 payment:				
Predistribution balances	$(40,400)	$(14,400)	$ 3,000	$(23,200)
Potential loss, $53,000†	21,200	21,200	(3,000)	10,600
Balances	$(19,200)	$ 6,800	–0–	$(12,600)
Potential loss, $6,800	4,533	(6,800)		2,267
Safe payments to partners	$(14,667)	–0–		$(10,333)
Computation of September 30 payment:				
Predistribution balances constitute safe payments to partners since no potential losses exist.				

* $64,000 noncash assets + $10,000 reserve for unrecorded liabilities + $6,000 capital deficiency of Pearson = $80,000.

† $46,000 noncash assets + $4,000 reserve for unrecorded liabilities + $3,000 capital deficiency of Pearson = $53,000.

The cash predistribution plan is prepared before the liquidation period and must be based on conservative assumptions about future events. Because future events might turn out to be inconsistent with those assumptions and as a precautionary confirmation of the decisions to distribute cash, it is wise to prepare a calculation of safe installment payments in support of each cash distribution. Illustration 17–12 presents this calculation for Slippery Walk Company.

Summary

This chapter describes the accounting problems and procedures associated with liquidation of a partnership. It includes coverage of both solvent and insolvent partnerships and partners, and it outlines the basic distributive rights of all equity interests in the partnership. Accounting techniques introduced in this chapter include the preparation of the basic schedule of partnership liquidation and two methods for dealing with installment distributions to the partners during the liquidation process. The installment distribution methods consist of cash predistribution plans and periodic calculations of "safe payments" each time an installment payment is to be made.

The schedule of partnership liquidation is the primary historical statement reflecting partnership transactions during the liquidation period. It involves recognition of the gain or loss on the final cash realization of all assets, as well as allocation of this gain or loss to the individual partners in the profit- and loss-sharing ratio. After the payment of liabilities (priority claims), any partners with debit capital balances should make payment to the partnership for the obligation. If partners with debit capital balances are unable to make payment, the debit balance is reallocated to the remaining partners in their relative profit and loss ratio. Although payments to partners are usually made first in respect to loans and then for capital and profits, it is important to remember that the right of "setoff" prescribes that a partner's loan be offset against a debit capital balance before any payment is made on the loan.

In a simple liquidation, the total gain or loss on the realization of assets, including the effects of liquidation expenses, is known before cash is distributed to partners. However, if the partners wish to make installment distributions during the liquidation period, a distribution procedure should involve periodic payments that may be made safely without undue risk of personal liability to the fiduciary. In the traditional approach to this problem, each time cash is to be distributed, the accountant estimates the largest potential loss that can be incurred in future realizations of noncash assets. This generally involves the assumptions that no cash will be realized on all noncash assets and no cash will be collected from partners with debit balances in their capital accounts. After these hypothetical losses are allocated to the partners, one or more partners will remain with credit balances in their combined loan and capital equity. In total, these credit balances equal the cash available for distribution to partners, and they constitute the "safe payments" for the period. A prudent extension to this calculation technique is to provide for estimated future liquidation expenses and unrecorded liabilities by treating them as additions to the potential assumed losses.

The cash predistribution plan is designed to show the order and amounts of payments that will be made to creditors and partners if, and when, cash becomes available during the liquidation period. Preparation of the cash predistribution plan involves three steps. First, each partner's loss-absorption potential is calculated. Second, using the order of equity extinguishment established in the first step, a schedule of loss absorption is prepared. In this schedule, losses are assumed in amounts that sequentially absorb each partner's equity. Finally, the cash predistribution plan is prepared from the information in the loss absorption schedule.

When partnership liquidation involves insolvent partners, the claims of the various creditor groups and the partnership itself against partners with a debit balance in their capital account depend on the legal doctrine applicable in the situation. Under the Uniform Partnership Act, the marshaling of assets doctrine prescribes that partnership assets, and individual assets constitute separate pools of resources against which partnership creditors and individual creditors, respectively, have initial and separate recourse. If the partnership is insolvent, partnership assets are completely exhausted in the partial settlement of partnership debts. If the partnership is solvent, creditors of individual partners have a claim against the remaining partnership assets to the extent of the partner's residual interest therein. Once individual creditors have satisfied their claims against individual assets, the partnership creditors may recover from the partners' separately owned assets to the extent of their unsatisfied claims, regardless of the equity status of the partner in the firm (debit or credit balance).

Questions

1. What are the main activities of a partnership during the liquidation process?
2. What is the order of priority for the distribution of assets under Section 40 (B) of the Uniform Partnership Act?
3. If after liquidation of the partnership assets, a partner has a debit balance in his or her capital account, what procedure is followed if the partner is solvent (i.e., holds enough personal assets to cover the capital deficiency)? What if the partner is insolvent?
4. Explain the rule of "setoff."
5. If one partner is assigned the role of managing the liquidation process and is to be compensated for this service by the partnership, how should the compensation be recorded in the records of the partnership?
6. If installment (periodic) payments are to be made during the course of liquidation, what factors might be of concern in determining the amounts of cash or other assets to be distributed?
7. Describe the role and usefulness of a schedule of safe (installment) payments.
8. How are loans from partners accounted for in the schedule of partnership liquidation and in the schedule of safe (installment) payments?
9. What hypothetical losses and/or hypothetical cash transfers are recorded in a schedule of partnership liquidation?
10. What is a cash predistribution plan? What are loss-absorption potentials?
11. To what extent does a cash predistribution plan show the actual gains or losses resulting from the liquidation of assets?
12. How should expected liquidation expenses and/or unrecorded liabilities be treated in proceeding with the process of liquidation by installments?
13. What events would cause the safe distribution of cash to differ in sequence from that indicated by a cash predistribution plan?
14. Briefly explain the marshaling of assets principle.

Exercises

Exercise 17–1   (Partnership Liquidation Schedule)

Ball, Ludick, and Thatcher are partners in BLT Company and have capital balances on January 1, 19X1, of $70,000, $35,000, and $52,000, respectively. After deciding to liquidate the business, the partners convert the noncash assets of $117,000 into $62,000 cash. All the liabilities, totaling $30,000, are paid, and the remaining cash is distributed among the partners. They share profits and losses: Ball, 60 percent; Ludick, 30 percent; and Thatcher, 10 percent.

Required:

Prepare a partnership liquidation schedule showing how cash is distributed.

Exercise 17–2   (Partnership Liquidation Concepts)

For each of the following, choose the one best answer that either completes the sentence or answers the question:

1. In terms of the legal definition of insolvency, a partnership is insolvent only when
   a. The partnership assets are insufficient to pay partnership obligations.
   b. The surplus of individual partners' assets over nonpartnership debts is insufficient, together with partnership assets, to pay partnership obligations.
   c. The partners' individual assets together with partnership assets are insufficient to pay partnership obligations.
   d. The partnership is declared bankrupt by court decree.
   e. None of the above.

2. In terms of the entity definition of insolvency, a partnership is insolvent only when
   a. Its recorded assets are insufficient to pay existing partnership liabilities.
   b. The surplus of the individual partners' assets over nonpartnership debts is insufficient, together with partnership assets, to pay partnership liabilities.
   c. The partners' individual assets together with partnership assets are insufficient to pay partnership liabilities.
   d. The partnership is declared bankrupt by court decree.
   e. None of the above.

3. If a partnership has only noncash assets, all liabilities have been properly recorded, and no additional liquidation expenses are incurred, the maximum potential loss of the partnership upon liquidation is
   a. The fair market value of the assets.
   b. The book value of the assets.
   c. The fair value of the assets less any proceeds that can be expected from selling the assets.
   d. The book value of the assets less recorded liabilities.
   e. None of the above.

4. If Simpson and Coolidge have equities of $75,000 and $60,000, respectively, and share profits and losses in the ratio of 6 : 4, their respective loss-absorption potentials are:
   a. $105,000 and $125,000.
   b. $125,000 and $150,000.
   c. $450,000 and $240,000.
   d. $75,000 and $60,000.
   e. $81,000 and $54,000.

5. XYZ Partnership is in the process of liquidation. The profit and loss ratio is 5 : 3 : 2 for X, Y, and Z, respectively. Preliquidation balances are Cash (Dr.), $10,000; Noncash Assets (Dr.), $25,000; Priority Claims (Cr.), $12,000; X, Capital (Cr.), $10,000; Y, Capital (Cr.), $7,800; and Z, Capital (Cr.), $5,200. The noncash assets are sold for $5,000, net of liquidation expenses. Cash distribution to partners at the conclusion of the liquidation process will be
   a. X, $0; Y, $1,800; and Z, $1,200.
   b. X, $833; Y, $666; and Z, $1,500.
   c. X, $5,000; Y, $3,000; and Z, $2,000.
   d. X, $1,000; Y, $1,000; and Z, $1,000.
   e. X, $0; Y, $0; and Z, $0.

Exercise 17–3   (Calculation of Safe Installment Payment)

The Nair, Rittenberg, and Weygandt Partnership has not been successful. Hence, the partners have sadly concluded that operations must be terminated and their partnership liquidated. Profits and losses are shared as follows: Nair, 45 percent; Rittenberg, 35 percent; and Weygandt, 20 percent. As the accountant placed in charge of this partnership, you have responsibility for the liquidation and distribution of assets. When you assume your responsibilities, the partnership balance sheet is as follows:

Assets		Equities	
Cash	$18,000	Liabilities	$12,000
Other assets	54,000	Loan from Nair	18,000
		Nair, capital	6,000
		Rittenberg, capital	30,000
		Weygandt, capital	6,000
Total assets	$72,000	Total equities	$72,000

During the first two months of your duties, the following events occur:

1. Assets having a book value of $40,000 are sold for $12,000 cash.
2. Previously unrecorded liabilities of $1,000 are recognized.
3. Before distributing available cash balances to creditors and partners, you conclude that a cash reserve of $1,000 should be set aside for future potential expenses.
4. Remaining cash balances are distributed to creditors and partners.

Required:

Prepare a schedule of partnership liquidation that covers all of the events described above.

Exercise 17–4   (Cash Predistribution Plan)

The balance sheet of the Oslo Company just before liquidation is as follows:

Assets		Equities	
Assets	$258,000	Accounts payable	$48,000
		Morton, loan	12,000
		Morton, capital	28,000
		McLain, capital	80,000
		Hirsch, capital	90,000
Total assets	$258,000	Total equities	$258,000

Morton, McLain, and Hirsch share profits and losses in the ratio of 1 : 4 : 5, respectively.

Required:

Construct a systematic plan showing how cash should be distributed to the various equities as it becomes available during the liquidation process.

Exercise 17-5   (Cash Predistribution Plan)

The XYZ Partnership is being dissolved. All liabilities have been liquidated. The balance of assets on hand is being realized by a comparatively slow conversion schedule. The following are details of partners' accounts:

Partners	Capital Account (Original Investment)	Current Account (Undistributed Earnings Net of Drawings)	Loans to Partnership	Profit and Loss Ratio
X	$10,000	$1,500 credit	$15,000	40%
Y	50,000	2,000 debit		40
Z	10,000	1,000 credit	5,000	20

Required:

Prepare a predistribution plan showing how cash payments should be made to the partners as assets are realized.

(AICPA adapted)

Exercise 17-6   (Calculation of Safe Installment Payments)

A, B, C, and D agree to dissolve their partnership. Their preliquidation capital and loan account balances are as follows:

	Capital	Loan
A	$28,000	$7,000
B	41,000	2,000
C	18,000	
D	12,000	2,000

They share profits and losses 40 : 30 : 20 : 10. Unpaid liabilities at the date of dissolution are $10,000; noncash assets total $105,000.

During the first month of liquidation, assets having a book value of $55,000 were sold for $31,000. During the second month, assets recorded at $32,000 were sold for $28,000. During the third month, the remaining unsold assets were determined to be worthless.

Required:

Prepare a schedule of liquidation indicating the cash distribution that is made at the end of each month of the liquidation period.

Exercise 17-7   (Cash Predistribution Plan)

Partners Jay, Jane, and John, who share profits and losses 50 : 30 : 20, elect to liquidate the partnership business. Their preliquidation capital balances are Jay, $25,000; Jane, $30,000; and John, $15,000. Partnership unpaid liabilities amount to $6,500.

Required:

Prepare a schedule indicating the distribution of cash as it becomes available in the realization process.

Exercise 17–8   (Cash Predistribution Plan)

Ball, Dean, and Vernon share profits and losses from their partnership in the ratio of 20 percent, 35 percent, and 45 percent, respectively. Capital and loan balances related to each partner are as follows:

	Loan to Partner from Partnership	*Loan to Partnership from Partner*	*Capital*
Ball		$10,000	$50,000
Dean	$7,000		28,000
Vernon		20,000	25,000

In addition to the loan to Dean, assets of the partnership include cash of $11,000, inventory of $36,000, receivables of $26,000, and plant and equipment of $71,000. Partnership liabilities to nonpartners amount to $18,000.

Required:

Prepare a plan showing how cash would be distributed in sequential payments if the business were liquidated.

Problems

Problem 17–9   (Cash Predistribution Plan)

On August 25, 19X1, Perry, Hill, and Stein entered into a partnership agreement to acquire a speculative second mortgage on undeveloped real estate. They invested $55,500, $32,000, and $12,500, respectively. They agreed on a profit and loss ratio of 4 : 2 : 1, respectively.

On September 1, 19X1, they purchased for $100,000 a mortgage note with an unpaid balance of $120,000. The amount paid included interest accrued from June 30, 19X1. The note principal matures at the rate of $2,000 each quarter. Interest at the annual rate of 8 percent computed on the unpaid balance is also due quarterly.

Regular interest and principal payments were received on September 30 and December 31, 19X1. A working capital imprest fund of $150 was established, and collection expenses of $70 were paid in December.

In addition to the regular September payment on September 30, the mortgagor made a lump-sum principal reduction payment of $10,000 plus a penalty of 2 percent for prepayment.

Because of the speculative nature of the note, the partners agree to defer recognition of the discount until their cost has been fully recovered.

Required:

a. Assuming that no cash distributions were made to the partners, prepare a schedule computing the cash balance available for distribution to the partners on December 31, 19X1.

b. After payment of collection expenses, the partners expect to have cash in the total amount of $170,000 available for distribution to themselves for interest and return of principal. They plan to distribute the cash as soon as possible so that they can individually reinvest the cash. Prepare a schedule as of September 1 showing how the total cash of $170,000 should be distributed to the individual partners by installments as it becomes available.

(AICPA adapted)

Problem 17–10   (Partnership Liquidation Schedule with Installment Payments)

Iris, Doug, and Dawn, partners in the Fast Copy Company, prepare to liquidate their business. On December 31, 19X1, the partnership account balances are as follows:

Cash	$ 5,430	Trade payables	$13,910
Other assets	61,870	Loans from partners:	
		Iris	8,000
		Doug	4,000
		Dawn	9,000
		Capital balances:	
		Iris	18,100
		Doug	3,090
		Dawn	11,200
	$67,300		$67,300

Iris, Doug, and Dawn share profits and losses 50 : 30 : 20.

It is agreed that cash made available during liquidation shall be distributed to the partners at the end of each month. However, an amount sufficient to provide for anticipated future expenses and unrecorded liabilities is to be withheld.

The following is a summary of transactions for the three-month liquidation period:

	Liquidation of Noncash Assets		Liquidation Expenses	Newly Discovered Unrecorded Partnership Liability	Estimated Future Expenses and Unrecorded Liabilities
	Book Value	Cash Realized			
January	$24,700	$18,180	$860	–0–	$3,000
February	33,170	26,810	800	$2,000*	3,350
March	4,000	3,200	200	–0–	–0–

* The partnership bookkeeper failed to record the property tax liability in December 19X1.

Required:

Prepare a partnership liquidation schedule indicating amounts of periodic cash distributions.

Problem 17–11   (Cash Predistribution Plan)

The partners of the Lomax Company agreed to dissolve their partnership on March 31, 19X1. Their preliquidation capital and loan account balances and the profit and loss ratio were as follows:

Partner	Capital	Loan	P & L Ratio
W	$16,000	$4,000	40%
X	29,000	7,000	30
Y	8,000		20
Z	9,000	1,000	10

The partnership had a cash balance of $2,000 and noncash assets of $90,000; obligations to outside creditors amounted to $18,000. Available cash was to be distributed at the end of each month during the period of liquidation. Assets were realized as follows:

	Book Values	Net Proceeds
April	$54,000	$26,000
May	26,000	14,000
June	10,000	2,000

Required:

a. On the basis of information available on March 31, prepare a plan for the distribution of cash.

b. Prepare a schedule showing how the April and May disbursements of cash were to be distributed.

Problem 17–12   (Legal Concepts for Partnerships)

A, B, and C formed ABC Company, a partnership, with A contributing $12,000 of capital, B contributing $8,000, and C contributing $6,000. In their partnership agreement, A, B, and C provided that the partnership was to exist for 20 years, but the partners made no provision as to the proportions in which profits and losses were to be shared. During the course of operating the partnership, A made a loan of $1,000 to the partnership that has not been repaid, and the partnership also owes outside creditors additional amounts that exceed the value of partnership assets by $3,000.

Required:

a. Under the Uniform Partnership Act, in absence of a specific agreement between the parties, how is the compensation and profit for each partner determined during the course of operating the partnership?

b. Under the Uniform Partnership Act
   (1) If A wishes to terminate the partnership but B and C do not, does A have the right to withdraw from the partnership? *Explain.*
   (2) If A, B, and C agree to terminate the partnership, how will losses be divided?

c. Discuss
   (1) The rule of "marshaling of assets."
   (2) The distinction between the "dissolution" of the partnership and the "winding up" of partnership affairs.

d. If D becomes a partner in ABC Company and replaces A, what is D's liability for obligations arising before her admission to the partnership?

(AICPA adapted)

Problem 17–13   (Insolvent Partners)

Newman, Jones, and Huber are partners in Newman Wholesale Company and share profits and losses 50 : 30 : 20. Their capital balances on January 1, 19X1, are as follows:

Newman	$ 5,000 debit
Jones	39,000 credit
Huber	24,000 debit

The partnership liabilities are $15,000. On liquidation, the noncash assets of $18,000 are converted into $4,000 cash. The nonbusiness (personal) assets and liabilities of each partner are the following:

Partner	*Assets*	*Liabilities*
Newman	$13,000	$20,000
Jones	17,000	6,400
Huber	18,000	3,200

Required:

Prepare a partnership liquidation schedule according to the provisions of
a. Bankruptcy law.
b. Uniform Partnership Act.

Problem 17–14   (Cash Predistribution Plan)

Mettlen, Cundiff, Jentz, and Nelson decide to dissolve their partnership. They plan a program of piecemeal conversion of assets in order to minimize liquidation losses. Partners share profits and losses as follows: Mettlen, 40 percent; Cundiff, 35 percent;

Jentz, 15 percent; and Nelson, 10 percent. The period of liquidation begins on June 1, 19X1, when the trial balance of the partnership is as follows:

Cash	$ 3,200	
Receivables	25,900	
Inventory (6/1/X1)	39,600	
Equipment (net)	19,800	
Accounts payable		$ 7,000
Mettlen, loan		6,000
Cundiff, loan		6,500
Mettlen, capital		20,000
Cundiff, capital		21,500
Jentz, capital		18,000
Nelson, capital		9,500
	$88,500	$88,500

Required:

a. Prepare a schedule as of June 1, 19X1, showing how cash will be distributed among partners as it becomes available.

b. On July 31, 19X1, cash of $12,700 is available for payment to creditors and partners. How should it be distributed?

c. Assume that the partnership decides to continue operations rather than liquidate. Following this decision, the partnership earns profits of $23,625. How should the profits be distributed if, along with the profit-sharing arrangement, Nelson is to receive a bonus of 5 percent of the net income from operations (with the bonus treated as a partnership expense)?

(AICPA adapted)

Problem 17–15   (Insolvent Partnership and Partners)

United Service Company, a partnership, prepared the following trial balance after realization of noncash assets but before distribution of cash to creditors or partners:

	Dr.	Cr.
Cash	$15,000	
Liabilities		$40,000
Ficken, capital	15,000	
Powell, capital		30,000
Carlson, capital	40,000	
	$70,000	$70,000

The individual financial status of each partner, excluding partnership capital balances, follows:

	Assets	Liabilities
Ficken	$40,000	$ 30,000
Powell	50,000	100,000
Carlson	90,000	30,000

The partners share profits and losses equally.

Required:

a. Prepare a schedule of partnership liquidation and a schedule indicating the partners' personal financial status under the provisions of the Uniform Partnership Act.

b. Calculate the amounts the partnership and the creditors of the separate partners would receive if the partners' obligations to the firm were judged individual liabilities.

Problem 17–16   (Insolvent Partnership and Partners)

Mathis, Overton, and Downey are partners sharing profits in the ratio of 4 : 3 : 2, respectively. The partnership and two of the partners are currently unable to make full payment of their obligations to creditors. The balance sheet of the partnership and a list of the assets and liabilities of the separate partners are as follows:

MOD PARTNERSHIP
Balance Sheet

Assets		Equities		
Cash	$ 500	Accounts payable		$37,000
Other assets	60,500	Capital:		
		Mathis	$9,000	
		Overton	7,500	
		Downey	7,500	24,000
Total assets	$61,000	Total equities		$61,000

Assets and Liabilities of Partners M, O, and D
Excluding Partnership Interests

Partner	Cash and Cash Value of Personal Assets	Liabilities
Mathis	$31,000	$22,000
Overton	9,450	11,900
Downey	4,000	5,000

Required:

a. Assuming that "other assets" are converted into $33,500 cash, prepare a partnership liquidation schedule *and* a complementary schedule indicating the distribution of partners' personal assets according to the provisions of the Uniform Partnership Act.

b. Calculate the miminum amount that must be realized from the sale of noncash partnership assets so that the personal creditors of Overton will receive full settlement of their claims.

(AICPA adapted)

Problem 17–17   (Cash Predistribution Plan and Calculation of Safe Installment Payments)

X, Y, and Z are the partners of the XYZ partnership. The profit- and loss-sharing ratio is 2 : 3 : 5. Immediately prior to liquidation of all noncash assets, the partnership has no cash, no liabilities, and noncash assets with a book value of $200,000. The capital balances of X, Y, and Z, are $35,000, $45,000, and $120,000, respectively.

Required:

a. Prepare a cash predistribution plan for the XYZ Partnership.

b. Assume that the ultimate loss on liquidation of noncash assets is $167,500. Compute the three capital account balances as the cash implicit in this amount of loss is paid in compliance with the cash predistribution plan and as the loss is allocated. Explain how a payment inconsistent with the cash predistribution plan will result in cash being received by a partner whose capital account subsequently becomes too small to absorb a loss allocated in the profit- and loss-sharing ratio (i.e., confirm the equity of the cash predistribution plan).

c. Now assume that monthly installment payments are to be made to X, Y, and Z. During the first month of liquidation, noncash assets with a book value of $60,000 are sold for $32,500. Compute the safe payment that can be made as of the end of the first month.

UNIT V # Fiduciary and Institutional Accounting

Accounting for Estates and Trusts

Chapter Outline

This chapter covers accounting for estates and trusts. It begins with a brief introduction to the topic of estate planning to provide a background for several topics related to estates and trusts. Subsequently, the roles of fiduciaries in both estate and trust administration are examined. The accounting procedures for estates and trusts are also covered in the chapter.

INTRODUCTION TO ESTATE PLANNING

Estate planning is meant to result in minimizing: (1) federal estate taxes, state inheritance (or estate) taxes, and federal and state gift taxes and (2) probate costs, subject to the overall goals of those owning the properties involved. These matters, as well as others, are discussed briefly below. We emphasize that this discussion is greatly simplified because estate planning is a complicated topic. Additionally, this discussion employs well-understood terms such as *estate, trust, probate,* and so on, without providing definitions. Subsequent portions of the chapter, which are more technical in nature, provide definitions of these, and other terms, as needed.

The federal taxation of estates is part of a unified transfer tax system which imposes a single tax on the sum of the values of (1) the taxable gifts made by an individual during his or her lifetime and (2) the property transferred at death (i.e., the estate). This sum is subject to progressive tax rates ranging from 18 percent on the first $10,000 to 55 percent on amounts over $3,000,000. Two important factors related to estate planning mitigate the taxation of this sum.

First, an individual, whether married or not, is allowed to transfer up to $10,000 annually to each of an unlimited number of donees without tax consequences. We emphasize that this provision applies in the case of married couples even if title to all the couple's property is held by one spouse. For example, suppose that Thomas Boatrey, a currently unmarried individual, begins a gifting program on January 1, 19X0, and gives both his son and his daughter $40,000 per year for 10 years (a total of $800,000). Of the $80,000 given each year, $20,000 is not subject to taxation because this amount is within his annual exclusion. On the other hand, $60,000 of the $80,000 given annually ($600,000 in total) is considered to be a taxable gift, although, as explained below, the tax paid on this amount may be zero. In any case, this example illustrates how a gifting program can be used in connection with the annual exclusion to minimize estate taxes. That is, it shows how the individual can exclude assets with values that might generate estate taxes from his or her estate without producing tax consequences. Note also that this technique can be used effectively in reducing estate taxes on appreciating or income producing assets. For example, assume that Boatrey gives only securities valued at $20,000 to his son and daughter during the fifth year of his gifting program and that these securities are worth $100,000 at the date of his death. In this case, he has reduced the value of his taxable estate through his fifth-year gift by $100,000, rather than only $20,000.

The second mitigating factor is the unified transfer tax credit. This credit of $192,800 equals the estate tax on an estate of $600,000, assuming no prior taxable gifts. Each individual is entitled to this credit, and its effect is to produce a tax of zero on the sum of the values of the individual's taxable gifts and estate, provided that this sum is less than, or equal to, $600,000. For example, assume the original data given above and that the value of Boatrey's estate at the date of his death is zero. In this case, the sum of the values of his taxable gifts and his estate simply equals the value of his taxable gifts—$600,000. Nevertheless, no tax is due at any time because of the unified transfer tax credit. That is, technically, Boatrey's taxable gifts of $600,000 yield a tax (over time) of $192,800, *assuming current tax rates*. However, this tax is offset by the unified credit (also over time); thus, the actual tax payable is zero.

Of course, the values of an individual's taxable gifts and estates often are sufficient to yield taxes which are due currently on gifts made prior to death or estate taxes. For example, assume now that the value of Boatrey's estate is $200,000 at date of death and, for simplicity, that the tax rate applicable to this incremental value is 35 percent. In this instance, the sum of the values of his taxable gifts and his estate is $800,000 ($600,000 + $200,000), and the tax on his estate is $70,000. This amount equals the tax on a $600,000 estate, plus 35 percent of the $200,000 excess of the sum of the values of Boatrey's taxable gifts and estate over $600,000 ($800,000 − $600,000), less the unified tax credit of $192,800 [$192,800 + 35% × ($800,000 − $600,000) − $192,800)]. Note also that the state in which the individual dies invariably imposes estate or inheritance taxes on the value of his or her estate. The various state laws may even require taxes to be paid on estates valued at less than $600,000. In any case, these laws, like the federal laws, are pertinent in devising strategies to minimize estate-related taxes and probate costs. Although only a few states have gift taxes, the related laws also are relevant in minimizing these taxes and costs.

Another important estate-planning technique is the use of trusts in connection with the unified tax credit. In this context, we emphasize that each spouse is entitled to a unified credit of $192,800. Thus, careful estate planning ensures that neither of these credits is lost. For example, assume that Don and Laura Willman, a married couple, have an estate valued at $1,200,000 as of the date of Don's death. Assume also that state law dictates that the value of Don's portion of the estate is $600,000 and that he wills this portion to Laura. Under federal law, the value of property passing from one spouse to another at death is not subject to estate tax. Thus, the value of the property willed to Laura is not taxable and, consequently, no estate taxes are due upon Don's death. However, assume that the value of Laura's estate at the date of her death is $1,200,000. Laura's unified tax credit of $192,800 prevents, in effect, $600,000 of her estate from being subjected to estate taxation. Unfortunately, the remaining $600,000 is taxed because the unified tax credit of only one spouse was utilized.

With skillful planning, the taxes on the remainder could have been avoided by utilizing both spouses' unified tax credits. For example, assume that Don arranged through his will, for his property to be placed in a trust at the date of his death, with the income of the trust being paid to Laura during the remainder of her life and its principal being distributed equally to their children upon her death. In this case, Don's portion of the $1,200,000 estate is, in effect, not taxed upon his death (even though it does not pass directly to Laura) because of his unified tax credit. Subsequently, Laura's estate of $600,000 is free of tax upon her death because of her unified credit. Thus, the estate-planning technique employed has allowed utilization of the unified tax credits of both spouses and, consequently, has reduced the taxes paid on the ultimate transfers of the spouses' properties significantly.

Careful planning also can reduce the costs of probating an estate. A basic estate-planning technique, which often reduces probate costs, is to draft a will which simplifies the probate process and facilitates an orderly distribution of estate assets. Another popular technique for reducing probate costs is to create a revocable trust (i.e., a trust which can be rescinded by the individual creating the trust). During his or her lifetime, the individual creating the trust acts as trustee; however, upon death, a new trustee of the decedent's choosing continues the administration of the trust and distributes its assets according to the decedent's wishes. Since all of the decedent's assets are in trust, complications which often arise during probate are avoided, and probate costs frequently are reduced accordingly.

ROLE OF THE FIDUCIARY IN ESTATE ADMINISTRATION

A *fiduciary* is a person or entity entrusted with the safekeeping, management, or distribution of the property of another. Thus, a fiduciary is accountable to various interested parties. Either an individual, partnership, or corporation may serve in this capacity. The fiduciary relationship is a stewardship, or custodial, arrangement that is important, among other things, in the administration of estates and trusts and in trusteeships related to financially distressed debtors (see Chapter 19 for discussion of the latter case).

Upon the death of an individual (the *decedent*), a personal representative of the deceased assumes the role of fiduciary and takes custody and control of the estate. If the decedent has executed a valid will, which indicates the choice of fiduciary, this selection normally controls. In this case, the decedent has died *testate;* he or she is referred to as the *testator;* and when confirmed by the court of appointment, his or her fiduciary is known as the *executor.* If a decedent failed to execute a valid will, then he or she has died *intestate,* and the representative, who is selected by the court, is known as an *administrator.* Also, if there is a valid will, the decedent's wishes usually govern the distribution of the estate's assets. If no will exists, or if the will is invalid, the various state laws of *descent and distribution* control the disposition of the decedent's property. The laws of descent govern the disposition of real property; the laws of distribution control the disposition of personal property.

The administration of estates normally comes within the purview of *probate, surrogate, orphan's,* or *county* courts. Before a will becomes effective, it must be *admitted to probate.* To probate a will is to prove its validity; that is, to prove that it was executed by a competent decedent without duress or other improper influence and that it represents his or her last expressions concerning the disposition of the property. Witnesses to the signing of the will may be called upon to testify concerning these, and other, matters as well as to the genuineness of the various signatures. Once the will is admitted to probate, the court appoints an executor. If the person named in the will is able and willing to serve, he or she usually is confirmed by the court and is issued *letters testamentary*—which evidences his or her formal authority to assume the fiduciary role. An administrator who is appointed is issued *letters of administration* empowering him or her to act as fiduciary.

Although acceptance of a fiduciary appointment is voluntary, once accepted, a fiduciary is obliged to faithfully discharge the related obligations. The fiduciary first discovers the assets of the decedent, takes legal possession of them, and inventories them. Subsequently, the fiduciary is charged with exercising reasonable prudence in caring for and managing the property. Consequently, the fiduciary is required to invest estate resources prudently, to liquidate the debts of the decedent (including estate and inheritance taxes), and to distribute the decedent's property according to the will or as prescribed by law.

Inventory of Assets

The fiduciary is required to submit an inventory of the assets of the decedent to the court of his or her appointment. This inventory contains, as a minimum, a complete description of all assets for which he or she is responsible. Some of these assets may have no apparent value, yet for completeness, they are included in the inventory, along with an indication of no value. Among the assets often included in an estate inventory are bank balances; jewelry, collections, and other valuables; securities; advances to legatees; accrued interest; dividends receivable; accounts and other receivables; judgments payable to the estate; and interests in jointly owned properties. The proceeds of life insurance policies to which the estate is the beneficiary also are included among the estate assets. If a beneficiary other than the estate is named in a life insurance policy, the proceeds are paid directly to the beneficiary and are excluded from the estate inventory. If the estate includes a partnership interest, this property right is disclosed in the inventory, and its value ultimately is determined. The value of a partnership interest generally is determined using procedures specified in the partnership agreement or through liquidation.

Real property of the testator usually passes directly by *devise* to the *devisees* identified in the will, with legal title vesting on the date of the decedent's death. However, all real property often is included in the inventory of the decedent's assets since the fiduciary frequently must include all real and personal property in various reports required by government agencies, including those submitted for federal estate and state inheritance tax purposes. Although not accountable for real property passing directly to devisees, the fiduciary may petition the court to allow the sale of such property to pay the debts of the decedent if the existing personal property is inadequate for this purpose.

Specific terms of personal property also are often allowed to pass directly to the distributees. These items often include household items, clothing, and other personal effects that are of special value to a surviving spouse and others. The legal title to personal property which does not pass directly vests with the fiduciary and necessarily is included in the estate inventory.

If assets for which the fiduciary is responsible are discovered subsequent to the filing of the inventory, the fiduciary files a supplementary report which describes these additions. The sum of the original and supplemental lists composes the *principal,* or *corpus,* of the estate as of the date of the decedent's death.

The valuation of estate assets also is the responsibility of the fiduciary who may be aided by (state) court-appointed appraisers. For example, the Texas Probate Code requires the fiduciary to provide an *appraisement* of the fair market value of each estate asset and to make these assessments with the assistance of court-appointed appraisers, if any.

Payment of Claims against the Estate

The fiduciary is obliged in most states to give public notice to those having claims against the estate and to request that they make a *presentment* of their claims within a specified period of time. Presentment may be made either to the fiduciary or to the court. The fiduciary considers the validity of the claims, rejecting those determined to be invalid. In this context, the fidicuary is required to exhaust all appropriate legal defenses, including the statute of limitations and the statute of frauds in determining whether claims are valid. The length of time allowed for creditors to file a claim against an estate varies among the states. The period frequently prescribed is one year, or less, from the date of public notice.

Once the validity of the claims presented is determined, the fiduciary establishes the *sequence of paying* the various obligations and begins their settlement. If the estate is solvent, the order of settlement is not especially important. However, for insolvent estates, state statutes dictate the priority sequence which the fiduciary must follow to avoid personal liability for improper distribution. The following order of payment is fairly typical:

1. Funeral and administration expenses.
2. Debts secured by a lien on the decedent's property.
3. Taxes, including estate and inheritance taxes.
4. Judgments in force that are a lien against property of the decedent at time of death.
5. Provable debts against the estate.
6. Wages due domestics or other employees.
7. Sustenance payments to the surviving spouse for a specified period of time.

Distribution of Remaining Assets

Once the debts of the estate are paid, legacies are distributed. A testator's bequest of personal property is a *legacy,* and its recipient is a *legatee.* Legacies are classifed as *specific, demonstrative, general,* and *residual.*

1. A *specific* legacy is a bequest of personal property (e.g., clothing, jewelry, and other personal effects; furniture; and securities) specified in the will.
2. A *demonstrative* legacy is a bequest payable from a designated fund or specified asset accumulation. A gift of cash payable from a designated bank account and the bequest of a quantity of grain from a specified granary are examples of demonstrative legacies.
3. A *general legacy* is a bequest of money or other property with no indication of the source of the asset to be distributed.
4. A *residual legacy* is the terminal distribution of personal property (the residue of the estate) occurring after all debts are paid and all other legacies are distributed. The residual legatee receives the residue of the estate.

Legacies are distributed in the preceding order. If there is insufficient property to satisfy all legacies, they are abated, or scaled down, in the reverse of this order. A legacy is not always paid, even though the estate is solvent. In such an instance, the default is termed a *failure* of a legacy. Failure may exist if the legatee dies prior to the testator, the property has deteriorated or has been destroyed, or related provisions in the will controvert public policy.

The statues of many states provide for bequests by *advancement* if the decedent dies intestate. That is, if the decedent, during his or her lifetime, made a gift of property to individuals (usually children or other lineal descendants) who otherwise would have been entitled to inherit a part of the estate, the gift may be regarded as an advancement in anticipation of the advancee's intestate share. However, all gratuitous transfers before death are regarded as absolute gifts, not advancements, unless contrary intent is demonstrated.

ROLE OF THE FIDUCIARY IN TRUST ADMINISTRATION

Individuals may specify that all, or some, of their property be placed in trust. A *trust* is an arrangement by which title to property is transferred to a *trustee,* either an individual or a corporation, who holds and manages (including investing) the property for the benefit of others. Although there are various types of trusts, two classes predominate—living trusts and testamentary trusts. *Living trusts,* or *trusts inter vivos,* are created and become operative during the lifetime of the creator. *Testamentary trusts* are created by provisions in wills. A trustee who is specified in the will is a *testamentary trustee.*

A trust is created or established by a *donor, trustor,* or *founder;* those expected to derive benefit from the trust are *beneficiaries.* The trust agreement may require, for example, that the principal of the trust be distributed eventually to one beneficiary and current income be paid to another. Of course, the principal and income beneficiary may be the same person. For example, a beneficiary may receive only the income of a trust until attaining majority, after which the principal is also conveyed to him or her. The income beneficiary is called a *cestui que trust*. A *life tenant* receives income for life. The recipient of the principal of the trust is the *remainderman*. A beneficiary who has the power to designate who will receive the income or the principal of a trust at some later date is referred to as having a *power of appointment*.

A trustee normally has only the authority conveyed by the trust instrument. This authority often includes the following:

1. The incurrence of costs and expenses necessary to preserve the trust principal.
2. The sale, exchange, or improvement of existing realty.
3. The settlement, totally or by compromise, of claims against the trust.
4. The making of new investments and disposing of existing investments.
5. The distribution of property to distributees as provided in the trust agreement.
6. The making of advances to beneficiaries.
7. The paying or expending of income for the benefit of minors.

A testamentary trustee is accountable as a fiduciary once trust property is conveyed to him or her. Legal title to real property customarily vests in the trustee upon the decedent's death. Title to personal property, however, passes to the trustee with the transfer of the property. The trustee is charged with exercising the degree of care in relation to trust property that he or she would exercise as a reasonably prudent business executive acting in his or her own self-interest. The creator of a trust may, by provision in the trust instrument, reserve the right to relieve the trustee of duties and liabilities otherwise imposed upon him or her. Similarly, by express provision in the trust instrument, the creator of the trust may add to, or impose new duties, restrictions, privileges, or powers on the trustee. The trustee may also be relieved of duties and restrictions by court action. The Uniform Trust Act specifically provides that a court may, for cause and upon notice to the beneficiaries, relieve a trustee from any or all duties and restrictions.

A trustee should carefully consider all options in investing resources in income-producing assets. If there is reasonable doubt about the propriety of an investment action, the trustee should seek the opinion of legal counsel. In this context, the trustee usually is allowed a reasonable period of time to make investments without penalty for uninvested funds. Note that the trustee is obligated to keep trust assets separate from his or her own assets, unless the trust instrument allows otherwise. We emphasize that courts have held trustees guilty of breach of trust when losses have resulted from the commingling of trust and other assets.

DUAL BASES OF ACCOUNTABILITY

In accounting for estates and trusts, the fiduciary maintains a dual basis of accountability. That is, he or she makes a distinction between initial principal and income and transactions subsequently affecting principal and income. The principal-income distinction is important for several reasons. First, a trustor may specify different principal and income beneficiaries or different times for the distribution of principal and income. Second, this distinction is important in the calculation of income taxes. This distinction is considered further below.

Principal (Corpus) and Income Distinguished

The principal-income distinction often is difficult to make because of the diverse provisions of state statutes and the special characteristics of these items. Nevertheless, in some cases, this distinction is not a problem. For example, a trustor may indicate, either in the will or in a trust indenture, the criteria to be used in distinguishing between principal and income. If these criteria are not apparent, courts follow state statutes in making the distinction. In any case, fiduciary accounting records are maintained so that the principal-income distinction is maintained for the reasons mentioned earlier.

The Revised Uniform Principal and Income Act defines *principal* essentially as property which has been set aside for a remainderman and income as the return in money or property derived from the use of principal which is set aside for an income beneficiary.[1] The rules for determining whether an item is principal or income are complex under this act and, therefore, are not within the scope of this book. Nevertheless, some of the elements of principal and income identified in this act are listed below since they are typical of the principal-income distinction in general.

Principal includes the following:

1. Consideration received from the sale or other transfer of property and receipts from the repayments of loans.
2. Proceeds from eminent domain proceedings.
3. Certain proceeds from insurance on property included in principal.
4. Stock dividends, receipts on liquidation of a corporation, and certain other corporate distributions.
5. Receipts from the disposition of corporate securities.
6. Royalties and other receipts from disposition of natural resources.
7. Certain receipts from principal subject to depletion.
8. Certain profits resulting from any change in the form of principal.

---

[1] This statute has been adopted in approximately 20 states.

Income includes the following:

1. Rent of real or personal property.
2. Interest on money lent.
3. Income earned during administration of a decedent's estate.
4. Corporate cash dividend distributions.
5. Accrued increment on bonds or other obligations issued at discount.
6. Receipts from business and farming operations.
7. Receipts from disposition of natural resources.
8. Receipts from principal subject to depletion.

In regard to certain transactions affecting principal and interest, the Revised Uniform Principal and Income Act also contains the following general provisions:

1. In general, expenses incurred in connection with the settlement of a decedent's estate, including debts, funeral expenses, estate taxes, interest and penalties related to taxes, family allowances, fees of attorneys and other personal representatives, and court costs are charged against estate principal.
2. Unless the will specifies otherwise, income from the assets of a decedent's estate, as well as related expenses, are distributed as follows:
   a. To specific legatees and devisees—(i) the income from the property bequeathed or devised to them respectively, less taxes, ordinary repairs, and other expenses of operating and managing the property and (ii) an appropriate portion of the interest accrued since the death of the testator and of taxes imposed on income (excluding taxes on capital gains) which accrue during the period of administration;
   b. To all other legatees and devisees, except legatees of pecuniary bequests not in trust—(i) the balance of the income, less the balance of taxes, ordinary repairs, and other expenses of operating and managing all property from which the estate is entitled to income and (ii) interest accrued since the death of the testator, and taxes imposed on income (excluding taxes on capital gains) which accrue during the period of administration, in proportion to their respective interests in the undistributed assets of the estate computed at times of distribution on the basis of inventory value.

The above generalizations are not sufficiently descriptive for a number of classes of items. These classes include accrued amounts, certain taxes, dividends received, partnership earnings, depreciation, repairs and maintenance, depletion, discounts and premiums on bond investments, and certain other expenses. These classes are discussed below in the order just given.

Special Problems

Accrued income on receivables and investments at the date of the decedent's death normally is regarded as estate principal. Such income accrued during tenancy is regarded as estate income. In regard to savings accounts and time deposits, accrued interest is regarded as either principal or income, depending on when the interest credit is made available to the depositor. *Accrued interest expense* normally follows rules similar to those described above. That is, interest accrued to the date of the testator's death usually is a debt of the estate and, accordingly, is charged to principal when paid. Interest incurred subsequently is charged ordinarily to income.

In most states, *accrued rent income* at the date of the decedent's death is included in the principal of the estate; the amount of rent earned during tenancy is regarded as income. Similarly, *accrued rent expense* payable at the date of death is a charge against estate principal, and similar accruals thereafter are charges against income.

Taxes on real property customarily are assumed not to accrue. Tax expense, rather, is regarded as relating to the period when the tax becomes a lien on the assessed property. If the lien becomes effective before the decedent's death, the tax expense is charged to estate principal. Alternatively, if the lien becomes effective subsequent to the decedent's death, the expense is a charge to income. As indicated earlier, *estate taxes* are levied against, and payable out of, estate principal. *Income taxes,* however, are identified with the elements making up the taxable base. The amount of income tax that relates to gains or losses on the conversion of principal assets is charged to principal, and the amount levied on normal operating income during the administration of the estate is charged against income. Income taxes for a fractional period prior to the decedent's death are payable out of the principal of the estate.

Ordinary corporate dividends generally are not accounted for on an accrual basis. Such dividends declared prior to the decedent's death usually are a part of the principal of the estate; declarations subsequent to death usually represent income of the estate. In some states, however, the significant identifying date is the date of record. In regard to dividends declared and received during tenancy, the statutes of various states also are not completely consistent. Some follow the Massachusetts rule, which generally provides that all cash dividends, whatever their magnitude and from whatever their source, are to be regarded as income accruing to the income beneficiary. *Stock dividends,* however, are regarded as additions to principal. In applying this rule, the *form* of the dividend controls. Other states follow the Pennsylvania rule, which emphasizes the *source* of the dividend. If the dividend—whether in cash or stock—is payable out of earnings accumulated prior to the creation of the trust estate, it belongs to principal. Alternatively, if it is paid from earnings accumulated subsequent to the formation of the trust, the receipt (including the market values of stock dividends) is considered income. If dividends relate partially to earnings accumulated prior to the creation of the trust estate and partially subsequent thereto, the fiduciary may apportion the receipt between income and principal. In this allocation process, the relative book values of the stock at the date of the decedent's death and at the date of the dividend payment are the deciding factors. If the book value after the dividend payment is less than the book value at date of the decedent's death, an amount equivalent to the reduction in value is credited to principal with the residual amount of the receipt regarded as income. Stock dividends are accorded parallel treatment, although the allocation is made in terms of shares of stock.[2] Note that the emphasis of the Massachusetts rules is reflected in the Revised Uniform Principal and Income Act.

The treatment of *partnership profits* depends largely on the partnership agreement. If it requires closing the books upon the death of a partner, the share of the profits assigned to the deceased partner for the fractional period prior to death normally is regarded as principal. If the agreement does not require such a closing, there is no consensus concerning the treatment of (all) profits earned during the period encompassing the partner's death. Exceptionally, if the partnership agreement provides for interest on partners' capitals, such interest prior to the decedent's death is included in principal, and the interest accruing subsequently is income.

Depreciation may or may not be charged against the income of an estate or trust during a period of tenancy. The resolution of this issue depends on the testator's intentions as indicated in the will or trust instrument (in regard to preserving the principal of the estate intact). In the absence of expressed testator intentions, state law controls.

Expenditures for repairs and maintenance, the effect of which is to materially improve or enhance the value of estate or trust properties, follow traditional rules of capitalization; that is, they normally are charged to principal. Expenditures which merely preserve the normal operating efficiency of depreciable assets are regarded as income charges. If the benefits relate partially to principal and partially to income, an apportionment of the expenditure is made based on estimates of benefits received.

If trust estate properties consist of wasting assets, that is, mineral deposits, timber, and so forth, the wishes of the testator or state law also control in regard to charges for *depletion*.[3] If the evidence shows that the testator intended to preserve the undiminished value of the original property for the remainderman, the fiduciary withholds income for the remainderman in an amount equal to the value of the exhaustion for depletion. However, if the evidence indicates that income, without reduction in amount for depletion, ought to accrue to the income beneficiary, principal is reduced accordingly—by the amount of cumulative depletion allowances.

---

[2] Stock rights that are a part of the decedent's estate at death, or that are acquired subsequently, are elements of principal. Accordingly, proceeds from the sale of such rights, reflecting conversion gains and losses, also are regarded as principal.

In most states, the courts have held that dividends payable from sources other than earnings relate to principal. Script and property dividends are accorded treatment equivalent to cash dividends. Liquidating dividends are accounted for by the fiduciary as in a commercial enterprise; that is, they are regarded as a return of capital and are accordingly classified as adjustments of principal.

[3] For example, the Revised Uniform Principal and Income Act provides, with respect to receipts for royalties for mineral interests, that 27.5 percent of gross receipts (but not to exceed 50 percent of net receipts before deducting depletion) is to be added to principal as a depletion allowance.

Corporate bonds held by the decedent usually are valued using market prices at the date of the decedent's death. To the extent that *premiums* or *discounts* are reflected in these prices, a question exists concerning amortization by the fiduciary. Of course, the wishes of the testator prevail in this context if they have been made explicit. In not, fiduciaries frequently choose not to amortize premiums and discounts under the view that estate principal is not changed as long as the bonds still are on hand and the periodic interest is classified as income. Under this view, the disposition of bonds is the focal point for recognizing changes in bond values resulting from approaching maturity and changes in interest rates as well as all related effects on estate corpus. If premiums and discounts are amortized, then periodic amortization logically affects income. Note also that premiums (discounts) on bonds acquired by the fiduciary usually are (are not) amortized. In these cases, the effects of amortization and bond dispositions are as described above. If amortization on bonds is recorded, brokerage expenses and transfer fees, which are elements of investment cost, also are amortized.

Expenses clearly pertaining to the conservation, management, or distribution of trust-estate principal are charged against principal; however, expenses related to the earning of income are charged to income. The Revised Uniform Principal and Income Act, for example, identifies various expenses that are charged to principal and others that are charged to income. Certain portions of this act are summarized below to provide an indication of the types of items that are charged against principal and income as well as some of the related considerations that often arise.

The following items are charged to principal:

1. Certain trustee's compensation not chargeable to income, special compensation of trustees, expenses reasonably incurred in connection with principal, court costs and attorney's fees pertaining to principal, and trustee's compensation computed on principal as an acceptance, distribution, or termination fee.
2. Costs of investing and reinvesting principal, payments on indebtedness principal, expenses of preparing property for rental or sale and, unless the court directs otherwise, expenses incurred in maintaining or defending principal.
3. Extraordinary repairs or expenses incurred in making a capital improvement to principal, including special assessments.
4. Taxes levied on profit, gain, or other receipts allocated to principal.
5. Estate and inheritance taxes, including interest and penalties, even though an income beneficiary also has rights in principal.

The following items are charged to income:

1. Ordinary expenses of administering, managing, and preserving property, including recurring taxes assessed against principal; water rates; premiums on insurance protecting the interests of the income

beneficiary, remainderman, or trustee; interest paid by the trustee; and ordinary repairs.

2. A reasonable allowance for depreciation on property subject to depreciation under generally accepted accounting principles (excluding property used by a beneficiary as a residence).

3. One half of court costs, attorney's fees, and other fees on periodic judicial accounting (unless the court directs otherwise).

4. Court costs, attorney's fees, and other fees related to accountings and judicial proceedings pertaining to the income interest (unless the court directs otherwise).

5. One half of the trustee's regular compensation (whether based on a percentage of principal or income) and all expenses reasonably incurred for current management of principal and application of income.

6. Any tax levied on receipts defined as income under this act or the trust instrument and payable by the trustee.

FIDUCIARY ACCOUNTS AND REPORTS

Fiduciary accounting emphasizes accountability related to delegated authority. Thus, the accounts of the fiduciary reflect measures related to his or her accountability and the extent to which it has been discharged. This emphasis on accountability yields the following fiduciary-related, fundamental accounting equation:

$$\text{Estate (trust) assets} = \text{Accountability}$$

Note that this equation reflects total assets without deducting the claims against the estate or trust. In this context, a fiduciary is accountable for all assets entrusted to him or her and payment of existing claims is one way he or she discharges that accountability. Note also that this equation emphasizes the type of stewardship orientation implicit in fiduciary accounting. This orientation is based on the master-slave relationship of Roman times. In that era, a slave was charged with funds advanced by the master and with the increase attributable to fortunate investments. Subsequently, the slave was discharged from accountability to the extent of repayment of advanced and accumulated resources and through other dispositions authorized by the master. Economic theories of income and asset valuation are not relevant to this type of stewardship orientation. Thus, income determination and so on are not a function of fiduciary accounting.

The accounts and reports of the fiduciary focus on the *dual* responsibility related to income *and* principal. Although state statutes provide criteria for distinguishing between income and principal, they often do not prescribe the exact form and content of the fiduciary's accounts and reports. The following discussion emphasizes typical accounting procedures and reports employed by fiduciaries in dealing with estates and trusts.

Overview of Record-Keeping for an Estate

Estate books are opened once the inventory of the decedent's assets is filed. The opening entry includes debits for the *assets,* and related values, shown in the inventory and a single offsetting credit to Estate Principal (or Estate Corpus). This credit reflects the fiduciary's initial accountability. If other *assets are discovered subsequently,* accounts are opened for them, and related credits are made to the Assets Subsequently Discovered account. This account is closed to Estate Principal at the end of the fiduciary accounting period. Note that *cash* related to principal is accounted for separately from cash related to income using Cash—Principal and Cash—Income accounts.

Liabilities of the decedent are not recorded by the fiduciary until paid. On settlement, the Debts of the Decedent Paid account is debited for the amount of the settlement. Settlements of debt constitute reductions in accountability; thus, debits to Debts of the Decedent Paid are equivalent to debits to Estate Principal. Ultimately, this account is closed to Estate Principal. With respect to both assets and liabilities, the amount of account detail (and the necessity for subsidiary records) is governed by the magnitude and diversity of assets in, and the number of claims against, the estate.

Gains (losses) on the conversion of principal assets increase (decrease) the accountability of the fiduciary in regard to the principal of the estate. Gains are credited to the Gain on Realization account, and losses are debited to the Loss on Realization account. Both accounts are closed to Estate Principal at the end of the accounting period. As implied previously, the increased (decreased) accountability of the fiduciary pertaining to gains and losses is not related to an attempt to measure income.

The accountability of the fiduciary also is decreased by *disbursements for funeral and administration expenses.* A single Funeral and Administration Expenses account often is used to record the related debits, or it may be desirable to use separate accounts for the various types of funeral and administrative expenses if they are numerous. Typical funeral and administration expenses are those related to the last illness; the funeral; the administrative services of the executor or trustee; accountants', attorneys', and appraisers' services; and court costs.

Other items which reduce the fiduciary's accountability with respect to principal are the *payment of estate and inheritance taxes* and the *distribution of legacies.* Estate and inheritance taxes are debited to the Expenses—Principal account when paid. If a legacy involves the distribution of specific assets, the values assigned to the assets in the inventory (or when discovered subsequently) constitute their accounting bases, regardless of their current market values. If there are relatively few legatees, a single acount—Legacies—may be sufficient for record-keeping purposes; however, if the number of legatees is large, the use of a separate account for each may be desirable. In either case, the pertinent legacy-type account is debited when a legacy is distributed. Note that if inheritance taxes are to be charged against the legatees (which often is the case), or the various legacies may be reduced for other reasons, record-keeping is facilitated by using separate legatee accounts.

Fiduciaries typically account for various items of *income* by crediting the Income account, although the use of separate income-type accounts facilitates record-keeping if there are numerous sources of income. *Expenses* chargeable to income are debited to the Expenses—Income account (or to several expense-type accounts which reveal the natures of the expenses). We emphasize again that fiduciary accounting requires the use of account designations which clearly associate items with income and principal because of the principal-income distinction. Although not expenses, *distributions to income beneficiaries* usually are charged to the Distribution to Income Beneficiary (or Beneficiaries) account. If there are numerous income beneficiaries, record-keeping again may be facilitated by using separate Distribution to Income Beneficiary accounts for each.

Basic Record-Keeping for an Estate

The following simplified case illustrates basic record-keeping procedures for an estate. Louis Martin died on June 1, 19X0. His will, admitted to probate on June 10, 19X0, names Paula Martin, daughter of the decedent, executor. The will stipulates specific legacies of $2,500 for both Andrea and Charles, grandchildren of the decedent. Also, $12,000 and the decedent's personal automobile are awarded to Paula. Pamela, (the surviving spouse), receives the personal effects of Louis. The remainder of the estate property, after payment of debts, expenses, and distributions to legacies, is placed in trust. The income from the trust is to be paid to Pamela during her lifetime, with the remaining principal being distributed equally to Andrea and Charles upon her death.

Paula Martin files the following inventory with the probate court on June 25, 19X0:

Cash in bank	$ 28,000
Personal effects	750
Life insurance policies payable to the estate	30,000
1,000 shares of Edens Company $50 par value common stock—at market	49,000
500 shares of Cincy, Inc., 6%, $30 par value preferred stock—at market	15,000
20 Burnett Corporation 5%, 30-year $1,000 bonds (interest payable March 1 and September 1)	19,600
Automobile	2,600
Dividend receivable (declared May 15, date of record May 20, payable July 15, Edens Company common)	1,500
Interest receivable (Burnett Corporation bonds)	250
	$146,700

On the same date, the fiduciary opens accounts for the estate of Louis Martin and records the inventory as follows:

Cash—Principal	28,000	
Personal Effects	750	
Life Insurance	30,000	
Edens Company Common Stock	49,000	
Cincy, Inc., Preferred Stock	15,000	
Burnett Corporation Bonds	19,600	
Automobile	2,600	
Dividend Receivable	1,500	
Interest Receivable	250	
Estate Principal		146,700

Other transactions, entries, and events related to the fiduciary in 19X0 are identified below. The related entries, which are discussed above in general, are elaborated on only when not self-explanatory.

June 28, 19X0—Public notice is given to creditors of the estate of the decedent to make a presentment of their claims.

July 15 19X0—Funeral expenses of $1,400 are paid.

Funeral and Administration Expenses	1,400	
Cash—Principal		1,400

July 16, 19X0—Dividends on the Edens stock are collected. These dividends are part of the estate's principal because both their declaration and record dates are before the date of death.

Cash—Principal	1,500	
Dividends Receivable		1,500

July 20, 19X0—Undeposited cash of $1,200 is discovered among the decedent's personal belongings.

Cash—Principal	1,200	
Assets Subsequently Discovered		1,200

July 31, 19X0—Proceeds from the insurance policies are received. The proceeds from these policies are included in the estate's principal because the estate is the beneficiary.

Cash—Principal	30,000	
Life Insurance		30,000

August 15, 19X0—One hundred shares of Cincy, Inc., stock are sold for $4,000.

Cash—Principal	4,000	
Cincy, Inc., Preferred Stock		3,000
Gain on Realization		1,000

September 1, 19X0—Interest on Burnet Corporation bonds is collected. One half of the interest on these bonds is included in principal (income) because it is available to the depositor before (after) death.

Cash—Principal	250	
Cash—Income	250	
Interest Receivable		250
Income		250

September 15, 19X0—Debts of the decedent of $2,950 are paid.

Debts of the Decedent Paid	2,950	
Cash—Principal		2,950

October 1, 19X0—Cash legacies are distributed.

Legacy—Paula Martin	12,000	
Legacy—Andrea Martin	2,500	
Legacy—Charles Martin	2,500	
Cash—Principal		17,000

October 3, 19X0—The automobile (current market value, $1,800) is delivered to Paula Martin.

Legacy—Paula Martin	2,600	
Automobile		2,600

October 3, 19X0—The decedent's personal effects are delivered to the surviving spouse.

Legacy—Pamela Martin	750	
Personal Effects		750

October 10, 19X0—Cash dividends of $1,000 on the Edens Company common stock are collected. These dividends are included in income because both their declaration and record dates are after date of death.

Cash—Income	1,000	
Income		1,000

October 15, 19X0—Attorney's fees of $1,000 and other administrative expenses of $2,500 are paid. Of the latter, $200 pertains to income.

Funeral and Administration Expenses	3,300	
Expenses—Income	200	
Cash—Principal		3,300
Cash—Income		200

October 30, 19X0—A 3 percent semiannual dividend on the Cincy, Inc., preferred stock is declared. These dividends are included in income because both their declaration and record dates are after date of death.

Dividend Receivable	450	
Income		450

November 1, 19X0—Income of the estate in the amount of $500 is distributed to the surviving spouse.

Distribution to Income Beneficiary—Pamela Martin	500	
Cash—Income		500

November 5, 19X0—Two hundred shares of Edens Company common stock are sold for $9,000.

Cash—Principal	9,000	
Loss on Realization	800	
Edens Company Common Stock (20% × $49,000)		9,800

December 1, 19X0—Interest of $250 is accrued on Burnett Corporation bonds (to December 1).

Interest Receivable	250	
Income		250

December 1, 19X0—The executor submits a charge and discharge statement, an accountability report, to the probate court.

Charge and Discharge Statement for an Estate

A report that reveals the details of the fiduciary's estate administration is prepared and submitted periodically to the court of jurisdiction. Such a report is the *charge and discharge statement,* and it may be interim or final, depending on the period required for the settlement of the estate. The general form of the statement usually is prescribed by state statute; however, there is no consensus concerning its form. The statement in Illustration 18–1 is typical of the reports presently used.

The charge and discharge statement lists the estate assets for which the fiduciary is accountable and describes the manner in which his or her accountability has been discharged. The responsibilities related to principal and income are reported separately in the statement. The initial section of the report (the As to Principal Section) first identifies the assets for which the fiduciary is *charged* (i.e., those for which he or she has accepted custodial responsibility). They include the following

1. Assets identified in the inventory.
2. Assets subsequently discovered.
3. Gains recognized on the conversion or other disposition of principal assets.

The next part of the As to Principal Section represents the discharge of the fiduciary's accountability; that is, it reflects items for which he or she is *credited.* The items discharged include the following:

1. Funeral and administration expenses.
2. Decedent's debts.

ILLUSTRATION 18-1

ESTATE OF LOUIS MARTIN
PAULA MARTIN, EXECUTOR
Charge and Discharge Statement
June 1, 19X0 to December 1, 19X0

As to Principal

I charge myself with:		
Assets per inventory		$146,700
Assets subsequently discovered		1,200
Gain on realization		1,000
Total		$148,900
I credit myself with:		
Funeral and administration expenses	$ 4,700	
Debts of decedent paid	2,950	
Legacies paid or distributed:		
Paula Martin	14,600	
Andrea Martin	2,500	
Charles Martin	2,500	
Pamela Martin	750	
Loss on realization	800	28,800
Balance as to principal		$120,100
Which includes:		
Cash		$ 49,300
Edens Company common stock		39,200
Cincy, Inc., preferred stock		12,000
Burnett Corporation bonds		19,600
Total		$120,100

As to Income

I charge myself with:		
Income collected or accrued		$ 1,950
I credit myself with:		
Expenses chargeable to income	$ 200	
Distribution to income beneficiary	500	700
Balance as to income		$ 1,250
Which includes:		
Cash		$ 550
Dividend receivable		450
Interest receivable		250
Total		$ 1,250

3. Estate and inheritance taxes.

4. Legacies.

5. Losses realized on principal assets.

To the extent that undistributed principal-related assets remain (as in an interim report or in a final report preceding the transfer of assets to a testamentary trust), the related accounts are identified in the third section of the statement.

With respect to income, the fiduciary is *charged* for income earned since the date of the decedent's death. These charges are shown in the As to Income section of the statement. The sources of the items of income are identified in the statement if they are significant. Dispositions of income for which the fiduciary is customarily *credited* in this section of the statement include the following:

1. Expenses chargeable to income.
2. Payments or other distributions to income beneficiaries.

The data pertaining to the estate of Louis Martin, in a typical charge and discharge statement, are presented in Illustration 18–1. If subsequent charge and discharge statements are necessary, they are prepared on a cumulative basis and, thus, continue to disclose the fiduciary's activities over the entire period of his or her accountability.

Closing Entries of an Estate

When an estate's activities are concluded, a final charge and discharge statement is prepared, and the fiduciary closes the estate accounts. With respect to principal, the closing process involves closing the accounts created representing increases or decreases in the fiduciary's principal-related accountability to Estate Principal. Accordingly, the Assets Subsequently Discovered, Gains and Losses on Realization, Debts of the Decedent Paid, Legacies Paid or Distributed, and Funeral and Administration Expenses accounts are closed to Estate Principal. Similarly, the accounts related to income are closed to the Income account; they include Expenses—Income and Distributions to Income Beneficiary.

The closing entries for the preceding case are presented in the next section since they involve a transfer of assets into a trust. The first two of these entries close the accounts pertaining to principal; the third entry closes the accounts related to income. The fourth closing entry closes the balances in the Income and Estate Principal accounts to the V. L. Ree, Trustee, account—which reflects the trustee's accountability immediately prior to final disposition of the estate's assets. Closing entries 5 and 6 record the transfer of the remaining assets pertaining to both principal and income into the trust.

Properties Transferred into Trust

As indicated, provision is made in the preceding case for the transfer of the remaining estate assets into a trust. Assuming that the transfer is made at the same time the charge and discharge statement is prepared (December 1, 19X0), the entries given in the following tabulation are required to close the books of the estate and to open the trust accounts. The closing entries were explained previously.

Note that entries 7 and 8 record the transfer of the estate assets pertaining to principal and income, respectively, into the trust. The trustee normally accepts fiduciary responsibility concurrent with the transfer of trust property. We empha-

Executor's Books—December 31, 19X0

1. Assets Subsequently Discovered	1,200		
Gain on Realization	1,000		
Estate Principal			2,200
2. Estate Principal	28,800		
Debts of the Decedent Paid			2,950
Funeral and Administration Expenses			4,700
Legacy—Paula Martin			14,600
Legacy—Andrea Martin			2,500
Legacy—Charles Martin			2,500
Legacy—Pamela Martin			750
Loss on Realization			800
3. Income	700		
Expenses—Income			200
Distribution to Income Beneficiary			500
4. Estate Principal	120,100		
Income	1,250		
V.L. Ree, Trustee			121,350
5. V.L. Ree, Trustee	120,100		
Cash—Principal			49,300
Edens Company Common Stock			39,200
Cincy, Inc., Preferred Stock			12,000
Burnett Corporation Bonds			19,600
6. V.L. Ree, Trustee	1,250		
Cash—Income			550
Dividend Receivable			450
Interest Receivable			250

Trustee's Books—December 31, 19X0

7. Cash—Principal	49,300		
Edens Company Common Stock	39,200		
Cincy, Inc., Preferred Stock	12,000		
Burnett Corporation Bonds	19,600		
Trust Principal			120,100
8. Cash—Income	550		
Dividend Receivable	450		
Interest Receivable	250		
Income			1,250

size that a testamentary trust usually becomes effective as of the date of death. Thus, in this case, the income of the estate is, in effect, income of the trust and, consequently, is transferred as income into the trust. In contrast, all income accrued prior to the creation of a living trust is included in trust principal, but income earned thereafter is distributable to income beneficiaries.

Once the trust books are opened, the trustee's accounting essentially parallels that of the executor. Thus, the Trust Principal account and the related Income account reflect the trustee's accountability related to principal and income, respectively. The trustee also renders periodic and final reports of his or her stewardship to the court recounting his or her activities as trustee. Although trustees' statements generally are not referred to as charge and discharge statements, their main feature, under the Uniform Trustees Accounting Act, is the disclosure of the trustees' financial activities related to principal and income, along with indications of how they have fulfilled their fiduciary responsibilities.

Summary

This chapter begins with an introduction to estate planning. Subsequently, it deals primarily with fiduciary accounting for estates and trusts. A fiduciary is a person or entity entrusted with the safekeeping, management, or distribution of the property of another. Thus, a fiduciary is accountable to various interested parties. Either an individual, partnership, or corporation may serve in this capacity. Because the fiduciary relationship is one of stewardship, fiduciary accounting focuses on the concept of accountability.

Upon the death of an individual, the fiduciary assumes the responsibility for the safekeeping, management, and distribution of the property of the decedent's estate. The fiduciary is required to submit a complete inventory of the decedent's property to the court of appointment. Generally, the fiduciary also gives public notice to those having claims against the estate. In this regard, the fiduciary determines the validity of the claims, establishes the sequence of payment of the various obligations, and settles the obligations. The decedent's bequests of personal property, called *legacies,* are distributed by the fiduciary to the various legatees after estate obligations are paid.

Another type of fiduciary relationship is related to trusts. A trust is an arrangement in which title to property is transferred to a fiduciary, the trustee, who manages the property for the benefit of others. The authority of the trustee is governed by the trust instrument. The trustee is charged with exercising the degree of care in managing trust property as would be executed by a reasonably prudent business executive acting in his or her own self-interest.

In accounting for estates and trusts, fiduciaries maintain a dual basis of accountability. That is, they make a distinction between initial principal and income and transactions subsequently affecting principal and income. The distinction between principal and income is important in making decisions regarding distributions to beneficiaries and in determining income taxes. *Principal* refers to the assets that are set aside by the donor in trust eventually to be distributed to a remainderman. Income represents the return in cash or other assets derived from the use of principal, which is set aside for an income beneficiary.

The accounts and reports of the fiduciary disclose his or her accountability and the extent to which it has been discharged. The fundamental fiduciary accounting equation is Estates (or trust) assets = Accountability. When the books of an estate are opened, the assessed values of the estate assets are debited to appropriate asset accounts with an offsetting credit to Estate Principal. Liabilities of the estate are recorded only when paid. Their payment reduces the accountability of the estate fiduciary. Gains (losses) on the conversion of principal assets increase (decrease) the accountability of the fiduciary with respect to the estate principal. Likewise, income (loss) increases (decreases) the accountability of the fiduciary with respect to estate income. The accountability of the fiduciary is further reduced by various expenses and distributions to legatees. The report which details the actions of the fiduciary in administering the decedent's estate is the charge and discharge statement. Trustee accounting, which pertains to trusts rather than estates, essentially parallels that of fiduciary-related estate accounting.

Questions

1. Briefly describe the responsibilities of a fiduciary (executor, administrator) in the administration of an estate.
2. What type of assets are frequently excluded from the fiduciary's inventory of assets?
3. What is a typical sequence of payments for the various estate obligations?
4. The fiduciary must distinguish in his or her records between the principal (corpus) and the income of an estate or trust. Why?
5. As a general rule, how are accruals of income and expense identified with the principal and with the income of an estate?
6. Should depreciation be charged against the principal or income of an estate?
7. What is the fundamental equation for fiduciary accounting? For what reason is this expression stated in terms of claims against the estate or trust?
8. Once an inventory of the decedent's assets has been filed, what accounts should be opened by the executor (administrator) in which to record the transactions for the estate?
9. What is the charge and discharge statement? What information does it provide?
10. In respect to an intestate decedent, what is meant by the expression "bequest by advancement"?

Exercises

Exercise 18–1   (Miscellaneous Estate and Trust Issues)

Each of the following relates to accounting for estates or trusts. Select the best answer in each expression:

1. To *probate* a will is to:
   a. Examine its provisions in respect to conformance with relevant model uniform laws if they are operative in the state.
   b. Review its fairness with respect to natural children and other lineal descendents.
   c. Prove its validity as to genuineness of the decedent's signature, his or her last expression of preferences, and his or her mental capacity at date of execution.
2. The executor, in respect to solvent estates, must accord *highest* priority to the following if he or she is to avoid personal liability for improper distribution:
   a. Wages due domestics or other employees.
   b. Provable debts against the estate.
   c. Taxes, including estate and inheritance taxes.
   d. Funeral and administrative expenses.
3. The legacy given first rank in order of distribution is
   a. Demonstrative legacy.
   b. Specific legacy.

    c. Residual legacy.

    d. General legacy.

4. The recipient of the principal of a trust is termed a

    a. Life tenant.

    b. *Cestui que trust.*

    c. Remainderman.

    d. Donee.

5. Income taxes payable by the executor of an estate during the period of his or her fiduciary responsibility

    a. Are chargeable against income of the estate.

    b. Must be identified with the elements making up the taxable base, that is, charges apportioned between income and principal.

    c. Are chargeable against the principal of the estate.

Exercise 18–2   (Journal Entries for an Estate)

Lloyd Carlisle died on January 18, 19X0. His will was admitted to probate on February 5, and Arthur Waddell was appointed executor of the estate. The following transactions relate to the executorial period, February 6 through July 1, 19X0:

1. Waddell filed the following inventory of Carlisle's assets with the court:

Cash on deposit, Second National Bank	$ 5,690
Undeposited currency	220
Common stock, Stuchell Corporation:	
1,000 shares (par, $10) at $27	27,000
6%, 20-year Harley Company debentures:	
10 bonds at $200	2,000
Automobile	4,300
Household furnishings	1,950
Life insurance, payable to the estate	10,000
Dividends receivable, Stuchell stock:	
Dividend declared January 15, 19X0	800
Interest receivable:	
Harley Company bonds (January 1 and July 1)	
January 1 to January 18	6

2. Funeral expenses of $934 were paid by Waddell.
3. Six $1,200 Arnheim, Inc., bonds, 5 percent payable November 1 and May 1, were discovered upon search of the decedent's personal belongings.
4. The life insurance policy was collected.
5. Notice was published for the presentment of claims against the estate, after which debts of the decedent amounting to $1,450 were validated and paid.
6. The dividend on Stuchell stock was collected.
7. All of the common stock of the Stuchell Corporation was sold for cash, $24,600.
8. Executorial fees were paid Waddell in the amount of $2,100.
9. The May 1 interest collection was made on Arnheim, Inc., bonds.

10. The automobile was sold for $3,100 cash.

11. According to the conditions of the will, a cash legacy was paid to Mary Carlisle, the widow, in amount of $10,000.

12. The July 1 interest collection was made on Harley Company debentures.

13. All income earned to July 1 was distributed to the surviving spouse; all other assets remaining in the estate were distributed equally to Tom and Barbara Carlisle, children of the decedent.

Required:

a. Journalize the above transactions on the books of Arthur Waddell, executor.

b. Make closing entries on July 1 to close the executor's books.

Exercise 18–3   (Journal Entries for an Estate)

Lisa Sims, attorney-at-law, died on July 1, 19X0. Her partner, Bradley Cee, was appointed executor of her estate and filed with the probate court on July 18 the following inventory of assets of the deceased:

Deposit balance, First State Bank	$ 4,800
4% RX bonds, interest payable April 1 and October 1	
(par, $40,000)	32,200
Accrued interest on RX bonds	400
6% cumulative Cleburne, Inc., preferred stock, 200 shares	
(par, $35,000)	19,300
100 shares of Bancroft-Benson no-par common stock	4,200
Value of properties established by court-appointed appraisers:	
Office building of the law partnership (separately owned	
by Sims)	46,000
Automobile	2,200
	$109,100

An additional 200 shares of Bancroft-Benson were discovered by the executor on September 1.

The office building was sold on September 14 to Bruegman and Sons, realtors, for $41,000; the 300 shares of Bancroft-Benson were sold on September 21 for $13,100. On October 1, interest was collected on the RX bonds.

During the three months ended October 1, 19X0, the executor made the following payments:

Funeral expenses	$ 2,500
Administrative expenses	1,900
Debts of the decedent	15,500

The will of the deceased provides that legacies and income be distributed as follows:

To widower, Albert:
  Cash, $17,000
  Cleburne stock
  Income of estate

To son, Arnold:
  Cash, $10,000
  Automobile

To daughter, Christine:
  Cash, $10,000
  RX bonds
  The residue

Required:

a. Prepare the executor's journal entries for estate transactions for the quarter ended October 1, 19X0.

b. Journalize the distribution of income and the distribution of legacies on October 2, making closing entries for the estate.

Exercise 18–4   (Different Types of Trust Income)

Read the following introductory facts and then denote whether each of the sentences is true or false according to the general principles of trust law, such as the Revised Uniform Principal and Income Act. If an answer is false, explain why it is.

Accountant Beth Smathers is trustee of a testamentary trust established by George Parker's will. The corpus of the trust consists of blue chip securities and a large office building subject to a mortgage. The will provides that trust income is to be paid to Parker's wife during her lifetime, that the trust will terminate on her death, and that the corpus is then to be distributed to the Brookdale School for Boys.

1. If Smathers receives a cash dividend on one of the trust securities, she may not use it to purchase additional securities for the trust corpus without compensating Mrs. Parker.

2. If Smathers receives a 5 percent stock dividend, she should distribute it to Mrs. Parker.

3. The cost of insurance on the office building should be deducted by Smathers from the income paid to Mrs. Parker.

4. Monthly principal payments to amortize the mortgage are deducted from Mrs. Parker's income.

5. Proceeds from fire insurance on the office building would be a part of the corpus.

(AICPA adapted)

Exercise 18–5   (Different Types of Trust Expenses)

Refer to the facts and the instructions of Exercise 18–4 to answer the following true-false questions:

1. The cost of exercising stock warrants is chargeable to trust income.
2. The Brookdale School is the remainderman of the trust created under Parker's will.
3. The beneficiaries of the trust have an equitable interest in the trust income and corpus.
4. The beneficiaries of the trust would have standing in court to proceed against the trustee for waste of the corpus.
5. If Mrs. Parker and the Brookdale School agree to terminate the trust and divide the corpus, Smathers would have to comply with their wishes.

(AICPA adapted)

Problems

Problem 18–6   (Journal Entries for an Estate)

Elizabeth Chase, partner in Chase-Dacey Farm Implements, died on March 31, 19X0. Nat Dacey was named executor of his partner's estate, which consisted of the following:

Cash	$ 25,100
Livestock	48,000
Ranch land and improvements including farm buildings, fencing, etc.—at appraised valuation	31,600
4% Gantry Company debentures, interest January 1 and July 1 (par, $60,000)	52,000
Interest receivable—Gantry Company debentures	600
150 shares Collegaire common stock (par, $30,000)	26,000
One-half interest in Chase-Dacey partnership— at appraised valuation	84,000
	$267,300

Legacies are to be distributed as follows:

1. Livestock and ranch properties to the spouse, Brian, together with the deceased's partnership interest in Chase-Dacey Farm Implements.
2. $30,000 par value of Gantry Company debentures to son, Richard.
3. Collegaire common stock to Fabens College.
4. Residual estate, after payments of funeral and administrative expenses, debts of decedent and other specific bequests, to Brian. Income of the estate, excluding partnership net income, is to be distributed as collected to the son, Richard. The interest of the deceased in partnership net income was 50 percent and is bequeathed to Brian.

Transactions of the executor were as follows:

Apr. 2 Filed the March 31 inventory of the deceased.
     15 Paid funeral and administrative expenses, $6,200.
     30 Sold $30,000 par value of Gantry Company debentures for $23,500 and accrued interest.
     30 Distributed estate income.
May 1 Paid debts of decedent, $9,400.
     10 Paid federal estate and state inheritance taxes, $28,700.
     20 Dividends declared on Collegaire stock on April 14 were received, $600.
     21 Distributed estate income.
July 1 Collected interest on Gantry Company debentures.
     1 Partnership profits for the second quarter of 19X0 are reported to be $7,000.
     1 Distributed estate income, legacies, and residual estate properties as provided in the will.

Required:

a. Prepare entries on the books of the executor through July 1, 19X0.

b. Journalize entries to close the books of the estate.

Problem 18–7   (Charge and Discharge Statement)

L. K. Daniel was appointed executor of the estate of Lucile Martin, who died February 6, 19X0, leaving the following assets:

Cash in the Last National Bank	$ 9,200
Investments in corporate stocks	69,500
Jewelry	21,250
Building	51,000
Life insurance payable to the estate	10,000

The above valuations for buildings, investments, and jewelry reflect market conditions on February 6.

Following probate of the will and upon review of other family commitments, it is determined that Lucile Martin, a widow at the time of her death, had advanced to her two surviving sons and one daughter the following amounts prior to death: Charles, $16,500; Stephen, $14,350; and Ellen, $7,650.

Payments made by Daniel during the executorial period were as follows:

Attorneys' fees	$1,950
Inheritance taxes	7,550
Debts of the decedent	1,200
Funeral expenses	1,450

The will of the deceased provided that any one of the surviving children should have an option to receive as a legacy her jewelry at a valuation of $25,000; Ellen exercised this option. The securities were sold for $72,000, and the building was purchased by a local realtor for $55,000. The life insurance was collected on May 15.

The residue of the estate was to be divided equally among the three children, given that the advances and bequests made previous to and during the executorial period be regarded as a portion of such distributive shares.

Final distributions were made, and the estate was closed on June 1.

Required:

Prepare a charge and discharge statement for L. K. Daniel on June 1, detailing by supporting schedule, the composition of the legacy to each child.

Problem 18–8   (Charge and Discharge Statement)

Bradley Charles was named executor of the estate of Ashley Nicole, who died on March 13, 19X0. On December 31, 19X0, the executor prepared the following trial balance:

ESTATE OF ASHLEY NICOLE
Trial Balance
December 31, 19X0

	Debit	*Credit*
Investments:		
Stocks	$18,500	
Bonds	42,000	
Accrued Interest Receivable	75	
Cash—Principal	10,850	
Cash—Income	2,125	
Household Effects	2,375	
Loss on Realization	650	
Gain on Realization		$ 1,200
Assets Subsequently Discovered		5,520
Debts of Decedent Paid	5,600	
Funeral Expenses	950	
Administration Expenses	2,570	
Estate Corpus		79,275
Income		3,575
Expenses—Income	380	
Distribution to Income Beneficiary	995	
Legacy—Zephra Nicole	2,500	
	$89,570	$89,570

Required:

Prepare a charge and discharge statement for the estate of Ashley Nicole.

Problem 18–9   (Charge and Discharge Statement)

Alex Dunn, Jr., died on January 15, 19X0; his records disclose the following estate:

Cash in bank	$ 3,750
6% note receivable, including $50 accrued interest	5,050
Stocks	50,000
Dividends declared on stocks	600
6% mortgage receivable, including $100 accrued interest	20,100
Real estate—apartment house	35,000
Household effects	8,250
Dividend receivable from Alex Dunn, Sr., trust fund	250,000
Total	$372,750

Twenty-five years earlier, the late Alex Dunn, Sr., had created a trust fund with his son, Alex Dunn, Jr., as life tenant, and his grandson as remainderman. The assets in the fund consist solely of the outstanding capital stock of Dunn, Inc., namely, 2,000 shares of $100 par each. At the creation of the trust, the book—as well as the market—value of these shares was $400,000 and at January 1, 19X0, was $500,000. On January 2, 19X0, Dunn, Inc., declared a 125 percent cash dividend payable February 2, 19X0, to shareholders of record January 12, 19X0.

The executor's transactions from January 15 to 31, 19X0, were as follows:

Cash receipts:			
Jan. 20	Dividends		$ 1,500.00
25	6% notes receivable		5,000.00
	Interest accrued on note		58.33
	Stocks sold, inventoried at $22,500		20,000.00
	6% mortgage sold		20,100.00
	Interest accrued on mortgage		133.33
28	Sale of assets not inventoried		250.00
29	Real estate sold		30,000.00
			$77,041.66
Cash disbursements:			
Jan. 20	Funeral expenses		$ 750.00
23	Decedent's debts		8,000.00
25	Decedent's bequests		10,000.00
31	Distribution of income to widow		500.00
			$19,250.00

Required:

Prepare a charge and discharge statement for the executor for the period from January 15 to January 31, 19X0.

(AICPA adapted)

Problem 18–10   (Charge and Discharge Statement and Supporting Schedules)

Janet Taine died in an accident on May 31, 19X0. Her will provided that all just debts and expenses be paid and that her property be disposed of as follows:

Personal residence—devised to Vernon Taine, spouse.

U.S. Treasury bonds and Puritan Company stock—to be placed in trust. All income to go to Vernon Taine during his lifetime, with right of appointment upon his death.

Seneca Company mortgage notes—bequeathed to Elaine Taine Langer, daughter.

Cash—a bequest of $10,000 to David Taine, son.

Remainder of estate—to be divided equally between the two children, Elaine Taine Langer and David Taine.

The will also provided that during the administration period, Vernon Taine was to be paid $300 a month out of estate income, calculated and reported on a cash basis. David Taine was named as executor and trustee.

An inventory of the decedent's property was prepared. The fair market value of all items as of the date of death was determined. The preliminary inventory, before the computation of any appropriate income accruals on inventory items, follows:

Personal residence property	$ 45,000
Jewelry—diamond ring	9,600
York Life Insurance Company—term life insurance policy on life of Janet Taine:	
Beneficiary—Vernon Taine, spouse	120,000
Granite Trust Company—3% savings bank account, Janet Taine, in trust for Frances Langer (grandchild), interest credited January 1 and July 1; balance May 31, 19X0	400
Fidelity National Bank—checking account; balance May 31, 19X0	143,000
$100,000 U.S. Treasury bonds, 3%, interest payable March 1 and September 1	100,000
800 shares Puritan Company common stock	64,000
700 shares Meta Mfg. Company common stock	70,000
$9,700 Seneca Company first-mortgage notes, 6%, 1982, interest payable May 31 and November 30	9,900

The executor opened an estate bank account to which he transferred the decedent's checking account balance. Other deposits, through July 1, 19X1, were as follows:

Interest collected on bonds:	
$100,000 U.S. Treasury:	
September 1, 19X0	$ 1,500
March 1, 19X1	1,500
Dividends received on stock:	
800 shares Puritan Company:	
June 15, 19X0, declared May 7, 19X0, payable to holders of record as of May 27, 19X0	800
September 15, 19X0	800
December 15, 19X0	1,200
March 15, 19X1	800
June 15, 19X1	800
Net proceeds of June 19, 19X0, sale of 700 shares of Meta Mfg. Company	68,810

Payments were made from the estate's checking account through July 1, 19X1, for the following:

Funeral expenses	$ 2,000
Assessments for additional pre-19X0 federal and state income taxes ($1,700) plus interest ($110) to May 31, 19X0	1,810
19X0 income taxes of Janet Taine for the period January 1, 19X0, through May 31, 19X0, in excess of amounts paid by the decedent on declarations of estimated tax	9,100
Federal and state fiduciary income taxes, fiscal years ending June 30, 19X0 ($75), and June 30, 19X1 ($1,400)	1,475
Federal and state estate taxes	58,000
Monthly payments to Vernon Taine: 13 payments of $300	3,900
Attorney's and accountant's fees	25,000

The executor waived his commission. However, he desired to receive his mother's diamond ring in lieu of the $10,000 specific legacy. All parties agreed to this in writing, and the court's approval was secured. All other specific legacies were delivered by July 15, 19X0.

Required:

Prepare a charge and discharge statement as to principal and income, and its supporting schedules, to accompany the attorney's formal court accounting on behalf of the executor of the estate of Janet Taine for the period from May 31, 19X0, through July 1, 19X1. The following supporting schedules should be included:

1. Original capital of estate.
2. Gain on disposal of estate assets.
3. Loss on disposal of estate assets.
4. Funeral, administration, and other expenses.
5. Debts of decedent paid.
6. Legacies paid or delivered.
7. Assets (corpus) on hand, July 1, 19X1.
8. Proposed plan of distribution of estate assets.
9. Income collected.
10. Distribution of income.

(AICPA adapted)

Problem 18–11   (Charge and Discharge Statement)

The estate of Gaylon Miles, deceased, consisted of the following assets that were appraised as required by the county court following admission of the will to probate and appointment of Nora Burns as executor:

	Appraised Value	Disposition under the Will
Miles building	$87,000	To his daughter, Mary.
6% mortgage, interest payable June 1 and December 1	35,000	To the widow, Margaret Miles, for life, and then to two of his children, Jeff and Alice, equally.
Vacant real estate:		
Lot 1	20,000	Cash to Jeff, Alice, and Mary,
Lot 2	18,000	$10,000 each, and the balance of the estate to the widow.
Home	29,000	
Household effects	1,500	
Cash	12,500	

At the time of death (June 30, 19X0), the accrued interest amounted to $175. Debts amounting to $2,400, funeral expenses of $1,450, and the probate expenses amounting to $900 were paid in cash. In September 19X0, Lot 1 was sold for $22,000, and by the consent of all parties, Jeff took Lot 2 in discharge of the bequest to him and paid the estate $9,000 in cash.

Margaret died on May 1, 19X1, at which date the accrued interest amounted to $875. She left her entire estate to Mary.

The interest on the mortgage was promptly collected on December 1, 19X0, and June 1, 19X1. All legacies were paid.

Required:

Prepare a charge and discharge statement for Nora Burns in respect to the estate of Gaylon Miles upon closing of the estate on July 15, 19X1.

Problem 18–12   (Accounting for an Estate and Charge and Discharge Statement)

The will of E. M Dodd, who died on December 31, 19X0, provided cash bequests of $40,000 to his wife, Susan Dodd, and $15,000 each to two children, the residuary estate to be divided equally among the three beneficiaries. Susan Dodd was appointed executor and trustee without fees or other emoluments.

By court order, Susan Dodd was to receive a family allowance of $4,000 a month, commencing January 1, 19X1, payable from income or from any cash principal available if the income should be inadequate. The estate never had enough cash available to pay the full allowance, nor could any part of the cash bequests be paid. Accordingly, a considerable liability to Susan Dodd had accumulated toward the end of 19X6 for the unpaid portion of the family allowance, as shown by the following trial balance of the estate ledger at December 31 of that year:

	Debit	Credit
Cash	$ 200	
Securities	20,000	
Building A	200,000	
Accumulated Depreciation		$ 36,000
Building B	160,000	
Accumulated Depreciation		38,400
Mortgage—Building B		32,000
Revolving fund—Building A	1,800	
Revolving fund—Building B	2,400	
Susan Dodd—Family Allowance		288,000
Susan Dodd—Paid on Account	178,000	
Estate Corpus		168,000
	$562,400	$562,400

The balance in the Estate Corpus account was made up as follows:

Appraisal of assets	$365,000
Deduct—funeral expenses, etc.	15,000
	$350,000
Add—income:	
Dividends received	6,000
Rentals, after deducting expenses and mortgage interest to date	100,000
	$456,000
Deduct—family allowance	288,000
Balance	$168,000

For want of cash, the beneficiaries decided to settle all liabilities by transfer of property, and they requested their attorney to petition the court for approval of the following agreement to take effect as of December 31, 19X6.

The building B and its revolving fund are to be conveyed to Susan Dodd subject to the mortgage. In turn, she agrees to waive all her claims against the estate for expenditures not refunded to her, including one of $5,000 for estate income taxes paid by her but not collected from the estate, and, to pay attorney's fees of $6,000 for the estate. Furthermore, all beneficiaries agree to have the family allowance discontinued after December 31, 19X6, and also to waive their claims to cash bequests.

The court gave its approval to the agreement and ordered an intermediary accounting by the trustee as of December 31, 19X6.

Required:

Based on the above information, prepare

a. A columnar work sheet showing the trial balance before and after adjustment.

b. A statement of Susan Dodd's account.

c. The trustee's intermediary accounting in the form of a charge and discharge statement.

(AICPA adapted)

Problem 18–13   (Accounting for an Estate)

James Roe died on December 31, 19X0, and left an estate that was to be divided equally among his four children, all legally of age:

Martha Roe Powell	Edward Roe
Albert Roe	Ethel Roe

All funeral expenses, doctor's bills, and other liabilities, including all death duties and estate taxes, were to be paid by the Cohasset Trust Company from a fund that had been provided by the deceased during his lifetime and was on deposit with the trust company. Any balance remaining in this fund, after all payments had been made, was to be retained by the trust company in payment for its services. The trust company agreed to accept that balance in full settlement.

Two trusts will ultimately be set up—one for Martha and the other for Ethel. The eldest son, Albert, was appointed sole executor and trustee of the estate and of the trusts to be created. The principal of each trust was to remain intact during the beneficiary's lifetime, but each beneficiary had the right of appointment (by this right, each daughter could direct to whom the principal of her trust should be paid at her death). The two sons, Albert and Edward, were each to receive their one-quarter share without any restrictions. The net income from the estate was to be distributed semiannually.

The inventory of the estate consisted of the following:

Cash in bank	$ 100,000
$400,000, 3³/₈% municipal bonds at market value	400,000
20,000 shares of no-par value stock of Roe Manufacturing	
Company, appraised at	5,400,000
1,000 shares Cohasset Trust Company stock of $100 par, market value $300 per share .	300,000
Waterfront property at Cohasset Bay, appraised at	800,000
	$7,000,000

The heirs decided to leave the estate undivided for the present under the trusteeship of Albert Roe who, with his brother Edward and his brother-in-law John Powell, continued the management of the Roe Manufacturing Company.

The coupons of the municipal bonds were payable on June 30 and December 31. The Roe Manufacturing Company continued to pay each month a dividend of 50 cents per share, and the Cohasset Trust Company paid a dividend of $12.50 per share, both on June 1 and December 1. No income was received from the Cohasset Bay property.

On July 1, 19X1, Ethel Roe was killed in an automobile accident. By the terms of her will, appointing Albert Roe executor, she left $500,000 in specific bequests, the balance of her estate to be equally divided among her brothers and sister. The estate of Ethel Roe consisted solely of her interest in the estate of her father, with the exception of cash in bank which was just enough to pay burial costs, death duties, and all other liabilities.

The executor of the estate of James Roe, with the consent of the court and of the other heirs, decided to advance to the estate of Ethel Roe the $500,000 required to pay the specific bequests and to charge the amount against her share in the estate of James Roe. It was likewise decided to grant the requests of Albert Roe for an advance of $200,000 and of Edward Roe for an advance of $100,000 against their shares in the latter estate. Both agreed to interest charges on these advances from July 1, 19X1, at a reasonable rate that would also be fair to the Martha Roe Powell trust, but no interest would be charged on the $500,000 advanced to the estate of Ethel Roe.

In order to provide the necessary cash funds on August 1, 19X1, the $400,000 municipal bonds and the 1,000 shares of Cohasset Trust Company stock were sold, for $420,000 and $320,000 net, respectively, after broker's commissions, taxes, and other selling expenses, and on that date the above advances were made.

No change in the executorship and trusteeship of Albert Roe was to take place on account of Ethel Roe's death, but with the consent of the court and of the heirs, her remaining interest in her father's estate was to be divided as of the date of her death in accordance with the terms of her will.

The trustee paid the following expenses in 19X1:

Incidental expenses for the year applicable in equal amounts to the six months before and after the death of Ethel Roe	$ 1,290
Taxes on real estate, payable in June and December	18,000

Trustee's commissions at the legal rates for "receiving and paying out" as follows:

5% on the first	$ 2,000
2½% on the next	20,000
1½% on the next	28,000
2% on the balance	

One half of these rates is for receiving and one half for paying. The same rates apply to principal and to income cash. These commissions are paid June 30 and December 31.

Required:

a. Prepare a columnar working paper to which the transactions in the six months before and after division of the Ethel Roe estate are posted so as to produce the balance sheets of the estate of James Roe immediately after the division of the estate of Ethel Roe on July 1, 19X1, and on December 31, 19X1. Show the calculation of the rate of interest charged to Albert and Edward Roe and give the reason why the use of that rate should be considered fair to the Mary Roe Powell trust.

b. Prepare the trustee's intermediary accounting as at December 31, 19X1, in the form of a charge and discharge statement, showing the payments to each beneficiary.

(AICPA adapted)

Problem 18–14   (Estate Planning)

Michael and Michelle Miller, a married couple, have property valued at $1,600,000 on January 1, 19X0. They wish to minimize federal estate taxes, using a combination of gifts and a trust, so that the value of the property they eventually pass on equally to their two children, Maxwell and Maxine, is as large as possible. State law dictates that one half of the value of the Miller estate belongs to each spouse. The Millers expect Michael, who is 90 years old, to die first at the age of 100. They also believe that the values of their estate assets will not change significantly over time since their funds are invested in bonds, certificates of deposit, and so on. The Millers wish to give the smallest equal amount possible to their children during the remainder of Michael's life (with no gifts to be made after Michael's death) and for Michelle to receive all the income from any remaining properties for the rest of her life.

Required:

Assuming that the Millers' expectations concerning the death of Michael and the values of their assets are correct, prepare a schedule indicating how they can transfer their entire estate to their children without incurring any taxes on gifts or estates and, at the same time, accomplish their various goals.

Financial Distress: Dissolution and Liquidation and Other Alternatives

Chapter Outline

This chapter discusses the accounting techniques related to corporate financial distress. The first topic considered is corporate dissolution and liquidation. This portion of the discussion emphasizes the Bankruptcy Reform Act and the preparation of the statement of affairs. Subsequently, the chapter deals with alternatives to dissolution and liquidation, including both nonjudicial and judicial remedies available to financially distressed corporations. Several of the more important remedies covered, at least briefly, are troubled debt restructuring, Chapter 11 reorganization, and quasi reorganization. In the context of Chapter 11 reorganization, trustee record-keeping procedures and the realization and liquidation account are emphasized.

CORPORATE DISSOLUTION AND LIQUIDATION

A corporation may be dissolved (and its existence terminated) either by *voluntary* or *involuntary* petition. Voluntary dissolution may be initiated by the incorporators if the corporation has not begun business or issued shares of stock. Subsequently, a corporation may be voluntarily dissolved with consent of its shareholders. In these cases, a primary reason for dissolution simply is lack of desire to operate as a corporation for economic or personal reasons. Involuntary dissolution may be initiated by the state of incorporation, the shareholders (or directors), or creditors. A state generally initiates dissolution only when state statutes are violated, fraudulent or felonious behavior is present, and so on. The major reason for involuntary dissolution by shareholders and creditors is financial distress and related insolvency. Dissolution results ultimately in the liquidation of the corporation.

As indicated, the corporation's (that is, the debtor's) financial distress may be related to *insolvency*. The distinction between insolvency in the equity and bankruptcy senses is important. *Equity insolvency* exists when a debtor is unable to pay debts as they mature. Under the national bankruptcy statutes, *bankruptcy insolvency* is a condition in which the aggregate of a debtor's property, at fair value, is less than the amount of the related liabilities (Section 101 (26)).[1] Given these definitions, insolvency in the bankruptcy sense often exists without equity insolvency. The converse is unusual; that is, finding a debtor insolvent in the equity sense but solvent in the bankruptcy sense is rare.

The distinction between state *insolvency* legislation and jurisdiction and federal *bankruptcy* legislation and jurisdiction also is important. Insolvency laws are the enactments of the states relating to the equitable distribution of the resources of a distressed debtor; the Bankruptcy Reform Act of 1978 is the controlling federal statute in such proceedings (see footnote 1). The federal law has superior

---

[1] Citations to national bankruptcy statutes in this chapter refer to Title 1 of the Bankruptcy Reform Act of 1978 unless otherwise noted.

constitutional status, and the insolvency laws must be consistent therewith. The state statutes remain operative to the extent that they do not controvert the federal act.

Overview of the Bankruptcy Reform Act of 1978

A business enterprise confronted with financial failure may undertake voluntary or involuntary reorganization or dissolution under the aegis of federal or state law. However, an insolvent debtor's action taken under state laws resulting in voluntary or involuntary receivership automatically provides a basis for legal action under the Bankruptcy Reform Act (BARA).

One of the purposes of the BARA is to provide for an orderly and equitable distribution of a distressed debtor's property among the related creditors. Once bankruptcy proceedings are terminated, the debtor is discharged of most of the unpaid debts (some are not dischargeable), after which steps may be initiated for financial rehabilitation and renewed business operations. Under the BARA, a debtor is any entity except a railroad, a domestic financial institution (e.g., an insurance company, bank, building and loan association, and credit union), or a foreign financial institution (Secion 109(b)).

A *voluntary* dissolution case may be initiated by an entity qualifying as a debtor filing a petition with the bankruptcy court. In regard to *involuntary* dissolution, a case may be initiated under the BARA if the following file a petition with a bankruptcy court:

1. Three or more entities, each of which is either a holder of a claim against such person that is not contingent as to liability or an indenture trustee representing such a holder, if such claims aggregate at least $5,000 more than the value of any lien on property of the debtor securing such claims held by the holders of such claims.[2]
2. One or more holders that hold in the aggregate at least $5,000 of such claims, if there are fewer than 12 such holders, excluding any employee or insider of such person (Section 303(b)).

A U.S. bankruptcy court is provided in each judicial district by the BARA (Title 2, Section 151).

Dissolution and Liquidation Sequence under the BARA

The progress of dissolution and liquidation related to a distressed debtor consists essentially of (1) the marshaling and protection of the debtor's property, (2) the conversion of the noncash assets into cash, (3) the equitable distribution of the proceeds from conversion to the creditors having provable claims in order of their priority, and (4) the formal discharge of the debtor. Items (1) through (3) are performed by a court-appointed trustee.

---

[2] The word *person* includes an individual, partnership, or corporation.

The trustee accepts custodial responsibility for the debtor's property for the purpose of preserving and protecting the interests of the creditors. Legal title to all, or some, of such property usually vests in the trustee when it is surrendered to his or her custody. In this context, the debtor must provide certain relevant information to the court or trustee. That is, under the BARA (Section 521), the debtor has a duty to

1. File a list of creditors and, unless the court orders otherwise, a schedule of assets and liabilities and a statement of the debtor's financial affairs.
2. Cooperate with the trustee, if one is serving in the case, as necessary to enable the trustee to perform his or her duties.
3. If a trustee is serving in the case, surrender to the trustee all property of the estate and any recorded information, including books, documents, records, and papers, relating to property of the estate.

A creditor having a claim against the debtor must file a *proof of claim* or interest. If the creditor does not file such a claim, the debtor may elect to file it. A claim or interest is deemed allowed unless an interested party objects. After notice and hearing, the court determines the magnitude of the allowable claim (Sections 501, 502).

As indicated, the trustee accepts custodial responsibility for the properties of the debtor (corporate or otherwise). In this context, a trustee may assume responsibility for managing a financially distressed business. The accounting techniques pertaining to this situation are described in a later section—Chapter 11 Reorganization. Certain classes of a distressed debtor's obligations must be fully satisfied before settlement is made with other creditors. The following is a partial list of debts and expenses that have priority status, and distribution is made in the indicated order (Section 507):

1. Administrative expenses, fees, and assessed charges.
2. Unsecured claims for wages, salaries, and commissions earned within 90 days before the date of filing of the bankruptcy petition (but only to the extent of $2,000 per individual).
3. Unsecured claims for contributions to employee benefit plans arising from services rendered within 180 days of the filing of the petition (but only to the extent of $2,000 per individual).
4. Unsecured claims of individuals arising from deposits for purchase, lease, or rental of property or services, limited to $900 per individual.
5. Unsecured claims of governmental units related to taxes.

In this context, mutual debts between a debtor and creditors may be offset with only the balance being paid (Section 553).

Following the conversion of a debtor's assets and the distribution of the proceeds among creditors, the debtor is released from provable debts. A discharge in bankruptcy releases the debtor from these obligations unless the debtor: (1) is not an individual, (2) has behaved fraudulently, (3) has concealed or withheld pertinent information, or (4) has failed to obey a court order (Section 727). The statement of affairs, which details the activities of the trustee, is described next.

The Statement of Affairs

We referred previously to the importance of the debtor behaving without fraud and providing all pertinent data to the court or trustee. Failure to perform satisfactorily in these and other contexts may result in the debtor's loss of discharge or other penalties. The *statement of affairs* includes information of special importance presented on behalf of the debtor. This statement, which details the resources expected to be realized from the conversion of the debtor's assets offset against the claims of secured and unsecured creditors, may be especially useful in helping the debtor to determine the extent of financial deficiency.

The statement of affairs exhibits some of the properties of the balance sheet; yet there are significant differences. Most important, the underlying assumption of business continuity is rejected in favor of a liquidation emphasis. This difference has implications for the valuation of corporate assets. In general, expected realizable values are substituted for unamortized costs. In order to assign these values to individual assets, however, the "liquidation concept" must be formulated precisely. For example, anticipated liquidation within three months often produces different estimates of realizable values than liquidation expected within six months. Thus, if the ultimate liquidation period is indefinite, disclosure often is enhanced by preparing more than one statement under different time assumptions.

In the statement of affairs, assets are classified according to their availability to creditors: (1) those pledged to fully secured creditors, (2) those pledged to partially secured creditors, and (3) those that are free or unencumbered. Similarly, liabilities are classified in terms of their legal preferences: (1) priority claims, (2) fully secured obligations, (3) partially secured obligations, (4) and unsecured claims. Thus, the statement of affairs is oriented toward the legal status of claims against the enterprise. In this context, stockholders' equity accounts lose their significance. In fact, they are included in this statement and a supporting statement (the deficiency account), primarily as an explanation of the insolvency condition. The following example illustrates a statement of affairs and the related treatment of stockholders' equity.

Assume that the balance sheet of Termitron Company on March 31, 19X0, is as follows:

TERMITRON COMPANY
Balance Sheet
March 31, 19X0

Assets

Cash	$ 1,850
Accounts receivable	21,200
Notes receivable	15,000
Merchandise	41,000
Arco common stock (60 shares at cost)	5,800
Land	6,500
Building (net of depreciation)	92,000
Machinery and equipment (net of depreciation)	43,000
Total assets	$226,350

Equities

Bank loan—First State Bank	$ 10,000
Notes payable	70,000
Accounts payable	90,625
Accrued wages	3,775
Accrued interest:	
Bank loan	375
Notes payable	600
Capital stock	150,000
Retained earnings (deficit)	(99,025)
Total equities	$226,350

Based on the expected liquidation interval, the land is appraised at $7,800, and the building has a current market value of $85,000. The machinery and equipment are valueless except as salvage and have a related value of $8,000. The merchandise has a realizable value of $20,000. On March 31, the Arco common stock is quoted on the security exchange at $110 per share. Receivables are estimated to be collectible according to the following schedule:

Notes receivable	100%
Accounts receivable:	
$10,000	100%
10,000	70%
1,200	Uncollectible

The First State Bank loan is secured by the Arco common stock, and the notes payable are secured by a first mortgage on the land and building.

The statement of affairs of Termitron Company is shown in Illustration 19–1. As indicated, a deficiency account (Illustration 19–2) frequently is appended to the statement of affairs. Among other things, this statement provides supporting detail related to estimated gains and losses on realization. The algebraic sum of

ILLUSTRATION 19–1

TERMITRON COMPANY
Statement of Affairs
March 31, 19X0

Book Value					Realizable Value
	Assets				
	Assets pledged with fully secured creditors:				
$ 6,500	Land	$ 7,800			
92,000	Building	85,000	$92,800		
	Notes payable	$70,000			
	Accrued interest	600	70,600	$22,200	
	Assets pledged with partially secured creditors:				
5,800	Arco common stock		$ 6,600		
	Bank loan—First State Bank	$10,000			
	Accrued interest	375	10,375		
	Free assets:				
1,850	Cash			1,850	
15,000	Notes receivable			15,000	
21,200	Accounts receivable			17,000	
41,000	Merchandise			20,000	
43,000	Machinery and equipment			8,000	
	Realizable value of uncommitted assets			$84,050	
	Liabilities having priority			3,775	
	Net free assets			$80,275	
	Estimated deficiency to unsecured creditors			14,125	
$226,350				$94,400	

Book Value			Unsecured
	Equities		
	Liabilities having priority:		
$ 3,775	Accrued wages	$ 3,775	
	Fully secured creditors:		
70,000	Notes payable	$70,000	
600	Accrued interest	600	
	Partially secured creditors:		
	Bank loan—First State Bank:		
10,000	Principal	$10,000	
375	Accrued interest	375	
		$10,375	
	Acro common stock	6,600	$ 3,775
	Unsecured creditors:		
90,625	Accounts payable		90,625
	Stockholders' equity:		
150,000	Capital stock		
(99,025)	Retained earnings (deficit)		
$226,350			$94,400

ILLUSTRATION 19–2

TERMITRON COMPANY
Deficiency Account
March 31, 19X0

Estimated losses:		Estimated gains:	
Accounts receivable	$ 4,200	Land	$ 1,300
Merchandise	21,000	Arco common stock	800
Machinery and equipment	35,000	Capital stock	150,000
Building	7,000	Retained earnings (deficit)	(99,025)
		Estimated deficiency to	
		unsecured creditors	14,125
	$67,200		$ 67,200

---

these gains and losses, when added to the total stockholders' equity reflected in the balance sheet, explains the impairment of capital—the estimated deficiency of the debtor to unsecured creditors.

The asset and equity sections in the statement of affairs in Illustration 19–1 are elaborated upon briefly below.

1. *Assets Pledged with Fully Secured Creditors*. This category includes each asset having a fair value equal to, or in excess of, the debt for which it is pledged as collateral.

2. *Assets Pledged with Partially Secured Creditors*. This class includes each asset having a fair value less than the amount of the debt for which it is pledged to secure.

3. *Free (or Uncommitted) Assets*. The assets in this category are unencumbered and are not otherwise identified with a specific liability (including the dollar portion of assets pledged with fully secured creditors in excess of the amount of the related liability).

4. *Liabilities Having Priority*. This category includes debts that must be liquidated before free assets are available for the payment of unsecured debts.

5. *Fully Secured Creditors*. The liabilities in this category are protected by pledges of specific assets that are expected to realize at least as much as the amount of the related obligations.

6. *Partially Secured Creditors*. The liabilities in this class are obligations of the debtor for which specific assets have been pledged, the estimated value of which is less than the related obligation. The amount of these liabilities not covered by secured assets reverts to the status of unsecured claims.

7. *Unsecured Creditors*. These debts have no designated legal priority, and no specific property is available as collateral to ensure their payment.

8. *Stockholders' Equity.* The balances of capital stock and retained earnings are entered only in the Book Value column for this category. They also are included in the deficiency account, thus indicating the extent to which estimated gains and losses on realization can be absorbed by the existing stockholders' equity.

Although the preceding class descriptions provide general indications of how balance sheet–related items are disclosed in a statement of affairs, a variety of problems exist. These problems, which are discussed briefly below, include reserves, contingent liabilities, accrued interest, prepaid insurance, and discount on capital stock.

Accountants tend to use more descriptive and meaningful terminology than the word *reserve*. Nevertheless, a reserve sometimes must be classified in the statement of affairs. The use of *reserve* to describe a valuation account indicates that the balance has been deducted from the related asset, with the net value of the asset extended to the Book Value column in the statement. In the case of liability "reserves" (i.e., estimated liabilities), the balances are classified consistent with the liability categories discussed above. Note that some "reserves" have a priority status—such as reserve for federal income taxes. Surplus reserves (i.e., appropriations of retained earnings) are elements of stockholders' equity and are reported along with retained earnings.

Contingent liabilities are not shown in the statement of affairs. Nevertheless, they are evaluated in terms of their probabilities of becoming actual liabilities from the perspective of this statement. For example, discounted notes receivable, which are unlikely to be dishonored, are omitted from the statement of affairs. If a discounted note is likely to be dishonored, its face value is reported in the unsecured creditors category. Other contingent liabilities are reported similarly.

Accrued interest receivable is added to the related obligation. If a note receivable is pledged to secure a debt, related accrued interest usually is considered as additional security and is reported as a complement to the note. Accrued interest on notes payable is similarly associated with the related notes.

The appropriate treatment of *prepaid insurance* in the statement of affairs depends on the circumstances. Although an insurance policy may have a cash surrender value, the related proceeds are not available unless the policy is canceled. Further, the policy may expire before the expected completion of the liquidation. Thus, if cancellation is not expected during the liquidation period, prepaid insurance is reported in the statement of affairs using book values. If cancellation is expected during this period, realizable values are reported.

If capital stock is sold at a *discount*, creditors often have a claim against the shareholders in the amount of the discount. If all, or a portion, of a discount is likely to be recovered from the shareholders, the expected realizable value is reported on the statement of affairs as a free asset, at least to the extent of the creditors' deficiency.

ALTERNATIVES TO DISSOLUTION AND LIQUIDATION

As an alternative to dissolution and liquidation, a distressed debtor may attempt to rehabilitate a financially floundering business through both nonjudicial and judicial remedies. Among the former are arrangements entered into with creditors to restructure troubled debt, composition agreements, voluntary assignments for the benefit of creditors, and creditor management committees. Judicial remedies usually involve formal reorganization under Chapter 11 of the BARA or quasi reorganization under the laws of various states.

Nonjudicial Remedies

As indicated, the usual nonjudicial remedies include troubled debt restructuring, composition agreements, voluntary assignments for the benefit of creditors, and creditor management committees. Each of these possibilities is discussed below. The discussions are brief because the topics typically are covered in related courses and because of space limitations.

An important nonjudicial remedy which often aids financially distressed debtors in avoiding dissolution is *troubled debt restructuring*. *Statement of Financial Accounting Standards No. 15* covers accounting for troubled debt restructuring.[3] Since this pronouncement is only tangentially related to corporate dissolution and liquidation and is covered in intermediate accounting, its major provisions are discussed here only briefly.

A troubled debt restructuring occurs when a debtor having debt-related financial distress is granted a concession(s) pertaining to debt by the related creditor. The concession(s) usually is (are) granted simply because the creditor will be better off economically after granting the concession than before. The debtor also is better off because of the receipt of a concession. Two types of events result in troubled debt restructurings under *Statement No. 15:* (1) the settlement of a debt at less than its carrying value and (2) the continuation of an existing debt with a modification(s) of its terms which favors the debtor. Typical term modifications are as follows:

1. Reduced stated interest rate.
2. Extended maturity date.
3. Reduced face value.
4. Reduced or deferred accrued interest.

One important feature of *Statement No. 15* is the requirement of symmetrical accounting for the gains of debtors and the losses of creditors for both type (1) and (2) events. That is, when a type (1) event occurs, the carrying value of the debt immediately prior to restructuring (i.e., the prerestructure value of the debt) exceeds the fair value of the consideration exchanged in discharging the debt.

---

[3] FASB, *Statement of Financial Accounting Standards No. 15*, "Accounting by Debtors and Creditors for Troubled Debt Restructuring" (Norwalk, CT: FASB, 1977).

Under these circumstances, the debtor has a gain and the creditor has a loss—both of which equal the difference between the prerestructure value and the fair value of the consideration exchanged. The debtor's gain is extraordinary, and the creditor's loss is ordinary (and often is charged to a pertinent allowance account).

The gain (or loss) related to a type (2) restructuring is the difference between the prerestructure value and the postrestructure value (i.e., the undiscounted total future cash flow from the restructured debt). If the prerestructure value exceeds the postrestructure value, the debtor has a gain and the creditor has a loss. Under these conditions, gains and losses are recognized and no interest is recorded in the future since the debt is considered to have been settled. In contrast, if the postrestructure value exceeds the prerestructure value, the debtor has a loss and the creditor has a gain—neither of which is recognized. However, an imputed (or effective) rate of interest is used in recording future interest. These procedures are used when the postrestructure value exceeds the prerestructure value because the debt is not considered to have been settled under these conditions.

Another possibility for forestalling liquidation is a *composition settlement*. *Composition settlement* refers to a contractual arrangement between the debtor, the creditors, and the creditors, themselves, in which the creditors agree to accept less than the full amounts of their claims in settlement. These settlements provide for ratable distribution of the debtor's assets among the creditors. When composition settlements are employed, the debtor usually is insolvent in the bankruptcy sense. Note that a composition settlement is not precluded even if some dissenting creditors exist, provided that the dissenting group receives full, or possibly preferential, settlement.

An insolvent debtor also may *voluntarily assign his or her property to a trustee or assignee for the benefit of his or her creditors*. The purpose of a voluntary assignment is to enable the debtor's representative to convert property into cash, as necessary, and to distribute the proceeds ratably among the creditors. If the creditors agree contractually, the assignment may result in the debtor being completely discharged from all debts. If undistributed assets remain, they are returned by the trustee to the debtor. Note that a voluntary assignment for the creditors' benefit constitutes an act of bankruptcy.

The *creditor management committee* is a form of debtor-creditor alliance providing for creditor committee management of the debtor's business for the purposes of rehabilitation, reorganization (see below), or liquidation. The control of the business rests with the committee—which may elect to contribute new capital if it appears financially and operationally feasible. Properties normally are returned to the debtor when obligations have been discharged or dealt with otherwise.

Judicial Remedies

As indicated above, several judicial remedies are available to a financially distressed debtor to forestall, or at least to postpone, liquidation. The remedies usually employed are reorganization under Chapter 11 of the BARA and quasi reorganization under the laws of various states. These procedures are considered next.

Chapter 11 Reorganization. Reorganization under Chapter 11 of the BARA begins with the debtor filing a petition for reorganization with the appropriate bankruptcy court. Subsequently, the court appoints a committee of creditors holding unsecured claims for management purposes. The creditor management committee normally consists of the creditors holding the seven largest claims against the debtor. The court also may appoint additional committees consisting of other creditors and shareholders at the request of interested parties. Assuming that a trustee is not appointed, the basic function of the committee(s) is to formulate a reorganization plan which leads to the profitable future operation of the debtor and ultimately to the maximum possible payment of existing debts. Whether or not a trustee is appointed, the plan usually must be approved by one half of the creditors in number and two thirds of the creditors in amount (of allowed claims) with respect to each class of creditor. In this context, the court also rules on the fairness and the legality of the plan. That is, the plan is not accepted unless the court judges it to be nondiscriminatory with respect to each class of creditor and to be consistent with the provision of Chapter 11 of the BARA.

The creditor management committee also may request that the court appoint a trustee (or examiner) to manage the financially distressed business when such appointment is not mandatory. The appointment of a trustee is mandatory if the debtor's fixed, liquidated, and unsecured debts (other than obligations for goods, services, or taxes) exceed $5,000,000. If a trustee is appointed, he or she is responsible for the reorganization plan and for accounting for the operations of the business while it is under his or her trusteeship.

Trustee Record-Keeping Procedures.   As indicated, a trustee may assume responsibility for managing a financially distressed business. In this context, legal title to all, or at least some, of the debtor's assets normally is conveyed to the trustee, who is accountable to the court, the creditors, the shareholders, and any other interested parties. In accounting for the debtor's assets and equities, the trustee may elect to use new accounting records or the existing records of the debtor. The debtor's records tend to be used in relatively uncomplicated circumstances.

The use of new records usually is desirable since they help the trustee to distinguish between the obligations of the debtor existing prior to his or her appointment and those created subsequently. In this context, previously existing debts are not recorded in new records. The trustee also is responsible only for debts created after his or her appointment, although he or she may be required to liquidate previously existing obligations. Similarly, the use of new records aids the trustee in distinguishing between the assets which are, and are not, conveyed to him or her. As implied, only assets that are conveyed to the trustee are recorded in the new records. With respect to assets, the trustee is completely responsible for asset acquisitions occurring after the appointment, although he or she is required only to manage prudently the previously existing assets falling under his or her purview. For example, the trustee is reponsible for collecting only those receivables existing prior to his or her appointment but also is responsible for granting credit and collecting receivables created under his or her management.

With respect to this discussion, the trustee's accounts usually indicate whether transactions pertain to "new" or "old" debts and assets. The record-keeping procedures of the trustee, which assume that new records are begun, are illustrated with the following case. The record-keeping procedures and illustrations related to this case are self-explanatory and, thus, are not discussed in detail.

Assume that the account balances of Insolvo Company on March 31, 19X0 are as follows:

Cash	$ 600
Accounts receivable	4,000
Notes receivable	5,800
Merchandise	18,000
Long-lived assets	24,000
Other assets	2,600
	$55,000
Allowance for doubtful accounts	$ 400
Accumulated depreciation	2,000
Accounts payable	21,000
Capital stock	40,000
Retained earnings (deficit)	(8,400)
	$55,000

Insolvo Company filed a petition for reorganization under Chapter 11, and Charles Louis was appointed trustee. Louis assumes responsibility on April 1. For the period April 1 through August 31, the following transactions and events occur.

1. All corporate assets are transferred to the trustee. Existing debts of Insolvo Company remain on the corporate records. New accounts are opened by the trustee for the transferred assets.
2. Merchandise purchased on account amounts to $40,000.
3. Credit sales amount to $69,000; cash sales are $4,000.
4. Collections of cash are as follows:

Notes receivable	$ 4,800
Accounts receivable (old)	2,100
Accounts receivable (new)	51,000

5. The following payments are made by the trustee:

Accounts payable (old)	$16,000
Accounts payable (new)	34,000
Operating expenses	2,500
Trustee's expenses	1,000

6. The trustee recorded these adjustments on August 31:

Depreciation (5 months)	1,200
Estimated doubtful accounts:	
Accounts receivable (old)	950
Accounts receivable (new)	1,600
Accounts written off:	
Accounts receivable (old)	400
Notes receivable	1,000

7. Both the trustee and Insolvo Company make closing entries on August 31; unsold merchandise on this date amounts to $16,000.

Entries for these transactions and events are journalized in Illustration 19–3. A working paper that combines the accounts of the corporation and the trustee (before closing entries) for the purpose of preparing conventional financial statements is shown in Illustration 19–4. The formal statements are easily extracted from this working paper.

Assuming that the trusteeship is terminated on August 31, the return of corporate management to Insolvo officials by Charles Louis is recorded by an entry in the records of the trustee as follows:

Insolvo Company—in Trusteeship	59,350	
Allowance for Doubtful Accounts (old)	950	
Allowance for Doubtful Accounts (new)	1,600	
Accumulated Depreciation	3,200	
Accounts Payable (new)	6,000	
Cash		9,000
Accounts Receivable (old)		1,500
Accounts Receivable (new)		18,000
Merchandise		16,000
Long-Lived Assets		24,000
Other Assets		2,600

The related entry on Insolvo Company books is as follows:

Cash	9,000	
Accounts Receivable	19,500	
Merchandise	16,000	
Long-Lived Assets	24,000	
Other Assets	2,600	
Allowance for Doubtful Accounts		2,550
Accumulated Depreciation		3,200
Accounts Payable		6,000
Charles Louis, Trustee		59,350

ILLUSTRATION 19-3

Trustee's Books			Corporation's Books		
(1) Cash	600		(1) Charles Louis, Trustee	52,600	
Accounts Receivable (old)	4,000		Allowance for Doubtful Accounts	400	
Notes Receivable	5,800		Accumulated Depreciation	2,000	
Merchandise, April 1	18,000		Cash		600
Long-Lived Assets	24,000		Accounts Receivable		4,000
Other Assets	2,600		Notes Receivable		5,800
Allowance for Doubtful Accounts			Merchandise		18,000
(old)		400	Long-Lived Assets		24,000
Accumulated Depreciation		2,000	Other Assets		2,600
Insolvo Company—in Trusteeship		52,600			
(2) Purchases	40,000		(2) No entry.		
Accounts Payable (new)		40,000			
(3) Cash	4,000		(3) No entry.		
Accounts Receivable (new)	69,000				
Sales		73,000			
(4) Cash	57,900		(4) No entry.		
Notes Receivable		4,800			
Accounts Receivable (old)		2,100			
Accounts Receivable (new)		51,000			
(5) Accounts Payable (new)	34,000		(5) Accounts Payable	16,000	
Insolvo Company—in Trusteeship	16,000		Charles Louis, Trustee		16,000
Operating Expenses	2,500				
Trustee's Expenses	1,000				
Cash		53,500			
(6) Depreciation Expense	1,200		(6) No entry.		
Bad Debts Expense	2,550				
Accumulated Depreciation		1,200			
Allowance for Doubtful Accounts					
(old)		950			
Allowance for Doubtful Accounts					
(new)		1,600			
Bad Debts Expense	1,000				
Allowance for Doubtful Accounts (old)	400				
Notes Receivable		1,000			
Accounts Receivable (old)		400			
(7) Sales	73,000		(7) Charles Louis, Trustee	22,750	
Merchandise, August 31	16,000		Income Summary		22,750
Merchandise, April 1		18,000			
Purchases		40,000	Income Summary	22,750	
Operating Expenses		2,500	Retained Earnings		22,750
Trustee's Expenses		1,000			
Bad Debts Expense		3,550			
Depreciation Expense		1,200			
Income Summary		22,750			
Income Summary	22,750				
Insolvo Company—in Trusteeship		22,750			

INSOLVO COMPANY—IN TRUSTEESHIP
Combined Account Working Paper
For Five Months Ended August 31, 19X0

	Trustee's Accounts	Insolvo Accounts	Eliminations Dr.	Eliminations Cr.	Income Statement	Balance Sheet
Cash	9,000					9,000
Accounts receivable (old)	1,500					1,500
Accounts receivable (new)	18,000					18,000
Merchandise (4/1)	18,000				18,000	
Long-lived assets	24,000					24,000
Other assets	2,600					2,600
Purchases	40,000				40,000	
Operating expenses	2,500				2,500	
Trustee's expenses	1,000				1,000	
Depreciation expense	1,200				1,200	
Bad debts expense	3,550				3,550	
Charles Louis, trustee		36,600		(1) 36,600		
	121,350	36,600				
Merchandise (8/31)	16,000					16,000
Net income					22,750	
					89,000	71,100
Allowance for doubtful accounts (old)	950					950
Allowance for doubtful accounts (new)	1,600					1,600
Accumulated depreciation	3,200					3,200
Accounts payable (old)		5,000				5,000
Accounts payable (new)	6,000					6,000
Capital stock		40,000				40,000
Retained earnings (deficit)		(8,400)				(8,400)
Sales	73,000				73,000	
Insolvo Company—in trusteeship	36,600		(1) 36,600			
	121,350	36,600				
Merchandise (8/31)	16,000				16,000	
Net income						22,750
			36,600	36,600	89,000	71,100

An additional statement related to the trustee's activities, the realization and liquidation account, is discussed below.

The Trustee's Realization and Liquidation Account.   Conventional financial statements reveal the managerial activities of the trustee and the income, and so on, of the entity. In the case of liquidation, a more important objective frequently is summarizing the liquidation and distribution activities of the fiduciary. A special report accommodating this goal is the *realization and liquidation account*. The reference to "account" in the title of this report accents its traditional format, which is illustrated below.

The realization and liquidation account is essentially a statement of accountability, reflecting the activities of the fiduciary in converting the debtor's noncash assets to cash and distributing the proceeds and other cash in settling the debtor's claims. The fiduciary's cash account normally is appended to this report. This supplementary report typically consists of three principal divisions depicted as follows:

Assets			
Assets to be realized	xxx	Assets realized	
Assets acquired		(conversion proceeds)	xxx
(or discovered)	xxx	Assets not realized	xxx

Liabilities			
Liabilities liquidated	xxx	Liabilities to be liquidated	xxx
Liabilities not liquidated	xxx	Liabilities incurred	xxx

Revenues and Expenses; Gains and Losses			
Supplementary charges	xxx	Supplementary credits	xxx

A summation of the debits in the three statement categories offset against the related summation of credits discloses any imbalance—which may be described as the net gain or loss for the liquidation period.

Using the data for the trusteeship previously discussed, the realization and liquidation account takes the form shown in Illustration 19–5. In this statement, net income is the algebraic sum of the debit and credit balances related to its 10 categories. The use of numerals in identifying elements in the realization and liquidation account indicates that the statement may be easily prepared by entering the transactions of the trustee directly into the relevant statement categories. These numerals would not appear in a formal report submitted to others. The related trustee's cash account is as follows:

Cash

(1) Balance, March 31	600	(5) Accounts payable (old)	16,000
(3) Sales	4,000	(5) Accounts payable (new)	34,000
(4) Accounts receivable (old)	2,100	(5) Operating expenses	2,500
(4) Accounts receivable (new)	51,000	(5) Trustee's expenses	1,000
(4) Notes receivable	4,800	Balance, August 31	9,000
	62,500		62,500
Balance, August 31	9,000		

Insolvo Company's stockholders' equity accounts are as follows:

Capital Stock

		(1) Balance, March 31	40,000

Retained Earnings

(1) Balance, March 31	8,400	Net income (April 1 to August 31)	22,750

The categories shown in the realization and liquidation account are elaborated upon briefly below.

1. *Assets to Be Realized.* The assets in this class existed on the date of the fiduciary's appointment (or at the beginning of the current period if the statement is not a cumulative record of fiduciary activities).

2. *Assets Acquired.* This category contains additional assets that are acquired (or discovered) during the period of fiduciary accountability.

3. *Assets Realized.* This category reflects the extent of the conversion of noncash assets into cash.

4. *Assets Not Realized.* This category summarizes the assets on hand at the date of the preparation of the statement, usually valued at the same amount indicated in the original statement of accountability under assets to be realized or assets acquired.

5. *Liabilities to Be Liquidated.* The obligations in this class are those existing at the date of appointment of the fiduciary (or at the beginning of the current period if the statement is not a cumulative record of fiduciary activities).

6. *Liabilities Incurred.* The liabilities in this category are the additional obligations assumed by the fiduciary during the period of his or her accountability.

7. *Liabilities Liquidated.* This class contains the debt cancellations occurring during the period, identified by creditor class.

8. *Liabilities Not Liquidated.* This category includes the unpaid claims existing at the end of the period.

9. *Supplementary Charges.* This category contains the expenses incurred during the period of trusteeship (ignoring amortization and losses on the conversion of noncash assets).

ILLUSTRATION 19–5

INSOLVO COMPANY
CHARLES LOUIS, TRUSTEE
Realization and Liquidation Account
April 1, 19X0 to August 31, 19X0

Assets to be realized:				**Liabilities to be liquidated:**			
(1) Accounts receivable (old)	4,000			(1) Accounts payable (old)			21,000
Less: Allowance for doubtful				**Liabilities incurred:**			
accounts (old)	400	3,600		(2) Accounts payable (new)			40,000
(1) Notes receivable		5,800		**Supplementary credits:**			
(1) Merchandise		18,000		(2) Sales			73,000
(1) Long-lived assets	24,000			**Assets realized:**			
Less: Accumulated depreciation	2,000	22,000		(4) Accounts receivable (old)			2,100
(1) Other assets		2,600		(4) Accounts receivable (new)			51,000
Assets acquired:				(4) Notes receivable			4,800
(3) Accounts receivable (new)		69,000		**Assets not realized:**			
Supplementary charges:				Accounts receivable (old)		1,500	
(2) Purchases		40,000		Less: Allowance for doubtful			
(5) Operating expenses		2,500		accounts (old)		950	550
(5) Trustee's expenses		1,000		Accounts receivable (new)		18,000	
Liabilities liquidated:				Less: Allowance for doubtful			
(5) Accounts payable (old)		16,000		accounts (new)		1,600	16,400
(5) Accounts payable (new)		34,000		Merchandise			16,000
Liabilities not liquidated:				Long-lived assets		24,000	
Accounts payable (old)		5,000		Less: Accumulated depreciation		3,200	20,800
Accounts payable (new)		6,000		Other assets			2,600
Net income		22,750					
		248,250					248,250

865

10. *Supplementary Credits*. The credits in this class include revenues earned during the period (ignoring realized unearned revenues and gains on the conversion of noncash assets).

The preceding category descriptions provide general indications of how the trustee discharges his or her accounting responsibilities. Nevertheless, a variety of related problems exist; they are considered briefly below.

1. *Sales and Purchases*. The fiduciary records merchandise purchased as either assets acquired or supplementary charges. Similarly, sales are recorded as either assets realized or supplementary credits. If operating transactions are relatively numerous, the use of the supplementary charge-credit categories generally facilitate record-keeping.

2. *Cash Discounts*. The fiduciary chooses between two alternative methods in recording cash discounts and allowances related to payables and receivables. For accounts payable, the amounts of the obligations, net of discounts and allowances, may be debited to liabilities liquidated when payments are made. Although the discount/allowance variance between liabilities to be liquidated and liabilities liquidated is not specifically identified by this treatment, this difference necessarily enters into the calculation of realization gain or loss—since there will be no remaining balance in liabilities not liquidated. If the fiduciary elects to debit liabilities liquidated with gross invoice amounts when payments are made, contra credits equal to the amounts of any discounts and allowances are recorded as supplementary credits. Thus, discounts and allowances again are factors in the calculation of realization gain or loss, although in this instance, their sum is identified separately. Treatments paralleling those described above may be applied to receivable balances and related sales discounts and allowances.

3. *Depreciation and Uncollectibles*. Depreciation expense and estimated bad debts usually are not separately identified in the realization and liquidation account. They are reflected, however, in the balances in the Accumulated Depreciation and Allowance for Uncollectibles Accounts balances at period-end—which are reported contra in the assets not realized category. These expenses, thus, are factors in the calculation of income or loss for the period.

4. *Accruals*. If the amounts of accrued income in the assets to be realized class are subsequently realized at larger amounts, two alternative treatments are available. The accountant may credit assets realized with the amount accrued at the start of the period, crediting the additional amount collected to supplementary credits. Alternatively, the increase in the amount of the accrual since the start of the period may be entered as accrued interest in assets acquired with a contra credit to supplementary credits. The subsequent collection is then recorded by a credit to assets realized. Comparable treatment may be applied to accrued expenses.

5. *Favorable or Unfavorable Settlement of Liabilities.* In the event that creditors agree to accept less than face value for their receivables, the settlement discount is reported preferably as a supplementary credit, with the total amount of the canceled obligation reported under the liabilities liquidated category. If a premium is required to liquidate an overdue indebtedness, accounting treatment parallels that of a discount settlement. Thus, the amount of the premium is entered in the supplementary charge class.

In measuring gains and losses on the favorable settlement of liabilities, recognition also is given to the reasonableness of the interest rate on the new debt. In this context, FASB *Interpretation No. 2*, "Imputing Interest on Debt Arrangements Made under the Federal Bankruptcy Act," states:

> *APB Opinion No. 21* applies to notes issued by a debtor in a reorganization, arrangement, or under other provisions of the Federal Bankruptcy Act. A note issued under such circumstances in exchange (in whole or in part) for an existing note or notes shall be considered a "note exchanged for property" for purposes of applying *APB Opinion No. 21*. In addition, an existing note shall be considered as originating in a reorganization, arrangement, or under other provisions of the Federal Bankruptcy Act and therefore as being a new note if its original terms are modified, altered, or otherwise changed as a part of the agreement with creditors. Accordingly, interest shall be imputed by applying *APB Opinion No. 21* if the new note does not specify interest or specifies an interest rate which is unreasonable in the particular circumstances.[4]

Quasi Reorganization.   A frequently used alternative to Chapter 11 reorganization is quasi reorganization. This procedure is available under various state laws if a corporation has a deficit in retained earnings. A quasi reorganization allows a corporation, in effect, to begin its operations again—to start over. In this context, a significant feature of a quasi reorganization is the elimination of the corporation's retained earnings deficit. Quasi reorganization, in general, and the elimination of the retained earnings deficit, in specific, are allowed because operating with such a deficit often is difficult for a corporation, which for one reason or another (e.g., the development of new products or the acquisition of a more capable management team) might operate profitably in the absence of its deficit. Operating with a retained earnings deficit is difficult, even for a company with improved future prospects, since, generally speaking, dividends cannot be paid if such a deficit exists which, in turn, makes it difficult for existing shareholders to sell their shares (in lieu of cash dividends) and for the company to raise new capital.

The more important features of a quasi reorganization under typical state laws are: (1) the adjustment of the carrying values of the corporation's assets to their fair market values; (2) the creation of an other contributed capital balance, which

---

[4] We presume that these comments apply to the 1978 BARA, even though they were made in relation to the prior bankruptcy act.

is used to absorb any deficit in retained earnings existing after asset revaluation (assuming that such a balance does not already exist); and (3) the disclosure of the existence, and the date, of the quasi reorganization by "dating" the retained earnings balance for at least 10 years. In addition, SEC *Regulation S-X* requires disclosure of the amount of the deficit eliminated for at least three years subsequent to reorganization on the balance sheet. The required additional paid-in capital balance can be created in a variety of ways, including reduction in the par value of the corporation's shares and the donation of treasury stock. The following example illustrates the entries for a quasi reorganization, assuming that the reorganization is accomplished by reducing the par value of the corporation's shares.

Assume that the Shakijo Company has a deficit in retained earnings of $200,000 at December 1, 19X0, even though its future is reasonably bright because of new product developments. Also assume that the company develops a quasi reorganization plan that is to be effective as of December 31, 19X0. The plan requires writing down the company's depreciable fixed assets by $65,000 (by decreasing fixed assets $100,000 and related accumulated depreciation from $35,000 to zero) and recording appreciation on its short-term marketable securities of $25,000. Also, the company's inventory is to be written down $10,000 because some of its components are salable only at scrap values. Shakijo Corporation has 10,000 shares of $40 par common stock authorized, issued, and outstanding. Its shares were issued at par. In this context, the reorganization plan calls for changing the par value of the company's shares to $10. The company's December 19X0 profit is $1,000, and it closes its books each month. The entries pertinent to the quasi reorganization, which are self-explanatory, are presented below.

Common Stock [10,000 × ($40 − $10)]	300,000	
Other Contributed Capital		300,000
Marketable Securities	25,000	
Accumulated Depreciation	35,000	
Retained Earnings	50,000	
Fixed Assets		100,000
Inventory		10,000
Income Summary	1,000	
Retained Earnings		1,000
Other Contributed Capital	249,000	
Retained Earnings ($200,000 + $50,000 − $1,000)		249,000

Shakijo Company's December 31, 19X0, stockholder's equity account balances subsequent to the quasi reorganization are as follows:

Common stock ($10 par, 10,000 shares authorized, issued, and outstanding)	$100,000
Capital from reduction in par value of common stock remaining after absorption of $249,000 retained earnings deficit	51,000
Retained earnings (accumulated since quasi reorganization on December 31, 19X0)	–0–
Total stockholders' equity	$151,000

Summary

This chapter begins by addressing corporate dissolution and liquidation. A corporation's existence may be terminated by voluntary or involuntary petition. Voluntary dissolution may occur if the corporation has not commenced business, has not issued stock, or the shareholders have agreed to do so. Involuntary dissolution, which often involves financial distress, may be initiated by the shareholders or directors of the corporation, the state, or creditors.

A corporation's financial distress may be related to insolvency. Equity insolvency exists when a debtor corporation is unable to pay its debts as they mature. Bankruptcy insolvency is characterized by the national bankruptcy statutes as a condition in which the fair market value of the debtor corporation's assets is less than the amount of its liabilities. In this context, the Bankruptcy Reform Act (BARA) of 1978 is intended to provide the orderly and equitable distribution of a distressed debtor's property among the debtor's creditors. When the bankruptcy proceedings are terminated, the debtor is discharged of most debts and may attempt to renew business operations.

Under the BARA, the process of dissolution and liquidation involves (1) the marshaling and protection of the debtor's property, (2) the conversion of the debtor's noncash assets into cash, (3) the equitable distribution of the proceeds from conversion to creditors having provable claims, and (4) the formal discharge of the debtor. The statement of affairs details the proceeds expected to be realized from the conversion of the debtor's assets contrasted with the claims of secured and unsecured creditors.

In the event that a trustee assumes responsibility for the business of a distressed debtor, the trustee may elect to use either the debtor's current records or new ones. If new records are maintained, only those assets subject to the fiduciary's accountability are recorded therein. Debts existing before the trusteeship remain on the books of the debtor. The trustee should clearly distinguish between the assets and liabilities existing before any reorganization and those assets and liabilities which come into existence during such reorganization. The trustee's accountability is reflected in the realization and liquidation account.

As an alternative to liquidation, a corporation may attempt to resolve financial difficulties through nonjudicial or judicial remedies. Nonjudicial remedies include debt restructuring, agreement to a composition settlement, voluntary assignment, and formation of a creditor management committee. Judicial remedies typically involve reorganization under Chapter 11 of the BARA and quasi reorganization.

Questions

1. Who may initiate a petition for the *voluntary* dissolution of a corporation? The *involuntary* dissolution of a corporation?
2. Distinguish between *bankruptcy insolvency* and *equity insolvency*.
3. What is the dissolution and liquidation sequence once a debtor has been determined bankrupt?
4. Certain classes of a distressed debtor's liabilities must be fully satisfied before other creditors can receive a settlement. What are they?

5. What is a statement of affairs? What distinguishes this statement from the conventional balance sheet?

6. How should contingent liabilities be reported in the statement of affairs?

7. What unique classification and descriptive distinctions should be made in the set of accounts that are prepared to record the actions of the trustee in a reorganization?

8. What purpose is served by the preparation of the realization and liquidation account? Identify the categories typically found in the realization and liquidation account.

9. Discuss the events leading to troubled debt restructurings, the symmetrical accounting required in accounting for such restructurings, and the calculation and disclosure of related gains and losses.

Exercises

Exercise 19–1   (Legal Issues Relating to Bankruptcy)

An accountant is often confronted with problems relating to bankruptcy proceedings. The following items relate to pertinent points of law with which the accountant should be familiar. Determine whether each legal conclusion is true or false according to bankruptcy law. For items which are false, explain why they are false.

1. Insolvency in the bankruptcy sense is a financial status in which the aggregate fair value of the assets of an entity is not sufficient to pay outstanding liabilities.

2. A preference in bankruptcy prefers one creditor over the others.

3. The Bankruptcy Reform Act specifically grants the exclusive original jurisdiction over bankruptcy proceedings to one of several bankruptcy courts.

4. The filing of a voluntary petition in bankruptcy does not automatically operate as an adjudication or determination that the petitioner is bankrupt.

5. The Bankruptcy Reform Act considers a partnership as an entity separate from the partners.

6. Federal, state, and local taxes are discharged by bankruptcy.

7. Insolvency in the bankruptcy sense is the same as insolvency in the equity sense.

8. A trustee in a bankruptcy proceeding is usually elected by the creditors.

9. A priority in a bankruptcy proceeding is given for administration costs including accountants' and attorneys' fees.

(AICPA adapted)

Exercise 19–2   (Legal Issues Relating to Bankruptcy)

Each of the following relates to points of bankruptcy law. Select the one best answer for each of the following items:

1. The highest priority for payment in full before general creditors' claims in a bankruptcy proceeding is assigned to

    a. Wages, in a limited amount, if earned within three months preceding bankruptcy.

    b. Wages owed to an insolvent employee.

    c. Administration costs of bankruptcy.

    d. Unpaid federal income taxes.

2. Under Chapter 11 of the Bankruptcy Reform Act, a plan to be accepted and confirmed by the court

    a. Must be accepted by all creditors.

    b. May be approved by a majority of creditors by number.

    c. May be approved by one third of the creditors by number if their claims equal two thirds of provable claims.

    d. Requires approval of a majority as to number of creditors and two thirds as to amount of claims of creditors where claims have been proved and allowed.

3. Which of the following statements best describes a composition agreement unanimously agreed to by all creditors?

    a. It provides for the appointment of a fiduciary to take over and operate the debtor's business.

    b. It is subject to approval by a federal district court judge.

    c. It provides for a discharge of the debts included in the composition agreement upon performance by the debtor.

    d. It binds only those creditors who do not subsequently withdraw from the agreement prior to its consummation.

4. Dexter had assets of $80,000 and liabilities of $100,000, all unsecured. He owed $25,000 to each of the following: Petrie, Dey, Mabley, and Norris. Petrie, Dey, and Mabley agreed with each other and with Dexter to accept 70 cents on the dollar in immediate satisfaction of their debts. Under these circumstances

    a. The agreement is void for lack of consideration.

    b. The agreement would not constitute an action justifying commencement of an involuntary case.

    c. Norris would be bound by the agreement.

    d. The agreement described is an assignment for the benefit of the creditors.

5. Ruth Dolson has filed a voluntary petition in bankruptcy. Her assets are listed as $4,200, and her liabilities, $18,750. Her creditors include (1) three employees who have not been paid wages for six weeks at $100 per week per employee, (2) the U.S. government for $6,900 in back income and social security taxes, (3) her former husband for a loan of $3,000, and (4) suppliers for goods purchased on open account for $7,050. In this situation

    a. All the debts in question are dischargeable in bankruptcy.

    b. Claims must be filed within three months of the filing of the petition in bankruptcy.

    c. The wage earners have the first priority after administration costs.

    d. The U.S. government claim will take precedence over the security interests of secured creditors.

(AICPA adapted)

Exercise 19–3   (Journal Entries Relating to Bankruptcy)

Cassens, Inc., experienced economic misfortune in respect to credit deficiencies during 19X0, after which its balance sheet disclosed the following on December 31:

Assets		Equities	
Cash	$ 1,506	Trade accounts payable	$265,000
Accounts receivable	96,183	Capital stock	100,000
Merchandise	176,021	Retained earnings	40,000
Long-lived assets—net	131,290		
Total assets	$405,000	Total equities	$405,000

Following the appointment of R. M. Guy, trustee, who was authorized to operate the business, the properties disclosed above were transferred to him; Guy insisted that accounts receivable and merchandise be written down to $76,300 and $145,055, respectively.

During the first six months of 19X1, the trustee collected old receivable balances, producing an additional loss of $5,035. During this period, credit sales were made for $185,000, of which $132,400 were collected. Trade accounts payable of $160,000 were paid by the trustee, as were trusteeship expenses of $36,100. Properties and related obligations, were returned to the Cassens management on July 1 after depreciation on long-lived assets was allowed to the extent of $6,563. The cost of unsold merchandise on July 1 was $18,460.

Required:

a. Prepare entries for both the trustee and Cassens, Inc., to record the transactions described above.

b. Submit to the management a balance sheet of Cassens, Inc., following the restoration of original custody.

Exercise 19–4   (Statement of Affairs)

Channel Service, Inc., has convened a meeting of its creditors to produce a composition settlement. The company's balance sheet discloses:

Assets		Equities	
Cash	$ 317	Accrued wages	$ 1,575
Accounts receivable	14,329	Accounts payable	41,585
Supplies	1,479	Mortgage on trucks	19,300
Trucks	28,770	Capital stock	5,000
		Deficit	(22,565)
Total assets	$44,895	Total equities	$44,895

Current value estimates for assets are as follows:

Supplies	$ 610
Trucks	22,500
Accounts receivable	12,500

Required:

Prepare a statement of affairs for the forthcoming meeting.

Exercise 19–5   (Statement of Affairs and Payment Schedule)

I. M. Train, toy manufacturer, on October 31, 19X0, prepared the following enumeration of resources and creditor claims:

Resources:
  Petty cash, $250, including expense vouchers for $119
  Cash, $2,615
  Accounts receivable, $3,680, of which $3,380 are believed to be collectible
  Toy materials and supplies, $12,000; estimated market value, $8,400
  Toys in process, $8,100; estimated market value, $2,000
  Building, $20,000; estimated market value, $9,000
  Display equipment, $11,800; estimated market value, $8,200

Claims:
  Accounts payable:
    Gem Supply Company . . . . $ 2,800
    Ornamental Trinkets, Inc.   6,300
    R. M. Brown 15,000
    A. K. Moyer   1,700
  Notes payable:
    American State Bank, $20,000. The display equipment is pledged as collateral.
    Texas Finance Company, $15,000. Unsecured notes receivable, $10,000 and warehouse receipts for finished goods are pledged as collateral. The finished goods (manufactured toys) have a book value of $8,000 and an estimated current value of $7,500. The notes receivable are estimated to be fully collectible.
    Accrued wages, $1,750.

Required:

a. Prepare a statement of affairs as of October 31, 19X0.

b. Prepare a schedule of payments to creditors on this date, indicating whether the amount of the settlement is a full or partial liquidation.

Exercise 19–6   (Concepts Relating to Involuntary Bankruptcy)

For several years, Marian supplied raw materials to Western, Inc., who processed the goods into a finished product for sale to retail customers.

Marian supplied goods to Western on credit terms, and to secure her claim for unpaid goods, she obtained and properly perfected a "floating lien" on all of the goods sold to Western.

Six months ago, Marian heard that Western, Inc., was in financial difficulty and stopped selling goods to the firm. Marian was not paid by Western for several shipments of goods and heard that recently Western made a general assignment for the benefit of its creditors. Also Marian heard that a group of Western's creditors may attempt to place Western into bankruptcy.

Required:

a. Under what circumstances may Western's creditors proceed to have it adjudicated an involuntary bankrupt?

b. Assume that Western's creditors may proceed to have it adjudicated an involuntary bankrupt. What action would they have to take in order to commence a bankruptcy proceeding?

c. Will the number of creditors required to commence an involuntary bankruptcy proceeding vary depending upon the number of Western's creditors? Explain.

d. How will Marian be treated in the bankruptcy proceedings if Western is declared a bankrupt? Explain.

(AICPA adapted)

Exercise 19–7   (General Bankruptcy Issues)

Indicate whether the following legal conclusions are true or false, according to general principles of bankruptcy law.

1. In order to be adjudged a distressed debtor under the Bankruptcy Reform Act
   a. A person must have debts totaling more than $2,000.
   b. There must be at least three creditors.
   c. A petition in bankruptcy must be filed by a majority of creditors.
   d. The creditor must agree to the commencement of bankruptcy proceedings.
   e. A petition in bankruptcy must be filed.

2. Bankruptcy proceedings may be instituted against any person or corporation, including
   a. A married woman.
   b. A domestic insurance corporation.
   c. A banking corporation.
   d. A building and loan corporation.
   e. A partnership.

3. Classes of claims that have priority under the provisions of the Bankruptcy Reform Act include the following:
   a. Expenses of bankruptcy administration.
   b. Wages earned within one year before the date of bankruptcy.
   c. Debts of less than $50.
   d. Taxes.
   e. Claims of creditors that are outstanding for more than three years.

4. Debts discharged by completion of bankruptcy proceedings and discharge of the debtor include the following:
   a. Contract obligations that are not due until three years following the filing of the petition.
   b. Trade accounts payable.
   c. Taxes.
   d. Fines or penalties to governmental units.
   e. A debt arising from the commission of a willful injury.

(AICPA adapted)

Exercise 19–8   (Alternatives to Bankruptcy)

In the course of examining the financial statements of Superior Systems, Inc., the financial vice president discloses that the corporation has a serious collection problem with one of its customers, Vizar Components, Inc. Vizar is approximately $10,000 in arrears; its checks have been returned for insufficient funds. Other creditors have similar claims against Vizar.

You have also learned that the principal creditors, including Superior, have held a meeting to consider possible alternative courses of action. During the meeting, an examination of the financial statements of Vizar revealed that it was in a difficult current position, but that it had sufficient assets to meet liabilities in the event of a bankruptcy proceeding. The meeting also revealed that Vizar's problems had built up over the past two years due to poor management. The company appears to have significant potential to return to profitability if properly managed.

Ignoring troubled debt restructuring and quasi reorganization, what are the viable alternatives to a bankruptcy proceeding? Explain.

(AICPA adapted)

Exercise 19–9   (Contrasting Voluntary and Involuntary Bankruptcy)

During the examination of the financial statements of Delta Corporation, you note that as of September 30, 19X0:

1. Current liabilities exceed current assets.
2. Total assets substantially exceed total liabilities.
3. Cash position is poor, and current payables are considerably in arrears.
4. Trade and secured creditors are pressing for payment, and several lawsuits have been commenced against Delta.

Further investigation reveals the following:

1. On August 31, 19X0, Delta made a $1,000 payment to Oliveros on a $20,000 mortgage indebtedness over one year in arrears. The fair market value of the mortgaged property is $35,000.
2. On September 20, 19X0, a trade creditor, Miller, obtained a judgment against Delta which under applicable law constitutes a lien on Delta's real property.
3. On September 22, 19X0, Delta paid a substantial amount to Helms, a supplier, on an account over one year old.
4. On September 27, 19X0, Delta executed and delivered a financing statement to Honea, a vendor, from whom Delta had purchased some new machinery six months earlier. Honea duly filed and perfected the financing statement.

Required:

a. As of September 30, 19X0, could the creditors of Delta file an involuntary petition in bankruptcy against Delta if a sufficient number of them having a sufficient amount of claims decide to do so? Explain.
b. Independent of your answer to requirement (a), assume the same facts set out above except that Delta's total liabilities exceed total assets and that on October 2, 19X0, Delta filed a voluntary petition in bankruptcy, and a trustee has been appointed.

(1) What are the rights, if any, of the trustee against each of the creditors involved in the four transactions stated in the problem? Explain.

(2) What are the general requirements for creditors to be entitled to vote on and participate in a bankruptcy proceeding? Explain whether each of the four creditors involved meets these requirements. Why?

(AICPA adapted)

Problems

Problem 19–10   (Statement of Affairs and Deficiency Account)

A receiver was appointed on September 30, 19X0, for Green, Inc. On this date, the following balance sheet accounts are available:

Assets

Petty cash			$ 120
Cash in bank			2,400
Accounts receivable	$32,000		
Notes receivable	20,000	$52,000	
Allowance for bad debts		340	51,660
Accrued interest, notes receivable			600
Merchandise			29,200
Prepaid insurance			240
Prepaid advertising			190
Building		$80,000	
Accumulated depreciation		21,000	59,000
Furniture and fixtures		$ 7,200	
Accumulated depreciation		1,600	5,600
Organization costs			1,740
Goodwill			4,000
Total assets			$154,750

Equities

Accrued wages	$ 2,800	
Accrued property taxes	1,810	
Accounts payable	79,800	
Notes payable	15,000	
Accrued interest payable	150	$ 99,560
Contributed capital:		
Common stock	$70,000	
Premium	2,000	
	$72,000	
Retained earnings:		
Deficit	(16,810)	55,190
Total equities		$154,750

It is estimated that conversion of assets will realize cash in the following amounts:

Notes receivable (with accrued interest)	$19,100
Accounts receivable	25,000
Merchandise	19,000
Building	25,000
Furniture and fixtures	2,000

Notes payable of $10,000 are secured by merchandise, the book value of which is $20,000. Notes payable of $5,000 are secured by the funiture and equipment. Interest expense is allocable ratably to all outstanding notes payable.

Required:

a. Prepare a statement of affairs as of September 30.

b. Prepare a supporting deficiency account or report on this date.

Problem 19–11   (Statement of Affairs and Estimated Settlement)

Noel Corporation is in financial difficulty because of a deficiency in sales volume. Its stockholders and principal creditors want an estimate of the financial results of the dissolution and liquidation of the corporation. The corporation's trial balance follows:

NOEL CORPORATION
Post-Closing Trial Balance
December 31, 19X2

	Debit	*Credit*
Cash	$ 1,000	
Accounts Receivable	20,500	
Allowance for Bad Debts		$ 350
Inventories	40,000	
Supplies Inventory	3,000	
Downhill Railroad 5% Bonds	5,000	
Accrued Bond Interest Receivable	750	
Advertising	6,000	
Land	4,000	
Building	30,000	
Accumulated Depreciation—Building		5,000
Machinery and Equipment	46,000	
Accumulated Depreciation—Machinery		
and Equipment		8,000
Accounts Payable		26,000
Notes Payable—Bank		25,000
Notes Payable—Officers		20,000
Payroll Taxes Payable		800
Wages Payable		1,500
Mortgage Payable		42,000
Mortgage Interest Payable		500
Capital Stock		50,000
Retained Earnings	29,100	
Reserve for Product Guarantees		6,200
	$185,350	$185,350

The following information has been collected in anticipation of a meeting of the stockholders and principal creditors to be held on January 2, 19X3.

1. Cash includes a $300 protested check from a customer. The customer stated that he would have funds to honor the check in about two weeks.

2. Accounts receivable include accounts totaling $10,000 that are fully collectible and have been assigned to the bank in connection with the notes payable. Included in the unassigned receivables is an uncollectible account of $150. The Allowance for Bad Debts account of $350 now on the books will adequately provide for other doubtful accounts.

3. Purchase orders totaling $9,000 are on hand for the corporation's products. Inventory with a book value of $6,000 can be processed at an additional cost of $400 to fill these orders. The balance of the inventory, which includes obsolete materials with a book value of $1,200, can be sold for $10,500.

4. In transit at December 31, but not recorded on the books, was a shipment of defective merchandise being returned by a customer. Mr. Noel, president of the corporation, had authorized the return and the refund of the purchase price of $250 after the merchandise had been inspected. Other than this return, Noel knows of no other defective merchandise that would bear on the Appropriated Reserve for Product Guarantees account. The merchandise being returned has no salvage value.

5. The Supplies Inventory contains charges for advertising literature, brochures, and other sales aids. These items could not be replaced for less than $3,700.

6. The Downhill Railroad bonds are recorded at face value. They were purchased six years earlier for $600, and the adjustment to face value was credited to Retained Earnings. At December 31, 19X2, the bonds were quoted at 18.

7. The Advertising account represents the future benefits of a 19X2 advertising campaign. Ten percent of certain advertising expenditures were placed in the account. Noel stated that this was too conservative and that 20 percent would result in a more realistic measure of the market that was created.

8. The land and building are in a downtown area. A firm offer of $50,000 has been received for the land that would be used as a parking lot; the building would be razed at a cost of $12,000 to the buyer. Another offer of $40,000 was received for the real estate that the bidder stated would be used for manufacturing that would probably employ some Noel employees.

9. The highest of the offers received from used machinery dealers was $18,000 for all of the machinery and equipment.

10. One creditor, whose account for $1,000 is included in Accounts Payable, confirmed in writing that he would accept 90 cents on the dollar if the corporation paid him by January 10.

11. Wages payable include year-end adjustments of $325 payable to certain factory employees for their overtime during the busy season.

12. The mortgage payable is secured by the land and building. The last two monthly principal payments of $200 each were not made.

13. Estimated liquidation expenses amount to $3,200.

14. For income tax purposes, the corporation has the following net operating loss carryovers (the tax rate is 50 percent):

19X0	. . . .	$10,000
19X1	. . . .	12,000
19X2	. . . .	8,000

Required:

a. Prepare a statement of affairs.

b. Prepare a schedule indicating the estimated settlement per dollar of unsecured liabilities.

(AICPA adapted)

Problem 19–12   (Deficiency to Unsecured Creditors)

Machine Manufacturing Company has been forced into bankruptcy as of April 30, 19X0. The following list of account balances was prepared by the company bookkeeper as of April 30, 19X0:

Cash	$ 2,700
Accounts receivable	39,350
Notes receivable	18,500
Inventories:	
Raw materials	19,600
Work in process	35,100
Finished machines	12,000
Supplies	6,450
Tools	14,700
Prepaid expenses	950
Plant and property:	
Land	20,000
Buildings	75,000
Machinery	80,900
	$325,250
Note payable to First Bank	$ 15,000
Notes payable to suppliers	51,250
Accounts payable	52,000
Accrued salaries and wages	8,850
Accrued property taxes	2,900
Employees' taxes withheld	1,150
Accrued wage taxes	600
Accrued interest on bonds	1,800
First-mortgage bonds payable	90,000
Accumulated depreciation—buildings	33,750
Accumulated depreciation—machinery	32,100
Common stock ($100 par value)	75,000
Deficit	(39,150)
	$325,250

Additional information:

1. Of the total accounts receivable, $10,300 worth, is believed to be good. The other accounts are doubtful, but it seems probable that 20 percent finally can be collected.

2. A total of $15,000 of the notes receivable have been pledged to secure the note payable to First Bank. All except $2,500 of these appear to be good. Interest of $800 is accrued on the $12,500 of good notes pledged, and $300 is accrued on the $15,000 payable to the bank. The remaining notes are not considered collectible.

3. The finished machines are expected to be sold for one third above their costs, but expenses in disposing of them will equal 20 percent of their sales price. Work in process can be completed at an additional cost of $15,400, of which $3,700 would be material used from the raw material inventory. The work in process, when completed, will probably sell for $40,000, and cost of sale will be 20 percent of sales price. The raw material not used will realize $8,000. Most of the value of tools consists of special items. After completion of work in process, the tools should sell for $3,000. The supply inventory, which will not be needed to complete work, should sell for $1,000.

4. Land and buildings are mortgaged as security for bonds. They have an appraised value of $95,000. The company recently purchased $20,000 of machinery on a conditional sales contract. It still owes $12,000 principal on this contract, which is included in the notes payable. These machines, having a current used value of $10,000, are repossessed. Machine Manufacturing Company remains liable for the unpaid obligation. Depreciation taken on these machines amounts to $1,800. The remaining machinery is believed to be salable at $10,000, but costs of selling it may be $1,000.

Required:

a. Prepare a statement showing the estimated deficiency to unsecured creditors, indicating clearly the causes of the deficiency. You need not consider any expenses of liquidation that are not stated in the information given.

b. Compute the percentage of probable payments to unsecured creditors.

(AICPA adapted)

Problem 19–13   (Statement of Realization and Liquidation)

The financial condition of Rawley Manufacturing Corporation was very unstable, although it has unimpaired contributed capital in the amount of $60,000 and accumulated earnings of $8,522. This condition was attributable to a deficiency of quick assets: cash, $265; and trade receivables, $4,062. Its current obligations to trade creditors amounted to $25,289. Other assets were raw materials, $16,000; work in process, $34,400; finished goods, $5,700; and machinery and dies, $33,384. In order to continue operations, it was necessary to obtain sufficient cash to meet current payrolls and to pay miscellaneous expenses.

At a meeting of the principal creditors, it was decided to advance $6,000 to Rawley Manufacturing Corporation to enable it to meet obligations presently due; additionally, it was decided to permit continuance of operations until the present in-process stock could be completed and sold. These operations were to be conducted by a trustee chosen by the creditors.

Transactions completed during the trusteeship were cash disbursements for labor, $16,625; for expenses, $4,530; and for additional dies, $750; raw materials purchased on account, $6,300; sales on account, $72,300; loss on collection of old accounts, $380; expenses incurred, on account, $15,000. Unliquidated account balances at the termination of the trusteeship period were as follows: Accounts Receivable (new), $3,382; Accounts Payable (new), $89; Raw Materials, $2,000; Finished Goods, $30,000; and Machinery and Dies, $34,134.

Required:

Prepare a realization and liquidation account with supporting schedules. Ignore the effects of depreciation in the determination of operating profit.

Problem 19–14   (Statement of Realization and Liquidation and Gain and Loss Account)

Boutique Company was unable to meet its obligations. As a result, Judy Nunn was appointed trustee on February 5, 19X0. The following accounts were taken from the books as of that date:

Cash	$ 560
Accounts receivable	6,210
Merchandise	16,536
Prepayment of expenses	704
Fixtures	12,942
	$36,952
Accounts payable	$16,100
Notes payable	3,500
Accrued wages, taxes, etc.	1,200
Accrued rent	600
Accumulated depreciation	3,803
Capital stock	10,000
Retained earnings	1,749
	$36,952

In the period from February 5 to April 30, 19X0, the trustee's actions resulted in the following:

1. An audit of the accounts receivable disclosed that there was an additional $237 of accounts receivable not recorded on the books.
2. Merchandise costing $7,500 was sold for cash.
3. A portion of the fixtures, which cost $5,376 and had accumulated depreciation of $942, was sold.
4. Accounts receivable totaling $1,882 were collected. Other accounts amounting to $741 have been determined to be worthless.
5. Claims have been approved and paid for $1,010 of the wages and taxes that were accrued at February 5. Wage claims for $125 that were unrecorded on February 5 have also been approved and paid. Other claims have not yet been paid.

6. Expenses for wages and supplies used in liquidating the business to April 30 amounted to $1,300. Fees for the trustee need not be considered.

7. Rent under leases has continued to accrue in the amount of $900. Interest of $70 has accrued on notes payable.

8. Cash receipts and cash disbursements show the following:

Cash receipts:	
Collection of accounts	$1,882
Sales of merchandise	8,300
Sale of fixtures	1,000
Cash disbursements:	
Accrued wages and taxes	1,135
Expenses of the trusteeship	1,300

Required:

Prepare a realization and liquidation account and related gain and loss account for the period ended April 30, 19X0.

(AICPA adapted)

Problem 19–15   (Statement of Affairs and Deficiency Account)

JONES, INC.
Balance Sheet, as of March 31, 19X5
(Prepared by the Company's Bookkeeper)

Assets

Current assets:			
Cash		$ 2,000	
Notes receivable	$ 4,640		
Less: Notes receivable discounted	4,640		
Accounts receivable		4,000	
U.S. Treasury bonds		10,000	
Inventories:			
Finished goods	$15,000		
Work in process	4,500		
Raw materials	6,000	25,500	
Total current assets			$ 41,500
Other assets:			
Subscriptions to capital stock			12,500
Investments			2,300
Property and equipment:			
Real estate	$45,000		
Factory equipment	24,000		
	$69,000		
Less: Accumulated depreciation	20,000		49,000
Total assets			$105,300

Liabilities

Current liabilities:
Notes payable:

To Manufacturers' Trust Co.	$10,000	
To Alex Smith	25,000	$35,000
Accounts payable		24,000
Accrued liabilities:		
Salaries and wages	$ 992	
Property taxes	460	1,452

Total current liabilities		$ 60,452

Long-term liabilities:

First mortgage on real estate	$15,000	
Second mortgage on real estate	20,000	35,000
Total liabilities		$ 95,452

Capital

Capital stock—authorized, subscribed, and		
issued, 50 shares, par $100 per share	$50,000	
Less: Deficit	(40,152)	9,848
Total liabilities and capital		$105,300

An analysis of the company's accounts disclosed the following:

1. Jones, Inc., started business with authorized capital of $50,000, represented by shares of $100 par value each. Of the 500 authorized shares, 375 were fully paid at par and 125 were subscribed at par, payment to be made on call.

2. Manufacturers' Trust Company holds $10,000 of U.S. Treasury bonds as security for its $10,000 loan; it also holds the first mortgage of $15,000 on the company's real estate, interest on which is paid through March 31, 19X5.

3. The real estate includes land, which cost $5,000, and a building erected thereon at a cost of $40,000. Of the accumulated depreciation, $5,000 is applicable to the building and $15,000 to the factory equipment. The realizable value of the real estate is estimated to be $30,000.

4. The note payable to Alex Smith is secured by a chattel mortgage on factory equipment and the inventories. Interest on the note has been paid through March 31, 19X5.

5. Alex Smith holds the second mortgage on the real estate.

6. The notes receivable, $4,640, which were discounted, though not yet due, are deemed uncollectible.

7. Of the $4,000 of accounts receivable, $2,000 are considered good; of the remaining $2,000, it is expected that one half will be uncollectible.

8. Inventories are valued at cost; finished goods are expected to yield 110 percent of cost. Goods in process cost $4,500 and have a realizable value, if scrapped, of $900. It is estimated, however, that the work in process can be completed into finished goods by the use of $1,200 of raw material and an expenditure of $1,400 for labor and other costs. The raw material deteriorates rapidly and is estimated to realize only 25 percent of cost.

9. The factory equipment, which cost $24,000 on April 1, 19X0, is considered to have a realizable value of $5,000 at March 31, 19X5.

10. The subscription to the capital stock for 125 shares at par is due from Wyman Jones, president of the company, and is fully collectible.

11. Investments include 15 shares (a 1 percent interest) of the common stock of Bourbon Company, acquired at a cost of $1,500, but with a market value of $3,390 at March 31, 19X5, and 20 shares of treasury stock for which the company paid $800.

12. Expenses of liquidation and accruals not specifically mentioned need not be considered.

The committee has called for payment of the capital stock subscription and has decided to have the goods in process converted into finished goods, which are expected to realize 110 percent of cost. Completion of goods in process can be done so quickly that no expenses other than those mentioned will be incurred.

Required:

a. Prepare a statement of affairs on March 31, 19X5.

b. Prepare a supporting deficiency account detailing estimated gains and losses.

c. Calculate amounts and settlement percentages for each class of creditors.

(AICPA adapted)

Problem 19–16   (Statement of Affairs and Settlement Estimation)

Neversink Corporation advises you, the company's CPA, that it is facing bankruptcy proceedings. The following are the balance sheet of Neversink Corporation at June 30, 19X0, and supplementary data:

Assets

Cash	$ 2,000
Accounts receivable, less allowance for bad debts	70,000
Inventory, raw material	40,000
Inventory, finished goods	60,000
Marketable securities	20,000
Land	13,000
Buildings, less accumulated depreciation	90,000
Machinery, less accumulated depreciation	120,000
Goodwill	20,000
Prepaid expenses	5,000
Total assets	$440,000

Liabilities and Capital

Accounts payable	$ 80,000
Notes payable	135,000
Accrued wages	15,000
Mortgages payable	130,000
Common stock	100,000
Retained earnings (deficit)	(20,000)
Total liabilities and capital	$440,000

Supplementary data:

1. Cash includes a $500 travel advance that has been expended.
2. Accounts receivable of $40,000 have been pledged in support of bank loans of $30,000. Credit balances of $5,000 are netted in the accounts receivable total.
3. Marketable securities consist of governmental bonds costing $10,000 and 500 shares of Bartlett Company stock. The market value of the bonds is $10,000, and the stock is quoted at $18 per share. The bonds have accrued interest due of $200. The securities are collateral for a $20,000 bank loan.
4. Appraised value of raw materials is $30,000, and finished goods is $50,000. For an additional cost of $10,000, the raw materials would realize $70,000 as finished goods.
5. The appraised value of fixed assets is land, $25,000; buildings, $110,000; and machinery, $75,000.
6. Prepaid expenses will be exhausted during the liquidation period.
7. Accounts payable include $15,000 of withheld payroll taxes and $6,000 of obligations to creditors who have been assured by the president that they would be paid. There are unrecorded employer's payroll taxes in the amount of $500.
8. Wages payable are not subject to any limitations under bankruptcy laws.
9. Mortgages payable consist of $100,000 on land and buildings and a $30,000 chattel mortgage on machinery. Total unrecorded accrued interest on these mortgages amounted to $2,400.
10. Estimated legal fees and expenses in connection with the liquidation are $10,000.
11. Probable judgment on a pending damage suit is $50,000.
12. You have not rendered an invoice for $5,000 for last year's audit, and you estimate a $1,000 fee related to liquidation.

Required:

a. Prepare a statement of affairs.

b. Compute the estimated settlement per dollar of unsecured liabilities.

(AICPA adapted)

Problem 19–17   (Quasi Reorganization)

Semided Company has a deficit in retained earnings of $100,000 at October 1, 19X0, although its future prospects are good because of an aggressive new management team. Because of its deficit, the company developed a quasi reorganization plan that is to be effective as of December 31, 19X0. The plan requires writing down the company's (1) depreciable fixed assets by $50,000 (by decreasing fixed assets $75,000 and related accumulated depreciation from $25,000 to zero) and (2) inventory by $15,000.

Semided Company has 20,000 shares of $30 par common stock authorized, issued, and outstanding. These shares were issued at par. The reorganization plans call for changing the par value of the company's shares to $20. The company's fourth-quarter profit for 19X0 is $2,000, and it closes its books quarterly.

Required:

Prepare the journal entries pertinent to the quasi reorganization and the related stockholders' equity section of the balance sheet.

State, County, and Municipal Governmental Units—General Fund

Chapter Outline

Chapters 20, 21, and 22 cover accounting for nonprofit entities. This chapter contains general discussions of accounting principles and concepts related to state, county, and municipal governmental units (i.e., state and local governmental units). It also explains the techniques used in accounting for the general funds of these units. Chapter 21 deals with the procedures used in accounting for other funds and account groups of state and local governments. Chapter 22 focuses on accounting techniques for colleges and universities, hospitals, and other nonprofit organizations.

FINANCIAL REPORTS OF STATE AND LOCAL GOVERNMENTAL UNITS—USES AND OBJECTIVES

In *Statement of Financial Accounting Concepts No. 4,* the FASB identifies the characteristics which it believes distinguish governmental and other nonprofit (or not-for-profit) entities from profit-seeking enterprises.[1] The FASB indicates that the major distinguishing characteristics of nonprofit entities are the following:

a. Receipts of significant amounts of resources from resource providers who do not expect to receive either repayment or economic benefits proportionate to resources provided.
b. Operating purposes that are other than to provide goods or services at a profit or profit equivalent.
c. Absence of defined ownership interests that can be sold, transferred, or redeemed, or that convey entitlement to a share of a residual distribution of resources in the event of liquidation of the organization.

Although the FASB views these qualities as applying to all nonprofit entities, a variety of environmental characteristics distinguishes state and local governmental units from other nonprofit entities.[2] Governmental Accounting Standards

---

[1] FASB, *Statement of Financial Accounting Concepts No. 4,* "Objectives of Financial Reporting by Nonbusiness Organizations" (Norwalk, CT: FASB, 1978), par. 6.

[2] The FASB indicates (par. 3) that its "Objectives of Financial Reporting by Nonbusiness Organizations" project included governmental units in its scope from the outset and that it is unaware of persuasive evidence indicating that the objectives set forth in *SFAC No. 4* are inappropriate for general-purpose external reports of governmental units. Nevertheless, the FASB deferred a final decision on whether these objectives apply to state and local governmental units because of the pending resolution of the appropriate structure for setting financial reporting standards for such units. The FASB also acknowledges that the objectives of general-purpose financial reporting by the federal government are the responsibility of others, although it sees no conceptual reason why the objectives of *SFAC No. 4* are not applicable to such reporting. The creation of the Governmental Accounting Standards Board (GASB) resolved the issue of the responsibility for identifying the objectives of financial reporting by state and local governmental units. The GASB currently is responsible for establishing these objectives for state and local governmental units, nonprofit entities whose financial statements are combined with those of such units, and public-sector entities dealt with specifically by a GASB pronouncement. Note also that the U.S. Comptroller General is responsible for establishing the financial reporting objectives of the federal government. As implied, the FASB is responsible for identifying the financial reporting objectives of all other entities.

Board (GASB) *Concepts Statement 1,* "Objectives of Accounting and Financial Reporting for Governmental Units," identifies these characteristics as follows:[3]

a. Primary characteristics of government's structure and the services it provides:
 (1) The representative form of government and the separation of powers.
 (2) The federal system of government and the prevalence of intergovernmental revenues.
 (3) The relationship of taxpayers to services received.
b. Control characteristics resulting from government's structure:
 (1) The budget as an expression of public policy and financial intent and as a method of providing control.
 (2) The use of fund accounting as a control device.
c. Other characteristics
 (1) The dissimilarities between similarly designated governments.
 (2) The significant investment in nonrevenue-producing capital assets.
 (3) The nature of the political process.

The differences between state and local governmental units and other nonprofit entities account partially for variations in the objectives of general-purpose financial reporting by these entities.

GASB *Concepts Statement 1* indicates that the objectives of state and local government financial reporting follow from the environmental characteristics listed above and the informational needs of all users of governmental financial reports (*Cod.* 100.174).[4] This statement identifies the primary users of such reports as "*(a)* those to whom government is primarily accountable (the citizenry), *(b)* those who directly represent the citizens (legislative and oversight bodies), and *(c)* those who lend or who participate in the lending process (investors and creditors)" (*Cod.* 100.130). The GASB's focus is on satisfying the information needs of user groups who are limited in their ability to obtain governmental financial information (*Cod.* 100.103). These groups need information, generally, for use in comparing actual financial results with the legally adopted budget; assessing financial condition and results of operations; determining compliance with finance related laws, rules, and regulations; and evaluating efficiency and effectiveness (*Cod.* 100.132).

---

[3] GASB, *Codification of Governmental Accounting and Financial Reporting Standards* (Norwalk, CT: GASB, 1990), Sec. 100.113. We refer to this *Codification* (abbreviated *Cod.*) in making references to authoritative governmental accounting pronouncements in Chapters 20 and 21 unless there is a need to refer to original pronouncements. The *Codification* is a synthesis of the effective accounting and reporting standards for state and local governmental units. The material in the *Codification* is drawn from GASB Statements, Interpretations, Technical Bulletins, and Concepts Statements; National Council on Governmental Accounting (NCGA) Statements and Interpretations; and the AICPA's Industry Audit Guide, *Audits of State and Local Governmental Units* (1974).

[4] The GASB acknowledges that governmental units undertake both governmental-type and business-type activities and indicates that its objectives apply to both types of activities.

From an overall perspective, the purposes of general-purpose financial reporting by state and local governmental entities are to assist users in assessing accountability and in making economic, social, and political decisions (*Cod.* 100.176). The specific objectives of general-purpose financial reporting by these entities are the following (*Cod.* 100.177–100.179):

.177   Financial reporting should assist in fulfilling government's duty to be publicly accountable and should enable users to assess that accountability.

a. *Financial reporting should provide information to determine whether the current-year revenues were sufficient to pay for current-year services. . . .*
b. *Financial reporting should demonstrate whether resources were obtained and used in accordance with the entity's legally adopted budget; it should also demonstrate compliance with other finance-related or contractual requirements.*
c. *Financial reporting should provide information to assist users in assessing the service efforts, costs, and accomplishments of the governmental entity. . . .*

.178   Financial reporting should assist users in evaluating the operating results of the governmental entity for the year.

a. *Financial reporting should provide information about sources and uses of financial resources. . . .*
b. *Financial reporting should provide information about how the governmental entity financed its activities and met its cash requirements.*
c. *Financial reporting should provide information necessary to determine whether the entity's financial position improved or deteriorated as a result of the year's operations.*

.179   Financial reporting should assist users in assessing the level of services that can be provided by the governmental entity and its ability to meet its obligations as they become due.

a. *Financial reporting should provide information about the financial position and condition of a governmental entity. . . .*
b. *Financial reporting should provide information about a governmental entity's physical and other nonfinancial resources having useful lives that extend beyond the current year, including information that can be used to assess the service potential of those resources. . . .*
c. *Financial reporting should disclose legal or contractual restrictions on resources and risks of potential loss of resources.*

Although the word *accountable* is used only once in these objectives, the concept of accountability is implicit in all of them. Thus, the accountability objective (stated in .177) is considered to be the paramount objective by the GASB and is the objective from which the remaining objectives flow (*Cod.* 100.176). Note also that the GASB believes that information cannot be effective in accomplishing the objectives without possessing the qualities of understandability, reliability, relevance, timeliness, consistency, and comparability (*Cod.* 100.162). The GASB defines these qualities by reference to the FASB's *Statement of Financial Accounting Concepts No. 2.*

HISTORICAL PERSPECTIVE ON AUTHORITATIVE PRONOUNCEMENTS

Prior to 1979, the main source of governmental accounting principles was *Governmental Accounting, Auditing, and Financial Reporting (GAAFR)*, published in 1968 by the National Committee on Governmental Accounting. The principles contained in this document were recognized as GAAP by the AICPA in its 1974 Industry Audit Guide, *Audits of State and Local Governmental Units*.

In 1974, the Municipal Finance Officers Association established the National Council on Governmental Accounting (NCGA), which consisted of 21 members serving four-year terms on a part-time, voluntary basis. In 1979, the NCGA issued *Statement 1*, "Governmental Accounting and Financial Reporting Principles," which restated and superseded *GAAFR*.[5] This statement contains 12 basic principles of accounting for state and local governmental units and remains an important authoritative pronouncement on governmental accounting. The AICPA, in its *Statement of Position (SOP) 80–2* (June 30, 1980), stated that financial statements presented in accordance with the NCGA's *Statement 1* are considered to be in conformity with GAAP. Between 1979 and 1984, the NCGA issued 7 statements:

Statement 1	"Governmental Accounting and Financial Reporting Principles."
Statement 2	"Grant, Entitlement, and Shared Revenue Accounting and Reporting by State and Local Governments."
Statement 3	"Defining the Governmental Reporting Entity."
Statement 4	"Accounting and Financial Reporting Principles for Claims and Judgments and Compensated Absences."
Statement 5	"Accounting and Financial Reporting Principles for Lease Agreements of State and Local Governments."
Statement 6	"Pension Accounting and Financial Reporting: Public Employee Retirement Systems and State and Local Government Employees"
Statement 7	"Financial Reporting for Component Units within the Governmental Reporting Entity."

Portions of *Statements 1* and *6* have been superceded by subsequent NCGA *Statements and Interpretations* and by GASB *Statements No. 1, 5,* and *6* (see below). Nevertheless, most parts of the seven NCGA *Statements* remain in effect.

During 1984, the GASB was formed by the Financial Accounting Standards Foundation. The GASB's function is to establish governmental accounting stan-

---

[5] Although *GAAFR* does not have authoritative status, this publication was updated in both 1980 and 1988.

dards, just as the FASB establishes reporting standards for profit-seeking entities and certain nonbusiness entities. Similar to the FASB, the GASB uses a due-process procedure in its standard-setting process to ensure that governmental reporting issues are studied thoroughly prior to the issuance of its standards and that all interested parties are allowed to participate in the process. Note also that Rule 203 of the AICPA's *Code of Professional Conduct* has been extended to encompass GASB pronouncements.

Shortly after its formation, the GASB issued *Statement No. 1,* "Authoritative Status of NCGA Pronouncements and AICPA Industry Audit Guide." This statement stipulates that all NCGA pronouncements in effect as of June 1984 remain effective until amended or superseded by a subsequent GASB pronouncement. As mentioned, portions of NCGA *Statements 1* and *6* have been superceded by GASB *Statements 1, 5,* and *6.* Between 1984 and 1992, the GASB issued 16 statements. These statements are as follows:

Statement No. 1	"Authoritative Status of NCGA Pronouncements and AICPA Industry Audit Guide."
Statement No. 2	"Financial Reporting of Deferred Compensation Plans Adopted under the Provisions of Internal Revenue Code Section 457."
Statement No. 3	"Deposits with Financial Institutions, Investments (including Repurchase Agreements), and Reverse Repurchase Agreements."
Statement No. 4	"Applicability of FASB Statement No. 87, 'Employers' Accounting for Pensions,' to State and Local Governmental Employers."
Statement No. 5	"Disclosure of Pension Information by Public Employee Retirement Systems and State and Local Governmental Employers."
Statement No. 6	"Accounting and Financial Reporting for Special Assessments."
Statement No. 7	"Advance Refundings Resulting in Defeasance of Debt."
Statement No. 8	"Applicability of FASB Statement No. 93, Recognition of Depreciation by Not-for-Profit Organizations, to Certain State and Local Governmental Entities."
Statement No. 9	"Reporting Cash Flows of Proprietary and Nonexpendable Trust Funds and Governmental Entities That Use Proprietary Fund Accounting."
Statement No. 10	"Accounting and Financial Reporting for Risk Financing and Related Insurance Issues."

Statement No. 11	"Measurement Focus and Basis of Accounting—Governmental Fund Operating Statements."[6]
Statement No. 12	"Disclosure of Information on Postemployment Benefits by State and Local Governmental Employees."
Statement No. 13	"Accounting for Operating Leases with Scheduled Rent Increases."
Statement No. 14	"The Financial Reporting Entity."
Statement No. 15	"Governmental College and University Accounting and Financial Reporting Models."
Statement No. 16	"Accounting for Compensated Balances."

The GASB also has issued several *Interpretations* and *Technical Bulletins* as well as its *Concepts Statement 1*. The pronouncements of the GASB constitute the highest level of authoritative support in the AICPA's state and local governmental accounting GAAP hierarchy. In decreasing order of authoritative support, the remainder of this hierarchy is as follows: (1) pronouncements of the FASB (including APB *Opinions* and CAP *Accounting Research Bulletins* which have not been superceded); (2) pronouncements of other bodies, composed of expert accountants, that follow a due-process procedure (including AICPA audit and accounting guides and *Statements of Position* and pronouncements of hospital, college and university, and nonprofit organization association committees); (3) practices or other pronouncements that are widely recognized as being generally accepted because they represent prevalent practice in a particular industry or the knowledgeable application to specific circumstances of pronouncements that are generally accepted; and (4) other accounting literature (e.g., textbooks and journal articles).[7]

As indicated, NCGA *Statement 1* contains 12 basic principles of accounting for state and local governmental units and remains an important authoritative governmental accounting pronouncement. The effective portions of this statement, along with parts of NCGA *Statement 7*, NCGA *Interpretation 5*, and GASB *Statements No. 5* and *6*, are integrated to form the vast majority of the *Codification's* "Part II. General Principles" and "Part III. Financial Reporting" (see footnote 3). The organization of these sections is based on the 12 basic principles

---

[6] GASB *Statement 11* is a very controversial document. Its effective date is for periods beginning after June 15, 1994. However, under a recently released exposure draft, this date would be extended two years beyond the issuance of a related implementation standard. Nevertheless, this text covers some of the features of GASB *Statement 11* because of their contemporary importance. Also, the problems and exercises of the text are designed to be consistent with both this standard and previously existing governmental accounting principles.

[7] AICPA, "The Auditor's Consideration of Accounting Principles Promulgated by the Governmental Accounting Standards Board: An Interpretation of SAS No. 5 . . . ," *Journal of Accountancy*, December 1984.

established in NCGA *Statement 1*. The following portion of this chapter identifies the 12 basic principles of state and local governmental accounting as summarized in Part II of the *Codification*.[8] We sometimes use footnotes to indicate how recently issued GASB *standards* have modified aspects of these principles. The remaining sections of this chapter and Chapter 21 contain discussions and examples related primarily to the 12 principles.

BASIC PRINCIPLES OF STATE AND LOCAL GOVERNMENTAL ACCOUNTING

The 12 principles of state and local governmental accounting provide the foundation for *fund accounting*—as practiced by these governmental units. The concept of a fund is defined and discussed below. For now, note that a governmental unit can have a variety of funds, depending on the nature of its activities. The 12 principles of fund accounting, as summarized in Part II of the *Codification*, are presented below. *Some of the terminology, and so forth, of governmental accounting is likely to be unfamiliar to you. Thus, we suggest that you acquaint yourself with the 12 principles by reading through them initially without being overly concerned if you fail to understand them completely. You can refer back to the principles when we discuss the concepts of governmental accounting subsequently.*

Accounting and Reporting Capabilities

.101   A governmental accounting system must make it possible both: (a) to present fairly and with full disclosure the financial position and results of financial operations of the funds and account groups of the governmental unit in conformity with generally accepted accounting principles and (b) to determine and demonstrate compliance with finance-related legal and contractual provisions.

Fund Accounting Systems

.102   Governmental accounting systems should be organized and operated on a fund basis. A *fund* is defined as a fiscal and accounting entity with a self-balancing set of accounts recording cash and other financial resources, together with all related liabilities and residual equities or balances, and changes therein, which are

---

[8] With few exceptions, the remainder of the effective state and local governmental accounting pronouncements is beyond the scope of this text. Detailed discussions of the remaining pronouncements and related techniques are found in texts devoted exclusively to the subject of governmental accounting. See, for example, Leon E. Hay and Earl R. Wilson, *Accounting for Governmental and Nonprofit Entities* (Homewood, IL: Richard D. Irwin, 1992).

segregated for the purpose of carrying on specific activities or attaining certain objectives in accordance with special regulations, restrictions, or limitations.

Types of Funds

.103   The following types of funds should be used by state and local governments:

a. Governmental funds

(1) *The general fund*—to account for all financial resources except those required to be accounted for in another fund.

(2) *Special revenue funds*—to account for the proceeds of specific revenue sources (other than expendable trusts or for major capital projects) that are legally restricted to expenditure for specified purposes.

(3) *Capital projects funds*—to account for financial resources to be used for the acquisition or construction of major capital facilities (other than those financed by proprietary funds and trust funds).

(4) *Debt service funds*—to account for the accumulation of resources for, and the payment of, general long-term debt principal and interest.

b. Proprietary Funds

(1) *Enterprise funds*—to account for operations (a) that are financed and operated in a manner similar to private business enterprises—where the intent of the governing body is that the costs (expenses, including depreciation) of providing goods or services to the general public on a continuing basis be financed or recovered primarily through user charges; or (b) where the governing body has decided that periodic determination of revenues earned, expenses incurred, and/or net income is appropriate for capital maintenance, public policy, management control, accountability, or other purposes.

(2) *Internal service funds*—to account for the financing of goods or services provided by one department or agency to other departments or agencies of the governmental unit, or to other governmental units, on a cost-reimbursement basis.

c. Fiduciary funds

(1) *Trust and agency funds*—to account for assets held by a governmental unit in a trustee capacity or as an agent for individuals, private organizations, other governmental units, and/or other funds. These include (a) expendable trust funds, (b) nonexpendable trust funds, (c) pension trust funds, and (d) agency funds.[9]

---

[9] GASB *Statement 6* eliminates special assessment funds from the list of types of funds for which financial statements are prepared under GAAP. Previously, these funds were classified as governmental funds. Nevertheless, financial reports still have to be prepared for these funds in some jurisdictions for purposes of legal compliance. See Chapter 21 for further discussion of special assessment funds. Also, see Chapter 21 for detailed discussion of the funds mentioned above, except the general fund.

Number of Funds

.104   Governmental units should establish and maintain those funds required by law and sound financial administration. Only the minimum number of funds consistent with legal and operating requirements should be established, however, because unnecessary funds result in inflexibility, undue complexity, and inefficient financial administration.

Accounting for Fixed Assets and Long-Term Liabilities

.105   A clear distinction should be made between (a) fund fixed assets and general fixed assets and (b) fund long-term liabilities and general long-term debt.

a. Fixed assets related to specific proprietary funds or trust funds should be accounted for through those funds. All other fixed assets of a governmental unit should be accounted for through the general fixed assets account group.
b. Long-term liabilities of proprietary funds and trust funds should be accounted for through those funds. All other unmatured general long-term liabilities of the governmental unit, including special assessment debt for which the government is obligated in some manner, should be accounted for through the general long-term debt account group.

Valuation of Fixed Assets

.106   Fixed assets should be accounted for at cost or, if the cost is not practicably determinable, at estimated cost. Donated fixed assets should be recorded at their estimated fair value at the time received.

Depreciation of Fixed Assets

.107

a. Depreciation of general fixed assets should not be recorded in the accounts of governmental funds. Depreciation of general fixed assets may be recorded in cost accounting systems or calculated for cost finding analyses, and accumulated depreciation may be recorded in the general fixed assets account group.
b. Depreciation of fixed assets accounted for in a proprietary fund should be recorded in the accounts of that fund. Depreciation is also recognized in those trust funds where expenses, net income, and/or capital maintenance are measured.

Accrual Basis in Governmental Accounting

.108   The modified accrual or accrual basis of accounting, as appropriate, should be utilized in measuring financial position and operating results.

a. *Governmental fund* revenues and expenditures should be recognized on the modified accrual basis. Revenues should be recognized in the accounting period in which they become available and measurable.[10] Expenditures should be recognized in the accounting period in which the fund liability is incurred, if measurable, except for unmatured interest on general long-term debt, which should be recognized when due.

b. *Proprietary fund* revenues and expenses should be recognized on the accrual basis. Revenues should be recognized in the accounting period in which they are earned and become measurable; expenses should be recognized in the period incurred, if measurable.

c. *Fiduciary fund* revenues and expenses or expenditures (as appropriate) should be recognized on the basis consistent with the fund's accounting measurement objective. Nonexpendable trust and pension trust funds should be accounted for on the accrual basis; expendable trust funds should be accounted for on the modified accrual basis. Agency fund assets and liabilities should be accounted for on the modified accrual basis.

d. *Transfers* should be recognized in the accounting period in which the interfund receivable and payable arise.

Budgeting, Budgetary Control, and Budgetary Reporting

.109

a. An annual budget(s) should be adopted by every governmental unit.

b. The accounting system should provide the basis for appropriate budgetary control.

c. Budgetary comparisons should be included in the appropriate financial statements and schedules for governmental funds for which an annual budget has been adopted.

Transfer Revenue, Expenditure, and Expense Account Classification

.110

a. Interfund transfers and proceeds of general long-term debt issues should be classified separately from fund revenues and expenditures or expenses.

b. Governmental fund revenues should be classified by fund and source. Expenditures should be classified by fund, function (or program), organization unit, activity, character, and principal classes of objects.

---

[10] GASB *Statement 11,* in effect, eliminates the phrases *modified accrual basis* and *available and measurable,* for governmental funds. Under this pronouncement, these funds are accounted for using a version of the accrual basis.

c. Proprietary fund revenues and expenses should be classified in essentially the same manner as those of similar business organizations, functions, or activities.

Common Terminology and Classification

.111   A common terminology and classification should be used consistently throughout the budget, the accounts, and the financial reports of each fund.

Interim and Annual Financial Reports

.112

a. Appropriate interim financial statements and reports of financial position, operating results, and other pertinent information should be prepared to facilitate management control of financial operations, legislative oversight, and, where necessary or desired, for external reporting purposes.

b. A comprehensive annual financial report covering all funds and account groups of the reporting entity—including introductory section; appropriate combined, combining, and individual fund statements; notes to the financial statements; required supplementary information; schedules; narrative explanations; and statistical tables—should be prepared and published. The reporting entity is the oversight unit and all other component units are combined in accordance with Section 2100, "Defining the Reporting Entity."

c. General-purpose financial statements of the reporting entity may be issued separately from the comprehensive annual financial report. Such statements should include the basic financial statements and notes to the financial statements that are essential to fair presentation of financial position and operating results (and changes in financial position of proprietary funds and similar trust funds). Those statements may also be required to be accompanied by required supplementary information, essential to financial reporting of certain entities.

d. A component unit financial report covering all funds and account groups of a component unit—including introductory section; appropriate combined, combining, and individual fund statements; notes to the financial statements; schedules; narrative explanations; and statistical tables—may be prepared and published, as necessary.

e. Component unit financial statements of a component unit may be issued separately from the component unit financial report. Such statements should include the basic financial statements and notes to the financial statements that are essential to the fair presentation of financial position and results of operations (and changes in financial position of proprietary funds and similar trust funds). Those statements may also be required to be accompanied by required supplementary information, essential to financial reporting of certain entities.

GENERAL CONCEPTS RELATED TO GOVERNMENTAL FUND ACCOUNTING

As indicated, a fund is, among other things, a fiscal and accounting entity that is authorized to carry on specific activities or to attain certain objectives in accordance with special regulations, restrictions, or limitations. For example, the *general fund* of a state or local governmental unit is authorized to administer the resources of the unit used in its general operations and in providing traditional services (e.g., police protection, fire protection, and street maintenance). Another example of a fund is a *special revenue fund*. Special revenue funds administer resources that are required by law, policy, or contractual agreement to be used in accomplishing specific purposes (e.g., operating a school district or a park system).[11] This section discusses several important concepts related to governmental fund accounting to provide a basis for examining the procedures used in accounting for the general fund as well as the funds and account groups considered in Chapter 21. The concepts covered are related to the 12 basic principles identified above and pertain to the reporting entity in general; funds and fund accounting in general; appropriations, allotments, and apportionments; general fixed assets and general long-term debt account groups; budgetary and encumbrance accounting; the various measurement focuses; the accrual and the modified accrual bases of accounting; intergovernmental revenues; and financial reporting. *Most subheading in this portion of the chapter contains a reference to the principle(s) which we believe you should read again in studying the contents of the section.*

The Governmental Reporting Entity (Principle .112)

Under the interim and annual financial reports principle, the financial reporting entity of a state or local governmental unit is the "oversight unit" (which is a component unit, itself) and all related "component units." In this context, the oversight unit is the unit which exercises oversight authority over the other component units, and the remaining units are governmental agencies, activities, organizations, and functions responsible to a single set of elected officials (*Cod.* 2100). The oversight unit generally is the primary unit of a government that is directly responsible to its chief executive and legislative body.

GASB *Statement 14* updates the concept of the financial reporting entity. This pronouncement defines the financial reporting entity as consisting of (1) the primary government, (2) organizations for which the primary government is financially accountable, and (3) other organizations whose relationships with the primary government are such that their exclusion would cause the reporting

---

[11] As shown in Chapter 21, the accounting procedures for special revenue funds usually parallel those of the general fund.

entity's financial statements to be misleading or incomplete. The major characteristic of a primary government is that it has a separately elected governing body. In this context, a primary government is any state government or general-purpose local government (i.e., a municipal or county government). A primary government also can be a special-purpose government (e.g., a school or park district), provided that it meets the criteria established by the GASB—including the existence of a separately elected body, legal separability, and fiscal independence. The financial data of the primary government and its component units are reported in accordance with the provisions of *Cod.* 2200 (and .112—which is under discussion).

A component unit, under GASB *Statement 14,* is a legally separate organization for which the elected officials of the primary government are financially accountable and any other organization whose relationship with the primary government is such that exclusion would cause the reporting entity's financial statements to be misleading or incomplete (e.g., governmental colleges and universities, governmental hospitals, and a variety of other organizations affiliated with governmental units). Component units are included in the reporting procedures of the financial reporting entity by "discrete presentation." That is, such units are reported in columns separate from that of the primary government. Note also that some component units are "blended" component units (e.g., a city redevelopment authority whose board members are essentially the same as the elected officials of the primary government) and that the GASB identifies criteria for identifying such units. These units, even though legally separate from the primary government, are so intertwined with this body that they are, in substance, part of the body and, consequently, their balances and transactions are reported in a manner consistent with those of this body. We emphasize that many of the subtleties of governmental financial reporting are not within the scope of this text. Thus, the illustrated financial statements and so on ignore topics such as blended component units.

Funds and Fund Accounting in General (Principles .101–.104)

Accounting is, among other things, the process by which the transactions of, and events affecting, entities are recorded, classified, summarized, and reported to users. Partnerships, corporations, and (corporate) affiliations are examples of profit-seeking entities to which the accounting process is applied. In governmental accounting, the primary accounting focus is the fund. Just as profit-oriented entities are accounted for separately from their legal owners, funds of governmental units are accounted for separately from those who provide their resources. Thus, the governmental accounting process summarizes, classifies, records, and reports the transactions and so on of individual funds viewed as separate entities.

The transactions of governmental units include, among other things, *revenue* transactions, *expenditure* transactions, and *expense* transactions. There is an important distinction between expenditures and expenses in governmental accounting. As explained more fully below, the focus is on accounting for financial resources expended (expenditures) for certain types of funds, and the emphasis is on accounting for expenses, including depreciation expense, for other types of funds.[12] In either case, the governmental accounting process classifies transactions consistently with the service efforts of the fund because of the service-oriented nature of governmental activities. Although the general fund invariably administers various activities, separate funds (e.g., a special revenue fund) often are utilized to record the transactions related to specific governmental activities. Each specific activity has its own particular underlying objectives. The specific activity and its objectives usually are based on special regulations, restrictions, or limitations, since the fund is a fiscal entity authorized by law to raise revenues and make expenditures. The set of accounts used in recording the transactions of each fund is self-balancing and may contain both *proprietary* and *budgetary* accounts. The proprietary accounts of funds are similar to the accounts of profit-seeking entities and include accounts such as revenues, expenditures (or expenses), assets, liabilities, allowances, reserves, and residual equities. The budgetary accounts of funds include estimated revenues and appropriations accounts. All of these accounts are discussed below.

Although funds are classified in a variety of ways (see principle .103 especially), the distinction between *expendable* and *nonexpendable* funds is important initially. An expendable fund is a fund whose resources can be expended in their entirety in achieving the objectives of the fund. The revenues of such a fund usually come from taxes, fees, licenses, permits, the provision of services, special assessments, proceeds of bond issues, interfund and intergovernmental transfers, and miscellaneous service charges. Common expendable fund expenditures include those for the services of employees and others, materials and supplies consumed, and fixed assets. Since the fixed asset purchases of an expendable fund are classified as expenditures, *fixed assets are not included in the assets of such a fund*. Important examples of expendable funds are general funds, special revenue funds, capital projects funds, and debt service funds (i.e., the funds classified as governmental funds in principle .103). Another example of an expendable fund is a trust fund established to expend the revenue, and principal if necessary, of an endowment provided by a donor for some specific purpose. A nonexpendable fund differs from an expendable fund in that its principal, or capital balance, is supposed to be preserved intact. Enterprise and internal service funds (i.e., the funds classified as proprietary funds in principle .103), which are meant to be managed so that they generate revenues sufficient to cover their operating expenses, are the primary examples of nonexpendable funds. Another

---

[12] In the remaining discussions of this chapter, our examples and so on emphasize funds for which the focus is on accounting for expenditures. We adopt this approach because the emphasis in accounting for the general fund is on expenditures. Nevertheless, much of what we say also applies to funds for which the emphasis is on accounting for expenses. Note also that expenditures generate expenses; thus, it also is proper to refer to the expenditures of a fund when the emphasis is on accounting for expenses.

example of a nonexpendable fund is a trust fund established to invest the endowment provided by a donor and use the related income for a particular purpose. This chapter emphasizes the accounting procedures for expendable funds since the general fund is an expendable fund. The procedures used in accounting for various types of nonexpendable funds, as well as additional expendable funds, are covered in Chapter 21.

Appropriations, Allotments, and Apportionments

Appropriations are the amounts of resources that can be expended by a fund on various specific activities (e.g., wages and salaries) in a given budget period (or fiscal period) as specified in its budget. The fund's total appropriation is the maximum amount it can expend during the period on all activities. Understanding the nature of appropriations is extremely important in dealing with the budgetary accounting procedures of governmental units. These procedures are explained in a subsequent section.

Allotments (state and local governments) and *apportionments* (federal government) are internal allocations of appropriations over subintervals of the budget period. They represent partial releases of appropriations for these intervals by the legislative or administrative body and are used in controlling expenditures. This type of control is designed to prevent over expenditure in the early part of the budget period; the goal is to eliminate the need for deficiency appropriations that might otherwise be required at the end of the period. When the number of administrative levels within a governmental unit is large (as, for example, in the federal government), both the terms, *allotment* and *apportionment,* may be used to describe the allocation process at different levels of the unit.

General Fixed Assets and General Long-Term Debt Account Groups (Principles .105–.107)

The fixed assets and long-term debts of proprietary and trust funds are accounted for in these funds. All other fixed assets and long-term debts of governmental units (i.e., their general fixed assets and general long-term debts) are accounted for in their *general fixed assets* and *general long-term debt account groups*. These account groups are self-balancing groups of accounts which provide (primarily) cost-based records of the unit's general fixed assets and general long-term debt. They differ from funds since, among other things, they do not represent fiscal entities with specific objectives and purposes. Accumulated depreciation may be recorded in the general fixed assets account group, although it is not recorded, for example, in the accounts of governmental funds (*Cod.* 1100.107). Depreciation expense and accumulated depreciation both are recorded in the accounts of proprietary funds. Further discussion of the general fixed assets and general long-term debt account groups and depreciation accounting for governmental units is provided in Chapter 21.

Budgetary and Encumbrance Accounting (Principle .109)

Authority for the operation of a fund related to a specific activity, or set of objectives, is provided formally when a legislature or city council adopts its *budget*. The budget is utilized for both planning and control purposes. Before adoption, the budget provides a basis for planning since it contains estimates of anticipated expenditures for specific items during a given period, or for a set of objectives, as well as identification of estimated revenues and related sources. Once the budget is adopted, the estimated expenditures become appropriations (i.e., the amounts that can be spent on specific items). At this time, the budget is transformed into a control device since it reflects mandated legal ceilings on expenditures and, therefore, is instrumental in prohibiting excess expenditures on items for which appropriations exist.

In governmental accounting, the authorized budget often is recognized formally in special *budgetary accounts* (i.e., the estimated revenues and appropriations accounts). These accounts constitute a formal record of the governmental unit's financial plan. In contrast, the unit's *proprietary accounts* (i.e., its revenue, expenditure (or expense), asset, liability, allowance, reserve, and residual equity accounts) are used in recording its *actual transactions*. Governmental units also may use *encumbrance* accounts to reveal the total future expenditures expected because of existing commitments (see next paragraph). Control is achieved using the balances in related budgetary, proprietary, and encumbrance accounts. For example, if year-end is near and the balance in the budgetary account, Estimated Revenues, exceeds the related balance in the proprietary account, Revenues, and all the revenues for the year have been recorded, a shortfall (deficit) may occur unless anticipated expenditures are reduced sufficiently to compensate for the difference. Likewise, an excess of expenditures over appropriations can be avoided by comparing the balance in the budgetary account, Appropriations, (which reflects authorized *total* expenditures) with the sum of the balances in the proprietary account, Expenditures (which reveals actual total expenditures to date), and the Encumbrances account (which reveals total committed expected future expenditures). As shown later, the procedures used in closing budgetary and certain proprietary accounts create a permanent record of the differences between budgeted and actual data. Note, however, that budgetary accounting is directed primarily at controlling the total expenditures of each fund, rather than at promoting efficiency. Additional analyses and controls are needed to promote efficiency in the sense provided by a standard cost system—which would allow comparisons of the standard costs of a fund's service accomplishments with the actual costs of these accomplishments.

As implied above, expenditure control is enhanced through the use of an *encumbrance system,* which reveals the fund's total future expenditures expected because of existing orders and contracts. In such a system, the account, Encumbrances, is debited and the account, Reserve for Encumbrances, is credited for the expected amount of an order or contract. Once the order or contract is satisfied and its actual amount is known, the entry for the encumbrance is reversed, and the actual expenditure is recorded in the proprietary accounts. Commitments for salaries and wages, bond interest, and other recurring expenditures usually are not encumbered when their payment is imminent.

Measurement Focus and Accrual Accounting (Principles .108 and .110)

Three measurement focuses (or objectives) exist in governmental accounting. The applicable measurement focuses pending the implementation of GASB *Statement 11* are: the *proprietary* (or businesslike) *measurement focus* and the *governmental measurement* focus. The former applies to proprietary funds, nonexpendable trust funds, and pension trust funds (see footnote 7 in Chapter 21) and encompasses *accrual accounting* procedures; the latter pertains to governmental funds, expendable trust funds, and agency funds and reflects the *modified accrual basis* of accounting. When implemented, GASB *Statement 11* will replace the governmental measurement focus with the *flow of financial resources measurement focus*. The latter also encompasses a version of accrual accounting. Among other things, the primary differences in the versions of accrual accounting related to the three focuses are discussed below. This discussion tends to emphasize GASB *Statement 11* because it reflects the most current thinking concerning the applicability of accrual accounting in governmental accounting. We emphasize again, however, that the implementation date of this statement is uncertain.

Under the proprietary measurement focus, accrual basis accounting implies that revenues and expenses are recognized and matched consistently with the financial accounting principles pertaining to business entities. Thus, this process includes, for example, the recognition of depreciation expense and the expensing of prepaid items and inventory when consumed (i.e., the use of what is referred to as the *consumption method in fund accounting*). As indicated, proprietary funds and fiduciary funds with a proprietary measurement focus (i.e., nonexpendable trust funds and pension trust funds) are accounted for using this version of accrual accounting. Accrual accounting is used in this context primarily to promote governmental operating efficiency rather than to produce the best possible measure of income.

As indicated, the modified accrual basis is used under the governmental measurement focus. Here, the general revenue recognition principle is that revenues are recognized in the period in which they become available and measurable. They generally are considered to be available if they are collectible within, or shortly after, the period. Also, depreciation expense is not recorded, and prepaid items and inventories may be accounted for using either the consumption or *purchases* methods. Using the latter, the costs of items acquired are considered to be expenditures in the period acquired. Under the modified accrual basis, revenues available to finance expenditures are matched with the related expenditures thus emphasizing control over planned revenues and expenditures.

GASB *Statement 11* considers the phrase *financial resources* as encompassing cash, claims to cash (e.g., debt securities and receivables), claims to goods and services (e.g., prepaid insurance), consumable goods (e.g., materials and supplies inventories), and marketable equity securities obtained or controlled as a result of past transactions or events. Under the flow of financial resources measurement focus, accrual accounting, which is applied to governmental funds and fiduciary funds having this focus (i.e., expendable trust funds and agency funds), emphasizes the matching of certain financial resources obtained during the period (governmental fund revenues) and related claims against financial resources incurred during the period (governmental fund expenditures). In general, this focus deemphasizes the timing of the receipt of cash.

Governmental fund *revenues* are increases in financial resources resulting from taxation and certain other nonexchange transactions and events (e.g., fines, fees, licenses and permits, and donations) and exchange transactions and events (e.g., charges for services and receipts related to investments and operating leases). Governmental fund *expenditures* encompass decreases in financial resources resulting from operating, capital, and debt-service expenditures related to operating debt. Most important, *operating expenditures* are decreases in financial resources resulting from claims against these resources arising from transactions and events other than capital asset acquisitions; general long-term, capital debt service; operating and residual equity transfers out; and other transactions reported as other financial uses. Note that the term *expenditures* as used here, does not encompass depreciation expense; thus, funds having a flow of financial resources measurement focus do not record depreciation expense.[13]

Ultimately, the flow of financial resources measurement focus is meant to provide a measure of *interperiod equity* reflecting the extent to which financial resources obtained during the period are sufficient to cover claims incurred against such resources during the period.[14] The governmental-fund-related notion of a measure of interperiod equity is roughly analogous to the business-related concept of a measure of net income. In this context, it emphasizes operating results, although not profitability.

GASB *Statement 11* requires two factors to be present for the recognition of *tax revenues* (which are considered to arise from nonexchange confiscatory transactions): (1) the underlying revenue-generating transaction or event has occurred (e.g., the use of properties over the pertinent period in the case of property taxes) and (2) there is a demand for the taxes as evidenced by the existence of a due date on or before the end of the period.[15] Revenues related to nonexchange transactions other than taxes (e.g., fines, fees for licenses and

---

[13] The treatment of depreciation expense is the major expenditures-related difference in the proprietary and flow of financial resources focuses.

[14] The major conceptual difference between this version of accrual accounting and the modified accrual method is that the former recognizes the financial effects of transactions or events even though their direct cash effects may not be felt until well into the future, while the latter focuses primarily on cash effects occurring during the year or shortly thereafter.

[15] Taxpayer-assessed taxes with a due date within two months after the end of the period are considered to have been demanded by the end of the period to allow for "administrative lead time."

permits, and donations) are recognized, in general, when the underlying revenue-generating events occur and the governmental unit has enforceable claims to assets, irrespective of when the related cash is received. The GASB's basic criterion for the recognition of revenues related to exchange transactions (e.g., those from charges for services, investments, and operating leases) is that the revenues must have been earned—where *earned* means that the governmental entity has performed its responsibilities related to the transactions. In this context, the receipt of cash again is not the governing factor in determining when revenue is earned.

Cash effects also are deemphasized in accounting for expenditures under the flow of financial resources version of accrual accounting. That is, operating expenditures (e.g., expenditures for salaries and utilities), capital expenditures (e.g., expenditures for capital assets acquired through purchase, construction, and capital lease), and debt-service expenditures related to operating debt (e.g., issue costs paid out of debt proceeds, attorney and rating agency fees, bond insurance, and interest expense at the effective rate) generally are recognized when the transactions or events resulting in claims against financial resources occur, regardless on when cash is disbursed.[16] Note that the proceeds and repayments of operating debt do not have operating statement effects (e.g., the reporting of the proceeds of such debt as another financing source).

In applying each of the three accrual bases of accounting, distinctions between transfers to and from funds (i.e., *interfund transfers*), which do and do not constitute revenues and expenditures, are needed. One class of interfund transfer is the operating transfer—including *operating transfers in* and *operating transfers out*. Operating transfers in and out are routine, frequently occurring transfers between funds required by law. For example, state law may require that taxes collected by one fund be used to accomplish the purposes of another fund. Thus, the first fund must transfer resources to the second fund. In recording such a transfer, a debit to Operating Transfers Out (an "expenditure-related" account) is made by the first fund, and a credit to Operating Transfers In (a "revenue-related" account) is made by the second fund. A second class of interfund transfer is the *quasi-external transaction*. Such a transaction involves a receipt (disbursement), or related accrual, which would be considered to be a revenue (expenditure) if the transaction were with an entity external to the governmental unit (e.g., a billing to or from an internal service fund—a proprietary fund). Accordingly, quasi-external transactions are recorded by crediting Revenues or debiting Expenditures. Another class of interfund transfer is the *reimbursement*. A reim-

---

[16] *Operating debt* is debt that is expected to be repaid from the resources of governmental funds and is unrelated to the acquisition of capital assets (including infrastructure) (e.g., revenue and tax anticipation notes and short-term and long-term debt issued to finance operations). *General long-term capital debt* (or general long-term debt) is debt that is expected to be paid using the resources of governmental funds and is related to (1) the acquisition of capital assets (including infrastructure) or (2) certain nonrecurring projects or activities that have long-term economic benefits (e.g., a toxic waste cleanup).

bursement is a transfer by one fund to another to repay the latter for an expenditure undertaken on behalf of the first. Thus, reimbursements are recorded as expenditures by the fund making the transfer and as reductions in expenditures by the fund receiving the transfer. A fourth class of transfer is the *residual equity transfer*—which is made to establish and eliminate funds. Such transfers are recorded as residual equity transfers in and residual equity transfers out. The more frequently encountered types of interfund transfers are illustrated in Chapters 20 and 21.

Intergovernmental Revenues

Intergovernmental revenues include *grants, entitlements, shared revenues,* and *payments in lieu of taxes.* The first three types of intergovernmental revenues are defined as follows (*Cod.* G60.501–505):

> .501 **Capital grant.**   A contribution or gift of cash or other assets restricted by the grantor for the acquisition or construction of fixed (capital) assets.
>
> .502 **Entitlement.**   The amount of payment to which a state or local government is entitled as determined by the federal or other government (for example, the Director of the Office of Revenue Sharing) pursuant to an allocation formula contained in applicable statutes.
>
> .503 **Grant.**   A contribution or gift of cash or other assets from another government to be used or expended for a specified purpose, activity, or facility.
>
> .504 **Shared Revenue.**   A revenue levied by one government but shared on a predetermined basis, often in proportion to the amount collected at the local level, with another government or class of government.

The definition of a grant encompasses capital grants. Grants other than capital grants are called *operating grants* (e.g., a grant for the operation of a social welfare program such as a food stamp program). The main difference between entitlements and shared revenues is the nature of the amounts being allocated. Entitlements are portions of fixed, appropriated amounts of resources, such as federal or state revenue-sharing appropriations. Shared revenues are portions of federal or state revenues that vary from period to period (e.g., gasoline, sales, and liquor taxes). Payments in lieu of taxes are amounts paid to one government by another government to reimburse the former for lost revenues because the latter does not pay taxes (e.g., property taxes).

Unrestricted grants, entitlements, shared revenues, and payments in lieu of taxes are recognized consistently with the above discussions of accrual basis accounting. Thus, the unrestricted intergovernmental revenues of proprietary funds and trust funds with a proprietary measurement focus are recorded using the accrual basis—with credits to nonoperating revenue accounts or contributed equity accounts, depending on whether the revenues are for unrestricted use or are restricted to the acquisition or construction of fixed assets. Similarly, the unrestricted intergovernmental revenues of governmental funds, agency funds, and trust funds with a governmental measurement focus are recorded under modified accrual procedures. *Restricted* grants, entitlements, shared revenues, and payments in lieu of taxes are recorded upon receipt as deferred revenues and are recognized as revenues when expenditures related to their intended purposes occur. Similarly, if the use of intergovernmental revenues requires compliance with legal requirements (e.g., cost sharing and matching requirements), the revenues are recorded upon receipt as deferred revenues and are recognized once the legal restrictions are satisfied.

Financial Reporting (Principles .111 and .112)

Three types of financial statements are used in reporting for state and local governments: *individual fund and account group statements, combining fund statements,* and *combined fund and account group statements.* Individual fund and account group financial statements report on the financial positions and operating results of individual funds and account groups. These statements, which are related to the component units of the reporting entity, are referred to as *component unit financial statements* (CUFS). They often are prepared on a standard comparative basis or provide comparisons between actual and budgeted data. Combining fund statements present financial data for all funds of a particular type (e.g., special revenue funds) in adjacent columns along with an all-funds total column. Combined fund and account group statements, which pertain to the reporting entity itself, are similar to combining fund statements, except that each statement of this type usually (1) contains a column for the financial data of each pertinent *type* of fund or account group (e.g., the all-funds total column from the combining funds statement for special revenue funds) or (2) contains a column for each relevant fund or account group. These statements also present memorandum totals for all funds combined; however, note that the effects of interfund transactions (including interfund receivables and payables) are not eliminated in arriving at these totals. Combined fund and account group statements are referred to as the *general-purpose financial statements* (GPFS) of governmental units (i.e., the reporting entities). For funds with a governmental measurement focus, the individual financial statements encompassed by the phrase *general-purpose financial statements* are (1) the balance sheet and (2) the statement of revenues, expenditures, and changes in fund balance (often with comparisons of actual and budgeted data).[17] For funds with a proprietary measurement objective, this phrase encompasses: (1) the balance sheet, (2) the statement of revenues, expenses, and changes in retained earnings (or fund balance in the case of pension trust funds), and (3) the statement of cash flows (except for pension trust funds).[18] We focus on

---

[17] Comparisons of actual and budgeted data are required for all funds which budget on an annual basis. General funds and special revenue funds almost always budget annually.

[18] GASB *Statement No. 9* requires the statement of cash flows for fiscal years beginning after December 15, 1989. Previously, the statement of changes in financial position was required. This standard also indicates that pension trust funds no longer are required to present a statement of changes in financial position and are not required to present a statement of cash flows.

the preparation of individual fund financial statements for the general fund (i.e., a fund with a governmental measurement focus) in this chapter.

As indicated in the 12th basic principle, each state and local governmental unit (i.e. reporting entity) is required to prepare a comprehensive annual financial report (CAFR). A CAFR includes the governmental unit's GPFS, combining fund statements, and individual fund and account group statements as well as related notes, supplementary schedules, narrative explanations, and statistical tables. Note that a governmental unit also may issue its GPFS (including related notes and so on) separately from its CAFR for users not requiring the detail provided by the latter.[19] We provide a comprehensive example of a governmental unit's GPFS in Chapter 21 (i.e., excluding related notes and so on). In summary, the reporting entity's CAFR and GPFS both usually encompass the following combined statements and related notes:

1. A combined balance sheet for all funds and account groups.

2. A combined statement of revenues, expenditures, and changes in fund balances for all governmental funds (with budgeted and actual values for general and special revenue funds and other similar funds with legally adopted budgets) and expendable trust funds.

3. A combined statement of revenues, expenses, and changes in retained earnings (or fund balance for pension trust funds) for all proprietary funds, nonexpendable trust funds, and pension trust funds.

4. A combined statement of cash flows for all proprietary funds and nonexpendable trust funds.

ACCOUNTING FOR THE GENERAL FUND—BASIC CONSIDERATIONS

As mentioned, the resources of the general fund of a state or local governmental unit are those used in the unit's general administration and in providing traditional services. In other words, the resources of a general fund are those that are not restricted for use in serving specific purposes and are not required to be accounted for in another fund. The general fund also is referred to as the *operating,* or *current, fund.* Many of the current operations of governmental units are financed by their general funds. Accordingly, various sources provide revenue for, and a wide range of activities are financed by, such funds. The primary revenue sources of general funds are taxes (e.g., property, sales, and income); licenses and permits; fines, penalties, and forfeits; and fees. Typical expenditures of general funds are those related to the services provided by fire, police, and sanitation

---

[19] Governmental units also may issue component unit financial reports and financial statements separately from their CAFRs. For discussion, see principle .112 and texts devoted exclusively to the subject of governmental accounting.

departments and those related to administrative and clerical activities. Additionally, general funds often finance capital outlays. In illustrating general fund accounting, we focus on recording the general fund's budget, recording its actual transactions, recording its encumbrances, closing its accounts (i.e., budgetary, encumbrances, and certain proprietary accounts), recording its nonencumbrance-related reserves and fund balance designations, and preparing its financial statements. Although we tend to emphasize general fund accounting for municipalities, the techniques illustrated apply with equal force to the general funds of other general-purpose governments.

Recording the Budget and a First Look at Closing Entries

The first step in accounting for the general fund is to record its budget in its budgetary accounts as follows:

Revenues	200,000	
Estimated Revenues		200,000
Appropriations	198,000	
Expenditures		198,000

The $198,000 credit to Appropriations implies that the governmental unit is authorized to spend a maximum of $198,000 in conducting the operations of its general fund. The $200,000 debit to Estimated Revenues records the budgetary estimate of $200,000 of revenues from sources such as property taxes, services, licenses, fees, and permits. The difference between these two amounts—the estimated increase in the fund balance (or estimated increase in residual equity)—is credited to Fund Balance. We emphasize that Estimated Revenues is debited and Appropriations is credited in the above entry. The entries to these accounts are recorded opposite to the way actual revenues and expenditures are recorded in *proprietary* accounts—by crediting revenues and debiting expenditures. In any case, the budgetary amounts are recorded for control purposes. More specifically, they are recorded to control actual expenditures so that a fund deficit is avoided. That is, as actual expenditures and encumbrances are made and actual revenues are earned, the Expenditures and Encumbrances accounts are debited and the Revenues account is credited. Throughout the period, total actual expenditures and encumbrances are compared with appropriations (the legal ceiling on expenditures) to ensure that expenditures do not ultimately exceed the maximum allowed. Similarly, actual and estimated revenues are compared to determine whether the budget is on target from the revenue perspective.

Consistent with the control procedures just described, the closing process in governmental accounting discloses differences in revenues and estimated revenues and expenditures and appropriations for further anlaysis. This process is introduced below assuming there are no differences in actual and estimated revenues and in expenditures and appropriations. In this simplified case, the closing entries, which do not affect the fund balance of $2,000, are as follows:

Revenues	200,000	
Estimated Revenues		200,000
Appropriations	198,000	
Expenditures		198,000

These entries reveal that the Budgetary, Revenues, and Expenditures accounts of a general fund are closed during the closing process. Note that if revenues exceed estimated revenues, the Fund Balance account is increased by the difference in these two amounts (with opposite results produced if estimated revenues exceed revenues). Similarly, if appropriations exceed expenditures, Fund Balance is increased by the difference (with opposite results occurring if expenditures exceed appropriations). Thus, as mentioned, differences in revenues and estimated revenues and expenditures and appropriations are highlighted in the closing process for further analysis.

Recording Actual Transactions

The general fund is accounted for currently using the modified accrual basis. Recall that under this basis: (1) depreciation expense is not recorded and (2) the consumption method may be used in accounting for prepaid items and materials and supplies inventories. Also recall that account groups for general fixed assets and general long-term debts are used to account for such assets and debts (i.e., the fixed assets and long-term debts of the unit that are not assignable to proprietary or trust funds) in governmental accounting systems. We emphasize that these items do not appear in the general fund accounts. Thus, for example, the purchase of a fixed asset through the general fund is accounted for as an expenditure.

In accounting for the general fund, its actual transactions are recorded in its proprietary accounts—its Revenue, Expenditure, Asset, Liability, Allowance, Reserve, Residual Equity, and so on, accounts. All of these accounts are general ledger accounts, and many of them (e.g., Revenues and Expenditures) are summary (or control) accounts which are supported by subsidiary ledger accounts that reveal their details. Note also that the fund's revenues and expenditures (as well as encumbrances) are classified by function (e.g., police, fire, and sanitation services). Functional classification allows comparisons of specific revenues and expenditures (and encumbrances) with their related budgeted amounts (which also are classified by function). The comparisons between expended (and encumbered) and appropriated amounts are especially important because they reveal the degree of compliance with the legally mandated maximum amounts that can be spent on specific items. Note that it is illegal to spend more than the amount appropriated for a given functional item unless authority for excess expenditure is obtained.

To begin illustrating the recording of general fund transactions in proprietary accounts, assume that property taxes of $150,000 are levied and collectible within, or shortly after, the budget period and that $10,000 of the taxes probably will not be received. Since the taxes satisfy the revenue criteria of the modified accrual basis, they are recorded when levied as follows:

Taxes Receivable	150,000	
Revenues		140,000
Allowance for Uncollectible Taxes		10,000

This entry is similar to the one a profit-seeking entity makes to accrue revenue, except that the allowance for uncollectible accounts is recorded simultaneously. Note that an entry is made in the Property Taxes Revenue account of the revenues subsidiary ledger so that the detail of the revenues recognized during the period is preserved.

A problem that arises in connection with tax revenues is delinquent taxes. The first step in dealing with such taxes is to transfer the amount of the delinquent taxes to the Taxes Receivable—Delinquent account and to transfer the balance in Allowance for Uncollectible Taxes to the Allowance for Uncollectible Taxes—Delinquent account. For example, assume that $20,000 of the taxes recorded above are delinquent at year-end. The entry to record the delinquent taxes is as follows:

Taxes Receivable—Delinquent	20,000	
Allowance for Uncollectible Taxes	10,000	
Taxes Receivable		20,000
Allowance for Uncollectible Taxes—		
Delinquent		10,000

The accounts that eventually are uncollectible are written off against the balance in Allowance for Uncollectible Taxes—Delinquent. If delinquent accounts ultimately are collected, the related portion of the Allowance for Uncollectible Accounts—Delinquent is closed to the Fund Balance account.

Assume next that wages and salaries amounting to $100,000 are payable at the end of December and that they are to be paid during the first week of January. Assume also that this amount has not been recorded as an encumbrance because it will be paid shortly after the end of December. The modified accrual basis entry to record the salaries and wages is shown below.

Expenditures	100,000	
Vouchers Payable		100,000

Similar to the revenue example, an entry is made in the Salaries and Wages Expenditures account of the expenditures subsidiary ledger to maintain the detail of the wages and salaries expenditures for the period. Note that the account title Vouchers Payable often is used in governmental accounting instead of the title Accounts Payable to describe current payables of an operating nature.

Another class of transactions recorded in the proprietary accounts is operating transfers—operating transfers in and operating transfers out. For example, assume that an operating transfer in of $5,000 from a governmental unit's school district fund is authorized and is received shortly thereafter. The pertinent entries are

Due from School District Fund	5,000	
Operating Transfers In		5,000
Cash	5,000	
Due from School District Fund		5,000

To illustrate further, assume an operating transfer out of $10,000 to a governmental unit's debt service fund is authorized and is paid subsequently. The related entries are as follows:

Operating Transfers Out	10,000	
Due to Debt Service Fund		10,000
Due to Debt Service Fund	10,000	
Cash		10,000

For a final introductory example, consider the acquisition of materials and supplies inventory. Recall that inventory may be accounted for using the consumption method under the modified accrual basis. Now, assume that the beginning inventory of materials and supplies under this method is $30,000 and that there is a related beginning-of-period credit balance in Fund Balance Reserved for Materials and Supplies of $30,000 (as explained below). Assume also that $25,000 additional materials and supplies inventory is acquired during the period for cash. The following are the consumption method entries to record this acquisition:

Materials and Supplies	25,000	
Cash		25,000
Fund Balance	25,000	
Fund Balance Reserved for Materials and Supplies		25,000

The second entry identifies the amount of the fund balance that is unavailable for expenditure because inventory has been acquired. At year-end, the following entries are required under the consumption method, assuming the cost of materials and supplies on hand at this time is $20,000:

Expenditures	35,000	
Materials and Supplies		35,000
Fund Balance Reserved for Materials and Supplies	35,000	
Fund Balance		35,000

The first of these entries records the cost of inventory consumed during the period as an expenditure and records the ending inventory of materials and supplies at $20,000 ($30,000 + $25,000 − $35,000). The second entry reduces the balance of Fund Balance Reserved for Materials and Supplies to $20,000 (also $30,000 + $25,000 − $35,000). The balance in this account at year-end identifies the portion of the fund balance, which is unavailable for expenditure because it already has been expended on materials and supplies. Note that the entry sequence given above implies that the balances of the Materials and Supplies and Fund Balance Reserved for Materials and Supplies accounts always are equal.

The entry sequence for the above example under the purchases method is illustrated below. Under this method, the beginning balances in Materials and Supplies and Fund Balance Reserved for Materials and Supplies necessarily are the same as those given above (as is implied by the following example). The following entry records the acquisition of the additional inventory:

Expenditures	25,000	
Cash		25,000

Thus, under the purchases method, the costs of materials and supplies acquired during the period are considered to be expenditures when the items are acquired. At year-end, the following entry is made:

Fund Balance Reserved for Materials and Supplies 10,000
    Materials and Supplies   10,000

This entry adjusts the balance in the Materials and Supplies account to its proper year-end amount of $20,000 ($30,000 − $10,000). It also reduces the balance in Fund Balance Reserved for Materials and Supplies from $30,000 to $20,000—an amount equal to the cost of the ending inventory. As under the consumption method, the balance in Fund Balance Reserved for Materials and Supplies identifies the portion of the fund balance which is unavailable for expenditure because it already has been expended on materials and supplies.

Note that both the consumption and purchases methods produce the same balances for Materials and Supplies and for Fund Balance Reserved for Materials and Supplies. After closing entries are made, the two methods also produce the same effect on the Fund Balance account even though inventory expenditures and inventory consumption are unequal. For example, assume a beginning fund balance of $50,000 under both methods. The following table shows the effects of the two methods on the Fund Balance account, assuming that no other items affected this balance during the period.

	Consumption Method	Purchases Method
Fund balance (1/1)	$50,000	$50,000
Entry made when inventory acquired	(25,000)	
Entry made at year-end	35,000	
Expenditures*	(35,000)	(25,000)
Fund balance (12/31)	$25,000	$25,000

* The Expenditures account affects the Fund Balance account because, as shown above, it is closed to the latter account.

Recording Encumbrances

Recall that budgetary control is enhanced through the use of an encumbrance system which reveals the fund's total future expenditures expected because of existing orders and contracts. In such a system, the account, Encumbrances, is debited and the account, Reserve for Encumbrances, is credited for the expected amount of an order or a contract. These accounts are offsetting *memorandum accounts* in the general ledger of the fund. When the order or contract is satisfied and its actual amount becomes known, the entry for the encumbrance is reversed, and the actual expenditure is recorded in the proprietary accounts. To illustrate, assume that an order is placed to purchase materials and supplies inventory for an estimated $11,000. Assume also that these items ultimately are billed at only $10,500 and that payment of this amount is expected within 30 days. The entries to record the original encumbrance and the related billing are as follows:

Encumbrances	11,000	
Reserve for Encumbrances		11,000
Expenditures	10,500	
Vouchers Payable		10,500
Reserve for Encumbrances	11,000	
Encumbrances		11,000

We emphasize again that salaries and wages, bond interest, and other recurring expenditures usually are not encumbered when their payment is imminent.

Closing the Budgetary, Proprietary, and Encumbrances Accounts

At the end of the fiscal period, the budgetary accounts, various proprietary accounts, and the encumbrances accounts of the general fund are closed, and the Fund Balance account is adjusted for differences in actual amounts and budgeted amounts. To illustrate, assume the following:

1. Actual revenues of $199,000.
2. Estimated revenues of $200,000.
3. Appropriations of $198,000.
4. Expenditures of $180,000.
5. Operating transfers in of $15,000.
6. Operating transfers out of $10,000.
7. A related fund balance of $2,000 ($200,000 − $198,000) (i.e., there is no beginning fund balance).
8. Remaining encumbrances of $15,000.

Under these conditions, the closing entries are as follows:

(a) Revenues	199,000	
Operating Transfers In	15,000	
Estimated Revenues		200,000
Fund Balance		14,000
(b) Appropriations	198,000	
Expenditures		180,000
Operating Transfers Out		10,000
Fund Balance		8,000
(c) Reserve for Encumbrances	15,000	
Encumbrances		15,000

(d) Fund Balance	15,000	
Fund Balance Reserved for		
Encumbrances		15,000

Entries *(a)* and *(b)* are similar to entries discussed previously, except that they also close the Operating Transfers In and Operating Transfers Out accounts. These entries, in combination with the existing Fund Balance of $2,000, produce an adjusted Fund Balance of $24,000. Entry *(c)*, which is new, closes out the remaining balances in both Encumbrances and Reserve for Encumbrances. Entry *(d)* reserves $15,000 (an amount equal to the remaining encumbrances) of the fund balance for specific appropriation in the following year to cover orders and so on placed in the current year.[20] That is, the account, Fund Balance Reserved for Encumbrances, reflects the portion of the year-end fund balance that must be appropriated next year to allow completion of transactions in process at the end of the current year. The remaining unreserved fund balance ($9,000) is available for new appropriations in the following year.[21] At the beginning of the next year, the encumbrances accounts are reopened as follows, provided that authorization to complete the transactions in process at the end of the prior year is given.

(a) Fund Balance Reserved for Encumbrances	15,000	
Fund Balance		15,000
(b) Encumbrances—Prior Year	15,000	
Reserve for Encumbrances—Prior Year		15,000

Nonencumbrance-Related Reserves and Fund Balance Designations

Segregations of the fund balance for purposes other than dealing with encumbrances also may be established by creating reserves and fund balance designations. One example of a nonencumbrance-related reserve is the Fund Balance Reserved for Materials and Supplies account discussed above. Another example of such a reserve is as follows. Assume that a $50,000 advance is made to a city's Printing Shop Fund (an internal service fund). Assume also that this advance is recorded by debiting Advances to Internal Service Funds and crediting Cash. The cash advanced to the print shop fund is not available for current expenditures; thus, a reserve, which reveals the related reduction in the fund balance, may be established with the following entry:

Fund Balance	50,000	
Reserve for Advances to Internal		
Service Funds		50,000

---

[20] Alternatively, this amount could be disclosed in the notes to financial statements.

[21] Prior to NCGA *Statement 1,* the encumbrances outstanding at year-end were treated as expenditures in fund financial statements. Under the *Codification* (and NCGA *Statement 1*) encumbrances no longer are reported as expenditures in these statements unless required legally.

Fund balance designations reflect administrators' expectations about future expenditures of funds, including expenditures in subsequent periods. For example, assume that a fund's administration wishes to designate $25,000 of the fund balance for expected equipment replacements. The following entry records this designation of the fund balance.

Fund Balance	25,000	
Fund Balance Designated for Equipment		
Replacements		25,000

Fund balance designations are analogous to unfunded appropriations of retained earnings by profit-seeking entities since resource transfers are not made in connection with these designations.

As a consequence of reserves and designations, the fund balance at any point in time may be split between reserved and unreserved fund balances. The unreserved fund balance consists of designated and undesignated fund balances. The undesignated fund balance, which is part of the fund balance, reflects the resources available for expenditure. Note that if assets reserved for a particular use are withdrawn from that use (through, for example, the repayment of an advance), or if a designation is deemed unnecessary, the original entry establishing the reserve or the designation is reversed.

General Fund Financial Statements

As mentioned, the individual financial statements of the general fund, which are encompassed by the phrase *general-purpose financial reporting,* include (1) the balance sheet and (2) the statement of revenues, expenditures, and changes in fund balance (virtually always with comparisons of actual and budgeted data). The balance sheet of a general fund is rather conventional. However, the assets shown consist of relatively liquid assets, such as cash, receivables, inventory, and advances to other funds because the fixed assets acquired by the general fund are recorded as expenditures and are included in the general fixed assets account group. Similarly, the related liabilities consist of short-term obligations because long-term debts incurred by the general fund are included in the general long-term debt account group. The remaining equities of the general fund's balance sheet consist of reserves, designations, and the fund balance. The general fund's statement of revenues, expenditures, and changes in fund balance includes sections for revenues, expenditures, other financing sources and uses of funds, and other changes in the fund balance (e.g., those related to increases in reserves).

COMPREHENSIVE ILLUSTRATION OF GENERAL FUND ACCOUNTING

The assumed post-closing trial balance for Cityville's General Fund at December 31, 19X0 is as follows:

GENERAL FUND—MUNICIPALITY OF CITYVILLE
Post-Closing Trial Balance
December 31, 19X0

	Debit	Credit
Cash	150,000	
Accounts Receivable	29,000	
Due from Federal Government (from grant)	260,000	
Taxes Receivable—Delinquent	75,000	
Materials and Supplies (consumption method)	38,000	
Allowance for Uncollectible Taxes—Delinquent		10,000
Vouchers Payable		185,000
Fund Balance		254,000
Fund Balance Reserved for Materials and Supplies		38,000
Fund Balance Reserved for Encumbrances		65,000
Totals	552,000	552,000

The 19X1 entries for Cityville's general fund are illustrated below. The entries considered are typical of general-purpose governments' general funds, although they are not intended to provide an exhaustive treatment of this topic. Prior to illustrating the general fund's closing entries, its 19X1 individual financial statements are presented.

The first set of entries for the general fund in 19X1 reopens its prior-year related Encumbrances and Reserve for Encumbrances accounts. These entries are as follows:

1. To zero out Fund Balance Reserved for Encumbrances and return the related amount to the Fund Balance account:

Fund Balance Reserved for		
Encumbrances	65,000	
Fund Balance		65,000

2. To reopen the prior-year related Encumbrances and Reserve for Encumbrances accounts:

Encumbrances—Prior Year	65,000	
Reserve for Encumbrances—		
Prior Year		65,000

The second set of entries records the portion of the city's budget related to the general fund, the fund's actual transactions for 19X1, and its 19X1 encumbrances. Prior to providing each entry, an explanation of the source of the entry is given.

1. The city council approves the budget for 19X1, which includes $2,200,000 in estimated revenues and appropriations of $2,150,000.

Estimated Revenues	2,200,000	
Appropriations		2,150,000
Fund Balance		50,000

2. Operating transfers of funds from the city's electric utility fund (an enterprise fund) in the amount of $165,000 are authorized in the budget.

Due from Enterprise Fund	165,000	
Operating Transfers In		165,000

3. Operating transfers to the city's debt service fund and capital projects fund of $300,000 and $200,000, respectively, are authorized in the budget.

Operating Transfers Out	500,000	
Due to Debt Service Fund		300,000
Due to Capital Projects Fund		200,000

4. Property tax statements are issued to property owners. The tax levy is 7 percent of total property valuations of $21,428,571. Uncollectible taxes are expected to equal 2 percent of the tax levy. Since the property taxes are available and measurable during 19X1, the modified accrual basis yields the following entry:[22]

Taxes Receivable	1,500,000	
Allowance for Uncollectible Taxes		30,000
Revenues—Property Taxes		1,470,000

5. Purchase orders for goods and services totaling $1,200,000 are issued.

Encumbrances	1,200,000	
Reserve for Encumbrances		1,200,000

6. Invoices for previously ordered goods and services totaling $1,160,000 are received. This total includes $75,000 for orders placed in the preceding year (estimated at $65,000) and $1,085,000 for orders placed in the current year (estimated at $1,070,000).

Expenditures	1,160,000	
Vouchers payable		1,160,000
Reserve for Encumbrances—Prior Year	65,000	
Encumbrances—Prior Year		65,000
Reserve for Encumbrances	1,070,000	
Encumbrances		1,070,000

---

[22] For illustrative purposes, we record revenues in specific accounts (e.g., Revenues—Property Taxes), rather than crediting them to the summary (control) account, Revenues.

7. Orders amounting to $20,000 are placed for additional materials and supplies inventory.

Encumbrances	20,000	
Reserve for Encumbrances		20,000

8. Services totaling $75,000 are provided for, and billed to, outside parties.

Accounts Receivable	75,000	
Revenues—Services		75,000

9. Property tax levies of $1,475,000 are collected (with $65,000 of this amount pertaining to the prior year). Also, other accounts receivable amounting to $45,000 are collected.

Cash	1,520,000	
Taxes Receivable		1,410,000
Taxes Receivable—Delinquent		65,000
Accounts Receivable		45,000

10. The city council authorizes the write-off of the remaining delinquent taxes ($75,000 − $65,000).

Allowance for Uncollectible Taxes—		
Delinquent	10,000	
Taxes Receivable—Delinquent		10,000

11. Payments for licenses, fees, permits, and other service charges totaling $235,000 are collected.

Cash	235,000	
Revenues—Licenses, Fees, Permits, and		
Other Service Charges		235,000

12. The inventory and invoice ($22,000) related to the earlier order (item 7 above) are received. As indicated by its December 31, 19X1, post-closing trial balance, Cityville uses the consumption method to account for general fund inventory acquisitions.

Materials and Supplies	22,000	
Vouchers Payable		22,000
Fund Balance	22,000	
Fund Balance Reserved for		
Materials and Supplies		22,000
Reserve for Encumbrances	20,000	
Encumbrances		20,000

13. Wages and salaries amounting to $200,000 are accrued. Cityville does not record accruals of this type as encumbrances because they are paid shortly after they become payable.

Expenditures	200,000	
Vouchers Payable		200,000

14. The transfer from the enterprise fund is received.

Cash	165,000	
Due from Enterprise Fund		165,000

15. Outstanding vouchers payable of $1,500,000 are paid.

Vouchers Payable	1,500,000	
Cash		1,500,000

16. The transfers out to the debt service fund and the capital projects fund are paid.

Due to Debt Service Fund	300,000	
Due to Capital Projects Fund	200,000	
Cash		500,000

17. Delinquent taxes in the amount of $90,000 are identified.

Taxes Receivable—Delinquent	90,000	
Allowance for Uncollectible Taxes	30,000	
Taxes Receivable		90,000
Allowance for Uncollectible Taxes—		
Delinquent		30,000

18. The grant due from the federal government shown on Cityville's December 31, 19X0, post-closing trial balance is received.

Cash	260,000	
Due from Federal Government		260,000

19. Materials and Supplies inventory on hand at the end of the year amounts to $32,000.

Expenditures	28,000	
Materials and Supplies		28,000
Fund Balance Reserved for Materials		
and Supplies	28,000	
Fund Balance		28,000

Once these entries are posted, the following trial balance is produced:

GENERAL FUND—MUNICIPALITY OF CITYVILLE
Trial Balance
December 31, 19X1

	Debit	Credit
Cash	330,000	
Accounts Receivable	59,000	
Taxes Receivable—Delinquent	90,000	
Materials and Supplies	32,000	
Expenditures	1,388,000	
Encumbrances	130,000	
Operating Transfers Out	500,000	
Estimated Revenues	2,200,000	
Allowance for Uncollectible Taxes—Delinquent		30,000
Vouchers Payable		67,000
Revenues—Taxes		1,470,000
Revenues—Services		75,000
Revenues—Licences, Fees, Permits, and Other Service Charges		235,000
Operating Transfers In		165,000
Appropriations		2,150,000
Fund Balance		375,000
Fund Balance Reserved for Materials and Supplies		32,000
Reserve for Encumbrances		130,000
	4,729,000	4,729,000

The general fund's individual financial statements, which are produced using this trial balance, are presented in Illustration 20–1. Note that if the purchases method had been used, the balances for both expenditures and fund balance would have been $6,000 higher. Consistently, Cityville's general fund statement of revenues, expenditures, and changes in fund balance would have shown expenditures of $1,382,000 and would not have incorporated the decrease in fund balance reserved for materials and supplies of $6,000. Thus, as shown previously, the consumption and purchases methods yield the same year-end fund balances.

The third set of entries for Cityville's general fund in 19X1 contains its closing entries. The closing entries close the budgetary accounts, certain proprietary accounts, and the encumbrances accounts of the general fund. They also adjust the Fund Balance account to the amount shown in the general fund's balance sheet. The closing entries for the general fund are as follows:

1. To close the Revenue, Operating Transfers In, and Estimated Revenues accounts to the Fund Balance account:

Revenues—Taxes	1,470,000	
Revenues—Services	75,000	
Revenues—Licenses, Fees, Permits, and Other Service Charges	235,000	
Operating Transfers In	165,000	
Fund Balance	255,000	
Estimated Revenues		2,200,000

ILLUSTRATION 20-1   General Fund Financial Statements

MUNICIPALITY OF CITYVILLE
General Fund Balance Sheet
December 31, 19X1

Assets

Cash		$330,000
Accounts receivable		59,000
Taxes receivable—delinquent	90,000	
Allowance for uncollectible taxes—delinquent	(30,000)	60,000
Materials and supplies		32,000
Total assets		$481,000

Liabilities and Fund Balance

Vouchers payable	$ 67,000
Fund balance reserved for materials and supplies	32,000
Fund balance reserved for encumbrances	130,000
Fund balance	252,000
	$481,000

MUNICIPALITY OF CITYVILLE
General Fund Statement of Revenues
Expenditures, and Changes in Fund Balance
For the Year Ended December 31, 19X1

Revenues:	
Taxes	$1,470,000
Services	75,000
Licenses, fees, permits, and other service charges	235,000
Total revenues	$1,780,000
Expenditures (Although not shown here, expenditures are subcategorized by governmental function. See Illustration 21–2 for an example of functional subcategories.)	1,388,000
Excess of revenues over expenditures	$ 392,000
Other financing sources (uses):	
Operating transfers in	$ 165,000
Operating transfers out	(500,000)
Total other financing sources (uses)	$ (335,000)
Excess of revenues and other sources over expenditures and other uses	$ 57,000
Other changes in the fund balance:	
Increase in fund balance reserved for encumbrances	(65,000)
Decrease in fund balance reserved for materials and supplies	6,000
Fund Balance—January 1, 19X1	254,000
Fund Balance—December 31, 19X1	$ 252,000

2. To close the Appropriations, Expenditures, and Operating Transfers Out accounts to the Fund Balance account:

Appropriations	2,150,000	
Expenditures		1,388,000
Operating Transfers Out		500,000
Fund Balance		262,000

3. To close the encumbrances accounts:

Reserve for Encumbrances	130,000	
Encumbrances		130,000

4. To transfer the portion of the fund balance representing amounts that must be appropriated next year to cover this year's outstanding orders and contracts to Fund Balance Reserved for Encumbrances:

Fund Balance	130,000	
Fund Balance Reserved for Encumbrances		130,000

The following trial balance is produced by posting the closing entries.

GENERAL FUND—MUNICIPALITY OF CITYVILLE
Post-Closing Trial Balance
December 31, 19X1

	Debit	*Credit*
Cash	330,000	
Accounts Receivable	59,000	
Taxes Receivable—Delinquent	90,000	
Materials and Supplies	32,000	
Allowance for Uncollectible Taxes—Delinquent		30,000
Vouchers Payable		67,000
Fund Balance		252,000
Fund Balance Reserved for Materials and Supplies		32,000
Fund Balance Reserved for Encumbrances		130,000
	511,000	511,000

Summary

This chapter contains general discussions of accounting principles and concepts related to state and local governmental units with emphasis on the techniques used in accounting for the general funds of these units. It begins by identifying the characteristics that distinguish governmental units from profit-seeking enterprises and other nonprofit entities. These differences account partially for variations in the objectives of general-purpose financial reporting by these entities.

GASB *Concepts Statement 1* indicates that the objectives of state and local government financial reporting follow from the characteristics of the environment in which governmental units operate and the informational needs of all users of governmental financial reports. This statement identifies the primary users of such reports as: (1) those to whom government is primarily accountable (the citizenry), (2) those who directly represent the citizens (legislative and oversight bodies), and (3) those participating in the lending process (investors and creditors). From an overall perspective, the objectives of general-purpose financial reporting by state and local governmental units are to assist users in assessing accountability and in making economic, social, and political decisions. Ignoring their details, the specific objectives of general-purpose financial reporting by these entities are: (1) to assist in fulfilling government's duty to be publicly accountable and to enable users to assess that accountability, (2) to assist users in evaluating the operating results of the governmental entity for the year, and (3) to assist users in assessing the level of services that can be provided by the governmental entity and its ability to meet its obligations as they become due. Although the term *accountable* is used only once in these objectives, the concept of accountability is implicit in all of them. Thus, the accountability objective [(1) above] is considered to be the most important objective by the GASB and is the objective from which the remaining objectives follow.

The GASB was formed in 1984 by the Financial Accounting Standards Foundation. The GASB's function is to establish governmental accounting standards. Shortly after its formation, the GASB issued its *Statement 1,* "Authoritative Status of NCGA Pronouncements and AICPA Industry Audit Guide." This statement indicates that all NCGA pronouncements in effect as of June 1984 remain effective until amended or superseded by a subsequent GASB pronouncement. Between 1984 and 1992, the GASB issued 16 statements. The GASB also has issued several *Interpretations* and *Technical Bulletins* as well as its *Concepts Statement 1*. The pronouncements of the GASB, including effective NCGA pronouncements, constitute the highest level of authoritative support in the AICPA's state and local governmental accounting GAAP hierarchy. The effective governmental accounting standards, as approved or promulgated by the GASB, are contained in the *Codification of Governmental Accounting and Financial Reporting Standards* (or in subsequently issued GASB pronouncements).

The *Codification* contains, among many other things, 12 basic principles of accounting for state and local governmental units. As indicated in this chapter, the 12 principles pertain to:

1. The accounting and reporting capabilities to be maintained.
2. The fund accounting requirement.
3. The types of funds to be used.
4. The number of funds to be used.
5. The methods to be used in accounting for fixed assets and long-term debts.
6. The valuation of fixed assets.
7. The use of depreciation accounting.
8. The use of accrual basis and modified accrual basis accounting.
9. The use of budgetary and encumbrance accounting.
10. The use of transfer, revenue, expenditure, and expense account classifications.

11. The use of common terminology and classifications.

12. Interim and annual financial reporting.

The 12 principles provide the foundation for state and local governmental unit fund accounting. In short, a fund is a fiscal and accounting entity with a self-balancing set of accounts which are segregated for the purpose of carrying on specific activities or attaining certain objectives in accordance with special regulations, restrictions, or limitations. An example of a fund is the general fund. The general fund of a state or local governmental unit is the fund which administers the resources used in the general operations of the unit and in providing traditional services.

After discussing the 12 basic principles, the chapter discusses several general concepts pertinent to governmental accounting to provide a basis for examining the procedures used in accounting for the general fund as well as the funds and account groups considered in Chapter 21. The concepts covered are related to the 12 basic principles identified above and pertain to the reporting entity; funds and fund accounting in general; appropriations, allotments, and apportionments; general fixed assets and general long-term debt account groups; budgetary and encumbrance accounting; the various measurement focuses; the accrual and the modified accrual bases of accounting; intergovernmental revenues; and financial reporting.

Subsequently, the techniques used in accounting for the general fund are illustrated. We illustrate general fund accounting primarily through the accounts of a typical municipality. Our focus is on recording the general fund's budget, recording its actual transactions, recording its encumbrances, recording its nonencumbrance-related reserves and fund balance designations, closing its accounts, and preparing its financial statements. The techniques illustrated apply with equal force to the general funds of all general-purpose governments.

Questions

1. Identify the characteristics that the FASB believes distinguish governmental and other nonprofit entities from profit-seeking enterprises.

2. Identify the environmental characteristics that distinguish state and local governmental units from other nonprofit entities.

3. Identify the primary users of governmental financial reports and the general reasons these groups need these reports.

4. Identify the general-purpose and the specific objectives of general-purpose financial reporting by state and local governmental units. Explain the role of accountability in the objectives. Ignore the detail of the specific objectives.

5. What type of accounting is used in governmental accounting and what is a fund in this context?

6. Identify and describe the uses of the funds that generally are needed in accounting for state and local governmental units.

7. Distinguish between expendable and nonexpendable funds.

8. Define *appropriation, allotment,* and *apportionment.* Identify the relationships among these terms.

9. Describe and explain the uses of account groups for general fixed assets and general long-term debt.

10. Identify the source of approval and the uses of a governmental unit's budget.

11. Distinguish between budgetary and proprietary accounts and indicate how these accounts are used in controlling the operations of governmental units.

12. Explain the operations of an encumbrance system.

13. Describe the measurement focuses and versions of accrual accounting operating in governmental accounting subsequent to the effective date of GASB *Statement 11.*

14. Identify the revenue and expense recognition criteria of governmental funds under the accrual basis of accounting.

15. Distinguish briefly among operating transfers, quasi-external transactions, reimbursements, and residual equity transfers.

16. Distinguish briefly among grants, entitlements, shared revenues, and payments in lieu of taxes.

17. Discuss the financial statements of state and local governmental units and the related financial reporting requirements.

18. Discuss the characteristics of the general fund, including the characteristics of its individual financial statements.

Exercises

Exercise 20–1   (Consumption Method)

The general fund of the city of Galston accounts for materials and supplies using the consumption method. The fund's beginning inventory of materials and supplies is $40,000, and there is a related beginning-of-period credit balance in Fund Balance Reserved for Materials and Supplies of $40,000. The fund purchases an additional $35,000 of materials and supplies inventory during the year for cash (with $37,000 encumbered). The cost of materials and supplies on hand at year-end is $30,000.

Required:

a. Prepare the general fund's journal entries for the year related to its Materials and Supplies account.

b. Explain the function of the Fund Balance Reserved for Materials and Supplies account.

Exercise 20–2   (Purchases Method)

Assume the information of Exercise 20–1, except now assume that Galston's general fund accounts for materials and supplies using the purchases method. With this change, complete the requirements of Exercise 20–1.

Exercise 20–3   (Closing Entries)

The account balances of the general fund of the city of Jinks reflect the following amounts: (1) actual revenues of $208,000, (2) estimated revenues of $210,000, (3) appropriations of $200,000, (4) expenditures of $190,000, (5) operating transfers in of $20,000, (6) operating transfers out of $15,000, (7) a fund balance of $4,000, and (8) remaining encumbrances of $18,000.

Required:

a. Prepare the fund's closing entries for the year.

b. Prepare the entries to reopen its encumbrances accounts at the beginning of the following year.

Exercise 20–4   (Closing Entries)

The trial balance of the general fund of the city of Paseo Ventoso contains the following accounts and balances: (1) Revenues—$320,000, (2) Estimated Revenues—$330,000, (3) Appropriations—$310,000, (4) Expenditures—$320,000, (5) Operating Transfers In—$30,000, (6) Operating Transfers Out—$35,000, (7) Fund Balance—$20,000, and (5) Encumbrances—$10,000.

Required:

a. Prepare the fund's closing entries for the year.

b. Prepare the entries to reopen its encumbrances accounts at the beginning of the following year.

Exercise 20–5   (Purchases Method)

Assume the information of Problem 20–13, except now assume that the city of Auston accounts for materials and supplies inventories using the purchases method. (This exercise assumes that Problem 20–13 has been solved.)

Required:

a. Prepare all entries that differ from those of Problem 20–13.

b. Identify the financial statement differences that are produced by the new assumption.

Exercise 20–6   (Purchases Method)

Assume the information of Problem 20–14, except now assume the city of Tulsi accounts for materials and supplies inventories using the purchases method. (This exercise assumes that Problem 20–14 has been solved.)

Required:

a. Prepare all entries that differ from those of Problem 20–14.

b. Identify the financial statement differences that are produced by the new assumption.

Exercise 20–7   (Purchases Method)

Assume the information of Problem 20–15, except now assume that the city of Armadillo accounts for materials and supplies inventories using the purchases method. (This exercise assumes that Problem 20–15 has been solved.)

Required:

a. Prepare all entries that differ from those of Problem 20–15.

b. Identify the financial statement differences that are produced by the new assumption.

Exercise 20–8   (Purchases Method)

Assume the information of Problem 20–16, except now assume that the city of Tuscon accounts for materials and supplies inventories using the purchases method. (This exercise assumes that Problem 20–16 has been solved.)

Required:

a. Prepare all entries that differ from those of Problem 20–16.

b. Identify the financial statement differences that are produced by the new assumption.

Exercise 20–9   (Encumbrances)

The statements below are based on the information from the following journal entries. Select the best answer for each statement.

The following entries were recorded in sequence in the general fund of the municipality of Huston:

1. Encumbrances	12,000	
Reserve for Encumbrances		12,000
2. Reserve for Encumbrances	12,000	
Encumbrances		12,000
3. Expenditures	12,350	
Voucher's Payable		12,350

1. The sequence of entries indicates that
   a. An adverse event was foreseen and a reserve of $12,000 was created; later the reserve was canceled, and a liability for the item was acknowledged.
   b. An order was placed for goods or services estimated to cost $12,000; the actual cost was $12,350, for which a liability was acknowledged upon receipt.
   c. Encumbrances were anticipated but later failed to materialize and were reversed. A liability of $12,350 was incurred.
   d. The first entry was erroneous and was reversed; a liability of $12,350 was acknowledged.
2. Entries similar to those for the general fund may also appear on the books of the municipality's
   a. general fixed assets group.
   b. general long-term debt group.

    c. trust fund.

    d. special revenue fund.

3. Assuming that appropriate governmental accounting principles were followed, the entries

    a. Occurred in the same fiscal period.

    b. Did not occur in the same fiscal period.

    c. Could have occurred in the same fiscal period, but it is impossible to be sure of this.

    d. Reflect the equivalence of a prior period adjustment had the entity concerned been one operated for profit.

4. Immediately after entry 1 was recorded, the municipality had a balanced general fund budget for all transactions. What would be the effect of recording entries 2 and 3?

    a. Cause no change to the balanced condition of the budget.

    b. Cause the municipality to show a surplus.

    c. Cause the municipality to show a deficit.

    d. Cause no change to the current budget but would affect the budget of the following fiscal period.

(AICPA adapted)

Exercise 20–10   (Fund Accounting and Related Accounts)

a. Reference frequently is made in governmental accounting to *budgetary and proprietary accounts.* Define these terms as they relate to the governmental entity. Do budgetary accounts have a parallel in the accounts of profit-seeking entities? Does the budget occupy the same role in both accounting systems?

b. The concept of a fund is inherent in governmental accounting systems. Discuss this concept, and distinguish the characteristics of the various equities which are implicit therein.

Exercise 20–11   (Revenue Recognition, Accounting Bases, Account Groups, and CAFR)

The accounting system of the city of Hemp is organized and operated on a fund basis. Among the types of funds used are a general fund, a special revenue fund, and an enterprise fund.

Required:

a. What basis of accounting should be used for each of the following funds? Explain.

    1. General fund.

    2. Special revenue fund.

    3. Enterprise fund.

b. How should fixed assets and long-term liabilities related to the general fund and to the enterprise fund be accounted for?

c. How should the balance sheets of the general fund, the special revenue fund, and the enterprise fund be handled when preparing the comprehensive annual financial report? Explain.

(AICPA adapted)

Exercise 20–12 **(Miscellaneous Topics)**

Select the best answer for each of the following.

1. Which of the following accounts of a governmental unit is (are) closed at the end of the fiscal year?

	Estimated Revenues	*Fund Balance*
a.	No	No
b.	No	Yes
c.	Yes	Yes
d.	Yes	No

2. Which of the following accounts of a governmental unit is credited when a purchase order is approved?
   a. Reserve for Encumbrances.
   b. Encumbrances.
   c. Vouchers Payable.
   d. Appropriations.

3. Repairs that have been made for a governmental unit, and for which a bill has been received, should be recorded in the general fund as a debit to an
   a. Expenditure.
   b. Encumbrance.
   c. Expense.
   d. Appropriation.

4. A debt service fund of a municipality is an example of which of the following types of fund?
   a. Fiduciary.
   b. Governmental.
   c. Proprietary.
   d. Internal service.

5. Which of the following funds of a governmental unit would use the general long-term debt account group to account for unmatured general long-term liabilities?
   a. Special assessment.
   b. Capital projects.
   c. Trust.
   d. Internal service.

6. Which of the following funds of a governmental unit uses the same basis of accounting as an enterprise fund?
   a. Special revenue.
   b. Internal service.
   c. Expendable trust.
   d. Capital projects.

7. Which of the following funds of a governmental unit could use the general fixed assets account group to account for fixed assets?
   a. Internal service.
   b. Enterprise.
   c. Trust.
   d. Special assessment.

8. A state government unit should use which basis of accounting for each of the following types of funds under GASB *Statement 11*?

	Governmental	Proprietary
a.	Cash	Modified accrual
b.	Modified accrual	Modified accrual
c.	Modified accrual	Accrual
d.	Accrual	Accrual

(AICPA adapted)

Problems

Problem 20–13   (Entries, Trial Balances, and Financial Statements—Consumption Method)

The post-closing trial balance for the municipality of Auston's general fund at December 31, 19X6, is as follows. (Note that this problem is integrated with Exercise 20–5 which deals with the purchases method.)

GENERAL FUND—MUNICIPALITY OF AUSTON
Post-Closing Trial Balance
December 31, 19X6

	Debit	*Credit*
Cash	180,000	
Accounts Receivable	40,000	
Due from Federal Government (from grant)	300,000	
Taxes Receivable—Delinquent	90,000	
Materials and Supplies (consumption method)	50,000	
Allowance for Uncollectible Taxes—Delinquent		30,000
Vouchers Payable		200,000
Fund Balance		300,000
Fund Balance Reserved for Materials and Supplies		50,000
Fund Balance Reserved for Encumbrances		80,000
Totals	660,000	660,000

Information related to the general fund's 19X7 budget, transactions, and encumbrances is provided below.

1. The city council approves the budget for 19X7—including $2,500,000 in estimated revenues and appropriations of $2,400,000.

2. The budget authorizes operating transfers of funds from the city's electric utility (an enterprise fund) in the amount of $200,000.

3. Operating transfers to the debt service fund and the capital projects fund of $350,000 and $225,000, respectively, are authorized in the budget.

4. Property tax statements are issued to property owners. The tax levy is 8 percent of total property valuations of $25,000,000 (with estimated uncollectible taxes based on 3 percent of the tax levy).

5. Purchase orders for $1,600,000 of goods and services are issued.

6. Invoices for goods and services previously ordered totaling $1,480,000 are received. This total includes $85,000 for orders placed in the preceding year (estimated at $80,000) and $1,395,000 for orders placed in the current year (estimated at $1,190,000).

7. Orders for $30,000 of additional materials and supplies inventory are placed.

8. Services are provided for, and billed at, $90,000 to outside parties.

9. Property tax levies of $1,950,000 are collected ($80,000 of this amount pertains to the prior year). Other accounts receivable amounting to $35,000 also are collected.

10. The city council authorizes the write-off of any remaining delinquent taxes.

11. Payments for licenses, fees, permits, and other service charges in the amount of $300,000 are collected.

12. The inventory and invoice ($32,000) related to the earlier order (item (7) above) are received.

13. Wages and salaries amounting to $250,000 are accrued. Accruals of this type are not recorded as encumbrances because they are paid shortly after they become payable.

14. The transfer from the enterprise fund is received.

15. Outstanding vouchers payable of $1,750,000 are paid.

16. The transfers out to the debt service fund and the capital projects fund are paid.

17. Delinquent taxes of $130,000 pertaining to the current year are identified.

18. The grant due from the federal government shown on the December 31, 19X6, post-closing trial balance is received.

19. The cost of materials and supplies inventory on hand at year-end is $40,000.

Required:

a. Prepare the general fund entries to reopen its encumbrances accounts in 19X7.

b. Make all entries related to the general fund's 19X7 budget, actual transactions, and encumbrances.

c. Prepare the general fund's trial balance at December 31, 19X7.

d. Prepare the general fund's 19X7 financial statements.

e. Record the general fund's 19X7 closing entries.

f. Prepare a post-closing trial balance for the general fund at December 31, 19X7.

Problem 20–14   (Entries, Trial Balance, and Financial Statements—Consumption Method)

The July 1, 19X6, trial balance of the general fund of the city of Tulsi is shown below. (Note that this problem is integrated with Exercise 20–6 which deals with the purchases method.)

Cash	60,000	Vouchers Payable		40,000
Taxes Receivable—		Fund Balance Reserved for		
Delinquent	40,000	Encumbrances		20,000
Allowance for Uncollectible Taxes		Fund Balance Reserved for		
Receivable—Delinquent	(30,000)	Materials and Supplies		30,000
Materials and Supplies	30,000	Fund Balance		10,000
	100,000			100,000

During the fiscal year ended June 30, 19X7, the following events and transactions related to the general fund occurred:

1. The general fund's annual budget was adopted—including estimated revenues of $400,000 and appropriations of $390,000.

2. The current year's tax levy amounted to $430,000 (of which $30,000 was estimated to be uncollectible).

3. Vouchers unpaid at the beginning of the year were paid. Orders for new equipment were placed in the amount of $40,000.

4. Delinquent taxes of $15,000 were collected. Related interest and penalties were $600. Delinquent taxes amounting to $18,000 were written off.

5. Cash of $30,000 was advanced to the general fund from the debt service fund.

6. The equipment ordered in (3) was received. The accompanying invoice was for $42,000.

7. Wages and salaries of $280,000 were accrued. Accruals for wages and salaries are not encumbered because these amounts are paid shortly after they become payable.

8. Materials and supplies with an estimated cost of $80,000 were vouchered. Encumbrances related to these items were not recorded because their delivery was imminent. The consumption method is used in accounting for materials and supplies.

9. Collections of $380,000 of current year taxes were made. Unpaid balances were transferred to the Taxes Receivable—Delinquent account.

10. Licenses and permits revenues amounted to $40,000.

11. Vouchers of $380,000 were paid.

12. Orders for $30,000 additional materials and supplies were placed.

13. The Materials and Supplies account and the related reserve account were adjusted to reflect materials and supplies of $20,000 on hand at June 30, 19X7.

14. Operating transfers were authorized and paid as follows: Operating Transfers In—City Gas Utility, $100,000, and Operating Transfers Out—Debt Service Fund, $90,000.

Required:

a. Prepare the general fund's entries to reopen its encumbrances accounts.

b. Make all entries related to the general fund's budget, actual transactions, and encumbrances for the current fiscal year.

c. Prepare the general fund's trial balance at June 30, 19X7.

d. Prepare the general fund's financial statements for the year ended June 30, 19X7.

e. Record the general fund's closing entries.

Problem 20–15   (Entries, Trial Balances, and Financial Statements—Consumption Method)

The post-closing trial balance for the city of Armadillo's general fund at December 31, 19X8, is as follows. (Note that this problem is integrated with Exercise 20–7 which deals with the purchases method.)

GENERAL FUND—CITY OF ARMADILLO
Post-Closing Trial Balance
December 31, 19X8

	Debit	*Credit*
Cash	200,000	
Accounts Receivable	30,000	
Due from Federal Government (from grant)	250,000	
Taxes Receivable—Delinquent	70,000	
Materials and Supplies (consumption method)	40,000	
Allowance for Uncollectible Taxes—Delinquent		9,000
Vouchers Payable		180,000
Fund Balance		301,000
Fund Balance Reserved for Materials and Supplies		40,000
Fund Balance Reserved for Encumbrances		60,000
Totals	590,000	590,000

The following information pertains to the general fund's 19X9 budget, transactions, and encumbrances.

1. The city council approves its budget for 19X9. The budgeted figures for estimated revenues and appropriations for its general fund are $2,000,000 and $1,900,000, respectively.

2. Operating transfers to the debt service fund and the capital projects fund of $125,000 and $150,000, respectively, are authorized in the budget.

3. The budget authorizes the (operating) transfer of $175,000 of funds from an enterprise fund (the city's electric utility).

4. Property tax statements are issued to property owners. The tax levy is 5 percent of total property valuations of $30,000,000. Uncollectible taxes are estimated to be 1 percent of the tax levy.

5. Purchase orders for $1,400,000 of goods and services are issued.

6. Additional materials and supplies with an estimated cost of $25,000 are ordered.

7. Services are provided for and billed at $80,000 to outside parties.

8. Invoices for goods and services previously ordered totaling $1,260,000 are received. This figure includes $65,000 for orders placed in the preceding year (estimated at $60,000) and $1,195,000 for orders placed in the current year (estimated at $1,150,000).

9. Property tax levies of $1,450,000 are collected. Of this amount, $60,000 is related to the prior year. Other accounts receivable amounting to $50,000 also are collected.

10. Delinquent taxes of $8,000 related to the prior year are written off.

11. Licenses, fees, permits, and other service charge revenues of $270,000 are collected.

12. The inventory and invoice ($27,000) related to item (6) are received.

13. The grant shown on the December 31, 19X9, post-closing trial balance is received.

14. The transfer from the electric utility is received.

15. The transfers out to the debt service fund and the capital projects fund are paid.

16. Delinquent taxes of $110,000 related to the current year are identified.

17. Wages and salaries amounting to $220,000 are accrued. Accruals of this type are paid shortly after they become payable.

18. $1,610,000 of outstanding vouchers are paid.

19. The cost of materials and supplies inventory on hand at year-end is $35,000.

Required:

a. Prepare the general fund's entries to reopen its encumbrances accounts in 19X9.

b. Make all entries related to the general fund's 19X9 budget, actual transactions, and encumbrances.

c. Prepare the general fund's trial balance at December 31, 19X9.

d. Prepare the general fund's 19X9 financial statements.

e. Record the general fund's 19X9 closing entries.

f. Prepare a post-closing trial balance for the general fund at December 31, 19X9.

Problem 20-16   (Entries, Trial Balance, and Financial Statements—Consumption Method)

The January 1, 19X4, trial balance of the general fund of the city of Tuscon is as follows. (Note that this problem is integrated with Exercise 20–8 which deals with the purchases method.)

Cash	70,000	Vouchers Payable	34,000
Taxes Receivable—		Fund Balance Reserved for	
Delinquent	30,000	Encumbrances	16,000
Allowance for Uncollectible Taxes		Fund Balance Reserved for	
Receivable—Delinquent	(15,000)	Materials and Supplies	20,000
Materials and Supplies	20,000	Fund Balance	35,000
	105,000		105,000

The following events and transactions pertaining to Tuscon's general fund occurred during the fiscal year ended December 31, 19X5.

1. The general fund's annual budget was adopted. The budget includes estimated revenues and appropriations of $350,000 and $345,000, respectively.
2. Taxes assessed during 19X5 amounted to $380,000 (of which $20,000 was estimated to be uncollectible).
3. All amounts encumbered at December 31, 19X4, were approved for payment. Orders for new equipment in the amount of $25,000 were placed.
4. The debt service fund advanced the general fund cash of $12,000.
5. Materials and supplies with an estimated cost of $60,000 were vouchered. Encumbrances were not recorded because delivery was imminent. The city accounts for materials and supplies using the consumption method.
6. Delinquent taxes of $10,000 were collected (along with related interest and penalties amounting to $400). Delinquent taxes of $8,000 were written off.
7. Collection of $320,000 of current year taxes was made. The remainder of the current year's taxes receivable was transferred to the Taxes Receivable—Delinquent account.
8. Wages and salaries of $170,000 were accrued but not encumbered because they will be paid very shortly.
9. The equipment ordered in (3) was received. The city was billed for $26,000.
10. Vouchers of $250,000 were paid.
11. Orders for $15,000 additional materials and supplies were placed.
12. Licenses and permits revenues of $30,000 were earned.
13. The Materials and Supplies account and the related reserve account were adjusted to reflect materials and supplies of $22,000 on hand at year-end.
14. The following transfers were authorized and paid: Operating Transfers In—City Electric Utility, $50,000 and Operating Transfers Out—Capital Projects Fund, $55,000.

Required:

a. Prepare the general fund's entries to reopen its encumbrances accounts.
b. Make all entries related to the general fund's budget, actual transactions, and encumbrances for the current fiscal year.
c. Prepare the general fund's trial balance at December 31, 19X5.
d. Prepare the general fund's financial statements for the year ended December 31, 19X5.
e. Record the general fund's closing entries.

Problem 20–17   (Entries and Fund Balance)

The following account balances were included in the January 1, 19X2, trial balance of the general fund of the city of Tallwood:

Fund Balance Reserved for Encumbrances	$20,000
Fund Balance (unreserved)	42,000

During the 19X2 fiscal year, the following transactions were engaged in by the general fund:

1. The budget for the 19X2 fiscal year was adopted, with estimated revenues of $300,000 and appropriations of $293,000.
2. The general tax levy for the year was $250,000; estimated uncollectible accounts amounted to $10,000.
3. Wages and salaries in the amount of $90,000 were approved for payment. (These expenditures were processed without prior encumbrance.)
4. Supplies ordered in 19X1 were received at a cost of $21,000. This transaction closes all purchase orders from the prior year. There are no beginning or ending supplies inventories.
5. Negotiations for the purchase of a building were completed, the construction cost of which was estimated to be $150,000. The city decided to account for this building purchase through the general fund rather than by setting up a capital projects fund.
6. Payment was made for the approved vouchers in (3) and (4).
7. Revenues of $55,000 from licenses and fees were collected.
8. Collections of current taxes of $200,000 were received.
9. The purchase of the building in (5) was approved for payment, the settlement price being $140,000.
10. Revenue of $10,000 was received for services rendered.
11. An invoice of $20,000 was received for gas and electricity from the city's power utility (an enterprise fund).
12. Orders were placed for supplies in the amount of $60,000.

Required:

a. Prepare journal entries to record the 19X2 transactions of the general fund and indicate what other funds, if any, are affected.
b. Prepare closing entries for the general fund.
c. Prepare an analysis of the Fund Balance account for 19X2.

Problem 20–18   (Changes in Fund Balance and Balance Sheet)

Sleepy Haven Township's adjusted trial balance for its general fund at June 30, 19X2, the close of the fiscal year, is as follows:

SLEEPY HAVEN TOWNSHIP
General Fund Trial Balance
June 30, 19X2

	Debit	Credit
Cash	1,100	
Taxes Receivable—Current (note 1)	8,200	
Allowance for Uncollectible Taxes—Current		150
Taxes Receivable—Delinquent	2,500	
Allowance for Uncollectible Taxes—Delinquent		1,650
Miscellaneous Accounts Receivable (note 1)	4,000	
Allowance for Uncollectible Accounts		400
Due from Internal Service Fund	5,000	
Expenditures (note 2)	75,500	
Encumbrances	3,700	
Revenues (note 3)		6,000
Due to Enterprise Fund		1,000
Vouchers Payable		2,000
Fund Balance Reserved for Encumbrances—		
Prior Year		4,400
Reserve for Encumbrances		3,700
Miscellaneous Revenue (note 4)		700
Appropriations		72,000
Fund Balance (unreserved)		8,000
	100,000	100,000

NOTE 1: The current tax roll and miscellaneous accounts receivable, recorded on the accrual basis as sources of revenue, amounted to $50,000 and $20,000, respectively. These items have been recorded on the books subject to a 2 percent provision for uncollectible accounts.

NOTE 2: Includes $4,250 paid during the fiscal year in settlement of all purchase orders outstanding at the beginning of the fiscal year.

NOTE 3: Represents the difference between the budgeted (estimated) revenues of $70,000 and the actual revenues realized during the fiscal year.

NOTE 4: Represents the proceeds from sale of equipment damaged by fire.

Required:

a. Prepare an analysis of changes in fund balance in columnar form for the year ending June 30, 19X2, with column headings: Estimated, Actual, and Excess or Deficiency of Actual Compared with Estimated.

b. Prepare a general fund balance sheet at June 30, 19X2.

(AICPA adapted)

Problem 20–19   (Entries, Trial Balance, and Financial Statements—Purchases Method)

The following balances are related to the general fund of the city of Valhalla on July 1, 19X8:

Cash	28,500	Vouchers Payable	12,000
Taxes Receivable—		Fund Balance Reserved for	
Delinquent	31,200	Encumbrances	14,000
Allowance for Uncollectible Taxes		Fund Balance Reserved for	
Receivable—Delinquent	(2,800)	Materials and Supplies	5,300
Materials and Supplies	5,300	Fund Balance (unreserved)	30,900
	62,200		62,200

During the fiscal year ended June 30, 19X9, the following transactions were completed:

1. The annual budget was adopted by the city council; it provided for estimated revenues of $325,000 and appropriations of $330,000.

2. The current year's tax bill was levied in the amount of $344,000, of which $14,000 of receivable balances was estimated to be uncollectible.

3. Vouchers for all encumbrances through July 1, 19X8, were approved. Orders for new equipment were placed in the amount of $28,000.

4. Receivables for $23,000 of delinquent taxes were collected, along with interest and penalties of $460. Delinquent taxes of $2,500 were written off.

5. Cash of $10,000 was advanced to the general fund by the debt service fund.

6. The equipment ordered in (3) was vouchered for $30,000.

7. Vouchers for wages and salaries of $225,000 were approved.

8. Vouchers for the purchase of $65,000 of materials and supplies were approved. Materials and supplies inventories are accounted for using the purchases method.

9. Collections of $318,000 of current-year tax assessments were made; unpaid receivable balances were transferred to the Taxes Receivable—Delinquent account.

10. Additional collections for the issuance of licenses and permits amounted to $33,000.

11. Vouchers of $330,000 were paid.

12. Orders for $20,000 additional materials and supplies were placed.

13. The Materials and Supplies account and the related reserve account were adjusted to reflect materials and supplies on hand of $12,000 on June 30, 19X9.

Required:

a. Prepare the general fund's entries to reopen its encumbrances accounts.

b. Make all entries related to the general fund's budget, actual transactions, and encumbrances for the current fiscal year.

c. Prepare the general fund's trial balance at June 30, 19X9.

d. Prepare the general fund's financial statements for the year ended June 30, 19X9.

e. Record the general fund's closing entries.

Problem 20-20   (Entries and Financial Statements—Purchases Method)

You were engaged to examine the financial statements of the Mayfair School District for the year ended June 30, 19X1, and were furnished the general fund trial balance given below.

Your examination disclosed the following information:

1. The recorded estimate of losses for the current-year taxes receivable was considered to be sufficient.
2. The local government unit gave the school district 20 acres of land to be used for a new grade school and a community playground. The unrecorded estimated value of the land donated was $50,000. In addition, a state grant of $30,000 was received, and the full amount was used in payment of contracts pertaining to the construction of the grade school. Purchases of classroom and playground equipment costing $22,000 were paid from general funds.

MAYFAIR SCHOOL DISTRICT
General Fund Trial Balance
June 30, 19X1

	Debit	*Credit*
Cash	47,250	
Taxes Receivable—Current Year	31,800	
Estimated Losses—Current Year Taxes		1,800
Temporary Investments	11,300	
Inventory of Supplies (purchases method)	11,450	
Buildings	1,300,000	
Estimated Revenues	1,007,000	
Appropriations—Operating Expenses		850,000
Appropriations—Other Expenditures		150,000
State Grant Revenue		300,000
Bonds Payable		1,000,000
Vouchers Payable		10,200
Due to Internal Service Fund		950
Operating Expenses:		
Administration	24,950	
Instruction	601,800	
Other	221,450	
Transfer to Debt Service Fund (principal and		
interest)	130,000	
Capital Outlays (equipment)	22,000	
Revenues from Tax Levy, Licenses, and Fines		1,008,200
Capital Fund Balance		87,850
	3,409,000	3,409,000

3. Five years ago, $1,000,000 worth of 4 percent, 10-year sinking fund bonds was issued so that school buildings could be constructed. Interest on the issue is payable at maturity. Budgetary requirements of an annual contribution of $130,000 ($90,000 principal and $40,000 interest) and accumulated earnings to date aggregating $15,000 were accounted for in separate debt service fund accounts.

4. Outstanding purchase orders for operating expenses not recorded in the accounts at year-end were as follows:

Administration	$1,000
Instruction	1,200
Other	600
Total	$2,800

No purchase orders were outstanding on July 1, 19X0.

5. The school district operates a central machine shop. Billings amounting to $950 were recorded in the accounts of the general fund but not in the internal service fund.

Required:

a. Prepare the formal adjusting and closing entries for the general fund.

b. The information disclosed by your examination was recorded only in the general fund. Identify the other account groups or funds that should be adjusted in connection with your examination.

c. Prepare a statement of revenues, expenditures, and changes in fund balance for the fiscal year ended June 30, 19X1, and a balance sheet at June 30, 19X1, for the general fund.

(AICPA adapted)

Problem 20–21   (Budget Variances and Balance Sheet—Purchases Method)

The following information pertains to the operations of the general fund of X County government. The functions of this government include operating the county jail and the county courts.

Funds to finance the operations are provided from a levy of county taxes against the various towns of the county, from the state distribution of unincorporated business taxes, from assessments for board of jail prisoners against the town and against the state, and from interest on savings accounts.

The balances in the accounts of the fund on January 1, 19X1, were as follows.

Cash in savings accounts	$ 60,650
Cash in checking accounts	41,380
Cash on hand (undeposited prisoners board receipts)	320
Inventory of jail supplies (purchases method)	3,070
Due from town and state for board of prisoners	3,550
General fund	108,970

The budget for the year 19X1, as adopted by the county commissioners, provided for the following items of revenue and expenditure:

(1) Town and county taxes	$20,000
(2) Jail operating costs	55,500
(3) Court operating costs	7,500
(4) Unincorporated business tax	18,000
(5) Board of prisoners (revenue)	5,000
(6) Commissioners' salaries and expenses	8,000
(7) Interest on savings	1,000
(8) Miscellaneous expenses	1,000

The general fund balance was appropriated in sufficient amount to balance the budget. At December 31, 19X1, the jail supply inventory amounted to $5,120, cash of $380 was on hand, and board of prisoners bills of $1,325 were unpaid. The following items represent all of the transactions which occurred during the year, with all current bills vouchered and paid by December 31, 19X1:

Item (1) was transacted exactly as budgeted.	
Item (2) cash expenditures amounted to	$55,230
Item (3) amounted to	7,110
Item (4) amounted to	18,070
Item (5) billings amounted to	4,550
Item (6) amounted to	6,670
Item (7) amounted to	1,050
Item (8) amounted to	2,310

During the year, $25,000 was transferred from the savings accounts to the checking accounts.

Required:

From the above information, prepare a working paper providing columns to show the following:

a. The transactions for the year.

b. Variances between budgeted and actual revenues and expenditures for the year.

c. The balance sheet of the general fund for December 31, 19X1.

(AICPA adapted)

Problem 20–22   (Entries, Trial Balance, and Financial Statements—Purchases Method)

The general fund trial balance of the city of Soulna at December 31, 19X0, was as follows:

	Debit	Credit
Cash	62,000	
Taxes Receivable—Delinquent	46,000	
Estimated Uncollectible Taxes—Delinquent		8,000
Stores Inventory—Program Operations	18,000	
Vouchers Payable		28,000
Fund Balance Reserved for Stores Inventory		18,000
Fund Balance Reserved for Encumbrances		12,000
Unreserved Fund Balance		60,000
	126,000	126,000

Collectible delinquent taxes are expected to be collected within 60 days after the end of the year. Any taxes remaining uncollected at that time are authorized to be written off by the city board of commissioners. Assume that Soulna uses the purchases method to account for stores inventory for simplicity. The following data pertain to 19X1 general fund operations:

1. *Budget adopted:*

Revenues and other financing sources:

Taxes	$220,000
Fines, forfeits, and penalties	80,000
Miscellaneous revenues	100,000
Share of bond issue proceeds	200,000
	$600,000

Expenditures and other financing uses:

Program operations	$300,000
General administration	120,000
Stores—program operations	60,000
Capital outlay	80,000
Periodic transfer to special assessment fund	20,000
	$580,000

2. Taxes were assessed at an amount that would result in revenues of $220,800, after deduction of 4 percent of the tax levy as uncollectible.

3. Orders placed but not received:

Program operations	$176,000
General administration	80,000
Capital outlay	60,000
	$316,000

4. The city board of commissioners designated $20,000 of the unreserved, undesignated fund balance for possible future appropriation for capital outlay.

5. Cash collections and transfer:

Delinquent taxes	$ 38,000
Current taxes	226,000
Refund of overpayment of invoice for purchase of equipment (equipment purchased during current year)	4,000
Fines, forfeits, and penalties	88,000
Miscellaneous revenues	90,000
Share of bond issue proceeds	200,000
Transfer of residual equity of a discontinued fund	18,000
	$664,000

(Note: The city board of commissioners authorized the write-down of the Estimated Uncollectible Taxes balance to 4 percent of the outstanding balance in Taxes Receivable. Since this write-down is to be made in the same accounting period as the initial estimate was recorded, the adjustment should be restored to revenue.)

6. Canceled encumbrances:

	Estimated	*Actual*
Program operations	$156,000	$166,000
General administration	84,000	80,000
Capital outlay	62,000	62,000
	$302,000	$308,000

7. Additional vouchers:

Program operations	$188,000
General administration	38,000
Capital outlay	18,000
Transfer to special assessment fund	20,000
	$264,000

8. Alfred, a taxpayer, overpaid his 19X1 taxes by $2,000. He applied for a $2,000 credit against his 19X2 taxes. The city board of commissioners granted his request.

9. Vouchers paid amounted to $580,000.

10. Stores inventory on December 31, 19X1, amounted to $12,000.

11. The remaining uncollected taxes receivable assessed for 19X1 and the related allowance account are to be reclassified as delinquent.

Required:

a. Prepare journal entries to record the effects of the above transactions.

b. Prepare a trial balance as of December 31, 19X1.

c. Prepare all closing entries. Any outstanding encumbrances should be reclassified as reserved fund balance.

d. Prepare a December 31, 19X1, balance sheet and 19X1 statement of revenues, expenditures, and changes in fund balance for the general fund.

(AICPA adapted)

State and Local Governmental Units— Other Funds and Account Groups

Chapter Outline

Chapter 20 discusses accounting principles and concepts related to state and local governmental units (i.e., state, county, and municipal governmental units) and applies them to the general funds of these units. This chapter applies the same principles and concepts to the other funds and account groups of these units. Thus, it emphasizes accounting for typical transactions of these funds and account groups and the related financial statements. The classes of funds and account groups dealt with in this chapter are governmental funds, proprietary funds, fiduciary funds, and the general fixed asset and general long-term debt account groups.

GOVERNMENTAL FUNDS

Governmental funds are expendable funds. Thus, their resources may be expended entirely in accomplishing their objectives. The governmental funds of state and local governmental units are their general funds, special revenue funds, capital projects funds, debt service funds, and (previously) special assessments funds.[1] Examples of special revenue funds are funds established to maintain streets, roads, and bridges; to operate libraries, parks, and school districts (or systems); and to account for grants. Examples of capital projects funds are funds established to acquire or construct buildings, highways, and bridges. Debt service funds are used to accumulate the resources needed to pay the principal and interest of general long-term debt and any related debt service charges. When required, special assessment funds usually are established to undertake projects (e.g., street widening and paving and providing sidewalks, gutters, and street lighting) or supply services which provide general benefits to the public and specific benefits to particular citizen groups. Accordingly, the particularly benefited groups tend to bear disproportionate shares of the special assessments required to complete the projects or provide the services of special assessment funds.

All governmental funds are accounted for very similarly. Perhaps the most important similarity is that governmental funds, which have a governmental measurement focus, are accounted for using the modified accrual basis. Under this basis, revenues available to finance expenditures are matched with the related expenditures. In this regard, Chapter 20 illustrates the financial statements of the general fund. Similar financial statements are prepared for each additional type of governmental fund. The pertinent financial statements are the balance sheet and

---

[1] Recall from Chapter 20 that GASB *Statement 6* eliminates special assessment funds from the list of types of funds for which financial statements are prepared under GAAP. We cover these funds in this section since their financial statements are required in some jurisdictions for the purposes of legal compliance. Note also that governmental units may levy special assessments even if the related projects are not undertaken by special assessment funds. As explained later, special-assessment transactions are accounted for in other funds under GAAP.

the statement of revenues, expenditures, and changes in fund balance. Although individual financial statements are not provided in the following examples, the financial statements of governmental funds, as well as those of other types of funds and account groups, are illustrated (at the end of the chapter) in the context of *the combined fund and account group statements presented in Illustrations 21–1 through 21–6.* The preparation of these statements is easy; nevertheless, *your knowledge of governmental accounting will be greatly enhanced if you study the financial statements of each type of fund and account group after carefully examining the various examples contained in this chapter.*

Special Revenue Funds—Additional Discussion and Illustrative Entries

Special revenue funds generally are used when legal or policy requirements dictate that special funds be created to serve purposes which, otherwise, could be served through general funds. Thus, they normally are required by statute or charter. As mentioned, special revenue funds are established for purposes such as maintaining streets, roads, and bridges; operating libraries, parks, and school districts; and accounting for grants.

As a rule, the number of special revenue funds utilized is minimized by financing activities of the types mentioned above using the general fund when possible. Minimizing the number of special revenue funds reduces the complexity of financial statements and facilitates planning. Once created, however, each special revenue fund is accounted for as a separate entity using the modified accrual basis. The accounting procedures for special revenue funds usually parallel those of the general fund. Thus, their budgets (usually) are recorded in budgetary accounts, their actual transactions are recorded in proprietary accounts, their ordered and contracted for items are recorded in encumbrances accounts, and their books are closed, creating a permanent record of differences between actual and budgeted amounts. Since special revenue fund accounting is so similar to general fund accounting, only a brief example of the former is provided below. The example illustrates some of the more common types of special revenue fund entries.

Assume that the city of Franklyn operates its library through a special revenue fund. The operations of the library are financed partially through a special property tax. The estimated revenue from the tax is $70,000 for the current year. In addition, $10,000 is provided annually from the city's general fund to cover library expenditures. The library's total appropriation, including the budgeted amount to be spent on books, is $77,000.

The entry to record the budget of the special revenue fund follows:

Estimated Revenues and Operating Transfers In	80,000	
Appropriations		77,000
Fund Balance		3,000

Assuming that the actual tax levy is $75,000 (with no taxes expected to be uncollectible for simplicity), the entries to record tax revenue and the amount due from the general fund are as follows.

| Taxes Receivable .... | 75,000 | |
| Revenues .... | | 75,000 |

| Due from General Fund .... | 10,000 | |
| Operating Transfers In .... | | 10,000 |

The following entry, which records orders for books that are expected to cost $26,000, is typical of the entries made to record special revenue fund encumbrances.

| Encumbrances .... | 26,000 | |
| Reserve for Encumbrances .... | | 26,000 |

Assuming that the books actually cost $27,500, the following are the related entries:

| Expenditures .... | 27,500 | |
| Vouchers Payable .... | | 27,500 |

| Reserve for Encumbrances .... | 26,000 | |
| Encumbrances .... | | 26,000 |

| Vouchers Payable .... | 27,500 | |
| Cash .... | | 27,500 |

Although not illustrated, the closing entries of special revenue funds usually are identical to those of general funds. Additionally, the encumbrances accounts of special revenue funds also are reopened as of the beginning of the next fiscal period. You may want to review the closing entries and the entries to reopen the encumbrances accounts of the municipality of Cityville presented in Chapter 20 since entries similar to all, or some, of these apply to all governmental funds.

Capital Projects Funds—Additional Discussion and Illustrative Entries

The acquisition and construction of major fixed assets often are financed through capital projects funds. Thus, these funds tend to be used in acquiring or constructing structures such as buildings, highways, and bridges. Such funds provide administrators with mechanisms for ensuring that revenues provided for capital projects are used solely for their intended purposes. Capital projects funds typically exist only until their purposes are satisfied (which may take more than one year).

The accounting procedures for a capital projects fund are similar to those of the general fund. Note, however, that budgetary accounts usually are not used in accounting for these funds. Thus, the accounts used for capital projects funds tend to be proprietary accounts and encumbrances accounts. Although recommended, even encumbrances accounts sometimes are not used in accounting for these funds. Note also that fixed assets acquired or constructed using capital projects funds are not accounted for in these funds; they are accounted for in the general fixed assets account group. Similarly, long-term debts incurred to acquire or construct capital project fund assets are accounted for in the general long-term debt account group.

Capital projects funds have three common sources of resources: (1) transfers from other funds—usually the general fund, (2) grants from other governmental units, and (3) proceeds of bond issues. Transfers from other funds are recorded as Operating Transfers In; grants from other governmental units are recorded as Intergovernmental Revenues. All, or part, of the proceeds of bond issues are credited to Proceeds of Bond Issues accounts (see below).

The issuance of bonds at a discount by governmental units frequently is prohibited by statute. If the proceeds of a bond issue, including any premium, are available for use on a related capital project, the entire proceeds of the issue are credited to the Proceeds of Bond Issue account. If only proceeds equal to the par value of the bonds are available for the project, the par value of the bonds is credited to this account, and the premium is credited to the Premium on Bonds account. The balance in this latter account recognizes an obligation of the capital projects fund to transfer proceeds from the bond issue equal to its premium to the related debt service fund (or other fund responsible for servicing the bonds). Note that, under GASB *Statement 11*, bond premium is considered to be an "other financing source" to a capital projects fund, even if unavailable for the project. Logically, if an amount equal to bond premium is transferred to a debt service fund, this transfer would be classified as an "other financing use." Frequently encountered capital projects fund entries are illustrated below.

Assume that the city of Bellair is going to construct a new city hall in 19X1 using a capital projects fund and that $4 million is authorized to construct the building. The city's general fund is to provide $500,000 of this amount, and $2 million of the needed amount is to be supplied by an agency of the federal government. The remaining $1,500,000 is to be raised through a general obligation term bond issue with a par value of $1,500,000.[2]

Given that the resources to be provided by the general fund and the federal agency are received immediately (they usually would be accrued otherwise), the related entry follows:

Cash	2,500,000	
Operating Transfers In		500,000
Intergovernmental Revenues		2,000,000

If the bonds are issued at a premium of $100,000 and proceeds equal only to the par value of the bonds are available for the project, the entry to record the issuance of the bonds is as follows.

---

[2] General obligation debt issues are backed by the "full faith and credit" of governmental units. Thus, they represent claims on all the revenues of these units. Such debts usually are issued by governmental units' general funds and capital projects funds.

```
Cash ...........................................  1,600,000
     Proceeds of General Obligation Term
          Bond Issue .............................              1,500,000
     Premium on Bonds  ...........................                100,000
```

Assuming that the Premium on Bonds account represents an obligation to the related debt service fund of the city, cash equal to the premium is transferred to this fund. The entry to record this transfer is as follows:

```
Premium on Bonds  ...........................    100,000
     Cash ......................................              100,000
```

Assume next that the construction project is initiated by engaging an architect. The estimated architectural fee is $120,000. Assuming that encumbrance accounting is used, the encumbrance for the estimated architect's fee is recorded below.

```
Encumbrances ...................................    120,000
     Reserve for Encumbrances .....................              120,000
```

Given that the architect completes her work and submits a bill for $127,500, the following entries are made.

```
Expenditures ...................................    127,500
     Vouchers Payable  ...........................              127,500

Reserve for Encumbrances  ........................    120,000
     Encumbrances ...............................              120,000

Vouchers Payable ...............................    127,500
     Cash ......................................              127,500
```

Entries similar to those illustrated for the architect would be made for most other project expenditures.

Assuming that the project's expenditures amount to $3,800,000 and that all construction activity occurs during the current period (as expected), the following closing entry is made.

```
Operating Transfers In .........................    500,000
Intergovernmental Revenues  .....................  2,000,000
Proceeds of General Obligation Term
     Bond Issue  ................................  1,500,000
          Expenditures ..........................             3,800,000
          Fund Balance  .........................               200,000
```

Once all vouchers related to the project are paid, the unexpended cash of $200,000 is transferred to the debt service fund for the newly issued bonds, and the capital projects fund is terminated. The following entry records these events.

```
Fund Balance  ..................................    200,000
     Cash ......................................              200,000
```

Debt Service Funds—Additional Discussion and Illustrative Entries

Debt service funds are used to accumulate the resources needed to pay the principal and interest of general long-term debts and related debt service charges. One type of general long-term debt is general obligation long-term debt. As indicated in footnote 2, general obligation long-term debt is backed by the full faith and credit of the governmental unit. Nevertheless, the phrase *general long-term debt* encompasses more than just general obligation debt. For example, the general long-term debt of governmental units includes all long-term debts which are guaranteed through taxes (i.e., all tax-supported debt) and the long-term debts arising in connection with special assessments.[3] In short, general long-term debt is the long-term debt of governmental units that is not serviced by proprietary funds or nonexpendable trust funds.

The accounting procedures for debt service funds are similar to those for the general fund. Thus, debt service funds usually record their budgets. In this context, debt service funds tend to service their debt via interfund transfers and fund earnings. In this case, the Estimated Revenues and Operating Transfers In account is debited for the budgeted resource inflows. Also, in recording the budget, the Appropriations account is credited for the period's expected debt service payments, including debt principal, interest, and debt service charges. The actual revenues and operating transfers in of the fund are credited to Revenues and Operating Transfers In accounts, and the Expenditures account is debited for the period's interest, principal reductions, and service charges. Liabilities for debt principal and interest are recorded as credits when the Expenditures account is debited. Debt service charges are recorded as expenditures when made. Typical entries of a debt service fund are illustrated below.

Assume that the city of Bellair has a debt service fund related to an issue of 6 percent general obligation serial bonds. These bonds, which have a par value of $1,100,000 outstanding on December 31, 19X0, were issued on January 1, 19X0. On January 1, 19X1, $100,000 of these bonds matures, and related service charges, which are estimated to be $500, are due on July 1, 19X1. The actual service charges turn out to be $750. Since the bonds pay interest on January 1 and July 1, interest on the bonds of $33,000 [50% × (60% × $1,100,000)] is due on January 1, 19X1, and interest of $30,000 [50% × (60% × $1,000,000)] is due on July 1, 19X1. The resources expected to be required in paying bond principal, interest, and service charges are provided by the city's general fund on January 1 and July 1. To ensure that sufficient amounts are available to pay bond principal as it becomes due, $10,000 of taxes are levied annually. The taxes are payable on July 1, 19X1. Assume for simplicity that all taxes are collected on this date.

On January 1, 19X1, entries are needed to record the debt service fund's budget, the transfer from the general fund, the assessment of the taxes, the

---

[3] An example of tax-supported debt that is not a general obligation debt is limited obligation debt. Such debt is secured by specific, rather than general, tax revenues.

obligations for bond principal and interest, and the related payments to bond-holders. In sequence, these entries follow:

Estimated Revenues and Operating Transfers In
($100,000 + $500 + $33,000 +
$30,000 + $10,000) 173,500
  Appropriations 163,500
  Fund Balance 10,000

Cash ($100,000 + $33,000) 133,000
  Operating Transfers In 133,000

Taxes Receivable 10,000
  Revenues 10,000

Expenditures 133,000
  Bonds Payable 100,000
  Interest Payable 33,000

Bonds Payable 100,000
Interest Payable 33,000
  Cash 133,000

On July 1, 19X1, entries are needed to record the transfer from the general fund for the payment of semiannual interest and the estimated debt service charges, the debt service fund's obligation to the remaining bondholders for interest, the payment of this interest, the payment of the debt service charges, and the collection of the taxes. These entries, respectively, are as follows:

Cash 30,500
  Operating Transfers In 30,500

Expenditures 30,000
  Interest Payable 30,000

Interest Payable 30,000
  Cash 30,000

Expenditures 750
  Cash 750

Cash 10,000
  Taxes Receivable 10,000

At year-end, the debt service fund's closing entry is as follows:

Revenues 10,000
Operating Transfers In 163,500
Appropriations 163,500
Fund Balance 250
  Expenditures 163,750
  Estimated Revenues and Operating
   Transfers In 173,500

Note that the December 31, 19X1, accrued interest of $30,000 is not recorded. Under GASB pronouncements, unmatured interest on general long-term debt is recognized by debt-service funds only when due unless resources have been provided for interest due early in the next period. If resources have been provided, expenditures and related liabilities may be recognized in the current period.

Special Assessment Funds—Additional Discussion and Illustrative Entries

Special assessment funds usually are established to undertake projects or supply services which provide general benefits to the public and specific benefits to particular citizen groups. Thus, the projects and services undertaken by these funds differ from those provided through the general fund. As indicated, financial statements for special assessment funds no longer are prepared under GAAP. Currently, special assessment transactions are reported under GAAP through other funds of the types illustrated in this chapter. Hay and Wilson provide the following summary of special assessment accounting under GAAP:

> Briefly the construction phase transactions of a project being financed in whole or in part by special assessments are to be reported in the same manner as capital projects financed with tax-supported debt. Transactions of the debt service phase of such a project are to be reported in the same manner as debt service of tax-supported debt if the government has some obligation to assume debt service in case property owners default; if the government has **no** obligation to assume debt service, but does collect the assessments and remit those collections to creditors, the transactions are reported in an agency fund.[4]

Since financial statements are required for special assessment funds in some jurisdictions, we illustrate special assessment accounting ignoring GAAP requirements below.

Ignoring GAAP requirements, special assessment accounting is similar to general fund accounting. Note, however, that if a special assessment fund's project (or services) is to be financed initially by a bond issue, the bond proceeds and the related liability are accounted for within the fund. Additionally, bond interest is accrued in special assessment fund accounting since the bonds of such a fund are not general obligation long-term debt. The assessments of the fund are used to pay bond interest and principal. Although long-term debt is accounted for in special assessment funds, fixed assets resulting from special assessment fund projects are not included in the assets of these funds. These assets are accounted for in the general fixed assets account group. Note also that special assessment fund budgets usually are not recorded. Special assessment accounting is illustrated below ignoring GAAP requirements.

---

[4] Leon E. Hay and Earl R. Wilson, *Accounting for Governmental and Nonprofit Entities* (Homewood, IL: Richard D. Irwin, 1992), pp. 272–273.

Assume that the city council of the city of Bellair authorizes a special assessment for the construction of sidewalks in a new subdivision on January 1, 19X1, and enters into a $200,000 contract for their construction on this date. The contract is 50 percent complete at fiscal year-end, and the contract calls for payment of 50 percent of the contracted amount to the contractor at this time. The property owners benefiting specifically from the sidewalks are to be assessed for their cost on January 1, 19X1. The assessments are to be paid in $100,000 installments at the end of each year for two years with 8 percent interest being charged on unpaid assessment balances (with interest payable on January 1). The special assessment fund is going to finance the project until all the special assessments are collected through the issuance of two-year, 10 percent bonds with a par value of $150,000 (with interest also payable on January 1). The bonds are issued at par on January 1, 19X1. The city's general fund is to advance its special assessment fund $25,000 for working capital purposes immediately. During the period, the latter expends $10,000 of this amount on miscellaneous items. The entries for Bellair's special assessment fund are given below.

On the first day of the fiscal year, entries to record the contract to construct the sidewalks, the receipt of the cash advance from the general fund, and the issuance of the bonds are made as follows.

Encumbrances	200,000	
Reserve for Encumbrances		200,000
Cash	25,000	
Due to General Fund		25,000
Cash	150,000	
Bonds Payable		150,000

On the same day, the special assessment levy of $200,000 on the property holders to benefit specifically from the sidewalks is recorded through the next entry.

Assessments Receivable—Current ($200,000/2)	100,000	
Assessments Receivable—Deferred	100,000	
Revenues		100,000
Deferred Revenues		100,000

Special assessment revenues of $100,000 are deferred because they pertain to the next fiscal year.

The following entries record the expenditures for miscellaneous items during the period. These entries assume that encumbrances are not recorded because the related invoices, and so on, are paid almost immediately.

Expenditures	10,000	
Vouchers Payable		10,000
Vouchers Payable	10,000	
Cash		10,000

On the last day of the fiscal year, the liability and the payment for 50 percent of the contracted amount are recorded as shown below (assuming there are no adjustments to the contract price).

Expenditures	100,000	
Vouchers Payable		100,000
Reserve for Encumbrances	100,000	
Encumbrances		100,000
Vouchers Payable	100,000	
Cash		100,000

Interest also is accrued on both the assessment receivables and the bonds payable on the last day of the fiscal period. These interest figures are recorded as follows.

Interest Receivable (8% × $200,000)	16,000	
Revenues		16,000
Expenditures	15,000	
Interest Payable (10% × $150,000)		15,000

The interest on the assessment receivables is accrued under the modified basis because it will be collected shortly after the end of the fiscal year on January 1, 19X2. The interest on the bonds is accrued even though it is not due because the bonds are not general long-term debt (i.e., the bonds are obligations of the special assessment fund).

The closing entries for the first year of the special assessment fund's operations are as follows:

Fund Balance	9,000	
Revenues ($100,000 + $16,000)	116,000	
Expenditures		
($100,000 + $10,000 + $15,000)		125,000
Reserve for Encumbrances ($200,000 − $100,000)	100,000	
Encumbrances		100,000

PROPRIETARY FUNDS

The proprietary funds of state and local governmental units are nonexpendable funds. Thus, the principal, or capital, balances of these funds must be preserved. The two types of proprietary funds are enterprise funds and internal service funds. Examples of enterprise funds are funds established to account for transportation systems, electricity and natural gas utilities, water and sewer systems, toll roads and bridges, parking lots and garages, public housing, airports, and recreational facilities. Typical internal service funds are automotive equipment funds, self-insurance funds, and stores (or supplies) funds.

Enterprise funds are financed and operated similarly to profit-seeking entities. They are established to provide goods or services primarily to the general public for fees. Because of their profit-seeking nature, enterprise funds have a proprietary measurement focus and are accounted for using the accrual procedures of business entities. As indicated, this focus emphasizes the matching of revenues and expenses (including depreciation expense) to enhance efficiency in governmental activities. Internal service funds also have a proprietary measurement focus and are accounted for analogously to enterprise funds. However, internal funds provide goods or services to other departments or agencies of the governmental unit on a user charge basis.

Like governmental funds, individual financial statements are prepared for proprietary funds. The financial statements that are pertinent to proprietary funds are the balance sheet; the statement of revenues, expenses, and changes in retained earnings; and the statement of cash flows. Examples of these statements are contained in Illustrations 21–1, 21–4, and 21–6 (at the end of the chapter).[5] The preparation of these statements is particularly easy because of the similarity between proprietary fund accounting and business-related accounting. Nevertheless, as indicated before, *your knowledge of governmental accounting will be greatly enhanced if you study the financial statements of each type of fund and account group after carefully examining the various examples contained in this chapter.*

Enterprise Funds—Additional Discussion and Illustrative Entries

Enterprise funds exist primarily to account for services rendered to the public for fees. As indicated, enterprise funds have a proprietary measurement focus and are accounted for accordingly. Thus, enterprise fund accounting procedures are essentially the same as those for business entities. For example, fixed assets acquired by enterprise funds are included in their accounts, and depreciation expense and accumulated depreciation are recorded on these assets. Note, however, that enterprise fund fixed assets (long-term debts) sometimes are listed first in the assets (liabilities) sections of the individual balance sheets of enterprise funds to emphasize the ongoing nature of these funds. Examples of typical entries of enterprise funds follow.

Assume the following data for the electric utility fund (an enterprise fund) of the city of Subrosa. These data pertain to the fiscal year ended December 31, 19X0.

---

[5] Note that Illustration 21–5 contains a combined statement of changes in financial position—all proprietary fund types and similar trust funds. GASB *Statement 9* requires the statement of cash flows for fiscal years beginning after December 15, 1989. Thus, Illustration 21–5 is presented primarily for historical perspective. Also, the data from this statement are used in developing Illustration 21–6. Illustration 21–6 ignores the governmental unit's pension trust fund since such funds are not required to present a statement of cash flows (or a statement of changes in financial position) under GASB *Statement 9*.

Billings to customers for sales of electricity:
   Billings to nongovernmental customers $500,000
   Billings to general fund of Subrosa 50,000
Collections from customers for sales of electricity:
   Collections from nongovernmental customers 450,000
   Collections from general fund of Subrosa 45,000
Customer electricity deposits:
   Billed and collected 1,000
   Refunded 300
Generating equipment purchased 50,000
Materials and supplies purchased 5,000
Uncollectible customer accounts at year-end 2,500
Customer deposits applied to unpaid bills 1,500
Expenses incurred:
   Depreciation expense (electricity plant) 240,000
   Customer accounts expense (i.e., bad debts expense)
     estimated 10,000
   Other operating expenses 290,000
Various payables liquidated 470,000
Year-end accruals for electricity service 20,000

The entries related to these data, along with explanations, are given below.

The following two entries record sales of electricity for the period and related collections. We emphasize that these entries, as well as several of the entries presented later, are summary entries for the period (rather than the actual entries made).

Customer Accounts Receivable 500,000
Due from General Fund 50,000
   Sales of Electricity 550,000

Cash 495,000
   Customer Accounts Receivable 450,000
   Due from General Fund 45,000

The next set of entries records customer electricity deposits billed, collected, and refunded. Note that the account, Customer Deposits, is a liability account; it reflects amounts due to customers upon termination of their services, provided that their accounts have been settled in full.

Customer Accounts Receivable 1,000
   Customer Deposits 1,000

Cash 1,000
   Customer Accounts Receivable 1,000

Customer Deposits 300
   Cash 300

Customer Deposits	300	
Cash		300

The next two entries record purchases during the period of several items: generating equipment and materials and supplies. The generating equipment is capitalized rather than recorded as an expenditure since the fund is an enterprise fund. For the same reason, the materials and supplies necessarily are accounted for using the consumption method.

Generating Equipment	50,000	
Cash or Accounts Payable		50,000
Materials and Supplies	5,000	
Cash or Accounts Payable		5,000

The next entry records the other operating expenses incurred during the period. This entry is consistent with the use of the consumption method on materials and supplies. The subsequent entry records payment of some of the accounts payable recorded in the operating expenses entry as well as accounts payable on the fund's books at the beginning of the year.

Other Operating Expenses	290,000	
Cash, Accounts Payable, Materials and		
Supplies, and So On		290,000
Accounts Payable	470,000	
Cash		470,000

The following entry applies customer deposits to uncollectible customer accounts and writes off the remaining uncollectible amounts. These amounts are debited to Accumulated Provision for Uncollectible Accounts.

Customer Deposits	1,500	
Accumulated Provision for Uncollectible		
Accounts	1,000	
Customer Accounts Receivable		2,500

The fund's year-end adjusting entries are given below. Note that depreciation expense is recorded since the fund is an enterprise fund. For the same reason, customer accounts expense is accrued.

Accrued Electricity Revenues	20,000	
Sales of Electricity		20,000
Depreciation Expense	240,000	
Accumulated Provision for Depreciation of		
Electricity Plant		240,000
Customer Accounts Expense	10,000	
Accumulated Provision for Uncollectible		
Accounts		10,000

The fund's closing entry, which includes a credit to Retained Earnings, is as follows. The use of the Retained Earnings account emphasizes the profit-seeking nature of enterprise funds.

Sales of Electricity	570,000	
Other Operating Expenses		290,000
Depreciation Expense		240,000
Customer Accounts Expense		10,000
Retained Earnings		30,000

Internal Service Funds—Additional Discussion and Illustrative Entries

Internal service funds, which also are referred to as *revolving funds, working capital funds,* and *intragovernmental service funds,* are established to provide goods (possibly manufactured) or services to the various segments of the governmental unit. An internal service fund may be financed initially by an advance from one or more other funds or by the sale of bonds. As in the case of enterprise funds, internal service funds have a proprietary measurement focus and are accounted for using accrual procedures. Thus, internal service fund accounting procedures also are analogous to those of businesses. Examples of typical entries of internal service funds are presented next.

Assume that the city of Oracal decides to acquire and to issue all supplies centrally through a stores fund. The city's stores fund is established by transferring cash of $190,000 and supplies costing $100,000 from its general fund. The sum of these two amounts, $290,000, is the beginning equity balance of the stores fund. The following entry records this initial equity transfer in and the related asset amounts.

Cash	190,000	
Inventory of Supplies	100,000	
Equity Transfer In		290,000

Assume next that part of the cash is used to purchase a warehouse and its site for $160,000 (with $40,000 of this amount allocated to land) and a delivery truck for $12,000. These acquisitions are recorded as follows.

Land	40,000	
Building	120,000	
Delivery Truck	12,000	
Cash		172,000

Subsequently, the stores fund issues supplies costing $60,000 to the city's general fund and supplies costing $10,000 to its electric utility fund. The stores fund's supplies inventory is accounted for using the consumption method since it is an internal service fund. Supplies issued are marked up 100 percent based on cost by the stores fund.[6] The account, Billings to Governmental Units, is a revenue account that is used to record issuances of supplies. The following entries record the issuances of the supplies and the assumed payments.

Cost of Supplies Issued	70,000	
Inventory of Supplies		70,000
Due from General Fund (2 × $60,000)	120,000	
Due from Electric Utility Fund (2 × $10,000)	20,000	
Billings to Governmental Units		140,000
Cash	87,500	
Due from General Fund		75,000
Due from Electric Utility Fund		12,500

Assume that the stores fund acquires additional supplies on credit for $20,000 and pays for this purchase shortly thereafter. These events are recorded via the following entries.

Inventory of Supplies	20,000	
Vouchers Payable		20,000
Vouchers Payable	20,000	
Cash		20,000

The following entries record the fund's administrative, warehousing, and delivery expenses for the period (except for depreciation expense) and the payments of the related vouchers.

Administrative Expenses	10,000	
Warehousing Expenses	15,000	
Delivery Expenses	20,000	
Vouchers Payable		45,000
Vouchers Payable	45,000	
Cash		45,000

Assume finally that depreciation expense of $8,000 is recorded at year-end and that there are no accrued revenues and expenses at this time for simplicity. Of the $8,000 in depreciation, $5,000 pertains to the fund's warehouse, and $3,000 applies to its delivery truck. The depreciation expense is recorded as follows.

Warehousing Expenses	5,000	
Delivery Expenses	3,000	
Accumulated Depreciation—Building		5,000
Accumulated Depreciation—		
Delivery Equipment		3,000

---

[6] Cost accounting procedures often are used in establishing the prices charged by internal service funds. The total expenditures of such a fund necessarily are limited to the amounts the various governmental segments are authorized to spend for its goods or services. Thus, there is no need for legislative bodies to restrict the expenditures of internal service funds through appropriations.

The stores fund's closing entries for the period are as follows:

Billings to Governmental Units	140,000	
Cost of Supplies Issued		70,000
Administrative Expenses		10,000
Warehousing Expenses		20,000
Delivery Expenses		23,000
Retained Earnings		17,000
Equity Transfer In	290,000	
Contributed Capital		290,000

FIDUCIARY FUNDS—TRUST AND AGENCY FUNDS

Trust and agency funds are used to collect, invest, or expend, in a fiduciary capacity, resources provided by individuals, private organizations, and other governmental units for various purposes. Trust funds are classified as nonexpendable trust funds, expendable trust funds, and pension trust funds. Nonexpendable trust funds are similar to proprietary funds, and expendable trust funds are similar to special revenue funds. An example of a nonexpendable trust fund is a fund established to maintain and to account for trust principal (or endowment or corpus) provided by a donor with the stipulation that the related income is to be used for a particular purpose (with the income transferred to an expendable trust fund). In contrast, an example of an expendable trust fund is a fund established to expend the revenue from an endowment established by a donor for some specific purpose. Examples of pension trust funds are funds which accumulate contributions to governmental units' pension plans, invest these resources, and make pension payments to qualified participants. Agency funds generally are established to account for assets (usually cash) received for, and payable to, other funds, although certain types of agency funds perform additional, more complex tasks. Examples of agency funds are deferred compensation agency funds (which account for employees' contributions to (tax) deferred compensation plans) and tax agency funds (which bill, collect, and disburse taxes and related penalties and interest of governmental units).

Nonexpendable trust funds and pension trust funds have proprietary measurement focuses; expendable trust funds have governmental measurement focuses.[7] Agency funds also have governmental measurement focuses. Thus, nonexpendable trust funds and pension trust funds are accounted for using the accrual basis and expendable trust funds and agency funds are accounted for using

---

[7] The accounting rules for pension trust funds are complicated and controversial. Under these rules, the tendency is to account for pension trust funds more or less consistently with funds with a proprietary measurement focus. Thus, for simplicity, we treat pension trust funds as proprietary in our discussions and do not delve into the complexities of accounting for these funds.

the modified accrual basis (although agency funds do not have revenues and expenditures accounts). Examples of the accounting procedures for nonexpendable and expendable trust funds and agency funds are provided below.

The financial statements that are pertinent to nonexpendable trust funds and pension trust funds are the balance sheet; the statement of revenues, expenses, and changes in retained earnings (or fund balance in the case of pension trust funds); and the statement of cash flows (except for pension trust funds). The financial statements that are relevent to expendable trust funds are the balance sheet and the statement of revenues, expenditures, and changes in fund balance. Only the balance sheet is pertinent to agency funds since they do not have revenues and expenditures accounts. All of these types of statements are illustrated, in essence, in Illustrations 21–1 to 21–6. *Your grasp of governmental accounting will be greatly improved if you examine the financial statements of the trust and agency funds found in these illustrations after carefully studying the following examples.*

Trust Funds—Illustrative Entries

Assume that Carlos Devine, a wealthy citizen of the city of Katalina, donates $500,000 to the city. The revenues from this endowment are to be used to cover the expenses of planting native trees and shrubs on city-owned properties. The city establishes two funds to account for the gift—a nonexpendable trust fund called the Devine Endowment Fund and an expendable trust fund called the Devine Endowment Earnings Fund. The first fund is used to account solely for the endowment provided by Carlos Devine; the latter fund is used to account for the revenues from the endowment and related tree and shrub expenditures.

The following entries pertain to the Devine Endowment Fund. In sequence, they reflect Carlos Devine's donation, the investment of the donation in revenue-generating securities, the receipt of the period's revenues (with no accruals needed at year-end), and the liability for, and related payment of, the endowment fund's earnings to the earnings fund. Note that budgetary accounts and encumbrances accounts usually are not used on nonexpendable trust funds.

Cash	500,000	
Devine Endowment Fund Balance		500,000
Investments	500,000	
Cash		500,000
Cash	30,000	
Dividend and Interest Revenue		30,000
Dividend and Interest Revenue	30,000	
Due to Devine Endowment Earnings Fund		30,000
Due to Devine Endowment Earnings Fund	30,000	
Cash		30,000

The following entries are related to the Devine Endowment Earnings Fund. The entries assume that $29,750 is spent on trees and shrubs during the period with the related liability being paid at year-end. They also assume that budgetary and encumbrances accounts are not used in accounting for the earnings fund for simplicity. However, note that the use of budgetary accounts may be required by law in the case of expendable trust funds.

Due from Devine Endowment Fund	30,000	
Transfers In		30,000
Cash	30,000	
Due from Devine Endowment Fund		30,000
Expenditures	29,750	
Vouchers Payable		29,750
Vouchers Payable	29,750	
Cash		29,750

The closing entry for the earnings fund follows:

Transfers In	30,000	
Expenditures		29,750
Fund Balance		250

Agency Funds—Illustrative Entries

Assume that the city of Hiko uses a tax agency fund to collect property taxes on behalf of its School District and Recreation Department. Assume further that the taxes to be collected during the year amount to $480,000. Of this total, $300,000 is to be paid to the Hiko School District; $180,000 is due to the Hiko Recreation Department. The following entries record the taxes receivable by the tax agency fund and the collections and subsequent remittances of the taxes to the Hiko School District and Recreation Department.

Taxes Receivable for Other Governmental Units	480,000	
Due to Other Governmental Units		480,000
Cash	480,000	
Taxes Receivable for Other Governmental Units		480,000
Due to Other Governmental Units	480,000	
Due to Hiko School District		300,000
Due to Hiko Recreation Department		180,000
Due to Hiko School District	300,000	
Due to Hiko Recreation Department	180,000	
Cash		480,000

Account Groups for General Fixed Assets and General Long-Term Debt

In governmental accounting, account groups for general fixed assets and general long-term debt are established as separate accounting (but not fiscal) entities of governmental units. These groups provide records of the general fixed assets and the general long-term debts of these units. Such records are needed to safeguard the units' general fixed assets and to ensure that their general long-term debts are serviced properly. The general fixed assets of a governmental unit are those which are not related to proprietary or trust funds. Similarly, the general long-term debts of a governmental unit are those that are not related to these funds.

Account groups for general fixed assets and general long-term debt are balancing sets of accounts. The primary financial statement pertinent to these groups is the balance sheet since they are maintained simply to provide records of the governmental unit's general fixed assets and general long-term debts. Note, however, that the balance sheet for the general fixed assets account group often is supplemented by a schedule revealing the descriptions and the dollar amounts of additions to, and deductions from, the various fixed asset classes during the period. Similarly, the balance sheet for the general long-term debt account group frequently is supplemented by a schedule revealing the changes in the various classes of general long-term debt during the period. Examples of balance sheets for these account groups are provided in Illustration 21–1. We believe that *your understanding of the general fixed assets and general long-term debt account groups will be facilitated if you examine this illustration after studying each of the following examples.*

The General Fixed Assets Account Group—Additional Discussion and Illustrative Entries

Governmental units' general fixed assets usually are acquired through the activities of their general funds (e.g., using general revenues or proceeds of general obligation bond issues) and capital projects funds, through special assessments, and through gifts. These assets are accounted for in general fixed assets account groups.[8] As mentioned, these account groups merely provide records of the general fixed assets of these units.

---

[8] General fixed assets also are acquired through leasing. In this context, the GASB accepts the FASB's criteria for capital leases. Thus, if these criteria are satisfied, assets related to capital leases are recorded in the general fixed assets account group. Related lease obligations are recorded in the general long-term debt account group (see below).

The general fixed assets of governmental units are recorded in general fixed asset group accounts at cost or, if acquired by gifts, at their fair values on the dates of the gifts. When general fixed assets are recorded, the offsetting credits are made to investment accounts—which reflect the sources of the fixed assets (e.g., Investment in General Fixed Assets—General Obligation Bonds, Investment in General Fixed Assets—General Fund Revenues, and Investment in General Fixed Assets—Gifts). Note also that most governmental accounting authorities recommend that transfers of fixed assets between funds or between funds and general fixed asset group accounts be recorded using book values rather than fair values.

As indicated in Chapter 20 (see principle .107), depreciation may be recorded in the general fixed assets account group. When depreciation is recorded in this group, the credits to Accumulated Depreciation are offset by debits to the related investment accounts. Dispositions of general fixed assets are recorded simply by reversing the entries made when the assets are acquired, assuming that depreciation is not being recorded. If depreciation is being recorded, dispositions require debits to the pertinent investment accounts equaling the unamortized costs of the disposed of fixed assets as well as the elimination of the balances in the fixed asset accounts and related accumulated depreciation accounts. In the following example, we assume that depreciation is not recorded for simplicity.

Assume that the city of Bellair maintains an account group for general fixed assets consistently with GAAP and that the current fiscal year is 19X1. Recall that Bellair completed its new city hall through a capital projects fund and partially completed sidewalks for a new subdivision through a special assessment during 19X1 (see above discussion and examples related to these projects).[9] Assume also that land with a fair value of $55,000 is donated to the city during 19X1 and that the city sells its (old) general fund administration building, which cost $250,000, for $100,000 during the year. The land can be used for any purpose, and the building was purchased using general fund revenues. Finally, assume that Bellair's city council decides in 19X1 that a city water utility fund building is going to be used in the future in housing the administrators of the city's general fund. The cost of this building is $300,000, and the related accumulated depreciation to date is $125,000. Accumulated depreciation has been recorded on the building because the water utility fund is an enterprise fund. The entries to record these events are provided below.

---

[9] We ignore the fact that a special assessment fund is used in constructing the sidewalks since financial statements are not prepared for such funds under GAAP. Thus, the entry given below to record the sidewalk construction in progress contains a credit to Investment in General Fixed Assets—Special Assessments—Property Owners rather than to Investment in General Fixed Assets—Special Assessments Fund—Property Owners.

The first two entries record the completion of the city hall and the partial completion of the sidewalks. Note that construction in progress is recorded in the general fixed assets account group.

Buildings	3,800,000	
Investment in General Fixed Assets—		
Capital Projects Fund—General Fund		
Revenues		300,000
Investment in General Fixed Assets—		
Capital Projects Fund—Federal Grant		2,000,000
Investment in General Fixed Assets—		
Capital Projects Fund—General		
Obligation Bonds		1,500,000
Construction in Progress	125,000	
Investment in General Fixed Assets—		
Special Assessments—Property Owners		125,000
Land	55,000	
Investment in General Fixed Assets—		
Gifts		55,000

The next entry records the disposition of the old administration building. Notice that the proceeds from the disposition of this building are not recorded in the general fixed assets accounts group. Such proceeds usually are recorded in general funds.

Investment in General Fixed Assets—General		
Fund Revenues	250,000	
Buildings		250,000

The final entry records the transfer of the water utility fund building to the general fixed assets account group at book value.[10]

Buildings	175,000	
Investment in General Fixed Assets—Water		
Utility Fund ($300,000 − $125,000)		175,000

The General Long-Term Debt Account Group—Additional Discussion and Illustrative Entries

Governmental units' general long-term debts usually arise through the operations of their general funds and capital projects funds. Speaking generally, however, the

---

[10] The water utility fund records a $175,000 loss on the transfer.

general long-term debts of governmental units are those that are not serviced through proprietary or nonexpendable trust funds. Such debts are accounted for using general long-term debt account groups. As mentioned, these account groups simply provide records of the general long-term debts of governmental units. Thus, they are not used to account for the proceeds of long-term debt issues or for related debt service.

Although the general long-term debt account group is not used for the purposes just mentioned, there are a variety of relationships between this account group and the other funds of a governmental unit. Several of these relationships are described below. First, at the time general long-term debt is issued, a liability account in the general long-term debt account group (e.g., Term Bonds Payable) is credited to record the liability. The offsetting debit is to the Amount to Be Provided for Payment of Debt account (e.g., the Amount to Be Provided for Payment of Term Bonds account). Second, at the time funds designated for principal reduction (e.g., a transfer in from the General Fund) become available to a debt service fund to reduce general long-term debt, the Amount Available in Debt Service Fund for Payment of Debt account (e.g., the Amount Available in Debt Service Fund for Payment of Term Bonds account) is debited for the anticipated principal reduction, and the Amount to Be Provided for Payment of Debt Account is credited for the same amount. Next, when the principal of general long-term debt is reduced via payment by the related debt service fund, the pertinent liability account is debited for the amount of the principal reduction and the Amount Available in Debt Service Fund for Payment of Debt account is credited for this amount. Finally, the Amount Available in Debt Service Fund for Payment of Debt account is debited for operating-related increases in the balance of the related debt service fund provided that such increases are designated for principal reduction. Such increases result, for example, from excesses of revenues over unreimbursed expenditures.[11] The related credits are to the Amount to Be Provided for Payment of Debt account. The entries just mentioned are illustrated via the following example.

Assume that the city of Bellair maintains an account group for general long-term debt consistently with GAAP and that the current fiscal year is 19X1. Recall from earlier examples the following effects of the city's general long-term debt-related transactions:

1. Constructed a new city hall in 19X1 partially through a new general obligation term bond issue with a par value of $1,500,000.

---

[11] Recall that the city of Bellair's debt service fund (considered above) increased by $9,750 during the period. This increase equals the excess of the fund's tax revenues ($10,000) over its unreimbursed debt service charges ($750 − $500).

2. Retired $100,000 of its 6 percent general obligation serial bonds, with funds provided by the city's general fund, through the related debt service fund. These bonds were issued on January 1, 19X0. The fund balance of the debt service fund increased $9,750 during the period because of an excess of revenues over unreimbursed expenditures.

Item (1) indicates that the city's general long-term debt increased by $1,500,000 during the period. As indicated above, such an increase is recorded in the general long-term debt account group by crediting a liability account and debiting an Amount to Be Provided for Payment of Debt account. Since the bonds are term bonds, the following entry is made.

```
Amount to Be Provided for Payment of
  Term Bonds  ...............................  1,500,000
    Term Bonds Payable  .........................              1,500,000
```

Item (2) reveals that $100,000 was transferred from the city's general fund to the debt service fund to be used in retiring the serial bonds. This transfer requires a debit to the Amount Available in Debt Service Fund for Payment of Debt account and a credit to the Amount to Be Provided for Payment of Debt Account.[12] The related entry follows:

```
Amount Available in Debt Service Fund for
  Payment of Serial Bonds  ......................  100,000
    Amount to Be Provided for Payment
      of Serial Bonds  ..........................              100,000
```

The second item also indicates that the city's general long-term debt was decreased by $100,000 during the period. When such a decrease occurs, the liability account is debited and the Amount Available in Debt Service Fund for Payment of Debt account is credited for the amount of the principal reduction. The pertinent entry is as follows:

```
Serial Bonds Payable  ...........................  100,000
    Amount Available in Debt Service Fund for
      Payment of Serial Bonds  ....................              100,000
```

Finally, item (2) indicates that the debt service fund related to the serial bonds increased during the period by $9,750 because of an excess of revenues over

---

[12] Note that an entry similar to the prior one is made on the issue date of the serial bonds (January 1, 19X0). The specific entry includes a debit to Amount to Be Provided for Payment of Serial Bonds for $1,100,000 and a credit to Serial Bonds Payable for the same amount. Thus, the balance in Amount to Be Provided for Payment of Serial Bonds will be zero once all the funds needed to retire these bonds have been provided. A similar observation applies to the Amount to Be Provided for Payment of Term Bonds account recorded above.

unreimbursed expenditures. This increase is recorded in the general long-term debt account group by debiting the Amount Available in Debt Service Fund for Payment of Debt account and crediting the Amount to Be Provided for Payment of Debt account. The specific entry follows:

Amount Available in Debt Service Fund for Payment of Serial Bonds	9,750	
Amount to Be Provided for Payment of Serial Bonds		9,750

FINANCIAL REPORTS OF STATE AND LOCAL GOVERNMENTAL UNITS

As indicated in Chapter 20, three types of financial statements are used in reporting for state and local governmental units: individual fund and account group statements, combining fund statements, and combined fund and account group statements. Recall that each combined fund and account group statement usually contains (1) a column for the financial data of each pertinent type of fund or account group or (2) a column for each relevant fund or account group. Recall also that these statements present memorandum totals for all funds combined (without eliminating the effects of interfund transactions) and that combined fund and account group statements are referred to as the *general-purpose financial statements* (GPFS) of governmental units. For funds with a governmental measurement focus, the individual financial statements encompassed by the phrase *general-purpose financial statements* are (1) the balance sheet and (2) the statement of revenues, expenditures, and changes in fund balance (often with comparisons of actual and budgeted data). For funds with a proprietary measurement objective, this phrase encompasses (1) the balance sheet, (2) the statement of revenues, expenses, and changes in retained earnings (or fund balance in the case of pension trust funds), and (3) the statement of cash flows (except pension trust funds). Ignoring Illustration 21–5, Illustrations 21–1 to 21–6 provide an example of the GPFS of a governmental unit (ignoring the related footnotes, and so on). This example illustrates the features of combined fund and account group statements mentioned above. Since each general-purpose financial statement illustrated contains (with minor exception) a column for each pertinent fund or group, Illustrations 21–1 to 21–4 and 21–6 also reveal the characteristics of the individual financial statements of the various types of funds and account groups. Remember that the GPFS of a governmental unit are only part (the major part) of its comprehensive annual financial report (CAFR). You may want to review the GPFS- and CAFR-related discussions found in Chapter 20 at this point.

ILLUSTRATION 21-1 Combined Balance Sheet—All Fund Types and Account Groups

NAME OF GOVERNMENTAL UNIT
Combined Balance Sheet—All Fund Types and Account Groups
December 31, 19X2

	Governmental Fund Types				Proprietary Fund Types		Fiduciary Fund Types	Account Groups		Totals (Memorandum Only)	
	General	Special Revenue	Debt Service	Capital Projects	Enterprise	Internal Service	Trust and Agency	General Fixed Assets	General Long-Term Debt	December 31, 19X2	December 31, 19X1
Assets											
Cash	$258,500	$101,385	$185,624	$659,100	$257,036	$29,700	$216,701	$ —	$ —	$1,708,046	$1,300,944
Cash with fiscal agent		—	102,000		—	—	—	—	—	102,000	—
Investments, at cost or amortized cost	65,000	37,200	160,990	—	—	—	1,239,260	—	—	1,502,450	1,974,354
Receivables (net of allowances for uncollectibles):											
Taxes	58,300	2,500	3,829				580,000			644,629	255,400
Accounts	8,300	3,300	—	100	29,130					40,830	32,600
Special assessments		—	458,930		—					458,930	420,000
Notes		—			2,350					2,350	1,250
Loans	—				—		35,000			35,000	40,000
Accrued interest	50	25	1,907		650		2,666			5,298	3,340
Due from other funds	2,000	—	—		2,000	12,000	11,189			27,189	17,499
Due from other governments	30,000	75,260		640,000	—		—			745,260	101,400
Advances to internal service funds	65,000	—			—					65,000	75,000
Inventory of supplies, at cost	7,200	5,190			23,030	40,000				75,420	70,900
Prepaid expenses		—			1,200	—				1,200	900
Restricted assets:											
Cash					113,559					113,559	272,968
Investments, at cost or amortized cost					176,800					176,800	143,800
Land					211,100	20,000		1,259,500		1,490,600	1,456,100
Buildings					447,700	60,000		2,855,500		3,363,200	2,836,700
Accumulated depreciation					(90,718)	(4,500)				(95,218)	(83,500)
Improvements other than buildings					3,887,901	15,000		1,036,750		4,939,651	3,922,200
Accumulated depreciation					(348,944)	(3,000)				(351,944)	(283,750)
Machinery and equipment					1,841,145	25,000		452,500		2,318,645	1,924,100
Accumulated depreciation					(201,138)	(9,400)				(210,538)	(141,900)
Construction in progress					22,713			1,722,250		1,744,963	1,359,606
Amount available in debt service funds									306,280	306,280	284,813
Amount to be provided for retirement of general long-term debt									1,889,790	1,889,790	1,075,187
Amount to be provided from special assessments									458,930	458,930	420,000
Total assets	$494,350	$224,860	$913,280	$1,299,200	$6,375,514	$184,800	$2,084,816	$7,326,500	$2,655,000	$21,558,320	$17,479,911

Liabilities and Fund Equity:

Liabilities:											
Vouchers payable	$118,261	$33,850	$ —	$49,600	$131,071	$15,000	$3,350	$ —	$ —	$351,132	$223,412
Contracts payable	57,600	18,300	—	119,000	8,347	—	—	—	—	203,247	1,326,511
Judgments payable	—	2,000	—	33,800	—	—	—	—	—	35,800	32,400
Accrued liabilities	—	—	—	10,700	16,870	—	4,700	—	—	32,270	27,417
Payable from restricted assets:											
Construction contracts	—	—	—	—	17,760	—	—	—	—	17,760	—
Fiscal agent	—	—	—	—	139	—	—	—	—	139	—
Accrued interest	—	—	—	—	32,305	—	—	—	—	32,305	67,150
Revenue bonds	—	—	—	—	48,000	—	—	—	—	48,000	52,000
Deposits	—	—	—	—	63,000	—	—	—	—	63,000	55,000
Due to other taxing units	—	—	—	—	—	—	680,800	—	—	680,800	200,000
Due to other funds	24,189	2,000	—	1,000	—	—	—	—	—	27,189	17,499
Due to student groups	—	—	—	—	—	—	1,850	—	—	1,850	1,600
Deferred revenue	15,000	—	555,000	—	—	—	—	—	—	570,000	423,000
Advance from general fund	—	—	—	—	—	65,000	—	—	—	65,000	75,000
Matured bonds payable	—	—	100,000	—	—	—	—	—	—	100,000	—
Matured interest payable	—	—	2,000	—	—	—	—	—	—	2,000	—
General obligation bonds payable	—	—	—	—	700,000	—	—	—	2,100,000	2,800,000	2,110,000
Special assessment debt with governmental commitment	—	—	—	—	—	—	—	—	555,000	555,000	420,000
Revenue bonds payable	—	—	—	—	1,798,000	—	—	—	—	1,798,000	1,846,000
Total liabilities	215,050	56,150	657,000	214,100	2,815,492	80,000	690,700	—	2,655,000	7,383,492	6,876,989
Fund equity:											
Contributed capital	—	—	—	—	1,392,666	95,000	—	—	—	1,487,666	815,000
Investment in general fixed assets	—	—	—	—	—	—	—	7,326,500	—	7,326,500	5,299,600
Retained earnings:											
Reserved for revenue bond retirement	—	—	—	—	129,155	—	—	—	—	129,155	96,975
Unreserved	—	—	—	—	2,038,201	9,800	—	—	—	2,048,001	1,998,119
Fund balances:											
Reserved for encumbrances	38,000	46,500	—	1,076,500	—	—	—	—	—	1,161,000	410,050
Reserved for inventory of supplies	7,200	5,190	—	—	—	—	—	—	—	12,390	10,890
Reserved for advance to internal service funds	65,000	—	—	—	—	—	—	—	—	65,000	75,000
Reserved for loans	—	—	—	—	—	—	50,050	—	—	50,050	45,100
Reserved for endowments	—	—	—	—	—	—	134,000	—	—	134,000	94,000
Reserved for employees' retirement system	—	—	—	—	—	—	1,426,201	—	—	1,426,201	1,276,150
Unreserved:											
Designated for debt service	—	—	256,280	—	—	—	—	—	—	256,280	325,888
Designated for subsequent years' expenditures	50,000	—	—	—	—	—	—	—	—	50,000	50,000
Undesignated	119,300	117,020	—	8,600	—	—	(216,135)	—	—	26,585	106,150
Total fund equity	279,300	168,710	256,280	1,085,100	3,560,022	104,800	1,394,116	7,326,500	—	14,174,828	10,602,922
Total liabilities and fund equity	$494,350	$224,860	$913,280	$1,299,200	$6,375,514	$184,800	$2,084,816	$7,326,500	$2,655,000	$21,558,320	$17,479,911

SOURCE: *Cod.* 2200.603, Copyright by Governmental Accounting Standards Board, 401 Merritt 7, P.O. Box 5116, Norwalk, Connecticut, 06856–5116, U.S.A. Reprinted with permission. Copies of the complete document are available from the GASB.

ILLUSTRATION 21–2 Combined Statement of Revenues, Expenditures, and Changes in Fund Balances

NAME OF GOVERNMENTAL UNIT
Combined Statement of Revenues, Expenditures, and Changes in Fund Balances— All Governmental Fund Types and Expendable Trust Funds
For the Fiscal Year Ended December 31, 19X2

| | Governmental Fund Types | | | | Fiduciary Fund Type | Totals (Memorandum Only) Year Ended | |
	General	Special Revenue	Debt Service	Capital Projects	Expendable Trust	December 31, 19X2	December 31, 19X1
Revenues:							
Taxes	$ 881,300	$ 189,300	$ 79,177	$ —	$ —	$1,149,777	$1,137,900
Special assessments	—	—	55,500	—	—	55,500	250,400
Licenses and permits	103,000	—	—	—	—	103,000	96,500
Intergovernmental revenues	186,500	831,100	41,500	1,250,000	—	2,309,100	1,258,800
Charges for services	91,000	79,100	—	—	—	170,100	160,400
Fines and forfeits	33,200	—	—	—	—	33,200	26,300
Miscellaneous revenues	19,500	71,625	36,235	3,750	200	131,310	111,500
Total revenues	1,314,500	1,171,125	212,412	1,253,750	200	3,951,987	3,041,800
Expenditures:							
Current:							
General government	121,805	—	—	—	—	121,805	134,200
Public safety	258,395	480,000	—	—	—	738,395	671,300
Highways and streets	85,400	417,000	—	—	—	502,400	408,700
Sanitation	56,250	—	—	—	—	56,250	44,100
Health	44,500	—	—	—	—	44,500	36,600
Welfare	46,800	—	—	—	—	46,800	41,400
Culture and recreation	40,900	256,450	—	—	—	297,350	286,400
Education	509,150	—	—	—	2,420	511,570	512,000
Capital outlay	—	—	—	1,939,100	—	1,939,100	803,000

Debt service:							
Principal retirement	—	—	115,500	—	—	115,500	52,100
Interest and fiscal charges	—	—	68,420	—	—	68,420	50,000
Total expenditures	1,163,200	1,153,450	183,920	1,939,100	2,420	4,442,090	3,039,800
Excess of revenues over (under) expenditures	151,300	17,675	28,492	(685,350)	(2,220)	(490,103)	2,000
Other financing sources (uses):							
Proceeds of general obligation bonds	—	—	—	900,000	—	900,000	—
Proceeds of special assessment debt	—	—	—	190,500	—	190,500	89,120
Operating transfers in	—	—	—	74,500	2,530	77,030	—
Operating transfers out	(74,500)	—	—	—	—	(74,500)	(87,000)
Total other financing sources (uses)	(74,500)	—	—	1,165,000	2,530	1,093,030	2,120
Excess of revenues and other sources over (under) expenditures and other uses	76,800	17,675	28,492	479,650	310	602,927	4,120
Fund balances—January 1	202,500	151,035	227,788	605,450	26,555	1,213,328	1,209,208
Fund balances—December 31	$ 279,300	$ 168,710	$256,280	$1,085,100	$26,865	$1,816,255	$1,213,328

ILLUSTRATION 21-3   **Combined Statement of Revenues, Expenditures, and Changes in Fund Balances with Budget/Actual Comparisons**

NAME OF GOVERNMENTAL UNIT
Combined Statement of Revenues, Expenditures, and Changes in Fund Balances—
Budget and Actual—General and Special Revenue Fund Types
For the Fiscal Year Ended December 31, 19X2

	General Fund			Special Revenue Funds			Totals (Memorandum Only)		
	Budget	Actual	Variance—Favorable (Unfavorable)	Budget	Actual	Variance—Favorable (Unfavorable)	Budget	Actual	Variance—Favorable (Unfavorable)
Revenues:									
Taxes	$ 882,500	$ 881,300	$(1,200)	$ 189,500	$ 189,300	$ (200)	$1,072,000	$1,070,600	$ (1,400)
Licenses and permits	125,500	103,000	(22,500)	—	—	—	125,500	103,000	(22,500)
Intergovernmental revenues	200,000	186,500	(13,500)	837,600	831,100	(6,500)	1,037,600	1,017,600	(20,000)
Charges for services	90,000	91,000	1,000	78,000	79,100	1,100	168,000	170,100	2,100
Fines and forfeits	32,500	33,200	700	—	—	—	32,500	33,200	700
Miscellaneous revenues	19,500	19,500	—	81,475	71,625	(9,850)	100,975	91,125	(9,850)
Total revenues	1,350,000	1,314,500	(35,500)	1,186,575	1,171,125	(15,450)	2,536,575	2,485,625	(50,950)
Expenditures:									
Current:									
General government	129,000	121,805	7,195	—	—	—	129,000	121,805	7,195
Public safety	277,300	258,395	18,905	494,500	480,000	14,500	771,800	738,395	33,405
Highways and streets	84,500	85,400	(900)	436,000	417,000	19,000	520,500	502,400	18,100
Sanitation	50,000	56,250	(6,250)	—	—	—	50,000	56,250	(6,250)
Health	47,750	44,500	3,250	—	—	—	47,750	44,500	3,250
Welfare	51,000	46,800	4,200	—	—	—	51,000	46,800	4,200
Culture and recreation	44,500	40,900	3,600	272,000	256,450	15,550	316,500	297,350	19,150
Education	541,450	509,150	32,300	—	—	—	541,450	509,150	32,300
Total expenditures	1,225,500	1,163,200	62,300	1,202,500	1,153,450	49,050	2,428,000	2,316,650	111,350

Excess of revenues over (under) expenditures	124,500	151,300	26,800	(15,925)	17,675	33,600	108,575	168,975	60,400
Other financing sources (uses): Operating transfers out	(74,500)	(74,500)	—	—	—	—	(74,500)	(74,500)	—
Excess of revenues over (under) expenditures and other uses	50,000	76,800	26,800	(15,925)	17,675	33,600	34,075	94,475	60,400
Fund balances—January 1	202,500	202,500	—	151,035	151,035	—	353,535	353,535	—
Fund balances—December 31	$ 252,500	$ 279,300	$26,800	$ 135,110	$ 168,710	$33,600	$ 387,610	$ 448,010	$ 60,400

SOURCE: *Cod.* 2200.605. Copyright by Governmental Accounting Standards Board, 401 Merritt 7, P.O. Box 5116, Norwalk, Connecticut, 06856–5116, U.S.A. Reprinted with permission. Copies of the complete document are available from the GASB.

ILLUSTRATION 21–4 Combined Statement of Revenues, Expenses, and Changes in Retained Earnings

NAME OF GOVERNMENTAL UNIT
Combined Statement of Revenues, Expenses, and Changes in Retained Earnings
Fund Balances—All Proprietary Fund Types and Similar Trust Funds
For the Fiscal Year Ended December 31, 19X2

	Proprietary Fund Types		Fiduciary Fund Types		Totals (Memorandum Only) Year Ended	
	Enterprise	Internal Service	Nonexpendable Trust	Pension Trust	December 31, 19X2	December 31, 19X1
Operating revenues:						
Charges for services	$ 672,150	$88,000	$ —	$ —	$ 760,150	$ 686,563
Interest	—	—	2,480	28,460	30,940	26,118
Contributions	—	—	—	160,686	160,686	144,670
Gifts	—	—	45,000	—	45,000	—
Total operating revenues	672,150	88,000	47,480	189,146	996,776	857,351
Operating expenses:						
Personal services	247,450	32,500	—	—	279,950	250,418
Contractual services	75,330	400	—	—	75,730	68,214
Supplies	20,310	1,900	—	—	22,210	17,329
Materials	50,940	44,000	—	—	94,940	87,644
Heat, light, and power	26,050	1,500	—	—	27,550	22,975
Depreciation	144,100	4,450	—	—	148,550	133,210
Benefit payments	—	—	—	21,000	21,000	12,000
Refunds	—	—	—	25,745	25,745	13,243
Total operating expenses	564,180	84,750	—	46,745	695,675	605,033
Operating income	107,970	3,250	47,480	142,401	301,101	252,318

Nonoperating revenues (expenses):

Operating grants	55,000	—	—	—	55,000	50,000
Interest revenue	3,830	—	—	—	3,830	3,200
Rent	5,000	—	—	—	5,000	5,000
Interest expense and fiscal charges	(92,988)	—	—	—	(92,988)	(102,408)
Total nonoperating revenues (expenses)	(29,158)	—	—	—	(29,158)	(44,208)
Income before operating transfers	78,812	3,250	47,480	142,401	271,943	208,110
Operating transfers in (out)	—	—	(2,530)	—	(2,530)	(2,120)
Net income	78,812	3,250	44,950	142,401	269,413	205,990
Retained earnings/fund balances—January 1	2,088,544	6,550	139,100	1,040,800	3,274,994	3,069,004
Retained earnings/fund balances—December 31	$2,167,356	$9,800	$184,050	$1,183,201	$3,544,407	$3,274,994

ILLUSTRATION 21-5   Statement of Changes in Financial Position—Working Capital Basis

NAME OF GOVERNMENTAL UNIT
Statement of Changes in Financial Position—All Proprietary Fund Types and Similar Trust Funds
For the Fiscal Year Ended December 31, 19X2

	Proprietary Fund Types		Fiduciary Fund Types		Totals (Memorandum Only) Year Ended	
	Enterprise	Internal Service	Nonexpendable Trust	Pension Trust	December 31, 19X2	December 31, 19X1
Sources of working capital:						
Operations:						
Net income	$ 78,812	$ 3,250	$44,950	$142,401	$ 269,413	$ 205,990
Items not requiring (providing) working capital:						
Depreciation	144,100	4,450	—	—	148,550	133,210
Working capital provided by operations	222,912	7,700	44,950	142,401	417,963	339,200
Cash from revenue bond construction account	127,883	—	—	—	127,883	743,800
Contributions	672,666	—	—	—	672,666	—
Total sources of working capital	1,023,461	7,700	44,950	142,401	1,218,512	1,083,000
Uses of working capital:						
Acquisition of property, plant, and equipment	324,453	7,000	—	—	331,453	842,812
Retirement of general obligation bonds	50,000	—	—	—	50,000	50,000
Retirement of revenue bonds payable	52,000	—	—	—	52,000	48,000

Repayment of advance from general fund	—	10,000	—	—	10,000	10,000
Net decrease in other current liabilities payable from restricted assets	8,946*	—	—	—	8,946	4,318
Net increase in other restricted assets	1,624†	—	—	—	1,624	414
Total uses of working capital	437,023	17,000	—	—	454,023	955,544
Net increase (decrease) in working capital	$ 586,438	$ (9,300)	$44,950	$142,401	$ 764,489	$ 127,456
Elements of net increase (decrease) in working capital:						
Cash	$ 119,276	$(20,300)	$ 4,310	$ 20,121	$ 123,407	$ 796,412
Investments	—	—	45,640	118,341	163,981	(84,286)
Receivables (net of allowance for uncollectibles)	(5,570)	(5,000)	—	—	(10,570)	2,396
Due from other funds	(6,000)	(8,000)	—	2,189	(11,811)	(4,923)
Inventory of supplies	11,250	14,000	—	—	25,250	(3,414)
Prepaid expenses	460	—	—	—	460	520
Vouchers payable	(72,471)	5,000	—	1,750	(67,471)	(42,427)
Contracts payable	551,653	—	—	—	553,403	(525,400)
Accrued liabilities	(12,160)	—	—	—	(12,160)	(11,422)
Net increase (decrease) in working capital	$ 586,438	$ (9,300)	$44,950	$142,401	$ 764,489	$ 127,456

* Assumed to pertain to deposits (see Illustrations 21–1 and 21–6).

† Assumed to pertain to construction in progress (see Illustrations 21–1 and 21–6).

SOURCE: *Cod.* 2200.607 (1987). Copyright by Governmental Accounting Standards Board, 401 Merritt 7, P.O. Box 5116, Norwalk, Connecticut, 06856–5116, U.S.A. Reprinted with permission. Copies of the complete document are available from the GASB.

ILLUSTRATION 21-6 Statement of Cash Flows

NAME OF GOVERNMENTAL UNIT
Statement of Cash Flows—All Proprietary Fund Types and Similar Trust Funds
For the Fiscal Year Ended December 31, 19X2

	Proprietary Fund Types		Fiduciary Fund Types	Totals (Memorandum Only) Year Ended	
	Enterprise	Internal Service	Nonexpendable Trust	December 31, 19X2	December 31, 19X1
Sources of cash:					
Cash flows from operating activities:					
Cash from customers	$683,720	$96,000		$779,720	$ xxx,xxx
Cash from interest			$ 2,480	2,480	x,xxx
Cash from gifts			50,000	50,000	xx,xxx
Cash paid to suppliers, employees, and lenders	(898,812)	(99,300)		(998,112)	(xx,xxx)
Net cash flows from operating activities	(215,092)	(3,300)	52,480	(165,912)	(xxx,xxx)
Cash flows from noncapital financing activities:					
Contributions	672,666			672,666	xxx,xxx
Repayment of advance from general fund		(10,000)		(10,000)	(xx,xxx)
Net decrease—deposits	(8,946)			(8,946)	(x,xxx)
Transfers out			(2,530)	(2,530)	(x,xxx)
Net cash flows from noncapital financing activities	663,720	(10,000)	(2,530)	651,190	xxx,xxx

Statement of cash flows (worksheet format). Columns left‑to‑right: first amounts, two adjustment columns, final amounts, and an illustrative format column.

	Amount	Adj.	Adj.	Amount	Format
Cash flows from capital and related financing activities:					
Cash from revenue bond construction account	127,883			127,883	xxx,xxx
Operating grants	55,000			55,000	xx,xxx
Retirement of general obligation bonds	(50,000)			(50,000)	(xx,xxx)
Retirement of revenue bonds payable	(52,000)			(52,000)	(xx,xxx)
Interest expense and fiscal charges	(92,988)			(92,988)	(xx,xxx)
Net cash flows from capital and related financing activities	(12,105)	—	—	(12,105)	(xx,xxx)
Cash Flows from investing activities:					
Acquisition of property, plant, and equipment	(324,453)		(7,000)	(331,453)	(xxx,xxx)
Interest revenue	3,830			3,830	x,xxx
Rent	5,000			5,000	x,xxx
Net increase—construction in progress	(1,624)			(1,624)	(x,xxx)
Purchase of investments		(45,640)		(45,640)	(xx,xxx)
Net cash flows from investing activities	(317,247)	(45,640)	(7,000)	(369,887)	(xxx,xxx)
Net increase in cash and cash equivalents	119,276	4,310	(20,300)	103,286	xxx,xxx
Cash and cash equivalents, January 1	137,760	2,000*	50,000	189,760	xxx,xxx
Cash and cash equivalents, December 31	$257,036	$ 6,310	$29,700	$293,046	$ 189,760
Reconciliation of operating income to net cash flows from operating activities:					
Operating income	$107,970	$47,480	$ 3,250	$158,700	$ xxx,xxx
Depreciation expense	144,100		4,450	148,550	xxx,xxx
Decrease in receivables (net)	5,570	5,000		10,570	xx,xxx
Decrease in due from other funds	6,000		8,000	14,000	xx,xxx
Increase in inventory	(11,250)		(14,000)	(25,250)	(xx,xxx)
Increase in prepaid expenses	(460)			(460)	(xxx)
Change in vouchers payable	72,471		(5,000)	67,471	xx,xxx
Decrease in contracts payable	(551,653)			(551,653)	(xxx,xxx)
Increase in accrued liabilities	12,160			12,160	xx,xxx
Net cash flows from operating activities	($215,092)	$52,480	($ 3,300)	($165,912)	($xxx,xxx)

* Assumed

Summary

This chapter applies the accounting principles and concepts related to state and local governmental units to the funds (except the general fund) and account groups of these units. It emphasizes accounting for typical transactions of these funds and account groups and their financial statements. The classes of funds and account groups covered are governmental funds, proprietary funds, fiduciary funds, and the general fixed assets and general long-term debt account groups.

The governmental funds of state and local governmental units are their general funds, special revenue funds, capital projects funds, debt service funds, and, previously, special assessment funds. All governmental funds are accounted for similarly using the modified accrual basis of the governmental measurement focus.

The two types of proprietary funds of state and local governments are enterprise funds and internal service funds. Enterprise funds provide goods or services primarily to the general public for fees; internal service funds provide goods or services to other segments of the governmental unit on a user charge basis. Because of their profit-seeking nature, proprietary funds are accounted for using the accrual principles of the proprietary measurement focus.

Trust and agency funds are used to account for the assets collected, invested, or expended by governmental units in a trustee capacity or as an agent for the specified purposes of individuals, private organizations, and other governmental units. In both cases, the governmental unit acts as a fiduciary. Trust funds are classified as nonexpendable, expendable, and pension. Nonexpendable trust funds and pension trust funds are accounted for under the proprietary measurement focus; expendable trust funds and agency funds are accounted for under the governmental measurement focus.

In governmental accounting, account groups for general fixed assets and general long-term debts are established as separate sets of accounts for governmental units. These groups provide records of the general fixed assets and the general long-term debts of these units. The general fixed assets and the general long-term debts of a governmental unit are those which are not related to proprietary or trust funds.

Ignoring Illustration 21–5, Illustrations 21–1 to 21–6 provide an example of the GPFS of a governmental unit (except the related footnotes and so on). These statements illustrate the features of combined fund and account group statements as well as the characteristics of the individual financial statements of funds and account groups. The GPFS of a governmental unit constitute a major part of its CAFR.

Questions

1. Discuss the uses and the characteristics of special revenue funds. Provide examples.
2. Discuss the uses and the characteristics of capital projects funds. Provide examples.
3. Discuss the uses and the characteristics of debt service funds. Provide examples.
4. Discuss the uses and the characteristics of special assessment funds. Include in your discussion the relationship between special assessment funds and GAAP. Provide examples.

5. Discuss the uses and the characteristics of enterprise funds. Provide examples.
6. Discuss the uses and the characteristics of internal service funds. Provide examples.
7. Discuss the uses and the characteristics of trust funds. Provide examples.
8. Discuss the uses and the characteristics of agency funds. Provide examples.
9. Discuss the general fixed assets of governmental units. Provide examples and identify the sources of these assets.
10. Discuss the uses and the characteristics of general fixed asset account groups.
11. Contrast the entries made in the general fixed assets account group when fixed assets are disposed of and *(a)* depreciation is being recorded and *(b)* depreciation is not being recorded.
12. Contrast general obligation long-term debt and general long-term debt.
13. Discuss the uses and characteristics of general long-term debt account groups.
14. Discuss the relationships existing between the general long-term debt account group and other funds of the governmental unit in terms of entries made in the long-term debt account group.

Exercises

Exercise 21–1   (Uses of Various Funds)

Select the best answer for the following:

1. The operations of a public library receiving the majority of its support from property taxes levied for that purpose should be accounted for in
   a. The general fund.
   b. A special revenue fund.
   c. An enterprise fund.
   d. None of the above.
2. The liability for general obligation bonds issued for the benefit of a municipal electric company and serviced by its earnings should be recorded in
   a. An enterprise fund.
   b. The general fund.
   c. An enterprise fund and the general long-term debt group.
   d. An enterprise fund and disclosed in the notes to the financial statements.
   e. None of the above.
3. The proceeds of a federal grant made to assist in financing the future construction of an adult training center should be recorded in
   a. The general fund.
   b. A special revenue fund.
   c. A capital projects fund.
   d. A special assessment fund.
   e. None of the above.
4. The receipts from a special tax levy to retire and pay interest on general obligation bonds issued to finance the construction of a new city hall should be recorded in a

    a. Debt service fund.

    b. Capital project fund.

    c. Revolving interest fund.

    d. Special revenue fund.

    e. None of the above.

5. The operations of a municipal swimming pool receiving the majority of its support from charges to users should be accounted for in

    a. A special revenue fund.

    b. The general fund.

    c. An internal service fund.

    d. An enterprise fund.

    e. None of the above.

6. The fixed assets of a central purchasing and stores department organized to serve all municipal departments should be recorded in

    a. An enterprise fund and the general fixed assets group.

    b. An enterprise fund.

    c. The general fixed assets group.

    d. The general fund.

    e. None of the above.

7. The monthly remittance to an insurance company for the lump sum of hospital-surgical insurance premiums collected as payroll deductions from employees should be recorded in

    a. The general fund.

    b. An agency fund.

    c. A special revenue fund.

    d. An internal service fund.

    e. None of the above.

8. Several years ago, a city provided for the establishment of a sinking fund to retire an issue of general obligation bonds. This year the city made a $50,000 contribution to the sinking fund from general revenues and realized $15,000 in revenue from securities in the sinking fund. The bonds due this year were retired. These transactions require accounting recognition in

    a. The general fund.

    b. A debt service fund and the general long-term debt account group.

    c. A debt service fund, the general fund, and the general long-term debt account group.

    d. A capital projects fund, a debt service fund, the general fund, and the general long-term debt account group.

    e. None of the above.

(AICPA adapted)

Exercise 21–2   (Uses of Various Funds)

Select the best answer for the following:

1. A city realized large capital gains and losses on securities in its library endowment fund. In the absence of specific instructions from the donor or state statutory requirements, the general rule of law holds that these amounts should be charged or credited to

 a. General fund income.
 b. General fund principal.
 c. Trust fund income.
 d. Trust Fund principal.
 e. None of the above.

2. The activities of a central motor pool which provides and services vehicles for the use of municipal employees on official business should be accounted for in
 a. An agency fund.
 b. The general fund.
 c. An internal service fund.
 d. A special revenue fund.
 e. None of the above.

3. A transaction in which a municipal electric utility paid $150,000 out of its earnings for new equipment requires accounting recognition in
 a. An enterprise fund.
 b. The general fund.
 c. The general fund and the general fixed assets account group.
 d. An enterprise fund and the general fixed assets account group.
 e. None of the above.

4. In order to provide for the retirement of general obligation bonds, a city invests a portion of its general revenue receipts in marketable securities. This investment activity should be accounted for in
 a. A trust fund.
 b. The enterprise fund.
 c. A special assessment fund.
 d. A special revenue fund.
 e. None of the above.

5. The activities of a municipal employee retirement plan, which is financed by equal employer and employee contributions, should be accounted for in
 a. An agency fund.
 b. An internal service fund.
 c. A special assessment fund.
 d. A trust fund.
 e. None of the above.

6. A city collects property taxes for the benefit of the local sanitary, park, and school districts and periodically remits collections to these units. This activity should be accounted for in
 a. An agency fund.
 b. The general fund.
 c. An internal service fund.
 d. A special assessment fund.
 e. None of the above.

7. A transaction in which a municipal electric utility issues bonds (to be repaid from its own operations) requires accounting recognition in
 a. The general fund.
 b. A debt service fund.
 c. Enterprise and debt service funds.

> > *d.* An enterprise fund, a debt service fund, and the general long-term debt account group.
> > *e.* None of the above.

8. A transaction in which a municipality issued general obligation serial bonds to finance the construction of a fire station requires accounting recognition in the
   a. General fund.
   b. Capital projects and general funds.
   c. Capital projects and the general long-term debt account group.
   d. General fund and the general long-term debt account group.
   e. None of the above.

9. Expenditures of $200,000 were made during the year on the fire station in item (8). This transaction requires accounting recognition in the
   a. General fund.
   b. Capital projects fund and the general fixed assets account group.
   c. Capital projects fund and the general long-term debt account group.
   d. General fund and the general fixed assets account group.
   e. None of the above.

(AICPA adapted)

Exercise 21–3   (Uses of Various Funds and Accounts)

The following items pertain to state and local governmental units. Select the best answer for each.

1. What type of account is used to earmark the fund balance to liquidate the contingent obligations of goods ordered but not yet received?
   a. Appropriations.
   b. Encumbrances.
   c. Obligations.
   d. Reserve for encumbrances.

2. Premiums received on general obligation bonds are generally transferred to what fund or group of accounts?
   a. Debt service.
   b. General long-term debt.
   c. General.
   d. Special revenue.

3. Self-supporting activities that are provided to the public on a user charge basis are accounted for in what fund?
   a. Agency.
   b. Enterprise.
   c. Internal service.
   d. Special revenue.

4. A city should record depreciation as an expense in its
   a. General fund and enterprise fund.
   b. Internal service fund and general fixed assets account group.
   c. Enterprise fund and internal service fund.
   d. Enterprise fund and capital projects fund.

(AICPA adapted)

Exercise 21-4   (Uses of Various Funds and Accounts)

The following items pertain to state and local governmental units. Select the best answer for each.

1. Authority granted by a legislative body to make expenditures and to incur obligations during a fiscal year is the definition of an
   a. Appropriation.
   b. Authorization.
   c. Encumbrance.
   d. Expenditure.

2. An account for expenditures does not appear in which fund?
   a. Capital projects.
   b. Enterprise.
   c. Encumbrance.
   d. Special revenue.

3. Part of the general obligation bond proceeds from a new issuance was used to pay for the cost of a new city hall as soon as construction was completed. The remainder of the proceeds was transferred to repay the debt. Entries are needed to record these transactions in the
   a. General fund and general long-term account group.
   b. General fund, general long-term debt account group, and debt service fund.
   c. Trust fund, debt service fund, and general fixed assets account group.
   d. General long-term account group, debt service fund, general fixed assets account group, and capital projects fund.

4. Cash secured from property tax revenue was transferred for the eventual payment of principal and interest on general obligation bonds. The bonds had been issued when land had been acquired several years ago for a city park. Upon the transfer, an entry would not be made in which of the following?
   a. Debt service fund.
   b. General fixed assets account group.
   c. General long-term debt account group.
   d. General fund.

5. Equipment in general governmental service that had been constructed 10 years before by a capital projects fund was sold. The receipts were accounted for as unrestricted revenue. Entries are necessary in the
   a. General fund and capital projects fund.
   b. General fund and general fixed assets account group.
   c. General fund, capital projects fund, and enterprise fund.
   d. General fund, capital projects fund, and general fixed assets account group.

(AICPA adapted)

Exercise 21-5   (Uses of Various Funds and Accounts)

The following statements refer to transactions of Brockton City. Select the best answer for each of the following items.

1. In preparing the general fund budget of Brockton City for the forthcoming fiscal year, the city council appropriated a sum greater than expected revenues. The action of the council will result in

  a. A cash overdraft during that fiscal year.

  b. An increase in encumbrances by the end of that fiscal year.

  c. A decrease in the fund balance.

  d. A necessity for compensatory offsetting action in the debt service fund.

2. Brockton City's water utility, which is an enterprise fund, submits a bill for $9,000 to the general fund for water service supplied to city departments and agencies. Submission of this bill would result in

  a. Creation of balances which will be eliminated on the city's combined balance sheet.

  b. Recognition of revenue by the water utility fund and of an expenditure by the general fund.

  c. Recognition of an encumbrance by both the water utility fund and the general fund.

  d. Creation of a balance which will be eliminated on the city's combined statement of changes in fund balances.

3. Brockton City's water utility, which is an enterprise fund, transferred land and a building to the general city administration for public use at no charge to the city. The land was carried on the water utility's books at $4,000, and the building at a cost of $30,000 on which $23,000 depreciation had been recorded. In the year of the transfer, what would be the effect of the transaction?

  a. Reduce retained earnings of the water utility by $11,000 and increase the fund balance of the general fund by $11,000.

  b. Reduce retained earnings of the water utility by $11,000 and increase the total assets in the general fixed assets account group by $11,000.

  c. Reduce retained earnings of the water utility by $11,000 and increase the total assets in the general fixed assets account group by $34,000.

  d. Have no effect on a combined balance sheet for the city.

4. Brockton City has approved a special assessment in accordance with applicable laws. Total assessments of $500,000, including 10 percent for the city's share of the cost, have been levied. The levy will be collected from property owners in 10 equal annual installments commencing with the current year. Assuming the use of a special assessment fund, recognition of the approval and levy will result in entries of

  a. $500,000 in the special assessment fund and $50,000 in the general fund.

  b. $450,000 in the special assessment fund and $50,000 in the general fund.

  c. $50,000 in the special assessment fund and $50,000 in the general fund.

  d. $50,000 in the special assessment fund and no entry in the general fund.

5. What would be the effect on the general fund balance in the current fiscal year of recording a $15,000 purchase for a new fire truck out of general fund resources, for which a $14,600 encumbrance had been recorded in the general fund in the previous fiscal year?

  a. Reduce the general fund balance $15,000.

  b. Reduce the general fund balance $14,600.

  c. Reduce the general fund balance $400.

  d. Have no effect on the general fund balance.

6. Brockton City's debt service fund (for term bonds) recorded required additions and required earnings for the current fiscal year of $15,000 and $7,000, respectively. The actual revenues and interest earnings were $16,000 and $6,500, respectively. What are the necessary entries to record the year's actual additions and earnings in the debt service fund and in the general long-term debt account group, respectively?

    a. $22,500 and $22,000.

    b. $22,000 and $22,000.

    c. $22,500 and $22,500.

    d. $22,500 and no entry.

7. Brockton City serves as collecting agency for the local independent school district and for a local water district. For this purpose, Brockton has created a single agency fund and charges the other entities a fee of 1 percent of the gross amounts collected. The service fee is treated as general fund revenue. During the latest fiscal year, a gross amount of $268,000 was collected for the independent school district and $80,000 for the water district. As a consequence of the foregoing, Brockton's general fund should

    a. Recognize receipts of $348,000.

    b. Recognize receipts of $344,520.

    c. Record revenue of $3,480.

    d. Record encumbrances of $344,520.

8. When Brockton City realized $1,020,000 from the sale of a $1 million bond issue, the entry in its capital project fund was

Cash	1,020,000	
Proceeds of General Obligation Bonds		1,000,000
Premium on Bonds		20,000

Recording the transaction in this manner indicates that

    a. The $20,000 cannot be used for the designated purpose of the fund but must be transferred to another fund.

    b. The full $1,020,000 can be used by the capital project fund to accomplish its purpose.

    c. The nominal rate of interest on the bonds is below the market rate for bonds of such term and risk.

    d. A safety factor is being set aside to cover possible contract defaults on the construction.

9. What will be the balance sheet effect of recording $50,000 of depreciation in the accounts of a utility, an enterprise fund, owned by Brockton City?

    a. Reduce total assets of the utility fund and the general fixed assets account group by $50,000.

    b. Reduce total assets of the utility fund by $50,000 but have no effect on the general fixed assets account group.

    c. Reduce total assets of the general fixed assets account group by $50,000 but have no effect on assets of the utility fund.

    d. Have no effect on total assets of either the utility fund or the general fixed assets account group.

(AICPA adapted)

Exercise 21–6   (Uses of Various Funds and Accounts)

Select the best answer for each of the following:

1. A building was donated to Palm City during 19X1. Its original cost to the donor was $100,000. Accumulated depreciation at the date of the gift amounted to $60,000. Fair market value at the date of the gift was $300,000. In the general fixed assets account group, at what amount should Palm record this donated fixed asset?

    a. $300,000.
    b. $100,000.
    c. $40,000.
    d. $0.

Questions 2 through 4 are based on the following data relating to Lily Township:

Printing and binding equipment used for servicing all of Lily's departments and agencies on a cost-reimbursement basis	$100,000
Equipment used for supplying water to Lily's residents	900,000
Receivable for completed sidewalks to be paid for in installments by affected property owners	950,000
Cash received from the federal government dedicated to highway maintenance, which must be accounted for in a separate fund	995,000

2. How much should be accounted for in a special revenue fund or funds?
    a. $995,000.
    b. $1,050,000.
    c. $1,095,000.
    d. $2,045,000.

3. How much could be accounted for in an internal service fund?
    a. $100,000.
    b. $900,000.
    c. $950,000.
    d. $995,000.

4. How much could be accounted for in an enterprise fund?
    a. $100.000.
    b. $900,000.
    c. $950,000.
    d. $995,000.

Questions 5 through 7 are based on the following data.

The city council of Vein City adopted its budget for the year ending July 31, 19X5, comprising estimated revenues of $30 million and appropriations of $29 million. Vein formally integrates its budget into the accounting records.

5. What entry should be made for budgeted revenues?
    a. Memorandum entry only.
    b. Debit Estimated Revenues Receivable Control, $30 million.
    c. Debit Estimated Revenues Control, $30 million.
    d. Credit Estimated Revenues Control, $30 million.

6. What entry should be made for budgeted appropriations?
    a. Memorandum entry only.
    b. Credit Estimated Expenditures Payable Control, $29 million.
    c. Credit Appropriations Control, $29 million.
    d. Debit Estimated Expenditures Control, $29 million.

7. What entry should be made for the budgeted excess revenues over appropriations?
    a. Memorandum entry only.
    b. Credit Budgetary Fund Balance, $1 million.

       c. Debit Estimated Excess Revenues Control, $1 million.

       d. Debit Excess Revenues Receivable Control, $1 million.

8. The following items were among Pain Township's general fund expenditures during the year ended July 31, 19X1:

Computer for tax collector's office	$44,000
Equipment for Township Hall	80,000

    How much should be classified as fixed assets in Pain's general fund balance sheet at July 31, 19X1?

    a. $124,000.

    b. $80,000.

    c. $44,000.

    d. $0.

9. Aerial Village issued the following bonds during the year ended June 30, 19X1:

For installation of street lights, to be assessed against properties benefited	$300,000
For construction of public swimming pool; bonds to be paid from pledged fees collected from pool users	400,000

    How much should be accounted for through debt service funds for payments of principle over the life of the bonds?

    a. $0.

    b. $300,000.

    c. $400,000.

    d. $700,000.

Questions 10 and 11 are based on the following data:

Alby Township's fiscal year ends on June 30. Alby uses encumbrance accounting. On April 5, 19X1, an approved $1,000 purchase order was issued for supplies. Alby received these supplies on May 2, 19X1, and the $1,000 invoice was approved for payment.

10. What journal entry should Alby make on April 5, 19X1, to record the approved purchase order?

	Debit	Credit
a. Memorandum entry only	—	—
b. Encumbrances Control	1,000	
Fund Balance Reserved for Encumbrances		1,000
c. Supplies	1,000	
Vouchers Payable		1,000
d. Encumbrances Control	1,000	
Appropriations Control		1,000

11. What journal entry or entries should Alby make on May 2, 19X1, upon receipt of the supplies and approval of the invoice?

	Debit	Credit
a. Appropriations Control 1,000		
Encumbrances Control		1,000
Supplies 1,000		
Vouchers Payable		1,000
b. Supplies 1,000		
Vouchers Payable		1,000
c. Fund Balance Reserved for Encumbrances 1,000		
Encumbrances		1,000
Expenditures Control 1,000		
Vouchers Payable		1,000
d. Encumbrances Control 1,000		
Appropriations Control		1,000
Fund Balance 1,000		
Vouchers Payable		1,000

(AICPA adapted)

Exercise 21–7   (Entries for Special Revenue Fund)

The city of Salpupa operates its library through a special revenue fund. The operations of the library are financed partially through a special property tax and through the city's general fund. The library has estimated revenues for the current year of $64,000 from the special property tax. The actual tax levy amounted to $65,000 (with no uncollectibles expected). The general fund's annual contribution to library operations is $15,000. The library's appropriations totaled $75,000. Items encumbered during the year by the library were: (1) books—$26,000, (2) supplies—$5,000, and (3) furniture and fixtures—$15,000. All of these amounts were vouchered and paid during the year (with the actual expenditure for books being $25,000). The library paid salaries of $25,000 during the year (ignore withholding taxes and related payroll taxes).

Required:

Record all entries for the special revenue fund for the year, including its budgetary account entries, encumbrance account entries, proprietary account entries, and closing entries.

Exercise 21–8   (Entries for Special Revenue Fund)

The municipality of Burnit uses a special revenue fund to operate its park system. The city's general fund provides $20,000 of the park system's operating budget each year. The remainder of its operating budget is provided through a portion of the city's sales tax. The park system's estimated revenues from the sales tax amounted to $80,000 for the current year. The actual taxes transmitted to the park system by the city's tax agency fund were $78,000. The park system's budget reveals appropriations of $95,000.

The following items were encumbered during the year: (1) supplies—$10,000, (2) park maintenance fees—$25,000, and (3) trees and shrubs—$5,000. All of these amounts were vouchered and paid during the year (with the actual expenditure for park maintenance fees being $24,000). Park employees were paid $50,000 during the year (ignore withholding taxes and related payroll taxes).

Required:

Record all entries for the special revenue fund for the year, including its budgetary account entries, encumbrance account entries, proprietary account entries, and closing entries.

Exercise 21–9   (Entries for Trust Endowment Fund)

Freda Wrich, a wealthy citizen of the city of Albakirk, donated $400,000 to the city. The revenues from this endowment are to be used to purchase library books for the city's library. The city uses a nonexpendable trust fund, called the Wrich Endowment Fund, to account for the endowment provided by Ms. Wrich.

Shortly after receiving the endowment, the entire $400,000 is invested in revenue-producing securities. During the period, the fund collects revenues of $37,500, records a related liability to the Wrich Earnings Fund (which is responsible for spending the revenues from the endowment), and transfers the appropriate amount to the Wrich Earnings Fund. There are no accrued revenues at year-end.

Required:

Record all entries for the Wrich Endowment Fund for the year.

Exercise 21–10   (Entries for Trust Earnings Fund)

Refer to the data of Exercise 21–9. Assume additionally that the Wrich Earnings Fund spends $36,000 on books during the year and that budgetary and encumbrances accounts are not used in accounting for the Wrich Earnings Fund.

Required:

Record all entries for the Wrich Earnings Fund for the year, including its closing entry.

Exercise 21–11   (Entries for Trust Endowment Fund)

The city of Windslow uses a nonexpendable trust fund, called the Eagle Endowment Fund, to account for an endowment given to the city on January 1 of the current year to provide revenues to cover repairs and maintenance on its city park. The endowment ($600,000) was raised by a local environmental group because the park is a bald eagle nesting ground.

Immediately after receiving the endowment, the entire $600,000 was invested in stocks and bonds. During the period, the fund collects revenues of $66,000 (with none accrued at year-end), records a related liability to the Eagle Earnings Fund (which is responsible for spending the revenues from the endowment), and transfers the appropriate amount to the Earnings Fund.

Required:

Record all entries for the Eagle Endowment Fund for the year.

Exercise 21–12   (Entries for Trust Earnings Fund)

Refer to the data of Exercise 21–11. Assume additionally that the Eagle Earnings Fund spends $64,000 on repairs and maintenance during the year. Budgetary and encumbrances accounts are not used in accounting for the Earnings Fund.

Required:

Record all entries for the Eagle Earnings Fund for the year, including its closing entry.

Exercise 21–13   (Entries for Tax Agency Fund)

The city of Santonio uses a tax agency fund to collect property taxes for its school district and its recreation department. The taxes to be collected during the year amount to $600,000. Of this total, $450,000 is to be paid to the Santonio School District, and $150,000 is due to the Santonio Recreation Department.

Required:

Record the taxes receivable by the tax agency fund and the collections and subsequent remittances of the taxes to the Santonio School District and Recreation Department.

Exercise 21–14   (Entries for Tax Agency Fund)

The tax agency fund of the city of Boda collects property taxes for its parks and library districts. Of the taxes collected, 60 percent is remitted to the parks district, and the remaining 40 percent is paid to the library district. The taxes to be collected during the year total $400,000.

Required:

Record the taxes receivable by the tax agency fund and the collections and subsequent remittances of the taxes to the Boda Parks and Library Districts.

Exercise 21–15   (Entries for General Fixed Assets Account Group)

The following events affected the general fixed assets account group of the city of Texican during 19X2.

1. The city constructed a new convention center through a capital projects fund. The resources used in constructing the convention center were provided by the city's general fund ($1,500,000) and a general obligation bond issue ($2,500,000).
2. The city partially completed sidewalks for a new subdivision through a special assessment. This project is approximately 60 percent complete at year-end. The construction costs to date are $75,000.
3. Land with a fair value of $95,000 was donated to the city. The use of the land is unrestricted.
4. The city sold an old warehouse, which was being used for general storage purposes, for $300,000. The cost of the warehouse to the city's general fund was $500,000.
5. Since 19X0, Texican's water utility (an enterprise fund) has provided water service and also has been responsible for the city's sewer system. Texican's city council decided to begin administering the operations of its sewer system through its general fund. Because of this change, an office building (cost $200,000 and accumulated

depreciation $50,000) and machinery and equipment (cost $25,000 and accumulated depreciation $10,000) were transferred from the water utility to the general fund.

Required:

Record the effects of the above events in Texican's general fixed assets account group.

Exercise 21-16   (Entries for General Fixed Assets Account Group)

Consistent with GAAP, the city of Wimperly maintains a general fixed assets account group. During 19X7, Wimperly constructed a new sports complex through a capital projects fund and partially completed sidewalks for an existing subdivision through a special assessment. The following tabulation provides details related to the resources expended on these projects during the year.

Sources of Funds	*Amount Provided*
Sports complex:	
General fund	$1,400,000
Federal grant	600,000
General obligation bond issue	400,000
Sidewalks:	
General fund	25,000
Property owners primarily benefited	75,000

The new sports complex is going to be administered by the city's parks and recreation fund, a special revenue fund.

During the year, land with a fair value of $150,000 also was donated to the parks and recreation fund. Additionally, the city sold its (old) general fund administration building for $200,000. This building had cost the general fund $750,000 10 years earlier. The city's general fund currently is being administered from its old sports complex, which was recorded on the books of its tourism enterprise fund. The complex cost $1 million, and the accumulated depreciation recorded on the complex through the date of transfer to the general fund was $750,000.

Required:

Record the effects of the above events in Wimperly's general fixed assets account group.

Exercise 21-17   (Entries for General Long-Term Debt Account Group)

The following events affected the general long-term debt account group of the city of Sanmarko during 19X2.

1. The city constructed a new convention center partially through a general obligation term bond issue of $2,500,000.
2. The city retired $300,000 of its 12 percent general obligation serial bonds, with funds provided by its general fund through the related debt service fund. The fund balance of the debt service fund increased $10,000 during the period because of an excess of revenues over unreimbursed expenditures.

Required:

Record the effects of the above events in Sanmarko's general long-term debt account group.

Exercise 21–18   (Entries for General Long-Term Debt Account Group)

Consistent with GAAP, the city of Rounroc maintains a general long-term debt account group. During 19X8, the city constructed a nature center in its city park partially through a general obligation term bond issue of $3,500,000. Also, the city retired $500,000 of its 10 percent serial bonds (using funds provided by its general fund) through the related debt service fund in 19X8. These bonds constitute general long-term debt but are not general obligation bonds. The fund balance of the debt service fund increased $12,000 during the period because of an excess of revenues over unreimbursed expenditures.

Required:

Record the effects of the above events in Rounroc's general long-term debt account group.

Problems

Problem 21–19   (Entries for Capital Projects Fund)

The city of Sadona is going to construct a new convention center in 19X1 using a capital projects fund. The authorized cost of the center is $6 million. The city's general fund is to provide $1 million of this amount, and $3 million of the needed amount is to be provided by an agency of the federal government. These amounts are received on January 1, 19X1.

The remaining $2 million needed to construct the convention center is to be raised through a general obligation term bond issue with a par value of $2 million. The bond issue also is sold on January 1, 19X1, at a premium of $200,000. Only proceeds equal to the par value of the bonds are available for the project. The Premium on Bonds account represents an obligation to the related debt service fund, and cash equal to the premium is transferred to this fund immediately. The city is to provide up to $500,000 at the end of each year from general fund revenues until an amount sufficient to retire the bonds is accumulated. The debt service fund's accounts reveal a $20,000 excess of revenues over unreimbursed expenses for the year.

The construction project is initiated by engaging an architect. The architect's fee is estimated to be $180,000, and this amount is encumbered once the related contract is signed. The architect's actual fee is $190,000. This amount is vouchered and paid upon receipt of the architect's invoice. All other costs related to the project also were encumbered. In sum, the remaining encumbrances recorded amounted to $5,700,000. By July 1, 19X1, the convention center is completed, and all of the remaining encumbrances have been vouchered and paid. Upon termination of the capital projects fund, the fund's unexpended cash is transferred to the debt service fund for the newly issued bonds.

Required:

a. Record all entries for the capital projects fund, including its encumbrance account entries, proprietary account entries, and closing entries.

b. Record any entries related to the city's general fixed asset account group and its general long-term debt account group.

Problem 21–20   (Entries for Capital Projects Fund)

The city of Talhassi is constructing a new administration building through a capital projects fund. The authorized cost of the building is $2 million. Construction is initiated on July 1, 19X5, by engaging a general contractor. The agreement with the contractor specifies a charge of $1,800,000 for the construction of the building provided that blasting is not required. The city will have to pay up to an extra $190,000 if blasting is required. The city council believes that blasting will not be required and decides to encumber $1,800,000 related to the building.

To ensure that sufficient funds are available to construct the building, the city's general fund is to provide $1,500,000 to the capital projects fund, and $500,000 is to be raised through a general obligation term bond issue with a par value of $500,000. The resources being provided by the general fund are received on July 1, 19X5. The bond issue also is sold on July 1, 19X5, at a premium of $20,000. Only proceeds equal to the par value of the bonds are available for the project. The premium on bonds account represents an obligation to the related debt service fund. Thus, cash equal to the premium is transferred to this fund on July 2, 19X5. The city is to provide up to $100,000 at the end of each year from general fund revenues until an amount sufficient to retire the bonds is accumulated. The debt service fund's accounts imply an excess of revenues over unreimbursed expenditures of $15,000 for the year.

The administration building is completed on December 15, 19X5. The final cost of the building is $1,900,000 since some blasting was required. This amount is vouchered and paid upon receipt of the contractor's invoice. Upon termination of the capital projects fund, the fund's unexpended cash is transferred to the debt service fund for the newly issued bonds.

Required:

a. Record all entries for the capital projects fund, including its encumbrance account entries, proprietary account entries, and closing entries.

b. Record any entries related to the city's general fixed asset account group and its general long-term debt account group.

Problem 21–21   (Entries for Debt Service Fund)

The city of Fluegervil has a debt service fund pertaining to an issue of 8 percent general obligation serial bonds. These bonds, which have a par value of $2,500,000 outstanding on December 31, 19X5, were issued on January 1, 19X5. On January 1, 19X6, $500,000 of these bonds mature, and related service charges, which are estimated to be $1,000, are due on July 1, 19X6. The actual service charges turn out to be $1,200. The bonds pay interest on January 1 and July 1. The resources expected to be required in paying bond principal, interest, and service charges are provided by the city's general fund on January 1 and July 1. To ensure that sufficient amounts are available to pay bond principal as its becomes due, $5,000 of taxes are levied annually. The taxes are payable on July 1, 19X6. All taxes are expected to be collected.

Required:

a. Prepare the January 1, 19X6, entries needed to record the debt service fund budget, the transfer from the general fund, the assessment of the taxes, the obligations for bond principal and interest, and the related payments to bondholders.

b. Prepare the July 1, 19X6, entries needed to record the transfer from the general fund for the payment of semiannual interest and the estimated debt service charges, the debt service fund's obligation to the remaining bondholders for interest, the payment of this interest, the payment of the debt service charges, and the collection of the taxes.

c. Prepare the debt service fund's closing entry.

d. Record any entries related to the city's general long-term debt account group.

Problem 21–22   (Entries for Debt Service Fund)

The municipality of Stillwall has general obligation serial bonds with a par value of $1 million outstanding on December 31, 19X1. These bonds have a stated interest rate of 10 percent and pay interest on January 1 and July 1. Stillwall's serial bonds mature in $100,000 annual installments beginning on January 1, 19X1. These bonds are serviced using a debt service fund. The debt service charges on the bonds, which are estimated to be $900 at January 1, 19X1, are payable on July 1, 19X1. The invoice for the actual service charges of $800 is received and paid on July 1, 19X1.

The resources needed to service Stillwall's bonds (except for the service charges) are provided by the city's general fund on January 1 and July 1 of each year. Also, $1,000 of sales taxes are transferred to the debt service fund on July 1 of each year from the city's tax agency fund to cover debt service.

Required:

a. Prepare the January 1, 19X1, entries needed to record the debt service fund budget, the transfer from the general fund, the assessment of the taxes, the obligations for bond principal and interest, and the related payments to bondholders.

b. Prepare the July 1, 19X1, entries needed to record the transfers for the payment of semiannual interest and the estimated debt service charges, the debt service fund's obligation to the remaining bondholders for interest, the payment of this interest, the payment of the debt service charges, and the collection of the taxes.

c. Prepare the debt service fund's closing entry.

d. Record any entries related to the city's general long-term debt account group.

Problem 21–23   (Entries for Special Assessments Fund)

The city of Laural uses special assessment funds in administering projects undertaken via special assessments. Contrary to GAAP, financial statements also are required for such funds; thus, complete sets of accounting records are kept for Laural's special assessment funds.

On January 1, 19X1, Laural's city council authorizes the establishment of a special assessment fund to be used in paving numerous streets in an older subdivision. The city's general fund is to advance its special assessment fund $20,000 for working capital purposes immediately. During the fiscal year, the latter expends $10,000 of this amount on miscellaneous items. Related encumbrances were not recorded.

The city also enters into a $400,000 contract for the paving on January 1, 19X1. The project is 25 percent complete at fiscal year-end (December 31, 19X1), and the contract calls for payment of 25 percent of the contract amount to the contractor at this time.

The property owners benefiting specifically from the paving are to be assessed for related costs on January 1, 19X1. The assessments are to be paid in equal beginning-of-year installments totaling $100,000 over four years (starting January 1, 19X1) with 10 percent interest being charged on unpaid assessment balances (with interest payable on January 1).

The special assessment fund is going to finance the project until all the special assessments are collected through the issuance of four-year, 12 percent bonds with a par value of $300,000 (with interest also payable on January 1). The bonds are issued at par on January 1, 19X1.

Required:

a. Record the contract to construct the sidewalks, the receipt of the cash advance from the general fund, and the issuance of the bonds on January 1, 19X1.

b. Record the special assessment levy of $200,000 on the property holders to benefit specifically from the sidewalks on January 1, 19X1.

c. Record the fund's expenditures for miscellaneous items during the period. Assume that encumbrances are not recorded because the related invoices and so on are paid almost immediately after they are vouchered.

d. Record the liability for, and the payment of, the amount due on the contract on December 31, 19X1, assuming there are no adjustments to the contract price.

e. Record the accrual of interest on both the assessment receivables and the bonds payable on December 31, 19X1.

f. Record the closing entries for the fund.

Problem 21–24   (Entries for Special Assessments Fund)

The city of Seebrook requires projects to be undertaken via special assessments to be accounted for in special assessments funds and the preparation of related financial statements (contrary to GAAP). On January 1, 19X5, Seebrook's city council authorizes the establishment of a special assessment fund to be used in improving the drainage in an existing subdivision. The property owners to benefit specifically from the improved drainage are to be assessed for related costs on January 1, 19X5. The assessments are to be paid in beginning-of-year installments over three years (with $83,333 due in 1986). Ten percent interest is to be charged on unpaid assessment balances (with interest payable on January 1).

Several other events related to the special assessment fund also occur on January 1, 19X5. First, the city enters into a $250,000 drainage improvement contract. The construction period specified in the contract is three years. Second, the city's general fund advances the special assessment fund $5,000 for working capital purposes. Finally, the special assessment fund is going to finance the project until all the special assessments are collected through the issuance of three-year, 8 percent bonds with a par value of $250,000 (with interest also payable on January 1). The bonds are issued at par on January 1, 19X5.

By fiscal year-end (December 31, 19X5), $4,000 of the advance has been spent on miscellaneous items. Related encumbrances were not recorded. Also, the drainage contract calls for year-end payments to be determined by applying the percentage of the construction completed during the year to the contract amount of $250,000. The contract is 30 percent complete at year-end. Any adjustments to the contract amount are to be made during the final year of construction.

Required:

a. Record the contract for the drainage improvements, the receipt of the cash advance from the general fund, and the issuance of the bonds on January 1, 19X5.

b. Record the special assessment levy of $250,000 on the property holders to benefit specifically from the improvements on January 1, 19X5.

c. Record the fund's expenditures for miscellaneous items during the period. Assume that encumbrances are not recorded because the related invoices and so on are paid almost immediately after they are vouchered.

d. Record the liability for, and the payment of, the amount due on the contract on December 31, 19X5.

e. Record the accrual of interest on both the assessment receivables and the bonds payable on December 31, 19X5.

f. Record the closing entries for the fund.

Problem 21–25   (Entries for Enterprise Fund)

The following data pertain to the water utility (an enterprise fund) of the city of Skyatuk for the fiscal year ended December 31, 19X8.

Billings to customers for sales of water:	
Billings to nongovernmental customers	$450,000
Billings to general fund of Skyatuk	45,000
Collections from customers for sales of water:	
Collections from nongovernmental customers	420,000
Collections from general fund of Skyatuk	42,000
Customer water deposits:	
Billed and collected	700
Refunded	600
Pumping equipment purchased	40,000
Materials and supplies purchased	4,000
Uncollectible customer accounts at year-end	3,000
Customer deposits applied to unpaid bills	2,000
Expenses incurred:	
Depreciation expense (water system)	180,000
Customer accounts expense (i.e., bad debts expense) estimated	9,000
Other operating expenses	280,000
Various payables liquidated	370,000
Year-end accruals for water service	18,000

Required:

a. Record the water sales for the period. Make summary entries here and below when appropriate.

b. Record the customer water deposits billed, collected, and refunded.

c. Record the equipment and materials and supplies purchased during the period.

d. Record the operating expenses for the period (except for those which usually would be recorded using adjusting entries) and the payments of accounts payable during the period.

e. Write off the uncollectible accounts applying customer deposits as appropriate.

f. Record the fund's adjusting and closing entries.

Problem 21–26   (Entries for Enterprise Fund)

The city of Emtyvee provides natural gas through its natural gas utility. The following data pertain to this utility for the fiscal year ended December 31, 19X4.

Billings to customers for sales of gas:	
Billings to nongovernmental customers	$200,000
Billings to general fund of Emtyvee	22,000
Collections from customers for sales of gas:	
Collections from nongovernmental customers	190,000
Collections from general fund of Emtyvee	21,000
Customer gas deposits:	
Billed and collected	900
Refunded	500
Storage equipment purchased	18,000
Materials and supplies purchased	1,500
Uncollectible customer accounts at year-end	2,000
Customer deposits applied to unpaid bills	1,500
Expenses incurred:	
Depreciation expense (gas plant)	95,000
Customer accounts expense (i.e., bad debts expense) estimated	6,000
Other operating expenses	140,000
Various payables liquidated	200,000
Year-end accruals for gas service	25,000

Required:

a. Record the gas sales for the period. Make summary entries here and below when appropriate.

b. Record the customer gas deposits billed, collected, and refunded.

c. Record the equipment and materials and supplies purchased during the period.

d. Record the operating expenses for the period (except for those which usually would be recorded using adjusting entries) and the payments of accounts payable during the period.

e. Write off the uncollectible accounts applying customer deposits as appropriate.

f. Record the fund's adjusting and closing entries.

Problem 21-27   (Entries for Internal Service Fund)

The council of the city of Tucakari has decided to begin issuing all supplies used by its segments through a stores fund. The city's stores fund is established by transferring cash of $250,000 and supplies costing $220,000 from its general fund. Part of the cash transferred in is used to purchase a warehouse and its site for $180,000 (with $30,000 of this amount allocated to land) and a delivery truck for $15,000. Depreciation expense for the period amounts to $20,000. Of this amount, $15,000 is related to the fund's warehouse, while $5,000 applies to its delivery truck.

The stores fund marks up supplies transferred to other segments 80 percent based on cost. During the period, it transfers supplies costing $90,000 to the city's water utility fund and supplies costing $60,000 to its electric utility fund (with related payments being received by year-end). Subsequently, the stores fund replenishes its supplies inventory by acquiring $90,000 of supplies on credit. These supplies are paid for before year-end shortly after being ordered.

The following tabulation summarizes the fund's administrative, warehousing, and delivery expenses for the period (except for depreciation expense). The various items are paid for before year-end shortly after they are vouchered.

Administrative expenses	10,000
Warehousing expenses	40,000
Delivery expenses	7,000

Required:

a. Record the initial transfers of assets to the stores fund.

b. Record the purchases of the warehouse and the delivery truck.

c. Record the issuances of supplies during the period and the related payments from the funds receiving the supplies.

d. Record the fund's purchases of supplies during the period and the related payments.

e. Record the fund's administrative, warehousing, and delivery expenses for the period (except for depreciation expense) and the related payments.

f. Record the fund's adjusting and closing entries.

Problem 21-28   (Entries for Internal Service Fund)

During the current year, the city of Rena began supplying automobiles to its various segments for use in travel required because of city business. The automotive services are provided through the city's automobile service fund. This fund was established by a $1 million transfer from the city's general fund.

The cash transferred to the automotive service fund was expended immediately on a fleet of automobiles costing $800,000. Depreciation expense for the period on the fleet is $40,000.

The automotive service fund charges $.40 per mile for automobiles provided to the city's segments. During the period, the city's general fund was charged for 250,000 miles driven, and its electric utility fund was charged for 150,000 miles driven.

The automotive service fund incurred the following expenses (except depreciation expense) during the period: administrative expenses—$40,000, repairs and maintenance expenses—$30,000, and gasoline expense—$20,000. These items were paid for before year-end shortly after they were vouchered.

Required:

a. Record the initial transfer of assets to the automotive service fund.

b. Record the purchase of the fund's fleet.

c. Record the billings to the funds using the automotive service fund's fleet during the period and the related payments from these funds.

d. Record the fund's administrative, repairs and maintenance, and gasoline expenses for the period (except for depreciation expense) and the related payments.

e. Record the fund's adjusting and closing entries.

Problem 21–29 (Effects of Events on Various Funds and Accounts)

The town of Sargentville uses budgetary accounts and maintains accounts for each of the following types of funds and account groups:

Symbol	Fund
A	Capital projects fund
B	General long-term debt
C	General fund
D	Property accounts (general fixed assets account group)
E	Debt service fund
F	Special assessment fund (required legally)
G	Special revenue fund
H	Trust and agency fund
S	Enterprise fund
T	Internal service fund

The chart of accounts of the general fund follows:

Symbol	Account
1	Appropriations
2	Cash
3	Due from Other Funds
4	Due to Other Funds
5	Encumbrances
6	Expenditures
7	Reserve for Encumbrances
8	Revenues
9	Revenues (estimated)
10	Vouchers Payable
11	Fund Balance
12	19X7 Taxes Receivable

The following transactions were among those occurring during 19X7:

1. The 19X7 budget was approved. It provided for $520,000 of general fund revenue and $205,000 of school fund revenue.
2. The budgeted appropriations for the general fund amounted to $516,000.
3. An advance of $10,000 was made from the general fund to a fund for the operation of a central printing service used by all departments of the municipal government. (This advance was not budgeted and is not expected to be repaid.)
4. Taxes for general fund revenues were levied, totaling $490,000.
5. Contractors were paid $200,000 for the construction of an office building. The payment was from proceeds of a general bond issue of 19X6.
6. Bonds of a general issue, previously authorized, were sold at par for $60,000 cash.
7. Orders were placed for supplies to be used by the health department—estimated cost, $7,500.
8. Vouchers approved for payment of salaries of town officers in the amount of $11,200. (No encumbrances are recorded for wages and salaries.)
9. The supplies ordered in item (7) were received, and vouchers were approved for the invoice price of $7,480.
10. Fire equipment was purchased for $12,500, and the voucher was approved.
11. A payment of $5,000 was made by the general fund to a fund for eventual redemption of general obligation bonds.
12. Of the taxes levied in item (4), $210,000 were collected.
13. Taxes amounting to $1,240, written off as uncollectible in 19X4, were collected.
14. $1,000 of the advance made in item (3) was returned because it was not needed.
15. Supplies for general administrative use were requisitioned from the store's fund. A charge of $1,220 is made for the supplies.
16. The general fund advanced $30,000 cash to provide temporary working capital for a fund out of which payment will be made for a new sewerage installation. Eventual financing will be by means of assessments on property holders on the basis of benefits received.
17. Equipment from the highway department was sold for $7,000 cash.
18. The town received a cash bequest of $75,000 for the establishment of a scholarship fund.
19. Previously approved and entered vouchers from payment of police department salaries of $6,200 and for the transfer of $500 to the police pension fund were paid.
20. Receipts from licenses and fees amounted to $16,000.

Required:

Prepare a table indicating for each transaction, by means of the appropriate numerals, the account debited and the account credited in the general fund. If a transaction requires an entry in any fund(s) other than the general fund, indicate the appropriate letter of the fund(s) affected.

(AICPA adapted)

Problem 21-30   (Entries for Various Funds and Accounts)

The following transactions represent practical situations frequently encountered in accounting for municipal governments. Each transaction is independent of the others.

1. The city council of Bernardville adopted a budget for the general operations of the government during the new fiscal year. Revenues were estimated at $695,000. Legal authorizations for budgeted expenditures totaled $650,000.

2. Taxes of $160,000 were levied for the special revenue fund of Millstown. Of this amount, 1 percent was estimated to be uncollectible.

3. *a.* On July 25, 19X1, office supplies estimated to cost $2,390 were ordered for the city manager's office of Bullersville. Bullersville, which operates on the calendar year, does not maintain an inventory of such supplies.

   b. The supplies ordered July 25 were received on August 9, 19X1, accompanied by an invoice for $2,500.

4. On October 10, 19X1, the general fund of Washingtonville repaid to the utility fund a loan of $1,000 plus $40 interest. The loan had been made earlier in the fiscal year.

5. A prominent citizen died and left 10 acres of undeveloped land to Harper City for a future school site. The donor's cost of the land was $55,000. The fair value of the land was $85,000.

6. *a.* On March 6, 19X1, Dahlstrom City issued 6 percent special assessment bonds payable March 6, 19X7, at face value of $90,000. Interest is payable annually. Dahlstrom City, which operates on the calendar year, will use the proceeds to finance a curbing project. The city is required legally to use special assessment funds in accounting for special assessments.

   b. On October 29, 19X1, the full $84,000 cost of the completed curbing project was accrued. Also, appropriate closing entries were made with regard to the project.

7. *a.* Carol Thamm, a citizen of Basking Knoll, donated common stock valued at $22,000 to the city under a trust agreement. Under the terms of the agreement, the principal amount is to be kept intact; use of revenue from the stock is restricted to financing academic college scholarships for needy students.

   b. On December 14, 19X1, dividends of $1,100 were received on the stock donated by Ms. Thamm.

8. *a.* On February 23, 19X1, the town of Lincoln, which operates on the calendar year, issued 6 percent general obligation bonds with a face value of $300,000 payable February 23, 19X6, to finance the construction of an addition to the city hall. Total proceeds were $308,000. The excess over par that was received was transferred to the fund responsible for payments of principal and interest.

   b. On December 31, 19X1, the addition to the city hall was officially approved, the full cost of $297,000 was paid to the contractor, and appropriate closing entries were made with regard to the project. (Assume that no entries have been made with regard to the project since February 23, 19X1.)

Required:

For each transaction, prepare the necessary journal entries for all of the funds and groups of accounts involved. No explanation of the journal entries is required. Use the following headings for your working paper.

Transaction Number	Journal Entries	Dr.	Cr.	Fund or Group of Accounts

Indicate in the last column which fund or group of accounts is affected using the coding below:

Funds:

General . . . . G

Special revenue . . . . SR

Capital projects . . . . CP

Debt service . . . . DS

Special assessments . . . . SA

Enterprise . . . . E

Internal service . . . . IS

Trust and agency . . . . TA

Group of accounts:

General fixed assets . . . . GFA

General long-term debt . . . . LTD

(AICPA adapted)

Problem 21-31   (Entries for Capital Projects Fund and Related Balance Sheets)

The city of Bel Air entered into the following transactions during the year 19X1:

1. A bond issue was authorized by vote to provide funds for the construction of a new municipal building which it was estimated would cost $500,000. The bonds were to be paid in 10 equal installments from a debt service fund, payments being due March 1 of each year. Any balance of the capital projects fund is to be transferred directly to the debt service fund.

2. An advance of $40,000 was received from the general fund to underwrite a deposit on a land contract of $60,000. The deposit was made.

3. Bonds of $450,000 were sold for cash at 102. It was decided not to sell all of the bonds because the cost of the land was less than was expected. All of the proceeds of the bond issue were available to the capital projects fund.

4. Contracts amounting to $380,000 were let to Michela and Company, the lowest bidder, for the construction of the municipal building.

5. The temporary advance from the general fund was repaid, and the balance on the land contract was paid.

6. Based on the architect's certificate, a check for $320,000 for the work completed to date was issued.

7. Due to changes in the plans, the contract with Michela and Company was revised to $440,000; the remainder of the bonds were sold at 101.

8. Before the end of the year, the building had been completed, and a check for $115,000 was issued to the contractor in final payment for the work.

9. Closing entries were made, and the balance in the fund was transferred to the debt service fund.

Required:

a. Record the above transactions in the capital projects fund using T-accounts. Designate the entries in the T-accounts by the letters which identify the data.

b. Prepare applicable fund balance sheets as of December 31, 19X1, considering only the proceeds and expenditures from capital projects fund transactions.

(AICPA adapted)

Problem 21–32   (Cash Budgets for Various Funds)

Cobleskill city council passed a resolution requiring a yearly cash budget by fund for the city beginning with its fiscal year ending September 30, 19X7. The city's financial director has prepared a list of expected cash receipts and disbursements, but he is having difficulty subdividing them by fund. The city is required legally to use special assessment funds in accounting for special assessments. The list follows:

Cash receipts:

Taxes:

General property		$ 685,000
School		421,000
Franchise		223,000
		$1,329,000

Licenses and permits:

Business licenses		$ 41,000
Automobile inspection permits		24,000
Building permits		18,000
		$ 83,000

Intergovernmental revenues:

Sales tax		$1,012,000
Federal grants		128,000
State motor vehicle tax		83,500
State gasoline tax		52,000
State alcoholic beverage licenses		16,000
		$1,291,500

Charges for services:

Sanitation fees		$ 121,000
Sewer connection fees		71,000
Library revenues		13,000
Park revenues		2,500
		$ 207,500

Bond issues:

Civic center	$ 347,000
General obligation	200,000
Sewer	153,000
Library	120,000
	$ 820,000

Other:

Proceeds from the sale of investments	$ 312,000
Sewer assessments	50,000
Rental revenue	48,000
Interest revenue	15,000
	$ 425,000
Total receipts	$4,156,000

Cash disbursements:

General government	$ 671,000
Public safety	516,000
Schools	458,000
Sanitation	131,000
Library	28,000
Rental property	17,500
Parks	17,000
	$1,838,500

Debt service:

General obligation bonds	$ 618,000
Street construction bonds	327,000
School bonds	119,000
Sewage disposal plant bonds	37,200
	$1,101,200
Investments	$ 358,000
State portion of sales tax	$ 860,200

Capital expenditures:

Sewer construction (assessed area)	$ 114,100
Civic center construction	73,000
Library construction	36,000
	$ 223,100
Total disbursements	$4,381,000

The financial director provides you with the following additional information:

1. A bond issue was authorized in 19X6 for the construction of a civic center. The debt is to be paid from future civic center revenues and general property taxes.

2. A bond issue was authorized in 19X6 for additions to the library. The debt is to be paid from general property taxes.

3. General obligation bonds are paid from general property taxes collected by the general fund.

4. Ten percent of the total annual school taxes represents an individually voted tax for payment of bonds, the proceeds of which were used for school construction.

5. In 19X4, a wealthy citizen donated rental property to the city. Net income from the property is to be used to assist in operating the library. The net cash increase attributable to the property is transferred to the library on September 30 of each year.

6. All sales taxes are collected by the city; the state receives 85 percent of these taxes. The state's portion is remitted at the end of each month.

7. Payment of the street construction bonds is to be made from assessments previously collected from the respective property owners. The proceeds from the assessments were invested, and the principal of $312,000 will earn $15,000 interest during the coming year.

8. In 19X6, a special assessment in the amount of $203,000 was made on certain property owners for sewer construction. During fiscal 19X7, $50,000 of this assessment is expected to be collected. The remainder of the sewer cost is to be paid from a $153,000 bond issue to be sold in fiscal 19X7. Future special assessment collections will be used to pay principal and interest on the bonds.

9. All sewer and sanitation services are provided by a separate enterprise fund.

10. The federal grant is for fiscal 19X7 school operations.

11. The proceeds remaining at the end of the year from the sale of civic center and library bonds are to be invested.

Required:

Prepare a budget of cash receipts and disbursements by fund for the year ending September 30, 19X7. All interfund transfers of cash are to be included.

(AICPA adapted)

Problem 21-33   (Adjusting Entries—Various Funds and General Fund Financial Statements)

You were engaged to examine the financial statements of the Mayfair School District for the year ended June 30, 19X1, and were furnished the general fund trial balance given below.

Your examination disclosed the following information:

1. The recorded estimate of losses for current year taxes receivable was considered to be sufficient.

2. The local governmental unit gave the school district 20 acres of land to be used for a new grade school and a community playground. The unrecorded estimated value of the land donated was $50,000. In addition, a state grant of $30,000 was received, and the full amount was used in payment of contracts pertaining to the construction of the grade school. Purchases of classroom and playground equipment costing $22,000 were paid from general funds.

MAYFAIR SCHOOL DISTRICT
General Fund Trial Balance
June 30, 19X1

	Debit	Credit
Cash	47,250	
Taxes Receivable—Current Year	31,800	
Estimated Losses—Current Year Taxes		1,800
Temporary Investments	11,300	
Inventory of Supplies	11,450	
Buildings	1,300,000	
Estimated Revenues	1,007,000	
Appropriations—Operating Expenses		850,000
Appropriations—Other Expenditures		150,000
State Grant Revenue		300,000
Bonds Payable		1,000,000
Vouchers Payable		10,200
Due to Internal Service Fund		950
Operating Expenses:		
Administration	24,950	
Instruction	601,800	
Other	221,450	
Transfer to Debt Service Fund		
(principal and interest)	130,000	
Capital Outlays (equipment)	22,000	
Revenues from Tax Levy, Licenses, and Fines		1,008,200
Capital Fund Balance		87,850
	3,409,000	3,409,000

3. Five years ago, $1 million of 4 percent, 10-year, sinking fund bonds were issued so that school buildings could be constructed. Interest on the issue is payable at maturity. Budgetary requirements of an annual contribution of $130,000 ($90,000 principal and $40,000 interest) and accumulated earnings to date aggregating $15,000 were accounted for in separate debt-service fund accounts.

4. Outstanding purchase orders for operating expenses not recorded in the accounts at year-end were as follows:

Administration	$1,000
Instruction	1,200
Other	600
Total	$2,800

No purchase orders were outstanding on July 1, 19X0.

5. The school district operates a central machine shop. Billings amounting to $950 were recorded in the accounts of the general fund but not in the internal service fund.

Required:

a. Prepare the formal adjusting and closing entries for the general fund. Note that this problem is identical to Problem 20–20, except for its requirements. Thus, if Problem 20–20 has been assigned, it may be desirable to require only item (b) below.

b. The foregoing information disclosed by your examination was recorded only in the general fund. Prepare the formal adjusting journal entries for the: (1) general fixed assets account group, (2) general long-term debt account group, and (3) internal service fund to correct the failure to record the relevant transactions of 19X1 and previous years.

c. Prepare a statement of revenues, expenditures, and changes in fund balance for the fiscal year ended June 30, 19X1, and a balance sheet at June 30, 19X1, for the general fund.

(AICPA adapted)

Problem 21–34 (Balance Sheet Working Paper for Enterprise Fund)

The city of Eau Claire provides electric energy for its citizens through an operating department. All transactions of the electric department are recorded in a self-sustaining fund supported by revenue from the sales of energy. Plant expansion is financed by the issuance of bonds, which are repaid out of revenues.

All cash of the electric department is held by the city treasurer. Receipts from customers and others are deposited in the treasurer's account. Disbursements are made by drawing warrants on the treasurer.

The following is the post-closing trial balance of the department as of June 30, 19X4:

Cash on Deposit with City Treasurer	$ 2,250,000	
Due from Customers	2,120,000	
Other Current Assets	130,000	
Construction in Progress	500,000	
Land	5,000,000	
Electric Plant	50,000,000*	
Accumulated Depreciation—Electric Plant		$10,000,000
Accounts Payable and Accrued Liabilities		3,270,000
5% Electric Revenue Bonds		20,000,000
Accumulated Earnings		26,730,000
	$60,000,000	$60,000,000

* The plant is being depreciated on the basis of a 50-year composite life.

During the year ended June 30, 19X5, the department had the following transactions:

1. Sales of electric energy—$10,700,000.
2. Purchases of fuel and operating supplies (on account)—$2,950,000.
3. Construction of miscellaneous system improvements financed from operations (on account)—$750,000.
4. Fuel consumed—$2,790,000.
5. Miscellaneous plant additions and improvements placed in service—$1,000,000 (depreciated $\frac{1}{2}$ year).
6. Wages and salaries paid—$4,280,000.
7. Sale on December 31, 19X4, of 20-year, 5 percent electric revenue bonds, with interest payable semiannually—$5,000,000.
8. Expenditures out of bond proceeds for construction of Steam Plant Unit No. 1 and control house—$2,800,000.
9. Operating materials and supplies consumed—$150,000.
10. Payments received from customers—$10,500,000.
11. Expenditures out of bond proceeds for construction of Steam Plant Unit No. 2—$2,200,000.
12. Warrants drawn on city treasurer in settlement of accounts payable—$3,045,000.
13. Warrants drawn on city treasurer for interest—$1,125,000. Interest on the bonds (issued 12/31/X4) during the construction period is capitalized as part of the cost of the steam plant.
14. Steam plant is placed in service June 30, 19X5.

Required:

Prepare a working paper for the revenue fund of the electric department showing:

a. The balance sheet amounts at June 30, 19X4.
b. The transactions for the year.
c. The balance sheet amounts at June 30, 19X5.

(AICPA adapted)

Problem 21–35   (Adjustments to Funds and Closing Entries)

The city of Happy Hollow has engaged you to examine its financial statements for the year ended December 31, 19X1. The city was incorporated as a municipality and began operations on January 1, 19X1. You find that a budget was approved by the city council and was recorded, but that all transactions have been recorded on the cash basis. The bookkeeper has provided an operating fund trial balance. Additional information, including the form of the working paper to be used in solving this problem, is given below:

1. Examination of the appropriation-expenditure ledger revealed the following information:

	Budgeted	Actual
Personal services	$ 45,000	$38,500
Supplies	19,000	11,000
Equipment	38,000	23,000
Total	$102,000	$72,500

2. Supplies and equipment in the amounts of $4,000 and $10,000, respectively, had been received, but the vouchers had not been paid at December 31.

3. At December 31, outstanding purchase orders for supplies and equipment not yet received amounted to $1,200 and $3,800, respectively.

4. The inventory of supplies on December 31 was $1,700 by physical count. The decision was made to record the inventory of supplies. A city ordinance requires that expenditures are to be based on purchases, not on the basis of usage.

5. Examination of the revenue subsidiary ledger revealed the following information:

	Budgeted	Actual
Property taxes	$102,600	$ 96,000
Licenses	7,400	7,900
Fines	4,100	4,500
Totals	$114,100	$108,400

It was estimated that 5 percent of the property taxes would not be collected. Accordingly, property taxes were levied in an amount so that collections would yield the budgeted amount of $102,600.

6. On November 1, 19X1, Happy Hollow issued $200,000 of 8 percent, 10-year, general obligation term bonds at 101.5. Interest is payable each May 1 and November 1. The city council ordered that cash equal to the bond premium be set aside and restricted for use in retiring bond principal. The bonds were issued to finance the construction of a city hall, but no contracts had been let as of December 3, 19X1.

7. The Happy Hollow working paper format is presented following the requirements:

Required:

a. Complete the working paper showing adjustments and distributions to the proper funds or groups of accounts in conformity with generally accepted accounting principles applicable to governmental entities. (Formal adjusting entries are not required.)

b. Identify the financial statements that should be prepared for the general fund.

c. Prepare closing entries for the general fund.

(AICPA adapted)

CITY OF HAPPY HOLLOW
Working Paper to Correct Trial Balance
December 31, 19X1

	Operating Fund Trial Balance	Adjustments		General Fund	Debt Service Fund	Capital Projects Fund	General Fixed Assets	General Long-Term Debt
		Debit	Credit					
Debits								
Cash	$238,900							
Expenditures	72,500							
Estimated revenues	114,100							
Equipment								
Encumbrances								
Inventory of supplies								
Taxes receivable—current								
Amount to be provided for the payment of term bonds								
Amount available in debt service fund—term bonds								
	$425,500							

Colleges and Universities, Hospitals, and Other Nonprofit Entities

Chapter Outline

This chapter focuses on accounting techniques for colleges and universities, hospitals, and various other nonprofit entities (not including governmental units). We use the phrase *nonprofit entity* (or *nonprofit organization*) to refer to entities that fall into these classes. The fund accounting procedures described in Chapters 20 and 21 provide a foundation for understanding the accounting techniques pertinent to nonprofit organizations. However, the procedures applied to these entities, and the related terminology, are different than those in the earlier chapters.[1]

FINANCIAL REPORTS OF NONPROFIT ENTITIES—USES AND OBJECTIVES

As indicated in Chapter 20, the FASB (*SFAC No. 4,* par. 6) indicates that the major characteristics which distinguish nonprofit entities from profit-seeking enterprises are the following:

  a. Receipts of significant amounts of resources from providers who do not expect to receive either repayment or economic benefits proportionate to resources provided.
  b. Operating purposes that are other than to provide goods or services at a profit or profit equivalent.
  c. Absence of defined ownership interests that can be sold, transferred, or redeemed, or that convey entitlement to a share of a residual distribution of resources in the event of liquidation of the organization.

From the FASB's perspective, these differences lead to variations in the orientation and the objectives of general-purpose financial reporting by nonprofit and profit-seeking entities.

SFAC No. 4 (pars. 9 and 30) indicates that the objectives of general-purpose financial reporting by nonprofit entities follow from resource providers' common interests in the services provided by the entities, their efficiency and effectiveness in providing the services, and their abilities in continuing to provide the services. Thus, according to the FASB, the focus of general-purpose financial reporting by nonprofit entities is resource providers—specifically those who generally are

---

[1] We encourage you to pay careful attention to the footnotes in this chapter. As mentioned, the chapter covers the accounting techniques of a variety of nonprofit entities. In order to streamline the chapter, we discuss several details of nonprofit accounting briefly in the footnotes and focus primarily on procedures in the main body of the text. Note also that some of the details discussed in the footnotes are covered in the chapter's Questions, Exercises, and Problems.

unable to prescribe the information they want from these entities. Under *SFAC No. 4* (pars. 35–55), the broad objectives of general-purpose financial reporting by nonprofit entities are to

1. Provide information that is useful to present and potential resource providers and other users in making rational decisions about the allocation of resources to those organizations.
2. Provide information to help present and potential resource providers and other users in assessing the services that a nonbusiness organization provides and its ability to continue to provide those services.
3. Provide information that is useful to present and potential resource providers and other users in assessing how managers of a nonbusiness organization have discharged their stewardship responsibilities and about other aspects of their performance.

The specific objectives, which are intended to lead to satisfaction of the general objectives, are to

1. Provide information about an organization's economic resources, obligations, and net resources.
2. Provide information about the performance, in terms of net changes in resources and service efforts and accomplishments, of an organization during a period.
3. Provide information about how an organization obtains and spends cash or other liquid resources, about its borrowing and repayment of borrowing, and about other factors that may affect its liquidity.
4. Provide explanations and interpretations to help users understand the financial information provided.

These objectives emphasize providing information that is useful in making economic decisions about nonprofit entities, that is pertinent in assessing the service accomplishments of these entities, and that is relevant in assessing their managers' performances. Pertinent information in these contexts is information about the entities' economic resources and obligations and the natures, sources, amounts, and so on, of their resource inflows and outflows.

As in the case of profit-seeking entities, the objectives of general-purpose financial reporting by nonprofit organizations are accomplished through the standard-setting process. In Chapter 20, we traced the historical development of governmental accounting principles. Since we deal with heterogeneous types of nonprofit entities in this chapter, we do not attempt to describe the historical development of the applicable standards. Instead, for the most part, we simply identify the current sources of GAAP for these entities.

AUTHORITATIVE PRONOUNCEMENTS—COLLEGES AND UNIVERSITIES

Colleges and universities (universities for short) may be governmental or nongovernmental. Currently, the distinction between these two types of universities is not well defined; however, the essential difference is that the former group receives significant governmental support, and the latter group is privately supported. As discussed in Chapter 20, the FASB is responsible for developing the accounting standards for all nonprofit entities other than those falling under the purview of the GASB. Thus, the GASB ultimately is responsible for the standards of governmental universities, and the FASB sets the standards of nongovernmental universities. This portion of the chapter deals with governmental universities following the GASB-accepted AICPA college guide model and GASB pronouncements (see below), although, with the exception of the treatment of depreciation, its discussions apply with equal force to nongovernmental universities operating under the FASB's purview. These discussions apply to FASB-related nongovernmental universities since the FASB also embraces the effective portions of the AICPA model. The reader can easily adjust for the differences in depreciation accounting existing in relation to the various universities (see below). We emphasize that most governmental universities and all nongovernmental universities follow the AICPA model. Thus, this portion of the chapter, in effect, covers the vast majority of signficant university accounting techniques. *We usually refer to the nongovernmental and governmental universities dealt with below collectively as universities for simplicity.*

Prior to the FASB's and GASB's interests in the accounting principles of nonprofit entities, the most authoritative pronouncements applying to universities were *College and University Business Administration (CUBA)* and *Audits of Colleges and Universities* (as amended by *Statement of Position 74–8*).[2] As discussed in footnote 2, these documents are largely consistent, although the former occupies a somewhat preeminent position because it is more comprehensive and because of the more recent publication date of its latest edition. In any case, these documents constitute GAAP unless a FASB or GASB standard is overriding. Note that GASB *Statement 15* allows governmental universities to

---

[2] National Association of College and University Business Officers (NACUBO), *College and University Business Administration (CUBA)*, 4th ed. (Washington, DC: NACUBO, 1982). Over the years, this document has been a primary comprehensive authoritative pronouncement for colleges and universities and has been refined several times. One of the more significant revisions occurred in 1974. This revision was the result of the efforts of a joint accounting group (JAG), which was drawn from the membership of NACUBO and the AICPA and was formed to reconcile differences between the 1968 version of *CUBA* and the AICPA's *Audits of Colleges and Universities* (Committee on College and University Accounting and Auditing, *Audits of Colleges and Universities* (New York: AICPA, 1973). The efforts of JAG also resulted in the AICPA's *Statement of Position 74–8* which, for the most part, made *Audits of Colleges and Universities* consistent with the 1974 version of *CUBA*. The latest version of *Audits of Colleges and Universities* was published in 1975.

follow either the AICPA college guide model or the governmental model.[3] Except for overriding GASB and FASB pronouncements, the former model is contained in *CUBA* and *Audits of Colleges and Universities*. The governmental model is contained in National Council on Governmental Accounting (NCGA) *Statement 1,* "Governmental Accounting and Financial Reporting Principles" (see Chapter 20 for discussion of NCGA pronouncements), except as superseded by subsequent NCGA and GASB pronouncements. As mentioned, most governmental universities and all nongovernmental universities follow the AICPA model.

The dual standard-setting approach described above has the potential for creating differences in the standards of nongovernmental and governmental universities. To date, only one significant financial reporting difference has developed. FASB *Statement No. 93* requires nonprofit entities to record periodic depreciation.[4] Under GASB pronouncements (GASB *Statement 8* and *Cod.* Co5), governmental universities following the AICPA college guide model are not supposed to change their treatment of depreciation in response to the issuance of *Statement No. 93.*[5] Thus, if not previously recording depreciation, they are not supposed to begin recording depreciation in compliance with this statement. Similarly, they are to continue their usual depreciation practices in regard to any proprietary-type funds employed and are free to continue to record depreciation in relation to the investment in plant funds subsection of plant funds if this option has been adopted (see later discussion). For simplicity, the following discussion and examples abstract from the treatment of depreciation through the assumption that depreciation accounting was not adopted when optional or because the funds employed are not proprietary type funds. As mentioned, the reader can easily adjust for the differences in depreciation possibilities existing in relation to the various universities.

FUND ACCOUNTING BY COLLEGES AND UNIVERSITIES

Funds are the accounting focus of universities. The following are the classes of funds frequently used by universities:[6]

1. Current funds (including unrestricted and restricted current funds).
2. Loan funds.

---

[3] GASB, *Statement 15 of the Governmental Accounting Standards Board,* "Governmental College and University Accounting and Financial Reporting Models" (Norwalk, CT: GASB, 1991).

[4] FASB, *Statement of Financial Accounting Standards No. 93,* "Recognition of Depreciation by Not-for-Profit Organizations" (Norwalk, CT: FASB, 1987).

[5] GASB, *Statement 8 of the Governmental Accounting Standards Boards,* "Applicability of FASB Statement No. 93, Recognition of Depreciation by Not-for-Profit Organizations, to Certain State and Local Governmental Entities" (Norwalk, CT: GASB, 1988).

[6] NACUBO, *Financial Accounting and Reporting Manual for Higher Education* (looseleaf).

3. Endowment and similar funds (including expendable, term, and quasi-endowment funds).
4. Annuity and life income funds.
5. Plant funds (including unexpended plant funds, funds for renewals and replacements, funds for retirement of indebtedness, and investment in plant funds).
6. Agency funds.

As explained below, the unrestricted and restricted current funds of universities are somewhat similar to the general and special revenue funds of state and local governmental units. Additionally, the loan funds, endowment and similar funds, annuity and life income funds, and agency funds of universities are similar to the fiduciary funds of these governmental units. Finally, universities' plant funds play roles similar to those of the general fixed assets and general long-term debt account groups of state and local governments. More specifically, investment in plant funds is used in accounting for the fixed assets of universities other than those held as investments by endowment and similar funds and annuity and life income funds. Also, funds for the retirement of indebtedness are used for debt service purposes in universities. All these types of funds are discussed below, and their frequently encountered accounting techniques are illustrated.

Current Funds—Discussion

Current funds are used in carrying on the day-to-day activities of universities performed in accomplishing their educational and scholarly objectives. These activities include their teaching, research, and public service activities as well as the operating activities related to their unions, student stores, food services, residence halls, and athletic programs. Universities' governing boards (e.g., a university's board of trustees) ultimately are responsible for administering these activities, although universities, like profit-seeking entities, have a variety of administrative personnel who oversee the day-to-day operations of their universities.

Current funds may be unrestricted or restricted. Portions of the resources that are available for unrestricted use by universities' governing boards in accomplishing their objectives are administered through unrestricted current funds. In contrast, portions of universities' resources whose uses are restricted by nonuniversity individuals or organizations (e.g., donors, grantors, and so on) are administered using restricted current funds. As mentioned, the unrestricted current funds of universities are similar to the general funds of state and local governmental units; the restricted current funds of universities are somewhat like the special revenue funds of such units.

Accounting for Unrestricted Current Funds

You will find the financial statements and accounting principles for unrestricted current funds to be familiar because of their similarity to those of state and local governmental units. The first similarity is that the *university* financial statements pertinent to these funds are the balance sheet; the statement of current fund revenues, expenditures, and other changes; and the statement of changes in fund balances.[7] *Note that the only university funds that recognize revenues and expenditures in a statement similar to an income statement are the current funds.* Examples of all of these statements are provided at the end of this major section in Illustrations 22–1, 22–2, and 22–3. These statements contain *individual sections for the various university funds.* The account balances for unrestricted current funds are presently first in university statements. For the most part, the accounts used for unrestricted current funds are similar to those of state and local governmental unit general funds or of profit-seeking entities. The account titles that are pertinent to our examples are explained below or are self-explanatory.

Second, budgetary accounting usually is required for the unrestricted current funds of universities receiving governmental funds to cover operating expenses. When budgetary accounting is used (voluntarily or not), encumbrances often are recorded formally using encumbrances accounts. Note, however, that universities may choose to keep track of encumbrances informally even when budgetary accounting is required. Our examples assume that encumbrances are not recorded for simplicity since encumbrance accounting is illustrated in Chapter 20. Note that the accounts used in university budgetary accounting are different than those used in accounting for state and local governmental units. The following entry illustrates the accounts used in university budgetary accounting.

Unrealized Revenues	XXX,XXX	
Estimated Expenditures	XXX,XXX	
Unallocated Budget Balance		XX,XXX

In university accounting, the balances in these accounts may be changed during the period given revisions in forecasts. Also, these accounts, along with any

---

[7] FASB *Statement No. 95* does not apply to nonprofit entities. Thus, they currently are not required to prepare a statement of cash flows. Nevertheless, a current FASB project is aimed at identifying uniform accounting standards for all nonprofit entities. In early 1989, the FASB added the issue of financial statement display (including the reporting of cash flows) to this project. An important input to the FASB's deliberations on financial statement display is the AICPA's position paper "Display in the Financial Statements of Not-for-Profit Organizations." This paper recommends, among other things, the adaptation of the statement of cash flows, as described in *Statement No. 95,* to nonprofit entities. After deliberation, the FASB will decide whether a financial reporting project related to nonprofit entities will be added to its agenda.

encumbrances memorandum accounts, are closed at year-end just as in state and local governmental accounting.

Third, the revenues of unrestricted current funds usually are recognized on the accrual basis. The main sources of revenues for these funds are tuition and fees; appropriations from governmental units; grants from governmental units; private gifts, grants, and contracts; endowment income; sales and services of educational activities; and sales and services of auxiliary enterprises.[8] Note that the current versions of the AICPA and NACUBO pronouncements dealing with colleges and universities recommend recognition of revenues and related expenditures applying to an academic term extending over two fiscal years in the fiscal year containing the majority of the term. Items of revenue are disclosed under the Revenues heading of the statement of current fund revenues, expenditures, and other changes.[9]

Fourth, the expenditures of unrestricted current funds also usually are accounted for on the accrual basis. Note that the term *expenditures* is used in accounting for these funds rather than the word *expenses*. Typical unrestricted current funds' expenditures are those made for instruction, research, public service, academic support, institutional support, operation and maintenance of plant assets, and scholarships and fellowships. Additionally, recall that FASB *Statement No. 93* requires universities under its jurisdiction to record depreciation expense, although GASB *Statement 8* indicates that universities under its jurisdiction should not revise their procedures in response to this pronouncement.

Fifth, university funds, like state and local governmental funds, make transfers out and receive transfers in. In the case of universities, transfers are classified as *mandatory* and *nonmandatory*. Mandatory transfers are those required legally; nonmandatory transfers are authorized by the governing board of the university. Examples of mandatory transfers pertaining to an unrestricted current fund are transfers of resources: (1) to be used by a retirement of indebtedness fund to service debt principal and interest, (2) for use by a renewals and replacements

---

[8] In general, nonprofit entities record donated properties and services at their fair market values on their receipt dates. The specific criteria applied to donated services for various types of non-profit entities are discussed further below. Note that the values of recorded donated services are reduced by the values of amenities (e.g., meals) provided to the donors. The fair value of donated property and services may be credited to operating or nonoperating revenue (or support) accounts, depending on the type of entity under consideration (and assuming that the fund under consideration recognizes revenues).

[9] The various funds of nonprofit entities may pool their resources for investment purposes. The resulting income (including gains and losses) must be allocated among the funds since the resources transferred to the pool by each specific fund cannot be identified with this fund once pooled. The most common allocation procedure is to allocate income among the funds pro rata on the basis of the market values of the assets in the pool as of the date of the latest transfer of assets to the pool. This pro rata allocation procedure is carried out using equity percentages (e.g., the market value of fund X's assets / market value of the pooled assets). The market values of the assets of the funds already in the pool are determined by applying their (old) equity percentages in the pool to the market value of the pool immediately prior to the transfer. After the transfer, new equity percentages are determined for the funds in the pool.

fund in renewing and replacing existing plant assets, and (3) to an unexpended plant fund for use in the initial acquisitions of plant assets. Since the transfers out of unrestricted current funds normally exceed the related transfers in, the net amounts of the transfers are reported in the Expenditures and Mandatory Transfers section of the statement of current fund revenues, expenditures, and other changes.

Finally, the assets and equities of unrestricted current funds are very similar to those of state and local governmental unit general funds or of profit-seeking entities. Typical assets of these funds are cash, investments, accounts receivable, inventories, prepaid expenses, and deferred charges. Note that fixed assets acquired through the resources of these funds are not accounted for in their records (i.e., they are accounted for in the investment in plant fund subcategory of plant funds). Note also that the investments of unrestricted current funds sometimes are carried at market value (provided that all investments of the university are accounted for similarly).[10] Typical equities of unrestricted current funds are accounts payable, accrued liabilities, students' deposits, amounts due to other funds, deferred credits, and fund balance.

The following example illustrates the basic accounting procedures related to the unrestricted current fund of a university which receives governmental assistance in financing its current operations. Recall that we assume that depreciation is not being recorded. We also assume that budgetary accounting is used and, as indicated above, that encumbrances are not recorded formally. Assume the following data for the unrestricted current fund of Texizona State University. These data pertain to the fiscal year ended December 31, 19X0.

Budgetary data:	
Unrealized revenues	$12,000,000
Estimated expenditures	10,275,000
Revenues (only tuition and fees are billed. All revenues but $50,000	
of tuition and fees are collected during the year.):	
Tuition and fees (including amounts unrealized	
at year-end)	9,000,000
Federal appropriations	1,000,000
State appropriations	750,000
Local appropriations	500,000
Private gifts	300,000
Endowment income	500,000
Sales and services of educational activities*	100,000
Sales and services of auxiliary activities†	75,000
Expenditures:	
Instructional	3,000,000
Research	1,500,000
Public service	1,400,000
Academic support	1,200,000

---

[10] Both *CUBA* and *Audits of Colleges and Universities* allow universities to account for their investments at cost or market value.

Student services	100,000
Institutional support	250,000
Operation and maintenance of plant	500,000
Scholarships and fellowships	350,000
Mandatory transfers:	
Retirement of indebtedness	375,000
Renewals and replacements	425,000
Loan fund	500,000
Nonmandatory transfers (all from unrestricted gifts):	
Loan fund	100,000
Endowment fund	250,000
Unexpended plant fund	300,000
Student deposits:	
Collected	75,000
Refunded	50,000
Unrealized revenues—tuition and fees:	
January 1, 19X0	50,000
December 31, 19X0	60,000
Inventories (the excess of beginning inventory over ending	
inventory is to be charged to Expenditures—Instructional.):	
January 1, 19X0	310,000
December 31, 19X0	180,000
Other data:	
Uncollectible accounts receivable—year-end	35,000
Accounts receivable estimated to be uncollectible amount	
to .5 percent of tuition and fees	

* From the sale of continuing education programs.

† From sales related to the merchandise or services provided by the university's bookstore, union, and student residences.

The entries related to these data, along with explanations, are given below.

The following entry records the university's budget for its unrestricted current fund for 19X0. We assume that the forecasts upon which the budgetary data are based are not changed during the year.

Unrealized Revenues	12,000,000	
Estimated Expenditures		10,275,000
Unallocated Budget Balance		1,725,000

The next four entries record the unrestricted current fund's revenues for the years as well as tuition and fees collections.[11] *We emphasize that these entries, as*

---

[11] Universities accrue tuition and fees at their full amounts even though portions of the accrued amounts are to be waived or refunded (e.g., because of tuition remissions (discounts) pertinent to employees, withdrawals, class cancellations, and scholarships and fellowships). Except for scholarships and fellowships, the waived or refunded amounts tend to be accounted for as contra revenue items. The current year's provision for bad debts usually is accounted for as an instructional expenditure (see below), although it sometimes is accounted for as a revenue deduction. Hospitals account for amounts to be waived similarly (see below). Hospitals treat the current year's provision for doubtful accounts as a revenue deduction.

well as many of the entries presented throughout this chapter, are summary entries for the period (rather than the actual entries made).

Accounts Receivable	9,000,000	
Revenues—Tuition and Fees		9,000,000
Cash	8,950,000	
Accounts Receivable		8,950,000
Cash	2,250,000	
Revenues—Federal Appropriations		1,000,000
Revenues—State Appropriations		750,000
Revenues—Local Appropriations		500,000
Cash	975,000	
Revenues—Private Gifts		300,000
Revenues—Endowment Income		500,000
Revenues—Sales and Services of		
Educational Activities		100,000
Revenues—Sales and Services of		
Auxiliary Activities		75,000

The following entries record the new student deposits received and the student deposits refunded.

Cash	75,000	
Student Deposits		75,000
Student Deposits	50,000	
Cash		50,000

The next entry records the unrestricted current fund's expenditures for the year. We assume that amounts expended for inventories are charged directly to the pertinent accounts during the year and that an appropriate adjusting entry is made at year-end to correctly state the Inventories account balance.

Expenditures—Instructional	3,000,000	
Expenditures—Research	1,500,000	
Expenditures—Public Service	1,400,000	
Expenditures—Academic Support	1,200,000	
Expenditures—Student Services	100,000	
Expenditures—Institutional Support	250,000	
Expenditures—Operation and		
Maintenance of Plant	500,000	
Expenditures—Scholarships and		
Fellowships	350,000	
Cash, Accounts Payable, etc.		8,300,000

The next set of entries records the mandatory and nonmandatory transfers for the period. They also record the related cash disbursements.

Manadatory Transfers—Principal and Interest	375,000	
Mandatory Transfers—Renewals and Replacements	425,000	
Mandatory Transfers—Loan Fund	500,000	
Due to Fund for Retirement of Indebtedness		375,000
Due to Fund for Renewals and Replacements		425,000
Due to Loan Fund		500,000
Due to Fund for Retirement of Indebtedness	375,000	
Due to Fund for Renewals and Replacements	425,000	
Due to Loan Fund	500,000	
Cash		1,300,000
Nonmandatory Transfers	650,000	
Due to Loan Fund		100,000
Due to Endowment Fund		250,000
Due to Unexpended Plant Fund		300,000
Due to Loan Fund	100,000	
Due to Endowment Fund	250,000	
Due to Unexpended Plant Fund	300,000	
Cash		650,000

The final set of entries records year-end adjustments, uncollectible accounts write-offs, and closing entries. Adjustments are needed for unearned tuition and fees, inventories, and uncollectible accounts expense. The closing entries close the budgetary, revenues, expenditures, and transfers out accounts.

Revenues—Tuition and Fees	10,000	
Deferred Credits		10,000
Expenditures—Instructional	130,000	
Inventories		130,000
Allowance for Doubtful Accounts	35,000	
Accounts Receivable		35,000
Expenditures—Instructional (.5% × $9,000,000)	45,000	
Allowance for Doubtful Accounts		45,000
Revenues—Tuition and Fees	8,990,000	
Revenues—Federal Appropriations	1,000,000	
Revenues—State Appropriations	750,000	
Revenues—Local Appropriations	500,000	
Revenues—Private Gifts	300,000	
Revenues—Endowment Income	500,000	
Revenues—Sales and Services of Educational Activities	100,000	

Revenues—Sales and Services of
    Auxiliary Activities   75,000

        Unallocated Budget Balance   215,000
        Unrealized Revenues   12,000,000

Estimated Expenditures   10,275,000
Unallocated Budget Balance   150,000
        Expenditures—Instructional   3,175,000
        Expenditures—Research   1,500,000
        Expenditures—Public Service   1,400,000
        Expenditures—Academic Support   1,200,000
        Expenditures—Student Services   100,000
        Expenditures—Institutional Support   250,000
        Expenditures—Operation and
          Maintenance of Plant   500,000
        Expenditures—Scholarships and
          Fellowships   350,000
        Mandatory Transfers—
          Principal and Interest   375,000
        Mandatory Transfers—
          Renewals and Replacements   425,000
        Mandatory Transfers—Loan Fund   500,000
        Nonmandatory Transfers   650,000

Unallocated Budget Balance   1,790,000
    Fund Balance   1,790,000

Accounting for Restricted Current Funds

The financial statements of restricted current funds are the same as those of unrestricted current funds. That is, the university financial statements pertaining to these funds are the balance sheet; the statement of current fund revenues, expenditures, and other changes; and the statement of changes in fund balances. Examples of the sections of such statements pertinent to restricted current funds are contained in Illustrations 22–1, 22–2, and 22–3.

    The accounts used in accounting for restricted current funds are similar to those used for unrestricted current funds, although fewer accounts usually are needed in accounting for the former. Frequently encountered asset accounts of restricted current funds are Cash, Investments, Accounts Receivable, and Unbilled Charges (e.g., for overhead, sometimes including depreciation, to be recovered from grantors). Fixed assets also are not accounted for in these funds. Typical equity accounts of restricted current funds are Accounts Payable and Fund Balance. The main revenue accounts of these funds tend to be those related to governmental grants and contracts and endowment income. Prime examples of expenditures accounts for restricted current funds are those related to instruction, research, public service, and scholarships and fellowships. *Although the accrual basis is used in accounting for unrestricted current funds, revenues are recog-*

nized in these funds only to the extent that related authorized expenditures have occurred. Unearned revenues are credited to the Fund Balance account initially.

The following example illustrates the basic accounting procedures related to universities' restricted current funds. We assume in the remaining university examples that budgetary accounting is not required and that encumbrances are not recorded formally. Assume the following 19X0 data for the Restricted Current Fund of Calivada State University.

Amount received from:*

Federal grants and contracts (including $50,000 for overhead†)	$500,000
State grants and contracts	200,000
Local grants and contracts	100,000
Endowment	50,000
Expenditures:	
Instructional	460,000
Research	175,000
Public service	125,000
Scholarships and fellowships	20,000
Investments purchased	15,000

---

* All amounts received expended except $5,000 received from the endowment.

† To be nonmandatorily transferred to the Unrestricted Current Fund.

The relevant entries and explanations are as follows.

The first entry records the cash provided to the restricted current fund during the year through contracts, grants, and the university's endowment. Note that the credit is to the Fund Balance account since the amounts received do not yet qualify for recognition as revenues.

Cash ($500,000 + $200,000 + $100,000 + $50,000)	850,000	
Fund Balance		850,000

The following entries record the fund's expenditures, purchase of investments, and recognition of related revenues.

Expenditures—Instructional	460,000	
Expenditures—Research	175,000	
Expenditures—Public Service	125,000	
Expenditures—Scholarships and Fellowships	20,000	
Nonmandatory Transfers Out	50,000	
Accounts Payable (assumed arbitrarily)		80,000
Cash		750,000
Accounts Payable	80,000	
Cash		80,000
Investments	15,000	
Cash		15,000

Fund Balance 845,000		
Revenues—Federal Grants and Contracts		500,000
Revenues—State Grants and Contracts		200,000
Revenues—Local Grants and Contracts		100,000
Revenues—Endowment		45,000

The closing entry for the restricted current fund is as follows:

Revenues—Federal Grants and Contracts 500,000		
Revenues—State Grants and Contracts 200,000		
Revenues—Local Grants and Contracts 100,000		
Revenues—Endowment 45,000		
Expenditures—Instructional		460,000
Expenditures—Research		175,000
Expenditures—Public Service		125,000
Expenditures—Scholarships and Fellowships		20,000
Nonmandatory Transfers Out		50,000
Fund Balance		15,000

The above entries reveal a $20,000 increase in the fund balance during the period. From the asset perspective, this increase is mirrored by increases in cash and investments of $5,000 and $15,000, respectively.

Loan Funds—Discussion and Accounting Procedures

University loan funds are used in making loans to students, faculty, and staff. Their resources typically are provided by gifts, grants, transfers from other funds, endowment revenues, and amounts realized from their own investments. Resources available for lending may be unrestricted or restricted. Unrestricted loan funds are subject only to the lending policies set by universities' governing boards; restricted loan funds are subject to the lending intentions of those providing the resources.

The university financial statements pertinent to loan funds are the balance sheet and the statement of changes in fund balances. Frequently encountered asset accounts of loan funds are Cash; Investments; Loans to Students, Faculty, and Staff; and Due from Unrestricted Funds. Typical equity accounts of loan funds are Fund Balance—Refundable Grants (e.g., federal government), Fund Balance—University Funds—Restricted, and Fund Balance—University Funds—Unrestricted. Loan funds' statements of changes in fund balances often contain receipt-related accounts such as Private Gifts, Grants, and Contracts—Restricted (or Unrestricted); Investment Income—Restricted (or Unrestricted); Realized Gains or Losses on Investments—Restricted (or Unrestricted); Transfers In—Mandatory; Unrestricted Gifts Allocated; and Interest on Loans Receivable (which is accounted for on the accrual basis). Examples of expenditures-related accounts shown in these funds' statements of changes in fund balances are Refunded to Grantors, Loan Cancellations and Write-offs, and Administrative and Collection Costs. Examples of the sections of university statements related to loan funds are contained in Illustrations 22–1 and 22–3.

The next example illustrates the basic accounting procedures related to the Loan Fund of Kansahoma State University. Assume the following 19X0 data.

Amount due or received from:*	
Private gifts (restricted)	$400,000
Unrestricted current fund (gifts allocated)	50,000
Refundable federal grants (restricted)	25,000
Repayment of loans (including interest of $5,000)†	50,000
Interest on investments†	15,000
Disbursements and related items:	
Investments acquired	100,000
Administrative and collection costs†	10,000
Loans made	360,000
Loans judged uncollectible†	25,000
New loans estimated to be uncollectible†	15,000

* All amounts received except $10,000 from the Unrestricted Current Fund.

† Assumed related to restricted university funds for simplicity.

The following entries and explanations pertain to these data.

The next three entries record the resources provided through restricted gifts, the unrestricted current fund, refundable federal grants, loan repayments, and interest.

Due from Unrestricted Current Fund	10,000	
Cash ($400,000 + $40,000 + $25,000)	465,000	
Private Gifts, Grants, and Contracts—		
Restricted		400,000
Unrestricted Gifts Allocated		50,000
Refundable Federal Grants and Contracts		25,000
Cash	50,000	
Loans to Students, Faculty, and Staff		45,000
Interest on Loans Receivable		5,000
Cash	15,000	
Investment Income—Restricted		15,000

The disbursements from the university's loan fund and amounts affecting its Allowance for Uncollectible Loans account are recorded as follows.

Investments	100,000	
Administrative and Collection Costs	10,000	
Loans to Students, Faculty, and Staff	360,000	
Cash		470,000
Allowance for Uncollectible Loans	25,000	
Loans to Students, Faculty, and Staff		25,000
Loan Cancellations and Write-Offs	15,000	
Allowance for Uncollectible Loans		15,000

The closing entries for the loan fund are given below. These entries are relatively uncombined for clarity.

Private Gifts, Grants, and Contracts—Restricted	400,000	
Unrestricted Gifts Allocated	50,000	
Refundable Federal Grants and Contracts	25,000	
Fund Balance—University Funds—		
Restricted		400,000
Fund Balance—University Funds—		
Unrestricted		50,000
Fund Balance—Refundable Grants—Federal		25,000
Interest on Loans Receivable	5,000	
Fund Balance—University Funds—		
Restricted		5,000
Investment Income—Restricted	15,000	
Fund Balance—University Funds—		
Restricted		15,000
Fund Balance—University Funds—Restricted	25,000	
Administrative and Collection Costs		10,000
Loan Cancellations and Write-Offs		15,000

Notice that we debit and credit accounts related to the statement of changes in fund balances initially in the above example and subsequently close the balances in these accounts to the appropriate fund balance accounts. We follow this procedure to emphasize the relationship between the statement of changes in fund balances and the balance sheet. An alternative procedure is to debit or credit the fund balance accounts initially. Under this procedure, subsidiary records are needed to determine the balances to be disclosed in the statement of changes in fund balances. This alternative procedure usually is illustrated in connection with loan funds and the university funds considered below in texts which deal exclusively with governmental and nonprofit accounting. We follow the alternative procedure below, except in the relatively simple case of annuity and life income funds. *Your understanding of the components of the statement of changes in fund balances will be greatly enhanced by examining the captions shown in the sample statement of changes in fund balances* (Illustration 22–3) *after carefully studying each of the remaining university examples.*

Endowment and Similar Funds—Discussion and Accounting Procedures

Endowment and similar funds are funds whose principal is invested to provide income for use in satisfying university objectives consistently with donor or university board stipulations. We often refer to these funds simply as *endowment funds* below. Endowment funds may be nonexpendable funds, term funds, or quasi-endowment funds. The first two types of funds are restricted, at least with respect to the use of principal. If an endowment fund is nonexpendable, its principal, which is provided by a donor, must be preserved intact (and the donor may even stipulate that some of the fund's income be added to principal). A term endowment fund allows the expenditure of principal, consistent with donor wishes, depending on the occurrence of some contingent event (e.g., the passage of a certain period of time as specified by the donor or the donor's death). Quasi-endowment funds are established by universities' boards to administer assets which are to be retained and invested in satisfying university goals. A quasi-endowment fund may be restricted or unrestricted, depending on whether the resources used in establishing the fund are restricted.

Like loan funds, the university financial statements pertinent to endowment funds are the balance sheet and the statement of changes in fund balances. The asset accounts of endowment funds tend to be only Cash and Investments. Their equity accounts often include Fund Balance—Endowment, Fund Balance—Term Endowment, Fund Balance—Quasi-Endowment—Unrestricted, and Fund Balance—Quasi-Endowment—Restricted. The accounts related to endowment funds' statements of changes in fund balances are similar to those of loan funds (but with no loan-related accounts). Examples of the sections of university statements relevant to endowment funds are provided in Illustrations 22–1 and 22–3.

An example that illustrates the basic accounting procedures for the endowment funds of universities is given below. The following 19X0 data pertain to the Endowment Funds of Arkarado State University. Assume the university's endowments are pooled for investment purposes.

Amount received:
  From a national accounting firm for establishment
    of a named professorship in accounting (gift) $1,000,000
  From the university's alumni association for
    use in maintaining athletic facilities* (gift) 3,000,000
  From unrestricted current fund† (gifts allocated) 200,000
  From restricted current fund‡ (mandatory transfer) 300,000
  Interest on pooled investments§ 800,000
Disbursements:
  Purchase of investments 3,500,000
  Interest on pooled investments:‖
    Endowment fund interest 200,000
    Term endowment fund interest 200,000
    Quasi-endowment fund:
      Unrestricted interest 200,000
      Restricted interest 200,000
Other data—Investments which cost $500,000 were sold for
  $700,000. The gain is allocated to the endowment funds on
  the basis of their equity percentages (assumed for simplicity
  to be equal—see footnote 9).

---

* At the end of five years this amount can be used on the construction of a new stadium.

† To be used for any university purpose.

‡ To be used exclusively in acquiring rare negatives for the university's photography center.

§ Allocated to the Endowment Funds using their equity percentages (assumed for simplicity to be equal—see footnote 9).

‖ These disbursements are assumed to be consistent with the provisions of the various endowments.

The next set of entries and explanations pertain to these data.

The following entries record the endowment funds receipts and the gain on the sale of related investments.

Cash ($1,000,000 + $3,000,000 +		
$200,000 + $300,000)	4,500,000	
Fund Balance—Endowment		1,000,000
Fund Balance—Term Endowment		3,000,000
Fund Balance—Quasi-Endowment—		
Unrestricted		200,000
Fund Balance—Quasi-Endowment—		
Restricted		300,000
Cash	800,000	
Income on Pooled Investments		800,000
Cash	700,000	
Investments		500,000
Fund Balance—Endowment		50,000
Fund Balance—Term Endowment		50,000
Fund Balance—Quasi-Endowment—		
Unrestricted		50,000
Fund Balance—Quasi-Endowment—		
Restricted		50,000[12]

The final entries record the endowment funds disbursements, including the purchase of investments and the distribution of the interest on the pooled investments. As indicated, the interest on the pooled investments is assumed to be distributed in accordance with the terms of the endowments.

Investments	3,500,000	
Cash		3,500,000
Income on Pooled Investments	800,000	
Cash		800,000

Annuity and Life Income Funds—Discussion and Accounting Procedures

Both annuity and life income funds make payments to their grantors, or other individuals, over specified time periods (e.g., a grantor's lifetime). Annuity funds make fixed payments (including principal) to such individuals; life income funds pay only income to them. At the ends of the specified time periods, the remaining fund balances are paid to current or endowment funds, depending on the grantors' stipulations.

---

[12] The gain of $200,000 is allocated between the Realized Gain on Investments—Unrestricted and Realized Gain on Investments—Restricted accounts for the statement of changes in fund balances. The allocated amounts are $50,000 and $150,000, respectively. Other accounts and amounts shown on this statement related to this example are Private Gifts, Grants, and Contracts—Restricted—$4,000,000; Unrestricted Gifts Allocated—$200,000; and Mandatory Transfers In—$300,000.

The university financial statements pertinent to annuity and life income funds are the balance sheet and the statement of changes in fund balances. Like endowment funds, the asset accounts of these funds tend to be only Cash and Investments. The equity accounts of annuity funds usually are Annuities Payable (the balances of which equal the present values of the expected payments to individuals) and Fund Balances—Annuity; the equity accounts of life income funds tend to be Income Payable and Fund Balances—Life Income. Commonly encountered accounts related to these funds' statements of changes in fund balances are Private Gifts, Contracts, and Grants—Restricted, and Adjustment for Actuarial Liability for Annuities Payable. The latter account is used in connection with annuity funds when actuarial assumptions appropriate for calculating the balances of Annuities Payable accounts change. Examples of the sections of university statements related to annuity and life income funds are presented in Illustrations 22-1 and 22-3.

The next example illustrates the basic accounting procedures for annuity and life income funds. The following 19X0 data pertain to the annuity and life income funds of Illihio State University. The first year the university received resources for these funds is 19X0.

Amount received:	
For annuity funds*	$ 500,000
For life income funds†	700,000
Income from annuity funds	35,000
Income from life income funds	60,000
Disbursements related to:	
Investments (all donated amounts invested)	1,200,000
Annuities payable	40,000
Income payable	60,000

* The donor is to receive $40,000 per year for life. The initial present value of the annuity payable is $200,000. The balance in the fund is to be transferred to the Unrestricted Current Fund upon the donor's death. At year-end, the present value of the annuity payable is determined to be $220,000.

† The balance in the fund is to be transferred to an endowment fund upon the donor's death.

The entries pertinent to these data are provided next.

The entries for the annuity funds, which are presented immediately below, record the donation of resources to the university, the investment of these funds, the receipt of related income, the annuity payment to the donor, and the adjustment of the Annuities Payable account.

Cash—Annuity	500,000	
Annuities Payable		200,000
Private Gifts, Contracts, and Grants—		
Restricted		300,000
Investments	500,000	
Cash—Annuity		500,000

Cash—Annuity	35,000	
Annuities Payable		35,000
Annuities Payable	40,000	
Cash—Annuity		40,000
Adjustment for Actuarial Liability for		
Annuities Payable	25,000	
Annuities Payable [$220,000 −		
($200,000 + $35,000 − $40,000)]		25,000

The next set of entries is related to the university's life income funds.

Cash—Life Income	700,000	
Private Gifts, Contracts, and Grants—		
Restricted		700,000
Investments	700,000	
Cash—Life Income		700,000
Cash—Life Income	60,000	
Income Payable		60,000
Income Payable	60,000	
Cash—Life Income		60,000

The closing entry for the annuity and life income funds is given below. Note that this entry is unaffected by life income fund operations.

Private Gifts, Contracts, and Grants—		
Restricted	1,000,000	
Adjustment for Actuarial Liability		
for Annuities Payable		25,000
Fund Balance—Annuity		275,000
Fund Balance—Life Income		700,000

Plant Funds—Discussion and Accounting Procedures

Universities' plant funds include unexpended plant funds, funds for renewals and replacements, funds for retirement of indebtedness, and investment in plant funds. Unexpended plant funds are used in initial acquisitions of universities' plant assets. In contrast, funds for renewals and replacements are used in renewing and replacing existing plant assets. Note that the phrase *renewals and replacements* pertains largely to betterments and improvements—which are capitalized in investment in plant funds accounts. Expenditures related to items which are strictly renewals and replacements usually are not capitalized. Funds for retirement of indebtedness are employed in servicing universities' long-term debts. Finally, investments in plant funds are used in accounting for universities' plant assets, except those held by endowment and similar funds and annuity and life income funds.

The university financial statements pertinent to plant funds are the balance sheet and the statement of changes in fund balances. Illustrations 22–1 and 22–3 provide examples of the sections of university statements related to these funds. The accounts pertinent to these funds are largely self-explanatory given the preceding discussions. Thus, since there are so many different types of plants funds, we do not elaborate on their accounts at this point. Note, however, that the fund balance accounts of these funds may be unrestricted or restricted, depending on the sources of their resources.

The following example pertains to the plant funds of Texizona State University in 19X0. Recall that the first example in this chapter provides illustrative entries for the unrestricted current fund of this university, including various transfers to its plant funds. For simplicity, we assume that all funds received from Texizona's unrestricted current fund also are unrestricted from the perspective of its plant funds. The following data are relevant to this example.

Amount received:
  From unrestricted current fund:
    Mandatory transfer—retirement of indebtedness $375,000
    Mandatory transfer—renewals and replacements   425,000
    Nonmandatory transfer—unexpended plant   300,000
  Gifts (which must be used for new plant assets)   400,000
  Issuance of bonds at par (for new building—construction
    begun and completed during year)   800,000
Disbursements:
  Building construction begun and completed during year   800,000
  Bonds retired (related to acquisition of land 5 years ago)   375,000
  Renewals and replacements* (from unrestricted funds)   400,000
  New building acquired from restricted funds   380,000
  New equipment acquired from unrestricted funds   275,000

* Installation of improved roofs on all university buildings.

The entries related to these data are given below.

The first set of entries is pertinent to the university's unexpended plant fund. These entries record the receipt of $300,000 from the unrestricted current fund, the receipt of $400,000 from restricted gifts, the purchase of new plant assets for $655,000, the issuance of the bonds for new construction, and the initiation and completion of this construction.

Cash	700,000	
Unexpended Plant Fund Balance—Unrestricted		300,000
Unexpended Plant Fund Balance—Restricted		400,000
Unexpended Plant Fund Balance—Restricted	380,000	
Unexpended Plant Fund Balance—Unrestricted	275,000	
Cash		655,000
Cash	800,000	
Bonds Payable		800,000

| Construction in Progress | 800,000 | |
| Cash | | 800,000 |

| Bonds Payable | 800,000 | |
| Construction in Progress | | 800,000 |

The next two entries are relevant to the fund for renewals and replacements. These entries record the receipt of $425,000 from the unrestricted current fund and the expenditure of $400,000 on renewals and replacements.

| Cash | 425,000 | |
| Fund for Renewals and Replacements Balance—Unrestricted | | 425,000 |

| Fund for Renewals and Replacements Balance—Unrestricted | 400,000 | |
| Cash | | 400,000 |

The following entries are pertinent to the fund for retirement of indebtedness. These entries record the receipt of resources from the unrestricted current fund and the related retirement of bonds.

| Cash | 375,000 | |
| Retirement of Indebtedness Fund Balance—Unrestricted | | 375,000 |

| Retirement of Indebtedness Fund Balance—Unrestricted | 375,000 | |
| Cash | | 375,000 |

The remaining entries for the plant funds of the university are related to its investment in plant fund. The needed entries record: (1) the acquisitions of the building and equipment from unexpended plant funds, (2) the construction of the building through the bond issue, (3) the renewals and replacements made through the fund for renewals and replacements, and (4) the effect of retiring the bonds through the fund for retirement of indebtedness.

Buildings	380,000	
Equipment	275,000	
Net Investment in Plant		655,000

| Buildings | 800,000 | |
| Bonds Payable | | 800,000 |

| Buildings | 400,000 | |
| Net Investment in Plant | | 400,000 |

| Bonds Payable | 375,000 | |
| Net Investment in Plant | | 375,000 |

Note that the last entry assumes that Land was debited for $375,000 and Bonds Payable was credited for this amount in the year the land was acquired. Thus, it assumes that the land already is recorded in the investment in plant funds accounts.

ILLUSTRATION 22–1   Educational Institution Balance Sheet

SAMPLE EDUCATIONAL INSTITUTION
Balance Sheet
June 30, 19—
(with Comparative Figures at June 30, 19—)

Assets	Current Year	Prior Year
Current funds:		
Unrestricted:		
Cash	$ 210,000	$ 110,000
Investments	450,000	360,000
Accounts receivable, less allowance of $18,000 both years	228,000	175,000
Inventories, at lower of cost (first-in, first-out basis) or market	90,000	80,000
Prepaid expenses and deferred charges	28,000	20,000
Total unrestricted	1,006,000	745,000
Restricted:		
Cash	145,000	101,000
Investments	175,000	165,000
Accounts receivable, less allowance of $8,000 both years	68,000	160,000
Unbilled charges	72,000	—
Total restricted	460,000	426,000
Total current funds	$ 1,466,000	$ 1,171,000
Loan Funds:		
Cash	$ 30,000	$ 20,000
Investments	100,000	100,000
Loans to students, faculty and staff, less allowance of $10,000 current year and $9,000 prior year	550,000	382,000
Due from unrestricted funds	3,000	—
Total loan funds	$ 683,000	$ 502,000
Endowment and similar funds:		
Cash	$ 100,000	$ 101,000
Investments	13,900,000	11,800,000
Total endowment and similar funds	$14,000,000	$11,901,000

Liabilities and Fund Balances	Current Year	Prior Year
Current funds:		
Unrestricted:		
Accounts payable	$ 125,000	$ 100,000
Accrued liabilities	20,000	15,000
Students' deposits	30,000	35,000
Due to other funds	158,000	120,000
Deferred credits	30,000	20,000
Fund balance	643,000	455,000
Total unrestricted	1,006,000	745,000
Restricted:		
Accounts payable	14,000	5,000
Fund balances	446,000	421,000
Total restricted	460,000	426,000
Total current funds	$ 1,466,000	$ 1,171,000
Loan funds:		
Fund balances:		
U.S. government grants refundable	$ 50,000	$ 33,000
University funds:		
Restricted	483,000	369,000
Unrestricted	150,000	100,000
Total loan funds	$ 683,000	$ 502,000
Endowment and similar funds:		
Fund balances:		
Endowment	$ 7,800,000	$ 6,740,000
Term endowment	3,840,000	3,420,000
Quasi-endowment—unrestricted	1,000,000	800,000
Quasi-endowment—restricted	1,360,000	941,000
Total endowment and similar funds	$14,000,000	$11,901,000

Assets

Annuity and life income funds:

	Amount	Amount
Annuity funds:		
Cash		$ 45,000
Investments		3,010,000
Cash	$ 55,000	
Investments	3,260,000	
Total annuity funds	3,315,000	3,055,000
Life income funds:		
Cash	15,000	15,000
Investments	2,045,000	1,740,000
Total life income funds	2,060,000	1,755,000
Total annuity and life income funds	$ 5,375,000	$ 4,810,000
Plant funds:		
Unexpended:		
Cash	$ 275,000	$ 410,000
Investments	1,285,000	1,590,000
Due from unrestricted current funds	150,000	120,000
Total unexpended	1,710,000	2,120,000
Renewals and replacements:		
Cash	5,000	4,000
Investments	150,000	286,000
Deposits with trustees	100,000	90,000
Due from unrestricted current funds	5,000	—
Total renewals and replacements	260,000	380,000
Retirement of indebtedness:		
Cash	50,000	40,000
Deposits with trustees	250,000	253,000
Total retirement of indebtedness	300,000	293,000
Investment in plant:		
Land	500,000	500,000
Land improvements	1,000,000	1,110,000
Buildings	25,000,000	24,060,000
Equipment	15,000,000	14,200,000
Library books	100,000	80,000
Total investment in plant	41,600,000	39,950,000
Total plant funds	$43,870,000	$42,743,000
Agency funds:		
Cash	$ 50,000	$ 70,000
Investments	60,000	20,000
Total agency funds	$ 110,000	$ 90,000

Liabilities and Fund Balances

Annuity and life income funds:

	Amount	Amount
Annuity funds:		
Annuities payable	$ 2,150,000	$ 2,300,000
Fund balances	1,165,000	755,000
Total annuity funds	3,315,000	3,055,000
Life income funds:		
Income payable	5,000	5,000
Fund balances	2,055,000	1,750,000
Total life income funds	2,060,000	1,755,000
Total annuity and life income funds	$ 5,375,000	$ 4,810,000
Plant funds:		
Unexpended:		
Accounts payable	$ 10,000	—
Notes payable	100,000	—
Bonds payable	400,000	
Fund balances:		
Restricted	1,000,000	1,860,000
Unrestricted	200,000	260,000
Total unexpended	1,710,000	2,120,000
Renewals and replacements:		
Fund balances:		
Restricted	25,000	180,000
Unrestricted	235,000	200,000
Total renewals and replacements	260,000	380,000
Retirement of indebtedness:		
Fund balances:		
Restricted	185,000	125,000
Unrestricted	115,000	168,000
Total retirement of indebtedness	300,000	293,000
Investment in plant:		
Notes payable	790,000	810,000
Bonds payable	2,200,000	2,400,000
Mortgages payable	400,000	200,000
Net investment in plant	38,210,000	36,540,000
Total investment in plant	41,600,000	39,950,000
Total plant funds	$43,870,000	$42,743,000
Agency funds:		
Deposits held in custody for others	$ 110,000	$ 90,000
Total agency funds	$ 110,000	$ 90,000

Source: *Audits of Colleges and Universities*. Copyright © 1975 by American Institute of Certified Public Accountants, Inc.

SAMPLE EDUCATIONAL INSTITUTION
Statement of Current Funds Revenues, Expenditures, and Other Changes
Year Ended June 30, 19—

	Current Year			Prior
	Unrestricted	Restricted	Total	Year Total
Revenues:				
Tuition and fees	$2,600,000		$2,600,000	$2,300,000
Federal appropriations	500,000		500,000	500,000
State appropriations	700,000		700,000	700,000
Local appropriations	100,000		100,000	100,000
Federal grants and contracts	20,000	$ 375,000	395,000	350,000
State grants and contracts	10,000	25,000	35,000	200,000
Local grants and contracts	5,000	25,000	30,000	45,000
Private gifts, grants, and contracts	850,000	380,000	1,230,000	1,190,000
Endowment income	325,000	209,000	534,000	500,000
Sales and services of educational activities	190,000		190,000	195,000
Sales and services of auxiliary enterprises	2,200,000		2,200,000	2,100,000
Expired term endowment	40,000		40,000	
Other sources (if any)				
Total current revenues	7,540,000	1,014,000	8,554,000	8,180,000
Expenditures and mandatory transfers:				
Educational and general:				
Instruction	2,960,000	489,000	3,449,000	3,300,000
Research	100,000	400,000	500,000	650,000
Public service	130,000	25,000	155,000	175,000
Academic support	250,000		250,000	225,000
Student services	200,000		200,000	195,000
Institutional support	450,000		450,000	445,000
Operation and maintenance of plant	220,000		220,000	200,000
Scholarships and fellowships	90,000	100,000	190,000	180,000
Total educational and general expenditures	4,400,000	1,014,000	5,414,000	5,370,000

Mandatory transfers for:			
Principal and interest	90,000		90,000	50,000
Renewals and replacements	100,000		100,000	80,000
Loan fund matching grant	2,000		2,000	
Total educational and general	4,592,000	1,014,000	5,606,000	5,500,000
Auxiliary enterprises:			
Expenditures	1,830,000		1,830,000	1,730,000
Mandatory transfers for:			
Principal and interest	250,000		250,000	250,000
Renewals and replacements	70,000		70,000	70,000
Total auxiliary enterprises	2,150,000		2,150,000	2,050,000
Total expenditures and mandatory transfers	6,742,000	1,014,000	7,756,000	7,550,000
Other transfers and additions (deductions):			
Excess of restricted receipts over transfers to revenues		45,000	45,000	40,000
Refunded to grantors		(20,000)	(20,000)	
Unrestricted gifts allocated to other funds	(650,000)		(650,000)	(510,000)
Portion of quasi-endowment gains appropriated	40,000		40,000	
Net increase in fund balances	$ 188,000	$ 25,000	$ 213,000	$ 160,000

SOURCE: *Audits of Colleges and Universities*, Copyright © 1975 by American Institute of Certified Public Accountants, Inc.

SAMPLE EDUCATIONAL INSTITUTION
Statement of Changes in Fund Balances
Year Ended June 30, 19—

	Current Funds		Loan Funds	Endowment and Similar Funds	Annuity and Life Income Funds	Plant Funds			
	Unrestricted	Restricted				Unexpended	Renewals and Replacements	Retirement of Indebtedness	Investment in Plant
Revenues and other additions:									
Unrestricted current fund revenues	$7,540,000								
Expired term endowment—restricted						$ 50,000			
State appropriations—restricted						50,000			
Federal grants and contracts—restricted		$ 500,000							
Private gifts, grants, and contracts—restricted		370,000	$100,000	$ 1,500,000	$ 800,000	115,000		$ 65,000	$ 15,000
Investment income—restricted		224,000	12,000	10,000		5,000	$ 5,000	5,000	
Realized gains on investments—unrestricted				109,000					
Realized gains on investments—restricted			4,000	50,000		10,000	5,000	5,000	
Interest on loans receivable			7,000						
U.S. government advances			18,000						
Expended for plant facilities (including $100,000 charged to current funds expenditures)									1,550,000
Retirement of indebtedness									220,000
Accrued interest on sale of bonds								3,000	
Matured annuity and life income restricted to endowment				10,000					
Total revenues and other additions	7,540,000	1,094,000	141,000	1,679,000	800,000	230,000	10,000	78,000	1,785,000
Expenditures and other deductions:									
Educational and general expenditures	4,400,000	1,014,000							

Auxiliary enterprises expenditures	1,830,000								
Indirect costs recovered		35,000							
Refunded to grantors		20,000							
Loan cancellations and write-offs			11,000						
Administrative and collection costs			1,000						
Adjustment of actuarial liability for annuities payable					75,000				
Expended for plant facilities (including noncapitalized expenditures of $50,000)						1,200,000	300,000		
Retirement of indebtedness								220,000	
Interest on indebtedness								190,000	
Disposal of plant facilities									115,000
Expired term endowments ($40,000 unrestricted, $50,000 restricted to plant)				90,000					
Matured annuity and life income funds restricted to endowment					10,000				
Total expenditures and other deductions	6,230,000	1,069,000	12,000	90,000	85,000	1,200,000	300,000	411,000	115,000
Transfers among funds— additions (deductions):									
Mandatory:									
Principal and interest	(340,000)							340,000	
Renewals and replacements	(170,000)						170,000		
Loan fund matching grant	(2,000)		2,000						
Unrestricted gifts allocated	(650,000)	50,000	50,000	550,000					
Portion of unrestricted quasi-endowment funds investment gains appropriated	40,000			(40,000)					
Total transfers	(1,122,000)	50,000	52,000	510,000			170,000	340,000	
Net increase (decrease) for the year	188,000	181,000	2,099,000	715,000	25,000	(920,000)	(120,000)	7,000	1,670,000
Fund balance at beginning of year	455,000	502,000	11,901,000	2,505,000	421,000	2,120,000	380,000	293,000	36,540,000
Fund balance at end of year	$ 643,000	$683,000	$14,000,000	$3,220,000	$ 446,000	$1,200,000	$260,000	$300,000	$38,210,000

SOURCE: *Audits of Colleges and Universities.* Copyright © 1975 by American Institute of Certified Public Accountants, Inc.

Agency Funds—Discussion and Accounting Procedures

Agency funds of universities, like those of governmental units, are used to collect, invest, or expend, in a fiduciary capacity, resources provided by others for various purposes. The only university financial statement pertinent to agency funds is the balance sheet (see Illustration 22–1). The asset accounts related to these funds usually are Cash, Accounts Receivable, and Investments. Agency funds do not have fund balance accounts; thus, their only equity accounts are liabilities to those for whom resources are held (such as associations of university professors and student organizations).

Our final university-related example pertains to the agency funds of New Mexitah State University in 19X0. The following data are relevant to this example.

Dues collected from faculty members for American Association of University Professors	$2,000
Amount of above used to purchase Treasury bills	2,000
Interest received from Treasury bills	150
Remittance to American Association of University Professors after maturity of Treasury bills	2,000

The entries related to the above data follow:

Cash	2,000	
Deposits Held in Custody for Others		2,000
Investments	2,000	
Cash		2,000
Cash	2,150	
Investments		2,000
Deposits Held in Custody for Others		150
Deposits Held in Custody for Others	2,000	
Cash		2,000

AUTHORITATIVE PRONOUNCEMENTS—HOSPITALS

Hospitals, like colleges and universities, may be parts of governmental units, or they may be nongovernmental. Governmental-type hospitals are accounted for as enterprise funds. Since enterprise fund accounting is illustrated in Chapter 21, we ignore these hospitals in this chapter. Thus, our focus is on nongovernmental hospitals.

Historically, the principal institutions involved in providing accounting guidance for nongovernmental hospitals have been the American Hospital Association (AHA), the Healthcare Financial Management Association (HFMA), and the

AICPA. Also, from the historical perspective, the principal authoritative pronouncements pertaining to nongovernmental hospitals have been the AICPA's *Hospital Audit Guide* and its *Statements of Position No. 78-1, 78-7, 81-2, 85-1, and 89-5.*[13] Recently, the AICPA issued *Audits of Providers of Health Care Services (APHCS).*[14] The latter pronouncement now is the preeminent authoritative pronouncement pertaining to hospitals and other providers of health care services (including, for example, clinics, health maintenance organizations, home health agencies, and nursing homes). This pronouncement is primary since the FASB requires nongovernmental hospitals to follow its reporting standards. Note also that *APHCS* is consistent with FASB *Statement No. 93* since both require nongovernmental hospitals to record depreciation.[15] As indicated, the hospital-related discussions and examples in this chapter deal with nongovernmental hospitals. *We usually refer to nongovernmental hospitals simply as hospitals below.*

Fund Accounting by Nongovernmental Hospitals

The accounting entities of hospitals, like those of governmental units and universities, are funds. The general classes of funds pertinent in hospital accounting are: (1) general funds and (2) donor-restricted funds.[16] The more important classes of donor-restricted funds of hospitals are specific-purpose funds, endowment funds, and plant replacement and expansion funds. The resources of hospitals' general funds can be used at the discretions of their boards; the resources of their donor-restricted funds must be used in accordance with their donors' or grantors' stipulations. Note that donor-restricted funds are classified as *permanently* or *temporarily restricted funds* under *APHCS,* although this distinction pertains only to endowment funds whose principals are, or are not, maintained in perpetuity. All these types of funds are discussed below, and pertinent accounting procedures are illustrated.

---

[13] American Institute of Certified Public Accountants, *Hospital Audit Guide* (New York: AICPA, 1985).

[14] American Institute of Certified Public Accountants, *Audits of Providers of Health Care Services* (New York: AICPA, 1990).

[15] Recall that enterprise funds record depreciation. Thus, governmental hospitals, which are accounted for as enterprise funds, also record depreciation. Note that the GASB also requires hospitals under its jurisdiction to follow the reporting standards contained in the AICPA pronouncements mentioned above.

[16] Note that a hospital's general funds is just one fund. Nevertheless, the plural, general funds, is used conventionally in referring to such a fund. Plurals are used in other hospital-related cases when it is possible for more than one fund of a particular type to exist. Hospitals also occasionally use resources related to agency relationships. Their use of such resources is similar to the use by universities. Under pronouncements existing prior to *APHCS,* hospital agency resources also were accounted for consistently with university accounting. Under *APHCS,* these funds are accounted for under the General Funds caption.

General Funds—Discussion and Accounting Procedures

The general funds of hospitals are used in carrying on their day-to-day operating activities. As indicated, the resources of hospitals' general funds are unrestricted. Unlike governmental units and universities, *all unrestricted hospital assets and liabilities (including long-term items) and all hospital revenues and expenses are recognized (under the accrual basis) in the financial statements of their general funds.* The hospital financial statements pertinent to their general funds are the balance sheet, the statement of revenues and expenses, the statement of changes in fund balances, and the statement of cash flows. Either the layered form (in which the various funds are shown separately) or the aggregated form of the balance sheet may be used under *APHCS*. Also, either the FASB's direct or indirect approach may be used for the statement of cash flows. Examples of these statements are presented on pages 1056–1060 in Illustrations 22–4, 22–5, 22–6, and 22–7. We illustrate only the layered form of the balance sheet and the direct approach to the statement of cash flows since these formats yield superior disclosure. The account titles and captions shown in these statements related to general funds are very similar to those of profit-seeking entities. Note, however, that the balance sheet of general funds may contain sections for assets whose uses are limited, for example, by debt or trust agreements under the provisions of *APHCS*. In such cases, the assets are shown under the Assets Whose Use Is Limited caption (see Illustration 22–4). Similarly, if liabilities are to be paid from assets whose uses are limited, they are segregated, under descriptive captions, in general funds' balance sheets.

The following example illustrates typical entries of hospitals' general funds. Assume the following data for the general funds of the Valleycrest Hospital for the fiscal year ended December 31, 19X0.

Revenues (all collected in cash during the year except $100,000 from daily patient services and the amounts related to revenue deductions):	
From daily patient services	$9,000,000
From nursing services	2,000,000
From other professional services	500,000
From specific purpose fund (transfer for cancer research expenses paid from general funds)	30,000
Other operating revenues (from hospital cafeteria ($240,000) and from restricted endowment fund ($10,000) to cover viral research expenses paid from general funds)	250,000
Unrestricted gifts	50,000
Revenue deductions (i.e., contra revenue items) except provision for bad debts:	
Contractual adjustments*	300,000
Charity services†	190,000
Discounts and allowances (patients and employees)	10,000
Expenses paid in cash:	
General services expenses	6,000,000
Fiscal and administrative expenses	1,500,000

Nursing services expenses	1,200,000
Other professional expenses	450,000
Research expenses paid through transfer from specific	
purpose fund (see above)	30,000
Property, plant, and equipment acquired:	
Fixed equipment acquired for cash	1,000,000
Major movable equipment purchased through plant	
replacement and expansion fund	250,000
Data for year-end adjustments, etc.:	
Accrued interest payable	50,000
Estimated bad debts expense (also a revenue deduction)	10,000
Accounts judged uncollectible	8,000
Depreciation expense:	
Buildings	500,000
Fixed equipment	200,000
Major movable equipment	50,000
Decrease in inventories (assumed pertinent to general	
services expenses for simplicity)	20,000
Increase in prepaid expenses (assumed related to fiscal and	
administrative expenses for simplicity)	5,000

* Reductions in patients bills covered by Medicare, Medicaid, and various hospitalization plans.

† The cost of services performed for those known unable to pay.

The entries related to these data, along with explanations, are provided below. We do not illustrate closing entries for hospital funds for brevity and because of the mechanical nature of these entries. Note, however, that the revenues and expenses of hospital general funds simply are closed to the Fund Balance account.

The three entries presented below are related to the general funds revenues for the year. The first two entries record revenues and related collections. The third entry records the revenue deductions for the year, except for the period's provision for bad debts. The provision for bad debts is recorded at year-end as an adjusting entry.

Accounts Receivable (assumed arbitrarily)	6,750,000	
Cash	5,080,000	
Revenues—Daily Patient Services		9,000,000
Revenues—Nursing Services		2,000,000
Revenues—Other Professional Services		500,000
Other Operating Revenues		
($30,000 + $250,000)		280,000
Nonoperating Revenues—Bequests		
and Gifts		50,000
Cash	6,150,000	
Accounts Receivable		6,150,000
Contractual Adjustments	300,000	
Charity Services	190,000	
Discounts and Allowances	10,000	
Accounts Receivable		500,000

The three entries presented below are related to the general funds revenues for the year. The first two entries record revenues and related collections. The third entry records the revenue deductions for the year, except for the period's provision for bad debts. The provision for bad debts is recorded at year-end as an adjusting entry.

Accounts Receivable (assumed arbitrarily)	6,750,000	
Cash	5,080,000	
Revenues—Daily Patient Services		9,000,000
Revenues—Nursing Services		2,000,000
Revenues—Other Professional Services		500,000
Other Operating Revenues		
($30,000 + $250,000)		280,000
Nonoperating Revenues—Bequests		
and Gifts		50,000
Cash	6,150,000	
Accounts Receivable		6,150,000
Contractual Adjustments	300,000	
Charity Services	190,000	
Discounts and Allowances	10,000	
Accounts Receivable		500,000

The next entry deals with the general funds cash expenses. We assume that amounts expended for inventories and prepaid expenses are charged directly to expense accounts during the year and that appropriate adjusting entries are made at year-end to correctly state the inventories and prepaid expenses account balances.

General Services Expenses	6,000,000	
Fiscal and Administrative Expenses	1,500,000	
Nursing Services Expenses	1,200,000	
Other Professional Expenses		
($450,000 + $30,000)	480,000	
Cash		9,180,000

The following entries record the period's property, plant, and equipment acquisitions. The first entry records the purchase of fixed equipment using cash. The second entry records major movable equipment purchased through the plant replacement and expansion fund. Note that nonoperating revenue in an amount equal to the cost of the major movable equipment is recognized in general funds accounts.

Fixed Equipment	1,000,000	
Cash		1,000,000
Major Movable Equipment	250,000	
Nonoperating Revenues—Transfers from		
Plant Replacement and Expansion Fund		250,000

The final set of entries records year-end adjustments and writes off the uncollectible accounts. Adjustments are needed for interest expense, bad debts expense, depreciation expense, inventory, and prepaid expenses.

Interest Expense	50,000	
Accrued Interest Payable		50,000
Provision for Bad Debts	10,000	
Allowance for Doubtful Accounts		10,000
Allowance for Doubtful Accounts	8,000	
Accounts Receivable		8,000
Depreciation Expense	750,000	
Accumulated Depreciation—Buildings		500,000
Accumulated Depreciation—Fixed		
Equipment		200,000
Accumulated Depreciation—Major		
Movable Equipment		50,000
General Services Expenses	20,000	
Inventories		20,000
Prepaid Expenses	5,000	
Fiscal and Administrative Expenses		5,000

Specific-Purpose Funds—Discussion and Accounting Procedures

As mentioned, the restricted funds of hospitals are used in administering resources which can be used only in accordance with their donors' or grantors' stipulations. Thus, hospitals' specific-purpose funds must be operated consistently with such restrictions. These funds are similar to the special revenue funds of state and local governmental units. They are similar in the sense that their operations often involve raising funds for specific purposes and disbursing the funds accordingly. For example, individuals often pledge amounts to hospitals to support certain types of research (e.g., cancer research) with the pledges being accounted for using specific-purpose funds. The (accrual basis) hospital financial statements relevant to their specific-purpose funds are the balance sheet and the statement of changes in fund balances (see Illustrations 22–4 and 22–7). The account titles and captions shown in these statements for specific-purpose funds are easily understood.

The next example pertains to hospitals' specific-purpose funds. Assume that Valleycrest Hospital's volunteer organization obtains pledges in 19X0 for $40,000 to be spent on cancer research, that all the pledges are collected during the year for simplicity, and that the pledges are accounted for in the hospital's only specific-purpose fund.[17] Recall also from the previous example that $30,000 was

---

[17] If uncollectible pledges are expected, an allowance for uncollectible pledges is established. Such an allowance is illustrated below in the context of a plant replacement and expansion fund.

transferred from the hospital's specific-purpose fund to its general funds to cover cancer research expenditures made during the year. The specific-purpose-funds entries for 19X0 follow:

Pledges Receivable	40,000	
Fund Balance		40,000
Cash	40,000	
Pledges Receivable		40,000
Transfers to General Funds—Research Expenses	30,000	
Due to General Funds		30,000
Due to General Funds	30,000	
Cash		30,000

Endowment Funds (Both Permanently and Temporarily Restricted)— Discussion and Accounting Procedures

Hospitals' endowment funds are similar to the endowment funds of universities. That is, these funds are established by donations, and their principal is invested to provide income for use consistent with donor restrictions or hospital board desires. Additionally, hospital endowment funds may exist indefinitely or for a fixed period of time contingent on the occurrence of some event (e.g., the donor's death or the passage of time). Those existing indefinitely are permanently restricted; those existing for a fixed period are temporarily restricted. The hospital financial statements relevant to endowment funds are the balance sheet and the statement of changes in fund balances (see Illustrations 22–4 and 22–7). The account titles and captions shown in these statements for endowment funds are self-explanatory.

If the use of the income from a hospital endowment is restricted by its donor, any unexpended income for the year is transferred to a specific-purpose fund or to the plant replacement and expansion fund, depending on the donor's desires. Alternatively, if the use of the income is not restricted, unexpended income is transferred to general funds. The principal of a hospital endowment is handled similarly upon the termination of the related fund. If the donor has placed restrictions on the ultimate use of an endowment (i.e., it is permanently restricted), the principal is transferred to an appropriately titled restricted fund. Alternatively, if the fund is temporarily restricted, its principal is transferred to general funds.

The following example is related to the (permanently or temporarily) restricted endowment fund of Valleycrest Hospital. This fund was established by a wealthy donor, who contributes $20,000 to the fund at the start of each year, with the stipulation that fund income is to be used to cover the hospital's viral research expenses to the extent possible. Any remaining income is to be transferred to the hospital's plant replacement and expansion fund. Recall that $10,000 was transferred from the endowment fund to the hospital's general funds to cover viral research expenditures made during the year. The fund's earnings for the year from investments in marketable securities amounted to $15,000. There is no accrued income receivable at year-end.[18] Valleycrest's endowment fund entries for 19X0 are presented below, assuming that contributions to the fund are invested in marketable securities.

Cash	20,000	
Fund Balance—Restricted		20,000
Marketable Securities	20,000	
Cash		20,000
Cash	15,000	
Due to General Funds		10,000
Due to Plant Replacement and Expansion Fund		5,000
Due to General Funds	10,000	
Due to Plant Replacement and Expansion Fund	5,000	
Cash		15,000

Plant Expansion and Replacement Funds—Discussion and Accounting Procedures

Plant expansion and replacement funds are used to account for donations, including pledges, that must be used to acquire or replace hospital plant assets. Nevertheless, fixed assets are not accounted for in plant expansion and replacement funds. When such assets are acquired through these funds, their Fund Balance accounts are debited. Although fixed assets are not accounted for in plant expansion and replacement funds, investments in securities are accounted for in these funds. Consistently, investment income and gains and losses on investments are closed to their Fund Balance accounts. The hospital financial statements relevant to their plant replacement and expansion funds are the balance sheet and the statement of changes in fund balances (see Illustrations 22–4 and 22–7). The account titles and captions shown in these statements for plant expansion and replacement funds also are easily understood.

The final hospital-related example pertains to hospitals' plant expansion and replacement funds. Assume the following 19X0 data related to the plant expansion and replacement fund of Valleycrest Hospital.

Pledges:	
Pledges obtained	$400,000
Pledges collected during the year	350,000
Pledges expected to be uncollectible	10,000
Pledges from prior year written off	8,000

---

[18] The accrual basis is applied to endowment funds and restricted funds in general. Thus, interest receivable, for example, is accrued in hospital accounting at year-end. The accrual of interest receivable is illustrated below in the context of a plant replacement and expansion fund.

Receipts other than from pledges:
Cash from investment income   30,000
Cash from sale of marketable securities with cost of
$80,000   100,000
Disbursements:
Purchase of marketable securities   150,000
Purchase of major movable equipment with
unrestricted use   250,000
Year-end accrued interest receivable   12,000

The entries related to these data, along with explanations, are provided below. The following entries record the pledges obtained and the related receipts.

Pledges Receivable   400,000
    Fund Balance   400,000

Cash   350,000
    Pledges Receivable   350,000

The next set of entries records the receipts of the fund generated through its investments. Note that both of these entries affect the Fund Balance account.

Cash   30,000
    Fund Balance   30,000

Cash   100,000
    Investments—Marketable Securities   80,000
    Fund Balance   20,000

The following two entries record the disbursements of the fund. Recall that an entry corresponding to the second entry below was recorded in the hospital's general funds.[19]

Investments—Marketable Securities   30,000
    Cash   30,000

Fund Balance   250,000
    Cash   250,000

The final set of entries records the year-end adjusting entries and writes off the uncollectible pledges. Adjusting entries are needed for accrued interest receivable and the estimated uncollectible pledges.

Accrued Interest Receivable   12,000
    Fund Balance   12,000

Fund Balance   10,000
    Allowance for Uncollectible Pledges   10,000

Allowance for Uncollectible Pledges   8,000
    Pledges Receivable   8,000

---

[19] This entry contains a debit to Major Movable Equipment for $250,000 and a credit to Non-operating Revenues—Transfers from Plant Replacement and Expansion Fund for the same amount.

AUTHORITATIVE PRONOUNCEMENTS—OTHER NONPROFIT ENTITIES

There are numerous types of nonprofit organizations other than universities and hospitals, including voluntary health and welfare organizations, civic groups, labor unions, cultural institutions, political parties, private schools, performing arts organizations, fraternal organizations, homeowners' associations, country clubs, religious organizations, and professional organizations. In this context, voluntary health and welfare organizations are unique. They are distinguished from other nonprofit organizations by their purposes (i.e., to meet community health, welfare, or other social needs), their voluntary nature (i.e., little or no fees are charged), and their resource providers (i.e., their resource providers are not the primary recipients of their services).

The primary authoritative pronouncement pertaining to voluntary health and welfare organizations is the AICPA's *Audits of Voluntary Health and Welfare Organizations*.[20] Although this audit guide is the principal authoritative pronouncement for these organizations, descriptions of their accounting techniques, which are based largely on the audit guide, are contained in *Standards of Accounting and Financial Reporting for Voluntary Health and Welfare Organizations* (or *Standards* for short).[21] Our discussions and examples of voluntary health and welfare organization accounting are based on the AICPA's audit guide and *Standards*. The principal authoritative pronouncement for the remaining nonprofit entities is the AICPA's *Audits of Certain Nonprofit Organizations (ACNO)*.[22] We do not provide examples related to these organizations because of their number and the similarity between their accounting techniques and those of voluntary health and welfare organizations. Nevertheless, the last major section of this chapter contains a brief discussion of certain accounting procedures pertinent to the remaining nonprofit entities.

FUND ACCOUNTING BY VOLUNTARY HEALTH AND WELFARE ORGANIZATIONS

The classes of funds often encountered in accounting for voluntary health and welfare organizations are: (1) current funds—unrestricted, (2) current funds—restricted, (3) land, building, and equipment funds, (4) endowment funds, and (5)

---

[20] American Institute of Certified Public Accountants, *Audits of Voluntary Health and Welfare Organizations* (New York: AICPA, 1988).

[21] The National Health Council, the National Assembly of National Voluntary Health and Social Welfare Organizations, and the United Way of America, *Standards of Accounting and Financial Reporting for Voluntary Health and Welfare Organizations* (Alexandria, VA, 1988).

[22] American Institute of Certified Public Accountants, *Audits of Certain Nonprofit Organizations* (New York: AICPA, 1981). This audit guide encompasses and expands on the principles set forth in the AICPA's *SOP 78-10*, "Accounting Principles and Reporting Practices for Certain Nonprofit Organizations."

ILLUSTRATION 22–4   Hospital Balance Sheet (Layered Form)

SAMPLE HOSPITAL
Balance Sheets
December 31, 19X7 and 19X6

Assets

	19X7	19X6
General funds		
Current assets:		
Cash and cash equivalents	$ 3,103,000	$ 4,525,000
Assets whose use is limited—required for current liabilities (notes 5, 7, and 8)	970,000	1,300,000
Patient accounts receivable, net of estimated uncollectibles of $2,500,000 in 19X7 and $2,400,000 in 19X6	15,100,000	14,194,000
Estimated third-party payor settlements—medicare (note 3)	441,000	600,000
Supplies, at lower of cost (first-in, first-out) or market	1,163,000	938,000
Other current assets	321,000	403,000
Due from donor-restricted funds, net		500,000
Total current assets	$ 21,098,000	$ 22,460,000
Assets whose use is limited (notes 5, 7, and 8):		
By board for capital improvements	11,000,000	10,000,000
By agreements with third-party payors for funded depreciation	9,234,000	6,151,000
Under malpractice funding arrangement—held by trustee	3,007,000	2,682,000
Under indenture agreement—held by trustee	11,708,000	11,008,000
Total assets whose use is limited	34,949,000	29,841,000
Less assets whose use is limited and that are required for current liabilities	970,000	1,300,000
Noncurrent assets whose use is limited	33,979,000	28,541,000
Property and equipment, net (notes 6 and 7)	51,038,000	50,492,000

Liabilities and Fund Balances

	19X7	19X6
Current liabilities:		
Current installments of long-term debt (note 7)	$ 970,000	$ 1,200,000
Current portion of capital lease obligations (note 7)	500,000	550,000
Accounts payable	2,217,000	2,085,000
Accrued expenses	3,396,000	3,225,000
Estimated third-party payor settlements—medicaid (note 2)	2,143,000	1,942,000
Deferred third-party reimbursement	200,000	210,000
Advances from third-party payors	122,000	632,000
Current portion of estimated malpractice costs (note 8)	600,000	500,000
Retainage and construction accounts payable	955,000	772,000
Due to donor-restricted funds	300,000	—
Total current liabilities	11,403,000	11,116,000
Deferred third-party reimbursement	746,000	984,000
Estimated malpractice costs, net of current portion (note 8)	3,207,000	2,182,000
Long-term debt, excluding current installments (note 7)	22,644,000	23,614,000
Capital lease obligations, excluding current portion (note 7)	500,000	400,000
Fund balance	69,310,000	64,567,000

Other assets:

	19X7	19X6
Prepaid pension cost (note 12)	85,000	35,000
Deferred financing costs	693,000	759,000
Investment in affiliated company (note 4)	917,000	576,000
Total other assets	1,695,000	1,370,000
	$107,810,000	$102,863,000

Commitments and contingent liabilities (notes 3, 6, 8, 12, and 13)

	19X7	19X6
	—	—
	$107,810,000	$102,863,000

Donor-restricted funds

Specific-purpose funds

Assets	19X7	19X6		Liabilities and Fund Balance	19X7	19X6
Cash	$ 378,000		Accounts payable		$ 205,000	$ 72,000
Investments, at cost that approximates market	728,000	455,000	Deferred grant revenue		92,000	—
Grants receivable	613,000	535,000	Due to general funds		—	255,000
			Fund balance		1,422,000	1,041,000
	$ 1,719,000	$ 1,368,000			$ 1,719,000	$ 1,368,000

Plant replacement and expansion funds

Assets	19X7	19X6		Liabilities and Fund Balance	19X7	19X6
Cash	$ 24,000	321,000	Due to general funds	$ —	345,000
Investments, at cost that approximates market	252,000	165,000	Fund balance	558,000	521,000
Pledges receivable, net of estimated uncollectibles of $60,000 in 19X7 and $120,000 in 19X6	132,000	380,000			
Due from general funds	150,000	—			
	$ 558,000	$ 866,000		$ 558,000	$ 866,000

Endowment funds

Assets	19X7	19X6		Fund Balance	19X7	19X6
Cash	$ 1,253,000	653,000	Fund balance	$ 5,259,000	$ 6,073,000
Investments, net of $175,000 valuation allowance in 19X7, market value $3,798,000 in 19X7 and $5,013,000 in 19X6 (note 9)	3,856,000	5,320,000			
Due from general funds	150,000	100,000			
	$ 5,259,000	$ 6,073,000		$ 5,259,000	$ 6,073,000

(notes not reproduced)

SOURCE: *Audits of Providers of Health Care Services.* Copyright © 1990 by American Institute of Certified Public Accountants.

ILLUSTRATION 22-5   **Hospital Statement of Revenues and Expenses**

SAMPLE HOSPITAL
Statements of Revenues and Expenses of General Funds
Years Ended December 31, 19X7 and 19X6

	19X7	19X6
Net patient service revenue (notes 3 and 7)	$92,656,000	$88,942,000
Other revenue	6,010,000	5,380,000
Total revenue	98,666,000	94,322,000
Expenses (notes 7, 8, 12, and 13):		
Professional care of patients	53,016,000	48,342,000
Dietary services	4,407,000	4,087,000
General services	10,888,000	9,973,000
Administrative services	11,075,000	10,145,000
Employee health and welfare	10,000,000	9,335,000
Medical malpractice costs	1,125,000	200,000
Depreciation and amortization	4,782,000	4,280,000
Interest	1,752,000	1,825,000
Provision for bad debts	1,010,000	1,103,000
Total expenses	98,055,000	89,290,000
Income from operations	611,000	5,032,000
Nonoperating gains (losses):		
Unrestricted gifts and bequests (note 11)	822,000	926,000
Loss on investment in affiliated company (note 4)	(37,000)	(16,000)
Income on investments of endowment funds	750,000	650,000
Income on investments whose use is limited:		
By board for capital improvements	1,120,000	1,050,000
By agreements with third-party payors for funded depreciation	850,000	675,000
Under indenture agreement	100,000	90,000
Other investment income	284,000	226,000
Nonoperating gains, net	3,889,000	3,601,000
Revenues and gains in excess of expenses and losses	$ 4,500,000	$ 8,633,000

(notes not reproduced)

SOURCE: *Audits of Providers of Health Care Services.* Copyright © 1990 by American Institute of Certified Public Accountants.

ILLUSTRATION 22-6　Hospital Statement of Changes in Fund Balances

SAMPLE HOSPITAL
Statements of Changes in Fund Balances
Years Ended December 31, 19X7 and 19X6

| | 19X7 | | | | 19X6 | | | |
| | | Donor-Restricted Funds | | | | Donor-Restricted Funds | | |
	General Funds	Specific-Purpose Funds	Plant Replacement and Expansion Funds	Endowment Funds	General Funds	Specific-Purpose Funds	Plant Replacement and Expansion Funds	Endowment Funds
Balances at beginning of year	$64,567,000	$1,041,000	$521,000	$6,073,000	$56,679,000	$933,000	$501,000	$5,973,000
Additions:								
Revenue and gains in excess of expenses and losses	4,500,000	—	—	—	8,633,000	—	—	—
Gifts, grants, and bequests (notes 10 and 11)	—	869,000	220,000	—	—	558,000	290,000	—
Investment income	—	62,000	20,000	—	—	50,000	15,000	—
Net realized gain on sale of investments	—	—	100,000	—	—	—	20,000	100,000
Transfer to finance property and equipment additions	243,000	—	(243,000)	—	255,000	—	(255,000)	—
	4,743,000	931,000	97,000	—	8,888,000	608,000	70,000	100,000
Deductions:								
Provision for uncollectible pledges	—	—	(60,000)	—	—	—	(50,000)	—
Capital contribution to Sample Health System (note 11)	—	—	—	—	(1,000,000)	—	—	—
Net realized loss on sale of investments	—	—	—	(639,000)	—	—	—	—
Unrealized loss on marketable equity securities (note 9)	—	—	—	(175,000)	—	—	—	—
Transfer to other revenue	—	(550,000)	—	—	—	(500,000)	—	—
	—	(550,000)	(60,000)	(814,000)	(1,000,000)	(500,000)	(50,000)	—
Balance at end of year	$69,310,000	$1,422,000	$558,000	$5,259,000	$64,567,000	$1,041,000	$521,000	$6,073,000
(notes not reproduced)								

SOURCE: *Audits of Providers of Health Care Services.* Copyright © 1990 by American Institute of Certified Public Accountants.

ILLUSTRATION 22-7 **Hospital Statement of Cash Flows (Direct Method)**

SAMPLE HOSPITAL
Statements of Cash Flows of General Funds
Years Ended December 31, 19X7 and 19X6

	19X7	19X6
Cash flows from operating activities and gains and losses:		
Cash received from patients and third-party payors	$ 90,342,000	$ 85,619,000
Cash paid to employees and suppliers	(89,214,000)	(81,510,000)
Other receipts from operations	6,042,000	5,563,000
Receipts from unrestricted gifts and bequests	1,122,000	905,000
Interest and dividends received	2,510,000	2,330,000
Interest paid (net of amount capitalized)	(1,780,000)	(1,856,000)
Net cash provided by operating activities and gains and losses	9,022,000	11,051,000
Cash flows from investing activities:		
Purchase of property and equipment	(4,728,000)	(5,012,000)
Transfer from donor-restricted fund for purchase of property and equipment	243,000	255,000
Investment in affiliated company	(394,000)	(425,000)
Capital contribution to Sample Health System	—	(1,000,000)
Cash invested in assets whose use is limited	(4,798,000)	(855,000)
Net cash used by investing activities	(9,677,000)	(7,037,000)
Cash flows from financing activities:		
Increase in retainage and construction accounts payable	183,000	175,000
Repayment of long-term debt	(1,200,000)	(1,630,000)
Payments from donor-restricted funds related to temporary loans	500,000	—
Payments on capital lease obligations	(550,000)	(600,000)
Temporary loans from (to) donor-restricted funds	300,000	(193,000)
Net cash used by financing activities	(767,000)	(2,248,000)
Net increase (decrease) in cash and cash equivalents	(1,422,000)	1,766,000
Cash and cash equivalents at beginning of year	4,525,000	2,759,000
Cash and cash equivalents at end of year	$ 3,103,000	$ 4,525,000

Reconciliation of Revenues and Gains in Excess of Expenses and Losses to
Net Cash Provided by Operating Activities and Gains and Losses

	19X7	19X6
Revenues and gains in excess of expenses and losses:	$ 4,500,000	$ 8,633,000
Adjustments to reconcile revenues and gains in excess of expenses and losses to net cash provided by operating activities and gains and losses:		
Depreciation and amortization	4,782,000	4,280,000
Provision for bad debts	1,010,000	1,103,000
Amortization of deferred financing costs	66,000	45,000
Loss on investment in affiliated company	53,000	—
Noncash gifts and bequests	—	(175,000)
Decrease in amounts due to third-party payors	(398,000)	(77,000)
Increase in liability for estimated malpractice costs	1,125,000	200,000
Increase in patient accounts receivable	(1,916,000)	(3,141,000)
Increase in supplies and other current assets	(193,000)	(118,000)
Increase in accounts payable and accrued expenses	303,000	301,000
Increase in interest earned but not received on assets whose use is limited	(310,000)	—
Net cash provided by operating activities and gains and losses	$ 9,022,000	$ 11,051,000

Supplemental Disclosures of Cash Flow Information
Sample Hospital entered into capital lease obligations of $600,000 for new equipment in 19X7.

SOURCE: *Audits of Providers of Health Care Services*. Copyright © 1990 by American Institute of Certified Public Accountants.

custodian funds.[23] We provide only a brief integrated discussion of the funds of these organizations because of the similarities between their funds and those of entities considered previously. We often refer to voluntary health and welfare organizations simply as *health organizations* below.

The unrestricted funds of health organizations are used in administering current assets whose uses are at the discretion of their boards of directors; their restricted current funds are used in administering current assets whose uses are subject to donor or grantor restrictions. Both types of current funds are used in financing health organizations' day-to-day operations. The land, building, and equipment funds of health organizations are used in accounting for their fixed assets, liabilities incurred in acquiring these assets, and current assets restricted by donors or grantors for fixed asset acquisitions or replacements. Their endowment funds are used in accounting for endowments that must be kept intact indefinitely or until some contingent event occurs. The operations of the four types of funds just mentioned are somewhat similar to those of corresponding university funds. The custodian funds of health organizations encompass assets which can be used only in accordance with the instructions of the individuals or groups making the assets available. The operations of these funds are similar to university agency funds.

The first four categories of funds are accounted for using the *accrual basis;* custodian funds are accounted for similarly to the agency funds of universities. The "revenues" of health organizations include *support, revenue, and fees and grants from governmental agencies.* Support is divided into *direct public support* and *indirect public support.*[24] The former category includes, for example, contributions, legacies, and bequests. Indirect public support consists of contributions obtained through other nongovernmental conduit organizations (e.g., from the United Way). The revenues of health organizations include items such as dues, sales of products and services, investment income and gains and losses, donated services, and program fees. Fees and grants from governmental agencies are disclosed separately because they tend to be partially support and partially revenue. The expenses, assets, and equities of these organizations are similar to those discussed previously. We emphasize that depreciation expense is recorded in accounting for health organizations. The financial statements pertinent to each of the funds of these organizations are the balance sheet; the statement of support, revenues and expenses, and changes in fund balances; and the statement of functional expenses. Examples of these statements are contained in Illustrations 22–8, 22–9, and 22–10. Expenses are classified using *program and support expenses classifications* in the statement of support, revenues and expenses, and

---

[23] The authoritative pronouncements for the "other nonprofit organizations" mentioned above do not require fund accounting. However, fund accounting usually is used by these entities if it is important to demonstrate accountability with respect to restricted resources (which frequently is the case).

[24] Support that is intended by donors for use in future periods is credited to deferred support accounts.

changes in fund balances; they are classified by *function* in the statement of functional expenses. As illustrated below, the recording procedures for health organizations produce the expense account balances for both of these statements.

Voluntary Health and Welfare Organizations—Accounting Procedures

The following example illustrates typical entries for the funds of certain types of health organizations.[25] The example deals with Caring Adults Serving Alcoholics (CASA). CASA's primary activity is alcoholism research—which is conducted through its unrestricted current fund. CASA also performs codependency research and stages codependency workshops. The resources expended on the latter activities are provided by donors who restrict the uses of their contributions to these activities. Thus, these activities are administered through CASA's restricted current fund.

Assume the data presented below for CASA's unrestricted current fund; restricted current fund; and land, building, and equipment fund for the fiscal year ended December 31, 19X0.[26] Also, assume for simplicity that: (1) there are no accrued revenues or expenses at year-end, (2) there are no unearned revenues or prepaid expenses at the beginning or the end of the year, (3) all pledges are expected to be collected, and (4) no inventory or supplies adjustments are needed at year-end.[27] Finally, assume that the program and support expenses classifications for CASA's statement of support, revenues and expenses, and changes in fund balances are (1) Program Services—Alcoholism Research, (2) Program Services—Codependency Research and Workshops, (3) Supporting Services—Management and General, and (4) Supporting Services—Fund-Raising.

Current fund—unrestricted:
  Direct support:
    Pledges (all but $50,000 collected during the year) 2,000,000
    Legacies and bequests 2,500,000
  Indirect support:
    United Way 400,000
    Alcoholics Anonymous 300,000

---

[25] Note that the transactions of other types of health and welfare organizations may be significantly different than those illustrated for our hypothetical organization.

[26] We do not illustrate the accounting procedures of the endowment and custodian funds of health organizations because of their similarity to the procedures for endowment funds and agency funds illustrated previously.

[27] As mentioned, accruals, prepayments, unearned revenues, inventories, and so on, are accounted for using the accrual method in health organizations' unrestricted current funds; restricted current funds; land, building, and equipment funds, and endowment funds. Accounting for uncollectible pledges is illustrated specifically in the above hospital plant expansion and replacement fund example.

Fees and grants from governmental agencies 800,000
Revenues:
   Sales of products 100,000
   Investment income 20,000
   Donated services 30,000
   Program fees—alcoholism research 300,000
Disbursements:
   Purchase of marketable securities 500,000
   Salaries and wages 1,500,000
   Professional fees 1,300,000
   Supplies used 50,000
   Rent 620,000
   Inventory (all sold) 50,000
   Transfers to land, building, and equipment fund for:
     Mortgage payments on building ($400,000 interest) 500,000
     Equipment purchased 1,250,000
     Other 100,000
Allocation of various expenditures for statement of support,
   revenues and expenses, and changes in fund balances:
     Program services—alcoholism research 2,153,000
     Supporting services—management and general 1,086,000
     Supporting services—fund-raising 381,000

Current fund—restricted:
  Direct support:
   Pledges (all but $5,000 collected)—codependency
     research and workshops 550,000
  Revenues:
   Program fees—codependency workshops 450,000
  Disbursements:
   Salaries and wages 200,000
   Professional fees 350,000
   Program costs—codependency research and workshops 300,000
   Rent 50,000
   Other 30,000
  Allocation of various expenditures for statement of support, revenues
   and expenses, and changes in fund balances:
     Program services—codependency research
      and workshops 622,000
     Supporting services—management and general 257,500
     Supporting services—fund-raising 50,500

Land, building, and equipment fund:
  Direct support:
   Pledges (all but $10,000 collected) 500,000
  Revenues—investment income 15,000
  Disbursements:
   Purchase of marketable securities 230,000
   Payments on mortgage on building ($400,000 interest) 500,000
   Purchase of equipment 1,250,000
  Data for year-end adjustments:
   Depreciation expense:
     Buildings 50,000
     Equipment 10,000

Allocation of various expenditures for statement of support, revenues
and expenses, and changes in fund balances:

Program services—alcoholism research	360,000
Program services—codependency research and workshops	40,000
Supporting services—management and general	20,000
Supporting services—fund-raising	40,000

The entries related to these data, along with explanations, are presented below.[28]
Various groups of entries are numbered in this case for clarity since CASA's data
are present all at once.

The first set of entries is related to CASA's unrestricted current fund. The
entries are as follows:

1. To record support, fees and grants from governmental agencies,
   revenues, and related collections:

Pledges Receivable (assumed arbitrarily)	1,700,000	
Cash	2,800,000	
Revenues—Contributions		2,000,000
Legacies and Bequests		2,500,000
Cash	1,650,000	
Pledges Receivable		1,650,000
Cash	1,500,000	
Allocation from United Way		400,000
Contribution by Alcoholics Anonymous		300,000
Fees and Grants from Governmental Agencies		800,000
Cash	450,000	
Sales of Products		100,000
Investment Income		20,000
Donated Services		30,000
Program Fees—Alcoholism Research		300,000

2. To record disbursements for marketable securities purchased; funds
   transferred to the land, building, and equipment fund for mortgage
   payments and equipment purchases; and expenses:

---

[28] Note that donated services are recorded by health organizations at their fair market values
when: (1) the services would have been performed by salaried personnel if not donated, (2) the organization directs the donor in providing the services, and (3) the value of the services can be
estimated reasonably.

Investments	500,000	
Cash		500,000

Fund Balance—Undesignated	1,750,000	
Cash		1,750,000

Salaries and Wages	1,500,000	
Professional Fees—Alcoholism Research	1,300,000	
Supplies Used	50,000	
Rent	620,000	
Cost of Products Sold	50,000	
Other	100,000	
Cash		3,620,000

3. To allocate the above expenses to the appropriate statement of support, revenue and expenses, and changes in fund balances classes:

Program Services—Alcoholism Research	2,153,000	
Supporting Services—Management and General	1,086,000	
Supporting Services—Fund-Raising	381,000	
Salaries and Wages		1,500,000
Professional Fees		1,300,000
Supplies Used		50,000
Rent		620,000
Cost of Products Sold		50,000
Other		100,000

4. To close the unrestricted current fund accounts:

Revenues—Contributions	2,000,000	
Legacies and Bequests	2,500,000	
Allocation from United Way	400,000	
Contribution by Alcoholics Anonymous	300,000	
Fees and Grants from Governmental Agencies	800,000	
Sales of Products	100,000	
Investment Income	20,000	
Donated Services	30,000	
Program Fees—Alcoholism Research	300,000	
Program Services—Alcoholism Research		2,153,000
Supporting Services—Management and General		1,086,000
Supporting Services—Fund-Raising		381,000
Fund Balance—Undesignated		2,830,000[29]

---

[29] Portions of the unrestricted current funds of health organizations can be designated for particular uses (e.g., for the purchase of plant and equipment). In general, the boards of directors of nonprofit entities have the authority to designate portions of *unrestricted fund balances* for specific uses. Designations are similar to appropriations of retained earnings by profit-seeking entities. See discussion of designations in Chapter 20.

The following entries are pertinent to CASA's restricted current fund. The entries for this fund are as follows:

1. To record support, revenues, and related collections:

Pledges Receivable (assumed arbitrarily)	400,000	
Cash	150,000	
Revenues—Contributions		550,000
Cash	395,000	
Pledges Receivable		395,000
Cash	450,000	
Program Fees—		
Codependency Workshops		450,000

2. To record disbursements for expenses:

Salaries and Wages	200,000	
Professional Fees	350,000	
Program Costs—Codependency		
Research and Workshops	300,000	
Rent	50,000	
Other	30,000	
Cash		930,000

3. To allocate the above expenses to the appropriate statement of support, revenue and expenses, and changes in fund balances classes:

Program Services—Codependency		
Research and Workshops	622,000	
Supporting Services—Management and		
General	257,500	
Supporting Services—Fund-Raising	50,500	
Salaries and Wages		200,000
Professional Fees		350,000
Program Costs—Codependency		
Research and Workshops		300,000
Rent		50,000
Other		30,000

4. To close the restricted current fund accounts:

Revenues—Contributions	550,000	
Program Fees—Codependency		
Workshops	450,000	
Program Services—Codependency		
Research and Workshops		622,000
Supporting Services—Management		
and General		257,500
Supporting Services—Fund-Raising		50,500
Fund Balance—Undesignated		70,000

The final set of entries is related to CASA's land, building, and equipment fund. The entries for this fund are as follows:

1. To record support, revenues, and related collections:

Pledges Receivable (assumed arbitrarily)	100,000	
Cash	400,000	
Revenues—Contributions		500,000
Cash	90,000	
Pledges Receivable		90,000
Cash	15,000	
Investment Income		15,000

2. To record disbursements for marketable securities purchased; the receipt of resources from the unrestricted current fund; disbursements for mortgage payments and equipment purchased from the resources transferred from the unrestricted current fund; and the reduction in fund balance—unexpended related to the latter disbursements:

Investments	230,000	
Cash		230,000
Cash	1,750,000	
Fund Balance—Unexpended		1,750,000[30]
Interest Expense	400,000	
Mortgage Payable	100,000	
Cash		500,000
Equipment	1,250,000	
Cash		1,250,000
Fund Balance—Unexpended		
($100,000 + $1,250,000)	1,350,000	
Fund Balance—Expended		1,350,000

---

[30] Note that the fund balances for land, building, and equipment funds are segregated into Fund Balance—Unexpended and Fund Balance—Expended Accounts. Resources transferred in from other funds are credited to the former. When assets are acquired or debt principal reductions are made from assets transferred in, Fund Balance—Unexpended is debited and Fund Balance—Expended is credited (see below). The Fund Balance—Expended account represents the fund equity in land, buildings, and equipment contributed directly or indirectly to the organization or financed through its operations. In contrast, the Fund Balance—Unexpended account represents the equity in the net current assets of the fund. Land, building, and equipment fund revenue and expense accounts are closed to the Fund Balance—Unexpended account. Finally, when assets are depreciated, the Fund Balance—Expended and Fund Balance—Unexpended accounts are debited and credited, respectively, for the amounts of the depreciation expense (see entries in (3) above). The credit to Fund Balance—Unexpended ultimately is offset through the fund's closing entries.

ILLUSTRATION 22-8   Health Organization Balance Sheet

FAMILY SERVICE AGENCY OF UTOPIA, INC.
Balance Sheet
For the Year Ended December 31

	Current Funds		19X2			19X1
	Unrestricted	Restricted	Land, Building, and Equipment Fund	Endowment Fund	Total	Total
Assets						
Current assets:						
Cash, including $115,000 and $123,000 in interest-bearing accounts	$121,100	$ 300			$121,400	$127,000
Short-term investments, at cost (approximates market)	100,000	7,100			107,100	121,700
Receivables:						
Program service fees, less allowance of $200 and $100	600				600	800
Pledges, less allowance of $11,200 and $9,700	58,900				58,900	46,000
Grants	1,000		$ 4,800		5,800	4,600
From affiliated organizations		1,000			1,000	1,000
Interfund receivable (payable)	2,000	(2,000)				
Inventory, at lower of cost or market	7,000				7,000	6,100
Prepaid expenses and deferred charges	13,800				13,800	9,600
Total current assets	304,400	6,400	4,800		315,600	316,800
Noncurrent investments (Note 3)	279,600			$194,800	474,400	430,700
Land, buildings, and equipment, at cost, less accumulated depreciation (Note 5)			174,800		174,800	168,500
Total assets	$584,000	$6,400	$179,600	$194,800	$964,800	$916,000

1068

Liabilities and Fund Balances

	Current Unrestricted	Current Restricted	Land, building, and equipment	Endowment	Total	Total (prior year)
Current liabilities:						
Accounts payable and accrued expenses	$ 39,300				$ 39,300	$ 46,000
Support & revenue designated for subsequent period	59,600				59,600	61,600
Total current liabilities	98,900				98,900	107,600
Mortgage payable, 6%, due 19XX (Note 11)			$ 3,200		3,200	3,600
Amounts payable under capital lease (Note 9)			10,200		10,200	
Total liabilities	98,900		13,400		112,300	111,200
Fund balances:						
Current unrestricted:						
Designated by the governing board for:						
Long-term investment	279,600				279,600	239,000
Purchase of new equipment	10,400				10,400	
Undesignated—available for general activities	195,100				195,100	207,300
Current restricted for:						
Professional education		$4,000			4,000	
Expansion of services		2,400			2,400	10,000
Land, building, and equipment:						
Unexpended restricted (Note 4)			4,800		4,800	2,100
Equity in fixed assets			161,400		161,400	154,700
Endowment				$194,800	194,800	191,700
Total fund balances	485,100	6,400	166,200	194,800	852,500	804,800
Total liabilities and fund balances	$584,000	$6,400	$179,600	$194,800	$964,800	$916,000

(notes not reproduced)

Source: United Way of America, *Accounting and Financial Reporting. A Guide for United Ways and Not-for-Profit Human Service Organizations* (Alexandria, VA, 1989). Reprinted by permission of the United Way of America.

FAMILY SERVICE AGENCY OF UTOPIA, INC.
Statement of Revenues and Expenses and Changes in Fund Balances
For the Year Ended December 31

	19X2					19X1
	Current Funds		Land, Building, and Equipment Fund	Endowment Fund	Total	Total
	Unrestricted	Restricted				
Revenues:						
Public support:						
Received directly:						
Contributions (net of estimated uncollectible pledges of $19,500 and $15,000)	$460,100	$ 6,200	$ 7,200	$ 200	$473,700	$500,400
Special events (net of costs of direct benefit to participants of $18,000 and $16,300)	10,400				10,400	9,200
Legacies and bequests	9,200			400	9,600	12,000
Donated services (Note 6)	8,000				8,000	7,000
Received indirectly:						
Collected through local auxiliary	4,000				4,000	7,900
Allocated by federated fund-raising organizations (net of their related fund-raising expenses estimated at $12,300 and $12,200)	223,500				223,500	222,000
Total public support	715,200	6,200	7,200	600	729,200	758,500
Revenues* and grants from governmental agencies		300			300	300
Other revenues:						
Membership dues—individuals	1,600				1,600	1,100
Program service fees	2,300				2,300	800
Sales of materials and services (net of direct expenses of $1,000 and $700)	400				400	300
Endowment and other investment income	30,500	700			31,200	26,000
Miscellaneous revenue	2,800				2,800	3,600
Gains (losses) on investments	(2,000)			2,500	500	27,500
Total other revenue	35,600	700		2,500	38,800	59,300
Total revenue	750,800	7,200	7,200	3,100	768,300	818,100

Expenses:

Program services:						
Adoption	195,100		700		195,800	185,000
Foster home care	131,200		600		131,800	121,600
Counseling	244,100	10,800	2,900		257,800	273,600
Total program services	570,400	10,800	4,200		585,400	580,200
Supporting services:						
Management and general	56,800		600		57,400	63,800
Fund-raising	65,000		400		65,400	54,600
Total supporting services	121,800		1,000		122,800	118,400
Payments to national organization (Note 10)	12,400				12,400	15,400
Total expenses	704,600	10,800	5,200		720,600	714,000
Excess (deficiency) of revenues over expenses	46,200	(3,600)	2,000	3,100	47,700	104,100
Fund balances, beginning of year	446,300	10,000	156,800	191,700	804,800	700,700
Other changes in fund balances:						
Acquisition of fixed assets	(7,000)		7,000			
Mortgage payment	(400)		400			
Fund balances, end of year	$485,100	$ 6,400	$166,200	$194,800	$852,500	$804,800

(notes not reproduced)

* The word *fees* usually is used in place of *revenues* in this caption.

SOURCE: United Way of America, *Accounting and Financial Reporting. A Guide for United Ways and Not-for-Profit Human Service Organizations* (Alexandria, VA, 1989). Reprinted by permission of the United Way of America.

ILLUSTRATION 22–10   Health Organization Statement of Functional Expenses

FAMILY SERVICE AGENCY OF UTOPIA, INC.

Statement of Functional Expenses
For the Year Ended December 31, 19X2
(with Comparative Totals for 19X1)

	Program Services				Supporting Services			Total Program and Supporting Services Expenses	
	Adoption	Foster Home Care	Counseling	Total	Management and General	Fund Raising	Total	19X2	19X1
Salaries	$ 33,600	$ 25,100	$126,900	$185,600	$33,100	$36,800	$ 69,900	$255,500	$243,300
Employee benefits	1,800	1,400	6,400	9,600	2,200	1,500	3,700	13,300	12,500
Payroll taxes, etc.	3,000	2,300	12,400	17,700	3,000	3,100	6,100	23,800	21,500
Total salaries and related expenses	38,400	28,800	145,700	212,900	38,300	41,400	79,700	292,600	277,300
Professional fees	63,000	300	61,200	124,500	2,600	800	3,400	127,900	125,300
Supplies	3,900	21,300	1,300	26,500	1,800	1,700	3,500	30,000	27,100
Telephone	9,500	1,000	1,100	11,600	1,500	2,300	3,800	15,400	16,800
Postage and shipping	2,900	1,300	8,900	13,100	1,000	9,000	10,000	23,100	18,000
Occupancy	2,550	21,100	11,250	34,900	1,500	1,350	2,850	37,750	36,300
Interest	—	—	100	100	800	—	800	900	200
Rental and maintenance of equipment	3,550	1,100	1,250	5,900	1,500	1,350	2,850	8,750	9,300
Printing and publications	5,400	400	6,400	12,200	300	1,600	1,900	14,100	15,800
Travel and transportation	12,500	2,000	2,200	16,700	2,300	3,000	5,300	22,000	31,300
Conferences, conventions, & meetings	3,700	7,100	2,000	12,800	4,500	400	4,900	17,700	20,600
Specific assistance to individuals	16,500	24,300	5,000	45,800	—	—	—	45,800	48,400
Membership dues	500	—	—	500	—	—	—	500	500

Awards and grants:									
To national organization	10,000	—	3,000	13,000	—	—	—	13,000	14,200
To individuals and other organizations	11,000	11,900	—	22,900			—	22,900	26,300
Insurance	10,450	10,100	5,100	25,650	600	50	650	26,300	21,000
Other expenses	1,250	500	400	2,150	100	2,050	2,150	4,300	5,600
Depreciation of buildings and equipment	700	600	2,900	4,200	600	400	1,000	5,200	4,600
Total functional expenses:	$195,800	$131,800	$257,800	$585,400	$57,400	$65,400	$122,800	$708,200	$698,600
Payments to national organization								12,400	15,400
Total expenses								$720,600	$714,000

(notes not reproduced)

SOURCE: United Way of America, Accounting and Financial Reporting. A Guide for United Ways and Not-for-Profit Human Service Organizations (Alexandria, VA, 1989). Reprinted by permission of the United Way of America.

ILLUSTRATION 22–11   **Library Balance Sheet**

SAMPLE LIBRARY
Balance Sheet
December 31, 19X1
(with Comparative Totals for 19X0)

Assets	Unrestricted Operating	Unrestricted Invest-ment	Unrestricted Total	Current Restricted	Plant	Endow-ment	Total	December 31, 19X0 Total
Current assets:								
Cash, including interest-bearing accounts of $600,000 in 19X1 and $400,000 in 19X0	$ 690,000	—	$ 690,000	$ 3,000	$ 7,000	—	$ 700,000	$ 411,000
Certificates of deposit	375,000	—	375,000	75,000	—	—	450,000	525,000
Grants receivable (Note 1):								
Governments	120,000	—	120,000	—	—	—	120,000	161,000
Other	30,000	—	30,000	27,000	8,000	—	65,000	35,000
Pledges receivable, at estimated net realizable value (Note 1)	15,000	—	15,000	—	—	—	15,000	15,000
Prepaid expenses and other current assets	70,000	—	70,000	—	—	—	70,000	85,000
Total current assets	1,300,000	—	1,300,000	105,000	15,000	—	1,420,000	1,232,000
Investments—at market (Note 2)	—	$920,000	920,000	—	165,000	$985,000	2,070,000	2,172,000
Land, buildings, and equipment—at cost, less accumulated depreciation of $90,000 and $79,000, respectively (Note 3)	—	—	—	—	1,525,000	—	1,525,000	1,491,000
Inexhaustible collections and books (Note 1)	—	—	—	—	—	—	—	—
Total assets	$1,300,000	$920,000	$2,220,000	$105,000	$1,705,000	$985,000	$5,015,000	$4,895,000

Liabilities and Fund Balances

Current liabilities:							
Accounts payable, accrued expenses, and current portion of long-term debt	$ 200,000	—	—	$ 10,000	—	$ 210,000	$ 130,000
Deferred restricted contributions, etc. (Note 6)	—	—	$105,000	5,000	—	110,000	100,000
Total current liabilities	200,000	—	105,000	15,000	—	320,000	230,000
Long-term debt (Note 4)	—	—	—	180,000	—	180,000	190,000
Total liabilities	200,000	—	105,000	195,000	—	500,000	420,000
Fund balances:							
Unrestricted:							
Designated by the board for:							
Investment	—	$920,000	—	—	—	920,000	740,000
Purchase of equipment	50,000	—	—	—	—	50,000	35,000
Undesignated	1,050,000	—	—	1,510,000	—	2,560,000	2,725,000
Restricted	—	—	—	—	$985,000	985,000	975,000
Total fund balances	1,100,000	920,000	—	1,510,000	985,000	4,515,000	4,475,000
Total liabilities and fund balances	$1,300,000	$920,000	$105,000	$1,705,000	$985,000	$5,015,000	$4,895,000

(notes not reproduced)

Source: *Statement of Position 78–10.* Copyright © 1978 by American Institute of Certified Public Accountants, Inc.

3. To record depreciation expense:

Depreciation Expense	60,000	
Accumulated Depreciation—Buildings		50,000
Accumulated Depreciation—Equipment		10,000
Fund Balance—Expended	60,000	
Fund Balance—Unexpended		60,000

4. To allocate the expenses recorded in (2) and (3) to the appropriate statement of support, revenues and expenses, and changes in fund balances classes:

Program Services—Alcoholism Research	360,000	
Program Services—Codependency Research and Workshops	40,000	
Supporting Services—Management and General	20,000	
Supporting Services—Fund-Raising	40,000	
Interest Expense		400,000
Depreciation Expense		60,000

5. To close the land, building, and equipment fund accounts:

Revenues—Contributions	500,000	
Investment Income	15,000	
Program Services—Alcoholism Research		360,000
Program Services—Codependency Research and Workshops		40,000
Supporting Services—Management and General		20,000
Supporting Services—Fund-Raising		40,000
Fund Balance—Unexpended		55,000

OTHER NONPROFIT ENTITIES—ADDITIONAL DISCUSSION

As mentioned, the primary authoritative pronouncement for the remaining non-profit organizations is the AICPA's *ACNO* (including *SOP 78–10*). The accounting procedures prescribed for these entities are similar to those of health organizations. Thus, accrual accounting is the basic accounting method applied to the remaining nonprofit entities. Additionally, the funds used in accounting for these entities (when used) generally are consistent with those of health organizations, including, for example, the use of unrestricted and restricted current funds as needed. The financial statements pertinent to the remaining nonprofit entities are the balance sheet, the operating statement (with a title and format appropriate for the entity), and the statement of changes in financial position. Examples of these statements for a library are presented in Illustrations 22–11, 22–12, and 22–13.

Although the remaining nonprofit organizations are accounted for similarly, there are several differences and subtleties worth noting. First, many of these entities are supported primarily by governmental resources. For these entities, *ACNO* is the governing authoritative pronouncement. Under this document, museums, libraries, and similar organizations are allowed to exclude art collections, rare book collections, historical treasures, and other assets from their balance sheets. Consistently, they are exempt from recording depreciation on these and similar assets (whether or not the assets are recorded).[31] Nevertheless, FASB *Statement No. 93* applies to the privately supported remaining nonprofit organizations. This statement requires nonprofit organizations to include all tangible assets (except "collections") on their balance sheet at cost or fair market value if donated. Note, however, that *Statement No. 93* (par. 6) does not require depreciation accounting on individual works of art or historical treasures whose useful lives are unusually long.

---

[31] See *ACNO* for a complete list of the assets which need not be recorded or depreciated.

ILLUSTRATION 22–12   Library Operating Statement

SAMPLE LIBRARY

Statement of Support, Revenues and Expenses, and Changes in Fund Balances
Year Ended December 31, 19X1
(with Comparative Totals for 19X0)

| | Year Ended December 31, 19X1 | | | | | | | Year Ended December 31, 19X0 |
| | Unrestricted | | | Current Restricted | Plant | Endowment | Total | Total |
	Operating	Invest-ment	Total					
Support and revenues:								
Support:								
Grants (Note 1):								
Governments	$ 150,000	—	$ 150,000	—	—	—	$ 150,000	$ 150,000
Other	25,000	—	25,000	—	—	—	25,000	—
Contributions, legacies, and bequests (Note 1)	350,000	$ 90,000	440,000	$75,000	—	—	515,000	490,000
Contributed services of volunteers (Note 1)	75,000	—	75,000	—	—	—	75,000	50,000
Use of contributed facilities (Note 1)	47,000	—	47,000	—	—	—	47,000	50,000
Total support	647,000	90,000	737,000	75,000	—	—	812,000	740,000
Revenues:								
Fees for services	50,000	—	50,000	—	—	—	50,000	45,000
Book rentals and fines	320,000	—	320,000	—	—	—	320,000	250,000
Investment income including net gains	25,000	93,000	118,000	10,000	—	—	128,000	103,000
Total revenues	395,000	93,000	488,000	10,000	—	—	498,000	398,000
Total support and revenues	1,042,000	183,000	1,225,000	85,000	—	—	1,310,000	1,138,000
Expenses (Note 7):								
Program services:								
Circulating library	390,000	—	390,000	75,000	$ 5,000	—	470,000	430,000
Research library	169,000	—	169,000	—	1,000	—	170,000	155,000
Collections and exhibits	49,000	—	49,000	10,000	1,000	—	60,000	50,000
Educational services	49,000	—	49,000	—	1,000	—	50,000	55,000
Community services	29,500	—	29,500	—	500	—	30,000	20,000
Total program services	686,500	—	686,500	85,000	8,500	—	780,000	710,000

Supporting services:								
General administration	315,500	3,000	318,500	—	21,500	—	340,000	290,000
Fund-raising	200,000	—	200,000	—	5,000	—	205,000	200,000
Total supporting services	515,500	3,000	518,500	—	26,500	—	545,000	490,000
Total expenses	1,202,000	3,000	1,205,000	85,000	35,000	—	1,325,000	1,200,000
Excess (deficiency) of support and revenues over expenses before capital additions	(160,000)	180,000	20,000	—	(35,000)	—	(15,000)	(62,000)
Capital additions:								
Contributions	—	—	—	—	40,000	—	40,000	95,000
Investment income including net gains	—	—	—	—	5,000	—	5,000	17,000
Contributed materials, equipment, etc. (Note 1)	—	—	—	—	10,000	—	10,000	—
	—	—	—	—	55,000	—	55,000	112,000
Excess (deficiency) of support and revenues over expenses after capital additions	(160,000)	180,000	20,000	—	20,000	—	40,000	50,000
Fund balances at beginning of year	1,270,000	740,000	2,010,000	—	1,480,000	$985,000	4,475,000	4,425,000
Mandatory transfers—principal of indebtedness	(10,000)	—	(10,000)	—	10,000	—	—	—
Fund balances at end of year	$1,100,000	$920,000	$2,020,000	—	$1,510,000	$985,000	$4,515,000	$4,475,000

(notes not reproduced)

SOURCE: *Statement of Position 78–10.* Copyright © 1978 by American Institute of Certified Public Accountants, Inc.

ILLUSTRATION 22–13   Library Statement of Changes in Financial Position

SAMPLE LIBRARY
Statement of Changes in Financial Position
Year Ended December 31, 19X1
(with Comparative Totals for 19X0)

| | Year Ended December 31, 19X1 | | | | | | | December 31, 19X0 |
| | Unrestricted | | | Current Restricted | Total | Plant | Total | Total |
	Operating	Invest-ment	Total					
Sources of working capital:								
Excess (deficiency) of support and revenues over expenses before capital additions	$(160,000)	$180,000	$ 20,000	—		$ (35,000)	$ (15,000)	$ (62,000)
Capital additions	—	—		—		55,000	55,000	112,000
Excess (deficiency) of support and revenues over expenses after capital additions	(160,000)	180,000	20,000	—		20,000	40,000	50,000
Add (deduct): Items not using (providing) working capital:								
Depreciation	—	—	—	—		11,000	11,000	11,000
Contributed equipment	—	—	—	—		(10,000)	(10,000)	—
Working capital provided by operations	(160,000)	180,000	20,000	—		21,000	41,000	61,000
Deferred restricted contributions and investment income received	—	—	—	$85,000		—	85,000	100,000
Sale of investments	22,000	245,000	267,000	—		—	267,000	110,000
Total sources	(138,000)	425,000	287,000	85,000		21,000	393,000	271,000

	Col1	Col2	Col3	Col4	Col5	Col6	Col7
Uses of working capital:							
Purchase of investments	—	—	—	—	165,000	165,000	—
Purchase of fixed assets	—	—	—	—	35,000	35,000	35,000
Reduction of long-term debt	—	—	—	—	10,000	10,000	10,000
Deferred restricted contributions and investment income recognized as support	—	—	—	85,000	—	85,000	100,000
Transfers between funds	10,000	—	10,000	—	(10,000)	—	—
Total uses	10,000	—	10,000	85,000	200,000	295,000	145,000
Increase (decrease) in working capital	$(148,000)	$425,000	$277,000	—	$(179,000)	$ 98,000	$126,000
Changes in working capital components:							
Increase (decrease) in current assets:							
Cash	$(129,000)	$425,000	$296,000	$ (7,000)	—	$289,000	$ (5,000)
Certificates of deposit	22,000	—	22,000	20,000	$(117,000)	(75,000)	61,000
Grants receivable	54,000	—	54,000	(8,000)	(57,000)	(11,000)	60,000
Pledges receivable	—	—	—	—	—	(15,000)	(5,000)
Prepaid expenses and other current assets	(15,000)	—	(15,000)	—	—	—	—
	(68,000)	425,000	357,000	5,000	(174,000)	188,000	111,000
(Increase) decrease in current liabilities:							
Accounts payable, accrued expenses, and current portion of long-term debt	(80,000)	—	(80,000)	—	—	(80,000)	15,000
Deferred restricted contributions, etc.	—	—	—	(5,000)	(5,000)	(10,000)	—
Increase (decrease) in working capital	$(148,000)	$425,000	$277,000	—	$(179,000)	$ 98,000	$126,000

SOURCE: *Statement of Position 78–10.* Copyright © 1978 by American Institute of Certified Public Accountants, Inc.

Summary

This chapter covers the accounting procedures of colleges and universities, hospitals, and various other nonprofit organizations. Its primary focus is on colleges and universities, nongovernmental hospitals, and voluntary health and welfare organizations. The accounting techniques for these organizations are similar to those discussed in Chapters 20 and 21.

The differing characteristics of nonprofit and profit-seeking entities lead to differences in the orientation and the objectives of general-purpose financial reporting by these organizations. The objectives of general-purpose financial reporting for the former are derived from resource providers' common interests in the services provided by the entities, their efficiency and effectiveness in providing the services, and their abilities in continuing to provide the services. They emphasize providing information that is useful in making economic decisions about nonprofit entities, that is pertinent in assessing the service accomplishments of these entities, and that is relevant in assessing their managers' performances. Pertinent information under these objectives is information about the entities' economic resources and obligations and the natures, sources, amounts, and so on, of their resource inflows and outflows. The objectives are accomplished through the standard-setting process.

The GASB is responsible for establishing the accounting principles of nonprofit entities whose financial statements are combined with those of state and local govenmental units, and the FASB is responsible for developing accounting standards for all other nonprofit organizations. Nevertheless, the GASB and FASB have been setting standards for nonprofit entities for only a short while; thus, their accounting principles are covered primarily in pronouncements other than those of the GASB and the FASB.

CUBA, Audits of Colleges and Universities, and pertinent GASB/FASB standards are the most important sources of college and university accounting principles. The college and university fund accounting principles covered in this chapter are consistent with these documents. The classes of funds frequently used in college and university accounting are the following:

1. Current funds (including unrestricted and restricted current funds).
2. Loan funds.
3: Endowment and similar funds (including expendable, term, and quasi-endowment funds).
4. Annuity and life income funds.
5. Plant funds (including unexpended plant funds, funds for renewals and replacements, funds for retirement of indebtedness, and investment in plant funds).
6. Agency funds.

The financial statements pertinent generally to college and university funds are the balance sheet; the statement of current fund revenues, expenditures, and other changes; and the statement of changes in fund balances.

The primary authoritative pronouncements pertaining to nongovernmental hospitals are the AICPA's *Audits of Providers of Health Care Services* and its *Statements of Position 78-1, 78-7, 81-2, 85-1,* and *89-5.* Under these documents, the fund accounting techniques of nongovernmental hospitals are similar to those of governmental units and colleges and universities. The major classes of funds encountered in nongovernmental hospital accounting are: (1) general funds and (2) donor-restricted funds. The restricted funds of these hospitals are specific-purpose funds, endowment funds, and plant replacement and expansion funds. The financial statements generally relevant to nongovernmental hospitals are the balance sheet, the statement of revenues and expenses, the statement of changes in fund balances, and the statement of cash flows. Recall that governmental hospitals are accounted for as enterprise funds.

The principal authoritative pronouncement for voluntary health and welfare organizations is the AICPA's *Audits of Voluntary Health and Welfare Organizations*. Although this audit guide is primary, descriptions of the fund accounting techniques for these organizations are contained in *Standards of Accounting and Financial Reporting for Voluntary Health and Welfare Organizations*. The classes of funds frequently encountered in voluntary health and welfare organization accounting are: (1) current funds—unrestricted, (2) current funds—restricted, (3) land, building, and equipment funds, (4) endowment funds, and (5) custodian funds. The financial statements pertinent to each of the funds of these organizations are the balance sheet; the statement of support, revenues and expenses, and changes in fund balances; and the statement of functional expenses.

There are numerous additional types of nonprofit organizations other than colleges and universities, hospitals, and voluntary health and welfare organizations, including civic groups, labor unions, cultural institutions, political parties, private schools, performing arts organizations, fraternal organizations, homeowners' associations, country clubs, religious organizations, and professional organizations. The primary authoritative pronouncement for these additional nonprofit organizations is the AICPA's *ACNO* (including *SOP 78-10*). The fund accounting procedures for these entities are similar to those of voluntary health and welfare organizations. The financial statements pertinent to the additional nonprofit entities are the balance sheet, the operating statement (with a title and format appropriate for the entity), and the statement of changes in financial position.

Questions

1. Identify the characteristics which, according to the FASB, distinguish nonprofit entities from profit-seeking entities.
2. Discuss the objectives of general-purpose financial reporting by nonprofit entities.
3. Distinguish between restricted and unrestricted funds.
4. Discuss the standard-setting bodies and the official pronouncements that govern accounting for colleges and universities. Explain why the standard-setting process may result in colleges and universities accounting for similar circumstances using different procedures. Provide an example and discuss the related differences.
5. Briefly describe the funds that are pertinent to colleges and universities and identify the financial statements that generally are relevant to these institutions.
6. Discuss the standard-setting bodies and the official pronouncements that govern accounting for hospitals.
7. Briefly describe the funds that are relevant to nongovernmental hospitals and identify the financial statements that generally are pertinent to these institutions.
8. Identify the characteristics that distinguish voluntary health and welfare organizations from other nonprofit organizations.

9. Identify the standard-setting body and the official pronouncements that govern accounting for voluntary health and welfare organizations.

10. Identify and describe the "revenues" of voluntary health and welfare organizations.

11. Briefly describe the funds that are relevant to voluntary health and welfare organizations and identify the financial statements that generally are pertinent to these institutions.

12. Identify some types of nonprofit entities other than colleges and universities, hospitals, and voluntary health and welfare organizations, the standard-setting body charged with establishing their standards, the official pronouncements that govern their accounting procedures, and the financial statements that generally are pertinent to these entities.

13. Discuss the procedures used by nonprofit organizations in accounting for donated services.

14. Discuss the procedures used by nonprofit organizations in accounting for art collections, rare book collections, historical treasures, and so on.

Exercises

Exercise 22–1   (Various Hospital Topics)

Select the best answer for each of the following. Questions 1 through 3 are based on the following data.

Under Abbey Hospital's established rate structure, the hospital would have earned patient service revenue of $6 million for the year ended December 31, 19X3. However, Abbey did not expect to collect this amount because of charity allowances of $1 million and discounts of $500,000 to third-party payers. In May 19X3, Abbey purchased bandages from Lee Supply Co. at a cost of $1,000. However, Lee notified Abbey that the invoice was being canceled and that the bandages were being donated to Abbey. At December 31, 19X3, Abbey had board-designated assets consisting of cash of $40,000 and investments of $700,000.

1. For the year ended December 31, 19X3, how much should Abbey record as patient service revenue?
   a. $6,000,000.
   b. $5,500,000.
   c. $5,000,000.
   d. $4,500,000.

2. For the year ended December 31, 19X3, Abbey should record the donation of bandages as
   a. A $1,000 reduction in operating expenses.
   b. Nonoperating revenue of $1,000.
   c. Other operating revenue of $1,000.
   d. A memorandum entry only.

3. How much of Abbey's board-designated assets should be included in the unrestricted fund grouping?
   a. $0.
   b. $40,000.
   c. $700,000.
   d. $740,000.

4. On May 1, 19X4, Lila Lee established a $50,000 endowment fund, the income from which is to be paid to Waller Hospital for general operating purposes. Waller does not control the fund's principal. Anders National Bank was appointed by Lee as trustee of this fund. What journal entry is required on Waller's books?

	Debit	Credit
a. Memorandum entry only		
b. Nonexpendable Endowment Fund	50,000	
Endowment Fund Balance		50,000
c. Cash	50,000	
Endowment Fund Balance		50,000
d. Cash	50,000	
Nonexpendable Endowment Fund		50,000

5. Glenmore Hospital's property, plant, and equipment (net of depreciation) consists of the following:

Land	$ 500,000
Buildings	10,000,000
Movable equipment	2,000,000

What amount should be included in the restricted fund grouping?
   a. $0.
   b. $2,000,000.
   c. $10,500,000.
   d. $12,500,000.

6. Depreciation should be recognized in the financial statements of
   a. Proprietary (for-profit) hospitals only.
   b. Both proprietary (for-profit) and not-for-profit hospitals.
   c. Both proprietary (for-profit) and not-for-profit hospitals, only when they are affiliated with a college or university.
   d. All hospitals, as a memorandum entry, not affecting the statement of revenues and expenses.

7. On July 1, 19X2, Lilydale Hospital's board of trustees designated $200,000 for expansion of outpatient facilities. The $200,000 is expected to be expended in the financial year ending June 30, 19X5. In Lilydale's balance sheet at June 30, 19X3, this cash should be classified as a (an)

    a. Restricted current asset.
    b. Restricted noncurrent asset.
    c. Unrestricted current asset.
    d. Unrestricted noncurrent asset.

8. An unrestricted pledge from an annual contributor to a voluntary not-for-profit hospital made in December 19X2 and paid in cash in March 19X3 would generally be credited to
    a. Nonoperating Revenue in 19X2.
    b. Nonoperating Revenue in 19X3.
    c. Operating Revenue in 19X2.
    d. Operating Revenue in 19X3.

(AICPA adapted)

Exercise 22–2   (Various Hospital Topics)

Select the best answer for each of the following.

1. Donated medicines which normally would be purchased by a hospital should be recorded at fair market value and credited directly to
    a. Other Operating Revenue.
    b. Other Nonoperating Revenue.
    c. Fund Balance.
    d. Deferred Revenue.

2. A gift to a voluntary not-for-profit hospital that is not restricted by the donor should be credited directly to
    a. Fund Balance.
    b. Deferred Revenue.
    c. Other Operating Revenue.
    d. Nonoperating Revenue.

3. During the year ended December 31, 19X3, Melford Hospital received the following donations stated at their respective fair values:

Employee services from members of a religious group	$100,000
Medical supplies from an association of physicians (restricted for indigent care and used for this purpose in 19X3)	30,000

How much revenue (both operating and nonoperating) from donations should Melford report in its 19X3 statement of revenues and expenses?
    a. $0.
    b. $30,000.
    c. $100,000.
    d. $130,000.

    Questions 4 through 7 refer to the accounts of a large nonprofit hospital which properly maintains four funds: operating, special purpose, endowment, and plant.

4. How should charity service, contractual adjustments, and bad debts be classified in the statement of revenues and expenses for the hospital?
    a. All three should be treated as expenses.
    b. All three should be treated as deductions from patient services revenues.

    c. Charity service and contractual adjustments should be treated as a revenue deduction; bad debts should be treated as an expense.

    d. Charity service and bad debts should be treated as expenses; contractual adjustments should be treated as a revenue deduction.

5. Depreciation on some hospital fixed assets, referred to as *minor equipment,* is not accounted for in the conventional manner. How is depreciation with respect to these assets accounted for?

    a. Ignored on the basis of immateriality.

    b. Handled in essentially the same manner as if assets were assigned to the activities of a city and were accounted for in its general fund.

    c. Determined periodically by inventorying minor equipment and writing the assets down to their value at the inventory date.

    d. Recognized only when minor equipment is replaced.

6. To ensure the availability of money for improvements, replacements, and expansion of plant, it would be most desirable for the hospital to

    a. Use accelerated depreciation to provide adequate funds for eventual replacement.

    b. Use the retirement or replacement system of depreciation to provide adequate funds.

    c. Sell assets at earliest opportunity.

    d. Transfer cash from the operating fund to the plant fund in amounts at least equal to the periodic depreciation charges.

7. The endowment fund consists of several small endowments, each for a special purpose. The hospital treasurer has determined that it would be legally possible and more efficient to pool the assets and allocate the resultant revenue. The soundest basis on which to allocate revenue after assets are pooled and to comply with the special purposes of each endowment would be to

    a. Determine market values of securities or other assets included in each endowment at the time of transfer to the pool and credit revenue to each endowment on that pro rata basis.

    b. Determine book values for each endowment at the time of transfer to the pool and credit revenue to each endowment on that pro rata basis.

    c. Apportion future revenue according to the moving-average ratio in which the various endowments have earned revenue in the past.

    d. Ask the trustee who administers the pooled assets to make the determination since he or she is in a position to know which assets are making the greatest contribution.

(AICPA adapted)

Exercise 22–3   (Various College and University Topics)

Select the best answer for each of the following:

1. For the spring semester of 19X4, Lane University assessed its students $3,400,000 (net of refunds) covering tuition and fees for educational and general purposes. However, only $3 million was expected to be realized because scholarships totaling $300,000 were granted to students, and tuition remissions of $100,000 were allowed to faculty members' children attending Lane. How much should Lane include in educational and general current funds revenues from student tuition and fees?

    a. $3,400,000

    b. $3,300,000.

 c. $3,100,000.
 d. $3,000,000.

2. The following funds were among those on Kery University's books at April 30, 19X4:

Funds to be used for acquisition of additional properties
  for university purpose (unexpended at 4/30/X4) $3,000,000
Funds set aside for debt service charges and for
  retirement of indebtedness on university properties 5,000,000

How much of the funds mentioned above should be included in the plant funds?
 a. $0.
 b. $3,000,000.
 c. $5,000,000.
 d. $8,000,000.

3. Which of the following should be used in accounting for not-for-profit colleges and universities?
 a. Fund accounting and accrual accounting.
 b. Fund accounting but not accrual accounting.
 c. Accrual accounting but not fund accounting.
 d. Neither accrual accounting nor fund accounting.

4. Which of the following receipts is properly recorded in a restricted current fund in the books of a university?
 a. Tuition.
 b. Student laboratory fees.
 c. Housing fees.
 d. Research grants.

5. During the years ended June 30, 19X2 and 19X3, Sonata University conducted a cancer research project financed by a $2 million gift from an alumnus. This entire amount was pledged by the donor on July 10, 19X1, although he paid only $500,000 at that date. The gift was restricted to the financing of this research project. During the two-year research period, Sonata's related gift receipts and research expenditures were as follows:

	Year Ended June 30	
	19X2	*19X3*
Gift receipts	$1,200,000	$ 800,000
Cancer research expenditures	900,000	1,100,000

How much gift revenue should Sonata report in the restricted column of its statement of current funds revenues, expenditures, and other changes for the year ended June 30, 19X3?
 a. $0.
 b. $800,000.

    c. $1,100,000.

    d. $2,000,000.

6. For the fall semester of 19X3, Cranbrook College assessed its students $2,300,000 for tuition and fees. The net amount realized was only $2,100,000 because of the following revenue reductions:

Refund occasioned by class cancellations and student withdrawals	$ 50,000
Tuition remissions granted to faculty members' families	10,000
Scholarships and fellowships	140,000

How much should Cranbrook report for the period for unrestricted current funds revenues from tuition and fees?

    a. $2,100,000.

    b. $2,150,000.

    c. $2,250,000.

    d. $2,300,000.

7. Which of the following is/are utilized for current expenditures by a not-for-profit university?

	Unrestricted Current Funds	*Restricted Current Funds*
a.	No	No
b.	No	Yes
c.	Yes	No
d.	Yes	Yes

8. In the loan fund of a college or university, each of the following types of loans would be found except

    a. Student.

    b. Staff.

    c. Building.

    d. Faculty.

9. On January 2, 19X3, John Reynolds established a $500,000 trust, the income from which is to be paid to Mansfield University for general operating purposes. The Wyndham National Bank was appointed by Reynolds as trustee of the fund. What journal entry is required on Mansfield's books?

    a. Memorandum entry only.

    b. Cash 500,000

        Endowment Fund Balance 500,000

    c. Nonexpendable Endowment Fund 500,000

        Endowment Fund Balance 500,000

    d. Expendable Funds 500,000

        Endowment Fund Balance 500,000

                                          (AICPA adapted)

Exercise 22–4   (Various Voluntary Health and Welfare Organizations Topics)

Select the best answer for each of the following. Questions 1 and 2 are based on the following data:

Community Service Center is a voluntary welfare organization funded by contributions from the general public. During 19X3, unrestricted pledges of $900,000 were received, half of which were payable in 19X3, with the other half payable in 19X4. It was estimated that 10 percent of these pledges would be uncollectible. In addition, Selma Zorn, a social worker on Community's permanent staff, earning $20,000 annually for a normal work load of 2,000 hours, contributed an additional 800 hours of her time to Community, at no charge.

1. How much should Community report as net contribution revenue for 19X3 with respect to the pledges?
   a. $0.
   b. $405,000.
   c. $810,000.
   d. $900,000.

2. How much should Community record in 19X3 for contributed service expense?
   a. $8,000.
   b. $4,000.
   c. $800.
   d. $0.

3. Cura Foundation, a voluntary health and welfare organization supported by contributions from the general public, included the following costs in its statement of functional expenses for the year ended December 31, 19X3:

Fund-raising	$500,000
Administrative (including data processing)	300,000
Research	100,000

   Cura's functional expenses for 19X3 program services included
   a. $900,000.
   b. $500,000.
   c. $300,000.
   d. $100,000.

4. A reason for a voluntary health and welfare organization to adopt fund accounting is that
   a. Restrictions have been placed on certain of its assets by donors.
   b. It provides more than one type of program service.
   c. Fixed assets are significant.
   d. Donated services are significant.

5. Which of the following funds of a voluntary health and welfare organization does not have a counterpart fund in governmental accounting?
   a. Current—unrestricted.
   b. Land, building, and equipment.
   c. Custodian.
   d. Endowment.

6. A voluntary health and welfare organization received a pledge in 19X2 from a donor specifying that the amount pledged be used in 19X4. The donor paid the pledge in cash in 19X3. The pledge should be accounted for as:
   a. A deferred credit in the balance sheet at the end of 19X2, and as support in 19X3.
   b. A deferred credit in the balance sheet at the end of 19X2 and 19X3, and as support in 19X4.
   c. Support in 19X2.
   d. Support in 19X3, and no deferred credit in the balance sheet at the end of 19X2.

   (AICPA adapted)

Exercise 22–5   (Allocation of Income from Pooled Investments)

On January 1, 19X2, three funds of Community Service Center, a voluntary health and welfare organization, pooled their individual investments. The costs and fair values of the investments on the pooling date were as follows:

	Cost	Current Fair Value
Unrestricted fund	$150,000	$170,000
Restricted fund	190,000	148,750
Endowment fund	90,000	106,250
Totals	$430,000	$425,000

During the year ended December 31, 19X2, the investment pool received dividends and interest totaling $51,000 and reinvested realized gains of $12,750.

Required:

Prepare journal entries for each of the three funds to reflect the results of the investment pool's operations during 19X2. Ignore the entry to record the sale of the investments.

Exercise 22–6   (Revenues and Contra Revenue Accounts of Hospitals)

National Hospital, a nonprofit organization, recorded patient service revenues of $7,500,000 for the year ended December 31, 19X1. National did not collect this amount because of various contra revenue items. During the period, National granted charity allowances of $1 million, recorded a provision for doubtful accounts of $225,000, and made contractual adjustments of $500,000 for third-party payers.

Required:

Prepare the journal entries to record the hospital's patient service revenues and the related items mentioned above.

Exercise 22–7   (Services Donated to Hospitals)

During 19X6, volunteer nurses' aides donated their services to Local Hospital at no cost. If regular employees had provided the services, their salaries would have been

$8,500. While working for the hospital, the volunteers received complimentary meals from the hospital cafeteria with a sales value of $700. The volunteers' services satisfied the criteria for donated services found in *SOP 78–10*.

Required:

Prepare the journal entry to record the donated services.

Exercise 22–8   (Revenues and Contra Revenue Accounts of Colleges and Universities)

For the spring semester of 19X6, Franklin University assessed its students $3,520,000 for tuition and fees. The net amount realized was only $3,020,000 because of the following reductions:

Refunds occasioned by class cancellations and student withdrawals	$ 80,000
Tuition remissions granted to faculty members' families	120,000
Scholarships and fellowships	300,000

Required:

Prepare the entries for Franklin University's unrestricted current fund for the items mentioned above.

Problems

Problem 22–9   (College and University Unrestricted Current Fund Entries)

Problems 22–9 through 22–15, which are independent numerically, deal with university funds in the same sequence they are illustrated in the text. Some of the problems are short enough to be considered exercises. Nevertheless, they are presented sequentially to aid you in obtaining an overview of university fund accounting.

The following data pertain to the unrestricted current fund of Arifornia State University for the fiscal year ended December 31, 19X0.

Budgetary data:	
Unrealized revenues	$14,000,000
Estimated expenditures	10,000,000
Revenues (only tuition and fees are billed.	
All revenues but $75,000 of tuition and	
fees are collected during the year.):	
Tuition and fees (including amounts unrealized at year-end—see below)	$11,000,000
Federal appropriations	3,000,000
State appropriations	1,000,000

Local appropriations	700,000
Private gifts	100,000
Endowment income	400,000
Sales and services of educational activities	200,000
Sales and services of auxiliary activities	100,000
Expenditures:	
Instructional	4,000,000
Research	1,750,000
Public service	1,000,000
Academic support	1,100,000
Student services	150,000
Institutional support	300,000
Operation and maintenance of plant	400,000
Scholarships and fellowships	550,000
Mandatory transfers:	
Retirement of indebtedness	400,000
Renewals and replacements	350,000
Loan fund	600,000
Nonmandatory transfers (all from unrestricted gifts):	
Loan fund	200,000
Endowment fund	150,000
Unexpended plant fund	350,000
Student deposits:	
Collected	100,000
Refunded	75,000
Unrealized revenues—tuition and fees:	
January 1, 19X0	70,000
December 31, 19X0	80,000
Inventories (the excess of beginning inventory over ending inventory is to be charged to expenditures—instructional.):	
January 1, 19X0	400,000
December 31, 19X0	220,000
Other data:	
Uncollectible accounts receivable—year-end	40,000
Accounts receivable estimated to be uncollectible amount to .6 percent of tuition and fees	

Required:

a. Record the unrestricted current fund's budget for the year.

b. Record the fund's revenues for the year and the related collections of tuition and fees.

c. Make any required entries for student deposits.

d. Record the fund's expenditures for the year.

e. Record the fund's mandatory and nonmandatory transfers and related cash disbursements.

f. Make any needed year-end adjusting entries and write off the uncollectible accounts.

g. Record the fund's closing entries.

Problem 22–10   (College and University Restricted Current Fund Entries)

Assume the following information for the Restricted Current Fund of Washigon State University for the fiscal year ended December 31, 19X0.

Amount received from:*
  Federal grants and contracts (including $60,000 for
    overhead†) $600,000
  State grants and contracts 150,000
  Local grants and contracts 200,000
  Endowment 25,000
Expenditures:
  Instructional 500,000
  Research 150,000
  Public service 100,000
  Scholarships and fellowships 70,000
Investments purchased 88,000

---

* All amounts received expended except $7,000 received from the endowment.

† To be nonmandatorily transferred to the Unrestricted Current Fund.

Required:

a. Record the cash provided to the restricted current fund during the year through contracts, grants, and the university's endowment.

b. Record the fund's expenditures, purchase of investments, and recognition of related revenues. Assume that $60,000 of accounts payable are recorded and are paid subsequently.

c. Record the fund's closing entry.

Problem 22–11   (College and University Loan Fund Entries)

The following data are pertinent to the Loan Fund of Virginisee State University for the fiscal year ended December 31, 19X0.

Amount due or received from:*
  Private gifts (restricted) $450,000
  Unrestricted current fund (gifts allocated) 40,000
  Refundable federal grants (restricted) 35,000
  Repayment of loans (including interest of $4,000)† 45,000
  Interest on investments† 17,000
Disbursements and related items:
  Investments acquired 125,000
  Administrative and collection costs† 12,000
  Loans made 350,000
  Loans judged uncollectible† 35,000
  New loans estimated to be uncollectible† 25,000

---

* All amounts received except $5,000 from the unrestricted current fund.

† Assumed related to restricted university funds for simplicity.

Required:

a. Record the resources provided to the loan fund during the year through restricted gifts, the unrestricted current fund, refundable federal grants, loan repayments, and interest.

b. Record the disbursements of the fund.

c. Write off the fund's uncollectible accounts and adjust its Allowance for Uncollectible Loans account.

d. Prepare the fund's closing entries.

Problem 22–12   (College and University Endowment Funds Entries)

Assume the following data for the Endowment Funds of Alasdakota State University for the fiscal year ended December 31, 19X0.

Amount received:	
From a computer company for establishment of a	
named professorship in computer science (gift)	$1,500,000
From the university's alumni association for	
use in maintaining recreational facilities* (gift)	2,750,000
From unrestricted current fund† (gifts allocated)	400,000
From restricted current fund‡ (mandatory transfer)	350,000
Interest on pooled investments§	900,000
Disbursements:	
Purchase of investments	$4,000,000
Interest on pooled investments:‖	
Endowment fund interest	225,000
Term endowment fund interest	225,000
Quasi-endowment fund:	
Unrestricted interest	225,000
Restricted interest	225,000
Other data—investments which cost $400,000 were sold for	
$500,000. The gain is allocated to endowment funds	
on the basis of equity percentages (assumed to be	
equal).	

* At the end of 10 years, this amount can be used on the construction of new racquet ball courts.

† To be used for any university purpose.

‡ To be used exclusively in acquiring rare books for the university's collection.

§ Allocated to endowment funds using equity percentages (assumed to be equal).

‖ These disbursements are assumed to be consistent with the provisions of the various endowments.

Required:

a. Record the receipts related to the endowment funds and the gain on the sale of related investments.

b. Record the disbursements from the endowment funds, including the purchase of investments.

c. Identify the balances for the following accounts for the statement of changes in fund balances: Realized Gain on Investments—Unrestricted; Realized Gain on Investments—Restricted; Private Gifts, Grants, and Contracts—Restricted; Unrestricted Gifts Allocated; and Mandatory Transfers In.

Problem 22–13   (College and University Annuity and Life Income Funds Entries)

The following data are related to the Annuity and Life Income Funds of Missisouri State University for the fiscal year ended December 31, 19X0. This year is the first year the university has received resources for annuity and life income funds.

Amount received:	
For annuity funds*	$ 550,000
For life income funds†	650,000
Income from annuity funds	40,000
Income from life income funds	55,000
Disbursements related to:	
Investments	1,200,000
Annuities payable	50,000
Income payable	55,000

* The donor is to receive $50,000 per year for life. The initial present value of the annuity payable is $230,000. The balance in the fund is to be transferred to the unrestricted current fund upon the donor's death. At year-end, the present value of the annuity payable is determined to be $250,000.
† The balance in the fund is to be transferred to an endowment fund upon the donor's death.

Required:

a. Record the initial donation of resources to the university's annuity funds, the investment of these resources, the receipt of related income, the annuity payment to the donor, and the necessary adjustment of the annuities payable account.

b. Make similar entries for the life income funds as needed.

c. Prepare the closing entry for the annuity and life income funds.

Problem 22–14   (College and University Plant Funds Entries)

The data provided below pertain to the Plant Funds of New Delashire State University for the fiscal year ended December 31, 19X0. Assume that funds received from the unrestricted current fund also are unrestricted from the perspective of plant funds.

Amount received:	
From unrestricted current fund:	
Mandatory transfer—retirement of indebtedness	$400,000
Mandatory transfer—renewals and replacements	375,000
Nonmandatory transfer—unexpended plant	325,000
Gifts (which must be used for new plant assets)	375,000
Issuance of bonds at par (for new building—construction	
begun and completed during year)	900,000

Disbursements:

Building construction begun and completed during year	900,000
Bonds retired (related to acquisition of land 5 years ago)	400,000
Renewals and replacement* (from unrestricted funds)	370,000
New building acquired from restricted funds	350,000
New equipment acquired from unrestricted funds	315,000

* Installation of improved wiring throughout the university.

Required:

a. Make all entries related to the university's unexpended plant fund, including entries to record the receipt of resources from the unrestricted current fund, the receipt of unrestricted gifts, the purchase of new plant assets, the issuance of bonds for construction, and the initiation and completion of the construction.

b. Make all entries relevant to the university's fund for renewals and replacements, including entries to record the receipt of resources from the unrestricted current fund and the expenditure for renewals and replacements.

c. Make all entries pertinent to the university's fund for retirement of indebtedness, including entries to record the receipt of resources from the unrestricted current fund and the related retirement of bonds.

d. Make all entries related to the university's investment in plant fund, including entries to record the acquisitions of the building and equipment from unexpended plant funds; the construction of the building through the bond issue; the renewals and replacements made through the fund for renewals and replacements; and the effect of retiring the bonds through the fund for retirement of indebtedness.

Problem 22–15   (College and University Agency Funds Entries)

Assume the data presented below for the agency funds of Main State University for the fiscal year ended December 31, 19X0.

Dues collected from faculty members for national Alliance of University Educators	$3,000
Amount of above used to purchase Treasury bills	2,750
Interest received from Treasury bills	100
Remittance to National Alliance of University Educators after maturity of Treasury bills	3,000

Required:

Make the entries pertinent to the university's agency funds, including entries to record the cash collected, the purchase of related investments, the sale of these investments, and the remittance to the association.

Problem 22–16   (Hospital General Funds Entries)

Problems 22–16 through 22–19, which are independent numerically, deal with hospital funds in the same sequence they are illustrated in the text. Some of the problems are short enough to be considered exercises. Nevertheless, they are presented sequentially to aid you in obtaining an overview of hospital fund accounting.

Assume the following data for the general funds of Hope Hill Hospital for the fiscal year ended December 31, 19X0.

Revenues (all collected in cash during the year except
  $100,000 from daily patient services and the
  amounts related to revenue deductions):
  From daily patient services $8,000,000
  From nursing services 3,500,000
  From other professional services 300,000
  From specific purpose fund (transfer for cancer research
    expenses paid from general funds) 50,000
  Other operating revenues (from hospital cafeteria ($260,000)
    and from restricted endowment fund ($20,000) to cover
    AIDS research expenses paid from general funds) 290,000
  Unrestricted gifts 80,000
Revenue deductions (i.e., contra revenue items) except
  provision for bad debts:
  Contractual adjustments* 320,000
  Charity services† 200,000
  Discounts and allowances (patients and employees) 20,000
Expenses paid in cash:
  General services expenses 6,500,000
  Fiscal and administrative expenses 1,000,000
  Nursing services expenses 1,600,000
  Other professional expenses 350,000
  Research expenses paid through transfer from specific-
    purpose fund (see above) 50,000
Property, plant, and equipment acquired:
  Fixed equipment acquired for cash 1,200,000
  Major movable equipment purchased through plant
    replacement and expansion fund 200,000
Data for year-end adjustments, etc.:
  Accrued interest payable 60,000
  Estimated bad debts expense (also a revenue deduction) 15,000
  Accounts judged uncollectible 11,000
  Depreciation expense:
    Buildings 550,000
    Fixed equipment 175,000
    Major movable equipment 75,000
  Decrease in inventories (assumed pertinent to general
    services expenses for simplicity) 30,000
  Increase in prepaid expenses (assumed related to fiscal and
    administrative expenses for simplicity) 7,000

---

* Reductions in patients' bills covered by Medicare, Medicaid, and various hospitalization plans.

† The cost of services performed for those known unable to pay.

Required:

a. Record the general funds revenues for the year and related collections. Assume that $5 million of accounts receivable are recorded initially when the revenues are recorded.

b. Record the general funds revenue deductions for the year, except for the period's provision for bad debts.

c. Record the general funds cash expenses.

d. Record the general funds property, plant, and equipment acquisitions.

e. Make any needed adjusting entries and write off the uncollectible accounts.

Problem 22-17   (Hospital Specific-Purpose Fund Entries)

Assume that Desert View Hospital's volunteer organization obtains pledges for the fiscal year ended December 31, 19X0, for $60,000 to be spent on heart disease research. All the pledges are collected during the year and are accounted for in the hospital's only specific-purpose fund. Assume also that $50,000 was transferred from the specific-purpose fund to its general funds to cover heart disease research expenditures made during the year.

Required:

Make all indicated entries for the hospital's specific-purpose fund.

Problem 22-18   (Hospital Endowment Fund Entries)

Healthcrest Hospital has a research-related endowment fund. This fund was established several years ago by a wealthy donor. The donor contributes $30,000 to the fund at the start of each year, with the understanding that the fund's income is to be used to cover the hospital's muscular dystrophy research expenses as far as possible. Contributions to the fund are invested in marketable securities. Any remaining income is to be transferred to the hospital's plant replacement and expansion fund. Assume that $20,000 was transferred from the endowment fund to the hospital's general funds to cover research expenditures made during the year. The fund's total earnings for the year amounted to $22,000. There is no accrued income receivable at year-end.

Required:

Make all entries related to the hospital's endowment fund, assuming that contributions to the fund are invested in marketable securities.

Problem 22-19   (Hospital Plant Expansion and Replacement Fund Entries)

Assume the following 19X0 data pertinent to Holy Health Hospital's plant expansion and replacement fund.

Pledges:
Pledges obtained	$450,000
Pledges collected during the year	425,000
Pledges expected to be uncollectible	12,000
Pledges from prior year written off	9,000

Receipts other than from pledges:
Cash from investment income	40,000
Cash from sale of marketable securities with cost of $70,000	110,000

Disbursements:
Purchase of marketable securities	175,000
Purchase of major movable equipment with unrestricted use	225,000
Year-end accrued interest receivable	15,000

Required:

a. Record the fund's pledges obtained and the related receipts.

b. Record the receipts of the fund generated through investments.

c. Record the fund's disbursements.

d. Make the fund's year-end adjusting entries and write off the uncollectible pledges.

Problem 22–20   (Voluntary Health and Welfare Organization Entries)

Citizens against Cocaine Use (CACU) is a voluntary health and welfare organization. CACU's primary activity is researching the addictive effects of cocaine. This activity is conducted through its unrestricted current fund. CACU also performs research and stages workshops meant to aid the family members of cocaine users. The resources for the latter activities, which are administered through CACU's restricted current fund, are provided by donors who restrict the uses of their contributions to these activities.

The data presented below pertain to CACU's unrestricted current fund; restricted current fund; and land, building, and equipment fund for the fiscal year ended December 31, 19X0. There are no accrued revenues or expenses at year-end, no unearned revenues or prepaid expenses at the beginning or the end of the year, and no inventory or supplies adjustments needed at year-end. All pledges are expected to be collected. As shown below, CACU's program and support expenses classifications are: (1) program services—addiction research, (2) program services—family aid research and workshops, (3) supporting services—management and general, and (4) supporting services—fund-raising.

Current fund—unrestricted:
Direct support:	
Pledges (all but $60,000 collected during year)	$2,225,000
Legacies and bequests	2,200,000
Indirect support:	
United Way	500,000
Association of Reformed Cocaine Users	300,000
Fees and grants from governmental agencies	750,000

Current fund—unrestricted:
  Revenues:
    Sales of products . . . . $ 300,000
    Investment income   25,000
    Donated service   20,000
    Program fee—addiction research   350,000
  Disbursements:
    Purchase of marketable securities   700,000
    Salaries and wages 1,600,000
    Professional fees 1,200,000
    Supplies used   100,000
    Rent   650,000
    Inventory (all sold)   60,000
    Transfers to land, building, and equipment fund for:
      Mortgage payments on building ($450,000 interest)   550,000
      Equipment purchased 1,100,000
    Other   150,000

Current fund—unrestricted:
  Allocation of various expenditures for statement of support,
    revenues and expenses, and changes in fund balances:
      Program services—addiction research 2,400,000
      Supporting services—management and general 1,100,000
      Supporting services—fund-raising   260,000

Current fund—restricted:
  Direct support:
    Pledges (all but $6,000 collected)—family aid research
      and workshops   600,000
  Revenues:
    Program fees—family aid workshops   350,000
  Disbursements:
    Salaries and wages   250,000
    Professional fees   325,000
    Program costs—family aid research and workshops   320,000
    Rent   40,000
    Other   50,000
  Allocation of various expenditures for statement of support,
    revenues and expenses, and changes in fund balances:
      Program services—family aid research and workshops   659,000
      Supporting services—management and general   240,500
      Supporting services—fund-raising   85,500

Land, building, and equipment fund:
  Direct support:
    Pledges (all but $20,000 collected)   530,000
  Revenues—investment income   20,000
  Disbursements:
    Purchase of marketable securities   240,000
    Payments on mortgage on building ($450,000 interest)   550,000
  Purchase of equipment 1,100,000
  Data for year-end adjustments:
    Depreciation expense:
      Buildings   75,000
      Equipment   15,000

Allocation of various expenditures for statement of support,
   revenues and expenses, and changes in fund balances:

Program services—addiction research	$ 440,000
Program services—family aid research and workshops	50,000
Supporting services—management and general	30,000
Supporting services—fund-raising	20,000

Required:

a. Make all entries related to CACU's unrestricted current fund, including its closing entry. Assume that $1,500,000 of pledges receivable are recorded initially when the fund's revenues are recorded.

b. Make all entries pertinent to CACU's restricted current fund, including its closing entry. Assume that $400,000 of pledges receivable are recorded initially when the fund's revenues are recorded.

c. Make all entries relevant to CACU's land, building, and equipment fund, including its closing entry. Assume that $350,000 of pledges receivable are recorded initially when the fund's revenues are recorded.

Problem 22–21   (Hospital General Funds Entries)

The following transactions and events, among others, affected the general funds of Public Hospital for the year ended December 31, 19X6.

1. Gross patient service revenue of $720,000 was billed to patients. Provision was made for indigent patient charity allowances of $35,000 (of which $23,000 was to be covered by Goodwill Welfare, Inc.). Contractual adjustments were allowed to Medicare totaling $36,000. Uncollectible accounts were estimated to be $30,000.

2. A donation of $15,000 was received by the Mark Wilson Restricted Fund (a specific-purpose fund). This fund is used solely to provide funds for the purchase of new equipment. The $15,000 was transferred to the fund responsible for acquiring new equipment, and $15,000 of equipment was purchased.

3. Volunteer nurses' aides donated services to the hospital with a total fair value of $72,000. Meals costing $1,800 were served to the aides at no charge by the hospital's cafeteria.

4. New pledges, due in one year, totaling $120,000 were received by the plant replacement and expansion fund from various donors. Collections on pledges amounted to $80,000, and the provision for doubtful pledges for 19X6 was $12,000.

Required:

Prepare the indicated 19X6 journal entries for Public Hospital. Identify the fund in which each entry is recorded.

Problem 22–22   (Statement of Revenues and Expenses for Hospital General Funds)

The following 19X6 events are related to the general funds of Goodwill Hospital.

1. Revenues from patient services totaling $20 million were recorded. The allowance for uncollectibles was established at $4,200,000. Of the $20 million in revenues,

$8 million was recognized under cost reimbursement agreements. These revenues are subject to audit and retroactive adjustment by third-party payers (estimated adjustments are included in the allowance account).

2. Patient service revenue is accounted for at established rates on an accrual basis.

3. Other operating revenue totaling $200,000 was recorded. Of this total, $120,000 was from specific-purpose funds.

4. The hospital received $280,000 in unrestricted gifts and bequests. They were recorded at fair market value when received.

5. The hospital's endowment funds earned $120,000 in unrestricted income.

6. Board-designated funds earned $120,000 in income.

7. Goodwill's operating expenses for the year amounted to $17,250,000. This total includes $625,000 in straight-line depreciation.

Required:

Prepare a statement of revenues and expenses for the general funds for the year ended December 31, 19X6.

(AICPA adapted)

Problem 22–23   (Allocation of Income from Pooled Investments)

The four funds of National Welfare Foundation, a nonprofit organization, formed an investment pool on January 1, 19X7. On that date, the costs and fair values of the pooled investment were as follows:

	Cost	Fair Value
Unrestricted fund	$ 35,000	$ 46,000
Restricted fund	25,000	25,300
Plant fund	50,000	57,500
Endowment fund	80,000	101,200
Totals	$190,000	$230,000

During the year ended December 31, 19X7, the investment pool reinvested realized gains totaling $20,000 and received dividends and interest amounting to $18,000. The interest and dividends were distributed to the participating funds.

On January 1, 19X8, the Heitman Life Income Fund entered the National Welfare Center investment pool with investments having a cost of $50,000 and a fair value of $70,000. At the time of this addition, the fair value of the investment pool was $280,000. During the year ended December 31, 19X8, the investment pool reinvested realized gains totaling $30,000 and received dividends and interest totaling $40,000. The dividends and interest were distributed to the participating funds.

Required:

a. Compute the following:
1. The equity percentages of the various funds on January 1, 19X7.
2. The revised equity percentages of the funds on January 1, 19X8.

b. Prepare journal entries on December 31, 19X7, for each of the four participating funds, to reflect the results of the investment pool's operations during 19X7.

c. Prepare journal entries on December 31, 19X8, for each of the five participating funds, to reflect the results of the investment pool's operations during 19X8.

Problem 22–24   (Balance Sheet for Voluntary Health and Welfare Organizaton Funds)

The December 31, 19X7, balance sheet for American Blood Donors Association is presented below:

AMERICAN BLOOD DONORS ASSOCIATION
Balance Sheet
December 31, 19X7

Assets

Cash	$ 470,000
Accounts receivable	160,000
Allowance for doubtful accounts	(30,000)
Pledges receivable	930,000
Allowance for doubtful pledges	(130,000)
Inventories	400,000
Investments	19,300,000
Land	1,300,000
Building and improvements	46,500,000
Equipment	2,700,000
Accumulated depreciation	(13,500,000)
Other assets	200,000
Total assets	$58,300,000

Liabilities

Accounts payable	$ 700,000
Accrued expenses	130,000
Deferred revenue—unrestricted	100,000
Deferred support—restricted	6,000,000
Deferred capital addition	1,600,000
Long-term debt	7,350,000
Total liabilities	$15,880,000

Fund Balances

Plant	$29,000,000
Endowment	3,850,000
Restricted	1,300,000
Unrestricted	8,270,000
Total fund balances	42,420,000
Total liabilities and fund balances	$58,300,000

Additional information concerning the balance sheet is as follows:

1. Except for $70,000 of cash, the endowment fund is made up of investments only. There are no liabilities.
2. The plant fund has no current liabilities and includes some investments and $15,000 in cash.
3. In addition to investments, the current restricted fund consists of the pledges receivable, $35,000 of accounts payable, and cash of $155,000.

Required:

Prepare a corrected balance sheet for the American Blood Donors Association at December 31, 19X7, using the following format.

Account titles	Current Unrestricted	Current Restricted	Plant	Endowment	Total
	$	$	$	$	$

(AICPA adapted)

Problem 22–25   (College and University Fund Entries)

The following transactions of Citizen College occurred during 19X7. The funds involved are the endowment fund, the annuity fund, the plant fund—unexpended, the plant fund—investment in plant, the loan fund, the unrestricted current fund, and the restricted current fund.

January 1

1. A gift of $10,000 was received from Sarah Waller. The principal was to be held intact and the income used for any purpose designated by the governing board.
2. Byron Scofield donated $20,000. The principal was to be kept intact and the income used for scholarships for worthy students.
3. Dan Persons donated $30,000. The principal was to remain intact; the interest was to be used for student loans. All income is to be loaned, and all losses from loans are to be charged against income.
4. A gift of $205,000 was received from Martha Bedwell. Semiannual payments of $10,000 are to be made to the donor during her lifetime. The fund is then to be used to purchase or construct a student residence. Ms. Bedwell has a life expectancy of five years, and investments are expected to earn 8 percent annually.
5. Julie Johnson donated 1,000 shares of BIM stock with a market value of $150. All income received from the shares is to be held intact, and the shares cannot be held over five years. Once the board sells the shares, all the proceeds are to be used to build a student hospital.

6. The assets of the Waller and Scofield Funds were consolidated into a pooled investment account by the governing board (in proportion to the principal accounts). Electric Power Company bonds worth $30,000 were purchased. The 12 percent interest was payable on January 1 and July 1.

7. The Persons Fund cash is used to purchase Great Company 10 percent bonds at par for $30,000. January 1 and July 1 are the interest dates.

8. $200,000 of 8 percent U.S. Treasury notes were purchased at par with cash from the Bedwell Fund. The interest dates are January 1 and July 1.

July 1

9. The interest has been received on all bonds and notes and has been transferred to the proper funds. Dividends of $4,000 are received from BIM stock.

10. The stipulated payment is made to Ms. Bedwell from the endowment fund.

11. Electric Power Company bonds bought for $20,000 are sold at 102. The gain is added to the principal.

12. A $300 student loan was made from the Persons Fund.

October 1

13. A notice of Martha Bedwell's death is received. There is no liability to her estate.

14. The Scofield Scholarship Fund awards a $200 scholarship.

15. $200,000 par U.S. Treasury notes are sold for $206,000.

December 1

16. Interest on bonds is received.

17. $100 of principal and $5 of interest were repaid on a student loan.

18. A building was purchased for $250,000 using the resources available from the Bedwell gift. The residence hall will have a 20-year mortgage payable to account for the balance.

Required:

Using the following format, record the journal entries necessary for each event. Ignore closing entries.

Event	Fund	Journal Entry

(AICPA adapted)

Problem 22–26   (College and University Unrestricted Current Fund Entries and Statements)

The current funds balance sheet of Big State University at the end of its fiscal year ended June 30, 19X6, is as follows:

BIG STATE UNIVERSITY
Current Funds Balance Sheet
June 30, 19X6

Assets

Unrestricted:

Cash	$210,000
Accounts receivable (less allowance for doubtful accounts, $9,000)	341,000
State appropriations receivable	75,000
Total unrestricted	626,000

Restricted:

Cash	7,000
Investments	60,000
Total restricted	67,000
Total assets	$693,000

Liabilities and Fund Balance

Unrestricted:

Accounts payable	$ 45,000
Deferred revenues	66,000
Fund balance	515,000
Total unrestricted	626,000

Restricted:

Fund balance	67,000
Total restricted	67,000
Total liabilities and fund balance	$693,000

The following transactions occurred during the fiscal year ended June 30, 19X6.

1. On July 7, 19X6, a gift of $100,000 was received from an alumnus. The alumnus requested that one half of the gift be used for the acquisition of books for the university library and that the remainder be used for the establishment of a scholarship. The alumnus further requested that the revenue generated by the scholarship fund be used annually to award a scholarship to a qualified disadvantaged student (with the principal remaining intact). On July 20, 19X6, the board of trustees resolved that the cash of the newly established scholarship (endowment) fund would be invested in bank certificates of deposit. On July 21, 19X6, the certificates of deposit were acquired.

2. Revenue from student tuition and fees applicable to the year ended June 30, 19X7, amounted to $1,900,000. Of this amount, $66,000 was collected in the previous year, and $1,686,000 was collected during the year ended June 30, 19X7. In addition, on June 30, 19X7, the university had received cash of $158,000, representing tuition and fees for the session beginning July 1, 19X7.

3. During the year ended June 30, 19X7, the university had collected $349,000 of the outstanding accounts receivable at the beginning of the year. The balance was determined to be uncollectible and was written off against the allowance account. On June 30, 19X7, the allowance account was increased by $3,000.

4. During the year, interest charges of $6,000 were earned and collected on late student fee payments.

5. During the year, the state appropriation was received. An additional unrestricted appropriation of $50,000 was made by the state but had not been paid to the university as of June 30, 19X7.

6. Unrestricted cash gifts totaling $25,000 were received from alumni of the university.

7. During the year, restricted fund investments of $21,000 were sold for $26,000. Investment earnings amounting to $1,900 were received (credit Fund Balance).

8. During the year, unrestricted operating expenses of $1,777,000 were recorded. On June 30, 19X7, $59,000 of these expenses remained unpaid.

9. Restricted cash of $13,000 was spent for authorized purposes during the year. An equal amount was transferred from the fund balance to revenue of the restricted fund.

10. The accounts payable on June 30, 19X6, were paid during the year.

11. During the year, $7,000 interest was earned and received on the certificate of deposit acquired in accordance with the board of trustees resolution (in item 1).

Required:

a. Prepare journal entries to record, in summary form, the transactions for the year ended June 30, 19X7. Use the following format in recording the entries.

		Current Fund				Endowment Fund	
		Unrestricted		Restricted			
Transaction	*Account*	*Dr.*	*Cr.*	*Dr.*	*Cr.*	*Dr.*	*Cr.*

b. Prepare a statement of changes in fund balances for the year ended July 30, 19X7.

c. Prepare a statement of revenues, expenditures, and other changes for the current fund for the year ended June 30, 19X7.

(AICPA adapted)

Problem 22–27   (Voluntary Health and Welfare Organization Entries and Activity Statement)

In 1950, a group of civic-minded citizens of Cityville organized a nonprofit sports club to benefit local youth. They called it the Cityville Sports Committee. Each of the committee's 100 members contributed $1,000 toward the organization's capital, and in turn, received a participation certificate. In addition, each participant agreed to pay dues of $200 a year for the organization's operations. All dues have been collected in full by the end of each fiscal year ending March 31. Members who have discontinued their participation have been replaced by an equal number of new members through transfer of the participation certificates from the former members to the new ones. The organization's trial balance as of April 1, 1982, is as follows:

	Debit	Credit
Cash	9,000	
Investments (at market, equal to cost)	58,000	
Inventories	5,000	
Land	10,000	
Building	164,000	
Accumulated Depreciation—Building		130,000
Furniture and Equipment	54,000	
Accumulated Depreciation—Furniture and Equipment		46,000
Accounts Payable		12,000
Participation Certificates (100 at $1,000 each)		100,000
Cumulative Excess of Revenues over Expenses		12,000
	300,000	300,000

Transactions for the year ended March 31, 1983, were as follows:

1. Dues collections from participants amount to $20,000.
2. Snack bar and soda fountain sales were $28,000.
3. Interest and dividends received totaled $6,000.
4. Additions to voucher register were
   House expenses—$17,000.
   Snack bar and soda fountain—$26,000
   General and administrative—$11,000
5. Vouchers paid totaled $55,000.
6. Assessments for capital improvements not yet incurred (assessed March 20, 1983; none collected by March 31, 1983; deemed 100 percent collectible during year ended March 31, 1984)—$10,000.
7. An unrestricted bequest amounting to $5,000 was received.

Adjustment data are as follows:

1. Investments are valued at market, which amounted to $65,000 on March 31, 1983. There were no investment transactions during the year.
2. Depreciation for the year:
   Building—$4,000
   Furniture and equipment—$8,000
3. Allocation of depreciation:
   House expenses—$9,000
   Snack bar and soda fountain—$2,000
   General and administrative—$1,000
4. Inventory on hand on March 31, 1983, was $1,000. The inventory is for snack bar and soda fountain operations.

Required:

a. Record the transactions and adjustments on a functional basis in journal entry form for the year ended March 31, 1983.
b. Prepare an appropriately titled all-inclusive activity statement for the year ended March 31, 1983, on a functional basis.

(AICPA adapted)

Index